THE CLASSICAL MUSIC LOVER'S COMPANION
TO ORCHESTRAL MUSIC

THE
CLASSICAL
MUSIC LOVER'S
COMPANION
TO ORCHESTRAL MUSIC

ROBERT PHILIP

YALE UNIVERSITY PRESS
NEW HAVEN AND LONDON

For information about this and other Yale University Press publications, please contact:
U.S. Office: sales.press@yale.edu   yalebooks.com
Europe Office: sales@yaleup.co.uk   yalebooks.co.uk

Set in Minion Pro by IDSUK (DataConnection) Ltd
Printed in Great Britain by TJ International, Padstow, Cornwall

Library of Congress Control Number: 2018954130

ISBN 978-0-300-12069-1

A catalogue record for this book is available from the British Library.

10 9 8 7 6 5 4 3 2 1

Contents

xii

Introduction

My earliest memories of listening to music, and to orchestral music in particular, go back to my grandmother's house in London. In the living room was a gramophone, housed in a huge walnut box with a great hinged lid. No modern household contains anything quite so magnificent and evocative. This was before the days of long-playing records, and the greatest excitement was to use the auto-changer. Onto the tall spindle you piled the five or six 78-rpm fragile shellac discs that made up the symphony or concerto you wanted to hear. If everything went according to plan, each disc in turn dropped with a light thump onto the turntable, the heavy 'tone-arm' settled in the groove, and off you went for another four minutes. When all the pile had been played, you turned the whole lot over and played the reverse sides. Sometimes four or five discs would crash down together – a heart-stopping moment until you discovered, as you usually did, that no damage had been done.

At home in Birmingham we had a little table machine with no sophistications, and just a few records – Schnabel playing Beethoven's 'Emperor' Concerto, Beecham conducting Rossini's *Silken Ladder* Overture and Handel's 'Arrival of the Queen of Sheba', Danny Kaye narrating *Tubby the Tuba*, the most enchanting of all 'Introductions to the Orchestra' (though the names of its composer, George Kleinsinger, and lyricist, Paul Tripp, are known only to aficionados of American song history). The needles barely lasted a few playings, and sometimes in desperation I took one of my mother's sewing needles and used it instead. This was not a good idea: the sharp, hard steel quickly gouged away inside the groove, and more than one record was ruined.

Setting off on the 'Emperor' Concerto was quite an adventure. As I approached the end of each side of the first movement, I knew there would be an emphatic chord, followed by the regular scraping noise that meant I should take off the record and put on the next side (our simple gramophone did not have an auto-changer). To this day, whenever I hear that movement, I mentally get up ready for the end of each side. It was years before I really pieced together the whole movement in my mind as a continuous flow.

Then we bought our first long-playing record player and our first LP records – Bach's Brandenburg Concertos and Beethoven's Seventh Symphony. All at once I could listen continuously to twenty minutes or more without stopping. I played these few records again and again, and they were my most important companions around the age of seven. I particularly remember the feeling as I set off into the Seventh Symphony, the sense of embarking on a great voyage of discovery. And the thing I discovered, which remains true many decades later, is that the sense of discovery does not diminish because you already know every step of the journey and its destination.

That, I think, is the most important thing I ever learned about music. It sounds like a cliché, but it is true: a work of music is a journey, and the great works of orchestral music are journeys of particular richness. In my later music studies and career, I have learned many other things about music, including the technical terms that music specialists use to describe structure, harmony, counterpoint, and all the rest. But I have never lost that basic sense of music as a journey, to which one can return again and again, each time refreshed as if one had never travelled it before.

Some music suggests a physical journey, but more important is the mental journey. The listener experiences nuances suggestive of the emotional twists and turns of life – expectation, hope, doubt, determination, struggle, conflict, disappointment, failure, resolution, acceptance, anger, confusion, dawning realization, sudden revelation. This is the starting point for my attempts to describe each piece of music in this book. Where is this music going? What is happening along the way? Is this a change of direction, or just an aside? Where have we heard this before? Is this an arrival, or is there still another hill beyond this one? How has the composer achieved all these events? As on a real journey, there is a multitude of different things to observe and savour along the way. But there is also the arrival, and the hope that this journey has added up to something that you can contemplate as a single event: that all the different elements add up to a coherent whole.

Of course all these things can be appreciated from recordings. But orchestras are made up of living human beings playing their instruments in a real space and co-ordinating in real time. Nothing is quite like being present in the concert hall when a great orchestra is making music together. I shall never forget the impact of a concert I attended at the Edinburgh festival in 1967, when I was twenty-two. George Szell had brought his Cleveland Orchestra. I knew almost nothing about him or them, but had read that they were then widely considered the finest orchestra in the world. They began with Weber's Overture to *Oberon*, a piece I had never heard before. The seventy-year-old Szell came to the rostrum, looking more like a bank manager than a conductor. With nothing more than a nod he set his orchestra going. There was a soft horn call, as if from the distance, answered even more softly by the strings. Another horn call, another answer with a poignant tug of the harmony from the cellos. Woodwind flitted by like a glimpse of fairies. The music became softer and softer, until there was suddenly an enormous bang of a full chord. Then we were into music of the most joyous energy, interspersed with moments of tenderness. It was irresistible, unforgettable, and a lesson for life that an orchestral concert could be a revelation of an emotional landscape. Thinking about it over the years, I came to realize that it was an extraordinarily sophisticated achievement. Musicians and critics often talk of 'balance' between different instruments. Yet what I heard that day was not just a balance of forces, but a blend of sound and purpose that seemed utterly natural and organic. Szell, I afterwards learned, was a tough and sardonic character. But the music-making that he and his orchestra created was something profoundly human and sympathetic. The only musical experience that capped that was to hear Carlos Kleiber conduct Verdi's *Otello* at Covent Garden in 1980. But that is a topic for another book.

It was around the same time as the Edinburgh concert that I started playing the bassoon in amateur orchestras, and I began to learn how an orchestra works from the inside. Later, I tried my hand at conducting. Of course an amateur orchestra is very different from a top professional orchestra, but I found myself gaining some important insights. There is, for a start, the matter of co-ordination. Some conductors are sticklers for ensemble, and will stop the rehearsal whenever it comes adrift. A professional orchestra has ways of keeping co-ordination under control, for which the leader, and the lead player in each section, take some responsibility. In the comparative looseness of an amateur orchestra, it requires much repetition, familiarity with the music, and the determination of the conductor to get it right. But 'playing together' is not just a matter of co-ordination. I learned that the surest way to precise playing is for the musicians to acquire a common sense of purpose. If the members of an orchestra have a strong sense of where the music is going at any moment, the resulting co-ordination will be more secure than if they are simply responding to demands to be accurate.

The psychology of accurate co-ordination is a subtle thing. I experienced a vivid illustration of this during my years of orchestral playing when I found myself volunteering to play the bass drum in Copland's *Fanfare for the Common Man* (a wonderfully cathartic experience). My job was to synchronize precisely with the timpanist. I learned very quickly that it was useless to watch his stick coming down on the drum. If I did, I was always early or late. The only way to do it was to watch his upswing, and then look away before the stick came down. That way I could synchronize with him every time. It's hopeless to try to synchronize with a point. You have to synchronize the move towards the beat, the dynamic expectation, the tension that leads to the release.

This is a tiny example of what applies across the whole spectrum of orchestral discipline: true co-ordination requires not just a desire to be accurate, but common understanding and impulse. Biologists have a word, entrainment, to describe the ability of flocks of birds and other creatures to act together, seemingly too quickly for any conscious thought to have been involved. Ethnomusicologists have started to use the term to describe the phenomenon of playing music together. Orchestras at their best are like a flock of birds. The members each have their own role, but they can function together as a single organism. The sense of common purpose becomes so strong that lightning reflexes are constantly adjusting the co-ordination to an extent that one might think impossible in a group of eighty people.

The sound of an orchestra is something very special – or rather the sounds, because it is the extraordinary range of sounds and their combinations that is remarkable. Composers have had very different ways over the centuries of exploiting the possibilities of the orchestras of their time, and the range of possibilities has changed as the orchestra has become larger and more diverse in its instruments and as the instruments themselves have developed. Some composers treat the orchestra rather like an organ, adding or subtracting groups of instruments like banks of organ stops to change the power and overall colour (Schumann, Bruckner, Franck, Elgar). Some composers place more emphasis on individual colours, with a great variety of different blends (Berlioz, Debussy), while others emphasize stark contrasts (Musorgsky, Borodin, Stravinsky). But every individual composer has a slightly different way of handling the instruments, and the music lover learns to recognize a particular composer's palette. Berlioz and

Haydn like to blend a violin line with a flute, to give it a silvery sheen; Janáček specializes in chords with the brass clustered at the bottom and woodwind and strings bunched at the top, a savage and powerful effect. Mozart's orchestra sounds subtly warmer when he adds clarinets (which Haydn rarely does). Brahms has a particularly expressive way of using wind instruments, so that they sound, as Gerald Abraham put it, 'not like an organ, but as that least musical of instruments would sound if it had any genuine power of expression'.[1]

These and other differences between composers rely on the members of the orchestra and the conductor to have their full effect. Standards in orchestras these days are extraordinarily high, worldwide. But their very competence makes it possible for orchestras to fall back on a 'default' blend of instruments that will cope with most situations – something often forced on them by limited rehearsal time. A conductor with an acute ear for balance and blend working with a highly responsive orchestra can make all the difference between blandness and a sound that really strikes the ear as individual. I have heard thoroughly competent performances of great works that have made me question whether they are as great as I thought they were; and I have heard performances that pin me to my seat just by the force of imagination represented in the sheer quality of the different combinations of sounds. Finding the right colour and blend of the orchestral sound is one of the prime functions of a good conductor. To the listener in the concert hall, this can seem mysterious. Claudio Abbado, for instance, was a conductor who said little in rehearsal and seemed to be doing little in performance. But the sound of his orchestras was constantly alive, because he had a way of making his musicians listen acutely. In a great performance, you can feel that the players are sensitive to what everyone else is doing, so that the relationship between a solo and an accompaniment, between the woodwind and the strings, even between the individual notes in a chord, achieves a balance that enables everything to acquire its proper force and expression. This is not easy to achieve in an ensemble in which each player has only their own part on the stand in front of them. In this way, the best orchestras are like giant chamber ensembles, in which the players have come to know exactly what is their place in the common endeavour at any moment. With such an orchestra, the route through a piece of music becomes like that journey through an endlessly fascinating landscape, in which every detail is clear, but the sense of direction is never lost.

The further back in history one goes, the more like a chamber ensemble the orchestra becomes. In the early eighteenth century, there was no clear distinction between chamber music and orchestral music. Works written for an orchestra could be played by a group of single instruments as chamber music. Until the establishment of the regular symphony orchestras in the nineteenth century, the size of an orchestra would depend on particular circumstances: the wealth of the church or court and the taste of its ruling members, the importance of the occasion, the availability of musicians. We might think that there is an ideal size of orchestra for music of a particular period, but it is not as simple as that. Corelli in the early eighteenth century sometimes directed orchestras of fifty or more players for special occasions, but usually had just a dozen or so. By contrast Brahms in the 1880s was used to the Vienna Philharmonic Orchestra with its eighty or more members, but he also worked happily with the Meiningen Court Orchestra which was half that size. In both cases, the success depended not so much on size as on the training of the orchestras: Corelli was renowned for insisting on a high standard of discipline in his orchestras, and Brahms particularly relished working with a small orchestra that had been meticulously trained by its conductor, Hans von Bülow, when standards in the Vienna Philharmonic were somewhat hit and miss.

This book covers the period from about 1700 to about 1950. This is not, of course, the complete history of orchestral music. It would be possible to go back to the court of Louis XIV with its *24 Violons du Roi* and the Renaissance bands before that. But Corelli is as good a place as any to start the history of orchestral music because we can hear in his concertos, if not the beginning, a gathering of forces that were to lead to the flowering of the orchestra and its music over the next two hundred and fifty years, and a way of writing that greatly influenced succeeding generations.

Orchestral music may in some sense have 'begun' with Corelli, but it certainly did not end in 1950. Many works for orchestra have been composed in the years since, in a bewildering range of styles and approaches. The trends and counter-trends, the arguments between those demanding intellectual rigour and those demanding an audience, between 'modernists' and 'post-modernists', 'serialists' and 'minimalists', between composers who regard developments in popular music as nothing to do with them and those who engage enthusiastically with them, have led to a melting pot of musical activity whose future is probably more uncertain than at any time in the history of music. Alex Ross has discussed these conflicting and inter-acting trends in his brilliant book, *The Rest is Noise*.[2] To examine this music in the sort of detail I have attempted with earlier music would have turned an already big volume into a huge one. So I have decided to leave recent developments for another day, and to restrict myself to what is still widely thought of as the 'core repertoire' of orchestral music. Even within the period 1700–1950 there have been difficult choices, and I have had to leave out many fine composers and works. But I hope that the music contained in the present volume does justice to this immense cultural heritage.

Anyone who visits an art gallery for an exhibition or the theatre for a play can expect to be given notes that explain the background and intentions of the artist or author, written in a manner that does not patronize, but does not contain unfamiliar technical jargon. This has been my approach in this book. I try to describe each piece of music so that listeners can find their way through it, hear the most important features and events, and gather a sense of what the whole piece consists of. I have aimed to include enough background and biographical information to illuminate what makes the composer tick, without loading down the reader with peripheral detail. I have tried to avoid technical terms as much as possible, but to explain them where they are unavoidable. Above all, I have tried to make everything clear, while not shying away from complexity. Some music is difficult, and there is no point in pretending that it is not. On the other hand, music that seems straightforward often contains subtleties that can easily be missed. My main task has been to find my way through the difficulties and to reveal the subtleties, to the point where I hope I understand what is going on in the music and can try to illuminate the composer's thinking to the reader.

The essays on each work vary considerably in length. But I would not like readers to think that there is a direct relationship between the length of the entry and the importance of the music. Some of the greatest works are so transparently self-explanatory that they need little from me beyond a few words about their background and particular subtleties. On the other hand, there are works that tie themselves in knots and need some unpicking, and others for which knowledge of the background is particularly important. I hope that I have struck the right balance, and that readers will find what they need.

The writing of this book has taken many years, and the development of my ability to write it stretches further back over decades and was encouraged by many people. It was in the 1970s that Robert Layton and John Lade first commissioned me to write and present scripts for BBC Radio 3. An author can have no better training than writing for speech. Radio demands clarity, simplicity, and vividness, and these are valuable qualities to carry over into the writing of books. At The Open University, where I was first a BBC producer and then a music lecturer, I found myself writing for an audience and readership who were enthusiastic about music, but had little or no training in it. At the same time, I worked not just with fellow music specialists, but with lecturers in history, literature, art history, and philosophy. Engaging with this broad range of experts really taught me how to think, and revealed to me the basic truth that clarity of writing is achieved first and foremost by clarity of thought.

At Yale University Press, I would like to thank Richard Mason for his helpful editorial suggestions and attention to detail. I owe a particular debt of gratitude to Robert Baldock. It was he who first suggested that I should write this book, and then waited patiently over the years as it grew to a volume six times the size of what was originally proposed. I hope it has been worth the wait, and justifies its length.

The vital shift from saying that I was writing a book to actually achieving it was encouraged most of all by my wife, Susan Tomes, who has been an inspiration to me throughout the process. Preparing programme notes for her concerts over the years and talking to her audiences has helped to focus my sense of what does and does not help the music-lover get to grips with the intricacies of classical music. And Susan's own books have taught me that, with a combination of acute musical sensitivity and a tireless search for exactly the right word, it is possible to describe the intangible essence of music more successfully than I had ever imagined.

JOHANN SEBASTIAN BACH
(1685–1750)

Music has an intellectual side and an emotional side, and people often talk as if the two are separate. But J. S. Bach demonstrates perhaps more clearly than any other composer the inseparability of intellect and emotion in music. He could write fugues of the most awe-inspiring complexity, and he could write an apparently simple melody of heart-aching beauty. But the most remarkable thing about his music is that the fugues are also beautiful and the melodies are also extremely clever. Perhaps his most famous melody of all, the Air from the Third Orchestral Suite (which used to be known as 'Air on the G string' because of a violin arrangement), is typical. It might sound like just a glorious melody. But if you listen to what is going on underneath, in the bass and the middle parts, you become aware that it is the interweaving of the different strands that creates the soaring effect of the melody. That is contrapuntal genius.

A word that often crops up in attempts to describe Bach's music is 'order'. But if this word will do, it is not in the sense of the abstract order of mathematics, but the organic order of life itself. The novelist Ian McEwan expressed it very well: 'No one before or since could make voices or instruments sing simultaneous melodies of such beautiful and interlocking separateness. Whether it is two, three or four melodic lines, solo piano or a whole choir and orchestra, when he unleashes the full glory of his contrapuntal genius, he conjures an ideal society, one we will never actually know, in which we can imagine our best selves, separate but harmonious.'[1]

With the revival of medieval and Renaissance music over recent decades, we now have a better understanding of the long tradition of counterpoint on which Bach drew. And it is clear from this tradition that Bach would have regarded the 'ideal society' as only part of the evocation that he was attempting. Complex counterpoint was, for hundreds of years, something like an act of worship. Learning how intricate patterns of notes could be fitted together to form a harmonious structure was a profound and mysterious art, part of the philosophical quest to express the nature of the universe, and the place of music, numbers, and human beings in it. That might seem high-flown for a consideration of the delightful secular music discussed here. But all of Bach's contrapuntal skill, and his seriousness of purpose, are in these works. And for Bach, a pious Lutheran (if a highly cantankerous one), the modern distinction between secular and sacred music would surely have had little meaning.

Bach spent the last twenty-three years of his life as the music director of St Thomas Church in Leipzig, and it was there that he wrote many of the great works on which his reputation now rests – the Passions, the Mass in B minor, the Christmas Oratorio, cantatas for every Sunday and festival of the year, and many volumes of organ music (Bach was more famous as an organist than as a composer during his lifetime). But the most celebrated of his instrumental works, the Brandenburg Concertos, date from an earlier period, 1717–23, when he was composer and *Kapellmeister* at the court of Prince Leopold of Anhalt-Cöthen. Here Bach had as happy a working environment as at any time in his life, at least until the prince married an unmusical and unsympathetic cousin in 1721. Leopold was an accomplished music-lover who played the violin, viol (viola da gamba), and harpsichord. For once in his career, Bach was not employed as a church musician. So, for a few years, his attention moved away from organ music and cantatas to secular instrumental music. Bach is thought to have composed many other concertos and other works during this period, but they are lost, and the only surviving parts are fragments that crop up in his cantatas.

The magnificent violin concertos were long assumed to be from his time in Cöthen, like the Brandenburg Concertos. But recent scholarship suggests that they are from a later period, when Bach was at Leipzig, where, as well as fulfilling the demanding role of Cantor of St Thomas Church, he worked with the Collegium Musicum from 1723 to the early 1740s (he took over as director in 1729). The Collegium Musicum was an established concert society of forty or more instrumentalists and singers, university students and professionals, who gave free concerts every week throughout the year at a coffee house in Leipzig. This gave Bach the opportunity to work on instrumental music and bring it to an appreciative audience, as he had done at Cöthen, and it also gave him an extra pool of good players who could augment the instrumentalists for church works. Two violin concertos and a double concerto survive, though, as with Bach's period at Cöthen, it is thought that many more concertos for violin were lost. There are also a number of harpsichord concertos which, although they are arrangements of earlier works, pioneered the keyboard concerto that was to become so important in succeeding generations.

Concertos
Brandenburg Concertos, BWV 1046–1051

In March 1721, Bach presented a magnificent set of six concertos, copied by himself, to the Margrave Christian Ludwig of Brandenburg, for whom he had played at his palace in Berlin two years earlier. This has led to the set being known as the 'Brandenburg Concertos'. But the presentation was a formality, in response to the Margrave's request for some of Bach's works. The concertos are more likely to have been conceived for his employer, Prince Leopold of Anhalt-Cöthen, who maintained an exceptionally fine group of instrumentalists at his court. The sixth concerto includes two viols, and since Prince Leopold played the viol the relatively straightforward parts may have been written with him in mind. The prominent harpsichord part in No. 5 was presumably played by Bach himself. The biggest question is whether Bach had access to a trumpeter who could play the dizzying part in No. 2, and scholars continue to debate the matter. Several movements of the concertos also exist in earlier versions – Concerto No. 1 started life with only three movements. It seems, therefore, that the presentation to the Margrave was a final revision of existing material, brought together to form a satisfying set of six concertos (six being the standard number for sets of works in the eighteenth century). As with other collections that Bach undertook (such as the *Art of Fugue* and the *Musical Offering*), the occasion itself was less important than the intellectual and musical significance of making the musical journey. Whatever the circumstances in which these concertos might have been performed, Bach was demonstrating the possibilities of the *concerto grosso* as he saw them.[2]

By the end of his career, Bach came to be regarded as a somewhat old-fashioned and 'learned' composer, but these concertos from his earlier years show that he took a keen interest in current musical fashions. His way of writing concertos was, as with his sonatas, based on fashionable Italian models by Vivaldi, Corelli, and others, and he had already arranged several Italian concertos for solo organ and harpsichord. Like the Italians, he based many of his movements on the ritornello form, in which the theme stated at the beginning returns from time to time, interleaved with episodes that introduce new material. In the Italian concerto, this is combined with alternation between passages for the whole group (the *ripieno*) and passages for one or more soloists (the *concertino*). But Bach's approach to this pattern was subtly different from that of the Italians. The solo episodes explore their themes more widely, venturing to more distant keys. And this sets up a very strong sense of homecoming when Bach returns to the opening *ripieno* theme in the original key, towards the end of the movement.

Bach's use of his instruments, and his command of textures, also vary from the Italian models. In two of the Brandenburg Concertos, the third and sixth, the distinction between the solo group and the *ripieno* is less clear-cut than in most Italian concertos. In the first movement of the sixth, all that happens in the solo sections is that the lower instruments drop out, leaving the two violas and two viols conversing on their own.

As for Bach's 'learnedness', this too brings a unique character to his concertos. His mastery of traditional counterpoint is heard throughout these works, in passages where the parts weave intricately round each other. In his approach to the concerto form, therefore, Bach puts his own original slant on the current fashion, and he is, as with so many great artists, forward-looking and backward-looking at the same time.

BRANDENBURG CONCERTO NO. 1 IN F MAJOR, BWV 1046
Duration: approx. 22 minutes

[Allegro]
Adagio
Allegro
Menuetto – Trio – Menuetto – Polacca – Menuetto – Trio – Menuetto

This is the biggest of the six concertos, both in length and in instrumentation. It is scored for three oboes, bassoon, two horns, '*violino piccolo*', strings, and continuo (that is, a keyboard with a bass stringed instrument). The horns are described in the autograph as '*Corni di caccia*', hunting horns, a term applied to the ancestor of the modern orchestral French horn, without the modern valves. The *violino piccolo* was a small violin tuned higher than the usual instrument, in this case a minor third higher, and is prominent in the third movement. The instrument fell out of use as the violin and its technique developed in the later eighteenth century.

As well as the final version of this concerto, as presented to the Margrave of Brandenburg, there is an earlier version that has only three movements (Sinfonia in F BWV 1046a, formerly BWV 1071). This lacks the third movement and the polonaise, and has no *violino piccolo* part.

The first movement has no tempo marking, but the time signature is two in a bar, not four, indicating quite a fast tempo. Nevertheless, the movement has a somewhat processional feel. This is partly because the instruments tend to move together, rather than dividing into elaborate counterpoint. There is, however, much interplay between the whole orchestra and the solo group, with the oboes and the horns often answering each other. In the *ripieno* sections that begin and end the movement, the horns play fanfares in a triplet rhythm that cuts across the predominant duple rhythm. This strikingly evokes a memory of horns as hunting instruments, and indeed the principal theme of the movement is based on a traditional eighteenth-century greeting call.[3]

The second movement is a beautiful Adagio, in which the oboe plays an elaborate singing line, answered by the violin, the two instruments then combining in duet. The other instruments mostly provide accompanying chords, but from time to time the bass line (cello, bass, and bassoon) also joins in with the melody, to haunting effect. The whole movement sounds like a meditation from one of Bach's church cantatas.

The third movement is in a sturdy, dancing metre. It is written almost like a concerto for the *violino piccolo*, whose part includes elaborate flourishes and chords. Two-thirds of the way through, the reprise of the opening is introduced by a few bars of Adagio, as if Bach wishes momentarily to remind us of the quasi-religious mood of the preceding movement. Several years later, he skilfully reworked this movement to form the opening chorus of a secular cantata: 'Vereinigte Zwietracht der wechselnden Saiten' ('United discord of changing strings', BWV 207), written to celebrate the inauguration of a professor of jurisprudence at the University of Leipzig in 1726. This brilliant chorus is such a successful transformation that it has been suggested that a yet earlier choral version might have formed the basis of the concerto movement, though there is no trace of it.[4]

The finale is a minuet with a rather formal mood evoked by the counterpoint between melody and bass. Alternating with the minuet are three 'trios'. Two of these are literally trios: the first continues the formality of the minuet with a demure, elegant trio for two oboes and bassoon. The second trio is a polonaise for strings, gentle in its stateliness, but with a sudden burst of energy in the second half. And the third trio features the two horns in a virtuoso extended fanfare, accompanied by the oboes.

BRANDENBURG CONCERTO NO. 2 IN F MAJOR, BWV 1047
Duration: approx. 12 minutes

[Allegro]
Andante
Allegro assai

This concerto is scored for trumpet, recorder, oboe, violin, strings, and continuo. The trumpet part is a high, virtuoso part, originally to be played on a trumpet in F without valves (valves, which make it possible to play all the notes of the chromatic scale, were only introduced on brass instruments in the nineteenth century). Although there were skilled trumpeters who specialized in high parts in Bach's day, this concerto is scored for an unusually high instrument even at the time – trumpets in D or C were much more common. It was not long after Bach's death before it was being suggested that the part could be played an octave down on a horn instead, and there is a lingering question among scholars as to whether Bach wrote the original with a specific player in mind, or whether he merely hoped that someone might one day be able to play it.[5]

The traditional skill of playing high baroque trumpet parts fell into disuse in the late eighteenth century, as the orchestra developed in new directions. It was only in the twentieth century that the art was revisited, at first on specially made short trumpets, which made the high notes more easily reachable. In recent years, the valveless, baroque trumpet has been revived, and specialist trumpeters have learned to play it (though with some minor adaptations that make it a little easier to play than the original instruments).

Playing such a high trumpet part is a great strain, and Bach has skilfully made it (more or less) possible by inserting plenty of gaps between trumpet entries, and by leaving the trumpet out of the slow movement altogether. Between two brilliant Allegro movements, the slow movement is a gentle trio for flute, oboe, and violin, over a walking bass in cello and harpsichord.

BRANDENBURG CONCERTO NO. 3 IN G MAJOR, BWV 1048
Duration: approx. 11 minutes

[Allegro]
Allegro

This concerto is scored for just strings and continuo, though in an unusual arrangement. There are three violins, three violas, three cellos, and continuo. In the first movement, the three trios of instruments act as separate 'choirs'. In the solo (*concertino*) sections of the movement, the choirs retain their separate identities, the theme passing from the three violins to the three violas, to the three cellos. In the *tutti* (*ripieno*) sections, the choirs come together. It is most exhilarating to sit close to a performance, as the theme leaps around the group from side to side (something of the same effect can be enjoyed on a stereo recording, but seeing the musicians pass the themes adds an extra dimension). The same applies in the second movement, except that all three cellos play the same music, so the textures are a little simpler than in the first movement. The exhilaration here is enhanced by the way in which the instruments imitate each other in quick succession, as in a fugue.

Between the two movements, rather than a slow movement there are two chords, marked Adagio, with a pause. It is not known quite what Bach intended by this, though it is widely assumed that he intended a moment of improvisation to link the two movements. Sometimes the harpsichord player will play a brief flourish. Adolf Busch, who pioneered the revival of these concertos in the 1930s, used to play a little cadenza on the violin. Some musicians insert a complete slow movement from another work of Bach, but he would surely have supplied a movement if this is what he had wanted.

Bach, like Handel, had no inhibitions about reusing movements when appropriate. In 1729 he added trumpet parts to the first movement of this concerto to provide the opening *Sinfonia* for a cantata for Pentecost, 'Ich liebe den Höchsten von ganzem Gemüte' ('I love the Highest with all my heart'), BWV 174.

BRANDENBURG CONCERTO NO. 4 IN G MAJOR, BWV 1049
Duration: approx. 16 minutes

Allegro
Andante
Presto

This concerto is scored for solo violin and two recorders, with strings and continuo. The autograph score unusually specifies 'Flauti d'Echo', usually taken to mean treble recorders, but the concerto is often played with the familiar 'transverse' flutes (which were also in use in Bach's day). Particularly with recorders, the texture of the first movement has a delightful, airy lightness.

Unusually for a *concerto grosso*, it begins with the solo group of two recorders and solo violin introducing the main theme, while the *ripieno* strings just provide punctuating chords.

Indeed, the whole movement reverses the priorities of the conventional concerto. The soloists predominate almost throughout, with the main body of strings only intervening from time to time to draw things together. The solo violin plays a virtuoso part, breaking into a cascade of rushing demisemiquavers halfway through the movement.

The slow movement is also unusual. Instead of a continuous interweaving of soloists, Bach presents a rather formal, dance-like movement like a sarabande, in which the whole group alternates with the three soloists.

The finale is an exhilarating, fast fugue. *Ripieno* sections alternate with passages for the three soloists (often without a bass line underneath). As in the first movement, the solo violin goes off on a virtuoso flourish of its own halfway through the movement. Bach brings all this accumulation of energy to a magnificent final climax.

Bach later arranged this work as a Harpsichord Concerto in F, BWV 1057, preserving the two recorder parts, but transferring the role of the solo violin to the harpsichord.

BRANDENBURG CONCERTO NO. 5 IN D MAJOR, BWV 1050
Duration: approx. 21 minutes

Allegro
Affettuoso
Allegro

If you look at the first page of the score, you would think that this concerto has only two soloists, flute and violin (Bach's autograph specifies 'transverse' flute, as opposed to recorder). But the harpsichord, which begins by playing continuo, emerges as a soloist in its own right ('*Cembalo concertato*', as the autograph states). In the solo (*concertino*) passages, the harpsichord part is fully written out. In the *ripieno* sections, only the bass line is given, with figures to indicate the chords (as is usual for a continuo part). At first in the *concertino* passages the flute, violin, and harpsichord play an equal role. But from time to time the harpsichord plays flamboyant rushing scales, and eventually it launches out into a long solo cadenza – an extraordinary display of virtuosity in the context of what might otherwise be a fairly conventional *concerto grosso*. This concerto dates from 1719. It was early in that year that Bach visited Berlin and played for the Margrave of Brandenburg. But his main reason for being in Berlin was to collect a new harpsichord for the court at Cöthen, made by the famous harpsichord maker Michael Mietke. This was described in the court inventory as 'a grand harpsichord with two manuals'. An earlier version of the concerto (BWV 1050a) has a shorter cadenza.

The slow movement is a gentle interweaving of three melodies – the flute, the violin, and the right hand of the harpsichord – over a bass line played by the left hand of the harpsichord with a stringed instrument. 'Affettuoso' means 'affectionate' or 'tender'.

The finale is a sprightly fugue in jig rhythm, in which the harpsichord again displays rapid scale passages. The rhythm in the score combines triplets with dotted rhythms, which, in some earlier recordings, used to be interpreted literally, giving a curiously stiff effect. But it is now generally accepted that Bach was using a French convention whereby the dotted rhythms were to be adjusted to coincide with the triplets, creating a simple jig rhythm.

BRANDENBURG CONCERTO NO. 6 IN B FLAT MAJOR, BWV 1051
Duration: approx. 18 minutes

[Allegro]
Adagio ma non tanto
Allegro

Like the third Brandenburg Concerto, the sixth is scored for strings and continuo. But here there are no violins, and the concerto is an ensemble of lower-pitched instruments: two violas, two *viole da gamba* (viols), cello, double bass, and harpsichord continuo. The viola and cello parts are elaborate, the viol parts less so. This has led to the suggestion that Bach wrote the viol parts bearing in mind the capability of his employer, Prince Leopold of Anhalt-Cöthen, a keen amateur musician.

In the joyful first movement of the concerto, the two violas in the *ripieno* sections create a canon by playing identical music half a beat apart from each other. In the *concertino* episodes, they interact in a looser manner, with moments of canon interspersed with free counterpoint. The second movement is, in effect, a trio sonata, in which the two voices of the violas interweave over a walking bass. The finale is a jig with an infectious swing. Sturdy sections of *ripieno* alternate with *concertino* episodes in which the two violas chase each other playfully.

Harpsichord Concertos

In the 1730s, while Bach was director of the Collegium Musicum in Leipzig, he composed seven harpsichord concertos, as well as a number of others for two, three, and four harpsichords. Presumably these were performed at the regular weekly concerts (see introduction to J. S. Bach), and there is a tantalizing clue as to why Bach might have started writing concertos for harpsichord at this time. In 1733 the start of a new season of concerts was announced in a Leipzig newspaper: 'Tomorrow, 17 June ... Bach's Collegio Musico will give the first of its weekly concerts, and will start with a fine concerto using a new clavicymbel of a kind that so far has not been heard here.'[6] Scholars continue to debate quite what this 'new clavicymbel' might have been. Conjecture includes an exceptionally large or fine harpsichord, a harpsichord with an extra set of strings an octave below pitch (a '16-foot' stop, rare at this time), or even one of the early pianos made by Gottfried Silbermann. This last idea is not widely supported, though Bach did later praise Silbermann's improved designs of piano, and famously played on them when he visited Frederick the Great in Potsdam in 1747.

Bach had already paved the way for a harpsichord concerto in the fifth Brandenburg Concerto, in which the harpsichord steps forward from its subsidiary role and takes centre stage in a flamboyant cadenza. Much earlier in his career, he had arranged violin concertos by Vivaldi and other Italian composers for unaccompanied harpsichord and organ. In 1735 he published his own 'Italian' Concerto for solo harpsichord, based on such Italian models. It was only a short step to put these different ideas together and create a true concerto for harpsichord and orchestra. This was, in effect, the start of the history of the keyboard concerto, which then proceeded via Bach's sons, particularly Carl Philipp Emanuel, and on to Mozart and Beethoven.

Whatever instrument Bach might have had available in Leipzig, his harpsichord concertos present particular problems for modern concert performance. They were written to be played with a very small orchestra in an intimate space, where there would have been no problem in making everything audible. They are, virtually, chamber music. In a large modern concert hall, a harpsichord with an ensemble of single strings can seem lost, little more than a distant jangle. The famous Wanda Landowska, pioneer of the revival of the harpsichord, had the firm of Pleyel build her a massive, iron-framed harpsichord with carrying power to overcome this problem. But such 'a-historical' instruments are now out of fashion, just as it would be thought improper to amplify the harpsichord. Alternatively, the concertos can be played on the modern piano, with a modern-sized chamber orchestra. This was how they were revived in the early twentieth century. Then, with the rise of 'authenticity' and period instruments, this too fell out of fashion, and the true chamber-music character of these works was rediscovered. In our more pluralistic times, Bach on the piano has become generally accepted again. The result is very far from what the composer would have expected. But Bach's music has an intellectual weight that does not rely strongly on particular instrumental colours; and, just as some of his music works equally well on organ, harpsichord or clavichord, so the adaptation of these harpsichord concertos to piano concertos can, in the hands of sensitive musicians, be very satisfying.

The harpsichord concertos are, in any case, already adaptations. They are, or in some cases are presumed to be, arrangements of existing works that Bach had originally written for other instruments, and several movements also crop up as sections of cantatas.

HARPSICHORD CONCERTO IN D MINOR, BWV 1052
Duration: approx. 21 minutes

Allegro
Adagio
Allegro

This concerto is thought to be derived from a lost violin concerto. There have been several editions reworking it as a violin concerto, and they confirm that much of the figuration sits naturally on the violin.

The outer movements are in that forthright style that is so characteristic of Bach's concertos in minor keys (such as the Violin Concerto in A minor, and the Concerto for Two Violins in D minor). The opening ritornello boldly throws down a theme in bare octaves. The soloist enters with flourishes and arpeggios over an unchanging bass note. These two features, the bare octaves and the passages with unchanging bass notes, recur throughout the movement, giving it a mood that is both somewhat austere and somewhat obsessional. In two episodes, insistent repetitive figures in the solo part resemble violin passages that alternate rapidly between two strings (reconstructions of the lost violin version demonstrate how 'violinistic' these passages are). The second of these episodes, again over an unchanging bass note, leads with hypnotic insistence into the main reprise of the opening theme.

The slow movement is in G minor, making this concerto unusual in being in minor keys throughout. It too begins with an orchestral theme of bare octaves, setting up a bass line with a pattern of pairs of repeated notes that underlies the whole movement (as in the slow movements of the solo violin concertos). Over this bass, the soloist seems to improvise a singing line, which increases in complexity and intensity as the movement progresses, creating one of Bach's spiritual, aria-like movements.

The finale is a brisk, energetic movement. The solo passages are highly rhythmic, often like a reminiscence of the first movement of the third Brandenburg Concerto, but in a minor key. Later, there are more passages with a violinistic 'crossing strings' effect over an unchanging bass note, and rapid runs and arpeggios that climax before the final reprise.

HARPSICHORD CONCERTO IN E MAJOR, BWV 1053
Duration: approx. 19 minutes

[Allegro]
Siciliano
Allegro

This is thought to be based on a lost oboe concerto. The first movement begins with a theme of simple arpeggio patterns, conveying an outgoing, joyful mood. The first solo entry of the harpsichord is particularly charming, with its opening phrase sauntering up a scale as if it is not quite sure where the theme begins. Soon the harpsichord line is decorated with elaborate runs and turns, which make it important not to set too fast a pace at the outset.

The slow movement is a siciliano – a lilting dance incorporating a characteristic little skipping dotted rhythm. At first the melody is in the strings, the harpsichord accompanying with running semiquavers, then the harpsichord takes over the theme, varying and decorating it extensively. As in the first movement, the elaboration of this line makes it difficult to set a pace that is both 'natural' and comfortable. The movement ends as it began, with the theme returning to the strings.

The finale's main theme returns to the simple but highly effective formula of the first movement, with vigorous arpeggio patterns, and the harpsichord dashing down and up the keyboard in triplet rhythm in the opening bars. It is these triplets that help to give the whole movement its great energy.

HARPSICHORD CONCERTO IN D MAJOR, BWV 1054
Duration: approx. 17 minutes

This is Bach's transcription of the Violin Concerto No. 2 in E major, BWV 1042. There are some fascinating changes of detail – added bass parts and decoration in the keyboard, partly to exploit the possibilities of the harpsichord, partly to compensate for its lack of sustaining power – but it is essentially the same concerto (see below under violin concertos).

HARPSICHORD CONCERTO IN A MAJOR, BWV 1055
Duration: approx. 14 minutes

Allegro
Larghetto
Allegro ma non tanto

This is thought to be derived from a concerto for oboe d'amore, but the original is lost. The first movement is a joyful Allegro – one could imagine it with baroque trumpets and drums, introducing a Christmas cantata. The opening figure in the violins is a building block throughout the movement, found as often in the bass as in the upper parts. For example, at the end of the opening ritornello, where the soloist launches into a new theme, the opening figure is there in the bass underneath it.

The slow movement, like several middle movements of Bach's concertos, has an almost continuous repeating motif in the orchestra, against which the soloist weaves an intricate melodic line like an aria. The unusual feature here is that this motif is not in the bass (as in the two solo violin concertos), but in the violins, occupying the same pitch range as the solo line, sometimes above it, sometimes below. This creates a particular sense of intimacy. The bass line is meanwhile in the left hand of the harpsichord, often without support from the cello and bass of the orchestra – a clear indication that Bach would have performed these concertos with a chamber group rather than an 'orchestra' in the modern sense.

The finale is a vigorous three-time movement. But the vigour lies in the decorative flourishes built into the theme (both in the violins and in the harpsichord). Too fast a tempo turns them into a scramble, as the 'ma non tanto' warns, and, as often in Bach, it is difficult to pinpoint a speed that achieves both bounce and poise.

HARPSICHORD CONCERTO IN F MINOR, BWV 1056
Duration: approx. 10 minutes

[Allegro]
Largo
Presto

This concerto is similar in character to the Violin Concerto No. 1 in A minor, and is presumed to be an adaptation of a lost concerto for violin or oboe (in G minor). It opens with another of those 'sturdy' minor-key first movements, with a theme whose first eight bars are built from insistent repetitions of a little cell. The potential doggedness of this theme is averted by the harpsichord, which echoes the end of each line and then breaks into flowing triplet patterns before the theme has finished, continuing in this vein with a new theme at the solo entry proper. Once the triplet genie is out of the bottle there is no stopping it, and it dominates the solo part throughout the movement, with the sturdy opening theme punctuating it at each of the orchestra's ritornelli.

The slow movement, in A flat major, is a singing line of increasing complexity accompanied by pizzicato strings. It is reminiscent of the slow movement of the Concerto for Oboe and Violin. And, indeed, this movement also occurs in a version for oboe, as the opening sinfonia of the Cantata No. 156, 'Ich steh' mit einem Fuss im Grabe' ('I stand with one foot in the grave'). In the sinfonia, the accompaniment is on bowed strings, over which the oboe has no difficulty in soaring. The pizzicato in the concerto makes the harpsichord more clearly audible. The sinfonia is often played as a concert piece, sometimes retitled 'arioso', both in its original form and in arrangements for various instruments. Like the slow movement of the Concerto for Oboe and Violin, this movement ends not in its home key of A flat major, but on an expectant chord of C major, ready for the finale to start in F minor.

The finale is a bustling presto. The theme incorporates a little echo phrase, as in the theme of the first movement, but here Bach instructs the musicians to play it as a real, *piano* echo, as if in imitation of the echo choruses and arias popular in baroque music.

HARPSICHORD CONCERTO IN F MAJOR, BWV 1057
Duration: approx. 17 minutes

This is an arrangement of the Brandenburg Concerto No. 4.

CONCERTO FOR TWO HARPSICHORDS IN C MAJOR, BWV 1061
Duration: approx. 18 minutes

[Allegro]
Adagio ovvero Largo
Fuga – Vivace

This is the best known of Bach's concertos for more than one harpsichord. The first movement has a bold character, and is dominated from the start by the two soloists. Alternations
between them begin immediately after the arresting opening two bars of ritornello and
continue throughout the movement with only the briefest of punctuations from the orchestra.

The orchestra falls silent for the slow movement, and the harpsichords play what is, in
effect, a meditation for four voices. Each hand plays one of the lines, and they answer each
other, creating a shifting pattern of textures – one voice, two voices, three and four voices in
counterpoint.

The finale takes the counterpoint a step further to create a fugue. This is both intellectual
and playful. The first harpsichord begins, stating the elaborate theme, and building up a
texture of three voices before the second harpsichord has played a note. The second harpsichord then enters, adding another three voices, as if we are to end up with a six-voice fugue
(which Bach was perfectly capable of writing, as in the six-part Ricercare in *The Musical
Offering*). But the first harpsichord soon drops out, and the movement turns out to be a teasing
sort of competition between the two instruments, each playing three-part fugal passages
pitted against each other. The orchestra takes little part in this, adding occasional supporting
chords, and from time to time joining in the fuguing with the keyboard players. Indeed, the
role of the orchestra in this concerto is so slight that it is perfectly possible for two keyboard
players to play the whole work on their own. This has led scholars to conjecture that it began
life as a concerto without orchestra (like the famous 'Italian' Concerto for solo harpsichord).

Violin Concertos

These concertos probably date from Bach's time at Leipzig, when he ran the weekly concerts
of the Collegium Musicum (see introduction to J. S. Bach). Two violin concertos and a double
concerto survive, though it is thought that many more concertos for violin were lost. Whoever
they were originally written for, Bach would probably have played them himself – his son
Carl Philipp Emanuel reported that, throughout his life, he played the violin 'cleanly and
penetratingly'.[7]

Bach's principal inspiration for these works was Italy, not only the home of great violins
and great violinists, but also the home of the violin concerto. Bach admired Vivaldi's concertos
and transcribed several of them for solo organ or harpsichord. Bach's own violin concertos to
a large extent follow the model of Vivaldi's, but with a concentrated energy in fast movements
and a lyrical intensity in slow movements that are entirely his own.

VIOLIN CONCERTO NO. 1 IN A MINOR, BWV 1041
Duration: approx. 14 minutes

[Allegro]
Andante
Allegro assai

The outer movements of this concerto have a particularly resolute energy, emphasized by the minor key and by Bach's use of very firm, often insistent, rhythms. After the opening ritornello, the solo violin enters with a decoration of the opening motif, but then develops it into an entirely new thought, with the main theme creeping in after a few bars underneath in the orchestra. Following another brief ritornello the soloist introduces a second important idea, incorporating a pair of energetic upward flourishes. Most of what the soloist plays throughout the movement is derived from these two ideas, and, as usual in this sort of Italian ritornello movement, they alternate with reminders from the orchestra of the main theme, passing through a variety of keys before returning home to A minor.

The slow movement in C major is an example of Bach's genius in taking the simplest of ideas and creating something subtle and complex from it. It opens with four bars, consisting of a bass line whose shape repeats with simple chords above it. The soloist enters with a decorative line for two bars, the bass line returns for another two bars. And so on throughout the movement, with the soloist sometimes pausing as the bass line repeats, sometimes continuing to meditate over it. Although the concerto was written for the pleasure of a public concert audience, this movement seems to occupy the same spiritual ground as the arias of the great religious works that Bach was writing during the same period.

The finale combines dance and learning in a characteristically Bach-like way. It has the swinging rhythm of a jig, but the theme enters in each part in turn, as in a fugue, creating the musical equivalent of a complex dance pattern. The soloist's entries are more straightforwardly playful, but with increasing flamboyant difficulty as the movement progresses. The brief orchestral ritornelli often have reminders of the opening fugue texture, but it is only at the end that the fugue returns wholeheartedly, to bring this marvellously forthright work to a close.

VIOLIN CONCERTO NO. 2 IN E MAJOR, BWV 1042
Duration: approx. 17 minutes

Allegro
Adagio
Allegro assai

The outer movements of the E major Concerto are written in the ritornello form usual in Italian concertos, in which passages for the orchestra alternate with solo passages. Most of the first movement is based on three distinct elements that appear within the first few bars: the three firm chords that start the movement, then the lively continuation, and finally the climax of the phrase, with its rapidly repeated notes and arpeggio. At the beginning of the movement these form a single, coherent theme. But as the movement progresses, each of them in turn steps forward and is elaborated and discussed. In the middle of the movement, there is a passage in C minor with new figuration and a moment of sustained, lyrical counterpoint in the orchestra. This feels almost like the middle section of an operatic 'da capo' aria – a beautifully subtle nuance to introduce into a concerto movement.

The slow movement is one of Bach's most sublime. Like the slow movement of the Concerto in A minor, it is built on a solemnly repeating bass line. But, unlike that concerto, here the bass line continues its repetitions, through various keys, almost throughout the movement. Over it, the soloist weaves a decorative line, creating a meditation of almost hypnotic cumulative effect. As in the first concerto, this movement conveys a strong sense that there was no clear distinction for Bach between church and concert music – it could almost be a transcription of a religious aria.

The finale is a dance with an energetic swing. Usually in a movement by Bach like this, the return of the opening ritornello goes on a journey through various keys. But that is not what happens in this movement. The solo passages adhere to type, venturing further afield and becoming more and more extravagant in their elaboration. But here, delightfully, the orchestral ritornelli refuse to budge from E major, reiterating again and again the dancing eight bars with which they began.

CONCERTO FOR TWO VIOLINS IN D MINOR, BWV 1043
Duration: approx. 15 minutes

Vivace
Largo ma non tanto
Allegro

Perhaps the best loved of all Bach's concertos, this work partly owes the development of its reputation in modern times to an early recording. In 1915, Fritz Kreisler and Efrem Zimbalist recorded the concerto with a string quartet (it being impossible with the recording technology of those days to record a full orchestra). This intimate performance came singing through the surface noise of the old shellac discs, and found its place in record collections across the world. The Double Concerto makes a fascinating comparison with Bach's concertos for single violin. Being in a minor key, it has much in common with the solo Violin Concerto in A minor – the sturdiness of the outer movements, the vocal quality of the slow movement. But throughout the concerto, the two violins are in duet and, furthermore, in counterpoint. With great energy in the outer movements, and great subtlety in the slow movement, the two parts chase each other, imitate each other, take it in turns to be the principal voice or the descant. Sometimes it is like listening to a vigorous two-part fugue, at other times it is like two voices singing a sublime duet from a cantata.

The fugal quality is evident straight away. In the opening ritornello, the voices enter in turn with a theme of a rising scale followed by leaps – the second violins, the first violins, the bass – setting up the soloists for their entry. When it comes, the soloists play a new theme that playfully reverses the shape of the opening theme – leaps followed by a descending scale. The whole movement consists of a dialogue constructed from the various elements of these two themes, teasing out their possibilities.

The slow movement consists of continuous two-part counterpoint for the two soloists, with the orchestra supplying an accompaniment of soft chords. There are at least four distinct thematic patterns – a falling line, repeated arpeggios, a rising and falling scale shape, a repeated pattern with falling leaps – but all woven so subtly and seamlessly together as to create a sense of a never-ending song.

In the finale, the fugal quality becomes even more intense than in the first movement, with the soloists at first chasing each other at a distance of only one beat, and then breaking into energetic triplet rhythm. But even in this highly energetic movement Bach finds time for moments of lyrical beauty, as one violin plays yearning phrases while the other maintains the vigorous momentum underneath.

CONCERTO FOR OBOE AND VIOLIN IN C MINOR, BWV 1060(R)
Duration: approx. 15 minutes

Allegro
Adagio
Allegro

This work survives in Bach's version for two harpsichords. But the range and character of the melodic lines have persuaded scholars that this is a transcription of a lost concerto for oboe and violin, and it is in that form that it is most often played. This beautiful concerto has many of the qualities of the Concerto for Two Violins. But (assuming the scholars are right about the instrumentation) a solo oboe brings out in Bach a particular vein of lyricism (as in the cantata 'Ich habe genug' and the slow movements of Brandenburg Concertos Nos 1 and 2). Putting the oboe in duet with a violin also has the effect of constraining the virtuoso element in the violin writing, giving the concerto a particular feel of chamber music – indeed, the oboe is, if anything, the leader of the two soloists.

The main theme of the first movement sets off with balanced pairs of phrases, which are formed of balanced pairs of sub-phrases, which in turn contain balanced rising and falling pairs of notes. This all adds up to a beautifully constructed theme with the poise of dance – very different in character from the more forthright movements that open Bach's other minor-key concerto movements (the Violin Concerto in A minor, the Concerto for Two Violins, the Harpsichord Concerto in D minor). The dance-like character persists through passages in which oboe and violin imitate each other in counterpoint, like a pair of dancers weaving patterns, hand in hand, through the corps de ballet.

If the first movement evokes dance, in the second the soloists seem to have left the ground. Over a gentle pizzicato accompaniment, the oboe floats a line that curls round in circles, falling without coming to rest, rising higher, falling a little, rising higher still, before the violin enters and the two airborne creatures weave an endless pattern round each other. Two-thirds of the way through the movement, the lines finally reach a point of rest. Here the accompanying strings change from pizzicato to sustained chords played with the bows, only the bass continuing to be plucked. Over this each soloist in turn sings a line, the other answering only with an accompanying phrase. This is a sublime moment, the finding of some kind of centre of calm. After a few bars, the pizzicato accompaniment resumes, the soloists reprise the opening of the movement, bringing it not to a full close in the movement's key of E flat major, but to a pause on an expectant chord of G major, ready to return to C minor for the finale.

After the floating of the slow movement, the finale is a joyful dance, faster and lighter than the first movement, and with passages in which the violin, for the first time, is allowed some virtuoso elaboration. It is these passages (preserved in the first harpsichord part of the surviving Concerto for Two Harpsichords) that most clearly indicate that this was originally a violin part.

CONCERTO FOR FLUTE, VIOLIN, AND HARPSICHORD IN A MINOR, BWV 1044
Duration: approx. 21 minutes

Allegro
Adagio, ma non tanto, e dolce
Alla breve

This concerto is scored for the same combination as Brandenburg Concerto No. 5, which, with its revolutionary deployment of the harpsichord as a soloist in a concerto, could be seen as the prototype for this work. But Bach derived his material for this concerto from quite different sources. The first and third movement take some ideas from a Prelude and Fugue in A minor for Solo Harpsichord (BWV 894), and the slow movement is taken from a Trio Sonata for Organ (BWV 527). The first movement is particularly intricate rhythmically – even more so than the first movement of Brandenburg No. 5 – with a theme that incorporates duplet rhythms, triplet rhythms, and dotted rhythms (though quite how the dotted rhythms are meant to be played against the triplet rhythms is a question that continues to exercise scholars). With all this profusion of events, the tempo, though notionally Allegro, has to be moderate, and the rhythms need to be clear and light, if the music is not to sound dense. Even more than Bach's other concertos, it works best as intimate chamber music, which is undoubtedly how it would have been heard at his Collegium Musicum concerts in Leipzig.

After the determined intricacy of the first movement, the second comes as a gentle refreshment. This is a transcription of a movement from one of Bach's Trio Sonatas for Organ. As in the fifth Brandenburg Concerto it is for the three soloists alone, but is in effect for four voices, the harpsichordist's right hand playing a treble part in counterpoint with violin and flute, the left hand playing the bass (Bach has cleverly adapted the three voices of the original organ piece to achieve this). The movement begins with a particularly beautiful texture, in which the harpsichord and flute play a duet, while the violin plays accompanying arpeggios pizzicato. Then the violin joins in with the bow, turning the duet into a trio. Throughout the movement, the violin alternates between accompanying pizzicato and solo bowed passages, creating an effect like the alternating ritornello and solo sections in the outer movements.

The finale (again like that of Brandenburg No. 5) begins like a fugue, but this is a 'double fugue', in which each entry of the theme is accompanied by a counterpoint in another part. Fugal passages for orchestra alternate with solo passages, as usual. But in this movement the focus is on the harpsichord, which breaks away from the solemnity of the fugue with flamboyant running triplets, and plays a cadenza before the final ritornello. The solo violin and flute stand back and accompany this display. It is quite an odd finale after the interaction of the solo trio in the earlier movements. We must imagine Bach himself, one of the great keyboard players of his time, relishing this opportunity to display his skills.

Orchestral Suites (Ouvertures), BWV 1066–1069

As with the violin concertos and harpsichord concertos, scholars' dating of these suites has changed over the years. They are now thought to have been composed, like the concertos, during Bach's period in Leipzig, for concerts of the Collegium Musicum. No. 1 in C major and

No. 3 in D major are the earliest, from around 1725, No. 4 in D major was composed a few years later, and No. 2 in B minor about 1739, which is likely to mean that it was Bach's last orchestral work (though there is some evidence for there having been an earlier version in A minor).

Bach called these Suites 'Ouvertures'. This term derives from the French overture first established by Lully to open his ballets and operas at the court of Louis XIV in the late seventeenth century. The French often grouped suites of dances together, preceding them with an overture, and this is the custom that Bach follows here. It is less confusing to refer to them as Suites, as is usual today, leaving the term Overture to refer to the opening movements.

The French influence in Bach's suites is evident not only in the dances themselves, but also in the overtures. These have the classic French format established by Lully, with a stately opening section incorporating assertive dotted rhythms, followed by a fast section in which the instruments enter in turn, as in a fugue, and often rounded off by a brief reprise of the stately opening. The dances that follow are a varied selection taken from the French repertoire, in many cases consisting of a pair of dances in which the first is repeated after the second (as in the 'Minuet and Trio').

In all four of the opening movements, Bach indicates that the fast section and the reprise of the slow section are to be repeated, but this makes for a long movement and the repeat is often omitted.

SUITE NO. 1 IN C MAJOR, BWV 1066
Duration: approx. 20 minutes

Overture
Courante
Gavottes 1 and 2
Forlane
Menuets 1 and 2
Bourées 1 and 2
Passepieds 1 and 2

This suite is scored for two oboes, bassoon, strings, and continuo. Of all the four suites, this is the one that is lightest on its feet, right from the delightful fast section of the overture. The oboes give an extra brightness to the sound, and, with the bassoon, feature from time to time as a solo group. In the overture, this wind trio plays solo sections that alternate with the more extended passages played by the full orchestra, like the alternations between solo and ritornello sections in a concerto. In the second of the gavottes, the oboes play a mellifluous duet against a fanfare-like motif in the strings. The second of the bourrées is a wind trio in the minor, contrasting with the delightfully sprightly first bourrée. And in the second passepied, the oboes play a swirling figure, like rustic bagpipes, while, below them, all the violins and violas play the melody of the first passepied in sonorous unison.

SUITE NO. 2 IN B MINOR, BWV 1067
Duration: approx. 20 minutes

Overture
Rondeau
Sarabande
Bourrées 1 and 2
Polonaise (lentement) and Double
Menuet
Badinerie

This suite is scored for flute, strings and continuo. It is the gentlest of the four suites, particularly when the flute is a baroque instrument – the modern flute has more cutting power, and can hold its own against a larger body of strings. Sometimes the flute plays as a soloist, but most often it plays along with the first violins, providing a silvery sheen to their tone (an effect that Haydn and Berlioz later relished). The flute was a favourite instrument of the French, and the elaboration of the melodic line in the opening section of the overture is very French in style. As in the first suite, concerto-like passages for solo flute punctuate the fast section of the overture.

The 'rondeau' was a favourite genre of French composers for harpsichord (Rameau, Couperin, and others), in which the opening strain recurs, interspersed with episodes of different material (as in the later 'rondo'). Here, the episodes also contain references to the opening theme, making for a subtly fluid form. In the rondeau and sarabande, the flute plays along with the violins. But in the second bourrée, the flute strikes out on its own, with playful running passages. The same happens in the 'double' of the polonaise. This has the melody of the polonaise in the bass, while the flute elaborates a flamboyant descant above it. But Bach is saving the most flamboyant display until last. After a poised minuet, in which the flute again joins the violins, the suite ends with an energetic 'badinerie' ('banter'): a fast dance movement, light as a feather, with playful syncopations in the violins against the virtuoso flute part.

SUITE NO. 3 IN D MAJOR, BWV 1068
Duration: approx. 20 minutes

Overture
Air
Gavottes 1 and 2
Bourrée
Gigue

This suite is scored for three trumpets, two oboes, timpani, strings, and continuo. With its trumpets and drums, this is a baroque orchestra on a grand scale, as in the largest of Bach's church cantatas written for festive occasions. After the splendid overture, there follows one of those heart-stopping moments when Bach does what you least expect. Instead of a courtly dance, Bach writes an 'air' for strings alone, which has become the most celebrated piece in his entire output. Over a treading bass line (which Bach certainly did not intend to be as reverentially slow as in some performances), a soaring melodic line gradually develops. Part of the secret of its beauty lies in the harmonies that underpin it. From the home key of D major, the music travels to the key of A major – the move up a fifth that is conventional at the end of the first section. But in the longer second section, it travels on an extensive journey – through E minor, B minor, touching briefly on A major and the home D major, then rising through a sequence of G major, A major, B minor, and E minor, touching again on the home key of D major, glancing sideways to G major, before finally deciding to head for home. It is a triumph of the art of expectations raised, delayed, and finally fulfilled, enhanced by a melody that responds sensitively to each stage of the journey, and inner voices that accompany with the most sensitive counterpoint.

The air is the one quiet movement in an otherwise boisterous suite that continues with a stately pair of gavottes, a dashing pair of bourrées, and a swinging gigue. It is tricky to pace and balance this suite so that the dances do not just seem like a sequence of rather similar movements after the serenity of the air.

SUITE NO. 4 IN D MAJOR, BWV 1069
Duration: approx. 20 minutes

Overture
Bourrées 1 and 2
Gavotte
Menuets 1 and 2
Rejouissance

This suite is scored for three trumpets, three oboes, bassoon, strings, and continuo, beating the grandeur of the third suite by one additional oboe. This might seem an insignificant difference, but the trio of oboes shows its effect straight away as the overture opens: the three oboes create a dialogue of equals with the three upper string parts (two violins and viola). Later, they play in unison with the strings. So they provide an extra richness both to the texture and to the counterpoint of the music. As in the other suites, there are also concerto-like solo passages for the woodwind. In the first of the bourrées, oboes and strings alternate (without trumpets), and in the second bourrée the bassoon provides a delightful running bass. The (single) gavotte is a stocky dance, which includes trumpets and timpani. The trumpets again fall silent for the two elegant minuets, the first doubling oboes and strings, the second for strings alone. Finally, trumpets and drums join in for the 'réjouissance' ('rejoicing'), a splendid dance in three-time, but with rather complex phrase structures that playfully throw the metre in doubt.

The overture to this suite also occurs as the opening movement of the Christmas cantata 'Unser Mund sei voll Lachens' (Cantata No. 110, 'Let our mouth be full of laughter'), in which, after the grand opening, the voices enter joyfully with running 'laughter' at the start of the fast section.

MILY BALAKIREV
(1837–1910)

Balakirev was one of the great galvanizers in the history of music. Drawing on the ideas of Glinka, who encouraged him as a young man, he promoted a distinctly Russian approach to composition, gathering around him a group of composers who became known as 'The Five' or 'The Mighty Handful'. The latter was the epithet given to them by the critic Vladimir Stasov, who was important in helping Balakirev and his circle to develop their ideas. The group included Musorgsky, Borodin, and Rimsky-Korsakov, all of whom received crucial encouragement and (often forceful) advice from Balakirev. One of them, César Cui, wrote that their early gatherings 'consisted of playing through everything that had been written by all the greatest composers, and all works were subjected to criticism and analysis in all their creative and technical aspects. We were young and our judgements were harsh. We were very disrespectful in our attitude toward Mozart and Mendelssohn; to the latter we opposed Schumann, who was then ignored by everyone. We were very enthusiastic about Liszt and Berlioz. We worshipped Chopin and Glinka.'[1] Balakirev was also one of the driving forces behind the establishment of a new Free School of Music in St Petersburg, of which he was first vice-president and then president. This was established in opposition to the German-trained Anton Rubinstein and the conservative, Germanic principles of his St Petersburg Conservatoire (which was also new), and the emphasis of the Free School on Russian choral and orchestral music gave a boost to developing a Russian school of composition.

One of the important elements in this development was the study of Russian folk song. Balakirev himself published an important collection of Russian folk songs in 1866, and in his own music showed how such material and its styles could be used convincingly in large-scale works (again, following the lead of Glinka).

During the 1870s his musical career was interrupted by a breakdown, and he worked for a time in a railway office and became devoted to the Orthodox Church. He did later return to head the Free Music School, but he had lost his reforming zeal and had become a more reactionary figure. His most important activity as a composer was now to complete major works that he had started in the 1860s. The most substantial of these were the symphonic poem *Tamara* and his First Symphony.[2]

SYMPHONY NO. 1 IN C MAJOR
Duration: approx. 43 minutes

Largo – Allegro vivo
Scherzo: Vivo – poco meno mosso – Tempo 1
Andante
Finale: Allegro moderato

Balakirev composed few large-scale works, but this symphony is undoubtedly his masterpiece. He started work on it in 1864. Two years later he had abandoned it, and it was not until the 1890s that he returned to the work, conducting the premiere in 1897 at a Free School concert in St Petersburg. This was his last appearance in public as a conductor. Despite the three decades from beginning to completion, there is nothing patchy or incoherent about the symphony. It is as 'Russian' as Borodin's symphonies, and as skilfully composed as Tchaikovsky's. It encapsulates Balakirev's passion for Russian culture but demonstrates the extent to which he had absorbed the styles and working methods of the great classical composers of Western Europe.

In August 1864, Balakirev wrote to César Cui, 'I hope, though I am not yet sure, that I shall bring the first *allegro* to Petersburg completed, introducing a Russian element of a religious nature, which is new ...'[3] According to Rimsky-Korsakov, by the time Balakirev set the score aside in 1866, 'About one third of the first movement was already written down in score. As well as this, there were sketches for a scherzo [which he subsequently moved to the Second Symphony], and also for a finale on the Russian theme "Sharlatarla from Patarla", which I was responsible for bringing to his notice. It had been sung to me by Uncle Pyotr Petrovich.'[4] This was a song that Rimsky published in his volume of 100 Russian Folk Songs in the 1870s. There are two other folk songs in the finale, the second of which Balakirev heard sung by a blind beggar while travelling by train in Finland.

The finale is the most obviously Russian of the movements, with its relatively straightforward deployment of the three folk songs. The earlier movements are much more complex. They too contain themes that suggest folk song, but Balakirev uses them very subtly. The first movement in particular is a very striking take on the classic symphonic first movement. Although it is based on traditional procedures of classical models, it treats them with great fluidity, and its landmarks are not nearly as obvious as in most symphonic movements. The composer who comes closest to Balakirev's method is Schumann, who was particularly (and unfashionably) admired by the Balakirev circle. Balakirev bases the whole movement on motifs that are presented at the beginning, and like Schumann he comes dangerously close to seeming obsessional about them. But in a good performance the movement can have an irresistible power.

The symphony opens with a very slow introduction. Two motifs alternate, and the entire movement is built from them. The first is a simple five-note shape played in stark octaves, like a fragment of an Orthodox chant – perhaps this is what Balakirev meant when he wrote of introducing 'a Russian element of a religious nature'. This is immediately joined by a little staccato counterpoint. To the end of this phrase the violas append a little curling shape – this is the second motif. The interweaving counterpoint of this passage also has quite a religious aura. The sequence is repeated, with the second motif rising to the first violins. After a few meditative bars in the woodwind, they set up a gentle pulsation, against which the first motif begins its long journey of exploration, passing from horn to oboe to violins to brass.

A build-up leads into the Allegro. Now the first motif is rounded off with a flourish to create a fast, vigorous theme. As it develops, it is also heard in counterpoint at half speed. Soon the second motif takes over, and passes from instrument to instrument. Eventually the first motif returns, builds to a climax, and fades to bring the first section of the movement to a close. The music has a fascinating character, mixing Russian and non-Russian influences. The reliance on simple repetition varied with different orchestration is very Russian, going back to Glinka's *Kamarinskaya*. But the persistence and development of motifs first declared in the introduction is very Schumannesque.

The Schumannesque method persists through the rest of the movement. The two motifs have already been varied and developed, and now that process is taken further. Having arrived in G major (the traditional arrival from a beginning in C major), trombone and tuba descend to E flat (a shift straight out of Schubert's 'Great' C major Symphony), and the development sets off in that key. The first motif continually changes character: at first the woodwind throw fragments around, then they halve it in speed over another pulsating triplet rhythm in the strings. As this rises in the violins, it breaks into a more determined four-square metre. The first motif (complete with its flourish) sets off pizzicato in the bass, and is answered by the cor anglais (Balakirev uses the plangent tone of the cor anglais very freely). Twice the music builds to a climax, and then, as it reaches a conclusive cadence, there is the feeling that some sort of turning point has been reached.

There is a sudden hush, and the second motif is wistfully recalled, as the music moves through a series of minor keys. The sense of nostalgia deepens, culminating in a beautiful passage for muted violins. From another moment of calm, forces begin to gather. The key continually shifts, until, over a sustained bass note and growing excitement, we find ourselves back in the home key of C major.

A horn calmly recalls the first motif in its simple form (this is the nearest we get to any sense of reprise in this very fluid movement). Woodwind answer with swirls that could have come out of Rimsky-Korsakov's *Scheherazade*, though it is impossible to know whether Balakirev thought of this touch before or after Rimsky. The first motif builds up, and then suddenly bursts into the return of an energetic fortissimo passage. From a sudden hush, the music once more builds gradually, using the second motif as its source of power. From another climax the music breaks into a faster tempo, and with one last ascent the movement culminates in a final peroration.

The scherzo in A minor was newly composed in the 1890s. At times it has the lightness of Mendelssohn's fairy music, but combines it with the vigour of Russian dance – the sort of blend for which Tchaikovsky was by now famous. The scherzo works away persistently at a little figure, which begins in the strings and is then tossed between them and the woodwind. A folk-song-like second melody passes from cor anglais to oboe and clarinet. The first theme returns, delicately at first in the woodwind, boldly in the strings, then combined with the second theme and reaching a blazing climax. In the final blaze, trumpets alternate between major and minor third, giving a powerful hint of menace.

The singing melody of the trio has a particularly Russian character as it floats ambiguously between different keys. It moves to the woodwind, with a charming, rather Tchaikovskian accompanying figure dancing in the violas. In the second half the melody is developed, moving through new keys. It returns to the home key (D minor) high in the violins, but subtly changed so that its ambiguities have been removed.

The scherzo is repeated, and then Balakirev adds a coda. Caught up in the final blaze, the melody from the scherzo gradually quietens. At the end, a piccolo wistfully mulls over the melody, adding a 'blue' flattened seventh, which gives a particularly poignant edge to the final bars.

For the slow movement, Balakirev moves to a remote key, D flat major. Over harp and murmuring strings, a clarinet sings a sustained melody that circles around a few notes over an unchanging bass note, evoking a traditional kind of free Slavic song (as Borodin had done in the slow movement of his Second Symphony). A middle strain takes the melody further afield, before clarinet and flute round it off with a return to the first part. This melody returns several times through the movement, interleaved with episodes. The first of these does not venture far, passing round a falling phrase from the middle strain of the theme, before clarinets and flutes bring the first phrase of the melody back, its final note drooping a semitone lower, and violins answering with the falling phrase. The next episode seems to enter new territory, with a singing cello theme. But it too is derived from the middle of the first theme, expanding its rise and fall in waves, and is then taken up passionately by the violins. As it subsides, the cor anglais touches on the first theme, and its opening phrase passes from instrument to instrument over shuddering tremolo, until it descends to a low bassoon.

There is a new start, in a new key. Cellos begin to embark again on the middle strain of the theme. But the other familiar elements intervene – the rising wave, the falling phrase – and these combine as they search through different keys. Eventually the music builds, turns a corner, and arrives back at the home key of D flat major. The violins and cellos embark on a full reprise of the theme, supported by a newly energetic pattern in the middle strings. There is a further series of waves, another diversion to a distant key, and a glorious final climax as the music returns to D flat major. Soon, the shuddering tremolo returns, over which the clarinet recalls the theme for the last time. But now the meditation is interrupted by sudden harp arpeggios, and with further shifts of harmony we are propelled into C major and straight into the finale.

The first of the three folk songs, provided by Rimsky-Korsakov's uncle, is a jovial patter-song in C major, whose humour derives from its repetition of three-bar phrases. If it seems comfortably at home here, this is partly because its opening phrase turns out to be an elaboration of the symphony's very first motif (though how Balakirev arrived at this neat link is unknowable). The tune starts in the bass (as if sung by an uncle), and then passes round the orchestra in a playful game of catch. Balakirev varies the orchestration in the classic style that originated with Glinka's *Kamarinskaya*, but he also varies and develops the tune in a sophisticated journey through different keys. It climaxes, fades, and hands over to the second song, in D major.

This tune, sung by the blind beggar, is introduced by a clarinet. It consists of repeated notes and swirls in an energetic jig rhythm, similar in its 'oriental' character to the last movement of Rimsky-Korsakov's *Scheherazade* – Balakirev had earlier begun his piano piece, *Islamey*, with a real Caucasian tune of this genre. The harmonies hover ambiguously between major and minor keys, like the trio of the scherzo. This tune too is thrown around the orchestra with delightfully varied accompaniments.

The metre steadies from jig to 'straight' rhythm, and the cellos play the third folk song, a sturdy tune with an offbeat kick. It is soon gone, giving way to a renewal of the second, jig tune, at first on blazing full orchestra and then dispersing into more playful banter. It fades, there is a moment of calm, and the first tune returns in the cellos and basses. Balakirev develops the theme, with sudden accents over held bass notes, surprising changes of key, and building in power. Before long this evaporates, and the second tune returns. This too is changed. It is high on muted violins, and it has acquired a scintillating accompaniment of rapid woodwind arpeggios, harp and triangle. It alternates with the 'straight' third tune. Then, over a held bass note and drum roll, the second tune begins to build. Bursts of the first tune are played against it by the brass. This climaxes in a full orchestral reprise of the first tune, followed after a moment of gathering by the second tune. The end must be near, but first there is another quiet moment in which the cellos return to the third tune, now very high, which emphasizes its rather plangent quality. Soon the metre changes to the stately three-time of a Polonaise, and in this new guise the first theme builds to a final climax to bring this exhilarating movement to a close.

SAMUEL BARBER
(1910–81)

Barber was one of a generation of American composers who grew up in a world of fragmenting modernism. But, like his slightly older contemporary, Aaron Copland, he was not afraid to offer an emotional experience through traditional means. In 1971 he said, 'When

I write an abstract piano sonata or a concerto, I write what I feel. I'm not a very self-conscious composer. It is said I have no style at all, but that doesn't matter. I just go on doing, as they say, my thing. I believe this takes a certain courage.'[1]

Barber composed across a wide spectrum: operas, symphonies, concertos, chamber music, choral works, and song. But he is famous for music that shows him as a master of direct and vivid evocation. His best-known vocal work, a setting of James Agee's 'Knoxville: Summer 1915' for soprano and orchestra, brings the text to life perfectly: 'It has become that time of evening when people sit on their porches, rocking gently and talking gently and watching the street and the standing up into their sphere of possession of the trees, of birds' hung havens, hangars … the talk is quiet, of nothing in particular, of nothing at all in particular, of nothing at all.' Barber's response to such a scene is perfectly judged. Of his orchestral works, by far the most frequently played is not a symphony or concerto, but a piece that lasts less than ten minutes.

ADAGIO FOR STRINGS, OP. 11
Duration: approx. 9 minutes

Barber's Adagio for Strings began life as the second movement of his String Quartet in B minor (1936). The conductor Arturo Toscanini had expressed interest in conducting a work by Barber (a rare honour – Toscanini included few contemporary pieces in his programmes). Barber sent him a new work – *Essay* – and an arrangement of the Adagio for full orchestral strings. The two works were broadcast by Toscanini and the NBC Symphony Orchestra on 5 November 1938. Olin Downes, music critic of *The New York Times*, wrote, 'The Adagio … is not pretentious music … This is the product of a musically creative nature … who leaves nothing undone to achieve something as perfect in mass and detail as his craftsmanship permits.'[2] But the broadcast and its reception sparked off a fierce debate in the letters column of *The New York Times* about tradition and modernism. One correspondent, Ashley Pettis, described Barber's music as 'utterly anachronistic as the utterance of a young man of 28, A.D. 1938!' Barber's partner and fellow composer, Gian Carlo Menotti, leapt to his defence: 'Must there be in art one "modern idiom"? … it was very amusing for Mr. Pettis' generation to be revolutionists. But now let them recognize that the younger generation is left with the thankless job of building on their ruins.'[3]

Barber's Adagio has suffered the same fate in the United States that Elgar's 'Nimrod' has undergone in Great Britain: it has become a piece to be wheeled out solemnly at funerals and ceremonies of remembrance. In a poll held in 2004 by the BBC's *Today* programme, it was voted 'the world's saddest music', beating Dido's 'Lament' from Purcell's *Dido and Aeneas* by a large margin. But, as with 'Nimrod', there was nothing funereal in the composer's mind. Barber wrote his String Quartet while staying in a gamekeeper's cottage with Menotti in an idyllic setting overlooking a lake in the Austrian Tyrol, in the summer of 1936. On 19 September he wrote, 'I have just finished the slow movement of my quartet today – it is a knockout!' Its enduring ability to move audiences was well summed up by Copland in a radio programme broadcast in 1982 after Barber's death: 'It's really well felt, it's believable you see, it's not phoney. He's not just making it up because he thinks that would sound well. It comes straight from the heart, to use old-fashioned terms. The sense of continuity, the steadiness of the flow, the satisfaction of the arch that it creates from beginning to end. They're all very gratifying, satisfying, and it makes you believe in the sincerity which he obviously put into it.'[4]

On paper, the Adagio looks simple. It consists of a slow chant-like melody that begins in the first violins, migrates to the violas, then to the cellos, and rises to a climax. At first it is supported by chords, then melodies develop in counterpoint in other parts. It has the appearance almost of a piece of Renaissance choral music. (Barber later arranged it for voices, setting the *Agnus Dei*, in 1967.)

The chord with which the Adagio starts gives us the impression that, rather than starting from the beginning, we have joined a process that has already been going on, or that we are returning to a previous thought – or perhaps that it is simply impossible to start from the beginning. In this it is reminiscent of some of Sibelius's beginnings, particularly the opening of *Tapiola*. Barber admired Sibelius, and had recently written a Symphony in one Movement modelled on Sibelius's Seventh Symphony. Sibelius, in turn, expressed his admiration for this work.

The harmonies of the movement – its 'harmonic rhythm' – are one of the features that make it work emotionally. From starting on a chord that seems not to be a beginning, the piece proceeds through a serious of wide-arching, undulating melodic shapes underpinned by chords that never truly settle. Phrases avoid coming to rest on the key-chord, but are always hovering ready to move on. The climax seems ready to reach a great resolution, but then moves firmly (and desolately) away to an unexpected chord, and breaks off in silence. Even the end of the movement fails to settle, ending not on the chord of the key, but on a half-close, an 'imperfect cadence'. So the Adagio is, for all its simplicity and traditional language, a carefully crafted expression of the attempt to reach a goal, but finding that there is no starting point, no resolution, and no end.

VIOLIN CONCERTO, OP. 14
Duration: approx. 22 minutes

Allegro
Andante
Presto in moto perpetuo

Barber's Violin Concerto was commissioned in 1939 by Samuel Fels, a wealthy industrialist who was on the board of the Curtis Institute of Music in Philadelphia. Fels had sponsored and adopted a brilliant young violinist from the Crimea, Iso Briselli, a pupil of the great Carl Flesch, who had taught at Curtis. A commissioned concerto from one of the rising stars among American composers would help to enhance Briselli's career (he was then twenty-six). Barber began work over the summer of 1939 in Switzerland. But the threat of war forced him to return to the United States, and he completed the concerto in Pocono Lake Preserve, Pennsylvania.

The planned premiere of the concerto the following January, however, did not take place. Briselli was pleased with the first two movements when Barber sent them to him. But his violin coach, Albert Meiff, thought that the music gave his pupil too little opportunity for display. He wrote a letter to the sponsor, Samuel Fels, in which he acknowledged that the concerto 'possesses beautiful romantic moods, many sombre and quite interesting parts typical of that composer', but went on, 'it is not a composition gratifying for a violinist to perform. The technical embellishments are very far from the requirements of a modern violinist, and this statement is very mild, because some of the parts are childish in details ...

After a long debate, I did succeed in proving to Iso that the composition has to undergo a "surgical operation" – only the violin part, that is understood ... We worked Sunday for four hours, mostly on the changes. Although I convinced Iso to accept my changes, it is necessary to get in touch with the composer to arrange a special meeting of the three of us.'[5] This intervention does not seem to have resulted in a meeting with the composer.

Meiff clearly saw himself in the line of great violinists who worked with composers on their concertos (indeed he mentions some of them in his letter). If this suggests that he was a man with an exaggerated idea of his own importance, there is delightful corroboration from the composer, Vernon Duke. Duke writes to the cellist Gregor Piatigorsky about the concerto that he is composing for him, and interjects a satirical sketch of Meiff: 'As I am writing this, I have before [me] the crazy countenance of Albert Meiff, whose real name, I understand, is Ascha Meifetz. It is not generally known that Jascha Heifetz has spent most of his life imitating my friend, Ascha Meifetz, and upon achieving some success he made it necessary for the poor man to change his name. It is said of Mr. Meifetz that whenever he plays in public he interrupts the proceedings to exclaim: "What tone!" '[6] Barber sent Briselli the completed finale, which consists of a short perpetuum mobile. Briselli told him (according to Barber's own account) that 'it was not very violinistic', and 'it did not suit musically the other two movements, it seemed to him inconsequential. He wished another movement written' (one can hear the voice of Meiff in all this).

As a result, Barber was released from his contract (though he seems to have been allowed to keep the 50 per cent advance), and the delayed premiere was given by Albert Spalding with the Philadelphia Orchestra under Eugene Ormandy in February 1941. The performance was enthusiastically received. The composer and critic, Virgil Thomson, wrote that the concerto 'cannot fail to charm by its gracious lyrical plenitude and its complete absence of tawdry swank'; but he added, 'the only reason Barber gets way with elementary musical methods is that his heart is pure'. The composer himself, in his notes for the premiere, described the concerto as 'lyric and rather intimate in character'.

Barber did make some minor revisions to the score after its early performances, but the fundamental character and substance of the three movements remained unchanged. His faith in his concerto was well placed: despite its rejection by the violinist for whom it was composed, it has become one of the handful of twentieth-century violin concertos to have established a firm place in the repertoire. It is scored for a modest-sized orchestra, with pairs of wind instruments. The only unusual addition is a piano. Sometimes this has a percussive role, as in Stravinsky or Copland, but more often it contributes to a sense of the concerto verging on chamber music.

The soloist enters straight away, announced by a spread chord of G major on the piano, and supported by strings and horns. The freely developing melody lies somewhere between chant and the improvisation of a folk musician. As it ascends, with the horns calling gently, its harmonies suggest memories of Vaughan Williams. The melody winds its way and comes to rest, the violin rises in a gentle flourish, and the second theme enters on a clarinet. This has a more explicitly 'folksy' character, with the tune enlivened by 'Scotch snaps' (often found in American traditional tunes). It would sound cheerful if it were not for the touch of melancholy in the harmonies and the high held note in the violins. The soloist takes up the melody, linking it with the figurations of the first theme. This prompts the strings to return to the first theme for a moment (now in E major). As it falls back, the soloist introduces a third idea, a vigorous, dancing theme. This settles into a pattern of arpeggios, and builds to a running ascent to bring the first section of the movement to a climax.

A passage for full orchestra injects a note of urgency. Soon it calms, leaving the clarinet remembering its second theme, now made more haunting by the tread of timpani and pizzicato cellos. From the quiet, a low chord on the piano pulls the music away from E major to B flat major. This takes us into the development. The soloist, in dialogue with the orchestra, meditates on the first theme, extending its improvisatory elements to build a broad span, meanwhile plotting a course back to the home key. The tread of the timpani persists as pizzicato. At first the mood is calm, but soon a touch of anxious tension enters, with the harmonies twisting, and the music begins to build. The tensions fall away, the second theme becomes a joyful fanfare on wind and piano, and the first theme returns fortissimo on full orchestra – an unclouded, climactic reprise typical of Barber's boldly traditional style.

From here, the music revisits the second and third themes. At the climax, the strings plunge down forcefully, and over a held E flat the soloist plays a brief moment of cadenza, at first dramatic and fortissimo, then rising and fading. Gently the harmony slips back to G major, and with wistful musings on the second theme, and a last farewell to the first theme, the movement comes to a gentle close.

The theme of the slow movement is again chant-like. Its key hovers ambiguously between E major and C sharp minor, warmer when tending towards E major, more melancholy when veering towards C sharp minor. The theme unfolds expansively on oboe, then moves to cellos, and on to clarinet. By now the key is shifting, and by the time the muted violins take up the theme, it is in B flat minor, accelerating a little and developing intensity. A horn rounds off the paragraph, and, over an expectant string chord, the soloist enters, rising up in a manner that has echoes of Vaughan Williams' *The Lark Ascending*.

A trill leads us to expect a chord of E major and a repeat of the theme from the soloist. But instead, the music turns suddenly to E minor, the opening shape of the theme becomes an assertive call from the wind, and with further harmonic twists we find ourselves in the more troubled middle section of the movement. The solo part now includes chords and more jagged lines. The violinist tries to regain serenity, but is unable to sustain it, and muted trumpets in the background add to a sense of unease.

The unease continues into a short cadenza, which builds to a conventional final trill, as if the soloist is determined to pull back to normality. And indeed, what follows is the reprise of the chant-like theme, now played on the lowest string (G string) of the violin, giving it extra warmth. Suddenly, over hushed tremolando strings, the melody takes a new direction, building in intensity until the full strings burst out to carry the theme to its climax, safely back in E major. Again the soloist takes the music away from safety, and the music builds up once more, this time to a climax in E minor. As it fades, the strings hold an expectant chord – the same chord over which the soloist first entered. This time, instead of ascending, the soloist leaps up, and descends dramatically. String chords tug tragically at the harmonies, the soloist sadly responds, and finds the way back to a serene final chord of E major.

Barber's final perpetuum mobile lasts no more than four minutes – less than half the length of the previous two movements. Early critics thought it insubstantial, but there is a precedent: Ravel's Piano Concerto in G similarly ends with a short, relentless Presto after a chant-like slow movement. It had first been performed in Philadelphia in 1932, when Barber was a student at the Curtis Institute – perhaps he was at the concert. Most of Barber's movement is in a rapid four-beat metre, with three notes per beat (as if the time signature were 12/8). But there are continual cross-rhythms within the pattern, as well as frequent changes of the metre itself. The violin keeps up an almost constant patter of triplet quavers, while the orchestra punctuates with sharp chords, many of them off the beat, occasionally joining in the scamper of quavers. This makes the movement very exciting when played with verve, but it also makes it incredibly difficult to co-ordinate – there can surely never have been a perfor-mance in which everything was exactly in place.

The timpani set the rhythm going, and the soloist enters with the theme. As the movement proceeds, the opening theme returns from time to time to create a rondo. But the rush of notes is so relentless that distinction between the 'theme' and the episodes is subtle. Entry into the episodes is felt mainly because of a sense of moving from one key to another (though even this is not straightforward). A first episode is announced by three loud chords, and soon after-wards a clarinet accompanies with little bursts of trilling. After a return to the opening, there is another episode in which the woodwind break across the prevailing metre with a little fanfare-like gesture. Then the music builds to a climax, at which the orchestral strings take over the return of the rondo theme. The episode that follows is full of little stumbles as the metre changes from bar to bar.

The next appearance of the theme is a simplified version tethered to a single harmony, with trumpet alternating with piano and clarinet. The woodwind then return to their little fanfare-like idea, which is thrown around from instrument to instrument. This provokes a build-up and general mayhem. Out of it steps the soloist with an even faster pattern of notes, and the concerto races to an exhilarating conclusion.

BÉLA BARTÓK
(1881–1945)

At the Budapest Academy, Bartók had a classical training in composition, and studied the piano under a pupil of Liszt – indeed, Bartók established a reputation as a pianist before achieving any success with his compositions. Having studied the music of Wagner and Liszt, and inspired for a time by the new works of Richard Strauss, he struggled to find his voice as a composer. The idea of developing a 'Hungarian' way of composing was in the air, and Bartók, like others, wrote settings of the popular tunes to be heard in the cafés of Budapest. Then, in 1904, he heard a servant girl from Transylvania singing to a baby a song about a fallen apple. Bartók was struck by what seemed its purity and beauty. The following year he set out into the countryside to collect Hungarian folk songs. A fellow pupil from the Academy, Zoltán Kodály, was working on a dissertation on Hungarian folk song. Over the next thirty years Bartók and Kodály carried out a project of collecting the music of rural Hungary and its neighbours, using a cylinder phonograph. By the 1930s they had amassed a collection of about 14,000 items. Many of their recordings still exist, and the characteristic rhythmic and melodic idioms of the music found their way into Bartók's own compositional style.

Bartók wrote: 'The right type of peasant music is most varied and perfect in its forms. Its expressive power is amazing, and at the same time it is void of sentimentality and superfluous ornaments. It is simple, sometimes primitive, but never silly. It is the ideal starting point for a musical renaissance, and a composer in search of new ways cannot be led by a better master.'[1] There was a political dimension to this enthusiasm. What began as a flexing of Hungarian cultural muscles within the Austrian Empire later took on a more urgent and bitter aspect. After the First World War, a socialist government in Hungary was followed by a communist dictatorship in 1919. This was in turn overthrown by conservative military rule. As Bartók wrote in 1920, 'The dictatorship of the military is crushing the intellectual life of the country, just as the dictatorship of the proletariat crushed its economic existence before.'[2] In these conditions the establishing of what seemed a 'true' Hungarian style took on an air of defiant determination.

In the late 1930s Bartók found himself trapped in Hungary, which had allied itself with Hitler. Bartók was a fervent opponent of fascism, but it was only on the death of his mother in December 1939 that he was seriously able to contemplate leaving his country. In the spring of 1940 he undertook a very successful tour of the United States, during which he played a concert with violinist Joseph Szigeti at the Library of Congress in Washington (the recording of this concert reveals a pianist of extraordinarily flexible expression). Then, in October 1940, he emigrated to the USA with his wife, Ditta. They arrived full of hope, but the success that his earlier concert tour had promised did not materialize. There was little interest in his music, and he was increasingly ill with what turned out to be leukemia. In June 1943 the conductor of the Boston Symphony Orchestra, Serge Koussevitzky, commissioned the Concerto for Orchestra, and this sparked off a new lease of life. Bartók composed sketches for a Viola Concerto and had almost completed a Third Piano Concerto by the time of his death.

Three aspects of the peasant music that Bartók collected made a particular impression on him. The first was what he considered the oldest type of song: a rhythmically free, highly expressive 'speaking' style, a sort of recitative. The second was the rhythmic complexity of much of the music. Metres were not just in the straightforward twos, threes, and fours familiar from Western 'art' music. Complex and subtle patterns of threes and twos in combination were widespread, forming groups of fives and sevens. And the third aspect was the scales or modes of the melodies. These old modes, Bartók, said, 'freed me from the tyrannical rule of the major and minor keys.'[3]

Bartók wrote pieces that set or incorporated actual folk tunes, the best known being the Romanian Folk Dances. But the influence of folk music goes much deeper than that. Bartók absorbed the complex rhythms, the phrasing, the insistent repetitions, the melodic inflections of the music that he encountered and collected, and used them as raw material to construct pieces using his classical training. The result of all these influences was a musical language that combines the sophisticated and the 'primitive', the modern and the traditional, the Western and the oriental in a very unusual way. He could be as 'modernist' as Schoenberg and Stravinsky, and some of his music is tough to listen to. This is because he uses a harmonic language that is often highly acerbic, giving a bitter edge to the folk-derived energy and complexity, while at the same time partly derived from it.

Because Bartók's musical language can be harsh and complex, it has often been played in a very hard-edged, aggressive manner. By contrast, the conductor Otto Klemperer wrote of Bartók's own piano-playing, 'The beauty of his tone, the energy and lightness of his playing were unforgettable. It was almost painfully beautiful. He played with great freedom, that was what was so wonderful.'[4] In the light of this, it is instructive to listen to Bartók's own recordings. He plays his music with a dance-like freedom, full of swirling energy, and with rhythm that is anything but mechanical. It is true that he said in a 1927 interview that the piano is an instrument whose inherent nature 'becomes really expressive only by means of the present tendency to use the piano as a percussion instrument'. But when Bartók plays percussively, it is the percussion of feet on the ground, not hammers on metal.[5]

CONCERTO FOR ORCHESTRA
Duration: approx. 37 minutes
Introduzione: Andante non troppo – Allegro vivace
Giuoco delle coppie: Allegretto scherzando
Elegia: Andante non troppo
Intermezzo interrotto: Allegretto
Finale: Pesante – Presto

The Concerto for Orchestra was composed in 1943 for Serge Koussevitzky and the Boston Symphony, who gave the premiere in 1944. It is a concerto in the sense that it is continually pitting strings, woodwind, and brass against each other, somewhat as in the baroque *concerto grosso*. But its overall shape is like a symphony with an extra movement. It is the most straight-forwardly enjoyable of Bartók's major works, dazzling in its orchestration, and vivid in its rhythmic and atmospheric effects. Because of the association in the 1940s of tough modern music with the fight against tyranny, there were some who thought Bartók had lost his bite and had sold out to populism. But denigrating a composer for accessibility is a game that, in the twenty-first century, has mercifully gone out of fashion.

The opening is dark and mysterious, with cellos and basses rising and falling in a pattern of fourths that is to be important throughout the work. Pianissimo trumpets intone a recita-tive, as if heard across the valley from some remote Hungarian or Romanian mountainside. The violins take it up in a passionate outburst. There is a gradual acceleration into the Allegro. This takes the rising and falling fourths from the opening, filling them in to create a vigorous theme full of abrupt energy. The second theme is a quiet, plaintively rocking melody on oboe and then clarinets. Soon the abrupt swirls of the first Allegro theme return, and we are into a development section, as in classical symphonic movements. The clarinet introduces a new, melancholy version of the rising and falling fourths. Then, with a sudden change of mood, the horns punch out a fanfare-like version, and this becomes the subject of a fugue, building to a massive climax. The movement ends with the first two themes in reverse order: first the gentle rocking theme on clarinet, then another acceleration that bursts into the abrupt theme with which the Allegro began, and a final blast of the brass fanfare.

The second movement in the published score is headed 'Giuoco delle coppie' (game of the couples), though Bartók had earlier marked it, 'Presentando le coppie' (presenting the couples). Pairs of instruments in turn take up a strain of the tune, like dancers stepping into the circle. Each pair plays a different interval apart. A teasing dance rhythm on the side drum introduces first a pair of bassoons, playing a sixth apart. They are followed by oboes a third apart. Clarinets are a seventh apart, flutes a fifth, finally, a mysterious tremolo in the violins intro-duces muted trumpets a second apart. This use of diminishing intervals was something that Bartók had come across in Dalmatian folk tunes, in a collection of Serbo-Croat music that he had recently been editing. In the centre of the movement is a stately brass chorale. Then the pairs return in the same order as before, but with the textures now made more complex by the addition of other instruments. The bassoons are joined by a third bassoon playing a witty running bass line. Oboes are joined by clarinets, clarinets by flutes, flutes by the rest of the woodwind. The muted trumpets are made to sound even more mysterious by harp glissandi. The movement ends as it began, with the pattern on the side drum fading away.

Most of Bartók's Concerto for Orchestra is fascinating and playful. But at its heart lies a beautiful, poignant Elegy, which takes up the atmosphere of the slow Introduction and intensifies it. It opens, like the Introduction, with a pattern of fourths, descending in the double basses, then rising with a chromatic twist in the upper strings. A high oboe plays a slow incantation, circling round three adjacent notes of the chromatic scale. It is accompanied by chromatic swirls on the clarinets, reminiscent of the lake of tears in Bartók's *Bluebeard's Castle*. Into this hushed atmosphere breaks the passionate folk recitative on violins from the Introduction. Here it is developed powerfully to form the climactic centre of the movement. After its first outburst it takes on a sense of ritual, as violas and then woodwind repeat a circling pattern again and again. The violins resume their recitative, higher than before, taking it to a yet greater climax, and descending ferociously as they had done in the Introduction, but at greater length and with even more intensity. Clarinet swirls reappear, taking the music back to the atmosphere from which it emerged, ending with a solitary piccolo, stranded in a dark and mysterious landscape.

The Interrupted Serenade is a gentle folk dance, a melody that once more circles round a few notes. There is Eastern pungency in its intervals, and a rhythm that varies between four and five quavers in a bar gives it a floating, unanchored feeling. First it passes among the woodwind instruments, then violas take up a version that is more expansive and less oriental-sounding. After a brief return of the original version, the rhythm stutters and then accelerates. A banal tune gets going in the clarinet. There is what sounds like a guffaw from the brass, then a cackle from the woodwind and grotesque glissandi from the trombones, and the vulgar little tune is hammered out by the violins. This, it turns out, is Bartók's unaffectionate homage to Shostakovich's Seventh Symphony, in which a somewhat similar tune is used to suggest the relentless destructive force of the German assault on Leningrad. After Bartók has satisfactorily vented his spleen, he returns gently to the opening material of the movement.

The finale begins with a horn call, yet another permutation of falling and rising fourths. This sets off a perpetuum mobile, beginning pianissimo, soon winding up to fortissimo. Abrupt rhythmic gestures are thrown insistently around, evoking a wild dance (these are related to the abrupt rhythm of the main theme from the first movement Allegro). The dance quietens and moves to the woodwind, then, after another powerful climax, bassoons take the opening horn call and seem to be starting an unlikely fugue. But this is a false trail, and it disperses into a few bars marked tranquillo in which the horn call is turned upside down and stretched out into a brief moment of meditation. The energy of the movement is not to be stopped for long. Woodwind lead a resurgence of the dancing and swirling. Trumpets play a new version of the horn call, and this leads to another massive climax. It too evaporates, there is a startling glissando on the timpani, and out of gentle harp chords emerges the trumpet fanfare again, now on violas.

This really does turn into a fugue. The peasanty stamping elaboration of the fanfare makes it sound anything but academic, but Bartók develops it in a mock-learned manner, including turning the theme upside down again. After a time, the rhythm becomes more agitated and complex, there are impatient interventions from the strings, and suddenly we are back at the pianissimo of the opening perpetuum mobile. From a mysterious undercurrent, fragments of the theme emerge, both ways up, slowly building to a magnificent climax on the full chorus of brass.

DANCE SUITE
Duration: approx. 17 minutes
Moderato – Allegro molto – Allegro vivace – Molto tranquillo – Comodo – Finale

Bartók was commissioned to write this work in 1923, as part of the celebration of the fiftieth anniversary of the union of Budapest (Kodály and Dohnányi also wrote new works for the occasion). Its Hungarian elements are, appropriately, unmistakable and celebratory.

There are six movements, played without a break, and linked by a recurring lullaby-like theme.

Dance 1 begins with truculent bassoons playing a dogged little phrase with lurching offbeat accents that Bartók described as 'rather Arabic in feeling'. There is then a series of accelerations that are halted in their tracks, before the whole orchestra breaks loose to a climax. The dance ends with a stolid tuba. Then a harp draws the curtain aside, Scheherazade-like, to reveal the gentle lullaby that links the dances.

No. 2 is fast and frantic, with a little figure repeated again and again with changing metre and cross-rhythms. The lullaby leads to No. 3, which consists of several dances alternating in the pattern of a rondo. A playful bassoon begins, a clarinet continues, and strings build to a climax. Then there is a dance in a wildly unstable metre. A piccolo returns to the playful dance, then the strings take up a highly energetic dance with a repetitive pattern. Without slackening the pace, woodwind allude to the lullaby without actually quoting it, and strings bring the series of dances to a rousing end.

No. 4 alternates slow, mysterious chords with a processional recitative on cor anglais and bass clarinet. The lullaby is briefly reprised high on violins. No. 5 remains subdued, built on the insistent repetition of a little figure with oriental-style glissandi, quiet at first, but climaxing in a loud stamping pattern before dying away again.

This leads straight in, without the lullaby, to No. 6, which is fast and energetic. Once again, a little phrase goes round and round, building up through sheer persistence in the brass. It metamorphoses back to the pattern of No. 1, and there is also a reminiscence of No. 3. This evaporates to a reprise of the lullaby for the last time, before the dance is resumed and builds up to a final, emphatic climax.

DIVERTIMENTO FOR STRINGS
Duration: approx. 26 minutes
Allegro non troppo
Molto adagio
Allegro assai

Bartók wrote his Divertimento for Strings in 1939 to a commission by Paul Sacher for his Basel Chamber Orchestra, for whom Bartók had composed the Music for Strings, Percussion and Celesta three years earlier. Sacher lent him a villa in the Swiss countryside, complete with a cook, where Bartók composed the work over the summer. In a letter to his wife, Bartók wrote, 'Divertimento indicates, loosely speaking, amusing, entertaining music. In any case, it entertains me; whether it will fare the same with the worthy audience, remains to be seen. Sacher had asked for an unpretentious piece; simplicity brings with it lightness', though he qualified this by admitting that the first movement includes 'a more sombre motif', and the second (slow) movement is not light at all.[6] It is certainly a more easy-going work than the Music for Strings, Percussion and Celesta, and reveals Bartók's love for baroque music. It is, in effect, a sort of *concerto grosso*, with contrasts between the full string orchestra and passages for solo strings, such as you would find in a concerto by Vivaldi or Corelli.

The first movement begins with stamping chords in a rhythm grouped in threes. But the tune is made up of irregular rhythmic groups that cut against the triple rhythm of the accompanying chords. And the melody keeps on circling around a single note, the fifth of the scale, with a recurrent flattened ('blue') seventh. All this gives a characteristically Bartókian sense of nervous energy and rustic wildness. The tempo eases a little for the second theme. This too plays with the rhythm, grouping a bar of eight beats into 3, 3, and 2. It suggests dancers coyly circling round each other, an effect enhanced by the way the solo strings and the full orchestra alternate bar by bar. This is short-lived, and the pace increases again, the music climaxing in assertive repeated octaves, alternating with quiet comment from the soloists. This first section winds down to a moment of calm. The opening theme returns, now developed further, and this leads on to an extended middle section of the movement in which all the thematic elements are explored with new contrasts, juxtapositions, and changes of pace. Despite the dance-like quality of much of the material, there are powerful climaxes, and hints of darkness or menace. When, finally, the opening chords and melody are reprised, it is with the shapes and textures varied once again as if improvised.

The second movement begins with a very slow and quiet violin melody that rises and then falls chromatically over a creeping accompaniment. The harmonies are strange and unsettled, the whole effect haunting. The melody is taken up by the violas in duet, and then by the cellos. This is interrupted by sudden fortissimo repeated notes, which lead on to an intense passage in which a melodic fragment with a snappy rhythm builds up to a climax. The mood of the quiet opening returns. But now the creeping accompaniment and the melody seem to have become transfixed, and they build up with shrieking trills and swoops to a terrifying climax. This collapses into the depths. Fragments of the opening melody alternate with fortissimo outbursts. The opening returns with rapid, ghostly tremolo in the accompaniment. Twice a fortissimo again bursts in, and the movement ends with a sense of lamentation.

The third movement has a repetitive 'peasant' theme, with alternations between soloists and the full orchestra (as in a *concerto grosso*). It starts in regular three-bar phrases, but then extends in irregular units. There is a second, wilder theme made up of insistent repeated notes ending with a fragment from the first theme. This is punctuated by a slapping pizzicato, in which the string hits the fingerboard (a speciality of Bartók). A little later there is a passage that begins to turn into a fugue. But this dissolves as first the solo cello then the solo violin play a melancholy recitative, which combines in an evocative way improvisatory styles of baroque Italy and the traditional recitatives that Bartók found on his collecting expeditions in Hungary and Romania. A return to the energetic first melody is decorated with trills and whoops. After another attempt to regain the original version of the theme, there is a sudden increase in pace to a frenzied rush. This peters out, and there is a surprising pizzicato little fragment that sounds as if it has stepped out of Johann Strauss's Vienna. The frenzied rush returns, and, with fits and starts, the movement stampedes to a conclusion.

THE MIRACULOUS MANDARIN
Duration: approx. 33 minutes

On 1 January 1917 there appeared in a Hungarian literary periodical a 'pantomine grotesque' called 'The Miraculous Mandarin', by the playwright Menyhért Lengyel. This script for a mimed drama fascinated Bartók: 'Just listen how beautiful the story is. In an "Apache" den, three tramps force a beautiful young girl to seduce men and to lure them into their den, where they will be robbed. The first turns out to be poor, the second likewise, but the third one is a Chinese. The catch is good, the girl entertains him with her dance, the Mandarin's desire is aroused ... but the girl recoils from him. The tramps attack the Mandarin, rob him, smother him with pillows, stab him with a sword, all in vain, because the Mandarin continues watching the girl with eyes full of desire and yearning. – Relying on her feminine ingenuity, the girl complies with the Mandarin's wish, whereupon he drops dead.'[7]

Bartók arranged to meet Lengyel, and the two men signed an agreement for Bartók to compose the score for a staged version of the pantomime. Bartók finished the piano score by June 1919, and Lengyel wrote in his diary, 'the other day Béla Bartók played for us on the piano the music of *The Miraculous Mandarin* ... Wonderful music! Incomparable talent!'[8] A version for piano duet was published in 1925, and sections of it were broadcast on Radio Budapest by Bartók and György Kósa in April 1926. The staged version with orchestra followed that November in Cologne. The conductor of the Cologne premiere, Jenö Szenkár, recalled, 'The uproar was so deafening and threatening that the safety curtain had to be lowered! We did not give up, however, and were not afraid even to go out in front of the curtain – at which the whistling redoubled!'[9] The mayor of Cologne intervened (Konrad Adenauer, later to be the German chancellor), and further performances were cancelled. It was staged in Prague in 1927, but performances in Hungary were banned, and it was not until December 1945, two months after Bartók's death, that it was staged in Budapest.

After the disaster of the premiere, Bartók prepared a concert version of the score. This is often referred to as a 'Suite', but it consists of about two-thirds of the score in a continuous run (with one small cut), from the opening to the point where the Mandarin catches the girl. Bartók wrote a few extra bars to bring it to a satisfactory conclusion. The full score of the stage version was not published until 1955, and even this did not include all of Bartók's music. The complete score was finally published in an edition by the composer's son, Peter Bartók, in 2000.

In an interview published in 1929, Bartók commented on the reception of the work at the staged premiere: 'There were ... various reasons for the demonstrations. Before the performance people had read the plot of the "Mandarin", and had made up their minds that it was objectionable. On the stage the action is carried out at a very brisk pace. From beginning to end the speed is almost breathless, and the effect, accordingly, is quite different from what had been imagined, apparently, by those who had been leisurely speculating upon the possibilities of the subject matter. The "Mandarin" is very much like an Eastern fairy tale, and contains nothing to which exception can be taken.'[10]

Bartók was perhaps being wise after the event. Although much of the work is very fast, the killing of the Mandarin, from the moment when the tramps attempt to smother him to the end where he finally dies, takes about ten minutes, which is hardly 'brisk'. As to what might be found objectionable, that is clearly something that has changed over the century since Lengyel and Bartók conceived the work. In 1926, when it was premiered, the violence and eroticism shown on the stage, and the dissonance of the score, would have been the main sources of objection. Audiences in those days, whether in Germany or in Hungary, would presumably not have been offended by the basic plot, in which a Chinaman with supernatural powers is seduced, taunted and killed. There was a long history in Europe of fearful superstitions about the Orient being used as the basis of drama (one could think of Puccini's *Turandot*, which reached the stage the same year as *The Miraculous Mandarin*). Nearly a century later, the torture and murder of a supernaturally weird Mandarin is a good deal more uncomfortable for audiences – as are the wicked moor, Monostatos, in Mozart's *The Magic Flute*, or the wheedling Jew in Musorgsky's *Pictures at an Exhibition*. But, as Bartók says, the story is basically a macabre rewriting of the classic fairy tale in which the girl takes pity on the bewitched beast (or frog), and her kiss enables him to regain his true identity as a handsome prince. Here, the release is not into life, but into death. Lengyel later observed, 'The true message of the Miraculous Mandarin, of course, is not the excess eroticism but the apotheosis of pure, almost unearthly desire and love.'[11] The pantomime's mixture of sordidness, violence, and unearthly strangeness inspired in Bartók a score to match. The music is as unsettling and vivid as Schoenberg's Five Pieces for Orchestra and *Erwartung* (both 1909), and like them it inhabits a tortured, 'expressionist' world. It has motifs and elements that recur, giving a sense of evolving structure. But the most striking thing about the score is the eerie sense of emotional dynamic, in which a scenario that starts as if it were a bleak comedy becomes a nightmare from which there is no escape.

While he was composing it, Bartók wrote to his wife, 'It will be hellish music if I succeed. The prelude before the curtain goes up will be very short and sound like horrible pandemonium, din, racket and hooting: I lead the honourable audience from the crowded streets of a metropolis into the apaches' den.'[12] The score begins with wild violin scales. Woodwind enter with an urgent, repetitive pattern. A trombone calls like a car horn, in a short–long (yá-daah) rhythm that is often found in Hungarian traditional music and is an important feature of Bartók's style. The 'pandemonium' increases, with the rest of the orchestra entering and the music becoming increasingly dissonant. As the climax falls away, the curtain rises. Over shuddering tremolando strings and drums, violas play a recitative as the first tramp searches his pockets for money, and the second rummages through the drawer of the table. The music becomes more threatening, with trombone glissando, and the third tramp 'advances on the girl and violently orders her to stand by the window to lure men in from the street for the tramps to rob' (stage directions are printed in the score). High violins plaintively echo the viola recitative as the girl refuses. As the other tramps join in the demand, she reluctantly agrees, and the violins descend over poignant chords as she goes to the window (this is the first of many moments where the harmonies are reminiscent of *Bluebeard's Castle*).

Over a low bass clarinet note and pianissimo cello tremolo, the 'First game of seduction' begins. A clarinet plays a free recitative, at first slower than that of the violas, with intervals that reach up tentatively, and then higher, with a flourish – a style inspired by the traditional 'peasant recitative' that so impressed Bartók. A second clarinet joins the first, the agitation increases, and an insistent rhythm, tapped with the wood of the bow on the strings, indicates that the first man is already coming up the stairs. The tramps hide, and a climactic chord gives way to grotesque trombone glissandi as a 'shabby old rake' enters and 'makes comic gestures of love'. The old man has no money, but 'what matters is love'. Cellos and violas play a mock-romantic duet, too dissonant to be the real thing. A seductive melody passes from cor anglais to oboe, then, as he 'becomes more and more importunate', to oboes and clarinets in dissonant duet, and then back to the cellos. As his ardour increases, the tramps 'leap out from their hiding place, seize the old rake and throw him out. They turn angrily to the girl and force her to go to the window again.' The agitation of the music refers back to the first time that the girl was threatened by the tramps.

The clarinet begins the 'second game of seduction', with another recitative, more elaborate and longer than the first. It reaches a height of urgency as the girl sees another man, and the tramps hide. 'A shy young man appears in the door. He is very confused.' An oboe plays a solo over anxious chords. Although he too has no money, the girl 'draws him towards her and dances – at first rather shyly'. Harp and high bassoon begin a tentative dance in an awkward five-time with repetitive phrases and references back to the old man's amorous melody, with its glissandi (the high bassoon and repetitions also evoke memories of *The Rite of Spring*). The melody passes to violins and flutes, then to a magical passage with trills on muted strings and flute. This is the most tender moment in the whole score. The girl is clearly drawn to the young man, and he responds passionately, with the melody on all the violins. This is not what the tramps had in mind, and they once again jump out from their hiding place and throw the young man out (violently agitated music as before). They urge her to have more sense, and to find someone suitable.

The 'third game of seduction' is immediately stranger than the previous two. Cellos and violas play the interval of a tritone (a classically weird interval), and their tremolo is played 'sul ponticello' (near the bridge, giving a glassy effect). The clarinet recitative explores wider and stranger intervals, and the violins punctuate it with sudden flashes of harmonics. The clarinet is joined by the piano, and the music becomes more and more threatening. 'Horrified, she sees a weird figure in the street, which can immediately be heard coming up the stairs.' The music acquires a relentless tread, with high woodwind trills and flurries (another passage reminiscent of *Bluebeard's Castle*). 'The Mandarin enters and remains immobile in the doorway; the girl flees terrified to the opposite end of the room.' There is a fearful climax, with trombone glissandi far more threatening than before. From savage dissonances emerges a simple minor chord: but there is nothing comforting about this sustained sound, which seems to represent the unflinching stare of the Mandarin. As the chord is held quietly by two horns, pizzicato in clashing keys suggests the 'general consternation'. As the girl overcomes her repugnance, and beckons to the Mandarin to come closer and to sit on a chair, tentative phrases are played by flute, clarinet, and oboe. There are brittle chords and flurries as she 'shudders and draws back'.

From this point on, it helps to go back to Lengyel's original script, which inspired Bartók, and which is much more vivid than the summary printed in the score. 'The Mandarin sits down. But fixedly, unrelenting, a darkly earnest look in his eyes, his set face never registering the least emotion, he continues to stare at the girl.' She sits on the Mandarin's lap. 'With the laughing woman lying, wriggling and tossing under his nose, the Mandarin slowly undergoes a peculiar transformation.' He trembles, blushes, starts to blink, and breathes with difficulty: 'His excitement mounts. Minute reflex actions burst forth – a twitch, a shudder passes over him – and a sudden hot rush of blood passing through him starts him shaking all over. The girl looks at him – and gets scared ... She stops laughing, jumps to her feet and backs away.

The Mandarin rises too. He stretches his arms and moves towards her. She flees … The Mandarin follows her, his eyes riveted on her, his face distorted and imploring like that of a sick animal.'[13] In Bartók's score, this passage begins with the most delicate, atonal web of sound with little fragments of yearning melody – a combination that could have come straight out of Schoenberg's Five Orchestral Pieces. The music then settles into a strange, slow waltz. It becomes agitated, settles again, becomes even more agitated, and then reverts to the harsh, statuesque music from the Mandarin's entry. From a quiet, tense moment, the music accelerates to a full-blown Viennese waltz, but with impossibly harsh harmonies together with a rhythm that keeps on breaking into five-time. It accelerates feverishly to a climax of trills (again referring back to the Mandarin's entry), as the girl embraces him and 'he begins to tremble with feverish excitement'. Muted trombones play a persistent, agitated solo, which accelerates into a stamping dance as the girl breaks free and the Mandarin chases her.

Once again, Lengyel's original is far more vivid than the directions printed in the score: 'He moves provocatively, starting to dance with fantastic movements. A strange, grating noise rises from his throat … He is crying – tears streaming down his cheeks … He is completely beside himself – spinning, whirling, with increasingly alarming speed … He is now like a huge spinning top, fanning a whirlwind around him.'[14] This is the most overtly Hungarian passage in the entire score, harking back to Bartók's *Allegro Barbaro*, and looking forward to the earthy dances of the Dance Suite. Its swirling melody derives from the earlier clarinet recitatives in the 'games of seduction'. It begins in the violas and cellos, and is taken up in turn by violins and woodwind as if this were the beginning of a fugue. As the dance becomes wilder, it is punctuated by bursts of the threatening trombone glissando. The Mandarin stumbles for a moment, and then the dance becomes yet more frantic, with increasingly irregular rhythms. At the wildest of climaxes, the Mandarin catches the girl and they fight. This is the point at which the concert version, or 'Suite', ends.

In the complete pantomime, the tramps leap out, and their familiar music returns. They tear the Mandarin from the girl, and strip him of his jewellery and his money. Dissonant brass chords and thumping drums announce their decision to smother him. As they do so, the orchestra plays slow, hideous versions of the swirling patterns and dance rhythms, culminating in shrieking chords. The tramps assume the Mandarin must be suffocated, and they move away as plaintive high woodwind play. 'Suddenly the Mandarin's head appears between the pillows and he looks longingly at the girl. The four shudder and stand aghast.' In a passage of the utmost strangeness, cellos play yearning fragments of melody (these can be traced right back to the melodic shapes associated with the girl at the beginning), while kaleidoscopic flurries of woodwind, harp, piano, celesta, and violin harmonics deepen the mystery. At last, the tramps master their horror, and, in their familiar rhythm, 'They drag the Mandarin out and grip him firmly. They discuss how he is to be killed.' Once more the brass blare out dissonant chords, as 'one of the tramps produces a rusty old sword and stabs the Mandarin three times'. As the music darkens, the Mandarin 'sways, totters, and almost collapses'.

The woodwind rise from the depths, as 'suddenly he draws himself up and leaps at the girl'. When the tramps grasp hold of him again, he 'looks longingly at the girl', as the celesta traces a delicate, otherworldly pattern. With a renewed outburst of violence, the tramps discuss how they are to get rid of the Mandarin, and decide to hang him. As they drag him to the centre of the room and hang him from the lamp hook, a new element of weirdness enters the music. As the timpanist plays a roll, the note slides up and down in a glissando (a new effect made possible by tuning pedals). Together with quiet glissandi in the trombones, cellos, and piano, this creates a truly horrifying effect underneath a slow, dissonant woodwind chorale. This is interrupted as the lamp falls to the floor and goes out.

Once again, Lenyel's original script conveys a disturbing horror that is only hinted at in the published score: 'Suddenly a dim and eerie light looms up in mid-air. The Mandarin's rotund belly – like that of a Buddha, a fantastical sphere floating in the air – begins to shine. The mystic light illuminates the whole figure of the man who has been hanged by his pig-tail – his big, yellow, round head, his eyes starting out of their sockets – eyes that, in a stubborn animal glare and with terrible desire, are turned on the girl like a pair of electric search-lights.' Suddenly the girl 'looks at the Mandarin – for the first time without fear – and smiles'.[15] A wordless chorus sings a mysterious, ritualistic chant, into which fleeting chords are dropped, like water dripping from the roof of a cave. The violas take up the pleading recitative with which the girl tried to resist the tramps right at the beginning. Now, as the Mandarin stares at her, it gradually rises and grows in strength, reaching a truly terrifying climax – the imagination with which Bartók twists and strengthens the harmonies in this passage is astonishing.

There is a silence as the tramps take the Mandarin down, and he falls on the floor. As he leaps up again, 'She resists no longer – they embrace.' This almost atonal passage builds to a passionate climax and falls back. The lowest instruments play a version of the mystic chorus, and chords again drip into the near-silence. 'The Mandarin's longing is now stilled, his wounds begin to bleed, he becomes weaker and dies after a short struggle.' Cor anglais and bass clarinet mournfully recall the swirling motif, and with a series of judders this extraordinary score comes to a close, and the curtain falls.

MUSIC FOR STRINGS, PERCUSSION AND CELESTA
Duration: approx. 28 minutes

Andante tranquillo
Allegro
Adagio
Allegro molto

This work was commissioned in 1936 by Paul Sacher, one of the great champions of new music in the twentieth century, to celebrate the tenth anniversary of his Basel Chamber Orchestra.

Bartók specifies that the strings are to be arranged in two separate groups, left and right of the stage, with the percussion between them and the double basses along the back. The interplay between these two groups in the fast movements gives the concerto echoes of the eighteenth-century Italian *concerto grosso*, a genre of music whose influence on Bartók was second only to that of folk music. The percussion instruments include assorted drums, cymbals, tam tam (gong), xylophone, harp (not often treated as part of the percussion section), and piano. A feature of the timpani part is the prominent use of glissando, achieved by adjusting the pedal-tuning mechanism while the note is sounding. Bartók was the first composer to make extensive use of timpani glissando, though Carl Nielsen had introduced the effect as early as 1916 in his Symphony No. 4. Bartók's highly evocative use of the percussion and the celesta in this work was a landmark in the history of percussion, revealing possibilities that have inspired composers through to the present day.

The piece can sound very different depending on the size of the orchestra playing it. With the full strings of a symphony orchestra, its impact is massive. But Bartók wrote it for a chamber orchestra, and although a chamber orchestra does not have the sheer weight of a full symphony orchestra, there is a gain in transparency of textures, and in the agility of rhythms. This sort of athletic transparency is presumably what Bartók had in mind.

Just looking at the score of the first movement, one might mistake it for an academic exercise. It is a slow fugue, with a complexity worthy of J. S. Bach in his *Art of Fugue*. The violas begin, then the first group of violins enters a fifth higher, then cellos a fifth lower than the violas, then the second group of violins a fifth above the first group, then double basses a fifth below the cellos, and finally a third group of violins a fifth higher than the second group. At the end of the movement the theme is turned upside down, and the entries are spaced closer together (a classic fugal technique called stretto). In the final bars, the original and upside-down versions of the theme are combined. But this is not just an intellectual exercise. It is a movement with a powerful atmosphere. 'Tranquillo' may be the heading, but the mood is unnervingly strange. The theme, though based around the note A, seems to float uncertainly, groping its way by unexpected intervals to find some sense of a key. As the voices enter, they resemble a crowd moving slowly around in total darkness. The fugue builds to a mighty climax, underlined by the first entry of timpani, rolling cymbals, and bass drum. Then the music falls away to pianissimo, with the celesta rippling mysteriously, as if a shaft of moonlight has momentarily revealed the strange scene below. At the end, the movement returns to the note A on which it started.

The shape of the fugue subject is used to form the theme of the second movement, though its character and mood are quite different. This is a punchy Allegro, a swirling, stamping dance, punctuated by strokes of the timpani and interventions of the piano. But the dance proceeds in fits and starts, with passages of fugue, sudden retreats and halts, and wild climaxes. At the centre of the movement, quiet pizzicato leads to a passage of reiterated, irregular rhythms, combining the piano with a pizzicato in which the string hits the fingerboard (a favourite device of Bartók's), the xylophone adding a hard edge. It is as if the whole orchestra has metamorphosed into one giant percussion instrument: Stravinsky surely had this passage in mind when he wrote the first movement of his Symphony in Three Movements a few years later. The tempo eases back into a quiet pizzicato passage that gradually subsides. The swirling re-emerges out of almost nothing and gradually builds up, the two string orchestras pitted against each other (a thrilling effect in the concert hall). Another easing, another acceleration, more fits and starts, and the movement rushes headlong to the end.

In the second movement, the xylophone had the role of focusing the attack. It is the xylophone that creates the atmosphere at the beginning of the third movement Adagio, with a high, expressively rhythmic recitative, like drops of water in a cave, with glissandi on the timpani adding a depth of mystery or even fear. The sense of recitative continues in a theme on violas and violins, a lament that seems full of words, even if the words themselves are left to the imagination. Over a night-time chorus of strange glissandi and trills, with dripping chords on the piano, a more coherent melody emerges high on violins, related in its strange chromatic intervals to the fugue of the first movement. Then the nocturnal background takes over, with rippling arpeggios on celesta, harp, and piano, the melody shuddering in the strings below. This builds up to a sudden explosion, which brings us back to the giant percussion instrument of the second movement. The nocturnal ripplings and the melody resume. The movement ends as it began, the quiet recitative retracing its steps back to the timpani glissandi, and the high xylophone leaving us alone in the darkness.

Of the four movements, the finale is both the most baroque and the most Hungarian in character, and it brings together material and moods from each of the preceding movements. In the outer sections, the choruses of strings answer and argue with each other, almost as in J. S. Bach's third Brandenburg Concerto. But the rhythms are like the wildest of Hungarian dance, with the principal theme breaking a very fast 8-metre into 2–3–3, in an exhilaratingly confusing manner. For a time, simpler rhythms and a more genial manner take over. Then the piano leads off an acceleration that becomes frenzied. At its climax, the pace suddenly drops, and the strings take us right back to the fugue theme that opened the work, but now changed into a sonorous chorale, and freed from its mysterious chromatic harmonies. Gradually the original atmosphere (and harmonies) return, and the music retreats into a shuddering reminiscence of the nocturnal recitative of the Adagio. Soon we are back to the exhilaration of the finale's first theme, and, after further reminiscences of earlier movements, the movement ends abruptly, as if a mood of celebration has finally been snatched from the dark thoughts that have threatened to engulf it.

PIANO CONCERTO NO. 1
Duration: approx. 25 minutes

Allegro moderato
Andante –
Allegro molto

Bartók composed his First Piano Concerto in 1926 at a time when he had become fascinated with Italian baroque music, transcribing a number of Italian works for his own performance (there are recordings of him playing Scarlatti Sonatas in 1929 with great flair). The interaction of piano with orchestra in Bartók's concerto sometimes evokes the baroque *concerto grosso*, but this is only one influence among several. There are echoes of Stravinsky, particularly his recent Concerto for Piano and Wind Instruments. And there is a 'primitive' percussive element that goes back to Bartók's own *Allegro Barbaro* for solo piano of 1911 – though by the 1920s it is impossible to separate this sort of primitivism from that of Stravinsky's *Rite of Spring*. And behind all this stands Bartók the virtuoso pianist, taught by a pupil of Liszt. The First Piano Concerto is a complex, tough work. Years later, having written his Second Piano Concerto, Bartók looked back at the First and concluded, 'I consider it a successful work although its writing is a bit difficult – one might even say very difficult! – as much for orchestra as for audience.'[16]

The orchestra is based on the standard large orchestra, with four horns, two trumpets, three trombones, two of each woodwind. But characteristically, Bartók asks for a large percussion section, needing four players: timpani, four cymbals, gong, high snare-drum, deeper side drum without snares, and bass drum. He gives detailed instructions on how the drums and cymbals are to be struck, and with what sort of stick or mallet, and asks for the percussion instruments to be placed immediately behind the piano, not in their usual place at the back of the stage. In this way, Bartók underlines the importance of the piano and percussion working closely together to provide the rhythmic life and force that drives the music forward. He also lays the groundwork for his Music for Strings, Percussion and Celesta, which was to follow ten years later.

The Concerto opens with a low B right at the bottom of the piano. A succession of timpani beats brings in low horns and trombones. The mood is of a sombre procession, which culminates in fortissimo horns blaring out a savage chant with a kicking syncopation. Bassoons answer with a more stately version of the chant, which curls round on itself. There is an unmistakable echo of Stravinsky's *The Rite of Spring*. Timpani and piano accelerate, and the piano breaks into hammered fortissimo repeated octaves. This is the beginning of the first real theme, though its main elements are drawn from the processional introduction: the repeated notes and the kicking syncopation, features that recur throughout the movement. As the piano develops momentum it is in continual dialogue with the orchestra, particularly the woodwind, in a manner that reflects Bartók's study of baroque music. But there is nothing 'neo-classical' about the mood: the music is possessed by a spirit of relentless drive and rhythmic combat.

This first paragraph culminates in double octaves and hammered, dissonant chords. From this climax emerges a quieter second theme on the piano, with a more playful, dancing character, whose melody is drawn from the savage chant in the introduction. The quiet moment is short-lived. Soon, the piano returns to its relentless rhythms and rushing scales, and the music builds to a second climax like the first. Again there is a sudden quiet. This is the beginning of the development section. The syncopated idea is combined in scales in opposite directions: a clarinet going up, and a bassoon going down. The piano's music becomes like an updated version of a Lisztian cadenza, full of virtuoso flourishes, but with acerbic dissonances. The chant builds from a quiet beginning, is knocked back, and builds again with raucous brass entries. Again the tempo is knocked back, and woodwind and piano exchange the repeated notes of the first theme. These signal the first attempt at a reprise, which becomes more and more violent. By now, the momentum has become unstoppable, and the second theme is dropped into the mix with little sense of easing. From here the music gradually builds to a huge climax, and a final fast dash brings the movement to an end.

The second movement is for piano, percussion, and wind, without strings – Bartók had recently heard a performance of Stravinsky's Concerto for Piano and Wind Instruments, and there are distinct echoes of it in this movement. It begins and ends as a piece for piano and percussion, and these two sections frame a central climax with the woodwind instruments. The opening is built from the simplest and starkest of material: timpani, side drum, and cymbal tap out a hypnotic three-beat rhythm and the piano responds with dissonant chords. The piano opens out to a more flamboyant moment, and then to a concentrated passage of bleak counterpoint. As the music sinks back to its opening simplicity, there are the first, tentative woodwind entries. Piano and percussion settle into another hypnotic tread, and a low clarinet begins a chanting line that seems related to the chant at the beginning of the concerto. Cor anglais and bassoon take up the chant in counterpoint (another moment that conjures up memories of *The Rite of Spring*, as well as Stravinsky's Concerto for Piano and Wind). As other woodwind and horns join in, and the tread of piano and percussion becomes more and more threatening, the chant builds to a powerful climax and falls away. After a moment of piano cadenza, delicate flutes and oboes return to the piano's earlier passage of counterpoint. The three-beat rhythms of the opening return, but now interspersed with pianissimo flourishes and lingering memories of the woodwind chant. Suddenly, the hypnotic side drum bursts into life with a vigorous new rhythm, muted trumpets and trombones enter with menacing glissandi, and we are propelled into the finale.

Over the relentless rhythmic stamping of the strings, the piano throws out fragments of a theme, answered by horns and timpani. These fragments are based on elements from the first movement – hammered repeated notes and rhythmic flurries that in time coalesce into smoother falling and rising shapes. A trumpet makes this into a jauntier tune, urged on by a side-drum rhythm. The texture becomes more complex, with swirling woodwind patterns and rattling piano scales. The music rises to a climax, and violent piano trilling pulls back the tempo, revealing a new version of the fall and rise, in grand octaves. This immediately accelerates, metamorphosing into a combative dance reminiscent of Bartók's *Allegro Barbaro*. Pounding timpani take us into the middle of the movement, in which the elements from the beginning of the movement are developed. The piano's flurries of notes coalesce once more into a continuous pattern, and the rising and falling pattern becomes a brazen call on horns and trombones. This develops into a web of counterpoint. Twice there is a climax. The second time there is a gong stroke, and the stamping rhythm of the opening returns. From this point on, Bartók reprises the elements from the first part of the movement, but all thrown into different relationships, as if the kaleidoscope has been shaken. The music becomes more and more frenzied, until the piano gathers its strength for one last dash.

PIANO CONCERTO NO. 2
Duration: approx. 29 minutes

Allegro
Adagio – presto – adagio
Allegro molto

This concerto was written in 1930–1, when Bartók was at the height of his reputation as a performer as well as a composer. He himself gave the first performance, in Frankfurt, in January 1933. Bartók described this concerto in an analytical note: 'I wanted to produce a piece which would contrast with the first [concerto]; a work which would be less bristling with difficulties for the orchestra and whose thematic material would be more pleasing. This intention explains the rather light and popular character of most of the themes of my latest concerto.'[17]

It is indeed less aggressive than the First Piano Concerto, but it still has those Bartók hallmarks of harmonic toughness and rhythmic energy, which are often in the foreground when he writes for piano. His emphasis on the piano as a percussion instrument is clear in this concerto, though, as in all Bartók, this can easily be taken too far in performance (the opening bars, for example, are marked forte, not fortissimo). Dance is at the root of the energy, as in the folk music and baroque concertos from which Bartók drew inspiration, and the best performances are those that make that clear. This is not easy in a concerto that demands extreme virtuoso technique. There exists a very faint and noisy private recording of extracts from a performance by Bartók himself. The orchestra is almost inaudible, but one can hear that Bartók plays with great dash and rhythmic swagger, not at all mechanically, and, in the slow movement, with a highly characteristic 'speaking rubato'.[18]

The first movement is scored for piano, wind, and percussion, without the strings. This, like the slow movement of the first concerto, is perhaps inspired by Stravinsky's Concerto for Piano and Wind Instruments. It begins with a tumultuous cascade of themes, with elements that are distinct – fanfare, scale, insistent repetition – but share a similarity of character. It reaches a climax, becomes even more frenzied, then slows to a delicate theme with rippling arpeggios. There is renewed frenzy, with hammered repetitions. This all has the feeling of a tussle between piano and wind, as if the piano is struggling to get away or the wind is struggling to hold the piano down. There is another easing, and a pause. The music becomes lighter and more humorous, with the woodwind to the fore – it is more like a dialogue now. Then a series of bravura developments and climaxes, punctuated by pauses, culminate in a massive cadenza. The wind re-enter, with the piano playing rushing scales below, and the movement comes to a climactic close. The overall impression is of a movement of fluctuating frenzy. But there is also a formal logic to it, with the themes that occur at the beginning providing material for discussion through the middle of the movement. At the end of the movement some of these shapes are turned upside down, and reversed. And they will recur in the third movement, giving a sense of unity to the whole work.

After this hyperactivity, the slow movement comes as welcome relief, with a slow, whispered chorale in the strings, marked to be played without vibrato. Its strange, haunting quality arises partly from the fact that the chords are made up of intervals of a fifth piled on top of each other, like the sound of open strings when an orchestra is tuning up (a succession of such chords occurred in one of the rare quiet passages early in the first movement). There is a nocturnal feel to this music, and indeed Bartók himself referred to such evocative passages as his 'night music'. This calm scene alternates with passages in which the piano plays a plaintive recitative, accompanied by rolling timpani.

In total contrast, the central part of the movement is a very rapid and increasingly wild scherzo, which begins pianissimo and gradually builds up to fortissimo. After a trumpet blast, the night music returns, but with the string chorale now rendered shimmering and glassy by bowing rapidly near the bridge, and with the piano playing trills and more agitated fragments. It is as if the intervention of the scherzo has made it impossible to regain the original sense of calm. There is a climax of fortissimo octaves, after which the calm does manage to return.

The finale has as its first theme a stamping, relentless folk dance. Soon the trumpet fanfare from the first movement joins it, and as the movement progresses it becomes increasingly clear that what we are listening to is a varied revisiting of material from the first movement, with the relentless dance as the driving force binding it all together.

PIANO CONCERTO NO. 3
Duration: approx. 23 minutes

Allegretto
Adagio religioso –
Allegro vivace

When Bartók emigrated to the United States in 1940, his final years were dogged by frustration and ill health (see introduction to Bartók). But Koussevitzky's commission of the Concerto for Orchestra sparked off a final burst of activity. Bartók composed a solo Violin Sonata for Yehudi Menuhin, and, following the successful premiere of the Concerto for Orchestra in December 1944, began work on two concertos simultaneously. The Viola Concerto was never completed, and had to be assembled from sketches after his death. The Third Piano Concerto, on the other hand, was virtually complete when Bartók made the final journey from his home to hospital. Only the last seventeen bars needed their orchestration filled in.

This concerto is very different from the previous two. Its style is lyrical and lucid, much less complex or acerbic even than No. 2. To an extent this new style was already audible in the Concerto for Orchestra. In the case of the Third Piano Concerto, there was an additional reason. Bartók composed it for his pianist wife, Ditta, to play, and she had found some of the previous concerto unplayable. It was the composer's hope that she would perform this new concerto and earn some money from it. She had taken part, with her husband, in the premiere of the Concerto for Two Pianos and Percussion (an orchestrated version of the Sonata) at Carnegie Hall in January 1943, the last occasion on which Bartók performed in public. But Ditta's experience of America had been even more unsatisfactory than her husband's, and as soon as she could, in 1946, she returned to Hungary, where she lived for another thirty-seven years. Although she did eventually play the concerto, its premiere was given in February 1946 by György Sándor with the Philadelphia Orchestra under Eugene Ormandy.

Over a shimmering accompaniment, the piano plays in simple octaves a theme in the 'peasant declamatory' style that Bartók derived from the traditional music of Hungary and the Balkans, and which he had made so much his own. The piano's flurries become more complex, metamorphosing into trills, and the violins take up the theme more powerfully. The piano continues with forceful running chords and double octaves in more traditionally grandiose concerto style. These in turn dissolve into a second theme, in which the rippling of the piano is answered by delicate staccato and a breeze-like swirl in the woodwind. The whole theme evokes sounds of nature, a premonition of the 'night music' that will form part of the slow movement. From here, the delicate staccato merges with patterns from the more conventional previous passage, and after a climax the first section of the movement comes quietly to an end in a mood of easy charm.

The opening notes of the first theme are heard, as if from the distance, on a muted horn. This is the signal for the middle section of the movement, a brief development. With a change of key, the piano launches into turbulent arpeggios, over which the woodwind play the first theme, smoothed out into a chant. The piano takes up this new version of the theme, and the violins echo it in counterpoint. Then the piano remembers the charming music that ended the first section, and this too is answered in counterpoint by flute, oboe, and clarinet in turn. The energy builds to a climax, out of which emerges a series of violin trills. As the trilling quietens, the piano enters with the first theme, and we are into the reprise. The main themes recur, but with almost every bar subtly rethought and re-orchestrated: the bass answering the first theme, and mysterious string glissandi accompanying the delicate second theme. There are no conventionally grandiose passages this time. Instead, the patterns become concentrated into a hypnotic interplay between piano and woodwind. And the movement ends with the first theme reduced to a haunting question and answer between flute and piano.

In his twenties, Bartók declared himself to be an atheist: 'If ever I were to cross myself,' he wrote, 'it would signify, "In the name of Nature, Art and Science".'[19] Later, he joined the Unitarian Church, but he was never conventionally religious, and the instruction 'religioso' occurs only this once in his music. There is a specific reason. Beethoven's late String Quartet in A minor, Opus 132, contains one of his most celebrated slow movements, with the title, 'Hymn of thanksgiving offered to the Deity by a convalescent'. When he wrote it, Beethoven had recently been seriously ill; Bartók was increasingly ill, though hoping to recover. Beethoven's movement conveys a sense of serenity emerging out of suffering, and it acted as the inspiration for Bartók's movement. Beethoven's hymn is interleaved with sections headed

'Feeling new strength', in which the music struggles to dance. In Bartók's movement, a serene start and finish are separated by one of the central inspirations of his life, the sounds of Nature.

The movement opens with a pianissimo chorus of strings in five-part counterpoint, in the clearest C major, made even more serene by the way in which the lines overlap and interweave. As it dies away on a discord, the piano enters with a simple chorale. Strings and piano alternate. From time to time the serenity of the piano's chorale is threatened by moments of dissonance, and, at its climax, by passionate Wagnerian chords, as if we have slipped for a moment into *Tristan und Isolde*. But the final benediction of the strings ensures that serenity has been restored. As the middle section of the movement opens, we enter Bartók's final example of 'night music'. Over shimmering violins, oboe, clarinet, flute, and piano evoke birdsong. The piano moves into floating arpeggio patterns, the orchestral texture becomes more complex, and the bird-calls become more insistent. At the climax of the passage, one specific call is heard again and again, that of the Eastern Towhey. Bartók had noted down its characteristic song in a letter to his son, Peter, from a sanatorium in North Carolina in April 1944, commenting, 'The birds have become completely drunk with the spring and are putting on concerts the like of which I've never heard.' This particular bird 'keeps on creating more and more variants'.[20] In this passage, Bartók does the reverse, starting with variations on the call, and culminating with the call itself at its most simple. The piano's cascades and arpeggios reach a climax and subside, simplifying into a pattern reminiscent of the end of the first movement. Then the opening chorale returns, this time in the woodwind. The piano, seeming to improvise, weaves a new counterpoint among the chords, at first almost ecclesiastically, and then breaking out into ecstatic runs as if Bartók is remembering the extravagant flourishes of Hungarian cimbalom-players. The climax of the chorale, with its *Tristan*-like chords, is given new intensity by the sudden entry of the strings. The piano responds with one of the most passionate climaxes in the whole of Bartók's music, the low chords darkened by strokes of a gong. It is the strings that bring us back to serenity, with a brief return to the weaving lines of the opening. In the last bar, the piano quietly moves from C major to a final chord of E major.

Without a break, a rush of arpeggios brings us into the finale. The theme has a sturdy three-in-a-bar swing with Hungarian-style rhythms and cross-rhythms in the accompaniment, giving it a downright character. It recurs from time to time through the movement, creating a sort of rondo. Subtly, the shape of its melody is drawn from the last few bars of the slow movement, now utterly transformed in character. It builds to a peak of ferocity, then dies away in drum strokes. The piano enters with a playful fugue subject. The orchestra gradually joins in, and by the time the trumpets have entered, we could be about to break into the fugue in the Concerto for Orchestra. But now the piano returns to the dancing first theme. Once again it dies away in drum strokes.

In the next episode, the piano plays a lyrical theme based on a rising scale, with surprisingly rich and conventional harmonies. The strings accompany it with fragments of counterpoint, as if wanting to continue the fugue. Suddenly, violas and cellos break in with a new fugue subject that breaks from the prevailing three-in-a-bar to two-in-a-bar. This builds up swiftly, and as quickly fades. The lyrical rising-scale theme resumes, with the theme in the horns and the piano playing the counterpoint. After some quiet rumination, the tension rises, and rushing woodwind and piano octaves lead to a renewal of the first theme, now on full strings, with powerful 'blue' harmonies that Bartók drew from Hungarian music. As the momentum builds, delicate passages alternate with further outbursts of the theme. There is a crescendo and a sudden silence. The piano begins a brooding pattern of chords, and there is a sense of forces gathering. Eventually these burst out into the first theme, thrown between brass and piano, and with a final rocket of Lisztian octaves, Bartók's swansong comes to an exuberant close.

ROMANIAN FOLK DANCES
Duration: approx. 7 minutes

Béla Bartók and Zoltán Kodály collected huge quantities of traditional music from Hungary and surrounding countries in the years leading up to the First World War. This music was to have a profound effect on Bartók's own style, and he also published arrangements of some of the tunes that he had collected. This sequence of six Romanian dances first appeared as piano pieces in 1915, and were then adapted for chamber orchestra in 1917, with strings, flutes, clarinets, bassoons, and horns. They are all based on fiddle tunes.

No. 1 *Joc cu Bâtă*: a stately dance with sticks. No. 2 *Brâul*: a rather coy dance, in which couples hold a cloth belt around their waists. No. 3 *Pe Loc* (In one spot): a slow version of a stamping dance, with a wistful piccolo solo. No. 4 *Buciumeana* (Dance of Buchum): this continues the wistful mood, with a solo violin and then full strings with flutes and clarinets. No. 5 *Poargă Românească* (Romanian polka): a fast children's dance with a stamping 3–3–2 rhythm. This leads straight into Nos 6 and 7 *Mârunţel*: a pair of fast dances with very small steps and quick movements. The second is urged on with flourishes from the flute.

VIOLIN CONCERTO NO. 1
Duration: approx. 22 minutes

Andante sostenuto
Allegro giocoso

In 1905, Bartók met Kodály for the first time, and they jointly established a project to collect Hungarian folk song, and to publish a 'complete' edition. The aim was to save this precious heritage that was in danger of being lost to the incursions of commercial light music. In 1907, Bartók toured Transylvania for the first time, recording traditional music on a pair of phonographs. This experience not only revealed to him the character and variety of folk music, but also persuaded him that it could form the basis of his own musical style.

While he was in Transylvania, Bartók started to write a Violin Concerto for a young violinist, Stefi Geyer, with whom he was in love. He planned a work in three movements, and wrote to her, 'The musical picture of the idealised Stefi Geyer is now done – it is heavenly, intimate; also that of the boisterous Stefi Geyer – it is humorous, witty, entertaining. Now the indifferent, cool, silent picture of Stefi Geyer has need of creation. But it would become ugly music.'[21] He came to dislike the idea for the third movement and abandoned it, leaving a concerto in two movements. Shortly after he finished it, in February 1908, Geyer ended their relationship. Bartók's letters, frank and sometimes patronizing, make it clear that they were fundamentally incompatible. Geyer never played the concerto, and Bartók adapted the first movement to form the first of his Two Portraits, Opus 5.

The concerto was not performed until after Bartók's death. It provides a fascinating glimpse of the composer at this stage of his career, just as his involvement with folk music was taking off. There is a certain tough edge to his language, but it is still rooted in traditional central European writing – particularly Richard Strauss. There is not yet much to be heard of the influence of folk music, except perhaps in the insistent rhythms of the second movement.

The concerto opens with the violin unaccompanied, playing a pattern of rising thirds, the 'Stefi motif'. This develops into a yearning solo line, joined in turn by the strings, building up a rich fugal texture in which the theme is sometimes inverted. Then the woodwind enter, and the music twice builds to a rich climax. Cor anglais, oboe, and muted strings meditate on inverted elements of the theme. The pace increases, building to a climax bigger than before, and the movement ends with another extended solo violin line, which regains the original form of the theme and culminates in a high pianissimo.

The violin opens the second movement with a theme of bold descending intervals and dotted rhythms that develop a motoric rhythm. A calmer second theme, in dialogue with the woodwind, is related to the descending version of Stefi's motif from the first movement. This takes time to work through, as if the preoccupation of the first movement cannot be shaken off, but eventually the rhythmic impetus returns. This begins by quoting Sancho Panza's theme from Richard Strauss's *Don Quixote*, ushering in further development of the opening theme. At one point the dotted rhythms are treated to Strauss-like fugal mockery, and there is a big orchestral climax. The violin continues to muse on the melancholy, Stefi-related theme. Then the first theme returns, and after a mysterious moment the concerto ends with a final dash.

VIOLIN CONCERTO NO. 2
Duration: approx. 38 minutes

Allegro non troppo
Andante tranquillo
Allegro molto

Bartók composed this concerto in 1937–8 at a time of growing tension in Europe, when he was already beginning to contemplate the possibility of exile from Hungary. The government, and much of the population, supported Hitler. As Bartók wrote to the conductor Paul Sacher in Switzerland, 'What is most appalling is the imminent danger that Hungary too will surrender to this system of robbers and murderers.' It was at this time that he wrote this concerto, which he had promised to Zoltán Székely, the Hungarian violinist with whom Bartók had played duo recitals for many years, and who had emigrated to Holland. Székely gave the premiere with the Amsterdam Concertgebouw Orchestra conducted by Willem Mengelberg in April 1939. Bartók had accepted Székely's commission as early as 1936, and some of the concerto's principal ideas date from that time. He had not composed a violin concerto for thirty years, and, wanting to update his knowledge of the repertoire, he asked his publisher to send him the concertos by Alban Berg, Kurt Weill, and Karol Szymanowski. But the composition of his own Violin Concerto was delayed by his work on the Sonata for two Pianos and Percussion, and it was not until August 1937 that he resumed serious work on the concerto. He finished it at the end of the following year.

Bartók had suggested a single-movement work in variation form, but Székely wanted a more conventional three-movement concerto. Bartók complied, but then wrote to Székely, 'the third movement turned out very well, actually a free variation of the first (thus I got the best of you, I wrote *variations after all*)'.[22] Quite apart from the links between the first and third movement, variation of themes is at the heart of this concerto. Yehudi Menuhin, who frequently performed the concerto, recalls a conversation he had with Bartók in New York in 1943. The composer asked his opinion of a passage in the first movement. ' "It's rather chromatic," I offered. "Yes, it's chromatic," he said, but then, nudging me towards the point he was making: "You see that it comes very often?" – which it does, some thirty-two times, never exactly the same. "Well, I wanted to show Schönberg that one can use all twelve tones and still remain tonal.'"[23]

The concerto opens with the harp quietly strumming chords of B major, a surprisingly intimate gesture, like the bard preparing to sing. Pizzicato strings pick out a bass line. The solo violin enters with a melody that is both lyrical and emphatic in an unmistakeably Hungarian way – even bard-like – and Bartók heightens its effect with characteristic, achingly 'blue' harmonies. The violin rises, elaborating the line as if in improvisation. As it descends it rushes off playfully, accelerating to a virtuoso climax. The orchestra takes up the melody, with the treble instruments echoed in the bass. A reflective moment for the soloist suddenly turns aggressive, with abrupt, awkward gestures thrown back and forth. The music calms and, over a quivering bass, the soloist floats a mysterious line, echoed *ppp* by the orchestral violins. This is the twelve-note row that Bartók mentioned to Menuhin, and variations of it fill this haunting passage. There is a sudden switch back to aggression, with fierce trilling in the orchestra answered by wild descending scale patterns from the solo violin. The music becomes increasingly dance-like until it is brought to a halt by a violent trombone trill.

The strumming harp returns, now in F major, and the soloist plays a melody drawn from the opening pizzicato bass. This is the start of a development section. The melody moves from instrument to instrument and from key to key, and the soloist plays ruminative decorations. The peace is broken by another sudden fortissimo, with rattling scales from the soloist and energetic syncopations from the wind and side drum. While the violin's scales continue, a horn reminds us of the lyrical opening theme. The music is tugged in three different directions, by scales, syncopated rhythms, and the lyrical element. At another sudden stop, the soloist turns the first theme upside down, against a magical texture of celesta, harp, and meandering violins. The aggressive dance rhythms return, building to another swift climax.

From this emerges the first theme, high on solo violin and back in its original key of B major. Is this the reprise? It seems so, but, this being Bartók, everything is transformed as it proceeds. The playful continuation of the theme soon arrives at a new, urgent orchestral passage. Out of this come the abrupt, awkward gestures. Three times these give way to calm moments, in which the twelve-note row is combine with the rhythm of the opening theme, the second time upside down. As before, fierce trilling in the orchestra shatters the atmosphere. This time the tumult is brought to a halt by the soloist scrubbing *ffff*, and then undulating in quarter-tones either side of a held D while fragments of the first theme seem like ghosts. From this develops a full-scale violin cadenza. From its complex two-part writing suddenly break rapid scales, and bassoons and horn enter with the energetic syncopated figure. As the violin scales develop momentum, the end seems in sight. But, in a glorious moment, the soloist draws back, and swings for a last time into an ecstatic reminiscence of the first theme, enhanced by harp glissandi. A powerful orchestral tutti propels the soloist into a final passage of bravura, during which the strings play 'Bartók pizzicato', plucked so that the string rebounds with a snap against the fingerboard. So a movement that began lyrically ends explosively.

The second movement is a set of variations on a theme. The strings unfold a soft chord of G major, touched in by harp harmonics. It could almost be the opening of Mahler's *Adagietto* from his Fifth Symphony. The solo violin enters with a gentle falling and rising melody, coloured by touches of plangency – it is in the Lydian mode, with its characteristic sharp fourth. Each phrase is punctuated by timpani. As the melody unwinds, it becomes more searching and more poignant in its accompanying harmonies, until the orchestra bursts out with a climactic phrase whose rich harmonies, bolstered by thrumming harp arpeggios, suggest a great depth of nostalgia. In Variation 1, the solo line flows in continuous semiquavers. At first it is accompanied only by timpani and pizzicato basses, picking out a chromatic bass line (Bartók's music requires pedal timpani, able to change pitch instantly). But then it is threatened by the scratchy sound of cellos bowing rapidly near the bridge ('sul ponticello') together with a drum roll. The nostalgic last bars rise higher, as if searching to regain serenity.

In Variation 2, flutes, later joined by violins, sustain a high note, and a harp, later joined by celesta, plays delicate runs. Against this peaceful background the solo line becomes more like a lament, evoking a pastoral scene of the shepherd singing sadly amid the tinkling bells of the flock. The final high harmonic is kicked away by the rude shock of Variation 3. This is reminiscent of the aggressive interruptions in the first movement, and consists of relentless two-part chord patterns, marked 'ruvido' (rough), accompanied by threatening horns. Only in the final bars does the soloist find more harmonious patterns, but the variation ends with its tensions unresolved.

Variation 4 is like an example of Bartók's 'night music'. Cellos and basses play a peaceful line that falls and rises alternately, while the soloist weaves a pattern of trills and swirls like a fluttering moth. Variation 5 is a moment of calm fugue, based on a phrase from the middle of the theme, distilled to the simplest of melodies. An echo of the climax of the theme is heard in the final bars, which gently fall in a series of similarly rich chords, but fading to *ppp*. There is another abrupt change of mood and pace to Variation 6. This is fast and energetic, peppered with cross-rhythms that are fiendishly difficult to co-ordinate between soloist and woodwind. Like Variation 3, it is reminiscent of rhythmic elements in the first movement, and it vanishes into thin air with a high piccolo. Variation 7 has a strutting, ironic character. The strut is established by pizzicato strings, sometimes playing normally, sometimes with the slapping 'Bartók pizzicato', with interjections from the side drum and the timpani played with wooden sticks. Over this, the soloist plays complex trills, swirls, and chattering repeated notes. Halfway through, the soloist breaks out of this ornamental display, and, as if remembering the seriousness of the matter, plays a lyrical line while the strutting pizzicato persists below.

Finally, Variation 8 returns to the tempo and metre of the theme, and to its original melody. The violin sets off serenely, even though the woodwind pull away with dissonances and towards other keys. Midway through the melody, the dissonances resolve and for a moment melody and accompaniment are harmonious, with the violas adding a counterpoint. But the way to the end is not straightforward: dissonances still lurk in the shadows, touched in by harp and celesta. In the final bars, where in the theme the strings burst out passionately, here the violins divided in four parts echo the last phrase pianissimo, as if searching in the darkness for a resolution. It finally comes with gentle taps on the timpani, as the melody and accompaniment converge on a unison G.

Bartók described the finale as 'a free variation of the first movement', and if you put the scores of the two movements side by side, it becomes clear how closely they follow each other.

The finale recognizably mirrors the main sequence of events of the first movement. The principal themes of the finale are derived from those of the first movement, drawing on the same melodic shapes, but giving them a different character so that they seem quite new, and with everything tightened to give the momentum of a finale. A series of abrupt scales propels the soloist forward for the first theme. This takes the opening shape of the concerto's lyrical first theme, and transforms it into an energetic dance in three-time, with ruggedly regular phrases. As in the first movement, the violin soon develops continuous patterns, now gritty and acerbic, and the orchestra takes up the theme, transforming it once more with thrusting cross-rhythms. The soloist throws in an abrupt gesture followed by aggressive, scrubbed repeated notes, which relate to the similarly aggressive elements in the first movement. And now comes the mysterious twelve-note passage, in which an eloquent violin line is echoed by a new twelve-note 'row' on the strings, high, muted, and pianissimo. As before, the calm is suddenly broken. The violin plays aggressive repeated notes and acerbic running scales, while the forces of the orchestra gather, the rhythms of a dance beginning to form in bass drum, side drum, and brass. This slowly develops power, becoming as much a threat as a dance, reaches a climax, and breaks off.

This is the point where, as in the first movement, the soloist meditatively turns the first theme upside down. Here, the background is a delicate, quasi-pastoral texture of string harmonics, tinkling celesta, and murmuring clarinets. There is an increase in pace, and the orchestra begins to drive forward again, with rhythms battling against each other two beats apart. At another cut-off climax, the soloist returns to the finale's first theme, the right way up, but not yet in the home key, and still in meditative mood. Is this the reprise? Again the pace picks up, and the orchestra drives to another climax. Out of it emerges the abrupt second idea, and we now know that we really are into the reprise. Soon, the music calms again, with new versions of the mysterious twelve-note line. Now there is a sense of forces gathering for the final assault, as the lower instruments mutter darkly with bass drum and gong, the wind try out staccato chords, and the soloist's gestures become more flamboyant. These culminate in rapid runs and trills, the abbreviated equivalent of the first movement's cadenza. The orchestra renews the dance, and, with only a passing moment of renewed reflection, this propels soloist and orchestra together headlong towards the conclusion. There are two endings. Bartók's original had the final climax left to the orchestra alone, with thrillingly daring glissando whoops in the trumpets. Székely asked Bartók to supply an alternative ending, in which the soloist is featured right to the end. This is the version almost always played, and it provides a more conventionally exciting and equally satisfying finish.

LUDWIG VAN BEETHOVEN
(1770–1827)

Of all the composers writing at the beginning of the nineteenth century, Beethoven was the giant from whom later composers drew most inspiration. Without him, the music of Schubert, Mendelssohn, Schumann, Liszt, Wagner and Brahms would have been very different.

There is a tendency to confuse Beethoven the man with Beethoven the composer. As a man he was difficult and truculent, refusing to give his aristocratic patrons the sort of respect they were used to, and becoming increasingly antisocial as he went deaf. One of the great virtuoso pianists of his time (before he went deaf), he would reduce a roomful of listeners to tears with his piano improvisations, then leap up and laugh at them. Famously, when a waiter brought him a plate of goulash by mistake, he threw it in the man's face.

How much of this character is in the music? You might think from the popular image that he constantly broke all rules, turned his back on all conventions, and never wrote a note of orthodox music in his life. It is true that he composed works of startling originality and power, stretching the musical language of the time, and the capabilities of players, in ways that astonished and sometimes puzzled his contemporaries. But Beethoven had immense respect for the great composers of the past – J. S. Bach and Handel in particular – and drew freely on their ideas and methods. Furthermore, the qualities of Beethoven's music cover a huge emotional and sonic spectrum, and that is really the point. The slow movements are as impressive as the fast and furious, the serene episodes at least as memorable as the violent. For every shock there are a hundred exquisitely turned phrases and a hundred delicate combinations of tone colours, using just the same instruments as Haydn and Mozart, but sounding like nobody but Beethoven. Because of this enormous range, for many listeners Beethoven is the composer who seems to convey in his music the greatest understanding of human life, in all its complexity.

One way in which he was a pioneer was in the importance that he attributed to himself and his art. It was a feature of Romanticism that the artist – musician, poet, painter – came to be regarded as a sort of priest, and art as a sort of religion. Humanity's sense of contact with ideas of creation, of the spirit, and of what later came to be known as the unconscious, was, by the early nineteenth century, a matter for artists as much as for conventional religion. Beethoven was the first great composer who declared his own stature as an artist, and whose music states unequivocally the importance of its task. This is partly a matter of emphasis and volume, partly a matter of length. Beethoven increased the dimensions of music, insisting that what was being undertaken was an immense task. An instrumental work of the scale of the Ninth Symphony would have been unthinkable to a Haydn or Mozart. It is this new grandiloquence that in later generations was to encourage the immense works of Wagner, Mahler, and Shostakovich.

Beethoven presents particular challenges to performers. Because of his unique place as a great icon of classical music, musicians approaching Beethoven often feel a sense of immense responsibility and the weight of hallowed tradition. In practice, this has tended to lead in two opposite directions. On the one hand, many performers have taken Beethoven very seriously indeed, emphasizing the massive and the awe-inspiring. On the other hand, in recent decades there has been a counter-movement to strip away all the baggage of tradition, to abandon the Romantic myth of Beethoven the Great, and to try to recreate his music as it might have sounded when it was fresh in his lifetime. Recordings of half a century ago tended towards a heavyweight approach to Beethoven. Many modern performances, particularly those on period instruments, tend to be fast and light-textured. For some years in the late twentieth century opinions were sharply divided between these two extremes, but now, in the early twenty-first century, there is a widespread (and healthy) view that neither approach presents 'the answer', and that there are many ways of performing this music.

Beethoven was one of the first composers to use the newly invented metronome to indicate tempo. Older generations thought many of his tempo markings impossibly fast. This stands to reason when you consider that he was deaf when he started using the metronome, and that he chose the tempi of his orchestral works by playing the music at the piano while somebody else operated the metronome, or by imagining the tempo, and not by measuring it while an orchestra played the music. In recent years some conductors have tried taking his metronome markings more literally, resulting in very fast tempi for some movements. It is a matter of opinion whether this works. One crucial element is how strictly conductors stick to the tempo once it has been set. This is another thing that has changed over time. An older generation (Furtwängler, Mengelberg, Richard Strauss) used to whip up the tempo in exciting passages, and let it relax in the lyrical moments. Some modern performances are so rigid that there is virtually no give and take. Conductors sometimes argue that the stricter modern approach is more 'authentic'. But the grounds for this are suspect, and there is nothing about Beethoven's character that suggests that he would have wanted it. He himself provided a strong clue in the autograph of a song, 'Nord oder Süd' (North or South), where, having given a metronome marking, he adds that this applies only to the opening bars, because 'feeling also has its tempo'.

Concertos

Beethoven's piano concertos are as varied as his symphonies. The first two are delightful and exuberant, the third is dark and intense, the fourth radiant, and the fifth grand and heroic. The range of the concertos, like that of his piano sonatas, also gives some idea of Beethoven as a pianist. He was widely regarded as the greatest pianist of his time, not just in his virtuosity but in his expressive power, which pushed the pianos of his day to their limits. He himself gave the first performance of four of his concertos. But by the time he came to write the fifth, the 'Emperor', his deafness was far advanced, and he left public performance of it to others. It is a sad thought that, if Beethoven had retained his hearing, he might have composed another five piano concertos.

PIANO CONCERTO NO. 1 IN C MAJOR, OP. 15
Duration: approx. 37 minutes

Allegro con brio
Largo
Rondo: Allegro scherzando

Beethoven published this concerto as 'No. 1', but it was written at least three years after 'No. 2', and first performed by Beethoven himself in Prague in 1798. Of all his piano concertos, this is the one that gives the most vivid impression of the dazzling young virtuoso, then at the height of his powers as a pianist. It has a spirit of carefree brilliance – indeed it marks the climax of his performing career. It was during the following year that Beethoven first became aware of the onset of deafness that was to cut short his career as a virtuoso.

The concerto begins with a fast march on tiptoe – more elfin than military at first, but with a confident swagger when it is taken up by the full orchestra. A quiet second theme suddenly moves to the warm key of E flat, and is in complete contrast in its gentle lyricism. When the orchestral tutti struts to a halt, the piano enters not with one of the themes already stated, but with something completely new and questioning. This is like the first entry in several of Mozart's concertos, and it is the orchestra that reminds the soloist of the principal theme, which the piano then elaborates with cascading arpeggios and runs. The end of the next orchestral tutti moves into E flat major (as the second theme did) to open the development section. This is a gloriously expansive fantasia, predominantly quiet and conversational, with the wind instruments in continual dialogue with the piano (another feature that Beethoven had learned from Mozart rather than from his teacher Haydn). This section ends very calmly, but is then interrupted by a brilliant fortissimo octave scale (which Beethoven would have played as a glissando – almost impossible on the modern piano), and the orchestra enters with the return of the first theme. The movement culminates in the usual cadenza, which Beethoven would no doubt have improvised. He later wrote out three cadenzas, the third of which illustrates his fearless command of the most brilliant pianistic effects.

The slow movement, though marked Largo, has two beats to a bar, and the tempo is therefore flowing. The melody that the piano unfolds is song-like but, even at its first appearance, quite elaborately decorated with turns and flourishes. As the movement proceeds, the melodic line, whenever it returns to the piano, becomes more and more intricately ornamented. But the effect is not flashy or gratuitous. It was the great genius of Beethoven the virtuoso pianist to be able to work his music to an increasing complexity that seems to become deeper and deeper, rather than, as in much of the conventional variation-writing of the time, shallower and shallower – a genius that was to culminate in the slow movements of his late piano sonatas, long after Beethoven was able to play the piano himself.

The finale is a delightful romp, sustaining a level of wit that is fully worthy of his great teacher Haydn, but with an extra edge of boisterousness unique to Beethoven. One of the episodes in the movement has a cheeky repeating phrase that sounds, to modern ears, like a samba – a startling effect in an eighteenth-century concerto. Near the end there is a brief cadenza. This is followed by a final reprise of the main theme by the orchestra, then a witty and very Mozartian exchange between piano and woodwind, a pause, and a brief fortissimo outburst from the orchestra to bring the work to an abrupt close.

PIANO CONCERTO NO. 2 IN B FLAT MAJOR, OP. 19
Duration: approx. 29 minutes

Allegro con brio
Adagio
Rondo: Allegro molto

This concerto was published in the same year as the concerto 'No. 1', 1801. But although it was given a later opus number, 'No. 2' was written earlier than the first. It is one of the works that Beethoven completed while studying with Haydn in 1793, though he had probably already been working on it before he moved from Bonn to Vienna in the previous year. When it was to be published, Beethoven described it to a rival publisher as 'one of my first concertos, and therefore not one of the best of my compositions'. This is probably not to be taken at face value, but as a sign that Beethoven was anxious to make it clear to a potential publisher that he had moved on since he wrote this concerto, and that his new works were in quite a different class. The second concerto was almost certainly the one performed by Beethoven at his first public appearance in Vienna as a virtuoso pianist-composer, at the Burgtheater in March 1795. He finished the final rondo only the day before the first rehearsal, which took place in his room. It turned out that the piano was a semitone flat, so Beethoven got the orchestra to tune their A to the B flat of the piano, and played the whole concerto a semitone up.[1]

The Concerto in B flat is on a more intimate scale than Beethoven's other piano concertos. The orchestra has no timpani or trumpets, and the style of writing is like chamber music on a large scale. In this sense it is closer to Mozart than Beethoven's later concertos. But the forthright character of Beethoven is evident right from the first theme, and the music covers an enormous emotional range during the opening orchestral passage, even before the soloist has begun. The first solo entry introduces new material, as Mozart often does, but with nonchalance and wit that are pure Beethoven. After a virtuoso elaboration of the first theme, the lyrical second theme also turns out to be something quite new, not previously introduced by the orchestra. And what the orchestra had presented as a second theme is not taken up by the piano until the middle of the movement. These subtleties, learned more from Mozart than from Haydn, are given Beethoven's own stamp, and developed into a movement of great concentration.

The slow movement is one of the earliest of those in which Beethoven takes a simple chorale, and develops it into a complex web of melodic elaboration. As it proceeds, passages that flow coherently are broken up by others in which speech seems inarticulate and hesitant. It is a sort of dramatic scene, part aria, part recitative, an experiment in a style that was to reach a climax in the ecstatic slow movements of piano works from the 'Hammerklavier' Sonata onwards.

Beethoven emerges from this meditation into a finale of pure high spirits. The cheeky offbeat accents of the piano's main theme are taken up enthusiastically by the orchestra. In between the appearances of this theme, there are episodes of different character, formed into an arch shape. The first leads to a tune of bouncing simplicity, sounding rather like the finale of the Quintet for Piano and Wind, another work from the 1790s. The second episode develops the offbeat accents of the main theme in new directions, creating the centre of the movement. The return to the main theme then leads back through the bouncy first episode to a final reprise. At the end, the piano playfully dallies in pianissimo trills, before the orchestra bursts out with a last fortissimo. It is tempting to imagine the young Beethoven at the first performance leaping up from his seat, and laughing in the face of his audience.

PIANO CONCERTO NO 3 IN C MINOR, OP. 37
Duration: approx. 36 minutes

Allegro con brio
Largo
Rondo: Allegro

Beethoven's first two piano concertos are works of the eighteenth century, and retain much of its elegance. In the Third Piano Concerto, Beethoven has not entirely turned his back on that world, but from its first bars the music is imbued with a new quality of serious purpose. This is partly to do with the key, C minor. Mozart had already used C minor to create some of his most sombre and powerful works, including a piano concerto, two fantasias, a piano sonata, a serenade for wind, and a mass. Beethoven took this significance of C minor a stage further. It was to become for Beethoven and later composers the key of heroic defiance, most famously in Beethoven's Fifth Symphony. There is already something of this spirit in the 'Pathétique' Sonata in C minor, and it was a year after writing that work that, in the summer of 1800, Beethoven began this concerto in C minor, though he continued working on it until after its first performance in Vienna three years later. Ignaz von Seyfried, who turned the pages for him at that concert, reported, 'I saw almost nothing but empty leaves; at the most on one page or the other a few Egyptian hieroglyphs wholly unintelligible to me scribbled down to serve as clues for him; for he played nearly all of the solo part from memory, since, as was often the case, he had not had time to put it all down on paper.'[2] Von Seyfried might be exaggerating for effect, but a glimpse at Beethoven's autograph is enough to demonstrate that turning pages for him would have been a nightmare.

The concerto opens with the orchestra quietly stating the first theme with its insistent dotted rhythms, first the strings in bare octaves, answered by the woodwind in harmony. It is fascinating to compare this with the opening of Mozart's Piano Concerto in C minor, which also starts with quiet, bare octaves. The Mozart is uncertain, keeping the listener guessing where the phrases are to come to rest, and where the harmonies might be going. Beethoven, despite the quietness, is absolutely firm, stating what has to be stated with no prevarication or ambiguity: this is the key, this is the rhythm, this is how the phrases go. Arguments about this material will be complex and far-ranging, but there is no doubt what is being argued about. The orchestral introduction already has a wide range, with an atmosphere of urgency generated by offbeat accents. There is a second, lyrical theme. But it is the assertive first theme that dominates, passing from strings to woodwind, from melody to bass, and being extensively worked out before the piano entry.

When the piano does enter, it is with a defiant flourish, and a restatement of the bare octaves and answering phrases from the opening. The pianist works through the material already presented by the orchestra, enhancing it with new twists and decorations, and with the accents rendered even more forthright by the percussive element of the piano. After another orchestral link, the development section of the movement enters new territory. The assertive main theme has become questioning, and the piano twice sets off on an extended meditation. This is the quiet centre of the movement, after which a more flamboyant passage leads to the fortissimo reprise of the main theme from the orchestra. Something of the meditative mood lingers in the piano's response, and leads naturally on into the lyrical second theme, and then builds to the pause for the cadenza. Beethoven wrote his own mighty cadenza for this movement, whose bravura effects and changes of mood give us some insight into how powerful his improvisations must have been. The end of the cadenza is masterly. From a series of quiet trills it evaporates to an unexpected chord, under which the timpani softly tap out the opening of the main theme. From this mysterious moment, the music builds to a great fortissimo, to bring the movement to a final gesture of defiance.

The slow movement opens with the piano on its own, singing very softly a song of great depth. This is Beethoven exploring to the full the quiet sonorities and expressive possibilities of the piano of his day. Whether the piano is period or modern, it is one of Beethoven's most heart-stopping passages, and when the orchestra comes in, it is difficult for them to equal it. The piano enters again with a melody highly decorated in thirds, which seems to be new. But the chords of the opening theme underpin this middle section of the movement, which turns out to be a greatly extended and elaborated variation on the theme. When the original version quietly returns, it too is subjected to more and more ecstatically complex decoration.

The finale returns to the definite rhythms and offbeat accents of the first movement. The sturdy rondo theme is cast in highly regular phrases, interrupted before the final strain by a pause and little cadenza. After an orchestral passage, a more playful episode follows. Then, after another forceful return of the main theme, there is a complete change of mood, as a clarinet ushers in a beautiful melody in A flat major. The piano answers and decorates it, and the melody extends to fill the centre of this movement with a relaxed beauty that contrasts strongly with the urgency of the surrounding material. After this, the main theme returns quietly as a fugue subject, building from the cellos upwards until the whole orchestra has joined in. But this peters out into repeated octaves, the key shifts upwards, and, as the piano enters again, we unexpectedly find ourselves back in E major, the key of the slow movement, with the main rondo theme transformed into a gentle melody. This moment too is short-lived: another side-step takes us back to C minor, and the rondo theme is restated, followed by the playful second theme that followed it at the beginning of the movement, and a final reprise of the rondo theme. This arrives at a pause and a brief cadenza. Out of it emerges a transformation of the rondo theme, now in C major and in a fast jig rhythm cheekily subverted by offbeat phrasing. This builds into a final flamboyant dash to the end.

PIANO CONCERTO NO. 4 IN G MAJOR, OP. 58
Duration: approx. 34 minutes

Allegro moderato
Andante con moto –
Vivace

For anyone who thinks of Beethoven only as the defiant, truculent hero, there is no better antidote than this concerto. It was written in 1805–6 and is one of his most serene works, exploiting all the poetic and lyrical possibilities of the piano of his time, just as the Violin Concerto, written during the same period, does for the violin.

The concerto opens with the most extraordinarily undemonstrative gesture: the piano plays a quiet chord of G major, then a pattern of repeated chords, elaborated into a phrase that ends with a question. It is like the beginning of an improvisation. The orchestra answers by quietly reiterating the piano's opening phrase, but in B major – the last key one would have expected. Soon it turns a corner back into G major, and the phrases build up to the first forte of the concerto. The second idea does not quite sound like a fully fledged theme: a little phrase of dotted rhythms is reiterated, subsides, and is overtaken by a reminiscence of the opening idea. This builds to another forte, dies down, and the piano enters again. It explores and elaborates the opening pattern of repeated notes, adding rapid scales, tricky patterns of thirds and arpeggios. But (as in the Violin Concerto) there is no impression of display. The predominant level is quiet and light. Any loud moments are quickly drawn back to a meditative tone. Eventually we reach a second theme – which did not occur in the orchestral introduction – played first by the strings, then elaborated by the piano. The improvisatory character of the piano writing, set at the opening, is sustained through to the end of this first section.

Then, after a brief orchestral tutti, the development begins. Again the piano enters quietly with its repeated notes, but it is now more halting and questioning, moving into more distant keys without settling in them. A sudden forte leads to the piano's first sustained loud passage, which, after a climax, subsides to a delicate pianissimo. Another gradual build-up leads to the return of the opening theme, now grand and sonorous, but again soon calming to a pianissimo. The reprise culminates in the expected cadenza. Beethoven supplied his own, which is most often played. It works to a powerful climax, then descends gently to lead out to a moment of deep calm, before a final build-up brings the movement to a close.

If the first movement is unusually meditative and expansive, the slow movement is unusually terse and concentrated, so short as to seem almost like an introduction to the finale rather than an independent movement. The strings play a brief passage of forceful dotted rhythms, like the introduction to a tragic operatic scene. The piano sings a plaintive hymn, very softly. Beethoven instructs the player to use the soft, *una corda* pedal (which on the Viennese pianos of his day really did mean that the hammer touched only one string, producing a much more delicate effect than the soft pedal on the modern piano). Assertive strings and pleading piano alternate, until the strings are eventually hushed. A brief fantasia develops to a troubled fortissimo, and is then calmed. Quiet reminiscences of the strings' dotted rhythms are answered by a final sorrowful phrase from the piano, and the movement is over.

The finale follows without a break. Pianissimo strings begin with a theme like a distant dance. The piano answers with a gentle elaboration, and there are further quiet exchanges. Then suddenly the full orchestra bursts out with the dance fortissimo. What follows is a wonderfully exuberant rondo. After the meditation of the first movement and the tragic simplicity of the slow movement, this seems like the perfect release. There are episodes of quiet exploration and poetry, but the predominant mood is one of delight, returning again and again to the whispered dance of the opening, and the inevitable outburst that never fails to follow it.

PIANO CONCERTO NO. 5 IN E FLAT MAJOR, OP. 73 ('EMPEROR')
Duration: approx. 39 minutes

Allegro
Adagio un poco mosso –
Rondo: Allegro

The Viennese first heard this concerto played by Beethoven's pupil Carl Czerny, because Beethoven by 1811 was too deaf to perform it in public. Czerny, in his commentary on Beethoven's piano works, adds a fascinating footnote to his description of this concerto: 'NB, In the latter Concertos of Beethoven it is most advisable to conduct the orchestra from a separate copy of the Pianoforte part, as the mode of performance cannot be gathered from the part belonging to the Violin.'[3] Orchestral scores were rarely available in the early nineteenth century, and orchestras were generally directed by the leader, or a pianist, or a combination of both. But Czerny's comment confirms that it would have been a tall order to achieve a co-ordinated performance of this mighty concerto without some kind of independent director.

The 'Emperor' (not Beethoven's title) is the most massive of his concertos. It provided the prototype for many later concertos in which piano and orchestra are pitted in battle against each other: Liszt, Brahms, Tchaikovsky, Prokofiev, Rachmaninoff. This 'barnstorming' aspect of the 'Emperor' is both its strength and, potentially, its weakness. The first movement in particular can seem relentless and overblown unless the pianist is also sensitive to the moments of delicacy and poetry. The movement opens, unusually, with a cadenza punctuated by fortissimo orchestral chords, in which the pianist declares the grandeur of the work ahead with a cascade of arpeggios and runs. Only then does the orchestra begin the tutti with the opening theme (until the early twentieth century, it was usual for the audience to applaud the soloist at the end of this cadenza, as modern audiences applaud the end of a jazz break). The first theme is a striding melody of the utmost confidence, almost march-like. A second theme, delicate and pianissimo, still has almost the tread of a march, but as a distant echo, to which horns answer with the first smooth melody of the movement. Many of the most telling passages of this movement are those where this material is transformed in character.

After the long opening tutti, the pianist enters with the first theme played quietly and 'dolce' (sweetly), an unexpected transformation of this march. A few bars later another confident arpeggio figure from the introduction is played meditatively, and in the minor. The delicate second theme is at first even more delicate than before, but when the orchestra takes it over, it is transformed into the snappiest of marches. Indeed, throughout the movement everything eventually comes back to the predominant heroic character of the opening.

The central development starts quietly and searchingly, but a gradual build-up leads to the most heroic passage of all, a mighty procession of double octaves that only gradually subsides. This passage, incidentally, contains one of Beethoven's occasional miscalculations, perhaps resulting from his deafness: in the background a bassoon intones the march rhythm, but it is barely audible against the octaves (even when the piano is a period instrument). After the double-octave passage comes another welcome moment of meditation, before a crescendo leads to the reprise. Here the bold opening cadenza returns, but in shortened form, before the orchestra repeats the first theme. Towards the end of the movement, the orchestra arrives at the pause where a full cadenza would conventionally be expected. Having started with a cadenza, Beethoven now subverts our expectations, and has only the briefest of flourishes before returning again to the delicate second theme. Having curtailed the expected cadenza, Beethoven now greatly extends what follows, rounding off the movement with a further excursion before bringing it to an emphatic close.

The slow movement begins in complete contrast, with muted strings singing a melody of the utmost calm, in a remote key (B major). Czerny tells us that Beethoven had in mind 'the religious songs of devout pilgrims'.[4] The piano enters with a meditative fantasia that seems new, but the quiet chords accompanying it are those of the opening hymn. After this free variation, followed by a moment of cadenza-like flourishes, the piano comes back to the opening theme, now playing a more explicit decorated variation of it. The woodwind take over the theme for a further variation while the piano accompanies them. This gradually settles to a moment of complete stillness, and the key of the music falls by a semitone.

The piano tentatively experiments with a rising pattern of chords, as if leading off into a new section of the slow movement. But this pattern then bursts out explosively to form the principal theme of the finale, which follows without a break. The rising chords of E flat are grouped in strangely truculent syncopation, with a kick on the final offbeat, so that it is only in the answering phrase that the underlying swing of the rhythm is allowed to surface. This movement is a rondo, in which the kicking theme recurs several times, with more delicate and expansive episodes between. The predominant mood is boisterous and, like the first movement, grandly sonorous, though with moments of great delicacy. These include the final pages, in which the timpani quietly repeat the dancing rhythm while the piano gradually winds down, before a final dash rounds off this most assertive of concertos.

CONCERTO FOR PIANO, VIOLIN, AND CELLO IN C MAJOR ('TRIPLE CONCERTO'), OP. 56
Duration: approx. 36 minutes

Allegro
Largo
Rondo alla Polacca

Beethoven composed this unusual concerto in 1804. The piano part is thought to have been written for Beethoven's pupil, the sixteen-year-old Archduke Rudolph, and it is much less demanding for the pianist than the concertos that Beethoven wrote for himself. The piano really acts as a foil for the violin and cello. The cello part, by contrast, is extremely difficult, involving virtuoso work high up on the fingerboard. It was probably written for Anton Kraft, the cellist for whom Haydn wrote his Concerto in D, who specialized in playing in high positions.

The concerto opens quietly with the orchestral cellos and basses trying out a phrase. This then develops into a fully fledged theme, with a dramatic crescendo to fortissimo. Indeed, 'dramatic' is a good word to describe the character of this concerto. It has a somewhat theatrical swagger, with pompous gestures giving way to moments of refined delicacy, such as the charmingly dancing second theme. The entry of the soloists is led by the cello, with a poetical version of the opening theme (the cellist is, throughout, the poet of the three players). Solo passages, by turns witty, assertive, and gentle, alternate with rather grandiose interpolations from the orchestra.

The opening of the brief slow movement is the emotional heart of the work, with the cello singing a melody that reaches higher and higher. Violin and piano then elaborate this theme, until a sustained moment of expectancy culminates in the cello reiterating a note, G, faster and faster. This extraordinary moment leads into a new, flowing melody, once again high on the cello. As it is taken up by the violin, then the orchestra, then the three soloists together, it begins to acquire more definite rhythm, and sounds more and more like a dance. Eventually the full orchestra reveals that it is a polonaise. So, without at first being aware of it, we have entered the finale. This, like the first movement, has a delightful swagger, enhanced by the extra verve and elegance of the polonaise rhythm. The movement is in the form of a rondo, with various episodes interspersed between the main polonaise theme. The first episode begins lyrically, and becomes more and more playful and skittish. The second is in the minor, with the polonaise rhythm very stately and assertive (like a foretaste of Chopin's polonaises). At the end of the movement, Beethoven converts the three-time of the polonaise to a fast two-time, for an exciting dash towards the close. But in a final surprise twist, the stately polonaise rhythm has the last word.

VIOLIN CONCERTO IN D MAJOR, OP. 61
Duration: 37–48 minutes

Allegro ma non troppo
Larghetto –
Rondo: Allegro

Beethoven began to compose a violin concerto in C major in the early 1790s, but only a fragment survives. In 1803 and 1805 he published two beautiful Romances for Violin and

Orchestra, and it has been conjectured that one of them might originally have been intended as the slow movement of the unfinished concerto. The two Romances are often played, but the pinnacle of Beethoven's music for violin is the Concerto in D major, which he composed in 1806. Virtuoso display concertos were all the rage during this period (to the displeasure of contemporary critics), and for that reason Beethoven's concerto was neglected during his lifetime. Unlike most other concertos of the time, it is not principally a display piece, but subtle and meditative (even though it also contains difficult virtuoso passages). It did not become part of the established repertoire until it was revived in the 1840s by the young Joseph Joachim – who himself combined deep seriousness of purpose with the qualities of a virtuoso. Beethoven's has come to be regarded as the greatest violin concerto of the early nineteenth century. He wrote it in the same year as another unusually contemplative concerto, his Fourth Piano Concerto. Later, Beethoven arranged the Violin Concerto for piano at the request of his publisher, but although it is occasionally played in this version it loses the essential quality of sustained lyricism that only the violin can provide (or perhaps this is another way of saying that Beethoven did not sufficiently rethink it so that it would really work on the piano).

The range for the duration given above might seem like a misprint. But there are few works that have been subjected to such contrasted extremes of tempo. The unusual nature of the concerto has led some players to take the first movement at a very leisurely tempo, in order to emphasize its deep spiritual qualities. This approach was most successfully taken by Yehudi Menuhin, and his example has been followed by many violinists since. But it is also a work of vigour and tight structure. The long first movement has a recurring motif of a march rhythm, announced in the opening bar by the timpani. It is the recurrence of this motif that binds the whole movement together, and too introvert or languishing a performance risks loosening it.

After the opening drumbeats, the woodwind, led by the oboe, sing a chorale-like first theme. This is followed by rising scales, and a moment of quiet, interrupted by the full orchestra with forceful, abrupt phrases developed from the drumbeats. This agitation leads in turn to a second chorale-like theme on the woodwind, at first still in the home key of D major, with violins tapping out the drum rhythm. But then the violins take up the second theme in D minor, expanding it into a sweeping melodic line. There is another moment of quiet, with the drumbeats transformed into warm string chords, a climax on full orchestra, and a tailpiece in the form of a rising lyrical melody, which seems to have grown out of the second chorale-like theme.

The violin enters quietly, feeling its way upwards in a gentle cadenza. The drum taps again introduce the first theme, now decorated by the violin. The sequence of themes and motifs follows as in the orchestral introduction – the rising scales, the second chorale theme with its development in the minor, and so on. Through all of this the violin weaves a lyrically virtuoso elaboration and exploration, teasing out the implications and possibilities of each theme in turn. This exposition ends with a big orchestral tutti, revisiting several of the elements forcefully and urgently. As the tutti dies down, the solo violin ascends again in another little cadenza to introduce the development section. Once more the first chorale theme begins, but now in B minor. Bassoons take it up, reiterating a little phrase in plangent duet, while the violin weaves a pattern of triplet arpeggios. These lead to a trill, quiet horns remind us of the drumbeat, and we reach the hushed and solemn heart of the movement. Over pianissimo strings, with drumbeats in the woodwind, the violin plays a series of rising phrases in G minor, which develop into a free, searching fantasia and a moment of repose. From this point the violin rises gradually, with the drumbeats now pizzicato on the strings; there is a sudden crescendo, and the full orchestra bursts in with the return of the first chorale theme. The reprise proceeds as before, with some abbreviation and variation, and an orchestral tutti leads to the cadenza, which Beethoven did not supply. A cadenza by Joachim is most often played, but perhaps the finest is by Fritz Kreisler, magnificently climaxing with the first and last themes combined in counterpoint. The end of the cadenza leads out into the second chorale theme, now sonorously on the lower strings of the violin. The bassoon (unusually prominent and lyrical in this concerto) sings the rising last theme, answered by cellos with violin decoration above. There is a final crescendo, and three chords bring this expansive movement to a close.

If the first movement has not been too drawn out, the slow movement has a magical, hypnotic, spiritual effect. This is a set of variations on a theme first played by the muted strings. It begins with short, hesitant phrases, and then blossoms into a long-breathed second half. The repetition of this pattern throughout the movement – hesitant searching followed by lyrical outpouring – gives the whole movement a wonderfully satisfying sense of cumulative, meditative discovery. In the first variation the melody is introduced by horns and taken up by the clarinet. The second variation has the bassoon playing the melody. Over these instruments the violin develops increasingly ecstatic decorations. The bassoon variation climaxes, and the strings, forte but still muted, reiterate the theme in its original form. The solo violin now enters a passage of profound meditation (as it had done at the centre of the first movement). At first it is cadenza-like, and then it settles into a brief, sonorous melody that breaks off into trills. As the violin rises higher, pizzicato strings bring in another variation of the theme, which the violin counterpoints and then joins. Further musing follows, eventually growing quieter and quieter. Muted horns begin what seems like another variation on the theme. But this is cut off by a sudden fortissimo from the strings, now unmuted, and a brief trill and cadenza lead without a break into the finale.

This is a rondo with strongly swinging rhythm (as is the 'Emperor' Concerto's finale, which followed three years later). The soloist begins, then the full orchestra takes up the theme fortissimo and extends it (again as in the 'Emperor' Concerto), sharpening the rhythm with the addition of trills and dotted rhythms. The first episode follows, in which the soloist introduces a new theme that becomes increasingly vigorous, with dashing arpeggio patterns and forceful chords – the most flamboyant writing in the whole concerto. The principal theme returns, once more followed by a fortissimo orchestral tutti. This time it soon moves away from D major, and the soloist takes over, moving into a singing melody in G minor. The two strains of the melody are each repeated by a bassoon, while the violin decorates with arpeggios. After this gentle interlude, the main theme returns in D major, followed again by an orchestral tutti and a repeat of the first episode, which ventures into new keys and eventually works round to a pause for a cadenza. As in the first movement, Beethoven left the soloist to supply it. The exit from the cadenza is quiet, and at first it gets lost in A flat major, gradually working back to the home key of D major. A final moment of repose is reached, at which the oboe with the other woodwind play a charmingly rustic version of the theme. From here the energy and volume gradually increase, and the movement ends with exuberant cross-rhythms, a playful last pianissimo ascent, and two emphatic final chords.

Overtures

CORIOLAN, OP. 62
Duration: approx. 8 minutes

Coriolan is a tragic drama by the Austrian playwright Heinrich von Collin, written in 1802 on the same subject as Shakespeare's *Coriolanus*. Coriolanus is a successful Roman general who, because of his arrogant disdain of the people, is banished from Rome. In revenge, he joins forces with the Volscians, and leads their army against Rome. As they reach the city walls, and are ready to invade it, Coriolanus is met by his mother, Volumnia, who pleads with him to spare the city. He gives way, and agrees to peace terms. In Shakespeare's version he is then killed by the Volscians, but in Collin's play he commits suicide (Collin did not know Shakespeare's version, and took the story straight from Plutarch's *Lives*, which Beethoven also knew).

Beethoven composed his *Coriolan* Overture not for the theatre, but as a concert piece. It was written in 1807, while he was still working on the Fifth Symphony, and it shares the same mood of determined struggle and heroism (and the key of C minor). The opening attacks, punctuated by silences, are as arresting as the famous opening of the symphony. These are followed by a darkly muttering figure that twice builds up to another silence before developing momentum, just as happens in the symphony. A second theme, with a gentle fall and a leap, has a quality of pleading (rather as the second theme of the symphony does), though the muttering of cellos continues unceasingly beneath it. The whole overture is built from the battle between these two opposing forces, the one associated with Coriolanus the defiant warrior, the other suggesting the desperate appeals of his mother. At the end, the overture returns to the defiant chords of the opening. But these falter, and the music peters out with dying phrases and a final pizzicato.

EGMONT, OP. 84
Duration: approx. 9 minutes

In 1809–10, Beethoven wrote incidental music for a revival in Vienna of Goethe's *Egmont*. The play is set in the sixteenth century, during the occupation of Flanders by the Spanish. Count Egmont is a champion fighting against the ruthless oppression of the people by the Duke of Alba, and is imprisoned and condemned to death. A rescue attempt by his lover fails, and Egmont is led to the block calling on his countrymen to fight for liberty, which they will achieve after his death. The themes of struggle, personal sacrifice, and liberation from tyranny, have obvious links with Beethoven's *Fidelio* (the first version of which, *Leonore*, he had completed several years earlier), and the mood of this overture has much in common with the overtures that he wrote for that opera.

Beethoven may have struggled to write an opera, but, as with the *Leonore* overtures, his genius for creating drama with an orchestra is obvious from the first notes of his overture to *Egmont*. The slow introduction starts with a stark, sustained note on full orchestra, followed by a defiant motif of dotted rhythms. On paper, you could see this as just another variant of the eighteenth-century slow introduction, derived from the stately baroque 'French Overture'. But Beethoven puts an entirely new stamp on it. This is music filled with the emotional conflict of Romanticism, fierce utterances giving way to melancholy questioning, repeated struggles resulting eventually in hard-won victory. As often with Beethoven, this sense of battling with conflicting emotions goes hand in hand with the careful structuring of the master craftsman. The anxious, descending line that is repeated over and over at the end of the slow introduction metamorphoses into the first theme of the Allegro, now extended downwards, and given a more confidently determined character. The dotted rhythms of the slow introduction are transformed into the fierce second theme of the Allegro, and, as before, they are answered by quiet comments from the woodwind. The third theme of the Allegro, a series of quiet falling phrases (first heard on the clarinet) derive from the repeated falling phrases of the slow introduction. After the reprise of the themes, the music comes to an abrupt halt, with solemn wind chords. From the silence, a new element in fast march tempo builds up, and the overture ends with a powerful evocation of Egmont's vision of the liberation to come.

OVERTURE TO *LEONORE* NO. 1, OP. 138
Duration: approx. 10 minutes

OVERTURE TO *LEONORE* NO. 2, OP. 72A
Duration: approx. 14 minutes

OVERTURE TO *LEONORE* NO. 3, OP. 72B
Duration: approx. 14 minutes

OVERTURE TO *FIDELIO*, OP. 72C
Duration: approx. 7 minutes

Beethoven completed only one opera, which went through lengthy rewriting and was staged in two different forms. In its first incarnation its title was *Leonore*. This was not a success when first staged, and Beethoven's friends did their best to persuade him to shorten it. Eventually, Beethoven completed a thoroughly revised version renamed *Fidelio*, and this is the form in which the opera is usually staged today. The plot concerns the rescue of a political prisoner, Florestan, who has been left to starve in a dungeon by the prison governor. Florestan's wife, Leonore, disguises herself as a young man called Fidelio and takes a job at the prison. While she is there, word reaches a minister of state that some of the prisoners have been wrongfully imprisoned, and an inspection is announced. The governor gives the order that the most important prisoner should be killed and buried before the minister arrives. Leonore, realizing that he is referring to her husband, accompanies the gaoler to the dungeon to help him dig the grave. At the very moment when she flings herself between Florestan and the gaoler's dagger, a trumpet sounds from the battlements, announcing the arrival of the minister. Florestan is saved, and the prison governor is arrested.

Beethoven wrote four different overtures. The first three are known as the Overtures to *Leonore* Nos 1, 2, and 3, but they were not composed in that order. Beethoven first wrote 'No. 2' for the Viennese premiere of *Leonore* in 1805. He revised and expanded this to create 'No. 3' for the revival the following year. 'No 1', a shorter version, was written for a performance in Prague in 1807, which never took place. The fourth overture is quite different from the other three, and is known as the Overture to *Fidelio*. It was composed for the revised opera, now retitled *Fidelio*, in 1814. This is a much terser piece, and the only one that works well in the theatre as an overture to the opera. The others are full-blown symphonic works, complete in themselves, and best suited to concert performance.

LEONORE OVERTURE NO. 3

This is the most famous, and the longest, of these overtures, with a wonderful sense of a mighty drama unfolding. For this reason, it is hopeless as an overture to a performance of the opera. Gustav Mahler, conductor of the Vienna Court Opera (later renamed Vienna State Opera) in the last years of the nineteenth century, used to perform it before the final scene of the opera, after Florestan has been rescued from his dungeon. But as it, in effect, retells the story of the rescue, it seems dramatically repetitive at that point.

The overture begins with a massive, slow introduction, which, with its opening descent, suggests the darkness of Florestan's dungeon. The hymn-like theme played by the woodwind is a quote from the beginning of Florestan's great aria in Act II, in which he sings of his lost youth and his imprisonment. By the end of the aria, he has gathered the strength for a final, delirious, vision of Leonore coming to rescue him – a vision that does indeed come true by the end of the scene. The overture is an orchestral portrayal of that journey from dark imprisonment to release.

After the slow introduction, the Allegro begins pianissimo with a theme full of aspiring, upward phrases that rises gradually to a climax. A horn reference to Florestan's theme ushers in a second, gentler theme. These ideas are extensively worked out, as in a traditional symphonic movement, until suddenly, just before the reprise, the music comes to a halt. Over a sustained note in the strings, an off-stage trumpet is twice heard playing a fanfare. In the opera, this is the signal that sounds just as Florestan is about to be killed, announcing that the minister has arrived, and that Florestan will therefore be saved. The overture continues with a reprise of the opening Allegro material, which works round for a final time to Florestan's theme. This peters out, and, after a moment's hesitation, the violins launch into a whirlwind of notes, in which the other strings join, building up to a chord marked *fff* (rare at this date, even in Beethoven), and a joyous return to the first theme of the Allegro. The journey from the dark opening of the overture to this point has been psychologically huge, and, in sheer time, has lasted a quarter of an hour. The fact that the composer originally wrote it to precede the opera is an eloquent demonstration of the fact that Beethoven, the great dramatist of orchestral music, had a far less confident grasp of what might or might not work in the theatre.

LEONORE OVERTURE NO. 2

This was the first of the overtures to be written. It follows broadly the same sequence of events as the better-known No. 3, though with almost every detail slightly different. The slow introduction is shorter, and it goes straight from the off-stage trumpet calls to the final Presto.

LEONORE OVERTURE NO. 1

This was the third overture to be written. At about ten minutes, it is much shorter than Nos 2 and 3. It has a different slow introduction, and a new, combative main Allegro theme, though it is also full of the aspirational rising phrases that characterize Overtures 2 and 3. Florestan's theme, which pervades Overtures 2 and 3, here occurs only as a meditative interlude before the reprise of the Allegro. And the reprise fights its way to a conclusion without an off-stage trumpet, and without breaking into the whirlwind Presto of Overtures 2 and 3.

FIDELIO OVERTURE

Having revised the opera as *Fidelio*, Beethoven wrote an entirely new overture for the 1814 production. It is more concentrated and condensed than its predecessors, and does not directly quote from the music of the opera itself. It is the shortest of the four overtures and, without attempting to convey the dramatic scope of the opera, does what a theatrical overture needs to do: it forcefully calls attention, and vividly conveys a sense of tension, anxiety, and the struggle ahead. It is a more unified work than the *Leonore* Overtures, with the opening call to arms also forming the main theme of the Allegro, and the laconic second theme hardly distracting from the energy of the whole.

Symphonies

SYMPHONY NO. 1 IN C MAJOR, OP. 21
Duration: approx. 27 minutes

Adagio molto – Allegro con brio
Andante cantabile con moto
Menuetto: Allegro molto e vivace
Adagio – Allegro molto e vivace

Beethoven's First Symphony was premiered on 2 April 1800 at a concert in the Court Theatre in Vienna. This was a highly significant event in Beethoven's career. He had moved to Vienna eight years earlier, but this was the first time he had held a large-scale concert devoted mainly to his own music, and for his own profit. A reviewer commented that the opera orchestra 'made a very poor showing', and their faults were 'all the more evident since B's compositions are difficult to execute'. However, he described the symphony as a work of 'considerable art, novelty and a wealth of ideas'.[5]

Beethoven took his time before presenting a symphony to the Viennese public. He had first achieved fame in the city as a virtuoso pianist, and most of his works so far had been built round that reputation and were designed for himself to play – piano trios and other chamber works, solo sonatas, and two piano concertos. It was only at the very end of the eighteenth century that he felt ready to embark on the two genres in which his great predecessors Mozart and Haydn were the undisputed masters, the string quartet and the symphony. He had written sketches for a symphony in 1794–5, but had never finished it. Now, at the age of twenty-nine, he finally took the plunge.

Although this is Beethoven's first symphony it is not a juvenile or immature work. It bursts with exuberance and self-confidence, and has much in common with the symphonies of his great mentor Joseph Haydn – a similar sense of wit and energy, though with just a touch of that truculence that surfaces so often in Beethoven. Of all his symphonies, No. 1 has the most consistent character throughout its four movements, as if one cast is acting out different scenes.

The first movement begins with a slow introduction, and with two woodwind chords that sound like a question. Indeed, the whole of the introduction seems to be feeling for a sense of direction, as the strings and wind interweave and echo each other. The answer to these searchings comes with the Allegro con brio, a fast-moving piece full of abrupt contrasts. A rapid scale tumbles into the first theme. It begins quietly with the violins working away persistently at a little motif of a rising fourth that ends in an upward arpeggio. Each phrase is answered by woodwind chords that seem to echo the introduction. Soon the energy builds to a vigorous tutti. Out of it emerges a second theme with a demure, falling scale that is passed between oboe and flute. After another brief tutti, the falling shape passes to the bass in a minor key, pianissimo, with an oboe counterpoint above, a surprising moment of darkness before the energy rebuilds to round off the first section.

After the repeat, the development takes the first theme, concentrating at first on the little repeating motif, then on the rising arpeggio, than the repeating motif again. All the while the music is moving through different keys, and the motifs pass rapidly between strings and woodwind. The music rises to a fortissimo, and fades as if we are to return to the quiet opening. But, with typical Beethovenian brusqueness, the reprise bursts in fortissimo. And, after the landmarks have been revisited, it is with an insistent fortissimo that the movement ends.

For the slow movement, Beethoven takes two little elements that were prominent in the first movement – an upbeat of a rising fourth, and a falling scale – and makes of them an elegant dance, too slow for a minuet, too fast for a sarabande. The phrasing emphasizes the upbeat, giving the dance a characteristic sway. It begins on second violins alone, and the other strings enter in turn, eventually joined by the woodwind and horns, as if characters from the energetic first movement are gradually joining in the dance. In the second paragraph, the interval of a fourth stretches higher, and the theme is rounded off with pointed dotted rhythms. These are tapped out by the timpani as violins and flute conclude with delicate running triplets. The section is repeated.

In the second part, the music moves into new keys, as the woodwind explore rising intervals over persistent dotted rhythms. When the reprise comes, the dance is accompanied by a running counterpoint. At the end, Beethoven extends the dance before rounding it off with horn calls.

The third movement is described in the score as a minuet, but it is much less like a real dance than the second movement and, as often in Beethoven, the pace is fast and furious. In the middle section the wind come to a standstill, quietly repeating chords while the strings swirl around them.

The finale, like the opening movement, begins with a slow introduction, a playful teaser in which an upward scale is gradually unfurled. At the Allegro molto, the scale takes off to introduce a theme of almost Rossini-like charm. A vigorous tutti leads into an equally poised second theme. The middle of the movement is particularly delightful, with the rushing scale thrown up and down, and combined to sound like a parody of a fugue. From a fierce fortissimo, the reprise of the delicate first theme emerges wittily, like one of Haydn's jokes. At the end of the reprise, Beethoven reaches a pause. More teasing with the scales leads on to another fortissimo and a march-like element that stiffens the rhythm. A final burst of scales in octaves brings this exuberant symphony to a close.

SYMPHONY NO. 2 IN D MAJOR, OP. 36

Duration: approx. 35 minutes

Adagio molto – Allegro con brio
Larghetto
Scherzo: Allegro
Allegro molto

The Second Symphony was finished in 1802, and it illustrates vividly the hazards of trying to draw too close an analogy between an artist's life and work. Despite increasing success as a composer, Beethoven was afflicted by the terrible realization that he was going deaf. He had noticed a deterioration in his hearing over the last three years, and had visited several doctors without significant improvement. Now he began to confront the bleak future ahead of him: 'I must withdraw from everything; and my best years will pass rapidly away without my being able to achieve all that my talent and my strength have commanded me to do.'[6] A student described him at this period as silent and morose, with occasional outbursts of extreme boisterousness.

Little of this is to be guessed from the Second Symphony. The tone is similar to that of the first, predominantly unbuttoned and vivacious, though the moments of reflection are more intensely meditative, the boisterousness has a harder edge, and the entire work is on a grander scale. Reports of the premiere on 5 April 1803 are mixed. One reviewer reported that the new symphony was 'voted very beautiful', like the first, which was played at the same concert. But another writer remarked on 'the striving for the new and surprising', and preferred the First Symphony, finding it 'less forced'.

Like the first, the Second Symphony starts with a slow introduction. It opens with an arresting call to attention on the note D, followed by a calm phrase on oboes and bassoons – this could be the beginning of a Haydn symphony. But soon the music moves away from D down to B flat, and we are in a new world of rushing scales exchanged between strings and woodwind. The tension increases, and the scales become rockets alternating between lower strings and violins, while the woodwind plaintively try to hold on to the serenity with which they started. This reaches a climax of fierce dotted rhythms in D minor – a moment that seems to look forward to the portentous opening of the Ninth Symphony. After a few bars of anxious anticipation, one last falling scale in the violins propels us into the Allegro con brio.

The Allegro seems to have emerged naturally from the scales of the introduction, with not so much a new theme as an organic growth. A quiet, agitated rising phrase in the lower strings is answered first by a swirling descent in the violins and then by the woodwind, still searching plaintively. But they are swept away by the full orchestra, combining the rising phrases and the swirling scales with brusque energy that sets the tone for the entire movement. Even the second theme, which you might have expected to relax (as in the First Symphony), is a march with a fanfare-like rising arpeggio, culminating in assertive dotted rhythms that recall the very opening gesture. A moment of quiet hesitation leads on a powerful falling phrase in D minor, which looks back to the fierce D minor dotted rhythms from the introduction.

After the repeat of the first part of the Allegro, the development continues in D minor, soon breaking into energetic counterpoint between upper and lower strings. The woodwind join in the counterpoint, sustained bass notes descend powerfully, while the agitated opening theme becomes an urgent obsession. A sudden quiet leads in a playful revisiting of the march-like second theme. But it is not long before this too builds in power. A climax of dotted rhythms falls away on a sustained C sharp. It is not at all clear where the music will go from here. But Beethoven, with a sly twist of the harmony, suddenly moves back into D major, and the familiar falling scale in the violins propels us into the reprise of the first Allegro theme.

This time round, the sequence of events is more compressed, giving an impression of an even greater level of energy than before. And at the end, the agitated opening phrases are worked up into the greatest climax of the movement. The theme is transformed into a triumphant rise and fall in octaves, as if this is what it had been wanting to become all along, and the final chords, with their sharp dotted rhythms, end in a simple declaration of the note D, returning the music to the point from which it started.

The slow movement is the one that reveals the greatest contrast with the First Symphony. This movement is much longer than its predecessor, beautiful in the textures of its orchestration, and with touches of anxiety giving it depth. The opening theme in A major is hymn-like, with each eight-bar phrase played first by the strings (without basses) and then answered by mellow clarinets and bassoons with the accompaniment delicately touched in by the strings (now with the basses). Then a charming second theme begins, with phrases again passing back and forth between woodwind and violins. But this turns out to be just the start of a long, exploratory continuation. The little theme darkens immediately from major to minor, a sudden fortissimo is answered by a delicate piano, and then the violins take wing. The mood is affectionate, becoming decorative, and then playful. After another burst of fortissimo, the playfulness develops into a dance, taking advantage of the three-time metre, and ends with a horn call evocative of huntsmen relaxing by the fire. Quite apart from this rural reference, the evolution of the movement to this point gives a hint of the expansive lyricism that Beethoven was to achieve in the slow movement of the 'Pastoral' Symphony No. 6.

After so much expansion and development, one might think that Beethoven is ready to return to the opening for the reprise. He does return to the first theme, but only in order to launch into a real development section, as in the first movement. At first it is in A minor, and decorated with little staccato runs. The key shifts again as the mood turns darker, with plaintive exchanges between strings and woodwind alternating with forceful passages. Eventually, a glorious climax (another portent of the 'Pastoral' Symphony) finds its way back to the home key of A major, and we arrive at the reprise of the first theme. This time, the woodwind answers are decorated by the violins with charming elaboration. With new touches along the way, the expansive paragraph arrives again at the unabashed dance and the horn call. The movement is rounded off with fragments of the first theme, echoed by flute arpeggios, and a firm final cadence.

The third movement is a scherzo, even faster than the 'minuet' of the First Symphony, and with an abrupt character that makes its dance origins scarcely recognizable. It is still in the three-time of a minuet, but broken into contrasted fragments, and punctuated by outbursts and swirls. There are subtle links to the first movement: the rising shape of the opening bars is a distillation of the first Allegro theme, and the swirls in the second half of the scherzo also evoke those in the first movement. The two statements of the scherzo are separated by a trio. Here, the elegant turns of phrase from the woodwind do remind us of a more conventional dance, but they are interrupted by aggressive growls from the strings, as if they are mocking the woodwind's old-fashioned courtliness.

The abrupt alternations of the scherzo continue into the finale, but now at virtuoso speed. It starts with a brusque gesture followed by a rapid muttering figure in the violins. Here too there is a subtle allusion to the first movement: the muttering figure contains within it the rising shape of the first Allegro theme. In the scherzo it was distilled, and now it is agitated. After these two elements have been worked up into a brief tutti, a smoother element moves up from the cellos through the upper strings to the woodwind – this too is a version of the rising shape. It soon gives way to a new theme in the woodwind, made up of simple falling arpeggios; this is a version of the march-like second theme from the first movement, turned upside down. Bassoon and oboe extend it in a lyrical line. From the next tutti emerges the bassoon, still playing arpeggios while the violins peck away at the opening gesture. This soon leads to a return to the first gesture and the muttering violins. It seems that this movement might be turning out to be a rondo, like many finales. But instead, the muttering turns to the minor, and the music enters a fierce development section. All of the thematic elements are drawn in to an extended battle. Suddenly it comes to a stop. Hesitant pecks from the violins bring us once again back to the brusque opening, and we are into the reprise.

The sequence of themes is revisited, and once again the bassoon arpeggios and the pecking violins emerge from the tutti. Surely we must be nearing the end. But now Beethoven embarks on a massive coda. It begins with another fierce tutti, as if the battles of the development are returning. There is a pause on an expectant fortissimo chord. A second, quiet string chord takes us away from D major. Where is this heading? The music sets off again in B minor, delicate pecking returns, and then sinks into mysterious sustained chords in G major. From the pianissimo hush blasts out a totally unexpected chord (in effect, an 'augmented sixth') with which we are wrenched back to D major. Beethoven has out-Haydned Haydn, and it is easy to imagine the shock that this chord would have produced in 1802. But he has still not finished. After a climactic tutti, he again reaches a pause, and again is diverted into B minor. But this time the pecking falters teasingly. With one last burst of full orchestra, the symphony comes to a brilliant close.

SYMPHONY NO. 3 IN E FLAT MAJOR ('EROICA'), OP. 55
Duration: approx. 50 minutes (including first movement repeat)

Allegro con brio
Marcia funebre: Adagio assai
Scherzo: Allegro vivace
Finale: Allegro molto

With the 'Eroica', written in 1803–4 and first performed in public in April 1805, we reach the Beethoven of myth and popular imagination – the composer who portrays in his music the struggles of life and the hard-won triumph of the spirit. It is difficult not to feel some truth in this picture when one hears the 'Eroica', and a reliable anecdote supports it. The symphony was inspired by Napoleon, and the title 'Buonaparte' was inscribed on the first page of the manuscript. But when Beethoven was told by his pupil Ferdinand Ries that Napoleon had proclaimed himself emperor, 'he flew into a rage and cried out: "Is he then, too, nothing more than an ordinary human being? Now he, too, will trample on all the rights of man and indulge only his ambition."' Beethoven tore up the title page, and gave the symphony the name 'Sinfonia Eroica' instead.[7]

After a semi-public performance in February 1805, a reviewer who declared himself one of Beethoven's 'sincerest admirers' had to confess that in this work 'he finds too much that is glaring and bizarre, which hinders greatly one's grasp of the whole, so that a sense of unity is almost completely lost'.[8] After the official premiere in April, another reviewer reported that only Beethoven's friends considered it a masterpiece, and that most of the public 'thought the symphony too heavy, too long, and himself too discourteous, because he did not nod his head in recognition of the applause which came from a portion of the audience'.[9] It is certainly a long and discursive work – it is one and a half times the length of the Second Symphony. And even for modern audiences there is a problem in sensing the overall coherence of the work. The first two movements are massive and deeply serious. The third is short and snappy, the fourth predominantly lightweight, and inclined to ramble. It takes a great deal of skill and concentrated energy for a conductor and orchestra to find a balance of tempo and weight between the four movements that really works, so that the audience does not feel a little disappointed by the finale.

The symphony begins with two abrupt chords of E flat major. They are followed by a quiet fragment of a melody in the cellos, which at first simply plays up and down the notes of that same chord of E flat. But immediately there are doubts. The melody droops downwards, the violins enter hesitantly. Soon the music pulls itself back to the cellos' opening phrase, now in the woodwind, but again it doesn't last for long. There are further hesitant exchanges of phrases, a build-up of sudden offbeat chords, and the cello phrase is stated fortissimo by the whole orchestra. This opening passage sets the mood – you might even say the problem – for the whole movement. Moments that seem assertive soon collapse, and are followed by searching, gathering of energy, another brief climax, another retreat, more questioning and searching. It is a movement of false trails, interruptions, and unexpectedly delayed outcomes. Writers have suggested that Beethoven derived some of the ideas for this movement from Mozart's Symphony No. 39 in E flat, whose first movement Allegro shares the same three-time metre and key, the contrast between lyricism and high energy, and even specific motifs. But what Beethoven set out to write was something representing far more of a struggle. In Mozart, the three-time gives it an element of dancing elegance. But in Beethoven, the sheer weight to the swing makes it much more portentous.

There are more relaxed elements. The first fortissimo gives way to an elegant little falling phrase that is passed between woodwind and strings. Then a passage of exuberant energy is rounded off with a phrase of simple repeated notes in the woodwind. This last element seems like nothing more than a linking passage, but its repeated notes will prove to be an important motif later in the symphony.

The opening section is packed with material and already long (and Beethoven as usual asks for a repeat, which most conductors observe today despite the length). In the central development, all of the elements and fragments from the first section contribute, often juxtaposed or combined together. The syncopations and offbeat accents from the beginning of the movement become an important feature. A climax builds up, in which aggressive accents again and again cut across the three-time rhythm, and culminate in a harmonic clash (between E and F) that must have been shocking to Beethoven's audiences. Out of this crisis emerges a quiet theme on oboes in E minor – a key utterly remote from E flat major, and yet a melody that seems subtly related to familiar lyrical elements. The music gradually struggles its way back closer to the home key. Once more the tension slowly develops, with the woodwind leading a crescendo in which the original cello theme is beautifully interwoven (touches of beautiful orchestration continually surprise in this symphony). After another climax, there is a moment of almost inaudible hush, with the violins marked *ppp* (like *fff* a rare marking in Beethoven). A horn quietly enters, playing the opening of the cello theme, but apparently too early – the harmony hasn't resolved, and the horn clashes with the violins. This is a moment that puzzled Beethoven's contemporaries: was it intended as a joke? Beethoven was in no doubt of its rightness. At the first rehearsal, his pupil Ferdinand Ries was standing next to him, and said, "'That damned horn-player! Can't he count? This sounds atrociously false!" I think I came pretty close to getting a box on the ear, and Beethoven did not forgive me for a long time.'[10] Beethoven's intention remains either a mystery or a stroke of genius.

The cellos regain their theme. But immediately the end of the cello phrase droops down not once but twice, pulling away to another surprising key (F major). Through a series of key changes, Beethoven wrenches the music back to E flat. From here, the reprise of the opening material proceeds much as before, through a similar trail of hesitations. The masterstroke comes at the end. After Beethoven seems more or less to have reached a conclusion, he adds an extended coda, starting with yet another sudden and surprising change of key. Just as we thought we had arrived safely back in E flat, the music lurches down to D flat, and then to C major. As the music subsides, we do gradually work back to the home key, and Beethoven asserts the fact with a final, and magnificently extended, crescendo, in which the three horns provide the mellifluous core (as the woodwind had done during the great crescendo in the middle of the movement). At the concluding climax, the hesitant little theme with which the movement began has finally blossomed into a great statement of triumphant homecoming.

The second movement is a funeral march in C minor. But it is far more than that. Processional in its rhythm, it has the scope and emotional range of a great funeral oration. The melody in the violins is given a sombre tread by the double basses, with flurries of grace notes suggesting muffled drums. This opening procession sometimes dies to a whisper, at other times is punctuated by sudden stabs of anguish. A second section warms into C major, with the oboe leading a gentle melody that begins with a simple rise over a chord of C major (this subtly links back to the cellos' outlining of a major chord at the beginning of the symphony). The effect is of consolation, but there are also emphatic climaxes, with trumpets lending a military edge. This is followed by a return to the quiet funeral march. After a few bars it turns away, and a solemn fugue begins. Gradually it builds up to reach a great tragic climax. But it breaks off almost brutally, and a fragment of the march is followed by further trumpet calls of menacing insistence. As these subside, the funeral march finally reasserts itself, but now emerging out of a complex texture, as if one has suddenly become aware of all the crowds lining the streets. At the end of the movement there is no neat finality. The music fragments, as if grief has robbed it of the power of expression.

If the funeral march ends in fragmentation, the scherzo begins with a sense of suppressed excitement, like a rumour circulating. An oboe enters with the theme, whose rapid repeated notes are like a speeded-up version of the repeated-note element in the first movement. Only after many bars do the mutterings form themselves into a real theme, and the whole orchestra relishes the sense of release. This section is repeated, and the trio follows. For once it really is a trio, of three horns playing hunting calls, at first in simple up-and-down arpeggios that relate to the beginning of the symphony. The mood is joyful, but the end of the trio introduces doubt (in a manner reminiscent of the way the opening theme of the symphony droops), and in the end it tails off, allowing the muttering of the scherzo to creep in and reassert itself.

The finale begins with a rushing call to attention, after which the movement consists of a loosely constructed set of variations. Its theme is taken from the finale of a ballet score that Beethoven composed in 1801, *The Creatures of Prometheus*. But the full theme does not appear immediately. At first pizzicato strings and woodwind play a simple bass line, and then two variations of it follow. It is only at Variation 3 that the oboe finally lays the melody on top of the bass. The rise and fall of its opening phrase relates closely to the first theme of the first movement (as well as to the trio of the scherzo). This is no coincidence. It seems that the intention of using this *Prometheus* theme was one of Beethoven's first ideas for the 'Eroica' Symphony. The first phrase of the theme has a climax of repeated notes, and perhaps this was the seed of the repeated note in the first movement, and the theme of the scherzo. It is characteristic of Beethoven's thinking that he should seek to bind a work together with such subtle relationships.[11]

After the oboe's statement of the theme, the movement becomes more rhapsodic, moving off into other keys, varying the length of each variation, and blurring the outlines of what started as a straightforward structure to become more of a free development. Variation 4 reverts to the bass line, making a little fugue out of the opening notes of it. In Variation 5, the violins and flute delicately elaborate the melody. A sudden interruption by all the strings leads into Variation 6, an urgent, thumping march in the minor (or is it more like a sturdy peasant dance?). Variation 7 begins with a reminiscence of the tune, but then reverts to another passage of fugue on the bass line, this time with energetic running scales as a counterpoint. This leads to a grand climax, back in the home key of E flat.

After a pause, the pace drops, and the woodwind transform the theme into a chorale. Its calm is disturbed by expressive accents, which, together with a rising scale in clarinet and oboe, suggest memories of the funeral march. This reminiscence is reinforced as the horns and trumpets join in, leading the theme to a powerful climax, as they did in the funeral march. After the climax subsides, the music seems to drift for a moment, and to begin setting off in a new direction and new key. But soon it quietens and becomes halting, with strings and woodwind tentatively exchanging pairs of notes (perhaps this alludes to the fragmentation at the end of the funeral march). Finally, the mood is shattered by an outburst from the whole orchestra, repeating the rushing call to attention with which the movement began, and the horns transform the theme into whooping hunting calls, like a carousing version of their trio in the scherzo. The rest of the orchestra joins them, and the symphony ends with chords of E flat emphatically hammered home again and again, finally laying all doubts to rest.

SYMPHONY NO. 4 IN B FLAT MAJOR, OP. 60

Duration: approx. 33 minutes

Adagio – Allegro vivace
Adagio
Allegro vivace
Allegro ma non troppo

The Fourth Symphony was composed in 1806 and first performed at a private concert in March 1807 given by Prince Lobkowitz, one of Beethoven's patrons. Like numbers one and two, it opens with a slow introduction. Yet this is no longer a gallant or stately gesture, but something much darker. The opening bars have almost the atmosphere of the 'Representation of Chaos' that begins Haydn's *Creation* – perhaps Beethoven was paying homage to his old teacher, consciously or unconsciously. The darkness is profound, the stillness punctuated by hesitant points of light. The music comes to rest, a massive crescendo brings in the whole orchestra in an outburst like a massive sneeze, and suddenly we are propelled into the Allegro, in which the points of light from the introduction have been formed into a joyful theme. The contrasts are great, the atmosphere is rumbustious. Even the gentler second theme, introduced by bassoon followed by oboe, consists at first of yet more staccato points, introduced by a flourish, though the flute then extends it into a sustained descending line (the first real melody in the symphony so far). The first section of the Allegro is repeated.

In the central development section of the movement, the staccato main theme at first predominates, then quietens, and, in the hands of the flute, moves off into D major. While the staccato motif continues, the strings play a rising melody, which is then passed back and forth between violins and woodwind. This seems entirely new, a delightful moment before a tutti breaks back to the exuberant mood. But this too soon evaporates into a mysterious pianissimo passage in which fragments from the earliest bars of the Allegro seem to be searching for a way forward, passing through the remote key of B major, then back to B flat, and finally building up to a fortissimo reprise of the main theme. From that point on, the movement is back on course, maintaining its exuberance to the final bars.

The slow movement also has a pointed motif running through it, a pattern of dotted rhythms stated immediately by the second violins. Over this, the first violins weave a long, singing melody, whose descending line perhaps derives from descending melodic fragments in the first movement. Later, in the most touching passage of the movement, a solo clarinet quietly turns this line upside down, ascending eloquently over the most delicate of accompaniments. Throughout this movement the accompanying figures, often derived from the opening dotted rhythms or variants of them, are highly active, while the melodic lines above them are simple and lyrical. It is difficult to get the balance of the contrasting elements right, so that the lines can sing, but all the detail of the accompaniments can fall naturally into place without becoming dogged. At the return of the opening theme, Beethoven decorates the violin line beautifully, in a manner that was to reach its climax in the slow movement of the Ninth Symphony.

The scherzo brings us back to the exuberant mood of the first movement. Cross-rhythms continually break up the three-time rhythm, as if a rival dance in two-time is fighting to gain the upper hand. There is a gentler trio, with elegant and simple phrases sung by the oboe, contrasting with the confusions of the scherzo. Unusually, the trio returns twice, and the horns momentarily threaten to bring it back a third time. But they are cut off abruptly.

The finale is a movement of irrepressible energy. The rapid opening figure is quiet at first, but soon punctuated by loud chords. This is a movement of strong contrasts, the perpetuum mobile of the semiquavers at one moment quiet and delicate, then suddenly aggressive and fortissimo, with offbeat accents. There is a song-like second theme, played by oboe and flute, and then descending to the cellos. But, as in the first movement, the exuberant elements allow little space for such musings. The central section of the movement culminates in an insistent, almost savage, series of accents, before the air clears to let through the reprise of the semiquaver theme, played by solo bassoon (and almost impossible to articulate at Beethoven's very fast tempo). This happens again towards the end, where clarinet and bassoon share the theme.

In the final bars, Beethoven slows the theme down, and introduces pauses as if something new is about to happen. But it was only a joke, and Beethoven rudely closes the movement with an aggressive gesture, like the raucous laugh with which he would sometimes end a piano improvisation.

SYMPHONY NO. 5 IN C MINOR, OP. 67
Duration: approx. 34 minutes

Allegro con brio
Andante con moto
Allegro –
Allegro

Beethoven began his Fifth Symphony in 1804 before composing his fourth, and then returned to it, working on it over several years while composing other major works. It was finally premiered in Vienna in December 1808 at the Theater an der Wien, in the same concert as the premiere of No. 6, the 'Pastoral'. The Fifth Symphony is a study in relentlessness. Beethoven takes a motif consisting of four notes – almost nothing – and constructs a whole movement out of it. Haydn had done similar things before him, but Beethoven hammers the point home with characteristic truculence. By lucky chance, the 'motto' theme turned out to be Morse Code for the letter 'V', and it was adopted as the symbol of Victory against the Nazis in the Second World War. This was fortuitous, but it is not what makes this symphony so powerful. It is that Beethoven maintains his determination right to the end, through four movements. There is less relaxation in this half hour than in virtually any piece of music. The impact is startling, and when performed well, it seems to express powerfully a spirit of endurance against the odds, of the ability to get through by sheer determination.

The first movement opens with two statements of the famous motto, separated by a pause: 'Thus Fate knocks at the door', Beethoven is supposed to have said (according to his unreliable pupil Anton Schindler). This music is so familiar that it is easy to take it for granted, and it takes some effort to imagine the impact it must have had in its day. This is compounded by the fact that in many modern performances the hammering of the motto is kept strictly in tempo, and the pause minimized, sometimes disciplining the music out of any real significance. An older generation was freer with it, often giving it portentous weight. This may now be unfashionable, but is perhaps closer to the spirit of Beethoven's music. The entire first movement is dominated by the motto. Even at moments of relaxation, during the brief melody that forms the second theme, the hammering is still there in the bass. And it is kept up right to the last bars in a sustained act of concentrated determination.

The second movement opens with a warm melody on the cellos, in the key of A flat major. It is almost like a slow dance, with its gentle dotted rhythms in three-time. But soon the music turns a corner, and we find ourselves back in C (C major, rather than the C minor of the first movement), with trumpets blazing a martial tune that in its rhythm resembles a slowed-down version of the 'Fate' motto. The movement becomes a struggle between these two elements, the gentle dance in A flat, and the fortissimo military theme in C. Twice the cello melody returns, varied with greater elaboration each time, and twice it is followed by the resurgence of the fortissimo C major theme. After a pause, there is a passage in which Beethoven seems to be searching for a solution to this conflict. Eventually it comes in the form of a magnificent fortissimo statement of the cellos' A flat melody, now on full orchestra, with the woodwind answering the violins in a contrapuntal interweaving of the theme. In this climax, the apparently irreconcilable elements seem to have been brought together.

But that is far from the end of conflict. The scherzo opens mysteriously, with pianissimo rising phrases in the bass and tentative pauses. The quiet is broken by yet another version of the 'Fate' motif, now hammered out by horns, and this movement too pits these violently contrasted elements against each other. A central trio section breaks into scampering scales, rising from the basses and cellos up to the violins. The little reiterated four-note phrase with which each build-up ends is another reminder of the 'Fate' motif. Modern performances sometimes repeat the whole of the scherzo and trio, this having been Beethoven's original intention (though he deleted the repeat before publication). The final return to the scherzo does not go as expected. The tentative opening is not brushed aside by fortissimo horns. Instead, a pianissimo version of the motif is accompanied by pizzicato strings, and subsides down to a low, held chord of A flat (the key of the slow movement). This is marked *ppp*, and in the distance the timpani quietly tap out the motif.

A massive crescendo leads without a break into the finale. Here all the struggle and martial implications of the preceding movements are released into an actual march, now reinforced by trombones and piccolo (the first time Beethoven has used these instruments in a symphony). The opening paragraph is capped by the horns playing bold phrases with a rising leap. In its shape this theme is strongly reminiscent of the cellos' gentle theme from the slow movement. Following this, the violins play a theme built from little scurrying four-note cells, another element drawn from the 'Fate' motif. The central section of the movement is built almost entirely from this cell, until a climax is reached and quickly dispersed, and we suddenly find ourselves back in a tentative reminiscence of the scherzo. Soon this settles, and a sudden crescendo returns us to the triumphal march. This time round, it ends in an acceleration to a Presto, in which reiteration of the march theme culminates in a series of relentlessly hammered final chords.

SYMPHONY NO. 6 IN F MAJOR ('PASTORAL'), OP. 68
Duration: approx. 43 minutes

Awakening of cheerful feelings on arriving in the countryside: Allegro ma non troppo
Scene by the brook: Andante molto mosso
Merry gathering of peasants: Allegro –
Thunder. Storm: Allegro –
Shepherd's song. Joyful and thankful feelings after the storm: Allegretto

Astonishingly, the Sixth Symphony was completed in the same year as the fifth, 1808, and was first performed in the same concert in December of that year at the Theater an der Wien. The two works could scarcely be more different: the sixth is Beauty to the fifth's Beast. While the fifth punches its way through all obstacles to eventual triumph, the sixth gently makes its way through an emotional landscape – though admittedly interrupted by one magnificent catastrophe. Perhaps Beethoven needed this total change of pace and mood as an antidote to the fifth.

The 'Pastoral' Symphony is a rare example in Beethoven of 'programme music' – music that has a declared narrative of a non-musical kind. This was a popular genre of composition at the time, which Beethoven only occasionally ventured into (as in the Piano Sonata 'Les Adieux', and *Wellington's Victory*). But Beethoven himself made it clear that he was not interested in the sort of naive musical representation other composers indulged in. He described this Pastoral Symphony as 'a matter more of feeling than of painting in sounds'.[12] There are representational elements in it, but it reflects most of all his deep love of the countryside, to which Beethoven retreated for long periods and in which he composed much of this symphony.

'Cheerful', in the title of the first movement, is the translation of 'heiter', a word used also to describe the weather as bright or clear. And there is an immediate sense of clarity in the music, with an airy, uncomplicated melody supported by the simplest of harmonies. This opening movement often used to be taken at a gentle amble. Modern performances, particularly those on period instruments, tend to be at more of a trot, and Beethoven's metronome marking suggests that this may be nearer to what he had in mind. Whether faster or slower, it evokes feelings of profound contentment, rather than mere cheerfulness. The gentle trotting (or ambling) phrase that opens the symphony recurs throughout the movement, with its motifs sometimes developing into expansive crescendos, like the sensation of one's spirits lifting on a warm summer's day. There are broader, lyrical developments also, and occasional moments where the main theme becomes almost boisterous. But the overall mood is genial and relaxed, expanding in the final moments into a joyful climax.

In the 'Scene by the brook', the first thing that strikes the ear is the rich texture: second violins, violas, and two muted cellos create a murmuring accompaniment with a gentle swing to the rhythm. Above them, first violins elaborate a melody, at first hesitantly and then opening out, handing it over to the clarinet and bassoon, responding with trills, and then finishing the melody off with the cellos echoing. It seems that a new theme might appear at this point, but instead the violins take up the melody again, now extending it, soaring higher and moving into new keys. Flute and bassoon add a new extension to the melody. Twice the strings build up a climax, and twice it subsides. Then, after a moment's hush, we move into more distant keys and the melody is taken up by the oboe, with flute answering, then by the clarinet. Another change of key, and back to the violins, very quietly. Another build-up, back to the flute, back to the violins. These constant repetitions and developments of the same melodic ideas might be boring (and indeed are if the movement is taken too slowly). But the delicate scoring, with the rich but transparent chords in the lower strings, the gently rocking rhythm, the dialogue with the woodwind instruments, and the continual venturing into new keys, give the movement a wonderful feeling of relaxed exploration, with new views of the familiar landscape opening out at each corner. At the end is a moment of imitation, of the kind that Beethoven generally avoided: the flute is labelled 'nightingale', the oboe 'quail', and the clarinet 'cuckoo', and they sing together, bringing the scene to a close with a moment of charming naivety.

The third movement is a rustic dance, at first delicate (or perhaps heard in the distance), and then bursting out fortissimo. Solo oboe, clarinet, and horn step forward in turn, the clarinet throwing in a flamboyant flourish. The bassoon dopily (or possibly drunkenly) supplies a few bass notes. Then the pace accelerates, and the crowd joins in, stamping out a square, stocky rhythm. There is a pause, then the opening section of the dance returns, and is followed again by the stamping set. Another return to the opening accelerates to a sudden halt, as distant thunder is heard and the first drops of rain begin to fall. We are into the fourth movement.

After a moment of gentle pattering accompanied by phrases of rising anxiety the storm bursts, with jagged descents and upward flashes of lightning, low rumblings, sudden cracks of thunder, and an impression of torrential downpour. But this powerful movement is not just impressionistic. It also has a musical shape. After the first phase of the storm has momentarily died down, the motifs from the opening of the movement are developed, the pattering rain in the violins combined with the anxious rising motif in the clarinet. A striding, descending line in the bass, with an offbeat accent, then carries us on through new keys until a great climax is reached, at which trombones join for the first time in reinforcing the fortissimo. As the climax subsides the striding bass line continues, with shuddering strings above. Distant thunder punctuates the conclusion, as a chorale on the oboe, together with a rising flute, leads straight into the fifth movement.

Shepherd pipes are heard, in clarinet and horn, and the violins quietly sing the shepherd's song, as if heard from the other side of the valley. The melody itself is like a distillation of the peaceful first movement, with its intervals like those of a natural horn and its simple harmonies. It passes from first violins to second violins to violas and cellos, quickly reaching a first climax (all the climaxes of this movement are bigger than those of the first movement, because of the addition of trombones). A more thrusting, joyful theme emerges, driving onwards until another climax. The quiet shepherd's melody is restated, now decorated with a trill and delicate little accompanying figures. A new, gently flowing melody follows, on clarinets and bassoons. This too leads to another build-up, after which the shepherd's song reappears, now elaborated into continuous semiquavers, and passing, as before, from first to second violins, and to violas and cellos, and followed once more by the joyful second theme and a climax. The whole of the rest of the movement consists of a thrice repeated reassertion of the shepherd's song, and of the home key of F major. The first time the song begins as a single line in cellos and bassoons, and builds up. The second time it is again in cellos and bassoons, but elaborated into semiquavers once more. This time the music swells to a glorious, and final, climax, slowly descending to pianissimo. Now, as a last farewell, fragments of the shepherd's melody are lovingly remembered. There is a distant, muted horn call, and two emphatic chords bring the symphony to a close.

It was perhaps on one of his walks in the country that Beethoven jotted down on a piece of paper, 'It seems as if in the country every tree said to me, "Holy! Holy!"' [13] And on a sketch for the last movement of the Pastoral Symphony he wrote, 'Lord, we thank Thee'.

SYMPHONY NO. 7 IN A MAJOR, OP. 92
Duration: approx. 40 minutes (including first movement repeat)
Poco sostenuto – Vivace
Allegretto
Presto
Allegro con brio

The Seventh Symphony was written in 1811–12, and first performed in Vienna at several concerts during 1813–14, at which it was paired with his popular *Wellington's Victory*. Beethoven himself conducted the concerts, despite his increasing deafness. Fortunately, orchestras in Beethoven's day were directed by the leader of the violins (in partnership with a keyboard player, if there was one), so Beethoven's ability to cause catastrophe was limited.

Nevertheless, there was one terrible moment during a rehearsal of the symphony, described by one of the violinists in the orchestra, composer Louis Spohr:

> It was easy to see that the poor deaf *Maestro* of the piano could no longer hear the quiet passages. This was particularly remarkable in a passage in the second part of the first *allegro* of the symphony. At that part there are two pauses in quick succession, the second of which is *pianissimo*. This, Beethoven had probably overlooked, for he again began to give the time before the orchestra had executed the second pause. Without knowing it therefore, he was already from ten to twelve bars in advance of the orchestra when it began the *pianissimo*. Beethoven, to signify this in his own way, had crept completely under the desk. Upon the now ensuing *crescendo*, he again made his appearance, raised himself continually more and more, and then sprang up high from the ground, when according to his calculation the moment for the *forte* should begin. As this did not take place, he looked around him in affright, stared with astonishment at the orchestra that it should still be playing *pianissimo*, and only recovered himself when at length the long expected *forte* began, and was audible to himself. Fortunately this scene did not take place at the public performance, otherwise the audience would certainly have laughed again.[14]

Of all Beethoven's symphonies, No. 7 is the one that creates the grandest of effects with the most economical means. The instruments of his orchestra are the same as in the First Symphony, but as the seventh begins, we know straight away that we are setting off on a great journey. Huge chords punctuate the opening bars of the slow introduction, and between them we hear the sound of oboe, then clarinets, then horns, like figures in an enormous, still landscape. There is a gathering of energy as quiet scales rise in the strings; then a crescendo to a fortissimo, with the oboe's theme now forcefully stated by the violins, and the scales driving them on, above and below. Eventually this introduction comes to a halt, the woodwind and the violins exchange hesitant phrases. These coalesce into a dancing theme on the flute, signalling the beginning of the Vivace. Another gathering of energy leads to a pause. And with a mighty swirl of the strings, we are finally off.

The little dancing flute theme has become an irresistible force. There are stops along the way through the movement – moments when the energy tails off, changes of key where we seem to have lost our way. But through it all, the dancing dotted rhythm of the flute theme persists. It seems generated by obsession – a determination to muster the effort to get through. This impression in the first movement lasts, in different ways, throughout the whole symphony. Each of its four movements is dominated by a rhythm that repeats endlessly. Richard Wagner called the symphony 'the apotheosis of the dance', and it certainly shows Beethoven at his most joyful and energetic. But as so often in Beethoven, there is a strong sense that the joy has to be won by sheer determination. The forces that defeat us may be out of sight in this symphony, but immense energy is needed to keep them there.

The second movement is based on a wonderfully simple idea: a solemn rhythmic tread begins quiet and low, and, through repetitions and accretions, grows until the air is filled with its sound, and then dies away. It suggests a procession coming gradually closer and receding (and it was this association that inspired the 'March of the Pilgrims' in Berlioz's *Harold in Italy*). The simple grandeur of the concept has in the past encouraged many conductors to make something massive and funereal of it; but Beethoven's marking is Allegretto, and the metronome marking (76 beats to the minute) is considerably faster than a slow march. Taken at something like Beethoven's suggested pace, it has a natural tread and an irresistible build-up of texture that is quite impressive enough.

After a rootless wind chord, the movement begins with just violas, cellos, and basses intoning the theme, with its simple reiterated motif (long-short-short-long-long). The second violins take up the motif, while violas and cellos sing a beautiful counterpoint against it. Then the treading motif passes to the first violins, the singing counterpoint to the second violins, with a new swinging accompaniment in violas and cellos, while a long crescendo grows in intensity. This culminates in a moment of sublime grandeur as the full orchestra joins in, with the treading rhythm in horns and woodwind, the singing counter-point high on the violins, and a more animated triplet rhythm cutting across in violas and cellos.

The procession subsides, there is a change from minor to major, and clarinets and bassoons sing a new, broad melody, while a fragment of the processional rhythm continues in the bass. After an expansive exploration of this melody, it is brought to an abrupt end, and the opening material returns. But now the mood is different. Instead of building, it remains muted, with the treading rhythm pizzicato in the bass, and a new agitated pattern in the strings. The procession evaporates, leaving a mood of anxiety. Pianissimo strings put the agitated pattern and the processional rhythm together, like the hesitant beginnings of a fugue. A sudden crescendo leads to an emphatic, fortissimo restatement of the processional theme in the whole orchestra. This soon subsides, and bassoon and clarinet begin their expan-sive theme in A major again. But this time it is short-lived. Fragments of the procession inter-vene, and the movement is brought to a close with the same rootless woodwind chord that began it.

The third movement bursts with energy. The scherzo itself alternates with a slower trio, in which woodwind reiterate little song-like phrases. Many conductors used to take this very slowly, like a solemn hymn. But, once again, Beethoven's marking is not particularly slow (two-thirds of the pace of the scherzo), and if his instruction is taken seriously (as it often is these days) the song has more of an easy-going, rustic character. Towards the end of this trio, a horn reiterates the rhythm of the song fragment very low under the sustained melody – an oddly hypnotic effect. These two sections alternate in a five-part pattern (scherzo – trio – scherzo – trio – scherzo), a pattern that Beethoven had used in the scherzo of the Fourth Symphony and had considered for the Fifth. At the end of the final scherzo section, it seems that we are returning to the trio yet again. But after two phrases of the song (now in the minor) it is swept aside by brisk chords.

The energy kicks up to an even higher level in a finale of sustained drive and determina-tion. A swirling figure, with a fierce accent on the offbeat, dominates the movement, inter-spersed with prancing dotted rhythms and exuberant horn calls. There are occasional quiet moments, but it is never long before we are back into the torrent. At the end, there is a long build-up of the swirling motif, below which cellos and basses obsessively repeat again and again a sawing pattern of two alternating notes, creating a hypnotic effect that harks back to the strange low horn in the third movement. Finally Beethoven breaks loose from this knot, and the symphony rushes headlong to its close.

SYMPHONY NO. 8 IN F MAJOR, OP. 93
Duration: approx. 26 minutes

Allegro vivace e con brio
Allegretto scherzando
Tempo di menuetto
Allegro vivace

Written in 1812, and premiered in Vienna on 27 February 1814, at first sight this symphony seems like a throwback. It returns to the scale of No. 1, and has none of the grandeur of No. 7. It is very concise, and contains no really slow music – no slow introduction, and no slow movement. But it is not just a return to an earlier style. This symphony has a highly concentrated character, with nervous and quirky rhythmic elements dominating each of its four movements.

It opens with a bang, as the first theme in F major is boldly stated by full orchestra. Like the first movement of the 'Eroica', it is in three-time, but it has none of the expansive exploration of that movement. Here the time signature gives the music the swing of a truculent dance. This truculence is emphasized by sharp accents, often off the main beat, and by insistent repetition of phrases. Even the quiet second theme is built from repetitions. We would normally expect this to be in C major (a fifth up from the home key of F), but here it is at first in D major, and is then, after a moment of hesitation, taken up by the woodwind in the more usual C major. This symphony is full of quirky harmonic twists of this kind.

In the centre of the movement the insistence become more and more obsessive as the music works towards a climax for the reprise. When the first theme does eventually return, it is at first in the bass, almost inaudible under the full orchestra, marked *fff*. The ending of the movement is particularly effective. After a climax, a bassoon quietly reiterates a familiar jumping figure, and a clarinet sets off into a completely new key (D flat major). It seems that we might be in for a substantial coda. But all of a sudden we are back in F major, there is more insistent hammering followed by quiet chords, and the movement ends with the first bar of the main theme played delicately, as if Beethoven is pretending that the whole thing was just a dance after all.

The second movement, with its almost continuous staccato chords in the woodwind, like a ticking clock, has long been taken to be a tongue-in-cheek tribute to Johann Nepomuk Mälzel, the inventor of the metronome. Beethoven's pupil and unreliable biographer, Anton Schindler, published a canon for voices, which sets this tune to the words 'Ta, ta, ta, liebe Mälzel', and which Beethoven was supposed to have invented at a dinner with Mälzel and others. It is a charming idea, but scholars have demonstrated that the canon was probably one of Schindler's many forgeries. The movement is charming and witty, with or without the story. Beethoven most likely intended it to evoke memories of the 'Clock' Symphony (No. 101) by his teacher, Joseph Haydn. There are several little themes, including one that almost becomes lyrical, but the ticking of the clock is never silent for more than a moment. The ending is a very Haydnesque joke, with hesitations and a sudden final lurch, like someone leaning on a door as it is opened from the other side.

The minuet is easy-going – the only real minuet in Beethoven's symphonies. But the frequent accents, often on offbeats, give it a surprising kick, like the accents in the first movement. The trio is charming and lyrical, with horns and clarinet in dialogue, over a tricky pattern of running triplets in the cellos.

The finale is extremely fast (according to Beethoven's metronome marking), with a theme consisting of little snatched phrases, played pianissimo by the violins. What is not obvious to the listener is that this is a speeded-up version of the opening of the second movement: rapidly repeated notes followed by three little curls. Nothing remains pianissimo for long in Beethoven. There is a rude outburst, an unexpected C sharp. Beethoven brusquely dismisses it at this stage, but it will come back to haunt him at the end of the movement. The theme takes off with the whole orchestra. There is a lyrical second theme in the violins, which, like the second theme of the first movement, starts in an unexpected key (A flat major), and is then taken up by the woodwind in the more usual C major.

Soon we are back to the nervous agitation of the opening. After a moment of hesitation, the development quickly builds up, with the motifs of the theme turned upside down and treated to energetic counterpoint. Out of the climax emerge straight-faced bassoon and timpani, and suddenly we are into a reprise of the opening. As before, the lyrical second theme begins in an unexpected key (D flat major), and is then pulled back to the home key for the woodwind. Once again, the reprise culminates in a hesitation. The theme attempts to get going. Against the fits and starts, a calm descending line begins in the woodwind, and then passes from instrument to instrument. This gradually builds rhythmic momentum, and a marvellously sturdy, sustained passage develops.

It sounds as if we have entered the final coda of the movement. But Beethoven has not finished with his surprises. Out of the climax again emerge the bassoon and timpani, and there is a second reprise of the opening theme. So this is turning out to be like a massively extended rondo. This time, the rude interruption of C sharp is reiterated. First it is a D flat (the same note as C sharp on the keyboard), and it seems that we might continue in D flat major. But this is immediately cut off by a loud C sharp, and we are in C sharp minor. More iterations of C sharp lead to a forceful statement of the theme in F sharp minor. After a few bars, with another harmonic wrench, we are dragged back to the home key of F major. The second theme follows, first on woodwind and then in the bass. There is another dramatic harmonic twist, another hesitation. Further fragments of the main theme lead on to persistent reassertions of the chord of F major. The last twenty-three bars of the score consist entirely of chords of F major and C major repeated again and again, just to ram home the message that we really have reached the end. It is a huge joke, and Beethoven no doubt laughed louder than anyone.

SYMPHONY NO. 9 IN D MINOR ('CHORAL'), OP. 125
Duration: approx. 68 minutes

Allegro ma non troppo, un poco maestoso
Scherzo: Molto vivace
Adagio molto e cantabile
Presto – Allegro assai

Beethoven's Ninth Symphony, composed between 1822 and 1824, and first performed in Vienna's Theater am Kärntnertor on 7 May 1824, has been burdened with iconic status. The famous 'Ode to Joy' from its last movement has become a political symbol, adopted as the anthem of the European Union, and the symphony was played at the falling of the Berlin Wall, at the reopening of Bayreuth after the Second World War, and before that on Hitler's birthday. No work of art could survive such treatment without scars. The important thing is to forget all that, and just to listen to it on its own terms. What you find, once you get to know the whole symphony, is that it has a sense of inevitability in its progress, which arises from the way that Beethoven has related the themes of the different movements. Once you spot this, you find that the 'Ode to Joy', when it finally arrives, is not just a random tune plucked out of nowhere, but the logical outcome of what has gone before.

The symphony opens mysteriously, with pianissimo horns and muttering strings. Fragments of a falling theme are heard, two notes at a time. They gather strength, bursting out into a jagged theme of tumbling dotted rhythms. But it is only at this moment that we realize we were previously in the 'wrong' key: Beethoven starts in A, with bare fifths, but the theme that eventually emerges is in D minor. The process is repeated, this time starting quietly in D minor and bursting out in B flat major, then finding its way back to D minor. The effect is to make it clear already that the symphony is going to involve a long struggle. As the first sustained fortissimo subsides, a lyrical rising and falling phrase is passed around the woodwind. Several other elements follow, but these first two – the jagged tumbling motif and the smooth rising and falling motif – prove to be the most important throughout the symphony. This first movement is long, exceptionally long for Beethoven's day (between thirteen and eighteen minutes, depending on how Beethoven's metronome marking is interpreted). It is a great journey, in which all the little motifs and arguments build into climaxes, subside, move into remote keys, build again, subside again.

At the end of the long first section of the movement (about five minutes in), there are gaps, and then Beethoven returns to the mysterious opening in A minor, just as it was before. It sounds as if he is beginning the conventional repeat of the opening section. But, for the first time in Beethoven's symphonies, there is no repeat, and he goes straight on into the central development section. After two short-lived build-ups and moments of hesitation, a fugal passage begins, in which the last phrase from the opening theme is passed from instrument to instrument, building to a climax and then subsiding. Further on, there is the biggest climax of the movement. Here, the jagged opening theme returns, but now subjected to a massive challenge. If the score is played as Beethoven wrote it, the theme in the strings is barely audible above the sustained fortissimo of wind and kettledrums. Some conductors over-correct this imbalance. But the whole point is that the theme struggles to be heard – as well as struggling to find the right key. The effect is huge and overwhelming, but the impression, once the storm subsides, is that the theme has not won through. There is unresolved tension that still has to be dealt with.

We are now into the third and last section of the movement. But it is even longer than the opening section. The themes and motifs from the opening reappear, but further developed in striking new ways. Twice a climax seems about to lead to a conclusion, but subsides again. Finally, there is a moment of hesitation and hush. Over a mysterious bass line, rising and falling chromatically in a wave, the dotted rhythms of the opening theme build to a final climax, brief and emphatic, and the movement comes to an end. It is a conclusion of sorts. But despite the time it has taken to reach this point, it is clear that there is a long way to go before we reach any sort of resolution.

The second movement is the scherzo, which in earlier symphonies had usually been placed third. The tumbling dotted rhythms, and the smoother rising and falling motif, have now been combined and transformed into a dance. The timpani are prominent, asserting themselves for a bar of the opening gesture. Later in the movement, they interrupt unexpectedly, then with an echo – a passage that provoked an outburst of applause at the first performance. An acceleration leads to the middle section (trio), in which the dancing three-time of the scherzo becomes a trotting two-time. Over the bassoons, the woodwind play another version of the smooth rising and falling motif, which is repeated again and again throughout the trio. There is, by the way, a problem about the tempo of this trio. Beethoven marks it Presto – faster, you would think, than the Molto vivace of the scherzo. But because of the way the beat of the three-time scherzo becomes the beat of the two-time trio, the trio usually sounds slower than the scherzo. Beethoven's metronome marking adds extra confusion by being an obvious misprint, being far too slow to be plausible. A solution has been proposed whereby, after the acceleration into the trio, a tempo exactly double Beethoven's printed marking is reached, by the device of preserving the value of the running crotchets. This seems very likely to be what Beethoven meant, but it produces such a startlingly unfamiliar effect that few conductors have yet adopted it.[15]

The third movement is a sublime Adagio, whose structure is two interleaved sets of variations – a form that Haydn used in several of his slow movements. Two sections, in different keys, alternate, becoming more elaborate at each repetition. The first, in B flat major, is a very slow, almost hymn-like theme, with a falling line followed by a rise and a curl, which is like a calm distillation of the opening jagged theme from the first movement. The second theme, in D major, is a little faster, rising and falling smoothly, like a great expansion of the rising and falling second motif from the first movement. The return of the first theme is elaborated, its big intervals now filled in with decoration. In this way it comes closer to the character of the second theme. Then the second theme returns, this time in the woodwind and now in G major. At the next return of the first theme, it is at first taken over by clarinets and bassoons, sounding like a sublime wind serenade, and now in a favourite wind-serenade key, E flat major. This proves to be a meditative fantasia, which moves through various keys before reaching the original opening key of B flat major.

Now the first theme is elaborated further by the violins, taking on that quality of ecstatic decoration that Beethoven had developed in his late piano sonatas and string quartets. From this point on there is no return to the second theme. Instead, the line passes to the woodwind, takes a sudden and unexpected turn of key, and there are loud fanfares on the whole orchestra. There is a moment of doubt, the elaborate violin line begins again, but there is another change of direction, another fanfare, and a marvellous plunge into a chord of D flat. Suddenly, it seems as if we might be faced with something quite unknown. But the decorated violin melody in B flat again reasserts itself, and the movement finds its way to a close.

The finale opens with a strident discord, and a rapid, fiercely insistent fanfare passage related to the jagged first theme of the symphony. Cellos and basses counter with a declamatory recitative, though there are, as yet, no words (instrumental recitatives increasingly feature in Beethoven's last works, such as the Piano Sonata, Opus 110, and the String Quartets). Again the wind insist, again the cellos and basses object. There are flashbacks to each of the preceding movements, as if searching for something. Cellos and basses comment on each. A decision is reached, and the cellos and basses are able to move on. What they play is a strikingly simple, four-square melody, like a hymn. But its relationship to the earlier music of the symphony is unmistakable: it is the gentle rising and falling second idea from the first movement, now extended and regularized into a real four-square melody. This theme is repeated three times, first with a lovely bassoon counterpoint, then filled out in a string chorale, and finally on full orchestra. This disperses, and we are taken back to the discordant wind fanfare, now on full orchestra. As before, a recitative answers it, but now sung by a real voice, the baritone: 'O Freunde, nicht diese Töne! ...' – 'Oh friends, not these tones! Rather, let us strike up more pleasant sounds, full of joy'. This introduces the setting of Schiller's 'Ode to Joy', which forms the rest of the movement. Beethoven casts it as a continuing set of variations on the theme we have already heard, at first proceeding straightforwardly, but later with interruptions and complications (in that respect rather like the slow movement, and with a similar pattern of changing keys).

The baritone calls to the chorus, 'Freude!' (Joy!), and the chorus answers. The baritone then leads off the first variation of the theme, with a counterpoint of woodwind, to the first verse of Schiller's poem:

Freude, schöner Götterfunken,	Joy, beautiful spark of the gods,
Tochter aus Elysium . . .	Daughter of Elysium . . .
Alle Menschen werden Brüder,	All humanity shall be brothers,
Wo dein sanfter Flügel weilt.	Where your gentle wing rests.

'Menschen' means 'people', all humanity, not just 'men' as it is usually translated, though the tone of the poem is inescapably masculine, with its 'brothers' and 'heroes' and their 'wives'. The chorus answers the last line in unison. Then the quartet of soloists sings the second verse, slightly varying the theme:

Wem der grosse Wurf gelungen,	Whoever has the great fortune
Eines Freundes Freund zu sein;	To be the friend of a true friend;

The chorus again answers. The next verse brings the first test for the soloists:

Freude, trinken alle Wesen	All creatures drink joy
An den Brüsten den Natur;	At the breast of Nature;

The soloists elaborate the theme in counterpoint, barely supported by the orchestra, with the soprano rising to a high B (after having waited three-quarters of an hour for this first entry). The chorus again answers, echoing the elaboration of the soloist. But then they add a stately repetition of the last line:

Und der Cherub steht vor Gott.	And the Cherub stands before God.

This ends on an unexpected fortissimo chord of F major (which echoes a similar surprise move in the slow movement). The sequence of variations has been interrupted, and there is a sudden silence.

Out of it emerges an unlikely sound: bassoons, contrabassoon, and bass drum, joined by the other wind, cymbals, and triangle. After the grand solemnity of the movement so far, we seem to have been transported to a village, where the local band is just getting going with a march – the sort of jolly, oom-pah band that abounds in Austria and Germany, with their characteristically buoyant rhythms. This episode can seem embarrassing. But Beethoven surely intended this simple, earthy variation on the theme to symbolize ordinary people everywhere joining in the celebration. His cue might well have been a line from the preceding verse of the poem, 'Even the worm is granted ecstasy'. The tenor sings the next verse:

Froh, wie seine Sonnen fliegen	Glad as the suns that fly
Durch des Himmels prächt'gen Plan,	Through the splendour of the heavens,
Laufet, Brüder, eure Bahn,	Go on your way, brothers,
Freudig, wie ein Held zum Siegen.	As joyful as a hero to his triumph.

It is essential to put out of one's mind all thoughts of the cataclysms of the twentieth and twenty-first centuries in order to open oneself to this grand and naive image, as the tenor and the chorus reach their enthusiastic marching climax. The orchestra too has been infected by it, and now turns the marching tune into a rollicking, scampering fugal development. When it runs its course, there is a moment's quiet, after which the chorus bursts out with the theme in its original, simple form, returning to the words of the first verse, 'Freude, schöner Götterfunken ...' ('Joy, beautiful spark of the gods ...'), while the orchestra still scampers below.

There is another sudden halt, followed by a solemn intoning of a new chant by the men of the chorus and trombones: 'Seid umschlungen, Millionen!' ('Be embraced, you millions!') This passage ends on a mysterious discord (a hushed version of the violent discord that started the movement), to the words:

Brüder, über'm Sternenzelt	Brothers, above the canopy of stars
Muss ein lieber Vater wohnen.	A loving father must dwell.

Then the three preceding elements are brought together. The sopranos of the chorus lead off the first verse to its original tune, but now swung into the rhythm of the marching band. Meanwhile, the altos sing the chant from the preceding section to its words, 'Seid umschlungen ...' ('Be embraced ...'). This develops into a complex fugal passage. At another sudden hush, the rhythm becomes fragmented, as at the opening of the whole symphony, and the section comes to a quiet end.

Scurrying strings and woodwind now introduce the solo quartet, which has been silent for some time. From this point on, Beethoven takes phrases and fragments of Schiller's poem, mostly from the first verse, and weaves them into a peroration leading to the final climax. The soloists begin, 'Freude, Tochter aus Elysium!' ('Joy, daughter of Elysium!') The chorus joins in. There are forceful repetitions of 'Alle Menschen' ('All people'), and then twice the pace suddenly slows. The second time, the soloists reach an ecstatic climax, and this is the last time they are heard. An acceleration in the orchestra brings in the final section of the movement. 'Seid umschlungen' ('Be embraced)', previously a solemn chorale, is now at a frenzied prestissimo, though with the same pattern of notes. There is a final great gathering at the climax, on the opening words of the poem 'Freude, schöne Götterfunken', and the orchestra races for the conclusion.

The effect of this movement can be overwhelming. In a good performance, the 'Ode to Joy' does not seem like a mere 'choral finale', tacked on to an instrumental work for a grand effect. It seems the logical outcome of what has gone before. And the more one understands how

Beethoven has built this symphony – with its two contrasting themes, the jagged and the smooth, recurring in each movement – the more inevitable the finale becomes. You could describe the joyous climax of the finale, with its hymn-like theme, as the triumph of the lyrical over the jagged, of peace over aggression. But the last notes the choir sings, to the word 'Götterfunken', and the last notes the orchestra hammers out, are not the smooth lyrical theme, but the jagged fifths that began and ended the first movement. Beethoven has brought these two hostile elements together: the lyrical and peaceful may be triumphant, but the 'aggressor' has been brought into the fold. *All* humanity shall be brothers, not just the peace-lovers – a naive but inspiring hope.

WELLINGTON'S VICTORY, OP. 91
Duration: approx. 15 minutes

Part 1: Battle
Part 2: Victory Symphony

This is Beethoven's least sophisticated orchestral work, but it was the greatest public success of his entire career, so it would be churlish to omit it. His increasing deafness had encouraged him to keep more and more out of the public eye. But in 1813 he suddenly scored a popular success with a work he wrote for a brilliant musical mechanic, Johann Nepomuk Mälzel, remembered today as the inventor of the metronome. In that year, Mälzel put on display an enormous mechanical orchestra called the Panharmonicon, and he persuaded Beethoven to collaborate with him by writing a grand symphony to be played by this machine. The symphony was to be a celebration of the Duke of Wellington's recent victory over the French at Vitoria in northern Spain, and Mälzel himself drew up detailed plans for the work, incorporating 'Rule Britannia' and 'God save the King' for the British side, and 'Marlbrough s'en va-t-en guerre' for the French (a tune known in the English-speaking world as 'For he's a jolly good fellow' or 'The bear went over the mountain'). Beethoven went on to arrange the symphony for live orchestra, and in this form it roused the patriotic fervour of the audience 'to the point of ecstasy', as one newspaper reported. The most successful performances were in the Redoutensaal in Vienna, whose long corridors were used to create the illusion of opposing armies approaching each other. One of these performances was given in November 1814 to a glittering audience including the King of Prussia. This was during the Congress of Vienna, at which all the monarchs of Europe, together with everyone else of political note, converged on the city to spend nine months bargaining over the frontiers of Europe following the end of the Napoleonic Wars. For once, Beethoven was in the right place at the right time, and was able to take full advantage of his status as the greatest living composer.

The work is scored for a large orchestra, with separate wind bands for English and French sides, each with trumpets and drums, including batteries of special drums to represent cannons. In the first printed edition of 1815, Beethoven included a preface giving detailed instructions on how the forces were to be deployed – the separation of the English and French bands, as large an orchestra as the hall will accommodate, the use of large theatrical drums to simulate cannons, and so on. The score indicates the precise timing of the cannon shots – which, with modern, electronically timed explosions, can be made all too realistic. Unfortunately, an excess of realism has the effect of making the sound of a huge orchestra seem insignificant.

Wellington's Victory is in two parts. Part 1 is the Battle. First, the English drummers are heard approaching, a fanfare is sounded, and their wind band plays 'Rule Britannia'. Then the French drummers, trumpets and wind band approach with 'Marlbrough'. There are fanfares from each side. Then the battle begins with the full orchestra and cannons firing from both sides. There is an increase of pace and change to a galloping rhythm, to indicate a charge. Eventually this subsides, leaving us to imagine a corpse-strewn battlefield. The occasional cannon still resounds, but now only from the English side.

Part 2 is the Victory Symphony. There is a celebratory march for full orchestra, interrupted in the middle by a solemn intoning of 'God save the King' by clarinets and bassoons. This breaks off, and the march resumes. 'God save the King' is again played, and fades into the distance. It is succeeded by a scurrying fugal passage in the strings, reminiscent of the end of the third *Leonore* Overture. This builds up into a final grand climax incorporating fragments of 'God save the King'.

ALBAN BERG
(1885–1935)

Born in Vienna, Berg was largely self-taught until he began studying with Arnold Schoenberg in 1904. Schoenberg reported that at this stage Berg was incapable of writing anything but songs. Later he developed a love of the most intricate instrumental writing, based on Schoenberg's twelve-note technique. But the quality that makes him by far the most widely appreciated of the 'Second Viennese School' is precisely that lyrical gift that Schoenberg identified when Berg first came to him. Despite this, and despite the fact that Berg was not a Jew, he found himself associated in his last years with what the Nazis deemed 'cultural Bolshevism' and 'degenerate art'. As he wrote in 1934: 'Although I have been living in Vienna for fifty years . . . I am considered here, *more than ever*, as not "indigenous", and am treated as I would be treated if I were, for example, a *Jew* and living in Germany. While here composers of whom one has never heard are becoming important . . . the likes of us are being suppressed in *every* respect. Indeed, I have it from the highest official quarter that the production some years ago of my *Wozzeck* was being regarded as a "desecration" of the Vienna Staatsoper.'[1]

Berg was only fifty when he wrote that letter, but it was to be the last year of his life. He died from an infected abscess after being stung by wasps.

Berg's greatest achievements were two operas. *Wozzeck* was first staged in Berlin in 1925, and soon established itself as one of the most important classics of twentieth-century music. *Lulu* remained incomplete when Berg died, with large sections unorchestrated. A truncated version of it was staged in 1937 in Zürich (performance in Germany or Austria being out of the question under the Nazi regime), and for many years this was all that Berg's widow would allow. It was not until after her death that the opera was finally completed, and it was premiered in Paris in 1979. *Lulu* has now joined *Wozzeck* in the short list of great twentieth-century operas.

Berg was a composer of fearsome intellect on a par with his teacher, Schoenberg. His operas and his other mature works are all composed using Schoenberg's twelve-note technique. But they are more immediately accessible to the listener than the twelve-note works of Schoenberg or Webern because they retain a little more connection with the 'old' world of familiar keys and harmonies. To the generation of young radical composers that followed him, such as Pierre Boulez, Berg was for a time regarded as a less rigorous composer than

Webern, and therefore of less importance. Compromise was not in fashion among the musical intelligentsia of the 1950s. But research into Berg's methods has revealed that he was as fearsomely methodical in his musical thinking as Webern. *Wozzeck* is constructed not just with twelve-note technique, but also with a complex interlocking of structures within structures related to more traditional forms – symphony, suite, passacaglia, rondo, and so on. This is not 'compromise', but synthesis of an astonishing order.[2]

THREE PIECES FOR ORCHESTRA, OP. 6
Duration: approx. 20 minutes

Präludium: Langsam (Prelude: Slow)
Reigen: Anfangs etwas zögernd – leicht beschwingt (Round-dance: At first somewhat hesitant – lilting)
Marsch: Mässiges Marschtempo (March: Moderate march tempo)

This was Berg's first large-scale work, a response to the criticism of his teacher, Arnold Schoenberg, for whom he had so far written only songs and pieces for small forces.

Berg finished the first and third pieces in August 1914, as the shocking brutality of the First World War began to unfold, and sent them to Schoenberg in time for his fortieth birthday on 13 September. The second piece was completed the following August. Berg wrote to Schoenberg, 'I really did try to give my best, to follow all your suggestions and advice', adding that, 'close study of your Orchestral Pieces proved infinitely helpful and continually sharpened my self-criticism'.[3] When the score was published in 1929, it bore the dedication, 'To my teacher and friend Arnold Schönberg with immeasurable gratitude and love'. Like Schoenberg's Five Pieces for Orchestra, composed in 1909, Berg's Three Pieces are for an enormous orchestra. Berg had already deployed almost as large an orchestra in his recent *Altenberg Lieder*, but using it mostly with delicacy and restraint. Freed from the need to let a voice be audible, Berg now gives his orchestra full rein. The eventual score includes six horns, four trumpets, four trombones, tuba, four of each woodwind, including piccolo, cor anglais, bass clarinet, and contrabassoon, and a battery of percussion including large and small gongs, side drum, bass drum, two pairs of timpani, cymbals, triangle, a large hammer, xylophone, glockenspiel, celesta, and two harps. The sound is huge, the textures dense and very difficult to make clear – indeed, half the effect is of things struggling to get out, like a sea full of writhing, drowning creatures. The first two movements, Präludium and Reigen, are short, about five minutes each; the March is almost twice as long.

Like Schoenberg's Five Pieces, Berg's Three Pieces are largely atonal, with only hints of keys or conventional harmonies. Berg makes complex use of little motifs or cells, some of which gradually reveal themselves on repeated listing. But the impact of the music is immediate and overwhelming. The mood is powerfully elegiac, and this sense arises from two sources. The first is Mahler, who had died in 1911, and whom Berg revered. The most recognizable of Berg's motifs are like reminiscences of Mahler, particularly of his Ninth Symphony, which Berg heard at its premiere in June 1912. To a later audience, the Three Pieces inevitably suggest a more general lament for a disintegrating world. Whether this was in Berg's mind or not, the idea is strongly evoked by music that seems rooted in engulfing chaos and destruction. Fragments of the familiar struggle to emerge from the forces surrounding them and are ultimately swamped.

The Prelude emerges from darkness with the sounds of gongs, drums, and cymbals, followed by flutter-tongued flute and muted horns. Yearning little fragments become discernible, evoking memories of the opening of Mahler's Ninth Symphony. A high trombone intones on a single note a rhythm that will recur. A deep brass chord breaks in ominously, with agitated strings below and fierce muted horns above. There is a brief, thunderous climax. Then the music falls back, and the yearning Mahlerian phrases begin to develop. The link to the Ninth Symphony is even more unmistakable, but cast adrift in a threatening nightmare. It gradually builds to a huge climax and falls away, the threat maintained by muted trumpets and a marching beat. This is followed by an eerie moonlit scene, with glockenspiel, xylophone, and celesta, a passage reminiscent of Schoenberg's *Erwartung* (which really is a nightmare). Flutter-tongued trumpet and flute bring us back to where we began, with the percussion alone.

Reigen (Round Dance) begins 'somewhat hesitantly'. The process is similar to that of the Prelude: fragments of melody and rhythm, many of them derived from the first movement, from time to time coalesce and are interrupted by outbursts and disintegration. After a while, the phrases of a waltz begin to emerge. But the 'lilt' of the waltz never breaks free from the nightmarish background: it is as if dancers are dimly visible in the smoking ruins of the dance hall. Berg has taken the Mahlerian use of dance in a new direction, subjecting it to fragmentation and destruction. The other composer that this movement strongly evokes is Ravel, whose *La Valse*, ending in chaos and destruction, was to follow six years later. Ravel and Berg came to admire each other's work, but it is unlikely that Ravel had heard or seen this piece. It ends with the strangest and most vivid of gestures: high, *pianissimo* trilling in the woodwind over a lumbering tuba, settling into an extraordinary, dissonant chord, over which muted horns and trumpets rise in a ghost of a fanfare.

The final movement is on a larger scale than the preceding pieces. It draws on another aspect of Mahler, his ironic use of the march, particularly in the Sixth Symphony, and subjects it to yet more levels of fragmentation and destruction. It even includes Mahler's hammer, used to give a mighty blow to the climaxes. The tread of the march begins quietly in the cellos. A clarinet plays a little motif with a leap and a trill that will recur in various transformations through the movement. A welter of competing lines quickly builds up and falls away. Horns take up the leap-and-trill motif, and a side drum starts up. It seems that the march is getting going. But it founders again, and solo violin, clarinet, and cello dolefully contemplate the scene. Suddenly the forces gather again, led by the brass, with the trill motif in horns and violins. Now a marching tune starts up that sounds like a parody of Mahler's parody, at first in the violins, and then shrieked out by the trumpets. A darker passage builds to a climax, Mahlerian yearning phrases in the violins call out, but the trumpets insist, and the power builds and builds, culminating in a huge climax that is dispersed by the hammer. There is a moment of quiet, but immediately the trumpets threaten again, and a more fragmented build-up culminates in further blows. There is another moment of quiet, with eerie chords recalling the end of the second movement. The brass enter with an insistent fanfare, which falls down to a gong stroke – another very Mahlerian moment. Now the music is quiet, with an extraordinarily menacing atmosphere created by trombones playing chords while hand-stopped horns mutter one of the motifs from the first movement. The menace grows, and falls away again. A pattering rhythm gradually rises, like the trapped desperately trying to flee. The silence is almost total, with only the pianissimo tapping of the celesta left. Suddenly the terrifying brass fanfares arise for the last time, and a hammer blow brings the work to a close.

VIOLIN CONCERTO
Duration: approx. 26 minutes

Andante – Allegretto
Allegro – Adagio

After the Nazis came to power in Germany in 1933, Berg, through his association with Jewish musicians and 'degenerate' music, was increasingly sidelined, and performances of his music became rarer both in Germany and in his native Austria. He was increasingly short of money, and his composition of the Violin Concerto began as a straightforward commission from the American violinist Louis Krasner, early in 1935. While he was working on it, he learned of the death of Manon Gropius, the beautiful eighteen-year-old daughter of Alma Mahler and Walter Gropius. He decided to dedicate it to her, and headed the score, 'To the memory of an angel'.

This was Berg's last composition, completed during the summer of 1935, and it was the work that, together with *Wozzeck*, established Berg as one of the greatest composers of the twentieth century. The Violin Concerto is much more approachable than much of the Schoenberg School. This is partly because Berg compromises between the extreme dissonance of Schoenberg's twelve-note technique and more traditional styles. It has distinct hints of keys and harmonies, and it includes a Bach chorale. The concerto has a strongly lyrical and expressive character, inspired by tragic memories.

The concerto is based on a twelve-note row. But before the main row is stated, there is an introductory passage with a pattern of fifths, up and down, which are to be almost as important as the main row itself. These are first played on clarinets, and then answered by the solo violin. The violin's answer consists of the four notes produced by the open strings of the violin. The pattern of fifths then rises and stretches to wider intervals, until the music arrives quietly at an unmistakable chord of G minor. This is the first of many moments in the concerto where, despite the atonal rootlessness of the language, we have a sudden glimpse of 'home', of the familiarity of a key. Berg uses these moments of familiarity to powerful emotional effect.

After this introduction, the solo violin plays the row of twelve notes that is to provide the main building blocks for the whole work. This consists of every note in the chromatic scale, but sequenced in intervals familiar from conventional music: first alternating minor and major thirds, and finally a succession of four notes in a whole-tone scale. The violin first presents this row ascending, then reverses it so that it descends. A web of fragmentary materials drawn from the row builds gradually to a climax and subsides. A pair of clarinets plays a new theme in gently dancing rhythm (Allegretto). The harmonies are mournful, combining the thirds of the tone row, and the effect is like the ghost of an Austrian *Ländler*. Throughout the remainder of the movement the different elements – the pattern of rising and falling fifths (and 'stretched' versions of it), the melodic thirds of the row (often combined in chords), the whole-tone scale, and this new dance element – come to the fore in turn, developing powerful climaxes and receding again. Towards the end, the dance rhythms take on a wistful element, and Berg quotes an Austrian folk song. The atmosphere of this movement is charged with the conflicting emotions generated by these different elements, the overwhelming impression being of a lament.

The second movement is, for much of its progress, faster and more violent. The dissonant opening chords and frantic violin passages are interspersed with the wind playing fragments of the *Ländler* theme. Moments of calm alternate with further outbursts. The violin line becomes freer, and sparsely accompanied: Berg specifies at the head of the movement that it should be 'always rubato, free like a cadenza'. It is disrupted by the most violent outburst so far, and the violin struggles to reassert itself against the fierce attack of the brass. This culminates in a mighty climax.

As it collapses, the whole-tone scale from the row metamorphoses into a chorale by J. S. Bach, 'Es ist genug', first in the solo violin, and then taken up by the clarinets (Adagio). In this very unusual chorale, the first four notes of the melody are those of a whole-tone scale, so that it seems to arise naturally out of Berg's note row (though of course he reverse-engineered the row to make the chorale seem like the natural outcome). The words set by Bach, the last verse of the chorale, are written into the score:

Es ist genug!	It is enough!
Herr, wenn es Dir gefällt,	Lord, when it pleases Thee,
so spanne mich doch aus!	grant me release!
Mein Jesus kommt:	My Jesus comes:
nun gute Nacht, o Welt!	now goodnight, O world!
Ich fahr' in's Himmels Haus,	I am going to the house of heaven,
ich fahre sicher hin mit Frieden,	I go from here confident with joy,
mein grosser Jammer bleibt darnieden.	my great misery remains behind.
Es ist genug,	It is enough,
es ist genug.	it is enough.

The remainder of the movement takes on the character of a meditation on this chorale, fusing its religious sentiment, the elegiac quality of the concerto as a whole, and the thematic link between the chorale and the row, into a powerful climax and resolution. The slowed dance rhythm of the *Ländler* and fragments of the Austrian folk song sound in the context like the rocking of a lullaby. The work ends with the violin taking the thirds of the row higher and higher to a sustained G, beneath which the orchestra settles on a final chord of B flat major.

HECTOR BERLIOZ
(1803–69)

Felix Mendelssohn met Berlioz in Rome in 1831, and wrote to his mother about his impressions of the composer and his recently performed *Symphonie fantastique*: 'He makes me sad because he is really a cultured, agreeable man, and yet composes so very badly . . . nowhere a spark, no warmth, utter foolishness.'[1] By contrast, Camille Saint-Saëns wrote about Berlioz, 'Whoever reads Berlioz's scores before hearing them played can have no real idea of their effect. The instruments appear to be arranged in defiance of all common sense, and it would seem, to use professional slang, that *cela ne dut pas sonner*, but *cela sonne* wonderfully. If we find here and there obscurities of style, they do not appear in the orchestra; light streams into it and plays there as in the facets of a diamond.'[2]

These two quotes represent the fiercely divided opinions that Berlioz's music has aroused over the years. It was really only in the second half of the twentieth century that he came to be generally accepted as a great composer, worthy to stand beside the nineteenth-century giants of Beethoven, Wagner, and the rest. He was an unorthodox figure. Although he did eventually study at the Paris Conservatoire, he was fearless in sticking to his own ways of doing things. He was full of grand schemes and ideas, constantly trying out yet more extreme and outrageous combinations of instruments. He was intensely self-dramatizing, as his effervescent *Memoirs* show.[3]

But he was far more than just an unorthodox maverick. There is a great deal of old-fashioned craft in his music. Some of his weird combinations of instruments do not really work, but his general command of orchestral sonorities is extraordinary. He wrote a series of articles on orchestration that were published together in 1843 as *Grand traité d'instrumentation et d'orchestration modernes*, a comprehensive study of up-to-date orchestration which has remained a standard reference book to this day. There are few composers who are so easily identifiable simply by the sound of the textures he creates. And despite the appearance of wildness, his music is also rooted in the past. His quiet music has a transparency of texture that sounds almost baroque – Gluck was a composer he particularly admired. He revered Beethoven, and learned a lot from him. Inspired by the massive scale of Beethoven's Ninth Symphony, Berlioz developed even grander ways of combining orchestra and voices – the *Grande Messe des Morts*, the Te Deum, *Roméo et Juliette*. And he also developed the dramatic narrative of Beethoven's music in ways that were to inspire Franz Liszt and later composers. From Beethoven's 'Pastoral' Symphony, with its rustic headings like chapters in a book, Berlioz developed his own highly pictorial musical language, notably in the *Symphonie fantastique*. This association of narrative and music in purely instrumental music – 'programme' music – was further developed by Liszt into the Symphonic Poem, an influence that extended to Tchaikovsky and Richard Strauss.

HAROLD EN ITALIE (*HAROLD IN ITALY*), OP. 16 (H.68)
Duration: approx. 43 minutes
Harold in the Mountains: scenes of sadness, of happiness and of joy (Adagio – allegro)
March of the Pilgrims, singing the evening prayer (Allegretto)
Serenade of a mountain-dweller of the Abruzzi to his mistress (Allegro assai – allegretto – allegro assai)
Orgy of brigands: memories of earlier scenes (Allegro frenetico)

On the title page of the score, Berlioz describes his *Harold in Italy* as a 'Symphony in four parts, with a principal viola'. He composed it in 1834, and it brought together three different influences: first, the great violinist Niccolò Paganini; second, Byron's poem, *Childe Harold's Pilgrimage*; and third, the period that Berlioz spent in Italy after winning the Paris Conservatoire's 'Prix de Rome', during which he spent some days with friends travelling on foot through the Abruzzi Mountains. Paganini had become an enthusiastic supporter of Berlioz after attending a concert of his music at the end of 1833. Berlioz describes in his *Memoirs* how Paganini told him that he had acquired a Stradivarius viola, and suggested that Berlioz write something for him to play on it. Rather than compose a virtuoso concerto, Berlioz decided to write an orchestral work incorporating a viola solo: 'My idea was to write a series of orchestral scenes in which the solo viola would be involved, to a greater or lesser extent, like an actual person, retaining the same character throughout. I decided to give it as a setting the poetic impressions recollected from my wanderings in the Abruzzi, and to make it a kind of melancholy dreamer in the style of Byron's Childe Harold.'[4]

The extent of the link with *Childe Harold* is as Berlioz describes it: it is in the 'style' of the Romantic wanderer and dreamer. There is no procession of pilgrims or orgy of brigands in Byron's *Childe Harold*. And although Berlioz himself encountered remote monasteries and rough peasants in his own wanderings through the Abruzzi, the source of these scenes is, as in the *Symphonie fantastique*, Berlioz's own imagination.

Paganini never performed the work, finding, according to Berlioz, that it gave the solo viola too little to play. But he did hear it at a concert conducted by Berlioz, after which (according to the *Memoirs*) he knelt and kissed Berlioz's hand, and sent him a gift of twenty thousand francs.

Harold in Italy has some similarities to the *Symphonie fantastique* from four years earlier. The orchestra, though large, is not quite so extravagant. Once again there is a recurring theme that appears in each movement like a reminiscence. *Harold*, like the *Symphonie*, begins with an evocative slow introduction, and ends with an orgy. And, despite the evocative descriptive titles of each movement, it is cast broadly in the form of a classical symphony – though coloured throughout with Berlioz's unique sense of orchestral textures and vivid imagination.

The slow introduction begins mysteriously, with a plangent bassoon over a darkly moving bass line. The main theme of the symphony is first heard in the minor key, from the wood-wind, building to a majestic climax. Then the solo viola sings the theme in its major form, accompanied by harp – a touch that gives a feel of the minstrel beginning a narrative (Berlioz drew this melody from his unsuccessful overture *Rob Roy*, written three years earlier). The orchestra takes up the theme. The Allegro follows, bursting with the joy in the movement's heading. Although there are plenty of solos for the viola, the orchestral passages are quite beyond what would be included in a conventional concerto. At the final section of the move-ment the pace increases, there is a reference back to the viola's main theme, and a huge climax builds up. Although the viola has a brief solo before the end, we feel that it has by now been cast in the role of observer. Perhaps this is a genuinely Byronic touch – the hero as witness of events, rather than in command of them.

The 'March of the Pilgrims' is one of Berlioz's most beautiful pieces, 'which', Berlioz writes, 'I sketched in a couple of hours one evening, musing by the fire'.[5] It is clearly inspired by the processional slow movement of Beethoven's Seventh Symphony, now tied to a specific image of pilgrims chanting. The phrases of the hymn repeat again and again, the interpolated rhythms of the woodwind adding an impression of muttered prayer. In a wonderfully evoca-tive touch, harp and horn punctuate the end of each strain of the hymn with a dissonant single note, like a church bell, which resolves as the new strain begins. The viola enters, and its theme is played in counterpoint with the hymn as it gradually builds in a crescendo and then dies away. The middle section of the movement is magical. A more solemn chant is sung, while the solo viola plays arpeggios 'sul ponticello', that is, near the bridge, producing a glassy tone that lends mystery to this passage. The original March of the Pilgrims returns, gradually fading away as the procession disappears into the distance, leaving the bell-like sounds of the harp lingering in the air.

The serenade is framed at either end by a cheerful rustic tune on oboe and piccolo, with an accompaniment in the violas that evokes the sound of a hurdy-gurdy. Between these sections the gentle serenade is sung first by the cor anglais. The solo viola enters, reminding us of its main theme again while the song continues. This develops into an impassioned duet between viola and woodwind. Only at the end does the viola play the serenade melody itself, over the top of the rustic dance rhythm, while the viola's own theme is taken up by flute and harp.

The finale begins with brief bursts of orgy-like music, interspersed (as in the finale of Beethoven's Ninth) with reminiscences of each of the preceding movements. The viola plays the melody of each reminiscence like a character lost in memories and reluctant to move on. Finally the orchestra breaks away, and from this point is unstoppable – the viola can only stand and listen. Twice the orgy reaches a great climax, with trombones majestically intoning a chorale-like fragment against awesomely unexpected harmonies, with high violins reiterating a desperately repeated pattern. Each time this collapses into pleading phrases, perhaps as if imagining the brigands' victims. Later the orgy breaks off, and there is a distant echo of the March of the Pilgrims, out of which the soloist reappears with a final plaintive melody. But the orchestra again sweeps all before it for the final assault.

Overtures

LE CARNAVAL ROMAIN (*ROMAN CARNIVAL*), OP. 9 (H.95)
Duration: approx. 9 minutes

First performed in 1844, this concert overture is based on material from Berlioz's opera *Benvenuto Cellini* (1836–8), whose libretto was adapted from parts of the celebrated *Memoirs* of the sixteenth-century Italian artist, musician, soldier, and larger-than-like-figure (it is easy to understand his appeal to the self-dramatizing Berlioz). Berlioz writes in his own *Memoirs*, 'I had been greatly struck by certain episodes in the life of Benvenuto Cellini. I had the misfortune to believe they would make an interesting and dramatic subject for an opera.' When he had composed the opera, it was rehearsed and performed at the Paris Opéra: 'I shall never forget the horror of those three months.' There were particular problems with the conductor, François-Antoine Habeneck: 'He could not catch the lively pace of the saltarello that is danced and sung in the Piazza Colonna in the second act. The dancers, put out by his sluggish tempo, complained to me. I kept on urging him, "Faster, faster! Put more life into it!" Habeneck struck the desk in his annoyance and broke his bow.'[6] The opera was a humiliating failure, and poisoned Berlioz's relationship with the Paris Opéra for the rest of his life. A few years later, Berlioz took this saltarello as the main theme of the Allegro in his *Carnaval romain*. He conducted the first performance of the overture himself, on 3 February 1844, with Habeneck in the audience: 'I started the allegro at the right tempo, the whirlwind tempo of the Roman dancers. The audience encored it; we played it again; it went even better the second time. On my return to the artists' room, I saw Habeneck standing with a slightly crestfallen air, and said casually as I went past, "That's how it goes". He did not reply.'[7]

The opera centres on the love of the sculptor, Cellini, for Teresa, daughter of the Pope's treasurer. They plan to use the confusion of the masked carnival to elope together. There is, of course, a rival for Teresa's hand, and the plot unravels. The overture is constructed from two elements taken from the opera. The bulk of it is based on the saltarello, which is the climax of the carnival scene in Act II. But before that gets going, there is the love song that Cellini sings to Teresa in Act I, having sneaked into her father's house, 'O Teresa, vous que j'aime plus que ma vie'.

The overture opens with a brief burst of carnival activity, but, with a flurry of trills, it soon comes to a halt. There follows the love song, one of Berlioz's most beautiful melodies, played first on the cor anglais accompanied by pizzicato strings, then on violas with a countermelody in the flutes (a typical Berlioz touch). Then, in an inspired stroke, cellos, violas, and bassoons sing the melody, and violins and upper woodwind join in, singing it in canon a beat later than the violins. This reproduces what Cellini and Teresa do in the opera, breaking into an ecstatic duet. Tambourine and triangle add a rhythmic accompaniment, bringing a premonition of the carnival dance to come.

When the love duet has run its course, a swirl of woodwind leads into the saltarello. It begins quietly, with the strings muted, as if coming from the distance. But soon it bursts out in the full orchestra. The dance is unstoppable, and the range of orchestral effects is dazzling. Berlioz deploys delicate strings, chattering woodwind, and sudden outbursts of brass and percussion, the whole piece expressing the most joyful exuberance. After the dance has been swirling for some time, it dies down to a moment of calm. As the violins quietly begin the rhythm of the dance again, over it the notes of the love song are intoned by bassoons, like a chorale. Trombones, then flutes and oboes, take up the chorale, while the rhythm of the dance continues, and a crescendo builds up. Soon we are back at the saltarello on full orchestra. But the climax is suddenly cut off, and once again we restart quietly on the strings. Beginning in the cellos, the theme works its way up through the strings, as if Berlioz is setting out on a fugue. But this is no time for such seriousness. The insistent rhythm of the saltarello pounds away while the trombones again intone the chorale. This time the rush of the dance really is unstoppable, and in a glorious blaze it tumbles headlong to a last, resounding chord.

LE CORSAIRE, OP. 21 (H.101)
Duration: approx. 8 minutes

In August 1844, Berlioz organized and conducted a concert with over a thousand performers at the end of a 'Grand festival d'industrie' in Paris. The strain of the preparations and concert completely exhausted him, so after the event he took the advice of a doctor and travelled to Nice to recuperate for a month. He describes in the *Memoirs* the joy of revisiting all the places he had seen thirteen years before on his way to Italy. One day he settled 'in a tower perched on a ledge of the Ponchettes rock, and feasted myself on the glorious view over the Mediterranean and tasted a peace such as I had come to value more than ever'.[8] It was while he was in Nice that Berlioz drafted this concert overture, giving it the title *The Tower of Nice*. He conducted it the following year, and then put it on one side for two years. Then he changed the name to *Le corsaire rouge*, the French title of James Fenimore Cooper's *The Red Rover*. Cooper's novels were very popular in French translation, and Berlioz particularly relished 'his pictures of untamed nature'. Finally he settled on the title *Le corsaire*, perhaps by allusion to *The Corsair* by another of Berlioz's literary heroes, Byron. Byron's poem is a passionate oriental tale of love, death, and chivalry, which is an entirely appropriate reference for this wildly extravagant overture.

A rushing theme on the strings is punctuated by the woodwind, playing in a chattering offbeat rhythm (very difficult to make clear at the breakneck tempo). As in *Le carnaval romain* (written a few months earlier), this frenzied activity soon peters out, to be followed by a slow section. This is a melancholy theme, rather like 'Juliet alone' in *Romeo and Juliet*, which develops a lamenting intensity. It reaches a close, and the woodwind tentatively suggest a return to the opening tempo. The strings join them, and we are back to the swirling opening theme. What follows is a fully worked-out movement, as in a symphony, complete with those traits for which Berlioz has been alternately admired and castigated – sudden outbursts, swings of mood, switches of key, leaps from one idea to the next, brazen climaxes and moments of delicacy intermingled in a kaleidoscopic manner. The overture needs to be played with fearless abandon if it is not to sound merely chaotic.

The initial swirling culminates in a fanfare-like gesture, in which trombones and tuba playfully dispute whether it is to be played on or off the beat. After a moment's indecision, the violins take it up, firmly on the beat, trying to develop it into a fully fledged theme. But, with characteristic volatility, Berlioz is not quite sure which direction to take. It fragments, regroups, changes key, and bursts out again fortissimo. As it once again peters out, fragments of the lamenting theme from the slow section are reiterated in the woodwind, and eventually the violins take this up as a second theme, adapted into the fast tempo. Musing on this theme occupies some time, reaching a very quiet low point, at which cellos and bassoons suddenly remind us of the rushing scales from the first theme, and the swirling strings and offbeat woodwind are back, followed (after some hesitant new twists) by the fanfare-like theme fortissimo in the violins. This is followed by another kaleidoscopic sequence of fragments of the fanfare theme, phrases from the lament, rushing scales, sudden outbursts and changes of key, until the fanfare theme once more is hammered out by the full orchestra. This is subjected to outrageous changes of key, more syncopated build-ups, and a final rush upwards in the violins. Even the penultimate bar is in a key you do not expect, so that the final blazing chord of C major is like the home you were beginning to think you were never going to reach.

ROMÉO ET JULIETTE, OP. 17 (H.79)
Duration: approx. 90 minutes (complete work)

The movements in parentheses are predominantly vocal, and are not discussed in detail below.

Part 1
Introduction: Combats – Tumulte – Intervention du Prince
(Prologue)
(Strophes)
(Scherzetto: Mab la messagère)

Part II
Roméo seul: Tristesse – Concert et bal – Grande Fête chez Capulet
(Nuit sereine) – Scène d'amour
Scherzo: La reine Mab, ou la fée des songes

Part III
(Convoi funèbre de Juliette)
Roméo au tombeau des Capulets
(Final)

In 1827, Berlioz attended performances of Shakespeare's *Hamlet* and *Romeo and Juliet* at the Théâtre de l'Odéon in Paris. He proceeded to fall madly in love with the actress who played Ophelia and Juliet, Harriet Smithson, and it was this passion that fuelled his ideas for the *Symphonie fantastique*. Their subsequent marriage, unsurprisingly, did not live up to that initial passion. But the love of Shakespeare that was ignited in Berlioz remained with him for the rest of his life. Berlioz writes in his *Memoirs*, 'Shakespeare, coming upon me unawares, struck me like a thunderbolt. The lightning flash of that discovery revealed to me at a stroke the whole heaven of art, illuminating it to its remotest corners. I recognized the meaning of grandeur, beauty, dramatic truth, and I could measure . . . the pitiful narrowness of our own worn-out academic, cloistered traditions of poetry. I saw, I understood, I felt . . . that I was alive and that I must arise and walk.'[9] The plays were performed in English, based on the eighteenth-century versions by David Garrick, and French translations were provided. Berlioz admits that he did not understand a word of English, and 'could only glimpse Shakespeare darkly through the mists of Le Tourneur's translation . . . But the power of the acting, especially that of Juliet herself, the rapid flow of the scenes, the play of expression and voice and gesture, told me more and gave me a far richer awareness of the ideas and passions of the original than the words of my pale and garbled translation could do.'[10]

Berlioz describes the work as a 'Dramatic Symphony', and his admiration for Beethoven's Ninth Symphony was obviously a central force in his writing of the piece. Beethoven's symphony consists of three instrumental movements, climaxing in a fourth with chorus and vocal soloists. Berlioz greatly expands the contribution of the singers, alternating instrumental and vocal sections throughout, and creating a highly unusual work that is (despite what the composer said) part symphony, part dramatic cantata. It is much longer than the Beethoven: an hour and a half, compared with Beethoven's hour or so. Berlioz conducted three performances of the newly composed work in 1839 at the Paris Conservatoire. They attracted a large audience, including the young Richard Wagner, who later recalled, 'For me this was a new world . . . The power and virtuosity of the orchestra were something I had never dreamed of and at first I was completely stunned . . . On the other hand numerous passages in *Romeo and Juliet* struck me again and again as empty and worthless, and the work itself suffered from its length and structure, but this pained me all the more as I was so overwhelmed by the many wonderful moments in the score that all criticism was rendered impotent.'[11] Twenty years later, Wagner presented Berlioz with a score of his own love tragedy, *Tristan und Isolde*, which he had inscribed with the words, 'To the dear and great author of Romeo and Juliet, from the grateful author of Tristan and Isolde'. Wagner was not only inspired by the wild and ambitious character of the work, but drew on the music for his own compositions, specifically the Overture to *Tannhäuser*, and the Prelude to *Tristan*.

Berlioz wrote in his *Memoirs*, 'The work is enormously difficult to perform. It poses problems of every kind, problems inherent in the form and in the style, and only to be solved by long and patient rehearsal, impeccably directed.'[12] The extent to which these problems can be solved, even in the finest performance, is debatable. This is because the purely orchestral sections are generally much more gripping and dramatic than the vocal sections. For example, the vivid orchestral introduction is followed by a quarter of an hour of vocal music, mostly in slow tempo. Here, Berlioz's chorus, with solo mezzo-soprano, outlines the tragedy that is to unfold. They paraphrase the brief introductions to Acts I and II of Shakespeare's play (where they are spoken by a 'chorus' of a single actor – these introductions had been cut in the production that Berlioz attended). Their role in the Berlioz is more like that of the ancient Greek chorus, and their evocation of what is to come includes the ball, the meeting of Romeo and Juliet, their death, and the reconciliation of the families. There is beautiful music in these sections, including a striking version of Mercutio's 'Queen Mab' speech, set for tenor, which was later to be revisited as an orchestral scherzo. But the sense of urgent drama that was instantly created by the Introduction has given way to something more like a ritual.

For this reason, the instrumental sections of *Roméo et Juliette* are generally played on their own.

The Introduction begins with a gambit that immediately demonstrates Berlioz's ability to adapt old techniques to striking new effect: he uses a fugue to suggest the households of the Montagues and Capulets quarrelling in the street (as in the first scene of Shakespeare's play). This is not a strict, 'academic' fugue: it is chaotic and irregular, more combative than the mock-fugue that ends the 'Witches' Sabbath' in the *Symphonie fantastique*. The violas begin it, and the theme itself is already at a high state of agitation with its rapid staccato and tense little trill. As others join in, the music quickly begins to lose its fugal character and move in broader thrusts. It reaches a climax, and the fight is halted by dramatic chords. Trombones (and ophicleides in the original score) declaim, 'proudly, and with the character of recitative'. This kind of instrumental recitative is clearly a reference to the finale of Beethoven's Ninth, which begins with a recitative played by cellos and basses. Here, it represents Prince Escalus, who rails at his 'rebellious subjects', threatening the warring families with death if they disturb the streets of Verona with fighting again. The recitative begins with the opening notes of the fugue subject, slowed to a stately tempo. Fragments of the fugue break through from time to time, showing that the fighters are reluctant to be calmed. The trombone recitative reaches an imposing climax. As the prince departs, mutterings suggest the scattering of the crowd.

Roméo seul (Romeo alone): In Shakespeare's original, Romeo is at first pining after a girl called Rosaline, and only forgets her when he sets eyes on Juliet at the Capulet's ball. In the version that Berlioz saw in Paris, which was based on Garrick's adaptation, references to Rosaline were cut, Romeo was already in love with Juliet from the first, and he was seen wandering on his own, pining for her. This helps to explain the character of Berlioz's 'Roméo seul', and its relationship with the ball scene to which it is joined. Wagner's debt to Berlioz is strikingly illustrated at the beginning of 'Roméo seul': the opening notes are the same as those of the Prelude to *Tristan und Isolde*. It is easy to hear the seeds of Wagner's intense melodic lines and harmonies in Berlioz's music, whose spare and wandering phrases powerfully evoke a sense of lonely yearning. After the vulnerable impression of the opening, the music settles into a sustained, gradually evolving melody on violins, richly accompanied. A middle part of the melody moves to the woodwind, and the opening part is reprised on the violins in a new key. As the melody sinks down to the violas and cellos, there is a sudden snatch of vigorous dance music, heard quietly as if from the distance. But it vanishes immediately, giving way to dark tremolando strings, with an echo of the dance rhythms in timpani and bass drum. Again the music turns a corner. Over harp-like pizzicato an oboe unfolds a tender serenade, drawn from the halting phrases that began the piece. From time to time, there is a distant echo of the dance rhythms in the drums. The oboe melody reaches a conclusion, and suddenly we are propelled into the ball of the Capulets.

With its agitated, tarantella-like rhythm, this is far more than just a dance. It conveys a swirl of turbulent emotions, from which dance music is struggling to emerge. A moment of disorientation, with dark trombone calls, suggests the threat of conflict lying beneath the surface. And then calm is restored with a moment of gentle elegance. The main theme passes to the woodwind with a new counterpoint on violins. In a sudden outburst, the oboe's sere-nade is heard on trombones. Then this is combined with the tarantella theme in a passage of sustained power, with thundering drums and cymbals. There is a moment of quiet uncer-tainty, as the winding chromatic melodies of 'Roméo seul' return. Gradually the music builds once more to a frenetic climax. There is one last look back to the plaintive oboe serenade, and with a final blast the dance is over.

Nuit serein (Serene night): Following the end of the ball, there is a brief choral scene in which groups of men disperse into the starlit night. Then follows the 'Scène d'amour' (Love scene), which Berlioz in his *Memoirs* called his favourite of all his pieces. This, the central scene of both Shakespeare's play and Berlioz's symphony, is rendered by Berlioz as a purely orchestral movement. He explained why, in the preface to the published score: 'As duets of this kind have been treated in vocal music a thousand times, and by the greatest masters, it seemed prudent, as well as unusual, to try another means of expression. In any case, the very sublimity of this love made its depiction so dangerous for its composer that he needed to give his imag-ination a latitude that the definite meaning of sung words would not have allowed, and thus to turn to the language of instrumental music – a language that is richer, more varied, less restricted, and by its very vagueness incomparably more powerful in such a case.'

If 'Roméo seul' gave Wagner some specific ideas, this 'Scène d'amour' must surely have been a major source of inspiration for the great love scene in *Tristan* (even though that is for voices as well as orchestra). Berlioz's outpouring is an extraordinary achievement – a contin-uous piece of music, lasting seventeen minutes (longer than most performances of the slow movement of Beethoven's Ninth Symphony), vividly depicting surging waves of passion, tenderness, regret, anxiety. Berlioz is right: it is as dramatic as any vocal duet. The darkness of the garden and a sense of heightened awareness are conveyed in the opening paragraph. Muted violas and divided cellos form a trio, deep and richly toned but delicate, while a gentle, regular rhythm is touched in by pizzicato basses, and violins play occasional, hesitant little phrases. It bears an uncanny resemblance to the slow movement of Schubert's C major String Quintet, which Berlioz could not have known (it was not yet published). From time to time the fragments of melody slide chromatically, reminding us of 'Roméo seul', but these are no more than a fleeting memory. The music rises and falls, and after a moment of disturbance, the cellos sing a yearning melody. This will be developed later, but now it falls back to a return to the opening. This rises again, a little higher than before, and sinks back. The cellos push forward in agitated steps, until they reach their yearning melody again, joined by the violas, and now higher and more impassioned than before. There follows a dialogue: oboe and flute play timid little phrases, and the cellos respond with a warm recitative, as if calming them (this clearly represents the first exchange between Juliet on the balcony and Romeo below). A long melody unfolds on flute and cor anglais, drawing on earlier phrases but greatly expanding them. The accompaniment below is, like the opening of the scene, both rich and delicate, with cellos divided, and a murmuring pattern in violas and second violins. The melody passes to the violins, with the simplest and sweetest of descants in the woodwind, then returns once more to the cellos and violas. The violins join in, with another sweet descant in the woodwind. Now the music moves in a new direction, by turns tender, passionate, impulsive, hesitant. Eventually it turns once more to the great melody, at first quietly on violins with the sweet descant in the woodwind. After another moment of hesitation, it passes to the clarinets, punctuated by ardent outbursts in the violins. There is another digression, another hesitation, another moment of ardour, and an agitated acceleration culminating in a brief renewal of the melody. And then a delicate series of hesitations and fond caresses brings the scene to an end: 'Parting is such sweet sorrow.'

'Scherzo: La reine Mab, ou la fée des songes' (Queen Mab, or the fairy of dreams): Mercutio's famous speech, describing the 'fairies' midwife' who 'gallops through lovers' brains' in impish and bawdy terms, occurs in Shakespeare's Act I, before the balcony scene. It was not to the taste of eighteenth-century England, nor to that of early nineteenth-century France, and was considerably softened in Garrick's version. Berlioz has already given a vocal version of the (rewritten) speech in Part 1 of *Romeo and Juliet*. Now he returns to it in this instrumental piece, to lighten the atmosphere after the 'Scène d'amour' and before the coming tragedy. It is, in outline, a scherzo and trio, and one can hear echoes of the scherzo from Beethoven's 'Eroica' Symphony, and of the fairy music from Mendelssohn's Overture to *A Midsummer Night's Dream*. But Berlioz's scherzo is uniquely evanescent and delicate in its scoring, with the strings muted.

It begins hesitantly, the music pausing on mysterious woodwind chords (the most obvious nod to Mendelssohn). When the scherzo gets going it is pianissimo and as light as a feather. It only occasionally rises to a forte and immediately falls back again, with continual cross-rhythms and tricky dialogue between strings and woodwind, at lightning speed. In the middle section (the trio in a conventional scherzo), flute and cor anglais (who figured in the 'Scène d'amour') play a wistful melody in the minor, whose opening notes are a slowed-down version of the scherzo's theme. Meanwhile the accompaniment maintains the fairy atmosphere, with the violins divided in four parts, trilling and playing high harmonics, *pppp*, and harp harmonics sounding almost like a celesta – this is Berlioz's scoring at its most magical and imaginative. The return to the scherzo begins in the cellos. New elements are introduced: horns play fanfares, referring to the soldier's dream of trumpets and drums in the version of the speech that Berlioz set earlier. A crescendo reaches a cymbal crash. After delicacy is restored, Berlioz returns for a moment to the mysterious chords of the opening (again echoing Mendelssohn's overture), and the scherzo ends with a rush to a final chord.

Part 3 of Berlioz's symphony is based on material from Garrick's version of Shakespeare's play that was excluded from the performances of the play in Paris, because of a ban on representing priests on the stage. Berlioz's music begins with the funeral cortège of Juliet, including a chorus of mourners. This scene was not in Shakespeare's original play, and was inserted by Garrick. It is followed by the final instrumental movement: 'Roméo au tombeau des Capulets' (Romeo at the tomb of the Capulets). In Garrick's version, Juliet wakes from her drug-induced sleep before Romeo has died from his poison, so that there is a final tragic love scene between them before Romeo dies and Juliet kills herself. Berlioz's piece opens with a passage of frantic despair. Then a series of dark and strange chords evokes Juliet's tomb. The solemn passage that follows is called 'Invocation'. Its mournful phrases (cor anglais, horn, and bassoon in unison) contain echoes of 'Roméo seul'. It descends into dark tremolando cellos as Romeo takes poison. Soft notes of a clarinet, *pppp*, evolve into fragments of the earlier love music, as Juliet awakes. 'Delirious joy' is expressed in the outburst for full orchestra. This too contains frenetic extracts from the love theme. But their joy is short-lived, and the music comes to an abrupt halt at the start of 'Anguish and death of the two lovers'. Romeo and Juliet die in a series of violent jerks, silences, and, on oboe, a final mournful snatch of 'Roméo seul'.

Berlioz's score ends with a crowd rushing to the tomb, and a final aria in which Friar Lawrence mourns the lovers, and urges the Montagues and Capulets to swear their reconciliation and friendship on the Cross. This they do in a grand final chorus which, though it has absolutely nothing to do with Shakespeare's sombre ending, is nevertheless impressive in its own right.[13]

SYMPHONIE FANTASTIQUE: ÉPISODE DE LA VIE D'UN ARTISTE (FANTASTIC SYMPHONY: EPISODE FROM THE LIFE OF AN ARTIST) OP. 14 (H.48)

Duration: approx. 55 minutes

Rêveries – Passions (Dreams – Passions): Largo – Allegro agitato e appassionato assai
Un bal (A Ball): Valse: Allegro non troppo
Scène aux champs (Scene in the Fields): Adagio
Marche au supplice (March to the Scaffold): Allegretto non troppo
Songe d'une nuit de sabbat (Dream of a Witches' Sabbath): Larghetto – Allegro

This famous work shows very clearly Berlioz's character, his debt to the past, and his wild sense of invention. It was his first major work to be performed in public, in May 1830, in the hall of the Paris Conservatoire. It is a symphony in five movements, like Beethoven's 'Pastoral', which certainly inspired its slow movement. Emotionally, the inspiration was Berlioz's love for the actor, Harriet Smithson, whom he first saw on the stage in 1827. Her entry into Berlioz's consciousness was, he writes, 'the supreme drama of my life ... An English company came over to Paris to give a season of Shakespeare at the Odéon, with a repertory of plays then quite unknown in France. I was at the first night of *Hamlet*. In the role of Ophelia I saw Harriet Smithson, who five years later became my wife. The impression made on my heart and mind by her extraordinary talent, nay her dramatic genius, was equalled only by the havoc wrought in me by the poet she so nobly interpreted.'[14] Berlioz's love of Shakespeare endured, and resulted twelve years later in his 'Dramatic Symphony' *Roméo et Juliette* (see above). His frenzied love for Harriet Smithson could scarcely result in a happy marriage, but while the flame was at its height it produced this extraordinary *Symphonie fantastique*. One of the most extraordinary things about it is the huge orchestra that Berlioz demands, including, as well as pairs of woodwind, four bassoons, four horns, two trumpets, two cornets, three trombones, and two ophicleides (a bass instrument with keys, like a giant keyed bugle, recently developed by a Parisian maker – these are usually replaced by tubas). He also requires four timpanists, who play four-part chords, and asks for 'at least' four harps, fifteen players on each violin part, and nine double basses.

Berlioz himself provided a detailed programme for the symphony.[15] Based on his own experience, it describes a young musician's passionate love for a woman who seems to embody his ideals. In a second version of the programme, Berlioz described the entire dream as having been provoked by a dose of opium. In the original version of the programme, the opium is only mentioned at the beginning of the fourth movement, the 'March to the scaffold', the earlier movements being daydreams. The following are abbreviated extracts from Berlioz's own programmes. In speaking of the 'vague des passions' (wave of passions), Berlioz is quoting Chateaubriand, who used the expression to describe the state of a young man subject to surges of passion that do not yet have a definite object – a mental situation that came to be associated with Byron.

Rêveries – Passions

'A young musician sees for the first time a woman who combines all the charms of the ideal being whom he has imagined in his dreams. The image of her is linked to a musical thought, passionate, noble and shy, that pursues him incessantly, like a double *idée fixe*. This is the reason for the constant appearance, in every movement of the symphony, of the melody that begins the first Allegro. The passage from this state of melancholy reverie, interrupted by occasional outbursts of groundless joy, to that of delirious passion, with its surges of fury, of jealousy, its return of tenderness, its tears, its religious consolations, this is the subject of the first movement.'

All of these fluctuations of mood are contained within a movement that is, in its basic design, classical: a slow introduction, followed by an Allegro loosely modelled in its structure on Beethoven's first movements. The first section of the Allegro is even repeated, as in classical symphonies. The slow introduction is unusually long in proportion to the Allegro – about five minutes, out of a total of fourteen or so. It drifts, meanders, is subject to sudden increases in speed, and sinks into further dreaming. The *idée fixe* melody, when it eventually arrives, is made up of phrases that leap up passionately and fall away. The scoring of the melody is characteristic of Berlioz – violins with a flute lending a silvery edge, together with impatient punctuations, like an irregular heart beat, in the strings below. After the theme, the tempo accelerates, bursting out in various fragmentary ideas rather than a clear-cut second theme. The middle section of the Allegro is the most extended, again full of changes of mood and volatile outbursts. The *idée fixe* is heard in new keys, and it too is fragmented under other material. Then a new, floating melody on the oboe gradually rises, with phrases of the main theme beneath it, until, after a long build-up, the main theme bursts forth fortissimo at a climactic reprise, before ebbing away to a quiet close.

Un bal (A Ball)

'He encounters the beloved at a ball, in the middle of a crowd at a brilliant carnival.'

Shimmering violins and rippling harps usher in a waltz. The violins sing the elegant melody. Berlioz was later to declare his admiration for Johann Strauss the elder, but this waltz was probably inspired by Weber's *Invitation to the Dance*, a sequence of waltzes for piano, which Berlioz later orchestrated. The beloved's theme is heard converted into waltz rhythm, over quietly shuddering chords. The dance continues, developing in verve, until it suddenly breaks off to reveal the beloved again, now alone on clarinet. Once more the dance swings into action and comes to a close.

Scène aux champs (Scene in the Fields)

'One evening in the country, he hears in the distance two herdsmen exchanging a *ranz des vaches* [an alpine horn-call]. He reflects on his isolation; he hopes he will soon not be alone any longer . . . But what if she deceives him! . . . This mingling of hope and fear, these ideas of happiness troubled by dark presentiments, form the subject of the Adagio. At the end, one of the herdsmen takes up the *ranz des vaches* again; the other does not answer . . . Distant sound of thunder . . . solitude . . . silence . . .'

The inspiration for the alpine horn call was probably Rossini, who incorporated a similar call into the Overture to *William Tell*, staged in Paris the previous year. But the atmosphere of the movement is more like that of the 'Scene by the brook' in Beethoven's 'Pastoral' Symphony.

A cor anglais is answered by an offstage oboe. The peace of the scene is underlined by the very sparse accompaniment of rustling violas. A long melody for violin and flute unwinds. After some development, this long melody is repeated in cellos, violas, and bassoons, with the violins decorating above (again, reminiscent of Beethoven's 'Pastoral'). A middle section is agitated, but eventually calms. The melody again winds its serene way, now in the second violins, with more elaborate decoration above. And at the end, the solitary cor anglais is answered, not by the oboe, but by rolls of thunder. These are played by four timpani, each playing a different note, one of Berlioz's famous innovations. Although the result is scarcely distinguishable as a 'chord', the effect is strikingly ominous and diffuse, as if coming from neighbouring valleys.

Marche au supplice (March to the Scaffold)

'Now certain that his love is not returned, the artist poisons himself with opium. The dose of the narcotic, too weak to kill him, plunges him into a sleep accompanied by the most horrible visions. He dreams that he has killed the woman he loved, that he is condemned, led to the scaffold, and witnesses his own execution.'

Berlioz's original orchestration for this movement includes not only the full array of woodwind, brass, and strings of other movements, but also extra percussion and two ophicleides (usually replaced by tubas today). The opening bars with their menacing rhythm are an example of Berlioz's highly inventive, and obsessively detailed, approach to orchestration. Two timpanists are instructed to play with sponge-covered sticks. The double basses are divided into four-part chords. These are so low in pitch that, with the addition of the drums, the listener is scarcely aware of the chords. But, as with the timpani chords in the slow movement, the effect is striking, producing a dark, dense texture. The horn players are instructed to change their notes by stopping the bell with their hand, rather than using the valves. This produces a muffled, semi-muted effect. The march is a magnificent demonstration of Berlioz's command of massed forces, building up terrific power, with the chords rooted into the ground with powerful, low trombone notes. At the end, the march breaks off, and a clarinet plays a few bars of the *idée fixe*, 'like a last thought of love interrupted by the fatal stroke', as Berlioz writes. A crash indicates the fall of the guillotine, and the crowd cheers.

Songe d'une nuit de sabbat (Dream of a Witches' Sabbath)

'He sees himself at the Sabbath, in the middle of a ghastly crowd of ghosts, sorcerers, monsters of every kind, gathered for his funeral. The beloved melody appears again, but it has lost its noble and timid character; it is no more than a dance tune, vulgar, trivial and grotesque; it is she, coming to the dance …'

The scene is set by muted violins and violas divided into eight parts, creating a shimmering, unworldly effect. The arrival of the vulgarized beloved is signalled by a high clarinet, playing the *idée fixe* transformed into a jig rhythm. After shouts of joy and general rejoicing, funeral bells introduce the *Dies Irae*, a medieval funeral chant, played on ophicleides (or tubas) and bassoons. Both this and the *idée fixe* are taken up enthusiastically by the whole orchestra. This leads to the 'Ronde du Sabbat' (Sabbath Round Dance), a cheeky little tune in the jig rhythm of the vulgarized *idée fixe*, treated with mock-solemnity as a fugue. In the final climax, the *Dies Irae* is combined with the dance tune, leading to a frenzied conclusion.

GEORGES BIZET
(1838–75)

B izet is, like Mozart and Schubert, one of those composers who died too young, at the height of their powers. He was only thirty-six, and died during the opening run of his great masterpiece, *Carmen*, too soon for him to have the slightest idea that it would become one of the most loved works in the history of music. If he had lived, he might well have become the leading French composer of the late nineteenth and early twentieth centuries, with a profound influence on the future of French music. His importance is principally as a composer of opera: *Les pêcheurs de perles* (*The Pearl Fishers*), *La jolie fille de Perth* (*The Fair Maid of Perth*), and above all, *Carmen*. For a play, *L'Arlésienne*, he composed incidental music, from which he extracted a Suite. Various suites from his stage works have been arranged by others.

Bizet worked for eight years on a symphony, which was inspired by his time in Italy as a winner of the Prix de Rome. It was performed only once during his lifetime, and Bizet planned further revision of it. The symphony was published after his death under the title *Roma*. While this has been largely neglected, a student symphony that Bizet never published has become one of his most popular works. This is the delightful Symphony in C major, composed when he was seventeen, and unknown until its discovery in 1933.

L'ARLÉSIENNE, SUITE NO. 1
Duration: approx. 18 minutes

Prélude
Menuet
Adagietto
Carillon

L'Arlésienne (*The Girl from Arles*) began as a short story by Alphonse Daudet that appeared in his Provençal collection, *Lettres de mon moulin* (*Letters from my Windmill*, 1869). With its evocative pastoral detail and unrequited passion, it has an atmosphere familiar in modern times from the books and films of Marcel Pagnol. The handsome young son of a farmer has fallen madly in love with a girl he met in Arles. His parents reluctantly agree to the marriage. But a man appears at the farm, and tells the father that the girl has been his mistress for two years, and had expected to marry him. Disconsolate, the young man eventually seems to have recovered, and never mentions the girl's name. But one day he climbs to the top of the granary and throws himself to his death in the courtyard below, watched by his mother. In 1872, Daudet was commissioned to adapt the story as a play. He elaborated the plot, with the death of the young man, Fréderi, taking place on the eve of his wedding to a local girl. A production of the play was staged in October 1872 at the Théâtre lyrique, with incidental music for a small orchestra by Bizet. The play was a failure, and it closed after twenty-one performances.

Bizet took some of the incidental music and arranged a suite of four pieces for full orchestra, and this was a great success when it was played a few weeks later. Four years after Bizet's death, the composer Ernest Giraud arranged a second suite of pieces, freely adapting and adding to Bizet's music. There is charming music in this hybrid second suite, but the first is pure Bizet.

The Prélude has three themes. The first is a traditional Provençal Christmas carol, 'The March of the Kings', played by strings and wind in powerful unison. Four variations follow. The first is played by a mellifluous woodwind chorus. The second has the tune in the wind with a restless string accompaniment below and a side drum, and proceeds in a series of dramatic crescendos. Variation 3 turns the carol into a gentle melody in the major, played by cellos in duet with a horn, while bassoons play the bass in a trotting triplet pattern. Finally, the carol goes back to its minor key, and is powerfully played by full orchestra with drum, ending with dark pianissimo chords. The second theme is a lyrical saxophone solo that was associated in the play with Fréderi's simple brother, known as L'Innocent. The third theme is a passionate melody associated with the doomed Fréderi himself, treated by Bizet with tragic intensity that looks forward to *Carmen*.

The minuet is sturdy and rustic. A middle section combines a broad theme with balletic running scales, over a bagpipe-like drone. The reprise of the minuet is delicate, rather than rustic as at the start.

The Adagietto is a tender, sad, heartfelt melody for muted strings, without double basses. It evolves quietly and gradually with seemingly natural grace, rising in the second half to an ecstatic climax, and falling gently away. It makes one ache for all the music that Bizet never survived to write.

In the outer sections of the Carillon, the horns insistently repeat three notes, like the ringing of bells. Over this a joyful tune unfolds. A quiet middle tune has a wistful, pastoral swing, with a duet of flutes joined by oboes and then strings. Over the end of this melody the horns quietly begin their ostinato, leading into a reprise of the Carillon.

SYMPHONY IN C MAJOR
Duration: approx. 32 minutes

Allegro
Adagio
Allegro vivace
Allegro vivace

The symphony by Bizet that is widely known today is not the work of his maturity, on which he struggled over eight years (see introduction), but a student work. He was a seventeen-year-old at the Paris Conservatoire when he wrote it in the autumn of 1855. He never published it, and it remained unknown until 1933, when the composer Reynaldo Hahn, a friend of Bizet's son, handed in a collection of Bizet's manuscripts to the library of the Paris Conservatoire. Two years later, Felix Weingartner conducted the premiere at Basel in Switzerland. It is a work of wonderful freshness, showing that Bizet at seventeen was worthy to stand beside the young Mozart and Mendelssohn. Indeed, the freshness of this symphony has a lot in common with that of the Octet that Mendelssohn composed when he was sixteen. But the immediate influence was Gounod, who taught Bizet for a time at the Paris Conservatoire. Gounod's First Symphony was performed and published in 1855, and Bizet had arranged it for piano duet. It was this symphony that Bizet seems to have used as a model when writing his own. The modest size of the orchestra, the thoroughly 'classical' shape of the movements, and the easy charm of its themes, are all shared with Gounod's symphony, and some of Bizet's themes are almost direct quotes from Gounod. The principal difference is that Bizet's symphony is a youthful masterpiece, whereas Gounod's is a pleasant but unremarkable work.

Bizet's first movement is built on a theme of bustling energy, beginning in the simplest possible way with arresting little phrases taken from the chord of C major. The second theme, on oboe, is a song with open-air quality, again consisting of little more than an arpeggio and a downward scale. Already the young Bizet shows his flair for taking the simplest ingredients and developing them in a way that is both obvious and satisfying – a talent that he was to develop into genius by the time of *Carmen*.

The theme of the second movement is already the work of a master. Once more the oboe steps forward, with a beautifully shaped arabesque. First the melody winds round itself, then leaps up and falls gently down, twisting chromatically as it does so. The second oboe rounds off the strain. Then the first oboe repeats its initial winding and leaps again, this time to a lower point over a different chord, and falling chromatically once more. The violins develop the melody upwards to a passionate climax. This really sounds like a rehearsal for *Carmen*, with its combination of elegant proportions, heartfelt passion, and a subtle suggestion of orientalism in its melody and harmonies. A middle section follows, which takes the dotted upbeat of the theme and delicately makes it into a fugue. If there is a touch of the student exercise about this passage, there is a reason. Gounod's First Symphony has a little fugal passage at this point in its slow movement, and Bizet seems to be paying homage to his teacher. The oboe's melody then returns, accompanied by more elaborate pizzicato patterns.

The third movement is a scherzo, light and airy, with a sudden flowering into a lyrical melody in its second half. Then a middle section (trio) changes key, and over a drone like a bagpipe or hurdy-gurdy the woodwind further muse on the theme of the scherzo, introducing more oriental-style harmonies as they develop the idea. The scherzo then returns.

The first theme of the finale is a delicious, rapid perpetuum mobile, with the violins on tiptoe. This becomes more march-like, and then introduces a lyrical second theme that sounds rather like a quote from Beethoven's *Coriolan* Overture. But the composer who most strongly comes to mind as an influence is, once again, Mendelssohn, who specialized in such 'airborne' music, notably in his *Midsummer Night's Dream* Overture, written at the same age. A return to the perpetuum mobile rounds off this first section, which is repeated. The second section takes the theme into new keys. Where the second theme recurs, it is accompanied by the perpetuum mobile in the second violins. A full reprise follows, and the movement is finished off with verve. This finale is a tour de force, an astonishingly fluent and seemingly easy creation for a seventeen-year-old. If it was ever played by his fellow students at the Paris Conservatoire, they would certainly have struggled with it. It is fiendishly difficult, and only a virtuoso orchestra can make it sound effortless, as the music demands.

ALEXANDER BORODIN
(1833–87)

The surname 'Borodin' was a convenient fiction: the composer was the son of Prince Luka Stepanovich Gedianishvili and his mistress, Avdot'ya Konstantinovna Antonova. In accordance with custom, the boy was given the surname of one of the prince's serfs. But he had a comfortable and privileged childhood, and grew up to be highly educated, with music as an important pastime. It proved to be so important that he became one of the group of

Russian composers known as 'The Five' or 'The Mighty Handful' – Rimsky-Korsakov, Cui, Borodin, Musorgsky, and Balakirev – whose aim was to build on the pioneering work of Glinka and develop a distinctively Russian school of composition. Borodin, like Musorgsky, was only a part time composer. His official career was as a chemist: he rose to become a distinguished professor of chemistry in St Petersburg, carried out important research on aldehydes, and established the first medical courses for women in Russia. As with Musorgsky and Rimsky-Korsakov, Borodin's most important musical influence was Balakirev, the centre of the circle that was to become 'The Five'. It was soon after meeting Balakirev in 1862 that Borodin, with Balakirev's help and encouragement, began his First Symphony in E flat, on which he worked over the next five years. Borodin started making plans for a Second Symphony in B minor. But his chemistry career, and work on the opera *Prince Igor*, meant that it too took him several years to complete. He was working on a third symphony when, at a grand medical ball, he suddenly collapsed, and died of heart failure.

Tchaikovsky was dismissive of Borodin's achievements: 'Professor of Chemistry at the Academy of Medicine, [he] possesses talent, a very great talent, which however has come to nothing for the want of teaching, and because blind fate has led him into the science laboratories instead of a vital musical existence . . . his technique is so poor that he cannot write a bar without assistance.'[1] Liszt, on the other hand, was very supportive. When Borodin visited him in Weimar in 1877, they played through his two symphonies in piano duet, and Liszt said to him, 'Generally speaking, the only advice I can give you is to follow your inclinations and listen to nobody. You are always lucid, intelligent and perfectly original.'[2] Liszt played an important part in helping to encourage performances of Borodin's music outside Russia, and Borodin dedicated to him his oriental tone poem, *In the Steppes of Central Asia*.

Borodin composed very little, very slowly, and his most important work, the opera *Prince Igor*, was unfinished when he died. Of the two symphonies that he completed, the first is fascinating, but struggles hard to find its own character. It is, in effect, a remarkable student work. His Second Symphony, on the other hand, is a work of mature and startling originality, with an absolutely clear purpose and sense of direction.

IN THE STEPPES OF CENTRAL ASIA
Duration: approx. 8 minutes

The Russian title is simply 'In Central Asia', but the longer version has become usual in English. Borodin composed it in 1880 for a series of twelve *tableaux vivants* to celebrate the twenty-fifth anniversary of the reign of Tsar Alexander II of Russia. However, the event was cancelled at short notice after an assassination attempt on the Tsar in the Winter Palace, and Rimsky-Korsakov conducted the concert premiere in St Petersburg in April 1880 instead. Borodin dedicated it to Liszt, who had befriended him and promoted his music.

This short but highly evocative piece was the most immediately successful of Borodin's orchestral works. It tapped into the Russian fascination with the East that helped to give a characteristic spice to the music of Russian composers from Glinka onwards. The Caucasus, which had been conquered in turn by Ottomans, Mongols, and Persians, became part of the Russian Empire in 1864 after half a century of war. Since it was Alexander II who had brought hostilities to an end, music with a mixture of Russian and oriental elements was appropriate for the occasion. Since Borodin's father was Georgian, Borodin himself had family roots in the Caucasus, so his feelings about the area may have extended beyond the usual 'orientalism'.[3]

Borodin supplied a note for early concerts, a shortened version of which also appeared in the published score in 1882. The original version is particularly interesting, because it includes a reference to Russia's military might, and to the peaceful coexistence of 'conquered and conqueror', calculated to please the Tsar (it would, of course, have been tactless to mention the mass ethnic cleansing that followed this conquest, even if Borodin had known about it): 'In the desert of Central Asia the melody of a peaceful Russian song is heard at first. The approaching tread of horses and camels is heard, together with the doleful sounds of an oriental melody. A native caravan guarded by Russian soldiers crosses the boundless steppe. It proceeds on its long journey trustingly and without fear under the protection of the victors' awesome military strength. The caravan moves further and further away. The peaceful melodies of both conquered and conqueror merge into a single common harmony, whose echoes long resound in the steppe before eventually dying away in the distance.'[4]

The music follows the narrative described in the note very closely. What makes the piece so vivid is Borodin's subtle and skilful orchestration. He uses it to build a coherent structure of variations out of the simplest of elements, in the tradition set by Glinka in his *Kamarinskaya* thirty years earlier. The empty scene is set by eerie, high violin harmonics, which are held throughout the opening section. The 'Russian' song is introduced first by a clarinet and then, in a different key, by a horn, while the still atmosphere is maintained by the violin harmonics, which persist as the key changes around them. In the bass, a treading pizzicato pattern begins, which continues through most of the piece, evoking the steady progress of the caravan. The cor anglais introduces the 'oriental' theme, a long, winding melody made up of curling shapes and decorations repeated and varied. The harmonics cease, and the Russian theme takes on a bolder character, first on woodwind chorus, then on horns with trombones, and finally on full orchestra, with emphatic chords suggesting military strength.

The treading rhythm returns to pizzicato strings, the high harmonics resume, and the cellos and cor anglais sing the oriental melody. This passes to the violins, and then the lower strings. As the melody returns to the violins, an oboe combines it with the Russian melody in counterpoint – Borodin has cleverly written his two contrasted themes so that they will fit together perfectly. Twice more they combine together gloriously, on horns and violins, then on upper and lower strings. As the pizzicato tread continues, fragments of the Russian melody linger in the air, and the caravan disappears into the distance, with the high harmonics re-evoking the atmosphere of emptiness with which the piece began.

SYMPHONY NO. 2 IN B MINOR
Duration: approx. 29 minutes

Allegro – Animato assai
Scherzo: Prestissimo – Allegretto – Tempo 1
Andante –
Finale: Allegro

Soon after the premiere of his First Symphony in 1869, Borodin started making plans for a Second Symphony in B minor. But his chemistry career, and work on his opera *Prince Igor*, meant that it again took him several years to complete it. He finished composing the piano score in 1873, and completed the orchestration two years later. The symphony received its premiere in 1877, and was not a great success. In his autobiography, Rimsky-Korsakov remembers that he and Borodin made a study of modern developments in brass instruments: 'Borodin was as enthusiastic as I over the fluency, the ease of handling the tones, and the fullness of the scale of chromatic brass-instruments.'[5] But Rimsky-Korsakov acknowledges that this enthusiasm led Borodin to score the brass too heavily and ambitiously, and two year later Borodin, with Rimsky's help, re-orchestrated the symphony. Rimsky-Korsakov successfully conducted the premiere of this revision, and, with Glazunov, also edited the symphony for publication. It drew on material Borodin had intended for *Prince Igor*, and the result is a work of tremendous strength, full of the character of Slavic traditional music, and with fashionably oriental touches perhaps derived from the opera's Polovtsians, invaders from the east.

The work begins with one of the most arresting opening gestures of any symphony: a series of stark, held octaves, alternating with a curt motto theme that curls round on itself like a fist. The mood is defiantly heroic. Borodin's first biographer, Vladimir Stasov, tells us that the movement 'depicts a gathering of Russian knights' (that is, of ancient Kievan Rus), and another friend of Borodin states that the theme was from a chorus of the invading Polovtsians taken from the (temporarily) abandoned *Prince Igor*.[6] The key of the piece is given as B minor, but this is immediately flung into uncertainty. The opening bars centre around the note B, but the powerful motto includes intervals characteristic of Arabic music (one of the 'exotic' elements often used by 'The Five'), which undermine the sense of key. After the second statement of the motto, the held note drops from B to A. After two more statements of the motto, the tempo increases, and the woodwind introduce a second, more dancing element, in D major. But this is short-lived, and after two phrases the opening motto reappears, dragging the music back to the opening tempo. Again the held Bs fall to A, and then to G, and the woodwind again attempt to introduce their dance, now in C major. Once more the attempt falters, and the motto reappears. But this time, instead of being dragged back to the opening tempo, the first four notes of the motto soften, and rise through the strings. Soon, the tempo eases slightly, and the cellos play a longer lyrical line, in D major. This is the second theme of the symphony, a melody that evokes the freedom of traditional Slavic song. A climax builds, the tempo accelerates, the motto reappears in the bass, and the opening section of the movement comes to a close in a mood of intense brooding.

What follows is less like a traditional 'development' and more like an operatic battle scene, with the familiar elements chasing each other in a struggle for supremacy. It begins with the opening motto darkly recalled by bassoons and lower strings. The softened version of the motto leads to a sudden surge of pace and energy. Over an insistent galloping rhythm, the motto, and a variant of it, move from key to key. The lyrical second theme is also drawn in, without dampening the energy. As the motto becomes concentrated in the brass, it takes on the character of a battle cry, echoing from instrument to instrument. There is a great build-up, and the entire orchestra bursts into the reprise of the motto, as it was at the opening, but now *fff*. The chords that punctuate it are different, giving it a more powerful sense of confrontation, and the tension lasts longer than before. When the woodwind do manage to pull the music into their dance, it leads more quickly on to the lyrical second theme, and the route to the end is swift. Threatening chords from trombones and horns announce the final triumph of the motto, which is stated starkly and simply for the last time.

After a first movement notionally in B minor, Borodin unusually leaps to F major for his scherzo. It was Balakirev who suggested linking these remote keys with the chord that opens the movement – though, if anything, this makes the effect even bolder. The scherzo is prestissimo, in a four-time so fast that it is notated as one beat per bar. There are two main elements. The first is set up by the horns' rapid repeated notes, and consists of a rising pizzicato in the strings answered by a chattering descent in the woodwind. A few bars with strange, bell-like harmonies lead to the second element, a series of breathless little stutters of melody syncopated against the continuing rapid repeated notes (an incredibly difficult rhythm to make clear at the tempo). This passes from the strings to the woodwind and then to both. After this pair of ideas has been repeated, the scherzo calms to the Allegretto middle section. It opens with a magical shift of key, to a chord of F sharp minor. An oboe plays a gently weaving melody, which hovers between D major and F sharp minor, and which is closely related to the second theme from the first movement. It passes to clarinet, then to oboe and flute in combination, joined by horns and changing key as it goes. The strings, low and dark, take up the melody, and it builds gloriously. The moment fades, and we are back into the rapid scherzo.

The slow movement opens with harp arpeggios and an evocative introductory phrase on clarinet. According to Stasov, the idea for this movement was suggested by the minstrel, Boyan, who appears in *The Lay of Igor's Campaign*, the medieval Slavic poem on which Borodin's *Prince Igor* was based, accompanying himself on the traditional *gusli* (a Slavic zither).[7] A horn unfolds a melody in D flat major, free in the shape and length of its phrases, richly accompanied by strings. Even without the reference to medieval minstrelsy, this melody strongly evokes traditional Slavic free song (a genre called *protyazhnaya*). It is repeated and extended on clarinet with woodwind choir, which seems to draw it closer to Orthodox chant. Horn and strings muse on the opening phrase of the melody, now with a more doleful falling interval. We are drawn into the middle section of the movement, with tremolando strings and a change of key. A sorrowful little fragment of melody passes among the woodwind and then briefly blossoms in horns and cellos. The doleful phrase returns, and builds to mighty chords. Now the pace increases, and a more hopeful phrase rises up from cellos to violins. This develops, alternating with the doleful phrase, until it reaches a climax. The sorrowful fragment of melody returns, and, with another change of key, we return to the D flat major of the opening, and all the strings reprise the horn melody. From here the movement slowly winds to a resolution through reminiscences of the various elements. It ends as it began, with the clarinet over harp arpeggios, and a final horn phrase.

Violins quietly hold over a bare fifth into the finale, which follows without a break. This is a lively, festive dance. Stasov tells us that it represents 'the knights' feast, the sound of the *gusli* (zither), and a jubilant throng of people'.[8] It bounds with rhythmic energy, very much like the overture to *Prince Igor*. It builds gradually, and when the dance bursts out, it has a characteristically Russian (or at least Slav) combination of offbeat accents and irregular metre, alternating three-time and two-time. After a while, a clarinet introduces a more lyrical melody, which draws its character from earlier lyrical themes in the symphony. This is passed around, building in energy, and it too – charmingly – is from time to time disrupted by irregular metre.

The festivities pause, and trombones solemnly intone a fragment of the dance tune, made threatening by its distortion into a whole-tone scale. It is as if the awe-inspiring hero has entered the hall. The dance resumes, tentatively at first, and then with increasing confidence. It is joined by a stamping version of the lyrical second theme. At a climax, this rounds a corner, and comes to a reprise of the dance in its original key (B major). After a time, this takes a new direction, and is joined by the second theme. There is a moment of quiet. Then the energy quickly builds again, and with one last burst of the dance tune, and a joyful trilling, the symphony is over.

JOHANNES BRAHMS
(1833–97)

The gruff, bearded figure of Brahms in his later years is so familiar from photographs and caricatures that it is easy to forget that he was once a striking young man. When he was twenty, trying to make his way as a composer and pianist, he went on a concert tour with a young Hungarian violinist, Eduard Reményi. While in Hanover, they visited the greatest of Hungarian violinists, Joseph Joachim. 'Never in the course of my artist's life,' wrote Joachim, 'have I been more completely overwhelmed with delighted surprise, than when the rather shy-mannered, blond companion of my countryman played his sonata movements, of quite undreamed-of originality and power, looking noble and inspired. His playing, so tender, so imaginative, so free and so fiery, held me spell-bound.'[1] Joachim introduced Brahms to Robert and Clara Schumann, who became his close friends and most ardent champions. When Robert Schumann died in an asylum three years later, Brahms rushed to Clara's side to help her run the household (which included six children). To Clara, he was 'the dearest friend I have in the world'. Brahms, always drawn to Clara, fell headlong in love with her, confessing to Joachim, 'I think I can't love a young girl any more, at least, I have entirely forgotten about them; after all, they only promise the heaven which Clara shows us unlocked.'[2] Although Clara was thirteen years older than Brahms, they might very well have married. But, for reasons that are not clear, their relationship cooled, and they went their separate ways. Their friendship, despite occasional quarrels and hurt feelings on both sides, was a rock for both of them over the years. They each remained single for the rest of their lives. The 'shy-seeming' Brahms matured into a bluff old (or old-seeming) bachelor, hiding his feelings beneath a crusty, bearded exterior and often clumsily offending his friends.

There are dangers in extrapolating from life to music, but it is tempting to see something of this character in his music. Brahms had a wonderfully easy lyrical gift, which he felt the need to cloak in serious, highly elaborated structures. At his best, he brings these two sides of his musical character together so that there is no mismatch: the lyrical and the complex combine to create music that evolves in a powerfully organic way. At other times, the struggle to rationalize his ideas can seem dogged. Alfred Maczewski, writing in the first edition of *Grove's Dictionary of Music and Musicians* in 1879, acknowledged Brahms as 'one of the greatest living German composers', but went on to say, 'There is (if the word may be allowed) an unapproachable asceticism about his genius which is opposed to all that is merely pleasing to the ear. He does not court understanding; he rather demands from it arduous and unwearied service.'[3] Understanding Brahms is a great deal less arduous in the early twenty-first century than it might have seemed in the 1870s. And, as with Beethoven, the process of struggle is an essential part of the musical and human picture.

Because of his association with Schumann, and his predominantly traditional approach to composition, Brahms came to be regarded as the leader of the 'classical' school of German music, the successor to Schumann and Mendelssohn, in opposition to the followers of Liszt and Wagner who styled themselves the New German School. In 1860, when they were in their late twenties, Brahms and Joachim unwisely drew up a manifesto publicly declaring themselves against the New German School: 'the undersigned ... regard the productions of the leaders and pupils of the so-called New German School ... as contrary to the innermost spirit of music, strongly to be deplored and condemned'.[4] When this manifesto was leaked to the press, before Brahms and Joachim had gathered the signatures of all their supporters, this immediately propelled Brahms into the forefront of the battle for German musical culture. His attack was aimed more at Liszt, whose music he deplored, than at Wagner, whose operas he came to admire; he once protested, 'Do you suppose that I am so limited that I cannot be delighted by the humour and greatness of *Die Meistersinger*?'[5] But, characteristically, it was Wagner rather than Liszt who retaliated with the greater antagonism. When Brahms composed his First Symphony, Wagner subjected it to a savage review: 'What had previously been dressed up as quintets and the like was served up as symphony: little chips of melody like an infusion of hay and old tea leaves, with nothing to tell you what you are swallowing but the label "best".'[6] Liszt, who was a more generous character than Wagner, continued to play Brahms's music, though he deplored the conservatism of some of his allies, 'the empty formulae of the objurations of our pseudo-classicists, who do their utmost to proclaim that art is being ruined'.[7]

This battle helps us to understand Brahms's unique place in music history. But we do not have to evoke the battles of the past whenever we listen to his music.

Concertos

CONCERTO IN A MINOR FOR VIOLIN AND CELLO, OP. 102
Duration: approx. 34 minutes

Allegro
Andante
Vivace non troppo

In 1884, Joachim and his wife Amalie separated after Joachim had become convinced that she was having an affair with Fritz Simrock, the publisher. Brahms was sure that she was not, and wrote a sympathetic letter to Amalie that was used as evidence in the divorce court. This resulted in a rift between Joachim and Brahms. Three years later, Brahms composed this double concerto as a peace offering to Joachim, dedicating it to him and the cellist Robert Hausmann for whom he had composed his second cello sonata the previous year. Brahms had frequently played chamber music with both of them, and he conducted the premiere and several other performances of the concerto with them in several cities. Clara Schumann attended an early rehearsal and wrote in her diary, 'Joachim and Brahms have spoken to each other for the first time in years.'[8]

The double concerto is shorter and more straightforward than the Violin Concerto or the two piano concertos. It was Brahms's last orchestral work, and although he gives full rein to the orchestra as usual, there is a brisk terseness that it shares with the chamber works he composed shortly before this concerto: the Violin Sonata in A, Opus 100, and the Piano Trio in C minor, Opus 101.

The concerto begins with a bold statement of the opening of the first theme on full orchestra, though not yet in the home key (this opening is in E minor, not A minor). It soon gives way to a passage of cello cadenza, 'in the manner of a recitative, but in strict tempo'. This dramatic way of starting a concerto has its origin in Beethoven's 'Emperor' Concerto, and had been adopted in recent years by Max Bruch in his First Violin Concerto, and by Brahms himself in his Second Piano Concerto. Here, it takes on a subtly new character, partly by starting in the 'wrong' key, and partly because this is a concerto for two instruments. The cello begins in a forthright manner, and ends meditatively. Woodwind and horns play a few bars of offbeat sighs, which will become the lyrical second theme. The solo violin enters, at first continuing the meditative mood, but soon becoming assertive. The cello joins in, and together they build to a brilliant climax, at which the orchestra bursts in to play the first theme, now in the home key of A minor. Brahms is rarely content just to state themes. This orchestral tutti explores the possibilities of the assertive first idea, with its contrast between hefty dotted rhythms and broad triplets (conflict between twos and threes is one of Brahms's favourite rhythmic devices.) Along the way it brings in other elements that will prove important: a vigorous syncopated idea that bursts into energetic triplet rhythms, followed by the offbeat sighs of the second theme, here in full vigour, and a final build-up from which emerges the solo cello once more.

In the cellist's hands the first theme takes on a broad sweep. The violin soon joins in duet. Together they develop the theme, and it leads on to energetic semiquavers, sturdy chords, and triplet arpeggios that begin assertively and become more thoughtful. This brings in the second theme, played by the cello. We have heard its offbeat sighs twice before, but now they are extended into a glorious lyrical line. Again the violin joins in, but rather than extending the theme further, the two soloists break off into a cascade of brilliant semiquavers. These are followed by a sudden burst of chords, and a reminder of the syncopated idea from the orchestral tutti. No sooner have they begun this than the orchestra takes it over, and we are into another vigorous tutti, bringing the first section of the movement to a close.

From the tutti the soloists emerge to develop the themes further. They begin with the first theme in duet, but it soon evaporates into a dialogue of playful running figuration, and a passage of trills. After a brief orchestral passage, the cello ruminates on the syncopated idea, and with the violin rises to a moment of serenity. From this, running scales build up quickly, and massive chords bring the orchestra in with the reprise of the opening theme. Brahms arrives more quickly than before at the second theme. This time the violin plays the lyrical line, the cello accompanying with a filigree of arpeggios. The music proceeds much as before, and the orchestra again takes over the syncopated idea. We half expect their tutti to culminate in the traditional cadenza for the soloists. But instead, Brahms gives them the first theme once more, and it develops into a sturdy coda to bring the movement to a close.

The Andante begins with horns and woodwind playing a gentle fanfare of two rising fourths. The soloists, an octave apart, take up this idea and extend it into a theme in D major. The melody is formal in its shape, with each half repeated, evoking the idea of a folk song, and the whole movement is constructed with clarity and simplicity. The melody, however, like the similar theme of the slow movement of the recent Piano Trio in C minor, has a wider range and greater harmonic richness than one would find in a real folk song. The theme draws to a close, the music moves into F major, and the woodwind play a chorale. Like the 'folk song', this is not quite as straightforward at it seems at first. The metre is ambiguous, and seems to shift as the soloists enter (this is one of Brahms's favourite confusions, as it was of his champion, Robert Schumann). Violin and cello exchange musings, and as these become more argumentative, the woodwind repeat their chorale, a phrase at a time. Again the music changes key, down from F to D flat major, as if it is about to venture further afield. But, as the orchestra swells to a brief climax, the harmonies swing beautifully back to D major, and, after a brief cadenza, the soloists reprise the opening theme. As the first strain repeats, they extend each phrase to allow time for the woodwind to sweep up and down an arpeggio. The second strain of the theme does not repeat. Instead, the soloists remember their music from the middle of the movement, while the woodwind quietly resume their chorale. The musing reaches a moment of great tenderness, there is a final reminder of the opening theme, and the movement comes to a peaceful close.

Like the folk(ish) tune of the slow movement, the main theme of the finale is typically Brahmsian in its ambiguity. Its rhythms suggest that it will be another Hungarian rondo, but it is not wholeheartedly Hungarian like the finales of Brahms's Violin Concerto or of Bruch's First Violin Concerto (or of Joachim's 'Hungarian Concerto', which established the fashion). The melody, working away at little staccato phrases in a repetitive rhythm, has a suggestion of searching or melancholy, despite its energy. After the cello and then the violin have played the theme, the continuation softens for a moment into major keys, before the energy builds up and the orchestra bursts in with more straightforward Hungarian vigour. After a few bars in which the soloists join in with this spirit, the music moves again to a major key (C major), and the cello plays a bold new theme in two-part chords, with the violin joining in. A brief linking passage takes us back to the opening theme. This time, the violin decorates it playfully, and hands it to bassoon, oboe, and flute, before it evaporates.

Now comes perhaps the most Hungarian moment in the whole piece. The two soloists together play an assertive theme that juxtaposes sharp dotted rhythms and smoother triplets (another version of Brahms's favourite conflict between twos and threes). This is decorated with flamboyant flourishes, and then alternates with subdued responses. The subdued element leads on to a thoughtful exchange of arpeggios, while the woodwind play a tune of offbeat chords – another hint of Hungarian dance. The soloists take up this offbeat dance enthusiastically, and then play a variation of it broken into arpeggios. The orchestra returns to the assertive dotted rhythms with which this episode began, and soon we are back at a full reprise of the opening theme. It follows on, much as before, to the second theme. But now the pace eases, the key warms from minor to major, and we enter an epilogue. This is the most subtle moment in the whole concerto. In the foreground, the soloists exchange delicate arpeggios, while in the background the woodwind play a smoothed-out version of the first theme (which now sounds wistful rather than Hungarian). The soloists extend and build up their figurations and fall back to pianissimo. Suddenly the music snaps back into its original tempo, and with a final burst of twos-against-threes, the work ends with a show of (not particularly Hungarian) confidence.

PIANO CONCERTO NO. 1 IN D MINOR, OP. 15
Duration: approx. 50 minutes

Maestoso
Adagio
Rondo: Allegro non troppo

Some pieces of music sound so inevitable, so exactly the way they should be, that it comes as a shock to discover the tortuous route by which the composer arrived at the final result. At the age of twenty, Brahms wrote three movements of a sonata for two pianos. But, after playing them over with Clara Schumann several times, he decided 'that they require even more than two pianos'.[9] Then he tried orchestrating the first movement, but still found it unsatisfactory. The following year he arrived at the solution and converted it into the first movement of a piano concerto, taking another year to complete the three movements, in 1858. The concerto was first performed in Hanover the following year, with Brahms playing the solo part and Joachim conducting, and was a complete failure. But with the encouragement of friends Brahms maintained his faith in it, made further minor revisions, and eventually it succeeded with the public and the critics.

The concerto is on a grand scale, longer even than Beethoven's 'Emperor'. It opens with a startling, Beethoven-like gesture: defiant phrases thrown up by the violins. Underneath is a held bass note and drum roll on D, but the key is at first uncertain. It might be in B flat, but there are disruptive trills on A flat. Eventually the storm quietens, we seem momentarily in D minor, but still the search for a key continues. Every time the music settles, it is either in a remote key, or in a state of flux. It is a long and tumultuous journey before the soloist enters, and early audiences might have wondered whether this was really going to be a concerto or a symphony. Finally, calm descends, and the soloist enters with an unassuming theme firmly in D minor, which sadly ruminates on the phrases with which the orchestral turmoil has just concluded. This soon builds up to the mighty trills from the orchestral opening. The quiet second theme is soon touched on, but this proves to be only a prelude to a new theme, a chorale in Brahms's most sonorous and expansive piano style. The tail-piece to the chorale is a reiterated phrase sounding like a gentle horn call. And indeed, a little later, a horn takes up this motif as the movement winds quietly to the end of its first section.

The piano begins the development by returning to the mood of the opening, with a burst of striding double octaves, the orchestra punctuating them with the defiant opening phrases. The quiet second orchestral theme is revisited, then another mighty build-up leads to the reprise. Here it is the piano rather than the orchestra that throws up the Beethoven-like gestures. The ruminating first piano entry is incorporated along the way, then the chorale, and this section winds down as before to the sound of a quiet horn call. Now the tempo increases, the grand double octaves return, and the tension builds. At its height, orchestra and piano are pitted against each other, but in a moment of characteristic Brahmsian synthesis, the climactic octaves are derived from the piano's gentle first entry, now transformed in character. As the movement thunders to its end, one can imagine the impression the shy young Brahms must have made playing this music.

The slow movement has an unmistakeably spiritual character, and a suggestion of the antique. Muted strings, in simple octaves, rise and fall in solemn, hymn-like procession, while bassoons in thirds weave a line that falls and rises in counterpoint. Brahms wrote on his score, 'Benedictus qui venit in nomine domini'. He had studied, and continued to study and perform, the choral music of the Renaissance and Baroque, and it was around this time that he began to collect the volumes of the new complete edition of J. S. Bach. But the words might refer to Beethoven's *Missa Solemnis*: the solemn prelude to the 'Benedictus' in that work could well have inspired the opening of this slow movement. After the opening chorale, the piano meditates upon it at length. Then further fragments of chorale are played pianissimo by the strings, the piano responding with hesitant and delicate decorations. These become more impassioned, and clarinets add a new melodious theme, which sounds very like a fragment of a song by Schubert ('Ständchen', Serenade). Further impassioned exchanges between piano and orchestra lead to the return of the chorale and responses of the piano. But the passionate tone cannot now be shaken off: pianissimo passages lead on to a fortissimo extension of the chorale in the woodwind, with forceful trills and arpeggios in the piano reminding us of the storms of the first movement. Calm returns, and further quiet musings in the piano bring one of Brahms's most poetical movements to a close.

The final Rondo is, in character and in plan, inspired by the finale of Beethoven's Piano Concerto No. 3 in C minor. It has a similarly brusque principal theme, which is subjected to similar treatment. At the same time, Brahms has derived the opening notes of this theme from the hymn-like second theme that the piano played in the first movement – the kind of subtle transformation that Brahms was to repeat throughout his career. There is a second, sonorous theme, which, again, seems new but derives from the shape of the first theme. In the centre of the movement there are further transformations: first a warmly lyrical melody in the violins, now in B flat major, then a teasing little moment of fugue, echoing a similar episode in Beethoven's C minor Piano Concerto. Towards the end of the movement there is the conventional pause for a cadenza. But this is sonorous and brief, quite unlike the showy cadenzas of most concertos, and leads into an expansive passage of reminiscence of the movement's themes. Rapid scales lead to a more animated tempo, and what seems like the final peroration. But there is another pause, another little cadenza, and only then does Brahms reach the home straight.

PIANO CONCERTO NO. 2 IN B FLAT MAJOR, OP. 83
Duration: approx. 50 minutes

Allegro non troppo
Allegro appassionato
Andante
Allegretto grazioso

After the bruising experience of his First Piano Concerto, it was more than twenty years before Brahms presented a Second Piano Concerto to the public. He began it in 1878 but took three years to complete it, having meanwhile written the Violin Concerto. The premiere in 1881, with Brahms at the piano, was a triumph. And yet this concerto is just as demanding for audiences as the first. It is just as long, and has four movements rather than the conventional three. Of all piano concertos, it is the one that comes closest to a symphony, not just in length, but in breadth of conception and concentration of musical argument.

It must surely be as a deliberate homage to Beethoven's 'Emperor' that the piano enters straight away, and then launches into a preliminary cadenza. But the effect could hardly be different. A horn plays a gentle rising phrase, the piano quietly answers. The horn plays a descending phrase, the piano answers. It is the most unassuming of openings. But after a few bars of woodwind continuation, the piano enters again with a commanding new motif of firm bass arpeggios and assertive dotted rhythms. This builds up to a climax, and (as in the 'Emperor'), the orchestra finally sets off on its journey, laying out the main themes of the movement. There are three themes that are to dominate: the horn theme already played in fragments at the opening and now on full orchestra, a lyrical second theme, whose yearning character arises partly because its key seems uncertain and fluctuating until its last phrase, and a third, strong element of dotted rhythms, derived from the opening piano cadenza. When the piano enters again at the end of the orchestral passage, it sets out on a revisiting of these different elements, with unexpected transformations and some new developments. The opening horn call is now treated to the most expansive of elaboration. The motif of arpeggios and dotted rhythms has changed, taking on a delicate, poised character. And the climax of this opening section is achieved by taking the orchestra's lyrical second theme, with its shifting harmonies, and transforming it into the grandest and most sonorous of solo passages. On through the forceful dotted rhythms, and to mighty trills with massive chords below, and the orchestra leads off into the middle section.

As the orchestra calms, the horn emerges playing the opening call, now in the minor. The development that follows is tumultuous, with the piano-writing ranging from strong and assertive to delicate and sparkling. This section comes to a firm end, with fortissimo chords on the orchestra, out of which rippling arpeggios in the piano quieten to pianissimo, while the woodwind reiterate phrases as if searching. This leads into one of Brahms's most beautiful moments of transition: from the delicate shimmering of the high piano writing emerges the quiet return of the horn call. The magically calm mood that this moment creates is not to be broken. The piano does not pound in with its sudden cadenza, as it did at the beginning. Instead, further quiet musings on the opening theme follow, and lead seamlessly on to arrive at the piano's grand version of the lyrical second theme. Indeed, despite all the delicate and lyrical passages, it is the grandeur of this movement that remains longest in the memory, the movement ending with a triumphant climax.

What could possibly follow this mighty opening movement? Brahms, with characteristic irony, described the second movement as 'a wisp of a scherzo'. In fact it is a massively passionate scherzo in D minor, the key of the First Piano Concerto, with which it shares a character of fierce determination. Urgent fortissimo passages alternate with delicate interludes, in which high woodwind intone a reiterated dotted-note figure, like a distant processional chant. In the centre, a great orchestral climax suddenly breaks out into a joyful new theme in D major, like a peal of bells, followed by dotted rhythms that seem to refer back to the woodwind's processional figure (or even to the dotted rhythms of the first movement). In the middle section, Brahms asks the pianist to perform the virtually impossible – complex pianissimo running figures, but in double octaves. Soon the piano is caught up in the jubilant mood set by the orchestra. The D minor scherzo returns. At the point where, the first time, the tension built up to the D major section, this time the music stays in D minor and builds powerfully, 'sempre più agitato' (with greater and greater agitation – in practice, faster and faster), and the movement thunders to a close.

Despite the massive power of the first two movements, it is the quiet slow movement that is the greatest achievement of this concerto. It is a companion piece to the lovely slow movement of the Violin Concerto, which Brahms had recently completed. There, a solo oboe was the companion to the violin. Here, a solo cello fulfils the same role. Its opening melody is among the most beautiful that Brahms ever wrote, the cello line supported by a warm chorus of accompanying cellos and violas, a magical descending violin counterpoint joining in at the second half of the melody. The piano enters, and quietly muses on the cello's theme, developing it into a fantasy of increasing power. At its climax, forceful trills remind us of the climactic trills in the first movement. The last climax subsides, the key shifts gently into F sharp major (a very long way from the B flat in which the movement started), and we enter a passage of complete stillness. A pair of clarinets, marked *ppp dolcissimo*, sustain an immensely slow-moving duet – comparable in its stillness to the slow movement of Schubert's String

Quintet – while the piano shadows them with delicate touches. The strings follow on from the clarinets, and the stillness deepens further. Out of almost complete silence, the solo cello emerges again, at first still in B major, and very high. It eventually finds its way back to B flat, and the movement ends with a reprise of the opening melody, while the piano decorates it lovingly with delicate cascades of arpeggios.

Brahms completes his concerto with the one element that has been missing: graceful dancing. This finale, like the first movement and the slow movement, is in the key of B flat. But Brahms avoids monotony by making the principle theme of his finale start in a somewhat uncertain E flat, only gradually working round to B flat. The little tune, delicate but in tricky octaves, passes from piano to strings and back again. Then a crescendo leads to a forceful outburst from the piano, with repeated dotted rhythms and bass octaves fortissimo. At this point it becomes clear how much the rhythmic shape of the themes in this part of the movement owe to the dotted rhythms of the first movement.

After a while an interlude follows in a broader rhythm, in A minor. This has almost the feel of one of Brahms's more sweeping Hungarian Dances. In the middle of this interlude comes a relaxed little tune in F major, which is delightfully decorated by the piano at its repetition. With fragments of the swinging Hungarian melody returning, the music winds round to repeat the opening theme, now on the oboe. But instead of simply repeating what happened before, Brahms elaborates this into a fully fledged development, the theme moving through different keys, now seeming whimsical, now searching, now declaimed forcefully by the orchestra and answered by the piano.

Eventually the music finds its way back to B flat, and a varied repeat of the opening section ensues, followed by a return to the Hungarian theme, now in D minor. Fragments of the main theme are tried out, until the pianist finally arrives at a faster variation on it, another technical challenge as Brahms transforms the theme into a delicate jig rhythm, but with the right hand playing rapid patterns of octaves. This coda develops irresistible momentum. The First Piano Concerto came to an end in a mood of fierce determination, but this coda brings the Second Piano Concerto to its close with a feeling of complete, but hard-won, joy.

VIOLIN CONCERTO IN D MAJOR, OP. 77
Duration: approx. 38 minutes

Allegro non troppo
Adagio
Allegro giocoso, ma non troppo vivace

Brahms's Violin Concerto marked the high point of his friendship with the great Hungarian violinist, Joseph Joachim. They had first met in 1853, when the young Brahms was on a concert tour (see introduction). Now in 1878, twenty-five years later, Brahms wrote a magnificent violin concerto for him.

He composed it not just for Joachim but also with him. Brahms was not a violinist, and although he had often written for strings he did not trust himself to write a violin concerto without the help of a virtuoso. So as soon as he had completed a draft of the first movement he sent the solo part to Joachim, with a letter asking him 'to make corrections, and not to have any scruples – neither a respect for music that is too good, nor the excuse that the score is not worth the trouble'.[10] Joachim found most of it manageable, but replied, 'whether it can all be played in a hot concert-hall I cannot say, before I've played it straight through'.[11] Brahms and Joachim worked on the concerto over the coming months, and Joachim played the premiere on New Year's Day 1879 in the Leipzig Gewandhaus, with Brahms himself conducting. Joachim had received the finished version of the violin part only four days before. The Leipzig audience, who had a habit of giving Brahms's music a cool reception, was polite rather than enthusiastic. But the performance in Vienna a few days later was a great success, as Brahms reported: 'Joachim played my piece better at each rehearsal, and the cadenza sounded so beautiful at the actual concert that the audience applauded it into the start of the coda.' The concerto is on a grand symphonic scale, with the solo violin and orchestra fully interwoven in texture and argument. This approach was quite unlike most concertos of the period, in which the orchestra was generally more subservient to the soloist. Brahms's model, however, was not the fashionable music of his time, but the concertos of Beethoven and, more recently, Bruch.

The opening orchestral tutti sets out important elements: a quiet falling and rising arpeggio that starts the movement; bold, sturdy octaves soon after; lyrical phrases with a dying fall; and finally assertive dotted rhythms (reminiscent of Beethoven's *Egmont* Overture) to announce the entry of the soloist. Each of these elements recurs through the movement, but often either changed in character or acting as an accompaniment to the violin. It is one of the most characteristic features of this concerto (as of Beethoven's) that the violin, though the soloist, is often in the role of decorating thematic material that is being played by the orchestra. This makes the interaction between soloist and orchestra unusually subtle and integrated.

The violin enters dramatically, in D minor, playing an energized and extended commentary on the smooth opening arpeggios. This gradually calms down (or rather is calmed down by the woodwind) until the violin settles into a beautiful statement of the opening theme, now back in D major. This leads on to what seems a new theme, in which the violin plays assertive chords on three strings. But underneath, in the cellos and basses, is the motif of bold octaves from the introduction. At last we do reach a genuinely new theme, a fully fledged lyrical melody that was not in the orchestral introduction. After a moment of calm, in which the orchestra reiterates the falling phrases from the introduction, the violin boldly states, again on three strings, the dotted-rhythm theme that had originally announced the arrival of the soloist.

Now it signals the culmination of the first section of the movement, and a grand orchestral tutti follows, leading on to the central development of the movement. This starts quietly, building on the falling motif. Assertive trills burst in, and a climax is reached at which the violin swoops up and down. This is based on the sturdy octave theme from the introduction, but now given added tension by overshooting to dissonant notes. A further great build-up leads to the return of the opening theme, now transformed into an exuberant orchestral outburst.

The reprise proceeds until a cadenza. Brahms left Joachim to provide this, and his is still the cadenza most often played. But there are many others that have been written since, notably a very fine one by Nathan Milstein. At the end of the cadenza, there is a quiet ascent to a hushed restatement of the opening theme. Now it is magically extended, rising higher, and interweaving with clarinet and oboe. This is a crucial moment for understanding what is to follow in the slow movement. Gradually the energy increases, and the movement ends emphatically.

Brahms originally planned four movements, as in his Second Piano Concerto. But he wrote that he was having problems with the middle two movements, and had abandoned them: 'Naturally they were the best! I am replacing them with a poor adagio.' This 'poor' Adagio is one of the most glorious movements Brahms ever wrote, beginning and ending with a beautiful oboe solo accompanied by the other wind instruments, like a homage to Mozart's sere-nades. This seems like a logical outcome of what has gone before at the end of the first movement, as if the oboe, musing further on the opening theme of the concerto, is given free reign to develop it into a fully fledged melody. The violin takes this up and meditates exten-sively on it, exploring all its melodic and emotional potential. The return of the opening melody is a beautiful moment. The oboe leads off the melody again, the violin weaving around it, and violin and oboe come back to their conversation to round off the movement.

In the finale, Brahms, like Bruch, pays affectionate homage to Joachim, who had already made a great success with his own 'Hungarian Concerto'. This movement is in 'Hungarian' style, with stamping dance rhythms alternating with melodies of intense sweetness. It is marked 'giocoso' – joyful – and it needs from the soloist immense confidence, and a certain sense of abandon. The gritty determination it sometimes receives tends to be much admired, but is not likely to be quite what Brahms meant.

Overtures

ACADEMIC FESTIVAL OVERTURE, OP. 80
Duration: approx. 11 minutes

This is one of a pair of concert overtures that Brahms wrote in 1880, the other being the Tragic Overture. Brahms dedicated the Academic Festival Overture to the University of Breslau, which had awarded him an honorary doctorate the previous year. Brahms himself described it as 'a jolly potpourri of student drinking songs à la Suppé',[12] and you might imagine from this a lightweight, even frivolous piece of music. But although this is Brahms at his most celebratory, it is at the same time a fully worked-out symphonic movement with a serious spine running through it. Brahms himself conducted the premiere at a ceremony at the University of Breslau in January 1881.

The idea of festivity is suggested right at the opening. A muttering march theme is accom-panied by quiet bass drum and cymbals, like the distant sound of a German band. But quite what is to come is uncertain: the march is in the minor key, there are mysterious flurries on clarinets, and there follows a touch of a serene chorale on strings and then horn, before a crescendo leads to a brief burst of a sturdy theme of dotted rhythms. Another hush makes way for a chorale on trumpets and woodwind (this is the student song 'We have built a stately house'), and a grand crescendo brings in the full orchestra, converting the opening mutterings into a triumphant flourish, and then developing further the 'stately house' song. When this dies down, there is another transformation of the opening march, which now becomes a quietly rolling melody on the violins. Further development leads to a soaring melody on violins, based on another student song, 'Father of the country'. And, a little later, two bassoons cheekily play a freshman's initiation song, the 'Fuchslied', which must have startled those members of the first Breslau audience who were expecting Brahms to remain solemn and dignified.

By now, Brahms has introduced all but one of his elements. A repeat of the 'Fuchslied' on full orchestra signals the beginning of the central section of the movement, in which frag-ments of several of the themes develop a powerful momentum. A sustained fortissimo passage climaxes in the 'stately house' chorale, which is now brought powerfully into the flow of the movement, and before we realize it, we are reprising the principal themes. This time around the sequence of events is abbreviated, and instead of the bassoons introducing the 'Fuchslied', a corner is turned, and a fortissimo statement of the tune culminates in a broad declaration of 'Gaudeamus igitur', the student song that Brahms was keeping up his sleeve, and, as it turns out, the only one that is still widely familiar today. On full orchestra, with rushing violins and crashing cymbals, it brings the overture to a close in the grandest possible manner.

TRAGIC OVERTURE, OP. 81

Duration: approx. 13 minutes

This is one of a pair of concert overtures that Brahms wrote in 1880, the other being the Academic Festival Overture. In contrast to that work, the Tragic Overture is dark and brooding, a marvellously satisfying symphonic movement on a grand scale. Brahms had no specific tragedies in mind, but it stands in a line of strong works in D minor, from Mozart's D minor Piano Concerto, through to Beethoven's Ninth Symphony (particularly its first movement).

The overture opens with a pair of Beethoven-style hammer blows, followed by a quiet string melody that rises and falls in two waves over a quiet drum roll. At first, the key of the piece is uncertain, hovering between D minor and F major, and taking a long time to resolve firmly into D minor. This gives an impression that this is not quite a beginning, as if we are joining ominous events that are already under way. This opening passage is full of sudden contrasts – fierce dotted rhythms, muscular string arpeggios, sonorous wind chords, and then, as the music quietens for a moment, the woodwind engage in urgent running exchanges, until another fortissimo builds up. Finally, the paragraph reaches a conclusion, with a cadence of D minor firmly stated three times. There is a strong sense of narrative running through all this, as if we are setting out against the odds, full of determination.

We have now reached the first sustained quiet passage. But it is an uneasy calm, with pulsating syncopated chords in the strings, over which horns intone bare fifths, and an oboe rises plaintively, phrase by phrase, to a pianissimo high note. High violins shimmer over solemn phrases on trombones, the music warms into F major, a horn calls as if from the distance, and the violins play the most sustained melody of the overture, a glorious rising theme, full of a feeling of consolation. This builds to a renewed struggle, with a return to the assertive dotted rhythms and arpeggios of the opening, which now push forward, on and on, with strings and wind often pitted against each other (very much in the vein of the Third Symphony, which was to follow two years later). This passage culminates in the return of the double hammer blow from the opening bars, and the music is suddenly quiet.

After a reminiscence of the opening string phrases, we enter the central section of the overture. Here, the pace is suddenly halved. There is a firm tread to the rhythm, over which the woodwind play dotted-rhythm phrases that seem quite new in the context. But they are a slowed-down version of phrases taken from the opening bars of the overture. After a while, this is elaborated into a hushed fugue-like passage, in which Brahms pays homage to a similar passage in the slow movement of Beethoven's Seventh Symphony. At the end of this section, there is a moment of sustained pianissimo, in which phrases familiar from the beginning of the overture are tentatively revisited. Eventually, a horn rises in an arpeggio, bringing the warmth of D major to the dark waves that opened the overture, and we find ourselves back at the glorious string theme, now on violas. As before, it culminates in a renewal of the struggle. This time it is prolonged even further, until, after a terrific climax, again it ends with emphatic cadences in D minor. Bare fifths in the horns suggest that we may be about to return to the quiet middle section again. But instead clarinets rise to a gentle climax, the music winds down, and a final burst of determination brings the overture to an emphatic close.

Serenades

SERENADE NO. 1 IN D MAJOR, OP. 11
Duration: approx. 45 minutes

Allegro molto
Scherzo: Allegro ma non troppo
Adagio non troppo
Menuetto I and II
Scherzo: Allegro
Rondo: Allegro

It was not until he was in his forties that Brahms challenged Beethoven on his home ground and composed his First Symphony. If we want some idea of the kind of symphony Brahms might have written in his twenties, the two serenades are as close as we can get – indeed, Joachim said of this first serenade that 'it declares itself to be a symphony'. It certainly is as long as a symphony, and the first and third movements are truly symphonic in scope. But the other movements are much shorter, and the whole work is in the tradition of Mozart's great serenades. To write such a piece and to call it a serenade in the 1850s was a bold act. It declared to the rival camps fighting over German musical culture that Brahms was firmly rooted in the classical tradition. One critic wrote of an early performance, 'Brahms has never, in our opinion, shown an inner inclination towards the futureless musicians of the future. We are persuaded that he has instead viewed the symphonic poems of Liszt, for example, with the disgust of a true musician.'[13]

In the autumn of 1857, while he was working on his First Piano Concerto, Brahms took a post as pianist, teacher, and conductor at the court of Detmold, where there was a thriving chamber orchestra and choral society. He spent three months of each year there, and it was for Detmold that he composed this Serenade. It began life as a nonet for strings and wind, and it was only later that Brahms adapted it for full orchestra.

The opening pays homage to Beethoven's 'Pastoral' Symphony, with its bagpipe-like drone bass and rustic calls on horn and clarinet. There is a characteristic moment of darkness before the whole ensemble takes up the theme. Another cloud crosses the sun before the music eases into the second, wide-spanning theme, first on violin then on cello, with beautifully relaxed triplet rhythms (a Brahms hallmark). The first section ends joyfully, and is repeated. The trotting triplets persist into the development as the music explores new keys, and as fragments of themes pass from strings to wind, eventually coming together in a climax. At the reprise, Brahms varies the harmonies in a masterly way, so that we hear the horn and clarinet calls in a new perspective. At the end, there is a beautiful coda in which the flute leads for the first time, drawing the movement to a delicate, wistful close.

The second movement is a surprisingly serious scherzo in a minor key – an ambivalent mood that Brahms was often to exploit in later works. The second strain of the scherzo expands warmly, illustrating how much Brahms learned from Schubert. The middle section (trio) goes halfway back to the pastoral mood of the opening movement, with a faster tempo and a persistently rolling rhythm.

The Adagio opens with solemn dotted rhythms warmly scored for lower strings and bassoon. Clarinets, and later flute, soar above. A second theme seems, once more, inspired by the peaceful brook from Beethoven's 'Pastoral' Symphony, with the melody gradually evolving above the murmuring accompaniment. As this wonderfully expansive paragraph comes to rest, we reach the end of the first section of the movement. The music moves on through new keys, as if through an ever-changing landscape, until, still in a remote key, the dotted rhythms of the opening are recalled, and the violin reprises the first theme. We round a corner, and return to the home key, and the violins elaborate the theme ecstatically. As it comes to rest, there is another change of direction, and an almost hymn-like moment, before we reach the second theme. This too rises gloriously, with new accompaniments. Over a long held bass note, the movement winds peacefully to a close.

Two miniature movements follow. The pair of minuets is miniature in instrumentation, as well as length. Minuet I is like Brahms's version of a Mozart divertimento for wind trio. A pair of clarinets plays a charming but slightly anxious melody in G major over a staccato bassoon. In the second half, a pizzicato cello and a flute join in, with some melting shifts of harmony. In the second minuet, which is in G minor, the melody is taken over by violin and becomes more lyrical, with the staccato moving to viola, and the bass in the cello. The lyricism becomes increasingly intense in the second half, enhanced by the clarinets, now supplying a warm counterpoint. Minuet I is then repeated.

The little scherzo and trio has distinct references to the scherzo of Beethoven's Second Symphony, and is perhaps intended as a gentle parody. The scherzo itself is based on a four-square hunting theme played by the horn. The two horns alternate in the trio, and underneath is a scurrying bass that moves up to the violins in the second half.

The final rondo is in that genial but persistent style that Brahms learned from Schubert (as in the Octet). The open-air dotted rhythms gradually build in energy, then, via a particularly Schubertian transition, relax into a more lyrical second theme. The lyricism is created not just by the violin melody, but by the running counterpoint in the viola. The opening dotted rhythms return, this time moving on to explore new landscapes. Indeed, the whole movement is like a country walk, in which familiar landmarks recur, but always seen from a different perspective, or in a different light. And when we return home, there is a moment of quiet contemplation, before the serenade comes to a decisive close.

SERENADE NO. 2 IN A MAJOR, OP. 16
Duration: approx. 32 minutes

Allegro moderato
Scherzo: Vivace
Adagio non troppo
Quasi menuetto
Rondo: Allegro

In the first serenade, Brahms showed his delight in sonorities that favour the lower strings and bring the woodwind and horns into the foreground. In the second serenade, he takes that approach one step further by dispensing with the violins altogether. He composed it in

1858–9, revising it in the 1870s. He sent it to Clara Schumann movement by movement as he wrote it, and dedicated it to her. Brahms himself was more satisfied with it than with his first serenade. As he was arranging it for piano duet (a routine procedure in the days before recordings), he wrote, 'I have seldom written music with greater delight. It seemed to sound so beautiful that I was overjoyed.'[14]

The Serenade opens with a gloriously rich theme, which several times rises in a series of steps, then falls gently. It begins on clarinets, then moves to the violas with the wind in counterpoint. This continual counterpoint between strings and woodwind is one of the chief sources of the rich quality throughout the work. A second theme returns to the clarinets, now in duet, with dancing dotted rhythms and with pizzicato strings to keep them light on their feet. At the end of the first section, Brahms returns to the opening theme. But rather than repeat the first section, he moves straight on into the development. Soon the triplet rhythms return and build. They are quietly combined with the opening, moving on through new keys and gathering intensity, then settling over a long held bass note. When the reprise comes, the first theme and the flowing triplets are combined, and throughout the reprise the familiar material is refreshed by new combinations of instruments. The movement ends with an extended meditation, in which woodwind and strings bid farewell to the various themes like old friends.

The scherzo has a delightfully Bohemian bounce, with persistent cross-rhythms. It is written in a fast three, but pairs of beats are grouped together to create a broader three-time metre. Only occasionally does this slip to reveal the underlying faster pattern. As the wind move seamlessly into the trio with a more sustained melody, the strings accompany with a dancing staccato. This playing with conflicting metres is just the sort of thing that Dvořák would later exploit in his Slavonic Dances.

When Brahms sent the Adagio to Clara Schumann for her comments, she wrote that it drew her towards it, 'as though I were to gaze at each filament of a wondrous flower. It is most beautiful! . . . The whole movement has a spiritual atmosphere; it might almost be an Eleison [that is, *Kyrie eleison*, the opening section of the mass].'[15] This quality is evident right at the start. Clarinets, flute, and oboe weave a chant-like melody in counterpoint. Underneath, the strings maintain a sombre bass line with a repeating pattern, like a ground bass or passacaglia, creating a processional character somewhat reminiscent of the 'Pilgrims' March' in Mendelssohn's 'Italian' Symphony. After a while, this devotional atmosphere is disturbed by agitated repeated notes and passionate chords, which open out lyrically. This leads on to a passage for wind alone, with a melody of consoling character. And this in turn develops further as the strings re-enter, the melody taken high by a clarinet, then passing to the cellos and reaching a resolution. The ground bass from the opening now returns, first in the violas then passing among other instruments, with a staccato counterpoint in oboe and flute. The chant-like melody returns, first in the horn, then, after a moment of uncertainty, in flute and clarinet, and the movement winds to a peaceful close.

Brahms marks the fourth movement 'Quasi menuetto'. But its gently swinging rhythm is part of a two-time metre, which has only the subtlest of dance elements in it. The trio is even further removed from that of a conventional minuet. It is composed of hesitant, even fearful, little phrases, against a persistently pulsating figure in the violas with pizzicato below.

The finale is a charming rondo in hunting style. Clarinets and oboes begin, and the hunting associations are soon reinforced by horns. Throughout the main theme, Brahms delights in alternations between a 'straight' two-time and a 'swung' jig rhythm, with three notes to each beat.

As the full orchestra joins in, a piccolo for the first time brightens the sonority of the violin-less texture. An episode begins with bassoons and clarinets in rather sombre counterpoint in a minor key, but soon this gives way to a charming tune in the major on the oboe that builds up to another tutti. A reprise of the hunting theme soon ventures off into new keys. The charming oboe tune reappears in the minor, and this is developed further. When the hunting theme recurs, it creeps in on clarinets at half speed – an enchanting moment. From here it builds up to full orchestra, with piccolo trills on top, and the music proceeds confidently on to a conclusion.

Symphonies

SYMPHONY NO. 1 IN C MINOR, OP. 68
Duration: approx 48 minutes (including first movement repeat)

Un poco sostenuto – Allegro
Andante sostenuto
Un poco allegretto e grazioso
Adagio – Allegro non troppo ma con brio

Brahms felt deeply the responsibility of writing a symphony, and he took many years to write one. It was the towering example of Beethoven that inhibited him, as he explained to the conductor Hermann Levi, 'I'll never write a symphony! You have no idea how the likes of us feel when we're always hearing a giant like that behind us.'[16] More than twenty years elapsed between his first attempts (which eventually transformed themselves into the first movement of his D minor Piano Concerto) and the work that was eventually performed as his First Symphony in 1876.

The symphony opens with a slow introduction, though surely not as slow as many conductors have taken it (Un poco sostenuto is the marking, not Adagio). It has a noble and solemn character, the timpani marking out the tread of the rhythm while a violin and cello line sweeps majestically above it. When we reach the Allegro, we find that the elements of the opening theme were all there in the introduction: a rising, chromatic phrase, a three-note rapid turn, and a leaping phrase that seems to signal the beginning of the main theme proper. After an extended agitated passage, the music calms to what might be thought of as a second theme, though this too reiterates the same elements. At the calmest moment clarinet and horn distil the essence of what has gone before, exchanging a simple rising and falling phrase. Then the agitation begins again, and carries us forward to the conclusion of the first section. A repeat of the first part of the Allegro is marked, but not always played.

The middle section of the movement develops all this material further (though, as often in Brahms, we have the impression that a lot of development has happened already). At its climax, chorale-like phrases remind us of the grandeur of the introduction. Another moment of calm arrives, with deep, quiet chords underpinned by a contrabassoon. The tension gradually mounts, until we are propelled into the reprise of the Allegro's opening theme. The revisited sequence of events leads to a climax even more agitated than before, with fierce cross-rhythms between strings and wind. Gradually the force ebbs away, the rhythm evens out, and the movement ends where it started, with a brief reminiscence of the introduction, warming at the very end from C minor to C major.

The second movement moves up a major third to E major, giving a particular radiance to the melody. It opens on violins, enriched by a bassoon. Then a solo oboe takes it higher. When the oboe hands the melody back to the violins, they develop it on and up still higher, reaching a glorious climax and descending again. Once more the oboe takes over, followed by the clarinet, elaborating the line over gently pulsating syncopations in the strings, as they move on through changing keys – C sharp minor, A flat major, D flat major. The mood becomes more agitated, and strings and woodwind combine to reach a climax, and then descend. Now the opening theme returns, at first on woodwind chorus, with the strings singing a counterpoint and the cellos playing pizzicato triplets. The violins finish off the melody. A solo violin then takes up the continuation that the oboe had originally played. This time the continuation is repeated on the horn, with the solo violin weaving arabesques round it. The orchestra seems reluctant to leave the melody, as violins, woodwind, and solo violin explore yet another corner, before the movement winds to a peaceful close.

From the E major of the slow movement, the third movement moves up another major third, to A flat major. This is one of Brahms's characteristic third movements, in which the usual scherzo is replaced by a piece more ambivalent in mood. It begins easily, with a smooth theme on clarinet, answered by gently dancing dotted rhythms in the other woodwind. After this is repeated, with typically Brahmsian elaborations, the strings start a more agitated rhythm, over which the woodwind line becomes more complex. The opening melody is briefly reprised. Now the music changes from a simple two-time to a swinging metre (6/8), and the key shifts to B major. The character of the music is more urgent than dance-like, with a motif of three repeated notes kept up more and more insistently. Eventually the original theme, in the original key, returns. The movement ends with a reminiscence of the repeated notes of the middle section.

The finale opens with a long slow introduction. With tragic intensity, a violin phrase reaches upwards and falls away. Hesitant pizzicato strings accelerate, coming to a sudden halt, and the opening phrase is repeated low on the violins. Again pizzicato strings accelerate to a sudden halt. This time, fragments of the opening phrase are quickly overwhelmed by rushing scales in the strings. There is a tempestuous build-up to a climax, and a timpani roll. From this dark moment arises a noble horn call, followed by a quiet chorale, in which trombones are heard for the first time. This seems to offer a resolution of the preceding tumult. And indeed, as the introduction gives way to the Allegro, we are greeted by a violin theme of splendid breadth and optimism. It begins with the phrase that was darkly prefigured at the opening of the slow introduction, and continues with a close resemblance to the 'Ode to Joy' theme from Beethoven's Ninth Symphony. Critics pounced on this obvious moment of homage, to which Brahms famously is supposed to have retorted, 'Any ass can see that.' As in the Beethoven, the regular breadth of the theme makes it difficult to move on, and there is a moment of 'gearchange' as Brahms propels the music forward. The more agitated episode that follows contains elements from the slow introduction and from the first movement. Eventually, it winds round to a reprise of the broad theme.

This time, it ends with a return to the pizzicato passage from the introduction, before launching into a longer, and even more turbulent second episode. This builds to a fierce climax, at which persistent, abrupt rhythms suddenly reveal the horn call from the introduction. Once more, this has the effect of providing a resolution, and the music calms for a moment. From here, Brahms doubles back to the first episode, and the momentum builds

again. There is a moment of relaxation that seems to be preparing for a return to the broad
main theme. But instead, there is a change of direction, with a dark chord underpinned by
contrabassoon, echoing a similar turning point in the first movement. Trombones quietly
remind us of the main theme against agitated figures in the violins. The pace increases,
and the music breaks into a joyful march tempo. The excitement builds, and climaxes in a
glorious return of the quiet chorale from the introduction, now fortissimo on full brass and
strings. A final, vigorous passage brings the symphony to a determined, very Beethoven-like
conclusion.

SYMPHONY NO. 2 IN D MAJOR, OP. 73

Duration: approx. 46 minutes (including first movement repeat)

Allegro non troppo
Adagio non troppo
Allegretto grazioso (quasi andantino)
Allegro con spirito

Brahms composed most of his Second Symphony during the summer of 1877, while staying
by a lake in southern Austria, the Wörthersee, and it was ready for performance in Vienna by
December. Not only did he find it much quicker to write than the First Symphony, but it also
had a more immediate success at early performances. It is easy to see why: this is Brahms at
his sunniest and most straightforwardly lyrical, the only one of his symphonies that is in a
major key in all four movements. (No. 3 is, on paper, in F major, but it spends much of its time
denying it.)

The first movement is a singing, expansive stretch of music. It opens with a falling phrase
in the cellos and basses, answered quietly by horns playing rising calls that one could imagine
played in the mountains on alpenhorns. These two motifs dominate the early part of the
movement, building to a first outburst of vigour. Playful woodwind lead in to the second
main theme. This is a duet for cellos and violas, is even more expansive, and is followed by a
contrasting theme of assertive dotted rhythms. This has a rather truculent air, enhanced by
the tempo being slightly held, but it soon develops a lyrical sweep of its own. Further quiet
musing on the second theme brings the first section to a close. Brahms marks a repeat at this
point, but he himself omitted it once the symphony became well known to orchestras and
audiences. It takes a firm command of the long spans of this music to observe the repeat
without making the movement seem too long.

The development opens with a lovely change of key down a major third from A major to
F major (one of Schubert's favourite shifts, as Brahms certainly knew). A horn quietly plays
the first phrase of the opening theme. The woodwind take up the last few notes of it, and this
develops into a passage of fugue-like counterpoint. The trombones enter, and the music
builds to a series of climaxes that struggle to find a resolution. The third and most powerful
of these eventually manages to break back to the home key of D major, the tension disperses,
and the opening theme creeps back on oboes and strings, with a delicate accompanying line
passing between violins and violas. The reprise soon moves on to the second theme, with
cellos and violas in duet as before, and on through the truculent dotted rhythms to the lyrical
continuation. We sense that the end is coming, but Brahms delays it beautifully. A horn returns
to musing on the opening theme, reiterating the oscillating notes of its third bar, drawing

them out into a lament that accelerates to a climax and falls away. The strings gently return to the opening notes of the theme and extend them into a warmly lyrical line. The playful wood-wind element returns for a last time, the strings answer pizzicato, and final echoes of the horn call bring the movement to a close.

The first theme of the slow movement is again given to the cellos, and is one of Brahms's finest melodies. Much of it consists of descending phrases, each of which is followed by upward leaps. This gives it a sense of combining peacefulness with striving – a very Brahmsian mixture. Underneath it is a rising bassoon line, a countermelody that adds to the striving quality. The theme ends with two particularly poignant leaps that do not wholly resolve. Instead, the violins enter to round off the melody by returning to its opening – a wonderfully simple way to bring the questioning to an end. Horn and woodwind exchange oscillating calls for a moment, and the strings bring in a passionate extension of the cello theme. As it dies away, the music changes metre, and a new, rocking theme enters on flutes and oboes over a pizzicato bass. This begins as a gentle interlude, but becomes far more than that. It soon begins to develop momentum, and moves into a minor key. Swirling string patterns accom-pany the woodwind and become turbulent, rising to a climax. As it falls away, the violins remember the opening theme. There is another burst of turbulence, and again the theme returns. At first it is hesitant, and uncertain of the key. But gradually it re-establishes itself, with the rising countermelody in the bassoons and the violins playing a graceful variation above it.

At the midway point of the theme there is a sudden hush as the violins return to the original, simple melodic line, but having shifted to a different key. This gives a quality of great tenderness as the melody rises to a climax, and the final phrases rise higher than before. Still the melody has not achieved resolution. After a few bars of the oscillating patterns, trumpets and trombones enter, and more swirling violin figures, varying the shape of the theme, drive the music to an impassioned climax (these violin variations of the theme seem to be paying homage to the slow movement of Beethoven's Ninth Symphony). For a few bars we are reminded of the turbulent middle section, but soon the first theme returns, and at last finds resolution – though ominous timpani strokes and piquant little surges in the cellos (drawn from the bassoon countermelody) keep the resolution in doubt until the very last chords.

As so often in Brahms, the third movement is not quite a conventional minuet or scherzo, but something that alternates elements of both. It begins with a gentle minuet-like dance in G major, but with an accent on the third beat that gives it a slightly rustic air (and the oboe solo sounds a bit rustic too). Then the speed doubles, and moves into two-time, producing a fleeting variation on the tune. This alternates between a light tripping and an enthusiastic stamping. Seamlessly we are back at a reprise of the 'minuet', but after eight bars the strings develop an obsession with the little triplet rhythm in the tune, which is repeated again and again. This gives the cue for the next fast section, in which this triplet finds itself transformed into a rapid dance in three-time, sounding rather like one of Mendelssohn's fairy dances. The tempo slows gradually, and winds beautifully round to another reprise of the minuet, but at first in a distant key (F sharp major). It never quite recovers from this, and explores a series of new turnings before reaching a wistful pause, and at last a cadence back in G major.

The final movement was perhaps inspired by the finale of Beethoven's Fourth Symphony. The tempo is rapid, and it begins in a hushed tone (*sotto voce*, under the voice), and gets even quieter before the full orchestra bursts out joyfully. There is a sense of unstoppable energy, which eventually gives way to a second theme, a lovely, rich melody on the violins. This builds up, culminating in a renewal of the energetic figures of the opening. At a sudden halt, Brahms plays one of his favourite rhythmic tricks, syncopating the rhythm so thoroughly that one loses track of where the beat is. A passage of snappy rhythms leads back to the opening of the movement, hushed as before. But this time it soon begins moving off into new keys, exploring unfamiliar territory. There is (as before) a sudden outburst, but now with punchy offbeat accents, as if infected by the earlier syncopations. This calms down to a passage where the first theme of the movement is turned into triplets, forming murmuring, reiterated phrases. The tempo becomes gradually slower, reaching a point of complete calm at which the opening theme returns for the main reprise.

Once more there is the joyful outburst, and this time the energy is sustained right up to the singing second theme, now satisfyingly full-toned, and scarcely interrupting the drive of the music. Again there are the syncopations, and the snappy rhythms. But this time there is a further build-up of syncopations. The murmuring triplet version of the first theme leads on to another climax, and the energy builds and builds. There is no acceleration marked, but only the most stolid of conductors will force an orchestra to stick rigidly to tempo. The drive to the ending is irresistible, and in the final bars blazing trumpets, horns, and trombones transform the second theme into a fanfare, bringing the energetic and singing elements of the music together in a final climax.

SYMPHONY NO. 3 IN F MAJOR, OP. 90
Duration: approx. 38 minutes (including first movement repeat)

Allegro con brio
Andante
Poco allegretto
Allegro

Brahms composed most of his Third Symphony in the summer of 1883, at a time when his inspiration was flowing freely. He was in Wiesbaden, staying for the summer in a converted painter's studio with a view over the Rhine: 'I live here quite charmingly, almost as if I were trying to imitate Wagner!' he wrote to a friend.[17] The premiere in December, played by the Vienna Philharmonic Orchestra conducted by Hans Richter, was a triumph with the audience, and the symphony was soon enjoying great success across Europe. The followers of Wagner (who had died in February) nevertheless continued to pour scorn on Brahms and his 'old-fashioned' symphonic approach. The young composer Hugo Wolf wrote about Brahms's three symphonies in an article in November 1884: 'Schumann, Chopin, Berlioz and Liszt, the leaders of the post-Beethoven revolutionary movement in music ... seem to have left no impression upon our symphonist. He was either blind or feigned blindness as the eyes of an astonished mankind opened wide and overflowed with tears in the glare of Wagner's radiant genius ... But this man, who has written three symphonies, and probably intends to follow them with another six, can remain unmoved and untouched by such a phenomenon! He is only a leftover of old remains, not a living creature in the mainstream of time.'[18] It was Wolf who was blinded by his adoration of Wagner to the fact that Brahms, more in this symphony than in earlier works, draws on ideas of theme-transformation from Liszt and Wagner. It may superficially seem like a traditional symphony, but the way Brahms links his themes, and creates a satisfying completion of the circle as the end returns to the beginning, is thoroughly 'modern'. It is a great synthesis of old and new ideas.

There are two sonorous chords from the wind, and then the violins declare the first theme of the symphony, which twice plunges down to a dotted rhythm, and twice rockets up. It seems highly confident, even heroic. But the harmonies immediately introduce an element of uncertainty. The first bar of the theme is in pure F major. But then the bass moves up to A flat, creating a minor chord. This harmonic ambiguity creates an important element of struggle, both in this opening movement and in the finale. Brahms has combined this harmonic move with another element that can easily be missed: the notes on top of the introductory wind chords move up, first by a third, and then by a sixth. This three-note, leaping motif turns out to be important throughout the symphony, and is one of the elements that binds it together. It is played again immediately in the bass under the violins' first entry (beginning with the rise from F to A flat), and a few bars later horns and trumpets take it up.

Another characteristic Brahmsian trick is the deliberate confusion in the rhythm of the violins' theme. At first it sounds as if it is in a big three-in-a-bar. But in the second half of the theme (where it rockets up), it suddenly switches to two-in-a-bar, while the length of each bar remains the same. In other words, 3x2 becomes 2x3. This is an affectionate homage to the opening of Schumann's Third Symphony, which does just the same. Brahms, like Schumann, loved rhythmic confusions and surprises, and this movement is full of them, giving it a partic- ular internal energy. In contrast to this energetic verve, the second main theme is a calm melody on the clarinet. But this is not straightforward either. It curls round, reiterating whole phrases and smaller groups of notes, like someone trying to find the right words. This gives it a floating, hesitant quality. Then there is another build-up with further confusions of rhythm to bring the first section to a close (this is usually repeated).

The energy generated by the cross-rhythms continues into the development. Here, Brahms transforms the clarinet's quiet circling theme into a powerful, surging melody in the minor, first on cellos and violas, then on violins. Eventually the mood subsides, there are hesitations, followed by a sudden calm. Deep chords sound, with a contrabassoon giving them organ-like depth, and above them a horn intones, in slow motion, the upward-leaping motif from the beginning of the symphony. This leads to a halting attempt at the opening main theme, and finally the two wind chords announce its return. The first section of the movement is reprised in varied form. And then, in a marvellously urgent coda, a final climax is reached. But the movement ends quietly, with a gentle restatement of the very opening.

The slow movement opens with the clarinet playing a calm melody that seems like a cousin of the second theme from the first movement, but which also, at the ends of phrases, alludes to the upward-leaping motif. The middle section of the movement is darker: a solemn chorale is sounded by the woodwind. It has a characteristically deliberate rhythmic tread, created by alternating groups of three notes (triplets) and two notes (duplets) – an idea linked to the rhythmic confusions of the first movement. The return of the clarinet's theme is at first elaborated by the cellos, with a passionate counterpoint above from the violins, and then the woodwind draw the movement to a close.

The third movement, in the place of the traditional minuet or scherzo, is a haunting melody in C minor on the cellos, like a distant memory of a dance. Its opening shape derives from the clarinet's second theme in the first movement, and its yearning upward leaps allude, more subtly, to the symphony's leaping motif. This is an example of a Brahms melody that starts in regular two-bar phrases, but then takes flight in a manner reminiscent of Schubert. A middle section has nervously reiterated little phrases from the woodwind, alternating with expansive phrases from the violins (again with upward leaps). A moment of quiet suspense brings in the reprise of the first melody, now on horn followed by oboe, and then passionately on violins. A reminder of the hesitations from the middle section brings the movement to a close.

The symphony is described as being in F major, but the prevalence of minor keys is strong in three of its movements. The finale also starts, and for much of the time remains, in the minor. One could trace this uncertainty between major and minor right back to the opening bars of the symphony, where a minor chord intruded on the second bar of the theme. The finale begins quietly, with a darkly wandering theme on strings and bassoons. This is followed by the sombre chorale from the middle of the slow movement, and then the whole orchestra bursts in with the leaping motif, now given an aggressive edge with sharp dotted rhythms. This calms down to a beautiful, surging theme on cellos and horns, which is closely related to the main theme from the third movement. A great battle of rhythms develops, with wind and strings, rhythms and counter-rhythms, battling until a brief quiet occurs. Then the tension mounts again, and in a moment of almost Wagnerian grandeur the brass enter with the chorale from the slow movement, now transformed into a call of determination around which the strings swarm fiercely, urging it to a mighty climax. The surging cello theme returns, and after a final burst of energy the music subsides, the opening theme of the movement spiralling down and slowing to a moment of profound calm. With the violins continuing to murmur quietly, the wind solemnly intone the chorale for the last time, extending it through new harmonies to a beautifully satisfying conclusion. One last leaping phrase from the horn, one last echo of the first descending theme from the violins, and the symphony comes to a quiet close.

Because of its quiet ending, this symphony is less often programmed in concerts than Brahms's other three. But it is the most powerful, complex, and subtle of his symphonies, as well as the most challenging to play and to pace.

SYMPHONY NO. 4 IN E MINOR, OP. 98
Duration: approx. 42 minutes

Allegro non troppo
Andante moderato
Allegro giocoso
Allegro energico e passionato

Brahms composed the last of his four symphonies over the summers of 1884 and 1885. He conducted the premiere with the Meiningen Court Orchestra in October 1885, and then toured with the orchestra for several weeks to introduce the new symphony across Germany and Holland. This was highly unusual in the 1880s, but the Meiningen Orchestra was no ordinary ensemble. Generously funded by the Duke of Meiningen, it was conducted by the eccentric but meticulous Hans von Bülow, and was able to rehearse more thoroughly than any other orchestra in Europe. Although the orchestra was much smaller than the major symphony orchestras, Brahms relished the opportunity to rehearse a new work thoroughly – it was not what he was used to in Vienna.

Each of Brahms's four symphonies opens completely differently, the first with tragic grandeur, the second with serenity, the third with a defiant challenge. With the fourth, it is as if we have come upon something that is already happening. Violins quietly play alternate falling and rising intervals, separated by rests. The alternating sighs and leaps have a quality of searching, underlined by the gentle offbeat chords in the wind and the flowing arpeggios in cellos and violas below. Gradually this idea evolves: the little phrases are elaborated, with running patterns in the woodwind, then the energy increases, until we reach a grand, sweeping phrase – the first continuous snatch of melody. From this emerges a completely new, second theme in the woodwind and horns, a sturdy, almost fanfare-like flourish, with one of Brahms's characteristic juxtapositions of a triplet with 'straight' dotted rhythms. As the dotted rhythms persist in the bass, the cellos and horns sing a noble, sweeping melody, as if taking their cue from the phrase that preceded the second theme. After a passage of pizzicato that reminds us of the opening, the woodwind play a new melody that seems to be musing on the second theme, with its triplet and dotted rhythms now expanded into a lyrical line. After this expansion comes a contraction: the fanfare-like opening of the second theme is reduced to sharp little gestures, at first quietly in the woodwind, and then with bold attack in the strings. This builds to the first fortissimo of the symphony, with the broad triplets and sharp dotted rhythms fighting against each other. From here, the music quietens, and the violins return to the opening theme. At first, it seems as if the whole of the opening section is to be repeated. But, for the first time in a symphony, Brahms has not indicated a repeat.

After a few bars of the sighs and leaps, the harmonies take a new direction, and it becomes clear that we are into the development. Suddenly, the rhythm stiffens, and fragments are thrown back and forth between strings and wind so that our sense of the metre is confused (this is a habit that Brahms shared with his great champion, Robert Schumann). From here, musings on the second and first themes alternate. A fortissimo outburst of the fanfare-like second theme softens, and the triplet rhythm extends into a new, floating line in the woodwind. There is a mysterious passage, in which a fragment of the first theme passes between strings and wind, the harmonies changing all the time. Eventually they settle back into the home key of E minor. Quietly, the woodwind play a slow version of the opening notes of the symphony. Then the violins gently take it up in tempo, and the reprise is under way. We arrive at the fanfare-like second theme sooner than before, and then proceed through the familiar elements and build up to a fortissimo. Now the tension heightens still more, and Brahms sets off on the final stage of the journey. The opening theme fights between bass and treble, and then strides forward with determination. This is a magnificently concentrated passage, culminating in a final cadence underpinned by the timpani.

Horns open the slow movement, repeating an austere, chant-like shape centring on the note E, the same as the keynote of the first movement. At first the key is uncertain, but then clarinets softly take over the phrase, warming it into E major and extending it into a theme. By now it has acquired a hint of the processional, with the tread picked out by pizzicato strings (there is an echo of the 'Pilgrims' March' from Mendelssohn's 'Italian' Symphony in this opening). After the theme has been extended and developed, it settles and metamorphoses into a warm melody on violins (now with their bows). The repetitions in the phrases take on a passionate character, and the woodwind break in with sturdy triplet rhythms. The music quietens, and the cellos transform the woodwind's triplets into a song-like new theme while the violins complement it with a delicate filigree of arpeggios. This too is quietly passed around and considered. The first theme returns as a viola duet, with woodwind arpeggios above. At first the tone is sweet, but then the woodwind enter forte, taking the theme back to the chant-like character of the opening. Now the strings inject a note of urgency, with rapid arpeggios in counterpoint to the chant. This builds to a fortissimo climax, at which the whole orchestra breaks into the sturdy triplet rhythms. The music quietens again, the violins sonorously reprise the cellos' second theme. Clarinets and bassoons remember the first theme, and there is a moment of mystery and a pause. With a last reminder of the opening chant, the music reaches a final resolution.

In the third movement Brahms gives us yet another take on the traditional minuet or scherzo. It is a fast dance, unlike the equivalent movements in his earlier symphonies, and in two-time not three, with a stamping, 'manly' rhythm, and with an offbeat kick that gives it tremendous energy. The addition of a triangle gives a joyful edge to some of the climactic chords. Brahms's way of structuring the movement is highly original. The dance has a lyrical second theme, and the return of the first theme then leads on to a passage in which the material is developed urgently. This calms down to what might seem to be the conventional 'trio' middle section. But instead of a new melody, this consists of the principal theme stretched out, and taken into new keys. Just as we are led to expect new developments, the opening theme bursts back, in mid flow, and we are into the reprise of the dance. This too is further extended, with a coda that develops tremendous momentum.

After such an energetic, even exhausting, third movement, it is difficult to imagine how Brahms can start his finale. The answer turns out to be a series of eight sustained, sonorous wind chords. These provide the framework for the entire movement that follows. The sequence of their harmonies forms the basis of a set of variations, on the model of the baroque passacaglia or chaconne, beloved of J. S. Bach and Purcell. Brahms had earlier arranged Bach's great solo violin Chaconne for piano left hand, and two years before starting work on the symphony had discussed the possibility of writing an orchestral work based on the chaconne in Bach's Cantata No. 150. This is exactly what he does in this movement. He takes Bach's rising bass, adds an extra chromatic note to give it a more dynamic thrust, and uses this as his melody. Under it, he puts a bass line that falls as the melody rises. This is a fine example of Brahms taking his love of old forms and investing them with new and powerful emotional significance. The opening eight chords are followed by thirty variations on them, each of which, in some way or other, preserves the harmonic shape, and often the bass line, of the chord sequence. They are rounded off by a coda. The result is not just a series of chunks, but a coherent, developing instrumental drama. It is an astonishing tour de force, bringing together ancient technique and modern expression, as Mozart's famous contrapuntal finale to the 'Jupiter' Symphony did a century earlier.

The theme of eight chords has a melody that rises upwards, and a bass that falls. It is followed by Variation 1, in which the theme is carried by pizzicato chords on offbeats, gradually quietening against stern horns and timpani. Variation 2: Above the pizzicato chords, a flowing countermelody begins in the woodwind. Variation 3: The flowing melody breaks into sturdy staccato. Variation 4: A noble, leaping melody is played by the violins. In Variations 5 and 6 it becomes more flowing, with woodwind counterpoints, reaching a low point at the end of Variation 5, and then rising through Variation 6. Variation 7 breaks into vigorous dotted rhythms, and Variation 8 into energetic semiquavers. They fade, only to burst out in even more energetic patterns in Variation 9. These too fade, giving way in Variation 10 to simple exchanges of mysterious chords between strings and woodwind. Tentative melodic fragments emerge in Variation 11, but these yield to a descending series of woodwind chords that come to rest.

With Variation 12 we have reached the quiet heart of the movement. In a slower tempo (or rather an extended metre) a solo flute plays a melody of halting phrases like a sorrowful aria, which rises to a climax and falls away. The bass (in horn and violas) is an unchanging E: only the changing chords retain the relationship with the theme. In Variation 13 the music moves for the first time from E minor to E major, with tender little phrases exchanged between clarinet and oboe. In Variation 14 trombones play pianissimo phrases of sonorous chords, joined in Variation 15 by the woodwind. A sorrowful descending flute scale brings this quiet section to a close.

Variation 16: Back in E minor, and in the original (faster) metre, trombones and wood-wind burst in with a return to the assertive opening chords, accompanied by a passionate descending line in the strings. There is new, urgent thrust to the music. In Variation 17 the woodwind call in short-breathed phrases over tremolando strings, in Variation 18 the horns enter with a firmer swing, and Variation 19 breaks into staccato, with strings answered by woodwind. Variation 20 breaks into vigorous triplets, and Variation 21 has rushing scales in the violins and harsh trombone calls. We seem to be approaching a climax. But the music evaporates in Variation 22 to chattering pianissimo triplet patterns fighting against duplet patterns, and exchanged between strings and woodwind. In Variation 23 this breaks into forte, as horns call out the original theme of the passacaglia. The energetic drive is wrenched under control. In Variation 24 horns and trumpets repeat a single E, and strings and woodwind hammer out on the offbeat their triplet-against-duplet rhythm. In Variation 25 agitated trem-olando violins play the melodic line taken from the woodwind in Variation 2. In a moment of calm in Variation 26, the quartet of horns plays the melodic shape of Variation 3 in a warm C major (there is a strong element of reprise at this stage of the movement). The warm mood (still in C major) persists through Variations 27 and 28, with delicate and elegant dialogue between strings and woodwind. In Variation 29 a mood of urgency (back in E minor) begins to return, with phrases across the beat in the woodwind, and offbeat pizzicato. In Variation 30 a plunging bass line is echoed a beat later in the violins, the tensions mounts, and the tempo is held back at a gathering point.

The pace suddenly increases as the wind declaim the chordal theme while the strings plunge downwards. This is the beginning of an extended coda, in which Brahms develops his theme, building towards the end. The chord sequence, rather than simply being repeated, builds up and up, until the trombones cut across the prevailing three-time metre, declaiming a bold rising phrase in a broader three-time. In this new metre the music grows in strength, based on the trombone motif. As the music reaches a climax, it suddenly switches back into the faster metre, and with unstoppable drive and determination the symphony comes to a powerful conclusion.

VARIATIONS ON A THEME BY HAYDN, OP. 56A
Duration: approx. 18 minutes

Chorale St Antoni: Andante
Variation 1: Poco più animato
Variation 2: Più vivace
Variation 3: Con moto
Variation 4: Andante con moto
Variation 5: Vivace
Variation 6: Vivace
Variation 7: Grazioso
Variation 8: Presto non troppo
Finale: Andante

After the disastrous premiere of the First Piano Concerto, and the success of the two Serenades, Brahms began in 1862 to write what eventually became his First Symphony. But he was beset by doubts, and did not complete it until 1876. Meanwhile during the 1860s he had composed several works for chorus and orchestra, including the German Requiem, which was an international success, and his two most substantial sets of variations for solo piano, on themes by Handel and Paganini. In 1873 he brought together his skill in composing variations with his developing expertise in orchestral writing to create one of his most perfect and popular works, which he published as Variations on a Theme by Haydn. Brahms's symphonies may be on a grander scale and display more obvious seriousness of purpose. But in these variations he is entirely at ease, matching his skill and powers of expression to the task in hand.

The theme is a movement from a Divertimento in B flat for Wind Instruments that was then attributed to Haydn, but is now thought not to be by him. It has the title 'Chorale St Antoni', and is possibly an earlier tune. It certainly has a processional tread, and it also has a very interesting structure, which must particularly have appealed to Brahms. The first half consists of two phrases that are each five bars long. The second half begins with two conventional four-bar phrases, and then reprises the last phrase of the opening, rounding it off with sonorous chords like the tolling of a bell. Both halves are repeated. In his variations, Brahms plays with wonderful fluidity on this template, with its shift from asymmetrical to symmetrical phrases, and back again. He also demonstrates his mastery of orchestral counterpoint, combining instruments and lines in rich and varied textures. There are eight variations, followed by an extended finale in the form of a passacaglia.

Brahms orchestrates the theme very much as it appears in the original work, with pairs of oboes and bassoons, two of his four horns (for most of the theme), and a contrabassoon below, to which he adds pizzicato bass. The prominence of the oboes is to be a feature throughout the work. Clarinets, which are often in the foreground in Brahms, are here in a supporting role.

Variation 1 continues the 'tolling' from the end of the theme, a little faster. Lower wind instruments, with timpani, use it to mark out the pattern of five- and four-bar phrases through the variation. Meanwhile the violins, which have been silent up to this point, enter with a sweeping, rising line. The rising violins play a two-note-to-a-beat pattern, while violas and cellos fall in a three-note-to-a-beat pattern. Then, for the second five-bar phrase, they swap. The interplay between the tolling wind and this two-against-three in the strings creates a wonderfully rich and complex texture throughout the variation – the first of many examples in the work.

Variation 2, a little faster still, is in the minor, and sets up new simultaneous patterns. Each phrase of five bars is announced by a loud bar. Clarinets and bassoons play a gently dancing falling line of dotted rhythms, while violins play a staccato falling phrase over pizzicato bass. The second half begins with the dotted-rhythm motif passing around, and rising higher, while the violins' staccato pattern now descends smoothly.

After two complex variations, Variation 3 is like a calm benediction. Brahms takes the two five-bar phrases and converts them into a single ten-bar phrase that pours out seamlessly. Oboe and bassoon sing the melody, while second oboe and bassoon accompany in smooth counterpoint. Rather than simply repeat these ten bars, Brahms varies them: violins and violas take over the melody and counterpoint, and flute and bassoon add a filigree of faster-moving patterns. The second half begins with a horn solo, rises to a little climax in the violins, and returns to oboes and bassoons, with flutes adding a touch of brightness. Again Brahms varies the repeat: while the melody passes between oboe and horn, lower strings play a faster-moving pattern. This then passes to the oboe, rising to a beautiful climax, before the melody returns to the violins with the filigree pattern in flutes and bassoons.

Variation 4 is slower. Oboe and horn play a sombre line in the minor key, with a flowing counterpoint in the violas and pizzicato bass. Once more, Brahms varies the repeat. The melody moves to violins and violas, in sonorous unison, with the flowing counterpoint now above in flute and clarinet. The second half begins with the melody back on oboe and horn, the counterpoint alternating between cellos and upper strings. And at the repeat, the melody is again in violins and violas (now an octave apart rather than in unison), with the counterpoint alternating between flute plus clarinet and bassoon.

Variation 5, back in B flat major and marked Vivace, is a mercurial scherzo, playful and virtuoso, with predominantly quiet, rapid staccato punctuated by sudden offbeat accents and cross-rhythms. It begins with the woodwind predominant and the strings accompanying, and reverses that for the repeat. The second half begins with the strings leading both times round. But the end of the section has a complex interplay between strings and wind that is reversed the second time.

Variation 6 is also marked Vivace, but its character is quite different, somewhere between a fast march and a stately gallop. The four horns begin quietly, almost like a hunting call, and are answered by the woodwind. The phrases are clear-cut and emphatic (though still in five-bar sections). The full orchestra joins for the second half, which is urgent and dramatic.

Variation 7 is in complete contrast. Marked Grazioso (gracefully), it has the gently swinging rhythm of a siciliano. A falling shape in flute and violas is answered by a rise in the bass. In the second five-bar phrase a fall in the violins and bassoon is answered by a rise in the upper woodwind. In the second half this rising and falling dialogue continues, while the violins soar upwards to a climax. And at the end, the music develops a beautiful network of cross-rhythms before the variation comes to a gentle close.

Variation 8 begins and ends pianissimo, and never rises above piano, with the strings muted. It is the ghost of a scherzo, with overlapping lines so fluid that the phrases blur into each other as if half-perceived through a mist. In the first half murmuring strings alternate with fleeting woodwind. The second half continues this pattern at first, and then combines strings and woodwind in a texture that is complex but still pianissimo.

Brahms's command of orchestral counterpoint has already been demonstrated throughout the variations. In the finale, he brings it to the fore with an extended passacaglia, a prototype of the movement with which he was later to conclude his Fourth Symphony. The theme is distilled into a five-bar bass, which repeats unceasingly, most often actually in the bass but sometimes migrating to the middle or even the top of the texture. At first the music builds up quietly, from cellos and basses through the strings and then woodwind in a web of counterpoint. Sturdy triplet rhythms soon begin to cut across the prevailing metre, and the music builds to a first climax. This dissolves into tender falling phrases from the violins. Hesitant offbeat utterances in the oboe move to the other woodwind, followed by smooth triplets from the flute. Suddenly the music turns from major to minor, as the oboe (which has been the leader of the woodwind throughout) takes up the passacaglia theme. This quickly builds to another rugged tutti. Out of this emerges the theme in its original form, in the woodwind, lightened by taps of a triangle. The rest of the orchestra joins in, as if recognizing an old friend, and a reprise of the chorale ensues, accompanied by joyful rushing scales in the woodwind. At the final tolling chords, these scales migrate to the strings, and become continuous. They gradually ebb away, to a moment of calm, before five final bars bring the work to an emphatic close.

BENJAMIN BRITTEN
(1913–76)

The composer with whom Britten most invites comparison is Aaron Copland. At a time when the musical establishment tended to take the view that music had to be difficult and challenging in order to be serious, both composers aimed to write in a manner that clearly expressed what they wanted to express, with no embarrassment about a direct way of achieving it. Britten aimed at a wide audience, not just the cognoscenti. The first Aldeburgh Festival in 1948, in the Suffolk seaside town where Britten lived, opened with his *Saint Nicolas*, a cantata that brought together professional instrumentalists, school choirs, and audience participation. As Philip Brett, writing in 2001, observed, this 'would have appeared ludicrous to the postwar avant garde', but 'it seems now as courageous and adventurous as the experimental music of the time'.[1] There was, however, nothing 'populist' about Britten. He was something of an outsider. He was a pacifist during the Second World War, and his partnership with the tenor Peter Pears was an open secret at a time when homosexual acts were still illegal in England (they were not legalized until 1967). Britten was a shy, prickly character, very sensitive to criticism, and uncomfortable with his own emotions and sexuality, in contrast to his flamboyant friends W. H. Auden and Christopher Isherwood (and the affable Copland). But in his quiet, determined way, he carved out for himself a position as the leading classical composer in Britain, rivalled in his generation only by Michael Tippett.

Britten and Pears were in America when the Second World War broke out, and they remained there until 1942. But although Britten had major successes he was increasingly homesick, longing for England and, specifically, for Suffolk. Although he admitted to finding New York 'intensely alive and doing', he basically found America a great disappointment: 'so narrow, so self-satisfied, so chauvinistic, so superficial, so reactionary, and above all so *ugly*'.[2] After the war, he settled with Pears in Aldeburgh, near where he was born on the Suffolk coast. There he established the annual Aldeburgh Festival, which hosted premieres of his works, but also supported contemporary composers and a wide range of the classics. He ended his life as Lord Britten, a status unthinkable to the young Britten, defiantly making his way in the 1930s.

Britten had a brilliant technical command of his forces, instrumental and vocal, and composed fluently, sometimes at incredible speed. The first work to make his name internationally, the Variations on a Theme of Frank Bridge, was completed in six weeks. This fluency made Britten an ideal composer for film, stage, and radio. But it also encouraged a view of him as facile and too clever. In the 1954 edition of *Grove's Dictionary of Music and Musicians*, Frank Howes wrote of Britten, 'Critical opinion, towards which his attitude is somewhat gunpowdery, is divided not so much on the question of his extraordinary talent, which can hardly be denied, as on the question how much is heart and how much is head. "Clever" is often applied to him with its usual pejorative implication [only a British writer could have written that sentence!]: there is universal agreement that Britten is extremely "clever", but the imputation is left that feelings do not go deep enough in his music.'

There is plenty of deep feeling in works that he wrote in the 1930s and 1940s: the searing funeral march in the Variations on a Theme of Frank Bridge, the evocation of powerful menace and isolation in his most celebrated opera, *Peter Grimes*, the overwhelming climax of his *Young Person's Guide to the Orchestra*, composed for an educational film in 1945. But it is undoubtedly true that his music has moments where judgements seem to have been made more for intellectual than for emotional reasons – a 'clever' piece of counterpoint, or the juxtaposing of contrasts in jarring ways. Listeners respond to these elements differently, some finding them wholly satisfactory, others left uncomfortable. 'Comfortable' is not a word to describe Britten himself, and it is not entirely fanciful to hear the tensions of his life reflected in his music.

PETER GRIMES: FOUR SEA INTERLUDES, OP. 33A
Duration: approx. 16 minutes

Dawn
Sunday Morning
Moonlight
Storm

In 1941, while Britten and Peter Pears were in California, they came across a copy of the BBC magazine, *The Listener*, in which there was the script of a radio talk by E. M. Forster about the Suffolk poet, George Crabbe (1754–1832). Crabbe was born in Aldeburgh on the Suffolk coast, not far from Britten's birthplace of Lowestoft, and close to the village of Snape where Britten had bought a converted mill in 1937. Forster talked about Aldeburgh, 'A bleak little place; not beautiful . . . and what a wallop the sea makes as it pounds at the shingle! Near by is a quay, at the side of an estuary, and here the scenery becomes melancholy and flat; expanses of mud, saltish commons, the march-birds crying.'[3] Forster singled out 'Peter Grimes', a poem in Crabbe's collection *The Borough*, published in 1810, and set in a fictionalized version of Aldeburgh. Pears tracked down a second-hand copy of Crabbe's poems in a bookshop in Los Angeles, and Britten was deeply affected by them. Homesick for Suffolk, 'I suddenly realised where I belonged and what I lacked. I had become without roots . . .'[4] He immediately made plans to return to England, and started thinking about an opera based on *The Borough*. Britten and Pears waited eight months before they obtained a passage across the Atlantic (this was during the war, when submarine attacks were a constant threat). The delay enabled Britten to attend a performance of his *Sinfonia da Requiem* by the Boston Symphony Orchestra. Its conductor, Serge Koussevitzky, learning that Britten was planning an opera, offered him $1,000 from the Koussevitzky Foundation, and promised to perform it at the Berkshire Festival. The premiere of *Peter Grimes* marked the re-opening of Sadler's Wells Theatre in London in June 1945. This was an exceptionally bold and controversial choice, but the opera was an immense success, and firmly established Britten as a major national and international figure. The American premiere followed the next year, conducted not by Koussevitzky, but by his young pupil, Leonard Bernstein.

'Peter Grimes' is the story of a cruel fisherman who acquires orphan boys from the workhouse as his apprentices. Savagely he beats and otherwise ill-treats them, and three successive boys die in suspicious circumstances. The third time, the court forbids Grimes to engage any more boys, and he works alone. Cast out from society, he is haunted by visions of the dead boys, and of his father (whom he also abused), until he becomes an object of pity, and dies in mental torment.

This grim story was subtly adapted by the librettist, Montagu Slater, with Britten and Peter Pears (the first Grimes). The brutality of Grimes becomes secondary to his role as an outsider in a community that is ready to condemn him on the basis of prejudice rather than evidence. The community comes together in powerful choruses that evoke comparison with Verdi and with Musorgsky's *Boris Godunov*. Only Ellen Orford, the schoolmistress whom Grimes hopes to marry, defends him against the mob. When another boy dies, Grimes is advised by an old sea captain, Balstrode, to take his boat out to sea and sink it. He does so, and the community gets on with its life.

Punctuating this drama are four 'Sea Interludes', which Britten adapted and reordered to make a concert suite.

The opera opens with a prologue, the inquest into the death of one of Grimes's boys. This is followed by the first of the interludes, which links to the early morning street scene of Act I, Scene 1, in which villagers and fishermen are going about their business. 'Dawn' begins with high, pianissimo violins in unison with flutes – a classic, silvery combination to suggest morning light, from Haydn's *The Creation* onwards. Here, the decorations and trills evoke the cries of seabirds, the answering arpeggios of clarinet, harp, and violas suggest the wind ruffling the surface of the water, and the solemn brass chords the deeps below. But there is anxiety in the bird calls, and menace in the brass chords, whose calm is threatened by dissonances. They rise once to a climax and fall away, leaving the strings hovering uneasily in the air, and setting up the tensions of the drama to come.

'Sunday Morning' leads into Act II, Scene 1, 'a fine sunny morning with church bells ringing'. Four horns set up a pattern of tolling bells, and woodwind join them with syncopated rhythms that are both playful and agitated. These pass to the strings, ending with the seabirds' chirrups and a whirling descent. While flute and piccolo continue the birdsong above, in violas and cellos a lyrical melody rises up, which Ellen Orford will sing at the opening of the next scene:

> Glitter of waves
> And glitter of sunlight
> Bid us rejoice
> And lift our hearts on high.

The tolling horns return, with trumpets joining the agitated rhythms, and a real bell begins to sound – combined with low tuba, gong, and harp, it has the solemn effect of a huge, continental bell rather than that of a village church. The lyrical theme returns, creating a three-layered texture with the bird-like flute and the tolling bell. Gradually, the elements disperse.

'Moonlight' follows the end of Act II in which Grimes's boy has fallen to his death down the cliff. The interlude is striking in its calm simplicity: a Sibelius-like chorale of low strings, with halting phrases in a slow, syncopated, rocking rhythm, like the coming and going of waves, is punctuated by falling droplets of flute and harp. The chorale rises to a climax, never losing its halting rhythm, and falls away.

The fourth interlude, 'Storm', occurs in the opera in the middle of Act I. Britten draws on a full range of stormy precedents to create a powerful effect. The urgent phrases at the beginning evoke memories of Debussy's *La Mer*. These recur, as in a rondo. Snarling trombones and trumpets recall the menace of Holst's 'Mars'. The return of the first element is accompanied by an urgent counterpoint in the horns. Next, high woodwind swirl in fragmented phrases, like Shostakovich at his most warlike, punctuated by savage low brass chords reminiscent of Janáček. The opening returns to build the climax of the storm, the theme now in the bass, battling against the frantic elements above. From here, the storm subsides, and from it rises a plaintive, yearning melody, interspersed with a nervous pianissimo chattering on full orchestra. This melody has earlier been sung by Grimes, as the storm threatened:

> What harbour shelters peace?
> Away from tidal waves, away from storms,
> What harbour can embrace
> Terrors and tragedies?
> With her there'll be no quarrels,
> With her the mood will stay,
> A harbour evermore
> Where night is turned to day.

This vision of life with Ellen is the music that Grimes will remember in the final act as, half-mad, he goes out to die in his sinking boat. Here, it fades, and as the nervous chattering continues, the first element returns, anxiously on the woodwind, and quickly builds to a last, violent climax.

SINFONIA DA REQUIEM, OP. 20
Duration: approx. 20 minutes

Lacrymosa
Dies Irae
Requiem aeternam

In the early months of the Second World War, Britten was asked by the Japanese government to write a substantial orchestral work, one of several pieces commissioned as part of the celebrations of the 2,600th anniversary of the Japanese Empire (the other composers who were invited included Richard Strauss and Jacques Ibert). Although Japan was not yet in the war, it had already been at war with China for two years, and relations between Japan and the United

States were deteriorating (no American composer was involved in the Japanese celebrations). It seemed unlikely that Britten, a pacifist, would accept such a commission. But he desperately needed the substantial sum that the Japanese were offering, and replied to his publisher with a cable, 'SOUNDS CRAZY BUT WILL DO.' It would have been obvious to anyone who knew Britten that he would not be writing any kind of traditionally celebratory piece. Strauss composed *Japanese Festival Music*, Ibert an *Ouverture de fête*. Britten's offering was 'a Sinfonia da Requiem, combining my ideas on war & a memorial for Mum and Pop'.[5]

Unsurprisingly, Britten's clearly expressed 'ideas on war' made the piece, in the words of the president of the Japanese Committee for the Anniversary, 'unsuitable for performance on such an occasion as our national ceremony', being 'religious music of a Christian nature' and 'melancholy in tone'.[6] It was not performed in Japan during the celebrations, but Britten was allowed to keep the money. Given the role that Japan was about to play in the war, it is probably a very good thing that Britten's work was rejected. Instead of being forever associated with Japan in wartime, it was given a highly successful premiere in Carnegie Hall by the New York Philharmonic Orchestra conducted by John Barbirolli, followed by a nationwide radio broadcast.

In hindsight, we can see the *Sinfonia da Requiem* as containing the seeds of one of the greatest works of Britten's later years, the *War Requiem*, composed for the consecration of the new Coventry Cathedral in 1962. This building stands next to the ruins of the medieval cathedral that was bombed in November 1940, at just the time that Britten was receiving the news that the Japanese had rejected his *Sinfonia da Requiem*. The work is headed 'In memory of my parents'.

Britten named the three movements after sections of the Requiem Mass, the Christian mass for the dead. The first, 'Lacrymosa', is part of the *Dies Irae*, the medieval hymn evoking the terrors of the Last Judgment: 'Tearful shall be that day, when from the ashes arises the guilty man to be judged.' It opens with great force, as timpani, piano, two harps, and pizzicato basses combine to create the effect of an enormous drum, beating a terrible warning over a sustained low bass note. As it fades, settling into a funereal tread, a melody tentatively emerges in the cellos, as if from ruins, reaching upwards in a rocking rhythm (this association of the 'Lacrymosa' with grief-stricken rocking goes back to Mozart's *Requiem*). As violas and woodwind take up the theme, the effect is of a procession of swaying figures. An alto saxophone joins them with an uncomfortable, leaping line, creating the impression of an intruder from another world. This has resonances of Vaughan Williams' *Job*, in which the saxophone represents the wheedling 'comforters' sent by Satan. Here the weirdness is less specific – perhaps the saxophone is the only living creature in this bleak scene. Muted strings take the music to its first climax, over the processional drums. Then, quietly menacing low trombone chords are answered by eerie, high flutes (the first of many suggestions of Holst's *The Planets*). Fragments of the rocking theme interleave with the increasingly ghostly chords. The saxophone reappears with its uncomfortable leaps as the tension rises. Now the strings remove their mutes, the brass take up the saxophone's leaps while the persistent rocking figure returns. The music builds powerfully, snarling brass reiterate the menacing chords. The great drumbeats of the opening return, and the music quickly reaches a massive, tragic climax. Slowly it recedes, and a high, sustained note links straight into the second movement.

The title of the hymn of the Last Judgment, *Dies Irae*, is taken from its opening words: 'The day of wrath, that day all time will dissolve into ashes.' The movement opens with a nervous, flutter-tongued little motif on flutes and piccolo, answered, pianissimo at first, by a frantic gallop in the strings. These two elements will drive the whole movement, punctuated by sudden snarls and grimaces. It rises to a first climax, with the flutter-tongued motif taking on a menace reminiscent of Holst's 'Mars'. Trumpets and horns play a mockery of military fanfares, and the threat grows ever more menacing. Suddenly, the saxophone returns with the first theme from the 'Lacrymosa', as if weeping at the destruction, and muted brass answer with brutal, syncopated little phrases. The galloping and the rhythmic cell return and build, punctuated by savage chords. From a final climax the music disintegrates into a series of whiplash glissandi, shrieks, and thumps, in which one can hear a fragmented mockery of the 'Lacrymosa' theme. Gradually the music slows and quietens, until the fragments coalesce onto a low D.

Harps and bass clarinet take us into 'Requiem aeternam': 'Grant them eternal rest, O Lord, and may perpetual light shine upon them.' A steady bass pattern begins, in a processional three-time. Over this bass, two flutes and a bass flute play a gentle, chant-like trio, answered by horns: this apparently new melody is, with masterly transformation, derived from the brutal, syncopated phrases that the brass played in the middle of the *Dies Irae*. The effect would be wholly soothing, if it were not for the dissonant intervals in the bass that undercut the calm. The procession winds to an end, and, over hushed tremolando, the violins embark on a melody drawn from the rocking shapes and yearning leaps of the 'Lacrymosa'. With sustained Mahlerian intensity and power, this rises to a great climax. As it falls away, the procession resumes, and, through uneasy dissonances, the music recedes, until all that is left is a pair of clarinets holding a dying harmony of D major: peace at last.

VARIATIONS ON A THEME OF FRANK BRIDGE, OP. 10
Duration: approx. 27 minutes
Introduction and Theme: Lento maestoso – Allegretto poco lento
Variation 1: Adagio
Variation 2: March (Presto alla marcia)
Variation 3: Romance (Allegretto grazioso)
Variation 4: Aria Italiana (Allegro brillante)
Variation 5: Bourrée classique (Allegro e pesante)
Variation 6: Wiener Walzer (Lento – Vivace)
Variation 7: Moto perpetuo (Allegro molto)
Variation 8: Funeral March (Andante ritmico)
Variation 9: Chant (Lento)
Variation 10: Fugue and Finale (Allegro molto vivace – Lento e solenne)

In 1932, Boyd Neel, a recently qualified doctor and gifted musician, founded Britain's first regular string chamber orchestra, drawn from young professional musicians emerging from London music colleges. The Boyd Neel Orchestra set new standards in music from the baroque to the twentieth century and rapidly became so successful that Neel was able to devote himself entirely to a musical career. In 1937 the orchestra was invited at short notice to play at the Salzburg Festival. Neel was asked to include the premiere of a work by an English composer:

As it was then May and the concert was to take place on August 27th, the prospect seemed well-nigh hopeless; but suddenly I thought of Britten (till then hardly known outside inner musical circles) because I had noticed his extraordinary speed of composition during some film work in which we had been associated [Britten wrote music for *Love from a Stranger* in 1936]. I immediately asked him if he would take on the Salzburg commission, and in ten days' time he appeared at my house with the complete work sketched out. In another four weeks it was fully scored for strings as it stands today, but for the addition of one bar. This was one of the most astonishing feats of composition in my experience. I saw at once that we had here, not just another string piece, but a work in which the resources of the string orchestra were exploited with a daring and invention never before known ... the work caused a major sensation, and was soon to be played all over the world.[7]

Britten's sheer inventive skill in writing for strings invites comparison with Bartók's Music for Strings, Percussion and Celesta, a work that Britten did not yet know (it had been premiered in Switzerland four months before Britten composed the Variations).

Britten dedicated the work to his teacher, Frank Bridge. He was not quite fourteen when he first met Bridge in 1927 at the Norwich Festival. He had been introduced by his viola teacher, and, Britten remembered: 'We got on splendidly, and I spent the next morning with him going over some of my music ... From that moment I use to go regularly to him, staying with him in Eastbourne or in London, in the holidays ... This was immensely serious and professional study, and the lessons were mammoth ... In everything he did for me, there were perhaps above all two cardinal principles. One was that you should find yourself and be true to what you found. The other – obviously connected to it – was his scrupulous attention to good technique, the business of saying clearly what was in one's mind.' Bridge became Britten's most important teacher, with whom he continued to study privately even during his years as a pupil of John Ireland at the Royal College of Music.[8]

The combination of technical brilliance, clarity, and personal directness that Bridge fostered is magnificently realized in Britten's first major work, the Variations on a Theme of Frank Bridge. He based it on a quotation from the second of Bridge's Three Idylls for String Quartet, composed in 1906, which he had already used five years earlier for a set of variations that he never finished. Other quotations from Bridge's music are scattered through the final fugue, and the dedication to him reads, 'A tribute with affection and admiration'. Britten presented a copy of the score to Bridge, in which each variation was headed with one of Bridge's characteristics – humour, depth, wit, and so on. Bridge was deeply touched: 'I don't know how to express my appreciation in adequate terms. It is one of the few lovely things that has ever happened to me, & I feel the richer in spirit for it all, including the charming dedication. Thank you & thank you, Benjie. What a great pleasure! And "ain't I glad" I love the work itself!'[9] Britten intended to include the personal characteristics in the published score, but Bridge and his wife persuaded him not to, preferring them to remain private.

Bridge's theme is a valse triste, full of poignant harmonies that hang unresolved. It consists of a sixteen-bar phrase played twice, the second time elaborated and with yet more poignant harmonies. The harmonies only succeed in resolving at the end of each phrase (both times into E minor). This harmonic tension is highlighted before the theme appears, in Britten's introductory bars, which are based on the clash that opens Bridge's theme. After a pizzicato chord of F major, the basses hold an insistent low C, while the upper strings play demonstrative fanfares and scales based on a chord of E major. This powerful battle between C and E subsides in pizzicato chords, out of which the theme quietly emerges. Britten increases the shyness of its opening by elongating each phrase, as if it is reluctant to be pulled into the light. And at the end of the theme, the bass descends through chromatic steps down to C for the beginning of the first variation.

Variation 1 (Adagio, 'His integrity', later changed to 'His depth'): Britten simplifies the theme into a series of slow, sonorous chords, over which the violins play fragments of an impassioned recitative.

Variation 2 (March, 'His energy') is a fast, brittle march that begins pianissimo, rises to a climax, and fades away. Again, the lower and upper strings have quite different roles: violas, cellos, and basses play the relentless march rhythms, while the violins play nervous fragments and trills. Only at the climax do all the instruments come together in the march rhythm.

Variation 3 (Romance, 'His charm') sees the violins almost revert to the slow waltz character of Bridge's theme, but persistent cross-rhythms try to give it a playful character.

Variation 4 (Aria Italiana, 'His humour', originally 'His wit') is an outrageous parody of a showy operatic aria over guitar-like strummed pizzicato.

Variation 5 (Bourrée classique, 'His tradition') is an update of a baroque dance nodding towards Stravinsky's *Pulcinella*, most directly in the central violin solo.

Variation 6 (Wiener Walzer, 'His enthusiasm', originally 'His gaiety') parodies not just a Viennese waltz but specifically the traditional way of playing it, with its coy hesitations and returns to tempo. It is by turns sturdy, wistful, and ghostly, sometimes with a hint of Ravel's *La Valse*. It was a bold parody to present to its first audience of well-heeled Austrians at the Salzburg Festival.

Variation 7 (Moto perpetuo, 'His vitality', originally 'His enthusiasm') is ferociously intense, with continuous, scrubbed double notes passing rapidly across the orchestra. This intensity prepares the way for the longest and most serious variation so far.

Variation 8 (Funeral March, 'His sympathy (understanding)'): This is a magnificent and tragic piece, with the poignant tug of a tearful melody supported by dissonant harmonies, and a drum-like beat below. From time to time the dissonances melt into warm chords, but not at the end, where a dying, unresolved chord is left hanging in the air.

Variation 9 (Chant, 'His reverence') is like a frozen version of Variation 1. Instead of recitative, there is a chant-like iteration on violas divided into three parts, while the rest of the orchestra sustains a barely changing bass note below and the cry of eerie harmonics above.

The work ends with an extended fugue and finale ('His skill' for the fugue, 'Our affection' for the slow conclusion). The fugue is based on a nervous and skittish subject that fragments the opening intervals of Bridge's theme. After a climax, the tempo increases, and a new swirling motif is added into the counterpoint. When the original fugue returns, the strings are muted and pianissimo. The fugue has become a ghostly backdrop, over which a solo quartet plays, in unison, a series of sustained quotations from other works by Bridge. Eventually the fugue vanishes into the sky, and all the strings come together on a fortissimo unison. This softens into the final section of the work, a reprise of Bridge's theme, now transformed into a lament. The melody is stretched out over sustained chords, so that, instead of being rootless, it struggles poignantly against the harmonic root that has been found for it.

Almost like Mahler in its tragic intensity, it seems like the fulfilment of what had been hinted at in the recitative of Variation 1. The melody becomes more and more impassioned, until it fades to a *ppp* whisper over tremolando. A series of mysterious harmonics finds final release in arpeggios that build a chord of D major, and the work ends on an affirmative, sustained D.

MAX BRUCH
(1838–1920)

Max Bruch, born and brought up in Cologne, first made his name as a composer of opera and choral works; and though his opera reputation faded, his reputation for choral music remained strong throughout his life. He also wrote large quantities of orchestral and chamber music. If he is remembered principally as the composer of his Violin Concerto No. 1 in G minor, this is because it is undoubtedly his finest work. Like his great contemporary, Brahms, Bruch allied himself with the 'classical' principles passed on from Mendelssohn and Schumann, and condemned the excesses of the New German School, led by Liszt and Wagner. Unlike Brahms, he survived well into the twentieth century, by which time musical styles had moved on. He remained true to his own way of working throughout his long career, and for this reason was increasingly neglected as modern developments passed him by. At the end of his life, several years after the premiere of Stravinsky's *The Rite of Spring* (1913), his style of composition was much the same as it had been when he wrote his famous First Violin Concerto half a century earlier. Having been regarded early in life as one of the major composers of his time, he died comparatively neglected – the same fate as that experienced by his contemporary, Saint-Saëns, and for very similar reasons. Sadly, Bruch himself came to acknowledge that his reputation would in the end rest on his G minor concerto, and on little else. He was asked in 1907 by his friend Arthur Abell how he thought his reputation would compare with that of Brahms in fifty years' time. Bruch replied, 'I predict . . . that, as time goes on, he will be more appreciated, while most of my works will be more and more neglected. Fifty years hence he will loom up as one of the supremely great composers of all time, while I will be remembered chiefly for having written my G minor Violin Concerto.'[1]

KOL NIDREI FOR CELLO AND ORCHESTRA, OP. 47
Duration: approx. 10 minutes

While he was in Berlin from 1878 to 1880, Bruch conducted the Stern'sche Gesangverein, an excellent choir. Many of its members were Jewish, and through them he got to know the cantor-in-chief at the synagogue, Abraham Jacob Lichtenstein. It was Lichtenstein who introduced Bruch to some of the music of Jewish tradition. Bruch wrote, 'Even though I am a Protestant, as an artist I felt deeply the outstanding beauty of these melodies and I am therefore glad to disseminate them through my arrangements.'[2] Chief among these melodies was Kol Nidrei, the ancient chant that begins the service on the eve of Yom Kippur, the Day of Atonement. The chant declares the annulment of vows, a declaration that came to be associated with times of persecution, but whose meaning is much debated. Its significance has come to attach less to its literal meaning than to its position at the beginning of the service celebrating the holiest day of the year. Part of that significance arises from the power of the

melody to which Kol Nidrei is traditionally sung. This is what attracted Bruch to the chant –
he is unlikely to have been interested in its religious significance, beyond his general feeling
for the power of traditional 'folk music'. There are many variants of the chant, and the version
that Bruch knew was the one that was currently in use in Berlin.

Kol Nidrei forms the basis of the first half of Bruch's work. The second half is based on a
melody from another collection that Lichtenstein introduced to Bruch. This is the Hebrew
Melodies of Isaac Nathan (1790–1864), an English composer whose father was a Polish cantor.
Nathan published a series of volumes of traditional melodies used in the synagogue, for which
Byron was persuaded to supply lyrics. Byron was very enthusiastic about the project, believing
that the melodies that Nathan had collected were, as he had implied, 'the real undisputed
Hebrew Melodies which are beautiful & to which David & the prophets actually sang the
"songs of Zion"'. In fact, only a few of the tunes had ancient origin, others being folk songs
from various times and places that had been incorporated into the traditions of the synagogue.

The song that Bruch quotes is 'Oh! Weep for those that wept by Babel's stream', which he
also set as one of his Three Hebrew Songs for Chorus and Orchestra. Byron's poem is based
on the opening verses of Psalm 137: 'By the rivers of Babylon, there we sat down, yea, we wept,
when we remembered Zion.' For the second part of Kol Nidrei, Bruch takes the melody of the
second stanza:

> And where shall Israel lave her bleeding feet?
> And when shall Zion's songs again seem sweet?
> And Judah's melody once more rejoice
> The hearts that leaped before its heavenly voice?

Bruch composed Kol Nidrei for the cellist Robert Hausmann, who played the premiere in
Liverpool where Bruch was the conductor of the Philharmonic Society.

It opens with pianissimo string chords, their unexpected shifts of key evoking the ancient
and mysterious. The cello enters with the opening phrases of the chant, made poignant by
their separation into individual sighs. A second phrase flows more smoothly, and prompts a
moment of lyrical outpouring, before the opening sighs return. Then a third phrase from the
chant is declaimed assertively by the strings, and answered with pleading phrases from the
cello. This new material is the trigger for a passage of declamation that grows more and more
urgent, until once more the sighs return, with unsettled tremolando below, and the cello line
winds down to a moment of rest.

The harp enters with three chords, and the music changes from minor to major. Over
shimmering string textures and harp arpeggios the woodwind play the melody from 'Oh!
Weep for those that wept by Babel's stream'. The beautifully spacious scoring here is very
similar to passages in Bruch's Scottish Fantasy, written shortly before Kol Nidrei. In the one
work, he seems to be evoking ancient Scottish bards, in the other the harp of the poet-king
David. The cello plays an elaborated version of the melody, which then blossoms into an
extended meditation. Gradually it becomes calmer, and suggestions of sighs return, without
any literal reprise of the opening chant. There is one more reminder of 'Oh! Weep', and the
cello ascends gently to a final high note.

SCOTTISH FANTASY, OP. 46
Duration: approx. 32 minutes
Introduction: Grave – Adagio cantabile
Allegro
Andante sostenuto
Finale: Allegro guerriero

Bruch's Second Violin Concerto had been premiered in 1877. Bruch considered its dramatic first movement even better than the one from his First Violin Concerto, but it never achieved the same success. The following September he moved to Berlin, where he stayed for two years. His reputation as a composer of choral music had led him to be appointed conductor of the Stern'sche Gesangverein, one of the most distinguished choirs in Germany. It was while he was in Berlin that Bruch composed another work for violin and orchestra which, though not quite in the same league as the First Violin Concerto, is highly effective and has remained popular with soloists and audiences. This is the Fantasy for the Violin with Orchestra and Harp, freely using Scottish Folk Melodies. That was the title in the edition published by Simrock, but it is generally known as the Scottish Fantasy. Bruch wrote it over the winter of 1879–80. He had been working on ideas for a dramatic cantata based on Sir Walter Scott's narrative poem, *The Lady of the Lake*. This was one of the most influential works in the nineteenth-century development of the Romantic image of Scotland, and Schubert had set several passages of the poem.

As for Scottish music, Bruch had first drawn on Scottish traditional tunes in his Twelve Scottish Folksongs for Voice and Piano (1863). His source was *The Scots Musical Museum*, a collection of six hundred songs compiled by James Johnson with the help of Robert Burns. Published over the years 1787–1803, it became the best-known source of Scottish tunes across Europe, with Haydn and Beethoven among the composers who arranged songs from it. By Bruch's time, the valuing of folk song, and the Romantic image of Scotland, had become major influences on European thought, and Bruch took this material very seriously: 'I would never have come to anything in this world, if I had not, since my twenty-fourth year, studied the folk music of all nations with seriousness, perseverance, and unending interest. There is nothing to compare with the feeling, power, originality and beauty of the folk song … here is the salvation of our unmelodic times.'[3]

Beyond the use of specific tunes, Bruch's Romantic evocation of Scotland also follows in the steps of Mendelssohn's *Hebrides* Overture and 'Scottish' Symphony. Soon after the premiere of the Scottish Fantasy, Bruch was offered the post of director of a projected new Conservatoire of Music in Edinburgh, but the plan foundered through lack of money and chaotic organization. At the time he wrote the Scottish Fantasy, he had never set foot in Scotland, and it was the combined influences of Sir Walter Scott, Scottish folk song, and Mendelssohn that inspired him to this evocative work.

Joseph Joachim, who had premiered the famous First Violin Concerto thirteen years before, again premiered the Scottish Fantasy in February 1881, in Liverpool, where Bruch was now conductor of the Philharmonic Society. According to Bruch, Joachim played 'very nervously, and with quite insufficient technique'.[4]

Nowhere is the influence of Mendelssohn stronger than in the opening bars. Like the introduction of Mendelssohn's 'Scottish' Symphony, inspired by the ruined chapel of

Holyrood in Edinburgh, Bruch's Fantasy begins with a solemn chorale. Brass instruments with harp evoke what might be an old Scots lament, with its minor key, dark chording, and sombre dotted rhythms. Over a quiet string chord, the soloist steals in pianissimo with a recitative, as if the bard is introducing his heroic tale (such an evocation would have been familiar to German audiences from the old harper of Goethe's *Wilhelm Meister's Apprenticeship*, whose songs Schubert set). Twice the recitative rises passionately and falls back. The second time, the darkness lifts from minor to major (marking the end of the Introduction and the beginning of the first movement proper), and with pianissimo chords that are both stately and airy the orchestra prepares for the entry of the first Scottish tune. This is 'Thro' the wood laddie' (not, as is often stated, 'Auld Rob Morris'). The violin plays it sonorously, with the rippling harp prominent in the accompaniment. The soloist develops the tune through the rest of the movement, with phrases in single notes alternating with two-part chords, and echoes of the stately introduction brought in. At the end, the brass chorus touches on the solemn introduction, as the soloist rises through trills to an ethereal high E flat.

The second movement, in G major, is based on 'Dusty Miller', a tune popular with fiddlers in the eighteenth and nineteenth centuries, and found in English as well as Scottish sources. In this movement it is as if Bruch has taken the idea of the fiddler and elevated it to high virtuosity. After a brisk introduction horns and violas play a drone of fifths, like a bagpipe. Over it, the soloist plays the first half of the tune in playful two-part chords. The second half of the tune is adapted to become more sentimental, ending with a flourish. The tune moves into the orchestral violins while the soloist plays rapid figurations against it. This leads into a vigorous orchestral tutti (which Jascha Heifetz and others used to shorten). The vigour carries through to the next solo passage, and to the next tutti. Here the orchestra sets up a repeating rhythm, taken from the first bar of the tune, over which the soloist meditates in a series of rising phrases, moving through different keys. A return to the sentimental second half of the tune leads on to another vigorous orchestral tutti. The soloist catches the excited mood, and with virtuoso flourishes returns to G major, and a reprise of 'Dusty Miller', with the lower instruments of the orchestra pursuing the upper ones a beat apart.

Again the solo violin returns to the sentimental second half of the tune. This time its phrases are answered by a flute, and the two instruments combine in a delightful, cadenza-like duet (very tricky to co-ordinate from opposite ends of the orchestra). Over the repeating rhythm of the tune, the soloist plays rising phrases as before. They culminate in a quick burst of orchestra bringing the movement to an abrupt end. But the violas hold a long note, which blossoms into a reminiscence of 'Thro' the wood laddie' from the first movement. The soloist takes it up, and, in another meditative passage, leads through different keys to A flat major, and without a break into the third movement.

The Andante is based on a Scottish tune first printed in the eighteenth century, 'I'm a' doun for lack o' Johnnie', and from it Bruch builds a substantial movement as beautiful as anything in the famous G minor concerto. The soloist plays the melody simply, repeating each strain an octave higher and accompanied first by strings then by woodwind. The tune is rounded off with echoing sighs in the woodwind, touched with a minor chord, like a wistful 'amen'. This is followed by a variation, in which the tune alternates between horn and woodwind, and then horn and cellos together, while the violin embellishes it with decorative figurations. This time, the sighing refrain moves on to a new key, the soloist's embellishments become more urgent, and the melody is taken up powerfully by violas and cellos enriched by harp arpeggios (its first entry in this movement). The soloist takes the theme on and on, rising passionately to a climax, and falling away to a tender cadence. The strings, now back in the original key, build once more, and again the soloist rises and falls gently to a conclusion.

The finale is based on a tune originally known as 'Hey Tuttie Tatie', a rousing melody traditionally supposed to have rallied the troops before Robert the Bruce led his army to victory against the English at the Battle of Bannockburn in 1314. Nearly five hundred years later Robert Burns used this ancient tune, re-imagining Bruce's address to his troops in the words, 'Scots, wha hae wi' Wallace bled'. This is the form in which the tune is best known, and which Bruch had set nearly twenty years earlier in his Twelve Scottish Folksongs.

Bruch appropriately marks the movement 'warlike'. It begins with the solo violin, accompanied only by harp, boldly setting out a phrase of the (adapted) tune in fortissimo three-part chords. A brief orchestral tutti is followed by another phrase of the tune, and after a further tutti the soloist launches into ferocious virtuoso variations – this is the violin as a weapon of war. Horns signal a calming of mood, and a change of key. The violin plays a lyrical, rather sentimental melody, which rises passionately in its second half. The orchestra re-injects energy into the music with a rather Mendelssohn-like passage, which the soloist then decorates. Running virtuoso scales are accompanied by fragments of 'Scots wha hae', and dissolve into a high trill. The full orchestra plays a phrase of the tune in a new key, and the soloist responds with the sentimental second theme. Alternations between orchestra and soloist pass through further keys, a tutti rises to a climax, and, back in the home key, the soloist bursts into a yet more complex variations on the tune. The Mendelssohnian link returns, together with the soloist's embellishment and extension of it. The sentimental second theme follows. This time, the soloist extends it into a more and more elaborate meditation, which, from a delicate high point, descends peacefully to a touching reminiscence of 'Thro' the wood laddie', the tune with which the work began. There is a rush upwards, a final burst of 'Scots wha hae', and the Fantasy is over.

VIOLIN CONCERTO NO. 1 IN G MINOR, OP. 26
Duration: approx. 24 minutes

Prelude: Allegro moderato –
Adagio
Finale: Allegro energico

In November 1865, Bruch wrote to the composer Ferdinand Hiller, 'My Violin Concerto is progressing slowly – I do not feel sure of my feet on this terrain. Do you not think that it is in fact very audacious to write a Violin Concerto?'[5] There had not been a major violin concerto by a German composer since Mendelssohn's in 1844. Furthermore, Bruch was known principally as a composer of choral music and opera, so it was natural that he should take his time with a violin concerto. He later wrote about the challenge, 'It is a damn difficult thing to do; between 1864 and 1868 I rewrote my concerto at least half a dozen times, and conferred with x violinists before it took the final form in which it is universally famous and played everywhere.'[6] Chief among the 'x' violinists were Ferdinand David (for whom Mendelssohn wrote his concerto) and Joseph Joachim (for whom Brahms would later write his). A first version of Bruch's concerto was tried out in the spring of 1866 in Coblenz. Bruch was dissatisfied, and sent it to Joachim with a list of questions to which Joachim replied with detailed answers. The most important was his agreement with Bruch that the orchestral passage that ends the first movement should be longer, and should be followed by a cadenza to link to the slow movement. This prompted Bruch to write the most powerful passage in the whole concerto.

The final version was premiered in Bremen in 1868 by Joachim, who then took it up enthusiastically, as did Ferdinand David, Leopold Auer, and Henri Vieuxtemps. The concerto has continued to be Bruch's greatest success. But he made very little money out of it – he sold it to a publisher for a one-off fee, and received no royalties when it turned into a major money-spinner. Shortly before his death in 1920, he allowed two American sisters to take the manuscript home, with the idea of selling it for him. He died full of hope that the sale would make a good legacy for his children, but all they received were some worthless German banknotes and a refusal to answer questions about the whereabouts of the manuscript.[7] This was the final insult after half a century during which Bruch had to face the fact that all his other music had been eclipsed by the concerto. His many fine choral works were largely forgotten, and even his two later violin concertos never became as popular as the first. The Second Violin Concerto begins with a long and beautiful slow movement, which Bruch considered publishing on its own. The Third Violin Concerto starts with a first movement that is powerful but also very long. All three concertos contain beautiful music, but the first is the only one of the three that is truly effective throughout. Bruch built on the example of Mendelssohn to create a serious, almost 'symphonic' concerto that was to influence Brahms when writing his violin concerto ten years later. This influence extended to the 'Hungarian' finale, which had in turn been inspired by Joachim's 'Hungarian Concerto' of 1857. Joachim's finale is a brilliant display of Hungarian fire and pyrotechnics. But it was Bruch who first showed how the Hungarian element could be used to build a really powerful conclusion.

There is a soft timpani roll, and the woodwind play a sombre phrase, like a fragment of a folk song. The soloist responds with a rising recitative, as if searching for the theme. The woodwind play again, in a different key, and the soloist searches again. Now the full orchestra takes up the woodwind's phrase, in its original G minor, and the movement has really begun. Over urgent tremolo and a pizzicato bass, the soloist declaims the first theme. It begins with chords in bold dotted rhythms, arpeggios, and a descending phrase, and develops as it goes, bringing in more fearsome chords and octaves. A burst of orchestral tutti leads into the second theme in B flat major. This begins sonorously on the solo violin and once more develops as it goes, turning into a sweet duet with oboe. The soloist rises higher, and as the extended theme winds to a conclusion the orchestra returns to the tremolo and pizzicato bass with which it began, and the soloist takes the opening theme in dramatic new directions.

The solo loosens into a rapid, virtuoso fantasia, and the pace gradually accelerates. The rhythm in the pizzicato bass becomes more continuous, and as the soloist's arpeggios reach a peak of virtuosity, the orchestra bursts into a ferocious fortissimo passage, with running violins over the insistent rhythm of the bass. Even the lyrical second theme gets pulled into the storm. The music reaches a climax, and fades to a reprise of the woodwind's sombre phrase from the beginning of the movement. The soloist again responds with a recitative, which becomes more cadenza-like and powerful. A rapid rising scale brings in the full orchestra, building the woodwind phrase into a passionate melody. It subsides to a held note in the violins, and, without a break, the slow movement begins.

The soloist plays the theme that, like the second theme of the first movement, develops from a sonorous, sustained opening to a sweeter and more flowing second idea. The melody then rises, becoming more impassioned and moving through different keys until it arrives at a trill. Horns and bassoons play a new theme of falling intervals like tolling bells, while the violin continues its ascent, then the soloist takes the new theme and decorates it with cascading arpeggios. From here, the music winds peacefully down to a reminder of the flowing second part of the first theme. We have reached the calm centre of the movement. The strings quietly play the opening of the first theme, down a major third, a warm change of key of which Schubert was particularly fond. The soloist takes up the theme, and then it moves to the cellos while the soloist adds a thoughtful counterpoint. As the soloist's musings become more intense, the theme moves to the violins, back in its original key, then, with increasing power, to woodwind and to all the violins. There is a climax, and the soloist moves straight on to the tolling second theme, with its cascading arpeggios. From here the music calms, and the movement ends with a last reminiscence of the first theme that rises to a final climax and falls away.

And so to the Hungarian-style finale. Over expectant tremolando violas a snappy rhythm gradually builds up, until it is taken up by the soloist and combined with chords to create a theme of splendid rugged strength that passes between soloist and orchestra. After a tutti, the soloist's running passages culminate in a second theme, a grand, sweeping line that first bursts out in the orchestra and is taken up by the soloist powerfully on the lowest string of the violin. As with earlier themes, it has a particularly charming second idea, which passes from soloist to orchestra, and then back to the soloist to be elaborated. While the elaborations continue, the snappy Hungarian rhythm creeps in below, and the music builds up to a powerful orchestral tutti. The soloist develops the theme at greater length, taking it into new keys, until a build-up culminates in the return of the sweeping second theme fortissimo in the orchestra. The elaborations of this theme once more build up to powerful reassertions of the first theme exchanged between soloist and orchestra. Then there is a gradual acceleration until a final dash brings the concerto to an exciting finish.

ANTON BRUCKNER
(1824–96)

Bruckner was the son of a schoolmaster and organist at Ansfelden, a village in Upper Austria. The father died when Anton was thirteen, and that year he became a choirboy at the Augustinian monastery of Saint Florian, near Linz, where he got to know the church music of Mozart and Haydn, and learned to love the music of Schubert. At first he followed the family tradition and worked for ten years as a schoolmaster at Saint Florian, where he began to compose choral works and developed a reputation as an organist. In 1855 he was appointed organist at the cathedral in Linz, and he was able to give up his teaching and become a full-time musician. But he lacked confidence as a composer, and combined his Linz post with studying counterpoint in Vienna. Still not satisfied, he followed that with further studies in orchestration and musical form with teachers in Linz. He attended the premiere of *Tristan und Isolde* in Munich in 1865, where he met Wagner. Inspired by this overwhelming experience, he composed his Symphony No. 1 in C minor. At last, in his forties, Bruckner began to compose with confidence. Three years later, he moved to Vienna, succeeding his teacher as professor of harmony and counterpoint at the Vienna Conservatory. But his attempts to establish himself as a composer were dogged by frustration. He had to wait until 1884 for a real success – the premiere of his Seventh Symphony in Leipzig, a triumph repeated in Munich and Vienna.

Before he moved to Vienna in 1868, Bruckner had enjoyed the support of the Viennese critic Eduard Hanslick in his early attempts at writing symphonies. But as his devotion to Wagner deepened, he found himself on the 'wrong side' of the battle raging between the supporters of Brahms (led by Hanslick) and the supporters of Wagner and Liszt with their 'Music of the Future'. Hanslick publicly poured scorn on Bruckner's ideas of the 'symphony of the future', which he saw as transferring to the symphony some of the methods and vision of Wagner.

Bruckner all his life spoke, dressed, and behaved as he had been brought up in rural Upper Austria, coming across as a quaint and awkward figure in the sophisticated world of Vienna. He wore voluminous trousers, which led a friend to ask him whether he had them made by a carpenter. He never married, despite continual attempts to find a suitable wife. Bruckner's ideas of 'suitable' raised eyebrows on more than one occasion. A letter survives, written when Bruckner was forty-two, in which he proposed marriage to a girl aged seventeen, a butcher's daughter, with whom he had fallen in love. Its combination of passionate naivety and respectful formality is touching and characteristic: 'May I hope for you, and ask your dear parents for your hand?'[1] Unsurprisingly, she rejected him, as did others. His diaries record numerous young women to whom he was attracted. But they also list his daily prayers. Brought up in the Roman Catholic Church, which retained a powerful hold over life in Upper Austria, he was unswerving in his faith.

Bruckner also had the misfortune to be drawn into political arguments. Like Wagner, he came to be associated with a strand of German nationalism that included a strong element of anti-Semitism (Wagner's own essay, 'Jewishness in Music', is a notorious contribution to it). Vienna had become a city riven by such issues, and this fostered musical divisions. Bruckner's most vociferous supporters saw him as a naive, true Austrian Catholic, a representative of Germanic culture at its purest and most conservative. This was in contrast to the liberal, intellectual, cosmopolitan Vienna in which Jews played so important a part, and whose musical leader was Brahms (who had many Jewish friends and associates).[2] Bruckner himself, though not a political thinker, was pulled into these battles. As with Wagner, associations with nationalism cast a long shadow over Bruckner's music in the twentieth century. From the 1970s onwards, however, as memories of these associations faded, the reputation of his music began to grow, and performance of his symphonies is now more frequent across the world than at any time since he composed them.

Any realistic assessment of Bruckner has to acknowledge the seriousness of some of the earlier criticism of him, from Hanslick onwards. Bruckner was no Beethoven or Schubert or Wagner, despite his indebtedness to all three of them. His methods are grandiose but naive. Since he was a deeply religious man, his symphonies are built from, and saturated with, his faith. The instrument at which he felt most at ease was the organ, on which he was a virtuoso and a brilliant improviser (he always prayed before playing the organ). He struggled long and hard to transfer this natural command to the composition of orchestral music. There is some truth in the claim that he uses the orchestra like an organ. You will not find in Bruckner the wealth of instrumental combinations that you find in his near contemporary, Brahms. In Brahms at his best, you sense the dialogue of human life. In Bruckner, you sense something more massive and, in some ways, more ancient: an attempt to express the splendour of God's creation, in which human beings are humble participants. In this, Bruckner has more in common with J. S. Bach, or even with Renaissance composers such as Palestrina or Tallis, than he does with his contemporaries.

Bruckner's weaknesses are obvious. Often in his symphonies an idea will peter out, and after a silence he will simply switch to a new idea in a different key. His immense paragraphs ratchet up the tension by shifting up a key, step by step, in a manner that has become a cliché in stage musicals and film scores (a method first made respectable by Liszt). Bursts of intricate counterpoint sometimes sound like academic exercises rather than part of a coherent argument. Critics, particularly Hanslick, ridiculed such procedures, and there are moments in Bruckner's symphonies that are undeniably clunky. But it is not always the people with the most sophisticated command of their arguments that most touch us. There is something immense about the way Bruckner struggles to build his great paragraphs and to pile up his enormous climaxes. It is easy to sense the depth of faith that lies behind them. And if the methods seem crude, they are the methods of a clumsy giant, and the resulting structures are unlike anything else in music.

SYMPHONY NO. 3 IN D MINOR (1873 VERSION)
Duration: approx. 70 minutes
Gemässigt, misterioso (in moderate tempo, mysterious)
Adagio: Feierlich (solemn)
Scherzo and Trio: Ziemlich schnell (quite fast)
Finale: Allegro

Bruckner worked on his Third Symphony from the autumn of 1872 to the end of 1873. While he was still writing it, he visited Wagner at Bayreuth and asked his permission to dedicate to him either this symphony, which was not yet complete, or its predecessor, No. 2. Wagner chose No. 3, and in May 1874 a presentation copy of the score was sent to Wagner, dedicated 'to the honourable Richard Wagner, the unattainable, world-renowned and sublime master of the poetical and musical arts, with the deepest reverence from Anton Bruckner'. Wagner's name, in elaborately decorated script, straddles the entire width of the page. Bruckner's name is a quarter of the size, modestly placed bottom right like the signature of a bank clerk.

The symphony came to be known as Bruckner's 'Wagner Symphony'. The links with Wagner, however, extend beyond the dedication. In his first version, which was sent to Wagner, Bruckner includes quotations from *Tristan* and *Die Walküre* in the first and last movements. This version of the symphony was never performed in Bruckner's lifetime, and the score was not published until 1977. Bruckner removed these quotations, as well as shortening the rest of the work, in revisions that he carried out between 1876 and 1878.

It was one stage of these revisions that was played at the disastrous premiere in Vienna in December 1877. Johann Herbeck, conductor of the Gesellschaft der Musikfreunde and one of Bruckner's staunchest supporters, had died in October, leaving Bruckner no option but to conduct the work himself. Although he was an effective choral conductor, Bruckner was out of his depth in front of an orchestra. Eduard Hanslick, who had previously been sympathetic to Bruckner, declared the failings of the new symphony: 'It is not our wish to harm the composer whom we rightly respect as a man and artist, for his artistic intentions are honest, however oddly he employs them. Instead of a critique, therefore, we would rather simply confess that we have not understood his gigantic symphony. On the one hand his poetic intentions were unclear to us – perhaps a vision of how Beethoven's Ninth made friends with Wagner's Valkyrie and ended up under her horse's hooves – and on the other hand, we could not grasp the purely musical coherence.' Members of the audience left in increasing numbers after the end of each movement, 'so that the Finale, which exceeded all its predecessors in oddities, was only experienced to the very end by a little group of hardy adventurers.'[3]

This humiliating experience added to Bruckner's insecurity and to his anxious revisiting of his scores. He continued making further revisions to the symphony over a long period, and a third version, prepared with his pupil Franz Schalk, was published in 1890. Discussions continue about which version should be performed, but, after many years in which only the later, cut versions were known, conductors have increasingly turned back to the original score of 1873. It is this version that is described here, with indications of the most important changes in later editions.[4]

The duration given above is, as with all Bruckner's symphonies, only the middle of a wide range. The duration of recordings varies from 58 minutes (Roger Norrington) to 77 minutes (Georg Tintner).[5] Most performances fall between these two extremes. The greatest differences are in the tempo for the first movement. There is a balance to be struck between maintaining momentum and allowing the monumentality of the music its full effect, and just where that balance lies is a matter of opinion. It is, however, a fact that Bruckner indicates a metre of two beats per bar, not four, so the most leisurely performances are unlikely to be what he had in mind.

As often in Bruckner, there are echoes not only of Wagner but also of Beethoven right from the start. The opening paragraph is built like the beginning of Beethoven's Ninth, but we might equally be in the forest of The Ring, with a light patter of strings outlining descending arpeggios like falling leaves. From the middle of this texture emerges a quiet trumpet call, the first theme of the symphony. The harmonies begin to shift, while the bass D remains constant. A falling pair of notes is reiterated again and again, the full brass of trumpets, horns, and trombones enter, and build until the full orchestra in octaves bursts out with two brusque falling phrases, separated by silence, and answered darkly by a chromatic rising string phrase. This passes between strings and woodwind, then, after a moment of forceful tutti, Bruckner returns to the forest murmurs of the opening, but now in A major (Bruckner is still shadowing Beethoven's Ninth). This time, the trumpet call is taken up by woodwind and horns, as the harmonies shift over the constant A, building with greater confidence than before. The outburst, when it comes, is cushioned by richer harmonies, and the quiet response leads into the second theme.

This is a warm string chorus, in which no single melodic line stands out as 'the theme'. The most important elements include a shape with a gently falling triplet, which begins in the violins. Bruckner's themes often mix duplet (two-note) and triplet (three-note) patterns – there was already a triplet in the opening trumpet call. This is combined with a more sustained rising line, which first appears in the violas, mirrored in the violins, and is then answered by a horn. Meanwhile the harmonies vacillate between major and minor. From this starting point, Bruckner sets out on a massively extended paragraph, as long as the entire movement so far. It begins as a meditation on the second theme, building over Bruckner's favourite sustained bass notes to stark outbursts in octaves, trumpet calls, and brass chorales, all permeated by the alternating duplet and triplet rhythms from the second theme. Gradually, through string textures that refer back to the forest-like opening, the music subsides to a moment of complete stillness, and a pianissimo string chord of F major.

We have arrived at the beginning of the development. Quietly, a horn plays the opening of the trumpet call over a chord of F minor. As the violins begin to resume their falling

arpeggios, the trumpet call is inverted in the bass, so that it rises. What follows is a characteristic series of interrupted attempts to move forward, changing key each time. The rising calls
overlap and begin to build, only to give way to the woodwind with the chromatic rising
phrase. At the third attempt, the horns take up a more sustained line, and the string patterns
become more determined. A more complex network of melodic fragments taken from the
various themes once more begins to build, until the harmonies twist back to D minor, and at
a huge climax the trumpet call is declaimed *fff* in octaves by the whole orchestra.

It seems as if we must be at the reprise. But this is only the beginning of a passage of great
splendour that veers away from the home key, and is once again interrupted by silences and
the woodwind rising phrase. It leads on to a warm passage for strings in F major that harks
back to their second theme, but with some of the lines inverted, and others changed in rhythm.
This too builds, and breaks off. It is not at all clear where we are heading. Over a soft timpani
roll, the woodwind play a moment of counterpoint whose theme, with its leap up and chromatic fall, is a quotation from Wagner's *Tristan* (while, at the same time, the chromatic fall
relates to the familiar rising chromatic rise that has punctuated the movement). The counterpoint disguises the quotation, but then the strings, *ppp*, play a series of chords that more
explicitly quote the 'sleep' motif from Wagner's *Die Walküre*. This creates a moment of great
mystery (these Wagner quotations were cut from later versions).

From the stillness emerge the falling arpeggio patterns of the opening, back in D minor.
Now we really are at the reprise, and the music builds as before to its brusque climax, with
startlingly changed harmonies, followed by the quiet rising response. This time, Bruckner
arrives sooner at the second theme, now in the home key of D (major). As before, it develops
into a long paragraph that rises to a climax, fades, and breaks off. The quiet string patterns
from the opening return together with the trumpet call, this time underpinned by a bass line
that repeats a descending chromatic scale – a clear homage to the coda of the first movement
of Beethoven's Ninth. The chromatic line then pulls upwards to a climax that, once again,
breaks off. The woodwind meditate for the last time on the rising phrase, and quiet string
chords lead into a final assault from the full orchestra.

The slow movement in E flat major alternates an Adagio with an Andante that itself has a
slower middle section. Bruckner shortened and simplified this scheme in his later revisions.

The first phrase for strings could be the beginning of one of Bruckner's church motets. But
then it rises up, and falls in a lingering series of sighs. The violins break into running scales
over harmonies that creep upwards (this has an echo of Mozart's *Don Giovanni*). A crescendo
comes to a stop. There is another quiet string phrase, like a cadence from a motet, then another
outburst of scales, and another ecclesiastical cadence. With further characteristic searching
and hesitations, including another poignant reference to Wagner's *Tristan*, Bruckner reaches
the end of the first Adagio.

The Andante section moves into B flat major, with not only a faster tempo but also a more
coherently flowing melody that begins in the violas and then moves to the cellos and basses.
As it does so, a syncopated counterpoint starts up in the violins, bringing an element of
urgency to the melody below. It begins to rise to a climax, but cuts off to a silence. The tempo
slows, and the strings, *ppp* and 'misterioso' in G flat major, play phrases that seem almost like
a halting memory of the ecclesiastical cadence. The woodwind respond with a more elaborate
phrase. Alternating phrases and silences search from key to key, eventually reaching a forte
passage of determined counterpoint.

Suddenly, the flowing melody of the Andante returns in the violas, now in C major, with a counterpoint of running semiquavers in the violins above. This time, the music rises to a fortissimo, at which trombones enter for the first time in the movement. But it quickly fades, and the opening Adagio returns, back in its original key of E flat major (Bruckner cut this reprise of the Adagio in later versions). The melody is now in flutes and oboe, with the syncopations in the violins and a new semiquaver pattern in the violas giving it more momentum than before. Moving through more distant keys, it too builds to a fortissimo that again cuts off. With a familar pattern of quiet responses and hesitations, Bruckner arrives at another pause, with more *Tristan*-like chords, and a reprise of the Andante follows.

The melody, now in G major, is in the cellos, answered in counterpoint by the woodwind, with the syncopated pattern persistent in the violins. The key soon veers back to the home key of E flat major, with the melody now in the basses and bassoons. This gives new confidence to the music, which begins to build. But it soon shies away to other keys, again the climax is thwarted, and after two attempts at a fortissimo it subsides once more. The halting 'misterioso' phrase is recalled in woodwind and brass, and there is another silence.

What follows is one of those moments that are most characteristic of Bruckner throughout his symphonic career. He returns to the Adagio of the opening with its chorale-like theme in E flat major, but now with agitated accompaniment that makes it clear this is the beginning of the final ascent. The theme is in the woodwind, with scale patterns in the violins taking on the syncopations that have become more and more dominant through the movement (here, the underlying rhythm is really too slow for the rapid syncopations to be discernible – if one notices them at all, they just sound slightly unco-ordinated). The music builds to a sustained fortissimo, and then *fff*. But even after this great struggle, the outcome cannot reach an easy resolution. Yet again the climax breaks off, and, over quietly trilling cellos, the strings play the quiet cadence. There are two more bursts of fortissimo, the second of which dissolves into the chords of the 'sleep' motif from Wagner's *Die Walküre* (which was quoted in the first movement). The movement ends by retreating to the calm of the ecclesiastical cadence, and the strings are finally able to resolve the movement into a quiet chord of E flat major.

Apart from Wagner and Beethoven, the other great composer who lies behind much of Bruckner's thinking is Schubert. The third movement seems directly inspired by the scherzo of Schubert's Ninth Symphony, which was unusually massive for its time. Bruckner's scherzo is enormous, not in its proportions but in its sonorities. It begins quietly, with a spinning pattern in the violins and pizzicato in the bass – this could be the introduction to a spinning chorus. But very quickly it builds, and the full orchestra thunders in to join what seems like a dance of giants, with fanfare-like shapes related to those of the first movement, and Bruckner's characteristic lurching through different keys. In the second strain of the dance, the spinning accompaniment is joined by graceful new elements, which predominate until the thunderous opening returns to round off the scherzo.

The trio is one of Bruckner's most charming inspirations, with a dialogue between violas and violins over pizzicato bass. Flute and oboe join in, like birds calling in the woodland. In the second half there is a very Schubertian key change down a major third (from E major to C major). The bird-like interventions spread to the other woodwind, and these persist as the violas and violins resume their dialogue. Mahler knew this work, and we can hear echoes of Bruckner's woodland scene in his music, particularly the First Symphony. After the trio,

Bruckner repeats the scherzo exactly as before. In one of his revisions he added a coda, but later thought better of the change and deleted it.

Hanslick was perhaps right to say that the finale is the most problematic of the four movements (though what he heard at the premiere was a cut-down version). None of the editions has quite the coherent sweep of some of his later finales. On the other hand, it has fascinating passages, and does, in the end, achieve some sort of resolution.

It opens with a whirlwind of eddying string patterns that rapidly grow from pianissimo to fortissimo – an echo of Beethoven's third *Leonore* overture. The home key of D is not going to be found easily. At first we seem to be in B flat, then as the brass enter, they do wrench away to a chord of D major. But it is soon gone in a gigantic trudging progress, rather than a real theme, which begins with forceful dotted rhythms that relate to the first movement's opening trumpet call, followed by a descending line. Bruckner charges through different keys until he arrives at a chord of A major. The pianissimo whirlwind starts again in that key, and again the brass wrench away. This time the passage does end on a chord of D, but with a seventh in it, as if we expect to modulate to G. There is a silence. Then, with absolutely no preparation, we are in F sharp major, and bass pizzicato introduces the second theme that combines two elements: a delicate polka, played by the strings, and a sustained chorale in the woodwind and horns that incorporates the descending line from the opening theme.

A reminiscence by Bruckner's friend August Göllerich sheds some light on the thinking behind this striking (and strikingly Mahlerian) idea. The two were walking together in Vienna when they heard dance music coming from a house. The cathedral architect had recently died, and his coffin was in another house nearby. Bruckner said to Göllerich, 'Listen! In that house there is dancing, and over there the master lies in his coffin – that's life. It's what I wanted to show in my Third Symphony. The polka represents the fun and joy of the world, the chorale represents sadness and pain.'[6]

The combined polka and chorale extend over a lengthy paragraph, with the chorale alternating between woodwind and horns while the polka continues in the strings, and vacillating unpredictably between various keys. This fades away to a moment of calm chords and a silence (Bruckner cut this hesitation in his revisions). It seems that something new is about to occur. But no, the polka and chorale resume (now in F major) and the wandering continues, rising to a forte and then thinning out until only the upper woodwind and upper strings are left (another passage that Bruckner later tightened up). The music slows to a quiet cadence that is interrupted by a return to tempo and the entry of the full orchestra, fortissimo. This is the third thematic element in the movement, an effortful attempt at striding, with the cellos and basses dragging half a beat behind the upper strings, while the brass play forceful dotted rhythms. A quiet passage is again interrupted by the full orchestra, and a very Wagnerian climax builds and is cut off. Soft wind chords take us to the end of the first section of the movement.

The development opens with a return to the opening whirlwind and the powerful entry of the brass. The whirlwind restarts, and builds to a hammering climax that again breaks off (we are now into another passage that was cut and replaced in later revisions). The delicate polka and chorale return, only to be interrupted by another brief burst of fortissimo. The polka and chorale resume, and, for the first time, the chorale moves to cellos (the later revision rejoins the original at this point). The two elements gradually disperse and fade. The opening whirlwind returns, and the reprise has arrived (in the revision Bruckner cuts the introductory whirlwind, so that the fortissimo reprise enters without warning).

After the two familiar build-ups, the second theme with its polka and chorale once again makes its leisurely progress through various keys. Then the third element follows, with its heavy syncopations and dotted rhythms. The harmonies take a new twist, a quiet passage ends calmly in D major, and there is another silence. Now the opening theme bursts in once more to announce the beginning of the final coda. This time, the harmonies firmly establish D minor, and then ratchet up semitone by semitone. The trumpets inject the call from the opening of the symphony.

Again we reach a sudden silence, and a moment of quiet meditation. Bruckner remembers fragments of the earlier movements – the second theme of the first movement, the first theme of the Adagio, the opening of the scherzo. This is homage to Beethoven in the finale of his Ninth Symphony, though the effect here is quite different – reflective rather than searching. For the last time, the full orchestra breaks into fortissimo, with the syncopations of the third theme, and a dramatic struggle to find resolution. This culminates in a cadence on full brass into D major, and all the uncertainties of the past hour are resolved as the trumpets declaim the call from the beginning of the first movement, *fff*, to bring this troublesome symphony to a glorious conclusion.

SYMPHONY NO. 4 IN E FLAT MAJOR, 'ROMANTIC'
Duration: approx. 66 minutes

(Tempo indications in 1880 score)

Bewegt, nicht zu schnell (animated, not too fast)

Andante, quasi allegretto

Scherzo: Bewegt (animated) – Trio: Nicht zu schnell (not too fast)

Finale: Bewegt, doch nicht zu schnell (animated, but not too fast)

Bruckner composed a first version of this Symphony in 1874. But his continuing dissatisfaction with it resulted in two major revisions over the next fourteen years. Arguments have raged about which version should be performed, but it is now widely accepted that the score of 1888 represents his most complete intentions, even though two pupils, Ferdinand Löwe and Josef Schalk, helped him with it.

This is the only one of Bruckner's symphonies to which he himself gave a title, 'Romantic', in the autograph score of the earliest version. To audiences brought up in Austro-German culture, the title would immediately have suggested artistic associations – the poetry of Goethe, the songs of Schubert, the operas of Weber, the paintings of Caspar David Friedrich – with their evocation of the sublime, and humanity's place in a world of powerful natural forces. Over the years, Bruckner was reported to have revealed more specific ideas lying behind the music. For example, one friend passed on this account of the first movement: 'Medieval city – Daybreak – Morning calls sound from the city towers – the gates open – On proud horses the knights burst out into the open, the magic of nature envelops them – forest murmurs – birdsong – and so the Romantic picture develops further ...'[7] This encompasses another theme of German Romanticism, medieval chivalry (as in Wagner's *Lohengrin*), though, as the end of that quote suggests, such specific images are not to be taken too literally.

Over a soft string tremolando chord of E flat major a horn calls and is answered by woodwind. The music grows in strength and a new line appears, ascending and descending in a determined two-plus-three pattern that was to recur again and again in Bruckner's symphonies. A grand fortissimo arises and comes to a conclusion on chords of F major. Horns hold the note F to lead in the second theme, a perky tune in D flat major (a very Schubertian change of key). Bruckner revealed that this melody was suggested not just by birdsong in general, but specifically by the call of the great tit. Against this theme is a singing countermelody in the violas. The music builds to a joyful passage that incorporates the descending figure from the opening, now in a straightforward striding rhythm, and further musing on the birdsong culminates in a grand reappearance of the original two-plus-three rhythm. Further peaks and troughs climax in a blazing brass call, and birdsong and its countermelody take the first section of the movement to a resolution over a sustained B flat and timpani roll.

Muted strings and new chromatic twists give the descending line an air of mystery. Then the opening horn call reappears quietly, and twice the music builds to powerful climaxes. The second time, a sudden quiet tremolo and the horn call suggest that we may be into the reprise. But we are not yet in the home key, and the journey has further diversions ahead. Once more trumpets and trombones enter fortissimo in the rhythm of the horn call, but now changed into a chorale. This fades away to a melancholy, rather Wagnerian meditation on the countermelody to the birdsong theme. It reaches a moment of intense calm, out of which the opening horn call reappears in the home key of E flat, accompanied by *ppp* arpeggios on flute and violins. This really is the reprise. After the familiar elements have been revisited, Bruckner delays the conclusion with a quiet and mysterious passage, interrupted by another burst of brass. Eventually, the horn again enters with its call, in the remote key of E major. This galvanizes the full force of the orchestra, a corner is turned back to the home key, and the movement ends with all four horns proclaiming their call magnificently.

Bruckner often evokes the spirit of Schubert, nowhere more specifically than in the slow movement of this symphony. Muted strings begin a tentative walk, as if stepping into the snow. Below, cellos sing a sorrowful melody in C minor that begins with the falling fifth of the horn call from the first movement, then rises phrase by phrase. This is surely Bruckner's homage to the trudging slow movement of Schubert's Piano Trio in E flat (which in turn is a companion of the walking song that opens his *Winterreise*). As the walk fades, the strings play a warm chorale, with interpolations of a dotted rhythm from the walking song keeping up the momentum. This too fades, and, surrounded by pizzicato chords, the violas sing a melody that seems as if it will never end – like a monk whose prayers are continually wandering to thoughts of the landscape outside. This drifts to a conclusion, and the full strings enter, no longer muted. They step out more confidently, now in A flat major, with the firm dotted rhythms in the bass. After a while, Bruckner combines three melodies in counterpoint, with the walking tune in the horn. This opens up warmly, with a spring in its step – one can hear how this vein of pastoral delight looks back to Beethoven and forward to Mahler – and the music rises to a glorious climax, then subsides to the reprise of the opening theme. This has plangent interventions from the woodwind, and moves straight on to the third theme, the wandering viola melody, without the intervening chorale. After a cadence of deep trombone chords, the opening theme returns once more, with an echo in flute and oboe and faster running patterns in the violins, creating a complex texture. Twice this rises to a fortissimo, the second climax blazing higher and for longer than the first. The end of the movement is quiet and sombre. Timpani beat out the tread of the walking theme, making it seem more like a funeral march, and a few fragments and pizzicato chords bring the movement to a close.

Bruckner's first version of the symphony included a third movement far too massive to sound like a scherzo. In his revision of 1878–80 he replaced it with an entirely new scherzo which he described as 'depicting a hunt'. Like the first movement, it opens with horns over a quiet tremolo. But now they are playing hunting calls that incorporate Bruckner's favourite two-plus-three rhythm. Trumpets and trombones join in the chase, with sudden switches of key and swift crescendos from pianissimo to fortissimo, as if groups in different parts of the forest are answering each other and then converging. The strings introduce a wistful second element, though not quite a new theme. In the second half of the scherzo, this wistful element predominates, at a slightly slower tempo, until the mood lightens and an acceleration leads to the reprise.

The trio is in the easy-going tempo of a *Ländler* and, according to Bruckner, represents 'a dance played by a huntsman on a hurdy-gurdy during lunch'.[8] The characteristic sound of the hurdy-gurdy is cleverly suggested by the combination of a drone bass and pizzicato chords. The melody is somewhat like a folk tune, but its sophisticated changes of key make it seem more like a nostalgic reminiscence rather than the thing itself. The scherzo is repeated unchanged apart from a few clangorous bars to round it off.

Bruckner made three attempts at a finale, and it is the third version of 1880, with or without a few later tweakings, that is most often played. The opening is sombre. A horn calls, as in the first movement, but in a dark B flat minor over an ominously repeated bass note. The call itself, from being a simple rise and fall of a fifth, has become a falling octave that then droops down a semitone – not at all like a traditional horn call. It is taken up by other instruments and becomes more insistent, cutting across the two-in-a-bar metre. The horns remember the two-plus-three hunting rhythm from the scherzo, and a crescendo leads to a stark declaration in massive octaves, in E flat minor, bringing together a version of the new horn call with the two-plus-three rhythm. A stormy passage struggles to throw off this threat, and eventually triumphs with a ringing declaration in E flat major of the original horn call, with its simple fifths restored. A second theme looks back to the opening of the slow movement, in the same key, C minor, with melancholy phrases in counterpoint over a steadily walking bass. The music moves into the major, with an increase in pace and energy, once again almost Mahlerian in its evocation of delight in nature (though it also evokes memories of Schubert's song, 'Ganymed', with the young boy bounding through the woods and being swept up by Zeus). There is a sudden outburst from the full orchestra, back in the severe B flat minor in which the movement opened. But when the onslaught is over, the Mahlerian-pastoral mood returns, and a tender little passage brings the first section of the movement to a close.

The development begins by returning to the opening in B flat minor, with the horn calls rising instead of falling. The key shifts constantly, until, in F sharp major, horns and trombones declaim a heroic chorale version of the stark octaves from the first climax of the movement. Again the pastoral mood is restored, the walking bass returns, and there is another massive interruption. This is the central crisis of the movement, with the brass raising the stark octave declaration upwards step by step, like Titans heaving mighty boulders, until a heroic climax fades into dark rumination and uncertainty. Again the full brass break in, with a renewal of the stark octaves in the home key of E flat (though minor at this point), and we are into the reprise. The second theme blossoms into pastoral delight and fades into a moment of stillness. The end is in sight. Over the dark shimmering of the strings, the horn call quietly sounds, simultaneously falling in the horns and rising in the woodwind. This is one of many of Bruckner's endings that owe their inspiration to the final build-up of the first movement of Beethoven's Ninth Symphony, greatly enlarged by the influence of Wagner's gigantic visions. Despite many a climax in Bruckner's later symphonies, there is no more sure-footed conclusion than this, as the power builds gradually and inexorably to a final glorious chord of E flat major.

SYMPHONY NO. 5 IN B FLAT MAJOR
Duration: approx. 75 minutes

Introduction: Adagio – Allegro
Adagio: Sehr langsam (Very slow)
Scherzo: Molto vivace (Schnell) (Fast)
Finale: Adagio – Allegro moderato

Bruckner composed his Fifth Symphony between February 1875 and May 1876. He later revised it (though not as radically as some of his other symphonies), completing the revision in 1878. But Bruckner never heard it played by an orchestra. A performance on two pianos was given in Vienna in April 1887, but it was only in 1894 that the orchestral premiere took place in Graz, conducted by Bruckner's pupil Franz Schalk. Bruckner, whose health was steadily degenerating, was too ill to travel. Schalk had introduced cuts and re-orchestration, including percussion and an off-stage band. This was the version of the symphony that was first published in 1896. But Bruckner had no hand in the revisions, and it is his own version of 1878 that is accepted as representing his wishes, and is generally performed.

Bruckner began work on the symphony at a time of despair. He had moved to Vienna eight years earlier in the hope of establishing himself as a composer. But so far there was nothing to show for it, as he complained in a letter: 'It'll all end with my getting into debt, and finally enjoying *the fruits of my labours* by going to jail, where I can descant to my heart's content on my folly in ever coming to Vienna.'[9] That was written the day before he started work on the symphony. Against this background, the struggling power of this symphony is all the more striking. Nothing is easy, nothing evolves smoothly, and the music seems continually to encounter obstacles. The result is a symphony that some people regard as a masterpiece, but others find lacking coherence.

The symphony begins with a slow introduction, the only one in Bruckner's symphonies. A solemn pizzicato tread of cellos and basses descends and then rises. The upper strings enter one part at a time, creating a web of ecclesiastical counterpoint reminiscent of chorale preludes by J. S. Bach (which Bruckner, as an organist, frequently played). This comes to a halt, and, with an abrupt change of key, there is a fortissimo thrusting, upward figure on strings and woodwind, which alternates with a fragment of chorale on the brass, changing key at each alternation. It is the bass line of the chorale, on bass trombone and tuba, that is to prove important. The tempo now increases, and a new web of counterpoint builds up, as second violins and cellos call to each other with a figure taken from the chorale's bass line, now at double speed. Its dotted rhythms drive the music on, and a crescendo leads to a grand reassertion of the Adagio tempo, with what was the bass line now forming the melody of the chorale. This hint of splendours to come soon fades.

Seamlessly, we enter the Allegro. Beneath pianissimo shimmering violins, violas, and cellos quietly announce the principal theme. Its dotted rhythm makes the link to the introduction clear. At first it is smooth, then spiky. After a crescendo, the theme is briefly taken up by the full orchestra, before fading away to a new pizzicato idea. The violins sing a sombre melody that rises and then falls back, in a series of phrases that seem unable to sustain themselves. Eventually it sinks down, giving way to arpeggios on clarinet and flute, which accompany sighing phrases in the horns. The violins make another attempt at their sombre melody, which once again falls back, its final phrases now troubled by syncopation. Woodwind introduce yet another melodic shape, under which the violins continue their syncopations, and cellos and basses play a dotted-rhythm phrase that refer back to earlier themes. Twice the music builds to fortissimo brass entries and falls back. Now the dotted-rhythm figure in the bass doubles in speed, and this leads to an energetic climax, with the dotted rhythms declaimed in octaves by the whole orchestra.

There is a sudden hush, the dotted-rhythm figure halves in speed again, and as it passes from instrument to instrument, changing key as it goes, we enter the central development section of the movement. This begins with a reminiscence of the Adagio introduction, with its ecclesiastical counterpoint, pizzicato bass, and thrusting upward figure. The Allegro tries to break in, and is pushed aside. When it does reassert itself, the principal theme predominates, moving between treble and bass, and played in counterpoint. Then it is combined with the thrusting figure from the introduction, building to a passage of great determination, welcome in a movement that has struggled to gain momentum. The second pizzicato idea is recalled, first on horns, then woodwind, and only then pizzicato. The brass chorale bursts in, as we first heard it, with the important dotted rhythm in the bass (though in a different key). Then a build-up leads to the reprise of the first Allegro theme. This arrives more quickly than before at the second, sombre violin melody. Once again, syncopations develop the energy to build to a climax. But this too is cut off abruptly. The pizzicato resumes, now in a more agitated pattern than before, and the music soon builds again. The thrusting upward figure is once more combined with the principal theme. After further moments of hesitation and doubt, the music suddenly finds its way back to B flat major, and to a splendid, but brief, reassertion of the home key.

The Adagio second movement, like the first, begins with quiet pizzicato, this time for all the strings. They outline the first four bars of a theme in D minor, then a solo oboe fills out that theme, cutting across the rhythm of the strings – the strings play three notes to the slow beat, the oboe plays two. The first two bars of the oboe's melody are smooth, but the third bar alternates widely spaced notes – high, low, high, low – and this is to be an important melodic shape as the movement proceeds. The woodwind, and then the strings, extend the theme, but it soon becomes wayward, and falters. Now the strings enter confidently, all using their bows for the first time, with a characteristically hymn-like theme. This too breaks off after a few bars. The opening phrase of the new theme leads off a passage of counterpoint, first delicately, and then increasing in power to a climax at which the trumpets take over the phrase.

After four bars of fortissimo, there is yet another sudden hush. Woodwind return to the opening oboe theme, with pizzicato below, and the cross-rhythms as before. This is the beginning of the middle section of the movement. After a few bars, the theme moves to the bass, while violins introduce a faster counterpoint above (six notes per beat – a further rhythmic complication). This develops into an extended passage that is full of stark contrasts, at one moment suddenly blazing fortissimo, the next echoing quietly. For a time, the widely spaced intervals are dominant, underlining a sense of struggle. Then the hymn-like second theme returns in the strings, now in the minor, and leads to a further build-up. But there is no real sense of a goal achieved, and the music again falters. Woodwind and horn enter with the reprise of the opening oboe melody, accompanied once more by a six-notes-per-beat violin counterpoint. It seems that we might finally be building to a real climax, but again the fortissimo is short-lived. The rest of the movement returns to the pattern of alternating blazes and whispers, until the music dissolves into pizzicato with fragments of the first theme above.

The third movement is a scherzo in rapid three-time, but a very unusual one. Throughout the nineteenth century, a scherzo had continued to be generally dance-like, not only in its metre, but also in its structure, with divisions into clear sections. Bruckner's beloved Schubert had extended it, Mendelssohn had given it a fluid and mercurial character. But Bruckner here presents a sort of deconstruction of a scherzo, as if, like the other movements of the symphony, it is struggling to find coherence – an approach that Mahler was to develop further. The strings begin quietly with the same pattern of notes that opened the slow movement, but now very fast, and played with bowed staccato instead of pizzicato. Over this pattern, woodwind play a snatch of melody that is almost like an elaboration of the oboe's theme from the slow movement. There is a rapid crescendo to full orchestra. But just as the music seems to be getting going, it comes to a halt. At a slower tempo, the strings play a new melody with the yodelling intervals of a *Ländler* (the opening pattern is now in the bass). The full orchestra joins in briefly, then the music accelerates back to the original tempo. It seems that the first theme will reappear. But instead fragments from it lead off in different directions, with persistent cross-rhythms, together with a new pattern of alternating high and low notes that again refers back to the slow movement. The music sinks down to *ppp* with a timpani roll.

In the second half of the scherzo ideas are developed further, moving into new keys. Again, there is a halt and change of gear, and the slower *Ländler* reappears. This time there is no acceleration. The *Ländler* hesitates and stops. The strings quietly begin the reprise of the opening. At first it proceeds as before, but then takes a new turn to end with a brief burst of brilliant D major – one of those moments of quickly snatched fulfilment that seem so difficult to achieve in this symphony.

A horn note announces the beginning of the trio. Flute, oboe, and clarinet play disjointed little phrases in two-time, as if trying out the steps of an unfamiliar dance. These phrases are in B flat major, but the horn note (G flat) keeps on pulling away from the key. Cellos and basses answer with the same tune upside down, and the key drifts around uncertainly. Just for a moment, the upside-down tune settles into a comfortable dance rhythm, and in a solid G major. Once again, the moment is short-lived, and the first strain of the trio ends in F major. The music continues with further tentative exploration. The opening dance steps return, to be answered with sudden savagery by trumpets and trombones. But eventually, the dance manages to settle in B flat – the key it was attempting to establish at the start of the trio.

Bruckner then repeats the whole of the scherzo, with all its sudden shifts of mood and tempo. Repeating the scherzo is conventional. But Bruckner's trio is so short (about two minutes) and the scherzo so long (about five minutes) that the trio seems like the briefest of moments in the middle of a somewhat bewildering search for a scherzo.

References to earlier themes were elusive in the scherzo, but at the beginning of the finale they become explicit, as if Bruckner is remembering the opening of the choral finale of Beethoven's Ninth Symphony. The movement opens as the first movement did, with pizzicato below and Bach-like counterpoint above. But as it proceeds, a clarinet plays a quiet, staccato falling octave, which turns out to be a portent of what is to come. The counterpoint softly comes to a close, and the clarinet loudly repeats the falling octave, linking it with a reminiscence of the dotted rhythms of the first movement. The strings ignore this interruption, and continue with a reminder of the first movement's Allegro theme. Again the clarinet interrupts. The strings remember the opening of the second movement. Two clarinets repeat their disruptive phrase. These interruptions have an unexpectedly cheeky effect – if this were Shostakovich, it would unleash one of his bitterly ironic passages. But irony is not in Bruckner's character, and he has a more straightforwardly serious purpose.

With heavy emphasis, cellos and basses take up the clarinet phrase and launch a passage of counterpoint. This soon peters out, giving way to a graceful second theme, whose rising intervals bear a distinct resemblance to the *Ländler*-like second theme of the scherzo. This is developed with warmth and delicacy, until the trumpets and trombones break in with a half-speed statement of the clarinets' phrase. This too fades away. Now the full brass solemnly intone a chorale fortissimo, answered quietly by strings (this has echoes of Mendelssohn's treatment of a Bach chorale in his *Hymn of Praise*). The music reaches a moment of expectancy. A horn plays the chorale theme, which is taken up by violas, with a countermelody in the woodwind. This is the start of a section in which the chorale theme is brought together with the livelier dotted rhythms of the clarinet theme to create a massive passage of fugue – in effect, a fugal development section. It reaches a climax, and is followed by a reprise of the graceful second theme. Now we are into the final stretch of the symphony, in which the clarinet theme is brought together with the theme from the first movement Allegro. After several attempts to build a climax, the full brass transform the clarinet theme into a grand statement. The chorale returns and is extended in a final blaze, at last bringing fulfilment to the long struggle that has dogged the whole symphony.

SYMPHONY NO. 6 IN A MAJOR
Duration: approx. 58 minutes

Maestoso
Adagio: Sehr feierlich (very solemn)
Scherzo: Nicht schnell (not fast)
Finale: Bewegt, doch nicht zu schnell (animated, but not too fast)

Bruckner started work on his Sixth Symphony immediately after finishing his String Quintet in the summer of 1879. As usual, he returned to it over a long period, during which he was also writing other works, and it was not until two years later, in September 1881, that he completed the score. The first performance, in a heavily cut and edited version, was conducted by Gustav Mahler in Vienna in 1899. A complete performance was given two years later in Stuttgart, conducted by Karl Pohlig, but it was not until 1935 that an edition based on Bruckner's complete autograph score was published.

The Sixth Symphony is a more compact and concentrated work than the fifth. Unlike the Fifth Symphony, which struggles to find momentum, the sixth opens with immediate self-confidence. The violins start a quiet, driving figure of a dotted rhythm and a fast triplet, beneath which cellos and basses declare a bold theme, firmly in A major for its first two notes, but then immediately exploring the possibility of other keys. The theme's broader triplet rhythm cuts against the regular pulse of the violins' pattern (did Mahler remember this opening when beginning his Second Symphony?). The continuation of this theme breaks into energetic dotted rhythms. Already, Bruckner has put forward the elements that will fuel the drive of this movement. The full brass enter, and the theme becomes a ringing declaration, with the accompanying rhythm set up by the violins continuing persistently. A sudden quiet brings in a second theme in E minor, which is a little slower. Under the violin melody, with its dotted rhythms now taking on a solemn character, the bass rhythm has three notes to each long beat. At first these conflicting rhythms coexist, but as the theme develops, the triplet rhythm becomes predominant, at times taking on an almost waltz-like swing. As the brass enter again, the rhythm is re-energized with dotted rhythms. The first section of the movement ends quietly with a flute gently murmuring fast triplet arpeggios, which continue into the development section.

The first theme is turned upside down, with its first interval rising an octave, and is echoed at a distance of half a bar, in an informal canon. This echoing persists as the trumpets enter, and then as the dotted-rhythm continuation takes over. All the while, the triplet accompaniment underpins these changing events. The energy builds up to a magnificent brass statement of the opening theme, at first in E flat major (far from the home key), but soon wrenching the harmony back to A major for the *fff* reprise. After the themes have run their course, the music builds in a series of waves, powered by the broad triplets from the opening theme, and driven on by the constant energy of the faster triplet accompaniment, until it reaches a blazing conclusion.

The slow movement will end serenely in F major, but for most of its quarter of an hour the home key is uncertain. The very first note is F, but the key of the opening theme seems at first to be in a much darker B flat minor (echoing the doubts cast on A major at the beginning of the first movement). The violin melody leaps downwards and then ascends gently, while the bass treads solemnly downwards. As the opening phrase recurs, an oboe plays a plangent little counterpoint that includes a dotted-rhythm motif from the first movement. The first climax comes and goes, by now in D minor. The four horns quietly turn a corner, and the strings play a second theme in E major (a long way, harmonically, from F and B flat minor). The cellos play the opening shape of the new theme, and the violins follow a beat later, halving the speed, and this contributes to a feeling of Wagnerian richness. At the same time, the opening of this theme is closely related to the first theme, with its leap downwards followed by gentle ascent. The music rises to a second climax, and falls away. Now the violins play a third theme, whose solemn dotted rhythms over a pizzicato bass evoke the character of a funeral march (this theme has features in common with the oboe's counterpoint right at the beginning of the movement). This theme is in C minor – distant again from the preceding E major.

When the funeral march has ebbed away, a horn repeats the opening phrase of the first theme in different keys, while the woodwind play the descending line that was originally in the bass and the violas supply a new counterpoint. This is the start of a brief development section that climaxes and falls back, brought to a close by the sighing phrases of an oboe. As two horns take up the reprise of the first theme, the sighing phrases reveal themselves to be the start of the oboe counterpoint from the opening. The theme and counterpoint then swap, the counterpoint taken by horns while the theme moves to the woodwind. During this passage, the strings keep up a more complex web of accompaniment, and these elements build to the biggest climax of the movement. When the second theme returns, it is now in the home key of F major – the first time the key has been established for more than a few notes at a time. But it too soon moves away, through a warm climax, to arrive at the third, funereal theme in F minor. The rest of the movement gently finds its way to the home key, first meditating on a rising motif from the second theme, over a timpani roll and a persistently repeated C in the bass, until this resolves onto a sustained F. Tender reminiscences of the elements that made up the first theme bring the movement to a close.

The scherzo is in a firm three-time, 'not fast', but there is a great deal of pent-up energy in its rhythms. Over the steady but quiet staccato beat in the bass, second violins and violas play a delicate, staccato triplet figure, answered by the woodwind, while the first violins throw incisive little fragments into the air. This explodes in a sudden fortissimo, in which trombones cut across the triplets with a descending phrase in duple rhythm. The key of the movement, A minor, is hinted at in these opening bars, but not stated unequivocally. The pattern is repeated, at greater length, and with exploration into new keys, until the first half of the scherzo climaxes in unambiguous chords of E major. The second half of the scherzo moves into warmer major keys, until a fortissimo outburst leads to the reprise of the opening. The scherzo ends with the full orchestra *fff* in chords of A major, just as the first half ended in E major. These are the only two moments of certainty in a movement that, like the first, spends much of the time searching for a key.

The trio is dominated by three horns who, at each appearance, begin with hunting calls in a firm C major, but then slide sideways into a warmer A flat major. This shift of key was a favourite of Schubert, but the trio of horns surely pays homage to Beethoven in the 'Eroica' Symphony. The woodwind answer the horns with a quotation from Bruckner's own Fifth Symphony. The certainty of the horn calls is surrounded, once again, by uncertainty of key, with the strings beginning tentatively and pizzicato. After the trio, the scherzo is repeated.

The first three movements have been characterized by a sense of searching – particularly for a stable key – but have been successfully driven forward with a balancing sense of confidence. In the finale, the confidence is under threat, and Bruckner struggles for coherence rather as he did in the Fifth Symphony. Opinion varies as to whether this finale is therefore a little weak after the preceding movements, or whether the fight for coherence gives it particular power.

The opening, with its quietly scrubbing tremolo in the violas and pizzicato descending bass, has a mood of urgent expectancy, evoking the stormy opening of Wagner's *Die Walküre*. This, like the scherzo, begins in A minor, but the violins' anxious descending line has phrases that end uncertainly. The brass burst in assertively, as if to bring the music firmly back to A major. But they too soon pull away with menacing, sliding phrases towards a darker B flat minor, first fortissimo, then pianissimo (this is the key in which the slow movement began). Another outburst, with dotted rhythms reminiscent of the first movement, wrenches the music to chords of E major, and a short-lived moment of triumph. There follows a delicate, charming second theme in the strings, in C major – another instance of that Schubert-like shift down a third to a warmer key. This is extended at some length, with Bruckner's characteristic counterpoint interweaving three different melodic shapes simultaneously.

We are by now in the central development section of the movement. Eventually the music builds up to another brief outburst of the brass's sliding phrase. Oboes and clarinets respond delicately with the dotted-rhythm motif, as if innocently unaware of the forces threatening them. The brass resume their menace, more insistently than before. Now it is the strings that innocently take up the dotted-rhythm motif, pursuing it in a passage that culminates, like the earlier brass entry, in a momentarily confident E major. At this point, the mood suddenly changes, and the tempo slows. In a spirit of lament, the cellos recall the descending opening theme (evoking memories of King Mark in Wagner's *Tristan*). The woodwind answer questioningly with the dotted-rhythm motif, over pizzicato. The strings play a melody that rises confidently, in contrast to their falling first theme. But despite another brief moment of confidence, the search for stability continues from key to key, and soon the descending line reasserts itself. With a sudden blast, the full brass enter with their dotted-rhythm fanfare, the strings respond anxiously, the brass repeat the fanfare in another key. Now the menacing shape reappears, at first in a solo horn. A mighty passage for full orchestra develops, with moments when some sort of resolution seems possible, only for the music to shift key yet again.

Out of this turmoil emerges the strings' delicate second theme, now in the home key of A major, and we realize that we are into the reprise, having sidestepped the first theme. After a time, the strings once more take up the dotted-rhythm motif, at first innocently, and then with more and more persistence as the music builds. There is a moment of hesitation, as oboe and clarinet delicately twist the dotted-rhythm motif over almost *Tristan*-like harmony. The strings continue their quest, as the harmonies lighten (though not yet in the home key), the music builds, and again halts. The opening returns, with the tremolando violas and pizzicato descending bass. But over it, instead of the violins' descending line, oboe and clarinet remember the menacing, sliding motif. Suddenly, the brass enter, in the home key of A major, and with dotted rhythms in full blaze. There is a last attempt to wrench the harmony away, but the home key is back, *fff*, and the work swiftly comes to a close, with trombones punching out the opening theme of the symphony in the unambiguous A major that has so long been elusive.

SYMPHONY NO. 7 IN E MAJOR
Duration: approx. 65 minutes

Allegro moderato
Sehr feierlich und sehr langsam (very solemn and very slow)
Scherzo: Sehr schnell (very fast) – Trio: Etwas langsamer (somewhat slower) – Scherzo da capo
Bewegt, doch nicht schnell (animated, but not too fast)

Bruckner began this symphony immediately after finishing the sixth, in September 1881. As usual, work was interrupted by other compositions, and it was not until September 1883 that he completed it. While he was writing the symphony, Bruckner visited Bayreuth for the first performance of Wagner's *Parsifal*. This was the last time Bruckner met Wagner, who is reported to have declared that Bruckner was the only composer of symphonies who measured up to Beethoven. Wagner also promised to conduct all of Bruckner's symphonies, a promise that was never fulfilled (even if he intended to carry it out), because Wagner died a few months later, in February 1883. Bruckner heard of Wagner's death while he was working on the Adagio of his symphony. He added a solemn ending to the movement 'in memory of the immortal and dearly beloved master who has departed this life'. The premiere in December 1884 in Leipzig's Gewandhaus was conducted by Arthur Nikisch, to raise money for a memorial to Wagner. Despite Hanslick's review, which described the work as 'a symphonic boa constrictor', the audience was enthusiastic, and the second performance, under Hermann Levi in Munich the following March, was a triumph. After all his struggles, Bruckner had finally achieved acclaim, at the age of sixty.

We do not have to wait until the Adagio to be reminded of Wagner. Under a shimmering violin tremolo, cellos and a horn open the symphony with a rising arpeggio of E major, evoking memories of the River Rhine at dawn at the beginning of *Das Rheingold*. This is just the opening gesture of a long, winding melody, which immediately begins to explore other keys before returning to E major. The theme moves to violins and woodwind, with the shimmering accompaniment below. Then oboe and clarinet introduce a second theme, which rises gently, with an elegant little turn and charmingly hesitant dotted rhythms. This melody is even more unstable in key than the first, with a series of phrases each a tone lower than the last. The theme is developed at some length, until the violins turn it upside down. Now it builds, with its dotted rhythms insistently repeated, to the first climax of the symphony. It breaks off, to give way to the third theme, pianissimo. This has a persistent, dogged rhythm, not quite like a dance, with a descending counterpoint on woodwind. Gradually the music builds to another climax, culminating in a mighty brass fanfare, then quickly fades away as the persistent dance-like phrases take us close to the world of Beethoven's 'Pastoral' Symphony.

The landscape empties for the beginning of the development. The opening arpeggio on clarinets, now falling rather than rising, alternates with an unaccompanied flute attempting to keep the dance-rhythm going. This passage has an almost Mahlerian sparseness. Cellos reminisce about the second theme, in its descending version, developing it into a passionate lament. After a moment of quiet, the full orchestra suddenly enters fortissimo in a solemn minor key, taking up the arpeggio theme. After this outburst, the music gradually works its way back to E major.

The opening theme, now in its original form, rises on cellos and a quiet trumpet, as a mirror-version descends in violins and oboe. The second and third themes follow, in varied shape and orchestration, reaching a climax that descends and fades away to a low E. Over a long drum roll, cellos and violas for a last time revisit the searchings of the first theme. They sink back, and trombones enter with a pianissimo chord of E major. The familiar, Wagnerian arpeggios, accompanied by faster, shimmering arpeggios in the violins, build up to a final, great climax.

The slow movement expresses homage not only to Wagner but also, more subtly, to Beethoven. As in Beethoven's Ninth Symphony, two themes alternate, the first solemn and in four-time, the second more flowing, and in three-time. The first sound we hear is a quartet of Wagner tubas – the instruments, combining characteristics of French horn and trombone, designed for Wagner, which he used to evoke the gods' palace of Valhalla in *The Ring*. They play a four-bar lament in C sharp minor of noble solemnity. The strings answer forcefully, with a determined, rising phrase. To Bruckner, a deeply religious man, this determination probably had more than musical significance. The same rising phrase figures prominently in the last section of his setting of the Te Deum, composed in tandem with the symphony, to the words, 'Let me not be confounded in eternity'. The theme extends, trying to find a way forward through characteristic moments of hesitation. It subsides, and gives way to the second theme in F sharp major. The reference here to the equivalent theme in Beethoven's great Adagio is very clear: not only does the tempo and metre change in the same way, but the offbeat opening phrase directly evokes Beethoven's melody. Violins lead the melody on, until it in turn subsides, and the Wagner tubas enter again with their lament. This time, the rising answer leads to a much longer exploration through different keys. It culminates in a stubborn reiteration of the rising phrase, each time in a different key – E flat, A flat, E, F, F sharp – until the trumpets enter, and the theme is released into a brief blaze of G major. The second theme returns, now in A flat major. Just as it seems to be embarking on another lengthy exploration, it pauses, and another moment of searching leads to the re-entry of the Wagner tubas with their lament, back in the original key of C sharp minor. This time they are accompanied by a swirling pattern in the violins, which persists through the rising answer and beyond. Inexorably, the power builds, and the harmonies progress with new confidence (the way they progress makes the link with the Te Deum absolutely clear). With a final wrench, the climax burst out in a glorious C major – perhaps the greatest climax in all of Bruckner's symphonies, overwhelming partly because the music has travelled so far (harmonically speaking) from the C sharp minor in which the movement began. The cymbal clash that marks the high point in most performances was suggested to Bruckner by his pupils after he had finished the symphony, but he seems to have given his consent. The climax fades, the harmony again moves sideways, and the Wagner tubas quietly take up the rising phrase. But it too has now been taken into a dark C sharp minor, as we enter the coda that Bruckner composed in memory of Wagner. Tragic power is followed by a moment of bleakness and a last statement of the tubas' lament, before the movement ends on a major chord, bringing a final note of consolation.

The first two movements are each twenty or more minutes long, and the slow movement is the emotional core of the symphony. The third and fourth movements are shorter and less intense, perhaps a relief after the outpouring of the slow movement. The rugged scherzo in A minor is built from three motifs. During the scherzo itself, the first two predominate: the reiterated figure with which the strings begin, and the cheerful fanfare played first by a trumpet. After the fanfare, the violins play a third ingredient, a phrase that descends with little leaps. From a quiet opening, the movement rises to fortissimo, and the dotted rhythms of the fanfare show their affinity to Wagner's 'Ride of the Valkyries'. The second half of the scherzo ventures into new keys, and the violins' leaping motif is for a time predominant (there is something quite Elgar-like about this idea and the way it is used, its liveliness tinged with melancholy). After another build-up, the opening returns.

The trio is in a slower tempo. Apart from occasional reminders of the dotted rhythms from the timpani, scarcely anything remains of the dance. The music sings throughout – closer to Wagner's *Siegfried Idyll* than to the traditional trio of a scherzo, and at times taking us back to the searching harmonic twists of the first two movements. After the trio, the scherzo is repeated.

The finale opens quietly, in a manner similar to the opening of the first movement. Beneath shimmering tremolo, violins play a theme with a rising arpeggio which, with its sharply dotted rhythms, sounds as if it has developed from the cheeky fugue subject of the finale of the Fifth Symphony. A second theme is simple and chorale-like, but each phrase has a harmonic shift that gives it a melancholy tinge. After this has been extended and repeated, there is a sudden outburst. The full orchestra, in bare octaves, transforms the opening theme into a stark, abrupt declaration. The first section comes to a quiet end.

The development begins peacefully, with fragments of the opening theme falling instead of rising, interspersed with bars of the chorale and moments of counterpoint. The full orchestra again bursts in with stark octaves. There is a dramatic silence, and, as if nothing has happened, we return to the chorale, with new touches of counterpoint. Is this the reprise? Bruckner makes that uncertain. It is only after another climax that the first theme quietly reappears in its original key (E major). Now we really are home, and the music builds up to the final blaze, ending with a glorious rising arpeggio, the fulfilment of the symphony's opening bars.

SYMPHONY NO. 8 IN C MINOR
Duration: approx. 80 minutes

Allegro moderato
Scherzo: Allegro moderato – Trio: Langsam (slow) – Scherzo da capo
Adagio: Feierlich langsam, doch nicht schleppend (solemnly slow, but not sleeping)
Finale: Feierlich, nicht schnell (solemn, not fast)

Bruckner worked on a first version of this symphony for three years, from 1884 to 1887. He then sent it to the conductor Hermann Levi, one of Bruckner's most dedicated supporters, who, after studying it, wrote to Bruckner's pupil, Josef Schalk: 'I am at my wits' end and I must appeal to you for advice and help. To put it briefly, I am completely at sea with Bruckner's Eighth Symphony, and haven't the courage to present it.' Levi was no doubt hoping that Schalk would break the news to Bruckner for him, but Schalk persuaded him that it would be better if Levi were to write to Bruckner himself. Levi did write to Bruckner, 'Dear and revered friend ...Never in my life have I found it so difficult to find the right words for what I need to say! But it can't be put off any longer...So: I find it impossible to perform the Eighth in its current form. I just can't make it my own! As much as the themes are magnificent and direct, their working-out seems to me dubious; indeed I consider the orchestration quite impossible ... Don't lose your courage, take another look at your work, talk it over with your friends, with Schalk, maybe a reworking can achieve something ... '[10] Levi's letter threw Bruckner into a state of dejection. But he soon set about revising the symphony and, by the following February, was able to write to Levi, 'I really ought to be ashamed of myself – at least on this occasion – about the Eighth. What an ass! It is already beginning to look quite different.' Bruckner completed a revised version, with the help of Josef Schalk, in 1890. Further revisions and cuts were later made by Schalk, and this was the version that was performed at the symphony's premiere in 1892. Modern performances generally follow the 1890 version (as edited by Nowak in 1955), or the Haas edition of 1935, which also includes elements from the 1887 original. The only substantial difference is in the Adagio, in which Haas restores an important passage that Bruckner later cut, though he also restores shorter, and less important, passages in the finale.

The premiere was conducted by Hans Richter on 18 December 1892 in Vienna, a city whose cosmopolitan audience was predominantly on the Brahms side of the Brahms–Wagner argument. For Bruckner, the most ardent of Wagnerites, this was unlikely to be a success to match the Leipzig premiere of the Seventh Symphony. Bruckner did not help matters by allowing his pupil, Josef Schalk, to supply the audience with a high-flown guide to the symbolism of the various themes in the symphony. This was perfect ammunition for the scathing Eduard Hanslick: 'we learned that the irksome humming theme of the first movement represents the figure of the Aeschylean Prometheus ... It was the composer himself who gave the scherzo the name of *Der deutsche Michl* ... With this authentic pronouncement before him, however, the commentator (Schalk) doesn't hesitate to find in the *Michl*-Scherzo "the deeds and sufferings of Prometheus reduced in parody to the smallest scale".' *Der deutsche*

Michel (or *Michl*) is a traditional embodiment of a German, whose character ranges from a naive victim of circumstances to a kind of peasant hero. It is quite plausible that Bruckner saw this figure as a reflection of himself, a simple man struggling to achieve great things, with overtones of the creator Prometheus. Hanslick also singles out Bruckner/Schalk's description of the Adagio as depicting 'the all-loving Father of Mankind in all His infinite mercy', and the finale as 'Heroism in the Service of the Divine'. Hanslick felt himself 'simply crushed under the sheer weight and monotony of this interminable lamentation' and 'the immediate juxtaposition of dry schoolroom counterpoint with unbounded exaltation'.[11] As with many another Viennese premiere, the audience was divided between Bruckner's enthusiastic supporters and the traditionalists, many of whom walked out during the performance.

Bruckner's earlier symphonies placed the greatest weight and length on the first and second movements, with the slow movement second. In the Eighth Symphony, Bruckner shifts that balance. The two shortest movements are first and second, with the scherzo second. The longest movements come third and fourth, with the deepest utterances reserved for the slow third movement. Bruckner's earlier first movements, with their massive triumphal climaxes, could almost function as finales. In the eighth, the opening movement could never be mistaken as anything but the beginning of a long journey. And although it contains big climaxes, there is no overwhelming triumph in them, and the movement ends quietly.

Under the familiar pianissimo tremolo, the lower strings embark on the brooding first theme. Hesitant utterances, separated by gaps, gradually rise higher and gain in confidence, ending with an emphatic descending shape that is to be important later. As at the beginning of the Third Symphony, there is more than a hint of the opening of Beethoven's Ninth, particularly in the rhythm, and, like Beethoven, Bruckner begins in the 'wrong' key. Indeed, there is no stable sense of key at all. A fleeting suggestion of the home key of C minor vanishes, and the music immediately moves off, searching without settling. The theme is repeated forcefully, building to a brief climax where, again, there is a moment of real C minor before the music subsides into doubt. A second theme rises warmly in G major, inverting the shape of the emphatic descent from the first theme, and with a yearning fall suggestive of *Tristan*. It moves to other keys, climaxes, and rounds off with an almost classical cadence. This theme is further extended, and then there is a third theme. This is a sombre, march-like melody in a minor key, intoned by horns and woodwind over triplet pizzicato (a very Mahlerian effect). It soon grows in force, and another climax is followed by a quiet reminder of the hesitant opening theme, bringing the first section of the movement to a close in a clear E flat major.

The development opens with fragments of the first theme – its drooping fall on Wagner tubas, and an upside-down version on violins and woodwind. Then the second theme is also inverted, falling instead of rising. Again it searches through different keys, and the tension builds to the greatest climax of the movement. As the harmonies twist powerfully above, the opening of the first theme is played in the bass, its final C emphasized by a burst of C major in the horns. Was this the reprise we have been waiting for? As the music moves off into further development of the theme, it is thrown into doubt. But then we arrive at the rising second theme, and it becomes clear that we really are into the reprise. The sombre, marching third theme follows, now in the home key of C minor, and builds to one last climax. This passage again suggests the final build-up of the first movement of Beethoven's Ninth. In his first version of the movement, Bruckner, like Beethoven, had ended with a further climax. But in his revision, unlike Beethoven, Bruckner puts the opportunity for powerful resolution on one side. Instead, he ends the movement by quietly reiterating the opening of the first theme, now over a sustained C in the bass. We are back in C, but this is just the end of the beginning.

After the dark ending of the first movement, the beginning of the scherzo is light and airy. Delicate shimmering phrases descend in the violins, beneath which cellos and violas set up a little one-bar motif that permeates the whole scherzo. Its swinging three-time, repeated endlessly, has an effect like church bells, at first heard in the distance, and then clanging fortissimo. Bruckner associated it with *Der deutsche Michel*, but the movement is predominantly joyful: it could be an Easter scene, though its mood swings also encompass the mysterious and the threatening. Violins over pizzicato begin the trio, with a lyrical melody whose opening phrase starts with yearning leaps and ends with a descent, reversing elements of the second theme of the first movement. A confident, almost military, climax develops, which dissolves into sweetly descending horn calls, accompanied by harps (Bruckner asks for three – this is the only symphony in which Bruckner includes harps). After a searching middle passage, the return of the melody again ends with the horn calls, and the scherzo is repeated.

The slow movement is the longest in the symphony, twice the length of the first movement, and is the emotional heart of the work. Over gently pulsating chords of D flat major, the violins begin a lament that shares elements of the opening theme of the first movement. It begins with hesitant phrases and then blossoms, first into a sorrowful descending line darkened by a bassoon an octave below, and then rising in an outburst. As this passage continues, the melody seems to want to pull the sustained bass note in a new direction, but it is unyielding. There is a sudden drop, with rich string chords that gradually soften, and only now the bass note changes. Enriched by harps, the melody ascends to an ecstatic moment. The opening theme returns, moves through different keys, and arrives again at an ecstatic conclusion. The cellos, joined by the violas, play a long, passionate new theme, whose opening phrase seems to have developed from the theme of the trio. Wagner tubas enter with a simpler, nobler phrase. This prompts the cellos to respond in kind, and to reach a powerful conclusion to their melody. A moment of contemplation for flutes, oboes, and clarinets leads to a reprise of the great opening violin theme, which immediately travels in new directions. It builds to the first great climax of the movement, which fades before any resolution.

Now the cellos and violas develop their second theme further, with more passion than before. There is a moment of almost dancing airiness, with violins and cellos in dialogue over pizzicato chords, and then the first theme returns for the last time. It is in the second violins, with first violins weaving a counterpoint above, and violas keeping up a quietly agitated accompaniment below, giving the theme a new momentum. It builds to a series of climaxes. At the first, horns quote Siegfried's motif from Wagner's *Ring*, and the full wind hammers out the opening phrase of the movement, its hesitancy now transformed into huge urgency. In Haas's restoration of a passage that Bruckner later cut, this subsides to a beautifully plangent transition to the next fortissimo. In Nowak's edition, representing Bruckner's later decision, the music cuts straight to that fortissimo, a less impressive effect. Either way, there are two more waves to go, before the movement reaches its final climax, and a cymbal crash. Now we are back at the sudden drop to rich string chords, and the harp-enriched moment of ecstasy. The violins quietly remember the cellos' second theme, the horns respond with the opening of the first theme, and, over warm tuba chords, the movement slowly unwinds in a mood of deep serenity.

The finale begins with the strings in a relentless gallop of repeated notes, which rapidly crescendo as if appearing over the horizon. Horns, trombones, and tuba enter with chords in a fierce pattern of dotted rhythms. Trumpets answer with fanfares. Then the theme is rounded off with brass chords in a stern descending phrase, and the galloping string figure gradually fades away. This passage suggests heroic escape from pursuit, and must surely have inspired Sibelius. At the same time, it seems to have grown out of the opening of the symphony, with its hesitant dotted rhythms that culminate in a descending line. And, as in the first movement, the key is at first unstable, only settling into C minor at the final, descending brass phrase. After a silence, a quiet second theme follows. This is a rather uncertain, extended interweaving of counterpoint, from which the descending line from time to time emerges. There is another silence followed by a third theme, a chant-like melody over a marching bass – clearly related to the third theme of the first movement. It begins to build to a climax, but is cut off. With a sudden change of key, the descending figure appears high over deep trombone and tuba chords, like a celestial vision. The music soon builds to a great blaze, announcing the end of the first section of the movement.

A quartet of horns gently reminisces about the dotted rhythms of the first theme, to lead into the development. A meditative passage culminates in three powerful statements of the descent that concluded the first theme, each one a tone higher than the last. There is further meditation on the theme and its rhythm, which all the time seems to be searching for a way back to the theme itself. Just as Bruckner is heading off in yet another direction, a corner is turned, the pace increases, and we are into the reprise, with its galloping strings and fierce brass chords. This time the struggle is longer. Three times the music reaches a blaze of *fff* brass, and then the quartet of horns leads in the second theme.

After a silence and a drum roll, the marching bass of the third theme appears, but with a new counterpoint instead of its chant-like melody. This gives the music new impetus, and a sudden crescendo leads to a mighty statement by trumpets and trombones of the first theme of the symphony, in the home key of C minor, and firmly secured to a thundering bass note of G. This is the breakthrough that finally opens out the route to a resolution. There is one last silence. Very quietly horns begin the final stage of the journey, with violins keeping up a gently insistent figure, and timpani tapping out a sombre beat. It is like an immense procession, or the progress of some great natural force. As it reaches a fortissimo, horns play a counterpoint of the scherzo's theme. In the last bars, Bruckner combines three themes in one huge fanfare: the scherzo on top, the Adagio's first theme in the middle, and, underpinning it all in the bass, the opening theme from the first movement. It is the end of this phrase that brings the symphony to a conclusion, hammered out in unison by the full orchestra.

SYMPHONY NO. 9 IN D MINOR
Duration: approx. 60 minutes

Feierlich, misterioso (solemn, mysterious)
Scherzo: Bewegt, lebhaft (animated, lively) – Trio: Schnell (fast) – Scherzo da capo
Adagio: Langsam, feierlich (slow, solemn)

Bruckner began work on his Ninth Symphony immediately after finishing the first version of his eighth in the summer of 1887. But although he was to live a further nine years, he never completed it. Having spent his whole working life battling against rejection and criticism, he became obsessed with revising his earlier works so as to give them the best possible chance of surviving after his death. He had completed three movements of the ninth by the end of 1894, but did not finish the finale. Substantial sketches survive (though others are now lost), and several attempts at completion have been published and recorded. Bruckner dedicated the symphony 'to beloved God – that is if he will accept it'.

Like the eighth, Bruckner's Ninth Symphony contains signs of homage to Beethoven's Ninth – how could it not? The key is Beethoven's, D minor, and it begins with quiet string tremolo, over which horns hesitantly try out the beginnings of a theme that then blossoms. But the manner in which it first does so, with distinctly Wagnerian twists of harmony, takes it a long way from Beethoven. A few bars later the theme builds to a massive *fff* statement, with the full orchestra in octaves. It then retreats to fragments in the woodwind over pizzicato. There is a characteristic silence, and the strings play a second theme, a singing melody in A major, with a beautifully lyrical countermelody. Gradually this rises, falls, and rises again, in expansive paragraphs. Bruckner then finds his way back to D minor (a strange thing to do so early in the movement) for a third theme. This has a solemn tread, a melody that begins with simple elaboration of the key chord – this gives it a clear relationship with the horn calls of the first theme.

As this reaches a climax then fades, we expect Bruckner to move on to a more or less conventional development section. But in this movement, the central section is more like a varied restatement of the opening two themes, during which new keys are explored. It begins with the fragmentary opening of the first theme, which twice reaches its Wagnerian bloom, though not the climactic statement in octaves. Over pizzicato strings, woodwind muse on a phrase taken from the third theme. After a silence, second violins play the countermelody of the second theme, now upside down. But the principal melody of the theme (also inverted) has been reduced to fragments that pass from oboe to horn, trumpet and flute. The energy builds and the tempo increases, until the full brass burst in with the climactic octaves of the opening theme, in the home key of D minor.

We are suddenly into the reprise. But Bruckner continues to develop and extend his material. The tempo drops to a march-like pace, the music builds again to the most urgent climax of the movement. It fades away, and a passage of solemn counterpoint leads into the reprise of the second theme, now with the principal melody on violas, and the countermelody above in the violins. The solemn third theme follows, and it too builds to a powerful climax. The woodwind play a delicate sequence of chords, followed by brass, and a timpani roll – this has distinct echoes of the equivalent point in Beethoven's Ninth, where a moment of calm precedes the final build-up. Over a held D in the bass, woodwind play the opening fragments of the first theme, while violins quietly reiterate a falling shape from the climax of that theme. The inevitable build-up culminates in massive octaves that rise and then fall decisively onto the keynote, D, and the movement ends with the stark power of D minor hammered home.

As in his Eighth Symphony (and as in Beethoven's Ninth), Bruckner places his scherzo second. It begins with mysterious chords and pizzicato. But soon this is overtaken by ferocious hammering of the keynote, D. This continues in the bass as a wrenchingly dissonant arpeggio descends, and then resolves into D minor to ascend. It is as if all the struggles to establish D minor in the first movement have been condensed into eight bars. Extremes alternate throughout the scherzo. Its second half begins with a charming oboe solo that is taken up by flute and clarinet. But the lightness of mood cannot be sustained, the tension soon builds, and the hammering returns. The violence and dissonance of this scherzo is new in Bruckner's music, and the trio is also very unusual. In earlier symphonies, Bruckner's trios have been slower than the scherzo. But this trio is in a faster three-time, with balletic lightness, and in a sunny major key. The tension rises, and the harmonies twist, but they culminate not in an outburst, but in nostalgic phrases in the violins, answered by oboe and clarinet. These are taken up at greater length in the second half of the trio, before the nimble opening returns. The scherzo is repeated, unchanged.

And so to Bruckner's last completed movement, the Adagio. Violins leap, overshooting the octave with poignant dissonance, and fall back. The line struggles upward, phrase by phrase, as string chords painfully try to find their way to some consonance. The resolution, when it comes, is a brief, shining chord of E major, the key of this movement. These seven bars could stand as a statement of Bruckner's entire life struggle and, more specifically, of his religious faith, filtered through the music of his greatest inspiration, Richard Wagner. There is no mistaking Bruckner's allusion to *Parsifal*, with its tortured harmonies evoking suffering (both of humanity and of Christ), and the serene motif associated with the Holy Grail, the cup from which Christ and his disciples drank at the Last Supper. In this Grail motif Wagner himself was quoting from the 'Dresden Amen', an eighteenth-century choral setting that was also quoted by Mendelssohn and others. So Bruckner, by putting this Amen at the heart of his final movement, alludes to his roots in German faith and culture. The moment of serenity is quickly over. Basses and cellos lead on into darkness. Forces gather, and trumpets call insistently over a chord that demands resolution, but does not get it. Instead, Wagner tubas gently descend towards the second theme. This is one of Bruckner's characteristically warm second themes, with a melody in violins accompanied by a countermelody below. String passages alternate with delicate, sorrowful woodwind. The strings rise passionately, the melody moves to the cellos, and four horns descend gently to a silence.

The first theme returns. This time, it is quietly repeated a tone higher, with a flute bleakly mirroring its shape. A sudden *ff* brass entry pronounces the rhythm of the opening theme, over a trudging bass line. The theme itself, with its leaping intervals, moves to cellos and basses. The tension mounts, until trumpets enter, over the same unresolving chord as before (now a tone higher). After a silence, we are back into the middle of the second theme. This rises higher, to another silence. Violins enter in the middle of the first theme, and this too rises to a climax, continuing with sorrowful woodwind, and another passionate entry from the strings. As the music moves forward, there is once again the sense of resolution being sought but not found. Suddenly, a trilling pattern in the second violins injects new anxiety, as the second theme returns over a pizzicato bass. The brass quietly enter, reducing the theme to a solemn procession of chords, and we begin to sense that forces are gathering for the final ascent. Yet the summit, when it appears, is no glorious release, but a discord more strident than previous unresolved climaxes. It breaks off, and out of the silence quiet tremolo and fragments of the first theme appear, like the 'still small voice' after the earth-quake and fire, with which God revealed himself to the prophet Elijah on the mountain. Gradually the music descends. In the final bars, Wagner tubas quote the first theme of Bruckner's Eighth Symphony, now drained of its sorrow, horns rise in a final arpeggio, like the opening of the Seventh Symphony, and the movement comes to an end on a serene chord of E major.

EMMANUEL CHABRIER
(1841–94)

Chabrier is a composer whose music is scarcely known today except for one or two concert pieces, but whose influence was profound. He earned his living as a civil servant until he was forty, composing in his spare time, and achieving little success with serious opera but rather more with operetta. His fortunes changed once he devoted himself full-time to composition. The Spanish rhapsody, *España*, made him a household name virtually overnight, and his opera *Le roi malgré lui (The king despite himself)* secured his reputation as a composer of powerful imagination and originality. Ravel once stated that he was more influenced by Chabrier than by Debussy, and particularly admired the comic opera, *Le roi malgré lui*, 'a work which I can play by heart from one end to the other', saying that he would rather have composed it than Wagner's entire *Ring*.[1] Its convoluted plot has prevented it from surviving in the repertoire, but, according to Ravel, its premiere in 1887 'changed the direction of harmony in France'.[2]

Like many French composers of his generation, Chabrier was steeped in Wagner. When he finally had the opportunity to attend a performance of *Tristan* in Munich in 1880, he famously broke into sobs as the Prelude was about to begin, explaining that he had waited ten years for this moment. But if he was one of France's most fervent Wagnerites, he was also the composer who most helped to show French composers the way beyond Wagner, particularly in the use of harmonies. Chabrier's harmonies can be complex, like Wagner's, but his entire style inclines towards lightness rather than density (somewhat following the lead of Gounod), and his music often floats evocatively in a manner that directly influenced Debussy and Ravel.

The other fashion that Chabrier encouraged was French composers' love affair with Spain. Bizet's *Carmen* reached the stage in 1875, but it was Chabrier, with his *España*, who demonstrated in 1882 how the latest orchestral resources could create an exhilarating Spanish evocation, without the need for voices.

ESPAÑA: RAPSODIE POUR ORCHESTRE
Duration: approx. 7 minutes

In 1882, Chabrier spent four months travelling across Spain with his wife. He made copious notes about the music that he encountered, but it was the whole interaction of life, culture, and music that enthralled him:

> We spend every evening in the *bailos flamencos*, the two of us surrounded by *toreros* in their town dress, their black felt hats split down the middle, jackets close-fitted at the waist, and tight trousers showing off sinewy legs and buttocks of the finest contour. And the gypsies singing their *malagueñas* or dancing the *tango*, and the *manzanilla* that is passed from hand to hand, and which everyone is obliged to drink. These eyes, these flowers in admirable heads of hair, these shawls tied around the waist, these feet that beat an infinitely varied rhythm, these arms that run quivering the length of a body always in motion, these undulations of the hand, these brilliant smiles, these wonderful Sevillian bottoms which turn in every direction while the rest of the body seems immobile – and all this to the cry of *Olé, Olé, anda la Maria! Anda la Chiquita!*[3]

A direct outcome of this trip was Chabrier's rhapsody for orchestra, *España*, which he first wrote as a piano score. The wife of the painter Auguste Renoir remembered, 'one day Chabrier came; and he played his *España* for me. It sounded as if a hurricane had been let loose. He pounded and pounded the keyboard. The street was full of people, and they were listening, fascinated. When Chabrier reached the last crashing chords, I swore to myself that I would never touch the piano again.'[4]

It was the conductor Charles Lamoureux who suggested that Chabrier should orchestrate *España*, and Lamoureux conducted the first performance in 1883. It was a dazzling success, and to satisfy the domestic market it was quickly published in versions for piano solo, piano duet, two pianos (for two or four players), and various vocal arrangements. It is easy to imagine the many attempts, from stumbling to expert, that filled the drawing rooms of France, transforming Chabrier into a popular composer. *España* was not, however, a success in Spain. Francis Poulenc, himself much influenced by Chabrier, observed that '*España* is a portrait of Spanish music by a dauber of genius. Albeniz detested this work and Falla, although he was more gallicised, did not care much for it. One must recognize that the *mantillas* of *España* have come straight from a Parisian department store. To my mind, it is exactly this that gives this brilliant Spanish adventure its true flavour.'[5]

Chabrier opens with playful cross-rhythms of the kind that abound in *flamenco*. Delicate pizzicato begins in what seems like a steady three-time. But within a few bars the metre shifts its subdivision, so that 3x2 becomes 2x3. These two patterns alternate as the forces gather, until the whole orchestra has joined in. From the climax emerges the main theme, a circling little tune on muted trumpet and bassoon shadowed by pizzicato cellos (one of Chabrier's typically witty combinations), basically in the 3x2 metre, but with teasing hints of 2x3. The tune moves to horn and the two harps, and then the harps alone. Just as it seems to be fading away, the entire orchestra bursts in with the tune. The horns and bassoons bring in a version expanded into a moment of full-blown melody in unambiguous metre, and the other brass and woodwind answer enthusiastically. Bassoons play a jolly solo, then violins and woodwind alternate. All through this opening passage, the bass and the simple pattern of harmonies have remained almost unchanged (as in a *flamenco* sequence), and this is, in effect, a loose set of variations. The last variation is a lyrical melody on violins, which gathers strength and rises to a climax to bring the opening section of the piece to a close.

For the first time the key shifts. Over rippling harps and string tremolo, trombones intone a version of the main theme that sounds like a bold declaration or recitative. Its rhythm begins four-square, contradicting the three-time, and in its second phrase broadens still further. This alternates with snatches of the original theme on woodwind, determined to hang on to its dancing rhythms. The trombone call is echoed by horns, and then builds to a climax, with new contradictory rhythms fighting with it.

The climax breaks off, and we are suddenly back at the beginning, with the original theme in its original key. The tune is played by woodwind, with the strings tapping their strings with the wood of the bow, evoking the sound of *flamenco* clapping. The horns' full-blown melody quickly follows, with the answers from brass and woodwind. Then there are more variations showing Chabrier's command of delightful orchestration: chattering flutes are echoed by violins, with the tune in the middle on bassoon and clarinet, then the chattering moves to the bass, sounding almost like a parody of the scherzo in Beethoven's Fifth Symphony. From this emerges the lyrical melody on violins, which builds to a climax as before.

The music subsides to a moment of suspense. Over a held bass note a tambourine quietly beats out a persistent rhythm. Horns and woodwind play the theme, interleaved with the trombone declaration. The brass entries come thick and fast, and the music builds to a great climax. There is one last moment of playful delicacy, and a final crescendo brings this most joyful of pieces to a close.

FRÉDÉRIC (FRYDERYK) CHOPIN
(1810–49)

Chopin is rivalled only by his contemporary, Liszt, for the title of the greatest pianist-composer after the death of Beethoven. Liszt and Chopin were friends for a few years, after they met as rival pianists in Paris. As a composer and public figure, Liszt was by far the more influential. He lived a long life, composed much orchestral as well as piano music, and together with Wagner became identified as one of the leaders of the 'New German School'. Liszt was a highly successful travelling virtuoso, very comfortable on the concert stage, achieving the sort of fame and status of a film star or rock musician. Chopin greatly admired Liszt as a pianist, admitting on one occasion, 'I wish I could steal the way he plays my own studies.' But Liszt's glittering public persona was something Chopin disdained, and in any case could never have aspired to. Chopin was more aloof and retiring, partly by temperament, partly because of his fragile health. He hated adoring crowds, gave few public concerts, and preferred to play in aristocratic salons in the company of knowledgeable connoisseurs. He was not yet forty when he died, and the compositions he left behind were almost all for solo piano, with just a few works for piano and orchestra, some chamber music (all with piano), and songs. And yet, as a composer, Chopin was at least as great as Liszt. His piano music, like Liszt's, requires a virtuoso, but the brilliance is founded on a much more sophisticated and powerful command of harmonies, subtle combinations of simultaneous voices (for which the dry word 'counterpoint' is insufficient), and a supreme gift for lyrical melody, its development and variation. There is as much variety and complexity in ten minutes of a Chopin Ballade for solo piano as in the forty minutes of Liszt's 'Dante' Symphony for huge orchestra.

Enthusiasts for Liszt's music might argue with that judgement. But there is no denying the quality of the music that Chopin was already writing as he completed his studies at the age of twenty. These include the pair of piano concertos with which he bade farewell to Warsaw in 1830, before setting off to make his name internationally in Paris. It was while he was in Stuttgart on his way to Paris that he heard that the uprising in Poland had been crushed by the Russians, and realized he must now remain an exile. The resulting sense of loss and yearning undoubtedly contributed to the character of his music. But, in essentials, Chopin's musical personality was fully formed by the time he left Poland.

His style of writing for the piano created a marvellous synthesis of contemporary and classical influences, at the same time drawing on specifically Polish traditions – the polonaises, mazurkas, and other dances that add spice to so much of his music. The contemporary influences included the brilliant piano style of Hummel, the nocturnes of John Field (a pioneer of the genre), and the decorative lyricism of Italian opera composers such as Bellini. Of the masters from the past that Chopin had studied, he was particularly drawn to Mozart and J. S. Bach for their mastery of melody, harmony, and counterpoint. Schumann went so far as to write, 'if a genius such as Mozart were born today, he would write concertos like Chopin's rather than Mozart's'.[1]

Chopin was a pianist of unique qualities. In the salons of Paris, his playing of his own music made a profound impression. Charles Hallé, the famous pianist and conductor, first heard Chopin play in 1836: 'I sat entranced, filled with wonderment, and if the room had suddenly been peopled with fairies I should not have been astonished. The marvellous charm, the poetry and originality, the perfect freedom and absolute lucidity of Chopin's playing at that time cannot be described . . . I could have dropped to my knees to worship him'.[2]

Of Chopin's two piano concertos, No. 2 was composed before No. 1. They acquired their numbers because they were published in that order, No. 1 in 1833, No. 2 in 1836. Both were premiered by Chopin in 1830, 'No. 2' in March, only a few months after he graduated from the Warsaw High School for Music, 'No. 1' in October. This was Chopin's last concert in Warsaw before he left for Vienna and then Paris, where he was finally able to establish his international name. One of the musicians who took part in that concert was a young singer, Konstancya Gladkowska, who had been a fellow student of Chopin's at the High School of Music in Warsaw. At the time Chopin was composing his piano concertos he was in love with her. In October 1829, when he was working on the first of the concertos ('No. 2'), he wrote to his old school friend Tytus Wojciechowski. Chopin had returned from a successful visit to Vienna, and reported that there was one pretty young pianist there, but she could not interest him: 'I, perhaps unfortunately, already have my own ideal, which I have served faithfully, though silently, for half a year; of which I dream, to thoughts of which the *adagio* of my concerto [in F minor] belongs, and which this morning inspired the waltz I am sending you'.[3] Before Chopin left Warsaw for good, Konstancya, who seems to have had no idea of Chopin's depth of feeling for her, wrote a farewell message in his album: 'strangers may esteem you more, reward you to the hilt, but they surely cannot love you more than we do'. Chopin later added sadly, 'They can, they can'.

These two concertos are the only large-scale works from this early period of Chopin's life to be regularly played today. Chopin never wrote another concerto, partly because he came to dislike playing in large public venues, partly because the fashion for piano concertos declined.

PIANO CONCERTO NO. 1 IN E MINOR, OP. 11
Duration: approx. 38 minutes

Allegro maestoso
Romanze: Larghetto
Rondo: Vivace

This was the second of Chopin's two concertos to be written. The opening movements of both works are 'maestoso' (majestic), but it is this E minor movement that has the greater swagger. The grand orchestral opening leads on to a gentler continuation, made particularly beautiful by the way the bass echoes the melody with a reference back to the beginning, so that we understand how the one has grown out of the other. Another surge soon relaxes into the second theme, in the major, a flowing melody that acquires a tinge of melancholy as the woodwind extend it. Bursts of fortissimo and moments of calm alternate, until a particularly peaceful passage is interrupted by the bold entry of the piano.

The opening theme is declared in *ff* octaves and then elaborated, before moving quickly on to the gentler continuation (interestingly, the piano changes the opening phrase from even to dotted rhythms, giving it the same shape as the opening phrase of the F minor concerto). The theme is extended and decorated, and leads into a new idea with a more continuous flow of semiquavers. From here the piano writing becomes more and more flamboyant, until it pauses and turns a corner into the lyrical second theme. This is followed by an exuberant virtuoso passage that leads into another orchestral tutti to bring the first section of the movement to a close.

The tutti ends peacefully, and the piano opens the middle part of the movement by musing on the second idea of the movement (still with its acquired dotted rhythms). It is decorated with Chopin's characteristic virtuoso delicacy, until it breaks into more assertive patterns. The piano continues with increasing flamboyancy, while the orchestra touches in reminders of the opening theme. This extended virtuoso passage culminates in the reprise of the first theme on full orchestra, back in the home key of E minor. This time, the piano entry omits the opening, cutting straight to the gentle continuation and taking a different direction until it finds the lyrical second theme. A final burst of virtuoso figuration brings us back to the home key for the brief orchestral ending.

The Romanze is in E major. One of the features of this concerto that makes it feel different from the F minor concerto is that all three movements are in E (minor, major, major), so that there is a sense of remaining closer to the home key. The muted strings open with a soft introduction, based on a rising phrase, echoed in the bass, which is reminiscent of the second theme from the first movement. When the piano enters, it is with a melody that seems, like the slow movement of the F minor concerto, almost like an aria. But the mood is more serene, and does not become quite so agitated. Chopin wrote about it to Tytus Wojciechowski, 'it should give the impression of gazing tenderly at a place which brings to the mind a thousand dear memories. It is a sort of meditation in beautiful spring weather, but by moonlight'.[4] The shape of the movement is a sort of rondo, in which the opening theme recurs twice, but the way in which it does so is wonderfully fluid and subtle.

The piano's opening melody begins with touching simplicity, and then takes a turn into B major and begins to develop greater complexity. As it does so, a bassoon joins it, anchoring the increasingly elaborate piano part to a simple counterpoint (judging by these two concertos, Chopin was particularly fond of the bassoon's tenor voice at this stage of his career). As in the best Italian arias of the time, the elaboration is not merely showy: in a good performance it achieves an ecstatic quality. When the first theme returns, the decoration of the preceding passage spills over into its opening phrases, and it takes several bars to recover its original poise. Now the piano embarks on another episode, this time in C sharp minor. This is the passage that approaches closest to the agitation of the F minor concerto's slow movement. Its emotional range, and the piano technique deployed to express it, are extraordinary in the writing of a twenty-year-old. Simple melodic lines, bold octaves, running thirds and sixths in complex patterns, spread chords and rushing scales, are used to create a mental landscape by turns troubled, forceful, sweetly melancholy, and determinedly passionate. With series of very delicate filigree arpeggios, the piano leads into the final reprise of the first theme. But, in perhaps the most beautiful passage in the whole concerto, Chopin gives the theme for the first time to the muted strings, while the piano pours over it a cascading counterpoint, as if the singer of the aria has been transformed into a nightingale.

The strings burst in abruptly, breaking the spell of the slow movement. Two years earlier, in 1828, the student Chopin had composed a brilliant *Rondo à la Krakowiak* for piano and orchestra, and it had been greeted with wild enthusiasm at the second of the concerts at which he introduced his F minor concerto in Warsaw. The Krakowiak is a popular Polish dance, and in this finale of the E minor concerto Chopin evokes its spirit again, teasing the audience by playing on the dance's traditional syncopations. When the piano first enters with the tune, it seems to consist of phrases that have two three-time bars followed by one two-time bar. It is only when the orchestra enters that it becomes clear that the music was in two-time all along. After playful alternations of piano and orchestra, the piano sets off in a new direction. A sustained passage of glittering virtuosity arrives at a gentle second theme in A major, with a shy, 'speaking' character. After moving wistfully through several different keys, it breaks back into virtuoso mode, and another passage of dashing brilliance takes us through to a return of the opening dance. At first this appears coyly, in E flat major, but it soon sidesteps nimbly back to E major for a proper reprise. Then the piano embarks on another virtuoso passage that develops great drive, wider-ranging in its arpeggios than before. Once again it arrives at the gentle second theme, now in B major. This time its travels through different keys bring it round to the home key of E major. Now a new, emphatically rhythmic element appears, which gives the momentum for the brilliant virtuoso dash to the finish.

PIANO CONCERTO NO. 2 IN F MINOR, OP. 21
Duration: approx. 32 minutes

Maestoso
Larghetto
Allegro vivace

Although it was published as No. 2, this concerto was the first of the two to be composed, in 1829 when Chopin was not yet twenty and about to graduate from the Warsaw High School for Music. Chopin's mastery is clear within a few bars. The melancholy first theme in F minor curls round and then descends gently. It begins unaccompanied, on first violins, and is then joined by second violins and violas, which also descend, but at a different rate, creating a counterpoint of poignant harmonies. The opening curl becomes more assertive, punctuated by *ff* chords. There follow at least three new ideas before we reach a major key for the second theme on the woodwind – just the sort of generosity of invention to be found in Mozart's piano concertos. The way the piano enters is also quite Mozartean. The orchestral introduction does not finish conclusively to 'announce' the soloist. Instead, inconclusive string chords fade to *pp*, and the piano enters unexpectedly with an *ff* descending flourish. This is not the start of a flamboyant first entry – indeed, it sounds like the end of a thought. Immediately, the piano softens to a repeat of the melancholy first theme. After a moment of elaboration, it introduces a new theme that, in its gentle descent, seems like a cousin of the first (again, it is very Mozartean for the soloist to introduce a new theme straight away). This is extended at greater length, and leads on to a brilliant virtuoso passage. It calms to reveal the second theme, which, like the piano's first entry, sounds not so much like a new beginning as a continuation, an 'answering' phrase. This is developed and elaborated with charming decoration. It leads on to another new element, a charmingly flamboyant, almost dancing idea in a minor key. This builds in grandeur to lead into the orchestral tutti that marks the end of the first section.

As the passage quietens, a bassoon emerges with a singing phrase drawn from the second theme. The piano answers with the opening phrase of the first theme, but now in a warm major key. This dialogue between piano and bassoon is a beautiful passage that will be echoed in the slow movement. The melodic fragments pass among other woodwind instruments and horn, while the piano meditates with more delicate elaboration. Then an extended virtuoso passage builds to a brief orchestral tutti to bring in the reprise. The piano plays the opening theme. But instead of extending it as before, and introducing the new theme, it takes a side-step to bring in the second theme straight away. This leads, via new elaboration, to the dancing element, now in the home key of F minor. From here, the music continues much as before, until it reaches a grand trill to bring in a final, brief tutti.

The second movement is in A flat major, a key to which the first movement often turned. A few bars of orchestra – really just a link between the two movements – leads in the piano. The first half of the theme is highly decorated, full of delicate tenderness. The second half has a simple dignity. The whole effect is like an operatic soliloquy – the heroine torn between love and duty, perhaps. This is just the sort of quasi-operatic style that Chopin was to develop in his Nocturnes. The theme repeats, with more flamboyant decoration, seems about to reach a conclusion, but instead veers away into the minor. Over urgent string tremolo, the piano plays a dramatic recitative. The fact that the piano plays only the melody, with the two hands an octave apart, gives a powerful impression of a human voice. When the passion of the recitative is spent, the most delicate descending passage leads into the reprise of the first theme. This is even more elaborately decorated than before, giving an ecstatic effect. Touchingly, as the dignified second half of the theme begins, the bassoon again answers, like the consoling tenor. With a return to the opening orchestral bars, and a final arpeggio, the movement comes to an end.

If the slow movement looks forward to later nocturnes, the finale draws on two dance genres that were to be important to Chopin: the waltz and the mazurka. The first theme is like a waltz in F minor. It begins rather seriously, contained within rising and falling scales, but then opens out, ending with a playfully syncopated flourish. The orchestra takes this as a cue to subvert the waltz with cross-rhythms. The piano finishes off the theme with yet more playful figurations, and the orchestra rounds it off with a brief tutti.

Cascading piano arpeggios announce the middle section of the movement. The piano soon settles into running triplet patterns (once more in A flat major), which the woodwind accompany with a simple rising and falling melody. With most composers, this florid piano-writing would be little more than 'passagework'. But Chopin's genius for melodic invention, which is always firmly tied to the progress of the harmonies, ensures that there is always a sense of unfolding events. A flute arabesque leads charmingly into a new theme. Tapping on the string with the wood of the bow (col legno), the strings set up another pattern of playful cross-rhythms. Over this, the piano plays a dancing mazurka. By turns charming and coy, and with another intervention from the bassoon, it ends by settling back into running triplet patterns. Exploring through a variety of keys, the piano seems to have forgotten the mazurka. But fragments of the dance begin to reappear, and, after a pause, the piano sets off with the running triplets in the treble and the mazurka theme in the bass. Again the music ventures through different keys, until, with a brilliant descent, it arrives on a chord of C major, with emphatic octave Cs in the orchestra.

The mazurka winds down, and, in a moment of calm, clarinets play a duet. With another descent, this time in a glittering pianissimo, the piano arrives at the reprise of the first (waltz-like) theme back in F minor. For a time this proceeds as before. But suddenly, in the middle of the waltz, the piano wistfully remembers the mazurka. The moment is soon over, and the end of the waltz theme brings in the familiar orchestral tutti. This comes to an unexpected stop on a major chord. An unaccompanied horn plays the opening phrase of the mazurka, now transformed into a posthorn call (marked in the score 'Cor de signal') – a charmingly naive touch. The piano sets off on a gallop of unstoppable triplet figurations, full of wit and bravura. Towards the end, it pauses for a wistful reminiscence of the mazurka, before bringing the concerto to an end with one last cascade and rocket.

AARON COPLAND
(1900–90)

Copland was two years younger than George Gershwin and, like him, was from a family of Russian-Lithuanian Jews and brought up in Brooklyn. They even shared the same composition teacher, Rubin Goldmark, for a time. But while Gershwin was making his name as a popular song composer, studying classical music on the side, Copland headed for France, the centre of the latest developments in classical music, where he studied for three years with the great Nadia Boulanger (a few years later, she was to refuse to take on Gershwin, on the grounds that her teaching would be no help to him). During the late 1920s and early 1930s, Copland was very energetic in the promotion of American composers old and new. But his own music, by turns brittly jazzy and aggressively dissonant, pleased only a narrow intelligentsia. It was during the Great Depression that his approach began to change. Drawn to the politics of the left, and to concern for the difficulties of ordinary people, he began to turn towards the idea of music that would be accessible to ordinary music lovers. During the 1930s his music became more accessible through what Copland himself called 'imposed simplicity'. He explained his change of approach in an essay published in 1939. He had begun 'to feel an increasing dissatisfaction with the relations of the music-loving public and the living composer. The old "special" public of the modern-music concerts had fallen away, and the conventional concert public continued apathetic or indifferent to anything but the established classics. It seemed to me that we composers were in danger of working in a vacuum. Moreover, an entirely new public for music had grown up around the radio and phonograph. It made no sense to ignore them and continue writing as if they did not exist. I felt that it was worth the effort to see if I couldn't say what I had to say in the simplest possible terms.'[1]

This new simplicity went hand in hand with a desire to find a way of writing truly 'American' music. Copland acknowledged Charles Ives as a pioneer in this quest, particularly in his incorporation of hymns and popular tunes, though he found his music disorganized (later he came to see Ives's music as 'a triumph of daring'). Copland's new approach was given a boost by visits to Mexico that began in 1932, at the invitation of composer Carlos Chávez. His impressions of Mexico, social and musical, had a deep effect on Copland and led to his first great success, the ballet *El Salón México*. The public response to this and the works that followed was enthusiastic. But some critics predictably took simplicity to mean a lack of seriousness compared with Copland's earlier, more 'severe' works. Copland had an answer: 'The inference is that only the severe style is really serious. I don't believe that . . . I like to think that . . . I have touched off for myself and others a kind of musical naturalness that we have badly needed ..'.[2] He was particularly successful in writing ballet scores on subjects drawn from the American past, and featuring the lives of ordinary people. He was a patriot of the left, most neatly summed up in the three-minute 'Fanfare for the Common Man' that he composed during the Second World War.

APPALACHIAN SPRING, SUITE
Duration: approx. 25 minutes

As early as 1931 the dancer Martha Graham had choreographed a dance solo, *Dithyrambic*, to Copland's Piano Variations. Copland admired Graham, and hoped that they would eventually collaborate on a stage work. In 1941, Graham suggested to him a ballet with the title, *Daughter of Colchis*, based on the ancient Greek story of the vengeance of Medea. But Copland declined the offer, finding the script 'rather severe'. Then, in July 1942, Copland was offered a commission by Elizabeth Sprague Coolidge, one of the great patrons of music in the twentieth century, to write a ballet score of about thirty minutes for Graham. This was an opportunity for a real collaboration, and he accepted it gladly.[3] Graham sent a first script with the working title, *House of Victory*, which underwent revision before Copland wrote his score. The ballet is set in a community of settlers in Pennsylvania in the early nineteenth century, and takes place in spring around a newly built farmhouse and the newly married couple who are to live in it.

At that stage the cast included an Indian girl representing 'part of the romance of our youth as a land', and a fugitive, 'the man who is hunted, persecuted', a type who 'is represented in the Civil War period by the slave' but who 'exists at all times'. At one point, the children play at a war game. The ballet, as originally conceived, therefore had powerful elements drawn from the Civil War, carrying resonance into the wartime in which the first performance took place. Copland wrote his music to this scenario, but found to his surprise that some elements had changed by the time he saw the finished ballet: the Indian girl was no longer included, and the fugitive had been replaced by a revivalist preacher who danced to music composed for the (scrapped) children's war play. But, Copland commented, 'that kind of decision is the choreographer's, and it doesn't bother me a bit, especially when it works'.[4]

The eventual title, *Appalachian Spring*, taken from a poem by Hart Crane, was chosen by Martha Graham shortly before the premiere, after Copland had completed the music. It premiered in 1944 at the Library of Congress in Washington, and won the Pulitzer Prize the following year. The character of Copland's music is, by turns, spacious, down to earth, and 'folksy', and draws on the tradition of American pastoral mythology seen in the paintings of Andrew Wyeth. But Copland subtly combines this feel with a rhythmic edge drawn from Stravinsky, and specifically from his ballet score *Les Noces* that depicts a traditional Russian wedding ceremony.

The original scoring is for thirteen instruments – strings, flute, clarinet, bassoon, and piano – and the ballet lasts about 35 minutes. Six months after the successful premiere, Copland arranged most of the music into a suite for orchestra, and this is the form in which the work is most often played. He shortened the score by removing the crisis of the ballet. In the scenario from which Copland worked, this included three episodes: 'Fear in the Night', in which the slave fugitive bursts in 'as though catapulted by fear', and dances a solo, 'awkward with the tragic awkwardness of the hopeless' (Graham replaced this with the revivalist preacher's solo); 'Day of Wrath', in which the Mother urges the citizen (that is, the husband) to furious action, the citizen dances an angry solo 'reminiscent of Harper's Ferry and John Brown', and the children play at war (Harper's Ferry was the site of a United States arsenal that John Brown raided in a doomed attempt to raise a slave revolt in 1859); and 'Moment of Crisis', in which the women dance with 'a barely suppressed hysteria' (later replaced by the Bride's solo). In cutting these episodes from the Suite, Copland removed the elements of conflict and darkness from the score, with the result that the most familiar version of the music has a much narrower emotional range than the original ballet. The suite is in eight sections, played continuously. In the following description, the quotations are from notes that Copland himself supplied for the premiere:

1. 'Very slowly. Introduction of the characters, one by one, in a suffused light.' Copland evokes an impression of purity and spaciousness with characteristically simple intervals, lightly spiced, over a sustained bass.

2. 'Fast. Sudden burst of unison strings . . . A sentiment both elated and religious gives the keynote to this scene.' The simple intervals, speeded up, are joined by playful running scales. Beneath them, a chorale twice begins to bloom (this is related to the song 'Simple Gifts' that will appear later).

3. 'Moderate. Duo for the Bride and her intended – scene of tenderness and passion.' The simple, shy phrases are twice interrupted by more troubled harmonies.

4. 'Quite fast. The Revivalist and his flock. Folksy feelings – suggestions of square dances and country fiddlers.' At first the dancing and playful phrases derive from the simple intervals and running scales of the introduction. The music takes on the rugged character of a square dance, though Copland characteristically plays with the four-square rhythm, introducing bars of five-time. At the end, there is another chorale-like reflection.

5. 'Still faster. Solo dance of the Bride – presentiment of motherhood. Extremes of joy and fear and wonder.' A movement of youthful energy, with nervous cross-rhythms cutting across the running scales.

6. 'Very slowly (as at first). Transition scene reminiscent of the introduction.'

7. 'Calm and flowing. Scenes of daily activity for the Bride and her farmer-husband. There are five variations on a Shaker theme, "Simple gifts", sung by a clarinet.' In the second variation, the tune is halved in speed and played in a sonorous canon between lower and upper strings. Before the final variation, the original ballet score includes the three darker episodes that Copland omitted from the suite: 'Fear in the Night', 'Day of Wrath', and 'Moment of Crisis'. In these, the music takes on a completely new, threatening character, rising to a height of tension, after which a mood of serenity is restored and the Shaker theme quietly re-emerges. The climactic final variation of the theme follows.

8. 'Moderate. Coda. The bride takes her place among her new neighbours. At the end the couple are left "quiet and strong in their new house".' Quiet rumination is followed by a gentle reprise of the chorale, and the 'pure' intervals of the introduction bring the work to a close.

BILLY THE KID (CONCERT SUITE)
Duration: approx. 20 minutes

Introduction: The Open Prairie
Street in a Frontier Town
Prairie Night: Card Game at Night
Gun Battle
Celebration after Billy's Capture
Billy's Death
The Open Prairie Again

Billy the Kid was composed for Ballet Caravan, a pioneering touring dance company, at the suggestion of its director, Lincoln Kirstein, and choreographed by Eugene Loring. Kirstein had suggested to Loring that a ballet could be made out of Walter Noble Burns's *Saga of Billy the Kid* (1925). It charts in vivid prose the exploits of the young William Bonney in the gang warfare in and around Lincoln, New Mexico, in the years 1878–81. In that last year Billy was shot by his friend, Pat Garrett, now the sheriff of Lincoln County, one of the resounding events in the history of the legendary American frontier. The following extract from Burns's book will give the flavour:

> Fate set a stage. Out of nowhere into the drama stepped this unknown boy. Opposite him played death. It was a drama of Death and the Boy. Death dogged his trail relentlessly. It was for ever clutching at him with skeleton hands. It lay in ambush for him. It edged him to the gallows' stairs. By bullets, conflagration, stratagems, every lethal trick, it sought to compass his destruction. But the boy was not to be trapped. He escaped by apparent miracles; he was saved as if by necromancy. He laughed at Death. Death was a joke. He waved death a jaunty good-bye and was off to new adventures . . . He died when he was twenty-one years old and was credited with having killed twenty-one men – a man for every year of his life.

Working from a number of different sources, and exploring attitudes to Billy and to the history and myth of the Western frontier, Loring developed a scenario. Copland worked closely with Loring, who recalled, 'the wonderful thing about Aaron was that he doesn't have the kind of ego that gets in the way. If you convince him that certain thematic material belongs somewhere else he is agreeable to that.'[5] Copland had been sent some published volumes of authentic cowboy songs by Kirstein, and in an article published shortly before the premiere, he wrote:

> To use or not to use cowboy songs as the basis for my ballet became a major issue. Mr. Kirstein said he didn't care – and quietly tucked two slim collections of Western tunes under my arm. I have never been particularly impressed with the musical beauties of the cowboy song as such. The words are usually delightful, and the manner of singing needs no praise from me. But neither the words nor the delivery are of much use in a purely orchestral ballet score, so I was left with the tunes themselves which, I repeat, are often less than exciting. As far as I was concerned, this ballet could be written without benefit of the poverty-stricken tunes Billy himself must have known.

Nevertheless, in order to humor Mr. Kirstein ... I decided to take his two little collections with me when I left for Paris in the summer of 1938. It was there that I began working
on the scenario as it had been outlined for me. Perhaps there is something different about
a cowboy song in Paris. But whatever the reason may have been, it wasn't very long before
I found myself hopelessly involved in expanding, contracting, rearranging and superim-
posing cowboy tunes on the Rue de Rennes in Paris.[6]

Although Copland used real cowboy songs, his evocation of the Wild West was inspired as
much by novels and Western cowboy films (a genre that reached a peak of popularity in the
1930s) as by any 'authentic' idea of the life of a cowboy. The ballet was first performed in
Chicago in a two-piano version on 6 October 1938, then in New York with full orchestra on
24 May 1939. Copland later said, 'I cannot remember another work of mine that was so unan-
imously well received.' Extracts performed as a suite usually omit two sections of the score:
Mexican Dance and Finale, and Billy in the Desert: Waltz.

The following description includes quotations from Copland's 'Notes on a Cowboy Ballet'
that appear at the front of the published score.[7]

'Introduction: The open Prairie'. The ballet opens with what Copland called 'a pastoral
theme' in bare fifths which 'gives the impression of space and isolation'. The effect is very
reminiscent of Stravinsky (as Copland often is), partly because of the scoring of high clarinets
over a low oboe. A processional rhythm begins, with piano and timpani emphasizing a
trudging offbeat pattern in the bass. The opening is joined by a rising call, halfway between a
fanfare and birdsong. Twice the music rises to a climax. The second time, it breaks off, and we
are in:

'Street in a Frontier Town': 'Familiar figures amble by. Cowboys saunter into town, some
on horseback, others with their lassoes.' First a piccolo 'nonchalantly' plays the first of the
cowboy songs, 'Great Grandad'. Other instruments join in, and there is a great deal of banter
with counter-rhythms and 'wrong' notes colliding. The energy increases, and the strings
vigorously play 'The Old Chisholm Trail' over a striding bass, with woodblock suggesting
horses' hooves. Two trombones (possibly drunk) sing 'Git Along Little Dogies' in duet. A little
later, the music breaks into five-time for a jarabe danced by Mexican women, with a trumpet
playing a distorted version of the song 'Trouble for the Range Cook'. Then the violins play a
broader tune, 'Goodbye, Old Paint', which builds to a great climax with thundering offbeats as
a fight develops: 'Attracted by the gathering crowd, Billy is seen for the first time as a boy of
twelve with his mother. The brawl turns ugly, guns are drawn, and in some unaccountable way
Billy's mother is killed. Without an instant's hesitation, in cold fury, Billy draws a knife from a
cowhand's sheath and stabs his mother's slayers. His short but famous career had begun.'

From this point on, 'In swift succession we see episodes in Billy's later life.' The first episode
is 'Prairie Night: Card Game at Night', in which Billy plays a quiet card game with his outlaw
friends. The rising call from the introduction, on oboe and bassoon, transports us back to the
prairie. This is the most peaceful section of the score, with first the violins and then a solo
trumpet meditating on 'The Dying Cowboy (Bury Me Not on the Lone Prairie)', with a
hypnotic rocking accompaniment like the murmuring of insects.

This is abruptly interrupted by the gun battle: 'Hunted by a posse led by his former friend
Pat Garrett, Billy is pursued. A running battle ensues. Billy is captured.' An insistent drum
rhythm, threatening muted trumpets, and tense, high violins, alternate in jagged fragments

and gradually coalesce to suggest the closing in of forces. At the end of the battle, the music again fragments, until the drum rhythm fades away.

'Celebration after Billy's Capture' depicts 'the townspeople rejoicing in the saloon, where an out-of-tune player piano sets the scene'. Piccolo and oboe start a cheeky tune that dominates the scene, and the out-of-tune piano is suggested by the oom-pah bass, which is in the wrong key. The tune builds to a climax, and a trumpet quietly holds a note over to the next episode. ('Billy in the Desert: Waltz' is omitted in the suite. In it, Billy, having escaped, dances with his Mexican sweetheart to an ironically distorted waltz version of the song 'Trouble for the Range Cook'. After falling asleep, 'he senses movement in the shadows. The posse has finally caught up with him. It is the end'.)

'Billy's Death' is a brief, sorrowful passage of slow chords, with a little figure of rapid repeated notes on solo violin, like a death rattle. Finally, the return to the prairie 'makes use of material from the introduction, but with different coloration to convey the idea of a new dawn breaking over the prairie'. The theme, with its bare fifths, begins on horns and builds to a mighty climax, marked to the end by the heavy offbeat rhythm of the drums.

CLARINET CONCERTO
Duration: approx. 17 minutes
Slowly and expressively – Cadenza – Rather fast

It was the bandleader Paul Whiteman who pioneered a bridge between jazz and classical music in the 1920s, most famously by asking Gershwin to write what was to become *Rhapsody in Blue*. Twenty years later, two of the great bandleaders of the 1940s, Woody Herman and Benny Goodman, again reached out to classical composers. In 1945, Herman commissioned Stravinsky to write the *Ebony Concerto* for his band. As early as 1919, Stravinsky had composed *Piano Rag Music* after studying sheet music of ragtime (which he had never heard played), and produced a grotesque, puppet-like piece full of mechanical syncopations. Although the syncopated style undoubtedly fed into the music of Stravinsky's 'neoclassical' works, the *Ebony Concerto* scarcely took any significant steps towards engagement with jazz. It is interesting in its quirkiness, but Herman's musicians were disappointed.

When Benny Goodman approached classical musicians, it was not to get them to write for his band, but to get them to write music that would raise his profile in the classical world. He had commissioned Bartók's *Contrasts* for clarinet, violin, and piano in 1938, which he performed and recorded with the composer and Joseph Szigeti. It has little or nothing to do with jazz, and is based on Hungarian and Romanian dance tunes. In 1947, Goodman asked Copland to write a clarinet concerto for him. Copland had long been an admirer of Goodman, 'and I thought that writing a concerto with him in mind would give me a fresh point of view'. So he took on this commission in preference to one offered by Herman a few months earlier.

Copland, unlike Bartók and Stravinsky, did embrace the spirit of jazz, and composed a finale for Goodman in a distinctly jazzy idiom. But he prefaced it with a serene first movement, which he linked to the finale with a cadenza. The scoring of the concerto is far removed from that of a jazz big band – string orchestra with harp and piano.

The opening has a spiritual calm reminiscent of *Appalachian Spring*, but it could as easily be French as American – perhaps Satie in his Olympian Greek mode (as in *Gymnopédies*). It is in a slow three-time with the second beat emphasized as in a sarabande, and with the harp picking out the treading bass and the second beat. The suggestion of a slow dance is confirmed by Copland, who said that he based the movement on an idea for a *pas de deux*. The music develops some elegiac, almost Mahlerian harmonies, and the suggestion of Mahler becomes stronger in the central section where the three-time breaks down and the beat falters.

Usually, a cadenza muses or elaborates on themes that have already been heard. But here, after a look back at the opening theme of the first movement, Copland develops fragments of themes that will occur in the following movement, like a jazz improviser trying out ideas.

The jazzy finale has much syncopation against the beat, but this varies between the feel of 'real' jazz and the sort of 'neoclassical' jazz pioneered by Stravinsky – one of the strongest influences in Copland's music. A theme marked 'with humor, relaxed' is a Brazilian tune that Copland heard in Rio de Janeiro, and is used to build the longest, and most charming, episode in the movement. The little tune begins nonchalantly, over a 'slap bass' (double bass plucked so that the string hits the fingerboard). Its elaboration is, by turns, languid and spiky, sometimes passing from instrument to instrument in witty interplay.

When Copland tried out the concerto with Goodman for the first time, he reported, 'Seems I wrote the last page too high "for all normal purposes". So it'll have to come down a step.'[8] As well as lowering the highest notes, Copland revised a passage towards the end where, in the final version, clarinet and piano banter with each other. This is delightful, but Copland originally intended Goodman to play all this passage by himself, in a continuous virtuoso burst of notes. Goodman was nervous about this, so Copland rewrote the passage to make it more playable. The original version, which survives in Copland's sketches, has been revived in recent years, and is exhilarating. The concerto ends with a glissando, in homage to the first ever jazz concerto, Gershwin's *Rhapsody in Blue*.

FANFARE FOR THE COMMON MAN
Duration: approx. 3 minutes

Copland's most famous piece was commissioned as one of a series of fanfares to open concerts of the Cincinatti Symphony Orchestra in their 1942–3 season, the first undertaken after the United States joined the Second World War (December 1941). The conductor, Eugene Goossens, hoped 'to make these fanfares stirring and significant contributions to the war effort'. Walter Piston wrote *A Fanfare for the Fighting French*, Goossens himself provided *Fanfare for the Merchant Marine*, and so on. Copland declared, 'if the fighting French got a fanfare, so should the common man, since, after all, it was he who was doing all the dirty work in the war'.[9] The inspiration for the title was a speech delivered in May 1942 by the vice-president, Henry Wallace, who was one of the chief drivers of Franklin D. Roosevelt's New Deal. In it Wallace looked forward to a world in which tyranny and enslavement would be defeated, and 'the common man' could enjoy a better and more just world: 'Some have spoken of the "American Century". I say that the century on which we are entering – the century that will come out of this war – can be and must be the century of the common man ... No nation will have the God-given right to exploit other nations ... there must be neither military nor economic imperialism. The methods of the nineteenth century will not work in the people's century that is about to begin.'[10] It was a vision of an ideal society that was to die all too soon, a vision that in the early twenty-first century seems all the more remote. Copland, deeply impressed by a speech that chimed with his own political sympathies, was later to find himself called to appear before Senator Joseph McCarthy's notorious committee to deny being a communist.

The *Fanfare for the Common Man* is scored for three trumpets, four horns, three trombones, tuba, timpani, bass drum, and tam-tam. Its powerful effect is achieved by the way Copland takes elements of a conventional fanfare and dramatizes them, enlarging them and letting them evolve in grandeur. It opens with an arresting gesture: two timpani, bass drum, and tam-tam beat a defiant, ceremonial pattern, leaving the sounds to vibrate. Over the vibrations rise the three trumpets in unison, the intervals stretching wider than in a conventional fanfare, and then falling. The drums beat again, this time without the tam-tam. The horns join the trumpets in duet, the bare fifths evoking the sense of open spaces familiar from Copland's ballet scores. Drums and tam-tam enter again. Now the trombones lead, the timpani echo the rhythm, and the fanfare expands into a grand chorale on full brass. The final fanfare expands yet further, creating a magnificent *fff* climax.

EL SALÓN MÉXICO
Duration: approx. 11 minutes

El Salón México was an important landmark in Copland's quest for a simpler, more direct style of writing. In its incorporation of popular Mexican tunes, it also helped him to find a way to express his respect for 'the people', and to make his music 'American' (even though the tunes here were American in the broad sense). He first visited Mexico in 1932, at the invitation of his friend, the composer Carlos Chávez, a prominent figure in Mexico's musical life. Copland was bowled over by revolutionary Mexico: 'The best is its people – nothing in them is striving to be bourgeois. In their overalls and bare feet they are not only poetic but positively "émouvant".'[11] It was during this stay that he visited a popular dance hall in Mexico City, *El Salón México*. In an article to mark the release of the first recording of the piece inspired by this visit, Copland remembered that he stayed at the dance hall all night until it closed at 5.00 in the morning. On the wall was a sign, 'Please don't throw lighted cigarette butts on the floor so the ladies don't burn their feet.' Copland recalled, 'in some inexplicable way, while milling about in those crowded halls, one felt a really live contact with the Mexican "peuple" – the electric sense one gets sometimes in far-off places, of suddenly knowing the essence of a people – their humanity, their separate shyness, their dignity and unique charm. I remember quite well that it was at just such a moment that I conceived the idea of composing a piece about Mexico and naming it *El Salón México*.'[12] Carlos Chávez conducted its premiere in Mexico City in 1937: 'Despite Chávez's enthusiasm, I still felt nervous about what the Mexicans might think of a "gringo" meddling with their native melodies. At the first of the final rehearsals that I attended, an unexpected incident took place that completely reassured me. As I entered the hall the orchestral players, who were in the thick of a Beethoven symphony, suddenly stopped what they were doing and began to applaud vigorously. What they were expressing, I soon realized, was not so much their appreciation of one composer's work, as their pleasure and pride in the fact that a foreign composer had found their own familiar tunes worthy of treatment.'[13] Copland himself drew an analogy between *El Salón México* and Chabrier's *España*. But a closer analogy is Milhaud's delightful collage of Brazilian tunes, *Le boeuf sur le toit*.

The music consists of a selection of Mexican tunes, which Copland obtained from published collections, juxtaposed to give a vivid sense of a dynamic crowd in festive mood.

Copland achieves this by weaving his material together with the freedom and skill of a film editor. He draws on at least nine tunes, a few of which recur to give a sense of coherence, as in a rondo. The traditional rhythms of Mexican music fuse with Copland's own Stravinskyan delight in rhythmic complexity to produce a work that sounds both unmistakably Copland and thoroughly Mexican.

It begins with a vigorous burst of the song 'El Palo Verde'. Then the pace slows, and a trumpet plays 'La Jesusita' in sultry style, alternating with extrovert clarinet flourishes. Bassoon and bass clarinet in duet play 'El Mosco' over a relaxed, syncopated beat. Violins answer with snatches of 'El Palo Verde', and then sing 'El Mosquito'. The energy and pace increase, until a reprise of 'El Palo Verde' on full brass punctuated by drums leads a sustained climax. The tune fragments, and the pace slackens again. The slow section that follows has snatches of several tunes, as if we are cutting between different groups of dancers, all half-asleep. The section includes a pair of waltzes, which Copland wittily signals by a combination of strings and horns, as if Richard Strauss has glimpsed into the room. After the waltzes recur, the pace increases again. Slowly the energy builds, and the beat becomes more insistent. The brass and drums return to 'El Palo Verde', exhilarating rhythms are repeated hypnotically, and a final thud brings the piece to an end.

ARCANGELO CORELLI
(1653–1713)

From time to time in the history of music, new developments in instrument-making spur on radical changes in the ways that composers write. Music from Mozart to Liszt would have been very different without the development of the piano. And the music of the early eighteenth century is unthinkable without the rise of violin-making in northern Italy over the preceding century. Corelli, Vivaldi, Locatelli, and other violinist-composers took this refined, powerful instrument, and used it to develop a brilliant style of writing that was to lay the foundations of instrumental music for the next hundred years and more. One of the indirect consequences of this development in violin-making was the rise of what we know as 'orchestral' music.

In France, an Italian violinist and composer, Jean-Baptiste Lully (originally Giovanni Battista Lulli, 1632–87), had been appointed superintendant of Louix XIV's Musique de Chambre in 1661. The king maintained what was, in effect, a string orchestra, the Vingt-quatre Violons du Roi. ('Violons' in this context ranged from what we know as violins through violas to bass instruments akin to cellos.) They played for ballets and operas and dinners at court. After Lully's death, his younger contemporary at court, Michel Richard de Lalande (or Delalande, 1657–1726), composed suites of several hundred pieces that were published under the title *Simphonies pour le souper du Roi*. The 'French' style of composition associated with Louis XIV's court at Versailles, with its emphasis on dances and stately overtures, was much imitated abroad. This was particularly so in England, where Purcell composed for Charles II's own Twenty-Four Violins, and in Germany, where J. S. Bach was one of many composers who wrote orchestral music somewhat in the French style.

But it was in Italy that the development of a separate strand of 'orchestral' music really took hold, and if anyone deserves the credit for its rise, it is Corelli. He was a pioneer on several fronts. As a violinist and teacher, he laid the foundations for later developments in violin-playing. As a director of musicians, he set standards of discipline and ensemble that remained exceptional until the late twentieth century. And as a composer, he was highly influential in the development of both chamber and orchestral music, and was the first prominent Italian composer to specialize in instrumental music.

It was in Rome that he acquired his reputation as a violinist in the 1670s. In 1681 he published his Opus 1, a set of twelve trio sonatas, and four other sets of sonatas followed over the next twenty years. His reputation as a composer of orchestral music rests on a single publication: the set of twelve *Concerti Grossi* that Corelli gathered together over the two years before his death, and that was published in Amsterdam in 1714. The concertos, like his sonatas, were immensely influential. They were particularly admired in England, where Handel took them as the models for his own set of concertos, Opus 6.

Concerti Grossi, Op. 6, Nos 1–12

Duration: 9–14 minutes each

Corelli's concertos, like his sonatas, are of two types: the *concerto da chiesa* (church concerto) and the *concerto da camera* (chamber concerto). This distinction arose from the different places in which sonatas were played. 'Church sonatas', suitable for playing during Mass in churches, contain more 'serious' contrapuntal movements, and few dance-based movements. 'Chamber sonatas' for domestic use were suites predominantly of dance movements, preceded by a prelude. Such suites had long been popular across Europe, but the development of orchestral suites is particularly associated with the court of Louis XIV, where Lully and Lalande worked. Of Corelli's twelve *Concerti Grossi*, Opus 6, the first eight are basically church concertos, the last four are chamber concertos. There is, however, some overlap between the two genres, and the distinction between them becomes increasingly blurred in the next generation of concertos composed by Vivaldi and Handel.

One feature that Corelli's concertos all share is their instrumentation. They are scored for two groups of instruments: the *concertino*, consisting of two solo violins and a solo cello with continuo (that is, an instrument playing chords – harpsichord, organ, lute), and the *concerto grosso*, consisting of two violins, viola, and bass (double bass or its baroque equivalent, the violone) with a separate continuo instrument. This arrangement had developed from a tradition of choral music in which a larger and smaller choir were contrasted, often each with their own group of instruments. In performance, there might be one or more instrument on each line of the *concerto grosso*. The word *ripieno* ('full') is also used as an alternative for *concerto grosso*, and *concerto grosso* is also the term generally used to describe this genre of concerto, with its contrast between 'full' orchestra and a group of soloists.

In 1789, Charles Burney wrote, 'The *Concertos* of Corelli seem to have withstood all the attacks of time and fashion with more firmness than any of his other works. The harmony is so pure, so rich, and so grateful; the parts are so clearly, judiciously, and ingeniously disposed; and the effect of the whole, from a large band, so majestic, solemn and sublime that they preclude all criticism, and make us forget that there is another Music of the same kind existing.'[1] Burney's reference to 'a large band' reflects the growing taste for larger orchestras in England (the Handel Commemoration of 1784 featured massed performances of Handel's concertos and oratorios). But the title page of Corelli's 1712 edition had already specified that the strings of the *concerto grosso* could be either omitted or doubled at will. So the concertos could be performed either as trio sonatas, by the *concertino* alone, or with an orchestra of single strings, or with a larger orchestra. An orchestra of a dozen or so players was usual in Rome, but Corelli himself sometimes led very large ensembles. Grand occasions would often command an orchestra of fifty or more, and the visit to Rome in 1687 of Lord Castlemaine, ambassador of James II of England, was marked by a concert with an orchestra of 150 strings. Corelli was greatly admired for the precision with which his ensemble performed his concertos. The violinist and composer Francesco Geminiani reported, 'Corelli regarded it as essential to the ensemble of a band, that their bows should all move exactly together, all up, or all down; so that at his rehearsals, which constantly preceded every public performance of his concertos, he would immediately stop the band if he discovered one irregular bow.'[2]

Although the collection was compiled at the end of Corelli's life, there is evidence that at least some of the concertos dated back several years. The German composer Georg Muffat, who visited Rome in about 1680, reported having heard concertos by Corelli 'performed with the greatest exactness by a large number of instrumentalists'. It is not possible to know whether any of these concertos found their way into the Opus 6 collection. Indeed, it is not always clear quite what is meant in reports by a 'concerto'. It was possible not only to perform concertos as trio sonatas, by omitting the *concerto grosso* parts, but also to perform trio sonatas as concertos, by simply doubling sections of each movement with extra instruments. Muffat, who had been so impressed by Corelli's concertos, published his own sonatas which, he explained, could be played as concertos in this way. These were the early days of 'orchestral' music, and the conventions and possibilities were rather more fluid than we are inclined to think from a distance of three hundred years.[3]

NO. 1 IN D MAJOR

Largo – Allegro
Largo – Allegro
Largo
Allegro
Allegro

The concerto opens with a sonorous Largo, incorporating one of Corelli's most characteristic features, a steadily walking bass. This leads into a lively Allegro, initiated by the solo *concertino*, in which the two violins pursue each other with leaping phrases while the cello plays running semiquavers. Twice this Allegro is interrupted by a bar of slow Adagio and then resumes – a rather operatic effect for a supposed 'Church Concerto'. A third Adagio brings the movement to a final cadence.

The next Largo is a gentle dance in three-time – one of many movements that blurs the distinction between *concerto da chiesa* and the dance-based *concerto da camera*. Depending on the tempo, a performance can make it sound more like a (faster) minuet or a (slower) sarabande. *Concertino* and *ripieno* alternate. Just at the moment when we expect a return of the *ripieno*, the music breaks into another Allegro. This reverses the texture of the first Allegro: now rapid semiquaver patterns are in the violins, with a bass of simple leaps. Soloists and orchestra play together throughout, with the rapid patterns alternating between first and second violins.

The following Largo is a lyrical duet in B minor for the two solo violins – the only movement not in the home key of D major. At first they play arpeggio patterns as the bass falls step by step. Then they play more sustained lines, often imitating each other half a bar apart, creating gentle clashes of harmony, and then combining a third apart. The orchestra accompanies, until all combine for the final bars.

The concerto ends with two movements headed Allegro, but they are very different in character. The first is a fugue, a genre whose formality is closely associated with sonatas and *concerti da chiesa*. But one of the pleasures of Corelli's fugues is their subtle informality. This one begins with the expected four entries of the subject, the first two played by solo violins alone, but the third and fourth joined by the orchestra. Various entries of the subject follow, sometimes in isolation, sometimes following after each other, but with changed intervals of time between each entry. A figure of running scales is worked into the counterpoint, and brings the first section of the movement to a close. Then the soloists begin a new phase of the fugue, but now with its subject simplified. The running scales are combined with this new version, and then with the original.

The final Allegro is a dancing movement that, if it were in a *concerto da camera*, might well be headed Giga (the same as Gigue or Jig). The two solo violins begin alone, with a lively pattern in duet. The orchestra rounds off their phrase with rather stately chords. The solo violinists and the orchestra alternate in this way. The effect is charming, like seeing rather serious parents in the company of their playful children. As the movement proceeds, the first violin's exuberance comes to dominate, until the more stately music brings the concerto to a close.

NO. 2 IN F MAJOR

Vivace – Allegro – Adagio – Vivace – Allegro – Largo andante
Allegro
Grave – Andante largo
Allegro

The opening sequence of movements might well have inspired Vivaldi in his naturalistic writing. In the brief Vivace introduction, the solo violins play bird-like trills. Then they fly off into the Allegro pursuing each other in playful imitation and combining in a duet of parallel thirds. Suddenly the poignant harmonies of an Adagio darken the mood. The first pair of sections returns, now in C major. This time the Allegro is extended, and soon finds its way back to F major. The Largo andante brings the movement to a solemn close.

The next Allegro is a fugue which, like that of the first concerto, begins with four entries of the subject, led by the solo *concertino*, and then becomes more informal. After the first paragraph, the solo violins begin a new set of entries, but the subject has changed, rising upwards instead of rising and falling. Towards the end of the movement, the original version of the subject reappears in the bass.

A short, sombre Grave introduces the Andante largo in D minor. The lines gently interweave in counterpoint, creating delicate harmonic clashes and resolutions.

The final movement has the four-square sturdiness of a gavotte. This is another example of a dance-like movement finding its way into a *concerto da chiesa*. It exemplifies just the sort of clean-cut simplicity in which Handel was to specialize.

NO. 3 IN C MINOR

Largo
Allegro
Grave
Vivace
Allegro

The first two movements form a pair, almost like a French Overture. In the Largo, bold dotted rhythms alternate with smoother, more lyrical phrases. The Allegro begins with four entries of a fugue subject, introduced by the soloists, and then loosens into an extensive pair of paragraphs in which the subject and other little elements are freely passed around in counterpoint. The whole movement has a sprightly air, despite the minor key, with playfulness and touches of lyricism in delightful coexistence.

The Grave is a masterclass in one of Corelli's favourite effects, the harmonic suspension. One note hangs over as a chord moves, causing a momentary dissonance that then resolves. Sequences of suspensions, as here, create a poignant melancholy.

The Vivace features another of Corelli's most characteristic devices, a walking bass. The whole movement is built over continuous quavers in the bass, with alternations between the *concerto grosso* and the *concertino*. Corelli knows just when to vary this pattern before it becomes monotonous: the second half has plainer rhythms in the upper parts, with more extended phrases.

The final Allegro is in jig rhythm (though not called 'Giga' in a *concerto da chiesa*). The triplets of the rhythm are set going by the solo violins, and then alternate with the bass. In the second half, the first violin comes to dominate, as if willing the music to metamorphose into a solo violin concerto, until the orchestra reasserts itself for a firm ending.

NO. 4 IN D MAJOR

Adagio – Allegro
Adagio
Vivace
Allegro – Allegro

Four bars of simple Adagio chords (with or without improvised elaboration) lead into the Allegro. This movement is like a walking-bass movement upside down: While the lower instruments play a relatively stately series of chord sequences, the two solo violins alternate in a continuous flow of rapid semiquaver patterns. It is the interplay between these two contrasted elements, rather than any intrinsic melodic interest, that makes the movement fascinating.

Similarly in the next Adagio, Corelli makes a virtue of simplicity. The movement is little more than a series of chords in B minor, given touches of poignancy by the frequent harmonic suspensions (see Concerto No. 3).

The Vivace is a minuet (though not so called) with a walking bass, and frequent alternations between soloists and full orchestra.

The final Allegro is predominantly in the familiar jig rhythm, as in the final movements of Concertos Nos 1 and 3. Corelli does, however, notate some bars in 'straight' rather than 'swung' rhythm. There is disagreement among scholars and players as to how this notation should be interpreted. In some performances, all the rhythms are swung, creating a whole movement in jig rhythm. In others, the 'straight' bars are played straight, creating a momentary calming of the rhythm (which can be charming). At the end, the music unexpectedly drops the jig rhythm and breaks into rapid semiquavers, and the concerto comes to an end with a rather Vivaldi-like display of orchestral energy.

NO. 5 IN B FLAT MAJOR

Adagio – Allegro
Adagio
Allegro
Largo – Allegro

The concerto begins with a brief Adagio of Handel-like dignity. This breaks straight into a lively Allegro in which playful virtuoso exchanges between first and second violins alternate with more sustained passages over a walking bass. During the latter part of the movement, the first solo violin comes to dominate, until a renewal of the sustained material ends with a return to the last phrase of the opening Adagio.

The next Adagio is a graceful movement that begins as a trio sonata for the *concertino* instruments with brief punctuation from the orchestra. Then the two groups come together in sustained sequences of Corelli's favourite harmonic suspensions, creating a succession of poignant dissonances and resolutions over a gently walking bass.

The Allegro begins as a double fugue – that is, a fugue in which two themes enter almost simultaneously. But, as usual, Corelli plays with this idea very freely. Other elements enter and are treated fugally, sometimes in the company of one of the original themes, sometimes not. Towards the end, Corelli seems to have abandoned his original themes, but the descending element of the first is still there in an elaborated and disguised form. The fugue ends with two Adagio bars that return to the final phrase of the Adagio that opened the concerto.

A brief and solemn Largo leads into the final Allegro. This is a charming movement, in which simple chord progressions are elaborated by the two solo violins. It is as if they were expecting to play a jig, but have found themselves confined to something like a gavotte and are determined to enliven it.

NO. 6 IN F MAJOR

Adagio
Allegro
Largo
Vivace
Allegro

The opening Adagio alternates forte and piano, with the solemn serenity that Handel admired and emulated. At each piano phrase, the second violins rise above the first violins – a subtle but telling effect.

The solo *concertino* launches the Allegro with vigorous semiquaver patterns in the violins over a firm bass line. As in the equivalent movement in Concerto No. 4, the violins' patterns are decorative rather than melodic, and it is the relationship between these and the bass line that creates the charm of the movement.

Fugues in Corelli's concertos are usually fast, but the Largo is a rare example of a slow fugal movement, in D minor. Its sonorities build up beautifully as each voice enters. For a time, the fugal entries give way to simpler answering phrases, until the theme enters again in the bass to bring the movement to an end.

The Vivace returns to F major in a dancing three-time. But this is not a simple dance: the two solo violin parts interweave in counterpoint, and when the orchestra joins in the entries of the different voices sound almost fugue-like. Throughout the movement, more subtle passages alternate with more straightforward episodes full of bustling semiquavers.

The final Allegro is a two-time dance. It has none of the decorative semiquavers of the earlier fast movements, but brings the concerto to a close in a mood of sturdy cheerfulness, with occasional touches of poignant harmony.

NO. 7 IN D MAJOR

Vivace – Allegro – Adagio
Allegro
Andante largo
Allegro
Vivace

The introduction, with its bold dotted rhythms, is marked Vivace – presumably 'vigorous' rather than 'fast' in this context. It leads straight into the Allegro, in which the violins play with figures in different note values – two notes per beat, then three, and, as everyone joins in, four. There is a spirit of celebration in which one could imagine trumpets and drums. Soloists and orchestra answer each other. As the music reaches a climax of energetic scrubbing, it is suddenly brought to a halt on a surprising chord. This is the beginning of the Adagio. Two halting attempts to move forward are resolved in a consoling cadence.

The next Allegro is based on one of Corelli's celebrated walking (or here running) basses. It is in two repeated halves, with alternations between *concertino* and *ripieno*. The second half moves into B minor before finding its way back to the home key of D major.

The Andante largo returns to B minor, and continues the walking bass (now definitely walking rather than running). Over it, the two solo violins exchange overlapping phrases, while the orchestra at first supplies punctuation, and later joins in the dialogue.

The next Allegro is a short fugue, treated with Corelli's characteristic freedom. It begins with each of the four voices entering in turn with the theme. But at the next set of entries the bass varies the shape of the theme, and at the end it plays yet another variation. So this is a fugue that evolves as it proceeds – even though it lasts scarcely more than a minute.

The final Vivace is a charming little dance in the style of a French minuet, with playful variation in the accenting of the three beats. Unadorned versions of the dance alternate with passages in which the violins elaborate the rhythm with semiquaver figurations. But it is the simple dance that concludes the movement, bringing the concerto to an unassuming end.

NO. 8 IN G MINOR, *FATTO PER LA NOTTE DI NATALE* ('CHRISTMAS CONCERTO')

Vivace – Grave
Allegro
Adagio – Allegro – Adagio
Vivace
Allegro
Pastorale ad libitum: Largo

A few bars of bold chords (Vivace) lead into a beautifully sustained Grave with interweaving counterpoint. Over the Grave, Corelli writes an unusual instruction: 'Arcate sostenute e come sta' ('sustained bowing and as written'). 'Come sta' is taken to mean that the movement was to be played without ornaments. And, since there was a prevailing stylistic convention of playing long notes with a swell to the middle of the note, 'Arcate sostenute' is thought to mean that the notes are to be played without such swells, creating a more organ-like effect.[4]

The Allegro combines two of Corelli's most characteristic ways of writing. The violins of the *concertino* play a two-part counterpoint that creates a continuous strand of suspensions (harmonies that clash and then resolve). Below, the bass keeps up a constant running pattern (Corelli's 'walking bass'). The combination of these two contrasted elements creates a movement that seems both free-flowing and firmly structured.

After an energetic movement in G minor there follows a peaceful Adagio in E flat major. It begins with ribbons of arpeggios in the solo violins over chords with a descending bass. Then the arpeggios move to the solo cello, while the violins play a sequence of suspensions above, as if remembering the previous movement. After a few bars, the music breaks into a brief Allegro with chord sequences formed into faster patterns. The moment is soon over, and the peaceful Adagio is repeated, coming to a tranquil close over another descending bass.

The Vivace returns to G minor for a gentle minuet, in which the solo *concertino* is delicately supported by the *ripieno*.

This is followed by a sturdy, gavotte-like Allegro. In the second half, there is a surprising moment when the first violin breaks into a swirling pattern in a minor key, like one of Vivaldi's evocations of the wind. The final phrase of the movement leads without a break into the piece that has made this the most celebrated of Corelli's concertos.

The final Pastorale in G major opens with violins in a gently rocking duet over a drone bass, evoking rustic bagpipes or perhaps a hurdy-gurdy. The continuation introduces more varied phrases and ventures into different keys without ever losing the pastoral character. The movement ends very peacefully, with a marking rare in Corelli, pianissimo. Corelli indicated that this Pastorale could be omitted: it is an unusual ending for a concerto, and was presumably composed especially for Christmas night. But it is precisely this optional movement that is the famous prototype of a Christmas pastoral genre that was to extend through Handel's *Messiah* to Berlioz's *L'Enfance du Christ* and beyond.

NO. 9 IN F MAJOR

Preludio: Largo
Allemanda: Allegro
Corrente: Vivace
Gavotta: Allegro
Adagio
Minuetto: Vivace

This is the first of the four *concerti da camera*, each consisting of a suite of dances with a prelude. The opening Preludio has something of the grandeur of a French Overture. But the dotted rhythms of the opening give way to a more sustained and lyrical style, giving the movement rather an ambiguous character somewhere between stateliness and a more muted solemnity.

The playful Allemanda (a dance named after its German origin) is invigorated by ribbons of semiquaver patterns that appear first in the solo cello, and then migrate to the two violins in turn.

The Corrente is a three-time dance, like a fast minuet, in which all the musicians play together with no separation between *concertino* and *ripieno*.

The Gavotta is brief and nimble, with passages for the solo *concertino* alternating with *ripieno* passages. It begins with regular phrases, but in the second half teasingly breaks the regularity with insistent repetitions.

The Adagio is no more than an introduction to the final movement, with pairs of chords separated by rests, no doubt intended to be filled out with improvisation by either a violin or a continuo instrument.

The final Minuetto is framed by a simple, clear-cut dance, which is played at the beginning and the end. In between is a section in which the two solo violins exchange lively patterns of arpeggios.

NO. 10 IN C MAJOR

Preludio: Largo
Allemanda: Allegro
Adagio
Corrente: Vivace
Allegro
Minuetto: Vivace

The opening Preludio features a gently walking bass. Over it, the violins play an interweaving duet with many poignant harmonic suspensions (moments of dissonance that resolve).

The Allemanda is an elegant dance in four-time, in which soloists and orchestra play together, and the melody is played throughout by the first violins, mostly accompanied by simple chords.

The brief Adagio in A minor consists of sonorous chords grouped in two-bar phrases, with a rest that invites some improvisation.

Back in C major, the Corrente (a dance like a fast minuet) features the solo cello, which keeps up a continuous, and tricky, pattern of arpeggios, while the violins play more sustained lines above.

In the Allegro, the focus moves to the solo first violin, which rattles away at fast patterns of alternating notes while the other players keep a steady pace below. Here too there are tricky jumping passages for the solo cello.

The final Minuetto is a movement of elegant regularity. Between its opening and closing statements in C major is a middle section that moves through different keys, with patterns of arpeggios in the first violin.

NO. 11 IN B FLAT MAJOR

Preludio: Andante largo
Allemanda: Allegro
Adagio – Andante largo
Sarabanda: Largo
Giga: Vivace

Sustained contrapuntal lines over a walking bass create a rich sonority in the Preludio.

The Allemanda transforms the dance into something like a movement of a cello concerto. Beneath a simple pair of violin lines, the solo cello plays a continuous stream of rapid figurations. But, unlike the solo part of a cello concerto, this is not the main melody but an elaboration of the bass line (a 'division', as Corelli's British contemporaries would have called it).

A brief Adagio consists of solemn pairs of chords, with rests that invite improvisation. It introduces the Andante largo in G minor. The violins interweave over a walking bass, with many poignant touches created by Corelli's favourite harmonic suspensions. It evokes memories of the opening Preludio – it even has some of the same melodic shapes.

The Sarabanda is an elegant, simple dance in three-time, with alternations between *concertino* and *ripieno*. Despite the marking, Largo, the tempo is not as slow as in the more elaborate and searching sarabandes of J. S. Bach (in Concerto No. 12, Corelli has an even faster sarabande, marked Vivace).

Corelli ends with a charming Giga, light and regular in its phrasing at the beginning and end, but with a hint of a frown in the middle as it moves through a series of minor keys.

NO. 12 IN F MAJOR

Preludio: Adagio
Allegro
Adagio
Sarabanda: Vivace
Giga: Allegro

In the Preludio the solo violins interweave in gentle counterpoint over Corelli's favourite walking bass. There are three paragraphs, in each of which the *concertino* begins, and the concerto grosso joins them to round it off.

The Allegro could pass for a movement of a violin concerto. The other members of the *concertino* and the *concerto grosso* merely support the first violin in its playful series of rapid and varied figurations.

The Adagio is a series of chords in D minor with a solemn pattern of repeated notes. It is followed (in F major) by the Sarabanda. By Corelli's day, there were faster and slower versions of this popular dance. Concerto No. 11 has a slower version (though not very slow), and this Sarabanda is faster. The solo violins play in duet over a walking bass.

The emphasis on the *concertino* continues into the cheerful final Giga, with the first violin dominating.

CLAUDE DEBUSSY
(1862–1918)

In discussion of modernism in music in the early twentieth century, the figure who is often seen as most revolutionary is Schoenberg. But Schoenberg was, in essence, a traditionalist, developing the chromaticism of Wagner and Liszt into a language without familiar harmonies but with its own fearsome internal logic. Debussy's revolution was of a different order. He preserved many conventional harmonies but threw the traditional relationships between them to the winds. In doing so he created a new sense of time in music, which, by the twenty-first century, is proving more influential and long-lasting than the innovations of Schoenberg's serialism. In traditional musical language before Debussy, time moves on inexorably, with the progression of harmonies pushing it forward like a stream. But with Debussy it is as if we have left the ground. There are still harmonies, many of them chords familiar from nineteenth-century music, others suggesting no specific key. But whether the chords are familiar or unfamiliar, they often seem to come into existence and evaporate, placed side by side without the next necessarily being the consequence of the last. The result is more like the motion of the air – sometimes static, at other times swirling in circles, changing course abruptly, rising or falling or coming to a stop. Debussy uses this new, evanescent language to create vividly evocative tone pictures.

This characteristic freedom of writing was inspired by many elements. They include the work of French poets, notably Stéphane Mallarmé, whose poem, *L'après-midi d'un faune*, an evocation of an erotic dream-world, inspired Debussy's *Prélude*. French poets, in their turn, were influenced by the writings of Edgar Allan Poe, who, more than half a century before Freud, had explored the world of subconscious fears and nightmares. Russian music, which Debussy had first encountered as a student in Russia (staying with Tchaikovsky's patron, Nadezhda von Meck) and at concerts of Russian music in Paris in the 1880s, helped to expand his ideas. Debussy's freedom of form, his use of scales and harmonies that create piquant and ambiguous effects unusual in Western music, and his complex and delicate orchestration, all show the influence of Russian composers such as Musorgsky, Borodin, Rimsky-Korsakov, and Balakirev, whose music, in turn, drew on central European and Eastern folk music. Some of Debussy's characteristic drifting harmonies are already to be found in the music of Chabrier – chains of seventh and ninth chords, in particular. Even Wagner had a powerful influence on Debussy. Although he took harmony in a different direction, Debussy's use of little motifs rather than traditional themes to construct musical forms owes much to Wagner's deployment of leitmotifs in his operas.

Debussy was greatly influenced by painting, and by images of all kinds. Sometimes a post-card or a wine label would be enough to set him off on a train of thought, and to give him what he needed to evoke an atmosphere. In this he was very different from most of the great Romantic composers of the nineteenth century, for whom the chief source of inspiration, apart from music itself, was almost exclusively literary. The association of colours and sound was in the air: several French writers in the early years of the twentieth century explored the analogies between the two, writing of painting as 'a music of colours without movement', and of Monet's landscapes as 'symphonies of luminous waves', while Debussy's music is 'Impressionism consisting of touches of sonority'. Debussy was certainly inspired by the Impressionists, but he disliked the term being applied to his own music. Writing about his orchestral *Images*, he said, 'I am trying to do something new, involving several kinds of reality – what the idiots call "impressionism".' For Debussy, J. M. W. Turner was 'the finest creator of mystery there could be in art'.[1]

Another encounter that fascinated Debussy was the Javanese gamelan that he heard and saw at the Paris World Exhibition in 1889. He spent hours listening to them, and wrote, 'Their conservatoire is the eternal rhythm of the sea, the wind among the leaves and the thousand sounds of nature which they understand without consulting an arbitrary treatise ... yet Javanese music is based on a type of counterpoint by comparison with which that of Palestrina is child's play. And if we listen without European prejudice to the charm of their percussion we must confess that our percussion is like primitive noises at a country fair.'[2] This is just one example of Debussy's openness to non-standard ways of creating musical effects and textures. In 1903, asked whether he would consider writing a history of orchestration, he replied, 'To be honest, you learn orchestration far better by listening to the sound of leaves rustling in the wind than by consulting handbooks in which the instruments look like anatomical specimens and which, in any case, contain very incomplete information about the innumerable ways of blending the said instruments with each other.'[3]

At the same time, Debussy was a master craftsman. The superficial effect may be of atmosphere, washes of sound, impressions. But his music is constructed with meticulous care through the deployment of motifs. Transformation of themes and motifs was a stock-in-trade of Liszt and Wagner, whose influence was felt in France as strongly as elsewhere. Debussy takes this art to a level of subtlety beyond any previous composer. In a lecture on modern music delivered in the United States in 1928, Ravel commented, '... is the symbolism of Debussy, his so-called Impressionism, at variance with the Gallic spirit? Quite the contrary, because beneath the fine and delicate lacework of atmospheric surface, one may easily find a refined precision of design, characteristically French.'[4]

IMAGES FOR ORCHESTRA
Duration: approx. 33 minutes

Gigues
Ibéria: 'Par les rues et par les chemins', 'Les parfums de la nuit', 'Le matin d'un jour de fête'
Rondes de printemps

Debussy wrote two sets of *Images* for piano. Between the two, in 1905, he started work on another set of *Images* for two pianos. But he soon decided to continue them as orchestral pieces. They were published as a set in 1913, in the order given above (in which they are usually performed). But Debussy had composed them over seven years in a different order: 'Ibéria' was completed in 1908, 'Ronde de Printemps' in 1909, and 'Gigues' in 1912. 'Ibéria' is often performed separately, and forms a satisfying twenty-minute, three-part work on its own.

'Gigues' is based on a Northumbrian folk song in jig rhythm, 'The Keel Row'. It was most likely familiar to Debussy from a song by Charles Bordes, 'Dansons la gigue', a setting of a poem by Paul Verlaine. In the song, the refrain, 'Danson la gigue' (Let us dance the jig) is accompanied by a wildly energetic performance of 'The Keel Row' on the piano. The verses between become increasingly nostalgic and intense as the singer remembers the eyes and kisses of the girl who 'has ways to devastate a poor lover'. Only with difficulty does he force himself back to the jig. Debussy's piece explores a similar tension between the jollity of the song and a nostalgic lament – he originally planned to call it 'Gigues tristes'. The plaintive voice is an oboe d'amore, an instrument halfway between oboe and cor anglais with a hauntingly plangent tone.

An introduction hints at 'The Keel Row' with fragments of the tune suspended over an atmospheric background of whole-tone harmonies. The oboe d'amore enters alone, playing not 'The Keel Row', but a lament whose bagpipe-style grace notes give it a distinctly rustic character (it could itself be a jig in slow motion). This alternates with further fragments of 'The Keel Row'. As the jig rhythm gathers energy in the orchestra, the lament of the oboe d'amore persists, creating a counterpoint on both a musical and an emotional level. 'The Keel Row' is continually quoted, but never played in its entirety, the shifting harmonies constantly subverting its cheerful character. The orchestra becomes infected by the oboe d'amore's melancholy, developing a nostalgic melody of its own. The music builds to a climax and collapses, and the piece ends in fragments, as it began.

André Caplet, who, according to some scholars, may have helped Debussy with the orchestration of 'Gigues', described the movement as '*Gigues* ... sad *Gigues* ... tragic *Gigues* ... painting of the soul ... A bruised soul whose modesty, however, is disturbed and frightened away by the overflowing of lyricism, so that it disguises its sobs beneath the mask and angular gesticulation of a grotesque marionette.'[5] There is certainly something mysterious and otherworldly about 'Gigues'. At the time Debussy wrote it, he was working on two opera projects based on Edgar Allan Poe, *The Fall of the House of Usher* and *The Devil in the Belfry*, neither of which were ever completed. In the latter, there was to be a scene in which the devil compels the crowd to follow him by playing 'a fantastic jig' that builds to a climax and then cuts off as the devil jumps into a canal. Whether or not 'Gigues' contains music planned for the scene, its blend of energy and mystery suggests an association.

In an essay on Debussy published after his death, the composer Manuel de Falla writes about the many works of Debussy inspired, more or less indirectly, by Spain.[6] He had visited Spain only once, on a day trip to San Sebastian to attend a bullfight. But, 'Debussy knew Spain from his readings, from pictures, from songs, and from dances with songs danced by true Spanish dancers ... The facts are that the character of the Spanish musical language had been assimilated by Debussy and this composer, who really did not know Spain, was thus able to write Spanish music spontaneously, perhaps unconsciously, at any rate in a way which was the envy of many who knew Spain only too well.'

In the first part, 'Par les rues et par les chemins', Falla writes, 'A sort of *Sevillana*, the generating theme of the work, suggests village songs heard in the bright, scintillating light.' Tambourine and castanets help to establish the scene, but it is the Sevillana rhythm, and the way the swirling fragments of melody cut against it, that give a depth of Spanish character. Impassioned violins lead into a darker middle section. The castanets falter and, over a drone bass, the swirlings take on a darker tone, low on clarinets, and the violins play an eerie pattern of harmonics. Into this strange atmosphere enter oboe and solo viola, singing a plaintive chant, evocative of the Andalusian *cante jondo* (deep song) that lies at the heart of flamenco.

As the chant develops, it is gradually engulfed by the growing energy in the rest of the orchestra, until the music bursts into a faster tempo. Horns and trumpets exchange fanfares. Twice the music builds over another drone bass. The first time, it is still haunted by the darkness of the chant. The second time it has a more affirmative mood, and leads on to a brief reprise of the opening Sevillana, until, with another touch of mysterious whole-tone harmony, the dance fades away.

Whole-tone harmonies also set the nocturnal atmosphere of the middle movement of *Ibéria*, 'Les parfums de la nuit'. There are languid fragments of chant from oboe and cor anglais. Flurries of notes on woodwind and celesta suggest a breeze getting up, and there are hints at the rhythm of a *habanera*. Over quiet, sonorous string chords, the chant becomes an extended, tender oboe melody. The mood becomes more still and concentrated, with scintillating touches of celesta and harp, as a horn takes up the chant. A brief outburst from the violins reveals the passion lying beneath the surface. Two low flutes in unison are followed by high bassoon and solo violin in unison, evocative expressions of tender melancholy. What now seems like a love scene develops further passionate intensity, before falling back to quiet memories of the opening of the movement. Distant bells sound, the high bassoon and solo violin (now with flute, 'soft and distant') sing a last couple of phrases.

At an early rehearsal of *Ibéria*, Debussy was particularly pleased with the transition to the final section: 'You can't imagine how naturally the transition works between "Les parfums de la nuit" and "Le matin d'un jour de fête". *It sounds as though it's improvised* ... The way it comes to life, with people and things waking up ... There's a man selling water-melons and urchins whistling, I see them quite clearly.'[7] Falla suggests that this section might evoke Debussy's visit to the bullfight at San Sebastian, where he remembered 'the light in the bull ring, particularly the violent contrast between the one half of the ring flooded with sunlight and the other half deep in shade'. Two factors contribute to the seamless join between the two sections: the speed of the beat is exactly doubled, so that there is no sense of pull to a faster tempo; and the little motif with which the new piece begins (two repeated notes and a higher note) is simply the final phrase of the old piece speeded up – indeed, this shape is closely related to motifs in the first movement, 'Par les rues et par les chemins', one of the many links that give a sense of organic unity to the whole work.

Debussy specifies that the opening of 'Le matin d'un jour de fête' is to be played 'in the rhythm of a distant march, alert and joyful'. The march begins very quietly, with the jingle of a tambourine. For a brief moment a fragment of the preceding slow melody is heard on flute, 'even more distant'. Then the march draws closer, with the tambourine joined by side drum. An excited crowd is suggested by swirling and chant-like fragments of melody, one of which is a faster version of the extended oboe melody from 'Les parfums de la nuit'. As the march settles in rhythm, this melody is played high by two clarinets in unison, suggesting the raucous effect of a bagpipe chanter or shawm. For a time, different elements come and go as if our attention is drawn to various groups in the crowd: there is a free, recitative-like melody on flute and bassoon, a trumpet reminds us of the slower melody from 'Les parfums de la nuit', a solo violin shows off like a juggler, punctuated by thwacks on the tambourine. The violin's melody (yet another version of the swirling shape) is enthusiastically taken up by oboe and cor anglais. This melody persists as the march tempo reasserts itself. 'Ibéria' ends with a burst of speed, and final whoops of joy from the trombones.

At the head of the score of 'Ronde de Printemps', Debussy placed a quotation from a poem:

Vive le mai, bienvenu soit le mai	Long live May, welcome May
Avec son gonfalon sauvage! (La Maggiolata)	With its wild banner!

This is a translation of a fifteenth-century Italian poem by Poliziano (Politian), sung and danced as part of the May Day celebrations in Tuscany. But this is no straightforwardly jolly piece. Like 'Gigues', it is evanescent, suggesting rather than stating its mood. And, also like 'Gigues', it draws on popular melody. 'Ronde de Printemps' incorporates two French traditional tunes: 'Dodo, l'enfant do', a lullaby, and 'Nous n'irons plus au bois', a children's round-dance. References to these tunes are even more fleeting and oblique than those to 'The Keel Row' in 'Gigues'. After a few bars of shimmering, with mysterious calls on bassoons and horns, hints at 'Dodo, l'enfant do' are played by flute and oboe. But these are soon over-whelmed by a web of sound as the agitation grows and then subsides. Clarinets enter with a pattern of dancing triplets. But they are in five-time, making it impossible to pin this music down. The tune 'Nous n'irons plus au bois' enters as a rapid theme on oboe, but soon disperses into fragments that are passed from instrument to instrument. The music slows and becomes more mysterious, developing motifs from the opening bars. Suddenly, the oboe returns to the rapid 'Nous n'irons plus au bois', and a game of musical catch ensues, becoming more and more energetic, with the horns playing the tune more slowly (and more recogniz-ably) than the other instruments. After a lull, the clarinets return to their rapid five-time triplets, and we are into a reprise of the opening. This soon takes a new turn, and 'Nous n'irons plus au bois' enters as a sustained chant on clarinets. This chant combines with a web of dancing rhythms, and the music develops energetic momentum to take it to a final rush of exuberance.

'Rondes de Printemps' prompted one of Debussy's most revealing comments about music in a letter to his publisher, Jacques Durand: 'The music of this piece is peculiar in the sense that it is immaterial and one therefore cannot handle it as though it were a robust symphony, walking on all four feet (sometimes three, but walking anyway). Generally speaking, I feel more and more that music, by its very essence, is not something that can flow inside a rigorous, traditional form. It consists of colours and of rhythmicized time . . . The rest of it's just a lot of nonsense invented by unfeeling imbeciles on the backs of the Masters, who in most cases were writing no more than the music of their period!'[8]

JEUX
Duration: approx. 17 minutes

Jeux (Games) was Debussy's last orchestral work, composed in 1912 as a ballet score for Sergei Diaghilev's Ballets Russes. The idea for the ballet was proposed by the dancer Vaslav Nijinsky while he was having lunch with Diaghilev and the designer Léon Bakst. According to the memoirs of the painter Jacques-Émile Blanche (largely corroborated in Nijinsky's diaries), Nijinsky declared, 'there should be no *corps de ballet*, no ensembles, no variations, no *pas de deux*, only boys and girls in flannels and rhythmic movements . . . a game of tennis was to be interrupted by the crashing of an aeroplane'. The idea was sent to Debussy by telegram, who replied, 'No, it's idiotic and unmusical. I should not dream of writing a score for this work.'[9]

Debussy was, however, seriously in need of money, and when the offer of a fee was doubled, he agreed to do it. The score was completed in three weeks in August 1912.

Nijinsky's original idea underwent revision and refinement. In the final scenario, there are three dancers in tennis clothes, a man and two women. The ballet opens in an empty park at night-time. A tennis ball lands on the stage, and a young man with a tennis racquet runs across the stage after it. Two girls timidly peer out, and then begin to dance. The young man surprises them, and at first they are alarmed and start to flee. But he gently coaxes them back. One of them dances with him, and they kiss. The other, a little jealous, mocks the man. Intrigued by her, he leaves the first girl and dances with the second girl with increasing passion. The first girl is upset. But the second girl comforts her, the man joins them, and the three dance together. Just as their dance culminates in an ecstatic triple kiss, another tennis ball lands on the stage. Surprised and frightened, they vanish into the dark.

This simple scenario in a modern setting was radically different from the conventional ballets of the time, with their exotic and antique scenarios and lavish costumes and sets. The premiere, on 15 May 1913, was not a success: the ballet was performed five times and then dropped from the repertoire. Debussy himself blamed the failure on Nijinsky's choreography, which was based closely on the 'Eurythmics' of the Swiss composer and educator Émile Jaques-Dalcroze. Seeing Nijinsky's choreography for the first time, Debussy wrote that he 'has given an odd mathematical twist to his perverse genius … This fellow adds up demi-semi-quavers with his feet, proves the result with his arms and then, as if suddenly struck with paralysis of one side, listens to the music disapprovingly. This, it appears, is called "the stylisation of gesture". How awful! It is in fact Dalcrozian, and this is to tell you that I hold Monsieur Dalcroze to be one of the worst enemies of music!'[10]

When the first concert performance was also unsuccessful the following year, Debussy wrote to the conductor, Gabriel Pierné, 'I had the impression the orchestra liked it much less than you did … I also felt the various episodes lacked homogeneity! The link between them may be subtle but it exists, surely? … And the last thing, by and large it's too loud.'[11] In an earlier letter, Debussy had written of the need in *Jeux* for an orchestra 'without feet', of an orchestral colour 'which seems to be lit from behind'.[12]

After being ignored for many years, *Jeux* has in recent decades come to be regarded as one of Debussy's finest works. It has been much discussed by analysts in search of the 'subtle links' to which Debussy referred. As often in Debussy, the thematic material consists of little motifs, never more than a bar or two long. *Jeux* is constructed from many different such motifs, which seem to flit by kaleidoscopically. The ballet score is like the most evanescent parts of *La Mer* extended into a seemingly free improvisation, with continual shifting of tempo and orchestration. But it is not entirely shapeless. Three of the motifs that occur at the beginning are important later on, and become prominent in the final climax. In the middle of the ballet, many other motifs come to the fore. Some of these are related to the opening motifs, in shape or rhythm, though it takes familiarity with the music for this to become clear. Overall, the ballet has a sort of arch shape, in which the motifs that occur at the beginning create a sense of return at the end. The satisfaction for the listener lies in the freedom and fantasy with which Debussy plays with the different elements, and constantly keeps us on our toes for the next turn of events.

There are few gaps in the music, and the landmarks are subtle and easy to miss. So timings are given in the description that follows, based on the classic 1958 recording by the Suisse

Romande Orchestra conducted by Ernest Ansermet.[13] This performance lasts 17 minutes. More recent performances are often closer to 19 minutes, so the timings of the landmarks are stretched out proportionately. The descriptions of the stage action are taken from the score.

Jeux begins with a slow introduction. Strings hold a sustained pianissimo note, against which harps and a horn haltingly touch in three notes of a rising chromatic scale. This is the first important motif. As it continues, mysterious wind chords fall (their whole-tone harmonies suggest an echo of the mysterious chords that open Dukas's *The Sorcerer's Apprentice*). The music breaks into a faster tempo, and an agitated little figure is played by low violas answered by cellos and bassoon – four repeated notes and a pattern falling down the chromatic scale. This is the second motif, and it gradually increases in energy as instruments gather over the next few bars. It is brought to a halt by a drum roll, and Debussy returns to the mysterious wind chords of the opening, with the rising and falling chromatic scale in the strings. Little calls on cor anglais and bassoon (again, three notes of a chromatic scale) take us back into the faster tempo. It introduces the third motif, a graceful little phrase on clarinet that ends on a rising scale. This, combined with the first two motifs, builds into a longer paragraph, until it is stopped by a sudden wind chord and descending flourish [1'50"]. At this point, a tennis ball drops onto the stage, and, in quick succession, the young man in tennis clothes leaps after it, and the two girls timidly peer out. The passage that follows, full of delicate trills and tremolo, is particularly like the 'Jeux de vagues' from *La Mer*. A bolder, falling motif in the violins introduces a moment of new warmth, but is soon overtaken by renewal of the third (rising) motif. This develops to a (modest) climax, with trumpets and woodwind calling [3'15"]. Here, one of the two girls dances by herself, with a high bassoon solo and swirls in the upper woodwind. The cor anglais repeats the bassoon solo, and the two girls alternate in a delicate passage with continually changing orchestration.

There is a sudden moment of hesitancy as the girls hear the sound of leaves rustling [4'30"]. The music rises agitatedly to a climax (trumpets and firm string chords) as the man steps out in front of the girls. After a timid little viola melody, the music becomes agitated again as the girls try to flee, then calmer as he gently brings them back, culminating in a moment of serene string chorus [5'20"]. He dances, to a high violin melody which begins as an elaboration of the bassoon solo that accompanied the first girl's dance. A passage constantly in flux, with scintillating runs in the woodwind, culminates in a little climax as the second girl runs towards him. As they begin to dance together [5'55"], the music of the man's solo returns, with the serene string chorus followed by the high violin melody. There is a trumpet solo as he asks her for a kiss, and a moment of coyness as she resists and flees. She rejoins him, consenting [quiet clarinets at 6'20"], and they dance together.

The music takes on a new passion, with harp glissandi and high woodwind arabesques adding a magical element to the strings. As it subsides to another moment of tenderness, an oboe recalls the timid viola melody from their first conversation [6'45"], and there is a moment of calm. A new agitated figure indicates the second girl's chagrin as she is left out; the motif of the falling chromatic scale appears in the piccolo. The couple, oblivious of her, continue their embrace, and the second girl renews her chagrin. After sour little calls on muted trumpets, she begins a mocking dance [7'30"]. Chords in the woodwind fall and rise in a chromatic scale over a reiterated pattern of pizzicato and staccato muted trumpet. The dance becomes more insistent and accelerates, until the rhythm steadies as the man becomes intrigued, leaves the first girl and joins the second girl. 'We'll dance like this', he indicates, with a clarinet solo that draws on the running scale of the third motif [8'00"]. At first the girl imitates him mockingly (brittle fragments of melody with pizzicato). But soon they dance together. They begin tentatively, but soon the music settles into an energetic waltz rhythm and becomes more and more passionate – this is the first really sustained passage in the ballet.

Suddenly they become aware of the first girl, who is upset and hides her face in her hands. The dance comes to a halt, with a high violin note marked 'éperdu' (desperate) [10'05"]. Fragments of melody, including a violin solo, suggest attempts at coaxing and the first girl's refusal. The scoring becomes warmer, with rich string chords, and eventually, to the sound of a trio of solo cellos, the second girl takes the first girl in her arms [11'25"]. The young man gently separates their heads, and urges them to surrender to the beauty of the night. Over the gentle beating of celesta chords, the waltz rhythm resumes, and the cor anglais plays the graceful third motif – the first time since the opening section that it has been heard clearly, in its original form. Other familiar motifs join it, and the dance builds in confidence, eases for a moment, then builds again. Soon [13'20"] the three are dancing together, with a sustained melody low on bass clarinet, bassoon, and horns. Gradually the dance grows in passion, the music evolving in a series of waves to a climax marked 'violent'. At its height, it gives way to a moment of quiet ecstasy, as the young man draws their three heads together in a triple kiss [15'50"].

The spell is broken by a pianissimo cascade of piccolos, flutes, and clarinets, as a tennis ball falls at their feet. With a harp glissando they vanish, surprised and frightened, into the darkness of the park. Finally, the music returns to the mysterious chords of the slow introduction, now unsettled further by rapid, murmuring patterns in the strings. The ballet ends with a tiptoeing descent down the familiar chromatic scale, and with one last chord, including a touch of xylophone and celesta, it is over.

LA MER
Duration: approx. 24 minutes

De l'aube à midi sur la mer (From dawn to midday on the sea)
Jeux de vagues (Play of waves)
Dialogue du vent et de la mer (Dialogue of the wind and the sea)

The premiere of Debussy's *La Mer* in Paris in January 1908 was conducted by the composer, and it was his first experience of conducting an orchestra. He could not have chosen a more difficult and complex work for his debut. But the orchestra had been well prepared by its chief conductor, Édouard Colonne, Debussy had the impression 'that I really reached the heart of my own music', and the result was a sensational triumph. The composer was called back to the platform ten times, and as he complied reluctantly he was made to feel like 'a freak showman or an acrobat at the completion of a dangerous act'.[14] Debussy had started composing the work in September 1903 at Bichain in Burgundy, where his wife Lilly's parents lived (he was to leave her the following year). He wrote from there to the composer André Messager, telling him that he was working on *La Mer*: 'You're unaware, maybe, that I was intended for the noble career of a sailor and have only deviated from that path thanks to the quirks of fate. Even so, I've retained a sincere devotion to the sea. To which you'll reply that the Atlantic doesn't exactly wash the foothills of Burgundy ...! And that the result could be one of those hack landscapes done in the studio! But I have innumerable memories, and those, in my view, are worth more than a reality which, charming as it may be, tends to weigh too heavily on the imagination.'[15] He completed the work in 1905 at the Grand Hotel, Eastbourne, from where he wrote to his publisher, Jacques Durand, 'It's a charming, peaceful spot. The sea unfurls itself with an utterly British correctness.'[16] There is nothing 'correct' about Debussy's vision of the sea. Of all his music, *La Mer* is the work that seems most to have been inspired by the powerful and mysterious seascapes of Turner. But it was part of a Japanese print, Hokusai's famous *The Great Wave off Kanagawa*, that Debussy chose for the cover of his score. In the original, three boats are caught in a huge wave, their crews tiny in the face of the great force of nature that seems about to overwhelm them.

Subtitled 'Three symphonic sketches', *La Mer* comes closer to being a symphony than anything Debussy ever wrote. At first hearing, it may seem formless, a succession of washes of sound, or a sort of 'stream of consciousness'. Its complex textures often sound like an echo of the gamelan music that so impressed Debussy at the Paris World Exhibition. But there is nothing vague or haphazard about his compositional methods. The whole work is carefully structured using a small number of motifs that recur and are transformed.[17]

'De l'aube à midi sur la mer' begins with a slow introduction, as if in darkness. Over a low, held bass note, two of the most important motifs are heard. First the cellos quietly play a rising, snappy two-note motif (short-long), then the oboe plays it rising and falling (a very similar motif is prominent in the earlier 'Sirènes', the third of Debussy's *Nocturnes*). The second motif is a slow triplet of repeated notes. This is played by the strange and haunting combination of muted trumpet and cor anglais, which extend it into a rising and falling chant. All this takes place over a delicate tracery of muted strings.

The pace accelerates, the strings remove their mutes, and rippling patterns emerge in cellos and woodwind. Four muted horns play a chant-like melody that seems related to the earlier chant of the trumpet and cor anglais. A flute plays another flowing melody, rising and falling in triplet patterns. An oboe elaborates the falling version of the snappy motif, with a solo violin in duet. The horns remove their mutes, and their chant becomes more insistent. Trumpets, still muted but now menacing, renew the first version of the chant, with its slow triplet and rise and fall, as the woodwind drive it on with their faster rippling triplets. The music rises to its first climax, at which the falling triplet is played slowly and forcefully and then scatters.

Now a new idea is generated: the cellos, divided into a four-part chorus, play the rising, snappy motif, and extend it into a dancing theme whose dotted-triplet rhythms inject new energy into the scene. This theme is taken up by the woodwind, then powerfully by the four horns. The music gradually calms, with the energetic dotted triplets persisting in the strings. As they continue, muted trumpet and cor anglais return to their haunting slow triplet chant from the beginning. The music becomes still, and cor anglais and two solo violas play a line that slowly falls and rises, seeming to distil all the rising and falling patterns into a moment of peace, though with a whole-tone scale that gives it a sense of uncertainty. Now we have reached the culmination of the movement. As two harps evoke scintillating wave patterns, the four horns, joined by trombones, solemnly intone the slow triplet from the chant, developing it into a chorale. This rises to a great climax, at which the snappy motif is reprised by the full brass, with cymbals, timpani, and gong adding to the awesome power. For the last time, the falling triplet is declaimed, and an *fff* chord swells and fades.

The second movement, 'Jeux de vagues', is a delicate and brilliant movement akin to a scherzo. After a few bars of evanescent touches, cor anglais, followed by oboe, play a rising flourish in a whole-tone scale, and then extend it into a chattering line. The rising flourish is like an expansion of the snappy motif in the first movement, and its extension relates to the familiar rising and falling shapes. The violins transform the chattering line into a dancing melody in three-time. Three horns play mysterious fragments of a chorale in whole-tone harmonies. Then, under flickering repeated patterns on flutes and clarinets, the cor anglais transforms the horn chorale into a flowing melody. A playful extension of it passes from clarinet to solo violin (all of this passage, with its exotic harmonies and evanescent textures, has quite a Russian sound).

Just as the music begins to build, the oboe quietly enters with a reprise of the opening flourish and chattering line. A little later, the flickering repeated patterns are taken up by horns and trumpets, and the cellos play the cor anglais's flowing melody, extending it further. As it sinks down, oboe and clarinet enter with a brief reminder of the opening flourish and chattering line. A trumpet fanfare sets off a new phase of dance, whose climax alludes to the snappy, two-note motif from the first movement. Now the dancing three-time melody from early in the movement returns. It is joined by a lyrical rising phrase that emerges from the middle of the texture to become dominant, its leaping shape driving the music on as it accelerates (this shape is clearly related to the dancing theme played by the chorus of cellos in the first movement). As the biggest climax of the movement is reached, trumpets and horns again remind us of the snappy two-note motif. The force quickly disperses, as elements from the beginning of the movement reappear – washes of harps and cymbals, the rising flourish, the horn chorale – and a movement that has been in almost constant, kaleidoscopic agitation finally comes to rest.

The finale, 'Dialogue of the wind and the sea', begins over a low drum roll with brusque muttering from cellos and basses: the flourish that started the second movement has become a menacing growl. They are answered by anxious woodwind and horns, with yet another version of the falling and rising motif that has undergone transformation throughout the work. Then two motifs return from the very beginning: the snappy two-note motif, and the muted trumpet's rising and falling chant. The music builds to a moment of violence. Then oboes and bassoon form the triplet from the chant into a plaintive melody, which rises and falls as the brusque muttering persists in a repeated pattern in the strings below. The agitation increases, the muted trumpet chant moves to the bass, in bassoons and pizzicato cellos, and a massive climax is reached. As it fades away, four horns solemnly intone the slow triplets, a reminder of the end of the first movement.

The music reaches a point of intense stillness. Violins hold a pianissimo high harmonic, and oboe and flute reprise the plaintive melody, extending it with a delicately falling pattern of repeated notes as the tempo ebbs and flows. This is taken up passionately by the strings, there is another quiet moment, and the tempo suddenly increases. Trumpets set up a pattern of fast triplets, over which a muted cornet plays a rapid version of the rising and falling chant. The chant, alternating with the snappy two-note motif, gradually builds in tension, driven on by the fast triplet pattern. The plaintive melody returns in the woodwind, as the surrounding texture becomes more complex and agitated, from bass drum at the bottom to piccolo at the top. From the middle of this web of sound emerges the solemn chorale from the end of the first movement, now majestic on full brass. This bursts into a scattering of the familiar motifs, and the movement hurtles to a tempestuous final climax.

NOCTURNES
Duration: approx. 24 minutes

Nuages
Fêtes
Sirènes

Debussy wrote the *Nocturnes* over several years in the 1890s. He originally intended to call them *Scènes au crépuscule* (*Twilight Scenes*), after poems by Henri de Regnier that evoke a dream-like, ancient landscape. Later they metamorphosed into a work for solo violin and orchestra. Finally in 1899 they reached their final form as the three *Nocturnes*. The sources of Debussy's ideas were, as usual, diverse, including not only de Regnier's poems but also the sight of clouds from one of the bridges of Paris, memories of a festival in the Bois de Boulogne, and (perhaps) the grand visit of the Russian Tsar Nicholas II and Tsarina Alexandra to Paris in 1896. But, as so often with Debussy, the atmosphere that the music evokes is impossible to tie down to such tangible origins. Debussy himself wrote that the title *Nocturnes* was intended to evoke 'all the various impressions and the special effects of light that the word suggests'.[18]

'Nuages' was inspired by 'night on the Pont de Solférino, very late. A great stillness. I was leaning on the railing of the bridge. The Seine, without a ripple, like a tarnished mirror. Some clouds slowly pass through a moonlit sky . . .' The music 'renders the immutable aspect of the sky and the slow, solemn motion of the clouds, fading away in grey tones lightly tinged with white'.[19] Clarinets and bassoons unfold a sinuous, drifting pattern. A cor anglais calls plaintively. Violins and violas, divided into many parts, take up the sinuous pattern, which evolves, rising to a climax, as the cor anglais repeatedly calls, punctuated by horns. The sinuous pattern evolves again into a repeating accompanying figure, as clarinets, bassoons, and oboes play a new, dark figure that gradually rises. Again a climax is reached, and again the cor anglais repeats its plaintive call. The opening sinuous figure briefly reappears on oboes, with a counterpoint on solo viola. The music settles, changing key to a quiet string chord. Over this, flute and harp play a rather oriental-sounding melody, rising and falling. This too evolves, on solo violin, viola, and cello, and then returns to flute and harp. The plaintive cor anglais returns, together with the horns, and over a *ppp* timpani roll and tremolando cellos and basses the piece winds quietly to a close. It ends with fragments of the sinuous figure on bassoons and flute, a final call of muted horns, an unresolved chord, and a last pizzicato B.

The modest orchestra of 'Nuages' is joined by trumpets, trombones, tuba, a second harp, cymbals, and side drum for 'Fêtes'. Debussy said that the piece was inspired by memories of an evening festival in the Bois de Boulogne: 'I have seen from afar, through the trees, lights approaching, and the crowd running towards the path where the procession is going to pass.'[20] But there is also a distinctly Mediterranean atmosphere created by the lively rhythm of a tarantella (as in the finale of Mendelssohn's 'Italian' Symphony). The violins burst in with the rhythm on repeated notes, like drummers, clarinets and cor anglais play a theme built of swirling scales finishing with a persistent little rhythmic tug, and a trumpet call cuts across the rhythm. These are the elements that, as in 'Nuages', repeat and evolve. The swirling theme moves from treble to bass as the momentum builds, but a stately brass fanfare interrupts. A rush of harps sets the woodwind chattering (their pattern has something in common with the drifting pattern at the start of 'Nuages', though the effect is very different), and the various elements join in a dance. There is a quiet moment, in which an oboe introduces a plaintive little phrase (again, this seems related to the cor anglais's calls in 'Nuages'), but the tarantella rhythm persists underneath. As the energy builds, woodwind play a more sustained melody that cuts across the prevailing rhythm. As the dance builds to a climax, it is suddenly cut off.

From the distance appears a marching procession, beginning very quietly on harps, timpani, and pizzicato strings (Stravinsky surely remembered this when he was writing *The Rite of Spring*). Pianissimo muted trumpets play a little fanfare that is a more stately derivative of the tarantella rhythm. The woodwind and the horns take up the march as it comes closer. Finally the march theme blazes on trumpets and trombones, as the tarantella rhythm persists on woodwind and side drum, and the strings play the swirling scales. Debussy breaks away from the procession as suddenly as he introduced it. We return to the original, faster tempo, and woodwind again take up the swirling theme. Against it, violins play a slower, forceful version of a phrase from the swirling. This leads on to a reprise of the woodwind chattering, which alternates with the swirling element. But soon the music quietens, a bassoon reminds us of the oboe's plaintive phrase from the opening section, and the tempo slows. Fragments of the swirling theme in slow motion pass from oboe to bassoon to flute, and the brass fanfare is dimly recalled. The tarantella rhythm resumes pianissimo, and, with a final distant sound of muted trumpets, the music vanishes.

'Sirènes', according to Debussy, 'depicts the sea and its countless rhythms, and presently, among the waves silvered by the moonlight, is heard the mysterious song of the sirens as they laugh and pass on.'[21] Several elements of this sea-painting were later to find their way into *La Mer*. The sirens are represented by a wordless chorus of sixteen female voices in two groups: eight sopranos and eight mezzo-sopranos. At first each group sings in four-part harmony, but later their parts simplify into lines in unison or octaves. The piece opens with horns calling languidly, and the sirens answering flirtatiously. Their falling two-note phrase is a version of the trumpet call that ended 'Fêtes'. Later, it persists with the two notes rising. The dialogue develops over a shimmering seascape of strings, woodwind, and harps. The cor anglais plays a plaintive phrase that curls as it falls – somewhat reminiscent of the calls of the cor anglais in 'Nuages'. This becomes a recurring motif that enlivens the sea-like texture. The choir sings a sinuous line that rocks over two notes and then rises and falls (this too seems to echo some of the drifting lines in 'Nuages').

The music builds in intensity and complexity, and subsides. At the quietest point, the choir sings a languid version of the falling cor anglais phrase, which now floats on a wave of voluptuously shifting harmonies. The orchestra responds by building to the most passionate climax of the movement. As it reaches its height, trumpets plays a rising and falling version of the sinuous line, now in a whole-tone scale (this evocative line was to become one of the most important elements in Debussy's *La Mer*). The music is still delicately agitated, with the rising two-note call from the opening, as the choir reiterates its sinuous rocking motif. From another low point, one more wave builds and falls. Over the final pages, the music becomes gradually more peaceful and mysterious, with whole-tone scales and harmonies culminating in a trumpet quietly repeating its version of the sinuous line. The ending is very quiet, with a *ppp* string chord of B major suspended in the air, anchored only by the lowest voice of the choir singing a low B.

PRÉLUDE À L'APRÈS-MIDI D'UN FAUNE
Duration: approx. 10 minutes

L'après-midi d'un faune is a poem by Stéphane Mallarmé that takes the ancient myth of the god Pan pursuing the nymph Syrinx, and develops from it an elusive dream-world, exploring the borderline between the conscious and the unconscious, reality and dream. A faun (half-human, half-goat), intoxicated by visions of an entwined pair of nymphs, tries to seize them, and as they flee, abandons himself to dreaming. That, at least, is the bald summary. But the whole poem is full of uncertainties, erotic but unspecific. Debussy's original plan was for several pieces of music that would be interleaved with a reading of the poem (Mallarmé always intended it to be read out loud). But in the end, Debussy decided to write a single piece. He described his *Prélude* as no more than 'the general impression of the poem'. But he added, 'As for the ending, it's a prolongation of the last line: "Couple, farewell. I shall see the shadow that you have become."'[22]

Debussy and Mallarmé were already friends at the time when the composer began work on his *Prélude* in 1892, but there are contradictory reports as to whether Mallarmé was or was not enthusiastic about Debussy's project. What is certain is that he was impressed when he heard the *Prélude*, first played by Debussy on the piano, and then at the orchestral premiere in December 1894. Afterwards he wrote to Debussy, 'I have just left the concert and am deeply moved: what a marvel! Your illustration of "L'après-midi d'un faune" presents no dissonance with my text, except that it goes further, truly, in nostalgia and light, with finesse, uneasiness and richness.'[23] Three years later, in 1897, Mallarmé presented Debussy with a copy of his poem, in which he had written a dedicatory poem:

Sylvain d'haleine première	Woodland spirit with primal breath
Si ta flute a réussi	If your flute has succeeded
Ouïs toute la lumière	Listen to all the light
Qu'y soufflera Debussy.	That Debussy will blow into it.

Prélude à l'après-midi d'un faune was Debussy's earliest international triumph, and it remains his most popular orchestral work. More than that, in its fluid treatment of its themes, which constantly evolve without ever quite repeating themselves, and in its floating harmonies, it created a precedent on which many composers were to draw into the twentieth century, just as Wagner's *Tristan* had opened the floodgates of feverish chromaticism thirty years earlier. Indeed, Debussy had been profoundly affected by his visits to Wagner's festival at Bayreuth in 1888–9, where he attended both *Tristan* and *Parsifal*, describing *Parsifal* as 'one of the most beautiful monuments ever raised to music . . . incomparable and bewildering, splendid and strong'.[24] In the fluid sensuality of his *Prélude* we can hear how Debussy had absorbed that powerful influence to create something uniquely his own.

The *Prélude* begins with a famous unaccompanied flute solo. This is a highly unusual beginning, and it could scarcely have existed without the great school of French flautists, Paul Taffanel and his pupils, that inspired Debussy's generation of composers. The flute's gentle arabesques immediately plunge us into harmonic uncertainty: the opening rise and fall extends from C sharp down to G natural, the interval of a tritone, making the melody hang in the air without any sense of a key. A horn quietly calls over sweeping harp glissandi. The flute melody then expands and becomes gradually more elaborate. As it winds to its highest point, the first flute is joined by the second flute, which then falls away as the melody descends. This is an example of the subtlety of orchestration that makes this music so fluid and fascinating. The clarinet introduces a more playful version of the melody, which is taken up by the flute. The oboe then brings in a simpler, more amorous simplification of the melody that builds to a climax and fades away.

From this still centre of the work emerges a broad melody. It seems quite new, but it is another evolution of the core theme. The previous version, the oboe melody, has now been simplified still further, its movements up and down transformed into passionate leaps. Here we are firmly in a key – D flat major – and for a glorious moment we seem at last to have found our bearings. The melody is played first by woodwind and then by the strings, rising to a sensuous climax. As it fades, a solo violin takes up the melody, until elements of the flute solo reappear, followed by a yet more playful reworking of the melody on oboe. These two elements alternate. As the pace slows, the opening melody returns to the two flutes at its original pitch, answered by two solo violins, and pianissimo touches on antique cymbals (tiny oriental bells) complete the magical atmosphere. In the final bars, two muted horns quietly remember the opening phrase for the last time, antique cymbals are echoed by harp harmonics, and three flutes hold a chord of E major over pizzicato cellos and basses.

FREDERICK DELIUS
(1862–1934)

What could be more English than the music of Delius? The vein of melancholy and nostalgia that characterizes the generations of English composers before and after the First World War found its most potent expression in his music. And yet, of all those composers (Elgar, Vaughan Williams, Butterworth, Gurney, Ireland, Warlock), Delius was the least English, and the least tied to England. His parents were German: his immigrant father was a prosperous wool merchant in Bradford, Yorkshire. And from his twenties until his death Delius lived abroad. The family was very musical, but Fritz (who later changed his name to Frederick) was obliged by his father to enter the family business rather than pursue music as a career. When he showed little interest or aptitude for the business, he was sent to Florida to manage an orange plantation. He stayed there for eighteen months, and it was in Florida that his desire to become a composer first developed. There he heard the spirituals and work songs of the African Americans. According to Eric Fenby, a young musician who worked with the composer as his amanuensis for the last five years of his life, Delius told him that he would sit up late into the night listening to their singing: 'They showed a truly wonderful sense of musicianship and harmonic resource in the instinctive way in which they treated a melody . . . and, hearing their singing in such romantic surroundings, it was then and there that I first felt the urge to express myself in music.'[1] In Florida he was taught music theory by an organist, Thomas Ward. Delius told Fenby, 'As far as my composing was concerned, Ward's counterpoint lessons were the only lessons from which I derived any benefit.'

After eighteen months in Florida, Delius was allowed by his father to study music at the Leipzig Conservatoire. From there he moved to France, where, apart from a period in England during the First World War, he lived for the rest of his life, first in Paris and then in his wife's house at Grez-sur-Loing, a village popular with artists near Fontainebleau. As a consequence of syphilis contracted in his twenties, he spent his last years paralyzed and blind. But he was able to continue composing with the help of Eric Fenby. After Delius's death, Fenby published a book, *Delius as I Knew Him*, which provides a vivid picture of a man of iron will and passionately held opinions.

Delius's musical style is difficult to place neatly. He drew on the post-Wagnerian harmonic language, as did his contemporaries in England. He clearly learned something from the fluidity of Debussy and other French composers. Perhaps most important was his admiration for Grieg, whose way of drawing folk song (real or imagined) into a contemporary musical style encouraged Delius in his own synthesis of the old and the new. The feature of Delius's music that is most distinctive is his harmony. He makes use of the intense harmonies of Wagner's *Tristan* and *Parsifal*, and many of the chords used by Debussy and Ravel. But in Delius the effect is particularly nostalgic and fleeting. He has a way of drenching a simple melodic line with strings of complex chords that are constantly in flux, and avoiding coming to rest on conventional cadences. Often it sounds like Grieg at his most melancholy. The character of Delius's music was well described by Philip Heseltine (who adopted the name Peter Warlock as a composer). Heseltine, more than thirty years younger than Delius, was an ardent admirer of his music, and kept up a long correspondence with him. On one occasion in 1919 he wrote to Delius's wife, Jelka Rosen, about a performance of *Brigg Fair*: 'I was very much struck on this occasion by the *richness* of the music: so much is happening all the time, one wants to linger over a bar here, a progression there. And I began to wonder whether one of the secrets of the wistful charm that pervades so much of Fred's music is not just this evanescence of beautiful things which appear for a moment, give one a glimpse of something perfectly lovely and then vanish, only to make way for another new glimpse.'[2]

Delius's music first had success in Germany. It was virtually unknown in England until, in 1907, Delius introduced himself to Sir Thomas Beecham after a concert in London. He engaged Beecham's orchestra to perform his *Appalachia*, which came as a revelation to Beecham. He wrote, 'What should have been evident at first hearing was the remotely alien sound of it, a note in English music stranger than any heard for over two hundred years, and the masterly and personal use of the orchestra.'[3] From this point on, Beecham became Delius's principal champion. He premiered *A Mass of Life* in London in 1909, and staged the opera *A Village Romeo and Juliet* during his first season at Covent Garden the following year. After Delius's death in 1934, Beecham also conducted many premiere recordings of Delius's music for Columbia Records' Delius Society.

Delius's music includes large-scale works – operas, concertos, choral works. But his lasting fame rests on a number of shorter orchestral pieces, to which his intense, fluid, melancholy voice is best suited. Of these, *Brigg Fair* is his masterpiece.

BRIGG FAIR: AN ENGLISH RHAPSODY
Duration: approx. 15 minutes

In 1905, at the North Lincolnshire Music Competition held in the market town of Brigg, Joseph Taylor, aged seventy-one, won the newly established folk song section with his performance of 'Creeping Jane'. The singing of traditional songs was in decline, and the Folk-Song Society had been founded in 1898 to collect them before they vanished. One of the Society's leading members was the composer Percy Grainger. He had encouraged the inclusion of folk songs in the Brigg competition, and was there to note them down. After the competition,

Taylor came to him and sang him 'Brigg Fair', which he had known since he was a child, and three years later Grainger recorded Taylor singing it, on a wax cylinder. Struck by the beauty of the song, Grainger arranged it for tenor solo with chorus, adding extra verses, and this version was performed at the Brigg competition in 1906. The following year, Delius was deeply impressed by Grainger's arrangement of 'Brigg Fair' and asked permission to use the tune as the basis of an orchestral work of his own. The result was this 'English Rhapsody', which Delius dedicated to Grainger. Joseph Taylor travelled to London to attend the first London performance in 1908 and stayed with Grainger and his mother, 'delighting us with his personality, which was every bit as sweet and charmful as his singing', as Grainger remembered. At the performance, 'When the "Brigg Fair" tune was given out at intervals by the English horn and other instruments of the orchestra, old Taylor gently "joined in" with his sweetly ringing tenor voice, to the amazement of the audience.'[4]

Delius's score, published in Germany in 1910, includes six stanzas:

It was on the fifth of August
The weather hot and fair
Unto Brigg Fair I did repair
For love I was inclined.

I took hold of her lily white hand
And merrily was her heart,
And now we're met together
I hope we ne'er shall part.

I got up with the lark in the morning
With my heart so full of glee,
Of thinking there to meet my dear
Long time I wished to see.

For it's meeting is a pleasure
And parting is a grief,
But an unconstant lover
Is worse than any thief.

I looked over my left shoulder
To see whom I could see
And there I spied my own true love
Come tripping down to me.

The green leaves they shall wither
And the branches they shall die
If ever I prove false to her,
To the girl that loves me.

Delius may or may not have known that only the first two stanzas were from the original song sung by Taylor. The rest had been assembled by Grainger from other traditional songs in order to make a more complete narrative.

Grainger, in a programme note for Delius's rhapsody, encapsulated the appeal to both composers of the melody and its (elaborated) text: 'a late-summer dream of morning freshness, love, peacefulness, quiet rural jollity, lazy church bells and the glowing English countryside'.[5] The words of the song are happy, and Joseph Taylor in his 1908 recording sings the opening verses with a dancing lilt. To musicians reared on major and minor scales, however, the melody has an ambiguity of mood, as so many songs in the old modes seem to ('Brigg Fair' is in the Dorian mode). It is this that both Grainger and Delius exploit to create music full of nostalgia and a sense of impermanence – the 'evanescence of beautiful things', as Philip Heseltine put it.

Delius's work is scored for large orchestra, including fourteen woodwind and six horns. These are used to provide a wide range of delicate effects, only occasionally coming together for grand climaxes. Most of the piece consists of a set of variations on the melody of 'Brigg

Fair', interspersed with contemplative passages. The opening sets a pastoral scene: a solo flute plays arabesques, accompanied by the lightest of harp arpeggios and *ppp* string chords. It inevitably calls to mind the opening of Debussy's *Prélude à l'après-midi d'un faune*, but the sensuousness of Delius's flute is less erotic, more rustic. As it continues it becomes more bird-like, and is joined by another flute and a clarinet as if from neighbouring trees. This gives way to the melody of 'Brigg Fair' on oboe, accompanied by clarinets and bassoons, followed by a set of variations on the theme. The flute takes it up, accompanied by strings, and the harmonies become more complex (they have had a nostalgic depth even from the opening bars). Then it moves to the strings in chorus, joined the next time round by flutes and clarinets. Now the melody begins to dance, with a tripping counterpoint in the violins. The counterpoint moves to flute and clarinet while horns take up the tune, and then a trumpet takes the melody to the first climax of the piece. The mood calms, and the opening flute arabesque returns for a moment.

This is the beginning of an interlude. Over quiet, sustained chords, the violins sing a rising phrase, as if stretching out the opening of 'Brigg Fair'. This little motif is repeated and developed. It passes to cor anglais, and then to a horn, all the while cushioned by the slowly shifting harmonies below. The effect is like a sustained meditation on a fine summer's day. From the calm emerges another variation of 'Brigg Fair' on clarinet, with its rhythm evened out and with counterpoint on cor anglais, bass clarinet, bassoon, and horns. The effect is mellow and even ecclesiastical – a bell sounds at the end of the tune. The strings join for the next variation, and the bell sounds again. The tune changes back to its original rhythm, but now in a broader three-time, and with a new counterpoint in the violins. This rises to a climax and falls away. The tune changes again, losing its swing, and becoming a solemn procession on trumpet and trombone, punctuated by string chords and the sounding of the bell ('slow: with solemnity'). The processional melody moves to the violins. Then there is another brief interlude, as reminders of the opening flute solo are interspersed with fragments of the tune. The woodwind return to the dancing lilt of 'Brigg Fair' ('gaily'). The cellos sing it, and the whole orchestra joins in. After a moment of hesitation, the music gathers energy, accelerates, and rises to a great climax at which the bells sound, and the tune is transformed into a blazing brass chorale. Gradually the climax falls away, an oboe gently plays the tune for the last time, and with a final reminder of the opening flute arabesques, the piece comes to a quiet close.

ANTONIN DVOŘÁK
(1841–1904)

Dvořák was brought up in a rural community in Bohemia. His father was an innkeeper and butcher, who intended his son to earn his living in the family trade. But by the age of sixteen Dvořák's musical talents were so obviously outstanding that his father was finally persuaded to allow him to pursue a career in music, with all its uncertainties. He studied at the Prague Organ School for two years. One of Dvořák's pupils recalled his description of the experience: 'At the organ-school everything smelt of mould. Even the organ . . . Anybody who wanted to learn anything had to know German. My knowledge of German was poor, and even if I knew something I could not get it out. My fellow-pupils looked a little "down their noses" at me and laughed behind their backs. When they discovered that I was composing, they said among themselves: "Just imagine that Dvořák! Do you know that he composes too?" And all those who laughed at me got on better than I did . . ."[1]

Dvořák's first professional engagement was as a viola player in a dance band. Later he played in the new orchestra of the Provisional Theatre in Prague that opened in 1862, the first theatre under Austrian rule to be allowed to stage Czech plays and operas. It was there that he first met Smetana, the great founder of the Czech national school of composition. Smetana conducted many Czech works at the theatre, including his own, and his influence on the young Dvořák was profound. Dvořák, building on Smetana's work, attempted to forge a style that brought together the dramatic 'New German' approach of Liszt and Wagner and the 'classical' methods of Mendelssohn and Schumann, at the same time drawing on traditional Czech songs and dances.

The turning point in Dvořák's career came in 1875, when, for the first of four years, he was granted an Austrian State Stipendium, which enabled him to devote more time to composition. In the second year, Brahms, one of the pillars of the Viennese musical establishment, was on the jury. He became Dvořák's most influential champion, recommending Dvořák's music to his publisher, and to the violinist and conductor Joseph Joachim.

Unlike Smetana, Dvořák rarely quotes actual folk tunes, but his music is full of lively dance rhythms and repeated melodic phrases that give it a pastoral, 'folk-like' character. From these deceptively simple ingredients he constructs substantial works with a powerful command of musical structures. This balancing act, between folk elements and the great German musical tradition, was not just a musical matter. Although Bohemia had been granted a limited autonomy within the Austrian Habsburg Empire in 1860 (hence the new Czech theatre in Prague), negotiating his way between the local Czech culture of Bohemia and the 'high' German culture of Austria was no easy matter for an aspiring composer. Dvořák had been brought up as a speaker of Czech (unlike the more prosperous Smetana, whose family spoke German), and his difficulties with German at the Prague Organ School were a portent of troubles to come. Brahms's support did not protect him from the prejudices of the Viennese. When his wind serenade and Slavonic Rhapsody No. 3 were performed at a Vienna Philharmonic concert in 1879, critics were divided. The critic Eduard Hanslick supported Dvořák, but a more conservative writer, Ludwig Speidel, wrote, 'The Slavic folk school is not loved in Vienna; when faced with it the Viennese feels himself to be decidedly German.' The conductor, Hans Richter, had already promised Dvořák the premiere of his Sixth Symphony in Vienna. But the orchestra delayed it, despite Richter's support, and the symphony was not played by them for another two years.[2] The skill with which Dvořák found his way through this minefield of conflicting pressures and interests is remarkable. His music so often feels, in an indefinable way, Bohemian and pastoral, but at the same time his major works are worthy to stand side by side with those of Brahms in the great Austro-German tradition.

Dvořák encountered another source of traditional music in the 1890s, when he was invited to spend three years in America as head of the newly founded National Conservatory in New York. There he encountered spirituals, work songs, and the music of Native Americans, and he brought elements of these into the works he wrote during his visit, notably the 'New World' Symphony. One of the reasons for the invitation to America was the hope that Dvořák, who had done so much to develop a characteristically Czech musical style, would help American composers towards a style of their own: 'The Americans expect great things of me and the main thing is, so they say, to show them to the promised land and kingdom of a new and independent art, in short, to create a national music!'[3] On one level, this might seem a naive hope on the part of his hosts. But there is no doubting the influence of Dvořák on American composers down to modern times. The music of Copland and Barber, the songs of the American musicals, and the 'wide open spaces' of American film scores, owe a great deal to Dvořák's sense of landscape and his interest in traditional dance and song.

CARNIVAL OVERTURE, OP. 92
Duration: approx. 9 minutes

Composed in 1891, *Carnival* is the second of a group of three concert overtures to which Dvořák gave the title *Nature, Life and Love*. He originally intended them to be played together, but then gave them separate titles, the other two being *In Nature's Realm* and *Othello*. *Carnival* has become by far the best known of the group, and it shows the same joyful spirit that fills his Eighth Symphony, composed two years before.

This is Dvořák's most brilliant overture, full of dancing energy and high spirits. It begins with full orchestra, including cymbals, tambourine, and triangle, in a dance that alternates whirling and stamping elements. The dance quietens briefly, but attempts to introduce a more chorale-like descending melody are soon brushed aside. Eventually the energy is reined in, and a beautiful second theme, in a minor key, is sung by the violins. After a time, this gives way to a new theme of dancing dotted rhythms, accompanied by the tambourine. At first these are delicate, but they generate a renewal of energy and, eventually, a climax.

This then gives way to an Andante middle section. The cor anglais sets up a murmuring pattern, over which flute and oboe combine in a pastoral theme, answered by clarinet, like a cuckoo calling from the woods. A solo violin takes up the theme, and then the murmuring pattern passes to the bass while all the violins join in the melody. Suddenly we turn a corner and find ourselves back in the fast opening tempo. But we are not yet back at the opening theme. Fragments of it are passed around, and its whirling elements become continuous, with other bits of the theme in counterpoint against them. This is the beginning of a substantial developing passage, which eventually builds up to a return to the first theme proper, complete with its percussion instruments. This time the dance is unstoppable. There is no yielding to the minor-key second theme, and the dancing dotted rhythms have now been subsumed into the headlong energy of the music. Eventually the pace becomes even faster, and the dance drives on to a wild conclusion, with trombones braying triumphantly.

Concertos

CELLO CONCERTO IN B MINOR, OP. 104
Duration: approx. 40 minutes

Allegro
Adagio ma non troppo
Allegro moderato – Andante – Allegro vivo

Cello concertos were written in the eighteenth and the twentieth centuries, but in the nineteenth century, the period of great piano and violin concertos, they were comparatively rare.

As orchestras became larger, and effects grander, composers shied away from the challenge of writing a concerto for a 'tenor' instrument that could easily be swamped by the orchestra. Although Schumann, Saint-Saëns, and Lalo all wrote distinguished cello concertos, it was Dvořák who really demonstrated what could be done with this problematic genre, writing what is widely acknowledged as the greatest of all cello concertos. He achieved it by bringing together elements in which he excelled: singing melodies, dance elements inspired by Czech traditional music, the development of such material in a manner that sounds natural rather than contrived, and great skill in his orchestration. The orchestral tuttis are powerful, but the passages that accompany the cello are written with great delicacy and finesse.

Dvořák composed his Cello Concerto while he was in America, in 1894–5. He had already made one attempt at such a work thirty years earlier, and his friend Hanuš Wihan, cellist of the Bohemian Quartet, had tried to persuade Dvořák to write a concerto for him. Dvořák had resisted, unpersuaded that the instrument (which he loved) was suitable for a modern concerto. But in March 1894 he heard Victor Herbert, the principal cellist of the Metropolitan Opera and a colleague of Dvořák at the National Conservatory, perform his own Second Cello Concerto (these days Herbert is most remembered as a composer of operetta). It was this that seems to have persuaded Dvořák that it was possible to write a concerto for cello with full orchestra. He composed a draft the following winter, then, during a return visit to Prague, he gave the score to Wihan for his comments. Wihan responded not only with the usual technical advice, but with more radical suggestions, composing a cadenza for the last movement. Dvořák rejected this idea, writing to his publisher, 'I told Wihan straight away when he showed it to me that it is impossible to stick a bit like this on. The finale closes gradually diminuendo like a sigh ... the solo dies down again to *pp* and then swells again, and the last bars are taken up by the orchestra and it finishes in stormy mood. That was my idea and from it I cannot depart.'[4] Naturally, Wihan was to give the premiere. The Philharmonic Society in London had offered a date in March 1896 during a forthcoming visit by Dvořák to England. But when it turned out that Wihan could not manage the date, the Society booked another cellist, Leo Stern, without consulting Dvořák. This very nearly caused Dvořák to cancel the visit entirely. But, in the end, Wihan agreed to give up the premiere and it went ahead with Stern playing and Dvořák conducting. Wihan first played the concerto three years later.

As in the 'New World' Symphony there are hints of American influence (spirituals and Native American music) that are impossible to disentangle from suggestions of Czech folk song. The very opening melody in B minor, on two clarinets in unison, has an insistent, doleful, quality that could have come out of an African American work song. With its short, memorable phrases and insistent dotted rhythms, it also lends itself well to development, and is soon built up into a powerful tutti. This winds down and eases into a second theme that is one of Dvořák's most beautiful inspirations, an open-hearted, lyrical melody in D major on the horn. These two themes supply most of the material for a long and satisfying movement. The different ways in which the cello develops the first theme are particularly striking. At the cello's powerful first entry, the theme is suddenly in the major, though still with a flat seventh that gives it a darker inflection. After a rhapsodic passage, energetic semiquavers take over, still retaining the shape of the theme. The momentum carries the music to a climax, with the original opening phrase high on the cello. From here it descends, easing into the beautiful second theme. Like the first theme, this soon develops into a more rhapsodic passage. It begins delicately then becomes more powerful, with the three horns urging the cello on to the next climax. A powerful orchestral tutti marks the end of the first section of the movement, taking the first theme through new keys to a passionate outburst high on the violins, and on to a quiet moment ready for the next entry of the cello.

By now the music is in a remote key (A flat minor), and as the cello enters with the first theme drained of its energy, we feel a long way from the insistence of its first appearance. The cello develops the theme into an extended lament, joined in a lovely duet by a flute, over quietly shuddering tremolando chords. Flute and oboe in unison transform it into one of those haunting, song-like melodies that could as easily be a Czech folk song as an African American spiritual. The cello accompanies this melody with quietly agitated figuration, which gradually becomes more dominant, culminating in a powerful run up in octaves that brings in a magnificent transformation of the second theme on full orchestra. Only when the cello takes up and continues the theme does it become clear that we are into the reprise, bypassing the opening theme. This proceeds much as before, through the build-up with the three horns, and into an orchestral tutti. The first theme is, for the only time, unambiguously in a confident B major. The cello takes this up, and in a powerful virtuoso passage builds to the final climax. The first theme, which began so dolefully, blazes in brass fanfares to bring the movement to a close.

The second movement opens with a woodwind chorus, led by clarinet, playing a melody whose broad span and delicate arabesques once more evoke traditional music and open spaces. The cello muses on this theme, first tenderly and then increasingly passionately. A passage for full orchestra breaks into a minor key, reminding us of the forceful rhythms of the concerto's opening theme. The cello responds with a soaring line that sounds as if it might refer to the second theme of the first movement. But it derives more directly from one of Dvořák's songs, 'Lasst mich allein' (Leave me alone). This was a favourite song of Dvořák's sister-in-law, Josefina, with whom he had been in love before marrying her sister. Josefina was dying as Dvořák was composing the concerto, and here, and at the end of the finale, he included this touching allusion to her.

This nostalgic passage builds to a climax, and falls away sorrowfully. There is another fortissimo orchestral passage. The song is developed further, again rising to a climax and falling away. A sonorous trio of horns brings us back to the opening theme of the movement, which is underpinned by drum-like patterns in the cellos and basses that introduce a sugges-tion of a funeral march. The cello enters, meditating on the theme and developing a cadenza-like passage, with first a flute and then other woodwind joining in. The end seems near, but the cello cannot let go of its memories (this is the effect of the music, with or without the personal background). Clarinets return to the first theme, the cello answers, again rises to a climax and falls away. One last paragraph brings the movement to a calm but sorrowful ending.

The horns open the finale, with music that has a march-like tread and builds up to welcome the cello. The cello declaims the theme forcefully, and the orchestra answers, making the march dance – there is something of the opening theme of the first movement in here, though it has been completely transformed. This is a rondo, in which this march-dance element recurs. The cello joins the celebration with rapid tremolo patterns and virtuoso flourishes, until the wood-wind repeat the theme and the orchestra rounds it off, leading into the first episode.

The cello begins to develop the theme, but soon falls into another meditation, in duet with a clarinet. The cello gradually recovers its virtuoso confidence, and the full orchestra returns to part of its previous tutti. The music calms, and the cello brings back the opening theme quietly (this moment is often played slowly, but the score says 'In tempo'). The orchestra takes up the theme joyfully, and then calms once more. A change of key brings in a new, gentle theme on the cello, which seems like a first cousin of the horn theme from the first movement, with the shapes turned upside down. This episode is extensive, and leads, via a high violin solo, to a climax at which the full orchestra returns to the opening theme. It seems as if we are approaching the end of the concerto. But there is one more passage of meditation to come, which, placed so near the end of the concerto, has (like the equivalent passage in the slow movement) almost the effect of an accompanied cadenza. There are wistful reminiscences of the opening theme of the concerto, and, once again, a fragment of Dvořák's song 'Lasst mich allein', played by solo violin. The cello descends gently, over soft string chords and touches of timpani, in a mood of the deepest nostalgia. It is with difficulty that the composer drags himself away from this sorrowful meditation. The full orchestra enters, maestoso (majestically), and accelerates with a final burst of energy to bring the concerto to a close.

VIOLIN CONCERTO IN A MINOR, OP. 53
Duration: approx. 35 minutes

Allegro ma non troppo –
Adagio ma non troppo
Finale: Allegro giocoso ma non troppo

Around the time that Joseph Joachim was performing the premiere of Brahms's violin concerto, Brahms's publisher, Fritz Simrock, suggested that Dvořák should also compose a concerto for Joachim. This followed on from the immense success of the first set of Dvořák's Slavonic Dances, published in 1878, which had made his name virtually overnight.

Despite Dvořák's new-found popularity, the project did not go smoothly. He wrote a first version of the concerto in the summer of 1879, sent it to Joachim, and then incorporated some of his suggestions. The following April he substantially rewrote it, presumably as a result of Joachim's further criticism. But that was not the end of the matter. It was not until September 1882 that Dvořák travelled to Berlin to play through the finished concerto with Joachim. He reported to his publisher, Simrock, that Joachim was delighted with it: 'I am very glad that it will be done with at last! The revised work lay a whole two years with Joachim. He was himself kind enough to make the alterations in the solo part. I must still only change something in the Finale and make the instrumentation more delicate in a number of places.'[5] Despite all this negotiation, Joachim, who played few new works by this stage of his career, never performed the concerto. The premiere was given in Prague by a brilliant young Czech violinist, František Ondříšek, who became its principal champion.

The roots of Dvořák's approach to this work lie not so much in Brahms's new violin concerto as in the concertos of Mendelssohn and Bruch. Mendelssohn had loosened the traditional format of a concerto's first movement, Bruch had taken this a step further, and now in Dvořák's concerto we get the impression of a first movement that is as much a fantasia as a conventional opening movement. The character of the music also owes something to Dvořák's great mentor, Smetana. From him Dvořák had learned how to integrate elements of traditional Czech music into a classical work while achieving a rhetorical freedom that has echoes of Liszt (Dvořák's early symphonies, which are not often played, are very 'Lisztian'). All of these currents combine to create a vivid, and highly characteristic, concerto.

The orchestra strikes up with a vigorous phrase, as if giving the call to attention for a dance. But instead of developing it into a theme they immediately give way to the soloist, who introduces a more thoughtful idea, followed by a brief flourish of cadenza ending on a high note. Again the orchestra plays the call to attention, more forcefully than before, and again the soloist responds with the same idea and a flourish. Now the orchestra does get going for a passage of tutti. But this is not the conventional statement of the principal themes. Instead, it starts by developing the violin's meditative idea more forcefully, and then the woodwind introduce a more sinuous melody. Suddenly the soloist returns, this time taking up the forceful idea with which the orchestra began, and developing it with bravura. Twice a more gentle idea begins to appear, but rather than settling, each time the soloist continues to pursue a virtuoso fantasy. Eventually the violin does settle, not with some new theme, but back where it started: the sonorous melody on which it meditated at its first entries, now brought together into a coherent theme.

After this has been developed with more virtuoso passages, an oboe returns to the sinuous melody from the first orchestral tutti. The soloist takes it up and extends it, until we arrive at the most peaceful melody so far. This, despite the wealth of ideas that have poured out, feels like the true 'second theme', though it has come far later than in a conventional movement. It reaches a lyrical climax, breaks into a dancing rhythm, and then gathers energy, with reminders of the ideas with which the concerto opened. This passage reaches a climax, at which the first theme bursts in fortissimo, first on the orchestra, then in the solo violin. This is the reprise, and from here there is only a short step until the soloist's flourishes reach a pianissimo high note. The tempo slows, and woodwind and solo violin join in a beautiful meditation on the opening theme. Without either a full reprise or a conventional cadenza, we have reached the end of the fantasy-like first movement, and an oboe descends to take us without a pause into the slow movement.

The dialogue with the woodwind continues as the violin sings a hymn-like theme. The orchestra warmly takes up the theme, and then the music moves from major to minor for the middle section of the movement. The violin plays a forceful new theme in octaves, answered by a horn. This alternates with a return to gentle music, with the violin playing bird-like decoration. The second of these gentle passages develops into an intense rhapsody, at the end of which the orchestra enters fortissimo with the forceful second theme, with trumpet calls. As the trumpets fade, oboe and clarinet quietly remind us of the lyrical first theme. Then the violins take up the theme, and the soloist weaves a lovely arabesque over it. The way that this develops is most touching, partly because the theme has not yet found its home key. That might seem a technical point, but the sense that the music has been searching becomes clear as, finally, the orchestra turns a corner into F major, and rises to the most glorious climax in the whole concerto. The journey does not quite end there. As the soloist enters again, the music turns away from the home key again, and the soloist must explore further in order to reach the final resolution that the orchestral climax promised.

After the subtle beauties of the first two movements, the finale comes as a breath of uncomplicated fresh, rural air. It is a rondo in A major in dance rhythm, like many finales of concertos. Joseph Joachim in his concerto had set a fashion for Hungarian finales, which Bruch and Brahms followed. Dvořák opts for a Slavonic dance, capitalizing on the immense success of his collection for piano duet. This is specifically a furiant, a fast dance with characteristically teasing cross-rhythms (like the first of his Slavonic Dances). It begins very quietly, with the soloist high up, supported only by violins. This alternates with joyful outbursts from the orchestra. The third outburst begins fortissimo, but after six bars there is a sudden change of key, and the woodwind take over with a new tune, as if the village band has just rounded the corner. This sets off a lilting rhythm in the strings, and as it quietens the soloist enters with playful staccato patterns. Against them an oboe plays yet another new dance tune. This begins in relaxed style, but gradually the violin figurations become more demonstrative, until a climax ushers in another tune (in yet another key). With its elegant, falling shapes, this is like a waltz. But it too soon develops power, with violin octaves and tumbling patterns.

After extensive exploration, the tune winds back to the home key, and the timpani announce the cross-rhythms of the rondo theme. Violin and orchestra alternate once again, until a horn ushers in a new episode. This is a more stately dance in a minor key, with its duple rhythms at first cutting across the horn's triplets. The very fact that this is a more measured dance gives the solo violin the space to elaborate it with increasingly complex two- and three-part chords – the sort of climactic elaboration you might expect in a cadenza (which, in this concerto, never comes). From a series of trills, the familiar rondo theme emerges. This leads to a full reprise of the opening section, with the sequence of themes leading from the wood-wind's 'village band' through to the waltz-like melody. The virtuoso climax fades, and as the soloist continues with staccato patterns a flute timidly plays the rondo theme, at first in A flat (the key in which the slow movement became magically lost). Gradually the home key is reasserted, and there is a silence. Out of it comes the stately dance from an earlier episode, now in A major, and assertively played in two-part chords by the soloist, while the strings persist with the three-time rhythm of the rondo theme. Three-time prevails, virtuoso octaves and arpeggios bring in a last burst of the rondo theme, and a final acceleration brings the concerto to a joyful conclusion.

SERENADE FOR STRINGS, OP. 22
Duration: approx. 27 minutes

Moderato
Tempo di Valse
Scherzo: Vivace
Larghetto
Finale: Allegro vivace

Early in 1875, Dvořák was awarded an Austrian State Stipendium for the first time. He was still struggling to earn a living and to make a name for himself, and this award gave him both valuable time for composition and a boost in self-confidence. He quickly composed a number of orchestral works, including the Fifth Symphony and this Serenade for Strings. Despite his success in the competition, he was almost unknown in the Austrian capital, Vienna, and had not yet been taken under the wing of Brahms and his publisher, Fritz Simrock. So the premiere of the serenade took place in Prague in December 1876, to great acclaim. Dvořák composed it in only two weeks, and it is easy to sense the fluency with which he wrote it. It has a lightness of spirit and directness of expression that make it one of his most appealing and popular works.

The serenade opens with one of those moments that show the genius of Dvořák in taking simple ideas almost like folk songs and developing complex structures out them. The violins quietly turn a phrase, the cellos and basses answer. From this emerges a great lyrical theme that frames the whole work, returning at the end of the finale. Within the frame, Dvořák runs a full spectrum of moods, rhythms, and textures. After he has let his opening theme blossom, he changes key and introduces a new theme. This is another simple idea: just up-and-down arpeggios in dotted rhythms. But, as with his first theme, Dvořák immediately starts developing its possibilities. At first it is pianissimo, like the distant sound of dancing. It changes key and swells a little. Then it returns to the original key and acquires a singing countermelody in the cellos. Another change of direction takes us to the reprise of the first theme, beautifully enriched with new scoring.

The second movement is a waltz, whose falling phrases and minor key give it a gentle melancholy. For a moment, at the end of the second strain, dancing dotted rhythms enter, like a reminder of the second theme in the first movement. The middle section is also based on a yearning falling phrase, but now in a warm major key, at least at first. There are moments of agitated counterpoint, and a climax of sturdy stamping rhythms. The waltz is repeated.

Dvořák labels the third movement a scherzo, but his treatment of the conventional scherzo and trio is wonderfully fluid. The scherzo theme begins quietly, with the violins chasing the cellos in canon, a bar apart. There is nothing academic about this canon: it simply adds to the sense of playfulness. The theme builds to a fortissimo and fades away, easing into a second theme. This takes the fall of the opening three notes of the scherzo and expands it into a heart-easing melody.

After a moment of intimate tenderness, the playful scherzo theme returns, in a minor key. But after a few bars, it yields to another lyrical theme, whose falling intervals give it a simple eloquence (and also relate it to the middle section of the waltz). This too rises to a climax, and fades into a return of the scherzo theme. It takes time to find its way back to the original key, but when it does so, it repeats the whole of its opening paragraph, and moves again into the second theme. For a moment, there is a haunting reminiscence of the third theme, then the music gathers strength for a final burst of the scherzo.

The Larghetto is a lament, based on a lonely sounding falling phrase like a memory of the middle section of the waltz and the third theme of the scherzo. At first it is very simple, its two-bar phrases supported just by rising viola chords. Then the chording becomes richer, and touches of counterpoint enhance the melancholy. All the while, the melody is developing, until it reaches a climax and falls away. Cellos take it up, answered by violins, and the music moves into new keys with more complex counterpoints. Suddenly it breaks into a moment of stately dance, over which the violins weave a high, lyrical line. A subtle reminiscence of the first movement brings us back to the opening. Cellos once again lead, answered by violins, and Dvořák takes this reprise to a more powerful climax than before. The movement ends in a spirit of deep consolation, *ppp*.

The serenade ends with a vigorous and dashing finale. Its opening call is another canon, with the violins echoed by the lower instruments. After a while it settles into a theme, with dotted rhythms and a falling shape (related to the falling themes in earlier movements). This is in a minor key, with no sign of the home key (E major). The opening calls return, and the music quietens to a second theme. This is made of more persistent dotted rhythms, with swirling patterns in the violas below, and is at last in the home key. It develops a dancing vigour, and fades. As hesitant fragments continue in the violins, cellos remember the lament from the slow movement. This is brushed aside by a renewal of the opening calls. The first theme is developed at greater length, and then the second theme, with its insistent dotted rhythms, builds to a powerful climax. As it calms, the music turns a corner, and we are back to the lyrical phrases of the theme that opened the serenade. It winds to a conclusion, as it did at the end of the first movement. Then the opening calls of the finale burst in at high speed, and the serenade comes to a confident, joyful conclusion.

Symphonies

SYMPHONY NO. 3 IN E FLAT MAJOR, OP. 10
Duration: approx. 33 minutes

Allegro moderato
Adagio molto, tempo di marcia
Allegro vivace

In 1869 the Czech poet Vitězslav Hálek wrote a patriotic poem, 'The Heirs of the White Mountain'. This was two years after the establishment of the dual monarchy of Austria-Hungary, a time when Czechs felt deeply frustrated in their hopes for greater autonomy. Hálek's poem was a rallying cry, culminating in a hymn celebrating the power of the Czech spirit to protect the motherland and lead her to freedom (the title of the poem refers to the Battle of the White Mountain, in which Czech forces were defeated by the army of the Holy Roman Empire in 1620). Dvořák set Hálek's hymn for chorus and orchestra, and its premiere in 1873 established him as a powerful voice in the Czech national cause.

Dvořák had already composed two symphonies, but neither had been performed. It was now eight years since he had written No. 2, and it was clearly the moment to capitalize on the success of his hymn with a third symphony. This was just at the time when Dvořák was attempting to find a way forward by synthesizing the fashionable methods of Liszt and Wagner with the more 'classical' approach of Mendelssohn and Schumann – a synthesis in which he was inspired by his great mentor, Smetana. It was Smetana who conducted the premiere of the Third Symphony in March 1874, to considerable acclaim. Three months later, Dvořák included the work in his portfolio when he applied for the first time for an Austrian State Stipendium, which he was granted.

The Third Symphony is therefore an important milestone on the way to the mature Dvořák. At times it is somewhat loose in its structure, and some of its big climaxes verge on bombast. But, as a critic wrote following the premiere, 'The composer has a wealth of ideas at his disposal, and he always offers them to us, his hands full, like some kind of Croesus . . . God willing, this young composer will attain greater serenity and will be more temperate in his deliberation in his subsequent symphonic works, and will thus achieve perfection in his musical creations.'[6] The version that was performed in 1874 was not quite what we know today. Dvořák revised the score more than a decade later (as he did Symphonies Nos 2 and 4), refining the orchestration and tightening some of its structure. The result is a work full of striking and beautiful ideas, and if there are weaknesses, they are those of a young(ish) composer already well on his way to greatness.

The idea of starting with a joyful awakening runs through five of Dvořák's symphonies (Nos 2, 3, 5, 6, and 8). Here in No. 3 it naturally seemed to the first audience that the composer of 'The Heirs of the White Mountain' was expressing patriotic awakening. The first movement has direct links to the hymn: it is in the same key (E flat major) with a similar, swinging metre, and the first phrase of melody even refers back to the opening of the hymn. But in the symphony Dvořák is expressing something both broader and more subtle. The sense of optimism is more akin to the opening of Beethoven's 'Pastoral' Symphony (though not as explicitly as in Dvořák's Fifth Symphony), with suggestions of love of countryside and the invigorating spirit of dance. Dvořák had attempted something similar in his Second Symphony, but now he achieves it with far more confidence.

Over murmuring strings and taps of the timpani, the opening theme unfolds, with a curl, a leap, and a confident ascent. It evolves as it goes, the full orchestra takes it up, and the curl becomes a swirl with energetic cross-rhythms (as in Dvořák's Slavonic Dances). In this seemingly straightforward paragraph, Dvořák shows his skill in developing his material, with the melody leaping higher, the harmonies varied, the key changing, so that there is always a sense of eager progress. The theme reaches a fortissimo climax, and a moment of mystery leads on to the second theme. This is a lyrical, descending line with a yearning leap (greater than the leap in the first theme), high in the violins, then in cellos and horns. The curl of the first theme accompanies it in the woodwind. Soon, the music returns to elements of the first theme, there is another brief climax, and tumbling arpeggios bring the opening section of the movement to a close.

The murmuring strings, timpani taps, and the opening theme return in the woodwind, now in E flat minor. Dvořák has been developing his themes ever since the start of the symphony, but this is the start of the formal development section. The opening bars of this development encapsulate in miniature Dvořák's particular genius for fluid harmonies and orchestral colours. The theme, low on oboes and flutes in unison, begins in E flat minor, but as it rises it takes a turn into G flat major (the key of the second theme), warmed by flutes and clarinets. Cor anglais and bassoon give the descending line of the second theme a processional tread for a moment. Then there is a swerve into E major as a horn, reinforced by cellos, introduces a moment of Wagnerian intensity. Immediately this is lightened by high violins and woodwind, delicately taking us into E minor. This little journey through a subtly shifting landscape has taken no more than thirty seconds, and seems effortless. But it is exactly this sure-footed grasp of harmonies and colours that enables Dvořák to build his larger structures with such conviction.

The evolving journey continues, with similar harmonic shifts and combinations of themes, until the full orchestra enters with a return to the dancing cross-rhythms from the opening. Again, the music turns in a new direction, and the descending line of the second theme takes on a searching quality, with a tug of the harmony pulling into different keys. The sense of mystery is heightened by a filigree of accompanying patterns. Trombones and horns call, and the power begins to build. Quietly, the cellos remind us of the opening theme, and the music rises to an *fff* climax. With a sudden shift back to E flat major, we descend into the reprise of the first theme.

Dvořák passes through new diversions and developments before he reaches his second theme. When he does so, the lyrical melody has become a glorious *fff* culmination of the entire movement. The movement comes to an end in a mood of joyful triumph.

The slow movement is a funeral march, a choice that inevitably invites comparisons with Beethoven's 'Eroica' Symphony. Dvořák's march, like Beethoven's, begins and ends sombrely, with a triumphant middle section, and it includes some direct references to the Beethoven. But the atmosphere is very different. It is in C sharp minor, a key remote from the home key of E flat major, and the mood of the outer sections is much more ambiguous than Beethoven's march, at times relaxing into something more akin to the slow movement of Schubert's Ninth Symphony. It seems more of a personal lament than a formal march.

This impression is given straight away by the sighing opening bars, in which the double basses are at first absent, touching in a pizzicato bass line only from bar three. The tread of the march is also softened by a recurring little curl of triplets on cor anglais and cellos (this refers back to the opening theme of the first movement). Dvořák develops from this material an expansive first section of the movement that is like a whole rondo in itself. The opening funeral march is interspersed with passages that float into other keys and introduce new material. A duet of clarinets in thirds has a particularly Schubertian tone. The whole span of this immense paragraph (about six minutes) is held together by Dvořák's gift for creating structure through shifting harmonies.

Low cellos bring in the middle section. The key changes from minor to major (D flat), and the woodwind begin a simple little march tune. This soon develops a Wagnerian richness, with swirling string figures. It passes through a lighter episode to a fortissimo return of the march tune (this passage can easily tip over into banality if too much is made of it). After some anxious wandering, another build-up collapses, and echoes of the march tune lead on to the reprise of the first section. This join is particularly beautifully handled, with a return not to the opening of the funeral march but to a later point, where the clarinet duet has given way to high woodwind. When the opening theme does return, it generates a passage of tragic force, which quietens to a new depth of sorrow. But at the end, the music warms into a gentle reminiscence of the central march tune, and the movement comes to a conclusion in a spirit of consolation.

For the only time in his symphonies, Dvořák omits the usual scherzo and goes straight into the finale. The main theme has persistent dotted rhythms and stabbing accents that permeate the whole movement, linking its ideas in an almost Haydn-like way. An expectant few bars of introduction lead to the theme itself, riding high over excited string patterns without the double basses, in a distinct echo of the 'Venusberg Music' from Wagner's *Tannhäuser*. The whole orchestra breaks in with a four-square second idea, still with the dotted rhythms predominant. A little later, another tutti introduces a third element, in which the dotted rhythms have been smoothed out (this too seems to echo *Tannhäuser*). After a delicate passage, the energy builds again, and leads to a ferocious fourth idea, which begins like the main theme but then rises step by step with fierce offbeat accents. When this has subsided, the key moves to C major for a fifth idea, in which oboe and piccolo transform the main theme into a demure little tune. This is developed at some length, until another surge of energy leads to a return to the main theme, back in E flat major, followed immediately by the square-cut second idea.

What follows is a sort of development section – though with this non-stop tumble of ideas there are no clear-cut divisions in this movement. The next passage moves through different keys before rounding a corner into the third idea (the other *Tannhäuser* reference). This too moves on into new keys, the music quietens, and the first theme passes from cellos to violins, to solo viola and cello, playfully modulating from key to key as it goes. The tension builds, and the rhythms broaden into a glorious climactic passage in E major. This is a long way, harmonically, from the home key of E flat major. But Dvořák suddenly steps sideways to E flat to bring in the third idea, and, before we know it, we are into the middle of reprise, having left out the first two ideas.

From the third idea, Dvořák goes straight on to the playful fifth idea – with typical insouciance he has again leapt sideways in key, to B major. More energetic development leads back to the main theme, at first in G flat, and then struggling back to E flat. By now, there is no letting go of it, or of the home key, and like a dog determined to kill his bone, Dvořák wrestles away to bring the symphony to an exhilarating, and exhausting, conclusion.

SYMPHONY NO. 5 IN F MAJOR, OP. 76
Duration: approx. 37 minutes

Allegro ma non troppo
Andante con moto
Scherzo: Allegro scherzando
Finale: Allegro molto

By March 1874, when Dvořák's Third Symphony received its successful premiere, he had already completed his Fourth Symphony. That had to wait until 1892 for its first complete performance. Meanwhile, it was in his Fifth Symphony, composed in the summer of 1875 and first performed in Prague in March 1879, that he really consolidated his characteristic style and way of working. Inspired by Smetana, Dvořák was continuing his search for a synthesis of the 'classical' methods of Mendelssohn and Schumann with the influence of the folk songs and dances of Czech and other Slavonic traditions, without losing the dramatic possibilities of the 'New German' manner of Liszt and Wagner. This symphony was one of the works that he submitted for an Austrian State Stipendium in 1876, which he was granted for the third year running. Brahms, who was on the jury, recommended Dvořák to his publisher, Fritz Simrock in Berlin, the following year, and his international success began. But the Fifth Symphony was not at first among the works published. It was not until 1888, after Symphonies Nos 6 and 7 had already been published, that Simrock issued No. 5, giving it a misleading opus number to encourage the impression that this was a 'mature' work (Dvořák had originally referred to it as Opus 24).

Dvořák had begun both his second and his third symphonies quietly, building to a joyful outburst. He does the same in No. 5, but with a distinct nod back to Beethoven's 'Pastoral' Symphony. Cellos set up a bagpipe-like drone of fifths, enlivened by murmuring violas, and two clarinets play a cheerful flourish somewhere between birdsong and the call of rustic pipes. The evocation of pleasure in a pastoral scene is as unmistakable as Beethoven's 'Awakening of joyful feelings'. The flourish passes to flutes, and is then given energy by the strings, building up to a second, striding idea, full of sturdy confidence. The striding idea is developed at some length, rising to a climax and falling away. Then violins, darkened by bassoon, introduce a new theme, a contemplative melody whose phrases rise and fall. As it sinks into the cellos, it acquires another of Dvořák's murmuring accompaniments in the violins, and as this too sinks down, the flutes delicately remind us of the sturdy second idea. This provokes a sudden fortissimo chord from the full orchestra. The quiet continuation is punctuated by more fortissimo chords, until a sudden crescendo brings in a stern, rather Wagnerian descending figure to take us to the end of the first section of the movement.

The score indicates a repeat of the first section, but Dvořák came to dislike these long repeats (see the Sixth Symphony below). The 'Wagnerian' descent quietens, and is surrounded by the murmuring accompaniment as we move into the middle of the movement. A flute brings back the opening theme, and its cheerful flourish forms the basis of a long exploratory passage as the music moves through different keys and from instrument to instrument. After a climax, an oboe plays the lyrical second theme, but this is soon followed by a return to the striding idea. As it softens, a horn quietly brings in the opening theme, in its original key. The clarinets answer, and we realize that we have arrived at the reprise. The sequence of themes is as before, but continually refreshed by new turns of harmony and orchestration. At the end, Dvořák lingers over the pastoral opening theme to bring the movement to a peaceful close.

The second movement is simple in form, but subtle in its detail. It begins and ends with a lyrical, rather melancholy theme in A minor, and the middle section, initially in A major, is more flowing and energetic. The opening theme on the cellos begins with two balanced two-bar phrases, almost like a folk song. But then it continues more freely, with six bars that climax with a leap up and then wind gently downward. The possibilities of the theme are explored further, first by the violins, joined by cellos, then by woodwind, until it returns peacefully to its opening. The whole of this paragraph, with its many subtle changes of direction, key, and orchestration, is like a single span.

For the middle section, the woodwind introduce a theme in A major over pizzicato accompaniment. It seems entirely new, with its simple falling pattern, but it is drawn from the opening shape of the first theme. Suddenly it becomes warmer as the violins take it up. Again and again the simple phrase is reiterated, blossoming into a passionate paragraph shaped by Dvořák's wonderful sense of harmony. Gradually it comes to rest, and the opening melody in A minor returns on the woodwind, accompanied by rippling accompaniment and a singing descant on violins. This time round, the theme builds to a powerful climax. It falls away, and reminiscences of both themes round off the movement.

Dvořák's instruction is that the next movement should follow after only a short pause. The cellos play a recitative-like passage remembering the slow movement, and finishing with expectant chords. It could be an introduction to a ballet scene. The woodwind delicately launch into the dancing scherzo that passes delicately from wind to strings and back again. But it is not quite ready to be fully established. It hesitates, and passes into distant keys, before finding the strength to return. At last the whole orchestra joins in fortissimo. This fades, and after a final chord, the trio begins, poised and charming, with a delicate dotted rhythm. As so often in Dvořák, it later reveals a much greater emotional range than it seemed to promise. There are moments of darker harmonies, the music builds to a climax, and fades to a wistful and lingering conclusion, before a return to the scherzo.

One of the most striking things about the finale is the amount of time it spends struggling to find the home key of F major. It begins with cellos and basses unaccompanied, playing a stormy theme in A minor (the key of the slow movement). The effect is reminiscent of the defiant cello and bass recitative that opens the finale of Beethoven's Ninth Symphony. The woodwind try the theme in G minor. After further struggle, the whole orchestra comes together and the violins play it fortissimo, still in A minor. The theme is tossed around, the music subsides to a passage of mysterious chords, and grows again. Only at the end of a long battle does the theme finally break into F major, now sounding defiantly cheerful (a persistent twist in the harmony makes sure that it never sounds straightforwardly cheerful).

Almost immediately the music calms, and shifts down from F to D flat major (the key of the trio in the third movement). For Dvořák, as for Schubert, this fall of a major third was one of his favourite key changes, creating a warm effect. Solo clarinet and violins share a sustained melody full of yearning leaps. The theme is stretched out by the violins, and is rounded off by a wind chorale. Then we enter a new period of struggle. The opening theme returns, and engages in combative counterpoint. The dotted rhythms at the end of the phrase take on a life of their own, at first fiercely, and then softening to an affectionate clarinet duet. The woodwind chorale returns, builds up once more, and leads to more combat with the first theme. There is a climax, with abrupt chords.

The tempo eases, and over horn chords, oboe and clarinet solemnly restate the first theme, back in A minor (where it started). This turns out to be the beginning of the reprise. The theme fights its way to F major, rather more quickly than before, and the music eases to the lyrical second theme, now on oboe. It unfolds gently, passed between woodwind and violins, and is followed once more by a moment of woodwind chorale. The music comes to a moment of complete calm, the first in the entire movement. The symphony could almost have finished there. But, with one more assault, Dvořák beats a more conventionally triumphant ending out of his main theme.

SYMPHONY NO. 6 IN D MAJOR, OP. 60
Duration: approx. 45 minutes

Allegro non tanto
Adagio
Scherzo (furiant): presto
Finale: Allegro con spirito

No. 6 was the first of Dvořák's symphonies to be published. He began work on it in the summer of 1880, when he was already a well-established composer. The conductor Hans Richter had given a performance of Dvořák's third Slavonic Rhapsody in Vienna the previous November, and after the concert held a dinner in his honour. Dvořák said that the performance had been 'incomparably fine', and promised Richter a symphony. He sent Richter the score when he finished it in October 1880 and Richter was delighted with it. For what seem partly to have been political reasons (see the introduction above), Richter and the Vienna Philharmonic then delayed the premiere, and in the end it took place in Prague in March 1881. Dvořák nevertheless dedicated the work to Richter.

The symphony was a tremendous success wherever it was performed, nowhere more so than in England, where Dvořák's reputation stood very high. In 1884 he conducted concerts at the Three Choirs Festival in Worcester – his *Stabat Mater* in the morning, and the Sixth Symphony at the evening concert on the same day. As the *Musical Times* reported, 'On his entry into the orchestra, the applause was so overwhelming that it was many minutes before he was allowed to give the signal for commencing.' A young violinist who played in that performance wrote to a friend, 'I wish you could hear Dvořák's music. It is simply ravishing, so tuneful and clever and the orchestration is wonderful; no matter how few instruments he uses, it never sounds thin. I cannot describe it; it must be heard!'[7] That violinist was Edward Elgar.

The first movement opens quietly and serenely, in a manner that evokes memories of Brahms's Second Symphony in the same key. Over gently pulsating horns, a simple rising phrase of two notes passes back and forth from upper instruments to lower instruments. What could be simpler? This blossoms, rising higher. So far, it could almost be a folk tune. But then Dvořák changes key, and extends the melody. A more lively rhythmic motif starts up and builds energetically, with dancing cross-rhythms. As this reaches a climax, the opening melody joins it, now in a fortissimo flood on full orchestra. This opening is Dvořák at his best and most characteristic: it is another version of the 'joyful awakening' that began the second, third, and fifth symphonies, using the simplest of ingredients, but creating a cumulative effect that has the most direct appeal. It sets the scene for a substantial movement. After the first climax dies down, there are several gentler elements: a singing second theme on cellos, an answering melody on oboe. A rhythmic element in this melody becomes persistent, and this (like the first melody), rises to a fortissimo climax, to bring the first section of the movement to a close.

This long section is, in the classical tradition, marked to be repeated. But Dvořák himself, in the score used for the premiere, crossed out this repeat mark and wrote 'Once and for all, no repeat!' The development that follows settles into a mood of deep calm, conjuring up images of Bohemian forests. At first Dvořák returns to the opening melody, though now in a different key, with its rise and fall extended in a calmly recurring pattern. More energetic elements then join in, at first firmly, then playfully, and building steadily towards a climax. Out of this emerges, quietly, the reprise of the opening theme, and the successive elements from the opening section are revisited. At the end, there is one last push to a grand climax, at which the opening theme is passed from trombones to horns in a glorious fanfare.

The slow movement is, like the first, based on a melody that seems simple, but is treated with great subtlety. It is sung by the first violins, but it is accompanied at every stage by other voices weaving counterpoints – first clarinet, then oboe, and, throughout, a beautifully constructed bass line. This melody occurs at the beginning, middle, and end of the movement. Between each occurrence, there are other episodes. This sounds like a simple structure, but, like the melody itself, it is more subtle than the bald description would suggest. Sometimes new material grows out of the main melody, sometimes there are contrasts – in particular, a sudden burst of dance-like activity. The music wanders through sequences of keys, and often we have the impression that we do not know quite where we are. Once more, rural images come to mind. It would not be surprising if Dvořák had been inspired to write this movement by a walk through a wooded valley. At first you see a view below you, and as you descend you lose your bearings. From time to time some landmark comes into view through a clearing. Then, as you ascend, you again see the view below, and catch sight of features that you passed some time before. It is, with or without this analogy, a masterly example of a movement whose structure and journey is rich, complex, and yet seemingly naive.

The third movement is a Slavonic dance. Specifically, it is a furiant, an exhilarating dance with insistent two-beat rhythms alternating with the three-time of the metre. There is much interplay between strings and woodwind, as if there are two groups of dancers. The central trio is slower and gentler. A version of a motif from the furiant is passed from instrument to instrument, and the piccolo plays a few bars like a peasant improvisation. This leads on to a more sweeping melody that is expanded and developed, before the tempo accelerates to return to the furiant. This time it ends with an acceleration, whipping up the tempo to the very last bar.

The finale begins quietly and genially, paying homage, like the first movement, to Brahms's Second Symphony. More sharply rhythmic elements gradually develop, until the theme bursts forth fortissimo. The music subsides, giving way to a more playful theme on clarinet. The dance element in this theme becomes infectious, until the whole orchestra takes up a rushing, stamping dance. Fragments of it continue on into new keys, leading into a substantial development section, with elements from both themes, swift changes of mood from gentle to forceful, and passages of determined argument building to climaxes. Eventually this leads to a statement of the first theme, transformed into a grand chorale, and in the minor. And, after a few bars, we are back at a quiet reprise of the theme itself, and then on to the dancing second theme. This time, a build-up leads to a rapid presto, in which the theme is reduced to a simplified rhythm, under which a scurrying accompanying pattern is played by the cellos. This passes wittily up through the violas to the violins, like a game of catch, until the whole orchestra is caught up in the energy, leading to an exhilarating finish.

SYMPHONY NO. 7 IN D MINOR, OP. 70
Duration: approx. 37 minutes

Allegro maestoso
Poco adagio
Scherzo: Vivace
Finale: Allegro

The early 1880s were a period of difficult decision-making for Dvořák. At a time of growing Czech nationalism, should he stay true to his roots, and risk the antagonism of the Austrian establishment, or should he aim for a more 'international' style, as friends in Vienna and Germany were encouraging him to do? Two of his greatest works date from this difficult period: the Piano Trio in F minor, and the Symphony No. 7 in D minor. Both of them have often been described as owing much to the inspiration of Brahms, and writers have debated the extent to which this helped or hindered Dvořák in the development of his mature style. But perhaps the important point is that people do not express their true natures only when doing what comes naturally. The very effort of struggling with other influences, and aiming at something that does not come spontaneously, reveals aspects of a personality that we might not otherwise have seen.

This is nowhere clearer than in the Symphony in D minor. Coming between two sunny and relaxed symphonies, Nos 6 and 8, No. 7 is dark and powerful, and in it Dvořák subjects his lyrical gift to rigorous organization. The influence of Brahms, or at least the desire to please him, is shown in a letter from Dvořák to his publisher in February 1885: 'The new symphony has been occupying me already for a long, long time, but something respectable should result, for I don't want to prove wrong the words Brahms spoke to me: "I imagine your symphony to be something quite different again from this D major one!" '[8] Dvořák wrote the symphony over the winter of 1884–5, to fulfil a commission from the Philharmonic Society of London. Its first performance was in London in April 1885, to great applause, with the composer conducting.

A sombre mood is established right away, with a dark, sinuous line in D minor in the cellos and violas, which ends with an ominously repeated little kick. It is this kick that generates much of the energy of the movement. At first the energy comes in short bursts, and there is a struggling first climax that reaches upwards to reveal a gentle melody in E flat major on horn answered by oboe (already quite far, in key and mood, from the sombre opening). Forceful dotted rhythms soon thrust this aside, and the opening theme re-establishes itself, now fortissimo on full orchestra, and with the kicks transformed into powerful dotted rhythms. This subsides, and the second main theme follows, a lyrical melody in B flat major. Its scoring, in which flutes give a silvery edge first to the clarinets and then to the violins, is typical of Dvořák at his most relaxed. But although the mood is far from the opening D minor theme, this sinuous melody also has something in common with it. It is allowed to expand gloriously, until the opening sombre melody reappears, and builds again, drawing in elements of the second theme, to round off the first section forcefully.

The development moves off into new keys, with a return to the hesitations of the opening. The second theme reappears, now in the minor, a new struggle involving the first theme develops, and this in turn subsides and breaks into fragments. Clarinets take up the first theme, mysteriously, and in a remote key. Further struggle leads to a magnificent reassertion of the opening theme, now fortissimo, and back in the home key of D minor. Is this perhaps the reprise? Eventually the reappearance of the lyrical second theme, now in D major, confirms that it is. When this has worked through its expansion, much as before, Dvořák moves on into a coda, in which the opening theme builds up into a final struggle. There is an acceleration, with turbulent cross-rhythms. The movement ends quietly, the opening theme given a tragic edge with yet darker harmonies, and evocative mutterings from the woodwind in the background, like wood sprites in the forest.

A combination of lyrical and tragic elements carries over from the first to the second movement. The opening theme, sung by a clarinet above a choir of woodwind, is like a folk song, but with evocatively poignant harmonies. Flutes and oboes expand and develop it over pulsating strings. A second theme is much darker, almost *Tristan*-like in its yearning falls and its punctuation by sombre trombones. The violins develop it in a great sweep. Woodwind take the yearning theme, and give it assertive dotted rhythms, to which the strings respond forcefully. As a tailpiece to this first section, there is a third theme, a noble horn call. A middle section begins with a great outburst in which the strings play a theme that seems new, but has a shape related to the clarinet's opening theme. Clarinet and oboe follow with a dialogue of falling and rising arpeggios, which pass to flute and bassoon. The violins take this up (is its falling opening phrase also related to the first theme?), and build it into a big climax. Dvořák takes his time winding through a transition, and some beautiful harmonic twists, to arrive at the return of the opening theme, now on cellos. The *Tristan*-like second theme returns, then the assertive dotted rhythms (previously in the woodwind) are taken up by the strings, and build to a final climax. Out of this emerges the horn, playing a half-remembered version of its earlier call. The movement ends with an evocative reminder of the opening theme, now on oboe over quietly shuddering strings.

The scherzo is full of delightful cross-rhythms, in which the six beats are sometimes divided into groups of three, sometimes into groups of two. Despite the playfulness, there is a serious, even ferocious, edge to it, partly because it is in D minor (like the first movement). Below the delicate opening tune is a singing countermelody in the cellos, which surfaces later in the violins, and later still in the woodwind. The central section (trio) of the movement is a little slower. There are rising calls on oboe, answered by trilling flute, over a rich web of strings, giving an almost forest-like atmosphere (like stretches of the slow movement). There is a second, perkier theme in which violins and woodwind answer each other over a pizzicato accompaniment. The rising calls return on clarinet, horn, and flute, and there is a fierce build-up. After this, the return to the quiet opening of the scherzo comes as even more delightful than before. The second time around, the scherzo ends with a passage of quiet meditation, culminating in another almost *Tristan*-like melody in the violas, before the opening theme returns to bring the movement to a wild conclusion.

The finale, like the earlier movements, is full of contrasts between tragic and lyrical, severe and playful. Cellos and horns leap up an octave, strike a dissonant accent, and descend sinu-ously. This theme takes us back to the sombre mood of the first movement, and timpani give an almost funereal tread to its continuation. But the mood soon becomes more agitated, with the opening octave transformed into a wild arpeggio. The violins take it up, and the full orchestra gives the theme a heroic edge, with trumpet calls. This culminates in a new theme like a defiant dance, still in D minor. The whole orchestra joins in, combining it with the wild arpeggio from the first theme.

As it quietens, a corner is turned, and a relaxed, sunny melody in A major is sung by the cellos. Soon the violins inject urgency into it, and it builds to a climax with insistent syncopa-tions from the horns. The middle section of the movement opens with the opening theme on tiptoe, pizzicato, and strange pianissimo chords in the trombones. Woodwind take up the theme anxiously, and a crescendo leads to a return of the defiant dance, now with a counter-point of almost Wagnerian calls in trombones and horns. There is a climax, and as it subsides the wild arpeggio from the first theme is recalled in the woodwind.

This provides the trigger for another crescendo, at the top of which the opening theme returns fortissimo on the violins, over a highly agitated accompaniment. It leads straight on to the cellos' sunny melody that again passes to the strings and builds to a fortissimo climax. This time the climax does not quieten, but leads on, via the assertive rhythms of the 'defiant' dance, to a coda that becomes gradually more and more agitated. At the final climax, the opening theme gets faster, as if it too is trying to be transformed into a wild dance. But at the very end the pace is suddenly held back, and the opening theme sings out for the last time, its anxious chromatic line now resolved into grand chords of D major.

SYMPHONY NO. 8 IN G MAJOR, OP. 88
Duration: approx. 37 minutes

Allegro con brio
Adagio
Allegretto grazioso – Molto vivace
Allegro ma non troppo

In February 1889, Dvořák scored a success with his opera *The Jacobin*, and later in the year was honoured by the Austrian Emperor Franz Josef with the Order of the Iron Crown, and admitted to membership of the Czech Academy of Science, Literature and the Arts. In celebration of this honour, Dvořák wrote his G major symphony, conducting the premiere in Prague on 2 February 1890. The following year he chose this symphony to conduct in Cambridge when he received an honorary doctorate from the university. Despite these academic associations, it is the least learned, the least forced, and the most straightforwardly delightful of all his symphonies.

The first movement, as usual in a symphony, falls into three parts, in which material is laid out, developed, and then reprised. But the character and variety of Dvořák's themes makes the effect of the movement anything but conventional. It is like a walk through a natural land-scape, in which there is something fresh or exciting at every new corner. The first melody, in the minor, is gentle and melancholy, scored for cellos, enriched by horns, bassoons, and clari-nets. Following on the end of it is a little tune in G major from the flute, its dotted rhythms and its simple arrangement of notes suggesting a shepherd's pipe, or even birdsong. It is this seemingly naive tune that turns out to be the main energetic force of the movement. Its dotted rhythms set off the first build-up, which climaxes with the shepherd tune on full orchestra – though not before yet another, broader, melodic element has crept in on violas and cellos almost as an aside. After the climax has died down, a new theme soon appears on clarinets and flutes, with an upbeat dotted rhythm that relates it to the shepherd tune. This leads to another climax, bigger than the first, at which the trumpets blaze out the outline of the shep-herd tune, now simplified into a fanfare.

As this in turn dies down, we find ourselves back at the beginning, with the gentle cello melody. We seem to be embarking on a repeat of the opening section. But as the flute begins its shepherd tune, a note from the horn, and anxious falling phrases from the cellos, make it clear that Dvořák is moving off in a new direction. The oboe answers the flute, there is a sudden fortissimo chord from the full orchestra, and the dotted rhythms of the flute tune gather energy. There is a reminiscence of a broader melody from the first part of the movement, on violas, and this is transformed into a snappy little phrase that is treated to a burst of fugue-writing. The effect is energetically rustic rather than academic, and with a counterpoint of forceful triplets an urgent climax is reached. Here Dvořák produces a masterstroke: the gentle cello melody from the opening blazes forth on trumpets to form the climax. It is only afterwards, as a cor anglais plays the shepherd tune, that we realize that the trumpet climax was also the beginning of the reprise. Some, but not all, of the earlier material is revisited, and Dvořák adds a coda full of the dotted rhythms that have dominated the movement, to bring it to a vivacious close.

The slow movement begins with a sonorous melody on the strings, with a sequence of phrases each beginning with a triplet of rising notes. This triplet upbeat is to dominate much of the movement. First the flute takes it up, adding a simple bird call reminiscent of the shep-herd tune from the first movement. Clarinets answer darkly, the flute reiterating the bird call again and again. As this dies away, a drum roll announces a forceful transformation of the triplet phrase, on woodwind and horns. Soon there is a further transformation. The triplet upbeat moves to the bass, horns play quiet staccato chords, and violins trip delicately down a scale. This sets up a continuous accompaniment, over which flute and oboe sing a new melody (though it too incorporates the rising triplet figure). A solo violin takes this up, and then the full orchestra, rising to a splendid climax. There is a sudden hush, the bird call is reiterated. The clarinets descend, leaving the strings playing solemn and mysterious chords very quietly.

The hush is broken by the horns, with the rising triplet figure. But now it is harsh and urgent, almost Wagnerian, with shuddering tremolo in the strings. This builds up fiercely. But at the climax the woodwind begin to chatter the triplet figure once more, the mood relaxes, and, sooner than expected, we are back at the delightful singing flute and oboe melody from earlier in the movement, now on the violins. This, with some extra excursions along the way, takes us gently to the end of the movement.

The third movement is one of Dvořák's happiest inspirations, almost like a waltz. The melody is made up of long phrases that gradually descend. But each phrase begins with a rising group of three notes, which give the melody a marvellous impetus (as well as linking to the rising triplets of the slow movement). Alternating with this melody is a haunting little interjection from the woodwind, which begins with the rising upbeats, but then falls in a staccato chromatic line that has a melancholy tinge. The middle section of the movement is, if possible, even more charming than the beginning. Flute and oboe sing a melody made up of a simple, lilting dotted rhythm that repeats again and again, rising and falling in an elegant line. Against this, the strings play a cross-rhythm that cuts across the two-bar phrases, and the cellos mutter a pattern of arpeggios. The strings then continue the melody to a climax. Oboe and bassoon repeat the melody, the strings repeat their climax. And then the strings themselves take on the melody for a final time. The first section of the movement is then repeated. And Dvořák rounds it off with a coda – not a conventional tailpiece, but a witty, chattering dance, led by oboes and bassoons, which (though it is not immediately obvious) is derived from the melody of the middle section.

The finale is announced by a trumpet fanfare. This is followed by a set of variations. The theme is a charming melody played by the cellos, each half repeated. The first variation develops force, led by cellos and basses, and is taken up in counterpoint by the upper strings. The second variation breaks loose, with a joyful outburst of dance on full orchestra, and whooping trills from the horns. The pace is maintained for the third variation, in which the flute plays a virtuoso solo. Then the joyful dance returns, after which the music moves to a minor key, and a strange little mock march on the woodwind.

The pattern of variations is broken at this point. The marching theme is developed, the tension builds up, and culminates in a great climax, at which the trumpets blaze the fanfare with which they introduced the movement. This gradually winds down, and we are back at the beginning, with the cellos playing their beautiful theme. This time the second half is richly harmonized, with delicate interventions from the flute. This is followed by two new variations, both wistful in character. Another variation begins, but soon loses its way in meditation, and comes to a halt. And then, as a final masterstroke, Dvořák interrupts the musing with a sudden return to the joyful whooping dance from the second variation, and wild accelerations bring the symphony to a brilliantly satisfying close.

SYMPHONY NO. 9 IN E MINOR ('FROM THE NEW WORLD'), OP. 95
Duration: approx. 41 minutes

Adagio – Allegro molto
Largo
Scherzo: Molto vivace
Allegro con fuoco

At the height of his fame in the 1890s, Dvořák spent three years in America as director of the new National Conservatory in New York. Over the winter of 1892–3 he read Henry

Longfellow's poetry, was captivated by its cadences, and had the idea that his epic poem *The Song of Hiawatha* could provide the theme for an opera libretto or a cantata. Then in the summer of 1893 he spent four months at Spillville, a little community, predominantly of Czechs, in the great plains of Iowa. 'It is very strange here,' he wrote, 'endless acres of field and meadow, and that is all you see. You don't meet a soul (here they only ride on horseback), and you are glad to see in the woods and meadows the huge herds of cattle which, summer and winter, are out at pasture in the broad fields.'[9] As for the music that Dvořák wrote while he was in America (this symphony, the Cello Concerto, a string quartet and a quintet), he wrote 'I should never have composed these works "just so" if I hadn't seen America.'[10] 'The 'New World' Symphony was commissioned by the New York Philharmonic Orchestra, and premiered by them under Anton Seidl in December 1893.

There was another important American influence on his music, the spirituals and work songs of African Americans, which Dvořák said were 'distinguished by unusual and subtle harmonies, the like of which I have found in no other songs but those of old Scotland and Ireland'. Although he did not make a habit of quoting particular songs, you can hear the influence of spirituals, and the sense of great open spaces, in the 'New World' Symphony. On the other hand, Dvořák's supposedly America-inspired melodies were not that different in character from those inspired by the folk songs and dances of his native Bohemia – such as the slow movement of the Piano Quintet, or the flute theme at the beginning of the Eighth Symphony, both of which were written several years before his visit to America.

The symphony opens with an Adagio introduction, which immediately conveys a sense of wide spaces, and of expectancy. As it becomes agitated, woodwind chirrups are interrupted by a rising and falling figure in horns, violas, and cellos. As the introduction ends, with a drum roll and violin tremolo, we discover that this is to be the first theme of the Allegro, now transformed into a horn call, and answered with a lively dotted-rhythm figure. This is the first of many instances during the symphony when Dvořák ties the music together by linking and relating themes across sections and movements. The material is worked up to a climax. As the energy subsides, the little dotted-rhythm motif is reiterated, smoothed out, and finally wound into a repetitive little figure in a minor key, with a character of folk dance that could equally be American or Czech in inspiration. This might well be the main second theme of the movement, but after further elaboration of this figure, the music subsides further to a moment of rest, at which a flute plays an entirely new American/Czech-style tune in the major – at least it seems entirely new, but its first phrase is an upside-down version of the horn call, falling instead of rising, and the dotted rhythm that follows is taken from the answer to the horn call.

The lull is brief, and a crescendo brings the first section of the Allegro to a close (the repeat that Dvořák indicates here is sometimes played, sometimes not). The middle part of the movement is based almost entirely on the opening horn call and its answer, developing an insistent rhythm and waves of increasingly intense climaxes. Eventually the horn call returns in its original form, and the events of the first part of the movement recur in the same sequence as before, varied in characteristically delightful ways. At the end, Dvořák caps a movement full of climaxes with one more, yet more urgent and compelling than all the others, to bring the movement to a resounding close.

Dvořák said that the slow movement was inspired by *Hiawatha*. People who knew Dvořák suggested two rival passages as sources for the movement: Hiawatha's journey to woo Minehaha, or the funeral of Minehaha in the forest. Scholars continue to debate which is the more likely, but the music itself, at first broad and serene, later troubled and melancholy, suggests that both passages might have inspired different parts of the movement. It opens with deep, solemn brass chords, beginning very quietly, moving mysteriously through unexpected changes of key, to end firmly on D flat major. Hushed strings take up the chord, and a cor anglais sings Dvořák's most famous melody. The strings take up the theme, musing on it, the cor anglais returns, and muted horns disappear into the distance.

The middle section of the movement begins with flute and oboe in unison (one of Dvořák's characteristically subtle colours), playing a more anxious melody that winds round on itself rather like the little minor-key folk dance from the first movement. This is answered by a more sombre and sustained melody, with the character of a lament. The anxious melody returns, and becomes more agitated, the solemn answer is repeated, and stillness descends. At this point an oboe quietly strikes up a cheerful piping, and is joined by trilling flutes and clarinets, unmistakably suggesting birdsong. The entire orchestra (the entire forest?) joins in, and a climax is reached from which the first movement's horn call sounds. As this joyful tumult dies down, the cor anglais takes up its theme again, the stillness becomes deeper, and the movement ends with the solemn brass chords, followed by high strings, and a last chord on double basses alone, like a gentle humming from the depths of the forest.

The inspiration for the scherzo was stated clearly by the composer himself: it was the Indian dance at Hiawatha's wedding feast. The poem describes how the handsome Pau-Puk-Keewis begins with 'a solemn measure', and then dances faster and faster, 'Whirling, spinning round in circles'. Dvořák's music has dances of various speeds, but arranged in the formal pattern of a scherzo and trio. The scherzo itself begins vigorously, with woodwind instruments chasing each other at two beats' distance, and with strong cross-rhythms that sound as much Czech as Native American. There is then a subsidiary, slightly slower, theme in the major, yet another melody that winds round itself. The faster dance returns briefly, and then quietens to the central trio. This is a slower, more stately dance, very Czech-sounding, though with strange echoing trills in its second half that are perhaps meant to sound Native American (or at least exotic). The scherzo returns, with its two dances, and is followed by a coda. Over shuddering strings, the horn call from the first movement sounds, and builds in power against fragments of the dance, as if we are being summoned to continue our great journey.

The finale sets off ferociously. The principal theme is announced by horns and trumpets like a fanfare. But the notes themselves are once again closely related to the minor-key folk melody from early in the first movement. This reaches a climax, at which the violins break the tune into the rhythm of a jig or reel, and in this form it proceeds energetically along. As it ebbs away, a clarinet spins a long-breathed melody, as if weaving a spell over the sleeping dancers. The violins take up the end of the tune, gather energy again, and transform it into another swinging dance. This becomes gradually more playful and more distant. At its quietest, flutes and oboes introduce a perky trilling motif, reminiscent of the trills in the trio of the scherzo, and horns respond with a reminder of the opening theme of the finale. To this is added a fragment of the cor anglais' tune from the slow movement. There is a climax, at which trumpets and trombones reassert the opening theme. This dies down and gives way to a reprise of the long clarinet melody, now on violins and cellos. There is no dance to follow, but a horn call leads into the final section of the movement, in which there is the greatest of the climaxes in the symphony, culminating with the brass and woodwind intoning the chords from the opening of the slow movement, fortissimo. There is a hush, followed by the last statements of the finale's opening theme, quietly and then on full orchestra, and a final rush to the end, concluding (surprisingly after such a head of power) with a long, held woodwind chord, dying away.

Reporting on the premiere in Carnegie Hall, the critic of the *New York Herald* wrote:

After the second movement, storms of applause resounded from all sides. [This was in the days before a reverent silence was expected between movements.] Everyone present turned to look in the direction in which the conductor, Anton Seidl, was looking. At last, a sturdily-built man of medium height, straight as a fir tree from the forest whose music he so splendidly interprets, was discovered by the audience. From all over the hall there are cries of "Dvořák! Dvořák!" And while the composer is bowing, we have the opportunity to observe this poet of tone who is able to move the heart of so great an audience. He has a dark complexion, dark hair, thin in front. His short, dark beard is beginning to turn grey. The large dark eyes are steady. His face is honest and friendly, and its expression reveals an open and guileless nature. Dr. Dvořák, hands trembling with emotion, indicates his thanks to Mr. Seidl, the orchestra and the audience, whereupon he disappears into the background while the Symphony continues.[11]

EDWARD ELGAR
(1857–1934)

Elgar is a composer who suffered for many years from a simplistic public image of his character. Photographs show him as an imposing figure with an impressive moustache, an upright gentleman clad in country tweeds. His most famous work is the first of his *Pomp and Circumstance* Marches, with its grand central melody, later set to A. C. Benson's patriotic verses 'Land of Hope and Glory'. This is sung every year in September at the last night of the Promenade Concerts (Proms) in London, and it has the effect of renewing Elgar's status as the imperial grandfather to the nation.

But scratch beneath the surface, and you find a complex character a great deal less comfortable than that of the image. Elgar always felt something of an outsider in the establishment of Edwardian Britain. He was a Roman Catholic, the son of a shopkeeper. In 1883, at the age of twenty-six, he was engaged to a Worcester girl, Helen Weaver. But her family could not contemplate her marriage to a Catholic, and the engagement was broken off. In 1889 he married Alice Roberts, nine years older than Elgar, and the daughter of a major-general. When she insisted on marrying a man of the wrong religion and the wrong class, her father disinherited her. Their marriage was undoubtedly happy, and Alice was a great support for Elgar. But there are strong clues, in his letters, reminiscences of those who knew him, and in his music, that he never achieved a real sense of ease with himself. Behind the facade of the English gentleman lay a man who was nervously witty, easily hurt, and who never felt that people really understood him. Although there is no suggestion that he was unfaithful to Alice, he became deeply attached to certain women other than his wife (particularly Alice Stuart-Wortley, whom he called his 'Windflower'), and to the few men friends in whom he could confide (particularly August Jaeger, at his publisher Novello, the subject of 'Nimrod' in the 'Enigma' Variations). His career as a composer was also far from easy. He struggled for years to make his mark, earning his living as a local music teacher, conductor, and organist around

Worcester. It was not until 1899, when he was forty-two, that Elgar first achieved real success as a composer with his 'Enigma' Variations.

The image of the comfortable Edwardian gentleman was therefore little more than a facade to hide behind. And there is a sense in his music, too, of passions lying beneath the surface, of feelings struggling to be expressed, of yearning for the unattainable or the lost. It is this aspect of Elgar's character that seems most English – a vein of things hinted at rather than stated outright – and it is perhaps this that makes it difficult for his music to make headway outside Britain. But it is once one taps into this side of Elgar that his music really comes alive. Like the man, the music is often conventional in outward appearance. It is often formed into long and overtly traditional works – symphonies, concertos, oratorios – and the music can sometimes seem a little stodgy. This is partly because of his orchestral palate. Elgar tends to use the orchestra rather like an organ. The strings are the foundation, to which he will add woodwind and brass like an organist pulling out more stops. There are few glorious wind solos (as there are throughout Brahms, for example). His music needs a great deal of under-standing to bring out the subtlety and the fluctuating passions that Elgar was attempting to express. He was often dissatisfied with other conductors' interpretations of his works, saying that he wanted them performed 'elastically and mystically' not 'squarely'. His own recordings, made in the decade before his death, have a drive and nervous intensity that has rarely been matched in later performances.

COCKAIGNE (IN LONDON TOWN), OP. 40
Duration: approx. 15 minutes

This exuberant concert overture was Elgar's first new work to follow after the dismal premiere of his oratorio *The Dream of Gerontius* in October 1900. It was a low point of Elgar's career. He was bitter at the failure of a work in which he had invested such depth of feeling. He was famous, but was not yet earning enough money from his compositions. Only three weeks after the *Gerontius* fiasco, Elgar was invited by the Philharmonic Society to submit an orches-tral piece for performance at one of their concerts. As this would actually cost Elgar money (there was no fee), he was at first reluctant. But he had already been working on this overture, and so he completed it, and conducted the first performance at a Philharmonic Concert in London in June 1901. It was an immense success, striking one critic as not only brilliantly written, but as a 'powerful expression of healthy & exuberant life'.[1]

Always ready to adopt a mask hiding his emotions, it is striking that, in the middle of this trough, Elgar was able to come up with this immensely cheerful work. He dedicated it to 'my many friends, the members of British orchestras'. Some of those members who took part in early performances of *Cockaigne* can still be heard playing in the two recordings that Elgar conducted many years later, in 1926 and 1933. The love of London's orchestral musicians for England's greatest living musician can easily be sensed in those warm and enthusiastic perfor-mances, even if they are, by modern standards, sometimes rough around the edges.

In any case, a little roughness is not out of place in this work. It is a Cockney overture, inspired by the street scenes and character of London. 'Cockaigne' is an imaginary land of luxury and idleness in medieval poetry, and it came to be ironically attached to London by association with Cockneys. Elgar wrote that the name 'calls up to my mind all the good-humour, jollity and something deeper in the way of English good fellowship (as it were) abiding still in our capital'.[2] The cover of the first edition of the score has a design with a delightful selection of appropriate scenes: Big Ben, St Paul's Cathedral, Piccadilly Circus, medieval jousting, archers, a golfer dressed in plus-fours, and a marching band.

The opening group of ideas, with their perky rhythms and lively switches of direction, immediately creates an impression of energy and bustle, as of a street scene. The overture begins quietly, but soon brings in the whole orchestra. Then there is a sudden change of pace, and a grander theme briefly makes an appearance. Elgar said that this theme had occurred to him one day while looking up at the roof of London's Guildhall: 'I seemed to hear far away in the dim roof a theme, an echo of some noble melody.'[3] After another moment of boisterousness, the mood becomes tranquil, and a lyrical second main theme is sung by the violins, and developed at length (Elgar called this a lovers' theme).[4] This theme is then cheekily doubled in speed, and brings the first section of the overture to a close.

The development begins with a quiet and evocative passage that brings together the grand 'Guildhall' theme and another version of the perky opening ideas. Gradually these come to predominate, and they build up to what Elgar might have called 'a splendid row', as if the street has filled with marching bands. As this dies away, there are lingering sounds of marching in the distance. Then the marching theme is smoothed out to give a period of quiet reflection. Into this tranquil scene the cheeky elements again begin to intrude, building up until we suddenly find ourselves at the reprise of the opening of the overture. The sequence of ideas is revisited, varied in detail and in keys. This time, the double-speed cheeky theme builds up into the 'splendid row', and from there to a great peroration of the Guildhall theme, underpinned by deep bass notes of the organ. A final flourish, the crowd wave their hats, and the overture is over.

Concertos

CELLO CONCERTO IN E MINOR, OP. 85
Duration: approx. 30 minutes

Adagio – Moderato –
Lento – Allegro molto
Adagio
Allegro – Moderato – Allegro, ma non troppo – Poco più lento – Adagio

Elgar wrote his Cello Concerto in 1919, eleven years after the Violin Concerto, and the two works are very different from each other. The Cello Concerto is scarcely half the length of the Violin Concerto and its musical language is more concise. It shares a certain melancholy tone, but it is less personally anguished, less introvert perhaps – less self-indulgent, some would say. Much had changed in the intervening years. The horrors of the First World War had affected Elgar deeply, and his relish for orchestral works on a massive scale had vanished. At the end of the war he had turned to chamber music, writing a violin sonata, string quartet, and piano quintet. The Cello Concerto has a transparency and spareness of scoring that takes it further towards chamber music than the Violin Concerto (though the orchestral forces are almost the same). At the same time it has elements of wit and lightness that are not found in the violin concerto, and are reminiscent of his *Falstaff* (1913). This was to be his last major work, though he lived for another fifteen years. It has a sense of elegy, of an epitaph for a vanished world.

The concerto opens with a bold, declamatory lament for cello. A clarinet answers, a sudden pianissimo in mid-phrase pinpointing the wistful melancholy that is to be a thread throughout the work. An unaccompanied rising scale on the cello leads into the principal theme of the movement, a gently rocking melody on unaccompanied violas, like a memory of a vanished pastoral scene. The cello takes it up, gradually increasing in force, until a powerful scale right up to the top of the instrument leads to a reprise of the melody on full orchestra. The cello gradually winds down to a held low note. Clarinets and bassoons play the second main theme, a rising and falling phrase in which a dotted rhythm brings a suggestion of dance. But the sense of lament persists, the cello answering with sighing phrases. A version of this melody ventures for a time into a major key, bringing a smile to the memory. Later, the cello moves seamlessly back to the first pastoral theme, then through another orchestral climax, and winds down as before. Over a held low note, the cello repeats the opening declamatory bars, pizzicato, and then toys with a phrase of rapid repeated notes. These are interspersed with more pizzicato chords, in the manner of a cadenza, and after further lamenting there is a pause.

This leads straight into the second movement, a scherzo in which the rapid repeated notes have been developed into a fully fledged theme. After a time the music pulls up, and a second theme emerges, a moment of rather grandiose singing to suggest for the first time the figure of Falstaff. The moment is short-lived, and we are soon back into the rapid repeated phrases. The Falstaff moment recurs later. This time, when the rapid repetitions reassert themselves, they remain pianissimo, taking on a ghostly character. Wisps of the Falstaff theme accompany it, first in clarinets, then in violins, before the movement accelerates to an abrupt close.

The Adagio is one of Elgar's shortest, simplest, and most inspired slow movements, in which the cello sings a heartfelt song, accompanied only by the strings, with occasional interjections from clarinets and bassoons. The melody begins with a series of questioning two-bar phrases. The answer comes in the form of a sustained line, full of rising intervals with an unmistakeably yearning character. This dominates the rest of the movement, twice rising to a great climax. The movement ends as it began, with the questioning opening phrases left suspended in mid-air.

The finale begins with a boisterous few bars from the orchestra, as if an important guest has been announced. But the cello interrupts with further declamatory lamenting, culminating in a defiant flourish to the highest notes of the instrument, sweeping the lingering melancholy away. The movement that follows is based on the boisterous theme announced previously by the orchestra, at first in more stately mode, then gathering energy. Its demeanour again reminds us, this time irresistibly, of Shakespeare's and Elgar's Falstaff. A second theme interrupts the progress with a moment of musing, at first lingering and sentimental, and in the next breath amused. The sentimental version predominates, and is enlarged upon.

After extensive rumination, the first theme returns, now spiked up by the woodwind (who rarely get much to play on their own in Elgar). This then moves back into more stately mode, and after a pause, becomes positively portly, emphasized by glissandi in the trombones (an effect that tends to be played down in fastidious modern performances). Material from the earlier part of the movement returns. But then the mood darkens, as if remembering past events, and we enter a passage of increasingly anguished meditation. It is based on an upside-down version of the theme of the slow movement, its rising chromatic melody now falling tragically. It becomes more intense, then more hushed, and at its quietest point recalls the beautiful continuation of the slow movement's theme. There is an expectant pause, and suddenly we are back where we started, with the declamatory lament that opened the concerto. But this is once again, and for the last time, swept aside, and the concerto ends with a determined reassertion of the solid, boisterous theme of the finale.

VIOLIN CONCERTO IN B MINOR, OP. 61
Duration: 41–53 minutes

Allegro
Andante
Allegro molto

Elgar began to sketch a violin concerto in 1905 and completed it in 1910, between his two symphonies (1908 and 1911). When he had nearly finished it, he wrote to a friend, 'It's *good!* awfully emotional! Too emotional, but I love it.'[5] Like the 'Enigma' Variations, the concerto has a mystery at its heart, for which a clue is given in a quotation on the opening page: 'Aquí está encerra [misprint for 'encerrada'] el alma de.....' ('Here is enshrined the soul of.....') This is a quotation from the eighteenth-century novel *Gil Blas* by Alain-René Lesage. In a preface, the hero, Gil Blas, tells a story of two students who find just such an inscription on an abandoned stone by the roadside. Under it one of them finds a purse full of gold pieces. The quotation in the score is followed by five dots rather than the usual three of an ellipsis. Alice Stuart-Wortley has long been thought the most likely candidate for this dedication. Elgar's relationship with her was very close; he called her his 'Windflower', and identified some of the most heartfelt themes in the concerto as 'Windflower themes'. (What Lady Elgar, also Alice, thought of all this is not recorded.) The name Alice has five letters, hence, perhaps, the five dots. But some think Elgar had in mind Helen Weaver, to whom he was engaged before he married the other Alice. Helen too has five letters. The truth is never likely to be known, but what is unmistakable is the sense of deep nostalgia that permeates the concerto. At the same time it is a virtuoso work, full of brilliant violin-writing. The difficulty in finding a good balance between emotional sensitivity and brilliance is reflected in the enormous range of durations in recorded performances.

The concerto has a convoluted early history of performance and recording. It was written for Fritz Kreisler, who gave the first performance in November 1910 in Queen's Hall, London, with Elgar conducting. There were attempts to get Kreisler to record it with Elgar, but they never came to anything. Elgar conducted a truncated recording in the pre-electric studio in 1916 with violinist Marie Hall. Many of the early performances were given by the violinist Albert Sammons, also with Elgar conducting. Sammons also made the first complete recording, though with Sir Henry Wood conducting rather than Elgar, because Elgar and Sammons were under contract to different recording companies. Finally, in 1932, at the age of seventy-five, Elgar did record the complete concerto, not with one of its established interpreters, but with a boy of fifteen who had never played it in public, and who met Elgar for the first time two days before the recording session. His name was Yehudi Menuhin, and he came to be associated with the concerto more than any other violinist. Menuhin seems to have encouraged Elgar to linger over the concerto more than he was accustomed to with Albert Sammons.[6] Sammons' own recording is generally faster and tighter than Menuhin's, and Elgar's recordings of his other works tend to be quite brisk. But he was clearly overwhelmed by the beauty of young Menuhin's playing, and deeply touched by the mature emotional understanding of the teenager. When, after subsequent concert performances, the critic Ernest Newman wrote that he found Menuhin's performance lacking 'English reserve and austerity', Elgar responded, 'Austerity be damned! I am not an austere man, am I?'[7]

The tone of the concerto is set in the opening orchestral tutti, which begins in a spirit of determined vigour, though with yearning leaps up and down in the first theme. Straight away it seems that there is an undercurrent of sadness to be overcome. This breaks the surface at the soloist's first entry. The violin reiterates the opening phrase, but now more slowly, and continues with a meditative, hesitant passage almost like a cadenza, before summoning the strength to move on purposefully. Similarly, the second theme, which in the orchestral intro-duction is a brief moment of quiet led by the clarinet, becomes a more extended meditation when taken up by the violin, once more with yearning leaps in the melody. In between these quiet moments, the music becomes agitated, and this culminates in a sustained outburst at the next orchestral section, marked 'con passione', and later 'strepitoso' (noisy, boisterous).

When the music calms down, the soloist embarks on a passage of sustained musing on the various elements from earlier in the movement. The mood is very volatile, ranging from the plangent, even desolate, to the animated and furious. Every few bars there is a change of pace, a hesitation or an acceleration. It is almost like a free fantasia or cadenza (in this respect, the concerto calls to mind Sibelius's Violin Concerto of 1903). The return to the opening theme creeps in underneath the soloist, and the other material from the early part of the movement follows much transformed and further meditated upon, until the movement reaches a defiant conclusion.

The first theme of the second movement is, by comparison with the volatile first move-ment, a straightforwardly lyrical theme in two-bar phrases. But it is not quite as it seems. It sounds as if it starts with an upbeat, but, as it appears in the score, this is actually the first beat of the bar. Elgar has shifted the rhythmic emphasis of the phrases by one beat in relation to the bar line. The soloist enters with a counter-theme conventionally phrased in accordance with the bar line, while the original theme continues underneath. This conjunction of two melodies with a different rhythmic emphasis gives a subtle sense of rhythmic ambiguity. The solo violin winds higher and higher, quieter and quieter, the highest notes given an ethereal quality by being played on harmonics. Then a hushed second theme enters in the strings, its yearning upward leaps giving it a clear relationship to the opening theme of the first move-ment. It leads on to a long central passage of passionate fantasy, full of accelerations and hesitations, like the central section of the first movement. At the return of the opening theme, the solo violin again rises higher and higher, this time culminating on a high D flat, which, in relation to the B flat major of the home key, has a magical effect.

The finale sounds at first almost like one of Mendelssohn's fairy scherzos, with a repeated swirling pattern in the solo violin. But within a few bars there is a hold-up, the mood turns assertive and dogged, and when the original tempo is regained, it is with a rugged, striding theme, against which the soloist plays more virtuoso patterns. Another hold-up leads to a melancholy second main theme, with another yearning upward leap featuring prominently.

The soloist continues with a complex, decorative passage, but all the time the melancholy theme is to be heard underneath, sustaining the ambiguity of mood that has permeated so much of the concerto. The opening sequence of themes returns, the striding theme now played forcefully by the soloist as chords on three strings. After the melancholy theme, high trills in the solo violin bring in a quiet, sonorous theme in the orchestra, with the familiar yearning upward leap. This is a reminiscence of the hushed second theme from the slow movement – though it therefore also has echoes of the very first theme of the concerto, making one realize how much the themes from different movements are interrelated.

There is a build-up, suddenly the soloist breaks back to the striding theme, and we sense that we are moving towards a final, satisfying climax. But it is not to be. The confidence evaporates, pianissimo strings, muted and tremulous, play a ghostly echo of the opening theme of the concerto. The soloist takes up another phrase from the theme (marked 'mesto', sad), and we are into an extended cadenza. Again and again the soloist looks back wistfully to the events of the past, occasionally breaking away for a moment of exuberant display, but always returning to fragments of themes that seem to haunt him. The orchestra does not fall silent, as in a conventional cadenza, but quietly underlines the poignancy of the mood with wisps of accompaniment, including a tremolando effect that Elgar instructs 'should be "thrummed" with the soft part of three or four fingers across the strings'. He told Alice Stuart-Wortley that in this cadenza, 'the music sings of memories and hopes'.[8] It is this part of the concerto more than any other that powerfully suggests a deep personal sense of regret and loss. Could this really be inspired by his friendship with Alice Stuart-Wortley, however close? Perhaps his long-lost fiancée, Helen Weaver, has the prime claim to the 'soul' of the concerto after all.

Eventually, all the pain and regret is worked through, the cadenza ends with a confident restatement of the opening theme of the concerto, followed by a determined reassertion of the bravura of the finale – though not without a sense that it has taken an immense effort of will to achieve the resolution.

FALSTAFF, OP. 68
Duration: approx. 35 minutes

Elgar was inclined to be protective and enigmatic about the thoughts and feelings behind his music. But in 1913 he did an uncharacteristic thing. A month before the premiere in Leeds of his 'Symphonic Study' *Falstaff*, he published in *The Musical Times* a long essay, in which he explained the background to the work, and provided a detailed breakdown of its episodes and themes and their relation to Shakespeare.[9] Even here, there are limits to what Elgar wishes to reveal. He writes, 'If we take the word "study" in its literal use and meaning, the composer's intention will be sufficiently indicated.' He goes on to say that the 'real' Falstaff is not to be found in Shakespeare's *The Merry Wives of Windsor*, which is the most familiar portrait to English playgoers (and the one taken by Verdi and his librettist Boito for their opera). Here, Falstaff is reduced to a caricature. The real Falstaff, according to Elgar, is the figure in the history plays, *Henry IV* parts 1 and 2, and *Henry V*. He quotes with approval an essay written in 1777 by Maurice Morgann, summarizing the complexities of Falstaff's character: 'He is a character made up by Shakespeare wholly of incongruities – a man at once young and old, enterprizing and fat, a dupe and a wit, harmless and wicked, weak in principle and resolute by constitution, cowardly in appearance and brave in reality; a knave without malice, a lyar without deceit; and a knight, a gentleman and a soldier, without either dignity, decency or honour.'

Why did such a figure particularly appeal to Elgar? For an answer to that, we have to read between the lines. Elgar quotes William Hazlitt's study of Falstaff: 'The true spirit of humanity, the thorough knowledge of the stuff we are made of, the practical wisdom with the seeming fooleries, have no parallel anywhere else … In one point of view they are laughable in the extreme, in another they are equally affecting – if it is affecting to shew what a little thing is human life.' Elgar was a man who hid his insecurity behind a dignified mask and defended his sensitivity with quips, and who, despite his exalted position in British music, felt misunderstood, and, by 1913, was beginning to seem like a figure from the past. Although he did not say so, it is easy to see that Elgar found some parallels between Falstaff and himself, and that, in writing what is, superficially, a portrait of a Shakespearean character, he was to some extent drawing on his own feelings about himself.

Although Elgar denied that *Falstaff* was 'programme music', like the tone poems of Richard Strauss, its various themes and episodes have a clear relationship to incidents in Shakespeare, which Elgar spells out in his essay. At the same time, these are woven into a large-scale and complex musical structure, like a one-movement symphony. It can seem rather long-winded and rambling unless a firm hand is kept on its narrative. Elgar's own recording of 1931–2 is characteristically brisk and to the point, though sometimes rather skimming over detail (the opposite of modern tendencies). As a critic commented of a concert performance by Elgar of his 'Enigma' Variations, 'Sir Edward has a drastic way of hacking at his music. All sorts of things which other conductors carefully foster, he leaves to take their chance. He cuts a way through in a manner both nervous and decisive. At the end we realize that detail and rhetorical niceties have been put in their right place, and that the essential tale has been vividly told'.[10]

Falstaff is in four sections, played virtually without a break. The second and third sections each end with a gentle interlude. Elgar provided the following headings, and the descriptions in quotation marks, in his essay:

Falstaff and Prince Henry (approx. 9 minutes)

'An apartment of the Prince's'. The awkward, lolloping theme in the cellos that begins the piece represents Sir John Falstaff, as Morgann describes him, 'in a green old age, mellow, frank, gay, easy, corpulent, loose, unprincipled, and luxurious'. The skittering theme that follows immediately is suggested by a quotation from Falstaff himself: 'I am not only witty in myself but the cause that wit is in other men.' This builds up to one of Elgar's characteristic 'nobilmente' themes, representing the prince 'in his most courtly and genial mood'. Another ambling theme in the cellos 'shows Falstaff as cajoling and persuasive'. Several themes recur and combine in an acceleration to a climax. There follows an extend passage of conversation, banter, argument. In among all this, during a fortissimo passage, there is another strangely awkward melody, 'gargantuan', with angular leaps, which exhibits Falstaff's 'boastfulness and colossal mendacity'. The mood quietens, then becomes highly agitated, and finally sweeps majestically into:

Eastcheap – Gadshill – The Boar's Head, revelry and sleep (approx. 10 minutes)

The change of scene to the bustle of Eastcheap is suggested by energetic patterns, punctuated by a tambourine. Elgar wrote that all of this 'should chatter, blaze, glitter and coruscate'. The whole passage was suggested by Prince Henry's escape to the 'teeming vitality of the London streets and the Tavern where Falstaff is monarch', with the Hostess and Doll Tearsheet evoked by a persistent, delicate theme with trills. A portly bassoon suggests the drunken Falstaff, who eventually falls asleep (the snoring is as realistic as anything in Richard Strauss's tone poems). Out of this sleep emerges an interlude, scored for small orchestra. 'Simple in form and somewhat antiquated in mood, it suggests in its strong contrast to the immediately preceding riot, "what might have been".' Falstaff is dreaming of the time when he was page to the Duke of Norfolk.

Falstaff's march – The return through Gloucestershire – The new king – The hurried ride to London (approx. 7 minutes)

A sudden awakening, and Falstaff is rallying his 'scarecrow army' for the Battle of Shrewsbury against the rebel Henry 'Hotspur' Percy. The march rhythm is accompanied by fragmented themes to suggest the motley assortment of down-and-outs that Falstaff has assembled. The noise of battle dies down, and gentler music evokes the return through Gloucestershire. This culminates in the second interlude, where rustic oboes and tambourines, and muted strings, suggest the peace of Justice Shallow's orchard. There is a sudden interruption, and a snatch of Prince Henry's theme – Pistol announces that Prince Hal has succeeded to the throne as King Henry V. Hasty preparations are made for the journey to London to greet his old friend: 'I know the young King is sick for me.'

King Henry V's progress – The repudiation of Falstaff, and his death (approx. 9 minutes)

This evokes the final scene of *Henry IV* part 2. 'Near Westminster Abbey the new King is to pass with his train; Falstaff and all his company await his coming among the shouting populace.' Various Falstaff-related and Hal-related themes build up to a great reprise of the prince's generous melody from part 1, as the king appears, 'Glittering in golden coat ... and gorgeous as the sun at midsummer.' Falstaff steps boldly forward and addresses the king. But he is rebuffed: 'I know thee not, old man. Fall to thy prayers. How ill white hairs become a fool and jester!' the procession moves on. 'In short phrases ... the decay of the merry-hearted one is shown. The broken man weakens until, with a weird, final attempt at humour ... we enter upon the death scene.' This is inspired by the Hostess's 'incomparable' description of Falstaff's death at The Boar's Head in *Henry V*: 'A' made a finer end and went away an' it had been any christom child; ... for after I saw him fumble with the sheets and play with flowers and smile upon his fingers' ends, I knew there was but one way; for his nose was as sharp as a pen, and a' babbled of green fields.' Here there are reminiscences of the interlude in the orchard. Falstaff dies to a quiet chord of C major. But Elgar adds a few bars of postlude: 'the King's stern theme is curtly thrown across the picture, the shrill drum again asserts itself momentarily, and with one pizzicato chord the work ends; the man of stern reality has triumphed.'

IN THE SOUTH (ALASSIO), OP. 50
Duration: approx. 20 minutes

In the winter of 1904 the Elgars spent several weeks at Alassio, on the Mediterranean coast in north-west Italy. There Elgar attempted, unsuccessfully, to make progress on a symphony in E flat (which, seven years later, was to become his Second Symphony). Elgar wrote in January to his friend August Jaeger, 'This visit has been, is, artistically a complete *failure* & I can do nothing: we have been perished with cold, rain & gales ... I am trying to finish a Concert overture for Covent Garden instead of the Sym . . .'[11] In March there was to be a three-day festival of Elgar's music at the Covent Garden opera house in London, a unique honour for a living British composer. The new overture that Elgar wrote for the occasion was given the title, *In the South (Alassio)*. It is a substantial work, lasting twenty minutes even in Elgar's brisk recording. Despite the weather, Elgar conjures up, from the very first notes, a joyful sense of Mediterranean light and splendour.

That, at least, is the impression. As often in Elgar's music, the direct inspiration for the first idea was something characteristically quirky. He had written the vigorous opening eight bars in the visitors' book of his friend George Sinclair in 1899, in honour of his bulldog, Dan (who had already featured in the 'Enigma' Variations). The fragment is labelled, 'triumphant (after a fight)'. But vigour is vigour, and the theme makes an immediate and arresting start to this Mediterranean overture. The effect is very like Richard Strauss in the openings of *Ein Heldenleben* and *Don Juan*, and that association is made all the stronger as the overture proceeds, with its brilliantly complex textures, and climaxes with heroic horns. There had been a Strauss Festival in London the previous year, and there is no doubting Elgar's debt to Strauss, in this work more than any other – even though he distanced himself from Strauss's ideas of 'programme music'.

Under a glittering torrent of tremolo and trills, the vigorous first theme rises up in the lower strings and horns, until, within a few bars, it takes over the whole orchestra. The violins then begin a more sustained melody, while the first theme continues underneath in cellos and horns. The two proceed together, until they give way to a rolling melody in the violins. These various elements eventually build up to the first great Straussian climax. When it dies down, two new elements appear: a gentle, pastoral phrase on clarinet (related to the earlier 'rolling' theme), and a melancholy drooping answer from the violins (whose rhythm is derived from the vigorous opening theme). A nostalgic mood develops, until there is a change of key, a slackening of pace, and a quiet melody in the violins, with Elgar's characteristic yearning upward leaps and dying falls. This extended gentle passage forms a complete contrast to the vigorous opening themes of the overture. As it draws to an end, the clarinet repeats its little pastoral phrase, with the drooping answer from the violins. But now these elements are developed and built up urgently.

There are trumpet fanfares, a sudden break, and we find ourselves confronted by something powerful and implacable. This is the central section of the overture, with the heavy tread of trombones, tuba, and drums, raw shifts of harmony, and a sense of unstoppable force. This passage was suggested to Elgar by a massive Roman bridge that he found awe-inspiring, and was intended 'to paint the relentless and domineering *onward force* of the ancient day and give a sound-picture of the strife and war ("the drums and tramplings") of a later time'.[12] The mighty procession gives way to a passage of frantic tumult. This in turn fades away, to leave behind a peaceful scene. A solo viola sings a melody, like a popular Italian tune, conjuring a reminiscence of the pastoral episodes in Berlioz's *Harold in Italy* (though it also incorporates elements from themes in the first part of the overture). In the middle of this scene, fragments of the overture's first theme appear, slowly and quietly, in the middle of the texture, before the viola takes up the melody again.

Then the vigorous opening theme does return, and we are into the reprise of the first section. Instead of building up to a great climax, this arrives quickly at the gentle, yearning theme, which had originally come later. Only then does the music begin to build up. This time, there is a long acceleration, culminating in a brilliant passage in which the chiming of a glockenspiel evokes memories of Strauss's *Don Juan*. Only then does the great rolling theme take over, rising to the final climax. The full brass section brays joyfully, and the overture comes tumbling precipitately to an end. The final bars are one of the trickiest of endings to make work. Getting the rhythm to tell, so that it really has its effect, is extremely difficult, and in Elgar's own recording it sounds perfunctory. You can see what Elgar meant: the long march to the climax has been accomplished, and it is rounded off with a final, daredevil flourish.

INTRODUCTION AND ALLEGRO, OP. 47
Duration: approx. 15 minutes

Even though he is remembered principally as a writer of massive orchestral and choral works, this Introduction and Allegro sums up Elgar's character and musical achievement as well as any of the bigger pieces. Into its fifteen minutes Elgar packs all his energy and aspiration. Unlike much of Elgar, it seems to express what it has to say with exactly the right number of notes, powerfully and economically. There are the familiar strands of melancholy, but the overall mood is optimistic and determined. Elgar wrote it in 1905, in response to a suggestion from his publisher August Jaeger ('Nimrod') that he might write a 'brilliant, quick scherzo' for the strings of the newly formed London Symphony Orchestra. But he also incorporated as its most strikingly melancholy element what he referred to as a 'Welsh tune', a melody inspired by singing that he heard in the distance on a holiday in Wales in 1901, and was then reminded of by another distant singer nearer home in the Wye valley. 'The work is really a tribute to that sweet borderland where I have made my home.'[13] At the same time, the Introduction and Allegro is a tribute to Handel, whose music Elgar greatly admired, and is cast somewhat in the form of the eighteenth-century *concerto grosso*. Like Handel's concertos, it has a group of solo strings (a string quartet) that interacts with the main body. The slow(ish) Introduction followed by an Allegro is also an eighteenth-century convention. But there the homage ends: this is in no sense a 'neo-baroque' work, but uses the full expressive range of the modern strings, in music that is deeply Romantic in spirit.

The introduction in G minor sets out almost all of the musical material from which the work is built. First, there is a fortissimo, plunging figure, one of the most arresting of Elgar's openings. From this emerges a quiet, anxiously rising figure on the solo quartet, answered by the lower strings of the orchestra with a smooth rising and falling phrase. This sequence of material is repeated, but now quietly, as if trying out the ideas. There is a hush, and the solo viola plays the haunting 'Welsh tune' – haunting because of the way it sadly repeats the same shape four times before it breaks out to a climax. This is then taken up by the full strings. A final statement of the plunging theme, a final strain of the 'Welsh tune', a brief pause, and the Allegro begins.

The first paragraph of the Allegro is built from the anxiously rising figure first heard in the quartet. This is followed by a new motif of rapidly repeated notes, in which quartet and full strings alternate. It builds to a climax, culminating in a big theme marked 'nobilmente', which is a spread-out and extended version of the first plunging figure. This leads to a yet greater climax, which then subsides to complete the first section of the Allegro. There is a reminiscence of the Welsh tune, very quiet, with a tremolando effect, suggesting the distant singing that Elgar first heard. After another pause, the music breaks into what Elgar referred to as 'a devil of a fugue'. It seems quite new, though it has some affinity to the rapid repeated-note motif, and it is soon joined by the smooth rising and falling phrase that first occurred in the bass in the Introduction. This climaxes and then winds down, and we find ourselves back at the beginning of the Allegro for the reprise. It proceeds much as before, until it reaches the grand 'nobilmente' theme. This time, instead of dying away, it builds to a mighty climax and a pause, and the Welsh tune is now played fortissimo by the whole orchestra. The wistful little melody is transformed into a great song of aspiration that carries the work through to its conclusion.

Pomp and Circumstance Marches Nos 1–5, Op. 39

Durations: 5–6 minutes each

The scholarship of recent decades has revealed to us the sensitive and troubled side of Elgar's personality, so that we are less inclined to think of him as a classic stiff-upper-lip Edwardian gentleman. The works that tend to bring us back to the old image are the five *Pomp and Circumstance* Marches, the first four dating from 1901–7, the fifth added in 1930. Elgar wrote in an article published in 1904, 'We are a nation with great military proclivities, and I do not see why the ordinary quick march should not be treated on a large scale in the way that the waltz, the old-fashioned slow march, and even the polka have been treated by the great composers ... I have some of the soldier instinct in me ...'[14] Many of the most swaggering themes in Elgar's major works are, in effect, marches, even though they are often subjected to doubt and struggle. Now the march character is given full rein. And yet, even here Elgar suggests some ambiguity. The title that he gave the marches comes from Shakespeare's *Othello*, at the point where the moor, tricked by Iago into thinking his wife unfaithful, bitterly expresses the feeling that his military prowess is now pointless:

> Farewell the neighing steed, and the shrill trump,
> The spirit-stirring drum, th' ear-piercing fife,
> The royal banner, and all quality,
> Pride, pomp, and circumstance of glorious war!

Elgar would certainly have known where the quote came from. Did he intend some irony or bitterness in his choice of title? If he had chosen it after the horrors of the First World War, which affected him deeply, that would have seemed an obvious inference. But in 1901 he gave no hint that any subtext was intended.

NO. 1 IN D MAJOR (1901)

Elgar began sketching ideas for the first two marches at the same time, at the beginning of 1901. He was particularly pleased with the trio (middle section) of No. 1, which was to become his most famous melody. Elgar enthusiastically declared to a visiting friend, 'I've got a tune that will knock 'em – knock 'em flat', and he described it elsewhere as 'a tune that comes once in a lifetime'.[15] He reused it a year later it in the *Coronation Ode* of 1902 (for Edward VII's coronation), setting words by A. C. Benson, 'Land of Hope and Glory', and it was this that cemented its fame. The effect of this melody in the march itself is enhanced by the outer sections, which have a restlessly energetic character, with phrases in short rhythmic bursts. The calm flow of the famous middle tune comes as an oasis of firm purpose in the midst of all the excitement. At the end of the reprise of the opening section, the famous tune returns to form a grand climax.

NO. 2 IN A MINOR (1901)

In a minor key, this has quite a different character from No. 1. In the outer sections, an urgent call to arms is followed by an insistently repetitive figure, almost like classic 'chase' film music. This gives way to a sonorous second idea, suggestive of bugle calls. The trio could have come out of one of Dvořák's Slavonic Dances, with its poised phrases over a repeating bass line.

NO. 3 IN C MINOR (1904)

Like No. 2, this is in a minor key, giving it a darker tone than No. 1. It begins in the distance, with a repetitive phrase punctuated by an offbeat drum. Twice this builds up to the full orchestra, before giving way to a delicate, rather pastoral-sounding trio. As in No. 1, this returns at the end, surprisingly transformed to create a forceful climax.

NO. 4 IN G MAJOR (1907)

Like No. 1, this march is in a major key, and shares its outgoing, confident character. Indeed, the opening section has a firm steadiness, without the restless short-windedness of No. 1. The tune of the trio is just as grand and sonorous as 'Land of hope and glory'. It too later had words added to it, first by Elgar's wife Alice, but, more famously, by A. P. Herbert during the Second World War. This was a 'Song of Liberty', with the refrain, 'All men must be free'. As in No. 1, this melody returns to form the grand climax of the reprise.

NO. 5 IN C MAJOR (1930)

This was composed many years later than Nos 1–4 and has an extrovert, almost sprightly character akin to the *Radetzky March* of Johann Strauss senior. The trio is another sonorous tune, though not as solemn or as singable as the trios of Nos 1 and 4.

SERENADE FOR STRINGS, OP. 20

Allegro piacevole
Larghetto
Allegretto

The Serenade for Strings is the earliest of Elgar's works to have become really popular. It was written in 1892, when he was struggling to make what income he could from teaching. He had been married for three years to Alice Roberts, whose well-to-do family had been appalled by her engagement to a Catholic musician with no prospects. When he finished the serenade,

Elgar wrote on the manuscript that his wife 'helped a great deal to make these little tunes'.[16] He sent the work to Novello, who refused to publish it on the grounds that 'this class of music is practically unsaleable'. Elgar then tried out the serenade with the Ladies' Orchestral Class that he ran in Worcester, and one of the players, Rosa Burley, left a reminiscence of that first rehearsal: 'One afternoon at the orchestral class Jessie and I found ourselves playing a work which was unfamiliar at any rate to me. I think I must have arrived late and commenced hurriedly, for I do not remember looking at the title. But I do remember the profound impression its rather Mendelssohnian slow movement made on me. "What is this?" I asked. "Oh, it's a thing he wrote himself," she said casually and quite without enthusiasm. "Wrote it himself?" I could scarcely believe it. "Oh yes. He's always writing these things and trying them out on us."'

Miss Burley wrote of Elgar at this period, 'The impression made on me at the outset was that he was extremely shy but that his shyness masked the kind of intense pride with which an unhappy man attempts to console himself for feelings of frustration and disappointment.'[17] Elgar's most obvious frustration was his inability to make any headway with his compositions, about which he was passionate. But perhaps there were also other sources of melancholy. His engagement to Alice Roberts was his second. His first, to Helen Weaver, had been broken off four years earlier. Despite its lightweight form, the serenade has dark currents of sadness running through it. It is tempting to think of them as in some ways biographical, but if they are, we can be sure that the intensely private Elgar never told anyone.

The violas open the first movement with a tripping dance rhythm that might seem to suggest light-heartedness. But as soon as the violins play their first melody in E minor it is clear that melancholy is to be the pervading mood. The phrases rise and fall elegantly, but cut off before they finish. A second theme is even more short-breathed: just pairs of staccato quavers answered by a three-note sigh. A middle section moves into E major, but its warmth seems sadly nostalgic, at first in an intimate pianissimo, later rising to a sudden climax at which the staccato second theme returns forcefully. The opening material returns, and it too rises to a climax where, for the first time, the music achieves a continuous flow of uninterrupted phrases. The confident moment is soon over.

The slow movement, in C major, takes the nostalgic mood of the first movement's middle section and explores it more deeply. It begins with yearning upward phrases, like the opening of Wagner's *Tristan* Prelude brought to a Worcestershire landscape. After a few bars the violins quietly sing the main theme, a cumulative sequence of rising phrases, reaching their peak pianissimo. A middle section recalls Grieg's *Last Spring* (another deeply nostalgic piece), with its high, quiet chords, and the cellos silent until they enter with a countermelody. The main theme returns very quietly, and now rises to a great climax, where all the pent-up emotion of the music is given full expression for the only time in the serenade.

The third movement is at first almost light-hearted. The yearning upward leap is still there, but now sounding more hopeful, in G major, and with a rolling succession of phrases developing. But this is short-lived, and soon the music of the first movement returns in E major, with the leaping phrases of the middle section, and, finally, the almost dance rhythm of the very opening ascending to a final chord, richly scored but diminishing to pianissimo.

Symphonies

SYMPHONY NO. 1, OP. 55
Duration: 46 (Elgar)–55 minutes

Andante nobilmente e semplice – Allegro
Allegro molto –
Adagio
Lento – Allegro

This symphony was first performed in 1908 in Manchester, by the Hallé Orchestra conducted by Hans Richter. It is dedicated to Richter, who had championed Elgar's music ever since conducting the triumphant premiere of the 'Enigma' Variations in 1899. Richter had urged Elgar to write a symphony, but he struggled to do so, and it was nine years before he completed it. Elgar described the work in a programme note as 'a composer's outlook on life', a characteristically laconic comment.[18] One gets a powerful sense of that 'outlook' from Elgar's own recording of the symphony, made in 1930 with the London Symphony Orchestra. Whereas many performances let the music roll out in a stately fashion, Elgar's interpretation blazes with intensity. The characteristic 'nobility', which sometimes seems the overriding character of his symphonies, is, in Elgar's performance, hard-won. Asked by his fellow composer Walford Davies whether there was any programme behind the symphony, Elgar replied, 'There is no programme beyond a wide experience of human life with a great charity (love) & a *massive* hope in the future.'[19]

The symphony begins with a slow introduction. After two tentative rolls on the timpani (rather like the opening of Haydn's 'Drumroll' Symphony, No. 103), violas and woodwind launch into a quiet, broad melody in A flat major, with a gently trudging staccato bass. This is repeated grandly by the full orchestra, and subsides again. Elgar wrote in a letter, 'the opening theme is intended to be simple ... noble and elevating ... & something above the everyday and sordid things'.[20] Beginning a symphony with a slow introduction is a classic procedure stretching back to Haydn and beyond. But here it is has a particular function. The theme (marked 'nobilmente') recurs in the first and last movements, helping to define their shape, and creating a dramatic frame for the whole symphony. Between these occurrences of the nobilmente theme are many powerful contrasts of musical and emotional character. Extending his analogy between music and life-experience, Elgar wrote, 'As to the phases of pride, despair, anger, peace & the thousand & one things that occur between the first page & the last ... I prefer the listener to draw what he can from the sounds he hears.'[21]

In the first movement, the nobilmente theme occurs four times: at the beginning, at the end of the first section of the Allegro (before the development), at the junction between the development and the reprise, and at the very end of the movement. The movement is long and complex (17 minutes in Elgar's own recording, usually longer in modern performances), and these recurrences help us to find our bearings.

After the slow introduction has subsided to a quiet, sustained A flat, the turbulent theme of the Allegro bursts out. It is turbulent not only in its agitated phrases: its harmony is also very unsettled (as it often is in Elgar's contemporaries, Mahler and Richard Strauss), though basically rooted in D minor – a key remote from the noble introduction in A flat. Over several pages the agitation builds up to a climax, and then settles back to a moment of rest. In this brief transition there are fragments of melodies that seem like mere passing thoughts, but which are to become important later on. The second main theme of the Allegro follows, a singing melody in F major in first violins, with characteristic aspiring leaps and gentle descents, accompanied by softly murmuring accompaniment. The overall mood is pastoral. The cellos take up the theme, the tension increases, and the agitation of the opening of the Allegro returns. Eventually this builds to a mighty climax, at which the horns blast out a menacing phrase. If this seems familiar, it is because it is derived from one of the passing thoughts that introduced the pastoral second theme. When this crisis has ebbed away, there is a ghostly reappearance of the nobilmente theme on muted horns and shimmering violas, marking the transition to the central development section of the movement.

Here the mood is at first tentative and anxious, with a little rising and falling phrase repeated over and over (like the earlier climax, this is derived from another passing thought that led into the second theme, but now turned upside down). The woodwind introduce a rapid motif, like a passing flight of birds, and the texture becomes more complex, in the manner of Richard Strauss. Soon, a bolder, striding motif appears, and builds up from the bass, almost like a passage of fugue: Elgar described this motif as 'restless, enquiring and exploring'. This develops power and energy, while a drooping phrase of two notes insistently accompanies it, taking over and leading to a turbulent passage. Again this settles to a quiet, anxiously nostalgic moment with solo violin, and further recalling of the little phrases that have dominated this section of the movement. Eventually, there is a brief, quiet reminiscence of the nobilmente theme, marking the end of the development section.

The anxious phrase that began the development now leads into the reprise of the opening D minor theme of the Allegro. The sequence of events then proceeds much as before, but with the important change that Elgar takes the music into new keys. The result is that, when we arrive at the pastoral second theme, it is in A flat major, the key of the nobilmente introduction. This may seem academic, but what Elgar is doing is to reconcile what were two sharply opposing keys (the A flat of the introduction and the D minor of the first Allegro theme). After the moment of calm, the tension builds as before to a great climax. This time it is sustained for much longer, the menacing rhythm blasted out again and again by the brass. Eventually it subsides, and from it emerges the nobilmente theme, first quietly, and surrounded by a halo – a harp flourish, and reminiscences of the different fragments that haunted the central section of the movement. Gradually the theme asserts itself, builds to a final climax, and again evaporates to give way to more reminiscence. It is with difficulty that the movement settles. In the final bars, a last whisper of the noble theme is interrupted by a ghost of the menacing climax, pulled suddenly into A minor, before the final chord of A flat major brings the movement to a close.

The second movement is a rapid scherzo. The lower strings set up a juddering rhythmic figure, over which first violins scamper hectically but pianissimo. Over the following pages the music seems to be searching for a coherent theme. Eventually this comes in the form of a jaunty little march, first on violas and clarinets, then moving through the orchestra and building to an urgent fortissimo. The scampering resumes, dies down, and gives way to a quiet contrasted passage, with flutes, solo violin, and harp creating a peaceful mood – Elgar in a rehearsal once said that it should sound 'like something we hear down by the river'.[22] The scampering figure returns, and the jaunty march again builds up to a fortissimo, wilder than before. Again the 'down by the river' passage returns, now more extended, and blossoming into something more nostalgic. There is more scampering, more river-music. Eventually, the mood of nostalgia becomes irresistible, even though the juddering rhythm still persists underneath. The tempo gradually slows, there is a final, slow-motion version of the march, the music disperses, and leaves the violins holding a lone F sharp. Without a break, this becomes the first note of the slow movement.

The movement that emerges from the scherzo is a heartfelt Adagio in D major. It is linked to the scherzo not just by the note that the violins hold. The first four bars of the slow, singing melody are, note for note, the opening of the scampering theme from the scherzo, slowed down. The conductor at the first performance, Hans Richter, described it as an Adagio such as Beethoven might have written. But there is something unmistakably Elgarian in the way that the melody seems to be searching with difficulty to express itself. The rhythm is irregular, the phrases halting, the harmonies slipping uncertainly from key to key, and only after several bars does it start to find a really coherent outpouring (at a point marked by Elgar 'sonore'). The great melody gives way to another characteristic passage of reflection. With its delicately touched-in phrases from strings and woodwind, and its harp accompaniment, it has something in common with the pastoral and 'down the river' episodes in the earlier movement. Soon, darker harmonic twists add a suggestion of Klingsor's magic garden in the second act of Wagner's *Parsifal*.

This leads into a second sonorous theme, with bolder leaps than the hesitant opening melody (and perhaps related to the striding motif from the middle of the first movement). More pastoral reflections follow, and more dark touches of harmony, and then the opening melody returns. This time, it leads straight on into a reprise of the second theme, which seems about to rise to a climax. But the climax soon peters out, leaving further reflection, and a deepening sense of nostalgia. This culminates quietly in the most haunting phrase of the movement, a simple utterance incorporating a yearning leap and fall. From all the searchings, hesitations, attempts at sonorous climaxes, Elgar seems to have found the essence that he was looking for. Further musing on this phrase enables him to bring the movement to a peaceful conclusion.

The finale opens with a slow introduction. This is very different from the broad, determined introduction to the first movement. From ghostly shimmerings emerge, first, a deep bass clarinet with a reminiscence of the striding motif from the first movement, then an ominous, treading staccato idea, which seems to have something in common with the nobilmente theme from the opening of the symphony. Amid an increasingly complex texture, a quiet reprise of the nobilmente theme itself emerges, accompanied by the ominous staccato. After a brief climax, these inconclusive searchings and musings are resumed, then brought to an abrupt halt, and Elgar launches into a forceful Allegro theme, rather Schumannesque in its insistent repetition of a dotted rhythm. This, like the first movement Allegro, is in D minor – remote from the 'home' key of the symphony, A flat major. A more comfortable theme emerges, first on violas and cellos, over a walking bass. After a build-up, the ominous staccato figure reappears, building ferociously.

The first theme continues, now more frenzied, and leading on to a sort of development, with the different themes combined in a relentless drive. As this dies down, there is a reminiscence of the nobilmente theme, which leads straight into a smoothed-out version of the ominous staccato element, showing clearly the relationship between the two. This builds up to a noble climax, as if opposing elements have for a moment been reconciled. But the agitated first theme, with its insistent dotted rhythms, is soon back, followed by the more comfortable second theme. Again, this is broken into by the staccato theme. It now leads on to a great and agitated build-up, with flurries of string arpeggios. Out of this emerges – or rather struggles – the great nobilmente theme. Obstructed all the way by the elements that are fighting against it, the theme ploughs on to approach a resolution in A flat – an achievement that seems to have been accomplished only with the utmost determination.

SYMPHONY NO. 2, OP. 63

Duration: 48 (Elgar)–58 minutes

Allegro vivo e nobilmente

Larghetto

Rondo: Presto

Moderato e maestoso

Elgar's Second Symphony was first performed in 1911, the year in which he was awarded the Order of Merit in King George V's Coronation Honours, and only a few months after the successful premiere of the Violin Concerto. Elgar himself conducted the performance in Queen's Hall, London, but the reception was cool. When the audience's applause was polite rather than enthusiastic, he turned to the leader of the orchestra, W. H. Reed, and said, 'What's the matter with them, Billy? They sit there like a lot of stuffed pigs.'[23] The reviews were good, though the critic of *The Telegraph* rightly observed, 'there are heights here that hitherto even Elgar himself had not touched, but we are doubtful if the greater public will realise the fact immediately.'[24] The Second Symphony is indeed emotionally more difficult to get to grips with than the first. You could describe its emotional landscape as a sort of reverse-impression of the First Symphony. The first is dominated by emotional turmoil out of which some sort of resolution is snatched. The Second Symphony has an overall mood of calm determination that undergoes threats, sometimes violently. Elgar himself described it as follows: 'The spirit of the whole work is intended to be high and pure joy; there are retrospective passages of sadness but the whole of the sorrow is smoothed out and ennobled in the last movement, which ends in a calm and, I hope and intend, elevated mood.'[25]

At the head of the score Elgar put a quotation from Shelley: 'Rarely, rarely comest thou, Spirit of Delight!' He suggested reading the poem to get near the mood of the symphony, and this confirms that the spirit of the music is far from just 'pure joy', and contains strong elements of yearning and nostalgia:

> Rarely, rarely comest thou,
> Spirit of Delight!
> Wherefore hast thou left me now
> Many a day and night?
> Many a weary night and day
> 'Tis since thou art fled away.

The work is dedicated to the memory of King Edward VII. But, despite this public gesture, it is as personal a work as the First Symphony.

The first movement launches straight into a bold theme in E flat major, which leaps up and plunges down confidently, accompanied by Richard Strauss-like whooping horns, and then settles to a rolling melody. This gradually becomes more and more animated, accelerating until it breaks off at a climax into jagged arpeggios and short phrases. Elgar instructs that this should return suddenly to the original, slower tempo. But he ignores this instruction in his own recording, which gives the passage a thrillingly reckless character. The climax ebbs away, and there follows a gentler second theme. This wavers uncertainly between G major and E flat major. For a moment it seems to have found its way to a sonorous E flat (as at the opening), but this dies down to leave the cellos playing a sorrowful theme in G minor, with yearning leaps and plaintive falls. The music builds again, through a passage in which the violins dash frantically up and down arpeggios, on through another acceleration to a mighty climax. This dies away, marking the end of the first section of the movement.

The development section begins, not with material already familiar, but with something new. Harp harmonics, like a quietly striking bell, introduce a motif in the violins, which rises and falls in mysterious harmonies – the harmonies of the whole-tone scale, often evocatively used by Debussy. This 'ghost' figure (as it was labelled in an early sketch) is interwoven with quiet reminiscences of the rolling opening theme, and the two alternate through an extended passage. Elgar reaches a moment of quiet intensity, where, over the quiet thrumming of bass drum and timpani, a complex texture is built up: the 'ghost' motif in violins, fragments of the opening theme in second violins and violas, fleeting chromatic scales in the flutes, and, singing through all this, a melancholy, sustained new theme on cellos (though it sounds new, it is distilled out of the shape and harmonies of the 'ghost' motif). This reaches a point of rest, musing nostalgically on earlier themes. Once more the 'ghost' motif returns, together with the cello song, more insistent bass drum, and with low trombones adding a hint of something sinister below the surface. This episode creates, at the heart of this confident, exuberant movement, an extended moment of doubt, quiet reflection, and mysterious complexity.

But then we turn a corner, and the rolling theme gradually builds up to a huge climax, majestically ushering in the reprise of the first theme. It proceeds, more briefly than before, through to the gentle second theme, on to the plaintive cello melody, and building once again to a frantic climax. This dies down, as before, to bell-like harp harmonics, as if we are to return to the 'ghost' episode. But instead, there is another brief moment of nostalgic reminiscence. It is soon brushed aside, and the movement ends forcefully, with a return to the mood of the opening, and a final confident flourish.

The slow movement begins with richly scored string harmonies, suggesting the sound of a choir chanting. This introduces a funeral march in C minor, solemnly intoned by trumpet and trombones. A middle part of the theme moves to the violins, sonorous in E flat major, and with melodic shapes that rise to a climax, evoking a memory of the confident opening theme of the first movement. There is also a suggestion of another famous funeral march in C minor – the second movement of Beethoven's 'Eroica' Symphony. After a sad little twisting version of the chant on woodwind, a new theme appears, beginning very quietly on the violins, with a counterpoint in the violas. This is a much more intimate moment, reminiscent of the deeply melancholy meditations of the Violin Concerto, written the previous year. With its yearning leaps it is also related, emotionally and in shape, to the melancholy cello theme from the first movement. It develops in scope and power, on through a complex web of different strands (rather like the complex treatment of the 'ghost' theme in the first movement), then focusing down to another sonorous violin line that builds to a sustained climax.

As it dies away, the funeral march returns. But this too is now elaborated in a complicated texture. The melody is in the horns, a weaving countermelody in the oboe, the tread of the drums enhanced by a halo of chords in the strings, with pizzicato bass. This complex pattern continues as the violins take up their sonorous continuation. It dies down to the intimate second theme. As before, this develops over a long build-up, but now it is more sustained, and reaches a climax of overwhelming intensity, the violins marked *fff*, vibrato, and 'glissez' (slide between notes). As the climax dies away, there is a melancholy little reminiscence of the very first theme of the symphony, which originally sounded so confident, followed by the sad, twisting version of the chant in the woodwind, a final snatch of the funeral march, and the movement ends as it began, with the choir of strings, and a final chord.

The third movement is a scherzo-rondo, in which the opening material returns several times. It is in a fast three-time, but its recurring opening section has cross-rhythms and fragmented phrases that give it a nervous, agitated character, as if frantically trying to escape. This impression is heightened by its unstable harmonies: it is notionally in C major, but the opening theme shifts rapidly up in major thirds, from C major to E major to A flat major, creating a 'whole-tone scale' effect that has echoes of the 'ghost' episode in the first movement. A second element is in complete contrast: regular and repetitive in rhythm, with all the strings co-ordinated in a firm fortissimo C minor. This is marked 'sonoramente', and in the only recording of Elgar rehearsing, he is insistent that this passage must be as sonorous as possible. The melody dies away, and the opening cross-rhythms return briefly, more delicate and fragmented than before. Another regular melody in the violins follows, a variant of the sonoramente theme, with an insistent little figure from the cross-rhythms persisting in the accompaniment. There is another build-up of the cross-rhythm material.

A gently singing phrase in the woodwind introduces a note of calm, and this leads in a gentler, rather pastoral episode. Eventually a touch of anxiety enters, with a quiet, chromatically sliding phrase in the strings, while the cross-rhythms return in the woodwind. This chromatic phrase is repeated again and again, while the rhythm in the background settles into a persistent pattern. It is at this moment that it becomes clear that this is a version of the 'ghost' theme from the first movement. So the hints of its whole-tone harmonies right at the beginning of the movement have come to fruition. As the rhythm builds up hypnotically in the wind and percussion, the ghost becomes a terrifying vision. The viola-player Bernard Shore remembered Elgar rehearsing this passage, telling the orchestra to imagine a man in a high fever, with a 'dreadful beating that goes on in the brain – it seems to drive out every coherent thought', and he wanted the percussion gradually to drown out the rest of the orchestra.[26] To a friend, Elgar said that it was inspired by a passage in Tennyson's monodrama *Maud* in which the narrator imagines his own burial:

And the hoofs of the horses beat, beat,
The hoofs of the horses beat,
Beat into my scalp and my brain.[27]

With or without these associations, this passage is the moment in the symphony where all the doubts and threats that have from time to time risen to the surface come together with overwhelming force.

Eventually the terrible apparition recedes. Out of the darkness emerges the violins' sono-ramente melody, though there is a persistent note of anxiety in the accompanying harmonies. The cross-rhythms return, then the mood calms as the variant of the sonoramente theme is recalled. Finally, the opening cross-rhythms return for the last time, building up into a moment of great agitation, as if still haunted by the destructive climax, and the movement comes to an emphatic close.

The finale returns to the mood of determination that characterized much of the first movement. The opening theme, on the cellos, is Falstaff-like in its ambling gait, in an unhur-ried three-time, and firmly in E flat major. It gradually builds up and leads straight into a second theme, a confident series of rising phrases whose four-square dotted rhythms and simple repetitions inject a ceremonial character, cutting across the three-time. This builds up into an extended paragraph, and at its climax is another of Elgar's characteristic nobilmente moments, which gradually ebbs away.

After this first section, there is a sudden change of key to D major, and the middle, devel-opment section of the movement begins. It takes the ceremonial second theme with its dotted rhythms, and subjects it to wild deconstruction, pitting it against increasingly frenzied arpeg-gios in the violins, until a piercing high B on the first trumpet signals the climax, and the tumult gradually subsides to fragments of the two principal themes. There follows an extended passage with a solemn tread – it would be march-like if it were not in three-time. Eventually, there is an unexpected twist of harmony, and we are back at the ambling first theme in the cellos.

The reprise of the opening section opens up much as before, but with greater emphasis, and a joyously extended climax. You might expect Elgar to go on from here to a great final peroration. But instead, like Brahms in his Third Symphony, he lets the music wind down to a mood of quiet reflection, in which fragments of the principal theme of the first movement are remembered, and, with a lingering cadence reminiscent of the end of Wagner's *Tristan*, the symphony concludes with a satisfying sense that all has been resolved.

VARIATIONS ON AN ORIGINAL THEME ('ENIGMA'), OP. 36
Duration: 27 (Elgar)–32 minutes

Elgar had the habit of improvising at the piano, trying out ideas. He was even persuaded to allow some of his improvisations to be recorded, and these give a vivid and touching impres-sion of the great man shyly exploring possibilities. According to Elgar himself, it was while he was improvising at home one evening in 1898 that his wife, Alice, said, '"What is that?" I answered, "Nothing – but something might be made of it ..."' This was the seed of an idea from which Elgar's most famous work grew. Still at the piano, he started trying out variations on the idea, as if played by his friends – a cellist, a woman with a characteristic laugh, a man with a habit of leaving the room abruptly, and so on.[28] This might have been nothing more than a parlour game, but it opened a door in Elgar's imagination, helping him to find ways to vary his musical material. Eventually, he composed a set of thirteen variations, plus a grand finale.

The work is 'dedicated to my friends pictured within'. Each variation is headed by a set of initials or a name, apart from one that has three teasing asterisks. And over the opening theme, Elgar writes the word, 'Enigma'. Elgar himself never revealed the meaning of this. In a letter quoted in the programme booklet for the premiere in 1899, he wrote, 'The Enigma I will not explain – its dark saying must be left unguessed.' And he went on, 'through and over the whole set another and larger theme "goes", but is not played'.[29] Scholars and others have spent much time and energy trying to uncover this 'missing' theme. Was Elgar referring simply to a melody that would fit against the opening theme? There have been a number of possible solutions to this, including, plausibly, 'Auld lang syne'. But if Elgar meant something so commonplace, why make an enigma of it? Alternatively (or in addition), it has been suggested that Elgar meant that there was some hidden meaning or reference behind the whole work. Given the declared theme of friendship, and Elgar's defensive, highly emotional character, it is easy to imagine some deeper love beneath the surface. But we will never know.

Elgar supplied some notes to accompany Aeolian piano rolls of the 'Enigma' Variations, and the descriptions that follow include extracts from them.[30]

Theme: This, the theme in G minor on which the variations are based, is the only section without a name attached to it. Elgar wrote that it expressed 'my sense of the loneliness of the artist'.[31] There is indeed something bleak about the way that it opens. Over simple, trudging chords, the melody proceeds in pairs of short phrases. The second of each pair is rhythmically the reverse of the first, and the placing of the high point of each phrase creates a sense of awkwardness against the regularity of the accompanying chords. The middle section of the theme breaks free from this awkwardness, and out into G major, with a succession of rising phrases in a regular rhythm, and with a sense of aspiration. Then the opening section in G minor returns, with, under its awkward melody, a poignant counterpoint in the cellos, with more aspirational leaps. Two mournfully falling bars link to:

Variation 1. C.A.E. (Alice Elgar, his wife). This is at the same pace, with the theme enmeshed in a complex and delicate texture. Oboes and bassoons intone a persistently reiterated phrase against the theme. As before, the middle of the variation ventures into a major key (E flat this time), but now a climax quickly builds up, and is soon gone, leaving the theme winding its way to the end, with a more hopeful conclusion in G major.

Variation 2. H.D.S-P. (Hew David Steuart-Powell). This pianist friend had the habit of warming up by running over the keys in a characteristic routine. Elgar arranges the rising and falling shape of the theme into a rapid, almost chaotic, pattern 'chromatic beyond H.D.S-P.'s liking'.

Variation 3. R.B.T. (Richard Baxter Townshend). An engaging eccentric. Elgar particularly remembered him playing the part of an old man in an amateur theatre production, 'the low voice flying off occasionally into "soprano" timbre'. His variation has a sprightly quality, with the 'low voice' suggested by the bassoon solo in the second half.

Variation 4. W.M.B. (William Meath Baker). 'A country squire, gentleman and scholar. In the days of horses and carriages it was more difficult than in these days of petrol to arrange the carriages for the day to suit a large number of guests. This variation was written after the host had, with a slip of paper in his hand, *forcibly* read out the arrangements for the day and hurriedly left the music room with an inadvertent bang of the door.' The rapid cross-rhythms of the speeded-up theme give the variation immense energy.

Variation 5. R.P.A. (Richard Penrose Arnold). He was the son of the poet Matthew Arnold and, according to Elgar, 'his serious conversation was continually broken up by whimsical and witty remarks'. A sombre variation in C minor, with a middle section that suddenly lightens in the major. It leads straight into:

Variation 6. Ysobel (Isabel Fitton). She was an amateur viola player in Malvern. Her variation is charming, and the middle section features a viola solo.

Variation 7. Troyte (Troyte Griffith). He was an architect in Malvern, whom Elgar tried to teach to play the piano. 'The uncouth rhythm of the drums and lower strings was really suggested by some maladroit essays to play the pianoforte; later the strong rhythm suggests the attempts of the instructor (E.E.) to make something like order out of chaos, and the final despairing "slam" records that the effort proved to be in vain.' Elgar's own 1926 recording takes it even faster than the already very fast metronome marking.

Variation 8. W.N. (Winifred Norbury). After spending variations 5–7 in C major, this variation returns to G major. It elegantly pairs rising phrases in the woodwind with falling phrases in the strings. The delicate middle section alludes to Winifred Norbury's characteristic laugh, though Elgar says that the variation was 'really suggested by an eighteenth-century house'. At the end, the music slows, and the violins hold a quiet, sustained note, G. With a magical change of key, we quietly enter:

Variation 9. Nimrod (August J. Jaeger). Jaeger was Elgar's editor at the music publisher, Novello, and his closest friend and advisor. 'Nimrod' is a play on his name: 'Jaeger' is the German for 'hunter', and Nimrod is the 'mighty hunter' listed as one of the great-grandsons of Noah in the book of Genesis. This is the emotional heart of the variations. As the very first chord quietly sounds, the note G from which it has emerged metamorphoses. It has been the keynote through most of the variations. Now the key shifts down a third to E flat major, with the note G as the third of that chord. This shift has a profound effect, as if Elgar has found the way into a previously unexpressed emotional world (there was a premonition of this shift in Variation 1, where the middle section moved briefly to E flat). A smoothed-out version of the theme proceeds slowly, in a series of great waves, to a mighty climax. The middle section here becomes a moment of doubt or questioning, which lends extra force to the final build-up.

But, after the long climb to the summit, the climax is short-lived, as if Elgar flinches away from it at the moment of its achievement. It suggests a man talking about his innermost feelings, and suddenly realizing what he has revealed. Whatever enigmatic meaning there might be behind this, it certainly has nothing to do with ceremonies of remembrance, with which 'Nimrod' has become associated over the years. Elgar and Jaeger were men in the prime of life (Elgar was forty-two, Jaeger three years younger). Elgar's metronome marking for 'Nimrod' is much faster than it is usually played today, and his own 1926 recording shows that it is intended to have an inexorable drive towards its moving climax.

The smoothing-out of the theme reveals a similarity to the slow movement of Beethoven's 'Pathétique' Sonata – Elgar remembered a summer evening when Jaeger had 'discoursed eloquently on the slow movements of Beethoven'.

Variation 10. Intermezzo: Dorabella (Dora Penny). Her tendency to stammer is delicately suggested in the reiterated phrases, and her character by a charming viola solo. After the cathartic intensity of 'Nimrod', this variation comes as a sudden relief. We are back in G major, as if the world of 'Nimrod' has been forgotten. But 'Nimrod' seems to have left an impact: this is the first variation in which the awkward shape of the theme has become completely unknotted. Nothing could be more regular than the delicate little phrases succeeding each other. It is as if 'Nimrod' has solved something at a profound level.

Variation 11. G.R.S. (George Robertson Sinclair). He was the organist of Hereford Cathedral, and had a bulldog called Dan. This tumultuous variation might suggest the vigorous pedalling of the organist, but Elgar tells us that it was inspired by an occasion when the bulldog fell into the river Wye, and paddled along to a place where he was able to scramble up, barking. Elgar's own dogs were very important to him (though his wife would not let them in the house).

Variation 12. B.G.N. (Basil G. Nevinson). Nevinson was an amateur cellist, who played trios with Elgar and Steuart-Powell, the subject of Variation 2. This is a particularly touching variation: 'a tribute to a very dear friend whose scientific and artistic attainments, and the whole-hearted way they were put at the disposal of his friends, particularly endeared him to the writer'. The variation begins and ends with a fragment of cello solo. At the conclusion, this leads without a break into:

Variation 13. Romanza (***). This delicate variation is headed by teasing asterisks instead of initials. It twice comes to a halt to quote Mendelssohn's overture *Calm Sea and Prosperous Voyage*, played very softly on the clarinet, while the timpanist plays a quiet roll with side-drum sticks. This effect simulates the sound of a ship's engine, and the crescendo suggests a mighty liner in the middle of the ocean. Elgar writes that 'The asterisks take the place of the name of a lady who was, at the time of the composition, on a sea voyage.' This is generally supposed to be a reference to Lady Mary Lygon, who emigrated to Australia while Elgar was working on the Variations. It seems that Elgar may originally have intended her as the subject. But Ernest Newman (who knew Elgar) was the first to suggest that the asterisks might stand for Helen Weaver, to whom Elgar had been engaged long before he married Alice (it is easy to imagine Alice's sensitivity about Helen, a good reason for the asterisks). She too had gone on a sea voyage, to New Zealand, after her engagement to Elgar was broken off.

Finale: E.D.U. This is a playful reference to Alice's pet name for Elgar, 'Edoo'. After all the portraits of (or perhaps by) his friends, here is a self-portrait. Or rather, it seems a portrait of the man who has weathered the emotional life suggested by the preceding variations. From the loneliness of the theme, through the bluff humour of the fast variations, the touching affection of the delicate ones, and the deep feelings of 'Nimrod', which are almost too intense to express, Elgar emerges with new swagger, facing the world with confidence – at least outwardly. The original version of this finale, performed at the premiere, was much shorter than the familiar version, ending with a quote from Variation 1 (his wife, Alice), and a final emphatic flourish. After the performance, Jaeger (Nimrod) reported that several people, including the conductor, Hans Richter, thought the ending perfunctory, and asked Elgar whether he would extend it. After much thought, Elgar agreed, adding a much lengthier build-up and acceleration to a final climax. The result is a magnificently convincing ending. The original, shorter version is sometimes performed (notably for Frederick Ashton's ballet), but if one is familiar with the revised version, it seems like a brutal amputation.

The 'Enigma' Variations finally established Elgar's reputation as a major composer, nationally and internationally. It remains his most perfect large-scale work. Everything seems to the point, emotionally accurate, without any unnecessary padding or struggle to create elaborate structures. Although it consists of a series of short pieces, they add up to a very satisfactory whole, with a powerful emotional trajectory. Elgar's own recording of it, made in 1926 with the Royal Albert Hall Orchestra, is one of his finest, and shows clearly how he envisaged the character of each variation (though his tempi were said to be very unpredictable, changing considerably from concert to concert). This clarity comes over despite the rough and ready character of some of the playing. Indeed, the sense of musicians being taken to the edge of their capabilities is part of the effect – few modern conductors would dare take Variation 7 ('Troyte') as fast as Elgar does.

MANUEL DE FALLA
(1876–1946)

Falla was the major Spanish composer of the twentieth century. Deeply influenced by traditional Spanish music – particularly the *cante jonda*, the melancholy gypsy song that underpins flamenco – he was also attracted to the new music coming from France. He spent several years in Paris, absorbing the new ideas of Debussy, Ravel, and Stravinsky, but returned to Madrid at the outbreak of the First World War. It was Falla who, after the death of Isaac Albéniz in 1909, led the development of Spanish music in the twentieth century, combining classical training with the influence of Spanish folk music and flamenco. It is the combination of these different influences that gives Falla's music its particular fascination.

NOCHES EN LOS JARDINES DE ESPAÑA (*NIGHTS IN THE GARDENS OF SPAIN*), G. 49
Duration: approx. 24 minutes
En el Generalife (In the Generalife): Allegretto tranquillo e misterioso
Danza lejana (Distant dance): Allegretto giusto –
En los jardines de la Sierra de Córdoba (In the gardens of the Sierra de Córdoba): Vivo

Falla dedicated this work to the great Spanish pianist Ricardo Viñes, who vigorously championed the music of Spanish and French composers. It was Viñes who persuaded Falla to turn what were originally planned as solo nocturnes (1909) into music for piano and orchestra, and the result (1915) is not quite a concerto, but what Falla himself called 'Symphonic impressions'. The orchestra is very large, including harp and celesta, and the piano seems at times to be part of the orchestra rather than a conventional soloist. The character of the music is very Spanish, based, as Falla said, 'on the rhythms, modes, cadences and ornamental figures which distinguish the popular music of Andalucia'. These include elements such as a scale with a flattened second – one of the 'Moorish' elements of flamenco song. Falla's music is not intended to describe in any literal way, but 'to evoke places, sensations and sentiments'.[1] But, Falla added, 'something more than the sound of festivals and dances has inspired these "evocations in sound", for melancholy and mystery have their part also'.

The first movement evokes the Generalife, the gardens of the Alhambra Palace at Granada, with its pools and fountains, its trees and its scented jasmine. It starts mysteriously with a reiterated figure played by violins bowing near the bridge ('sul ponticello'), and the harp adding guitar-like punctuation. The piano entry adds an impression of rippling fountains to the scene. The melodic figures, which twirl repetitively round each other, suggest the calm of the night, with evocative high violins, horns and woodwind reminding us that Falla learned some of his Spanish style from Debussy and Ravel. The piano bursts into Spanish dance, in which the rhythmic patterns almost constantly suggest the guitar. A song-like theme rises to a climax. The mysterious atmosphere returns, and passages of cadenza alternate with moments of evocative, processional music. Eventually the opening returns, this time with the strumming piano taking over the role of guitar, and it rises to another passionate climax before sinking back into the peace of the garden.

The 'distant dance' opens with mysteriously swirling patterns (rather like the famous 'Ritual Fire Dance' from *El amor brujo*). The dance is highly volatile in mood and pace, sometimes accelerating to a climax, sometimes slowing for reflection. The end of the movement is very still, but with high violins and a cymbal roll injecting tension into the air. With its whole-tone harmonies, this passage has more than a hint of the opening of Paul Dukas's *The Sorcerer's Apprentice* (1897).

From the eerie calm the piano breaks out into the vigorous finale, set in the hills of Córdoba, which quickly builds up to a frenzied orchestral dance. The determined repetitions of the rhythm and the piquant harmonies have a distinctly 'moorish' tinge. A second theme has the piano singing a swirling flamenco-style recitative. The orchestral dance builds up again, and this leads on to an extended song-like exchange between piano and orchestra. Mysterious harmonies (again reminiscent of *The Sorcerer's Apprentice*) lead on to the piano quietly reflecting on its earlier flamenco recitative. There is a final orchestral climax (evoking the grand Russian tradition as much as anything Spanish) and the music subsides to a quiet conclusion.

EL SOMBRERO DE TRES PICOS (THE THREE-CORNERED HAT)

This is one of two fine ballet scores by Falla, the other being *El amor brujo* (*Love the Magician*). *El amor brujo* is best known for its powerful 'Ritual Fire Dance', and *El sombrero de tres picos* for two concert suites that Falla extracted from the score.

Between 1915 and 1917, Falla wrote the music for a humorous mime play in two tableaux called *El corregidor y la molinera* (*The Magistrate and the Miller's Wife*), scored for a chamber group. Sergei Diaghilev got to know it during a visit to Spain, and asked Falla to enlarge it as a two-act ballet, with full orchestra. Renamed *El sombrero de tres picos* (the title of the novel by Pedro Antonio de Alarcón on which it was based), this was one of the successes of Diaghilev's Ballets Russes season in London in 1919, with choreography by Léonide Massine and designs by Pablo Picasso. It tells the story of the magistrate's attempt to seduce the miller's wife, and his eventual humiliation.

Act I begins with the miller and his wife trying to teach a pet blackbird to tell the time (one of the more unlikely openings to a ballet). The magistrate (*corregidor*), who has his lecherous eye on the miller's wife, is passing by on his daily walk, wearing his three-cornered hat, and the miller and his wife decide to play a trick on him. As the miller hides, the wife entices the magistrate with a dance and offers him some grapes. As the magistrate takes them, she runs away and he chases after her. The miller leaps out from a bush and beats the magistrate with a stick. In Act II the miller dances for his guests, but is interrupted by the magistrate's bodyguard, who has come to arrest him. With the miller out of the way, the magistrate comes at night and creeps into the miller's bed. The miller, having escaped from prison, finds him there asleep, and dresses in the magistrate's clothes. The magistrate wakes up, and dresses in the miller's clothes. Predictable mayhem ensues, with the bodyguard attempting to arrest the magistrate, and the ballet ends with the magistrate being tossed in a blanket.

This naive tale is enlivened by a score steeped in the atmosphere and sounds of Spanish traditional music, with singers, castanets, and hand-clapping. Falla took the most important sections of the ballet and formed them into a pair of concert suites, the first derived from Act

I and the second from Act II. The suites omit the singers and the more discursive, narrative sections of the ballet.

Suite No. 1

Mediodía (Afternoon)
Danza de la molinera (Dance of the miller's wife)
El corregidor (The magistrate) – La molinera (The miller's wife)
Las uvas (The grapes)

Duration: approx. 10 minutes

After a fanfare, a dreamy introduction evokes a sunny, sultry Andalucian scene, though with an element of nervous expectation created by a reiterated violin pattern, bowed near the bridge ('sul ponticello'). Characters come and go until suddenly we are thrown into the 'Dance of the miller's wife'. This is a fandango, a dance with held accents on the end of the bar and alternating rhythmic patterns of 3x2 and 2x3. Accompanying flourishes evoke flamenco dancing, and an oboe evokes the plangent singing.

A brief bassoon solo perfectly suggests the magistrate walking by, a man who thinks he is dignified and has no idea how ridiculous he looks. This leads straight into a moment of elegant dance, as the miller's wife entices him. It is in that charming, neo-baroque style beloved of French composers of the time.

It ends with a flirtatious little flute solo and a trill, to take us into 'The grapes'. This is the most extended dance in the first Suite, in which the magistrate chases the miller's wife. It has a delightfully skittish character, with more of the alternations between 2x3 and 3x2 that are so characteristic of flamenco. After several teasing halts and pauses, it leads into a reprise of the miller's wife's first dance, and comes to an emphatic conclusion as the magistrate is beaten.

Suite No. 2

Danza de los vecinos (Neighbours' dance): Seguedillas
Danza del molinero (Miller's dance): Farruca
Finale: Jota

Duration: approx. 13 minutes

The neighbours dance a gentle seguedillas. Like sections of the first suite, this plays with changing patterns within three-time, the sinuous lines of the opening melody giving way to livelier dance rhythms, followed by another plangent oboe solo. The opening section returns, and is brought to a peaceful end.

A fortissimo horn and a swirling cor anglais, again evoking flamenco song, introduce the miller's dance, a farruca. This is a dance with assertively stamping rhythms and violent contrasts, vividly suggesting masculine threat. A plaintive oboe line and other delicate episodes are in turns thrust brusquely aside, and the dance ends in a fearsome accelerando. The final dance is a jota, a proud, energetic dance that again plays with combinations of twos and threes within a three-beat bar. This is an extended movement, with several sections in different metres. The excitement and the tempo build up, and are twice brought back with a powerful restraining force to the original jota. It is a joyous movement that draws on the full repertoire of orchestral effects derived from the Russian-French tradition popularized by Diaghilev (Rimsky-Korsakov, Stravinsky, Debussy, Ravel), and it builds to a grand climax.

GABRIEL FAURÉ
(1845–1924)

Unlike most prominent French composers of his time, Fauré wrote very little orchestral music and only one fully fledged opera. He never completed a symphony, and despite the fact that he trained as a pianist he never composed a piano concerto: his only work for piano and orchestra is the Ballade, an arrangement of a solo piano piece. He is principally renowned as the composer of a haunting Requiem, and a large quantity of subtle and beautiful piano music, chamber music, and songs. His one attempt at a full-scale opera, *Pénélope*, was a success when it was staged in Paris in May 1913. But it was Fauré's misfortune that, in the very same theatre, Stravinsky's *The Rite of Spring* received its scandalous premiere a few days later. The two productions alternated, and nobody paid much attention to the subtleties of Fauré. *Pénélope* is full of beautiful music, but lacking traditional drama it has never established itself in the repertoire.

Fauré did not study at the Paris Conservatoire, where generations of French composers learned to concentrate their attentions on opera and orchestral composition. He was sent as a nine-year-old child to the newly established boarding school in Paris, the École Niedermeyer, which principally offered training for organists and choirmasters, intended to raise the standards in French churches. Fauré stayed at the school for eleven years. As well as studying piano and organ, he got to know a wide range of repertoire including Gregorian chant and the choral music of the Renaissance – Josquin des Prez, Palestrina, Victoria – composers largely ignored in the mainstream studies at the Paris Conservatoire. This music had a profound effect on him that lasted throughout his life. From it he developed a love of the melodic shapes and modal harmonies of chant, and an understanding of the fluid and complex interweaving of Renaissance counterpoint.

It was at the École Niedermeyer that Fauré met Saint-Saëns, who joined the school in his twenties as the principal piano teacher. Saint-Saëns did more to further Fauré's career than anyone. In 1871, ten years after first meeting Fauré, Saint-Saëns founded the Société Nationale de Musique, to provide a platform for new works by French composers. His intention was to encourage the composition of music in the classical tradition of Beethoven and Schumann, as a counterblast to what Saint-Saëns saw as the French obsession with Wagner and his music drama. Following the performance of Fauré's first violin sonata in 1875 at the Société, Saint-Saëns wrote a glowing review in which he identified Fauré as a potential leader of a renaissance in French music. Fauré himself later acknowledged that it was this encouragement that directed him towards chamber music: 'the truth is that, before 1870, I would never have dreamed of writing a sonata or a quartet'. It is in these chamber works that we can hear the passionate complexities and subtleties of Fauré's musical character more clearly than in any of his other music. And it is this passionate subtlety that also characterizes Fauré's few orchestral works.

Despite his non-Conservatoire training and his lack of operatic credentials, Fauré in later life became one of the most respected figures in French music. He was appointed Director of the Paris Conservatoire from 1905, where he resolutely set about modernizing and reforming an institution that had been deeply conservative for decades. By the end of his life, musical tastes had moved on. The fashionable mood of 1920s France was acerbic and witty, and Fauré, the grand old man of French music, was completely out of tune with the times. Undeterred, and despite serious hearing loss and aural distortions, he continued to compose in his own way to the end of his life. He died an honoured figure, accorded a full state funeral.

MASQUES ET BERGAMASQUES, OP. 112
Duration: approx. 14 minutes

Ouverture: Allegro molto vivo
Menuet: Tempo di minuetto – Allegretto moderato
Gavotte: Allegro vivo
Pastorale: Andantino tranquillo

Fauré's songs often set poems by Paul Verlaine, and the title of this work, *Masques et Bergamasques*, comes from one of them, 'Clair de lune', the first poem of Verlaine's *Fêtes galantes* (1869), which Fauré had set in 1887:

Votre âme est un paysage choisi	Your soul is an exquisite landscape
Que vont charmant masques et bergamasques	Where masqueraders and bergamasquers come and go
Jouant du luth et dansant et quasi	Playing the lute and dancing and almost
Tristes sur leurs déguisements fantasques!	Sad beneath their fantastic disguises!

A bergamasque is a rustic dance, the name deriving from the Italian town of Bergamo. By giving an 'almost sad' slant to the dancers and masked figures, Verlaine evokes a wistful memory of the paintings of Antoine Watteau, specifically his haunting portrait of Pierrot, the sad clown, pining for the love of Columbine. It was this evocation by Verlaine that inspired this whole work, and the theatrical performance of which it was part.

In September 1918, Fauré wrote to his wife, Marie, that the director of the Monte-Carlo Theatre, '(who was inspired, I'm sure, by Saint-Saëns!) has requested for next winter a small musical tableau for which Fauchois would work out a scenario; and it would consist of some of my previous pieces . . . to which I would only need to add two or three little dances: minuet, gavotte . . . in short, a more comprehensive recreation of what happened at Madeleine Lemaire's house some ten or twelve years ago.'[1] Madeleine Lemaire, who fancied herself as a painter of flowers, held regular salons in Paris, and was one of the main inspirations for the absurd hostess, Mme Verdurin, in Proust's *À la recherche du temps perdu*. Fauré had contributed music for a divertissement at her house entitled *Fêtes galantes* – just the sort of refined entertainment designed to appeal in such circles. Now, at Monte Carlo, the playwright René Fauchois worked this idea up into something more elaborate.

The programme for the two performances first given in 1919 at Monte-Carlo contained the following note, probably supplied by Fauchois: 'The story of *Masques* is very simple. The characters Harlequin, Gilles and Colombine, whose task is usually to amuse the aristocratic audience, take their turn at being spectators at a '*fêtes galantes*' on the island of Cythera. The lords and ladies who as a rule applaud their efforts now unwittingly provide them with entertainment by their coquettish behaviour.'[2]

Fauré was delighted by the combination of his 'somewhat evocative and melancholy' pieces with the stage performance: 'In fact it really is the impression given by Watteau, and of which Verlaine has given so good a definition: "Playing the lute and dancing and almost sad under their fantastic disguises" ... [the composer] Reynaldo Hahn says it is as if Mozart had *imitated* Fauré!'[3]

From the score of eight pieces, Fauré selected four to create the orchestral suite. The Ouverture and Gavotte are the oldest of the pieces, composed when he was in his early twenties. The Menuet is of more recent date, and the Pastorale was freshly composed for the occasion.

The light and lively Ouverture could almost be by Chabrier or Bizet, if it were not for Fauré's characteristic way of taking the harmonies in unexpected directions, particularly in the bass line. The cheerful opening gives way to a broader second melody. Then the opening idea is further developed, and slips effortlessly into a reprise.

The Menuet is an evocation of eighteenth-century manners, opening with a woodwind ensemble and continuing with strings. Under the naive melody lurk charming and character-istic touches of counterpoint. The trio is bolder, with stamping beats, teasing cross-rhythms, and playful modern spicing in the harmonies.

The Gavotte is delightfully quirky in its harmonies and contrapuntal lines and in its playing with metre and phrase lengths. There is a gentler middle part with soulful inter-weaving melodies that are regular interrupted by echoes of the Gavotte.

The newly composed Pastorale takes us straight into the haunting world of late Fauré, in which strange, floating harmonies blend modern dissonances with suggestions of ancient modes. The middle section is yet more piquant, with its whole-tone harmonies. The opening of the Pastorale returns, but then suddenly blossoms into a nostalgic reminiscence of the Ouverture, and the Suite ends on quite a melancholy note.

PAVANE, OP. 50
Duration: approx. 6 minutes

In a letter of September 1887, Fauré writes that, with all his teaching commitments, he strug-gles to find time to compose: 'The only new thing I have been able to compose during this shuttlecock existence is a Pavane – elegant, assuredly, but not particularly important.'[4] This 'unimportant' piece was to prove Fauré's most popular orchestral work. After composing the orchestral score, Fauré added a chorus. Having done so, he created a presentation copy for his wealthiest patron, the Countess Elisabeth Greffuhle. He told her that her cousin, Count Robert de Montesquiou, had set a 'delightful' text to the chorus parts, so that it could be both danced and sung: 'If the whole marvellous thing with a lovely dance in fine costumes and an invisible chorus and orchestra could be performed, what a treat it would be!'[5] If this sounds quite Proustian enough, it is worth adding that the Count was the model for Proust's outrageous Baron de Charlus in À la recherche du temps perdu. The Count's text is in an antique pastoral style inspired by Verlaine, and the Pavane was performed with chorus and dancers at a night-time party held by the Countess on an island in a lake in the Bois de Boulogne in July 1891. In 1917, Léonide Massine choreographed a ballet to the Pavane for Diaghilev's Ballets Russes.

The chorus adds an air of theatrical antiquity that is charming. But it also obscures some of the detail of Fauré's orchestral score, which is delicate and subtle, so the music is really better without the singers. Over steadily treading pizzicato, a flute plays a solo in the low register that, ever since Debussy's *Prélude à l'après-midi d'un faune*, had (without the need for any chorus) conjured images of mythical antiquity. The flute is answered first by oboe and clarinet, then by clarinet and bassoon, with Fauré's characteristic ancient-and-modern harmonies deepening the atmosphere. After an extended second strain of the melody, the violins take it up with a sonorous new counterpoint on bassoon, and are answered by a chorus of woodwind.

The central section changes key dramatically. Assertive string phrases become chant-like, interleaved with a slower chant on solo horn. Solemn repetitions of this dialogue, dropping in key each time, take us back to the second strain of the flute solo. When we arrive at the reprise of the first strain, it is enriched with beautiful new counterpoints, and is lovingly extended into a long coda.

PELLÉAS ET MÉLISANDE, CONCERT SUITE, OP. 80
Duration: approx. 17 minutes

Prélude: quasi adagio
Fileuse: andantino quasi allegretto
Sicilienne: allegro molto moderato
Mort de Mélisande: molto adagio

In March and April 1898, Fauré was visiting London, where he was introduced to the actress Mrs Patrick Campbell. She was planning the first English-language production of Maurice Maeterlinck's play, *Pelléas et Mélisande*. She had asked Debussy to supply incidental music, knowing that he had finished an opera on *Pelléas*. She assumed that he would be able to draw on the opera to create music for the play. But Debussy's evanescent score was not suitable for such treatment (it had not yet been staged, so the music was not widely known). And in any case Debussy, having conceived his work as a musical drama, could not bring himself to unpick it for use in the play. He expressed his reasons for refusing in elliptical terms worthy of Maeterlinck himself: 'I always prefer something in which, in some way, action is sacrificed to the expression which has long been sought by the feelings of the soul.'[6] By the time Mrs Campbell approached Fauré, the production was less than two months away. To get the music completed in time, Fauré made use of some existing pieces, and asked his pupil, Charles Koechlin, to orchestrate the score.

The production, with designs by the pre-Raphaelite artist Edward Burne-Jones, was a great success. Maeterlinck attended the first night together with his friend, the poet Charles van Lerberghe, who reported that it was finer than the original French staging: 'The production put on in Paris and Brussels gives no idea of what we've just seen. The Mélisande is pure Burne-Jones and the Pélleas [Martin Harvey] is an actor of genius. Maeterlinck was bowled over. His little masterpiece, with actors like that and ravishing scenery, has been a real triumph. I heard it with a beating heart and tears in my eyes. It was so beautiful!'[7] Mrs Campbell wrote that Fauré 'had grasped with the most tender inspiration the poetic purity that pervades M. Materlinck's lovely play'.[8] The London production was followed by a run in the United States. When the music proved successful, Fauré created a concert suite from four of the movements, making minor revisions to Koechlin's orchestration.

Following the success of the production and of Fauré's hand in it, Debussy received a letter from his publisher reproaching him for turning down the commission and thereby letting

Fauré claim the first musical link with *Pelléas*. Debussy replied, 'The impact of [Fauré's] music seems to me hardly likely to survive the current production and, if I may boast, I don't think there can be any confusion between the two scores, at least in the matter of intellectual weight. In any case Fauré serves as the music-satchel for a band of snobs and fools who will never see anything in or do anything for the other *Pelléas*.'[9] (He here refers to the Proustian circle of aristocratic patrons who supported Fauré and disdained the modern tendencies of Debussy.)

The plot of Maeterlink's play is simple in outline, but rendered complex and mysterious by things that are left unsaid and implied. Prince Golaud is out hunting when he comes across a terrified young woman, Mélisande, alone and abandoned in the woods. He takes her home and marries her. Mélisande and Golaud's young stepbrother, Pelléas, fall in love. Their love is, it seems, innocent, but the enraged Golaud cannot believe it and kills Pelléas. The play ends with the death of Mélisande after she has given birth to Golaud's child.

Fauré's Prelude reflects essential elements of Maeterlick's play: a sense of inevitable tragedy arising from passions that lurk beneath the surface but are not to be suppressed, and a haunting vagueness of age and passing time. It opens with a four-part chorus of strings alone, which play gentle, chant-like phrases that hover between G major and E minor – a characteristic ambiguity that, with touches of counterpoint in the inner voices, echoes Fauré's love of Renaissance choral music. This theme develops and builds in a series of waves. After a particularly strong climax, cellos introduce a broader melody. This too builds gradually to a climax. As it falls away, oboe and clarinet step forward to bring us back to the first theme, which rises to a final, passionate outburst. A quiet horn call suggests the distant hunting party of Golaud. The harmonies acquire a poignancy reminiscent of Wagner's *Parsifal*. And the Prelude ends with a return to its first phrase, coloured with a new harmonic twist that makes it particularly touching.

'Fileuse' is the Prelude to Act III of the play, which reveals Mélisande at her spinning-wheel (a scene cut in Debussy's opera). The muted first violins keep up pianissimo whirling triplets while the lower strings, unmuted, accompany with pizzicato chords. Over this persistent pattern, an oboe sings a lullaby-like melody, in duet with a bassoon. Like the themes of the Prelude, this melody is full of harmonic ambiguities that give it a restless quality despite its surface calm. The music moves into a minor key, and low clarinet and horn bring in a darker melody. Other instruments join in a subtle strengthening of the line, but the oboe soon returns to the major to bring in a reprise of the first theme. This is now developed and extended while the spinning theme persists beneath. For a glorious moment, the spinning violins join in with the melody, taking it to a climax before it falls peacefully away.

Fauré used a Sicilienne composed in 1893 for the scene in which Pelléas and Mélisande meet at the fountain, and Mélisande loses her wedding ring in the water. A flute plays a solo accompanied by harp arpeggios. The melody has beautifully balanced phrases, the first built from a rising arpeggio, the second a demure answer in the classic lilting rhythm of the baroque siciliano. Once again, it is Fauré's subtle harmonies, veering unpredictably between minor, major, and modal, that turn this from a pleasant tune into something more evocative. Muted violins take up the melody, then continue it, unmuted, into a second strain. The opening returns. Then the key shifts down a third for the middle section of the piece. Here, the siciliano rhythm continues in the flute, and over a sustained bass, cellos introduce a broader melody in counterpoint with it (as often in Fauré, it is impossible to say which is the principal melody, and which the counterpoint). When the reprise of the first section comes, it jumps straight to the second strain. The opening flute solo then returns, with new touches of counterpoint in the second flute, and the Sicilienne draws to a close.

'The Death of Mélisande' originally formed the entr'acte into the final act in which Mélisande dies, only the final bars being repeated at the very end of the play. The music is sombre and tragic, but, this being Fauré, it is something more than that. It has the tread and incisive dotted rhythms of a traditional funeral march; but this is not a march, because it is in three-time. So it hovers somewhere between a funeral march and a slow dance, perhaps a sarabande. The melody begins low on two flutes in unison, a particularly haunting sound.

After the first strain of the melody, the music lightens to a moment of sad serenity, with a rising phrase on the muted strings. This is a quotation from a song that Mélisande sang in Act III, at the end of her spinning-wheel scene. The music soon returns to the march-sarabande, which several times rises to a climax and falls back. As it increases in intensity, the role of the flutes is taken over by a low trumpet, adding an organ-like pungency to the mixture. The piece ends with a return to Mélisande's gentle song, rounded off by a flute rising up a scale to the keynote of the last chord.

In November 1924, 'The Death of Mélisande' was played as Fauré's coffin was carried from the church of La Madeleine in Paris, where he had played the organ for ten years, to the waiting horse-drawn hearse outside, with crowds lining the streets for his state funeral.

CÉSAR FRANCK
(1822–90)

Franck was born in Liège, in what was soon to become Belgium, but moved to Paris with his family in 1835. Although he was a brilliant pianist and organist, and a composer of obvious talent, he struggled to make any mark on the cultural scene in the capital. A devout Roman Catholic, he composed a number of religious choral works. But what brought him fame was his appointment in 1858 as organist at the new basilica of Sainte Clotilde in Saint-Germain-des-Prés in Paris, when he was thirty-five, a post that he kept until the end of his life. A magnificent organ by Aristide Cavaillé-Coll was inaugurated by Franck the following year, and he developed a reputation for the remarkable improvisations that he played at the ends of services, some of which were developed into published organ works. One of his pupils, Vincent d'Indy, described the experience of being in the organ loft listening to Franck improvise: 'that rapt profile, and the intellectual brow, from which seemed to flow without any effort a stream of inspired melody and subtle, exquisite harmonies, which lingered a moment among the pillars of the nave before they ascended and died away in the vaulted heights of the roof'.[1]

In 1872, Franck was appointed organ professor at the Paris Conservatoire. He had already begun to attract a group of composition pupils, known as the 'Bande à Franck', and this evolved into a campaigning group that favoured a 'modern' (broadly speaking, Wagnerian) approach to music, and in particular promoted Franck's own works and ideas. A bitter battle developed in French musical culture. The Societé Nationale de Musique had been founded by Saint-Saëns in 1871 to promote the music of living French composers. Among its members there soon developed differences of opinion about the direction in which French music was heading. Leading the 'conservative' wing was Saint-Saëns himself, the doyen of French composers, who emphasized the importance of the classical values of Mozart and Beethoven. He regretted the rise of a generation of young composers for whom these values were increasingly irrelevant, largely because of their devotion to Wagner, and this put him at odds with Franck's pupils (notably Henri Duparc and Vincent d'Indy). In the end, Saint-Saëns was to lose this battle. He found himself increasingly sidelined, while Franck gained support in his role as the leader of the pro-Wagnerian 'progressive' group.

The orchestral music for which Franck is best known was written in the last ten years of his life, when he had finally achieved fame as a composer. In his two best-known works, the Symphonic Variations of 1885 and the Symphony in D minor of 1886–8, the strong influence of Wagner (and Liszt) is clear in two aspects of his compositional style. The first is his harmonies. Although his music is still rooted in the major and minor keys of classical music, the harmonies are in a constant state of flux and uncertainty. This gives his music a characteristic fluidity and passionate restlessness, often directly evoking Wagner's *Tristan*, though with a particular kind of quasi-religious ecstatic intensity that sometimes recalls *Parsifal*. The second aspect is a different kind of fluidity. Themes, or motifs, transform themselves and reappear, so that his material evolves as the music proceeds. Themes recur in later movements, either in their original form, or in one of these transformations. There is nothing entirely new about this procedure, which can be found as far back as Mozart and Beethoven. But Franck takes it to new lengths, building on the methods of Liszt and Wagner, so that his best pieces seem like satisfyingly organic structures.

SYMPHONY IN D MINOR
Duration: approx. 37 minutes

Lento – Allegro non troppo
Allegretto
Allegro non troppo

Franck wrote his only symphony over a period of three years, between 1886 and 1888, and it was first performed in the concert series of the Paris Conservatoire in February 1889. Rehearsed without enthusiasm, and subjected to acerbic and partisan comment from the 'conservative' wing of French musical opinion (see introduction), it had to wait until after Franck's death before it was accepted as the remarkable work that it is.

The symphony opens with a slow introduction, a feature of many classical symphonies from Haydn onwards. But it is not merely introductory: it presents the most important themes in the symphony. First, questioning phrases rise up in the lower strings. Then the violins answer with a falling, sinuous melody, with evocatively chromatic harmonies. Over shuddering string tremolo, wind instruments solemnly intone the rising theme, its key changing as it rises further, reaching a climax. This introduction sums up several of the preoccupations and influences of Franck's life. The mood is intense and dramatic, but solemn, even religious – it could be an introduction to an act of Wagner's *Parsifal*. The orchestration combines instruments rather as an organist combines stops: the strings on one keyboard, the woodwind on another. When the wind take over the first theme, Franck combines bass clarinet, bassoons, and horns in unison, giving a peculiarly organ-like sonority. And the build-up to the climax is like a grand crescendo on Franck's beloved Cavaillé-Coll organ.

As the Allegro begins, we hear Franck's technique of theme transformation at work. The opening theme, now much faster, has become forceful and assertive, and the answering falling phrase has acquired sharply dotted rhythms. The music begins to move on into new keys, as if embarking on some large-scale adventure, but suddenly it is halted in its tracks. The opening Lento returns. It proceeds much as before, but now up a third in F minor. Again it reaches a climax, and bursts once again into the Allegro.

This time, the Allegro does move on, leading to a sweet second theme in the major, made up of smoothly rising phrases. It gradually gains power, until it culminates in a third theme, still in the same key. This is played fortissimo, as if on 'full organ', the theme reinforced by trumpets, its simple up-and-down phrases repeated insistently. It comes dangerously close to banality (as Franck's critics were quick to point out), but, in a good performance, it takes on a quality of religious fervour. Eventually, the fervour is spent, and the movement pauses for a moment of calm reflection.

There follows the traditional development section. This is the most orthodox part of the movement, with several elements from the main themes in dialogue, the dotted rhythms of the first theme and the smoother lines of the later themes fighting for dominance. Eventually, a build-up culminates in a sudden slowing of pace, and we are back at the Lento introduction. This is now on full orchestra, fortissimo, sounding massively Wagnerian, in contrast to the opening that sounded mysteriously Wagnerian. The outburst into the Allegro is more frenetic than before, plunging into new keys. When it subsides into the sweet second theme, we have reached the home key of D – an altogether classical thing to do at this stage, and the security of the key is emphasized as the music reaches the fervent fortissimo of the third theme. After the descent to the moment of reflection, there is one last build-up, culminating in a final *fff* statement of the rising theme with which the movement began, and a triumphant chord of D major.

Even critics who find the outer movements of the symphony heavy-handed admit the beauty of the central movement. It is basically a slow(ish) movement, but incorporating passages with the lightness of a scherzo, and it therefore has the effect of combining the two usual middle movements of a symphony in a single piece. A tread of harmonies in B flat minor is laid down by pizzicato strings and harp, as if this were the start of a passacaglia. Then, over this, a beautiful cor anglais solo is played. The melody sounds entirely new, but its opening notes trace the shape of the very opening phrase of the symphony – one of Franck's most subtle transformations. Violas join in with a counterpoint to the cor anglais melody, and then it is taken up by horn and clarinet in unison (again, an organist's combination – most composers would have chosen one or the other).

The pizzicato accompaniment in B flat minor now gives way to a rich texture of bowed strings in the major, and the violins embark on a new melody. This is not entirely new either, because the repeated semitone interval of its opening phrases are based on the ecstatic third theme from the first movement, but, like the cor anglais solo, it is completely transformed in character. The broad, warm melody soars further and further, its second strain incorporating a falling chromatic shape that is also drawn from the third theme of the first movement. Eventually, the melody comes quietly to rest, and the cor anglais briefly reprises its solo, now an octave lower, to round off this first section of the movement.

There is (as at a similar point in the first movement) a moment of reflection. A pianissimo tremolando figure in the violins steps tentatively forward, and is answered by the woodwind, with the same repeated semitone interval drawn from the first movement. Twice this happens, and comes to a halt. Then the tremolo gets under way, with the pizzicato harmonies from the first part of the movement under it. As the tremolo breaks into little running scales, we suddenly have the sense of having been drawn, without realizing it, into a rapid scherzo, superimposed over the harmonies of the slow movement (so the passacaglia feeling of the opening was not far-fetched). After a time, this gives way to another of Franck's warm, sweeping melodies, which explores far and wide before coming to rest.

Then the tremolando scherzo theme returns, and this time the cor anglais reprises its solo over it. So the 'slow movement' and the 'scherzo' have combined – a brilliant stroke, of which Franck was justifiably proud. The two elements go forward together, exploring new keys. Then the two warm secondary themes are also interleaved, the melody from the first part of the movement played by the woodwind, the strings answering with the sweeping melody from the second part of the movement. Eventually, the strings take over the first of those melodies from the woodwind, and it is with this that the movement winds to a peaceful conclusion.

The finale is joyful and outgoing. Its opening theme on cellos and bassoons, with its repeated phrases, is derived from the ecstatic third theme of the first movement, but rendered even more breezy by being opened out into arpeggios, and having its chromatic elements removed – it is as straightforwardly in the home key of D (major) as any theme by Haydn or Mozart. It quickly builds up to fortissimo on full orchestra, moving on through various keys, and subsiding to a second theme. This is a quiet chorale on the brass, with the rather low trumpet line marked 'dolce cantabile'. The effect is peculiarly French, once more conjuring up the effect of the Cavaillé-Coll organ on which Franck played. The phrases of the chorale are answered by rising, yearning phrases from the strings and woodwind. This too moves on through various keys, entering a passage with a rather Wagnerian uncertainty of direction. Soon the destination becomes clear: over the strings' quiet pattern, the cor anglais enters with its solo from the second movement. Fragments of the finale's outgoing first theme reappear, and gradually they coalesce to build to a climax. But at the climax itself, the melody which is played is not that theme, but the brass chorale, now blazing confidently. It dies away to another of those moments of reflective pause that occur in all three movements. Fragments of the cor anglais melody, the brass chorale, and other less defined phrases halt the music several times. Eventually, the music moves on again, with the cor anglais theme and anxious chromatic fragments from the strings alternating.

With almost *Tristan*-like passionate haste, this builds up, until once more the bold opening theme of the finale bursts out on full orchestra. But this too is soon overtaken by a reminiscence of the cor anglais theme, now, rather startlingly, blaring fortissimo on trumpets (the least subtle of Franck's transformations). It dies away to another passage of pianissimo searching, which eventually finds its way back to the ecstatic second theme from the first movement, now warmly on violins and then clarinet, and dying away on high violins. A moment of tense hush follows. Over rippling harp and a persistent bass note (the third of the chord, a favourite effect of Franck's), fragments of the very opening phrase of the symphony are heard. They alternate with fragments of the ecstatic theme, until the finale's own first theme reasserts itself, and the symphony plunges on, with full brass, to a blazing conclusion.

VARIATIONS SYMPHONIQUES (SYMPHONIC VARIATIONS) FOR PIANO AND ORCHESTRA
Duration: approx. 15 minutes

Franck wrote this work in 1885, dedicating it to the pianist Louis Diémer (the teacher of Alfred Cortot, whose 1933 recording of the work has a particular poetry). Diémer had recently given the successful premiere of Franck's symphonic poem for piano and orchestra, *Les Djinns*. The Symphonic Variations, an intimate and subtle work, made much less impression at its early performances than the more extrovert and straightforward *Les Djinns*, but it is these Variations that have stood the test of time. The work is a sort of miniature piano concerto in a very fluid form. It breaks down into recognizable sections, which are played continuously: an introduction, a theme and variations, and a finale. But all the material in the work is closely related, so that elements from the theme also form the basis of the introduction, and the finale is, in effect, another variation. All of this is knit together with passages of free fantasia, and these too incorporate elements of the theme. The whole piece has the character of a structured improvisation, and is the most successful of Franck's attempts to create a fluid and unified form, drawing on the methods used by Wagner in his operas and Liszt in his symphonic poems and piano works.

Despite these influences, the first bars of the introduction pay homage, unmistakably, to Beethoven. As in the slow movement of Beethoven's Piano Concerto No. 4, assertive dotted rhythms in the orchestra alternate with plaintive answers from the piano. The music gradually gathers pace, and becomes more continuous, reaching a climax. Then a new element is heard: a pizzicato phrase, answered by a smooth phrase, and rounded off with pizzicato. This is the first time we have heard what is to become the theme of the Variations (though its shape has already been hinted at). The piano launches into an extended passage of fantasia, based on its opening solo. There is another passage of alternation between dotted rhythms low in the orchestra and lyrical responses from the piano. The music reaches a climax, dies down, and hesitates.

Then the solo piano launches into the theme that forms the basis of the Variations. This is like a distillation of the opening bars, incorporating some of the rhythms and intervals we have heard, but now shaped into a lyrical and coherent theme. In Variation 1, orchestra and piano alternate (as at the beginning of the piece), with a gentle elaboration of the theme. In Variation 2, the theme is sung by violas and cellos, while the piano plays a delicate pattern of chords above. Variation 3 is more energetic, with the piano breaking into semiquavers, accompanied by pizzicato strings. These become louder and more agitated, culminating in the entry to Variation 4. Here the orchestra reverts to the assertive dotted rhythms of the opening, with the piano answering forcefully. This variation is extended beyond its expected length, with the piano playing double octaves and building to a climax. Gradually this subsides, and slows to enter Variation 5. This is a beautiful, dreamy variation, with the melody low in the cellos, and the piano playing a delicate, murmuring pattern above. Like Variation 4, this variation is extended, with the cellos (now muted) meditating on the plaintive phrase that began the piano's very first entry. The piano continues its delicate murmuring of chord patterns.

Eventually, trills announce the beginning of the final Allegro non troppo. This transforms various phrases from the introduction and theme into a bubbling, extended finale. At one point, the piano breaks into what sounds almost like a popular song, a delightfully relaxed transformation of the dotted-rhythm phrases that began the piece. As in a conventional concerto, near the end the pianist breaks off into a solo cadenza. But the moment is short-lived, the woodwind soon bring the piano back to the principal theme of the finale, and the work winds to a joyful and exuberant conclusion.

GEORGE GERSHWIN
(1898–1937)

The brothers George and Ira Gershwin, together with a younger brother and sister, were the children of Russian and Lithuanian Jewish immigrants to New York, brought up in Brooklyn. When George was twelve, the family acquired a piano for his older brother Ira, but it was George who took to it and began having piano lessons. His most important teacher, Charles Hambitzer, recognized an exceptional talent, describing him as 'a genius', fostered his love of classical music and encouraged him to attend concerts. Gershwin later recalled, 'I had gone to concerts and listened not only with my ears, but with my nerves, my mind, my heart. I had listened so earnestly that I became saturated with the music. Then I went home and listened in memory. I sat at the piano and repeated the *motifs*.'[1] This cemented a love of classical music that Gershwin retained throughout his life, and he became knowledgeable about music over a wide span of periods and genres. In a 1929 interview he talked about the balance between heart and brain that makes a great composer: 'Tchaikovsky (although he was a good technician) was apt to stress the heart too much in his music; Berlioz was all mind. Now Bach was a glorious example of the unity of the two.' As for modern composers, 'I admire Ravel intensely. He is a superb master of technique. But he has never known great inspiration.' On the other hand, 'Debussy is one of the most profound composers of his time. Look at *Pelléas and Mélisande*.'[2] Gershwin was only fifteen when he took a job as a 'song plugger', playing and singing songs for customers at one of the publishers on Tin Pan Alley. From then on, he spent his career in two camps, continuing with his classical studies while earning a living in popular music. By the age of twenty he was already known as a composer of songs, several of which had appeared in Broadway shows. His great breakthrough occurred in 1919, when Al Jolson heard him sing 'Swanee' at a party, and decided to perform it in his shows and record it. Within a year, it had earned Gershwin $10,000 in royalties.

Gershwin's unique appeal was his ability to inhabit the classical and popular fields with equal ease. There were other classically trained emigrés who had brought the skills of the classical composer to Broadway, but Gershwin had aspirations in the opposite direction. He became increasingly interested in composing concert pieces that brought popular song elements into classical music. He studied harmony, counterpoint, and other skills with the Hungarian Edward Kilenyi, and later went to the composers Henry Cowell and Rubin Goldmark and took courses on orchestration and music history at Columbia University. In 1927 he visited Paris, hoping to study with Ravel. But Ravel told him that 'it would probably cause him to write bad "Ravel", and lose his great gift of melody and spontaneity'. Ravel recommended Gershwin to Nadia Boulanger, describing him as 'a musician endowed with the most brilliant, most enchanting, and perhaps the most profound talent ... Would you have the courage to take on this awesome responsibility?' But Boulanger too recognized the risk of tampering with Gershwin's natural genius, and turned him down: 'I told him that what I could teach him wouldn't help him much . . . and he agreed. Never have I regretted the outcome. He died famous.'[3] The climax of Gershwin's career in large-scale works was his great 'American folk opera', *Porgy and Bess*.

The end was sudden and shocking. Suffering from dizzy spells, he suddenly lost consciousness. An emergency operation to remove a brain tumour was unsuccessful, and he died at the age of thirty-eight, at the height of his powers.

AN AMERICAN IN PARIS
Duration: approx. 18 minutes

In April 1926, four months after the premiere of his piano concerto, Gershwin gave the first hint that he might be thinking of a Parisian theme for his next large-scale work. Following a short stay in Paris, he sent a postcard to his hosts that included a little tune with the title, 'An American in Paris'. Nearly two years later, Gershwin remembered this fragment, but at first had difficulty knowing what to do with it. It was at home in New York, as he gazed at the Hudson River, that he found the way forward: 'I love that river, and I thought how often I had been homesick for a sight of it, and then the idea struck me – an American in Paris, homesickness, the blues. So there you are. I thought of a walk on the Champs Elysées, of the honking taxi . . .'4

After he had made this breakthrough, he developed the ideas further while he was in Europe for an extended visit in the spring and summer of 1928. He described the opening part as being 'developed in typical French style, in the manner of Debussy and the Six, though the themes are all original [almost all, as it turned out]. My purpose here is to portray the impressions of an American visitor in Paris as he strolls about the city, listens to the various street noises, and absorbs the French atmosphere . . . The opening gay section . . . is followed by a rich "blues" with a strong rhythmic undercurrent. Our American friend, perhaps after strolling into a café, and having a few drinks [this was the time of prohibition in America], has suddenly succumbed to a spasm of homesickness.' Finally, 'the spirit of the music returns to the vivacity and bubbling exuberance of the opening part with its impressions of Paris. Apparently the homesick American, having left the café and reached the open air, has downed his spell of the blues and once again is an alert spectator of Parisian life. At the conclusion, the street noises and the French atmosphere are triumphant.'5

Gershwin was determined to incorporate authentic street sounds, so while he was in Paris he went from shop to shop trying to find taxi horns that would sound specific notes. He composed most of the piece in Paris and Vienna, and almost completed the orchestration on the ship back to New York. *An American in Paris* was premiered by the recently amalgamated New York Philharmonic Symphony Orchestra under Walter Damrosch in December 1928. It rapidly became one of Gershwin's most successful scores, and in 1951 it reached new audiences as the ballet centrepiece of the film *An American in Paris* choreographed by, and starring, Gene Kelly.

Gershwin sets out with an irresistible spring in his step. It is as if the 'cheerful feelings' of Beethoven's 'Pastoral' Symphony have metamorphosed into the high spirits of a twentieth-century boulevardier. There's also a hint (here and later) of Elgar's portrait of London, *Cockaigne*, with its more Edwardian swagger. Part of the charm of Gershwin's tune is the way it is surrounded by other strands that come and go, particularly a descant of a long note and flourish, first on flute and bassoon then on solo violin. There are sudden cross-rhythms, as if the stroller is having to dodge round people and cars. A sturdier second strain is accompanied by taxi horns at different pitches. There is a brief moment of quiet, delicately reiterating a phrase of repeated notes from the theme, then the tune starts off again with new harmonies. These include the sort of sliding, parallel harmonies beloved of Debussy, and there is even a quote from Debussy's 'Fêtes'. This is swiftly followed by, on trombones, a snatch of a French popular song, 'La Mattchiche' ('La Maxixe' is a Brazilian tango-like dance in march rhythm). A flute gives the long-note-and-flourish descant a whole-tone twist, and the clarinets respond

with a raucously humorous variant on a phrase from the main tune. In a kaleidoscopic procession of characters and shifting perspectives, reminiscent of the fair scene in Stravinsky's
Petrushka, the music builds to a climax, and comes to a halt with a horn call.

With muted strings playing more Debussyan chords, cor anglais and oboe quietly muse on
the opening phrase of the tune, elongating its first note (this gives a first hint of the melody
that is to come in the middle of the piece). After a moment of calm, as if looking around, lost
in reverie, the jaunty tempo resumes, the trombones inject a new, vigorous phrase, and old
and new elements are thrown around in another virtuoso passage of orchestration. Once
again this culminates in a climax and a sudden stop, and the cor anglais muses on the trombone's new idea. A brief burst of renewed energy soon fades out again, a celesta and a solo
violin lead the way into a more extended meditation, and the music reaches a peaceful chord
of F major. A trombone slyly introduces the seventh into the chord, and, in B flat major, a slow
but insistent rhythm starts up, with wood block and brushed side drum. Over it, a trumpet,
playing into a felt crown (as in the piano concerto), sings an unashamed blues (this is the
melody hinted at by cor anglais and oboe a little earlier). The way this melody develops is one
of Gershwin's most masterly touches. The violins take it up, and as the ardour increases,
moments of surge in the accompanying rhythm suggest that wine is fuelling this outburst of
nostalgia. As the violins finish the melody, there is a lovely moment of transition from one key
to the next, where Gershwin touches in a descending bass with pizzicato, drawing attention to
a link between this blues and J. S. Bach's famous Air in D. Now strings and trumpet combine
for a reprise of the blues. The tempo pushes on, the tipsy passion becomes frenzied, until one
last snatch of blues breaks through the mood, and the solo violin, which introduced this
episode, brings it to a close.

Out of the calm steps a cheeky, jazzy trumpet, strutting a cheerful twelve-bar blues with a
Charleston kick. This is taken up with relish by the whole orchestra, and accompanied by
swooning violins (another Americanized touch of Debussy). Eventually, the great nostalgic
blues melody sweeps in majestically. As it subsides, again the solo violin creates a transition,
followed by solo tuba. With a sudden switch of mood, the opening returns, though not yet
quite as it was. A burst of energy and exploration quickly finds the way back, and the opening
tune emerges, in its original key, but only for a moment. A rapid climax leads to one last burst
of the blues tune, as if to say that it is possible to be nostalgic and happily adventurous at the
same time. And on this optimistic note, almost like the overture to a show, the piece comes to
an end.

PIANO CONCERTO IN F MAJOR
Duration: approx. 31 minutes

Allegro
Adagio – Andante con moto – Più mosso – Tempo I
Allegro agitato

The conductor of the New York Symphony Orchestra, Walter Damrosch, who had got to
know Gershwin through his daughter, attended the concert in 1924 at which Gershwin played
the premiere of his *Rhapsody in Blue*. He then commissioned Gershwin to compose a full-
scale piano concerto. Gershwin had never written for full orchestra – *Rhapsody in Blue* had
been scored by Paul Whiteman's orchestrator, Ferde Grofé – but Damrosch wanted a work

entirely by Gershwin himself. This was before Gershwin's studies with Henry Cowell, and he claimed that, on his way to London for a new show, he took 'four or five books on musical structure to find out what the concerto form really was'. Gershwin himself said, 'Many persons had thought that the *Rhapsody* was only a happy accident. Well I went out, for one thing, to show them that there was plenty more where that came from. I made up my mind to do a piece of absolute music. The *Rhapsody*, as its title implied, was a blues impression. The Concerto would be unrelated to any programme.'[6] Gershwin started sketching some ideas for the concerto in the spring of 1925, composed it over the summer as a score for two pianos, noting some of the ideas for instrumentation. He sent a few trial pages of orchestration to Damrosch and to William Daly, a friend and Broadway music director, for comment, and completed the orchestration by November. Gershwin then hired a fifty-five-piece orchestra under Daly to try it out, with Damrosch attending, and made some revisions. He later said, 'You can imagine my delight when it sounded just as I had planned.' Gershwin, Damrosch, and the New York Symphony Orchestra performed the premiere at Carnegie Hall on 3 December 1925.

The concerto is written for a large classical orchestra, with extra percussion contributing to the jazzy elements, including a wood block and a slapstick. It is clearly not the work of someone who had quickly learned how to write a concerto from a few books. Whatever he may or may not have read in the months before he started composing it, Gershwin was well steeped in the classics, which he had studied and loved ever since his early days learning with Charles Hambitzer. His concerto makes it clear that he was at ease with a whole range of classical techniques, including how to vary and transform themes, how to use changes of key to structure the music, and that he had a sensitive ear for orchestral effects. His harmonic style brings together blues-inflected chord progressions with the modern classical language of Debussy and Ravel. Indeed, there are striking links between Gershwin's and Ravel's piano concertos. But here the influence is the other way round: Ravel did not start writing his piano concerto until 1929.

Because of the hybrid style, critics and others varied greatly in their views of the piece. This was a time when jazz could still be condemned as 'the music of the savage, intellectual and spiritual debauchery, utter degradation', in the words of a Baptist minister, Dr John Roach Straton, a few months after the premiere of Gershwin's Concerto.[7] Even among liberal-minded people, the marrying of jazz with a classical genre could scarcely be expected to reap universal praise. Olin Downes in *The New York Times* thought it 'a dubious experiment'. But Carl Engel in *Musical Quarterly* hailed it as 'of a newness to be found nowhere except in these United States'. The composer Morton Gould described the reception at the premiere as 'thunderous. All around me people marvelled at the originality and strength of the work.'[8] Gershwin performed the concerto many times across the United States, and after his death it became accepted into the classical repertoire.

Whatever the truth about Gershwin's previous knowledge of concerto-writing, his own take on the genre was highly individual, nodding towards traditional ways of working, but treating them with a great deal of fluidity. If, as commentators often state, Gershwin's concerto suffers from being too 'rhapsodic', it might be pointed out that it is no looser in its rhapsody than the concertos of Liszt or Chopin: the cadenza-like passages in the Gershwin are positively ascetic compared with those of Liszt. If the structure of Gershwin's concerto often sounds rather loose in performance, this is because it tends to be played rather loosely.

Gershwin himself had a straightforward approach to playing his music. Indeed, his recordings and piano rolls can seem rather too cut and dried for the expressive content of the music (like the playing of another twentieth-century composer-pianist, Sergei Prokofiev). But self-indulgent pianists could certainly learn something from it.

In an essay in the *New York Herald* published before the premiere, Gershwin described the first movement as 'quick and pulsating, representing the young, enthusiastic spirit of American life'.[9] It is the longest of the three, and the most complex and subtle in construction. It is possible to discern the conventional shape of a first movement – the exposition of themes, a development section, and a reprise – but Gershwin plays with this convention, continually developing and transforming his themes throughout, and delaying any sense of reprise until very late.

Four timpani strokes announce the opening of the movement. Two ideas follow in quick succession: four bars of a theme in Charleston rhythm, answered by a rising and falling pattern of dotted rhythms on bassoon. Gershwin immediately begins to develop these ideas, until the two rhythms combine (dotted rhythms above, Charleston syncopations below) and build to a moment of climax and suspense. The piano enters with a third idea: a languid melody in a blues-inflected F minor. When the piano repeats the theme, viola and cor anglais play a poignant counterpoint. At the height of the theme, the piano breaks off. After a moment of reflection, the orchestra begins a repetitive rhythmic idea – perhaps new, but with its roots in the Charleston rhythm, and with its high point referring back to the high point of the piano's languid theme. The piano enters with the Charleston, the excitement builds. Then, after another reflective moment, the strings burst in with the languid third theme, now given a passionate sweep, and with the piano playing the counterpoint. A brief moment of piano cadenza rounds off the first section of the movement.

The Charleston returns, at a slightly faster tempo (Gershwin's precise tempo relationships are carefully calculated), with a quiet exchange between woodwind and piano. A wood block taps out the syncopated rhythm, and the dotted-rhythm second idea is combined with it. At a change of key, the piano combines the dotted rhythms and the syncopation in another variant, with repeated phrases as in the strings' earlier variation. This is developed, with playful piano-writing moving through different keys, until the music calms. The strings, with cor anglais, play a consoling melody, like a love song or lullaby. It is in a pure E major (a key remote from the F major in which the piece started). This too might seem new, but its gentle, repeated syncopations are drawn from the Charleston, its high point again refers back to the piano's languid theme, and the conclusion is full of dotted rhythms. The piano accompanies delicately, and, a second time round, pulls the orchestra to a climax. There is another sudden change of tempo. Over an insistent bass, the piano combines the Charleston rhythm with the dotted rhythms, as they first appeared in the bassoon. A slap-stick marks the syncopations. The music moves rapidly from key to key – E minor, D minor, G minor, F minor. The tempo steadies, and the piano plays a new, playfully syncopated idea. But soon it is combined with fragments of the strings' love song. The music builds energetically, and slows to a climactic reprise of the languid third theme, with the melody on strings and trumpet, the counterpoint on horns, and the piano accompanying with forceful chords. This is the climactic point of the movement, but it is in B flat minor, not yet the home key. It fades, giving way (as it did at its first appearance) to the repetitive, Charleston-based idea. There is an interruption from the timpani, reprising the opening strokes of the movement. From here the music builds in brilliance and speed, until persistent Charleston rhythms in F major bring the movement to a conclusion.

In his essay, Gershwin described the slow movement as 'almost Mozartean in its simplicity', with 'a poetic, nocturnal tone. It utilizes the atmosphere of what has come to be referred to as the American blues, but in a purer form than that in which they are usually treated.'[10] Two bars of a dreamy muted horn (Adagio) are followed by a mellow trio of two clarinets and bass clarinet (Andante con moto). Over the trio, a solo trumpet plays a blues lament. Gershwin specifies that the trumpet should play into a 'hat with felt crown', producing a hauntingly muffled resonance. An oboe takes over the middle section of the melody, and then it returns to the trumpet. The piano enters with a delicate, perky tune, lightened by flicking grace notes. This might seem new, but it is an elaboration of the second phrase of the trumpet solo, over a similar rising bass. At the second strain of this tune, the woodwind play a little undulating counterpoint that will be important later. The new tune is discussed at length, first in playful dialogue with the woodwind, then with the violins playing the tune and the piano accompanying. As the ideas are thrown around, different elements become prominent in turn. The music develops vigour, and then subsides to a wistful violin solo. The clarinet trio and trumpet solo return, with a new counterpoint on flute derived from the middle-section tune. There is a short piano cadenza, which ends by meditating on the little undulating phrase that the woodwind played earlier. Then the strings launch into a wholehearted song theme. Its character is new, but it is based on those same undulating phrases, and the high points of the theme are like cousins of the high points in the first movement's great song. After another meditative linking passage, the piano takes up the new theme, and piano and orchestra develop it to a passionate climax. It breaks off suddenly. Quietly, the piano remembers the clarinet trio with which the movement began, a flute delicately touches in the trumpet solo, and the movement comes to a peaceful close.

In January 1925, Gershwin had begun sketching a Prelude in G minor. He never finished it, but he remembered it when he was working on the concerto, and turned it into the principal theme of this finale. It is a toccata of rapid repeated notes, with a syncopated kick at the end of each phrase. The energy of the toccata is given an extra twist as its two-time metre occasionally breaks into three-time. It is a virtuoso movement for everyone. Making the kick 'tell' is one of the most difficult things to achieve in the whole concerto – impossible if the movement is taken too fast. And the quick-fire interplay between piano and orchestra demands the lightening rhythmic responses more often found in the best jazz big bands than in a large symphony orchestra. The toccata theme is interleaved with other elements, most of them from earlier in the concerto, creating a rondo structure.

The first dash of toccata gives way to the languid big theme from the first movement, but now given an insouciant air in the rapid tempo of the finale. A second burst of toccata leads on to a new tune with a jazzy swing, on muted trumpet (it opens with the same shape as the bassoon theme right at the beginning of the first movement). This too is interrupted, by a brief swooning two bars of slower three-time. Woodwind follow on with playful runs, and the piano incorporates the toccata into the new tune, the two elements vying for dominance. When the full orchestra returns to the toccata, the swooning interruption has strange chords, like a sudden glimpse of Stravinsky's *The Rite of Spring*. The next stretch of toccata is overlaid with another reminiscence, of the song-like theme from the slow movement. The piano rounds this off with another return to the jazzy trumpet tune, which is taken up by the brass in a burst of swaggering counterpoint.

The piano breaks back into the toccata, and is joined by a xylophone. As the piano continues with glittering figurations, the strings bring in another reminiscence: the perky tune from the middle section of the slow movement. Again the piano returns to the jazzy trumpet tune, followed by a brief reminder of the Charleston rhythm, which we haven't heard since the first movement. The next return to the toccata is on full orchestra, with driving octaves in the piano. Quickly the tension builds, and then pulls to a halt. Out of the silence a gong strikes. With magnificent theatrical drama, the full orchestra bursts into the great song theme from the first movement, the piano accompanying with pulsating chords. It subsides, the piano emerges with sweeping glissandi, and launches a final attack on the toccata. The orchestra joins in, and climaxes with a return to the timpani strokes with which the concerto began. The work ends with brassy trills, and the piano plays octaves in a rising and falling pattern that refers back to the jazzy trumpet tune, and from there back to the bassoon theme at the beginning of the first movement. Right to the end, Gershwin demonstrates that he is not just a popular showman, but a musical intellectual who can hold his place in the most exalted company.

RHAPSODY IN BLUE
Duration: approx. 17 minutes

The band leader, Paul Whiteman, was one of the first musicians to attempt the task of making jazz more 'respectable' by encouraging composers to write jazz-inspired works employing classical techniques – what we would now call works of crossover or fusion. There had been a number of successful experiments in which jazz items were performed in concert halls, but this was something new. Whiteman approached Gershwin, already famous as a songwriter and pianist, and asked him to write a concerto-like piece for piano and band, for performance at a concert in February 1924. Gershwin, who had never composed such a piece before and was working on a musical, *Sweet Little Devil*, initially refused. It was his brother, Ira, who spotted in the *New York Tribune* of 4 January an article about Whiteman's forthcoming concert, which was to be called 'An experiment in modern music'. Whiteman claimed, 'George Gershwin is at work on a jazz concerto, Irving Berlin is writing a syncopated tone poem, and Victor Herbert is working on an American suite.'[11] When Gershwin phoned Whiteman, he was told that the band leader Vincent Lopez also had plans for a 'symphonic jazz' concert, and it was this that persuaded Gershwin to find the time to write his piece. Gershwin recalled to his biographer Isaac Goldberg in 1931 that the first ideas for the piece occurred to him on the train to Boston for the premiere of the musical: 'It was on the train, with its steely rhythms, its rattley-bang that is so often stimulating to a composer . . . I frequently hear music in the very heart of noise. And there I suddenly heard – and even saw on paper – the complete construction of the Rhapsody from beginning to end. No new themes came to me, but I worked on the thematic material already in my mind and tried to conceive the composition as a whole. I heard it as a sort of musical Kaleidoscope of America – of our vast melting pot, of our unduplicated national pep, of our blues, our metropolitan madness. By the time I reached Boston I had a definite *plot* of the piece, as distinguished from its actual substance.'[12] He composed the piece in three weeks during January 1924.

The concert included such famous pieces as 'Alexander's Ragtime Band' and 'Limehouse Blues', and new pieces by Jerome Kern and Victor Herbert. Gershwin's *Rhapsody* occupied pride of place as the penultimate work, and the concert ended with Elgar's first *Pomp and Circumstance* March. For the occasion Whiteman had augmented his band, with extra classically-trained string players, accustomed to sight-reading difficult scores. One of them, the violinist Kurt Dieterle, remembered, 'at the very first rehearsals, the brass – Henry Busse [trumpeter] and the different players – they were such big shots. They'd come in with derby hats, raccoon coats, and those floppy shoes, but when they had to play "Rhapsody in Blue" they didn't do so well. So those of us with a classical background had a big laugh.'[13]

Although Gershwin was famous as a popular song composer, he had a wide knowledge of classical music and had loved it since he was a child. His classical skills would be demonstrated more thoroughly in his piano concerto, but already *Rhapsody in Blue* shows a fluent use of classical techniques. He employs several themes and ideas, extending and developing them. But its structure is (in classical terms) quite loose. Gershwin begins and ends in B flat major, and the music passes through a great variety of keys between those two points. But there is no real sense that the music is structured by its keys, more a feeling of a fluid sequence from one point to the next. Indeed, this is the overall character of the music, particularly the extensive passages for solo piano that have an improvisatory quality.

It has often been said that the *Rhapsody* is too loose in structure to sustain its length. Some musicians, notably Leonard Bernstein, have played shortened versions. But Bernstein's cuts remove important orchestral passages that punctuate the rhapsodic piano writing, so that the effect is to make the work seem still looser, even though shorter. Gershwin's two recordings, made in 1924 and 1927 with Whiteman's band, were savagely cut, but that was so as to fit the work onto two sides of a single 78-rpm disc. It is best to accept the work as it is: an experiment, full of brilliant and touching ideas, and if it rambles somewhat it is worth sinking into its leisurely progress and enjoying the journey. Needless to say, its rambling has not prevented it becoming the most famous and popular piece in the history of attempts at 'symphonic jazz'.

The original 1924 version performed by Whiteman's band was orchestrated by Ferde Grofé. Grofé made other arrangements for different forces, including a version for theatre orchestra (published 1926), and a version for full symphony orchestra (published 1942). This last version is the one most often played. Gershwin was in discussion with his publisher about making his own orchestration shortly before he died.

The premiere took place on 12 February 1924, with Gershwin playing the piano, and Paul Whiteman conducting his Palais Royal Orchestra. It was Abraham Lincoln's birthday, cleverly chosen by Whiteman as the day for a concert of 'Symphonic Jazz'. In the audience at the premiere were the composers Igor Stravinsky and Sergei Rachmaninoff, violinists Jascha Heifetz and Fritz Kreisler, and conductors Leopold Stokowski, Willem Mengelberg, and Walter Damrosch. Of these, Damrosch, conductor of the New York Symphony Orchestra, was to prove the most significant, because it was he who, soon after the concert, proposed that Gershwin should write a piano concerto.

Rhapsody in Blue opens with one of the most striking and original effects in music. A clarinet plays a low trill and an upward scale that becomes a cheeky glissando. Kurt Dieterle remembered, 'George had written an ascending scale, and it was extremely difficult. So Ross [Gorman], who could make incredibly odd sounds with his instrument, started experimenting. Finally, he just made a whooping slide up the scale right to the top. George loved it, and that's the way it's been played ever since.'[14] From the clarinet glissando emerge, in quick succession, three ideas. The first is the clarinet's melody, demonstrative and wide ranging. The second idea is, at first, little more than a tailpiece to the clarinet solo, repeated rhythmic shapes over a held bass note. The first theme is taken up by muted trumpet, with a 'wha wha' mute. Again there is a little tailpiece, the third idea, which is another rhythmically repetitive muttering from the solo piano. The full orchestra responds to this modest piano entry (a striking idea in itself) by declaiming the opening phrase of the clarinet's theme in a brash fortissimo. The piano at first seems unaffected by this, and continues exploring the modest third idea. But soon it becomes emboldened, and quasi-improvisational phrases build up over a reiterated E in the bass, until they arrive at the first theme, now in A major. In classical terms, it would be most odd for the soloist to repeat the opening theme a semitone lower than at the start; this sort of harmonic 'drift' is one of the features that gives *Rhapsody in Blue* its unusual, rhapsodic character.

The first theme alternates with the 'tailpiece' third idea, and then, as the piano continues its solo, a fourth idea briefly appears, a series of rising phrases. More piano 'improvisation' leads into another brash *ff* orchestral statement of the first theme. The new fourth idea is pulled into it, and the trombones and horns bring the paragraph to a climax, ending with raucous flutter-tonguing trumpets. This bursts into a fifth idea, a cheerful tune on trumpets, in C major, enlivened by syncopations in piano, bassoons, and violas. As a tailpiece to this tune, the clarinet plays a jazzier version of the rhythmically repetitive second idea. Then the whole orchestra takes this idea up fortissimo, extending it into a fully fledged sixteen-bar tune. Bluesy phrases from clarinet, trumpet, and trombone (again with wha-wha mutes) form another tailpiece, and four *ff* chords propel us into a sixth idea, in G major. This is another syncopated sixteen-bar tune with bluesy harmonies in the bass and regular chords above, its second half rising up on a trombone solo. The tune is extended and builds up, until it breaks off. This has been the longest continuous orchestral passage in the piece, and its end signals the start of what, in a classical piece, might be termed the development section – though there's nothing quite so definite about this passage in the *Rhapsody*.

Throughout the orchestral tutti, the piano has played the supporting role, but now it emerges again for an extended solo. It begins playfully, then becomes meditative. Every thematic idea is considered and mulled over (except the cheerful fifth idea). When the piano suddenly breaks into a fortissimo statement of the opening theme, the orchestra is prompted to join in for a few bars. But they soon drop out, and the piano re-enters the meditative mood. The syncopated sixth idea builds to a climax and a moment of almost Lisztian cadenza. But then mysterious pianissimo chords take us to a pause. Gently, strings and woodwind launch into a new, seventh idea, in E major. This, like one of Gershwin's famous love songs in his musicals, creates the emotional core of the piece. Astonishingly, it seems that (like 'Somewhere over the rainbow' in *The Wizard of Oz*) this famous and heart-warming tune nearly got cut. At rehearsals, Gershwin feared that it would extend the piece too much. According to Dieterle, 'He felt it impeded the rhapsody's momentum. Ferdé said, "No, George – that's your best theme." He was responsible for keeping that important strain in the "Rhapsody".'[15] Although the warmth of the tune is obvious, it is subtly constructed. It is built out of just one two-bar shape that rises, drops, and rises again. In the first phrase of the tune, this shape is followed by three long notes, which each last for two bars and rise a semitone at a time, accompanied by a reiterated, murmuring pattern in the horns. This makes an eight-bar phrase. At the second phrase, the shape is followed by two long notes, so that the phrase is six bars long. And at the third phrase, the shape is immediately repeated, then followed by a wistful violin solo to make up eight bars. The murmuring accompaniment is fascinating in itself: it consists of a three-note cell that is reiterated again and again within a regular four-beat pattern, creating a gentle effect of syncopation. The whole tune is repeated fortissimo, this time ending by continuing to repeat the shape quietly. The piano takes up the murmuring pattern, and reprises the whole of the tune. This time the final bars extend with more repetitions of the shape, and arrive at an expectant pause.

The piano breaks into a rapid, accelerating toccata, which consists of the modest little third idea (with which the piano first entered) converted into an insistent repeating pattern – the original version of this idea breaks through at one point, to remind us of the link. As the piano continues its brilliant toccata, horn and trombone play the opening shape of the big tune at the new, fast tempo. All of the brass join in, building to a brilliant climax, and an expectant chord with flutter-tonguing. But we are not there yet. The piano continues alternating the third idea with the toccata patterns, the orchestra again builds to a climax and breaks off. Now, over a march beat, the piano plays the second idea in grand double octaves. These build to become full chords, and the piano, with full orchestra *fff*, break into a reprise of the opening clarinet theme. The piano remembers the second idea for one last time, in the grandest of chords, and a final crescendo brings the *Rhapsody* to a resounding end.

MIKHAIL IVANOVICH GLINKA
(1804–57)

Glinka was from a wealthy Russian family, and worked for several years as a civil servant. But he gave it up to devote himself to music, and took advantage of his financial independence to travel to the musical centres of Europe. It was while he was in Italy, immersing himself in the world of opera and trying to write in the fashionable Italian manner, that he began to sense his true vocation:

> It cost me a great deal of effort to counterfeit the Italian *Sentimento brillante*. We inhabitants of the North feel differently. With us it is either frantic jollity, or bitter tears. With us, even love, that wonderful emotion which brightens the entire universe, is always bound up with sadness. There is no doubt that our melancholy Russian songs are children of the North, perhaps owing something to the East.
>
> All the pieces written by me to please the inhabitants of Milan only served to convince me that I was not following my own path, and that I could not sincerely be an Italian. A longing for my own country led me gradually to the idea of writing in a Russian manner.

What Glinka meant by a 'Russian manner' was to have a profound effect not only on the next generation of Russian composers – Borodin, Musorgsky, Rimsky-Korsakov, Balakirev, Tchaikovsky – but right through to Stravinsky, Shostakovich, and beyond. In essence, Glinka was the first major composer to take characteristics of Russian folk song – its repetitions, terse phrases, rhythmic insistence, sometimes 'oriental' scales – together with the extremes of jollity and melancholy he saw in the Russian character, and create a musical expression of them that cut through conventional, Austro-German or Italian ways of developing extended pieces of music. It was the beginning of a genuine 'Russian accent' in music.

His chief works were his two operas: *A Life for the Tsar* (1836) and his masterpiece *Russlan and Ludmilla* (1842). They are full of vivid effects and daring contrasts, providing a 'blueprint' for Rimsky-Korsakov and later Russian composers of opera. The Overture to *Russlan and Ludmilla* is one of the virtuoso showpieces of the concert hall. But for composers of orchestral music, Glinka's importance is summed up in a short piece that he composed in 1848, *Kamarinskaya*. In it, we can hear how skilfully he performed a tricky balancing act, using his conventional classical training to create something beautifully and coherently structured out of 'folk' material.

KAMARINSKAYA

Duration: approx. 7 minutes

Kamarinskaya is one of three colourful orchestral pieces that Glinka wrote after meeting Berlioz in Paris in 1844. The two composers greatly admired each other's music. Glinka was particularly impressed by Berlioz's evocation of national character, as in the overture *Le carnaval romain* and the Hungarian March from *La damnation de Faust*, and set out to do something similar. Two of Glinka's three pieces are Spanish in flavour, but *Kamarinskaya*, composed in 1848, is emphatically Russian, and soon came to acquire a national importance to his fellow Russians that Glinka could hardly have imagined.

Tchaikovsky wrote about Glinka's *Kamarinskaya* and its influence in his diary in June 1888: 'Without intending to compose anything beyond a simple, humorous trifle, he has left us a little masterpiece, every bar of which is the outcome of enormous creative power. Half a century has passed since then, and many Russian symphonic works have been composed; we may even speak of a symphonic school. Well, the germ of all this is contained in *Kamarinskaya*, just as all of an oak tree is in an acorn. For many years to come Russian composers will drink at this source, for it will take much time and much strength to exhaust its wealth of inspiration.'[1]

Glinka's method is simple and brilliant. He takes a Russian folk tune and repeats it again and again, changing the instrumental colours, chording, harmonies, and counterpoints at each repetition. It is a technique inspired by the traditional Russian bands that used to play on festive occasions, particularly weddings, in which a fiddle-player or other instrumentalist would improvise variations on a tune. Glinka himself liked to do this in piano duet, with a friend playing the tune and Glinka improvising below. His formalization of this method in *Kamarinsaya* has been used, as Tchaikovsky predicted, by Russian composers over many years: the hypnotic repetitions in Stravinsky's *The Rite of Spring* employ what is essentially the same technique. It has often been said that the use of folk tunes presents a problem for composers of long pieces of music, because traditional tunes are complete in themselves, not susceptible to the 'development' of classical music. Glinka's technique confronts this problem head on: he makes no attempt to develop the tune, but instead presents it in ever varying contexts, like someone on a sleigh travelling through an ever-changing landscape.

Kamarinskaya is based on two traditional tunes, a gentle wedding song followed by 'Kamarinskaya', a fast dance tune of the kind often accompanied by an athletic squatting dance. Glinka himself described in his memoirs how he came to choose these two themes, and the significance of the choice: 'Quite by chance I noticed a kinship between the wedding song, "From the mountains, the high mountains", which I used to hear in the country, and the dance song, "Kamarinskaya", which everyone knows. All at once my imagination took fire and ... I wrote a piece for orchestra with the title, "A Wedding Song and a Dance Song". I can assure the reader that I was guided in composing this piece solely by my innate musical feeling, thinking neither of what goes on at weddings, nor of how our orthodox populace goes about celebrating . . .'[2] The similarity that Glinka had spotted between the two tunes was in the opening rise and fall of the slow wedding song, which, embellished, also occurs in 'Kamarinskaya'. This helps to give a sense that the two tunes belong together in Glinka's piece, even though the reason might not be obvious to the listener.

The wedding song acts as an introduction. After a portentous few bars, the strings play the tune unaccompanied. Then three variations follow. First, the woodwind embellish it with counterpoint. Then the tune moves into the bass, with counterpoints above. Then, still in the bass, it is stated fortissimo. A few bars lead to a climax, the pace increases, and the music changes key. The violins repeat a little flourish, like a fiddler announcing that he is about to start, and launch into 'Kamarinskaya'.

The tune consists of two three-bar phrases, the second of which is, apart from its upbeat, identical to the first. This little tune is repeated many times during the piece, so that it becomes hypnotic in its effect. There is a great deal of sophistication in the way Glinka varies the tune. He begins with six straightforward variations, with countermelodies sometimes above, sometimes below the tune, and the tune itself moving from treble to bass and back again. But then the tune disappears for eight variations, while the pattern of three-bar phrases comtinues, with its bass and chords – as if the fiddle-player has put down his instrument and left the band to carry on without him. Teasing variations of the melody appear, which reveal the affinity with the wedding song that started the piece. The key shifts from major to minor, the mood and pace relax, and the music returns to the wedding song itself, in its original key, with a shortened reprise of the introduction.

Flourishes from a clarinet announce the return of 'Kamarinskaya'. At first this is still in the key of the wedding song, and for several variations Glinka again teases us by leaving out the melody. With a climax and a joyous wrench of the harmony, the strings take up the tune in the 'proper' key (these changes of key are part of Glinka's subtlety as a composer – this is not just a simple set of variations). The tune is now repeated many times by the violins. But although the tune itself continues unchanged, the harmonies around it are more destabilizing than before. Sustained notes from the horns, and harmonies from the high woodwind, seem to be tugging the tune away from its key. But the violins persist, and eventually the harmonies are pulled into line to a triumphant climax (this destabilizing and resolution of harmonies is another mark of Glinka's subtlety). After the climax, the violins drop to pianissimo, their tune is interrupted by horn chords, and the music slows. There is a sudden final dash, and the piece comes to an end with an abrupt chord. You can almost see the fiddler and the band flinging down their instruments and reaching for their glasses.

EDVARD GRIEG
(1843–1907)

Grieg was the first Norwegian composer to achieve an international reputation. A fine concert pianist, who lived long enough to make a few recordings, he was one of the great pianist-composers in a line from Mozart and Beethoven through Mendelssohn and Schumann to Brahms. But, unlike these composers, he did not achieve his fame through symphonies and other major orchestral works. After Grieg had left the Leipzig Conservatory, the Danish composer Niels Gade, a friend of Schumann and Mendelssohn, encouraged him to attempt a symphony. But it turned out that Grieg's particular talent was for encapsulating a mood or a concentrated emotional narrative in a short piece. In this respect he was closest to Schumann, whose music he got to know as a student at the Conservatory. His many 'Lyric Pieces' for piano have similarities to Schumann's and Mendelssohn's short piano works.

What enabled Grieg to develop a distinctive approach to the genre was his exposure to Norwegian folk music and the Norwegian nationalist movement, which he first encountered in the 1860s. It was the young composer Rikard Nordraak who encouraged Grieg with the idea of creating distinctively Norwegian music, drawing on folk music. After the early death of Nordraak, it was Grieg who became the focus of Norwegian musical nationalism. In his many collections of short pieces, Grieg sometimes quotes actual folk tunes, but more often he reinvents through the imagination of a nineteenth-century pianist. His *Holberg Suite* and incidental music for *Peer Gynt* consist of pieces of this type, transferred to the orchestra. His only large-scale orchestral work to have achieved success is his early piano concerto, a magnificent piece that he was never able to equal in later life.

HOLBERG SUITE, OP. 40
Duration: approx. 21 minutes

Praeludium: Allegro vivace
Sarabande: Andante
Gavotte: Allegretto
Air: Andante religioso
Rigaudon: Allegro con brio

The year 1884 was the bicentenary of the writer Ludvig Holberg (1684–1754). Born in Norway but working mostly in Denmark, Holberg is celebrated for the satirical comedies that he wrote for the new Danish-language theatre in Copenhagen in the 1720s and 1730s, leading him to be known as 'The Molière of the North'. For the bicentenary celebrations Grieg was commissioned to write the Holberg Cantata for male voices. It was while he was working on it that he composed a set of piano pieces, subtitled 'From Holberg's Time: Suite in olden style'. The following year he arranged it for string orchestra, and it is in this form that it is best known, usually referred to in English as the *Holberg Suite*. It takes as its inspiration the baroque suite of Holberg's time.

The five movements are based on baroque models, and as in a baroque suite they all share the same tonality, G (G major except for the Air and the middle section of the Rigaudon, which are in G minor). The music is not pastiche, but an evocation. Late nineteenth-century composers often evoked earlier music – Tchaikovsky famously did so in his Variations on a Rococo Theme. But Grieg's *Holberg Suite* is a particularly deft example of the approach, which set a model for later composers. Echoes of it can be heard clearly in Ravel's *Le tombeau de Couperin* (indeed, Ravel went so far as to say, on a visit to Norway in 1926, 'I have never till this day written a single work that was not influenced by Grieg').[1]

The original version of the Praeludium has rapid broken-chord patterns that fit neatly under the hands of the pianist, evoking harpsichord preludes of the eighteenth century. But the patterns do not fit under the hand of a violinist, and Grieg substitutes repeated notes. This loses the baroque evocation, but replaces it with an energetic galloping rhythm that is equally effective, adding strong accents and crescendos that heighten the dramatic potential. Over these sounds a haunting melody that falls in a series of steps, with delicate flourishes and a trill. After this section is repeated, the music moves into new keys and becomes operatically stormy, with tumbling cascades and then, in complete contrast, quiet violin chords gently falling over delicate pizzicato (this is another completely new effect in the string version; in the piano original the chords simply emerge from the broken-chord pattern). A flamboyant descent brings the music back to its home key, and to the reprise, disguised by a new violin line above. The movement ends with the grandest of chords.

The orchestration of the Sarabande greatly expands the scope of the original piano version. It begins without the basses, who join in halfway through the first strain with pizzicato, bringing a firmness to the slow dance rhythm. The second half continues in similar fashion, until the melody moves to a solo cello. Then two more solo cellos join in, over a solo pizzicato bass, creating an intimate moment of cello trio. As the rest of the strings enter, they build to a spacious fortissimo, with new touches of poignancy in the harmony, before the music subsides to the conclusion.

The melody of the Gavotte begins with exactly the same shape as the Sarabande. Now it is extended in a rising sequence that gives a delightful lift to the rhythm. There are many subtle touches. Part of the charm of the opening lies in its asymmetry: the first phrase is four bars long, the second five bars. Under this opening, the first violins sustain a gentle drone on their open G string. When these bars return for the last time at the end of the Gavotte, Grieg adds a gentle offbeat pizzicato. Between the two statements of the Gavotte, the middle section is a Musette, in which the bagpipe-like drone has become persistent, with equally bagpipe-like circular patterns above (the Musette derives its name from a kind of bagpipe popular at French courts in the eighteenth century).

The Air is marked Andante religioso, but its melancholy seems more personal than that might imply. It evokes the balletic expressiveness of J. S. Bach at his most poignant. Its melody consists of a series of long held notes blossoming into ornamental arabesques. Obviously this echoes baroque ornamentation, but, more importantly, it uses the ornaments to intensify the expression as they vary in their elaboration, and as the harmonies shift underneath. There is a particularly Bach-like moment in the first half where the melody moves to the bass, as it does at some of Bach's most touching moments. In the second half, a little rocking motif becomes predominant, passing between violins and solo cello and leading to a climax. This falls gently away, the reprise of the opening is played by all the cellos, with the rocking figure continuing in the violins above, and the music builds to a final climax.

The Rigaudon is a lively French dance popular in the eighteenth century. Grieg gives its rapid figurations to solo violin and viola, with the full orchestra entering only in the final bars, as if to suggest the baroque *concerto grosso* with its solo *concertino*. The full orchestra plays a gentler middle section in G minor, which develops unexpectedly powerful harmonies in its second half. The Rigaudon is repeated, bringing the suite to an energetic conclusion.

PEER GYNT: INCIDENTAL MUSIC, OP. 23

Henrik Ibsen wrote *Peer Gynt* as a dramatic poem in 1867. It is a rambling, dizzying journey through the life of an adventurer, from his beginnings as a headstrong young farmer's son who abducts a bride on her wedding day, through travels to the kingdom of the trolls, to Morocco as a maverick businessman and Bedouin prophet, to Egypt as a historian, and back to Norway as a broken old man where he is reunited with the woman who, despite everything, has waited for him through all his years of absence. There are echoes in it of Goethe's *Faust*, Byron's *Childe Harold*, and even Cervantes's *Don Quixote* and Swift's *Gulliver's Travels*, but its mixture of fantasy, philosophy, and satire is entirely Ibsen's own. As he wrote, 'It is reckless and formless, written with no thought of the consequences – as I could only dare to write when far from my own country'[2] (Ibsen wrote it in Italy). Some of the wildness and self-willed determination of *Peer Gynt* derives from Ibsen's own character, as he himself admitted: 'Everything I have written has the closest possible connection with what I have lived through, even if it has not been my own personal experience; in every new poem or play I have aimed at my own spiritual emancipation and purification – for a man shares the responsibility and guilt of the society to which he belongs.'[3] On the other hand, when audiences and critics began to examine the allegory and satire in *Peer Gynt*, Ibsen himself tended to downplay the symbolism of Peer Gynt's life and character. He wrote to his publisher soon after the first publication of the work, 'I learn that the book has created great excitement in Norway. That does not trouble me in the least, but both there and in Denmark they have discovered more satire in it than was intended by me . . . But if the Norwegians of today recognize themselves, as it would appear they do, in the character of Peer Gynt, that is the good people's own affair.'[4]

Seven years after its first publication, Ibsen decided to revise and shorten *Peer Gynt* to make it practicable as a stage play. In January 1874 he wrote to Grieg inviting him to compose incidental music for the first production. This proved to be a major project consisting of twenty-six numbers, and it was not until eighteen months later that Grieg completed the score. The revised play, with Grieg's music, was premiered on 24 February 1876 in Christiania (Oslo). The production was an enormous success. It was performed thirty-seven times that year, and the run would have continued if the theatre had not burned down in January 1877.

Grieg's complete incidental music is rarely performed, but he extracted from it two orchestral suites in 1888 and 1891, which contain some of his best-loved music.

Suite No. 1, Op. 46
Morning Mood: Allegretto pastorale
The Death of Åse: Andante doloroso
Anitra's Dance: Tempo di Mazurka
In the Hall of the Mountain King: Alla marcia e molto marcato
Duration: approx. 15 minutes

'Morning Mood' is one of Grieg's most beautiful pieces, simple in its effect, but accomplished with great subtlety. A flute plays a tune like a folk song in the pentatonic (five-note) scale common to many musical traditions across the world. Act IV of Ibsen's play is set in Africa, but this could equally well be Norway. In either case we probably imagine a shepherd playing a pipe at dawn. The tune is echoed by an oboe, as if from the opposite hill. But this is not a simple echo: the oboe moves the melody on into a new key (something that would not happen in traditional music), and we realize that this is the beginning of an emotional journey. Passed again to flute, and back to oboe, the melody finds its way back to the original key, and the full strings sweep it away: Grieg imagined 'the sun breaking through the clouds at the first *forte*.'[5] Three times the music builds to a fortissimo, and at each climax cascading arpeggios give way to a singing cello line. As the music calms, a horn takes up the melody accompanied by the arpeggios, with distinct echoes of the 'Forest Murmurs' from Wagner's *Siegfried*. Gradually the music becomes more and more peaceful, with the tune joined by trilling birdsong, the flute echoed by a bassoon, and the piece ends as serenely as it began.

'The Death of Åse' accompanied the scene in which Peer Gynt is with his mother, Åse, as she dies. Together they remember the game they used to play when he was a child, pretending to ride on a sleigh to the mythical Soria Moria Castle. He embarks on a fantasy, in which he takes her there again, St Peter forbids her entry, but God overrules him. It is only as the music stops that Peer realizes that his mother has died. 'The Death of Åse' is even simpler than 'Morning Mood', but no less subtle. Muted strings play a series of slow four-bar phrases. Six times the phrase rises, becoming gradually louder, then four times it falls as it becomes quieter. The power of the music lies in the way the chords change. In the first rising phrase the chords are simple. But in the second phrase they twist, twice arriving at a poignant dissonance (an 'augmented sixth'). The third phrase is again consonant, the fourth contains the same dissonances, and the pattern repeats in the fifth and sixth phrases. This repetitive device is heart-rendingly effective, building to a climax made even more piercing by the fact that the power of the strings is restrained by their mutes. As the music then falls away, each part of each phrase begins with this very same dissonance, which resolves onto a simple major chord. So the tension that was gradually built towards the climax now gradually falls away.

Anitra is the daughter of a Bedouin chief. Peer Gynt is himself disguised as a Bedouin, and has been mistaken for a prophet. Anitra dances for him, and Peer is strangely fascinated. At night, he attempts to abduct her, but she tricks him out of his money and steals his horse, leaving him alone in the desert.

The dance is scored for muted violins with the rest of the strings mostly pizzicato, and with the occasional delicate touch of a triangle. 'Tempo di Mazurka' might seem an odd instruction for a Bedouin dance. But there is nothing straightforwardly logical about the juxtapositions of *Peer Gynt*, and Grieg treats the dance with a haunting delicacy that seems entirely right for this scene. The piece begins simply, but with alternation between bowed and pizzicato playing giving it subtle variety. The second half opens with the violins playing a yearning phrase in duet. Then the opening phrase of the dance returns, echoed in the violas, and rising step by step to a climax over a sustained line in the cellos. The counterpoint between violins and cellos continues into the reprise of the opening, giving it a plaintive intensity.

The Mountain King is the king of the trolls. Peer has wooed his daughter, who has brought him on the back of a giant pig to her father in the hall of the trolls. The king, thinking Peer to be a prince, expects him to marry her. But the trolls threaten to kill Peer, and they dance this increasingly wild dance. Grieg deliberately created something crudely trollish, but as he wrote to a friend, 'I literally can't bear to listen to [it] because it absolutely reeks of cow-dung, exaggerated Norwegian nationalism, and trollish self-satisfaction! But I have a hunch that the irony will be discernible!'[6] In the original version for the stage production, Grieg included a chorus of trolls, and as the piece reaches its climax, it is cut off by a shout from the king ordering them to stop.

It was one of the first numbers that Grieg composed, and the opening shape of its melody was later echoed both in Anitra's Dance and in Solveig's Song (the final movement of the second suite). The simple, three-part theme begins quietly with pizzicato cellos and basses alternating with bassoons in taking the tune, punctuated by bass drum and a menacing note on hand-stopped horns. Then pizzicato violins alternate with oboes, accompanied by offbeat chords given a shudder by the violas, as the crescendo begins and the pace starts to increase. Now the strings take up the theme, with rapidly scrubbed tremolo, and on full orchestra the savage dance accelerates to a manic climax.

Suite No. 2, Op. 55
Abduction of the Bride – Ingrid's Lament
Arabian Dance
Peer Gynt's Homecoming (Stormy Evening at Sea)
Solveig's Song
Duration: approx. 18 minutes

In Act I of *Peer Gynt*, the young wastrel Peer is mocked by his mother for his useless fantasies. If only he had played his cards right, he could have married Ingrid, the daughter of a rich farmer. Ingrid is to be married to someone else the next day, and Peer goes to the wedding to try his chances. First his eye falls on Solveig, but when he asks her to dance, she refuses, fearing the disapproval of her father. Peer gets drunk, and seizes the opportunity to abduct Ingrid and carry her into the mountains. By the following morning he has tired of her, realizing that it is Solveig he wants, and he cruelly abandons Ingrid to find her way home.

Frantic outbursts give way to a lamentation, made all the more poignant by being played by all the violins on their lowest (G-) string, shadowed by cellos and basses – Grieg comes close to Sibelius at such a moment. The lament passes to high violins, with sliding chromatic harmonies in the woodwind and the middle strings increasing the intensity. As it reaches its climax, timpani thud out a doleful rhythm, which then accelerates to two further outbursts, and a last, solemn chord.

The 'Arabian Dance' preceded Anitra's dance (see Suite No. 1) in the scene in which Peer Gynt is posing as a Bedouin. Anitra, the daughter of a Bedouin chief, together with a group of girls, dances for Peer while he drinks coffee and smokes a long pipe. The style of Grieg's dance is in the long tradition of Westernized 'Turkish' music stretching back to the eighteenth century. Drums and triangle set up a march-like rhythm, over which a pair of piccolos play a jaunty tune. The woodwind respond with a more 'Arabic' turn of phrase. As the rest of the orchestra and extra percussion join in, the music acquires a delightful energy. Part of its charm lies in the fact that many of the phrases are three bars long, rather than the four bars more usual in dances and marches. In a middle section, the violins and cellos play a sultry duet over pizzicato accompaniment. For a moment there is a charming reference back to the earlier dance, but with all the exoticism drained from it, as if Peer's Bedouin costume has slipped to reveal the Norwegian inside. Then the duet returns, with the violins high in octaves. The 'Arabic' woodwind announce the reprise of the first section. At the end, it fades to leave only the drums that began the piece.

After many years of travel and adventures, Peer is a bearded old man and has reached a state of despair. On a ship bound for Norway, a storm gathers and he is shipwrecked. 'Peer Gynt's Homecoming' begins with a fortissimo chord over which high woodwind call urgently, answered by dark, muttering clarinet and bassoon. The first part of the storm is built from these two motifs. Later, the music quietens and a flute introduces a fearful descending scale – a touch drawn from the storm in Beethoven's 'Pastoral' Symphony. This builds up to a renewal of the opening, which bursts with increased ferocity. Then the different motifs all combine. The storm dies away, and the woodwind play chords to link directly to the next movement – Grieg added this connecting passage for the suite.

At the end of Peer's exploits in the desert, culminating in his failed attempt to abduct Anitra, he discards his Bedouin costume, rejects all his life so far, and resolves to become a historian. As he reflects on the empty and faithless ways of men and the inconstancy of women, we see his faithful old love, Solveig, 'now a fair and handsome middle-aged woman', sitting spinning outside her hut in the Norwegian forest while her goats feed in the sunshine. Solveig sings of her constant faith that Peer will return: winter and spring may pass, then summer and the whole year. But one day you will come, and I shall be waiting for you as I promised. This is the best known of all Grieg's songs, and he arranged it for orchestra to create this movement in the suite. By placing it as the last movement, perhaps he intended it also to evoke the end of the play, where Peer and Solveig, both now old, are finally united, Peer buries his face in Solveig's lap, and she sings as she rocks him to sleep.

Grieg acknowledged that, in this song, 'an echo of folk song may be detected'. The verses of the song are in a minor key, and, as often in Grieg, part of the character of the melody lies in unexpected phrase lengths: each of the first two phrases is three bars long, with a chord held for a fourth bar. After this opening the song becomes more elaborate in its yearning, introducing chromatic notes and harmonies that pull further away from the folk song. Between each of the two verses, the music shifts into the major key, and the gently lilting rhythms evoke the Norwegian *Halling* dance, like a memory of happier days (in the original song, Solveig hums these sections). In Grieg's orchestration of the song for the suite, the voice part is played by muted violins that, in the second verse, rise higher and play in octaves. They are accompanied by delicate chords in strings, woodwind, and harp. After the second major-key passage, the music returns for a last time to the minor-key music that introduced the song, and a final pianissimo chord leaves the aching sense of hope hanging in the air.

PIANO CONCERTO IN A MINOR, OP. 16
Duration: approx. 30 minutes

Allegro molto moderato
Adagio
Allegro moderato molto e marcato – Presto

While he was a teenage student at the Leipzig Conservatory, Grieg heard Robert Schumann's widow, Clara, play Schumann's Piano Concerto. Ten years later, in 1868, he wrote his own piano concerto, his only major orchestral work. It takes Schumann's concerto as a model, with its intimate and poetic qualities, and adds to it a dash of virtuoso flamboyance, an admixture of tunes influenced by Norwegian folk music, and a subtle way of transforming the character of themes. The transformations and the virtuoso elements owe something to Liszt, who encouraged Grieg and suggested changes to the manuscript. Despite these diverse influences, the result is a coherent masterpiece. It is a shame that, though he wrote a number of substantial chamber works, Grieg never followed up this orchestral success in later life. He continued to refine the orchestration of the concerto throughout his life, and it is in its final form that we know it today.

The opening is one of the most dramatic of any concerto: from silence a pianissimo drum roll crescendos to a crashing chord of A minor on full orchestra. The piano simultaneously makes a grand entrance, as in Schumann's concerto, and Grieg develops this idea into a bold cadenza more reminiscent of the opening of Beethoven's 'Emperor' Concerto. At the same time, the falling intervals of the piano's first entry are suggestive of Norwegian folk song (a semitone and a major third, a melodic shape Grieg was particularly fond of). This melodic shape might seem just like a rhetorical flourish, but it is a cell that recurs in different forms throughout the concerto. The flamboyant opening is followed by an overflowing succession of themes. First the woodwind play a tune that begins as a gentle dance and then expands lyrically upwards. The piano takes this up, adding a rich texture of arpeggios, and then breaks into a faster, more brilliant idea, which, in its falling intervals, harks back to the opening cadenza. This too has a lyrical tailpiece, which leads into the singing second main theme, played by the cellos (Grieg's 1872 manuscript reveals, rather shockingly, that at that stage it was to be played on trumpet). Again the piano takes up the melody and elaborates it meditatively. This builds up to a climax, and the full orchestra enters, rounding off the first section of the movement with what might seem to be new material, but is once again drawn from the falling first phrase of the piano's opening cadenza, followed by the shape of the woodwind's first theme.

As this tutti fades away, what follows is a development section that, in its emotional logic and brevity, is worthy of any of the great classical composers. First, the opening woodwind theme is taken up by flute and horn, but now with added melancholy in its harmonies, underpinned by restless arpeggios in the piano. The same theme turns suddenly more urgent, with the piano leading it on through new keys and culminating in fortissimo cascades of notes, and a return to the forceful descending octaves that opened the concerto. Soon the energy ebbs away, and the woodwind lead in the reprise of their opening theme. The succession of themes proceeds much as before, but now culminates in a substantial cadenza. This takes the woodwind's opening theme, starting pianissimo, and builds it up to a magnificent climax (it is easy to hear how this cadenza might have influenced Rachmaninoff). Eventually the great tumult dies away, and the orchestra enters quietly. The piano joins them, builds up again, and ends with a return to the grand octaves with which the concerto opened.

The slow movement is in the key of D flat major – unusually remote from the A minor of the outer movements. The effect is that we feel we are entering quite a different world as the violins begin their beautiful, expansive theme. The form of the movement could not be simpler. The violins sing a melody, the piano plays an interlude, and then repeats the violin melody. But within this simple structure there is a great deal of subtlety. The shape of the opening phrase is built from a semitone and a rising third. This is an inversion of the shape that opened the concerto (a falling semitone and third). Is this a deliberate hidden reference? An analyst would say so. What is certain is that the piano's first entry – a wistful falling cascade – is like a distant dream of the concerto's opening cadenza. This is followed by a gradual build-up, after which the piano takes up the violin's melody, now transformed into a grand and heroic utterance. A French horn plays a prominent role, pulling the piano towards a more nostalgic mood, until the movement ends quietly.

Dancing woodwind chords link back to A minor, and, with a dashing flourish from the piano, we are into the finale. This has the characteristic kicking accents of the ancient Norwegian dance, the *Halling*, with patterns suggestive of traditional fiddle-playing. The dance is set going by the piano, and taken up fortissimo by the orchestra. The piano continues with a second strain of the dance, more intricate than before. After a moment of calm, the dance builds to a pitch of wild intensity, the piano part becoming more and more virtuosic.

An orchestral transition ebbs away, and a solo flute plays another gentle, folk-like melody (this too incorporates the opening shape of falling semitone and third). This is decorated and extended by the piano, with more of Grieg's beautifully nostalgic harmonic subtleties. Then the opening dance sequence is reprised. This time, it culminates in a Lisztian virtuoso piano cadenza. The dance continues, but now in a lively three-time (ending a concerto with a burst of three-time is a tradition stretching back to Mozart). The excitement builds, and at the climax Grieg reveals a final Lisztian transformation. The gentle flute tune from the middle of the movement has now become a great peroration, and it is with this grand effect that the concerto comes to a close.

GEORGE FRIDERIC HANDEL
(GEORG FRIEDRICH HÄNDEL)
(1685–1759)

Of all the composers from continental Europe who settled in England over the centuries, Handel was the one who achieved the greatest celebrity, becoming established as a quintessentially 'English' composer. He first became famous as a writer of operas in Germany and Italy, then moved to England in 1712 and never left, developing an enormous reputation as a composer of operas, church music, and the type of dramatic religious music known as oratorio. In recent decades, Handel's operas have increasingly been staged again after a long period of neglect. But it was his oratorios that left the most lasting impression after his death. They formed the highlights of the great Handel Commemoration held in Westminster Abbey and The Pantheon, London, in 1784, twenty-five years after his death, at the instigation of King George III. *Messiah*, performed in monumental style by mass choirs and orchestras, became the mainstay of every choral festival in Britain through the nineteenth and on to the mid-twentieth century. In the late twentieth century, the early music revival restored this and his other oratorios to a scale, and liveliness, more likely to be recognized by Handel and his contemporaries.

Handel also wrote a large body of instrumental music: sonatas for domestic use, and concertos and suites for public concerts, including his two famous works composed for royal occasions, the *Water Music* and the *Music for the Royal Fireworks*. Many of Handel's concertos were composed for performance in the intervals of his own oratorios. These include organ concertos that Handel himself performed, and two sets of *concerti grossi*. The first set was a compilation by his publisher rather than a new composition, but the second set of twelve concertos, published as Opus 6, is largely new, and is a wonderfully inventive and varied group. The concertos represent Handel's response to the Italian *concerti grossi* that were then fashionable. Handel was always ready to take advantage of the latest trend, but, being a consummate musician, he could be guaranteed to make something highly original and personal out of the genre.

Concerti Grossi, Op. 6, Nos 1–12, HWV 319–330

Durations: each concerto 11–16 minutes

In 1734, Handel's publisher, John Walsh, issued as Handel's Opus 3 a set of six concertos compiled and arranged from his existing works. The *concerto grosso* had become a popular genre following the appearance of Corelli's Concertos, Opus 6, in 1714, and it was natural that Walsh would wish to take advantage of the fashion. Handel himself frequently reused his music, and although he may have had no hand in Walsh's edition of his 'concertos', he is not known to have objected. Handel's run of success as a composer of Italian opera was coming to an end, through a combination of competition and changes in fashion, and so he transferred his energies to the composing of English oratorios. As an added attraction, Handel took to performing organ concertos during his oratorios, and in 1738, Walsh published a set of them as Handel's Opus 4. It was a logical step for Handel to follow with his own original set of *concerti grossi*.

He completed the set of twelve by the end of October 1739, and Walsh published them as Handel's Opus 6, in a subscription edition. This was a publication of the highest prestige, whose subscribers included members of the royal family. Four of the concertos were entirely new – Nos 2, 3, 6, and 10. No. 11 and two movements of No. 9 were based on existing organ concertos, and the others were a mixture of new and reworked material. The result is a set of brilliant and varied concertos, far superior to the Opus 3 compilation, and more than worthy to stand beside Corelli's famous Opus 6. As Charles Burney put it, 'Handel sports with a band, and turns it to innumerable unexpected accounts, of which neither Corelli nor Geminiani had ever the least want or conception.'[1] The style of the movements is extremely varied, including French Overtures, fugues, English, French, and Italian dances, movements almost like operatic arias, and sets of variations. Handel composed the entire collection in little more than a month, and they were first performed during his oratorios at the theatre in Lincoln's Inn Fields, London, over the 1739–40 season.

The set of concertos includes many borrowings from Handel's own works and those of other composers. This was entirely normal practice in the eighteenth century, when the musical world shared material freely without the modern obsession with 'originality' (or the modern protection of copyright). The concertos are scored for strings with basso continuo: that is, a bass instrument with harpsichord or organ (or both) filling out the chords indicated by figures. As in Corelli's concertos, the strings are divided between a *concertino* group (two solo violins and cello) and the *ripieno* (full orchestra). Handel himself also added oboes when they were available, but they are not included in the published scores.[2]

CONCERTO NO. 1 IN G MAJOR

A tempo giusto – Allegro – Adagio – Allegro – Allegro

The opening of this first concerto immediately shows how far Handel has travelled from his Italian models. Stately passages alternate with elegant, sighing phrases from the solo *concertino*. So far, so conventional. But then the harmonies take a surprising turn, as if this is to develop into a much longer movement. There is a sudden hush, the dotted rhythms lose their confidence, and the music darkens to a series of sombre chords, ending in suspense. Unsurprisingly, this is taken from a dramatic work, an early draft of the overture to Handel's opera *Imeneo*, on which he was working at the time. Burney vividly expresses the impression of this movement on a listener of the late eighteenth century: 'Nor did I ever know so much business done in so short a time; that movement contains but thirty-four bars, and yet nothing seems left unsaid; and though it begins with so much pride and haughtiness, it melts, at last, into softness; and, where it modulates into a minor key, seems to express fatigue, languor, and faintness.'[3]

The second movement springs into life with a jaunty melody over one of Handel's typical walking basses (a favourite device of Corelli). Within the vigorous mood there is a great deal of lively interplay between different elements, and the journey sounds almost like a prototype miniature symphony movement.

The Adagio, in E minor, begins with the two solo violins in solemn counterpoint over a repeated, tiptoeing phrase in the cello. This alternates with stately passages on full orchestra. Eventually, the tiptoeing bass is satisfyingly incorporated into the stately music. Declamatory final bars take another surprising turn of harmony, preparing for a return to G major in the next movement.

The fourth movement is a playful fugue, whose subject is announced by the solo violin. The playfulness extends not just to the subject itself, but to the way in which Handel treats the conventions of fugue. Instead of pursuing the subject rigorously, he throws in new ideas to create a series of episodes that alternate with the main fugal business. At the end, there is a sudden pause, followed by two final bars pianissimo – a delightful ending to a movement that never takes itself seriously.

The final Allegro releases all this playfulness into an energetic jig in two parts, each repeated. It draws on a harpsichord piece by Domenico Scarlatti, No. 2 of his *Essercizi per Gravicembalo*, which had recently been published in London (Handel quotes another of these pieces in the fifth concerto).

CONCERTO NO. 2 IN F MAJOR
Andante larghetto – Allegro – Largo – Allegro, ma non troppo

The opening Andante larghetto is flowing and serene, with the voices of the solo trio occasionally calling like shepherds from the mountainside. At the end is a series of three Adagio phrases that seem to invite some intervening decoration from one or more of the soloists.

The second movement is particularly tricky. The soloists announce a pointed little figure that passes between the two violins and is then pursued relentlessly throughout the entire movement in an almost obsessive manner.

The Largo alternates two contrasted elements. The first has bold dotted rhythms, with the *concertino* answering the *ripieno*. The second is a flowing idea with rich harmonies.

The last movement starts off like an energetic fugue. But this turns out to be just the first of two ideas that, once again, alternate. The second idea is a simple pattern of rising notes over gently pulsating chords. When the fugal section returns for a third appearance, we discover that the rising pattern of the second idea was designed to fit with the fugue subject, and the two combine to bring the concerto to an end.

CONCERTO NO. 3 IN E MINOR
Larghetto – Andante – Allegro – Polonaise – Allegro, ma non troppo

The concerto opens with the solemn tread of a sarabande, alternating *ripieno* and *concertino* – it could almost be Purcell.

The Purcell-like boldness continues into the Andante. This is a fugue on a subject reminiscent of 'And with his stripes we are healed' from *Messiah* (which followed two years later).

Its fourth note creates a clash with the counter-subject until it resolves on the fifth note – this is surprising enough today, and must have been shocking to eighteenth-century listeners.

Following two Purcell-like movements, the Allegro could almost be Vivaldi. After an opening of sturdy octaves, the violinist of the *concertino* emerges with elaborate figuration, as if trying to turn this into a violin concerto. But the solo episodes are outnumbered by the material for full orchestra, as if Handel is once again playing with our expectations.

Handel describes the fourth movement as a 'Polonaise', but it has nothing of the traditional character of that dance. Instead it is like a rather stately minuet, with a hint of something more rustic in the drone bass with which it begins.

The brief finale is in the metre of a jig, but with rather a serious demeanour and one or two surprising harmonies. It leaves us feeling that, throughout the concerto, Handel has been determined to keep us guessing.

CONCERTO NO. 4 IN A MINOR
Larghetto affettuoso – Allegro – Largo, e piano – Allegro

'Affettuoso' means 'affectionate'. The caressing sighs of Handel's theme dominate the movement, increasing in poignancy as the music develops and moves through different keys, sometimes with surprisingly disorienting harmonies.

The second movement is a fugue. The theme is bold and energetic, and Handel sustains this character unflinchingly through a surprisingly long movement. Just as he might be in danger of running out of ideas, Handel once more introduces new twists of harmony, together with moments of dialogue between *concertino* and *ripieno*, and maintains the interest right to the end.

The third movement is one of those simple, sublime movements for which Handel is famous. Over a walking bass, the two violin parts sing a duet in solemn counterpoint, their harmonies discreetly enriched by the violas.

The final movement is a remarkable example of Handel's genius for reinvention. He takes an aria, 'É si vaga del tuo bene' ('She cares so much for your happiness'), from the opera on which he was working, *Imeneo*, and creates from it an instrumental movement that is more dramatic than the aria. Both versions open with a theme that insistently repeats short, edgy phrases. In the opera, these introduce a fairly conventional da capo aria. But in the concerto, Handel builds the whole Allegro out of this opening material, to create a movement that seems driven almost obsessively. There are occasional interventions of the solo *concertino*, as if to remind us of the entries of the singer, but part of the obsessional effect relies on the whole orchestra persisting most of the time. Once again, there are surprises of harmony and mood, including, near the end, two unexpectedly hushed moments, but the overwhelming impression is of music of concentrated seriousness and power, to bring one of the finest of Handel's Opus 6 to a close.

CONCERTO NO. 5 IN D MAJOR
Ouverture – Allegro – Presto – Largo – Allegro – Minuet

Handel's title 'Ouverture' for the first movement reveals that this is a French overture – Charles Burney considered it 'the most spirited and characteristic of all the music written by HANDEL or any other composer, on Lulli's model of Opera Overture'.[4] It is a more dramatic rewriting of the first part of the overture to Handel's 'Ode for Saint Cecilia's Day', composed shortly before the concertos. That, in turn, bears a striking resemblance to a Courante from one of Gottlieb Muffat's recently published harpsichord suites, *Componimenti Musicali*. The assertive flourishes in dotted rhythm dominate the whole movement, climaxing in a descent of wall-to-wall trills that land on a surprising harmonic shift. The mood is wonderfully confident and celebratory – a brilliant contrast to the stern preceding concerto.

The Allegro is an energetic movement that, like many a second movement of an 'Ouverture', begins as a fugue and then becomes only loosely contrapuntal, with alternations between *ripieno* and *concertino*. This was originally the second part of the overture to the same Ode.

The Presto, in a rapid three-time, sounds almost like a much later symphonic scherzo as its busy figurations develop. By contrast, the following Largo in B minor looks firmly back to Corelli, with the two solo violins alternating with the *ripieno* in a duet of serene counterpoint darkened by touches of plangency.

The fifth movement is even more forward looking than the scherzo-like Presto. Burney (writing nearly fifty years later) described this Allegro as 'a very early specimen of the symphonic style of Italy', its subject 'modern, marked and pleasing'.[5] A pattern of rapidly repeated notes, which first occurs as a passing comment, eventually comes to dominate the movement, to exciting effect. What makes this more than just an effect is the firm progress of the harmonies that underpin the repeated notes: as Burney put it, 'the base accompaniment of his iterations [is] bold and pleasing'. It is difficult to imagine the movement having been conceived for anything but orchestra. Yet Handel's starting point was No. 23 of Domenico Scarlatti's harpsichord pieces, *Essercizi per Gravicembalo* (he had already quoted No. 2 in the first concerto). It is the rapid repeated notes, newly added by Handel, that transform the piece.

Handel finishes the concerto with the minuet that ended his overture to the 'Ode for Saint Cecilia's Day'. It is in the simple, elegant style for which Handel was (and is) so much admired. The first playing of the Minuet is followed by two variations. In the first, a running bass supports the melody, and in the second, the melody itself is elaborated.

CONCERTO NO. 6 IN G MINOR

Larghetto e affetuoso – Allegro, ma non troppo – Musette – Allegro – Allegro

The concerto opens with a solemn movement in slow three-time, like a sarabande. As it begins, Handel's listeners would have thought themselves in the familiar world of Corelli's concertos. But four phrases later there is an unexpected harmonic shock, more like Purcell. The movement develops at much greater length than the conventional first movement, taking on a quality of tragic nobility.

The second movement is a terse fugue. Its theme falls through a chromatic scale, then rises through another, creating a disorientating effect until the phrase is resolved. Burney was most struck by this fugue subject, 'which is so unobvious and difficult to work, that no composer of ordinary abilities, in this learned species of writing, would have ventured to meddle with it, if such an unnatural series of sounds had occurred to him'.[6]

Burney was also full of praise for the following Musette in E flat, writing that it 'was always in favour with the composer himself, as well as the public; for I well remember, that HANDEL frequently introduced it between the parts of his Oratorios, both before and after publication'.[7] Handel's most familiar musette is the serene 'Pastoral Symphony' in *Messiah*, where its bagpipe-like drone evokes a rustic scene. In this concerto movement, composed two years earlier, the genre is developed into something far more wide-ranging. It begins with the violins, low and sonorous over a drone, intoning a theme that mingles stylized bagpipe flourishes with hymn-like solemnity. This theme recurs, as in a rondo, interleaved with a series of episodes. In the first, the pastoral mood continues, as soloists and the *ripieno* answer each other. In the second episode, the rhythm is enlivened with 'Scotch snaps', first in the violins and then in the bass, while a more sustained line creates the gentlest of counterpoints. A third episode moves into C minor, with a sudden surge of energy. The violins vie with each other in an exchange of lively figuration, as if they have suddenly remembered that this is a concerto. This makes it all the more touching when the bagpipe theme, together with the Scotch snaps, returns, bringing the movement to a serene close.

The following Allegro returns to G minor with the brisk energy of a Vivaldi violin concerto. But at the point where one would expect the solo violin to enter, the orchestra continues. From time to time, the solo violin does step forward with some elaborate figurations, but these seem oddly incidental to a movement that is overwhelmingly orchestral.

For the final Allegro, all the violins combine in a single line, over simple viola and bass parts. This is a sturdy dance in three-time, with a rugged – in some performances even truculent – character.

CONCERTO NO. 7 IN B FLAT MAJOR
Largo – Allegro – Largo, e piano – Andante – Hornpipe

The seventh concerto is the only one of the set in which the full orchestra plays throughout – there are no solo passages for the *concertino*.

It opens with a brief Largo in which Handel uses the lowest range of the violin to create rich sonorities. This is followed by an unusually playful fugue. The theme consists of a single note repeated at increasing frequency: twice in the first bar, four times in the second, and eight times in the third, after which the spell is broken and it breaks into an ongoing pattern. The effect is tongue-in-cheek, but Handel develops this whimsical idea into a fugue of determined energy.

The Largo, e piano is unusually contrapuntal for a Handel slow movement, with the two violin parts weaving around each other, and the bass also drawn in, creating a rich harmonic tapestry.

The Andante is more straightforwardly melodic. The elegant opening theme gives way to a second idea that is dominated by chains of sighing pairs of notes over a simple accompaniment of repeated chords. Shifting harmonies create a somewhat floating, unpredictable effect. The two ideas alternate through the movement until, at the end, the sighing pairs of notes are drawn into the final reprise of the first theme.

The final Hornpipe is a most intriguing take on an English dance. Traditional three-time hornpipes often feature cross-rhythms, but Handel peppers the entire piece with syncopations and extended phrases, so that it acquires the sort of rhythmic sophistication more often associated with baroque courantes (as in Handel's own harpsichord suites). Handel based the piece on a Hornpipe from one of Gottlieb Muffat's *Componimenti Musicali* for harpsichord, but took the process of 'courantization' much further than Muffat.

CONCERTO NO. 8 IN C MINOR
Allemande – Grave – Andante allegro – Adagio – Siciliana – Allegro

The opening movement is a greatly extended version of an Allemande from one of Handel's harpsichord suites. Its opening phrase is soon taken over by the bass, where it provides a foundation for the violins' elaboration above. The music has a conventionally elegant, courtly style. But at the end of each half of the dance Handel subverts the comfortable impression with a harmonic shock: twice the cadence lands on a surprising chord, provoking a timid echo of the opening phrase before the music reaches its resolution.

Strangely dramatic chords introduce the slow but brief Grave, in which soloists and *ripieno* alternate. This is followed by a lively movement, whose pointed flourishes over a walking bass are taken from a vocal quartet in the first act of Handel's opera, *Agrippina* (composed in Venice in 1709, it had never been heard in England). While the walking bass continues, the solo violins introduce a duet of simple counterpoint. These two ideas at first alternate, and later intermingle with characteristic subtlety.

The poignant Adagio quotes one of the most beautiful of Handel's operatic arias, with which much of his audience in London would have been familiar: Cleopatra's lament 'Piangerò la sorte mia' from *Giulio Cesare (Julius Caesar)*.

The gentle rhythmic swing of the Siciliana has a pastoral atmosphere, but its minor key gives it a melancholy tinge. The three soloists of the *concertino* alternate with the full orchestra in a gentle conversation. As the dance seems to be nearing its end, the violins introduce running passages that re-energize it. But when the simple opening theme returns, it stops in its tracks. There is a series of pianissimo chords, as if the music has become lost. Eventually, strength returns, and a last strain of the theme brings the movement to a confident close.

The final movement is a quirky Allegro, a dance in three-time whose phrases promise to be straightforward, but are unbalanced by rhythms that never do quite what we expect.

CONCERTO NO. 9 IN F MAJOR
Largo – Allegro – Larghetto – Allegro – Minuet – Gigue

The opening Largo is little more than a succession of chords, with sudden contrasts of piano and forte and fragments of melody with dramatic leaps, accompanied by harmonic surprises. It sounds very much like the opening of an operatic aria, perhaps with the heroine alone, struggling to come to terms with tragic developments. But, as far as scholars have been able to determine, it was newly composed.

The second and third movements are based on two movements of Handel's Organ Concerto in F major, HWV 295, known as 'The Cuckoo and the Nightingale', though extensively reworked. In the Allegro, the full strings of the *ripieno* alternate with the soloists of the *concertino* in charming dialogue. The 'cuckoo' calls of the original are replaced by simple repeated notes, echoing between first and second violins (still quite bird-like), and the nightingale-like effects in the solo organ have been replaced by more conventional concerto figurations in the solo first violin. Later in the movement these are taken up by all the violins to create the climax of the movement.

The Larghetto has the lilting rhythm of a siciliano (as in the eighth concerto). But here Handel puts an offbeat emphasis in the second half of the bar, creating a touch of hesitation, and making the metre ambiguous. The ambiguity is resolved as we get used to the rhythm, and this is part of the charm of the movement.

The fourth and fifth movements are taken from the newly completed overture to *Imeneo*. The Allegro is a delightful fugue. Its energetic theme bustles away for three bars of continuous semiquavers, creating a subject quite unsuitable for a conventional fugue. And indeed, after its second entry Handel soon discards most of the semiquavers, and concentrates on the vigorous opening figure.

The Minuet is in the minor, giving it a delicate melancholy. Only in its final strain does it break into the major – an unusual and striking effect.

The concerto ends with a newly composed Gigue, set going by the solo *concertino*. It begins very much like the Giga that concludes the last concerto in Corelli's Opus 6 set. But what makes this thoroughly Handelian is the subtle way in which the parts interact as the movement develops, so that a piece that is straightforwardly cheerful is also satisfying at a deeper level.

CONCERTO NO. 10 IN D MINOR
Ouverture – Air – Allegro – Allegro – Allegro moderato

As far as we know, this concerto was newly composed throughout, and it is one of the finest of the set. It is in the style of a classic French suite, a genre most familiar through J. S. Bach's Orchestral Suites, and consisting of a French overture and a sequence of dances. The 'Ouverture' is formed of two movements. The first is in the grand French style, with flurries of notes in sharp dotted rhythms, and a satisfying progression of harmonies. This leads straight into an Allegro, a brilliant movement in fugal style, full of vigour and playful counterpoint, ending in six slow bars with Purcell-like touches of poignant harmony.

The Air is gentle and sad, in stately three-time. Again, it has echoes of Purcell's theatre music. It is followed by an Allegro in the style of an Allemande. This is another movement full of playful counterpoint, and with a lightness of rhythm that keeps it dancing.

The fourth movement is a more elaborate Allegro, in which the full *ripieno* and the solo *concertino* alternate, passing back and forth several different ideas to create a vigorous contrapuntal dialogue.

For the final Allegro moderato, Handel breaks from D minor into D major. This is a movement of sunny charm, the first Allegro in the concerto to shed elaborate counterpoint in favour of a simple, dancing style (again, it could easily take its place in one of Purcell's theatre scores). The two parts of the dance are repeated. Then Handel plays the whole movement once more, elaborating it with pairs of repeated notes (in a French suite, such an elaborated repeat is often called a 'Double').

CONCERTO NO. 11 IN A MAJOR
Andante larghetto, e staccato – Allegro – Largo, e staccato – Andante – Allegro

Four of the five movements of this concerto are shared with the Organ Concerto in A major, HWV 296, which Handel had recently composed. The first movement opens with a vigorous theme made up of dotted rhythms and leaps. Throughout the movement this alternates with a contrasting idea, in which repeated notes creep upwards, semitone by semitone. In later occurrences, the rate of these repetitions multiplies dramatically. Their transfer from solo organ to violins is particularly successful – they could have stepped out of Vivaldi's *Four Seasons* (Charles Burney described this movement as 'uncommonly wild and capricious for the time when it was composed').[8]

The second movement (which is not in the organ concerto) is a short fugue. The theme, in bold quavers, begins on second violins, and is joined in its second half by rapid interjections on violas and cellos. This combination of two elements gives the fugue unstoppable energy. Towards the end, the energy is increased still further, as the quavers of the theme break into semiquavers.

The Largo, e staccato is no more than a brief introduction to the fourth movement (in the organ concerto these two are reversed, so that the Largo introduces the final movement). The Andante is a dance in a gentle three-time. Its theme seems a prime example of Handel's command of elegant simplicity, but is really an example of Handel spotting elegant simplicity: it is quoted from the third sonata of *Frische Clavier Früchte* ('Fresh keyboard fruits') by Johann Kuhnau, J. S. Bach's predecessor as Cantor at St Thomas, Leipzig. In a series of episodes, the solo first violin breaks into triplet figurations, and finally into semiquavers. The charm of the movement lies in the way that the tread of the dance is never lost, and the gentle original theme is always ready to restore calm after these flights of fancy.

The final movement is in an Italian concerto style reminiscent of Vivaldi. It opens with a forthright theme, four bars long, which recurs in varied form throughout the movement. This is interspersed with solo passages, sometimes in quick repartee, at other times in extended virtuoso figuration. One episode moves to a minor key, creating a sixteen-bar middle section, after which the whole of the earlier part of the movement is repeated.

CONCERTO NO. 12 IN B MINOR
Largo – Allegro – Larghetto, e piano – Largo – Allegro

The final concerto opens with a movement of subtle ambiguity. It has the traditional dotted rhythms of a French Overture, but they are contrasted dramatically with moments of meditation.

The Allegro is one of Handel's most brilliant movements. It could almost be Vivaldi, with its vivacious interplay between soloists and full orchestra, and its restless energy never flags for a moment.

The Larghetto, e piano is one of the most renowned of Handel's movements, a sonorous melody in a gentle three-time over a steadily treading bass, with a beautifully interwoven viola part filling out the harmonies. It is followed by a 'Variatio', in which the bass breaks into walking quavers, and then the quavers move into the melody itself.

A brief Largo, with poignant harmonies, leads into the final Allegro. This is a fugue on a lively, even impudent, theme made up entirely of dotted rhythms. As it proceeds, its energy is enlivened further by running triplets. Touchingly, Handel took the first two bars of the theme of this fugue from a Suite in B minor by Friedrich Wilhelm Zachow, the teacher who had first nurtured his talent in his home city of Halle.

WATER MUSIC
Duration: approx. 55 minutes

In 1714, George, Prince-Elector of Hanover, succeeded to the British throne as King George I following the death of Queen Anne. He was a contentious figure from the start. There were fifty or more relatives of Queen Anne who had a stronger claim to the succession, but they were all Roman Catholics. A recent British law banned Catholics from the throne, and so George became king. On the day of the coronation there were riots across England, and the following year a rebellion attempted unsuccessfully to have George replaced by the Catholic James Francis Edward Stuart, Queen Anne's half-brother. Quite apart from the contested succession, George was not a figure who inspired popular support. His command of English was poor, and he was reluctant to speak it. He had no interest in pageantry and disliked appearing in public. Furthermore, he was increasingly in conflict with his son, the Prince of Wales, who encouraged political opponents of the king.

It was against this background that it was suggested to the king that, in order to enhance his public image, one of the royal progresses in the summer of 1717 should take the form of a grand procession up the River Thames on a royal barge. Handel was asked to provide music for the occasion. He was well known to the king: Handel had been employed by George at the court in Hanover from 1710. His contract there had allowed him extensive periods of travel, but when Handel decided to remain in London he was dismissed (the reasons for the abrupt dismissal are not entirely clear). Nevertheless, George retained a love of Handel's music, continued the pension that had been paid him by Queen Anne, and regularly attended his operas in London.

This grand event took place on 17 July 1717, and was reported two days later in the *Daily Courant*:

> On Wednesday Evening, at about 8, the King took Water at Whitehall in an open Barge ... And went up the River towards Chelsea. Many other Barges with Persons of Quality attended, and so great a Number of Boats, that the whole River in a manner was cover'd; a City Company's barge was employ'd for the Musick, wherein were 50 instruments of all sorts, who played all the way from Lambeth (while the Barges drove with the Tide without Rowing, as far as Chelsea) the finest Symphonies, compos'd express for this Occasion, by Mr Hendel; which his Majesty liked so well, that he caus'd it to be plaid over three times in going and returning. At Eleven his Majesty went a-shore at Chelsea, where a Supper was prepar'd, and then there was another very fine Consort of Musick, which lasted till 2; after which, his Majesty came again into his Barge, and return'd the same Way, the Musick continuing to play until he landed.[9]

A letter from a representative of the Prussian court in London confirms the number of musicians, and adds that they 'played on all kinds of instruments, to wit trumpets, horns, hautboys [oboes], bassoons, German flutes, French flutes [recorders], violins and basses'. He also confirms that the music was repeated three times, 'although each performance lasted an hour – namely twice before and once after supper', and that the weather 'was all that could be desired for the festivity'.[10]

Handel's music was an immense success, circulated in numerous manuscript copies during the eighteenth century, and it remains his most popular instrumental work to this day.

Unusually for Handel, no autograph score survives. Details of the original ordering of the music are uncertain. There are twenty or more pieces (depending on how you count the pairs of dances), most of them in one of three keys, F, D, and G (major and minor). This suggests a grouping of the pieces in three suites, one in each of those keys, and recordings of the work are often divided in this way for convenience. This has the effect of separating the different instrumentations. The 'suite' in F, by far the longest group, contains all the pieces with horns but not trumpets. Horns were a rarity in England at this date, and would probably have been played by Bohemian musicians who specialized in the instrument. The group in D has all the pieces with trumpets – D major was the most common key for trumpets in England. The group in G has flute and recorder, but not horns or trumpets. This quiet ensemble would have been rather lost outdoors on the water, and is perhaps part of the 'very fine Consort of Musick' that was played during the king's supper.

However, the earliest manuscript copy, which dates from within two years of the original performance, begins with the sequence of (mostly) F major pieces, and then interleaves the trumpet pieces in D with the quiet pieces in G. Perhaps, as scholars have suggested, this was the original order, but it is impossible to know. To complicate matters further, two movements in D, with trumpets, also exist in a version in F with horns but no trumpets. So it is possible to include these two movements in either 'suite'.[11] But we do not really have to worry about these different possibilities. Handel would surely have laughed at any idea of establishing a fixed or 'authentic' form for his music, particularly music composed for a ceremonial event lasting several hours. We are therefore free to take movements from the *Water Music* in any selection that makes musical sense and suits the occasion.

The descriptions that follow are grouped in the three notional suites in F, D, and G. The column on the right of the list indicates the position of each movement in the earliest manuscript, which is also the order followed in the complete Handel Edition of 1886.

Suite in F, HWV 348

Overture: Largo – Allegro	(1)
Adagio e staccato	(2)
Allegro	(3)
Andante	(4)
Presto [?]	(5)
Air	(6)
Minuet for the French Horn	(7)
Bourrée	(8)
Hornpipe	(9)
[Andante]	(10)

Suite in D, HWV 349

[Allegro]	(11)
Alla Hornpipe	(12)
Trumpet Minuet	(22)
Lentement	(16)
Bourrée	(17)

Suite in G, HWV 350
[Minuet]   (13)
[Rigaudons I and II]   (14 and 15)
Minuet   (18)
Minuets I and II   (19)
Country Dances I and II   (20 and 21)

Suite in F

Handel begins with what could broadly be called a French Overture. But its opening Largo has, instead of the dotted rhythms of most French Overtures, a persistent pattern of skittering upbeats, which, together with the harmonies, evokes the great Purcell. The Allegro begins as a fugue, first on two solo violins, and then with full orchestra, including oboes and bassoons but not yet horns. Passages of loosely fugal writing alternate with passages in which an oboe joins the two violin soloists. Later, the violinists break into playful semiquavers, which are then taken up by the orchestra. This part of the overture is much more in the mould of the composer who most influenced Handel's concerto-writing: Corelli.

The second movement, Adagio e staccato, consists of an oboe solo accompanied by string chords – the 'staccato' of the heading presumably refers to these chords, not to the solo. The oboe part is written as a simple succession of melodic patterns, most of them falling. An oboist of Handel's day would have understood the part as a framework on which to build a more elaborate melody. There is a particularly beautiful moment halfway through when the violins break away from their staccato chords to play an overlapping sequence of falling shapes, to which the oboe then responds.

The next Allegro brings in the pair of horns for the first time. Their calls, with repeated notes and trills, immediately evoke military and hunting scenes, and the entire movement is based on them. In the days before horns had valves, they could not modulate to different keys without changing crooks (sections of tubing). Handel is a master of the art of enlivening the music with subtle invention while staying close to the key (F major). Oboes and bassoons alternate with the horns, and the movement is punctuated by passages for full orchestra. After one of these passages, there is a delightful moment when the melody moves to the bassoon in unison with violins and violas. A little later, just as we might begin to tire of the familiar material, Handel suddenly breaks into the syncopations of a hornpipe, and this injection of new energy sparks off a cascade of running semiquavers, not just in the violins but also two octaves below in bassoons and cellos.

The Andante moves into D minor, and the horns are silent so that the music can modulate freely into different keys. The movement starts as a trio for two oboes and bassoon. The strings begin to repeat the opening, and the oboes and bassoon join them a bar later, holding notes over the chord changes to create poignant suspensions – a favourite device of Corelli. The middle of the movement modulates briefly to F major, with strings and wind playing the opening phrase in overlapping echoes. When the music returns to D minor, this overlapping continues, and then the violins rise higher to create a climax of yet more poignant harmonic suspensions. After the Andante, the preceding Allegro is often repeated, as suggested in some of the early sources.

The fifth movement has the marking 'Presto' in one eighteenth-century source, but the tricky rhythmic details and trills in the horn parts make it unsuitable for a very fast tempo.

The horn calls have here moved from the parade ground to the dance, in a swinging three-time like a fast minuet. Each section of the dance is played by full orchestra, with the final six bars echoed by the pair of horns, unaccompanied. A middle section moves into D minor, without the horns. Its graceful simplicity is a welcome contrast before the return to the first section in F major.

It comes as a surprise to find that the famous Air that forms the sixth movement is also marked 'Presto' in several eighteenth-century sources. Christopher Hogwood remarks that this 'will be more than welcomed by generations of listeners bored by the sentimental and even funereal tradition'. This is perhaps going too far – and, indeed, Hogwood's own recording, although it is faster than most, takes the movement at no more than a tripping Andante.[12] With its gentle dotted rhythms and repetitions, it has the character of a pastoral interlude in an opera or oratorio. The first statement is played by the strings alone. Then the oboes join in, together with the horns, each in turn holding a sustained high note, which has the effect of putting the familiar melody in an entirely new context.

The Minuet for the French Horn begins, in some sources, with the entire first section of the dance played unaccompanied by the pair of horns. They then repeat their duet while the rest of the orchestra joins them. This is followed by a middle section in F minor without horns. Here the main melody is on bassoon, second violins, and violas, with a descant above in the first violins. This has a charming effect – Handel clearly appreciated the lyrical, plangent tone of the bassoon in its tenor register. The Minuet with horns is then repeated.

The Bourrée is one of the most delightful movements in the Water Music, and for once the marking 'Presto' is unambiguous. It is to be played, '3 times, 1st all the Violins, 2nd all the Hautboys, 3rd all together'. 'Violins' here means all the strings, and 'Hautboys' means all the oboes and bassoons. The delight of the piece is subtly contrived. It is in regular four-bar phrases, with a lot of repetition of little cells – a two-note fall and a faster three-note rise. Handel keeps up this repetitiveness throughout, while the overall shape of the melody rises and falls. In the second half, the harmonies take us rapidly through new keys, and the fast three-note rise is echoed half a bar later. At the end, the expected return of the opening four bars is charmingly extended to six bars.

The Hornpipe is to be played '3 times in the same manner' – strings, then woodwind, then everyone. It is constructed from little cells much like those in the Bourrée, and it goes through a similar succession of keys. It has a particularly buoyant character because of the way that Handel plays with the rhythm within the three-beat bar. At times the metre is unambiguous, but elsewhere there are two-beat cross-rhythms within it, sometimes obviously, sometimes subtly.

The final movement of this 'suite' is in D minor (the minor key most closely related to F major), still without horns, and is the most substantial piece since the Overture. Without being a formal fugue, it is full of the most inventive counterpoint. There is a single theme, a classic shape with repeated notes followed by a little curl, but it is varied during the move-ment, with the curl often becoming a descending scale. The trio of two oboes and bassoon begins, with the bassoon launching a walking bass that persists throughout the movement and ensures its momentum (though the bass sometimes joins in the counterpoint too). The relationship between woodwind and strings is very fluid. When the strings first enter, they repeat the first woodwind entry, with the wind filling in harmonies above. Then the strings play alone, and the wind join in with counterpoint. A new variant of the theme in the wood-wind is echoed in the strings. And so the movement continues, progressing through a succession of keys, with the music constantly enriched by subtle changes of relationship between the instruments and between the occurrences of the theme. One could easily imagine this movement adapted as a chorus in one of Handel's oratorios – and indeed Handel later simplified it to form the basis of the vocal trio, 'The flocks shall leave the mountains', in *Acis and Galatea*.

This is a fine movement, but it could hardly act as the finale of the supposed suite in F major, being in D minor and without horns. Musicians wanting to provide a plausible conclusion to the suite have the option of adding the alternative versions of the first two movements of the 'Suite in D', which are in F major with horns but not trumpets.

Suite in D

All movements of this suite have pairs of trumpets and horns (the horns having swapped their F crooks for D crooks). It is the first two movements that also exist in a version in F.

The opening Allegro is a movement of simple splendour. It opens with a trumpet call in military style, answered by the horns. This is one of Handel's many borrowings from the music of the German composer Reinhard Keiser, taken from his 1700 opera, *La forza della virtù* (*The Power of Virtue*). The movement is little more than a succession of such calls, passed back and forth and varied in rhythm, with energetic scales and a sturdy bass in the strings, culminating in a tutti. At the end, string chords modulate to a new key, inviting some elaboration, perhaps from the first oboe.

The 'Alla Hornpipe' combines the military style of the preceding Allegro with the rhythms of a hornpipe. The result is a splendidly vigorous piece, in which passages for strings and woodwind frame the calls from the trumpets and horns, giving the movement a coherent shape. There is a middle section in B minor without trumpets or horns. It takes the repeated notes from the hornpipe, and uses them as a persistent motif, building over them a wonderfully inventive structure passing through various keys, with the strings and oboes combining in beautifully varied textures. A return to the opening hornpipe rounds off the movement. The first part of this hornpipe is derived from an aria in Handel's opera, *Amadigi di Gaula*, staged in London in 1715.[13]

The Trumpet Minuet is a minuet in regal style, simple and grand in its rhythms and in the sweep of its melody and harmonies. It is to be played '3 times, 1st Trumpets & Violins, 2nd Horns & Hautboys, 3rd all together' ('Violins' means all the strings, and 'Hautboys' indicates oboes and bassoons). This is the movement that, in the earliest source, is placed at the very end of the *Water Music*.

The next movement, 'Lentement', again quotes Reinhard Keiser, transforming a pastoral jig from his opera, *Claudius*, into the slow French gigue known as a loure.[14] This dance has a rather stately progress, with a characteristic dotted rhythm within a three-time metre. The effect is particularly grand here, with the full orchestra, including trumpets and horns, following the rhythm of the melody.

The last piece with trumpets is a lively Bourrée. It is similar in character to the Bourrée in F major, but with a breezy straightforwardness of phrasing and rhythm. One eighteenth-century source instructs, 'This Aire is to be play'd thrice', presumably with the same varied instrumentation as the Trumpet Minuet.

Suite in G

In order to understand why Handel's music was so popular in his lifetime, one need do no more than contrast the brilliant trumpet pieces with the gentle dance that opens the G major 'suite'. This is a sort of demure minuet, with an emphasis on the second beat as in a sarabande. The phrasing is very regular, with groups of four bars throughout. In the hands of a lesser composer it would be dull. But Handel knows just how to vary the repetitions of the phrases, and to enliven them by subtle shifts of harmony, so that the ear is drawn on through to the end. The relationship between melody, middle parts, and bass is finely judged. The second half of the opening section is particularly beautiful. After a trill and a descending scale, we might expect the opening of the melody to return. Instead, the next bars include a leap down from a high note, while the bass moves calmly upwards, and sustained notes in the second violin draw attention to the changing key. This a moment of subtle genius, and Handel returns to it just before the end of the movement.

The untitled next movement is a pair of rigaudons (or bourrées – the dances are very similar). They are marked, in one eighteenth-century source, 'Presto', like the famous Bourrée in the suite in F. The music is written for strings, without separate parts for the wind. But the same source suggests that in the first bourrée the flute should double the first violin, and that the second bourrée should be played by two oboes, viola, and bassoon. Another source suggests that oboes should double the violins in the first dance. Modern musicians are free to choose from these options.

The charm of the first bourrée lies partly in its unusual phrase lengths. It begins with a pair of three-bar phrases, the first running down a scale, the second repeating a snappy little turn. It continues with another three-bar phrase, but then a fourth phrase extends to six bars, so that the first half of the dance is fifteen bars long. After the repeat of the first half, the second half of the dance falls into a more usual pattern of four-bar phrases, while it ventures into new keys. This creates a fascinating little journey, from the quirky to the regular. The second bourrée is in G minor. This has yet another pattern: it begins with a four-bar phrase, the last bar of which includes the snappy little turn from the first bourrée, then it continues with what sounds as if it will be another four-bar phrase; but at the last moment, the snappy turn extends upwards to create an eight-bar phrase. A variation of this pattern forms the second half of the dance. The first bourrée is then repeated.

A minuet in G minor follows, scored for three-part strings – all the violins, violas, and bass instruments – though several sources suggest adding the bassoon to the bass line. In contrast to the preceding bourrées, this minuet is positively demure in its regular four-bar phrases, until, at the end, a trill leads on to an extended final phrase.

The following movement is a pair of minuets, the first in G minor, the second in B flat major, scored for strings with the violin melody doubled by a recorder an octave higher. This takes regularity to a micro-level: the melody consists mostly of reiterated two-bar shapes, leaps up and down in the first minuet, and a gentle fall and a leap up in the second minuet, supported by an equally repetitive pattern in the bass. The effect is curiously hypnotic, coloured by slightly odd harmonies, which are suspended from one bar to the next.

The 'suite' in G concludes with a pair of 'Country Dances'. These are jigs – the rollicking English jig rather than the less sturdy gigue of French suites. In the first dance in G minor, recorders are again an octave above the violin melody. The second dance is in G major, and the melody moves to bassoons and middle strings, with a descant above in the violins. The effect is enchanting – it could have been composed two centuries later as an evocation of 'Merrie England'.

FRANZ JOSEPH HAYDN
(1732–1809)

Haydn and Mozart are often paired together as the two greatest composers of the late eighteenth century. But comparison between them is often to Haydn's disadvantage. Haydn is acknowledged as a composer of endless invention and brilliance, while Mozart is widely thought of as the deeper of the two. However, judged by the impact that they had on the course of musical history, Haydn is by far the more important. Over a long career (he lived more than twice as long as Mozart) Haydn developed new ways of writing instrumental music, particularly the symphony and the string quartet, and it was largely because of his influence that these two genres of composition acquired such importance in the next generation, paving the way for the orchestral music of the nineteenth century. He is often described as the 'father' of the string quartet and the symphony, and though, like all great composers, he developed ideas that were already in circulation, it was Haydn who really demonstrated the dramatic possibilities of such works.

Most of his symphonies were written while he was employed as a court composer. The earliest were composed for Count Morzin, for whom he worked for about four years until 1760. Then in 1761, at the age of twenty-nine, he was engaged as Vice-Kapellmeister by Prince Anton Esterházy, head of an extremely wealthy family with a castle in Eisenstadt and a palace in Vienna. Five years later, when the old Kapellmeister died, Haydn took the position and became head of the family's musical establishment. By now, Prince Anton had been succeeded by his brother, Nikolaus, who was a great enthusiast for music and himself an accomplished musician. There was a court orchestra, which increased in size from about fifteen players in the 1760s to twenty-five or so in the 1780s. When a grand new summer palace was built in the Hungarian marshes, the prince included an opera house in the plans. From 1768, Haydn was in charge of the annual season of opera productions, which included operas composed by himself.

Although Haydn's music was gradually becoming known outside the Esterházy family, his fame greatly increased when, from 1779, he was allowed to compose to commissions from outside the family. He rapidly became the most celebrated composer in Europe. The climax of his public career came in the 1790s when, following the death of Prince Nikolaus, Haydn was given permission to travel to England. There he was greeted as a celebrity, and the new symphonies that he composed for his two visits were rapturously received at public concerts. He was invited by the king to stay permanently in England, but Haydn decided to return to Austria, where a new Prince Esterházy had plans to revive the family's musical establishment. By the time Haydn left England at the end of his second stay in 1795, he had earned 24,000 florins, a vast sum that multiplied his capital twelve times or more since he had first arrived in England five years earlier.

The twelve 'London' Symphonies that Haydn composed for his time in England have become mainstays of the orchestral repertoire. With few exceptions, these were for many years virtually the only ones of the 104 catalogued symphonies by Haydn that were regularly played. But with the growth of Haydn scholarship in the late twentieth century, and particularly the monumental chronicles of his life and works by H. C. Robbins Landon together with a complete edition of his symphonies, the full set has gradually become more widely known.[1] It turns out that, far from having just a 'late flowering', Haydn had been composing symphonies of genius for many years (a fact that would have come as no surprise to lovers of his string quartets). The scope and expressive range of the symphonies is extraordinary. Haydn himself acknowledged that his long years in isolation with the Esterházy family had had a peculiarly concentrating effect on him: 'My prince was always satisfied with my works. Not only did I have the encouragement of constant approval, but as conductor of an orchestra I could make experiments, observe what produced an effect and what weakened it, and was thus in a position to improve, to alter, make additions or omissions, and be as bold as I pleased. I was cut off from the world; there was no one to confuse or torment me, and I was forced to become original.'[2]

Originality is certainly a strong feature of Haydn's musical personality. He is witty, surprising, sometimes actually funny (a rare thing in music). But he is also a composer of intellectual rigour and emotional depth. He does not have the persistent vein of melancholy that makes Mozart's mature works so touching. But he can, in the middle of good-humoured music, suddenly take one's breath away with a turn of phrase or harmony. He draws on the widest possible range of techniques and sources to create his musical dramas. One moment he will be pursuing the discipline of fugue, the next moment he will introduce a popular song or a gypsy dance. And 'drama' is an essential key to it all. Haydn was, like Mozart, a fine opera composer. The symphony, as Haydn encountered it as a young man, had developed out of the opera overture. Composers, since the time of Vivaldi, had employed dramatic effects in instrumental music. But it was Haydn more than any other composer who revealed how it was possible to create a compelling four-movement drama out of purely instrumental music. It was this that laid the foundations for the explosion of orchestral music that was to follow – Mozart, Beethoven, Schubert, and on through the nineteenth century.

Haydn's opinion of Mozart as the greatest living composer is often quoted. Despite the age difference between them of twenty-three years, the two became close friends. Mozart's debt to Haydn in his own works is obvious. And Mozart's opinion of Haydn is summed up in a quote that, though it was published seven years after his death, rings true: 'He alone has the secret of making me smile and touching me at the bottom of my soul. There is no one who can do it all – to joke and terrify, to evoke laughter and profound sentiment – and all equally well: except Joseph Haydn.'[3]

Concertos

Mozart wrote concertos, particularly piano concertos, throughout his working life. Haydn wrote concertos only sporadically, and most of them date from the 1760s, his earliest years in the service of the Esterházy family. There are a number of reasons for this. Mozart was one of the first great pianists, and it was important for him to have a supply of new works to play at concerts. Haydn was an accomplished violinist and keyboard player, but he did not have a reputation as a virtuoso, and when he wrote a concerto it was for others to play. The musicians at Esterházy included some fine virtuosi, and no doubt in his early years as Kapellmeister, Haydn was called upon to furnish them with concerti. As he became more established, and his fame spread, he was freer to concentrate on what he wanted to write, notably his incredibly inventive series of symphonies and string quartets.

But the fact that Mozart regularly wrote concertos, and Haydn did not, also points to an important difference between them in the way they liked to write large-scale works. Haydn's symphonies and string quartets, particularly their first movements, are tight musical arguments. The possibilities of the material – often little more than a phrase or two – are exhaustively discussed and explored, and reach a logical conclusion. Mozart sometimes works like this too, but more often he gives the impression of setting off on an emotional journey, in which new material and new directions can come into view at any stage. For Mozart, to have a soloist along on the journey is like having a companion to share it with. For Haydn, a soloist is something of a restraint, imposing the need to work with alternations between orchestral and solo passages, as was the convention of the time.

CELLO CONCERTO IN C MAJOR, HOB. VIIB:1
Duration: approx. 25 minutes

Moderato
Adagio
Allegro molto

Haydn's C major Cello Concerto dates from his earliest years with the Esterházy family. It is an extremely lively and charming work, which demonstrates to the full what an eighteenth-century virtuoso cellist was capable of. Specifically, it shows what a fine cellist Prince Esterházy's orchestra had in Joseph Weigl. Weigl became a close friend of Haydn, and Haydn and his wife were godparents to one of his children. Weigl played in the Esterházy orchestra for eight years from 1761, and, as the only regular cellist, would have played the beautiful cello solos Haydn wrote in some of his early symphonies. This concerto was written for him in the early 1760s, at roughly the same time as symphonies Nos 6–8, and it is an exceptional work for the time. The fact that cello concertos of the period are so rare suggests that virtuoso cellists were also rare. One of them, Luigi Boccherini (ten years younger than Haydn), was to compose several concertos and quintets with virtuoso cello parts, and Haydn himself wrote a second concerto for the instrument twenty years after his first, but neither Mozart nor Beethoven wrote a cello concerto. This concerto was lost for nearly two centuries. Haydn had written the opening in his catalogue of works in 1765, but there was no trace of the score until a copy was discovered in Prague in 1961.

The opening theme, played by the orchestra, has an almost baroque stateliness with its snappy dotted rhythms and elegant curls. To describe it as a 'theme' is really inadequate, because it consists of half a dozen ideas, by turns sturdy, elegant, pointed, and flowing, which form a seamless paragraph. The soloist enters and explores this rich supply of material, extending the ideas lyrically and introducing playful running passages. In the centre of the movement, the solo part becomes more virtuosic, with rapid repeated notes and arpeggios. Pairs of oboes and horns fill out the orchestral tutti, but are silent during solo passages.

The slow movement is scored for cello and strings without the wind instruments. The melody, introduced by the violins, not only takes its elegance from the first movement, but draws on specific elements from earlier thematic ideas. The cello steals in with a long note that blossoms into an echo of the theme – a favourite device of Boccherini. The movement is in three sections, each of which begins in this way. Each time, the cello extends and develops the melody. In the middle of the movement it moves into minor keys, adding a touching note of plangency to what had previously been a serene line.

The finale is a joyful movement. As in the first movement, the orchestra sets out a richly varied paragraph. It begins with a witty, pointed idea and then develops energy. For a quiet moment, the music is darkened by a more melancholy idea in a minor key, but this is soon thrust aside to make way for an exuberant resolution. Once again the cellist enters stealthily over a long note, before running up a scale to announce that this is going to be a movement of brilliant virtuosity. The writing is full of rapid patterns and chords, always underpinned by elements of the material that the orchestra laid out at the beginning. The middle section of the movement progresses into minor keys. But rather than introduce the touch of melancholy that occurred in the opening orchestral passage, this adds an element of steely determination. At the end of the movement, the mood returns to the light-heartedness of the opening, and the concerto ends with delightful exuberance.

CELLO CONCERTO IN D MAJOR, HOB. VIIB:2
Duration: approx. 25 minutes

Allegro moderato
Adagio
Rondo: Allegro

Haydn's second cello concerto was written in the 1780s, twenty years after the first, for Anton Kraft, a Bohemian cellist and composer who was Prince Esterházy's principal cellist from 1778 to 1790. Haydn gave him composition lessons, and Kraft himself wrote concertos and sonatas for cello. Indeed, although this concerto was published 'd'après le manuscrit original de l'auteur' in 1804, it was thought for over a century to have been written by Kraft. The manuscript had disappeared, and in 1837 an article stated with apparent authority that Kraft was the composer. It is very likely that Kraft did indeed advise Haydn about the writing: its technical difficulties and figurations are very different from the C major Concerto, favouring high positions as in Kraft's own compositions. But the rediscovery of the manuscript in 1951 established Haydn once and for all as the composer. It is a charming work, and its technical demands give ample evidence that Kraft must have been a cellist of exceptional skill. But it is surprising to think that this concerto is roughly contemporary with Haydn's 'Paris' Symphonies (Nos 82–87), and with Mozart's mature piano concertos. For Haydn, a concerto was principally a vehicle for the soloist, and the level of interaction between soloist and orchestra is much more like that in Boccherini's concertos than in Mozart's. The scoring is as in the first concerto, with pairs of oboes and horns and strings.

Compared with the earlier concerto in C major, however, the opening orchestral tutti does declare that this is to be a more 'modern', symphonic movement. The contrast between different elements is stronger. The first theme begins quietly and mellifluously, and then becomes bold and develops energy. A second theme starts quietly, and then rises to forte in a fashionable crescendo. When the cello enters, the writing is predominantly higher than in the first concerto – the cello plays the first theme at the same pitch as the violins do at the opening. As in the orchestral opening, the writing is at first mellifluous and then energetic, with rapid scale passages covering a wide range. After a brief orchestral passage, the cellist begins the second theme a sixth below the violins in duet. This is followed by more elaborate virtuoso passages and chords.

Another orchestral passage leads into the centre of the movement. This is the most remarkable part of the concerto. It is more extensive than Haydn has led us to expect, and has something of the character of the development section in his symphonies. The soloist begins by returning to the opening theme. But then it moves off into predominantly minor keys, in which virtuoso passages acquire a determined and earnest character, drawing from time to time on elements of the themes. The reprise returns to the earlier combination of mellifluous and energetic virtuosity, and a cadenza (which Haydn did not provide) leads to a final orchestral tutti.

The Adagio has a simple structure, with the theme played three times and interleaved with brief episodes. The song-like melody is played first by the soloist, and then taken up warmly by the strings and oboes (but not horns). In the first episode the cello-writing rises higher and becomes more elaborate, and when it returns to the first theme, it is an octave higher than before. A second episode begins with the orchestra in a minor key, and continues with the cellist in the major, both with a new version of the opening phrase. The movement ends with a return to the theme, a cadenza, and a final farewell from the orchestra.

The principal theme of the finale is an innocent, pastoral melody in a lilting metre, gently presented by the cellist. Its appearances are interleaved with episodes with lively scales and arpeggios, chordal passages, and explorations of the high register (Anton Kraft's speciality). A later episode, like the middle of the first movement, shifts to a minor key, a section formally marked 'Minore' in the score. Here, tricky passages in octaves are added to the repertoire of virtuoso effects. The music emerges into the 'Maggiore' for a final reprise of the theme and a cheerful conclusion.

KEYBOARD CONCERTO IN D MAJOR, HOB. XVIII:11
Duration: approx. 20 minutes

Vivace
Un poco adagio
Rondo all'Ungharese

It was perhaps the example of Mozart's first Viennese piano concertos that prompted Haydn to publish this Concerto in D major in Vienna in 1784, though it may have been composed several years earlier. Mozart by the 1780s was in effect a freelance composer with a growing reputation as a virtuoso pianist. Haydn, with his more traditional role as court composer to the Esterházy family, had less reason to write keyboard concertos. Apart from its publication, nothing is known about the circumstances that prompted Haydn to write this keyboard concerto, the only one to achieve popularity in his lifetime. Although it may have been inspired by Mozart's success as a composer of concertos, its style is somewhat more traditional. It was described on the title page as a concerto 'for harpsichord or fortepiano', as Mozart's concertos were. Many households in 1780s Vienna still had harpsichords rather than the new pianos, and publishers did not want to discourage harpsichord-owners from buying the latest concertos. Mozart's subtle nuances and textures meant that a harpsichord, with its limited expressive flexibility, was in practice unsuitable for his concertos. By contrast, Haydn's keyboard-writing in this D major Concerto is much more straightforward, and really can be played satisfactorily on harpsichord as well as piano.

The first movement is a sturdy Vivace, with brilliant passages and lively rhythms, similar in style to the opening movements of Haydn's cello concertos. The slow movement, at first elegant in its decorative line, develops a plangent expression that is almost operatic – and here the piano certainly has an advantage over the harpsichord.

The finale, 'in Hungarian style', was a great success with early audiences. Like Haydn's famous 'Gypsy Rondo' for piano trio, it contains elements of the wild gypsy music that Haydn would often have heard around the Esterházy palace in Hungary, with swirling figures and trills, accented grace notes, and insistent dance rhythms.

TRUMPET CONCERTO IN E FLAT MAJOR, HOB. VIIE: I
Duration: approx. 14 minutes

Allegro

Andante

Allegro

Until the invention of valves in the early nineteenth century, trumpets, like horns, were restricted to the notes of the harmonic series. This meant that they could not play continuous melodies except in the upper registers, where the notes fell close together. There had been, in the time of Handel and J. S. Bach, a tradition of high 'clarino' trumpet-playing, but it had fallen out of practice by Haydn's time. During the late eighteenth century there were various attempts to make the trumpet capable of playing more of the notes of the chromatic scale. These included a design of trumpet that enabled the player to place a hand in the bell to adjust the pitch, a 'hand-stopping' technique used by horn-players. An alternative was to make holes in the tubing and open and close them with keys. It was in 1793 that Anton Weidinger, a trumpeter in the Vienna Court Orchestra and a friend of Haydn, invented an improved version of this keyed trumpet.

When Haydn returned from his second visit to London in 1795, he composed a concerto for Weidinger. Four years elapsed between Haydn's completion of the work in 1796 and its premiere in Vienna in 1800, perhaps because Weidinger was still working on modifications to the instrument. The *Wiener Zeitung* announced that Weidinger wished 'to present to the world for the first time ... an organized trumpet which he has invented and brought – after seven years of hard and expensive labour – to what he believes may be described as perfection: it contains several keys [actually five] and will be displayed in a concerto specially written for this instrument by Herr Joseph Haydn.'[4] Responses to Weidinger's trumpet were mixed, one reviewer regretting the loss of the characteristic tone, another particularly admiring its ability to play softly. The softening of the tone was inevitable, as the opening of the holes interfered with the brightening effect of the bell, as did hand-stopping. But, as we have learned in modern times, a skilled player can use the softness to advantage (as with the earlier cornett of Monteverdi's time). Indeed, one might argue that the later development of valves tends to encourage a bold, brassy style that can obscure some of the subtleties of Haydn's concerto.

Haydn's Trumpet Concerto is fascinating partly because it is his only concerto from his later years, composed after his last symphony (though there is also the delightful Sinfonia Concertante for oboe, bassoon, violin, and cello, composed in 1792 while Haydn was in

London). It makes one wonder what a late keyboard or cello concerto by Haydn could have been like. The use of the orchestra is much richer and more varied than in his earlier concertos, and he deploys the chromatic possibilities of the keyed trumpet with touching simplicity.

The orchestral introduction opens with strings and horns playing a quiet, rising melody, answered by the woodwind, and followed by a trumpet call from the full orchestra (including conventional trumpets, and a first note from the soloist). A more sustained tutti is interrupted by a poignant little descent over a chromatic scale, enhanced by a high flute. The soloist enters with the first theme. Soon, it is adding little chromatic touches to show the versatility of the instrument, and it extends the melody lyrically, to link to the chromatic descent from the introduction. Throughout the concerto it is these simple, lyrical moments that are the most telling, as if the keyed trumpet is more suited to these passages than to conventional trumpet figurations (as indeed it is).

The development section ventures into new keys, and the trumpet is able (for once) to follow. Virtuoso runs culminate in a high note, followed by a quiet low note rising and falling over a semitone – this dark, un-trumpety effect must have sounded particularly striking in the 1790s. A moment of quiet anticipation brings in the reprise. This includes not only runs of semiquavers, but also leaps and arpeggios more associated with the old baroque trumpet concerto. A cadenza (which Haydn did not supply) and a brief tutti bring the movement to a close.

The slow movement is brief but lovely. Violins, joined by a flute an octave higher, play a melody in A flat major with the lilting rhythm of a siciliano. The solo trumpet repeats the melody. Then the violins continue, as if starting the second strain. But when the trumpet enters, it takes it in quite a different direction, via a chromatic scale to C flat major. The strings take the melody on to D flat minor, and then, with a consoling little flourish, back to A flat major for the reprise. This miniature development is like a glimpse of another world, just the sort of touch that shows the mastery of the mature Haydn.

The last movement is a rondo as inventive as any in a Haydn symphony. It begins quietly on the strings, and then continues on full orchestra with the muscular sound of trumpets, horns, and drums. The introduction ends with a vigorous horn call to bring in the soloist. After the trumpet has played the theme, the strings move off into the first episode. The soloist takes up a phrase from the opening theme, and extends it with tricky little turns incorporating trills – an example of detail designed specifically for the keyed trumpet. A pause, perhaps with a moment of cadenza, announces the return of the rondo theme. This time a flute echoes the solo trumpet in counterpoint. As the trumpet moves off into a new key, the echo passes to a bassoon. These echoes with quiet instruments suggest the potential delicacy of the keyed trumpet's tone.

After a moment of counterpoint in the strings, the music winds round to E flat again for the reappearance of the theme on the trumpet. This time, the continuation builds to a virtuoso moment of arpeggios and leaping octaves. The end is in sight, but not before Haydn has teased us with delicate moments, more trumpet trills, a dramatic burst of fortissimo on full orchestra, and a pianissimo tremolo. After a silence, the trumpet revisits the theme for the last time, accompanied by poignant touches of a minor chord in the strings, before a last fanfare with the horns and trumpets brings the concerto to an exhilarating close.

Symphonies

The complete list of Haydn's symphonies drawn up by Eusebius Mandyczewski in 1908 includes 104 symphonies. Research since then has added a few more, and has corrected the dating of others, but the original numbering is still in general use. The symphonies are works of extraordinary invention, many of them written during the thirty years (1761–1790) when Haydn was in the service of the Esterházy family and directed the court orchestra. For twenty of those years he was obliged to compose only for his employers, though his music was widely disseminated. From the 1780s, Haydn was allowed to accept commissions from abroad. Symphonies Nos 82–87 were composed for Paris, where his music was already well known, and his last symphonies, Nos 93–104, were written for his visits to London. From works composed for a court orchestra of no more than fifteen players in the 1760s, Haydn found himself writing in the 1780s and 1790s for much larger orchestras playing to a public audience, and he took full advantage of the challenges this presented.

The descriptions that follow cover a selection of thirty-four of the works from each period of Haydn's symphonies. This is only a third of the total, and a different writer would probably have made a different selection, certainly of the earlier works. But the selection does include all those that are generally acknowledged as Haydn's finest.[5]

Haydn's symphonies range from some early works that are little more than opera overtures lasting ten minutes or so to substantial pieces lasting more than half an hour. But the duration in practice varies considerably depending on the conductor's attitude to Haydn's repeat markings. The repeats of the second halves of movements, in particular, are often omitted (though they are more often played today than they used to be). Durations of individual symphonies are therefore not given here.

SYMPHONY NO. 6 IN D MAJOR, 'LE MATIN'

Adagio – Allegro
Adagio – Andante – Adagio
Minuet and Trio
Finale: Allegro

This symphony and its two companions, No. 7, 'Le midi', and No. 8, 'Le soir', were the first that Haydn composed after being engaged in 1761 as Vice-Kapellmeister by Prince Paul Anton Esterházy at the family castle at Eisenstadt. According to an early biographer, it was the prince who suggested the three titles to Haydn, and the symphonies were probably first performed in the Esterházy palace in Vienna. Haydn was in charge of the orchestra, in which he played violin. It consisted of a small group of excellent musicians who included the violinist Luigi Tommasini, the concertmaster, and cellist Joseph Weigl, for whom Haydn wrote his first cello concerto. The virtuoso make-up of the orchestra is reflected in the scoring of these symphonies, which have solo parts for a violin, cello, and double bass. As the bass player was also one of the two bassoonists, there is only one bassoon part, together with one flute (two in 'Le midi'), two oboes, two horns, strings, and harpsichord. The first of the group, 'Le matin', is the most fascinating of the three.

The fashion for evocations of natural phenomena in the baroque period reached its most famous expression in Vivaldi's *Four Seasons*. By comparison, the allusions to times of day in these three works are slight. But 'Le matin' does open with six bars of unmistakable sunrise beginning with pianissimo violins and building to the full orchestra – a miniature forerunner of the glorious sunrise that Haydn was to compose nearly forty years later in *The Creation*. The Allegro opens with a charming theme on the flute, formed of a simple shape like a horn call and a rising scale, which is rounded off by the oboes. The opening shape continues in the wind as the violins bustle in, forte. A second theme is equally simple, though quirky – falling intervals with snappy echoes, and a sigh. More bustling forte, with a number of new ideas, brings the first half to a close (in symphonies of this period, both halves of the opening Allegro are invariably repeated).

The flute opens the second half, reversing the direction of the scale, and the oboes playfully echo this inversion. There is a hush, and the violins rise mysteriously through a chromatic scale. There are more bustling scales, followed by sonorous wind chords. Suddenly a horn bursts in with the opening of the first theme, making it into a real horn call, before the flute takes it over and completes it – this unexpected moment sounds like a premonition of the famous (and much more dramatic) 'wrong' horn entry in the first movement of Beethoven's 'Eroica' Symphony. An abbreviated reprise of the opening section, without the quirky second theme, brings the second half to a close.

The slow movement in G major begins and ends with a short Adagio. Its pianissimo string chords, with a rising scale, seem like a memory of the sunrise. But then the solo violin asserts itself with a pattern of repeated notes. Is this intended as a dramatic intervention, or a joke? Richard Wigmore suggests that it parodies a violin lesson.[6] Immediately, however, the violin elaborates the rising scale elegantly, and exchanges arpeggios with the other violins of the orchestra. The central part of the movement, Andante, continues the elegant mood and the asserting of virtuosity. It is a gentle, tiptoeing courtly dance in three-time. The solo violin elaborates with arpeggio patterns, joined in duet, towards the end of the first half, by solo cello. In the second half, cello and violin exchange solo passages before once more joining in duet. Both halves of the Andante are repeated. Then the Adagio returns. If the first Adagio hinted at a violin lesson, now we seem to be in a counterpoint class: in the violins the scale rises and falls, while the lower strings provide a classic, elaborate counterpoint.

The minuet has a strikingly dark sonority, with oboes and violins rather low in unison. From this emerges the flute, elaborating the line with trills and running triplets in a manner that evokes the solo violin in the slow movement. The sonorities of the trio are even more unusual. The bassoon is joined in duet by solo double bass, with solo cello later joining to form a trio. There is once again a suggestion of humour, but the minor key ensures that the music remains at least mock-serious.

The rising scale that featured in the opening two movements becomes the first element of the lively finale. It passes rapidly between flute, strings, and solo violin. Then the solo cello joins in with virtuoso passages similar to parts of Haydn's first cello concerto (composed around the same time). A simpler, falling shape emerges in the wind, and the music comes to a pause on an unexpected chord before rattling to the end of the first half. In the second half, the solo violin begins with the familiar scale, but then launches into a virtuoso display of complex arpeggios and two-part writing. The reprise of the opening begins with the flute, and follows with the solo cello. But then the sequence of running scales is powerfully extended. There is another unexpected pause, and the movement comes to an end in high spirits.

Adagio
Presto
Menuetto and Trio
Finale: Presto

This symphony is dated 1764 on the surviving autograph. It has a most unusual scoring: two cor anglais, two horns, and strings. Haydn uses this combination to create a fascinating blend of the antique and the new. The first movement has an almost baroque, ecclesiastical character, and all four movements are in the same key, as in many of the old *concerti grossi*. And yet, as always in Haydn, he uses these old methods to create something entirely fresh. It had acquired its nickname, 'The Philosopher', by 1790.

The first movement is in two sections, the second much longer than the first. Each section is repeated. Over a quiet walking bass, fortissimo horns intone a chorale, answered by the two cor anglais. So far, the movement evokes a solemn chorale prelude of an earlier generation. But after a couple of answering phrases, the muted strings follow on with delicate falling phrases. Suddenly the music seems not simply ecclesiastical, but more like an operatic scene – perhaps a procession watched by elegantly dressed onlookers. In the second section, the delicate strings continue over the walking bass, taking up the phrases of the chorale and interweaving them with a counterpoint. This contrapuntal development carries on through different keys, with occasional chorale phrases from horns and cor anglais, until the music arrives back in the home key for the reprise.

The strings remove their mutes for the second movement, which is a fast and furious Presto. As often throughout Haydn's career, the principal theme metamorphoses into various subsidiary ideas, without any sense that there is a clear second theme.

The minuet has rather a formal air and, in subtle ways, refers back to the opening movement. The theme opens with the same shape as the first phrase of the chorale, and the staccato bass reminds us of the walking bass of the first movement. In the trio, the two cor anglais join the horns in a rich-toned ensemble, evoking the sort of music that horns might play as the company relaxes after the hunt.

The finale evokes the hunt itself, an early example of the sort of galloping finale that Haydn and other composers were to return to in later years. The level of energy is almost constant, with the cor anglais valiantly answering the horns' hunting calls, as if trying to keep up with them in the chase.

SYMPHONY NO. 26 IN D MINOR, 'LAMENTATIONE'

Allegro assai con spirito
Adagio
Minuet and Trio

In Roman Catholic countries, including the Habsburg Empire of Haydn's day, there was a long tradition in churches of chanting the Gospel accounts of the passion and crucifixion of Christ in the week leading up to Easter. Different singers would take the words of Christ and the Evangelist (narrator), and the congregation would join in as the Voice of the People. This symphony early acquired the title 'Lamentatione' because Haydn uses extracts from such chants as themes. He composed it for Easter week of 1768, or possibly 1769 – several years after Symphony No. 31 (see below). Its scoring has a certain austerity: there is no flute, which Haydn so often uses elsewhere to provide moments of lightness and charm. And the austerity is heightened by the fact that it is one of the earliest examples of a Haydn symphony in a minor key – only No. 34 in D minor (which dates from 1765) precedes it. These symphonies in minor keys came to be associated with the early Romantic literary movement known as *Sturm und Drang* (Storm and Stress). This term, derived from a play of 1776, is used to describe a genre of literature in which the focus of attention is the personal struggle with turbulent emotions. The most famous example of the genre is Goethe's *The Sorrows of Young Werther* of 1774, a work that cast its influence far into the nineteenth century. But the association of Haydn's minor-key symphonies with *Sturm und Drang* literature is not one that he would have made in the 1760s, a decade before the term was in use. The character of these works has more to do with musical tradition. The depiction of raging storms in music goes back through Vivaldi's *Four Seasons* to seventeenth-century opera. Gluck's 'Dance of the Furies' from his ballet *Don Juan* (1761) was a recent example of the type. Haydn, a brilliant reinventer of fashions and styles, took this tradition of ferocious, minor-key music and used it to create a new, powerful type of symphony, combining it with other traditions that came to hand. So in this 'Lamentatione' Symphony, he brings together minor-key ferocity with the austerity of chant to create a strikingly new synthesis.

The first theme features persistently repeated patterns of syncopated notes, over a treading bass, at first forceful and then quiet and anxious. Soon the music moves to a major key, and oboe and second violins intone a chant, with an accompanying staccato pattern on first violins. The first strain is taken from the chant of the Evangelist. The quieter, calmer phrase that follows sets the words of Christ. And the louder conclusion is The Voice of the People. Violin arpeggios bring the first section of the movement to a close in a more familiar symphonic style. The development that opens the second section concentrates on the syncopated opening. At the reprise, the chanting second theme again breaks into a major key, and the movement never returns to the D minor of its opening. So the turbulence of the opening has resolved into a cheerfully energetic conclusion.

The slow movement draws on another chant, not from the passion narrative but from the Lamentations of Jeremiah, appointed to be chanted on the Thursday of Easter Week. As in the first movement, violins and oboe intone the chant in unison. The first violins play a charming counterpoint to it, beautifully devised so as to sound like a theme in its own right. After the first strain of the chant, the first violin line breaks into a delicate pattern in triplet rhythm, and this continues as the chant re-enters. The most striking moment comes halfway through the second section of the movement. The chant is reprised by the two oboes together, and the two horns fill out the harmonies, creating a warm texture.

The finale is very far from a conventional minuet. It has a mood of anxiety alternating with forcefulness that links back to the first movement. And this is heightened at the end when bass and treble play the melody in canon a bar apart – a procedure as 'antique' in a symphony as the incorporation of chant. The more playful trio in D major comes as a moment of relief.

To conclude a symphony with a minuet is highly unusual, and this movement has a subtle ambiguity of mood that could have stepped out of Haydn's later chamber music (his Piano Trio in F sharp minor, Hob. XV:26, composed nearly thirty years later, concludes with an equally anxious Tempo di menuetto). This unusual finale has led writers to conjecture that this symphony might have been composed for a specific context, such as a prelude to a ceremony of Holy Week. But in that case, a minuet seems an even stranger choice for a finale.

SYMPHONY NO. 31 IN D MAJOR, 'HORNSIGNAL'

Allegro
Adagio
Minuet and Trio
Finale: Moderato molto

This symphony dates from 1765, three years before No. 26 (see above), and marks the end of a period when the Esterházy orchestra had only two horn players. Prince Nikolaus engaged two more, and Haydn took advantage of this horn quartet in several symphonies of this period. No. 31 is the most striking of them, rivalled only by the (misnumbered) No. 72, which is in a very similar style and format. Like earlier symphonies, No. 31 also includes extensive solos for the virtuoso string players of the Esterházy orchestra – violin, cello, and violone (double bass). It is known as the 'Hornsignal' for reasons that are immediately obvious as the work begins.

The symphony opens dramatically, with a forceful horn call from all four horns in unison. A single horn then plays a call that leaps up and down an octave. From this, the horns fall into the background for a more conventional orchestral tutti, with running scales interspersed with more graceful phrases. A solo flute emerges with charming rising scales, and the first section of the movement ends quietly. The four horns call again at the start of the second section. The reprise goes straight into the solo horn call, with its leaping octaves. Haydn saves the reprise of the forceful opening call for the final bars, so that the movement ends as dramatically as it began.

The slow movement is in the lilting rhythm of a siciliano. A violin solo, full of graceful elaboration, is answered by a pair of horns, and then by solo cello, with pizzicato accompaniment. The other two horns open the second section with flamboyant scales and arpeggios, and solo violin and cello combine in duet.

The full orchestra plays the robust minuet. The trio opens with what might be a horn call, but played on two oboes rather than horns. The horns later take up the melody, first combined with violins, and then with flute.

You might expect a hunting finale to round off the symphony, but instead Haydn concludes with a set of variations. The theme is a demure little tune for strings, scored simply for violins with a bass line. The first variation adds a mellifluous combination of two oboes and two horns. The second variation is a virtuoso cello solo, written for Joseph Weigl, the principal cellist of the Esterházy orchestra, for whom Haydn composed his first cello concerto. Variation 3 is for solo flute, with an elaborate pattern of running triplets. Variation 4 brings in the horn quartet, with the first horn reaching into the highest register, and the violins an octave below. Variation 5 returns to the virtuoso style of Variation 2's cello solo, now on solo violin. Variation 6 returns to the simplicity of the original theme, but now with the harmonies richly filled in by horns and woodwind. Variation 7 is another virtuoso solo, surprisingly for violone (double bass) – an even greater challenge than the cello solo of Variation 2. This is followed by an anxious little linking passage in D minor. From it bursts out a final Presto, an exuberant release of energy that ends with the four horns returning in full cry to the call with which the symphony began.

SYMPHONY NO. 39 IN G MINOR

Allegro assai
Andante
Minuet and Trio
Finale: Allegro di molto

Haydn's own catalogue of his works lists this symphony as having been composed in 1768, probably the same year as No. 26 in D minor. The two works share that troubled, minor-key character that is often given the label *Sturm und Drang* (see No. 26 above). No. 26 has only two horns, No. 39 has four. But the purpose of having four horns is quite different than in Symphony No. 31. Instead of a glorious horn quartet, Haydn has here arranged the parts so that he can have two horns playing for most of the outer movements. The two pairs of horns are pitched in different keys – horns 1 and 2 in high B flat, horns 3 and 4 in G. They rarely play together, but horns 3 and 4 play when the music is in G minor, and horns 1 and 2 play when the music is in B flat, as it often is.

The first movement is dominated to an unusual extent by the insistent little phrase with which it opens. Twice the music stops, as if looking nervously over its shoulder, before it can achieve momentum. Once it is under way, the theme drives all the way through the first section, with almost no material that does not seem to have arisen from this single idea. In the second section, the theme develops into a concentrated passage of counterpoint, before we find ourselves back at the nervy opening once more.

The second movement in B flat major is for strings alone. It is an elegant, rather demure dance, punctuated by sudden, bold gestures. Almost all of it is scored very simply, as nothing more than melody and bass. This makes the final bars all the more touching, as second violins and violas shyly step forward to fill out a four-part texture.

The simple melody and bass continue into the minuet in G minor, though the two parts create poignant harmonic touches on their own, with only occasional interventions from a pair of horns. By comparison, the trio in B flat major seems warm and rich, with high horns joined by the pair of oboes.

The finale is fast and ferocious, with leaps and rushing scales, scrubbing tremolo in the middle parts, and bold contrasts between loud and soft passages. A brief moment of anxious quiet opens the second section, but the emotional storm soon resumes, and continues unabated to the end.

SYMPHONY NO. 41 IN C MAJOR

Allegro con spirito
Un poco andante
Minuet and Trio
Presto

This is Haydn at his most splendid, one of a series of a dozen symphonies in C major with trumpets, high horns, and timpani that he composed over a thirty-year span, from the 1760s to the 1790s. This one was written in 1768 or 1769. The key of C was one of the most common for the natural (valveless) trumpet of Haydn's day, and it was trumpets in C that Haydn chose for his most festive music (though he sometimes wrote for trumpets in other keys in later symphonies).

At first the trumpets and drums punctuate smoothly rising and falling violin phrases. But soon the festive spirit takes over, with a wide range of effects: vigorous dotted rhythms, rushing scales, tremolo (rapidly scrubbed) double notes. From this grand tutti emerge delicate staccato violins, and an elegant second theme to bring the first section of the movement to a close. The second section opens quietly and mysteriously, and becomes even quieter. Before we know it, we are back at the opening theme. But this is not as it seems. There is a surprising chord and a pause; and then the rapid tremolo returns, taking us dramatically through new keys. The staccato violins again emerge, and take us to the reprise – and this time Haydn means it.

The slow movement is one of those in which Haydn seems to be the heir of Handel, in his ability to compose music that is touching in its naive simplicity. The trumpets are silent, and a flute enters for the first time. All the violins in unison play a melody full of elegant gestures, like a dance of shepherdesses. The pastoral impression is enhanced when the flute takes a falling arpeggio from the violins' melody and makes a continuous pattern of it, while an oboe plays a more sustained line. The violins respond with tiptoeing that is elaborated into an iterated murmuring, and more flute arpeggios round off the first section. In the second section, first violins develop the melody further, while the murmuring pattern continues in the second violins, until a pause brings in the reprise.

The flute exits and the trumpets re-enter for the minuet. Like the first movement, this is Haydn in festive mood, an impression enhanced by rather baroque-sounding trills. The trio features stratospherically high horns in unison with oboes and violins.

The finale is a Haydn speciality, a Presto in galloping, chattering jig rhythm. There are sudden contrasts between soft and loud, touches of wistful harmonies in the lower parts, and bursts of high horns. It all adds up to a finale full of delight, almost like the high-speed conclusion of a comic opera.

SYMPHONY NO. 44 IN E MINOR, 'TRAUERSYMPHONIE'

Allegro con brio
Menuetto: Canone in diapason, and Trio
Adagio
Finale: Presto

This symphony was composed around 1771. The early 1770s were a time of enormous productivity for Haydn. Within a period of five years he composed four operas, two masses, twelve string quartets, and sixteen symphonies, as well as piano sonatas, Prince Nikolaus's favourite trios with baryton (a kind of viol with extra strings for plucking), and numerous other works. Although they were neglected for many years, the symphonies of this period are of astonishingly high quality, matched only by the six Haydn wrote for Paris (Nos 82–87) and the twelve he composed for London (Nos 93–104). They were much appreciated and performed in Haydn's lifetime. The composer himself was reported to have asked for the slow movement of No. 44 to be played at his funeral. In the event it was not, but the story of Haydn's request probably gave the work its title: 'Trauersymphonie' ('Mourning Symphony').

The opening movement is full of defiant gestures echoed by doubts. When it does develop momentum, the rushing semiquavers are accompanied by persistent memories of the first idea. The first section ends with another moment of doubt, a touching hesitation before the defiant first theme returns. After the themes have been developed and reprised in the second section, this moment of doubt returns as a ghostly few bars of fugue, before reassertion brings the movement to a close.

Unusually the minuet follows second. The melody is played in canon, the bass following a bar after the treble ('Canone in diapason' is an antique term for 'Canon at the octave'). It is as if the little moment of fugue just before the end of the first movement has sparked this more thoroughgoing movement of counterpoint. And there is another feature that links this minuet with the first movement. The contrasts between piano and forte seem to echo the earlier contrasts between assertion and doubt. This is particularly striking in the middle of the second section, where there is a sudden quiet, and a drooping phrase is echoed in the bass, not one bar late, but two bars late. This echo persists until the last few bars of the minuet, where the opening phrase of the canon is recalled. From elements of the minuet evolves the trio, with a lovely duet between the two violin parts enriched by a high horn.

Just as aspects of the minuet seem to have been sparked off by an event in the first movement, so the falling theme of the slow movement seems to have grown out of the melody of the trio. Muted strings sing a gently unfolding melody. Its many evolutions seem entirely natural without conforming to expectation. In the second half, which develops the melody further, there never comes a moment when we return to the opening of the theme in a conventional reprise. Instead, the music returns to the climax of the theme, where the wind enter, and then develops further before finally coming to rest.

The finale is exceptionally terse, full of determination, and with not a redundant note. There is really only one theme, but it is subjected to a great range of treatments. First it is stated in stark, staccato string octaves, which give way to delicate interplay between violins and bass. This sets off a stretch of vigorous counterpoint, with the theme in the bass and countermelody above, which develops and breaks up into yet more vigorous scrubbed repeated notes. As in the first movement, the vigour dissolves into a questioning moment to bring the first section to a close. After the repeat, the second section becomes even more persistently vigorous and contrapuntal. Like the slow movement, it avoids a reprise where one might expect it. Instead, the energy breaks up into another questioning moment. Only after this, in the very last bars of the movement, does the theme return, now in the bass, to bring the symphony to a defiant end.

SYMPHONY NO. 45 IN F SHARP MINOR, 'FAREWELL'

Allegro assai
Adagio
Minuet and Trio: Allegretto
Finale: Presto – Adagio

The story of the 'Farewell' Symphony comes down to us from Haydn's earliest biographers, who obtained it from the composer himself. One of them, Georg August Griesinger, tells it as follows:

In Prince Esterházy's orchestra, there were several vigorous young married men who in summer, while the Prince was in residence at Esterháza Castle, were obliged to leave their wives behind in Eisenstadt. Contrary to his custom, the Prince once wished to extend his stay at Esterháza by several weeks. The affectionate husbands, utterly dismayed by this news, turned to Haydn and pleaded with him to do something. Haydn had the idea of writing a symphony (known as the Farewell Symphony) in which one instrument after another falls silent. This symphony was performed at the earliest opportunity in the presence of the Prince, and each of the musicians was instructed, as his part came to an end, to snuff out his candle, pack up his music, and with his instrument under his arm, to leave. The Prince and his audience understood the meaning of this pantomime at once, and the next day came the order to depart from Esterháza. This is how Haydn related the occasion for the Farewell Symphony to me.[7]

According to the date on the autograph manuscript, this happened in 1772. Quite apart from the charming story, the symphony is a remarkable work in its own right, and in Haydn's own lifetime it was deservedly one of the most popular of his symphonies. It is thought to be the only symphony in F sharp minor to have been composed during the eighteenth century. Haydn ordered special slides to extend the length of the horns' G crook by a semitone, so that they could play in this unusual key (Symphony No. 46 in B major would also have used these slides). In practice, it is only in the minuet and trio, which is in F sharp major, that these crooks become necessary. In the other movements, the horns are pitched in A and E, allowing them to play many of the harmony notes of F sharp minor and related keys, giving the orchestration of the tuttis in the outer movements an unusually rich texture.

The first movement has all the hallmarks of what is often referred to as Haydn's *Sturm und Drang* style, a style that has at least as much to do with the recent history of opera and ballet music as it does with parallels in literature (see Symphony No. 26). Those hallmarks include the minor key, sharp accents, agitated leaping figures, syncopations in the inner parts, and scrubbing tremolo bowing. All of these are heard within the first few bars, creating a mood of tragic urgency. The music is immensely varied in detail, with continual jolts of harmony and changes of articulation, but there is really only one theme, or maybe one group of thematic ideas. This is normal in Haydn. What is not at all normal is what happens in the second section. It begins, as usual, by developing the ideas further and moving into new keys. But then there is a pause and a silence. Out of nowhere comes a quiet new theme which, though in a major key, has a sad, wistful effect in the context of such a stormy movement. Commentators sometimes describe Haydn as having displaced the conventional second theme to the central development section of the movement. But its effect is much more like an interlude, a moment of troubled calm in the midst of turmoil. The melody goes through its own thoughtful development, and reaches another silence. Without warning the stern opening returns, fortissimo. And that is not the end of the surprise. Rather than just a reprise of the first section, with the usual minor changes, what follows is a wholesale further development of the thematic material, bringing an extra level of dramatic urgency to the music.

Adagio was not a very slow marking in Haydn's day, as it was later to become. Here, it is more helpful to think of the everyday Italian meaning of the word: 'gently'. It is a movement of grace, but with long moments of extraordinary poignancy and tension, like a genial conversation that becomes unexpectedly serious from time to time. Muted violins sing a melody in

A major full of delicately flicked grace notes, which give it something of a dance-like character. (Did Mozart remember this music when writing the slow movement of his Symphony No. 40 in G minor?) The melody unfolds without hurry, until the harmonies begin to twist, and the music arrives at a pause. There is a sustained moment of dissonant anxiety, until the tension is released, the grace notes return, and the oboes join the strings to bring the first section to a close.

In the second section, the conversation ventures further, reaching an even more anxious pause on the most unlikely of chords. At the reprise, the horns enter for the first time, bringing welcome warmth to this delicate music. When the pause is again reached, it takes an agonizingly long time to be resolved, as if unable to tear itself away from a painful memory. In the final bars, oboes and horns enter again, enabling the music to end with elegant resolution.

The minuet in F sharp major is also unconventional. Its quiet, elegant start is interrupted by a jolting bass note in the third bar. And at the end of each half, a phrase droops down, so that it is unclear where one section ends and the next begins. In the minuet, the horns, able to play in F sharp major with their specially ordered slides, provide warm support. In the trio, they lead with a gentle duet.

Back in F sharp minor, the Presto is sturdy and insistent rather than dancing. It proceeds with Haydn's characteristically concentrated energy to the point where it seems to be heading for the end. But suddenly there is a pause, and the music returns to the key of the slow movement, A major, and begins another graceful Adagio. Is this going to be an interlude (like the unexpected new melody in the middle of the first movement), after which the Presto will return? No, this is the surprising conclusion, in which the instruments gradually fall silent. First to leave are the first oboe and the second horn. They are followed a few bars later by the bassoon, then the second oboe and the first horn. The double bass plays a solo, and then leaves. At this point there is a magical change of key: the music shifts from A major to F sharp major. Next to go is the cello, then two of the four violins. Two muted violins and viola are left, and soon the viola falls silent. In the final bars, the two remaining violins (originally Haydn and his concertmaster, Luigi Tommasini) continue in the most delicate duet, until they fade to pianissimo.

SYMPHONY NO. 46 IN B MAJOR

Vivace
Poco adagio
Minuet and Trio: Allegretto
Finale: Presto e scherzando

Like the 'Farewell' Symphony, No. 46 was composed in 1772, and it too is written in a most unusual key, B major. As in that symphony, the horn players would have used the specially ordered extension slides to lower their instruments by a semitone, in this case lowering their C crooks to B.

As often in Haydn, the theme is at first deceptively straightforward. Bold and delicate phrases alternate, leading on to a more energetic second element. Then the opening phrase is combined with a running counterpoint in the second violins. This is all in the major, and has a genial tone. But suddenly the forceful second element breaks into the minor, fortissimo, and there is a dark passage for strings, echoed quietly. After this moment of *Sturm und Drang* drama, the music kicks back into the major to bring the first section to a close.

As the second section begins, the opening of the theme passes quietly between upper and lower strings. Suddenly we are back in the home key, and it seems that we might already be into the reprise. But a shift into F sharp minor takes us into a further, sustained paragraph of dramatic development based on the second element. Eventually, through a series of anxious key changes, the music arrives at the bold reprise of the opening. But this not quite 'home' as we remember it. The genial opening material cannot shake off the darker, dramatic events of the development. A nervous passage combines the echoing of upper and lower strings with the running counterpoint, and this culminates in an outburst in the minor, with a low F sharp held by basses and bassoon, and the opening phrase drawn into this darker drama for the first time in the movement. The emergence back into B major is only a brief moment of relaxation before the second element breaks back into a forceful B minor, with high oboes increasing the tension. As the movement reaches its final bars, again in B major, there is a feeling that the geniality of the opening has been severely tested.

Something of the anxiety generated by the first movement seems to hang over the second. This is in the lilting rhythm of a siciliano, like the slow movement of the 'Hornsignal' Symphony (No. 31). But whereas that movement has a serenade-like quality, this has a more brooding character, partly because it is in B minor (the minor version of the home key of the symphony). Muted strings play an elegant pair of phrases that end with tiptoeing staccato, echoed in the bass. The staccato semiquavers come to dominate this first paragraph. Then there is a smoother continuation, ending with a return to the staccato semiquavers that are, rather surprisingly, taken up by the horns. This first section has arrived in D major. But the run of semiquavers turns a corner back to B minor without coming to rest.

The second time around, this leads on to a passage in which the violins rise higher in a smooth line over the staccato accompaniment, with sustained oboes adding to the lyrical intensity. Soon we arrive at the reprise. But (as so often in Haydn), it is as if the theme has learned from its journey. After the first pair of phrases, staccato semiquavers continue in first violins and the bass, while the oboes and second violins play a beautiful sequence of harmonic suspensions, each creating a dissonance that resolves on the next beat. After the staccato semiquavers come to rest, the smoother continuation is more poignant this time round, being in a minor key. And a moment later, the oboes again intensify the mood with high, plangent harmonies. The last murmuring turns of melody from the violins, and a last tiptoeing from the cellos and basses, bring the movement to close.

The minuet is composed of rippling melodic shapes that rise and then fall elegantly. The beginning of its second strain is enhanced by the oboes playing more of the harmonic suspensions that intensified the slow movement. The trio, in B minor, is pared down to something like a chant, but with sudden fortes that give it a mysterious air. At first it is austerely in two parts, with violins playing the chant and lower strings touching in a bass, then it warms into a three-part chorus. The second half begins with the oboes entering in pure thirds, and ends with the harmonies again becoming enriched. The trio is a simple and haunting interlude between the two statements of the cheerful minuet.

The finale is Haydn at his most playful, reminding us, as often in his symphonies, of his reputation as a writer of comic opera. The tripping little theme begins on two-part violins alone. The rest of the orchestra twice joins them to round it off, first quietly, and then in loud octaves. There is a sudden silence. The violins continue with mock anxiety, in the minor, and the orchestra responds with mock force (not so much *Sturm und Drang* as storm in a teacup).

Alternations between piano and forte take the music to the end of the first section, where the violins are left looking around in bewilderment, and there is another sudden silence.

After the repeat, the music shifts abruptly into a new key, with what might be a burst of outrage. There is another silence, and the quiet tripping resumes. It finds its way back surprisingly quickly to the home key for a reprise of the theme, and proceeds on through the forceful passages to another silence. What happens next is the last thing we expect: the violins pick up the minuet halfway through, and it continues on as if the finale had never existed. Instead of coming to an end, it dissolves into a moment of quiet chords, and a pause. Then the orchestra breaks back into the finale, as if the return of the minuet was an aberration. Soon it peters out once more. Silence. The violins try out a phrase at half speed. Another silence. The horns lay down a low octave B, and a few pianissimo bars take us to a final pair of fortissimo chords.

This is obviously intended to sound like the end. But, if Haydn's repeat is observed, this is just another of the comic silences, and the music returns to the movement's second half, complete with the interruption of the minuet. The second time round, the end really is the end.

SYMPHONY NO. 47 IN G MAJOR, 'THE PALINDROME'

[Allegro]
Un poco adagio, cantabile
Minuet and Trio al roverso
Finale: Presto assai

This symphony, sometimes nicknamed 'Palindrome' after its minuet, was composed in 1772, the same year as the 'Farewell' and No. 46. It is one of Haydn's finest works, combining intellectual brilliance and emotional depth in a rare combination.

If this were a symphony with trumpets and drums, the dotted rhythms at the opening would have that festive character of Haydn's many symphonies in C major. But here, with high horns in G and no trumpets or drums, the effect is jaunty, even ironic. This is partly because the phrases are not in orderly four-bar lengths: the distance from the first forte chord to the next is nine bars, and the following phrase is three bars long. This is a movement that is continually throwing up the unexpected. When Haydn reaches the first sustained forte, he drops the irony and subjects the theme to a moment of serious-sounding counterpoint. But then there are running triplets that sound almost like Rossini in their bubbling energy – the nearest Haydn comes to a second theme.

The second section of the movement begins with the first theme creeping up a semitone at a time, as if on tiptoe. A little later, the Rossini-like triplets are explored further, until they reach a cadence that leads us to expect the reprise of the first theme. This is the greatest surprise of the movement: the theme bursts out ferociously in G minor, as if we have slipped into one of Haydn's so-called *Sturm und Drang* symphonies. Perhaps this is not the reprise, but a continued development. Yet when the running triplets follow, we realize that we really are back, and from this point on the movement proceeds to its conclusion in high spirits.

The slow movement is one of Haydn's most masterly – it would undoubtedly be as famous as that of the 'Surprise' if the symphony had a more fetching nickname. Muted violins play an elegant melody, and, following half a bar later, lower strings and bassoon answer with a bass line in contrapuntal dialogue. As in the first movement, the unusual phrase lengths – five bars each – are part of the charm. There is a mini-interlude, in which first the horns and then the horns and oboes support the violins with the most delicately scored accompaniment. Then the opening ten bars are repeated, but with the parts reversed: the lower strings begin with the leading melody, and the violins answer above with what was the bass.

This is followed by four variations that adhere to the same pattern. Variation 1 is in flowing semiquavers. Variation 2 breaks into delicate triplets, Variation 3 into more elaborate patterns. Each time, the little interlude brings in the horns and the oboes as in the theme. Up to this point, most of each variation has been played by the strings, the oboes and horns entering only for the interlude. But in Variation 4, the last of the set, the oboe joins the violins an octave above, and throughout the variation oboes and horns enrich the string texture. The effect of this is extraordinarily touching, the high oboe brightening the melody like a shaft of light in a Renaissance painting illuminating the baby Jesus. An equally touching final few bars comes gently to rest, as if tiptoeing away from this vision.

The Minuet 'al roverso' gives the symphony the name by which it is sometimes known: 'Palindrome'. The autograph score presents just the first half of the minuet, and the first half of the trio (both to be repeated). The musicians are to create the second halves by playing the first halves backwards. The minuet is in forthright style, with bold contrasts between forte and piano bars. Twice there are forte accents on the first beat of the bar. When the music is reversed, these fall on the third beat of the bar, creating quirky offbeat accents. The trio opens with a horn duet, and therefore finishes with it when the music is reversed. Haydn was clearly pleased by this playful and clever piece of writing: he reused it the next year in a keyboard sonata (in A major, Hob. XVI:26). It is not known why he chose to play this intellectual game in this particular symphony, but here is an idea: this symphony dates from the same year as the 'Farewell', No. 45. If the musicians were becoming restless at being kept longer than usual at the summer palace, perhaps Haydn decided to amuse his musicians by enlivening a symphony with devices that only they would fully appreciate.

After the drama of the first movement, the intellectual and emotional beauty of the second, and the tour de force of the third, the finale is without any contrapuntal elaboration. At a rapid tempo it places side by side a quiet and simple, even naive, opening idea, with a rough and vigorous second idea, and the contrast between the two sustains the whole movement. It is perhaps an unremarkable ending for such a symphony. But the sheer refreshment of such music after the intellectual complexities of the earlier movements has its reward.

SYMPHONY NO. 48 IN C MAJOR, 'MARIA THERESA'

Allegro
Adagio
Minuet and Trio: Allegretto
Finale: Allegro

The nickname arises from a long-held belief that this symphony was composed for the visit of the Austrian Empress Maria Theresa to Esterháza in 1773. But a copy of the score written out by Haydn's copyist at Esterháza, Johann Elssler, discovered in the 1950s, has the date 1769. The symphony may nevertheless have been played during the empress's visit. It is certainly in Haydn's festive C major style, and was published in the 1780s with parts for two high horns, two trumpets, and timpani. But the 1769 copy does not have trumpets or timpani. Some scholars think that Haydn must have approved the additional parts for publication, others that they should be omitted. The horns are high in the outer movements, creating on their own a particular kind of strenuous excitement. The addition of trumpets at the same pitch masks this effect, creating instead a more familiar kind of brilliance. Some conductors opt for horns with the additional timpani, but not trumpets, which is a thoroughly effective compromise.

The symphony opens with brisk and cheerful horn calls (with or without trumpets), and this sets the predominant tone for the first movement. Haydn is often very economical with his themes, but here he gives us half a dozen ideas. Immediately after the opening salvo, there is a moment of hesitant wistfulness, and other thoughtful moments occur later, but they are soon swept away and the overall character is vigorous and bustling.

The slow movement is in Haydn's favourite pastoral mood, in a gently swinging metre, with muted violins. The horns are now in the lower key of F, and their intervention soon after the opening is consoling rather than strenuous. The music could be a pastoral interlude in an opera, with the elegant turns of its violin melody and the murmuring accompaniment in the second violins. This comes to dominate, gently migrating to the melody itself and extending it in new directions.

Haydn's ability to stretch the moment, like a long summer's day, is extraordinary. The melody reaches a cadence and a pause, where an unexpected chord brings enchanting suspense before the music gently winds its way to a resolution. As the second section opens and the music explores further afield, venturing into new keys, there comes another point where time seems suspended. Horns and oboes quietly enter with a sustained note, then the horns turn this into a reprise of their consoling entry from the beginning of the movement. This heralds a return to the violins' pastoral melody, which calmly winds its way, through another moment of suspense, to a peaceful conclusion.

The horns take up their high C crooks again for the minuet that combines vigour with persistent, almost baroque, little ornaments. The second half is particularly striking, culminating in severe fortissimo drummed octaves (with or without actual drums) before ending elegantly. The trio moves into C minor, the persistent ornaments move to the upbeat, and the mood becomes darker.

Running scales create a celebratory atmosphere in the finale, with the oboes chattering brightly and the horns sustaining joyful high notes. Forte and piano passages alternate. But there is no moment of darkness until the second section. Here there are a few bars of creeping minor harmonies, but they are soon over, and the opening scales burst in to take the celebration forward confidently to the conclusion.

SYMPHONY NO. 49 IN F MINOR, 'LA PASSIONE'

Adagio
Allegro di molto
Minuet and Trio
Presto

This was one of the most widely performed of Haydn's symphonies in his lifetime. The earliest known use of the title 'La Passione' dates from a performance in Germany in 1790, when it was played during the week leading up to Easter. Whether it was, like Symphony No. 26, associated with the Passion of Christ when it was first performed at the Esterházy court in 1768 is unknown. An undeniable mood of tragic intensity permeates the symphony. This has led writers to regard it as one of Haydn's *Sturm und Drang* symphonies, again like No. 26. But there are also deliberately 'antique' references in the music, most obviously in its overall format. Every movement is in the same key, F minor, and the symphony begins with a substantial slow movement. This refers back to the old 'church sonata' format that, in the previous generation, was common not only to trio sonatas but also in some *concerti grossi* (see entry on Corelli). As usual, Haydn blends the old and the new in a fascinating way. There are pairs of horns and oboes, but no flute or trumpets to brighten the mood.

The opening Adagio is like the prelude to a tragic scene in an opera, but on an expansive scale – if both sections are repeated (which they rarely are) the movement lasts about twelve minutes. The sombre opening rises eloquently, and then falls haltingly. Then the melodic line becomes more troubled, its meditation giving way to outbursts, at first forte and then fortissimo. The occasional entries of the horns and oboes are telling. The horns are pitched in F, which enables them to play the keynote F and the fifth, C, but not A flat, the third of the home chord. But when the music has chords of D flat major and A flat major, the horns can play the third of the chord (F and C respectively). Haydn uses this fact to inject sudden fullness and warmth to these chords as the music moves through different keys.

The second movement opens with an almost Handel-like gesture. Against a running bass, the violins declaim a strong theme with leaping intervals like a baroque fugue subject – it brings to mind the chorus 'And with his stripes we are healed' from Handel's *Messiah*. But this is only an opening declaration, not a fugue, and the music soon breaks up into agitated, syncopated patterns, followed by half a dozen further elements, most of them energetic and urgent. The opening gesture returns to signal the start of the second section, and after extensive development of the various elements it returns again at the reprise. In the final bars the leaping intervals are played at double speed, heightening the energy as the movement comes to a close.

The minuet, still in F minor, has clear links to the first movement, both in its sombre character and in its melody: the first three notes are the same in each case. In quiet moments, the violas fall below the cellos, creating chords of dark richness. The trio is in F major, and with its high first horn part brings a welcome moment of relief.

The finale is fast and furious, with abrupt, short phrases, and rapidly bowed repetitions. It has subtle links to earlier movements, without directly quoting them. The first theme begins with a variant of the opening notes of the symphony, and later there are leaps that relate to the Handelian theme of the second movement. These subtleties may not seem obvious, but they contribute to the sense of this symphony as having an unusually 'organic' unity, not only in mood but in the details of its structure.

SYMPHONY NO. 56 IN C MAJOR

Allegro di molto
Adagio
Minuet and Trio
Prestissimo

This symphony was composed in 1774. Like Nos 41 and 48, it is one of Haydn's series of festive symphonies in C major, with high horns, trumpets, and timpani. It is widely regarded as one of the very finest in this genre, on a par with his later symphonies for Paris and London.

What is most striking in the first movement is the range and subtlety of expressive devices brought together within a basically celebratory piece. The full orchestra opens with a bold, simple falling arpeggio of C major. The strings give a quiet, thoughtful answer, with subtle suggestions of counterpoint. The full orchestra plays another rising and falling arpeggio, this time with sharp dotted rhythms, and follows it with a repeat of the original falling arpeggio, but now made doubly assertive with rapid tremolo bowing. The strings again answer thoughtfully. Then there is a more sustained passage for full orchestra. This is just as vigorous as the opening, with more tremolo bowing, but the music develops complexity. Instead of proceeding in a block, it now has three independent lines, with sudden tensions created by the pull of the harmonies and touches of minor chords. What began as a simple assertion of C major now has an element of struggle, as if the music is having to exert more energy in order to ward off doubt and to maintain its cheerfulness. This sense of potential conflict in overtly festive music is one of the hallmarks of Haydn at his greatest – a feature that Mozart was just beginning to develop in a highly personal way (his Symphony No. 29 in A major is contemporary with this symphony). There is a pause, and the strings develop their original, quiet thought into a second theme in a gentle, serenade-like style. Strings and full orchestra alternate, until a final tutti rises gloriously to a climactic high G to round off the first section of the movement.

In the second section, the potential conflict hinted at earlier is brought to the surface. The strings' thoughtful idea becomes more anxious, taking the music into minor keys, and the full orchestra's brusque replies become more threatening. The development culminates in another sustained tutti in the minor, in which the sense of conflict is at its most severe. The anxious response of the strings turns a corner, and we emerge into the sunlight for the reprise back in C major. This proceeds much as before, but with wonderful additional touches: a high oboe joins the violins for their thoughtful answer, which is then developed further. And at the very end of this complex and subtle movement, the simple arpeggio of C major is asserted one last time. Nowhere in Haydn's earlier symphonies has the sense of homecoming been so welcome, the culmination of a journey so dramatically and convincingly constructed.

Like the first movement, the Adagio in F major extends far beyond the implications of its opening. The strings, with violins muted, play a warm, consoling six-bar phrase with a characteristically elegant little turn, and this is answered by oboes. A solo bassoon follows, extending the melody by ten bars. An oboe slows the melody, holding long notes and gradually creeping upwards, while the barest of accompaniments adds touches of poignant harmony. A sudden forte, with a duet of oboes, pushes this bleakness aside for a moment. But then it returns, an oboe suspended motionless as the bass inches forward to a cadence: Haydn has the second oboe overlap with the first to make the suspense seamless. The violins finish off the first section with a smoothly elaborated flow of notes, as if needing to reassure us.

The strings open the second section by returning to the opening melody. Then, like the earlier bassoon, they extend it. It reaches a minor key, and the wind join in to take it to a climax – the wind and strings moving in opposite directions create a particularly plangent effect. Still in the minor, the long oboe notes return, but these too develop in a new direction, so that the music once again warms towards the home key of F major, and prepares us for the reprise of the opening theme. This leads on to another bassoon solo, more playful than before, but its lightness is immediately contradicted by the return of the oboes bleak long notes. Once again this is pushed aside, once again the bleakness returns, and for a final time the violins elaborate a consoling conclusion.

The minuet is in Haydn's grandest style, opening, like the first movement, with a gesture simply and boldly asserting C major. Rushing scales and tumbling triplet patterns alternate with piano phrases for strings as naive as those of a village dance band. In the second half, there is a teasing silence before the reprise. In the trio, violins play a sweet melody with an oboe an octave above – Haydn was fond of this combination at this stage of his career, and it creates a particularly tender effect.

In the finale, Haydn seems to have decided that the tumbling triplets from the second half of the minuet can be used to create an entire movement. With this extreme economy he creates an impression like the last scene of a comic opera, as if the characters are running helplessly around, doomed to live with the consequences of their foolish actions. At the start of the second section there is a moment of anxiety, and later the music comes to a sudden halt, as if everyone is looking around in bewilderment. As they try to move forward, the reprise bursts in unexpectedly, and without further ceremony the ending is dispatched.

SYMPHONY NO. 60 IN C MAJOR, 'IL DISTRATTO'

Adagio – Allegro di molto
Andante
Menuetto and Trio
Presto
Adagio (di Lamentatione)
Finale: Prestissimo

Prince Nikolaus Esterházy was an enthusiast not only for music but also for the theatre. As well as staging operas, for which Haydn was responsible, he also brought theatre companies to Esterháza to perform a wide range of drama, including Shakespeare, whose plays were just becoming known in German adaptations. For a period of five years from 1772 to 1777 the prince engaged the well-known Carl Wahr troupe. Haydn had a close relationship with Wahr, and supplied incidental music for many of his productions, including Shakespeare's *Hamlet* (according to contemporary reports, though the music has never been found). It is to the Wahr troupe's visit in 1774 that we owe this Symphony No. 60. Among the works that they performed that year was a German translation of *Le Distrait* (*The Absent-minded Man*), a play written in 1697 by Jean-François Regnard, who was, after Molière, the most celebrated French writer of comedy in the seventeenth century. For this production, Haydn composed an overture, four entr'actes, and a finale. A report in the *Pressburger Zeitung* commented on the music, 'connoisseurs consider it a masterpiece. One notices the same spirit that elevates all of Hayden's [sic] work, this time in a musical-comical caprice. His masterly variety excites the admiration of experts while delighting ordinary listeners, for Hayden knows how to satisfy both parties.'[8]

Léandre is a well-meaning but scatterbrained young man whose absent-mindedness is the principal catalyst for comedy in the play. The trouble this leads him into ranges from simple farce, such as searching for gloves that he is already wearing, to more serious gaffes, notably forgetting that he has signed a marriage contract as a condition of inheriting his uncle's fortune. When it comes to Haydn's music, the details of the plot are neither here nor there. What matters is that this symphony gives us insight into the wit and charm that Haydn brought to theatre music.

Trumpets and drums announce the opening of the Adagio, and a few elegant bars lead into the Allegro di molto (Presto in one early source). This has the lively energy of many of

Haydn's first movements. But a second theme gets stuck after four bars, repeating the same chord and getting quieter, until it is rescued by a burst of fortissimo. This is the first 'absent-minded' moment in Haydn's score, a device that he wittily uses again to lead in the reprise.

The second movement is in Haydn's characteristic ambling style, with ironic touches. The violin melody is quiet, but it is punctuated by loud quasi-fanfares from the horns and oboes, like the entry of a character who has an exaggerated view of his own importance. Leading on from this theme there is a moment of canon, in which the melody is echoed one bar later in the bass. This too seems mock-serious. After a genuinely serious moment, the first section ends with a rather lumpy dance, with awkward cross-rhythms. As these elements interact in the second half of the movement, it is not always clear when Haydn intends to be serious.

The minuet is rather stately, with, at the beginning of the second half, a surprising moment of serious counterpoint. The trio is in the minor, austere at first, and then with oboe and violins picking their way up and down a scale, over a held drone. Some writers suggest that this is another 'absent-minded' moment, others suggest it has the character of Balkan folk song (perhaps Haydn meant both).

The Presto features Hungarian tunes. Most of it is in C minor and is for strings and oboes only. But after a passage of high-energy tremolo bowing, the music breaks into C major, the trumpets, horns, and drums join in, and the movement ends in high spirits.

The fifth movement is headed Adagio (di Lamentatione). The first violins play a gentle melody, while the second violins play a flowing accompaniment over a pizzicato bass. It is one of Haydn's loveliest movements; but it is interrupted by a sudden outburst of military-style horns, trumpets, and drums. This is probably a reference to the Chevalier, a ridiculous soldier who is in love with the woman whom Léandre is contracted to marry. At the end, the music accelerates to a sudden conclusion, as if this entr'acte was intended to lead straight into a comic scene.

Finally, there is rapid Prestissimo, which presumably would have been played at the end of the play. It begins with a moment of pure farce: after a few bars, the music stops, and the violins find that their bottom string, G, is tuned to F, and they must retune it. Then the movement restarts, and, interrupted only momentarily by another Balkan-style tune, it rattles helter-skelter to a witty conclusion worthy of Rossini.

Symphonies Nos 82–87, the 'Paris' Symphonies

In 1779, Haydn's contract as Kapellmeister to Prince Esterházy was renewed. The most important change was an omission: the previous contract stated that Haydn's compositions were reserved exclusively for the prince, and that he was not to compose music for anyone else without the prince's permission. This clause was removed from the 1779 contract. This was perhaps an acknowledgement that such restraints were impossible to enforce. Copies of Haydn's works, licit and illicit, were to be found all over Europe, his music was often performed in far-away countries, and he was internationally famous. His principal task at court during the period 1775–84 was to supervise opera productions, the prince's current obsession, and Haydn had less time to write symphonies, string quartets, and other instrumental works. Perhaps the prince's concentration on opera, and the eminence of his Kapellmeister, persuaded him that it could only enhance the reputation of his court if Haydn were to be allowed greater freedom to exploit his works.

Whatever the reason, the relaxing of Haydn's contract was to bear spectacular fruit within a few years. His symphonies and string quartets had been regularly performed in Paris for a decade or more when, in 1784, he received a commission to compose a set of six symphonies (Nos 82–87) for *Le Concert de la Loge Olympique*. This organization held series of concerts played by a large orchestra made up of some of the best professional and amateur musicians in Paris, including forty violins and ten double basses. A young aristocrat, the Comte d'Ogny, was responsible for engaging Haydn for the *Concert*, and the success of the new symphonies was so great that he went on to commission a further three, Nos 90–92.

Haydn composed his six 'Paris' Symphonies over 1785–6, and they were first performed in Paris in 1787 to great acclaim. The critic of the *Mercure de France* had particularly perceptive things to say about the new works: 'one admires more and more the output of this great genius, who, in each of his works, is able to make so much of a single subject, to draw out such rich and varied developments; so different from those sterile composers, who continually pass from one idea to another, not knowing how to create variety from a single idea, and mechanically pile effect on effect, without coherence and without taste'.[9]

SYMPHONY NO. 82 IN C MAJOR, 'THE BEAR'

Vivace assai
Allegretto
Minuet and Trio
Finale: Vivace

This is Haydn in splendid, quasi-military mood, with horns, trumpets, and drums – a style well calculated to go down well in Paris. Mozart had composed his Symphony No. 31 in D for Paris eight years before, and that too has a distinctly military splendour. The Parisian musicians were particularly noted for their attack – the *premier coup d'archet* – and Haydn launches straight in with a bold arpeggio, followed by insistent fanfare flourishes. But this is just the beginning. Haydn takes this opening material and builds a dramatic paragraph from it, culminating in Beethoven-like discords. A second theme is light and elegant, but elements of the dramatic music continue to break through before the first half of the movement finishes quietly.

The second half opens with these elements being placed in new relationships with each other. The contrasts between the lyrical and the assertive are increasingly dramatic, and the changes of key create a sense of an ongoing journey. In a quiet moment, the lyrical elements combine in counterpoint. But then the fierce discords return, and we are back to the opening in C major for the reprise. This time the second theme is charmingly coloured by a bassoon. Towards the end there is a moment of quiet suspense, with plangent harmonies, before a further outburst of fanfares brings the movement to a festive conclusion. Both halves of the movement are marked to be repeated, but many performances omit the second repeat.

The second movement is a Haydn speciality, a set of double variations: that is, a set of variations on alternating themes, one in the major, the other in the minor. The first theme in the major, on strings alone, begins as a tiptoeing dance, naive (or maybe ironic) in its simplicity. But its second part twice passes through touches of poignant harmony before returning to the naive opening. The second theme is (as often in Haydn) closely related to the first, but darkened by being in the minor. The tiptoeing alternates with brusque forte phrases. The first major-key variation is varied only in instrumentation. A flute joins the violins in playing the melody, at first an octave above and later in unison, with other wind instruments below. The first minor-key variation is a sudden change. The sequence of harmonies remains, but the melody has vanished to be replaced by a running bass line. The second major-key variation returns to the simplicity of the original theme, but now with a bassoon colouring the melody an octave below the violins. Later the flute again joins the violins, and the tune is decorated with playful grace notes. The variation comes to an end, and we might expect another pair of variations. Instead, Haydn develops an extended coda to round off the movement. This climaxes in a passage evoking a country dance with offbeat accents – a premonition of what is to come in the finale – before the music winds to a close with the same naivety with which it began.

The minuet is full of contrasts. Its basic character is sturdy, with trumpet (or horn) calls. But the first half finishes with a demure phrase on the oboe, and in the second half this idea is developed by the violins. The trio begins with phrases whose naive, charming character is like that of the opening of the second movement. But in a similar way, Haydn surprises us in the second half. The music turns more serious, moving into the minor first on woodwind then on strings. There are further explorations before the naivety of the opening is restored.

The principal theme of the finale gives the symphony its nickname. It is an evocation of a rustic dance, with the drone and flicking grace notes of a bagpipe. This prompted an imaginative early nineteenth-century piano arranger to come up with the title, 'Le Danse de l'Ours' (dancing bears were a common feature of the time).[10] It begins quietly, and then bursts out and extends into a vigorous paragraph. This is interrupted only momentarily by a perky second theme on woodwind. The second half of the movement takes the 'Bear' theme and treats it seriously, moving through different keys and using a web of counterpoint to maintain momentum. There is a sudden cut-off, and the reprise enters quietly. This time the forte outburst culminates in a more insistent assertion of the drone, joined by horns or trumpets, bassoons, and oboes. Once more it cuts off, and a final build-up ends with the timpani thundering fortissimo.

SYMPHONY NO. 83 IN G MINOR, 'THE HEN'

Allegro spiritoso
Andante
Minuet and Trio: Allegretto
Finale: Vivace

This is the odd one out of the 'Paris' Symphonies. It is the only one with its first movement in a minor key, less obviously designed for popular appeal than the others. It is often described as a throwback to the tempestuous symphonies of Haydn's so-called *Sturm und Drang* period a decade earlier. But Haydn never lost his capacity to come up with bold, even shocking Romantic gestures. Three years after he composed this symphony, Haydn composed a Piano Trio in E minor (Hob. XV:12) whose first movement has very similar nervous drama. The scoring of the symphony includes two horns, but not trumpets.

It opens with brusque phrases separated by silences. Each phrase rises, with every note accentuated, to a discord on the third note, and then falls in urgent dotted rhythms. After the third silence, the phrase extends into a paragraph of great power and urgency, with the dotted rhythms supplying fierce energy. Eventually this gives way to more fanfare-like patterns and then to a relaxed, humorous, second theme with pecking staccato and grace notes. This is the theme that gives the symphony its nickname, but it could equally well evoke comic opera. Soon it is joined by an oboe renewing the dotted notes, which gives the theme an even more

chicken-like character. The violins take up the dotted rhythms, and it is these that triumphantly bring the first half to a close.

The second half throws the fierce opening and the witty second theme in strong contrast
with each other. Then the first theme is combined with another pattern from the opening into
a powerful passage of counterpoint. This breaks off once again in a dramatic silence. The first
theme is held in a moment of mysterious suspense, before bursting out forte to bring in the
reprise. This time, after the third silence, Haydn suddenly breaks into G major, and we are
soon at the humorous second theme. The next forte arrives at an unexpected pause. Then,
after a moment of questioning, the movement comes to an end with the dotted rhythms reasserting themselves.

The Andante is a lyrical movement punctuated by sudden shocks that the famously attacking
Paris orchestra must surely have enjoyed. The melody gently unfolds in the first violins, and then
moves to the second violins with the firsts playing an elegant counterpoint, and then back to the
first violins. The final few bars of the theme are a duet between the two violin parts. Now comes
the first interruption, a rapid descending scale. Four bars of quiet suspense, getting quieter and
quieter, are interrupted by a sudden scrubbing fortissimo. Then a new elegant idea continues as
if nothing unusual has happened, and the first half of the movement comes to a demure close.
The pattern continues into the second half as the music moves into new keys, and the lyrical
theme is again interrupted by sudden outbursts. After the third outburst, there is a particularly
beautiful moment, as a subsidiary phrase from the first part of the movement is developed into
an extended passage of counterpoint. This brings us to the reprise of the first part.

The minuet in G major is vigorous. Its opening phrase already contains a playful cross-
rhythm, and at the end of the minuet Haydn has fun with it, throwing the metre into confusion. The trio, by contrast, is sweet and serene. The sweetness is heightened by Haydn's
characteristic uses of the flute. At first it plays an octave above the violins, at the beginning of
the second half it is in unison with the violins, and it finishes once again an octave above – a
simple but utterly charming effect.

The finale, with its tarantella-like swinging rhythm in G major, is very reminiscent of the
famous 'Joke' finale of the Quartet in E flat major Opus 33, No. 2, in E flat, composed three years
before. There is really only one theme, though it has several different elements, with continual
contrasts between delicate piano and bustling forte and an overall spirit of boundless energy.
The second part of the movement, as usual, moves into new keys. After a moment of anxious
questioning it breaks into a perpetuum mobile in the violins, with savagely accented chords on
each half-bar – the most insistently tarantella-like passage in the movement. Suddenly the wildness is over, and the quiet reprise begins. At the end, there are three hesitations – quizzical
rather than funny – before the momentum is regained and the dance hurtles to a conclusion.

SYMPHONY NO. 84 IN E FLAT MAJOR

Largo – Allegro
Andante
Minuet and Trio: Allegretto
Vivace

Like No. 83, this symphony is scored with two horns, but not trumpets. It opens with a broad,
slow introduction. Immediately we can hear Haydn's feeling for beautiful string sonorities, as

the upper strings sing in chorus, and the bass line and violins interweave in dialogue (this is, after all, the great composer of string quartets). The wind instruments also have the first of many sonorous moments. The Allegro begins quietly and delicately, with a demure violin melody over running staccato. The full orchestra enters twice, the second time launching out into increasingly energetic patterns in both melody and bass. Just at the moment when we have arrived in a new key, and might expect a second theme, the woodwind instead return to the first theme, taking it in a slightly different direction. There is a brusque interruption from the full orchestra, followed by some surprising harmonic twists, before vigorous arpeggios round off the first half of the movement. In the second half, the main elements vie with each other in new dramatic turns. The surprising harmonic twists are sustained for longer than before, so that the music seems suspended, until a return to energetic patterns brings in the reprise.

The second movement is a set of variations. If the opening of the theme seems to evoke a memory, it is because it echoes the shape of the melody at the beginning of the symphony's slow introduction. The theme is like a slow dance, in a lilting metre (6/8) that Haydn loved, with offbeat accents giving an unexpected tug. At first violins and violas play the theme in simple octaves over the bass, but then touches of harmony creep in to warm it – a typically subtle idea. The first variation is in the minor, with full orchestra entering brusquely (an unusually dramatic change so early in a set of variations). The severe sound of the forte contrasts with sad piano passages. The second half is particularly beautiful, with the phrases answering each other in sombre counterpoint. The second variation returns to the major and to the strings, with delicate elaborations of the melody. Again, Haydn saves something special for the second half, where the theme moves to the second violins while the firsts play a lovely descant above it.

The full orchestra enters for the third variation, with the melody on top and running elaboration of the bass below. In the second half, treble and bass answer each other. The high horns give a splendid, celebratory character to the texture. Instead of finishing, the variation reaches an inconclusive pause. From here, the music moves to the sort of cadence that, in a concerto, would herald a cadenza for the soloist. And indeed what follows is a miniature cadenza, played by the wind instruments in mellifluous counterpoint over accompanying pizzicato. After another pause, the movement is rounded off with a simple return to the theme.

The minuet is invigorated by its upbeats, with a persistent 'Scotch snap' – Haydn was to do the same thing in the famous 'Lark' String Quartet, Opus 64, No. 5, four years later. The second half begins with bassoon and violas adding a sonorous countermelody. Then there is a charming moment of hesitation before the music finds its way to a conclusion. A bassoon is again prominent in the trio, joining the violin melody an octave below. Each upbeat of the melody is accented, and in the second half this offbeat emphasis develops a rustic persistence.

The finale opens with Haydn's characteristic good humour – a simple, regular melody on the violins that becomes more complex in its second half, followed by an extended burst of vigorous tutti, with the melodic line broken into energetic pairs of repeated notes. As the forte gives way to piano there is a moment of mystery, and then a hint of a second theme. But it is scarcely more than a link to the equally vigorous tutti that finishes the first half.

The second half begins simply with the first strain of the theme, and then breaks forcefully into the minor, and on into other keys, with different possibilities of the theme explored. The explorations culminate in a renewal of the energetic repeated notes. From here the music calms to the mysterious passage, now elongated into an extended moment of suspense. Out of it emerges the reprise of the theme. All seems as before, until Haydn plays with our expectations, introducing another moment of suspense before the full orchestra enters. Now there is nothing more to impede the music's joyful progress to its conclusion.

SYMPHONY NO. 85 IN B FLAT MAJOR, 'LA REINE'

Adagio – Vivace
Romance: Allegretto
Menuetto and Trio: Allegretto
Presto

Royalty and nobility used to attend *Le Concert de la Loge Olympique*, including Queen Marie Antoinette, who particularly liked No. 85. When the set was published in Paris in 1788, this symphony was given the title 'La Reine de France'. This is a rare instance of a Haydn symphony receiving its nickname soon after its composition, and it has been known as 'La Reine' ever since. Like Nos 83 and 84, it has horns but not trumpets.

The slow introduction bears a family resemblance to the traditional baroque 'French Overture', with its forceful dotted rhythms and scales (stately or vigorous, depending on how they are performed). Perhaps it was this allusion that first struck the French queen. The Vivace begins with an idea that seems almost naked in its simplicity. But Haydn's genius is to use this seemingly unpromising material as the principal theme with which to build the movement. After the modest opening, there is a brief tutti, with energetic scales (echoing those in the slow introduction). Then the opening theme returns, with harmonies delicately touched in, together with responses from the woodwind. There is a more extensive tutti, in which the energy of the subsidiary idea develops momentum. At one point, the music breaks into a minor key, becoming severe and urgent, before warming into the major, in preparation for (we might think) a second theme. But, as often in Haydn, what we get is another variant of the first theme, with an oboe playing the melody, and new touches of harmony giving it a plangent nuance. Another vigorous tutti concludes the first section of the movement.

The second section continues energetically, but then quietens to yet more variation of the main theme. Haydn develops an extended paragraph from it, with delicate echoing and overlapping phrases, once again almost in baroque style. After another tutti outburst, we reach the reprise of the theme, with horns and flute providing yet more subtle variation.

Four years before the premiere of Haydn's 'Paris' Symphonies, a rustic 'hamlet', complete with mill and farm, had been built for Queen Marie Antoinette in the grounds of the Palace at Versailles, as a place of retreat from the formality of the court. She liked to dress as a shepherdess, and took part in pastoral tableaux in the little theatre in the nearby Petit Trianon. The theme of Haydn's slow movement is just the sort of naive pastoral song that would have appealed to the queen, and which she might even have sung on the stage. Carl Friedrich Pohl, who published the first major study of Haydn in the late nineteenth century, stated that this melody was an old French song, 'La gentile et jeune Lisette'. But it is uncertain whether it really is old, or whether these words were added to Haydn's melody – a common practice of the time.[11] The theme is played by strings alone. In Variation 1, each half begins demurely as before, with the strings joined in the first half by a flute and in the second half by horns. Each half ends with the mock-dramatic entry of the full orchestra. Variation 2 is in the minor and played by strings alone, with lovely interplay between first and second violins. Variation 3 returns to the major, with a charmingly decorative descant on the flute. In Variation 4, the violins are joined by a bassoon an octave below, giving a wry tone to the elaboration of the melody. In the second half, the other woodwind join in, and the movement ends with the full orchestra, but pianissimo.

The minuet of Symphony No. 84 was enlivened by upbeat 'Scotch snaps'. Here, in No. 85, Haydn sprinkles Scotch snaps around in a playful manner. By contrast, the trio is evenly mellifluous, with a bassoon enriching the violin melody an octave below.

The theme of the Presto finale is light and carefree, though the bassoon an octave below the violins, as in the minuet, adds a touch of mellowness (or perhaps mock-seriousness) to the mix. This movement is a rondo, in which three occurrences of the theme alternate with two episodes. Rather than introduce new themes, the episodes develop the main theme in new directions: a striking example of Haydn's ability, as the Parisian critic put it, 'to make so much of a single subject, to draw out such rich and varied developments'. The first episode is by turns forceful and airy, the airiness enhanced by Haydn's characteristic use of the flute. The second episode breaks in before the rondo theme has quite finished, and develops an almost Beethoven-like momentum and intensity. Eventually the intensity evaporates into a passage of teasing suspense, and the final reprise of the rondo theme brings the movement to an ending as carefree as its beginning.

SYMPHONY NO. 86 IN D MAJOR

Adagio – Allegro spiritoso
Capriccio: Largo
Minuet and Trio: Allegretto
Finale: Allegro con spirito

This symphony begins with one of Haydn's most striking slow introductions. It opens very delicately, with oboes and violins over pizzicato chords. A few bars later, the full orchestra enters with the grandest of effects – trumpets, horns, and timpani, violin scales rushing downwards, bass scales rushing upwards. A few delicate bars are interrupted by a dramatic chord, with more trumpet calls. And the surprises do not end there. The slow introduction moves seamlessly into the Allegro spiritoso, with a theme whose harmonies suggest that it has started in the middle. Only when the full orchestra enters again are we securely, and splendidly, in D major. After a brief return to the opening theme, Haydn introduces a new, shy little theme, before the first section ends with another splendid tutti.

The second section begins with one of Haydn's most searching developments. It starts by exploiting the uncertain harmony of the first theme to venture off into new keys. By the time the full orchestra joins in, we are in F sharp minor, and the shifts of key take on dramatic urgency. This searching quality also infects the shy second theme, which lingers uncertainly. Eventually, the journey takes us back to D major. The reprise of the opening theme, with its surprising harmonies, once again sounds more like a continuation than the beginning of a theme. By the time the movement ends, with the splendour of trumpets and drums, we have the sense that this has been an exceptionally bold and far-ranging journey.

Haydn occasionally used the term Capriccio to suggest music with a somewhat improvisatory character (like the more familiar Fantasia). This, like the first movement, is unusually exploratory music. The sombre opening bars could be the introduction to a dark operatic scene. When the violins begin to unfold a delicate, elaborate melodic line, it sounds like the meditation of the heroine – and, once again, she seems to be continuing a line of thought, rather than starting at the beginning. There are three great paragraphs of the meditation, each introduced by the sombre opening bars. The first, predominantly delicate, ends with a dramatic outburst. The second is less obviously the voice of the 'heroine', and begins by developing the sombre introductory bars in new directions and into new keys. Again, a sudden dramatic outburst leads back to the opening bars, and to the third great paragraph. This is a reprise of the opening paragraph, but varied and extended. The slow movements of Haydn's later symphonies often have an aria-like quality, but this fully developed 'scene' is unusual. He must have had great confidence in the Paris orchestra's ability to do justice to it.

The third movement is the most splendid type of minuet, with trumpets and drums. But, in this symphony full of surprises, it is no ordinary minuet. It begins fairly conventionally, but the second half after a few bars suddenly moves quietly into a minor key, and for an extended, poignant moment it is as if we are embarking on the sort of development that belongs in the middle of a first movement. After this astonishing minuet, the trio, with its charming doubling of the tune by bassoon and oboes, comes as a naive contrast.

If the slow movement is like the outpouring of a tragic heroine, the finale is pure comic opera. The insistently regular little phrases of the opening theme are like the mannerisms of a ridiculous pedant, at first delicately precise, and then in a rage. After an extended tutti, there is an attempt at a second theme, but it is as if the first theme has been reduced to incoherent stuttering, with much comic use of 'Scotch snaps'. In the second section of the movement Haydn develops these different elements playfully. And just before the end of the movement, there is a final moment of stuttering, so incoherent as to seem like someone reduced to virtual speechlessness. A final burst of full orchestra brings this extraordinary work to a close.

SYMPHONY NO. 87 IN A MAJOR

Vivace
Adagio
Minuet and Trio
Finale: Vivace

This symphony has no trumpets, but the fanfare-like opening nevertheless sets a festive tone straight away. The bold, bustling style is in line with many other symphonies and operatic overtures of the day. But the way it dissolves into a moment of doubt, sliding into an unexpected key before reasserting its self-confidence, is pure Haydn. There is a second theme, delicate and staccato, and a further bold tutti, but it is an echo of the staccato second theme that brings the first section to a surprisingly quiet close. In the second section, the fanfares of the opening take on a darker, more aggressive character, pushing their way through new keys. The moment of doubt reappears, made more poignant by a delicate countermelody on flute. And the staccato second theme is also extended, hesitating before turning back to A major for the reprise of the opening theme.

The Adagio features the woodwind, in a manner that suggests something between concerto and opera scene – the instruments seem almost like characters singing (or perhaps dancing) to express their personal emotions. The strings set the scene with eight solemn bars. As these are repeated, the first 'character', a flute, sings over them a delicately embellished line. Oboe and bassoon respond in duet, and then the line moves to the violins. As the various woodwind join in, the music becomes more and more like an opera ensemble. This culminates in a trio for flute and two oboes, in effect a miniature cadenza, to bring the first strain of the movement to a close.

The strings take the opening bars in a new direction, the harmonies becoming more plangent. Quite soon, the music returns to its original key for the reprise of the opening strain. Once again the ensemble coalesces into a cadenza. This time, it begins as a trio for two oboes and violins, then the flute introduces running embellishments and is answered by oboe and bassoon. A trill brings the cadenza to an end, and the movement finishes with a return to the opening bars, with the flute charmingly lightening the solemnity with its rising scales.

The minuet is one of Haydn's most playful. The playfulness lies in a combination of old and new. The little flourishes that accentuate the main beats are like traditional baroque ornaments. But they are brought into music with thoroughly modern surprises and developments. The trio features an oboe, playing a charming pastoral solo.

The quiet principal theme of the finale has regular phrases that evoke popular song, interspersed with passages of bustling energy. What is most striking in this movement is the way that Haydn develops this 'naive' material in the second section. The music becomes highly contrapuntal, almost like a passage of fugue, but with a sense of great energy rather than anything academic. Having passed through several keys, it arrives back in D major. But Haydn does not reprise the theme at this point, and we seem to be approaching a final climax without it. Then, after a pause, the theme does sneak back in, before a final burst of energy rounds off the movement.

SYMPHONY NO. 88 IN G MAJOR

Adagio – Allegro
Largo
Menuetto and Trio: Allegretto
Finale: Allegro con spirito

Following the enormous success of the six 'Paris' Symphonies, and the greater freedom that his employer now allowed him, Haydn established relationships with publishers in Paris, Vienna, and London. His next five symphonies, Nos 88–92, were composed with Paris in mind. Nos 88 and 89 were put in the hands of Johann Tost, a violinist in the Esterházy orchestra, who was travelling to Paris to try to establish business as an entrepreneur. He was an unscrupulous (though ultimately successful) figure, who not only sold Haydn's new symphonies to a publisher in Paris but also tried to pass off symphonies by another composer as the work of Haydn. Haydn complains of the difficulty of getting Tost to pay him the money due to him. No. 88 is a particularly fine symphony. In English-speaking countries it is sometimes referred to as 'Letter V', a pointless nickname that derives from nothing more interesting than an old publisher's cataloguing letter. In German-speaking countries it is the Symphony 'Mit dem Dudelsack' (with the bagpipe), referring to the drone in the trio of the minuet.

The slow introduction begins with a formal call to attention, within which the violins weave moments of elegant decoration. These suggest the elaborate gestures of dance, or the decoration of an opera singer. Then the Allegro opens with a theme like a horn call, but quietly on violins. Only when it is repeated forte do the horns join in. This little theme, particularly its rhythm, dominates the entire movement, without any real second theme. Characteristically, Haydn subjects the theme to highly imaginative variation. An energetic semiquaver pattern soon joins it, at first in the bass, then in the violins, and this drives the movement forward. Where the energy eases off for a quiet moment, you would expect a second theme. But instead, Haydn preserves the pointed rhythm of his first theme, combining it with a falling chromatic accompaniment that gives it a plaintive character. In the centre of the movement, the pointed rhythm and the energetic semiquaver pattern combine to build up an insistent passage of counterpoint that develops great energy. When the horn-call theme returns, it cannot shake off the semiquavers, which are wittily combined with it, first on flute, then on violins.

The theme of the slow movement is a lovely, singing melody for solo cello with oboe (Brahms was reported to have said, 'I want my ninth symphony to be like this!').[12] Its three-time gives it the poise of a very slow dance. This melody is treated to beautiful decoration and variation. Violins accompany it with a delicate, tripping counterpoint that seems to have stepped out of the opening bars of the symphony. Later, the violins take up the melody itself, then they add running scales to it. Later still, it is the turn of the oboe to add touches of counterpoint. The other, and most startling, feature of this movement is the interruption of all this beautiful melody by trumpets and drums. They were silent throughout the first movement, but now, when they are least expected, they add a stern, warlike tailpiece to the melody, hammering out the beats of the bar – one, two, three, one. The second time the trumpets and drums intervene, in the middle of the movement, they lead the music into a new key, where the melody acquires a rich sonority, low on the violins.

The third movement is a sturdy minuet (Allegretto, not Allegro), with a twiddle on each upbeat giving it an insistent, rather baroque emphasis, and the timpani adding a ceremonial tread. The trio has drones in the bass, suggestive of bagpipes, over which the woodwind and violins dance demurely.

The finale is very short and delightfully witty. The theme is on violins with bassoon an octave below, later joined by a flute an octave above. Like the first Allegro, the whole movement is dominated by this tripping theme. In between its opening and closing appearances it is taken on an excursion, with the upper and lower strings pursuing each other in mock-serious counterpoint – first with the lower strings one beat ahead of the upper, then with the upper strings one bar ahead of the lower. The return to the original tune is playfully delayed, and the symphony ends in high spirits.

SYMPHONY NO. 92 IN G MAJOR, 'OXFORD'

Adagio – Allegro spiritoso
Adagio
Minuet and Trio: Allegretto
Presto

Composed in 1789, this is the last and most impressive of the three symphonies (Nos 90–92) commissioned by the Comte d'Ogny following the great success of the 'Paris' Symphonies. It acquired its nickname because it was performed in Oxford when Haydn visited in July 1791 to receive an honorary doctorate. Haydn wrote in his notebook, 'I had to pay 1½ guineas to have the bells rung at Oxforth [sic] in connection with my doctor's degree, and 1/2 a guinea for a robe.'[13] The event was celebrated with concerts over three days, and on the second, Haydn brought forward this symphony, which had not been performed before in England. The *Morning Herald* reported, 'The new Overture of Haydn, prepared for the occasion, and previously rehearsed in the morning, led on the second Act, and a more wonderful composition never was heard.'[14]

The symphony begins quietly, with strings only. But the texture is given added richness by a separate cello line above the bass (cellos at this time usually spent most of their time following the bass line). And what sounds at first straightforwardly gentle becomes unexpectedly poignant, with chromatic notes creating suspensions and clashes. The introduction comes to a halt in mid-air, with an unresolved phrase. The Allegro begins by answering this question, reaching a resolution at the first forte, where the wind and timpani enter. This gives the main theme a very unusual character of a response, rather than a new start, and we are reminded of this throughout the movement whenever Haydn returns to it. The thematic material that follows the opening phrase is full of spirit, with pointed leaps and bustling semiquavers, and passes between treble and bass. Twice Haydn returns to his opening phrase and the tutti resolution. At the first recurrence, the violins are accompanied by the wind, with a high flute joining the tune. The tutti response then moves emphatically to new keys, so that when Haydn reaches a third occurrence of the opening phrase, it is in D, rather than the home key of G. This shift of key would usually signal the arrival of a new theme, so Haydn is playing with his audience's expectations by returning to his original theme yet again. Only at the very end of this section of the movement does Haydn finally supply a second theme, which is scarcely more than a droll little tailpiece, rather than a fully fledged theme.

The central development of the movement at first takes up this new theme, but then spends the rest of the time exploring the possibilities of the original opening phrase, turning it upside down, combining this with the original version, making it chase its own tail in elaborate counterpoint, and then hammering out the rhythm against vigorous semiquavers. When the reprise of the opening arrives, something of the spirit of this middle section lingers on, as the flute (later the bassoon) answers the violins in counterpoint. This time round, there are extra twists. Just when we expect Haydn to be heading for home, he starts toying with the little 'tailpiece' theme prematurely, then returns to his opening phrase, and another tutti, before reprising the tailpiece theme properly. Then there are further surprises, including a sudden lurch into E flat and back again, before he finally finds a way of drawing the movement to an end.

The slow movement is an outpouring of song from the violins, who are then joined by the oboe, and later the flute. The oboe is wonderfully subtle in its interventions, sometimes playing the melody, sometimes weaving a counterpoint, and sometimes magically melting from one to the other. The middle section is suddenly stern and in a minor key, alternating between outbursts of the whole orchestra and more delicate moments from strings, and then woodwind. The return of the opening melody culminates in a moment of hesitation, which seems to be remembering how the first movement introduction ended without resolution. Then the woodwind muse for a moment on a little phrase from the middle section of the movement, and the strings take this up to bring the movement to a close.

The minuet is a firm Allegretto. At first it seems very straightforward, but its second half contains some more moments of surprising hesitation, with poignant harmonies. The trio begins with a horn call across the beat, and these cross-rhythms become a feature, to the extent that they become deliberately confusing in the second half.

The finale is Haydn at his cheekiest, with the insistently four-square phrases of the opening tune giving it a humorous character, underlined by the accompanying bass octaves in bassoon and horn. You could imagine this as a song sung by a comic peasant in an opera. As so often, Haydn combines wit and learning, subjecting the tune to mock-serious counterpoint in the middle of the movement. And, as in the preceding three movements, there are moments of surprising hesitation, which here add to the impression of wit.

The 'London' Symphonies: first visit, Nos 93–98

When Prince Nicolaus Esterházy died in 1790, his son Anton disbanded the court orchestra, and Haydn, though still retaining the title of Kapellmeister and a substantial pension, had no formal duties. He was fifty-eight, famous, and had no need to exert himself to live comfortably. He moved to Vienna, and might have stayed there if it were not for Johann Peter Salomon. Salomon was a German violinist and impresario who organized important series of public concerts in London. He offered Haydn a lucrative contract to travel with him to London and to provide new symphonies for performance at Salomon's concerts in the 1791 season.

Haydn and his music were rapturously received in England, and he stayed for two seasons, risking the wrath of Anton Esterházy who had only granted him leave of absence for one year. Haydn's very first concert with Salomon's orchestra, on 16 May 1791 in the Hanover Square Rooms, London, was described by the historian Charles Burney: 'Haydn himself presided at the piano-forte [this was in the days before conductors, when responsibility for leading the orchestra was shared between a keyboard-player and the leader of the violins]: and the sight of that renowned composer so electrified the audience, as to excite an attention and a pleasure superior to any that had ever, to my knowledge, been caused by instrumental music in England. All the slow middle movements were encored; which never happened before, I believe, in any country.'[15] Haydn returned to London for another pair of seasons in 1794–5. To these visits, and to the enterprise of Salomon, we owe the twelve symphonies that crowned Haydn's career as a composer for orchestra.

SYMPHONY NO. 93 IN D MAJOR

Adagio – Allegro assai
Largo cantabile
Minuet and Trio: Allegro
Finale: Presto ma non troppo

This was the first of Haydn's new symphonies to be performed in Salomon's 1792 season, and the enthusiasm for Haydn and his music continued to grow. *The Times* reported, 'Such a combination of excellence was contained in every movement, as inspired all the performers as well as the audience with enthusiastic ardour. Novelty of idea, agreeable caprice, and whim combined with all *Haydn's* sublime and wonted grandeur, gave additional consequence to the *soul* and feelings of every individual present.'[16]

The opening is as arresting as that of any of Haydn's symphonies: the full orchestra, including trumpets and rolled drum, hold a fortissimo D. This bold and novel effect was to be imitated by Beethoven, notably in his Symphony No. 2. The introduction that follows is grand and elegant, with a sudden darkening of mood in the middle as it shifts sideways up a semi-tone. The Allegro is in a bold, swinging three-time, like a giant waltz, rather reminiscent of Mozart's Symphony No. 39 in E flat written three years earlier. Even more dance-like is the playful, delicate second theme. Most of the development section is taken up with a phrase from this second theme, worked up into vigorous counterpoint.

The theme of the Largo proceeds with touching hesitation from one phrase to the next. Unusually, it begins on a quartet of solo strings, then the full strings join in with bassoon adding a plaintive sonority to the melody. The middle of the melody suddenly turns to the minor, with the whole orchestra creating a grand effect like a French Overture. The middle section of the movement brings in an accompaniment of delicate running triplets. These persist even when the first theme returns, and it never quite regains its original character. After a time, the music gradually peters out to a standstill. In the middle of the silence, the bassoons play a rude fortissimo bottom C – a surprise even more startling than the more famous 'surprise' in Symphony No. 94 – after which the tune quickly recovers its dignity, and comes to a conclusion as if nothing had happened to disturb it.

Despite its Allegro marking, the minuet has an unmistakably stately character. The most surprising element is heard in the central trio. The trio of a minuet is often a gentle oasis between the two statements of the minuet. But here the trio begins with a brusque one-note fanfare from brass and drums (on the keynote, D, which began the whole symphony). The strings try to introduce a gentle element, in a different key, but the brass are determined to stick to their note, and the strings are obliged to join them.

As so often in Haydn, the spirit of comic opera seems to lie behind the finale. The theme is charming and witty. And it is subjected to all manner of detours, interruptions, changes of texture and key, as if characters are bustling about on the stage, new characters arrive unexpectedly, and revelations are made.

SYMPHONY NO. 94 IN G MAJOR, 'SURPRISE'

Adagio cantabile – Vivace assai
Andante
Minuet and Trio: Allegro molto
Finale: Allegro di molto

This symphony was the sensation of the concert on 23 March 1792, and it soon acquired its nickname. The slow introduction starts with two hymn-like bars, rising and falling, played by the wind and answered by flowing strings. This pattern is repeated, then some darker harmonies develop, with the bass sliding chromatically. The Vivace has an opening phrase with a rising and falling shape similar to the opening of the introduction. This is in a jig rhythm (6/8) more often associated with finales than with first movements (Haydn was to do the same in Symphonies Nos 101 and 103). The character of the music alternates between graceful and vigorous, and in the central development the sliding chromatic harmonies that appeared in the introduction drive the music to new regions.

The Andante is a set of variations on a naive little theme. It proceeds on tiptoe for eight bars, then even more furtively, with pizzicato bass, for another eight bars. This is followed by a crashing chord for full orchestra. This is the 'surprise' of the nickname. It would certainly have made Haydn's audience jump, though the rude bassoons in the slow movement of the preceding symphony would have been just as surprising (see Symphony No. 93). After this, the tune is rounded off in an orderly fashion. The first variation puts the tune in the second violins, with an elegant counterpoint above, in first violin and flute. The second variation begins in stern octaves in the minor key, answered by violins who wish to hold on to the elegance. The second half becomes more agitated, with full orchestra, running scales, and dotted rhythms. Variation 3 returns to the delicacy of the opening, but with the note values subdivided in violins and oboes to give a charming, chattering effect. This gives way to the simple version of the theme, now with charming counterpoint in flute and oboe above. Variation 4 brings in the full orchestra, with the melody in the wind, including trumpets (who join in with the notes they can play without valves) and agitated patterns and offbeat chords in the strings. After a gentler string passage in the middle of the theme, this full version rounds off the variation. Finally, a little tailpiece brings the set of variations to a conclusion, with the harmonies adding a surprising mournful tone.

The minuet is fast, with a vigorous swing. The trio, rather than introducing new material, draws on some of the running patterns of the minuet, and reforms them into a gentler version of the dance, with a bassoon following the violins an octave below.

The theme of the finale sounds almost as naive as that of the slow movement. It opens quietly, and maintains its composure for a surprisingly long time, like a conspirator in a comic opera, before the full orchestra bursts in. This loud tutti is, in turn, maintained for a long time, getting a lot of agitation out of its system. A second naive theme follows, and another brief tutti, before the first theme returns, followed by another tutti that takes us off into new keys. The final pages of the movement are, once again, surprising. We think we are winding to a close when a timpani roll announces a lurch into E flat. From this, Haydn deftly winds the harmony back to the home key, and the symphony ends with vigorous self-confidence.

SYMPHONY NO. 95 IN C MINOR

Allegro moderato
Andante cantabile
Menuet and Trio
Finale: Vivace

This symphony is unique among Haydn's London Symphonies in two ways. It launches straight into an Allegro without a slow introduction; and it is the only one in a minor key (his last minor-key symphony was No. 83, written in 1785). Its opening movement has a forthright, serious character, evoking the spirit not of comic opera, as so often, but the tragedies of Gluck (as in Haydn's so-called *Sturm und Drang* symphonies from twenty years earlier). The fortissimo opening bars are followed immediately by an anxious-sounding theme, with agitated dotted rhythms. Later, the dotted rhythms are used to make an elegant second theme in a major key. It is the contrast between these three elements that gives the entire movement its drama and narrative.

The second movement returns to more familiar ground, with one of Haydn's singing, elegant themes in E flat major, on which he builds a set of variations. The first variation alternates solo cello and violins, with playful running triplets. Variation 2 is in the minor key, with warm modulations, and sudden interventions from fortissimo wind. Variation 3 returns to the major, with running counterpoints in the violins. The tug of chromatic harmonies suggests that we are starting a fourth variation, but this turns out to be no more than an evocative little tailpiece, and Haydn soon recovers the geniality of the original mood to end the movement.

The minuet returns to C minor, and, like the first movement, has a serious, and at times stern, character, with trumpets and drums giving an almost military spine to the music. A solo cello again features in the trio, playing a concerto-like part against pizzicato accompaniment. This is a tricky passage, and has to be taken at a moderate pace. This in turn causes difficulties in pacing the minuet itself (which has no tempo marking). Should you take it almost at the same pace as the trio, in which case it becomes portentously slow, or do you slow down for the trio, with the danger that the two parts will not seem to relate to each other? It is one of the moments in Haydn for which there is no ideal solution.

The last movement begins almost like a 'normal' Haydn finale, in C major, with a genial theme that combines sustained melody with witty little touches. But the first tutti immediately develops quite an intensely contrapuntal texture, reminding us of the serious mood of the opening movement. Later, there is an outburst of C minor, to remind us of it even more forcefully. But this is soon over, and peace is restored. Then, while we might be wondering what Haydn has next up his sleeve, the movement is suddenly over, one of his shortest finales at three and a half minutes.

SYMPHONY NO. 96 IN D MAJOR, 'MIRACLE'

Adagio – Allegro
Andante
Minuet and Trio: Allegretto
Finale: Vivace assai

The nickname 'Miracle' has nothing to do with the music, or indeed with this symphony. The story goes that, at the end of the first performance in London, the audience crowded towards the stage to get a better view of Haydn, and at that moment a chandelier at the back of the hall crashed to the floor without hurting anyone. Contemporary reports of this event relate to the premiere of Symphony No. 102 in 1795. The name 'Miracle' has nevertheless stuck to No. 96.

This symphony has a particularly beautiful introduction. Bold descending octaves give way to a violin line that rises serenely. The octaves return, and the music moves into a warmer region of harmonies, with a sustained oboe above. After these hints of dark complexity, the Allegro that follows has a brisk open-air quality, punctuated by trumpets and drums. The running staccato accompaniment is so prominent through the movement that it seems almost as 'thematic' as the violin theme that is played above it.

Like many of Haydn's slow movements, the Andante has a formally decorated style akin to an opera aria. As in the first movement, running staccato lines are a feature. In the middle section of the movement, this combination of elements is developed into a powerful contrapuntal build-up. When the melody returns, it too becomes a running staccato line. Then a pair of solo violins take it over, still keeping the delicate staccato going, and the music undergoes surprising harmonic progressions before the movement comes eventually to an end.

The third movement is a large-scale minuet for full orchestra, with rapid rising violin scales adding a ceremonial flourish. Most of the trio is a delicate oboe solo (on older recordings, a trumpet joins the melody at one point, but this was inserted by an early twentieth-century editor).

In the finale, a pointed rhythmic pattern is repeated and examined again and again. It is like an operatic scene in which a character reiterates his appalling situation, the others from time to time bursting in with expressions of outrage. There are occasional moments of darker anger, but they never last long, and are not to be taken seriously.

SYMPHONY NO. 97 IN C MAJOR

Adagio – Vivace
Adagio ma non troppo
Minuet and Trio: Allegretto
Finale: Presto assai

This is less well known than the symphonies with nicknames, but it is as substantial and satisfying as any of them. A bold octave of C opens the symphony. Anyone who knows Haydn's *Creation* is likely to be reminded of the opening of the mysterious 'Representation of Chaos', which has the same pitch, and a very similar scoring, with trumpets and drums. And indeed there is something mysterious about this introduction. The note C is reiterated persistently, while harmonies shift and melody weaves around it. After a few bars, the flute joins in unison with the violins on the melody – one of Haydn's favourite and most beautiful combinations.

The Vivace that follows is a striking example of Haydn taking the simplest material and embarking with it on a great journey. The first theme for full orchestra is nothing more than an arpeggio of C major for full orchestra, including trumpets and drums, in which a pair of notes is hammered out repeatedly, creating a ferocious fanfare. This develops into an exhilarating tutti. There is much exploration, with some surprising twists, before we arrive at a delightfully poised second theme with a pizzicato bass. The glory of this movement is the central development. Flute and oboes weave an almost ecclesiastical web of counterpoint, which the strings quietly punctuate with reminders of the military fanfare. The counterpoint is then taken up forcefully by the whole orchestra, with running scales driving it energetically forward. At the reprise, we arrive once more at the poised second theme. Then, with a subtle reminder of the repeating Cs of the introduction, we enter a series of wonderful modulations into unexpected keys, until we emerge to a triumphant final reiteration of the military fanfare.

The slow movement is a set of variations on an unusually substantial and subtle theme. The theme is in two halves, each of which is repeated. The first part alternates pairs of contrasted phrases, the first divided into distinct little gestures like a delicate dance, the second flowing smoothly, more like a hymn. The second half of the theme becomes more consistently hymn-like, and extends further than we expect. As we approach the end of the melody, a phrase repeats, with a bass note trying to move it into a new key, but it reaches a conclusion without doing so, and then this whole pattern is itself repeated. This has a most touching effect, like a memory that one is reluctant to let fade.

In the first variation, the melody breaks into delicate staccato triplets, though the contrast between the dancing first phrase and hymn-like answer is maintained in the lower parts. In this variation, the two halves of the theme are played only once. The second variation is in the minor key, and is punctuated by threatening outbursts from the whole orchestra. Here the two halves are repeated. The harmonies at the end of each half are particularly beautiful. In the first half, they modulate consolingly to a major key. In the second half, they wind chromatically through a sinuous path before arriving back in the home key. The third and final variation is back in the major key, and the theme is broken into lively semiquavers. This is marked to be played 'al ponticello', that is, bowed near the bridge. This is an effect used much later to produce a scratchy, ghostly effect in quiet music. It is most unusual in eighteenth-century music, and here it is applied to running semiquavers. It is difficult to know quite what effect Haydn was looking for. Perhaps he meant the passage to sound rough, like a village band (this instruction was missing from published editions until the mid-twentieth century, and even today not all conductors observe it). At the end, instead of immediately finding a resolution, it extends into a long coda, which culminates in plaintive phrases from flute and oboe, over harmonies that sound as if they come from a later era – Schubert, perhaps.

The minuet is unusually grand and extensive. Its two halves are not just repeated, but slightly varied at the repetition. The first half is forte the first time round, piano and staccato the second time. The second half is unusually extended, with the final strain taken higher, to create a climax. The trio has oboe and bassoon joining the violins, and a tune with snappy little grace notes over a persistent staccato accompaniment. This gives a suggestion of rural dance instruments, perhaps a hurdy-gurdy (though without the drone). The final bars have a solo violin playing an octave above the others, with a specific instruction: 'Salomon solo ma piano'. Johann Peter Salomon, the organizer of the concert series in London, was also the leader of the orchestra, and Haydn wrote this delightful little moment specially for him.

The last movement is one of Haydn's joyous finales, the product of the wise old mind that sees humorous weight and context in the simplest of ideas. Part of the wit lies in the fact that the tune is obvious and symmetrical almost to the point of banality. It is subjected to extension and excursions, moments of unexpected harmonic twists and vigorous intervention, but nothing can stop it resurfacing just as it was before, with the bassoon faithfully following along an octave below the strings (this colouring helps to give Haydn's humour a straight-faced character). At the end of the first outing of the tune, a tailpiece seems almost like a second theme, and this develops into a sustained passage of counterpoint. The next outing of the tune turns to the minor, and to another vigorous tutti, with a humorous interruption in the middle. The tune returns yet again, and a pause seems to indicate that we are heading for the end. But Haydn has several more tricks up his sleeve, including another false ending, before he does finally wind it all up in high spirits.

SYMPHONY NO. 98 IN B FLAT MAJOR

Adagio – Allegro
Adagio
Minuet and Trio: Allegro
Finale: Presto – Più moderato

The Adagio begins with bare octaves, outlining a theme based on an arpeggio of B flat minor. First this is bold and staccato, then quiet and smooth with a shift of key. When the Allegro arrives, we discover that this was not just an introduction, but the theme that is to be the main material for the whole movement. At the opening of the Allegro, the arpeggio is simply speeded up, and put into B flat major. There are often subtle links between the introduction and the Allegro in Haydn's symphonies, but such an obvious transformation of material was unusual in the eighteenth century – though it was to become a favourite 'unifying' device in the nineteenth century. Immediately the Allegro introduces little touches of counterpoint, and then bursts into an energetic tutti. Near the end of the first section, the oboe interrupts the tutti to intone four long notes in a chromatic pattern. This seems to come out of nowhere, but is subtly related to a melodic shape that has occurred, seemingly incidentally, both in the Adagio introduction and in the opening theme of the Allegro. The development section begins with a sustained passage of vigorous counterpoint. At the end of this, the oboe again intones its long notes. And towards the end of the reprise, it does so again, answered by the flute, before a final burst of energy brings the movement to a close.

The slow movement opens with four hymn-like bars, which will have struck the London audience as sounding like their national anthem, 'God save the King'. But this is just the beginning of a long melody which, while preserving its slow three-in-a-bar, becomes elaborately decorated, full of beautiful touches of harmony, with dialogue between violins and woodwind. In the middle of the movement, there is one of Haydn's characteristic passages of sustained counterpoint in a minor key, with the opening notes of the theme (at first in the bass) pitted against vigorous semiquaver triplets in the other voices. In this minor version, the theme reveals itself as closely related to the oboe's motif of four long notes from the first movement. So, once again, Haydn is subtly linking his thematic material.

The minuet is lively, with little flourishes emphasizing its cheerfulness. The trio begins with Haydn's favourite mellifluous combination of violins with bassoon an octave below, and continues with his other favourite, violins and flute in unison, with the oboe also joining in.

The finale has the easy-going buoyancy of a jig. After an extended tutti, a second theme has a light staccato wit that could be mistaken for Rossini. At the end of the first section there is a sudden halt, followed by a startling change of key, and a passage of solo violin (which would have been played by Salomon). At the next reprise of the first theme, it is the solo violin that starts it going. The symphony ends with a section that reverses what happened at the beginning of the first movement: the main theme is suddenly brought down to a slower pace (più moderato). But soon the pattern of quavers, which has dominated the movement so far, is broken down into semiquavers, so that the music becomes even more energetic. There is one final surprise, of a personal nature. At early performances of his symphonies in London, Haydn presided at the fortepiano, sharing the directing with the leader, Salomon. Here, for the only time in his symphonies, Haydn inserts a modest little keyboard solo, nothing more than a pattern of arpeggios. This must have been a very charming moment – though with the modern large orchestras and halls, it becomes difficult to make much point of it.

'London' Symphonies: second visit, Nos 99–104

In 1793, at the age of sixty-one, Haydn planned a second trip to London. At first his employer, Prince Anton Esterházy, was reluctant to let him go, despite the fact that he had disbanded the court orchestra three years earlier and had little practical need of Haydn's service. The attraction of England was very powerful. Quite apart from popular success, Haydn had made a great deal of money out of his first visit, and he had already agreed to write six new symphonies for London, Nos 99–104. The prince finally agreed to release him, and Haydn left for London on 19 January 1794. Symphonies Nos 99–101 were first performed at Salomon's Concerts in 1794. But Salomon cancelled his 1795 season, because (it has been assumed) he was unable to secure enough excellent soloists during the continuing war with France. But there was a new concert series, the Opera Concerts, held fortnightly at the King's Theatre, under the direction of the celebrated Italian violinist, Giovanni Battista Viotti. Salomon took part in these concerts, and the 1795 season included the premieres of Haydn's last three Symphonies, Nos 102–104.

SYMPHONY NO. 99 IN E FLAT MAJOR

Adagio – Vivace assai
Adagio
Minuet and Trio: Allegretto
Finale: Vivace

This symphony was first performed a few days after Haydn's arrival in London in February 1794 at one of Salomon's Concerts in the Hanover Square Rooms.

Right from the first bars of the introduction, the sound of this symphony has a particular fullness and warmth. This is partly because Haydn has, for the first time in a symphony, added clarinets to the wind. The beginning, with its rich chords in E flat major alternating with quiet descending violin lines, is rather reminiscent of the opening of Mozart's Symphony No. 39 in the same key, written five years earlier, which also has clarinets. The introduction (like Mozart's) ventures further, and at greater length, than most introductions of this period, After a pause, the music is taken into the remote key of E minor, and then, by a series of modulations, comes to rest on a chord of G major. By this time, we have quite forgotten what key we started in, and it is a shock when the wind instruments quietly remind us that we are supposed to be in E flat major.

The Allegro can then begin, with a bustling theme that is explored at length, both quietly and tutti. After all this activity, the first section comes to a close with a much simpler tune (though over the same tripping accompaniment as before), in which the clarinet doubles the violins, followed by the oboe (a subtle contrast between cooler and warmer tone colouring). The development begins with fragments of the first theme. But it is the simpler second theme that eventually gets under way. At first it passes between oboe and flute over the violins, but then it is used to build up a passage of counterpoint, soon giving way to the bustle of the first theme. This energy spends itself and reverts to the simple tune, which leads into the reprise of the opening.

The slow movement is one of Haydn's beautifully decorated arias. The woodwind are particularly prominent. The opening theme alternates between strings and flute, then the woodwind take it over entirely, the tune moving from oboe to bassoon with counterpoint weaving round them. The strings then finish up the first section with a tailpiece that is virtually a separate theme in itself. The middle section begins with a passage where Haydn modulates from key to key, before settling into the 'tailpiece' theme, and ending on an agitated flurry of activity. The reprise begins much as it did before, with the first theme passing from violins to flute. But then the theme is further elaborated with running scales and contrapuntal entries, still within the singing, quiet string sonority. The 'tailpiece' theme is then built up to a fortissimo passage, with trumpets in almost military mode, before it settles back to a final reprise of the same theme, with violins and high oboe on the tune, repeated woodwind chords and pizzicato strings below. So what seemed at first a mere tailpiece turns out to be the dominant theme of this movement.

The minuet is firmly poised, its thematic material formed from staccato arpeggios. By the end of its first section, it has developed a peasant swing. The second half is unusually extensive, venturing into new keys, and passing around fragments of the theme, until suddenly it is back at the beginning of the minuet without quite realizing it. The trio is delicate and elegant, with the oboe brightening the violin line.

The finale is one of Haydn's most virtuoso movements. Like the opening movement, it evokes memories of the dashing finale of Mozart's Symphony No. 39. But Haydn's carefree wit and high spirits are of rather a different order from Mozart's. The music is full of surprises and deadpan humour, with the jaunty little tune at one moment self-sufficient in its simplicity, the next moment being drawn into mock-serious counterpoint. The tune may be simple in character, but 'simple' is not the word to describe the movement from the performer's point of view. It is extremely difficult, demanding immense technical command that has to be worn lightly. Only an orchestra of the highest accomplishment can make it sound joyful rather than laborious. It would be fascinating to be able to hear how Salomon's orchestra coped with it.

SYMPHONY NO. 100 IN G MAJOR, 'MILITARY'

Adagio – Allegro
Allegretto
Minuet and Trio: Moderato
Finale: Presto

This symphony was first performed in March 1794 at the Hanover Square Rooms at Salomon's eighth concert of the season, with Haydn presiding at the keyboard as usual. It scored one of the greatest triumphs of his career, and soon came to be known as the 'Military' Symphony. The name refers to the second movement, in which the trumpets and timpani from the first movement are joined by triangle, cymbal, and bass drum – 'Turkish Music', evoking the Janissary bands of the Ottoman Empire.

The work begins innocently enough, with an Adagio introduction. The violins weave a melody that 'speaks' almost like the introduction to a dramatic scene. A few bars in, there is an ominous drum roll and crescendo, giving a hint of things to come. But this is followed by the sunniest of Allegros. The fact that the time signature has two beats to a bar, rather than four, encourages some conductors to take it very fast indeed. But this is a mistake, because it is full of delightful detail and wit that need enough time to have their full effect. The first theme is introduced by gentle flute and oboes, and taken up by the strings before bursting out exuberantly on the full orchestra. A second theme is made up of cheeky repetitions of a little phrase (writers have suggested that it might have inspired the rather similar main theme of the *Radetzky March*, written by Johann Strauss senior half a century later). As usual in a symphony of this period, the first section of the Allegro is repeated. It comes round to its conclusion for a second time. And then? Nothing. There is a startling silence of two bars. Then the strings restart in the surprise key of B flat, revisit the second theme, and use its little phrases to set off on a journey of unpredictable turnings and Beethoven-like outbursts, until Haydn eventually winds round to the home key, and the reprise of the opening theme on flute and oboes.

It is the second movement in C major that led to this symphony being nicknamed the 'Military'. Turkish-style percussion had been used for exotic effect in operas, by Haydn and Mozart (most notably Mozart's *Die Entführung aus dem Serail*), but bringing it into a symphony was quite new. We are used to large percussion sections in symphony orchestras these days, so it is difficult to recapture the shock this caused. When the symphony was first performed in 1794, Britain was at war with Napoleon, and Austria had been at war with the Ottoman Empire. At early performances in London, the audience was enraptured by the bold stroke of bringing 'Turkish Music' into this movement, and demanded an encore. What the audience would not have known is that this was a recycled piece of music. Haydn had taken a movement from a piece he had written for the King of Naples a few years earlier. This was a concerto for a sort of hurdy-gurdy incorporating little organ pipes. Haydn obviously did not want to let such a charming piece go to waste, so he reused it, virtually note for note, in this symphony, keeping its clarinets (which do not play in the other movements of the symphony), and adding the percussion. The movement is a gentle Allegretto, with a hint of a processional tread. When the music moves into the minor (as it did in the original concerto), the cymbals, bass drum, and triangle unexpectedly join in, turning the charming procession into something much more threatening. Eventually, the movement seems to draw to a close (at the point where the original movement ended). But Haydn has one more shock up his sleeve. A trumpet plays a military fanfare, there is a crescendo on the timpani, and the whole orchestra, with percussion, comes crashing in on a fortissimo chord of A flat. This soon dissipates, the music returns to its home key of C major, and comes to a peaceful conclusion.

After a slow movement that is not particularly slow, there follows a minuet that is not particularly fast. Haydn marks it moderato. This used to lead conductors to adopt an extremely sturdy, grand manner, but the tendency nowadays is to take it flowingly. It does, however, possess an inherently stately character, with its trumpets and drums, and the firm counter-point of its bass line. The trio begins as a real dance, with demure elegance. But in the second half the trumpets and drums again threaten for a moment.

This is followed by a final Presto, a virtuoso tour de force. Like the first movement Allegro, it is full of unexpected silences, contrasts, sudden changes of key. In a fast and delicate performance, these can seem witty and evanescent. In bigger or slower performances, they take on a more truculent, Beethoven-like character. At the end, the Turkish percussion from the second movement join in, to bring the symphony to an exuberant conclusion.

SYMPHONY NO. 101 IN D MAJOR, 'CLOCK'

Adagio – Presto
Andante
Minuet and Trio: Allegretto
Finale: vivace

This symphony was first performed in March 1794 at Salomon's fourth concert of the season at Hanover Square, amid the usual mixture of arias, duets, and concertos by other fashionable composers of the day. The *Morning Chronicle* published an enthusiastic review:

> As usual, the most delicious part of the entertainment was the grand new Overture by Haydn: the inexhaustible, the wonderful, the sublime Haydn! The first two movements were encored; and the character that pervaded the whole composition was heartfelt joy. Every new overture he writes, we fear, till it is heard, he can only repeat himself; and we are every time mistaken. Nothing can be more original than the subject of the first movement; and having found a happy subject, no man knows like Haydn to produce incessant

variety, without once departing from it. The management of the accompaniment of the andante, though perfectly simple, was masterly; and we never heard a more charming effect that was produced by the trio to the minuet – it was Haydn; what can we, what need we say more?[17]

The contrast between the slow introduction and the Presto of the first movement could not be greater. The introduction is very sombre, growing mysteriously out of its quiet opening note, D. There are moments of consolation, but the overall mood is tragic. This is Haydn at his most intense, writing in a style that greatly influenced Beethoven (notably in his *Leonore* overtures). The Presto is the last thing we expect after this: the sort of cheerful, sparkling jig-rhythm music more usual as a finale. Even when Haydn arrives at a second theme, it too is happily outgoing, growing naturally out of the insistent dance rhythm of the tutti that precedes it. The development takes this second theme, and subjects it to a characteristic passage of counterpoint. This intensifies the mood without really darkening it. When the reprise reaches this second theme, it passes between cellos and violins, leading to an extended further discussion. A solo flute reminds us of the opening theme, and the whole orchestra bursts in for a final joyful tutti.

Pizzicato strings and bassoons open the Andante, with the ticking that gives the symphony its nickname. The demure melody is in the violins, later joined by a flute – a typically Haydnesque touch. One little feature that helps to give this movement its quirky character is the way that, each time the tune returns, it begins with a bar of ticking, instead of going straight into the tune itself. This gives a charming dislocation – a sense that an extra bar has been added. The first statement of the theme is interrupted by a vigorous passage in the minor that develops determined seriousness of purpose. This middle section ebbs away to leave the violins returning to their demure melody. But now the ticking is in bassoon below and flute above, so that the melody is sandwiched between them – a delightful variation. There is a sudden silence, and the ticking and the melody resume in the strings, but now in the wrong key. It takes a brief, forceful intervention to bring the music back home. Now the whole melody is reprised forte, but with the notes broken into vigorous triplets, and this further variation of the theme brings the movement to a close.

The minuet is bright but stately, with some teasing cross-rhythms. In the trio, the strings reiterate chords pianissimo, and a solo flute climbs up a scale of D major. The first time, the strings fail to change the harmony where they should, but the second time they 'wake up' and do so (some editions and recordings correct this joke). In the second half, flute and bassoon answer each other. These are simple devices, but, as the *Morning Chronicle* reported after the first performance, 'we never heard a more charming effect'.

Having written a first movement Presto that is almost like a finale, Haydn ends the symphony with almost the substance of a first movement. The opening theme has a relaxed grace, but soon gives way to a tutti that drives forward energetically. We then expect a second theme, but what Haydn gives us is really a development of the original theme. After another tutti, there is more development, leading into a reprise of the theme itself, but now varied in shape. A stormier tutti follows, in the minor. When this comes to an abrupt halt, Haydn quietly returns to the theme, but now worked up to a passage of mock-baroque counterpoint, almost like a fugue. Finally, the whole orchestra takes up the theme, and the symphony comes to a joyful close.

SYMPHONY NO. 102 IN B FLAT MAJOR

Largo – Vivace
Adagio
Minuet and Trio: Allegro
Finale: Presto

Twice the keynote, B flat, is sounded quietly by the full orchestra, and twice it is answered by ethereal high strings (this could almost be Verdi). The second time, the music moves on, becoming more intense and searching, and then coming to rest. There is a sweet little flute cadenza, and we are into the Vivace. This tumbles out irrepressibly, and when it eventually comes to a halt, two bare octaves are sounded fortissimo, reminding us of the sustained notes that opened the symphony. This time, they are interleaved with phrases of a perky little second theme. These are answered by another burst of tutti, which brings us to the end of the first section of the movement.

Another fortissimo unison announces a change of key as we enter the development. This switches its attention between the first and second themes. A passage of counterpoint develops into an intense struggle, with sharp accents and dissonances, sounding almost like a passage from Beethoven's Ninth. All of a sudden it stops, and a flute quietly plays the first theme. But we are not yet back to the home key, and the development is not over. More struggle follows, gradually working round to the home key, and then joyfully bursting into the opening theme on full orchestra, and on into the bustling tutti. We move on through the fortissimo octaves and the perky second theme, and seem to be approaching the end. There is another sudden moment of Beethoven-like fierceness, out of which the violins and flute timidly attempt to re-establish the first theme. But this peters out, and with great vigour the whole orchestra brings the movement to an emphatic conclusion.

The Adagio also appears as the slow movement of one of Haydn's piano trios (in F sharp minor, Hob. XV:26). It is delicately florid, with a rather improvisational style. This conveys an intimacy of character which might make one suspect that the trio was written first, though it has generally been assumed that the orchestral version was the original. The florid line rests on a foundation of three very slow beats, often with sustained wind chords, and it is this coexistence of the florid and the sustained that creates the beautiful richness of the movement. Part of its subtlety lies in Haydn's favourite combination of violins and flute on the melody. At first the violins are alone, then the flute joins them an octave above, then in unison. The relationship keeps changing from unison to an octave apart, and the result is a continual shift from a warmer to a brighter sonority. As the movement continues, it develops a subtly increased darkness and weight: the return of the theme is accompanied by trumpets and timpani, both muted. Towards the end, these become more threatening, though without breaking the elegant thread of the melody.

From time to time during the minuet bare octaves are stamped out – this is perhaps a reminder of the octaves that featured in the first movement. There are also moments of delicacy and hesitation, but the overall character is downright and straightforward. The trio is in complete contrast, a sweet melody sung by oboe and bassoon.

The finale is one of the wittiest in all of Haydn. The wit depends partly on making a great deal out of almost nothing. First, two bars go up, then two bars come down. This happens again, but heads for the wrong key. There is a sudden crescendo, and a four-bar phrase to round off the paragraph. And all this happens in the first ten seconds. What can Haydn do but repeat it? The woodwind interject a comment, the strings play around with the opening phrase, looking at it from all different directions, before ending up more or less where they started. Another repeat, and then the full orchestra enters with a sudden fortissimo, and some new, energetic material. Between the reappearances of the little tune there are events that we come to expect in Haydn – an outburst in the minor, a passage of mock-serious counterpoint – but these are devices that, in Haydn, never fail to have their dramatic effect. The whole movement could be a Feydeau farce. It is full of surprises, unexpected events, expected events that do not materialize, things that begin but get nowhere. Towards the end, it becomes comically hesitant, like a character nervously putting his head around the door hoping not to be seen. You can tell that there is one more surprise in store. The astonishing sequence of chords that Haydn then produces – like a premonition of Mahler – puts the cap on a work of sheer brilliance.

SYMPHONY NO. 103 IN E FLAT MAJOR, 'DRUMROLL'

Adagio – Allegro con spirito
Andante più tosto Allegretto
Minuet and Trio
Finale: Allegro con spirito

For once, this symphony justifies its nickname in the first bar, which consists of a drum roll on the keynote, E flat. Different sources suggest that it should either swell and die, or start fortissimo and die. Either way, there is something quietly stately about what follows: a solemn bass line on lower strings and bassoon. It is as if a passacaglia is beginning, and we can expect variations over this bass. And indeed, after a few bars the bass moves into the first violins, with each half-beat etched out in the second violins. Then it settles into a series of mysterious chords, ending with a simple pair of notes, G and A flat, rocking back and forth (just as the opening notes of the introduction did). This provides the seed for the Allegro's first theme, which takes these notes and uses them as the start of a lively tune in 6/8 jig rhythm, first quietly, and then on full orchestra. The first section of the movement is rounded off by a delightful melody like an Austrian *Ländler*, with a dancing accompaniment and pizzicato bass.

The development begins with the opening phrase of the first theme elaborated into a passage of counterpoint. There is a sudden pause, after which the bass line continues, quoting the opening notes of the introduction but now at the fast tempo of the Allegro. It becomes clear how closely this is related to the first theme of the Allegro as the music builds up, using fragments of melody that relate to both themes. There is a moment of hesitation. The music proceeds to search among fragments of the main Allegro theme, at one point answering it very charmingly with the dancing second theme, which then builds up into a tutti. After another pause, we are back at the reprise of the main theme. This proceeds swiftly on to the dancing second theme, but then takes a dramatic turn, with a fiery outburst and chords that suggest we are heading in a new direction.

That direction turns out to be a complete surprise: the drum roll announces a return to the slow introduction, a return that used to be a feature of the French Overture earlier in the eighteenth century, but is highly unusual in a symphony. The two strains of the solemn bass line are played, and the cadence at the end of the second leads straight back into a brief Allegro to finish off the movement. This final tutti begins not with the Allegro theme, but with the opening of the solemn bass line from the introduction, now transformed into a vigorous melody. The horns then play the 'real' Allegro theme, so bringing the two themes together in a final joyful synthesis.

The tempo instruction, 'more Allegretto than Andante', makes it likely that many conductors take the second movement too slowly. It consists of a double set of variations – that is, variations on two separate themes which alternate. Haydn was fond of this form (he used it two years earlier in his wonderful Andante and Variations in F minor for keyboard). The first theme is in C minor, with a rather furtive, staccato tread, the second theme is in C major, with a more open-air, confident manner. Both are based on Croatian folk songs, and are quite similar in shape, adding to the sense of a coherent movement. The first is scored for strings alone. It begins with a bare accompaniment, but tentatively fills in chords in the second half. When the opening returns, the tune is in the bass, sounding even more furtive than it did on the violins. The second melody, in the major, has the oboes doubling the violins, adding to the bright effect of the major key. The first variation of the first theme has the tune played much as before, but with the addition of plaintive wind counterpoints – first an oboe, later also flute and bassoon (perhaps surprisingly, the clarinets do not play in this movement – Haydn does not seem to have shared Mozart's love of clarinet solos). The first variation of the second tune returns to the strings, with a charming solo violin elaborating the tune into running triplets.

The second variation of the first tune is for full orchestra, with trumpets, horns, and drums punctuating in military rhythm. The second variation of the second tune begins with oboes (as in the theme), with bassoon genially bouncing up and down in the bass and the flute playing arpeggios above. Then the whole orchestra joins in, and, after a pause, the wind charmingly round off the theme. The rest of the movement is an extended coda. This begins with beautiful string counterpoint, then a hush and a crescendo leads to a surprising change of key, and a moment of uncertainty as oboes and flute play fragments of the second theme. Soon they find their way back to C major, the full orchestra reprises the second tune, and the wind round it off as before.

The minuet has a slightly 'folksy' character too, because of grace notes and insistent 'Scotch snaps' in the rhythm. Haydn had published some arrangements of Scottish folk songs in London three years earlier, so these rhythms may indeed have been intended to sound Scottish. The movement has a bright, open-air character, accentuated by the trumpets. The trio is an object lesson in creating beautiful textures by simple means. At first, the clarinets (which have not been prominent so far) double the violins, creating a strangely veiled tone colour. The second half begins with high strings, then the cellos join in with a countermelody while the basses play pizzicato below.

The finale opens with the two horns playing a simple rising and falling hunting call, which seems to refer back to the last few notes they played at the end of the minuet. After a pause, they repeat it, and the violins add an incisive countermelody, which falls and rises as the horns rise and fall. This countermelody turns out to be the theme on which the whole of the movement is based. Sometimes the music concentrates on the repeated opening notes, sometimes on the fall and rise. Haydn finds so many possibilities in this material that he has no need of a second theme. At important landmarks the horn call reappears with it. And the repeated notes come to form a buoyant carpet on which much of the movement flies. For music that is essentially carefree and airy, this movement has an extraordinary amount of counterpoint in it. At almost every point, a phrase of the theme is answered in another voice, or pairs of voices interweave with each other, so that the whole piece takes on the character of a virtuoso piece of embroidery – light as a feather, but intricate in every detail.

SYMPHONY NO. 104 IN D MAJOR, 'LONDON'

Adagio – Allegro
Andante
Minuet and Trio: Allegro
Finale: Spiritoso

This is Haydn's last symphony, 'The 12th which I have composed in England', as he wrote on the first page of his autograph score.[18] It has come to be known individually as the 'London' Symphony, even though it has no greater claim to this title than the other eleven that he wrote for London. Its premiere was the climax of a long line of ecstatic receptions of Haydn's work in England. The *Morning Chronicle* reported that, 'for fullness, richness and majesty, in all its parts, [it] is thought by some of the best judges to surpass all his other compositions.'[19]

The full orchestra, with trumpets and drums, begins with fortissimo octaves, declaiming in a forceful dotted rhythm the interval of a fifth, D to A. This interval is a motif that links all movements of the symphony, in a way that is sometimes obvious, sometimes subtle. Three times the interval is declaimed in the introduction. Between each occurrence, the music takes on a character of tragic uncertainty, with falling phrases building up, culminating in the plaintive voice of the oboe. The Allegro banishes all anxiety, with a theme of quiet confidence, which soon bursts out into an exuberant tutti. As in several earlier symphonies, where we expect a second theme Haydn continues to explore his first theme. It is only near the end of the first section that he finally introduces a new melody, almost as an afterthought. This features a falling phrase of three notes, outlining the interval of a fifth that was stated at the opening of the symphony. Much of the development is taken up with a phrase of staccato repeated notes from the first theme, which Haydn explores with his usual ingenuity. At the reprise he takes particular delight in returning to this same phrase, hammering it out joyfully.

The slow movement begins with a poised, elegant melody in G major like a slow dance. It seems wholly new, but its opening phrase is cleverly built from much the same shape as the Allegro's first theme. It incorporates a falling fifth – a reference to the 'motto' fifth of the introduction. In the latter part of the theme, the violins are joined an octave below by the bassoon – one of Haydn's favourite combinations. The woodwind lead on to the middle section of the movement. An agitated tutti in a minor key gives way to a sorrowful reminiscence of the opening theme. Then a bolder tutti in the major leads eventually to a reprise of the opening section. But the dance-like melody is not as untroubled as it was. Some of the agitation of the middle section lingers, so that it develops spiky dotted rhythms, with the intervention of the whole orchestra. After a silence, the dance theme resumes, settling into its stride, and being elaborated with flowing triplets. But soon it begins to lose its way, drifting into new keys, and pausing on a chord of D flat major – far away from the home key of G. A flute shyly attempts to modulate to other keys, twice pausing, before the strings take up the melody again, and find their way back to the home key and the last reprise of the theme. This passage, in which the music seems to wander, is one of the most haunting in Haydn's symphonies, an effect that was to be echoed in different ways by many later composers, from Beethoven onwards.

The minuet has a distinctly rural bluffness, with a stamping emphasis on the third beat of the bar. This culminates in a startling silence in the second half. The trio is surprisingly in B flat, not the home key of D. It is charmingly delicate, with gently running scales in which violins are joined first by an oboe and then by a bassoon.

Haydn's last symphonic finale is indeed spiritoso ('spirited'). The melody is based on a Croatian folk tune, 'Oj Jelena', over a drone bass that gives it an immediately rustic feel. The tune contains a subtle reference to the motto interval of a fifth: the first phrase falls a fifth, and then rises a fifth. Haydn finds quite enough in this lively tune to supply material for the whole movement without the need of a second fully fledged theme. But there is at least a second important element – a yearning leap and gradual descent, which first occurs as we approach the end of the first section. This provides welcome moments of tenderness, but it is the general exuberance that marks this last finale.

PAUL HINDEMITH
(1895–1963)

Hindemith was a virtuoso player before he established a reputation as a composer. As a violinist he became the leader of the Frankfurt Opera orchestra during the First World War when he was only nineteen. Later, having switched to the viola, he played in the famous Amar–Hindemith String Quartet. When he did make headway as a composer in the 1920s, he was a leading member of a group promoting what was termed *Gebrauchsmusik* ('Utility Music'). Hindemith encapsulated its philosophy in 1927: 'The composer today should write only if he knows for what purpose he is writing. The days of composing only for the sake of composing are perhaps gone for ever.'[1] This movement laid emphasis on music written to be playable by amateurs and children. But even when not pitched at an amateur level, much of Hindemith's music has a down-to-earth practicality. He was constantly writing solo and chamber music for all sorts of instruments, providing useful additions to the repertoire not just for the obvious violinists, cellists, and pianists but also for trombonists, bassoonists, harpists, and others. This was linked to an anti-Romantic and anti-expressionist artistic movement in Germany, *Neue Sachlichkeit* (New Objectivity). This in turn was in tune with the socialist ideas of Bertolt Brecht, which were a powerful force in the arts of Germany between the two World Wars. However, there was also a strong streak of Romanticism and spirituality to Hindemith's character, which finds freest expression in his large-scale orchestral works and operas. It was this, and a reluctance to embrace Brecht's communist principles, that led the two men to fall out in 1930.

When Hitler's National Socialists came to power in 1933, much of Hindemith's music was placed on the list banned for exhibiting 'cultural Bolshevism'. In reaction to this artistic isolation, Hindemith started work on an opera, *Mathis der Maler*, based on a fictionalized account of the life of the sixteenth-century painter, Matthias Grünewald. He saw that the story, with its conflict between artistic necessity and political necessity, had the potential to reflect something of his own situation as a musician in Nazi Germany.

While starting to work on the opera, Hindemith was asked to write a new orchestral work by Wilhelm Furtwängler, conductor of the Berlin Philharmonic Orchestra and the State

Opera. Hindemith composed a symphony that incorporated music later used in the opera. Although Furtwängler's proposed premiere of the opera at the Berlin State Opera had been banned by the Nazis, he was allowed to conduct the symphony in March 1934. Its success inflamed the Nazi persecution of Hindemith further, and a stream of attacks on him appeared in the press. Furtwängler took the bold step of publishing an article, 'The Hindemith Case', in which he defended Hindemith in defiance of the Nazis, declaring, 'Given the incredible paucity of really creative composers in the world today, we cannot afford to turn our backs like this on a man of the calibre of Hindemith.'[2] The audience at the Opera supported Furtwängler with an ovation the day following the publication of the article. Joseph Goebbels, the Nazi Minister of Propaganda, responded two days later in a characteristically chilling speech, renewing the condemnation of Hindemith: 'Purely German his blood may be, but this only provides drastic confirmation of how deeply the Jewish intellectual infection has eaten into the body of our own people ... Certainly we cannot afford, in view of the deplorable lack of truly productive artists throughout the world, to turn our backs on a truly German artist. But he must be a real artist, not just a producer of atonal noises.'[3] Furtwängler, the most prominent musician in Germany, resigned from his posts, though a few months later he returned, having reached an uneasy, and controversial, accommodation with the Nazi regime. By 1936, Hindemith's music had been banned in Germany. He finally emigrated, first to Switzerland in 1938 and then to the United States in early 1940, becoming an American citizen in 1946.

During the period in the late 1930s when he was restricted in his activities by the Nazis, Hindemith wrote an important theoretical work, *The Craft of Musical Composition*. In it, he analyses harmony and melody in relation to the harmonic series, and considers the degree of consonance or dissonance of different intervals and chords. He attempts to find a way of retaining music's relationship to its fundamental origin in the harmonic series, while allowing freedom from the conventions of the traditional keys. In his own music, he arrived at a language that has some relationship to his theories, but is not constricted by them. It is a highly personal style, with a rather quirky combination of the traditionally harmonious with the acerbically dissonant. Sometimes it has the effect of seeming to be quite traditional but with added 'spice', sometimes it is harsh and combative. Hindemith can seem rather cold, even pedantic. But he can also blossom into unexpected warmth. His best works put these elements in a satisfactory balance.

SYMPHONIC METAMORPHOSIS OF THEMES BY CARL MARIA VON WEBER
Duration: approx. 20 minutes

Moderato – Lebhaft (Lively)
Turandot, Scherzo: Moderato – Lebhaft (Lively)
Andantino
Marsch

Soon after Hindemith emigrated to America in 1940, the choreographer Léonide Massine suggested that he should compose a ballet on themes by Weber. They had worked together two years earlier on a successful ballet about the life of Saint Francis, *Nobilissima Visione*, which had premiered in London. In March 1940, Hindemith started the new project by arranging for solo piano two of Weber's piano-duet pieces that he and his wife used to play together. The collaboration foundered when Hindemith learned that Massine intended to involve Salvador Dalí as designer: in 1941, Hindemith saw Dalí's designs for Massine's ballet to the Bacchanale from Wagner's *Tannhäuser*, and found them ridiculous. But the idea of working on Weber's music had sparked Hindemith's interest, and he went on to write the Symphonic Metamorphosis, using his piano arrangements as the basis of the first and third pieces. The whole work was finished by August 1943, and premiered the following January by the Philharmonic-Symphony Orchestra of New York conducted by Arthur Rodzinski. It was a great success, its brilliant and sometimes brash scoring well calculated to show off American virtuoso orchestras and to appeal to audiences.

Three of the four movements are based on piano duets by Weber, and one is from an overture. Like Stravinsky in *Pulcinella*, Hindemith uses not just themes but whole pieces, transforming them into something quite new.

The first movement is taken from the fourth of Weber's Pieces for piano duet, Opus 60. The original is a brisk march with rather Turkish-sounding offbeat accents. Hindemith stays quite close to the original, while using the resources of the orchestra to add a kaleidoscopic wealth of changing colours and little counter-melodies, often with a characteristic touch of harmonic spice. The march has a rumbustious swagger, until relieved by the delicate middle section. Here the melody is given to an oboe, and then to clarinet, piccolo, and glockenspiel.

Soon after, the first march tune returns, at first quietly in a combination pioneered by Ravel in his *Boléro*. Violas, clarinet, flute, and piccolo play the melody together; but violas and clarinet play it at pitch, while the flute plays it an octave and a fifth above, and the piccolo two octaves and a third above. This is an effect used in organ 'mixtures', adding higher notes of the harmonic series to the basic note. If balanced well, the effect is an intriguing tone colour, rather than audible chords. With a lurch into an unexpected key, the music bursts out in a final blast. The audience at the first performance must have realized with a shock that this German composer, with his reputation as an intellectual and theoretician, was capable of writing music that was unashamed fun.

Hindemith based the second piece on an overture by Weber from his incidental music for Schiller's adaptation of Carlo Gozzi's *commedia dell'arte* play, *Turandot* (the same story that was to form the basis of Puccini's opera). Weber uses a (supposedly) authentic Chinese melody, brought from China by a Jesuit missionary, which appeared in Jean-Jacques Rousseau's *Dictionnaire de Musique* (1768). The tune is, like many traditional tunes from around the world, in a pentatonic (five-note) scale, with intriguingly irregular phrases. Weber's overture consists mostly of variations on the Chinese melody, and he gives it a quirky effect in line with ideas of the 'oriental' fashionable in the late eighteenth and early nineteenth centuries. Hindemith redoubles the quirkiness in a wholly twentieth-century manner by altering the tune: he repeats its two phrases, and adds a harmonic twist to each of them, moving away from the basic scale in the middle and returning at the end. Hindemith's relentless and virtuoso set of variations is, again, reminiscent of *Boléro*, though the origin of this style of variations is essentially Russian, beginning with Glinka – the tune remains the same throughout, but colourful orchestration provides an ever-changing background. The movement opens with an atmospheric introduction, in which flute, piccolo, and clarinet try out the tune. Then the pace increases, and cellos and basses start the series of variations. The music rises to a raucous climax, and fades to give way to a jazzy, syncopated new theme on the brass.

This too builds to a climax, then the brass hand the baton to the woodwind, then on to the percussion, and then to the strings. The original tune returns in the bass, with a counterpoint above. There is one more brash climax, and then the percussion take the tune to a fade, and a last string chord.

The third piece is based on the second of Weber's *Six Pièces Faciles*, Opus 10, for piano duet. Hindemith flavours Weber's gentle piece, giving it a nostalgic, pastoral atmosphere with an almost Delius-like use of modal harmonies that slide chromatically. The outer sections are in a minor key, the middle section is in the major. Here Hindemith gives the tenor tune to the cellos, changing its continuation to give it a much darker feel. When the first section returns, the flute adds a delicately elaborate counterpoint.

The final March returns to the same source as the first piece: it is an expanded version of the seventh of Weber's Pieces for Piano Duet, Opus 60. Hindemith gives Weber's march a dark undercurrent, accompanying it with string rhythms coloured by chromatic harmonies, and then having it burst out on all the strings. In the middle section, Hindemith takes the obvious hint from the horn calls in Weber's piano duet and gives them to four horns, and then builds to a brilliant orchestral tutti worthy of a cowboy film set in the Wild West. The opening theme returns, on sombre trombones. But the urge to return to the exuberance of the second theme proves irresistible, and the piece ends in a blaze, like the sheriff's posse riding bravely to the rescue.

SYMPHONY *MATHIS DER MALER*
Duration: approx. 27 minutes

Engelkonzert (Concert of Angels): Ruhig bewegt (flowing peacefully) – Ziemlich lebhafte Halbe (moderately lively, in two)

Grablegung (Entombment): Sehr langsam (very slow)

Versuchung des heiligen Antonius (The Temptation of Saint Anthony): Sehr langsam, frei im Zeitmas (very slow, free in tempo) – Sehr lebhaft (very lively)

Hindemith's opera, *Mathis der Maler*, is based on a fictionalized account of the life of the painter, Matthias Grünewald (*c.* 1470–1528). It draws on suggestions that Grünewald was sympathetic to the cause of the peasants in their rebellion against serfdom. In the opera, Grünewald gives up painting in order to join the peasants in their fight, but becomes disillusioned because of their violence. He takes refuge in a forest, where he dreams that he is St Anthony. St Paul the Hermit tells him that it was wrong to abandon his God-given artistic gift. He must 'bow humbly before your brother and selflessly offer him the holiest creation of your inmost faculties'. Grünewald returns home, and spends the rest of his life in a burst of artistic activity.

Hindemith composed this symphony while working on the opera, drawing in music that would later appear as interludes or form the basis of scenes (see introduction to Hindemith, above, for the circumstance of composition). The titles of the movements relate to three panels of Grünewald's Isenheim Altarpiece, painted in 1515 for an Antonine monastery in Alsace. The monastery looked after victims of a terrible disease known then as 'St Anthony's Fire', but later identified as ergotism, a disease caused by a fungus that leads to violent skin eruptions. It was believed that praying to St Anthony could cause a miraculous recovery, and the Antonine Order of monks was founded to provide hospitals to care for sufferers.

The altarpiece is constructed in three layers as a series of unfolding panels. The outer central panel is a particularly vivid depiction of the Crucifixion, with Christ's ulcerated body (a reference to ergotism) writhing in agony. When the outer panels are opened, an inner central panel is revealed, depicting the Nativity, in which Mary and the baby Jesus are attended by a concert of angels. At the back of the group of angels is one covered with feathers, with distorted, claw-like hands, who looks up to the heavens with an expression of horror or fear. It is suggested that this is Lucifer, the fallen angel who became Satan. So this scene includes a reference to the fight against evil, and perhaps the fight against disease.

Hindemith's 'Concert of Angels' opens with pianissimo string chords of G major, with peaceful rising phrases in the woodwind. Then follows the melody associated with the title of the movement: 'Es sungen drei Engel einen süssen Gesang' ('Three angels sang a sweet song'), a traditional carol whose text appears in the early nineteenth-century collection, *Des Knaben Wunderhorn* (a frequent source of inspiration for Gustav Mahler). Trombones intone the seventeenth-century tune most often associated with the words (this is different from the melody that Mahler composed for them in his Third Symphony). The accompanying rising and falling string line, as often in Hindemith, seems partly to harmonize with the melody, partly to conflict with it. The melody moves to the horns, and then to the trumpets, building to a climax and falling away. The peaceful rising phrases from the opening return, bringing the introductory section of the movement to a close.

The tempo increases ('moderately lively'). Flute and violins play a melody that trips downwards and then rises in a series of steps. If it were in a conventional key, it would seem innocent and charming. But Hindemith's characteristic touches of harmonic contradiction give it a delicately pungent character. The theme is passed around, in quite a classical manner, until the tempo eases ('peaceful'). There is a reminder of the quiet chords from the opening (though now spiced up), and the violins play a new, more lyrical theme. This too is developed, and begins to build up, until a flute introduces a more playful third theme. This injects energy into the music for a time, until the first theme re-enters below the violin figurations, and again the music comes to a halt with pianissimo string chords. The first theme sets off again, but immediately gives way to the second theme, now transformed into a sturdy fugue subject. Both themes are combined freely, and the music gradually becomes more complex and builds up. At the moment when it seems to be heading for a climax, there is a sudden quiet, and the trombones softly intone 'Es sungen drei Engel' again. As before, it passes to the horns, while strings and woodwind continue their contrapuntal build-up round them. At the climax, the tempo pulls back, and the trumpets smooth the carol into a broad chorale. This is both the climax of the movement and the reprise of the opening. The climax fades, and is followed by the first theme of the 'moderately lively' section. Here, it is remembered wistfully, passing between the woodwind and reaching a pause. The lively tempo is renewed, and Hindemith jumps to the third of the 'lively' themes. As before, it energizes the music, and soon the first theme joins in. Then, as the music builds once more, the missing second theme appears, now cheerfully in the woodwind and glockenspiel, like a ring of bells. With fragments of brass chorale, and a final bold statement of the first theme, the movement comes to a grand close.

The base of Grünewald's altarpiece (the predella) shows the entombment of Christ, the body as starkly depicted as it is on the Cross in the central front panel. Three women mourn over the body (traditionally 'the three Marys', including Mary Magdalene). Hindemith's

'Entombment' is a simple, tender movement. Its first theme, on muted strings, is halting, like a memory of a funeral march. As it grows in strength, it is interrupted by a sorrowful pianissimo phrase on strings, answered by a flute that rises bleakly (Hindemith is close to Shostakovich at such moments). Over quiet pizzicato, flute and oboe entwine in dialogue. The funeral march returns and builds to a climax. A sorrowful, leaping phrase passes from clarinet to flute to violins, reaching a poignant climax, and fading to a final, resolving chord.

The innermost panels of the Isenheim Altarpiece are dedicated to the monastery's patron, St Anthony. On either side of the sculpted central panel are two paintings by Grünewald. On the left is the meeting between St Anthony and St Paul the Hermit. And on the right is 'The Temptation of St Anthony', in which the saint is shown lying on the ground, being tormented by monstrous creatures. In Hindemith's opera, Grünewald dreams that he is St Anthony, and that he is tormented by demons, together with characters from his life, for having abandoned his artistic gift. The dream ends with St Paul the Hermit urging Anthony (Mathis) to return to his art, and together they sing an Alleluia.

The final movement of the symphony is headed by a quotation from Athanasius's fourth-century *Life of Saint Anthony*, which appears in the bottom right-hand corner of Grünewald's painting of the *Temptation of St Anthony*:

Ubi eras bone Jhesu ubi eras,	Where were you good Jesus, where were you,
quare non affuisti ut sanares vulnera mea?	why were you not there to heal my wounds?

Hindemith's movement opens with an introduction, a sorrowful, powerful recitative. This gives way to a fast section ('very lively'). A broad melodic line is driven onwards by a persistent galloping rhythm ('Your worst enemy is inside yourself', sings the chorus to this melody in the opera). This reaches a climax and halts abruptly, leaving a solitary flute. While the galloping rhythm continues to mutter in the strings, a new, anxious, searching theme moves from oboe to clarinet and to oboe, flute, and piccolo in combination. Hindemith's quirky, almost medieval way of playing the melody in parallel fifths here is particularly characteristic. Again the tension mounts, and again the music cuts off. A new theme appears, an arresting, falling figure, which in the opera is sung to the words 'Wir plaugen dir' ('We torment you'). This provokes a powerful crisis, which comes to a halt leaving a high violin trill.

This is the beginning of a central slow section of the movement. Under the tormenting trill, the cellos play a long, pleading line, which rises to a height and then melts as it falls. William Walton recognized this as one of Hindemith's most touching moments, quoting it in his Variations on a Theme of Hindemith. The violins take up the pleading theme. After a final descent to a low cello note, the brass break back to the lively tempo with a taunting version of the powerful falling motif. A climax is reached, and as the energy passes to chattering woodwind the violas take up the pleading cello theme. A yet bigger climax is reached, and again cuts off. The strings begin an agitated passage of fugue, based on the shape of the galloping theme. From this complex texture emerges a chorale, played by the woodwind. This is the thirteenth-century hymn, 'Lauda Sion salvatorem' ('Sion, praise the saviour'). Amid the increasing tumult, the hymn calmly sings out, until, at a final halt, the full chorus of brass bursts in with a blazing *Alleluia*, sung in the opera by St Anthony (Mathis) and St Paul.

GUSTAV HOLST
(1874–1934)

Like his contemporary, Vaughan Williams, Holst was a pupil of Stanford, a composer and teacher who remained true to the great classical tradition epitomized by Brahms. But, also like Vaughan Williams, Holst embraced a wide range of influences beyond that tradition – English folk music (inspired by Vaughan Williams' enthusiastic collecting), the English madrigalists, Purcell's *Dido and Aeneas* (which Stanford had conducted at Purcell's bicentenary in 1895), the latest scores by Stravinsky and Schoenberg. At the same time he read and thought widely beyond music. He joined the Hammersmith Socialist Club and conducted its choir, read books by William Morris and attended lectures by George Bernard Shaw, embracing the socialist philosophy that art should be available to everyone. This took practical form in his work at Morley College where, from 1907 to 1924, he taught predominantly working-class students (their high-quality concerts included the first modern performance of Purcell's *The Fairy Queen*, in an edition prepared with the students).

Holst became interested in Indian religious texts and oriental mysticism, and learned Sanskrit so as to be able to prepare his own translations (the chamber opera *Savitri* is the most impressive result). His understanding of the orchestra was, in part, learned from the inside, as a professional trombonist. Like Vaughan Williams and Elgar, he struggled to make a name as a composer, devoting much of his time to teaching. His music was performed, and achieved patchy success. But it was *The Planets*, composed in his forties, that established his name as a composer of international status.

THE PLANETS, OP. 32
Duration: approx. 50 minutes

Mars, the Bringer of War
Venus, the Bringer of Peace
Mercury, the Winged Messenger
Jupiter, the Bringer of Jollity
Saturn, the Bringer of Old Age
Uranus, the Magician
Neptune, the Mystic

The young Adrian Boult first conducted *The Planets* in front of an invited audience in the Queen's Hall, London, in September 1918, and then gave the official premiere (of five movements) the following February. The first public performance of the complete work was not given until 1920. Inevitably, the first movement, 'Mars, the Bringer of War', came to be associated with the horrors of the First World War, which had just come to an end. But Holst had written 'Mars' during the summer of 1914, and although the threat of war was already looming, he always denied that this lay behind the piece. Does 'Mars' at least reflect the spirit of the time? It is impossible to say, without making glib links between music and the state of the world. Similar questions hang over Stravinsky's *The Rite of Spring* (1913) and Schoenberg's Five Pieces for Orchestra (1909 – Holst admired the work enough when he heard it in January 1914 to acquire the score). What is certain is that, on holiday in the summer of 1913, the writer Clifford Bax (brother of the composer Arnold Bax) had introduced Holst to astrology.

Holst, already attuned to mystical subjects, became fascinated, and began to read about astrology and horoscopes.[1] Holst himself emphasized, in a letter to the music critic, Herbert Thompson, 'that the pieces were suggested by the astrological significance of the planets and not by classical mythology'.[2]

The response of the audience at the first performance was enthusiastic. But not all the critics were so impressed. They pointed to obvious sources for Holst's effects: Dukas's *The Sorcerer's Apprentice* for 'Uranus', Debussy's 'Sirènes' for 'Neptune', Hagen's motif from Wagner's *Ring* for 'Mars'. These references are not without foundation, but a century later they do not undermine the force of the music, any more than Elgar's debts to Richard Strauss or Vaughan Williams' to Ravel. Holst took the available musical language of his day and made something powerful with it, crafting his music with skill, but ensuring that the basic ideas were simple enough for any music lover to understand.

'Mars, the Bringer of War' is a relentless march, made doubly threatening by being warped into five-time. It opens with the rhythm that will dominate the whole piece, tapped out on the note G quietly by strings *col legno* (with the wood of the bow), timpani with wooden sticks, and harps, washed with a pianissimo gong roll. Over this already unnerving pattern, bassoons and horns play a three-note motif: it rises a fifth, G to D, as if beginning a fanfare, but then droops down a semitone to D flat, to create a dissonant 'tritone' against the G in the bass. The tritone had long been treated as a dangerous (in early times, forbidden) interval, and nineteenth-century composers such as Wagner, Liszt, and Saint-Saëns used it to evoke associations with evil and the infernal. This is just the start of a piece that is full of clashing dissonances. When the music rises to its first climax, the rhythmic bass moves from G to C, and the D flat of the tritone jars harshly against the C. Now a second motif emerges in trombones and horns, a line that rises and falls sinuously in an attempt to impose a more regular rhythmic pattern over the continuing five-time. As the music moves into more distant keys, tenor tuba and trumpets exchange fanfares. The mood seems more optimistic, until there is a flurry of rapid scales on strings and woodwind, and a crashing halt on a heavy, sombre chord.

The rising and falling second theme returns, quietly and persistently in the bass, as the side drum taps out fragments of the five-time rhythm. The air of menace grows, and eventually the music bursts into a reprise of the opening five-time rhythm, hammered out on its original note, G, by full brass, woodwind, and strings with side drum. The various elements return, with renewed power, and reach a huge, climactic chord, in which the orchestra is joined by full organ. The opening motif becomes a cry of anguish, which echoes and falls away. The scattering flurry of scales returns, over a crescendo of gong and timpani. Full brass and the two timpani players hammer out the rhythm in fragments, with the dissonant tritone at the top of the chord. Mercilessly the chord is struck again and again, *ffff*, slowing for greater emphasis. Finally the tension is released in a last sustained chord. After all the dissonance, the resolution is a bleak fifth, C and G. It is as if the force that began so quietly has torn itself to pieces, leaving nothing but desolation behind it.

'Venus, the Bringer of Peace' is in complete contrast to 'Mars'. The orchestration is airy and transparent, subtle in its combinations of instruments. It includes four flutes, six horns, and two harps, and this enables Holst to create textures that are both rich and delicate. A solo horn quietly plays a high, rising line, and a chorus of four flutes and three oboes answers with a falling line. Like Vaughan Williams, Holst in such quiet music evokes a sense of the pastoral and the mystical, by the combination of traditional, modal scales and harmonies with chromatic shifts from one key to another (a method that owes much to Ravel). After the dialogue between horn and woodwind, the rising line moves to the bass, and quiet rocking chords gently oscillate in harps, horns, and flutes, with delicate touches of glockenspiel and celesta.

The solo horn returns. As the violins hold a high note, the key changes round it. A solo violin emerges with an innocent, pleading melody, soon joined by all the violins. This passage has a distinct feel of human passions, evoking thoughts of Venus as the goddess of love. A new, yearning phrase is introduced by the oboe, and passes to solo cello. Then the rocking chords return, followed by the rising solo horn. The orchestration here is particularly delicate, with a solo flute and violins divided into eight parts. Once again the key changes over a held violin note, and the innocent melody reappears, higher and more mysterious than before, and accompanied only by the four flutes. The rocking chords return for the last time, gently animated by murmuring patterns on harp and low woodwind, with the falling line reiterated above. Over the remaining paragraph, this rich texture gradually lightens and becomes transparent, until we are left only with high strings and flutes and the silvery touch of the celesta.

'Mercury, the Winged Messenger' is a fleeting scherzo. With its muted strings and its cross-rhythms at high speed, its most obvious precursor is the 'Queen Mab' scherzo from Berlioz's *Romeo and Juliet*, but 'Mercury' has a mysterious quality of its own. Holst, in his note for the public premiere in 1920 wrote, 'Mercury is the symbol of mind.' The sense of mystery is created straight away, as the opening alternates rapidly between two distant keys: half a bar in B flat major, then half a bar in E major. It is no coincidence that the interval B flat–E is a tritone, the threatening interval that dominated 'Mars'. Here it gives a sense of floating weightlessness. Everything about this scherzo is rapid and changeable: the six quavers of the bar are grouped sometimes in two beats of three, sometimes in three beats of two, and sometimes both together, creating a sense of quick nervous energy. Strings and woodwind alternate at high speed, trading arpeggio patterns and flurries of scales, while the key is also shifting and uncertain.

Under a high violin harmonic, the rhythm coalesces into a sturdier dance. Out of this steps a solo violin, playing a swirling melody. The little phrase is three bars long, and in its persistent repetition with varied orchestration it sounds thoroughly Russian – an example of the favourite variation technique first popularized by Glinka in his *Kamarinskaya*. The beginning of the scherzo returns, with new developments and variations of orchestration, until, under another high violin harmonic, the phrases fragment, and the piece evaporates with one last chord of E major, resolving the ambiguity that began the movement.

If 'Mercury' owes something to Berlioz, 'Jupiter' has more than a touch of Elgar. It has a shape and character similar to a *Pomp and Circumstance* March, with a hymn-like centre, and rumbustious outer sections. But, although the tempo is that of a fast march, there is nothing military about its character. It bursts with high spirits, such that the music seems at first too excited to settle to a beat. Beneath the chattering of the violins (which itself contains cross-rhythms), a joyful, syncopated tune is played first by the six horns, then by the full brass with woodwind joining the chattering. The horns introduce a new element, a fanfare of rising fourths, which a trumpet immediately corrupts to give a reminder of the tritone that dominated 'Mars'. But this is not the time to dwell on that memory. Soon the horns establish a firm theme, with just enough rhythmic irregularity in it to emphasize its jollity (the first three notes are taken from the chattering pattern that began the piece). Then the return of the rising fourths on trumpet leads into a new theme on horns, in a swaggering three-time. It has the feel of a traditional English folk dance or drinking song, and it is (like the 'Russian' tune in 'Mercury') repeated again and again, with more and more members of the orchestra joining in. The music accelerates, and is released into a great chord.

From its dissolution emerges the hymn that forms the centre of the piece. It seems new, but its opening rise comes from the second theme played by the horns (which in turn came from the opening chattering pattern). In his 1920 programme note on 'Jupiter', Holst contrasted 'jollity in the ordinary sense' with 'the more ceremonial type of rejoicing associated with religions or national festivities', which he celebrates in this hymn. As with Elgar's 'Land of hope and glory', it is difficult to hear this melody without imagining the words with which it later came to be associated. In 1921, Holst used it to set a patriotic poem by a diplomat, Cecil Spring Rice, 'I vow to thee, my country', which he then further adapted to become a hymn. Together with Hubert Parry's 'Jerusalem' (1916), it came to form one of the trio of uplifting, patriotic songs that express pride in Britishness (and specifically Englishness) and remain popular to this day. But the original melody, as it appears in 'Jupiter', is already deliberately hymn-like. It is perhaps an expression not just of ceremonial rejoicing, as Holst said, but of the spirit of community, and community music-making, which was important to Holst, just as it was to Vaughan Williams.

The hymn builds, and then evaporates without reaching a conclusion. The opening section returns, revisiting each of its themes, varied in order and in orchestration. Once again, the swaggering three-time theme, repeated many times, builds to a climax. This time, the climax breaks into a majestic passage in which strings, woodwind, and harps sweep up and down while, below them, the hymn from the centre of the movement is intoned in the bass, and then by trumpets. There is a final dash, in which the pattern of fourths forms a peal of bells to bring the movement to a joyful close.

Holst in his 1920 note wrote, 'Saturn brings not only physical decay, but also a vision of fulfilment.' The fulfilment is hard won. Flutes and harps set up a pattern of two chords that oscillate, like the tolling of a bell or the swinging of a pendulum. This echoes the oscillating chords in 'Venus'; but the effect here is very different. Each chord has as its top two notes the tritone, and when the double basses creep in below it is with a variant of the first motif from 'Mars'. Very quiet, rootless, and at a slow tempo, the effect is bleak. Violins, oboe, and cellos in turn repeat the end of the motif, like a long sigh. And then it is repeated by an unfamiliar instrument, the bass oboe, dark and plangent. The oscillating chords are replaced by a pizzicato repeating pattern in the bass, and the three trombones play a solemn dirge that rises heroically and falls away (there are echoes of the finale of Tchaikovsky's 'Pathétique' Symphony here).

The three flutes return, playing a mysterious chant that is given processional weight by offbeat chords below. Gradually this increases in power, reaching an enormous climax punctuated by clanging bells, the return of the tritone chords, and the variant of the 'Mars' motif below. The bleak vision of the opening has reached its terrifying consummation. As it ebbs away, the sighing phrases (including another appearance of the bass oboe) lead on to a lifting of mood. The tritone chords give way to warmer harmonies, with a gentle repeating pattern on harp harmonics. Double basses play an unthreatening variant of the 'Mars' motif. This is the beginning of the 'vision of fulfilment' of which Holst wrote, and at first it recalls the 'In Paradisum' that concludes Fauré's Requiem. As the music builds to a final, ecstatic wave, it might remind us of the dawn from Ravel's Daphnis et Chloé. It is indeed a fulfilling end to the great arc that began with the chill of the tritones.

'Uranus, the Magician' opens with a four-note spell, fearsomely intoned by trumpets and trombones. Notes two and three form the tritone, adding to the sense of threat. The spell is repeated, accelerating, on tubas and timpani. But then, as three bassoons start a galumphing dance, we become aware that this magician is a grotesque, even humorous figure. Thoughts of Dukas's *The Sorcerer's Apprentice* come to mind – Holst is very likely to have heard it at concerts in London following its premiere in 1899. The mock-magical themes of 'Uranus' have subtle connections to motifs from earlier movements. The bassoons' dancing theme opens with a version of the first 'Mars' motif upside down, which develops chaotic energy. The mood lightens to reveal a second dancing theme, which begins with a shape taken from 'Saturn' and rounds off the phrase with another from 'Venus', both transformed almost beyond recognition. This too builds, culminating in a third theme. It has a powerful swing, with horns and strings in unison, and almost sounds like another dance inspired by English folk music; but this sense is subverted by building the melody from the whole-tone scale, with prominent notes that once again outline the dreaded tritone. The music reaches a mighty chord, closely related to the climactic chord of 'Mars'. The music scatters, with reminders of the four-note spell, and the protesting screech of piccolos.

From this chaotic moment the dance rhythm reappears, as if the bassoons are trying to re-establish their first theme. Instead, tubas start up a new, march-like tune, but one in which the phrases are irregular and the harmonies wayward, with more touches of whole-tone harmonies. The mood seems mock-serious, but the march nevertheless builds into the biggest climax of the piece, with every section of the orchestra *fff*, culminating in a huge chord, with a glissando on full organ, and a sudden break. From this cataclysm emerges a mysterious pianissimo string chord. Harp harmonics outline the four-note spell, and the magician seems to have broken through to some real magic after all. For a moment the bassoons renew their dance, tubas intone the spell, and the timpani accelerate wildly, provoking one last spell and a massive chord (the mysterious chord over a new bass). Again the music evaporates, finally reaching a quiet resolution.

'Neptune: the Mystic' is the simplest and yet most subtle of the seven movements, clearly indebted to the influence of other composers and yet utterly original in its effect. It is a virtuoso piece of orchestration – pianissimo throughout, but with a seemingly infinite variety of delicate effects and combinations, washed by harps and celesta, and joined in its final pages by an offstage chorus of women's voices.

The use of a wordless chorus evokes memories of Debussy's 'Sirènes', the third of his *Nocturnes*, which Debussy had conducted in London in 1909. But equally important was Holst's own experience of writing for female chorus and harp, in the third group of his *Choral Hymns from the Rig Veda*, composed in 1910. Many of the chordal and harmonic effects in 'Neptune' are to be found there. Another source of inspiration for new effects was Schoenberg's Five Pieces for Orchestra. Holst had first heard them at a Promenade Concert in London, where they provoked laughter and boredom, but Holst was fascinated enough to obtain the score. The third of Schoenberg's pieces, 'Farben' (Colours), consists of low, dissonant chords that rarely rise above *ppp*, shifting subtly in their instrumentation, and creating a sense of static uncertainty. Holst was never drawn to Schoenberg's extremes of atonality, but what he learned from this experiment in orchestration helped to create the motionless effect of 'Neptune'.

The movement opens with a duet of flute and alto flute, in another rocking pattern that opens up into an arpeggio. In each bar, chords of two distant keys alternate, E minor and G sharp minor. This is reminiscent of 'Mercury', whose opening alternated between B flat major and E major. But 'Mercury' was fleeting, whereas 'Neptune' is almost static. The sense of floating is increased by the fact that the music is in five-time – like 'Mars', but in slow motion and to quite different effect. The two chords (E minor and G sharp minor) share one note, B, which Holst exploits to give them a sense of a mysterious link to each other, like a doorway between two different universes. He uses this combination of distance and connection as the foundation of the entire movement. The original rocking alternation returns and extends, and the two chords come together to create a clash of the two keys. Other patterns develop, more akin to the chant-like melodies from earlier movements. The music drifts through these various elements, while the sense of limitless space is created by a range of instrumental effects: high harp tremolo, delicately cascading arpeggios, and deep brass chords that bring the two original chords together, or form other bitonal clashes.

Gradually the scintillating background textures simplify. The celesta plays a repeating, rising pattern formed from the notes of the first two chords. This becomes a yet simpler rising scale pattern in the woodwind, led by the bass oboe, over held string chords. While this continues, we gradually become aware of what seems to be a new instrument sounding a long, held G. This steady, motionless sound, like the aural equivalent of a distant star, is created by the offstage chorus. As the woodwind scales fall silent, the chorus takes them over, further simplifying them into fragments of chant that overlap with each other. There is one last mysterious, profound dissonance from the low brass and woodwind. The chorus renews the weaving of its overlapping patterns, simplified still further until the music is reduced to two chords, rocking back and forth. They continue singing, while the offstage door is gradually closed, until the voices disappear into the eternal distance and silence of the universe.

CHARLES IVES
(1874–1954)

Charles Ives, one of the great figures of American music, spent most of his life in musical obscurity as a spare-time composer, earning his living in an insurance business. Indeed, he was much more famous during his lifetime for his work in insurance than his work in music, making important contributions to modern concepts of estate planning. He regarded this not as cold business, but 'participating in a great movement for the benefit of humanity at large', as his boss at Mutual Life had put it during an investigation into unscrupulous practices.[1] Ives may have been naive to swallow such statements whole, but it was a good basis on which to set up his own insurance partnership, free of the taint of corruption.

Naivety was an essential part of Ives's appeal, particularly when it came to his music. He embraced music in all its manifestations. And if his experimentation was daring, this too he partly attributed to his experience in the business world: 'My business experience revealed life to me in many aspects that I might otherwise have missed. In it one sees tragedy, nobility, meanness, high aims, low aims, brave hopes, faint hopes, great ideals, no ideals, and one is able to watch these work inevitable destiny. And it has seemed to me that the finer sides of these traits were not only in the majority but in the ascendancy . . . It is my impression that there is more open-mindedness and willingness to examine carefully the premises underlying a new or unfamiliar thing, before condemning it, in the world of business than in the world of music.'[2] His father was a professional bandmaster and music teacher – he had been the youngest bandmaster in the Union army during the Civil War – and Ives received from him not only his first training in harmony and counterpoint and music history but also a love of popular music, songs, and hymns, and a taste for experimentation. His father introduced him to novel musical sounds and effects – quarter-tones, bitonality (a tune played or sung in one key with the accompaniment in another), and the sound of bands playing different marches simultaneously. Although these were introduced in a spirit of boyhood fun, they were to become material for serious musical thinking later in life. Charles Ives was also an idealistic thinker on a grand scale, declaring that a composer 'must never be timid or afraid of trying to express that which he feels is far above his power to express'.[3] Despite never earning his living as a composer, Ives was far from untrained. He acquired a wide range of musical knowledge from his father, and was a professional organist from the age of fourteen. At Yale University he studied harmony, music history, and composition with Horatio Parker.

One of the chief sources of inspiration for Ives was the repertoire of nineteenth-century American hymns that he first got to know as a boy, when his father led the singing at religious camp meetings. Ives's devotion to them goes a long way to explain the mood of mystical fervour that lies at the heart of his music:

> [A man] may find a deep appeal in the simple but acute 'Gospel Hymns of the New England camp meeting' of a generation or so ago ... These tunes have, for him, a truer ring than many of those groove-made, even-measured, monotonous, non-rhythmed, indoor-smelling, priest-taught, academic, English, or neo-English hymns (and anthems) – well-written, well-harmonized things, well-voice-led, well-counterpointed, well-corrected, and well O.K.'d by well-corrected Mus. Bac. R.F.O.G.s ... – in a word, those proper forms of stained-glass beauty, which our over-drilled mechanisms – boy-choirs are limited to. But if the Yankee can reflect the fervency with which 'his gospels' were sung – the fervency of 'Aunt Sarah', who scrubbed her life away for her brother's ten orphans, the fervency with which this woman, after a fourteen-hour work day on the farm, would hitch up and drive five miles through the mud and rain to 'prayer meetin'' – he may find there a local colour that will do all the world good. If his music can but catch that 'spirit' by being a part with itself, it will come somewhere near his ideal – and it will be American too, perhaps nearer so than that of the devotee of Indian or Negro melody.[4]

The composer who most invites comparison with Ives is Mahler. Mahler's famous remark that 'the symphony must be like the world, it must embrace everything' could equally well have been spoken by Ives. Mahler, like Ives, brings into his music popular song, marching bands, jarring and ironical contrast. Ives may have heard Mahler conduct his music in New York (he certainly attended a concert conducted by Mahler), but there is no evidence that Ives had any extensive knowledge of Mahler's works. Nevertheless, the two composers, coming from very different cultures, reached conclusions that have important elements in common.

When Ives's music started to become widely known from the 1960s, it became clear that he had pioneered new approaches to music. This applies particularly to the use of chaotic combinations of sonorities giving the effect of indeterminacy (though, in the case of Ives, such effects are notated in detail). One of the composers most closely associated with the later development of indeterminate music was John Cage. In a BBC interview in 1966, Cage described what he was doing, in setting up indeterminate performances that could last for hours, in contrast to the longest works of the past: 'I connect those works of Mahler, Bruckner and Wagner and so forth with the industrial business. They're big machines. I'm not making a machine. I'm making something far more like weather.'[5] This thinking has something in common with Ives. His music does not seek resolution of contrasts, but simply allows them to exist, often in jarring cacophony.

Like Sibelius, Ives stopped composing several decades before his death. In 1927, according to his wife, Harmony, 'he came downstairs one day with tears in his eyes and said he couldn't seem to compose any more – nothing went well – nothing seemed right'.[6] He left uncompleted a *Universe* Symphony, a work even more complex than his Fourth Symphony.

SYMPHONY NO. 4
Duration: approx. 30 minutes

Prelude: Maestoso
Comedy: Allegretto
Fugue: Andante moderato con moto
Finale: Largo

Ives worked on his Fourth Symphony for many years, from about 1910 to the early 1920s. The first two movements were performed, with a reduced orchestra, in New York in 1927, but the symphony had to wait until 1965, eleven years after Ives's death, for a complete premiere.[7]

The symphony begins with a slow Prelude lasting about three minutes. As Ives expressed it, the sense of the Prelude is 'the searching questions of "What?" and "Why?" which the spirit of man asks of life. The three succeeding movements are the diverse answers in which existence replies.' Although the Prelude is short, it is spacious and complex. The orchestra is divided into two groups: the main ensemble, and a distant group of four violins and harp, labelled 'distant choir (angelic host)'. The two groups begin together, but after a few bars the main orchestra increases tempo, while the distant group continues at the original, slow tempo, which is now unrelated to the main orchestra's tempo (hence the need for a second conductor). The distant group is instructed to continue playing until a general bar of silence is reached, repeating their music if necessary, and playing very quietly throughout. They reiterate a phrase from the hymn, 'Nearer my God to thee', a tune that Ives quotes very often in his music, and which will return in the finale. Meanwhile, the main orchestra begins with an arresting fortissimo played by low strings and piano, with a muted trumpet call. As the two tempos diverge, a solo cello ('or violin') plays a meditative, hymn-like solo. After a bar of silence, a choir sings the hymn 'Watchman, tell us of the night', revealing that this was the melody on which the cello was meditating. The quiet, rich texture of the orchestra is brightened by the sound of a celesta, which plays in a rhythm unrelated to anything else, creating yet another layer of rumination. As the chorus concludes with the words, 'See, see, oh see!', they are instructed to die away 'in a half kind of humming, like a cloud'.

The second movement was based on an earlier piano piece, 'The Celestial Railroad', which in turn was partly derived from a movement of Ives's *Concord* Sonata. The inspiration and the title came from a short story by Nathaniel Hawthorne, a satirical reworking of Bunyan's *Pilgrim's Progress* that attacks the easy and comfortable Christianity of modern times compared (by implication) with that of the Pilgrim Fathers. As in Bunyan, the narrator falls asleep and dreams. His journey begins at the City of Destruction, where a convenient railroad has been built from there to the Celestial City. He falls in with Mr Smooth-it-away, 'a director of the railroad corporation and one of its largest stockholders', who acts as his guide through the journey. They board the train in the company of 'parties of the first gentry and most respectable people in the neighbourhood setting forth towards the Celestial City as cheerfully as if the pilgrimage were merely a summer tour'. From the windows of the train, they catch sight of 'two dusty foot travellers in the old pilgrim guise, with cockle shell and staff, their mystic rolls of parchment in their hands and their intolerable burdens on their backs. The preposterous obstinacy of these honest people in persisting to groan and stumble along the difficult pathway rather than take advantage of modern improvements, excited great mirth among our wiser brotherhood. We greeted the two pilgrims with many pleasant jibes and a roar of laughter; whereupon they gazed at us with such woeful and absurdly compassionate visages that our merriment grew tenfold more obstreperous.' After a stay in the decadent city of Vanity Fair, they reboard the train and reach Beulah land on the banks of the River Jordan. Here they are amazed to see, on the far side of the river, that the two poor pilgrims have arrived before them, emerging from the water and being greeted by a celestial choir. The narrator boards the ferry to cross the river to the Celestial City. Too late, from the water the narrator sees Mr Smooth-it-all laughing on the shore, as fire darts from his eyes and smoke from his mouth and nostrils. He realizes that he has been tricked by a devil, rushes to leap off the boat, but is drenched by a deadly cold splash of water from the paddle-wheel, and wakes from the dream.

For the first performance of this movement in 1927, a programme note, thought to derive from Ives himself, states, 'Indeed this work of Hawthorne's may be considered as a sort of incidental program in which an exciting, easy, and worldly progress through life is contrasted with the life of the Pilgrims in their journey through the swamp. The occasional slow episodes (of the symphony movement) – pilgrims' hymns – are constantly crowded out and overwhelmed by the former. The dream, or fantasy, ends with an interruption of reality – the Fourth of July in Concord – brass bands, drum corps etc.'[8] Thomas M. Brodhead, who prepared an edition of Ives's 'The Celestial Railroad', demonstrates that the piano piece and the orchestral movement are closely related, and that both are not just loosely inspired by Hawthorne's story, but can be shown to follow through some of its episodes, beginning from the train whistle, and ending with the abrupt awakening into reality.[9]

This is the longest movement of the symphony (about eleven minutes), and is immensely complex. The huge orchestra is from time to time divided into different groups that proceed at different speeds, coming together at certain points. This gives a sense of multi-layered simultaneous events that relate to the story: the speed of the train, the groups of passengers on board, the weary trudging of the pilgrims, and the jeering reaction of the passengers as they see them. The movement opens to reveal a bleak and bewildering landscape, full of strange and threatening sounds. This is the City of Destruction (the weird mood evokes memories of Schoenberg's *Erwartung*, though Ives probably did not know it). Out of this chaos quietly emerges a hymn tune played by two violins in unison. This represents the two pilgrims, who are trudging through the swamp rather than board the train. It continues steadfastly as low string glissandi with piano chords evoke the sound of the train getting into motion, and the pace gradually accelerates. The train whistles (high woodwind), and the brass shout with delight. The pilgrims continue to sing their hymn, but they are only audible in moments of quiet.

Most of the next few minutes are given up to raucous jollification on board, with a welter of brass, shrieking high woodwind, playful clarinets. Popular tunes are thrown around with increasing enthusiasm, as the passengers have a wild time and jeer at the pilgrims. Eventually the music calms, and the violins play a sweet melody that in the piano piece 'The Celestial Railroad' was specifically associated with Mr Smooth-it-away. This is the start of a quieter episode as the travellers enjoy the delights of Vanity Fair. A pair of violas play a gentle melody that circles round and round in its own tempo, like a half-remembered version of 'In the sweet by and by'. Ives in a note writes, 'a take off here on polite salon music. This is sweetie sweet stuff – violet water, pink teas in Vanity Fair social life.' Trumpets and trombones announce the resumption of the train journey. More raucousness breaks out, and rival tunes compete with each other. There is one last burst of speed, and a sudden halt. From the mayhem emerges the sweet sound of a solo violin, set against a strange, ethereal landscape including (optionally) a piano tuned in quarter-tones, as the passengers reach Beulah Land and the river. Finally, there is a blast of full orchestra, with conflicting marching tunes, as the narrator wakes with a shock and finds himself in the midst of Fourth of July Celebrations. Rather than reach any conclusion, this simply peters out, leaving the violas straggling in the final bars.

The third movement provides the second 'answer', which Ives described as 'an expression of the reaction of life into formalism and ritual'.[10] He returns to the formal counterpoint that he was taught by his father and by his teacher Horatio Parker. The movement is a fugue, lasting almost as long as the tumultuous second movement. There is a bold naivety about it that, out of context, could scarcely succeed. But this is Ives, and after the mayhem of 'The Celestial Railroad', it comes across as a curiously touching statement of faith in old verities. Like the second movement of the symphony, it had its origins in an earlier work, the first movement of his first string quartet, composed in student days. The fugue is based on the hymn 'From Greenland's icy mountains', woven together with 'All hail the power of Jesus' name'. A trombone introduces phrases from 'Joy to the world', and it is with a resounding return to this hymn that the fugue ends.

The finale, according to Ives, is 'an apotheosis of preceding content, in terms that have something to do with the reality of existence and its religious experience'. He thought it, 'the best, compared with the other movements, or for that matter with any other thing I've done'.[11] At its heart lies the hymn tune 'Nearer my God to thee', which was quoted in the Prelude. Once again it is layered in different groups at different distances and in independent metres: as well as the main orchestra, a percussion group, a distant choir of violins and harp (as in the first movement), and a wordless vocal choir. It begins with quiet bars of drums and gong, which persist throughout the movement. The double basses begin to hint at the hymn tune. The forces gradually gather to an immense climax. As they fall away, a wordless chorus returns to 'Nearer my God to thee', and the movement dies away to the gentle sounds of percussion with which it began.

THREE PLACES IN NEW ENGLAND (ORCHESTRAL SET NO. 1)
Duration: approx. 19 minutes
The 'St Gaudens' in Boston Common (Colonel Shaw and his Colored Regiment)
Putnam's Camp, Redding, Connecticut
The Housatonic at Stockbridge

Ives composed this work over a long period, from about 1908 to 1920, and then revised and rescored it for chamber orchestra in 1929, after an invitation from Nicolas Slonimsky to compose something for his Boston Chamber Orchestra (with new dissonances added, according to Elliot Carter who saw him at work). Slonimsky conducted the premiere in January 1931 at New York Town Hall, and this was the first time that a major orchestral work by Ives had been performed complete. When Slonimsky was to conduct the set again in Paris the following June, Ives wrote to him, 'Just kick into the music as you did in the Town Hall – never mind the exact notes or the right notes, they're always a nuisance. Just let the spirit of the stuff sail up to the Eiffel Tower and on to Heaven.'[12]

The 'St Gaudens' in Boston Common (Colonel Shaw and his Colored Regiment)

This piece, which Ives originally called 'Black March', was inspired by a bronze relief sculpture by Augustus St Gaudens commemorating one of the famous acts of tragic heroism during the Civil War. Colonel Robert Gould Shaw, a twenty-six-year-old white man, commanded the 54th Massachusetts regiment, one of the first to consist entirely of black volunteer soldiers. After marching for two days, they took a leading part in the unsuccessful charge on Fort Wagner, a Confederate bastion near Charleston, South Carolina, in July 1863. Shaw was killed on the parapet, urging his men on, and more than a hundred of them died in the battle. The victorious Confederates buried the colonel in a mass grave with his black soldiers – an act intended as an insult, but seen by Shaw's father as an honour: 'We can imagine no holier place than that in which he lies, among his brave and devoted followers . . .'[13] The monument is in the heroic style of classical military bas-reliefs, with Shaw mounted on horseback, his men marching beside him, weary but determined.

Ives composed the piece c. 1915–17, and prefaced it in the 1935 published score with his own poem:

> Moving, – Marching – Faces of Souls!
> Marked with generations of pain,
> Part-freers of a Destiny,
> Slowly, restlessly – swaying us on with you
> Towards other Freedom!
> The man on horseback, carved from
> A native quarry of the world Liberty
> And from what your country was made.
> You images of a Divine Law
> Carved in the shadow of a saddened heart –
> Never light abandoned –
> Of an age and of a nation.
> Above and beyond that compelling mass
> Rises the drum-beat of the common-heart
> In the silence of a strange and
> Sounding afterglow
> Moving, – Marching – Faces of Souls!

From dark and mysterious dissonances begin to emerge fragments of music from the Civil War, beginning with a ghostly glimpse of 'The Battle Cry of Freedom'. Later we will hear touches of 'Marching through Georgia'. But at first nothing is clearly defined – the music seems to be shrouded in mist. The tempo marking is 'Very slowly', and there is only the occasional suggestion of a march-tread. After a while, there is a slight increase in pace and a firming of the rhythm, which Ives has marked with a characteristically evocative note: 'From here on, though with animation, still slowly and rather evenly. Any holding-back and variation should be of a cursory kind. Often when a mass of men march uphill, there is an unconscious slowing up. The Drum seems to follow the feet, rather than the feet the drum.' From here the music gradually builds, struggling through dissonances, until it reaches a climax on a great chord of C major – virtually the only pure consonance in the whole piece. The moment is soon gone, and the music retreats back into elegiac darkness. A solo flute plays the clearest reminiscence of 'The Battle Cry of Freedom', followed by a clarinet with 'Marching through Georgia', and the movement ends unresolved, with the sense of tragic aspiration hanging in the air.

Putnam's Camp, Redding, Connecticut

For this movement, Ives incorporated material from two earlier works, 'Country Band March' and Overture and March '1776', both composed in 1903. He completed the movement in 1912.

General Israel Putnam was one of the most renowned officers of the American Revolution, with the sort of reputation for fighting spirit that creates legends. At the Battle of Bunker Hill (17 June 1775), he is reported to have issued the famous order, 'Don't fire until you see the whites of their eyes.'

The score is prefaced by an explanatory essay:

Near Redding Center, Conn., is a small park preserved as a Revolutionary Memorial; for here General Israel Putnam's soldiers had their winter quarters in 1778–1779. Long rows of stone camp fire-places still remain to stir a child's imagination. The hardships which the soldiers endured and the agitation of a few hot-heads to break camp and march to the Hartford Assembly for relief, is part of Redding history.

Once upon a '4th of July', some time ago, so the story goes, a child went there on a picnic, held under the auspices of the First Church and the Village Cornet Band. Wandering away from the rest of the children past the camp ground into the woods, he hopes to catch a glimpse of some of the old soldiers. As he rests on the hillside of laurel and hickories, the tunes of the band and the songs of the children grow fainter and fainter; – when – 'mirabile dictu' – over the trees on the crest of the hill he sees a tall woman standing. She reminds him of a picture he has of the Goddess of Liberty – but the face is sorrowful – she is pleading with the soldiers not to forget their 'cause' and the great sacrifices they have made for it. But they march out of the camp with fife and drum to a popular tune of the day. Suddenly a new national note is heard. Putnam is coming over the hills from the center – the soldiers turn back and cheer. The little boy awakes, he hears the children's songs and runs down past the monument to 'listen to the band' and join in the games and dances.

The repertoire of national airs at that time was meagre. Most of them were of English origin. It is a curious fact that a tune very popular with the American soldiers was 'The British Grenadiers'. A captain in one of Putnam's regiments put it to words, which were sung for the first time in 1779 at a patriotic meeting in the Congregational Church in Redding Center; the text is both ardent and interesting.

This is a march in 'Quick Step Time', which immediately flings us into the most exuberant Fourth of July celebration, combining in rapid succession popular marches of Ives's youth with tunes dating back to the time of the Revolution, sometimes in different metres and keys simultaneously. These include 'The Girl I Left Behind Me', 'Yankee Doodle', 'The Arkansas Traveller', 'The Battle Cry of Freedom', 'Hail Columbia', 'Columbia, the Gem of the Ocean', 'Tramp! Tramp! Tramp!', and others. After two minutes of joyous confusion, the music quietens, descending to a single low note on the double basses. Mysterious chords introduce a plangent oboe solo, with fragments of 'The British Grenadiers' on trumpet. The spell is soon broken by the resumption of march tempo, and a combination of keys; the bass is firmly on E flat, the brass play a fanfare in A major, the flute plays 'The British Grenadiers' in A major, but soon swerves to G major. From here the music builds to a climax of amazingly daring mayhem, flinging itself at a final dissonance.

The Housatonic at Stockbridge

Ives wrote that the piece 'was suggested by a Sunday morning walk that Mrs Ives and I took near Stockbridge the summer after we were married [in 1908]. We walked in the meadows along the river and heard the distant singing from the church across the river. The mists had not entirely left the river and the colors, the running water, the banks and trees were something one would always remember. Robert Underwood Johnson, in his poem, *The Housatonic at Stockbridge*, paints this scene beautifully.'[14] Ives started writing the piece as soon as they had returned, completed it in 1911, and then revised and orchestrated it 1912.

Johnson was one of Ives's favourite poets, and he prefaced the score with part of that poem, which had appeared in *The Atlantic Monthly* in July 1896:

Contented river! In thy dreamy realm –
The cloudy willow and the plumy elm . . .

Thou hast grown human laboring with men
At wheel and spindle; sorrow thou dost ken; . . .

Thou beautiful! From every dreamy hill
What eye but wanders with thee at thy will,
Imagining thy silver course unseen
Convoyed by two attendant streams of green. . . .

Contented river! And yet over-shy
To mask thy beauty from the eager eye;
Hast thou a thought to hide from field and town?
In some deep current of the sunlit brown
Art thou disquieted – still uncontent
With praise from thy Homeric bard, who lent
The world the placidness thou gavest him?
Thee Bryant loved when life was at its brim; . . .

Ah! There's a restive ripple, and the swift
Red leaves – September's firstlings – faster drift;

Wouldst thou away! . . .
I also of much resting have a fear;
Let me thy companion be
By fall and shallow to the adventurous sea!

'Bryant' refers to the Boston poet, William Cullen Bryant (1794–1878), author of 'Green River'.
Ives's movement is purely instrumental, but in 1921 he used some of the music to set an
extract from Johnson's poem as a song.

The marking is Adagio molto (Very slowly). A suggestion of mists and running water is
created by a complex combination of swirling patterns – groups of three in the violas, groups
of four in lower violins, groups of ten spilling over the bar line in upper violins, with middle
violins playing delicate tremolo and the piano playing isolated notes like droplets of water.
From this shimmering background begins to emerge a hymn-like melody, first in cellos and
bassoon, then, with greater definition, in cor anglais and violas. This is derived from an actual
hymn tune, Isaac B. Woodbury's 'Dorrnance' (not 'Dorrance', as frequently misprinted), a tune
that was sung to several texts. It is not known which text Ives might have had in mind, but
there is a clue in a letter from an old friend, George A. Lewis, who attended the first performance in 1931. He wrote to Ives the following day that he 'was deeply touched to find . . . that
the hymn about the cross was struggling to rise above the sound of the waters and express
itself'.[15] The tune is never completely formed, but comes and goes, as if half-remembered or
half-heard (as in Ives's description of hearing singing from the church across the river). The
melody moves to the violins and the density of the texture increases. There is a massive
crescendo, and an acceleration to Allegro moderato. This culminates in a moment of tumultuous exultation, with the melody in the brass, climaxing on a final discord. When this is cut
off, delicate *ppp* strings are left playing one last haunting, unfinished phrase.

LEOŠ JANÁČEK
(1854–1928)

Now acknowledged as the most important Czech composer of the early twentieth century,
Janáček spent many years of his life scarcely known outside his native Moravia. He was
the leading musical figure in Brno, where his opera *Jenůfa* was premiered in 1904. But the
Prague Theatre refused to stage it, and it was not until the opera was performed in Prague in
1916 and in Vienna in 1918 that Janáček's international reputation was finally established. He
was by now in his mid-sixties, and the remaining ten years of his life produced an extraordinary outpouring of great works, including several operas, among them *Kátya Kabanová* and
The Cunning Little Vixen, together with two string quartets and the wind sextet *Mládi* (Youth).

This late flourishing was greatly inspired by Kamila Stösslová, a married woman thirty-
eight years younger than Janáček whom he first met at a spa in 1917, and with whom he
developed a one-sided passion. Janáček and his wife had a difficult relationship, and this was
not the first time he had fallen for another woman. What was extraordinary was the way that
the two couples, Janáček and his wife and Kamila and her husband, sustained a friendly relationship over ten years. During this period, Janáček wrote more than seven hundred letters to
Kamila, and she responded while fending off his passionate obsession. She was the leading
inspiration for the central figures of his operas *Kátya Kabanová*, *The Cunning Little Vixen*,

and *The Makropulos Case*, and for the figure of the gypsy woman in *The Diary of One Who Disappeared*.

Janáček's musical language was highly personal. It was influenced specifically by the folk music of Moravia, where he was born and brought up. He was a leading collector of Moravian traditional music, which became fundamental to Janáček's own style of musical composition (as Hungarian and Rumanian music became to Bartók's music). He found in Moravian songs a powerful and natural form of expression: 'a vital ebullience, a heartfelt outcry, a jubilation, a lament', whose variety of moods and rhythmic freedom he regarded as deriving from speech-rhythms: 'The proof that the songs originated from words lies in the special character of their rhythm. There is no possibility of organising them within barlines. The rhythm of these folk songs, unbelievably rich in variety, can be put into order only by the words.'[1] From this basis Janáček developed a profound interest in the sounds and inflections of Czech speech, together with the calls of birds and animals, and used them to create the shape of his music like no other composer. Janáček was, in his musical style, a loner, and while this partly accounts for his lack of recognition during his lifetime, it is also his great strength. Within a few bars of his mature works you know exactly who is speaking – and 'speaking' is at the heart of it. This is obvious in his operas and other vocal works, but it is also true of his instrumental music.

SINFONIETTA

Duration: approx. 24 minutes

Allegretto – Allegro – Maestoso (Fanfares)
Andante – Allegretto (The Castle)
Moderato (The Queen's Monastery)
Allegretto (The Street)
Andante con moto (The Town Hall)

Janáček's Sinfonietta originated as a commission for the 1926 mass gymnastics meeting of Sokol (Czech for 'falcon'), a gymnastics association that had been founded in Prague in 1862, and had developed into an empire-wide and then an international movement. Always a focus of national pride, it was particularly so after the founding of independent Czechoslovakia in 1918. Every few years, Sokol held a *slet* (Czech for 'flock of birds'), a mass celebration in Prague. The 1926 *slet* was the eighth, held at the newly built Strahov Stadium, holding over 100,000 spectators. As many as 15,000 participants at a time took part in mass callisthenic performances, folk dancing, military drills, gymnastic competitions, children's games, and grand marches.

Janáček was commissioned to compose fanfares for this great occasion (Josef Suk had written a march for the previous *slet* in 1920). But as well as fulfilling this commission, he developed the fanfares into a five-movement Sinfonietta. Artistic events took place at various locations in Prague during the *slet*, and Václav Talich conducted the Czech Philharmonic Orchestra in the premiere of the Sinfonietta.

Janáček referred to the work as his 'Military Sinfonietta', and dedicated it to the Czechoslovak Armed Forces (to whom he had previously dedicated his rhapsody, *Taras Bulba*). It is scored for a huge orchestra, including an extra brass contingent of nine trumpets, two bass trumpets, and two tenor tubas, which play fanfares in the first and last movements. These were inspired by a military band display that Janáček and Kamila heard in a park in

Písek (where Kamila and her husband lived). Janáček said to Talich that he wanted these fanfares to have the cutting sound of a military band, as opposed to the more refined tone of orchestral players.

The other movements were partly inspired by reminiscences of the town of Brno, where he had been a chorister from the age of eleven. For the Prague premiere Janáček supplied titles for the five movements: 'Fanfares', 'The Castle', 'The Queen's Monastery', 'The Street', and 'The Town Hall'. He had developed a particular love of Brno after Czech independence in 1918. In an essay called 'My Town' published in a Prague journal in 1927, Janáček wrote of 'the glow of freedom' and the rebirth of the town: 'I saw myself in it, I belonged to it. The blare of the victorious trumpets, the holy peace of the Queen's Monastery [where he had been a chorister] . . . the shadows of the night, the breath of the green hill and the vision of the secure growth and greatness of the town arose in my Sinfonietta from this recognition, from this town, Brno.'[2]

The opening fanfares have a uniquely powerful effect. The tenor tubas set up a pattern of bare fifths. Under it, timpani and bass trumpets play an abrupt little two-bar phrase. This is a 'mirror rhythm', a rhythm that is the same forwards and backwards, a favourite ingredient of Moravian traditional music. The nine trumpets extend the phrase to three bars, then to four, then five, enriching the harmony as they go. As the phrase expands again, it breaks into a faster tempo. All through this development, the timpani and bass trumpets keep up their dogged repetition of their original two-bar phrase. Then the trumpets bring in a broader melody that quotes a Moravian Christmas song. The fanfares end with this tune gloriously echoing fortissimo between the groups of trumpets, over the persistent drumming of the mirror rhythm.

The second movement ('The Castle') opens with an agitated pattern in the clarinets and low muted trombones. Over staccato trombones, woodwind play a sort of folk dance, which is then taken up by the violins. This is a mixture of the jaunty and the strange – it is typical of Janáček that it is impossible to put one's finger on the character, which seems both ancient and modern, dark and light, cheerful and haunting. The music slows, and oboe and flute in unison sing a calmer melody, while the agitated pattern accompanies. Cellos and bassoon answer. By now, one might think this is going to be one of those scherzo-like movements with a simple alternation of faster and slower sections. But soon it develops into something much more complex. The pace increases again, and, over urgent rhythmic patterns, the violins take the melody higher and higher. The tension increases, driven by the rhythms that began the movement, until the brass enter majestically with phrases reminiscent of the opening fanfares. The music calms for a moment, the grand fanfare enters once more, and calms again. Harp and oboe introduce a new folk-song-like tune that refers back to the first theme of the movement. The brass answer with a muted echo of their fanfare. With a sudden chord, we are back at the beginning, with a reprise of the opening woodwind tune over muted trombones. But this is soon brought to an abrupt stop, and the movement is over.

The third movement ('The Queen's Monastery') begins with a gentle melody on muted violins over a sustained bass note in the tuba. The melody passes to cor anglais, then oboe, back to violins (higher and no longer muted), then to a quartet of flutes. Throughout, the theme is accompanied by Janáček's characteristic reiterated patterns. Trombones and tubas enter with a determined new idea with a solemn tread, answered by swirls of flutes and piccolo. The violins briefly reprise their opening melody. Then a trombone plays a jaunty new tune, with abrupt phrase endings that hark back to the mirror rhythms of the first movement.

This idea is reiterated and developed with enormous tension, with insistently repeated horn whoops driving the music on to a great climax. Brass and swirling woodwind recall their earlier exchange, and the tension eases. The movement ends with oboe and cor anglais briefly remembering the first melody.

The fourth movement ('The Street') is short. Three contrasted ideas are pitted against each other simultaneously: the repetitive little 'folk fanfare', with which the trumpets begin (including the mirror rhythm of the opening fanfare), the plodding bass line with which the cellos and basses answer, and the sweeping phrases that the violins play while the first two elements continue to vie for attention. These three ideas pass from instrument to instrument, until the folk fanfare on muted trumpets dissolves into a chorale-like phrase. This is twice interrupted and repeated, before the reiterated folk fanfare is taken up again. As in the previous two movements, this moment of reprise is brief, and the movement is brought to an abrupt end.

The final movement is 'The Town Hall'. This opens with an easy-going melody on three flutes, answered with another of Janáček's anxiously repeated motifs on violins. The anxious motif rises in tension, resisting the attempts of the flutes to calm it. A high clarinet enters with a more plaintive version of the flutes' melody, in a strange duet with piccolo. As the oboe takes up the theme, the piccolo continues above, with trombones below. After an impassioned violin entry, the music breaks into a faster metre, and a nervous, swirling motif begins in the flutes, answered by clarinets. Once more the tension builds, and over savage trombone chords another high clarinet plays wailing phrases. This sets off the final build-up of the work. The tension reaches its height and the massed brass enter, reprising their opening fanfares, as the violins and woodwind continue to trill, bringing the work to a splendid and triumphant conclusion.

FRANZ LISZT
(1811–86)

By the time he was in his thirties, Liszt was widely regarded as the greatest pianist of all time. From the 1780s, when the piano first became popular, through to the 1840s, the instrument had developed in power and tonal range, and a succession of famous virtuosi had developed with it, from Mozart through Beethoven and his pupils and rivals, to Chopin and Liszt. The urge to take piano technique to yet a new level was generated by Liszt's encounter in 1832 with the great virtuoso of the violin, Niccolò Paganini. By this time there were many piano virtuosi, but Liszt set himself the task of achieving on the piano what Paganini had done on the violin, bringing together all the aspects of contemporary technique and synthesizing them to reveal all the possibilities of the modern piano. His success was phenomenal. As he toured Europe he attracted adoring crowds, who reached a state of ecstatic excitement more like that of late twentieth-century pop fans than of a nineteenth-century audience (though with an element of spirituality not common at pop concerts), and he was accepted in the highest aristocratic circles, living with, as mistresses, first a countess and then a princess.

But at the height of his fame, at the age of thirty-five, Liszt decided to retire from his career as a touring virtuoso. Some years earlier, he had been offered a post as Kapellmeister at the court in Weimar, and in 1848 he took it up in order to devote himself to composition and conducting. He stayed at Weimar until 1861, and during this period he composed most of his orchestral works, including twelve symphonic poems, three piano concertos, and symphonies based on Dante and on Goethe's *Faust*. Liszt already had a reputation as a composer of phenomenally difficult piano music, and had conducted from time to time, but he had had little experience of writing for orchestra. It was a period of experimentation, made possible by having an orchestra on hand with which Liszt was able to try out ideas. Joachim Raff, a gifted young composer whom Liszt had helped to establish a career, came to Weimar as his assistant. Raff undoubtedly helped Liszt to develop his skills, orchestrating his piano scores so that Liszt could try them out with his orchestra. But Raff, an ambitious young man, later exaggerated his role, claiming that much of the orchestration of Liszt's music was in fact by him. It was not until the early years of the twentieth century that it was established that Raff's claims were false. Liszt had simply used Raff's scores as a learning tool, revising and rewriting them a great deal until he was satisfied with the result. The orchestration of the published scores is overwhelmingly by Liszt.[1]

Like his piano music, Liszt's orchestral music relies on bold, dramatic gestures, barely contained within forms that are, in comparison to those of his great god, Beethoven, very free. His most important contribution to orchestral music was the 'symphonic poem'. Liszt was the first composer to give orchestral pieces this title, and they take the form of a greatly expanded concert overture, usually taking some literary source as its inspiration, and constructed in a fluid and highly dramatic manner. In his expansion and breaking down of classical methods Liszt was in tune with the writers and artists of the Romantic movement, who saw themselves as attempting to express things beyond the rational and the knowable – the forces of nature, destruction, and renewal, the fleeting and the eternal, the universe and humanity's place in it, the mysteries of imagination and the supernatural. Since it was impossible to express such things with completeness, a sense of failing to express them, a sense of things glimpsed but not fully encompassed or ordered, became desirable in itself. Liszt's take on this was to write music that breaks down traditional forms and procedures. Often movements are incomplete, breaking into the next without warning. Classical working out and developing of themes and their relationships are largely replaced by a looser assembly of themes that repeat and are transformed. This 'transformation of themes', used freely, is central to Liszt's music and to his influence on later composers. It was not a new technique. Themes in Mozart and Beethoven are often closely related to each other in shape, helping a long work to achieve a feeling of unity. An unusually bold example of linked themes is Schubert's 'Wanderer' Fantasy, the work that was the prime model for Liszt's thematic transformation, and which he arranged for piano and orchestra. Liszt made this process of transformation obvious to the listener, often simply slowing down or speeding up a melodic shape (though he used subtler forms of transformation too). Together with more straightforward repetition of themes, this helps to give a sense of logic to music that would otherwise seem to sprawl shapelessly.

Many contemporaries and later composers seized on this as a way of developing a new musical practice. Wagner's technique of using *Leitmotiven* ('guiding motifs') to bring structure to his enormous music dramas owes a great deal to Liszt. Richard Strauss's symphonic poems (or 'tone poems') are thoroughly Lisztian. Liszt's influence extended into the twentieth century: the fluid, subtle thematic transformations of Debussy can be seen as the grandchildren of Liszt. Practitioners of Liszt's methods came to be known in the 1860s as the 'New German School', who were declared to be composing 'the Music of the Future', as distinct from those supposedly backward-looking composers (principally Brahms) who adhered more closely to the classical procedures of Mendelssohn and Schumann. A great amount of heat and ill-feeling was generated between these rival camps – more often by their followers than by the principals themselves. Liszt, who, in life as in his music, never did things by halves, was the prime target for attack. His critics considered (and still consider) his musical structures shapeless, and his reliance on transformation of themes inadequate to create a real sense of form. Gerald Abraham draws a delightful analogy between this technique and the 'music-hall science known, if I remember rightly, as "chapeaugraphy", by which a black felt ring ingeniously twisted into the shapes of various characteristic hats enabled the performer to impersonate now Napoleon, now a Non-conformist minister'.[2]

Liszt's orchestration, though bold and effective, often relies on a relatively simple application of melody-and-accompaniment and block chordal writing that could easily be imagined as a transcription of piano music; it is rarely as complex as the (quite different) orchestral styles of Berlioz or Brahms, or as rich as that of Wagner, though it undoubtedly has moments of great beauty (particularly in *A Faust Symphony*). Liszt also has a limited sense of harmony. He uses all the repertoire of 'advanced' harmonies of his day, sometimes to a daring extent. But he often falls back on repetition of the most obvious dramatic effects, particularly the 'diminished seventh' – a chord that is immediately striking, mysterious, and uncertain, sometimes terrifying, but which, if used too frequently, easily seems to be crying wolf. But, whatever one thinks of his grand effects and his fluid structures, Liszt was undoubtedly a great spirit. He had the highest aspirations in his music, he was generous in his support of other composers, and even his failures are impressive Romantic gestures.

Concertos

PIANO CONCERTO NO. 1 IN E FLAT MAJOR
Duration: approx. 18 minutes

Allegro maestoso. Tempo giusto
Quasi adagio –
Allegretto vivace –
Allegro marziale animato

Liszt sketched the opening theme of this concerto as early as 1832, but it was not until 1855, after several revisions, that he first performed the work, in a concert at Weimar conducted by Berlioz. Although it is in four movements, the last three are connected without a break. Fortissimo strings state the principal theme, punctuated by chords of full brass and woodwind. The rhythm of the theme is fiercely assertive, but it descends through five notes of the chromatic scale, from E flat to B natural, so that we immediately lose any sense of key. Boldness is undermined by uncertainty – a Romantic-tragic declaration typical of Liszt. The piano enters with double octaves, and embarks on the first of the concerto's cadenzas. Twice it seems to come to an end, and the orchestra renews its playing of the theme, but each time the cadenza continues. Eventually the piano settles into a rippling pattern, over which a clarinet sings a rising arpeggio. The piano responds with a gentle falling line in C minor. This second theme is discussed in duet, first with clarinet then with violins. As the piano becomes more impassioned, breaking once more into arpeggios, fragments of the first theme reappear below, building to a climactic restatement of the theme, and thundering double octaves. Further alternations between the theme and passages of piano cadenza lead eventually to a quiet close back in the home key of E flat major.

For the theme of the slow movement, Liszt takes a turn of phrase from the first movement's second theme and extends it into a singing line – this movement in particular owes
much to Chopin, in turn inspired by Italian opera arias. The piano develops the theme, unaccompanied, and follows with a passage of more agitated recitative over string tremolo (this
passage in particular echoes a moment in Chopin's Piano Concerto No. 2 in F minor). Over a
piano trill, a flute plays a charming new melody. This seems like the middle of the movement,
and when a clarinet begins to play the opening theme, we expect a reprise. But instead, the
piano breaks off from its trilling, and a triangle delicately announces the beginning of the
scherzo.

This is fairy music, full of playful cross-rhythms and cascading flurries – mercurial delicacy was always one of the specialities of Liszt's piano-playing. Its theme is a subtle example
of Liszt's theme-transformation: it is related to the opening of the slow movement's theme,
turned upside down. As the delicate cascades continue, the flute joins in with a lively new idea
of trills and dotted rhythms. The piano part becomes more elaborate as the themes are taken
up by the orchestra. Then the piano turns a corner into a moment of cadenza, in which it
remembers the first theme of the concerto, and the music builds to a blaring restatement of
the theme on trombones. The piano responds with its opening double octaves, the charming
second theme from the slow movement enters at a brisk tempo, and a climax is reached.

The final section is a march, based on transformation of material from the slow movement. It begins with the first phrase of the melody, now revealed as a jolly, even cheeky tune.
The trombones burst in with the second phrase, which the piano incorporates into its double
octaves, before drawing in the second theme. Reminiscences follow of the scherzo, with figuration that becomes more and more brilliant. Over this, the violins combine familiar motifs
into a singing line – a falling chromatic scale followed by yearning leaps. The pace accelerates,
the opening motto theme reappears beneath the piano, and the concerto comes to a conclusion in an unashamed display of pianistic fireworks.

PIANO CONCERTO NO. 2 IN A MAJOR
Duration: approx. 22 minutes

Adagio sostenuto assai –
Allegro agitato assai –
Allegro moderato –
Allegro deciso –
Marziale un poco meno allegro –
Allegro animato

As with the First Piano Concerto, Liszt began this work while he was still pursuing his virtuoso
career. He drafted it during 1839–40, and later, in Weimar, repeatedly revised it. Liszt's pupil,
Hans von Bronsart, gave the first performance in 1857 in Weimar, with Liszt conducting.

In the First Piano Concerto, the division between four movements was clearly defined,
and the orchestra was (as in Chopin's concertos) little more than an accompanist to the piano.
The Second Piano Concerto is rather different. The piano part is still massively assertive and
virtuosic, but orchestra and piano are much more equal partners in the dialogue. The listing
of sections with different tempi hardly helps the listener. These are not clearly defined movements: the music flows almost continuously from first note to last, like a free fantasia, seeming

to give way to each mood and tempo as it arises, and held together only by the recurrent and transformed themes.

The concerto begins gently, with a soft, falling theme on clarinet over woodwind chords, the second of which is a melting surprise (Liszt loves the floating effect of harmonies that refuse to settle in a key). The piano enters modestly with accompanying arpeggios as the strings take up the theme. For a moment, the theme moves boldly to the bass of the piano, a portent of things to come. But for now, the gentle mood continues. As the piano part begins to glitter, a horn plays a second theme with falling and rising leaps. Oboe and solo cello allude to the first theme as the piano part becomes more elaborate, cascading down in thirds to arrive at a climactic restatement of the opening theme.

Then the horn's theme is transformed into a stately march with ominous drum-flourish effects, first in the bass of the piano, then in strings and timpani. This accelerates to another climax with cascading double octaves. The rhythm of the march becomes a terse, forceful theme with bold leaps, as if the intervals of the horn theme have been forced violently apart (Allegro agitato assai). The music becomes increasingly agitated, culminating in an orchestral tutti, built from a rapid version of a phrase in the horn theme, followed by more double octaves.

Suddenly they break off, and after a few quiet arpeggios the strings slow the agitato theme to play a warm, rich melody (Allegro moderato). A rippling moment of piano cadenza leads in a cello solo reprise of the first theme, with arpeggio accompaniment as at the beginning. Cello solo alternates with meditation from the piano. As the piano becomes more determinedly lyrical, a new singing phrase develops passionately, and an oboe joins in. Delicate chords of high woodwind and two solo violins touch on the first theme, and there is a moment of piano cadenza.

Now the determined tread of the march returns, faster than before, with the agitato theme below (Allegro deciso). This builds to a great climax with the leaping motif in the bass, more double octaves, and a profusion of Liszt's favourite dramatic chords ('diminished sevenths'). Gradually the music loses power and becomes delicate. Over a sustained bass note, it builds again to a grand restatement of the opening theme on full orchestra in march rhythm (Marziale, un poco meno allegro). After more glittering and powerful display, the music breaks off again. For the last time, the piano quietly rhapsodizes on the first theme. The orchestra delicately joins in, and a moment of quiet cadenza arrives at a pause. The piano, accompanied by flutes, plays a brilliant new variant that plays delicately with the opening notes of the first theme (Allegro animato). This quickly builds up, the march theme enters, and with a last burst of bravura, the concerto rises to its final grand climax.

LES PRÉLUDES
Duration: approx. 15 minutes
Andante – Andante maestoso – Allegro ma non troppo – Allegro tempestuoso – Allegretto pastorale – Allegro marziale animato – Andante maestoso

Les Préludes was published as 'Symphonic Poem No. 3' in 1856, and is by far the most frequently performed of Liszt's symphonic poems. Some of its thematic material was taken from a much earlier set of four choruses with the title, *Les quatre élémens* (*The Four Elements*), which Liszt composed in 1844–5 to poems by Joseph Autran. The poems are 'Les aquilons' ('The North

Winds'), 'La terre' ('The Earth'), 'Les flots' ('The Floods'), and 'Les astres' ('The Stars'), in reference to the ancient Greek elements of Earth, Air, Fire, and Water. Liszt never published the choruses, but instead reworked their themes as the basis of this symphonic poem. He originally gave it the title, *Les Préludes (d'après Lamartine)*, in reference to a celebrated poem of that title by Alphonse de Lamartine from his *Nouvelles Méditations Poétiques*. At the head of the first edition of the score is a preface, loosely drawn from Lamartine by Liszt's partner, Carolyne zu Sayn-Wittgenstein:

> What else is our life but a series of preludes to that unknown Hymn, the first and solemn note of which is intoned by Death? – Love is the glowing dawn of all existence; but what is the fate where the first delights of happiness are not interrupted by some storm, the mortal blast of which dissipates its fine illusions, the fatal lightening of which consumes its altar; and where [is] the cruelly wounded soul which, on issuing from one of these tempests, does not endeavour to rest his recollection in the calm serenity of life in the fields? Nevertheless man hardly gives himself up for long to the enjoyment of the beneficent stillness which at first he has shared in Nature's bosom, and when 'the trumpet sounds the alarm', he hastens to the dangerous post, whatever the war may be, which calls him to its ranks, in order at last to recover in the combat the full consciousness of himself and entire possession of his energy.[3]

Lamartine's long poem is a great deal more subtle and complex than this purple prose would suggest. But the preface identifies the themes, or emotional states, that give the broad outline of Liszt's structure: a questioning introduction; a lyrical love episode; the storm of life; recovery in serenity; and the call to arms leading to victory. This might seem a naive scheme for a piece of music, but Liszt brings it a little closer to the subtlety of the poem by the way he transforms his basic theme, making continual use of the three-note motif that opens the work – a little fall and a greater leap. At the same time, he alludes to the traditional form of a symphony's first movement, with (after the brief introduction) a decisive opening theme, a lyrical second group of themes, a stormy 'development', and a reprise of the opening ideas culminating in a triumphant conclusion.

The 'question' is posed quietly at first by the strings, the three-note motif followed by rising and falling arpeggios, and echoed by the woodwind. Step by step the music rises in pitch and gathers in strength, until it bursts out in a majestic fortissimo (Andante maestoso). Here, the motif has been transformed into a powerful theme in the bass, led by trombones, with energetic arpeggios in the strings above and trumpet calls – the mood is heroic.

Soon this gives way to the 'love' episode, which has two themes. The first, also beginning with the motif, is a singing melody, at first on cellos and violins, later on violins and horns. The second is a chorus of four horns, evoking memories of Schumann and Weber (the horn, associated with hunting and woodland, was a favourite instrument of the Romantics). Here the link to the motif is subtler: to begin with, the melody oscillates around the first, narrow interval before leaping upward. It passes to the woodwind, increasing in passion as the violins take it over. There is a long moment of ecstatic contemplation, culminating in a quiet woodwind chord.

Then we hear the dark muttering of the approaching storm (Allegro ma non troppo). This too begins with the motif, in the bass, which now disperses into swirling chromatic scales under quiet tremolo. The tension rapidly increases, as the music rises through a series of diminished seventh chords, until the storm is upon us (Allegro tempestuoso – this evokes memories of the 'Wolf's Glen' from Weber's *Der Freischütz*). From this turbulence emerges another heroic theme incorporating the motif, on trumpets and then violins, over an agitated accompaniment. This calms, to a reminiscence of the 'love' theme on oboe, which passes tenderly to the violins (marking the 'recovery in serenity').

The mood becomes pastoral (Allegretto pastorale) as a horn call passes to oboe and clarinet. A playful passage culminates in a reprise of the horn chorale, now on violins, with the playful accompaniment continuing below. As it moves to the cellos and the texture becomes fuller, the pace begins to accelerate, until, accompanied by dashing violins, trumpets and horns enter, transforming the first of the 'love' themes into a confident fanfare (Allegro marziale animato – 'the trumpet sounds the alarm', but our hero is clearly up to the task). The excited agitation of this passage strikingly recalls the Venusberg music from Wagner's *Tannhäuser*, which Liszt conducted at Weimar. Finally, the tempo steadies to a climactic reprise of the majestic theme from the opening (Andante maestoso), whose heroism is now underlined by side drum, bass drum, and cymbals.

A FAUST SYMPHONY IN THREE CHARACTER PORTRAITS (AFTER GOETHE)
Duration: approx. 75 minutes

Faust

Gretchen

Mephistopheles – Chorus Mysticus

It was Berlioz who first introduced Liszt to Goethe's *Faust* in Paris as early as 1830, at the beginning of their friendship. Berlioz had been enraptured by Part I of *Faust* when he had first read it (in French translation) two years earlier. According to Berlioz, Liszt soon came to love it as much as he did. Years later, both composers developed major works inspired by *Faust*. Berlioz's 'dramatic legend', *La damnation de Faust*, was first performed in Paris in 1846, and the score was dedicated to Liszt. By this time, Liszt had already begun seriously thinking about composing a work based on *Faust*. In 1852 he held a Berlioz week at Weimar, during which Berlioz again conducted his *La damnation de Faust*. Two years later, Liszt completed his own *Faust Symphony*, which he dedicated to Berlioz.

Weimar was a city steeped in Goethe: the poet had lived and worked there for fifty-seven years, becoming the most revered figure in German literature. After so many years contemplating the idea of *Faust*, Liszt was inspired to write his symphony very quickly in only two months in 1854. While he was composing it, he wrote in a letter, 'I am working like a being possessed.'[4] Three years later, he added a choral ending in which he set the final words of Goethe's *Faust*.

Liszt conducted the premiere in Weimar in September 1857, as part of a Goethe–Schiller festival at which statues of the two poets were unveiled (Schiller being the other figure who had made Weimar a centre of literary pilgrimage). Liszt's pupil and son-in-law, Hans von Bülow, conducted another performance four year later. But the symphony was neglected for many years, and it is only in recent decades that the work has been revived with any frequency.

A Faust Symphony is Liszt's most substantial and impressive orchestral work. The methods of theme-transformation, the building of climaxes and other dramatic effects, are much the same as in his symphonic poems but on a larger scale. Of all his works, it contains the most striking passages of orchestration, sometimes suggesting the world of Wagner's *Ring*, and Liszt's harmonies specifically point the way towards Wagner's *Tristan*. Liszt had played some of his draft material for the symphony to Wagner on the piano, when he visited him in Zürich in 1853, and Wagner would certainly have remembered Liszt's most striking ideas – it was shortly after this visit that he began the composition of *Das Rheingold*, the first music drama of the *Ring* cycle.[5] Distinct echoes of the symphony can be heard in Mahler, particularly the choral ending.

A *Faust Symphony* is a very long work, and nearly half of its length is taken up by the first movement. Massive paragraphs are interspersed with brooding, meditative passages, full of dramatic silences (another Lisztian tactic that Wagner adopted wholeheartedly). There are perhaps too many of them to sustain the length of the symphony. But, if one has the patience to sink into Liszt's world, it is certainly an all-embracing experience.

Goethe's *Faust* is one of the central works of German literature and of Romanticism. Goethe worked on it over a period of sixty years, and the scope of the drama and the range of issues it explores are vast. A brief summary of its plot will give some idea:

Faust, a scholar frustrated in his attempts to understand nature through scientific and magical means, strikes a pact with Mephistopheles. Mephistopheles will give him the knowledge and power he seeks in this life, in exchange for Faust's soul in the afterlife. Part I of Goethe's play is dominated by the tragedy of the young girl Gretchen (Margaret), whom, with Mephistopheles's help, Faust seduces and makes pregnant. Gretchen goes mad, drowns her newborn child, accidentally kills her mother with a sleeping draught given her by Faust, and is condemned to death. Part II extends far and wide, in time and space. Faust is granted the ultimate sexual experience, union with Helen of Troy. By old age he has become a great and ruthless landowner. But in his last hours, remorse and a desire to benefit humankind enable him to be saved from his pact with Mephistopheles. In the final, mystical scene, the spirit of Gretchen invokes the intercession of the Virgin Mary, and angels bear Faust's soul to heaven.

Liszt makes it clear in his title for the symphony that he is not trying to follow any plot or narrative. The symphony consists of three 'character portraits' of Faust, Gretchen, and Mephistopheles. The first movement uses the conflicting aspects of Faust's character to create the contrasting themes for a substantial musical structure. 'Gretchen' is a portrait of Gretchen as the innocent young woman who first falls in love with Faust – Liszt is not concerned with her later betrayal and destruction. 'Mephistopheles' is a movement full of demonic energy, which owes something to the 'Witches' Sabbath' from Berlioz's *Symphonie fantastique*. Liszt's original ending was purely instrumental, with a return to one of Gretchen's themes. But he found this inadequate, and added a setting of the final passage from Part II of Goethe's drama, in which the Chorus Mysticus sings of salvation and the power of the Eternal Feminine (represented by the soul of Gretchen).

Richard Pohl, one of Liszt's most devoted champions, wrote an essay in 1862 analysing the symphony. Probably on the basis of what Liszt had told him, he gave the principal themes titles relating to the three characters: 'magic', 'doubt', and so on.[6] These are not to be taken too literally, but they help in finding one's way through the music, and they are used in the description that follows.

The symphony opens with a slow introduction. Muted violas and cellos play a fortissimo A flat, which immediately fades, and a mysterious pattern follows made up of rising three-note cells. The mystery is in their intervals: the three notes are a major third apart from each other, outlining an augmented chord (the first consists of G, B, and E flat). Without a resolution, these chords have no suggestion of a key. Instead of resolving the first three-note cell, Liszt repeats it three times, shifting down a semitone each time. So the four rising cells contain all twelve notes of the chromatic scale (a fact that has absolutely nothing to do with Schoenberg's later development of 'twelve-note technique'). The woodwind respond with a sad falling phrase that is also based on augmented intervals. Pohl identifies the strings' opening as the 'magic' theme, and the woodwind answer as 'doubt'. Clearly, this relates to the first appearance of Faust in Goethe's play, alone at night in his study, dejected by the thought that he under-stands nothing. Wagner certainly remembered this introduction: its mysterious yearning, expressed in halting phrases, sounds like a premonition of the prelude to *Tristan*.

There is a brief outburst of rage, with the 'magic' theme blasted out by the brass, and then, after a silence, a bassoon dolefully playing the 'doubt' theme. Then there is a further outburst, more sustained this time, with an agitated melody that is more clearly in a key, C minor. This is the 'passion' theme. Its anguished first chord is the same as the famous first chord of *Tristan* (though notated differently, and resolving onto a chord of C minor, which Wagner avoids). From this turmoil emerges a falling line on oboes and clarinets over string tremolo: this is 'yearning'. It alternates between woodwind and low strings, until it eventually slows and fades.

Now one of the most beautifully orchestrated passages opens out, with quiet, sustained wind chords enlivened by rippling patterns in the strings – another very Wagnerian effect. Through a series of harmonic shifts, this leads on to a passage of urgent sighs, and into the gentle 'love' theme on horn and clarinet. This is a transformation of the doleful 'doubt' theme, but now in E major (very remote from the home key of C minor). Its falling seventh has taken on a consoling character, answered sweetly by a rising curl on solo cello. As these alternate, they are joined by the descending line of the 'yearning' theme. There is a passionate accelera-tion, a moment of expectant tremolo, and the full brass burst in with a grand transformation of the 'doubt' motif into a confident, swaggering theme in E major, 'pride' (we have to switch off memories of all heroic film scores in order to avoid hearing such grandiosity as banal).

From here, the music gradually accelerates and becomes more agitated again. The 'doubt' motif pushes onward assertively. Then the tension builds, with the frantic semiquavers of the 'passion' theme in the strings combined with a bold reference to the 'magic' theme in the brass. We have entered the development section of the movement without realizing it. The music slows for a moment, as if struggling for breath. Then 'passion' reasserts itself, driving forward with increasing desperation. After a mighty climax, ending with trumpet fanfares, a string tremolo fades, and we find ourselves back at the slow introduction, with the 'magic' motif answered by 'doubt' in the woodwind, exactly as it was at the opening of the symphony. This is the beginning of the reprise. Bringing back the slow introduction in the middle of a move-ment to mark significant points in the structure is something that Beethoven occasionally did, notably in the 'Pathétique' piano sonata. But it is highly unusual in a symphony.

As the solo bassoon descends for a second time, we expect the sudden outburst that orig-inally followed. But instead, with only a slight increase in pace, Liszt combines the 'magic' motif in the bass with the 'doubt' motif in the woodwind, followed by 'yearning' in the strings, as if Faust is painfully trying to assemble all his thoughts and drag himself out of his dejected state. Gradually, the music begins to build. After a moment of hesitation there is a particularly striking moment of hushed orchestration, where the atonal 'magic' theme is played on clarinet with pizzicato violas, while flutes and high, tremolando violins sustain chords. The music resumes its crescendo, to reach a sustained climax on a chord of pure E major. Just as this moment of triumph seems unassailable, the anguished first chord of the 'doubt' theme breaks the spell, and the reprise resumes its tumult in C minor.

More quickly than before, it twists back to E major for the 'love' theme. The exchanges between woodwind and strings proceed as before. But, as at the beginning of the reprise, Liszt once again prolongs the moment. The violins rise higher until, with a sidestep of harmony, the music arrives in C major (the major of the home key), and cellos tenderly take up the 'love' theme. The violins wind down to a moment of profound calm. Pizzicato cellos and basses hesitantly try out the 'pride' theme. A brass chorus takes it up, a trumpet plays the theme, answered by the woodwind. But the darkness is not banished. Under ticking violas, the 'doubt' theme (from which the 'pride' transformation was derived) appears ominously on cellos. There is another gradual acceleration and crescendo, and full orchestra play the 'pride' theme *fff*.

Soon the agitated 'doubt' theme breaks in again, and there is a moment of sustained tension as 'pride' tries to regain the upper hand. There is one last agitated build-up to a climax, with the 'magic' theme persisting ominously in the brass. After a silence, one last defiant outburst collapses, and the movement ends in darkness with 'doubt' and final taps of the timpani.

The portrait of Gretchen opens with a delicate quartet of two flutes and two clarinets, whose interleaving curls contain echoes of the solo cello in the earlier 'love' theme. This is the first of many instrumental combinations in this movement that have an intimate quality of chamber music. Another follows immediately: a solo oboe plays a lyrical melody in A flat major accompanied by flowing semiquavers on a solo viola. This is Liszt evoking a sense of innocent purity, and sounding distinctly like Mendelssohn (the melody specifically resembles a theme in the finale of Mendelssohn's Piano Trio in D minor). Its opening strain is taken up by clarinet and flute, then a middle section moves to a small ensemble of strings. There is a lovely moment when, with a melting change of key to D major, the oboe enters again. This passage has an atmosphere of enchanted exploration, and it leads on to a moment of little hesitant phrases. These are clearly intended to evoke the scene when Gretchen is in the garden with Faust, takes a flower, and plucks the petals, saying 'He loves me, he loves me not.' At the final 'He loves me', Liszt slips tenderly back into A flat major, and the first part of the theme returns, now on full strings (though without double basses – Gretchen's music is more intimate without them).

Delicately wandering violins lead on to a second theme that, in its simplicity, seems to confirm Gretchen's naive love for Faust. The curling shape from the introduction rounds off each phrase. After it is played by strings, and then woodwind, another wandering passage leads down to the sudden reappearance of Faust's 'doubt' theme, ominously on horns, and back in the C minor of the first movement. The threat of this dark theme continues until, once again, the oboe leads in a melting change of key, back to D major. Three flutes play rippling arpeggios, and the descending line of the 'yearning' theme enters on cellos. This ecstatic passage reminds us that Faust (unlike Mephistopheles) is convinced that he is experiencing true love, not mere lust. The 'love' theme (itself a transformation of 'doubt') enters, and develops irresistible entreaty. Then the music becomes more agitated, as the 'passion' theme is transformed into an urgent declaration of love. It reaches a climax, and dissolves into a moment of great tenderness, with delicate harp harmonics.

A silence is followed by a reprise of Gretchen's first theme in the home key of A flat major, on a quartet of solo violins and with a new flowing descant. Woodwind gently join in, and then the full strings (but without the basses). This time, the oboe's delicate intervention leads on to another silence. Pianissimo violins rise, and the woodwind play the 'love' theme. This descends down to the return of Gretchen's second theme, on strings and then woodwind. The movement ends in complete tranquillity.

The 'Mephistopheles' movement begins with a quick-witted introduction in which the 'doubt' motif is touched in by horns and bassoon and then pizzicato strings. A savage outburst is followed by the series of augmented chords that make up 'magic'. After a hush, the movement begins in earnest, with the 'passion' theme in a jerky jig rhythm, and in C minor as it was in the first movement. With 'doubt' in the bass, it builds to a wildly jubilant passage – 'Hell celebrates a feast-day', wrote Richard Pohl.[7] Further touches of 'doubt' and 'magic' quieten to an ominous moment with pairs of knocks on timpani and horns. This is a quotation from one of Liszt's pieces from the 1830s for piano and strings, *Malédiction* (*Curse*). It sets the violas off on an extension of 'doubt', full of agitated cross-rhythms, and this then becomes the subject of a fugue (Berlioz had included a demonic fugue in the finale of his *Symphonie fantastique*). It gradually breaks up, and then builds to an ironically jaunty version of the bombastic 'pride' theme (this is in E major, as it was in the first movement).

There is a sudden silence, from which emerge fragments of 'passion', the mysterious chords of 'magic', and the knocking of the curse. Another outburst of 'pride' follows. Just as it reaches a terrific climax, it breaks off. Beneath a high pianissimo tremolo, an oboe sings Gretchen's first theme. This replaces Faust's 'love' theme at this point, and, symbolically, this is the only theme that Mephistopheles's distortions cannot touch. Liszt reminds us that it is Gretchen's enduring love for Faust, even at the moment of death, that enables his soul to be saved. The vision is soon over, and after a tentative moment of cursing, the mayhem resumes with the transformed 'passion' theme. This time, there is a further acceleration. Over an expectant, sustained bass note, woodwind return to the 'pride' theme. Gradually the tension builds to a final climax, at which the rhythm of the curse is hammered out. Soon, the agitation dissolves into a mysterious series of descending chords (these seem to anticipate the 'magic sleep' motif in Wagner's *Ring*).

The harmonies settle, and a solo cello reminds us of Gretchen's theme. There is a silence. Over an organ chord of C major, with gently pulsating strings, the men's chorus sings a simple chant, to the words of the Chorus Mysticus that ends Goethe's drama:

Alles Vergängliche	Everything transitory
Ist nur ein Gleichnis;	Is only a parable;
Das Unzulängliche,	The unachievable
Hier wird's Ereignis;	Will come to pass;
Das Unbeschreibliche,	What cannot be described
Hier ist es getan;	Will be accomplished.

The chords gradually shift to A flat major – Gretchen's key – and the tenor soloist enters with the final lines, sung to Gretchen's first theme:

Das Ewig-Weibliche,	The Eternal Feminine
Zieht uns hinan.	Draws us upward.

Chorus and tenor alternate. The tenor's third entry has a falling line related to Gretchen's second theme (and to 'yearning' from the first movement).

Brass and organ enter and, with the utmost grandeur, the chorus takes the chant to a climax (this climax, and the approach to it, surely inspired Mahler at the end of his setting of this scene in his Eighth Symphony, and earlier, at the end of the Second Symphony, the 'Resurrection'). There is a moment of meditation, with solo violin and harp arpeggios. Then the music builds for the last time to a final great chord of C major.

GUSTAV MAHLER
(1860–1911)

Mahler was a composer whose immense aspirations can really only be compared with Wagner's. But unlike Wagner, he put his principal energies into composing symphonies rather than operas. He was also a fine composer of songs and song cycles (*Lieder eines fahrenden Gesellen*, *Rückert Lieder*, and *Kindertotenlieder*).

The ingredients for his major works are taken from an enormous range of sources. When he met Sibelius in 1907, they famously disagreed about what a symphony should be. According to Sibelius, he told Mahler that he admired a symphony's 'strictness and the profound logic that creates an inner connection between all the motifs'. Mahler replied, 'No, the symphony must be like the world. It must embrace everything.'[1] The 'everything' in Mahler's symphonies includes folk song, marches, laments, cataclysms, and encompasses moods from childlike innocence to bitter irony, despair, and triumph. In this his great model was Beethoven's Ninth Symphony, with its struggle between opposing forces, its slow movement of spiritual ecstasy, and climactic choral finale encompassing everything from a solemn hymn to a village marching band. As the philosopher and music theorist Theodor Adorno wrote of Mahler, 'With the freedom of a man not entirely overwhelmed by culture, in his musical vagrancy he picks up the fragment of glass that he finds on the road and holds it up to the sun so that all its colours are refracted ... Every bar in Mahler's music opens wide its arms.'[2] But the juxtaposing of extreme opposites in Mahler's music is much more than just an assembly of every possible ingredient. The 'world' that Mahler is really concerned with is the interior world of the human mind as it grapples with the experiences of life, and struggles to find sense in its surroundings – and often fails.

In 1910, at a crisis in his relationship with his wife Alma, Mahler consulted Sigmund Freud. Freud left an account of this meeting, during which Mahler described a particularly telling incident from his childhood: 'His father, apparently a brutal person, treated his wife very badly, and when Mahler was a young boy there was an especially painful scene between them. It became quite unbearable to the boy, who rushed from the house. At that moment, however, a hurdy-gurdy in the street was grinding out the popular Viennese air, "Ach, du lieber Augustin". In Mahler's opinion, the conjunction of high tragedy and light amusement was from then on inextricably fixed in his mind, and the one mood inevitably brought the other with it.'[3] This incident by itself can hardly account for the range of bizarre juxtapositions in Mahler's music, but it is highly suggestive nevertheless.

Another great source of inspiration for Mahler was his fascination with the 'folk' poetry of *Des Knaben Wunderhorn* (*The Boy's Magic Horn*), a collection published in the first decade of the nineteenth century. Like other collections of the period, it was a publication aimed at the cultured reader of the time, with genuine traditional poems adapted and new examples added in order to provide an evocation of the people's literature, fit, as Goethe put it, to 'find its place in every household'. Its influence on Mahler was profound. It was one of the chief sources of that well of nostalgia that runs through Mahler's music, a way to express not only the simple and naive, but the longing for a time and place that is out of reach, and perhaps never existed. In his first four symphonies, and in his songs, he makes specific use of material from *Des Knaben Wunderhorn*. In his later symphonies, the nostalgia acquires a harder edge and a more bitter tone.

The contrast between Mahler's and Sibelius's view of the symphony might be taken to mean that Sibelius was a more intellectual composer than Mahler. But Mahler's music, despite its overwhelming effects, is extremely carefully constructed. Mahler's methods are just as 'classical' as Sibelius's, with much use of Beethoven-like development and cross-referencing by motifs. It was partly for this reason that Mahler was revered by the younger radicals that formed the 'Second Viennese School', Schoenberg and his pupils Berg and Webern. They admired Mahler's perfectionism and his refusal to compromise in the teeth of sometimes vicious opposition, and Mahler in turn supported them. There are also in late Mahler, and particularly in the Ninth Symphony and the incomplete Tenth Symphony, some of the seeds of the tortured chromaticism that was to lead the younger Viennese generation to strike out towards atonalism and a new way of ordering music. Mahler at his most intensely chromatic is miles away from this break. He is nevertheless, of all the composers active in Vienna, the one who forms a bridge between the great symphonists of the nineteenth century and the intensity and strangeness of the Second Viennese School.

Mahler was not just a great composer, he was also an exceptional conductor. He was appointed as artistic director at the Vienna Court Opera in 1897, where, over a period of ten years, he swept away slovenly routines, set new standards of rehearsal and performance, and brought in revolutionary designers from the Vienna Secession (strangely, despite his supremacy as an opera conductor, he never wrote an opera in his mature years).[4] In 1907 he left Vienna, worn down by opposition to his perfectionism and autocratic control. Anti-Semitism undoubtedly formed part of the Viennese opposition to Mahler (he had converted to Roman Catholicism in 1897, but this was because Jews were barred from the directorship of the Vienna Opera). Mahler himself, according to his wife Alma, declared, 'I am thrice home-less . . . as a Bohemian among the Austrians, as an Austrian among the Germans, and as a Jew throughout the world. Everywhere an intruder, nowhere welcomed.'[5]

Mahler spent four years in America, as conductor of the New York Philharmonic Society. There too storms brewed, his health broke (brought on by heart disease), and in February 1911 he went to Paris for treatment, and from there back to Vienna to die. The Viennese establish-ment, which had rejected him four years before, welcomed him with vast quantities of flowers, overflowing from his sanatorium room into the corridor. When he died in May, the critic Paul Stefan, one of Mahler's staunchest supporters against his Viennese enemies, wrote bitterly, 'Now, of course, everyone's conscience was awakened, and in the flood of oratory that poured over Mahler's bier were to be heard expressions of respect, regret, and affection . . . Gustav Mahler was dead; he could disturb no more; he might be as great a man as people pleased.'[6]

Mahler composed ten symphonies, of which the last was incomplete at his death. They are immensely varied, and the biggest and most ambitious of them stretch the nineteenth-century concept of a symphony to breaking point. Nos 2, 3, and 4 all include singers, and No. 8, known as the 'Symphony of a Thousand', is really a giant dramatic cantata. Apart from the symphonies themselves, there is also *Das Lied von der Erde* (*The Song of the Earth*), which is both a song cycle with orchestra and a symphony.

DAS LIED VON DER ERDE (THE SONG OF THE EARTH)
Duration: approx. 62 minutes

Das Trinklied vom Jammer der Erde (The Drinking Song of the Earth's Lamentation)
Der Einsame im Herbst (The Solitary One in Autumn)
Von der Jugend (On Youth)
Von der Schönheit (On Beauty)
Der Trunkene im Frühling (The Drunkard in Spring)
Der Abschied (The Farewell)

The score of *Das Lied von der Erde* is subtitled 'A Symphony for tenor, contralto (or baritone) and orchestra'. It consists of settings of Chinese poems from the Tang Dynasty (seventh–tenth centuries), which Mahler had got to know through a 1907 collection in German translation called *The Chinese Flute*, compiled by Hans Bethge. This was the year in which Mahler had suffered three major blows: his eldest daughter, Maria, died of scarlet fever and diphtheria, Mahler himself was diagnosed with heart disease, and he resigned bitterly from his position as director of the Vienna Court Opera, taking up a post at the Metropolitan Opera in New York. Back in Austria for the summer of 1908, he worked on *Das Lied von der Erde*, completing it the following year.

Of the six songs, Nos 1, 3, 4, and 5 are taken from poems by Li Bai, No. 2 from a poem by Qian Qi, while No. 6 combines poems by Meng Haoran and Wang Lei, with an ending written by Mahler himself. This was only the most significant of Mahler's changes to the poems. Mahler selected, adapted, and added to the texts, to enable him to create musical settings of characteristic intensity. He had chosen poems that contrast the beauty of the earth with the pain of human sorrow, culminating in 'Der Abschied' ('The Farewell').

The first performance was given in November 1911, six months after Mahler's death, by the Vienna Philharmonic Orchestra conducted by Mahler's faithful protégé Bruno Walter. It was Walter who also conducted the first recording of *Das Lied von der Erde* in 1936, a live concert performance recorded in Vienna with the Vienna Philharmonic. This recording is an exceptionally moving document to a vanished era. Not only Walter but also members of the orchestra had worked with Mahler, and the Jews among them (including Walter and the leader, Arnold Rosé, Mahler's brother-in-law) knew that their life in Austria might be coming to an end. Hitler's annexation (the *Anschluss*) was to follow two years later, shortly after another document had been created, a live recording of Mahler's Ninth Symphony, again with the Vienna Philharmonic Orchestra conducted by Walter. In both works, one can sense the intensity of musicians holding on for dear life to something precious that was about to be taken from them. The tension of the situation was, however, even more complex than that: the twenty or so members of the orchestra who were either wholly or partly Jewish were roughly equalled by the number who had voluntarily joined the Nazi Party. Vienna was as divided in 1938 as it had been in Mahler's day.

Bruno Walter left this reminiscence of Mahler at the time of the composition of *Das Lied von der Erde*: 'When he spoke to me of *Das Lied von der Erde* for the first time, he called it a

Symphony in Songs. It was to have been his *Ninth*. Subsequently, however, he changed his mind. He thought of Beethoven and Bruckner, whose *Ninth* had marked the ultimate of their creation and life, and did not care to challenge fate. He turned the manuscript over to me for study … When I brought it back to him, almost unable to utter a word, he turned to the *Abschied* and said: "What do you think? Is it to be endured at all? Will not people make away with themselves after hearing it?" [7]

Songs for tenor and contralto soloists alternate. The contralto songs can, as the score suggests, be sung by a baritone. This is occasionally done, but it has never been a popular option. There is a peculiar poignancy in the combination of a woman's contralto voice in combination with Mahler's orchestra, and a man's baritone can sound inappropriately sturdy, particularly in the last, intensely yearning song.

Das Trinklied vom Jammer der Erde (The Drinking Song of the Earth's Lamentation) (tenor)

This movement has a structure common to many songs: two verses that share similar music, an interlude that explores further afield, and a third verse returning to the opening music. But it is no coincidence that this is also the form of the classical first movement of symphonies by Haydn and Mozart: an exposition that is repeated, a development that explores further afield, and a reprise. Mahler also employs another classical device, the use of motifs that link movements. Most obviously, this song is full of falling two-note sighs. These are evoked poignantly in the last movement, 'Der Abschied', particularly in its last moments, 'ewig … ewig', evoking a sense that the end somehow resolves something that was posed at the beginning. It is typical of Mahler to have composed music of such immediate impact that is also intellectually subtle.

The song begins with four horns in unison calling against a background of agitated flurries and muted trumpets. Violins and violas take the horn call and make of it an emphatic theme. The tone is defiant, with an edge of desperation. The tenor enters with a hesitation on the upbeat, like a bitter parody of the upbeat to a Viennese waltz (this whole movement is in three-time):

Schon winkt der Wein im gold'nen Pokale,	The wine sparkles in golden goblets,
Doch trinkt noch nicht, erst sing' ich euch ein Lied!	But before you drink, I'll sing you a song!
Das Lied vom Kummer soll auflachend in die Seele euch klingen.	The song of sorrow will ring like laughter in your soul.

The music quietens, and as it becomes more reflective, the melody is full of sighs: the words 'stirbt die Freude, der Gesang' ('joy and song die') are set to pairs of falling sighs, which will be echoed poignantly in the last movement, 'Der Abschied'. The verse ends with a sustained, falling refrain: 'Dunkel ist das Leben, ist der Tod' ('Dark is life, dark is death'), which seems to concentrate the ache of the song into a single line.

The horn call returns to announce the second verse. This time there is a more extended struggle before the voice enters, and the quieter passage is also longer, with new warmth in the words:

Die Laute schlagen und die Gläser leeren,	To strike the lute and drain the glasses,
Das sind die Dinge, die zusammen passen.	These are the things that go well together.

Again the verse ends sorrowfully with the refrain, 'Dunkel ist das Leben, ist der Tod'. In Mahler's very fluid key scheme, this refrain is a semitone higher each time it occurs.

Now the music moves on to a new key for the middle section of the song (the equivalent of a development section). The horn call moves to muted trumpet and cor anglais. Violins extend the theme further, in duet with a clarinet. The trumpet, now unmuted, takes it up, leaping to a high note that generates a climax in the violins followed by a collapse. The tenor enters sadly, with sighing phrases:

Das Firmament blaut ewig, und die Erde	The heavens are blue for ever, and the earth
Wird lange fest steh'n und aufblüh'n im Lenz.	Will stand firm and blossom in the spring.
Du aber, Mensch, wie lang lebst denn du?	But you, human being, how long do you live?
Nicht hundert Jahre darfst du dich ergötzen	Not a hundred years may you delight
An all dem morschen Tande dieser Erde!	In all the rotten trinkets of this earth!

The tension rises, the harmonies twist painfully, and suddenly we are into a wild, savage reprise of the opening:

Seht dort hinab! Im Mondschein auf den Gräbern	See down there! In the moonlight on the graves
Hockt eine wild-gespenstische Gestalt –	Squats a wild, ghostly figure –
Ein Aff'ist's! Hört ihr, wie sein Heulen	It is an ape! Hear how his howls
Hinausgellt in den süssen Duft des Lebens!	Ring out in the sweet fragrance of life!

Now is the time to drink, and for the last time the tenor sings the refrain, 'Dunkel ist das Leben, ist der Tod'. There is a final burst of the horn call, and the song ends with all the low wind and pizzicato strings clustered together in a last, savage chord.

Der Einsame im Herbst (The Solitary One in Autumn) (contralto)

Muted violins play a meandering pattern, and an oboe plays a lament that begins with the falling sigh and continues with the same intervals as the opening horn call. The marking in the score is 'exhausted'. The singer wanders sadly in an autumn landscape:

Herbstnebel wallen bläulich überm See;	Bluish autumn mist drifts over the lake;
Vom Reif bezogen stehen alle Gräser;	Every blade of grass stands covered in frost;
Man meint, ein Künstler habe Staub von Jade	As if an artist had scattered jade-dust
Über die feinen Blüten ausgestreut.	Over the delicate flowers.

The voice's melody is soft and even, as if drained of energy. It is in the orchestra that we hear the poignancy of the scene, with the plangent oboe, a dark horn solo, and a sudden outburst of passionate longing in the violins. As the second verse subsides, the music becomes bleaker, and the voice sings:

Mein Herz ist müde. Meine kleine Lampe	My heart is weary. My little lamp
Erlosch mit Knistern, es gemahnt mich an den Schlaf.	Goes out with a crackle, and I feel the urge to sleep.

For a moment, the voice warms into a major key as she sings 'Ich komm' zu dir, traute Ruhestätte! ('I come to you, trusted resting-place') But soon the meandering violin line returns, and a bassoon leads in a reprise of the opening oboe melody. Suddenly the voice bursts out passionately, echoing the earlier violin outburst:

| Sonne der Liebe, willst du nie mehr scheinen, | Sun of love, will you never shine again |
| Um meine bittern Tränen mild aufzutrocknen? | And gently dry my bitter tears? |

The music sinks back into exhaustion, a bassoon echoes the first voice entry, the meandering violins and oboe lament return for the last time, and the song ends in darkness, with a deep chord of horns and clarinets.

Von der Jugend (On Youth) (tenor)

This is the first of a pair of songs that, unlike the other four, take pleasure in the good things in life with scarcely a hint of melancholy reflection. This song is the only one with an obviously 'Chinese' flavour: the flute and oboe start with a pattern in a pentatonic (five-note) scale characteristic of Chinese music (though also common in traditional music worldwide). The tenor enters with a cheerful tune evoking a Chinese scene:

Mitten in dem kleinen Teiche	In the middle of the little pond
Steht ein Pavillon aus grünem	Stands a pavilion of green
Und aus weissem Porzellan.	And white porcelain.
Wie der Rücken eines Tigers	Like the back of a tiger
Wölbt die Brücke sich aus Jade	The jade bridge arches
Zu dem Pavillon hinüber.	Over to the pavilion.

With a change of key, the melody in voice and violins becomes more flowing as the singer describes the friends sitting and chatting in the little pavilion. The music slows, returning to its original key, as the tenor sings of the scene reflected in the still water. Suddenly, with a stroke of the triangle, the tempo recovers, and the song ends with a reprise of the opening music, as violins and high woodwind ascend into the sky of the imagination.[8]

Von der Schönheit (On Beauty) (contralto)

Delicate flutes and high, muted violins play a charming little trilling theme that seems to have grown out of moments of trilling in the first song. The contralto sings a melody which, with its fluid metre and stresses, is not as simple as it seems:

| Junge Mädchen pflücken Blumen, | Young girls gather flowers, |
| Pflücken Lotosblumen an dem Uferrande. | Gather lotus flowers at the shore's edge. |

As the second and third strains of the song unfold, they are embellished by a high violin descant and delicate touches of a glockenspiel, evoking the naive spirit of Mahler's Fourth Symphony. But everything changes as the poem continues:

O sieh, was tummeln sich für schöne Knaben	O see how handsome lads dash about
Dort an dem Uferrand auf mut'gen Rossen ...	There by the shore on spirited horses ...

This unleashes the force of Mahler in mock-heroic mode, with full brass and cymbals, and an accelerating gallop gathers force, dragging the poor contralto with it. The music becomes wilder and wilder, until suddenly, as if nothing had happened, it returns to its gentle opening. As the fairest of the girls sends longing glances at one of the boys, the song acquires yearning leaps, and the violin descant becomes yet more tender. The song ends demurely, but:

Ihre stolze Haltung ist nur Verstellung.	Her proud bearing is only a pretence.
In dem Funkeln ihrer grossen Augen,	In the flash of her large eyes,
In dem Dunkel ihres heissen Blicks	In the darkness of her ardent gaze
Schwingt klagend noch die Erregung ihres Herzens nach.	Beats the longing agitation of her heart.

The singer may not reveal this passion, but it is there in the lingering sweetness of the orchestral postlude.

Der Trunkene im Frühling (The Drunkard in Spring) (tenor)

Like the first song, this is a setting of a drinking song by Li Bai, alternating between wild exuberance and sentimental melancholy. If this work is a symphony, then this movement is a second scherzo, in which the sentimental episode is like the conventional trio. The opening combines two elements familiar from earlier songs: trilling flourishes and a horn call. As in the first song, the tenor enters with a hesitating emphasis, as if proposing a toast:

Wenn nur ein Traum das Leben ist,	If life is only a dream,
Warum denn Müh' und Plag'?	Why all this toil and torment?
Ich trinke, bis ich nicht mehr kann,	I drink until I can drink no more,
Den ganzen, lieben Tag!	The whole, blessed day!

Already after the second line, the violins play a yearning, falling motif, introducing a sentimental lurch into the drunkenness. A second verse follows, in which the twisting dissonances reach a peak of desperation. The poet falls asleep, and a solo violin wakes him:

Was hör' ich beim Erwachen? Horch!	What do I hear on waking? Listen!
Ein Vogel singt im Baum.	A bird sings in the tree.
Ich frag' ihn, ob schon Frühling sei,	I ask him if spring is already here,
Mir ist als wie im Traum.	It's as if I'm in a dream.

The music slows, an oboe transforms the horn call into birdsong, the solo violin takes up the yearning motif, and a piccolo responds (Mahler had a particular feeling for the nostalgic possibilities of the piccolo). For a moment the original tempo resumes as the bird tells him that spring is indeed here. But the singer responds with the yearning, falling phrases, and the tempo slows once more. In the violins, Mahler indicates long glissandi to underline the dreamy sentimentality, and the piccolo again adds to the poignancy. The original tempo resumes, and the tenor, singing the yearning phrases with renewed energy, refills his cup. This is the reprise of the opening section, with its edgy exuberance. The persistence of the yearning fall adds to the sense of desperation, rising higher and higher:

Was geht mich denn der Frühling an?	What does spring matter to me?
Lasst mich betrunken sein!	Let me be drunk!

Der Abschied (The Farewell) (contralto)

The final movement, taking nearly half an hour, is as long as the previous five songs combined. It is perhaps Mahler's finest achievement, a lingering farewell to the earth and its beauties. Mahler chose and carefully edited poems by two authors, Meng Haoran and Wang Wei. For the ending, he added lines of his own, evoking an ecstatic vision of an earth that constantly renews itself, while the human heart 'awaits its hour' – a vision that can be heard as a response, musically and spiritually, to the *Liebestod* that concludes Wagner's *Tristan*.

Like a tolling bell, contrabassoon, horn, pizzicato basses, harps, and gong intone a low C. An oboe plays a solo with melancholy flourishes, as if the birdsong of the previous movement has transformed itself into a lament. Beneath it, horns bring in the falling sighs, and the violins extend them into a plaintive line. There is a brief outburst in the high woodwind, like a moment of disorientation, and the music sinks back to a low C.

The contralto enters with a recitative, accompanied by melancholy flourishes now on a solitary flute:

Die Sonne scheidet hinter dem Gebirge.	The sun departs behind the mountains.
In alle Täler steigt der Abend nieder	In all the valleys the evening descends
Mit seinen Schatten, die voll Kühlung sind.	With its deeply cooling shadows.

The flute sinks back. Now the sighs become a repeating pattern, first on clarinets then on horns, while the oboe returns to its lament. Suddenly, from a melancholy C minor, the singer rises into C major with new warmth:

O sieh! Wie eine Silberbarke schwebt	Look! Like a silver ship the moon
Der Mond am blauen Himmelssee herauf.	Sails in the blue lake of heaven.

But the glorious moment is soon over, as the music returns to C minor, and with further melancholy flourishes reaches another low resting point.

Now the mood lightens into F major as, over a rocking accompaniment in harp and clarinet, the oboe lamentation takes on a more peaceful, pastoral tone. It peters out in mid-phrase and the contralto enters, with a flute taking over the oboe's role in a meditative descant:

Der Bach singt voller Wohllaut durch das Dunkel.	The brook sings so melodiously through the darkness.
Die Blumen blassen im Dämmerschein.	The flowers fade in the twilight.

The violins, always the most poignant voice throughout the work, intervene, rising to a moment of anguished yearning and falling away again. Calm descends once more, and with the oboe as her companion the singer resumes:

| Die Erde atmet voll von Ruh' und Schlaf. | The earth breathes, full of rest and sleep. |
| Alle Sehnsucht will nun träumen. | All longing aspires to dream. |

On this line, the violins again enter over a poignant chord, rise, and fall away. This pattern repeats, the singer's evocation of the deepening twilight punctuated by moments of anguish and lapses into silence. The music arrives at a reprise of the singer's opening recitative with the solitary flute:

Es wehet kühl im Schatten meiner Fichten.	There is a cool breeze in the shadow of my fir trees.
Ich stehe hier und harre meines Freundes;	I stand here and wait for my friend.
Ich harre sein zum letzten Lebewohl.	I wait for his last farewell.

The flute once more falls into silence. Ten minutes into the song, this is a turning point, and in retrospect we can hear that everything up to this moment has been an extended introduction. The repeating pattern of the harps is joined by touches of a mandolin – a reference to the lute that is mentioned later in the poem. Tentatively, flutes try out a rising motif (this has the intervals of the opening theme of the first movement, in reverse). For the first time in the movement, the violins develop a continuous melody that brings together the falling sighs, yearning leaps, and flourishes into a coherent flow, in a warm B flat major, but with aching harmonic shifts (not for the first time, the music is reminiscent of the Adagietto from Mahler's Fifth Symphony). The singer enters:

Ich sehne mich, o Freund, an deiner Seite	I long, my friend, to enjoy the beauty
Die Schönheit dieses Abends zu geniessen.	Of this evening at your side.
Wo bleibst du?	Where are you?

Passionate climaxes give way to high, pianissimo violins and a renewal of the patterns in the flutes, harps, and mandolins, then the music builds again to a yet more poignant climax:

| O Schönheit! O ewigen Liebens – Lebens – trunk'ne Welt! | O beauty! O world forever drunk with love and life! |

This central outpouring comes to an end, and the music lapses into fragmentation. Over shuddering tremolo the gong sounds, and the music returns to its starting point in C minor, with the lament now on cor anglais.

This reprise is the halfway point of the song, and the beginning of a long orchestral interlude. At first it struggles to find a way forward. Eventually, the clarinets resume their repetitive pattern of falling sighs, and flutes and oboes sing a melancholy line. Gradually, with weary effort, the music finds its way to a dark climax, and then back to the deep C and gong stroke with which the movement began.

The contralto returns to her opening recitative, with the words of the second poem:

| Er stieg vom Pferd und reichte ihm den Trunk | He dismounted from his horse and offered him the drink |

| Des Abschieds dar. Er fragte ihn, wohin | Of farewell. He asked him where |
| Er führe und auch warum es müsste sein. | He was going, and why it had to be. |

Through dark sonorities and harmonies, the music keeps returning to its resounding deep C, warms for a moment, then sinks back as the friend answers:

| Wohin ich geh'? Ich geh', ich wandre in die Berge. | Where am I going? I go to wander in the mountains. |
| Ich suche Ruhe für mein einsam Herz. | I seek peace for my lonely heart. |

For the last time, the music lapses into silence. The familiar oscillations emerge, with the flourishes on muted violins and flute, the singer returns to her rising phrases in a major key as the friend continues:

Ich wandle nach der Heimat! Meiner Stätte.	I am heading for home, where I belong.
Ich werde niemals in die Ferne schweifen.	I shall never stray far.
Still ist mein Herz und harret seiner Stunde!	My heart is calm, and awaits its hour!

By now we are into lines added by Mahler himself. There is a long moment of suspense, and the singer returns for the last time to the heart-easing melody that first appeared a quarter of an hour ago, in a serene C major that resolves the troubled C minor with which the song began:

Die liebe Erde allüberall blüht auf im Lenz und grünt	The dear earth everywhere blossoms in spring and is green
Aufs neu! Allüberall und ewig blauen licht die Fernen!	Anew! Everywhere and for ever the distance shines blue!
Ewig … ewig …	Forever … Forever …

Deep trombone chords, harp oscillations, silvery celesta arpeggios, the falling repetitions of 'ewig … ewig', the rising repetitions of the woodwind, come together in a long, lingering moment, an evocation of humanity contemplating the everlasting universe. The voice line does not in the end resolve, but is left hanging above the keynote. It is left to the orchestra to bring the work to a final resolution.

Symphonies

SYMPHONY NO. 1
Duration: approx. 55 minutes

Langsam, schleppend (Slow, dragging) – Immer sehr gemächlich (Very leisurely throughout)

Kräftig bewegt, doch nicht zu schnell (Moving energetically, but not too fast) – Trio: Recht gemächlich (Rather leisurely)

Feierlich und gemessen, ohne zu schleppen (Solemn and measured, but without dragging) – Sehr einfach und schlicht, wie eine Volksweise (Very simple and plain, like a folk tune) – Wieder etwas bewegter, wie im Anfang (Again somewhat faster, as at the beginning)

Stürmisch bewegt (In a stormy tempo)

It took Mahler a decade from first draft to final score to complete his First Symphony. The starting point was a song, one of his *Lieder eines fahrenden Gesellen* (*Songs of a Wayfarer*), which he composed in the early 1880s to his own texts, in the evocative 'folk' style of *Des Knaben Wunderhorn*. The song, 'Ging heut' Morgen übers Feld' ('This morning I walked through the fields'), supplied much of the material for the first movement of the symphony. Mahler conducted the premiere of the first version of the work in 1889, at which stage it was a five-movement 'symphonic poem' in two parts. After the failure of this first performance, Mahler revised it for a second performance in 1893, and called it '*Titan*: a tone poem in symphonic form'. *Titan* was the title of a novel by Jean Paul (pen name of Johann Paul Friedrich Richter), one of Mahler's favourite authors. But he found that the reference merely confused audiences, and decided to drop the title (it nevertheless often appears on modern concert programmes and recordings). More useful is the programme note that he supplied at this stage, identifying the opening as the awakening of Nature, and the slow movement (which eventually became the third movement) as having been inspired by a picture, 'The Huntsman's Funeral', in a children's book. By the time Richard Strauss conducted the third performance, in 1894, Mahler had dropped the original second movement ('Blumine'), and the symphony had reached the four-movement form that, with yet more revision, was finally published in 1899.

Whatever literary associations Mahler may originally have had in mind, the opening of the first movement gives an unmistakable impression of nature coming to life. Indeed, over the first bars Mahler writes 'Wie ein Naturlaut' (Like a sound of nature). The strings play sustained, high harmonics, while a phrase gently falls in the woodwind, establishing a scene of almost silent expectancy, evoking memories of the opening bars of Beethoven's Fourth and Ninth Symphonies. Clarinets, and then offstage trumpets, play a distant hunting call (Austro-German Romanticism had long associated hunting calls with the peace of the countryside). A cuckoo is heard on clarinet – it sings the same interval as the opening woodwind phrase (a falling fourth). The horns play a chorale, the lower strings begin to stir, and there is a sense of gradual awakening. The cuckoo becomes more insistent, until its call forms the opening interval of a tune. This is the song that Mahler reused from his *Lieder eines fahrenden Gesellen*, 'Ging heut' Morgen übers Feld': 'This morning I walked through the fields, with the dew on the grass, the call of a chaffinch declaring that the world is beautiful.' This too has a sense of gradual awakening, as the young man strides into the field. The tempo increases, culminating in a joyful fortissimo. The melody of the song has several different elements in it, from the delicate, trotting start with its cuckoo interval, through more elaborate (indeed chaffinch-like) phrases, to a sturdier element. There is no distinct second theme as in a conventional first movement of a symphony. However, Mahler does move from the opening D major to end the first section in A major, as in a classical symphony, and he asks for the conventional repeat of this opening section.

The second time round, we return to the stillness and high harmonics of the introduction, with poignant wisps of melody on the cellos, and the chaffinch-like call from the song, together with the cuckoo. The music emerges very gradually from this dream and finds its way back to D major. The horns quietly signal the reprise with a hunting chorus that incorporates the call of the cuckoo. Mahler anticipates this moment with wonderful pianissimo chords, in which the trombones enter for the first time together with all seven horns. The chaffinch call returns in the flute, the song is taken up at a mid-point by cellos and then violins, and its different elements are revisited, with exploration through different keys and with new descants and accompaniments. This time, as the music builds up it turns darker, with more insistent march-like figures coming to the fore (these will reappear at the end of the finale). There is a tremendous climax, at which the horns break out into their hunting chorus, ending with whoops of delight. This sets off the whole orchestra in a sustained outburst of *joie de vivre*. There is an acceleration, until the timpani bring it to an abrupt halt. After two stuttering false starts, the movement finally achieves an exuberant finish.

The second movement is a sturdy *Ländler* introduced by yodelling phrases. The opening melody is very like that of the song from the first movement, now recast in a dancing three-time. The first half of the dance is repeated. The second half begins with an excursion into more threatening territory, with darker harmonies and sinister muted horns. The reprise of the dance begins in a whispered pianissimo, but then quickly builds to a massive tutti, accelerating to a culmination with the horns in full cry. The middle section of the movement (trio) is very warm and lilting, with falling intervals and glissandi that underline a sense of yearning and nostalgia. The second half of the trio, like the second half of the first section, ventures further afield into new keys, with vigorous rhythms giving way to more extended melodic phrases. The first section returns, abbreviated.

The slow movement is based on a children's song, known in German as 'Bruder Martin' and in French as 'Frère Jacques'. In his programme note Mahler tells us that its inspiration was a well-known illustration in a children's book, 'The Huntsman's Funeral', which shows the animals of the forest – hares, deer, boar, foxes, birds – escorting the bier of the huntsman, in a mixture of mock-solemn and comic attitudes. Mahler, characteristically, takes this simple tune and makes it sound strange, putting it into D minor, and having it played on a muted solo double bass, with nothing but the tread of timpani accompanying it. Other low-pitched instruments join in canon: bassoon, cellos, tuba, bass clarinet. Over this solemn procession an oboe plays a cheeky staccato tune, as if mocking the solemnity of the others. More instruments join in 'Bruder Martin', and oboe and clarinet again puncture their seriousness. The procession winds to an end. A pair of oboes enters with a lament in distinctly Jewish style. This is taken up and turned into a march by clarinets with bass drum and cymbals (Mahler specifies 'Mit Parodie'). Lament and parody alternate, until the tap of the timpani brings back a brief moment of the opening procession.

Then the music quietly warms into G major, and the violins sing a simple melody 'like a folk tune' over a persistent, rocking bass. This is taken from another of Mahler's settings from *Des Knaben Wunderhorn*, 'Die zwei blauen Augen' ('The two blue eyes'). As it proceeds, the melody acquires nuances of nostalgia and regret, with pungent twists of harmony. It gradually winds down, ending in darkness with touches of gong, timpani, and harp, and the flutes mournfully above, quoting 'Die zwei blauen Augen'. The opening procession resumes, but now in the distant key of E flat minor. The textures are heavier than before, with horns and cor anglais mournfully in low octaves, and the contrast with the cheeky clarinets and oboes even starker than before. The trumpets play a new lament, and the clarinets again launch into their march-parody with cymbals and bass drum. Suddenly the music slips back into D minor, and, with an increase in pace, the trumpets' lament and the march-parody come together in a collision that could have come from Charles Ives. The lamenting is resumed, and the movement ends very quietly and darkly, with the tread of the procession left hanging in the air.

Without a break, the 'stormy' finale begins. A cymbal crash, a dissonant chord on high wind, a drum roll, and frantic arpeggios on the violins unleash a mighty crisis (Mahler described this as 'the sudden erupting of a heart wounded to its depths'). Trumpets and trombones enter with one of the march figures from the end of the first movement, and the woodwind answer with a menacing little descending figure. These elements struggle with each other for some time, until the music settles into a steady, driven march, with the wind on the melody and rapid figures in the violins. This is not in the home key of the symphony (D major), but in F minor, and it will take a long struggle to reach home. The march is developed at length, until it collapses in a series of shocks. With a quiet chord, there is a complete change of mood. The violins embark on a long, singing melody in D flat major, which seems to draw together all the nostalgic elements from earlier in the symphony in one great span. Very gently it comes to rest, and, over a low, held bass note (D flat), a creeping figure begins to emerge, the falling intervals from the very beginning of the symphony sound quietly on clarinets, the horns tentatively remind us of the march theme, and muted trumpets play the menacing little descending figure.

Now the music bursts out again, returning to the struggle of the opening of the movement. There is a sudden hush, and the march turns to a major key (C major), and is played very quietly by muted trumpets, as if in the distance. For the first time, we sense that there might be eventual triumph to be gained out of all this turmoil. After another passage of struggle, this potential triumph becomes more explicit, with the seven horns declaiming a confident extension of the march, incorporating the falling intervals from the beginning of the symphony, and back in the home key of D major. However, this is only the halfway point of the movement, and the climax soon dissolves.

After the horns' reference to the opening intervals, the music now turns back to the mood of the introduction. The pace halves, and we hear the slow descending intervals under a held note, and quiet hunting calls on the horns, now joined by the menacing figure, together with bird calls. There is a lingering moment of nostalgic reminiscence, with several elements from the first movement recalled. These reminiscences drift toward the great nostalgic melody from the finale, and this prompts an outburst, as the violins suddenly remember this theme with passion. The moment is soon over. Then the violas, with an impatient gesture, galvanize a return to the march. This soon builds to a tutti, and long-anticipated triumph is upon us. Mahler instructs the seven horns to stand as they again declaim their confident march, and the symphony comes to a blazing close.

SYMPHONY NO. 2, 'RESURRECTION'
Duration: approx. 85 minutes
Allegro maestoso. Mit durchaus ernstem und feierlichem Ausdruck (With utterly grave and
    solemn expression)
Andante moderato. Sehr gemächlich. Nie eilen (Very leisurely. Never rush)
In ruhig fliessender Bewegung (In gently flowing tempo)
Urlicht: Sehr feierlich, aber schlicht (Primal Light: Very solemn, but simple)
In Tempo des Scherzos (In the tempo of the scherzo) – Langsam (Slow) – Allegro energico
    – Langsam: misterioso

Mahler composed the first movement of his Second Symphony in 1888 as the single-movement 'Todtenfeier' (Funeral Rites) while he was still working on the first version of his

First Symphony. Mahler later wrote, 'it is the hero of my [First] D major Symphony whom I am bearing to the grave, and whose life I, from a lofty vantage point, reflect in a clear mirror'.[9] The second and third movements followed in 1893. Mahler wanted to conclude with a choral finale, as in Beethoven's Ninth, but it took him a long time to find a text. The inspiration came at the memorial service for the conductor Hans von Bülow in February 1894. Bülow had been a great support to Mahler in his career as a conductor (though he had not understood his 'Todtenfeier' when Mahler played it to him on the piano). At the service, Klopstock's 'Resurrection' Hymn (1758) was sung by a children's choir: 'Rise again, yes, you shall rise again, my dust, after a brief rest.' Mahler wrote to the critic Arthur Seidl, 'It flashed on me like lightning, and everything became plain and clear in my mind.'[10] Mahler took the opening lines from the hymn to begin his choral finale, and wrote the rest of the text himself.

He finished the symphony that summer at Steinbach, adding the song 'Urlicht' ('Primal Light' from *Des Knaben Wunderhorn*) as a fourth movement to introduce the choral finale, and orchestrated it over the winter. It was first performed complete, at Mahler's expense, in Berlin in December 1895, with the composer conducting. As with the First Symphony, Mahler supplied a programme for the premiere, which he subsequently withdrew, and from time to time made other attempts to describe what lay behind the music.[11] The first movement unsurprisingly represents a funeral, but also raises questions, 'What is life? – and what is death? Have we any continuing existence? Is it all an empty dream or has this life of ours, and our death, a meaning?' The second movement, a *Ländler*, remembers happy times in the life of the dead hero. The third movement draw on a song about St Anthony preaching to the fishes to evoke a sense of life as meaningless activity. The fourth movement appeals to faith in God to release us from this meaninglessness. And the finale moves from an initial cry of anguish to find transcendent renewal. Mahler did not, however, intend these indications of his thinking to become permanent descriptions, nor did he give the symphony the title 'Resurrection'.

The symphony is scored for a massive orchestra including ten horns, eight to ten trumpets, and seven percussion players, a group of whom form an offstage band in the finale. There are gongs, higher and lower, which alternate at the final climax, an organ, contralto soloist, and chorus.

If we wonder why Mahler withdrew his attempts to describe the ideas behind this symphony, the reason becomes clear as soon as the first movement gets under way. Lasting more than twenty minutes, this is far more than a funeral march. It begins with an urgent fortissimo tremolo, below which cellos and basses attack with rushing, fragmented phrases *fff*. Gradually these settle into more regular patterns, and subside. Over them, oboes, cor anglais, and clarinets intone a solemn, chanting march in C minor. The violins take it up, and it builds to a powerful descent of dotted rhythms, culminating with *fff* trumpets, the rhythm hammered out by horns, trombones, and timpani. The element of funeral march is unmistakable, but so is a ferment of emotions – anger, desperation, grief, determination. Once again the music subsides, first with falling phrases in oboes and clarinets, and then, as the key changes to E major, with a tender rising melody in the violins. This is the main second theme of the movement, and the contrast between the violent opening music in C minor and this yearning, rising melody in E major gives the first glimpse of the emotional trajectory of the symphony. When the melody has risen to a climax and wound to a close, there is another sudden change back to C minor, and a return to the opening tremolo with fragmented phrases in the bass.

Now the pace accelerates. The woodwind chant becomes more urgent, the brass enter, and once again the sharp rhythms from the opening develop to another climax which subsides, with plangent woodwind phrases drawing the music back to a slower tempo, the march rhythms reduced to a steady tread. This marks the end of the first section of the movement. The central development of the movement is entered with the violins' rising second theme, now in C major. This begins a long passage in which melodies, many of them drawn from earlier themes, pass quietly from instrument to instrument – horns, cor anglais, oboe, clarinets – over held bass notes. There is a strong sense of reminiscence and nostalgia. Then the sharp dotted rhythms of the march enter quietly in the cellos and basses, and cor anglais and bass clarinet join in with renewed chanting. The music builds up again, continually changing direction, striving without success towards some sort of resolution. In a quiet moment, a flute delicately takes up the rising second theme and is joined by solo violin. The mood lightens as trumpets, woodwind, and horns play march fragments pianissimo, now drained of their menace. The pace accelerates, and the music arrives at a point of rest over a quiet timpani roll. Suddenly, the strings enter with their *fff* rushing phrase. With crashes of gongs, high and then low, this is like a nightmare recollection of the opening. It fades away with sinister pianissimo tremolo on the strings (played near the bridge, giving an insubstantial, glassy effect).

Slowly and tentatively, cellos and basses set off in marching dotted rhythms, as if trying to find their way back. But the key, E flat minor, is remote from the C minor in which they started the movement, and there is a long way to travel. They are joined by other instruments, some with familiar fragments, others with new versions of the chanting lines and, in the horns, a distinct suggestion of the *Dies Irae* (the medieval chant evoking the Day of Judgment). Gradually these fragments coalesce into another enormous build-up. For a time, the mood turns triumphant, but this impression is soon destroyed by another onslaught of dark struggle, and we reach a great crisis. It is only at this point that the music is able to break back to its original C minor.

Now the reprise can begin, setting off with the familiar march fragments in the bass, and the chanting of the woodwind above. The progress to the second theme in E major is shorter than before, and when it arrives, it too is only briefly touched on before it drifts off into another passage of nostalgic reminiscence like that at the centre of the movement. This fades away into a moment of 'almost inaudible' tremolo. And now for the last time the cellos and basses, with the two harps, set off with a repetitive, trudging bass, as the instruments above them gradually gather. Slowly they accumulate, as if heading for another great climax. But it turns out that the force of the movement has already been spent, and the music descends again into quietness, with a last plangent sigh from major to minor. There is one last rapid downward scale, like a gesture of futile defiance, and the movement ends with two pizzicato chords. In the score, Mahler asks for a break of at least five minutes before continuing.

The second movement is a *Ländler*, the Austrian waltz-like dance that Mahler often uses to evoke a particular vein of rustic nostalgia. The dance is interrupted by two episodes that journey far beyond the warm cosiness of the *Ländler*. This is a particularly easy-going version of the dance, superficially simple in its scoring for strings, but beautifully varied in detail. The melody begins as a duet for the violins, moves to the cellos, then up via the violas back to the violins. The harmonies move subtly in and out of other keys, and Mahler intensifies the nostalgic character of the dance with occasional glissando. The first section of the *Ländler* comes to an end, and the first episode follows. The violins move from major to minor, breaking into the most delicate *ppp* triplets. The rest of the strings join them, still *ppp*, like the entry of a troupe of fairies. Over this delicate ballet clarinets and then other woodwind play melancholy phrases reminiscent of the *Ländler* tune. The *ppp* triplets persist, sounding almost like the ghost of the scherzo from Beethoven's Ninth. Sudden sharp accents and silences bring this episode to a close, and the *Ländler* returns.

This time it is accompanied by a singing counterpoint on the cellos, which enhances the tenderness of the dance. At the end of this section, the strings again break into triplets for the second episode, but now *fff*. What was before delicate has become urgent, and the melancholy woodwind phrases, now on horns and trumpets, have become threatening. Again it ends with sharp accents and silences, and with more acerbic harmonies than before. The *Ländler* returns for the last time, pizzicato, punctuated by staccato comments from the flutes. Eventually the tune moves to clarinets and flutes, and the violins take up their bows to play a yearning descant, an elaboration of the counterpoint played earlier by the cellos. The lower strings then take the melody, with the violins still descanting above, and the movement winds to a conclusion in a spirit of the utmost tenderness.

Mahler elaborated the third movement from one of his settings of a poem from *Des Knaben Wunderhorn*, 'Des Antonius von Padua Fischpredigt' ('St Anthony of Padua's Sermon to the Fishes') – he composed the song and the movement at the same time. The text of the song describes the fish rushing to hear St Anthony's sermon, after which they behave exactly as they did before. The irony is here developed into something far darker, and Mahler's indication, 'In gently flowing tempo', gives little idea of the movement's character. Like the song, it begins as a sort of perpetuum mobile in C minor. It is announced by drumbeats, and then the woodwind set a three-time rhythm going, like a trot or a sleigh ride, an impression enhanced by the crack of a whip. The violins enter with the theme, a smooth and unrelieved line of semiquavers. As it passes seamlessly from instrument to instrument, it gives a sense of something inescapable. It could almost be a *danse macabre*, with death in the saddle. Mahler drew an analogy to try to explain what he was getting at: 'if, at a distance, you watch a dance through a window, without being able to hear the music, then the turning and twisting movements of the couples seem senseless, because you are not catching the rhythm that is key to it all. You must imagine that to one who has lost his identity and his happiness, the world looks like this – distorted and crazy, as if reflected in a concave mirror.'[12]

After a brief fortissimo outburst, the music moves into F major, and for a time is halfway back to the mood of a *Ländler*. But another outburst brings it back to C minor, and the tapping of the whip reasserts the insistent mood. As the music slips delicately into C major, there is a coy staccato reference to the scherzo of Beethoven's Fifth Symphony. But this is pushed aside by a sudden fortissimo in which trumpets and horns enter with a mock-heroic phrase (this injection of a deliberately banal element must surely have inspired Shostakovich). After a further outburst, the music warms to an extended moment of tenderness, with the trumpets singing in E major (the continual shift from one key to another is one of the ways in which Mahler creates a sense of being on an unpredictable, uncontrollable journey). This develops into a reverie, which is broken by a return to C major, with the Beethoven-like staccato semiquavers in the bass, and threatening brass chords bring us back to a reprise of the opening in C minor, followed by the F major episode. Suddenly the mock-heroic trumpets are back. The pace accelerates, culminating in an awe-inspiring dissonant chord with rolling drums which, with almost Wagnerian splendour, gradually resolves and settles. After this 'cry of despair', as Mahler called it, nothing can be quite the same. The C minor opening returns briefly, with its tapping whip, but it soon comes to an uneasy halt with a final, deep gong stroke.

For the short fourth movement, Mahler turns once again to *Des Knaben Wunderhorn*, setting the poem 'Urlicht' ('Primal Light') for contralto in the key of D flat major (very remote from the home key of C minor). The poem speaks of humanity's pain, and the yearning for heaven:

Ich bin von Gott und will wieder zu Gott!	I came from God, and shall return to God!
Der liebe Gott wird mir ein Lichtchen geben,	The loving God will grant me a little light,
Wird leuchten mir bis in das ewig selig Leben!	Which will light me into that eternal blissful life!

After the opening words, 'O Röschen rot!' ('O little red rose!'), the brass solemnly intone a chorale-like phrase, which is answered by the singer and rounded off tenderly by an oboe. The tempo increases as an angel bars the way, and for the only time in the movement there is a suggestion of the supposed 'folk' origins of the poem – clarinets over a drone bass, a solo violin, then a pair of piccolos (Mahler has a characteristic way of using piccolos for plaintive effect, which Shostakovich later exploited). The music becomes urgent as the singer will not be denied – 'Ich bin von Gott und will wieder zu Gott!' – and the movement finishes in the solemn mood with which it began. The fifth movement follows without a break.

The finale is the longest of the five movements, lasting more than half an hour. There are two distinct sections. The first is like a complete symphonic movement in itself. It begins by returning to the great crisis of the third movement, 'wildly bursting out', like a gigantic version of the outburst that begins the finale of Beethoven's Ninth Symphony. As the music gradually settles and disperses, we hear fragments of themes that will become important in the choral section to come. There is a moment of silence, out of which sounds an offstage horn call. Mahler asks for this to be played by as many horns as possible, very loudly, but very far away. They evoke the sound of the Last Trump. There follow attempts to find our way in the darkness. At first, plaintive woodwind calls lead to a moment of urgency. This subsides to a brass chorale that opens quietly with the first four notes of the *Dies Irae* (as in the first movement), but then rises to an affirmative climax full of trumpet calls and brilliant trills. This too fades away.

There is a huge rolling crescendo of drums and gongs, and a fast march begins. At first it is frantic, as if the funeral march of the first movement has been taken over by demons. But soon a turn from minor to major brings a sense that the music is striving mightily toward a goal. Into this struggle enters again the transformation of the *Dies Irae* motif, and a huge climax is reached that breaks up in crisis, to be followed by another hushed moment. There are further plaintive calls on trombone and woodwind (the falling semitone is the same as the first two notes of the *Dies Irae*). These develop into a reminiscence of a yearning melody from the first movement, while, in the distance, offstage fanfares are heard. There is another great crisis. As it fades away, the fragments of themes we heard early in the movement return. Again the distant horns call, answered by trumpets, and melancholy piccolo and flute seem to improvise a duet.

Into this scene – mystical, somewhere between serene and desolate – quietly steps the chorus. They sing the opening lines of Klopstock's 'Resurrection Ode':

Aufersteh'n, ja aufersteh'n	Rise, yes rise again,
Wirst du, Mein Staub,	Will you, my dust,
Nach kurzer Ruh'!	After a short rest!
Unsterblich Leben! Unsterblich Leben	Immortal life! Immortal life
wird der dich rief dir geben!	Will He who called you give you.

As this last sentence is extended, the soprano solo emerges, rising above the chorus like an angel leading them on. After a moment of quietly ecstatic fanfares, the chorus enter for the remainder of the extract from Klopstock:

Wieder aufzublüh'n wirst du gesät!	You are sown to bloom again!
Der Herr der Ernte geht	The Lord of the harvest goes
und sammelt Garben	and gathers in the sheaves,
uns ein, die starben!	us who have died!

Again the soprano rises over the chorus at the final words, and the orchestra quietly rounds the verse off with a lingering cadence over a held bass, with the familiar rising line dominant.

The words from this point on are Mahler's own. First, the solo contralto returns to the plaintive sighing phrases, over anxious tremolo:

O glaube, mein Herz, o glaube:	Oh believe, my heart, oh believe:
Es geht dir nichts verloren!	Nothing will be lost to you!
Dein ist, ja dein, was du gesehnt!	Everything that you have yearned for,
Dein, was du geliebt,	What you have loved,
Was du gestritten!	Struggled for, is yours!

The melody rises passionately and falls back. Then the soprano solo enters more confidently:

O glaube	O believe
Du wardst nicht umsonst geboren!	You were not born in vain!
Hast nicht umsonst gelebt, gelitten!	You have not lived and suffered in vain.

The chorus continues, very quietly at first: 'Was entstanden ist/Das muss vergehen!' ('What was created/Must perish!'), and forcefully, 'Was vergangen, aufersteh'n!' ('What has perished must rise again!'), quietly at 'Hör' auf zu beben!' ('Cease from trembling!'), and once more forcefully at 'Bereite dich zū leben!' ('Prepare to live!'), with the contralto rising over the chorus at the final phrase. This propels the music forward, and the soprano and contralto sing in duet, with almost *Tristan*-like passion, of the end of pain, the conquering of death, and the wings of love that will take us to the light. The chorus takes up these words, at first with the voices entering in turn in almost Handelian style. But soon the immense forces come together, including organ and bells, and with a powerful series of wrenching harmonies, the great goal is attained:

Aufersteh'n, ja aufersteh'n	Rise, yes rise again
Wirst du, mein Herz, in einem Nu!	My heart, you shall arise in an instant!
Was du geschlagen	And your conquest
Zu Gott wird es dich tragen!	Will bear you to God!

Mahler wrote: 'The increasing tension, working up to the final climax, is so tremendous that I don't know myself, now that it is over, how I ever came to write it.'[13]

SYMPHONY NO. 3

Duration: 95–105 minutes

Part I
Kräftig. Entschieden (Vigorous. Resolute)
Part II
Tempo di Menuetto
Comodo. Scherzando. Ohne Hast (Without haste)
Sehr langsam – Misterioso. Durchaus leise (Light throughout)
Lustig im Tempo und keck im Ausdruck (Cheerful in tempo and cheeky in expression)
Langsam – Ruhevoll – Empfunden (Slow – Peaceful – Deeply felt)

Mahler finished a draft of his Third Symphony in the summer of 1894 at Steinbach, in his study by the lake, and completed the score two summers later. He conducted the first complete performance in June 1902. It is a massive work in two parts. Part 1 consists of the first movement, lasting about half an hour. Part 2 comprises the other five movements, totalling 60–70 minutes.

As with his first two symphonies, Mahler described a programme lying behind the symphony, which he later withdrew.[14] He said that the best overall title for the symphony would be *Pan*, in both Greek senses, meaning the god, and 'All'. He suggested titles for the individual movements:

1. Pan Awakes – Summer Marches In (Bacchic procession)
2. What the Flowers in the Meadow Tell Me
3. What the Animals in the Forest Tell Me
4. What Humanity Tells Me
5. What the Angels Tell Me
6. What Love Tells Me

A seventh movement, 'Heavenly Life', was originally planned, but then moved to the Fourth Symphony. By the time of publication (1898), Mahler had abandoned all these titles.

The symphony begins with the eight horns in unison, fortissimo, playing a punchy theme that pays unmistakable homage to the finale of Brahms's First Symphony. But soon the horns separate into a dark four-part chorus, underpinned by deep contrabassoon. Bass drum and trombones set up the rhythm of a funeral march which, over the next five minutes, moves slowly forward, punctuated by fragments of thematic ideas: sinister calls on muted trumpets, a leaping phrase in the woodwind, a rushing upward scale in the strings, awkward calls from the horns like a gigantic creature coming to life (there is more than a hint of Wagner's giant-dragon,

Fafner, in this music). This effortful passage struggles to develop energy, and eventually sinks back to the rhythm of the bass drum. There is a change to a spring-like mood, as quiet string trills and woodwind chords introduce a gentle melody on oboe and solo violin. This is stridently interrupted by high clarinets, and it seems as if the music might be gathering energy. But again it collapses down to the sound of the bass drum. The rhythm of the funeral march returns, over which a solo trombone plays a solemn incantation, developing the awkward, giant-like phrases of the earlier horn calls. Three more trombones and a tuba bring the solo to a forceful conclusion, and the muted trumpets renew their sinister fanfare. With another change of mood, the spring-like trills and high woodwind chords return. This time a momentum develops, with a march-like tread, distant at first but then becoming bold, even swaggering, and the horns bring in a rousing version of their opening tune. In this joyful, unbuttoned passage, Mahler evokes memories of the marching band in Beethoven's Ninth.

A climax is reached and elements of the struggle return, with the gigantic call moving from horns to trumpets. As the music quietens, the solo trombone returns, now developing the more plaintive elements of its earlier melody, and answered by cor anglais. The quietly trilling violin accompaniment takes us back once more to the spring-like music, with another violin solo evoking birdsong. There is distant marching, and more bird calls from a piccolo, accompanied by constant, quiet trilling. Then this softens to a more lyrical, yearning passage, with solo violin and horn in duet. As it begins to develop a sunny mood it is cut short by abrupt rhythmic interventions. A marching bass starts up, joined by the strident little figure on high clarinets and oboes setting an ironic tone. The street seems to be filling with a crowd of marching, gesturing, cheering groups. Rowdy percussion bring in a separate marching band of horns and trumpets, like something out of Charles Ives. Eventually the colourful scene empties, leaving the sound of a distant side drum receding into the distance.

All of a sudden, we are back at the beginning, with the eight horns intoning their magnificent Brahms-like melody. Once more the funeral march begins, and soon the solo trombone enters again with its solemn incantation, rounded off by the cellos. After a hesitation, the cellos and basses set the march going again. As before, it begins quietly, with a spring in its step, and then develops swagger. Touches of acerbic harmony and strident high wind give a mocking edge to the march, and it brings the movement to an end in a mood of noisy triumph that seems both joyful and ironic.

Part II of Mahler's enormous plan begins with a minuet in A major, which he originally called 'What the Flowers in the Meadow Tell Me'. It had the title 'Flower Piece' when it was premiered, before the rest of the symphony, in 1896. Of course, this being Mahler, it is far more than a minuet, consisting of several sections in different metres, all strictly related to each other so that the joins are seamless. The minuet begins very delicately, on oboe with the lightest pizzicato accompaniment. So far, this could almost be an evocation of the baroque. But then the atmosphere becomes subtly mysterious, as the pizzicato moves to the harp and the melody moves to high violins in F sharp minor, becoming more elaborate. After a few bars, this blossoms into a yearning phrase in the violins, back in A major, and the harmonies take a poignant turn. But soon, the poise of the minuet is restored, and brought to an elegant conclusion.

There follows what, in a conventional minuet, would be a first trio. Returning to F sharp minor, the music breaks into a faster three-time, its lively rhythm suggesting a children's game, with the melody chased from instrument to instrument. For a time the music breaks into two-time, as if another group has suddenly appeared. Then the three-time chase returns, with another change of key and with renewed vigour (two delicate taps on the glockenspiel are a typical Mahler touch). The tempo eases for a moment, and a renewal of yearning phrases in the cellos brings us to a reprise of the minuet, followed again by the 'children's game' episode in F sharp minor. This is sharper-edged than before, and soon moves to new keys. After the break into two-time, and then back to three-time, the two- and three-time metres are combined playfully. The scene fades, leaving a solo violin, and, for the last time, the music eases seamlessly back into the minuet. This time the violins lovingly decorate the melody, as if some of the playful character of the preceding episode has brushed off on it. These decorations become more elaborate, and are combined with a singing counterpoint in the cellos. The movement ends very quietly, with high violins weaving the most tender of lines, as if recalling the sweetest of memories.

Just as the second movement is much more than a minuet, the third movement is much more than a scherzo. It is almost twice the length of the minuet, but most of the additional length is taken up by meditative interruptions, rather than the scherzo itself. Like the scherzo of the Second Symphony, this movement is inspired by a text from *Des Knaben Wunderhorn*, which Mahler had set a few years earlier, 'Ablösung im Sommer' ('The Changing of the Guard in Summer'). The song asks who should entertain us through the summer now that the cuckoo has fallen to its death. The answer is Frau Nightingale. The scherzo, like the song, opens with an ironical little tune in C minor, played by piccolo over pizzicato accompaniment, and warms into the major at the moment where the nightingale is mentioned (running violins, and a cheerful tune on oboe and clarinet). With the braying of a donkey in the violins, a robust new dancing theme appears. It becomes quite aggressive for a time, but ends charmingly. With a turn back to the minor, the first tune returns. It is varied with new counterpoints, and it too becomes dark and aggressive, culminating in a fierce descending scale on the brass. This is immediately followed by a quiet return to C major, with that section also varied with new orchestration and harmonies.

With the violins' donkey-bray, we expect the return of the robust dance. But instead there is an expectant passage over a drum roll, and the scherzo fades away. From the far distance, we hear the sound of a flugelhorn (a bugle-like instrument). It plays an extensive solo, 'in the manner of a posthorn', mostly in fanfare style, but sometimes falling into what might be fragments of folk songs. Over the quietest of violin chords, the effect is magical, reminding us of an early title for the symphony, 'A Midsummer Noon's Dream'. Twice we think the solo has ended, but after a few bars it is renewed. The second strain ('approaching a little nearer') is joined by two horns. After a delicate reminder of the first theme, a third strain is joined again by two horns for a longer passage, the violins maintaining the spell with very quiet sustained notes.

Suddenly a trumpet breaks in with a fanfare, and the scherzo returns, with yet more variations and developments. The fierce descending scale now leads in a forceful version of the C major episode, with six horns *fff* and persistent cross-rhythms (Mahler marks this 'coarse!'). For a time the music becomes frantic. But suddenly a trumpet fanfare sounds, tremolando strings bring back the magical atmosphere, and the distant flugelhorn returns. This time the high violins, divided into eight parts, join in with the singing melody, and then the trio of flugelhorn and horns brings the section to a close. For the last time, the dance is renewed, faster than before. But just as it is getting going, a mighty chord intervenes, with solemn horn calls – a moment of crisis like those in the first and second symphonies. After this portent of things to come, the scherzo comes to a brisk and noisy conclusion.

Mahler originally called the fourth movement 'What Humanity Tells Me'. In it, a solo contralto sings the Midnight Song (Zarathustra's Roundelay) from Nietzsche's *Also sprach Zarathustra*: 'O Mensch! Gib Acht!' ('Oh human! Take heed!'). The song speaks of the depth of the world, the depth of its pain and its joy. Joy, according to Zarathustra, is the great force that encompasses and demands everything else, and the poem ends with the words, 'But all joy seeks eternity, deep, deep eternity.'

The movement is very slow, predominantly very quiet, evoking the sense of timeless eternity ('eternal recurrence' is one of the main themes of *Also sprach Zarathustra*). The music looks both forwards and backwards – back to a gently rocking figure from the first movement, and forward to the ecstatic world of the Fourth Symphony (whose finale Mahler originally intended for this symphony). For long stretches the harmony is suspended over a continuous drone in the cellos and basses, and the slow-moving rhythm is marked by the gentle plucking of harps, high and low, giving an almost bell-like effect. After a very spare accompaniment for the first half of the song, the violins enter very quietly, with a melody rising upwards (as in the slow movement of the Fourth Symphony), and the voice later joins the violins in this phrase at the words, 'Doch alle Lust will Ewigkeit!' ('But all joy demands eternity!')

The short fifth movement (originally 'What the Angels Tell Me') follows without a break. The children's choir enters, singing 'Bimm, bamm', and instructed to sound like bells, while actual bells are played at the same time. A three-part women's chorus, later joined by the solo contralto, sings a poem from *Des Knaben Wunderhorn*, 'Es sungen drei Engel einen süssen Gesang' ('Three angels sang a sweet song'). The angels rejoice because Saint Peter has been absolved from sin. Christ declares that those who have sinned must love God forever, and then they will attain heavenly joy. There are phrases that Mahler will use again in the vision of heaven in the Fourth Symphony: a cheerful rising phrase at 'Du sollst ja nicht weinen' ('But you must not weep' – a line that Mahler himself added), and the solemn chords that follow it, like a medieval hymn, 'Ich hab' übertreten die zehn Gebot!' ('I have violated the ten commandments'!) These contrasting elements are all contained within an angelic children's march, as if the marching of the first movement has been washed of its aggression and rendered heavenly.

The power of love to cleanse sin is the message of the poem, and Mahler draws this message into the finale, which he first called 'What love tells me', heading his draft with the words, 'Father, behold my wounds! Let not one soul be lost!' But the voices have fallen silent, and this huge Adagio in D major (twenty-five minutes) is for instruments alone. It begins as a solemn string chorale that touchingly refers back to two of the profoundest moments in Beethoven: the slow movement of his final string quartet, Opus 135, and the funeral march from the 'Eroica' Symphony. Its broad paragraphs extend for several minutes before a new phrase with a rising leap appears, and the pace begins imperceptibly to increase. Other instruments enter, first an oboe then a horn, and the mood becomes anguished. Before a real crisis can develop, calm is regained and the cellos lead a return to the string chorale. As they reach a reprise of the opening strain, the woodwind join with a descant. After a few bars, there is a change of key to C sharp minor, and another slight increase in pace (this subtle alternating of slightly different tempi probably alludes to the slow movement of Beethoven's Ninth). Again the power builds and the pace accelerates for a moment, but then recedes to another change of key (A flat minor, very far from D major). Again the music builds up, leading to the first real climax of the movement. But, despite further wrenching changes of key, there is no reso-lution, and the music sinks back again.

There is a moment of hush, and we are back in D major at the original tempo, with a reprise of the string chorale. Once more the music builds, and as it begins to do so Mahler pays passing homage to another great work on the theme of sin and redemption, Wagner's *Parsifal*. Now the music reaches a full-blown crisis, and once again it slowly sinks down. A flute plaintively recalls the chorale, and there is a moment of searching *ppp* violin tremolo. Very quietly, trumpets and a trombone intone the chorale, now cleansed of any sense of doubt. Gradually, the music builds in a series of enormous waves, which encompass lingering memo-ries of the anguish through which it has passed, to a culmination of the utmost splendour. Mahler's indications on the final page are significant: The drum strokes are to be played 'not with raw power, but with full, noble tone', the strings and woodwind are fortissimo, the trum-pets, horns, and trombones merely forte. This is intended not as a vulgar, clamorous climax, but a satisfying, complete resolution of everything that has gone before.

SYMPHONY NO. 4
Duration: approx. 55 minutes

Bedächtig. Nicht eilen (Deliberately. Do not hurry)
In gemächlicher Bewegung. Ohne Hast (At a leisurely pace. Without haste)
Ruhevoll (Peacefully): Poco Adagio
Sehr behaglich (Very comfortably)

After the great expanses of the second and third symphonies, the Fourth Symphony returns to the more modest length of the first. It is, on the face of it, the most straightforward of Mahler's symphonies, scored for the lightest orchestra (there are no trombones or tuba). He began it in the summer of 1899 and completed it in August 1900, but continued to revise the score over the years until his last concerts. He started by writing the finale in 1892, while revising the First Symphony. This is a setting of a poem from *Des Knaben Wunderhorn*, 'Das himmlische Leben' ('Life in Heaven'), originally composed as a separate song for voice and piano, and then orchestrated (the poem, like many in 'folk' collections, was probably written in the eighteenth century). Mahler planned to use this song in his Third Symphony. Instead, he saved it for his fourth, not only using it as the finale, but letting it provide inspiration and thematic material for the whole of the work. He himself was reported as saying that it formed 'the tapering, top-most spire of the edifice of this Fourth Symphony', and that from it the entire symphony was developed.[15]

Even before we reach the finale, the symphony gives the impression of harking back to a time and place in which people sang and danced and poured out their feelings in a natural way, without the inhibitions of self-doubt. The fact that such a time is a myth is part of the point. Just as Goethe wrote poems that were mistaken for folk songs, and Schubert set them as if they were, so Mahler evokes a time of innocence, and with it, the nostalgia and anxiety that arise from knowing that such innocence is rarely if ever to be found. Here, more strongly than in any other symphony, one can sense Mahler's connection to that great tradition of folk music and folk literature that runs through German and Austrian culture from the late eigh-teenth century onwards. In the first three movements he finds his way, sometimes anxiously or painfully, towards the vision that is represented in the finale. Mahler conducted the premiere in Munich in 1901.

The symphony begins with the sound of sleigh bells and flutes. But the effect is not straightforwardly joyful. The music is not in a major key: it begins with bare fifths, and when the clarinets enter, the key reveals itself as B minor. So these are wistful sleigh bells, perhaps a distant memory. They are to recur throughout the first movement, and again in the finale, and they are always in a minor key. It is only when the tempo eases, and the violins begin their melody, that we enter G major, the home key of this movement. On a visit to Amsterdam, Mahler was reported to have asked the orchestra to play this easing of tempo 'as though we were beginning a Viennese waltz in Vienna'.[16] The melody, however, is in four-time, not three, combining lyrical elegance with an almost polka-like poise generated by perky repeated chords in the accompaniment. The theme passes to the lower strings, developing sturdiness, then to horn, to violins, to oboe and clarinet. As the melody arrives back at the beginning, violin and viola play it in duet, half a bar apart. Cellos and basses introduce tripping semiquavers, and the theme develops further. We arrive at a bracing new element, with clarinets playing a little fanfare like shepherds' pipes. Soon the tempo eases again, and the cellos play the second main theme, which is broad and singing, with a yearning leap at its apex. This theme develops, arriving at a little climax, with the violins leaping much higher, and falling gently away. Now the oboe plays a rustic tune with accented flurries 'suddenly slow and deliberate' (Mahler's markings are very detailed and specific). This too is extended, with more toing and froing of tempo, and winds down.

The opening sleigh bells return, with the 'Viennese' theme, and for a moment we might think that the whole opening section is to be repeated (as in the classical symphony). But the jogging rhythms are halted in their tracks by the cellos, who sing another nostalgic melody, in which each phrase ends with a yearning upward leap, marked to be played with a glissando. With this the first section of the movement finally draws to a gentle close. The sleigh bells start up again, and a solo violin leads the theme in a new direction. This is the beginning of the central development section of the movement. Having taken five minutes or so to lay out his predominantly naive and nostalgic material, Mahler spends about the same amount of time challenging this vision, as if it has been too easily assumed. The familiar elements pass through different keys, and from instrument to instrument. At one point four flutes in unison introduce a new 'shepherds' call', constructed from elements of the other themes. There are excursions, rises and falls of tension, in which dark and sinister colours and harmonies test the seemingly naive material. Eventually, an accumulation of these tensions leads to a massive climax, with a sense of terrible foreboding that could never have been predicted from the first part of the movement. The trumpets call menacingly, and the harmony gives even the flutes and sleigh bells an edge of anxiety. But the climax soon falls away to a sudden silence.

And then, as if nothing significant had happened, the violins pick up the middle of the opening theme ('very leisurely and comfortable'). It takes determination to re-establish the spirit of the opening. The different elements are there, but put together with heavier weight. The cellos' singing second theme is now played forcefully by violins and violas (*Schwungvoll* – 'full of verve'), firmly supported by horns. Once more we reach the rustic tune, now on clarinet, and the reappearance of the sleigh bells. But a roll of the bass drum disturbs the calm, and the violins go off at a tangent, with new and anxious variants of a familiar idea. It seems that we may be heading for another climax. But suddenly the mood lightens, and we arrive at the cellos' final, nostalgically leaping theme. This time the violins respond with a line that rises high, until a mood of serene calm is established. A horn calls. Out of the silence, the violins slowly and very gently approach their first theme for the last time. Gradually it gathers pace and strength, and the movement comes to an end with a reassertion of joyful energy.

The second movement is a dance in three-time, an Austrian *Ländler*, a characteristic Mahler substitute for the traditional scherzo or minuet. It features a solo violin, tuned a tone higher than usual. This gives the instrument a tight, bright sound, and Mahler instructs that he wants it played 'like a [folk-] fiddle'. Although Mahler indicates a 'leisurely' pace, the movement is not a straightforward *Ländler*. It begins in a minor key, and the fiddle is accompanied by voices that have a nervy, independent life of their own, with sudden accents and stings of discord, so that the accompaniment seems to be competing with the melody for attention. It is this that gives the movement an edgy character, even though its elements are as 'folksy' as those of the first movement.

The movement is constructed as a dance with two trios, the second longer than the first. The main dance is set going by a horn, and the oboes respond with a quirky staccato, like a twisted version of the opening sleigh bells. The solo violin enters with its equally quirky fiddle tune. The first time, the violin plays the melody all the way through for sixteen bars. But this is the only time it is allowed to do so. Through the rest of the movement, the soloist is continually breaking off or being interrupted in mid-phrase, adding to the sense of fragmentation. This first section of the movement has a middle part, in which muted strings play an up-and-down arpeggio shape in a major key, which would sound more easy-going but for the 'ping' of a high harp in the last note of each phrase. The solo violin returns with the first theme in the minor, even more fragmented than before.

The pace eases a little, and the first trio begins. A clarinet plays a rustic-sounding tune, full of trills and staccato. As this is passed to the oboes, the violins play a soft, dreamy line, rising to form a lyrical melody, with tender glissando. The contrast between the bucolic woodwind and the dreamy violins creates an impression of intense nostalgia. The horn returns with its opening phrases, the tempo increases, and the first dance is reprised, with an insistent horn competing with the solo violin. When the middle section arrives, with its violin arpeggios, the solo violin joins the harp with its sudden 'pings' at the end of each phrase. This section is rounded off with the return of the first melody, with its competing horn.

A trumpet call announces the arrival of the second trio. Again the pace eases, and again there is a contrast between the woodwind, with rustic trills and staccato phrases, and the violins, which once again seem lost in a reverie of their own, joined by solo violin and viola. The melody moves to the basses, and the key changes to the minor, as if we expect the return of the first dance. But instead, there is a magical change of key to D major, and the mood of nostalgia deepens further. With many unashamed glissandi, the violins remember fondly their lovely melody from the first trio, as the clarinets burble bucolically in the background. As this finishes, the melody once again passes to the basses, and a reprise of the first dance begins hesitantly, taking time to reach its original pace. With further exploration of the quirky possibilities of the dance, the movement comes to an end.

After the anxiety and quirkiness of the second movement, the opening of the third comes as a haven of peace. The movement consists of a loosely constructed set of variations in G major, twice interrupted by darker, more passionate episodes in minor keys, and culminating in a crisis. The sustained serenity of the variations, and the way they are challenged from time to time, evoke memories of Beethoven in the slow movements of his Ninth Symphony and last piano sonata, opus 111. Over a pizzicato bass and a string chorus, cellos sing a sustained line that rises and falls in two arcs. The pizzicato bass repeats, and the violins join in counterpoint with the cellos. Then the bass repeats again, as the violins rise high, and a plaintive oboe joins them. It is like the beginning of a passacaglia; but only the first half of the bass repeats, and after the entry of the oboe and the climax of the melody high in the violins, the music seems rooted to the spot by the beauty of the dream. Horns and bassoons enter, and then the music winds gradually down, and reaches a halt.

An oboe, often the most plaintive member of Mahler's orchestra, begins a lamenting new melody in E minor, over a reminder of the pizzicato bass in the bassoon. The violins take up the melody, and it becomes more passionate, with a series of glissando leaps, each greater than the last. The oboe returns to the lament, and it takes a new direction, triggering a crisis. The violins' passionate melody builds to a full-blown climax. As it dies away, the pizzicato bass returns, and there is a prolonged moment of musing on it. The harmony quietly turns a corner, and we are back in G major.

Over the pizzicato bass, faster than before, the cellos play a variation of the rising and falling melody, now with a lilting rhythm ('moving gracefully', Mahler instructs). At the next variation, the oboe and violins join in counterpoint with the cellos. Then the violins become more animated. The melody extends with new harmonies, and eventually winds to a moment of uneasy calm. The oboe, once more in a minor key, muses on its earlier lament, with cor anglais and horn. Violas and violins join in, and the music again becomes passionate. Twice it rises to climaxes on full orchestra. The second climax fades away, and once more the music slips gently back into G major. With a swooping ascending glissando, the cellos resume their singing, over the pizzicato bass. But now the melody is in a gentle three-time. Then, 'without the slightest anticipation of the new tempo', the music quietly clicks into a waltz (or perhaps a *Ländler*), in a moment of great charm. Suddenly the tempo and the metre switch again, breaking into a fast two-time. The music becomes more and more urgent. The violins race away, and the music becomes more and more frenzied. But with a cymbal crash the mood is broken.

There is a last variation on the opening theme, with the bass now bowed rather than pizzicato, and the violas playing in counterpoint with the violins. The music settles into the deepest calm, with a final reminder of the pizzicato bass. It sounds like the end, in the original G major. But suddenly there is a vigorous upbeat from the violins, and a tremendous crashing chord of E major from the full orchestra. Timpani beat out a tattoo of the pizzicato bass, four horns, with their bells in the air, blaze out a fanfare, reminding us of the 'shepherds' call' played by four flutes in the middle of the first movement, and trumpets play a descending scale drawn from earlier in the first movement. Again the power gradually ebbs away, the violins quietly remember their passionate melody from earlier in the movement, the music finds its way back to G major, and dies away on a high chord of violins and flutes.

The finale opens pianissimo in G major, with a clarinet picking up the climactic fanfare of horns and trumpets from the end of the preceding movement, and turning it into a gentle, pastoral tune – 'sehr behaglich' (very comfortable, or easy), writes Mahler. More important is his instruction to the singer, who enters a few bars later: 'To be sung with childlike, serene expression, with no trace of parody'. The poem is 'Das himmlische Leben' ('Life in Heaven'). Mahler separates the four verses with interludes of the sleigh-bell motif from the first movement, always starting in their original B minor. Verse 1 adopts the genial clarinet theme in G major, describing the peaceful heavenly life that includes dancing and singing. Saint Peter looks on – a moment of chorale-like solemnity. The sleigh bells then intervene for an orchestral interlude. The second verse develops out of this interlude, with a new melody in E minor. Lambs and oxen go patiently to their death at the hands of butcher Herod, wine is free, and the angels bake the bread – another moment of solemn chorale.

A brief interlude of sleigh bells brings the music back to G major, and the next verse reprises the theme from the first verse. There are vegetables and fruit in abundance, and hare, deer, and fishes run and swim up to be caught. Saint Martha is the cook – a third moment of solemn chorale. The sleigh bells begin for the last time, but soon the music quietens and modulates to E major. The harp sets up a peaceful, low rhythmic pattern. Violins and flute together elaborate the melody from the first verse, like improvising shepherds (or angels). This continues meditatively as the soprano sings the last verse: 'Kein' Musik ist ja nicht auf Erden' ('There is no music on earth that can compare to ours'). The peaceful mood deepens to the end, with most of the verse over an unchanging bass. And so the symphony, which began in G major, ends in E major, the key of the outburst near the end of the slow movement. It is unusual for a symphony to end in a key remote from the one in which it began. Clearly Mahler wanted to give the impression that the arrival at this point of serene innocence was an arrival somewhere new, not a return.

SYMPHONY NO. 5
Duration: 60–70 minutes
Trauermarsch: In gemessenem Schritt. Streng. Wie ein Kondukt (Funeral march: With measured step. Severe. Like a cortège)
Stürmisch bewegt. Mit grösster Vehemenz (Moving stormily. With the greatest vehemence)
Scherzo: Kräftig, nicht zu schnell (Vigorous, not too fast)
Adagietto: Sehr langsam (Very slow)
Rondo-Finale: Allegro – Allegro giocoso

Mahler composed the Fifth Symphony over a tempestuous and highly significant period in his life. This was sparked off by meeting Alma Schindler in November 1901 at a dinner party full of Viennese artists and intellectuals. It was not the first time he had met her, but it was the meeting that changed his life. She was twenty-two (he was forty-one), the daughter of a distinguished painter, Emil Schindler, and a composition pupil of Alexander Zemlinsky. Mahler found her sitting between the artist Gustav Klimt and Max Burckhard, former director of the Burgtheater. The conversation was very lively, and Mahler had already been struck by Alma's beauty and 'acerbic and direct' style of conversation. Soon Mahler and Alma were in a furious row about a ballet by Alma's teacher, Zemlinsky (with whom she was having an affair at the time), which had been submitted to Mahler as artistic director of the Opera, and which he had kept for a year without a decision.[17] Four tumultuous months later, Mahler and Alma were married.

Mahler's symphonies are full of struggle, disappointments, glimpses of what might be and what might have been, and eventual hard-won triumph – fleeting or not. Connections with Mahler's own life are impossible to untangle, and the music exists in its own right without the need for such conjecture. As for this Fifth Symphony, it begins with a funeral march, goes through struggle to a moment of serenity, and ends in triumph. How much this has to do with Alma is impossible to know. But her presence in his life certainly unleashed a sustained burst of inspiration, of which the Fifth Symphony was one of the major fruits.

Mahler wrote most of the symphony in the summers of 1901 and 1902 in the composing cottage he had had built near his villa at Maiernigg, in the woods above the Wörthersee. He began it in the year that he also composed three of the *Kindertotenlieder* (*Songs on the Death of Children*), four Rückert songs, and 'Der Tamboursg'sell' ('The Drummer-Boy', his last *Wunderhorn* song), all of which are quoted in the symphony. It was a period in which he was studying the works of J. S. Bach. In March 1901, recovering from an operation in a sanatorium, he studied Bach's scores, and wrote to his friend, Natalie Bauer-Lechner, about one of the cantatas, 'this miraculous freedom of Bach's, which probably no other musician has ever attained and which is based on his unparalleled skill and command of technique. In Bach, all the vital cells of music are united as the world is in God; there has never been any polyphony greater than this!' Already in the Fourth Symphony (as revised after his Bach studies) there is a new polyphonic freedom in Mahler, and this has become even more pronounced in the rich complexities of the Fifth Symphony.

The premiere took place in Cologne, and after the first rehearsal Mahler wrote to Alma, 'Heavens, what is the public to make of this chaos in which new worlds are forever being engendered, only to crumble into ruin the next moment? What are they to say to this primeval music, this foaming, roaring, raging sea of sound, to these dancing stars, to these breathtaking, iridescent, and flashing breakers?' Despite this 'chaos', the symphony is in some ways Mahler's most traditional so far. It is purely instrumental, unlike Nos 2–4, it makes only glancing reference to song as inspiration, and although it is in five movements, and scored for a large orchestra, it is not as huge a symphony as Nos 2 or 3. Its length, however, varies considerably in performance, from about an hour (Bruno Walter) to seventy minutes or more (Bernard Haitink, Leonard Bernstein, Valery Gergiev, and others). This is partly because of the wildly different approaches to the famous Adagietto, which, like Elgar's 'Nimrod', has taken on tragic associations that seem never to have been intended by the composer.

The first movement is a funeral march in C sharp minor, a genre to which Mahler returned again and again – he had already placed a funeral march at the beginning of his second and third symphonies. But whereas those were both long and complex movements, this is shorter, starker, and more clear-cut. The main march theme is interleaved with two contrasted episodes. The march is announced by the solemn call of a trumpet, which seems to refer back to the crisis at the heart of the first movement of the Fourth Symphony. After a few massive bars the music settles into a quiet tread, over which violins and cellos sing a lament. This has something in common with the last of Mahler's songs from *Des Knaben Wunderhorn*, 'Der Tambourg'sell', which he wrote at the time he was beginning work on the symphony. It is the song of a former drummer-boy, who bids farewell as he is taken from his prison cell to the gallows. Bleakness is one end of the emotional spectrum in this movement. Once more the trumpet brings in the opening call, which subsides to a renewal of the lament on violins and woodwind, with a new counterpoint on cellos. For a moment the lament moves into a major key, with more consoling woodwind phrases. But soon the violins bring it back to a darker tone, and the march comes to the end of its first section.

The trumpet call begins again, but is now cut off with an abrupt break into B flat minor at a faster tempo, marked 'Leiderschaftlig, Wild' ('Passionate, Ferocious'). A swirling descending figure in the violins fights for supremacy with an assertive trumpet melody. The music becomes increasingly tense, with the six horns cutting across the rhythm with their own whooping line. A second great wave culminates in a climax, and as it disintegrates the trumpets renew their opening call. The tempo gradually settles, and the funeral march returns, with the melody, somewhat changed, now in the woodwind, joined by trumpet in counterpoint (the wind scoring makes this sound much more like a military band than before). A more consoling element enters again, and the timpani are left tapping out the march rhythm.

Now there is another change of key, to A minor, and a new lament, full of yearning upward leaps. The tension soon builds, and there are poignant references to a moment from one of Mahler's *Kindertotenlieder*, in which the sun rises despite the tragedy that has occurred during the night. The next climax is less violent, but more disorientated. As it fades away, the trumpet once more calls insistently. Gradually it too fades away, its final fanfare taken by the flute, and a pizzicato brings the funeral march to a close.

The first movement consisted of a funeral march interrupted by a passionate episode. The second movement, which is a little longer than the first, reverses that. It is a 'stormy' and 'vehement' movement interrupted by returns to the character of the funeral march. These alternations are straightforward at first, but become more complex and confused later, until the music takes an unexpected turn towards a glimpse of triumph. Some elements of the first movement reappear throughout the movement, in varied form, most prominently the lament, and phrases with upward leaps that here become insistent.

Cellos, basses, and bassoons start the movement with thrusting phrases, accompanied by brusque punctuating chords. The violins then launch into several pages of frantic energy, with the brass in pursuit, beginning with the first of many wild leaps upwards. When this settles the violins play a more sustained theme that, at this fast tempo, seems to be trying to recall the lament from the first movement. But the moment soon passes and a further passage of frantic activity works itself out, until there is an abrupt halt, leaving a timpani roll. Now the tempo switches back to that of the funeral march. There are a few bars in which the woodwind play phrases that combine the upward leap with a sighing fall. And then the cellos sing a variant of the lament from the first movement, with a counterpoint in the clarinets, together with more of the leaping and sighing phrases. The lament is developed further, until the music suddenly breaks back to the 'stormy' tempo. This explores new territory, and new keys, before once more coming to an abrupt halt with a quiet drum roll. Over the drum roll, at the slower tempo, the cellos search for a way forward, trying out phrases with different leaps and sighs. Eventually they settle into a narrow, repetitive pattern, over which the horns play the new version of the lament, while a solo violin interjects leaping phrases. In this passage we notice most clearly how Mahler is writing with more complex counterpoint than in his earlier symphonies.

The tension rises and the pace increases, until the 'stormy' tempo is resumed. But this soon retreats, and development of the lament is renewed. In the woodwind are reminders of the consoling second theme from the first movement. This passage, too, is short-lived, transforming itself into a mock-triumphant march. It's as if we have been grasped by the shoulders, and marched along without knowing where we are going. We round a corner, and suddenly there is a triumphant blaze of major-key chords (most of this movement has been in minor keys). But we only get a glimpse of this before we are back in the 'stormy' music from the beginning. Soon the lament theme is drawn into it, though faster than before, and this is built up to a climax. It struggles with the stormy material for supremacy, until, out of the blue, the triumphant music that we glimpsed a little earlier becomes a glorious chorale in D major, its intervals seeming to have evolved from those of the lament. It will return in the finale. This moment of glory is soon gone, the stormy music reappears, and it fades away into the distance. With a few more leaping and sighing phrases, the movement comes to a quiet close.

After two very intense movements, Mahler asks for a long pause. And indeed it is essential, if the symphony is not to seem relentless. This is because what follows is not the slow movement that one might have expected, but a mighty scherzo in D major (the key of the climax of the preceding movement). It has an effect somewhat akin to that of the scherzo in Brahms's Second Piano Concerto, which is similarly massive after a big first movement. Mahler's scherzo is particularly gruelling for the first horn, who has an 'obbligato' (in effect, solo) part. It requires unusual stamina after playing the earlier movements, so an extra 'bumper' first horn is often brought in to relieve the player elsewhere. The movement has the usual alternations of scherzo and trio (though not labelled) with a slower tempo for the trio. But both sections have long excursions within them, making this the longest of the five movements.

With a debonair flourish, four horns set the movement going, the first horn takes up the melody, and the woodwind join in counterpoint. Already in these first few bars the character of the movement is declared: a robust dance, with an almost waltz-like swing, counterpoint with cross-rhythms, and sturdy instrumentation dominated by the horns, and topped with the brightness of a triangle (later also a glockenspiel). The violins enter with a new dancing element, with the horn in counterpoint. Several other elements get thrown into the mix. Violas and cellos start up a staccato accompanying figure, over which three clarinets (with their bells in the air) take turns to play a cheeky little phrase. The mood becomes more changeable, acerbic for a moment, with more combative counterpoint, then returning to the opening playfulness. Momentum develops, which is suddenly halted by the horns.

The strings begin the first of the gentler trios, with a *Ländler*-like swing. This too has a complex texture, with the violins joined in counterpoint by the cellos, and other pairings following. Once more, just as momentum is developing, there is a sudden switch of tempo, and a trumpet announces the return to the scherzo. This time, elements are developed at greater length. The staccato figure now extends into a long paragraph, joined by smoother elements in the horns. Eventually, the pace is again slowed, and the solo horn emerges, meditating on this new element, at first in dialogue with the cellos, and then hauntingly echoed by a muted horn. This is analogous to the passage in the preceding movement where the cellos were trying out leaping and sighing phrases, and a sighing semiquaver interval is prominent in the horn's phrases here. The meditation leads into a pizzicato passage, in which the strings tentatively experiment with the horn's meditative ideas. An oboe suggests a return to the strings' *Ländler* theme, but the horn meditation predominates, passing to the clarinet, now in a major key, and developing into an extended lyrical passage – the most sustained quiet music in this otherwise rumbustious movement, though other elements are continually threatening it.

Eventually, the episode comes to an end with the solo horn. Over more pizzicato, the violins renew their *Ländler*. But this soon accelerates to the scherzo tempo, building in power. Another sudden cut, and the horns announce the return to the scherzo proper. This time it is even more exuberant than before, with more instruments joining in the complex web of counterpoint. After a time, it takes a new direction. The smoother element from the last episode returns, moving darkly to the lower brass instruments. But this subdued moment is brief, and the energy of the scherzo returns. It builds up to a splendid chord, out of which the solo horn emerges, and the meditation is revisited. A last moment of quiet, a drum roll, and with a yet faster tempo the scherzo dashes to a wildly exuberant finish, with five horns punching the air like triumphant footballers.

What follows could not be a greater contrast. The fourth movement is the famous Adagietto in F major for strings and harp. It pays homage to the poignant Adagietto from Bizet's *L'Arlésienne*, and, as with Bizet, the title indicates a brief Adagio, not a tempo faster than Adagio: Mahler specifies that it should be 'very slow'. The effect of this quiet, slow movement at this late stage of the symphony is far more than just relief or relaxation. Its long melody seems like a resolution of the tensions of the past, specifically a resolution of the great lament from the first movement, whose elements have recurred in the second and third movements. The Adagietto, too, is full of those sighing semiquavers, up as well as down, that have been such a feature of the symphony. And the central section of the movement, where the music turns darker and more struggling, culminates in insistent downward leaps of ninths and sevenths (one note more and less than an octave), mirroring the upward leaps of earlier movements.

The scoring is simple but masterly. The relationship between the five string lines is as subtle as in Schubert or Mozart (another sign of Mahler's increasing command of counterpoint), and the harp provides more than just atmosphere. Its simple arpeggios range freely, often with three notes to a beat against the violins' two, and often without a note on the beat itself. The effect is as if improvised, as if the orchestra is a singer accompanying itself on the harp. The harp drops out for the middle section – appropriately, because this sounds more like an impassioned appeal than a song – and then returns for the reprise.

The impact of all this in the context of the symphony suggests, without the need for further evidence, affirmation rather than lament, even though the music evokes tensions and doubts on the way to resolution. And, despite the Adagietto's modern use in funereal contexts and as the soundtrack to the film of *Death in Venice*, there is evidence strongly suggesting that death was far from Mahler's mind when he wrote it. The conductor Willem Mengelberg, a great champion of Mahler who kept notes of many of his comments during rehearsals, claimed that both Mahler and his wife, Alma, told him that the Adagietto served as a declaration of love for her – though it is not clear whether he wrote it for her, or whether it was already written when he decided to use it in this way. At the same time, the music is unmistakably related to a song that Mahler composed while he was working on the symphony: 'Ich bin der Welt abhanden gekommen' ('I am lost to the world'). The words are by Rückert, and they end:

Ich bin gestorben dem Weltgetümmel,	I am dead to the world's tumult,
Und ruh' in einem stillen Gebiet!	And I rest in a quiet realm!
Ich leb' allein in meinem Himmel,	I live alone in my heaven,
In meinem Lieben, in meinem Lied!	In my love, in my song!

Relationships between life and art are never simple, and there is a danger of making too much of the 'declaration of love' story. But it seems clear that the movement should not sound funereal. Mahler, in his own performances, took between seven and nine minutes to conduct the movement, as, on recordings, did his close associates Bruno Walter and Willem Mengelberg.

This must be closer to Mahler's intentions than the tragedy-laden twelve minutes or more of some later conductors.[18]

Mahler instructs that the Rondo-Finale should follow straight after the Adagietto without a break. The melody of the Adagietto ends on A (the third on top of a warm chord of F major). The first horn picks up the A, and, after a moment of hesitation, a bassoon plays a cheeky tune in D major under it (A is the fifth of D major). After the exhausting intensity of the first three movements and the resolution of the Adagietto, it is as if all the struggle and tension has been finally cleansed, and we are back in the world of Mahler's First Symphony and *Des Knaben Wunderhorn*. The cheeky tune quotes Mahler's song, 'Lob des hohen Verstandes' ('Praise of High Intellect'), about a bet between the cuckoo and the nightingale as to who is the finer singer. The donkey (no doubt a Viennese critic) awards the prize to the cuckoo. The cheerful jauntiness of the song is not a just a passing element but informs the whole character of the finale. The struggles and anguish that surfaced in previous movements (even to some extent in the Adagietto) have been put behind us, and the music strides out with a spirit of joyful reawakening. The horns and woodwind set the movement going, over a bagpipe drone. This is the principal theme of the rondo, and the strings join in enthusiastically. The theme comes to an end with a suggestion of the donkey's bray.

The cellos start up a rapid patter that recalls a similar staccato element in the scherzo. Here Mahler plays at fugue-writing, soon bringing in the song theme in counterpoint, any danger of seriousness being pushed aside by uncouth blasts from the brass. The music eases for a moment, then horn and violins bring in the first reprise of the main theme. With a change of key, the pattering bass follows, with assertive horn phrases over it. Soon this leads into a familiar melody. It is the theme of the Adagietto, now speeded up, so that its yearnings and leaps take on a joyful character. There follows an extended passage in which the different elements of the movement are developed into an elaborate and energetic web. Eventually the Adagietto theme returns, higher and more assertively passionate than before. This is followed by another passage in which elements jostle with each other in counterpoint. One of the energetic motifs that keeps on recurring is taken from the Adagietto theme, though one would scarcely recognize it in its bold new character.

The music builds and builds, until suddenly we are back at the rondo theme, now elaborated and filled out. The energetic patter element joins, and the energy increases over a drum roll. Just as we expect the climax, the music draws back again, and a delicate passage intervenes. Soon the Adagietto theme returns, and this provokes another build-up. This time the climax does arrive, in the form of the glorious chorale that we glimpsed at the end of the second movement. Mahler gives it its head for a moment, topped by the brightness of a glockenspiel (a favourite touch of Mahler and Richard Strauss). But instead of a grandiose ending, there is a final burst of energy, a last interrupting blast from the brass, a scattering of the crowd, and, with the horns whooping their delight for the very last time, the symphony is over.

SYMPHONY NO. 6

Duration: 80–90 minutes

Allegro energico, ma non troppo. Heftig, aber markig (Vehement but sturdy)

Andante moderato

Scherzo: Wuchtig (Heavy)

Finale: Sostenuto – Allegro moderato – Allegro energico

Mahler composed his Sixth Symphony over the summers of 1903–4 and finished the orchestration the following May, though, as was his habit, he continued to revise it. He conducted the premiere in Essen, in May 1906. The period of composition was an exceptionally happy time in his life. He had married Alma in 1902, their first daughter (Maria) was born that November, and their second daughter (Anna) in June 1904. At Mahler's insistence, Alma had put her own composing career to one side, and had, at least for the time being, settled into the role of wife and mother, enabling Mahler to devote himself to his work. One might imagine Mahler composing his sunniest music during this period. But the Sixth Symphony is the most tragic of his symphonies. The finale culminates in mighty blows that are reinforced by a hammer. Alma in her reminiscences claims that Mahler described this as the fall of a hero, who 'is dealt three blows, the third of which fells him like a tree'. She tried to make sense of the writing of this work at this time by describing it as 'prophetic', with the three blows anticipating those that were to strike Mahler himself, all in 1907: the death of Maria, at the age of four, from scarlet fever and diphtheria; the diagnosis of Mahler's heart disease; and his resignation from the Vienna Court Opera. This is a very dramatic theory, but it was constructed in retrospect; and Alma was presumably unaware that Mahler originally planned five hammer blows in the finale, not three (and in his final revision he reduced them to two).[19] Nevertheless, Mahler was very tied up emotionally with this symphony. Alma, more convincingly, describes his state of mind at the end of a rehearsal two days before the premiere in Essen: 'After the rehearsal, Mahler paced up and down in the dressing room sobbing and wringing his hands, completely beside himself.'[20] He used to refer to the work as his 'Tragic' symphony, and it was given this title at the second performance, in Munich, though never again.

Mahler changed his mind about the order of the second and third movements. Originally, the scherzo came second, and the Andante third. It was only during rehearsals for the premiere in 1906 that Mahler decided that the Andante should come before the scherzo, and this was how the score was published. After Mahler's death, Alma told Willem Mengelberg, conductor of the Concertgebouw Orchestra in Amsterdam, that the original order should be restored. It is impossible to know whether she was reporting Mahler's last wishes, but many have subsequently agreed that the scherzo, a bitter parody of elements in the first movement, works best if played immediately after it.

The first movement is long – twenty-five minutes if the repeat is observed. It is a fierce march in A minor, one of many marches in Mahler's music, but this one has a particularly relentless tread. After an extensive passage full of fierce determination, wild leaps, and plunging descents, the first statement of the march comes to an end with a stern rhythm beaten out by timpani over a side-drum roll, followed by a loud trumpet chord that slips from major to minor as it fades – a clouding of harmony that forms a motif throughout the symphony (the oboes crescendo while the trumpets fade, creating a subtle shift of tone as the harmony changes). This is followed by a pianissimo woodwind chorale, which would sound ecclesiastical except for its haunting chromatic slips of harmony – it is rather like Bruckner at his most searching. As the chorale comes anxiously to rest, the violins burst in with a passionate new theme in F major, which could have stepped out of the middle of the Fifth Symphony's Adagietto. The link is perhaps not coincidental: Alma reported that Mahler had tried to express her in this theme, just as he had presented the Adagietto to her as a love token. Surprisingly, it dissolves into a return to the march, jauntier than before, and the passionate new theme has to push it back, building to a climax that brings the first section of the movement to a gentle end. The whole of this opening exposition is repeated – the only symphony apart from the first in which Mahler asks for this.

After the repeat, the development begins with a sinister return to the march. This moves into new keys, with darker and more acerbic harmonies, and the more threatening mood is accentuated by a xylophone. There is an extended passage of nervous exploration, until suddenly a strange calm is reached. There is the sound of distant cowbells, with chords on celesta and tremolando violins. Muted horns recall the woodwind chorale. It is like a sudden vision of the mountains, or, as Mahler put it, 'The last greeting from earth to penetrate the remote solitude of the mountain peaks'. Out of this emerges a gently rising melody in the woodwind, which seems to have been distilled out of the violins' passionate theme, but is also reminiscent of the second theme in his Second Symphony. The violins quietly take it up, with a horn in counterpoint. A solo violin emerges, then a bass clarinet as the cowbells return, and this long moment of meditation comes to an end.

Suddenly, the march tempo is resumed. It struggles to find its way back to the home key and the opening theme, and when it does so, it is with extra vehemence. And when the woodwind chorale arrives it is at double speed, with pizzicato violins and celesta adding a sense of floating anxiety. The passionate string theme does not burst in, but gently arises, never quite regaining confidence, and sinks back. The march resumes, but now with solemn trombones and gong strokes, as if it is metamorphosing into a funeral march. Suddenly horns and trombones snap back to the march tempo 'as if enraged'. The last few minutes of the movement are like a nightmare in which all the elements struggle and mock each other. Out of this builds a sort of climax that seems conflicted between rage and parody. It ends with a phrase taken from the passionate theme flung in the air with a gesture of defiance or exasperation.

In Mahler's revised order, the Andante comes next, but originally the scherzo followed after the first movement (see introduction). The Andante opens with a beautiful violin melody, whose melancholy flow is subtly shaped and orchestrated. The phrases begin regularly, with an echo of the 'Child's vision of heaven' from the Fourth Symphony, but they then become irregular, creating a sense of wandering. The melody passes between first and second violins, to oboe and back to the violins. The woodwind writing that interleaves with the strings is darkened by a bass clarinet. The harmonies are also subtle. The key is E flat major, but continually tinged by touches of minor, echoing the clouding from major to minor that the trumpets first introduced in the opening movement. The theme is explored further, moving away from the home key and back again, with subtle exchanges between strings and wind, eventually settling back to conclude quietly in E flat major.

There is a change of mood and key: high violin and flute chords take us to the remote key of E minor, and an oboe continues to explore the rising and falling interval that has been a recurrent feature of the theme. The sonorities become grander, there is a sense of emerging into open spaces. Suddenly the music moves into E major, and horns and trumpets call. The cowbells return, closer than before. It is as if the clouds on the mountain have parted for a moment. But the vision is soon over. The music quietly falls away, and reverts to E flat major. The opening theme is reprised by oboe, then horn and bassoon, while the violins play a haunting descant. The melody winds to a conclusion, and once more the music ventures into new territory. We enter a quiet C major, with serene, almost chorale-like, wind chords. The serenity deepens with a shift to A major, with touches of harp and celesta. The mood and key darken again, and the music builds once more, this time climaxing back in the home key of E flat major, and the grand vision of serenity is affirmed. As the climax fades, the major-to-minor harmonies darken the sky once more, but the movement nevertheless finishes calmly.

The scherzo (originally placed second) returns to the A minor of the first movement. It takes the parody elements of the march and forces them into three-time to create a bitter and insistent dance in three-time, like a premonition of Shostakovich. The rhythm, counterpoint, and orchestration are heavy and stumbling, pierced by shrieks of trilling high woodwind and the rattling of a xylophone. The dance calms to a quieter episode. An oboe timidly tries out a dance step, unsure whether it is in three-time or two-time, and the strings develop it awkwardly. Mahler gives this the unusual marking, 'altväterisch' (old-fashioned), as if wanting to evoke glimpses of an old Viennese ballroom. There are interruptions by timpani, sudden accents and disruptions from which the timid dance re-emerges. The sense of timidity is increased by moments of hesitant counterpoint. Timpani and horns signal a return to the scherzo, but at first ironically and sinisterly slow. Soon it speeds up and the original character is renewed, with the xylophone more prominent than before.

Dark trombone chords and a deep undulating tuba line take us into a second episode. It is disturbed – sometimes it is a sort of awkward dance, then the dark undulating trombone chords resurface, there is an abrupt accent, a trumpet call, more tiptoeing dance, a snarl of horns. Eventually the oboe returns with a charming little dance in A major. But even this is uncertain, moving between bars in different metres, with sudden loud pizzicato alternating with gentle phrases. The tempo sometimes surges forward and then retreats again. There are nostalgic little glissandi, as if a *Ländler* is about to begin, but it seems that nobody can quite remember how anything goes, or what anything means. Solemn timpani strokes and sinister creeping horn chords lead into a yet slower passage on woodwind, with the strings tapping out the rhythm with the wood of the bow. The menacing energy of the scherzo returns for the last time. Again the sinister horn chords resurface, and from here the music fragments, ending with low mutterings from bass clarinet and contrabassoon, and final dismal taps on the timpani.

Of all Mahler's symphonic movements, the finale is the one that presents most challenge to the listener, looking forward to the musical cataclysms of the later twentieth century. No wonder that Schoenberg's pupils Berg and Webern so admired the symphony. Berg wrote that it was 'the only Sixth – despite the *Pastoral*', and one can easily hear how this finale might have inspired the violent climaxes of Berg's opera *Wozzeck*, and the final march of his *Three Orchestral Pieces*.[21] Mahler's finale is half an hour of relentless and often disorientating music. The one guide to cling onto as one submits to it is that the music of the slow introduction recurs to introduce each of the main sections of the movement: before the development, before the reprise, and at the start of the final coda. Everything else is like a wild nightmare – the nightmare with which the first movement concluded has finally come true. The famous hammer blows (originally intended to be five, then three, becoming two in the final revision) come in the middle of the movement. For the hammer blow, Mahler gives an instruction doomed to failure: it should be 'brief and mighty, but dull in resonance and with a non-metallic character (like the fall of an axe)'. It accompanies a chord of full orchestra, and, although conductors have tried all kinds of solutions to the problem, it rarely achieves a distinctive effect in the concert hall beyond what is already produced by bass drum and cymbals.

The introduction begins with a low C and a stroke of the bass drum, from which a chord of wonderful strangeness is swept upwards by celesta and harp over woodwind and muted strings. The first violins, fortissimo, declaim a recitative that includes a memory of 'Alma's theme' from the first movement. But there is no consolation to be found in it. Other memories and half-memories come back in fragments: a portentous rhythm beaten out by the timpani, cries of the woodwind from the scherzo, a horn attempting to reprise more of the 'Alma' theme, funereal march rhythms, and a solemn wind chorale. Eventually the introduction climaxes in a glorious blaze of C major, but the trumpets quickly darken it to C minor, as in a familiar recurrent moment from the first movement. Another fierce march begins, which soon accelerates to a fast pace. The march is frenetic in character, at moments like a hero battling, sometimes desperate, sometimes seeming to be mocked. The alternation of major and minor harmonies continues to recur. The horns introduce a more solemn element that quickly turns mock-heroic. The march quietens to give way to a second theme in D major. Led again by a horn fanfare, this has a positively relaxed and cheerful character. As the march rhythm reasserts itself, it seems as if some sort of triumph might be possible after all. But once more the harmonies darken, the march comes to a halt, and the violins renew their passionate recitative from the introduction.

The distant cowbells return. We seem lost for a moment, and it is not clear where this music is heading. Once more the march rhythms start up in the bass, with cries from the woodwind. Again heroic elements build up, with violin and horn lines competing for supremacy (a battle that could be Richard Strauss as easily as Mahler). Through a long struggle full of twisting harmonies, we arrive at a mighty climax in D major, at which the first stroke of the hammer falls. The expected cadence veers off in another direction, and the climax is frustrated. Further striving and struggling ensues, with moments that seem to grasp at serenity, others that seem heading towards triumph, with the familiar elements – march, chorale, woodwind cries, major-to-minor chords – jostling with each other in waves of increasing frenzy. One such wave breaks into a moment of grandeur, with sweeping string lines that reach a point of calm and build up again. Once more we reach a climax that is topped by a second hammer blow. A mighty brass chorale combines with frantic string scales, and with stately dotted rhythms a moment of resolution is reached.

Suddenly we are back at the sweeping chord of the introduction, and the violins renew their plaintive recitative. All the elements of the introduction are revisited, including the cowbells. An oboe and a solo violin gracefully revive memories of the 'Alma' theme; there is another huge build-up, and once more we glimpse the possibility of triumph. But as the frenzy increases there seems no way out of the struggle. Eventually we reach a steadier build-up, and a fade to a moment of calm. For the last time, the strange first chord of the introduction sounds, and the violins lament. The ominous timpani rhythm leads into a dark chorale of trombones. We hear a desultory call from the horns, and halting fragments of the march rhythm in the bass. There is an almighty crash of A minor from the whole orchestra, the timpani thunder out the ominous rhythm one more time, and the symphony lapses into oblivion with a final pizzicato and stroke of the bass drum.

SYMPHONY NO. 7
Duration: 70–80 minutes
Langsam (Adagio) – Allegro risoluto, ma non troppo
Nachtmusik I: Allegro moderato. Molto moderato (Andante)

Scherzo: Schattenhaft. Fliessend aber nicht zu schnell (Shadowy. Flowing but not too
    fast). Trio
Nachtmusik II: Andante amoroso
Rondo-Finale

Mahler began his Seventh Symphony in the happy summer of 1904 in his composing cottage
in the woods on the shores of the Wörthersee. He composed the two 'Night-music' movements while he was still working on the finale of the Sixth Symphony, and it would be difficult
to imagine a greater contrast with the tragic turbulence of that movement. The following
summer, back at the lake, he could not find the inspiration for the other movements. He
remembered this blockage in a letter to Alma several years later: 'For two weeks I tortured
myself into a state of depression, as you may surely remember – until I escaped to the
Dolomites! There the same struggle, until finally I gave up and went home, convinced that
this summer had been wasted.' On his return, he stepped into the ferry to cross the Wörthersee:
'With the first stroke of the oars, the theme (or rather the rhythm and style) of the introduction to the first movement came to me – and within four weeks the first, third and fifth
movements were ready!'[22]

In the summer of 1908, Mahler and Alma were back in Europe after a season in New York,
where Mahler was music director of the Metropolitan Opera. Mahler had resigned from the
Vienna Court Opera in March 1907, and with the deterioration of his relations with Vienna
and the Viennese, a premiere of his new symphony in Vienna would certainly have presented
an opportunity for a hostile and anti-Semitic reaction. Mahler did not think that New York,
with its deeply conservative audience, was ready for it either. So the premiere took place in
Prague, during a festival marking the sixtieth year of the reign of Franz Josef as Emperor of
the Austro-Hungarian Empire.

Mahler's Seventh Symphony took longer to be widely appreciated than any of his other
symphonies. But one musician who was enthusiastic about it from the start was Arnold
Schoenberg. He heard the symphony performed in 1909 in Vienna, and wrote to Mahler
comparing his reaction to previous encounters with Mahler's symphonies: 'I had less sense
than previously of something extraordinarily sensational, something that immediately excites
and works one up ... What I felt this time was a perfect repose based on artistic harmony ...
an attraction such as guides the planets, letting them travel along their own courses, influencing these, yes, but so evenly, so entirely according to plan, that there is no longer any
jarring, any violence ... From minute to minute I felt happier and warmer. And it did not let
go of me for a single moment.'[23]

The first movement opens quietly in B minor with a solemn, persistent dotted-rhythm
figure. This has the suggestion of a funeral march so familiar in Mahler's symphonies. A tenor
horn calls (a military band instrument known in Britain as the baritone horn, with a full tone
like a bolder French horn). When we know that the atmosphere of this opening came to
Mahler as he was being rowed across the lake, it is possible to imagine the regular lapping of
water, and a ship's horn sounding from the distance out of the darkness. The uncertain
harmony of the opening chord suggests a continuation rather than a beginning, rather like
the openings of several of Beethoven's late quartets. A slightly faster, more overtly march-like
theme starts in the woodwind, accelerates to a climax and falls away. The tenor horn call reappears. There is another acceleration and build-up. This time there is no going back. Against

the driving rhythms, four horns declaim a new call (which had already been buried in an earlier climax) and, with its thrusting rhythms, this becomes the first theme of the Allegro, in the key of E minor.

A struggle develops between march-like and more lyrical forces. Eventually the music calms, and the violins play a quieter second theme in a warm C major. This is a typically Mahlerian long, searching melodic line, full of impassioned rising and falling and great leaps, but to be played 'Mit grossem Schwung' (With great verve). This builds, and suddenly snaps back into the march rhythm. Further struggles with the march elements slow to the funereal tempo of the introduction, the tenor horn call returns, and the first section of the movement comes to a close with a delicate reminiscence of the passionate second theme played out against the march rhythms.

The pace increases again, thrusting us into the central development of the movement. At first, this takes the sort of journey we have come to expect in the middle of Mahler's long movements, with battles between the different march elements developing enormous energy. But suddenly there is a halt, and the violins play a quiet, high, sustained tremolo. Trumpets very delicately play fanfares, and flutes and oboes call almost like birds. Below, a chorus of violas and cellos, with lower woodwind, play solemn phrases extracted, in slow motion, from a march theme in the introduction. A solo violin muses on the passionate violin melody, in counterpoint with the Allegro march on cor anglais. The high violin tremolo returns, and again trumpets sound distant fanfares, there are calls in the woodwind, sometimes quasi-miltary, sometimes more bird-like (there are echoes of the nature sounds of the First Symphony here), with the fragments of solemn march chorale below. There is a sweep of a harp, and the violins recall their passionate melody, now in B major, against a tapestry of woodwind trills and calls. It rises ecstatically, and plunges down. There is sudden quiet, and the melody resolves not into B major, but into B minor, with the funeral rhythm of the introduction.

The reprise is under way, more troubled than before, with a trombone aggressively challenging the tenor horn. When the Allegro march arrives, it is similarly fiercer than before, and the succeeding struggle is wilder. The passionate violin melody begins from a higher level of tension than the first time, and soon increases in intensity to snap back into the march rhythm. The triumph of the march is in no doubt from now on, but its energy and brightness are never free of darker twists in the harmony, and the final burst of B major seems more like a defiant gesture than a real resolution.

The first 'Night-music' movement opens with horns calling to each other. Mahler specifies that the first calls forte and the second answers piano and muted, as if from the distance. Elements of the horn calls are then drawn into a complex web of sound, first with oboe, clarinet, and cor anglais, then with the other woodwind. The intricate tripletatterns and trills evoke the sounds of birds and insects, another of Mahler's 'nature-scapes', and the calls themselves evoke memories of the tenor horn at the start of the first movement. The chattering reaches a climax and falls away. The horn call becomes a more formal melody on a trio of horns, incorporating a major-minor shift with an almost blues-like effect. From it emerges a cheeky bass line in march rhythm, and a characteristically mocking passage develops. This too fades away, and a sweeping cello melody follows.

At first, the march rhythm seems to have been put aside, but it soon resurfaces. This time the mood is not so much mocking as straightforwardly cheerful. This too fades away, and the horns renew their call and answer. As they do so, the sound of cowbells is heard in the distance, evoking, as in the Sixth Symphony, flocks grazing in the alpine meadows. The trio of horns renews its melody, now muted, and with more ambivalent cheerfulness than before, the continuation comes to rest.

This is the central point of the movement. Until now, it has been predominantly in C major and C minor. Now there is a change of key, and, accompanied by trills, a pair of oboes sings a melancholy theme in F minor. Even this soon acquires a touch of marching jauntiness, and another complex web of sound develops, with the rising horn call building up, and falling away as a chord slides from C major to minor. This is another echo of the Sixth Symphony, and rather as there, this harmonic shift was already foreshadowed in the melody of the horn trio. Over a quiet, but distinctly military, march rhythm, two solo cellos take up the oboes' melancholy duet. The mood is once again ambivalent, the melancholy tune supported by the rather jaunty march rhythm. It too fades away, and a touch on the harp signals another change of key.

There is a moment of uncertainty, but then the horn-trio melody reasserts itself back in C major, with woodwind, brass, and strings all joining in. This develops in new directions, once more with touches of mockery, mostly good-humoured, but sometimes acerbic. There is another fade, another corner is turned, and in a warm A flat major a new melody emerges in the violins, with descant in flute, oboe, and clarinet. This develops a real swing, brightened by glockenspiel, and with the cowbells onstage, as if the herd has wandered on from the wings. There is another fade, and a muted horn renews its call. Delicately the march restarts, its fragility buffeted by sudden accents. Over a drone, the 'natural' web of triplet patterns and trills returns, and the movement ends with a final major-minor chord, preserving to the end its ambivalence of mood.

At the centre of the symphony is a scherzo, the shortest of the five movements, which Mahler instructs should be 'shadowy' in character. As to tempo, he writes that it should be 'flowing but not too fast', adding, 'the opening bars somewhat hesitant'. Indeed, this movement is full of hesitation, fragmentation, and unexpected arrivals and changes of direction. Almost nothing is allowed to develop without being knocked off course. Everything is indeed 'shadowy', like things momentarily glimpsed or imagined in darkness or semi-darkness – another kind of 'Nachtmusik'. The movement opens with alternations between timpani and pizzicato cellos and basses, which gradually form a regular rhythm as low wind instruments join in. The effect is reminiscent of the opening of the scherzo in the Fourth Symphony, but here the effect is stranger and darker. The pairs of notes alternate between two pitches only a semitone apart, the timpani's A and the pizzicato B flat. And when the muted violins play a theme in D minor over the rhythm, it is a wispy, fleeting line, a ghost of a melody. It soon gathers intensity, climaxing in a weird downward glissando, more like a frightened wail than the nostalgic glissando Mahler so often uses. As the wispy line becomes a continuous element, a more sustained, sighing melody arises in the woodwind (again reminiscent of the Fourth Symphony).

The violins play a bolder tune in D major, as if attempting to jolt the music into a more familiar *Ländler*. But its yodelling leaps soon stretch and acquire alarming glissandi, culminating in another wailing downward slide. The music is again reduced to a bass rhythm with strange intervals, and the wispy theme develops in new directions. The violins repeat their D major *Ländler*, with more vigour than before, and this time they manage to force their way through to a more or less coherent melody. The wispy figure returns for a few bars, and then a pair of oboes sings a more relaxed melody, like a slow waltz, in dialogue with a solo violin.

This is the middle section of the movement, the trio (Mahler gives it the traditional label). Although it is in D major, there are many minor harmonies along the way, giving a typically Mahlerian melancholy, which is enhanced by accelerations and hesitations in the tempo. The second strain of the melody moves to solo viola and then to all the first violins, and the harmonies become yet darker. This 'valse triste' gathers alarming strength, until cellos, bolstered by horns, summon a final heart-felt outburst to bring the trio to an end.

The wispy, fleeting element and the sighing woodwind melody from the scherzo return. But this is only a false start, which soon collapses. It is only after further hesitation that the reprise gets under way. The scherzo is even more troubled than before, each moment of coherent melody accompanied and interrupted by forceful stabs and aggressive counter-phrases. The dark interventions of the tuba give a particularly bottom-heavy weight to the texture. The scherzo undergoes disintegration, and its disjointed phrases end with a mournful bassoon and a final thwack on the timpani.

The second 'Night music' has the character of a serenade, with solo violin, guitar, and mandolin. Finally, Mahler achieves a sense of real relaxation, with music of loving charm. From time to time, however, it rises to ecstatic climaxes, one of which (towards the end of the movement) quotes the famous Adagietto from the Fifth Symphony. This raises the possibility that Alma Mahler, to whom Mahler seems to have dedicated the Adagietto, might also have (at least partly) been the inspiration for this Nachtmusik. Its ending is almost Mendelssohnian in its delicacy – this could be Midsummer Night.

Mahler called his fifth movement a 'Rondo-Finale', as if it were cast in a classical mould. Indeed, it does have the basic feature of a rondo, in that material from the beginning recurs from time to time, interspersed with other material. But it is so wild and extravagant that all one can do is submit to its seventeen or so minutes, as if one were a surfer riding a great wave. If the finale was suggested by the idea of 'the full light of day', as Mahler said, it comes not with the dawn one might expect, but with immediate impact, like the shock of sudden awakening, full of boisterousness and confusion.

The movement is full of references and parodies, most prominently Wagner's *Die Meistersinger*. What reason might Mahler have had for putting a parody of that opera at the focus of this finale? *Die Meistersinger*, which evokes the ceremonial traditions of medieval Germany, ends with the triumph of the unorthodox genius, and a plea for tradition to keep its heart open to the inspiration of the new (e.g. Wagner himself). Mahler, the genius who faced such conflict and discrimination amid his triumphs, takes Wagner's music and makes a jolly romp of it, as if to say that real life is not that simple, and all one can do is laugh and fight.

Timpani and trumpets open the movement with military splendour. This is followed by a grand brass chorale (the first suggestion of *Die Meistersinger*), which is soon accompanied by frantic woodwind scales. The opening paragraph ends with the strings taking on the sort of frenzy usually reserved for the end of a symphony. But now a wind chord slides from C major to A flat major, and a gentler episode ensues. With trilling woodwind and a jog-trot rhythm, we glimpse the imagined pastoral world of the Fourth Symphony. Back in C major, a burst of Wagnerian chorale intervenes, soon coming to an abrupt end. A dancing figure starts up in the violins, in counterpoint with a broader melody in the woodwind (there is a hint of Wagner's 'Dance of the Apprentices' from *Die Meistersinger* here). This develops for a moment, and then comes back to the opening brass chorale. The dancing elements soon return, and lead on to a new episode in A minor, with delicate dotted rhythms. We round a corner straight into a brief reprise of the brass chorale, and immediately into a sturdier version of the 'Dance of the Apprentices', and on to a delicate renewal of the pastoral style, with trills and sentimental glissandi.

The 'Apprentices', the chorale, and the drum rhythm fight it out. There is a build-up to a huge climax, which collapses back to the pastoral trills, moving from key to key, and developing energy again. This fades away, and the brass enter with a grand reprise of their opening material, now in B flat. Another halt, another new element: with the assistance of bass drum and cymbals, the 'Apprentices' music has metamorphosed into 'Turkish' music, as if from Mozart's *Die Entführung aus dem Serail*. This is subjected to a moment of counterpoint and a burst of energy, and with a sly, pseudo-baroque trill on the trumpet changes back into a courtly dance, with ironic glissando. It undergoes a bizarre series of transformations and changes of pace, from the grand to the cheeky, the ferocious, and back to the delicate. From time to time, fragments of a familiar theme surface – the march from the first movement. Eventually, the opening trumpet call comes bursting in once more, back in its home key of C major. The final build-up is upon us, crowned by bells and the first-movement march. Its climax sounds dangerously like Mahler mocking the great climax of his own Second Symphony. But before we can be too sure, there is a return to the frenzy that ended the introduction to the movement, a questioning brass chord fades, and the symphony concludes with a final thwack from full orchestra.

SYMPHONY NO. 8, 'SYMPHONY OF A THOUSAND'
Duration: 75–85 minutes

Part I: Hymn: *Veni Creator Spiritus*
Part II: Final Scene from Goethe's *Faust*

Having suffered a prolonged attack of composer's block in the summer of 1905, Mahler had planned to start the summer holiday of 1906 revising the orchestration of his Seventh Symphony, without any thoughts of composition. But, as Mahler later recalled, 'On the first morning of my holiday, I went up to my cottage in Maiernigg firmly resolved to be lazy (I needed it so badly) and gather my strength. As soon as I entered my old, familiar workroom, the *Spiritus creator* took hold of me, shaking me and scourging me for eight weeks, until the main part was finished.'[24] He jotted down a plan for a four-movement work, beginning with 'Veni Creator', and ending with 'Creation through Love, Hymn'. On the back of the sheet he wrote the first theme for 'Veni Creator', with its bold opening interval of a falling fourth.

In its final version, the symphony consists of two parts: I. *Veni Creator Spiritus*, II. The final scene from Goethe's *Faust*. It is a work for voices and orchestra throughout. Mahler's biographer, Richard Specht, remembered a conversation with Mahler in August 1906, when he had just completed the basic work of composing the Eighth Symphony. Mahler told him that he had long intended to set the final scene of Goethe's *Faust*, but had put it to the back of his mind. Then, 'I happened upon an old book. I opened it to the hymn *Veni Creator Spiritus*, and immediately the whole thing was there: not only the first theme, but the entire first movement.' The work of composing went, for once, very quickly: 'It was a vision that struck me like lightning, the whole immediately stood before me; I had only to write it down as if it were being dictated to me.' He described it as 'a completely new symphony, something that makes all my other works seem like mere preludes'.[25] Not only was the process of composition unusually easy, but the premiere in Munich in September 1910 was also a triumph. There were two performances, and the large audience included Richard Strauss, Webern, Saint-Saëns, and Thomas Mann. It was the last of his symphonies whose premiere Mahler conducted himself: he was to die eight months later.

The debate about what Mahler really meant by his Seventh Symphony, particularly its finale, continues. There is no such debate about the Eighth Symphony, because Mahler's intentions are absolutely clear. It is a setting of two texts, separated by nine centuries, but united by the themes of divine creation, divine love, and human redemption through love (both divine and human).

Goethe's *Faust* explores the legend of the frustrated scholar who strikes a pact with Mephistopheles. The devil will give him the knowledge and power he seeks in this life, in exchange for Faust's soul in the afterlife. Part I of Goethe's play is dominated by the tragedy of the young girl Gretchen, whom, with Mephistopheles help, Faust seduces and makes pregnant. This is the part of the play that Liszt used as the basis of his *Faust Symphony*. Mahler sets the final scene from Part II. Full of remorse, Faust has been saved from his pact with Mephistopheles. The soul of Gretchen invokes the intercession of the Virgin Mary, and angels bear Faust's soul to heaven.

The text for Part I of Mahler's symphony is the ninth-century 'Veni Creator Spiritus', a Latin hymn for Pentecost, the festival that celebrates the coming of the Holy Spirit to Jesus's disciples after his death and resurrection. Mahler would have been familiar with earlier settings of the hymn, including the original Gregorian chant, its adaptation by Luther as the hymn 'Komm Gott Schöpfer', and J. S. Bach's settings of Luther's hymn. And, as we shall see, certain words in the text struck him as crucial in creating a link with *Faust*.

The work is scored for two four-part choirs, children's chorus, and two groups of four soloists. This multi-voice writing pays homage to the great choral composers of the past – the Gabrielis, Heinrich Schütz, J. S. Bach, Handel. But this influence also comes via the great Germans of the nineteenth century, Beethoven in his Choral Symphony and *Missa Solemnis*, and Mendelssohn in his Hymn of Praise. Like Beethoven, Mahler places huge demands on his singers, and, as in the *Missa Solemnis*, it takes choirs and soloists of immense stamina to do the work full justice. Even with the finest singers, the listener cannot hope to hear all the words in performance; Mahler could be accused of sacrificing clarity to impact, but it is the impact that matters.

The first section, *Veni Creator Spiritus*, is a vigorous twenty-three minutes or so (Part II is more than twice as long). It is like a giant motet with orchestra, though it also adheres somewhat to the traditional form of a symphony's first movement, with its opening material developed in the middle of the movement, and a reprise at the end. It has passages of fugal and more loosely contrapuntal writing, as in Beethoven and Mendelssohn, but the overwhelming impression is of a movement constructed from great slabs, like some vision of an ancient monument. It opens with a chord of E flat major on full organ, to which the choirs respond with a joyous shout, 'Veni, Veni creator spiritus' ('Come, come creator spirit'). This recurs at the end of the first section, and again at the end of the whole movement.

The overall structure of the movement, and its relation to the words, can be summarized as follows:

Veni creator spiritus (Come creator spirit, choirs *ff*): first theme
Imple superna gratia (Fill with supreme grace, soloists *p*, choirs join): second main theme
Veni creator spiritus (choirs and soloists *ff*): reprise brings first section to an end
(Instrumental passage): start of development
Infirma nostri corporis (The weakness of our bodies, choirs *p* with violin solo, soloists joining)
(Instrumental passage)
Infirma nostri corporis (soloists *f*)
Accende lumen sensibus (Inflame light into our senses, choirs and soloists *ff*)
Veni creator spiritus (choirs and soloists *ff*): reprise
Gloria Patri Domino (Glory to the Father, our Lord, soloists *ff*, then choirs *ff*)

Apart from the sheer impact of the massed voices, the most striking, and most touching, moment comes quietly at the heart of the movement. After a brief instrumental passage, the soloists repeat the words, 'Infirma nostri corporis/Virtute firmans perpeti' ('The weakness of our bodies/Fortify with perpetual strength'). Out of this emerges the next pair of lines: 'Accende lumen sensibus/Infunde amorem cordibus' ('Inflame light into our senses/Pour love into our hearts'). Mahler places the word 'lumen' (light) first, and at the end of the phrase, the tenor is left softly reiterating 'lumen, lumen'. At the final rehearsal for the premiere, Mahler told Webern, 'The passage *Accende lumen sensibus* forms the bridge to the final section of Faust. This spot is the cardinal point of the entire work.' The violins rise quietly to an ecstatic high note, and the soloists tenderly finish the line. Then the horns enter decisively, and the couplet is repeated, with the words in their original order, by the full chorus, fortissimo, with maximum energy, and joined by the children's choir.

The forward thrust through the next verses is unstoppable, the most sustained power of the entire movement, including a complex fugue (Mahler, like Beethoven, uses fugue not as an academic exercise, but to build momentum). The great wave of sound culminates in a return to 'Veni creator spiritus' and a reprise of the opening stanzas. From their climax follows a blazing instrumental passage, with full organ and brass, to introduce the final verse, 'Gloria Patri Domino' ('Glory to the Father, our Lord'). This soon takes over the theme of 'Veni creator', with timpani beating out its opening bars. The movement ends with the full glory of all the forces together, as mighty scales well up from below. This is, surely, a moment of direct homage to Beethoven: a very similar (though quiet) combination of sustained chords with rising scales below ends the Credo of his *Missa Solemnis*.

Part II is a setting of the final scene of *Faust*. In the previous scene, Faust's soul has been rescued at the moment of death from Mephistopheles by angels. The final scene is set in a landscape of 'Mountain gorges, forest, rock, wilderness'.

Prelude
Mahler evokes the awesome scene. Below a violin tremolo, cellos and basses play pizzicato, and above, woodwind answer. The first of these elements, with its falling interval, refers back to the first theme of 'Veni creator spiritus', and the second, with its smooth line, echoes the second theme. These two elements, in turn, supply material for the whole of the rest of the symphony. The atmosphere is spare, bleak, opening into moments of solemn chorale, with horns, bassons, and contrabassoon. A sudden outburst brings a surge of anguish, with more than a hint of Wagner's *Parsifal*. After a moment of quiet, the violins burst out again with a

more agitated surge, which develops further. Soon this is interrupted by a quiet procession of woodwind, a solemn moment of brass chorale, and with a return to the bass pizzicato and woodwind above, we arrive at the first chorus entry.

Choir and Echo: Holy anchorites (hermits), scattered about the ravines, form two choruses (tenors and basses). They sing of the forests, rocks, and caves of Love's holy hermitage, in a quiet, staccato version of the second theme from the Prelude. After a moment of deep chorale, they are joined by altos.

Pater Ecstaticus (baritone, the first of the anchorite fathers, who 'floats in the air'): He sings of the eternal fire of rapture, the shattering power of Love, developing the two themes into an impassioned line.

Pater Profundus (bass, 'in the depths'): He sings, at greater length, of the powerful forces of nature – raging waters, purifying lightning – that are Love's heralds. His soul struggles to free itself, and he prays to God for light.

Choir of Angels (sopranos and altos): Soaring in the high atmosphere, they bear Faust's immortal soul. Faust has been redeemed by striving, and by the power of Love. They are soon joined in joyful counterpoint by:

Choir of Blessed Boys: They accept the soul with holy fervour.

Choir of Younger Angels: In a gentler passage, they sing that victory over devils, even over Mephistopheles himself, was won by strewing roses from the hands of loving and holy penitent women. A brief orchestral interlude leads to:

More Perfect Angels (sopranos, altos, and tenors, later joined by basses and alto solo): There is still an earthly element, from which the soul can be separated only by the power of eternal Love. This sombre passage is accompanied by elaborate viola and violin solos, which refer back to the violin solo in Part I at the words 'Infirma nostri corporis' ('The weakness of our bodies'). The atmosphere warms at the entry of the alto solo, singing of the power of Eternal Love to release the soul.

The Younger Angels (sopranos and altos): They see a host of holy boys who feast their eyes on the spring and flowers of the celestial world. This dancing passage accelerates until the choir is joined by:

Doctor Marianus (tenor, an anchorite father, dedicated to the Virgin Mary, 'in the highest, purest sphere'): He sees the Queen of Heaven in a circle of stars. She has the power to command us to courage or to peace through the sacred joy of Love. Doctor Marianus is accompanied for a time by the Choir of Blessed Boys, who sing that the soul of Faust already grows tall and fair in this holy life. Doctor Marianus continues with an extended solo. This culminates in a solemn moment where he praises the Virgin Mary, accompanied softly by basses and then the whole of the first choir. Horns enter with the first theme, the atmosphere opens out, and after a silence the violins begin a very slow, quiet melody of profoundest calm, accompanied by horn chords and harp arpeggios. This is the emotional turning point of the scene, where the possibility of redemption begins to become reality. Softly, the second choir enters, then the first, appealing to the matchless powers of the Virgin Mary: All those who have succumbed to lusts of the flesh can turn to her, but the way is steep and treacherous.

The music builds, until, at a climax, a solo soprano (second soprano) enters. This is Una Poenitentium (The One Penitent), who in life was Gretchen, and she joins the choir in their pleas to the Virgin.

Further appeals to the Virgin follow, from three more penitents: Magna Peccatrix (the Great Sinner) (soprano), the woman who anointed Jesus' feet with her tears and ointment, and dried them with her hair; Mulier Samaritana (alto), the Samaritan woman at the well, whom Jesus asked for water; and Maria Aegyptiaca (alto), St Mary of Egypt, who, having led a dissolute life, was struck by remorse at the Church of the Holy Sepulchre in Jerusalem, and lived the rest of her days as a hermit in the desert.

The three penitents each sing a solo, in which they tell of the experience that brought them to penitence. Then they sing together, first in elaborate counterpoint, then in sweet harmony, praying to the Virgin for her grace.

Una Poenitentium (Gretchen) re-enters. She joyfully receives her former love, now purified, and asks for the Virgin's grace. The Blessed Boys sing with her:

Doch dieser hat gelernt,	His soul increases in strength,
Er wird uns lehren.	And he will teach us.

Una Poenitentium (Gretchen) sings:

Sieh, wie er jedem Erden bande	His soul strips away each husk
Der alten Hülle sich entrafft,	Of his former self,
Und aus ätherischem Gewande	Until he steps forth
Hervortritt erste Jugendkraft!	In the strength of youth!

At the moment where she sings of the celestial vestments in which the soul of Faust will be clothed, she evokes the very first phrase of the *Veni Creator Spiritus*.

Now, as horns and trumpets solemnly intone, there is a quiet, celestial shimmering (played by the celesta). The voice of Mater Gloriosa (The Glorious Mother, that is, The Virgin Mary) is heard, very softly (sometimes offstage in performance). In her only utterance, Mary invites Gretchen to ascend to higher spheres. The soul of Faust will be drawn upwards with her.

Doctor Marianus and the chorus urge them on:

Blicket auf, zum Retterblick,	Look up to the redeeming gaze,
Alle reuig Zarten ...	All penitent, tender souls ...
Jungfrau, Mutter, Königin,	Virgin, Mother, Queen,
Göttin, bleibe gnädig!	Goddess, be ever merciful!

There is a first choral climax, a long moment of quiet orchestral interlude, and once again the combined choruses ('Chorus Mysticus') enter pianissimo:

Alles Vergängliche	All transitory things
Ist nur ein Gleichnis;	Are nothing but allegory;
Das Unzulängliche,	The unattainable
Hier wird's Ereignis;	Is now achieved;
Das Unbeschreibliche,	The inexpressible
Hier ist's getan;	Is accomplished;
Das Ewig-Weibliche	The Eternal Feminine
Zieht uns hinan.	Draws us upward.

The great climax is slow in coming, overwhelming when it arrives. And in a mighty orchestral postlude, it seems as if the medieval hymn and the heavenly vision of Goethe have become united, in a final, massive statement of the eternal beyond this transitory life.

SYMPHONY NO. 9
Duration: 70–90 minutes

Andante comodo

Im tempo eines gemächlichen Ländlers. Etwas täppisch und sehr derb (In the tempo of a
  leisurely *Ländler*. Somewhat clumsy and very coarse)

Rondo-Burleske: Allegro assai. Sehr trotzig (Very defiant)

Adagio. Sehr langsam und noch zurückhalten (Very slow and held back even more)

After the death of his four-year-old daughter Maria in 1907, Mahler could not bear the associations of the villa on the shores of the Wörthersee. So he and Alma acquired a new summer retreat, at Toblach (Dobbiaco) in the mountains in South Tyrol on the border between Austria and Italy. The death of Maria was not the only blow of this period. There had also been Mahler's diagnosis of heart disease, and his bitter resignation from his post at the Vienna Court Opera. But he wrote to Bruno Walter early in 1909 that the crisis of the preceding eighteen months had provoked in him a strange sort of rebirth: 'sometimes I wouldn't be surprised to find myself in a new body (like Faust in the final scene). I am thirstier for life than ever, and find the "habit of existence" sweeter than ever'.[26] It was in his new retreat in the mountains that Mahler composed *Das Lied von der Erde* in 1908, the Ninth Symphony in 1909, and the incomplete Tenth Symphony in 1910. He drafted most of the Ninth Symphony over the summer of 1909, dating the completion of the finale as 2 September.

Of these works, *Das Lied von der Erde* is most obviously valedictory, culminating as it does in the long and heart-rending 'Der Abschied' ('The Farewell'). But, wordlessly, the Ninth Symphony encompasses a similar emotional world, from bittersweet clinging to life to final resignation. Alban Berg wrote about the first movement of the symphony that it is 'the expression of an unheard-of love for this earth, the longing to live in peace upon it, still to enjoy Nature to her profoundest depths – until death comes. For it comes irresistibly. This entire movement is based on a presentiment of death'.[27] Bruno Walter made a direct link with *Das Lied von der Erde*, writing that 'the title of the last song, "Der Abschied", could stand at the head of the Ninth'.[28]

It was while Mahler was drafting the symphony that he wrote a letter to Alma in which he highlights the importance of a human being's life above his or her works:

> The 'works' of this person or that ... are, properly speaking, the ephemeral and mortal part of him; but what a man makes of himself – what he becomes through the untiring effort to live and to be – that is permanent. This is the meaning, my dear Almschi, of all that has happened to you, of all that has been laid on you as a necessity of the growth of the soul and the forging of the personality. And you still have a long life before you ... What we leave behind us is only the husk, the shell, no more, properly speaking, than our bodies are. The Meistersinger, the Ninth, Faust – all of them are only the discarded husk! No more, properly speaking, than our bodies are! I don't of course mean that artistic creation is superfluous. It is a necessity of man for growth and joy, which again is a question of health and creative energy. – But what actual need is there of notes?[29]

This was in reply to a letter from Alma – perhaps she had expressed frustration at having produced so little music herself because of the demands of life since being married to Mahler. But Mahler's letter is striking, expressing the tension between art and life, engagement and detachment, and, ultimately, life and death. Many of these tensions are to be found in the Ninth Symphony, which was the last work that Mahler completed.

The symphony was premiered in Vienna in June 1912, a year after Mahler's death, by the Vienna Philharmonic Orchestra conducted by Mahler's faithful disciple and champion, Bruno Walter. Twenty-six years later, in January 1938, Walter and the Vienna Philharmonic performed the symphony at another concert in Vienna, with many of the players who had taken part in the premiere. This was the last time Mahler was played by the orchestra before Hitler's troops marched into Vienna and Walter and the Jewish members of the orchestra were forced to flee. The concert was recorded, and, like the recording of *Das Lied von der Erde* from two years earlier, it provides an intense and moving experience.

The first movement is an expansive, gradually unfolding Andante lasting 25–30 minutes. It is broadly in the shape of a conventional first movement – exposition, development, reprise, and coda – but Mahler's characteristic way of developing and varying his material as he goes makes this a very fluid experience.

The movement opens quietly and hesitantly. Cellos and a horn alternately reiterate a single note, A. The harp plays a solemn pattern of four notes, like the tolling of bells, which is to become a motto through the movement. A muted horn calls. Violins enter with a timid melody in D major – not the first violins, as one might expect, but the second violins. It is only after several bars that the first violins join them. This is one striking feature of this movement: the prominent, separate role of the second violins, and the duet, often of equals, that they sing together with the firsts. The melody is anchored on chords of D major, almost like a drone. Its first phrase consists simply of two notes, falling in a sigh. It recalls the similar sigh that Mahler set to the word 'Ewig' (always) in 'Der Abschied', the last song of *Das Lied von der Erde*, composed the previous year. Mahler himself wrote 'Leb' wohl' (farewell) over this sigh in the draft of his symphony, suggesting also a reference to the opening of Beethoven's Piano Sonata No. 26 ('Les Adieux'), with its motif of three falling notes. Each of the phrases that follows is short-breathed, an upbeat and a downbeat, a breath in and a breath out. But their shape changes as the melody rises, the in-breath sometimes falling, sometimes rising, sometimes consisting of two or three notes. When the first violins join in, the melody rises further, with wider leaps. This process of evolution is, on a larger scale, what happens throughout this movement. And this subtle way of developing material is matched by subtlety of orchestration and counterpoint. As the second violins begin, a horn plays a counterpoint. When the first violins join in duet, the cellos are also in counterpoint, playing another version of the theme. The gradually evolving theme comes to rest, but then there is a turn to the minor. The violin melody becomes more agitated, rising higher. The trumpets play a sort of drooping fanfare, strangely anxious, and at the first climax of the movement, the music breaks back to D major, with the violins, still in duet, determinedly striving to regain the serenity of their theme. Slowly the mood calms and the music settles.

Once more there is a switch from D major to minor, and an increase in agitation. The violin melody starts as it did at the earlier D minor entry, but now it moves on more passionately, and is joined by the anxious trumpet fanfare. A complex web of strings, brass, and woodwind builds up, the violin line culminates in a moment of heroic declaration (whose shape is derived from the trumpets' drooping fanfare), and the full brass respond with blazing calls. The first section of the movement is over.

A timpani roll quietens, linking to the development section of the movement. This begins with a reminder of the very opening, with the hesitant rhythm in the horns, and the harp's tolling pattern tapped out by the timpani. The tone becomes threatening as muted horns play the sighing motif, and trombones take over the tolling pattern. Violins and then cellos try to develop the principal theme, but always there are threats in the background, and this passage has a sense of hopelessness. The harp sets up a persistent rhythm, and the strings very quietly and sorrowfully edge their way back to the theme, together with a horn. For a moment the old serenity is remembered. But sinister trumpet calls (which seem to be quoting Mahler's First Symphony) provoke another twist of agitation, which builds up to a full-blown crisis. As the elements battle with each other for supremacy, the violins again manage to climax with their heroic phrase. But this time there are no responding trumpet calls, and the music collapses darkly. Once more the violins attack their agitated line, by now in the remote key of B flat minor. This leads to another struggling build-up and another collapse. Trombones darkly intone the anxious trumpet fanfare, horns turn the sighs into a lament. For some time, there seems no way forward. But from uncertain trills and fragments emerges a violin solo, and something of the serenity is recalled. The music builds up, at first with a spirit of determined optimism, climaxing with the trumpets playing the violins' heroic phrase. But the moment of triumph breaks in disarray. Trombones fiercely play the opening rhythm, timpani pound out the tolling pattern, and a mood of despair has taken over. But still elements of the old world persist, and eventually the violins, once more in duet, find their way back to the opening theme, at last back in D minor, and the reprise is under way. But the old serenity cannot be recaptured: there is a sense of clinging on to its memory as the duet struggles its way forward. Compared with the opening section of the movement, these last minutes suggest a sort of disintegration. There are moments of wistful violin solo, intimate woodwind passages, memories of warmth, but always with a bitter tinge. The ending, with its solitary flute and violin solo, and the reiterated sighs, bring strongly to mind that other farewell, the last movement of Mahler's *Das Lied von der Erde*.

The second movement returns to Mahler's favourite *Ländler*, but with a heavy application of irony. It begins with a slow *Ländler* in C major, introduced by staccato bassoons with violas, answered by a trio of two clarinets and bass clarinet. The mood is mock-rustic. The violins enter 'heavily', with savage trills on horns and the clarinet trio trying to interrupt. The dance moves to the basses and cellos, lightly for a moment, then turns savage again. At least three versions of the *Ländler* seem to be trying to establish themselves, as if a drunk is assailed by conflicting images of the dancers. After this first dance fades away, a second dance bursts on the scene, faster and in E major. At first this might seem jovial, but its increasingly acerbic harmonies, the thumping of the timpani, and the wild leaps of its melody show that it is just a continuation of the nightmare in a different guise. At its height, trombones and low strings give it an elephantine character. Then the opening staccato of the first *Ländler* appears in the horns, without breaking tempo, as if trapped in the ongoing rush.

Eventually the mayhem subsides, giving way to a third *Ländler* in F major, slower than the first. This is the gentlest music in the movement so far, and its melody is made up of the falling sighs that began the first movement. The woodwind recall the staccato beginning of the first *Ländler*, then the sighing theme returns. This leads into another burst of the fast second dance, now more relentlessly jovial than before, though the splashes of cymbals and sinister sliding harmonies in the horns add to the sense that it is still part of some sort of terrible dream. There is another sudden braking of the tempo, and the slow third *Ländler* returns.

There is a rare moment of genuine tenderness, and suddenly we are back at the beginning of the first *Ländler*, with the staccato bassoons. Its constituent parts have been reassembled, so that we never know who is going to play what – a fragile piccolo, bold horns, sturdy cellos, solo violin, each suddenly stepping forward and equally suddenly giving way to someone else. The tempo increases, and the second dance is back, developing a brutal swagger, with a desperate high violin line. Over this the woodwind play a rather banal tune, which is taken up by trumpet and violins (a combination of the banal with the aggressive that particularly appealed to Shostakovich). The tempo increases, the music becomes wilder, and in a bizarre collision of elements a trumpet recalls the sighing phrases, to be cut off by an abrupt return to the tempo and music of the opening *Ländler*. But now it is as if nobody can quite remember how anything fits together any more. The rest of the movement gives the impression of trying to find a way out, revisiting all the relevant fragments, until piccolo and contrabassoon, four octaves apart, spot a chink in the door, and slip out.

If the second movement has moments of wildness, the savage abandon of the third movement is on a different level. Mahler calls it a Rondo-Burleske, but if there is humour in it, it is of a dark and bitter kind (again, this is just the sort of Mahler that most inspired Shostakovich). The marking is 'very defiant', and it is like one of Mahler's habitual marches wound up to a frenetic level of energy. But, in all the welter of competing elements and contrapuntal elaboration, it is not at all clear whether the 'defiant' marcher is in control, or is being whipped along by some demonic force. It opens with abrupt fragments hurled at us, tiny motifs out of which almost the entire outer sections of the movement are constructed. The abruptness rarely settles into anything truly coherent: if the music is continuous, it is because there is so much going on at once, with the thematic elements in simultaneous layers, at times almost like a fugue, at other times more like a battle. Brass and strings, in particular, seem to be at war with each other.

A few minutes into the first section of the movement, there is a passage where the tension lightens somewhat, becoming almost playful. But the savagery soon returns. This first section climaxes in a sudden crash of cymbals. Out of this emerges what we least expect: a trumpet plays a serene curl of melody, a slow-motion version of one of the fragments that opened the movement. Out of this Mahler builds a sustained moment of sanctuary, almost as if meditating on a hymn (he seems extraordinarily close to Charles Ives at this moment). The vision is interrupted by a forceful chord and a harp glissando. Clarinets cheekily play the hymn-like melody double speed. For a time there are attempts to hang on to the moment of serenity, but eventually the savage march breaks through. The reprise is yet more violent than before, and in the final bars it accelerates to destruction.

The violence of the third movement usually provokes a stunned silence after it has finished. Out of the silence, the violins embark on a great lament in D flat major to begin the finale. Its introductory bars contain two elements taken from the serene centre of the third movement, the trumpet's curl of melody, and a falling phrase (which surely relates to 'Leb' wohl', or 'Lebe wohl'). These are the two elements from which the Adagio is built. It is, after the nightmarish complexity of the third movement, music of passionate simplicity. The lines, predominantly played by the strings, weave around each other with Mahler's accustomed counterpoint, and with twisting harmonies full of the elusive search for resolution. But the same ingredients keep on recurring, the curling phrase often in one voice while the descending line, together with yearning leaps, is in another. Several times this lament returns. Between each paragraph, there are episodes of spare, otherworldly music. The first, brief suggestion of this is a solitary bassoon, with bleak rising phrases in a minor key. But this is cut off by another impassioned outburst, more anguished than before, which rises to a climax and suddenly evaporates. Contrabassoon and cellos take up the rising phrases, which are combined in ethereal, high, pianissimo counterpoint with the other elements. The next, yet more impassioned, statement of the lament takes longer to reach a climax, and to die away.

Again the music quietly moves into the minor, and over delicate harp patterns, a cor anglais introduces another mournful melody, in counterpoint with oboe, flute, and clarinet, with variants of the falling, rising, and curling elements combining. The strings return with their lament for a last time, twice rising to climaxes. The final climax evaporates, the music becoming insubstantial and bleak. From this emerges a final, *ppp* violin line, curling and rising, then falling, like an echo of earlier climaxes. Drawing together the familiar elements, Mahler creates at this moment a specific memory, from his song cycle on the death of children, *Kindertotenlieder*. The fourth song poignantly expresses the hope that the children have simply gone ahead, on a walk into the hills, and that we will meet them again up there in the sunshine. It is the last line that Mahler quotes in the dying moments of this symphony: 'Im Sonnenschein, der Tag ist schön/Auf jenen Höh'n' ('In the sunlight, the day is beautiful/On those heights'.) Although Mahler never said so, it seems very likely that he meant this as a memory, if only a private one, of his four-year-old daughter, who had died two years previously. And perhaps, as the quotation arises organically from the earlier elements in the movement, the whole movement was at least partly inspired by her.

SYMPHONY NO. 10
Duration (edition by Deryck Cooke, 1976): approx. 75 minutes

Adagio
Scherzo
Purgatorio: Allegretto moderato
[Scherzo]
Finale: Einleitung (Introduction [Adagio]) – Allegro moderato

Mahler drafted most of his Tenth Symphony in the summer of 1910, at a time of great turmoil in his life. He had discovered that his wife Alma had started an affair with the young architect Walter Gropius, while taking a cure at the spa of Tobelbad. Urged by Gropius to leave Mahler, Alma decided to remain with her husband, while continuing the affair with Gropius in secret (she married him after Mahler's death). Torn between despair and his love for Alma, Mahler consulted Sigmund Freud (see introduction). Something of the state of his mind can be deduced from the highly emotional annotations that Mahler wrote in his draft of the symphony, some of them addressed directly to Alma. The couple returned to the United States for Mahler's last season as conductor of the Metropolitan Opera and New York Philharmonic. He collapsed after a concert in February, and was diagnosed with streptococcal endocarditis (inflammation of the heart), for which there was then no cure. With Mahler terminally ill, they returned to Vienna in April, where he died on 18 May 1911.

At the time of Mahler's death, the five-movement symphony was drafted in short score, mostly on four staves. He had begun the work of orchestrating the first movement, and, to a more limited extent, the second and third movements. But some passages of composition were only sketched out, and the later movements had only occasional indications of orchestration. Nevertheless, the surviving material does amount to at least a draft of a complete symphony. There have been several attempts to complete it, beginning with the composer Ernst Krenek, who was asked to try to make sense of it by Alma Mahler in 1924. But it was not until the 1960s that a workable version of the whole symphony was achieved, by Deryck Cooke. This began as a BBC project, which was broadcast in 1960. Alma Mahler, then in her eighties, was advised by Bruno Walter not to allow further performances. But when she heard a recording of the broadcast, she wrote to Cooke to say that she was so moved by it that she gave him permission to have his completion performed worldwide. After Alma's death in 1964, her daughter Anna gave Cooke access to further sketches for the symphony that had not been published, and, together with composers Colin and David Matthews, Cooke revised his edition, and this revision was performed in 1972 and published in 1976.

There have been other completions since Cooke's death that year, but his version remains the best known. Some conductors continue to perform the first movement on its own, arguing (as Bruno Walter did) that it is the only movement complete enough in Mahler's autograph to indicate his intentions reliably. Cooke described his work as 'a performing version of the draft of the Tenth Symphony', not a completion, knowing that Mahler would certainly have revised his draft extensively if he had lived. As such, it gives an insight into Mahler's thinking at this stage of composition, as well as being a satisfying experience in itself.

The symphony begins with a fragile, unaccompanied viola line (marked Andante), uncertain in its key, full of searching chromatic twists and leaps (there is more than a hint of the Prelude to Wagner's *Tristan* at the opening). With sudden warmth, the full strings enter with an Adagio theme in a clear F sharp major, in which huge leaps, up and down, predominate. The continuing twists of harmony create a characteristic mood of intense yearning, enriched by trombone chords and the horn's falling countermelody, both clearly indicated in Mahler's autograph score. The texture lightens, with the violins in duet and pizzicato below. The Andante unaccompanied viola line returns, followed again by the full strings Adagio in F sharp major. This time the yearning is yet more intense and prolonged, culminating in anguished, high violins, which descend. Again the texture lightens a little, but with more struggle in the harmonies than before. Then once more the unaccompanied viola line returns.

This time, there is no return to the F sharp major theme. Instead, woodwind and strings, including a solo violin, embark on further exploration of the lighter, second group of ideas, with the various elements thrown around and combined in a characteristically complex, nervous kind of chamber music. The violins introduce references to the passionate Adagio theme from time to time, and eventually this tugs the music back to F sharp major and to the theme itself. Again there is a return to the lighter material, which goes through further exploration before another return to the F sharp major theme (it is unusual for Mahler to punctuate a long movement with such persistent returns to the home key). This time, the great theme is halted in mid-flow, giving way to a ghostly, pianissimo passage for violins in duet. Mahler marks this 'somewhat hesitating', and it is as if the music has suddenly lost its way. But as the duet peters out, the full orchestra enters with a mighty chord of A flat minor. This leads to a huge climax on a violently dissonant chord, pierced by a sustained high trumpet. Out of this crisis emerges a further return to the F sharp major theme, but its strength seems spent. The rest of the movement revisits all the earlier elements, as if trying to find its way back. There are moments of serenity, but as if half-remembered, and the movement ends with a high, quiet chord of F sharp major.

Mahler's draft of the second movement is mysteriously labelled 'Scherzo – Finale', but he also numbers it clearly as the second movement, so he probably changed his mind about its position in the symphony. The metre is continually shifting between four, three, and even five beats to the bar. Mahler's scherzi are often nervous and edgy, but this fluctuating metre, together with the shifting harmonies, gives the music a particularly unstable character, like an attempt to dance on hot coals. The orchestration is less completely indicated than in the first movement, but the characteristic prominence of the horns is very clear in the draft. The first section of the scherzo is on a large scale. It includes a lighter, more dancing middle passage, in which woodwind are dominant. After a brief return to the opening, the music moves without a break into a contrasting section (trio). This is a haven of stability after the disruptive metre of the scherzo. It is in a straightforward three-time, and in E major (though it ventures into various keys as it proceeds). Its warm, *Ländler*-like melody reaches upwards in a clear reminiscence of the great Adagio theme from the first movement. The opening music returns. Then there is an attempt to recapture the warm stability of the trio. But this time it is elusive, and hesitant. After more of the scherzo music, there is a further, nostalgic attempt to get back to the trio, before the scherzo returns to bring the movement to a surprisingly triumphant conclusion.

Mahler heads the short third movement, 'Purgatorio' (originally 'Purgatorio oder Inferno', but he crossed out 'Inferno'). Its muted perpetuum mobile accompaniment over a persistent bass note evokes memories of a song from *Des Knaben Wunderhorn*, 'The Earthly Life', a tragic tale of a child whose mother makes him wait for food until he dies (Mahler had made similar use of another song, 'St Anthony of Padua's Sermon to the Fishes', in the Second Symphony). There is a sense of something ghostly and inescapable. In the middle of the movement there are phrases of increasing intensity and longing. Here Mahler has written a series of annotations in his manuscript: 'Death! Transfiguration!', 'Mercy!', 'Oh God! Oh God! Why hast thou forsaken me!', and finally, 'Thy will be done!' There is a strong sense that this music is connected to Mahler's personal anguish – though he would scarcely have intended these annotations to become public, and this fleeting movement conveys only an echo of such powerful emotions. The ghostly perpetuum mobile returns, and ends inconclusively in darkness.

From the elusive to the devilish. At the front of his short score of the fourth movement, Mahler wrote:

The devil joins me in the dance
Madness, seize me, the accursed one!
Destroy me
That I may forget that I exist
That I may cease to be
That I for . . .

Like the second movement, this is a kind of scherzo, but quite different in character. The earlier scherzo was nervous and unstable in metre. This movement, even without Mahler's annotation, might well seem like a 'Totentanz' (*danse macabre*), with its lumbering three-time rhythm that veers from the violent to the seductive. There are episodes of yearning, which include world-weary phrases from the first song of *Das Lied von der Erde*, 'Das Trinklied vom Jammer der Erde' ('The Drinking Song of the Earth's Lamentation'). And there are also frequent moments of waltzing, sometimes specifically labelled 'Tanz' in the autograph, for which Cooke's version convincingly brings in a solo violin (as in Saint-Saëns's *Danse macabre* – the association of a violin with the devil goes back many centuries). There are very few indications of instrumentation in Mahler's short score, and the overall impression is of a movement that begins powerfully and then fragments. Fragmentation is one of Mahler's most characteristic processes, but it is impossible to know to what extent the rather loose trajectory of the latter part of this movement represents finished thinking, and how much Mahler would have revised and tightened it.

The end of the fourth movement and the beginning of the finale are linked by muffled drum strokes. According to Alma Mahler, this sombre passage was inspired by the funeral procession of a New York fireman, whose heroism had been reported in the newspapers. The cortège halted underneath their hotel window, there was a roll of muffled drums and a silence, and then it moved on. 'I looked anxiously at Mahler's window. But he too was leaning out and his face was streaming with tears.'[30] At the end of the fourth movement, Mahler scrawled lines, presumably addressed to Alma, which perhaps refer to this:

You alone know what it means . . .
Farewell my lyre!
Farewell!
Farewell!
Farewell!

After three shorter movements, the finale is on the scale of the first movement, lasting over twenty minutes. Of this, a third is a slow introduction, whose opening and closing passages are punctuated by the impressive thud of the muffled drum. A low instrument (Cooke specifies tuba, but others have suggested contrabassoon or solo double bass) climbs dolefully between each drum stroke, and horn calls answer. Over soft strings, a flute (specified by Mahler) rises in a lament. It is as if the fragile viola line with which the symphony began has found its voice. The line is taken up by the violins in the first moment of serenity in the whole work. The climax increases in poignancy, the harmonies twisting beneath it, and the opening drum, tuba, and horn calls (now on trumpet) return.

The horn calls set the Allegro moderato going, a characteristically brisk march, delicate at first, with a mixture of rising and falling phrases and distinct references to the *Purgatorio* movement. Soon the violins sing an impassioned version of the falling phrase (which emphasizes its origin in the opening viola line), and this becomes an important element. Some of the serenity of the introduction builds up again, and then the brisk march returns. But it is soon interrupted by a return to the crisis of the first movement, with an anguished dissonance pierced by a sustained high trumpet. This collapses into a moment of uncertainty, before a return to the serene music of the introduction, which rises high over a sustained bass note, and back to the key of F sharp major on which the first movement was based. 'All the violins', Mahler specifies as the melody intensifies, recalling (whether coincidentally or not) the love music from Richard Strauss's *Ein Heldenleben*. Mahler's symphony, and his entire life of composition, end in what sounds like a final declaration of love, in a mood of ecstatic, hard-won serenity. A few bars before the end, he writes, 'To live for you! To die for you!' There is one last leap, like a sob, and a last descending line, beneath which is a final annotation: 'Almschi!'

BOHUSLAV MARTINŮ
(1890–1959)

Martinů spent the first twelve years of his life living at the top of a church tower in the town of Polička, in the hills of eastern Bohemia. His father, a cobbler, was also the Town Keeper, with the duty of keeping watch for fires – a disastrous fire had destroyed much of the town in 1845. So the entire Martinů family, including three children, lived in a room over the bell-chamber and clock. Because Bohuslav was a frail child, until the age of six when he started school he rarely descended to ground level. It is tempting to imagine that the proximity of the bells (which his father rang for services) and the heavily ticking clock exerted a strong influence on his musical development. Certainly, his music is full of insistently repeated phrases and obsessive rhythms. But Martinů himself remembered most of all the view from the tower: 'On one side there's the lake, on the other the cemetery and village stretching further and further into the distance. To the north there's flat, unwooded country, and below, the town itself, everything in miniature, with tiny houses and tiny people moving, creating a kind of shifing pattern.'[1] 'Shifting patterns' is a very good phrase to describe much of Martinů's music.

Like his great Czech predecessor, Smetana, Martinů was in his thirties before he found his feet as a composer and began to attract international attention. He studied at the Prague Conservatoire, joined the Czech Philharmonic Orchestra as a violinist, and was already composing substantial works during the First World War. At the end of the war, he studied for a time with Josef Suk. But it was his move to Paris in 1923 that gave him the stimulation that he needed. He soaked up ideas avidly: he studied with Albert Roussel, was attracted by the neo-classical ideas of Stravinsky, was captivated by the rhythmic energy of jazz, and was influenced by Bartók's powerful absorption of Eastern European folk music.

Over his lifetime Martinů composed a huge quantity of music in many different styles and forms. After emigrating to the United States in 1941, encouraged by its well-funded orchestras, he took to composing symphonies. But his most powerful and distinctive orchestral work dates from the difficult years before his emigration, as Europe descended towards chaos and war.

DOUBLE CONCERTO, FOR TWO STRING ORCHESTRAS, PIANO, AND TIMPANI (H. 271)
Duration: approx. 22 minutes

Poco allegro
Largo
Allegro

Martinů's Double Concerto was commissioned by Paul Sacher, conductor of the Basel Chamber Orchestra. He began composing it in the summer of 1938 in France. Then in July, as always, he went to Prague for the annual Sokol festival, a great celebration of gymnastics and dance (which had inspired Janáček's Sinfonietta in 1926). Czechoslovakia was rearming against the threat of Hitler, following the German annexation (*Anschluss*) of Austria in March. Nevertheless, travelling back through Germany on his return to Paris, Martinů reported, 'Nothing about the journey through Germany indicated that we were so close to the tragedy which was to hit our country within a few months and later the whole world. Here and there we saw an aeroplane or a soldier guarding the track which led to the frontier.'[2]

In September, Martinů and his wife accepted an invitation from Sacher to spend some time in Switzerland. In an article published in a Czech newspaper in New York during 1942, Martinů wrote:

> We lived in the mountains, almost completely isolated from the outside world – in a coun-
> tryside full of sunlight and the song of birds – while somewhere in Europe the great tragedy
> that was approaching the frontiers of my homeland was being prepared. With anguish we
> listened every day to the news bulletins on the radio, trying to find encouragement and
> hope that did not come. The clouds were quickly gathering and becoming steadily more
> threatening. During this time I was at work on the Double Concerto; but all my thoughts
> and longings were constantly with my endangered country, where only a few months
> before I had been filled with such hope and joy by the unforgettable moments of the Sokol
> Festival. Now, in the lonely mountainous countryside, echoed the sound of my piano, filled
> with sorrow and pain but also with hope. Its notes sang out the feelings and sufferings of
> all those of our people who, far away from their home, were gazing into the distance and
> seeing the approaching catastrophe ... It is a composition written under terrible circum-
> stances, but the emotions it voices are not those of despair but rather of revolt, courage, and
> unshakable faith in the future.[3]

There is another circumstance that might well have nurtured the emotional intensity of the Double Concerto. Martinů's visit to Czechoslovakia was spent in the company of his pupil, Vítězslava Kaprálová, and her family, while his wife remained behind in Paris. Kaprálová, a composer and conductor, was a woman twenty-five years younger than Martinů, and their affair developed to the point where Martinů was ready to leave his wife and move back to Czechoslovakia to join her. It was the outbreak of war that prevented this. It is easy to imagine that the personal turmoil that Martinů was undergoing, as he wrestled with the decision whether or not to leave his wife for Kaprálová, might also have contributed to this work's mood of intense struggle. In the end, Martinů and his wife were to leave together for America early in 1941. By this time Kaprálová had been briefly married to someone else before dying from tuberculosis at the age of twenty-five.

Sacher's orchestra, after the first play-through, at first refused to rehearse the Double Concerto further, saying it was too complicated. But Sacher insisted that it was a masterpiece, and they worked on it over a period of six months before the premiere.

The Double Concerto is one of several works that Martinů composed in the 1930s that were inspired by his love of the baroque *concerto grosso*. But the way he uses the two orches-tras is scarcely 'neo-baroque' in any meaningful sense. Only occasionally does Martinů have them answering each other, as in the contrasts between solo group and orchestra of the Corelli and Vivaldi *concerti grossi*. He uses the two orchestras to create a complex web of sound, in which they often tug against each other – an effect that is particularly powerful in concert performance. The clearest influences in Martinů are often Stravinsky and jazz. But here there is a strong flavour of Bartók, whose Music for Strings, Percussion and Celesta had been commissioned by Paul Sacher two years previously. Bartók was steeped in the pungent melodic and harmonic ingredients of Hungarian traditional music, enabling him to develop a dark and combative musical language. The Czech Martinů seems in this concerto to be glancing with more than usual concentration towards Bartók, and particularly towards Bartók's ways of combining strings with piano and timpani (though the piano is often prominent in Martinů's orchestral scores). The Double Concerto is a challenging work, for both musicians and listeners, but the more one listens to it, the more transparent the language becomes, and the clearer the elements that create a work of coherent power.

Under a rapid violin tremolo, the lower strings begin an agitated theme full of offbeat rhythms. This provides most of the material for the first movement, and for much of the finale. It opens more or less in D minor, but the alternations between A flat and A natural create a sense of uncertainty that will be one of the most persistent features as the movement develops. The theme builds and transforms itself over the powerful opening paragraph as the two orchestras confront each other, urged on by piano and timpani, culminating in a fiercely reiterated dissonance and a powerful chord of D minor – the first consonant harmony we have heard. From this the theme re-emerges as a more sustained fugue subject. Other voices join in, creating a dense web of sound that then relaxes as the piano plays mysterious chords. Nervous touches of the theme combine with haunting, sustained lines, building to rich chords and subsiding mysteriously.

Then a new tiptoeing variant of the theme begins, pointed by dissonances in the piano and with a sustained viola line below. As the two orchestras answer each other, phrase by phrase, the piano breaks into agitated semiquaver patterns, and these move into the cellos while fragments of the theme persist in the violins. The semiquavers become more and more dominant, propelling the whole orchestra on in a fearsome acceleration. Suddenly we arrive at a unison D, and we are into the reprise of the opening. All the energy and determination of the movement seems concentrated in these last two minutes, with the offbeat theme, rapid semiquavers, dense chords, and plaintive melodic lines leading on until they burst out in a snatched final chord of D major.

The slow movement opens with tragic chords, and a repeated motif of rising notes. Then the two orchestras echo each other in a continuous exchange of the rising motif, beginning slowly, then accelerating and becoming more complex, reaching a massive climax and falling away. The rising motif continues darkly in the bass, and then the piano enters, playing the rising motif with a bleak counterpoint above. The motif returns briefly to the cellos and basses, and the piano enters again. It elaborates on the motif, and develops a powerful cadenza-like paragraph, full of the percussive alternation of notes characteristic of the Hungarian cimbalom, with its two hammers.

Over the piano's low, dissonant shuddering, the orchestras enter powerfully with the rising motif. The piano sets up a solemnly treading bass, and over this the strings play the motif in counterpoint, at single and double speed, in two-note patterns that conflict with the three-note pattern of the treading bass. This is reminiscent of eerie passages in Bartók, particularly the Music for Strings, Percussion and Celesta. The music twice rises to powerful climaxes, and the second time the orchestras revert to echoing each other, as if trying to tear the music apart. This culminates in a return to the great cry of the opening chords. The music collapses, as if exhausted. The motif persists in dark counterpoint, and the movement ends with a desolate exchange of phrases between piano and strings, the clash of harmonies resolving only on the last, peaceful chord.

With a jolt, the finale knocks us back to the nervous energy of the first movement. Not only that, it returns to the motifs that made up the opening theme; but it is now as if they have been smashed with a hammer, so that they spread out over a wider span of notes. The violent impression is heightened by accompanying trills and rapidly repeated notes, like a swarm of angry wasps. Eventually, the trills move to the piano, over which the two orchestras exchange nervous little phrases of the rapidly repeated notes. The strings take up the trills, and the piano plays a spiky version of the main motif with new cross-rhythms. There is an angry build-up, and the spiky version of the motif is played pizzicato, alternating with the piano.

The violins introduce a more sustained line against the staccato piano. This too builds up, the sonorities become heavier and denser, and the music becomes unstoppable in its power and momentum. Just as it seems that it could not become any more intense, it accelerates to high speed, in a passage of relentless destructive force. Then, as the energy begins to fade, the sombre motif of rising notes from the slow movement enters in the bass and piano. The upper strings take this theme and weave it into a solemn fugal passage. Gradually it increases in intensity, over the heavy tread of the piano and timpani, until it becomes a hymn of enormous elegiac power. At its height, it breaks back into the tragic opening chords of the slow movement. The final chord fades, suspended in the air, as piano and pizzicato cellos and basses tap out a last, emphatic bass.

FELIX MENDELSSOHN
(1809–47)

Mendelssohn, like Mozart, was an immensely gifted child prodigy, both as a pianist and as a composer, and in his teens he was already writing music of great character and maturity. Unlike Mozart, he was highly successful internationally during his lifetime – indeed, he was the first German Jewish composer to achieve this. His elder sister, Fanny, was also a highly gifted composer (as was Mozart's sister), and if she had been a man she might have achieved similar fame. But that is another story.

As well as composing, Felix Mendelssohn was prominent as conductor of the Leipzig Gewandhaus Orchestra (he was one of the first to use a baton), he founded the Leipzig Conservatoire, led the revival of the music of J. S. Bach, notably his St Matthew Passion, and in England was entertained by Queen Victoria and Prince Albert. Mendelssohn was a man of great energy and charm, and the composer Hubert Parry wrote that 'He was too full of occupation to brood over the troubles of the world, or to think much of the tragedies and the stern workings of fate; but all moods must have their expression in art, and those which were natural for him to express he dealt with in the most delicate and artistic way, and the results have afforded healthy and refined pleasure to an immense number of people.'[1]

Reading between the lines, it seems that Parry is saying that Mendelssohn lacked depth and seriousness. This is a benign version of a view that was encouraged soon after Mendelssohn's death by critics with their own agenda, led by Wagner. Playing the anti-Semitic card, Wagner argued that Mendelssohn could not be regarded as the great leader of German musical culture that he had aspired to be in his lifetime, because, as a Jew, he had merely 'borrowed' German culture. This was part of Wagner's ruthless campaign to remove competitors to his own position at the centre of German musical life, and does not deserve to be taken seriously. It is, however, true that much of Mendelssohn's music, particularly that written for the drawing room, has an easy charm and fluency that has gone in and out of fashion: one generation's 'healthy and refined' is another generation's 'comfortable and unchallenging'. But much of his music has *joie de vivre* and a haunting beauty, and he certainly did not deserve the century of comparative neglect that he suffered until the late twentieth century. Several of his greatest works were written for orchestra.

Concertos

PIANO CONCERTO NO. 1 IN G MINOR, OP. 25
Duration: approx. 20 minutes

Molto allegro con fuoco
Andante
Presto – Molto allegro e vivace

Mendelssohn composed two piano concertos, but No. 1 is by far the more successful and more frequently performed of the two. He played the premiere in Munich, on 17 October 1831. By happy coincidence, one of the most vivid letters to his family dates from eleven days before, when he was already in Munich preparing for the concert. At the age of twenty-two, he had a brilliant career, was feted wherever he went, and was thoroughly enjoying life:

> It is a glorious feeling to wake in the morning and to know that you are going to write the score of a grand allegro with all manner of instruments, and assorted oboes and trumpets, while bright weather holds out the hope of a cheering walk in the afternoon ... I scarcely know a place where I feel as comfortable and domesticated as here. Above all it is very pleasant to be surrounded by cheerful faces, and to know your own is the same, and to be acquainted with everyone you meet in the street.
>
> I am now preparing for my concert, so my hands are pretty full; every moment my acquaintances interrupt me in my work, the lovely weather tempts me to go out, and the copyists, in turn, force me to stay home.[2]

Mendelssohn had arrived in Munich after spending several months in Italy, and it was there that he had conceived the idea of a piano concerto. But it was during his stay in Munich that he composed most of it, and this was no doubt why the copyists were keeping him at work completing the orchestral score, so that they could prepare the orchestral parts.

The concerto opens with the boldest and most confident of gestures. Over just a few bars, the orchestra builds a dramatic sense of expectation. Then in bursts the soloist with pounding double octaves and scintillating decoration, like an operatic hero rushing in to declare his triumph. The clearest precedent for this fantasia-like opening was Weber's *Konzertstück*. Weber's opening, however, is quiet, and it was Mendelssohn who set the model for later concertos in which the pianist breaks in dramatically and expounds the first theme (as in Schumann, Grieg, Tchaikovsky, and others).

The orchestra continues the triumphant mood, the piano accompanies and then emerges with more octaves. Eventually, the music calms to a lyrical second theme. It searches for a moment and then settles in D flat major, an utter contrast to the ferocious G minor of the opening, with a warm, even sentimental melody. At the end of the theme, the music breaks back to the minor with more octaves. These settle into rippling patterns as clarinets and bassoons take up the second theme. The rippling evolves into brilliant and scintillating passages, mostly delicate, but then building to a reminder of the forceful elements. From time to time fragments of the lyrical second theme are brought in. This brief passage of development reaches a quiet moment, and the orchestra reprises its quasi-operatic opening. But instead of the piano breaking in with its octaves, as before, it muses further on the second theme. Gradually another brilliant passage develops, culminating in powerful octaves again. An orchestral tutti seems to be preparing for a conventional ending. But instead, a trumpet call announces a change of key, the music calms, and with a moment of meditative cadenza, the piano leads straight into the slow movement (this fantasia-like link again echoes Weber's *Konzertstück*).

The piano searches for a moment in a minor key. Then the cellos take the piano's phrase and extend it into the first half of a hymn-like theme in E major. This is a particularly beautiful example of Mendelssohn's skill in orchestration: the cellos are supported not just by a conventional accompaniment of strings, or strings doubled by wind. Mendelssohn carefully interleaves one horn, one bassoon, and violas, with a second group of cellos playing the bass line – a combination that is both rich and delicate. The piano repeats and embellishes the line, and continues it into a second half. Here the leaps stretch higher, and the line becomes more florid. Under a piano trill the cellos enter with a repeat of the first phrase. It winds beautifully towards a conclusion, but then takes a new direction, with runs and arpeggios – a style of elaboration that again looks back to Weber, and that Mendelssohn's young contemporary, Chopin, was exploiting in his two piano concertos at much the same time. As the fantasy reaches a climax and drifts upwards, the cellos return with the theme, now without the wind, while the piano decorates above. The piano then takes the melody in simple octaves – a touching moment after all the decoration – and the movement winds to a peaceful close.

Trumpets and horns renew their call from the end of the first movement, and an expectant orchestral passage brings in a torrent of piano arpeggios. This leads into the main rondo theme of the movement, a straightforward, square-cut tune, whose dotted rhythms have a family resemblance to those in the first theme of the first movement. The rather blunt opening of the theme gives way to a lighter, more scherzo-like continuation – by far the most charming part of the theme – and this leads on to a second theme with yet more glittering patterns for the first episode of the rondo. Many brilliant semiquavers later, the rondo theme returns on full orchestra. At the end of this tutti there is a change of key, and more exploration of the glittering second theme.

All of a sudden, the piano reintroduces the rondo theme, quietly and coyly, and explores its sentimental possibilities for a moment. But soon it returns to the second theme, with delightful interplay between piano and orchestra. A burst of double octaves brings in the rondo theme on the orchestra again. As the piano continues, a little phrase gradually changes into a quote from the second theme of the first movement, and there is a moment of quiet reflection, and a pause. But this is not the time for deep thought, and with a bang we are into a volley of octaves (in the left hand) and brilliant semiquaver patterns (in the right). Soon the irresistible second theme breaks through again, and with a final burst of double octaves and arpeggios the concerto comes to a thunderous conclusion.

VIOLIN CONCERTO (NO. 2) IN E MINOR, OP. 64

Allegro molto appassionato –

Andante

Allegretto non troppo – Allegro molto vivace

In July 1844 Mendelssohn was back in Germany, relaxing in the countryside after a brilliant and hectic visit to England. He wrote to his sister Fanny, 'my family improves every day in health, and I lie under apple-trees and huge oaks ... the contrast of these days with my stay in England is so remarkable that I can never forget it. There, not one hour was free *three weeks* ahead, and here, all the bright, livelong days are free, without a single occupation of any kind, except what I choose for myself (and those alone are fruitful and worthwhile) and what is not done today is done tomorrow, and there is leisure for everything ... Further, I sketch busily, and compose still more busily.'[3]

Twenty-two years earlier, the thirteen-year-old Mendelssohn had composed a violin concerto for his violin teacher, Eduard Rietz, in a confident and at times eloquent style. That remained unpublished until Yehudi Menuhin prepared an edition in 1951. The work that everyone knows simply as 'Mendelssohn's Violin Concerto' is this later masterpiece from 1844. It was during this summer that Mendelssohn wrote it for his violinist friend Ferdinand David, and its character combines just the qualities of relaxation, concentration, and spontaneity that Mendelssohn describes in that letter. But, as with Mozart, the very qualities that make it sound so natural also make it extremely difficult to play, and particularly to start. The soloist has to launch straight in, without any opening orchestral introduction, playing a sweeping melody elegantly, and faultlessly in tune, and this leads without a break into rushing figurations and tricky passagework, with octaves extending high up on the instrument. Of other well-known violin concertos, only the Sibelius concerto has quite such a challenging start (and that must surely have been modelled on Mendelssohn's).

After the violin's first solo, the full orchestra repeats the opening theme and leads it onward – a very effective reversal of the usual way of starting a concerto. The soloist enters again, developing a little tailpiece with which the orchestra finished its tutti. Further brilliant passages eventually calm, and while the violinist holds a pianissimo low G, the woodwind sing the beautiful second theme. It sounds like a chorus of four clarinets. But in fact the two clarinets have been joined by two flutes, beautifully balanced and interwoven to create a light and mellifluous texture. This is an example of Mendelssohn's subtle skill as an orchestrator, to rival the 'four horns' effect in the third movement of his 'Italian' Symphony.

There are other places in the movement where Mendelssohn does something quite unusual, but with such subtlety that it seems entirely natural. The join between the opening section of the movement and the development is seamless. A climax is reached, at which the soloist forcefully repeats the opening phrase of the concerto, high up. After a descent, the soloist revisits the little 'tailpiece' that occurred at the end of the first orchestral tutti, and it is this that leads on to the development. At first, there is more elaboration from the violinist as the woodwind reiterate the opening phrase, then a quiet passage that builds up to a cadenza. The cadenza usually comes near the end of the movement, but Mendelssohn has placed it in the centre, so that it acts as a link between the development and the reprise (another feature that Sibelius adopted in his concerto). And when we later reach the point where composers usually place the cadenza, Mendelssohn gradually increases the pace, until fortissimo chords clear to reveal a solitary bassoon, holding a sustained B. This shifts up to C, other instruments quietly assemble chords around it, the music settles to a rocking figure in C major, and the slow movement has begun.

The violin unfolds one of Mendelssohn's most beautiful melodies. At each of its climaxes, a chorus of clarinets and bassoons mellifluously take over the accompaniment from the strings. There is a middle section in which the melody continues serenely, but with more agitated figuration below it, both in the solo violin and in the orchestra, as if a breeze has sprung up to propel the sails forwards. The movement winds beautifully to an end. But the violin moves on immediately to a questioning little passage almost like a wistful recitative.

Trumpets, horns, and timpani sound a fanfare, and we have entered the finale. Like the first movement, this sounds deceptively simple in a good performance. But catching the buoyant lightness of the music is extremely difficult – Mendelssohn writes under the opening solo, 'sempre pp e leggiero' ('always pianissimo and light'). When the soloist achieves this, we can hear the delightful relationship between the violin line and the delicate accompanying woodwind. The opening solo eventually gathers power, and culminates in a march-like theme on the orchestra, which is then thrown into the mix as the soloist continues. A little later, a broader melody is brought in by the soloist, while elements of the opening theme accompany underneath. Then, the next time the soloist returns to the opening theme, the strings play the broader theme in counterpoint below. From here, the march theme returns, and the energy increases to the end. The final pages are brilliant, but Mendelssohn never loses the sense of charm and lightness with which the movement began.

THE HEBRIDES (FINGAL'S CAVE) OVERTURE, OP. 26
Duration: approx. 10 minutes

This overture, like the Symphony No. 3, was inspired by a visit to Scotland in the summer of 1829. Mendelssohn was taken by boat to the tiny island of Staffa, where he saw the great cavern of basalt columns known as Fingal's Cave. Keats and Wordsworth wrote poems about it, and Turner painted it, but it was Mendelssohn who created the most potent evocation of the place with what is perhaps his finest single piece of music.

Inspiration is rarely simple, and Mendelssohn had already formed in his mind a Romantic idea of Scotland, based on the novels of Walter Scott and, in this case, the poem Fingal, supposedly by an ancient Scottish bard, Ossian, but actually the work of James Macpherson. Macpherson, drawing on traditional tales and legends, published 'translations' of ancient poems in the 1760s, and their evocative, epic style caught the imagination of a wide readership across Europe. To visit what had become known as 'Fingal's Cave' was a sort of pilgrimage to this idea of Scotland. Mendelssohn had already jotted down ideas for the opening of his overture before seeing the cave, but the grandeur of the site spurred him to work these ideas up into a magnificent piece of music. Immediately after his visit, Mendelssohn sent his family a brief letter that included the opening bars of the overture. He excused himself for the brevity of the letter by saying, 'the best that I have to tell you is described exactly in the above music . . . '[4]

Mendelssohn evokes the sea, waves crashing on the rocks, the sky, by means that one might think obvious, even naive: repeating patterns ebbing and flowing, rising and falling shapes like a great ocean swell, drum rolls, and so on. But his genius (like that of Schubert in his songs) is to create out of this naturalistic material a deeply satisfying musical narrative and structure, which does not depend on knowing the source of the inspiration. The overture opens with a wave-like motif on lower strings and bassoons. This is the most important element, and it changes in character. It soon develops into the first fully fledged melody. Then it forms a murmuring background as the woodwind continue the theme, expanding it upwards. The music moves into a major key, and the second main theme surges up from the deep, in cellos and bassoons, and then moves to the violins. The wave motif becomes sharp-edged and urgent, driving the music to the first fortissimo climax. Trumpet calls signal the end of the first section of the overture.

Mendelssohn now develops his themes, creating vivid new aspects of his seascape. The trumpet calls are followed by woodwind calls, forte over a shimmering pianissimo background – it is easy to imagine these as echoing sounds in the great cave. There is a moment of calm. Then the wave motif becomes light and pointed, and the energy quickly builds to an extended, stormy passage. As it quietens, the opening motif returns in the cellos and violas, and we are into the reprise.

Still Mendelssohn continues to shift the perspectives. The melody rises to a new climax. As it falls away, a high, sustained oboe note sounds above the strings. This is such a simple, evocative touch: it is like that moment at the end of a stormy day, when the ocean and sky have calmed, and the sun breaks through for a few minutes before sinking below the horizon. Over the stillness, the second theme rises, transformed into a tranquil, floating melody on clarinets. Suddenly, the sea awakes again, and the music drives on to one last surge of power. It reaches a climax, and suddenly the power is spent. A clarinet quietly plays the wave motif, and the overture ends with calm restored.

A MIDSUMMER NIGHT'S DREAM: OVERTURE, OP. 21, AND INCIDENTAL MUSIC, OP. 61
OVERTURE, OP. 21

When we think of musical child prodigies, the first name that comes to mind is inevitably Mozart. But unlike Mozart, Mendelssohn had by the age of sixteen already written one of his greatest works, the Octet for strings. According to Mendelssohn's sister, Fanny, the scherzo of the Octet, composed in the autumn of 1825, was inspired by the dream scene from the 'Walpurgis Night' in the first part of Goethe's *Faust*. This is a strange, satirical episode, in which a cast of spirits (including a theologian and a shooting star) perform a play of 'Oberon and Titania's Golden Wedding'. What caught Mendelssohn's imagination was not the satire, but the four lines with which the scene ends:

The flight of clouds and veil of mist
Are lighted from above;
Breeze in the leaves and wind in the reeds –
And everything has vanished.

The following year, the Mendelssohn family moved into a grand house in Berlin with an enormous garden, ideal for the family pastime of plays, charades, and musical entertainments. For Mendelssohn's mother's birthday in March 1826, the children devised a masquerade that featured, among other figures, Titania and Oberon. It was around this time that Mendelssohn became acquainted with Schlegel's German translation of Shakespeare's *A Midsummer Night's Dream*, which had recently been reissued, and he and Fanny had been taken to a performance in Berlin. This inspired Felix to compose his first orchestral masterpiece, the Overture to *A Midsummer Night's Dream*, completed in August 1826. Brother and sister first played the overture to an audience at home on two pianos. The composer Carl Loewe conducted the first public performance at Stettin in February 1827, when Mendelssohn was just eighteen. The overture is not just an astonishing achievement for a teenager. It is also remarkable as having set a trend for concert overtures, that is, overtures that are designed to be played as separate concert pieces, not as the preludes to operas. Mendelssohn himself followed it up with several others, including the famous *Hebrides* Overture. Later in the nineteenth century, the genre was to enlarge, and then evolve into the symphonic poem.

In 1833, Mendelssohn's publisher, Breitkopf and Härtel, asked him for a note about the ideas behind the overture for a performance in Leipzig. Mendelssohn responded by outlining the relationship between the overture and the play in some detail: 'I think it will be enough to remember how the King and Queen of the elves, Oberon and Titania, with all their attendants, continually appear throughout the piece, now here, now there; then comes Prince Theseus of Athens who goes hunting with his wife, then two pairs of fond lovers, who lose and then find each other, and finally a troop of clumsy, coarse tradesmen, who ply their ponderous amusements, and then the elves, who tease everyone – and on this is built the piece. When, at the end, everything has turned out well, and the principal characters leave, fortunate and happy, the elves return, and bless the house, disappearing as morning breaks. So ends the play, and also my overture.' Mendelssohn ended by saying that the audience did not need such a detailed explanation: 'the music can speak quietly for itself, if it is good; and if it is not, then the explanation certainly will not help'.[5]

The overture opens with four quiet chords that evoke an air of mystery. They begin with the gentle sound of two flutes, then the chords expand outwards as the treble moves upwards and the bass moves downwards, adding clarinets, then bassoons and a horn – a chord darkened by a change to the minor – and finally, a major chord on full woodwind, with horns low in the bass and flutes high in the treble. The violins, divided into four parts, enter pianissimo with another minor chord, and this breaks into a quiet, scampering pattern, like the flitting of fairies. Twice it is interrupted by mysterious woodwind chords, and finally the full orchestra bursts in with a joyful new theme. This is presumably the prince and his retinue, and galloping rhythms soon enter the music to suggest the element of hunting. The fairy element has not gone away – towards the end of this passage the scampering pattern is drawn in. As the music quietens, clarinets begin a song-like theme, answered by a tender falling phrase in the violins (presumably the theme of the lovers). Twice it is punctuated by the rhythm of the hunt. The theme builds, and over a stamping bass there is a loud, 'rustic' theme that incorporates the unmistakable 'hee-haw' of a donkey. A brief snatch of the prince's theme rounds off this first section.

The middle section opens with a return to the quiet scampering of the fairies. Mendelssohn now develops this idea, creating a sense of the mystery deepening. It wanders off into new keys, with little touches of woodwind and timpani and sudden horn calls, as if we are being drawn deeper into the forest. The music reaches a point of stillness, with shimmering violin tremolo and delicate pizzicato below, as if our senses are heightened in the darkness. The violins quote the lovers' theme, but now wearily and in the minor. The music comes to a halt, the mysterious opening chords return, and the reprise comes in with the scampering violins. Mendelssohn changes this reprise, as if the dark events in the forest have left lingering effects.

Beneath the scampering are low notes of bassoon, horn, and tuba (ophicleide in the original score), and taps of the timpani. There is no return of the prince's theme at this point, and the music goes straight into the song-like lovers' theme, and on into the 'rustic' theme, and only then the prince's theme.

The overture might well have ended here, but instead Mendelssohn returns one last time to the scampering fairies. They are interrupted by woodwind, which now reach a peaceful resolution. Quietly, the violins remember the prince's theme, and the overture ends, as it began, with the magical four chords. The house has been blessed, the fairies have departed, and dawn is about to break.

INCIDENTAL MUSIC, OP. 61

No. 1 Scherzo
No. 7 Nocturne

Seventeen years after the composition of the overture, Mendelssohn had become one of the principal figures of the German musical establishment as director of the Leipzig Gewandhaus. He was in favour with the new King of Prussia, Friedrich Wilhelm IV, who wanted Mendelssohn to participate in a revived Academy of Arts in Berlin. Although this project came to nothing, Mendelssohn went on to found a Conservatoire in Leipzig. Meanwhile, the king appointed Mendelssohn to the post of Kapellmeister, and commissioned him to write music for theatrical performances at the New Palace in Potsdam. The first of these, in 1841, was Sophocles's *Antigone*, in a version by Ludwig Tieck, for which Mendelssohn composed choruses. The second, in 1843, was Shakespeare's *A Midsummer Night's Dream*, also in a version by Tieck. After the performance at Potsdam, the production moved to a theatre in Berlin, where it was greatly admired.

The claim that Mendelssohn never equalled the music of his youth is greatly exaggerated. It is true that he sometimes wrote music that seems a little glib or sentimental. But the fact that he was still capable of writing music of brilliance and power in his mature years is demonstrated by his incidental music to *A Midsummer Night's Dream*, as it is by the Violin Concerto that followed a year later. The incidental music consists of fourteen numbers, some with voices, others purely instrumental. It begins with the reused overture, which, of course, was not designed as a theatre overture, and is perhaps rather long for the purpose. Mendelssohn then recaptures the freshness of the overture to a remarkable extent in the numbers that follow, particularly in the scherzo and nocturne. He planned the music for Shakespeare's five acts. In the production at Potsdam and Berlin, Tieck compressed the play into three acts, so that the music did not fit quite according to Mendelssohn's plans.

Scherzo
By the time he wrote the scherzo, Mendelssohn had successfully revisited the idea of 'fairy music' in several different works, and this is a marvellously evocative example. The scherzo was planned as an intermezzo between Acts I and II, between the first meeting of the 'mechanicals' and the first entry of Puck, and it is beautifully judged to make that transition. It opens with woodwind, in a light, dancing rhythm that dominates the entire piece. They are answered by the strings. This is an incredibly difficult piece to play, requiring accuracy and lightness of rhythm, and a matching of approach between woodwind (for whom incisiveness is easier

than lightness) and strings (for whom lightness is easier than incisiveness). At first the music is in a minor key, like the fairy music in the overture (and the spirit-inspired scherzo of the Octet). It is as if a minor key is more able than a major key to suggest the element of mystery needed for fairies. But this scherzo is more than just a fairy dance. It contains witty allusions to other elements in the play. As the first paragraph approaches its end, with tricky cross-rhythms, there are sly little accents reminding us of the 'hee-haw' from the overture, and looking forward to Bottom's transformation. They prompt a rather jolly passage (in a major key) that suggests more the dance of the 'mechanicals' than that of fairies. This soon evaporates, in a delicate upward tripping of violins, to bring in a return to the woodwind opening. It develops in a new direction, with dramatic crescendos interspersed with chattering interaction that passes from flute to clarinet and to strings (a fiendishly difficult passage to co-ordinate). The 'rustic' second theme reappears, and is also developed. Clarinets remind us of the opening theme, and after a moment of suspense, another delicate upward tripping takes us to the woodwind reprise. Mendelssohn's imagination takes this in yet new directions, until the theme metamorphoses into a continuous run of notes on the flute – a challenging virtuoso passage. At a final ascent, the opening bars are touched in for one last time, to bring the scherzo to a delicate conclusion.

Nocturne

The nocturne was intended for the end of Act III. After their wild chase through the forest, the two pairs of lovers collapse exhausted on the ground, and fall asleep. Puck squeezes juice into Lysander's eyes, to make him return to his true love. At this point of resolution, Mendelssohn produces one of his most magical scores. A beautiful horn solo is supported by two bassoons – a more delicate version of a horn trio, which enables the solo horn to predominate while playing quietly. When, after a pause, the opening of the melody repeats, the violins enter for the first time with two held notes, pianissimo – the simplest of touches to enhance the magic. Then the violins take the first phrase of the horn melody in a new direction, in a minor key, the agitation suggesting a memory (or a dream) of the turmoil that has brought the lovers to this point. The moment when the agitation settles is particularly beautiful, with a pair of flutes turning a phrase of the melody into a gently rocking accompaniment, as the horn re-enters with its solo. An oboe joins the horn, and the melody twice rises higher than before. After its second climax, there is the most tender of lingerings as the music comes to a peaceful close.

Symphonies

The numbering of Mendelssohn's symphonies is confusing, and does not represent the order in which they were composed. Symphony No. 1 is a charming apprentice work composed when he was fifteen. 'Symphony No. 2' is a symphonic cantata, *Lobgesang* (*Hymn of Praise*). The first real symphony of Mendelssohn's maturity is the one published after his death as No. 5 and known as the 'Reformation'. Mendelssohn intended it to form part of the celebrations in June 1830 of the 300th anniversary of the presentation of the Augsburg Confession, one of the most important documents of the Lutheran Reformation. But the symphony was not completed in time for it to be included in the celebrations in Berlin. Mendelssohn did conduct a performance two years later, but he later declared it to be a work of 'youthful *juvenilia*', and it was not published until 1868. There are many beauties in the first three movements, but it is somewhat let down by its finale, based on Luther's hymn, 'Ein feste Burg' ('A mighty fortress is our God'). In the *Lobgesang* (and in his second piano trio), Mendelssohn used chorales to powerful effect, but his inspiration does not rise quite so high in the 'Reformation' Symphony. After a long period of neglect, however, the work is increasingly performed.

That leaves two acknowledged masterpieces among Mendelssohn's symphonies, Nos 3 and 4, whose published numbering reverses the order of their composition.

SYMPHONY NO. 3 IN A MINOR, OP. 56, 'SCOTTISH'

Duration: approx. 42 minutes

Andante con moto – Allegro un poco agitato

Vivace non troppo

Adagio

Allegro vivacissimo – Allegro maestoso assai

Through the folk ballads published by Herder, the novels of Sir Walter Scott, and the poems of the supposedly ancient bard Ossian (really the work of James Macpherson), Germans of Mendelssohn's generation had learned to think of Scotland as a land of antique mystery. Mendelssohn first conceived the idea of writing a 'Scottish' symphony on his visit to Scotland in 1829. But unlike the *Hebrides* Overture, which was finished the following year, the symphony remained in the back of his mind for more than a decade, and it was not until 1842 that it was first performed. Visiting Britain again, Mendelssohn conducted the London premiere in June that year, and dedicated the symphony to the young Queen Victoria. In his letters, he left a delightful description of his visits to Victoria and Albert, during which the queen sang beautifully and the prince played the organ (little trace of this musical talent survives in their descendants).[6]

The symphony is in the conventional four movements, but played without a break. Like the *Hebrides* Overture, the work is highly evocative but not crudely pictorial. Indeed, of all its changing moods, only that of the Andante introduction is known to have been inspired by a specific scene. In a letter home, Mendelssohn described his visit to Holyrood Palace in Edinburgh in 1829: 'The chapel below is now roofless. Grass and ivy thrive there, and at the broken altar where Mary was crowned Queen of Scotland. Everything is ruined, decayed, and the clear heavens shine in. I think today I have found there the beginning of my "Scottish" Symphony.'[7]

This opening shows Mendelssohn's mastery of orchestration, with a darkly scored wind ensemble over which the sombre melody is played by violas and oboes in unison (how utterly different in effect from the light wind scoring of the Violin Concerto). Into this austere scene enter the violins, with a recitative-like series of phrases that become gradually more passionate, until eventually they are combined with the opening woodwind theme to bring the introduction to a close. The Allegro that follows begins quietly, its gently swinging melody suggesting a Scottish folk song. But its outline is clearly an elaborated version of the woodwind theme that began the introduction. Indeed, everything in this movement seems related to the opening theme or its folk song transformation in some way. Fragments are reiterated to form new melodies, interspersed with agitated passages. The most haunting theme emerges almost as an afterthought, as the first section of the movement winds down, and a rocking figure rising up in the violins, supported by a beautiful cushion of wind instruments and a held note in the bass. This, more than anything in the symphony, conjures up a sense of Scottish land-scape, with its bare mountains and great vistas. The moment occurs twice more, each time at a point of transition: once towards the end of the development, as the music quietens towards the reprise, and again near the end of the movement. After this last appearance, a final stormy climax rises up and dies down. But instead of coming to a halt, it leads straight into a reminder of the sombre woodwind introduction.

The scherzo follows without a break. This has something of the lightness of Mendelssohn's famous scherzos, in the Octet and *A Midsummer Night's Dream*, but with an extra rugged edge. The first theme is on the clarinet, and its swirls, dotted rhythms, and four-square phrasing give it a suggestion of a Scottish reel. At first the accompaniment is very delicate, but the energy of the tune gradually takes over the whole orchestra, and a vigorous dance develops. Once more, Mendelssohn's orchestration is dazzling, with the full orchestra contrasted with pianissimo chattering woodwind. Like Mendelssohn's other well-known scherzos, this one evaporates to nothing, leading straight on to the slow movement.

This could be one of Mendelssohn's *Songs Without Words*, and, as so often in his melodies, the most beautiful bars are those that round it off – a rising phrase that seems like a cousin of the principal themes of the first movement. A second theme is quite different in character, with a sombre tread of dotted rhythms, like a slow march, building up to fortissimo. When the opening melody returns, it is on cellos and horns, with a delicate filigree counterpoint in the violins, and pizzicato in between (again, this seems almost like the texture of one of Mendelssohn's piano pieces).

The finale could almost be a second scherzo, with its fast pace and its snappy dotted rhythms. The vigorous march-like tread is unrelenting, and although two other themes make an appearance, we never seem far away from the character of the opening. After various excursions and developments, a seemingly final climax is reached. But, as in the earlier move-ments, it does not reach a conclusion. Instead, it is followed by a slower coda, with a swinging melody that is closely related to the opening themes of the first movement. Like them it has the character of a Scottish folk tune, now in the major, and rising up confidently to a fortis-simo. It is capped by the horns, with a warlike cry of such bald simplicity that it is in danger of sounding banal – and indeed does so if this coda is taken too slowly and grandly.

SYMPHONY NO. 4 IN A MAJOR, OP. 90, 'ITALIAN'
Duration: approx. 29 minutes

Allegro vivace
Andante con moto
Con moto moderato
Saltarello: Presto

Mendelssohn began to think about this symphony during a happy time he spent in Italy, from October 1830 to the following July. He wrote from Rome to Fanny in February 1831, 'I have once more begun to compose with fresh vigour. The Italian Symphony makes rapid progress; it will be the most amusing piece I have yet composed, especially the last movement. I have not yet decided on the adagio, and think I shall reserve it for Naples.'[8] But it was another two years before he completed it, and Mendelssohn conducted the premiere in London in 1833.

He then revised it, was still not satisfied, and never managed to complete the revisions before his death. It is difficult to imagine what he can have been dissatisfied with, because, together with his Octet and Violin Concerto in E minor, this is one of the works of Mendelssohn that seem perfect in every detail. He wrote it with the exuberance of Haydn, and for a Haydn-size orchestra, with pairs of wind instruments. The exuberance is emphasized by the fact that both first and last movements are in the skipping rhythm of a jig (6/8) – not unusual in a finale, but, by Mendelssohn's time, rather unusual in a first movement. This, again, is a Haydnesque trait. As for the 'Italian' title, Mendelssohn never referred to it by this name once he had composed it, and the label was attached to the symphony after Mendelssohn's death. Calling the finale a saltarello seems like a clear Roman connection. But other associations with Italy, and particularly the traditional labelling of the slow movement as a 'Pilgrims' March', are conjectural, based on Mendelssohn's letters from Italy.[9]

The opening movement, Allegro vivace, is often taken very fast (or as fast as the wind can tongue the repeated notes), but it is rhythmic verve rather than sheer speed that gives the joyful character of the movement. Over the chattering woodwind, the violins' first theme is made up of bold, leaping phrases. After the full orchestra has taken it up fortissimo, the violins subside into pianissimo fluttering in Mendelssohn's famous scherzo mode. The second theme that emerges, first on woodwind, is based on the leaps and rhythms of the opening, but now softened into a more elegant shape. The first section of the movement ends with a return to the first theme, and quite an extensive linking passage to take us back to the opening of the movement for the repeat.

The second time around, Mendelssohn continues on into the middle of the movement with another passage of delicate scherzo-like writing in the strings. Against this, a new theme appears, with an insistently repeated little grace note providing a 'snap'. This passes quietly from instrument to instrument, in the manner of a playful fugue, and then rises to a forte and is joined by the assertive rhythm of the opening theme. A fortissimo climax, emphasizing the 'snap', dies down to a beautiful passage in which fragments of the first theme appear tentatively, until a gradual increase in energy takes us back to the opening for the reprise.

Here, Mendelssohn reworks his material charmingly. The second theme, which was originally on woodwind, is now on violas and cellos, with a filigree of accompanying arpeggios in the woodwind. After this, the 'snap' theme reappears, sounding fairy-like in the woodwind. This is combined with the opening theme, and as the pace accelerates, all the elements of the movement come satisfyingly together to bring the movement to a close.

The slow movement, in D minor, has the character of a procession. Mendelssohn's letters from Italy describe a number of religious processions that he witnessed, though the prototype for this quasi-processional style of slow movement was Beethoven's Symphony No. 7, a work that Mendelssohn greatly admired. Over a treading bass line, a somewhat chant-like melody is intoned by oboe, bassoon, and violas, a 'tenor-heavy' combination that helps to evoke the atmosphere of solemnity. But when the melody is taken up by the violins, the mood is lightened by the most beautiful counterpoint of two flutes weaving round each other, as if children have begun mingling with the procession. The processional theme alternates with a lovely melody in the major. At the end of the movement, the procession fades into the distance.

The third movement is in three-time, like the conventional minuet, but its gently undulating melody has almost none of the character of a dance, and is more like one of Mendelssohn's *Songs Without Words* (Brahms was to take up this idea of a wistful third movement in his works). In the middle section – what would be the trio of a minuet – quiet horn calls evoke the atmosphere of Mendelssohn's music for *A Midsummer Night's Dream*. This is an example of his skill in orchestration: the effect is of four horns playing together, but this is achieved by interleaving two horns and two bassoons.

The finale returns to the skipping jig rhythm of the first movement, but now with a ferocious edge and at a faster tempo. It is a saltarello, a Roman dance akin to the Neapolitan tarantella, which incorporates jumping rhythms and obsessively repeated figures. Mendelssohn's letters describe the overwhelming experience of the carnival in Rome, at which he recounts being pelted by sweets and flowers, and witnessing elaborate masquerades and horse races.[10] Whether or not this inspired Mendelssohn to write this movement, there is no denying its wild excitement. Fortissimo passages alternate with others of great delicacy, sometimes pitting the skipping rhythms against a 'straight' four-time. Towards the end, there is a magnificent build-up to full orchestra, and then the revellers seem to disperse, before the movement ends with a final fortissimo flourish.

OLIVIER MESSIAEN
(1908–92)

Messiaen was a unique figure among twentieth-century composers. His precocious talent at the age of ten is illustrated by the fact that his first harmony teacher gave him, as a leaving present, the score of Debussy's *Pelléas et Mélisande*, a work which, in 1919, was still regarded as extremely difficult and, in Messiaen's words, 'the height of daring'. It pointed the young pupil 'in the direction he wanted'. But modernity of outlook was not what made Messiaen unique; it was his deeply held faith as a Roman Catholic. At the age of only twenty-two he was appointed as organist at the church of La Trinité in Paris, one of the great positions in the musical world of the capital, and he remained there until his death sixty years later. Charles Tournemire, a senior figure in the organ world, wrote in a letter of recommendation that Messiaen was 'a transcendent improviser, an astonishing performer, and a *biblical* composer ... With Messiaen, all is prayer.'[1]

Over a long career, Messiaen wrote music for organ, solo piano, voice and piano, orchestra, and a famous chamber work, *Quatuor pour la fin du temps*, composed and first performed in a German prisoner-of-war camp in 1940–1. His music covers a huge range of expression, but Tournemire was not far wrong when he wrote, 'With Messiaen, all is prayer.' Meditation on death, redemption, and divine love provided endless inspiration for his work. But his sources extended far beyond the narrowly religious, because he saw everything as a manifestation of God's love.

While Messiaen was a student at the Paris Conservatoire, he came across an article on Indian music in Albert Lavignac's recently published *Encyclopédie de la Musique*. He was particularly struck by the table of traditional Indian rhythms, *deçi-tâlas*, recorded by a thirteenth-century musician, Sharngadeva. Messiaen became particularly fascinated by rhythms that did not have the metrical regularity that had formed the basis of 'Western' rhythm for many centuries. He came to see these 'free' rhythms as having a profound connection to the natural (and hence divine) world, and he drew on them to create music liberated from the human straitjacket of conventional metre. He developed from his studies of Indian music a repertoire of rhythmic devices that enabled him to create a fluid, non-metrical, effect.

These included 'additive values': that is, distortion of a metrical rhythm by the lengthening of a note, or the addition of a shorter note. 'Augmentation' involves repeating a rhythm with the durations of the notes lengthened. A sense of controlled acceleration or deceleration is created by making the lengths of the notes gradually shorter or longer, either by the same proportion each time or by changing proportions. Rhythmic 'palindromes' are the same values played backwards or forwards.

Messiaen drew on sources other than Indian music to develop such methods. Ancient Greek rhythm, which he also studied at the Conservatoire, contains some of the same 'irregularities' as Indian music. Birdsong, by which Messiaen became fascinated in the 1950s, added a further repertoire of free rhythms to his musical language. Stravinsky's *The Rite of Spring*, a work that was an important inspiration for Messiaen, is full of 'additive values' that break up any sense of regular metre (though these derive from traditional Eastern European rather than Indian music). Messiaen, like Stravinsky, sometimes uses these irregular rhythms moving together to create a sense of frenzy or ecstasy. But he also, unlike Stravinsky, layers unrelated rhythms on top of each other, so that several lines move freely and independently at the same time – an effect that has something in common with the experiments of Charles Ives in the early years of the twentieth century, in which separate groups move at different tempos. Messiaen's idea of counterpoint liberated from metre was further enhanced in the 1930s by his encounter with Balinese gamelan. Debussy and Ravel had come across Javanese gamelan at the Paris World Exhibition in 1889, prompting Debussy to observe that Javanese music 'is based on a type of counterpoint by comparison with which that of Palestrina is child's play'.[2] Messiaen probably heard Balinese gamelan at the *Exposition Colonial Internationale de Paris* in 1931, and developed a complex use of percussion to enrich his Indian-inspired rhythmic language, a synthesis that reached its climax in the *Turangalîla Symphony*.

TURANGALÎLA SYMPHONY
Duration: approx. 80 minutes

1. Introduction
2. Chant d'amour (Song of love) 1
3. Turangalîla 1
4. Chant d'amour (Song of love) 2
5. Joie du sang des étoiles (Joy of the blood of the stars)
6. Jardin du sommeil d'amour (Garden of love's sleep)
7. Turangalîla 2
8. Développement de l'amour (Development of love)
9. Turangalîla 3
10. Final

In the 1940s, Messiaen turned to the myth of Tristan and Isolde. This story of fatal and irresistible love provoked by a love potion entered European literature in medieval times, and was the subject of Wagner's great opera. Messiaen's interest was not in a reworking of Wagner, but in the symbolism of the story, as part of his broader concern to celebrate the functioning of divine love in the cosmos: 'I've preserved only the idea of a fatal and irresistible love, which, as a rule, leads to death and which, to some extent, evokes death, for it is a love that transcends the body, transcends even the limitations of the mind, and grows to a cosmic scale.'[3] Together with the Tristan legend, Messiaen drew on a wide range of sources related to love and death, ranging from Edgar Allan Poe and Prosper Mérimée to traditional stories from Greek, South American, and Celtic sources. All were drawn together to create a meditation on love and death that was deeply connected to Messiaen's Christian faith.

As early as 1944, Messiaen jotted down in his diary ideas for an orchestral work that contained the seed for his *Turangalîla Symphony*. Then, in October 1945, he noted, 'Write a symphonic work for Koussevitzky.' This was the result of an unusually generous commission from conductor Serge Koussevitzky to 'choose as many instruments as you desire, write a work as long as you wish, and in the style you want.' The work evolved over the next two years, beginning as a four-movement symphony, and gradually expanding to a massive work in ten movements. In February 1949 three of the movements (3, 4, and 5, entitled *Trois Tâla*) were premiered in Paris. Critics were struck by their novelty, but not entirely convinced. One wrote, 'This is a difficult work, with its complex and confusing rhythms, its ultra-modern sounds, and its extraordinary orchestral writing. But Messiaen is a man on the move.' Another observed that it 'recalls the cinema screen . . . Everything here is games with prisms, montage, slow-motion, speeding-up, zooming in on motifs which grow, or shrink, or are caught by surprise . . . This listener finds it all like an extraordinary musical toy, complicated, polyphonic and polyrhythmic.'[4]

After ten rehearsals, the complete symphony was first performed by the Boston Symphony Orchestra under Leonard Bernstein on 2 December 1949, and repeated by them in New York a week later. Critical reaction was generally hostile, with descriptions including 'futile', 'empty', and 'tawdry'. But its commissioner, Koussevitzky, kept faith with the project, describing the premiere as 'a big day in music'. One New York critic acknowledged the symphony as 'one of the most radical extensions of orchestral range, color and expressivity contrived by any modern composer'. The first performance in France took place in Aix-en-Provence in July 1950, after which Francis Poulenc wrote to Darius Milhaud that he had had a ferocious argument with fellow composer Georges Auric about it. Auric defended the work, but Poulenc thought it 'atrocious', and described himself as 'at the end of my tether about the dishonesty of this work, written to please both the crowd and the élite, the bidet and the baptismal font . . . people surrounded us as if they were at a cock-fight'.[5]

Messiaen wrote extensive notes about the symphony for the premiere and for subsequent recordings. He derived the title *Turangalîla* from two Sanskrit words: *turanga* signifying ideas of time, 'time that runs, like a galloping horse', and 'time that flows, like sand in an hourglass'; *lîla* conveys cosmic ideas of 'play' or 'dance', and 'love'. The two words combine to give Messiaen a vast canvas on both a cosmic and a human scale, involving love, death, fate, and the eternal forces that order everything. As for the construction of the work, he wrote:

> Besides numerous themes relating to each one of the ten movements, the *Turangalîla-Symphonie* has four cyclic themes, which reappear pretty well all through the work . . . The first cyclic theme, in weighty thirds, nearly always played by trombones *fortissimo*, has that oppressive, terrifying brutality of Mexican ancient monuments. For me it has always evoked some dread and fatal statue (one thinks of Prosper Mérimée's *La Venus d'Ille* [a short story in which an ancient statue of Venus comes to life and kills a man with her embrace]). I call it the 'statue theme'. The second cyclic theme, assigned to caressing clarinets in a *pianissimo*, is in two parts, like two eyes reflecting each other . . . Here the most

appropriate image is of a flower. One might think of a delicate orchid, a florid fuschia, a red gladiolus, an excessively pliant convolvulus. I therefore call this the 'flower theme'. The third cyclic theme is the most important of all. It is the 'love theme'. The fourth cyclic theme is a simple chain of chords. More than a theme, it is a pretext for different sound strata ... whether it is hurled into the depths in heavy bundles of blackness, or distributed in fine strokes, in airy arpeggios, this 'chord theme' embodies the formula of the alchemists' doctrine: 'dissociate and coagulate'.[6]

As well as the all-pervading influence of Indian music, Messiaen's fascination with gamelan permeates the symphony in its rhythms and complex textures, particularly in the ninth movement, 'Turangalîla 3'. Throughout the symphony, piano, celesta, vibraphone, glockenspiel, and metal percussion (triangle, cymbals, tam-tam, and bells) form what Messiaen called 'a small orchestra within the large orchestra, the sonority and function of which are reminiscent of the Balinese gamelan'. The score includes five different kinds of cymbals, temple blocks and wood block, maracas, several types of drum, and tubular bells.

Besides a large body of strings, woodwind, and brass, there are two instruments that play an unusually prominent role. The first is the piano, which sometimes functions as one of the percussion instruments, but also has extensive cadenzas, often formed of birdsong. The other quasi-solo instrument is the ondes Martenot. This electronic instrument was invented in 1928 by a cellist, Maurice Martenot, and is a more sophisticated development of the theremin (invented by a Russian in 1920). The ondes Martenot generates an eerie tone from vacuum-tube oscillators. The note can be played with vibrato, and the player slides a ring along the front of the keyboard in order to produce a continuous glissando. Such effects, whether produced on these instruments or their electronic successors, have become familiar in popular music, film, and television to create a spooky atmosphere (Radiohead have famously used the ondes Martenot). One has to rid oneself of these modern, and by now clichéd, uses to appreciate how novel the instrument would have sounded in early performances of the *Turangalîla Symphony*. Not everyone appreciated its effect at the time: Messiaen's outspoken pupil, the young Pierre Boulez, told him that a performance of three of the movements in 1949 made him 'vomit'.[7]

1. Introduction
A few frenzied bars, a cymbal crash, and the first, weird entry of the ondes Martenot signal the appearance of the 'statue theme' on blaring trombones: a stark, lumbering sequence of chords evoking memories of the catacombs in Musorgsky's *Pictures at an Exhibition*. After more frenzied activity, the music quietens to a reminiscence of Stravinsky's *The Rite of Spring*, out of which emerges a pair of clarinets, repeating a gentle curling phrase 'in tender arabesques'. This is the 'flower theme'. A wild piano cadenza culminates in deep bass notes, from which the orchestra bursts forth. Woodwind, strings, brass, piano, and percussion combine several different evolving rhythmic patterns to create a sense of immense power on the move, like a sustained earthquake. There is a sudden silence, the trombones return with the 'statue theme', and the movement comes to a thunderous end.

2. Chant d'amour 1
This movement evokes 'two violently contrasted aspects of love: passionately carnal love, and tender and idealistic love.' These two elements form a refrain, rather as in a rondo or a song,

interspersed with other material. The movement begins with a few wild, fragmentary bars held together by sustained strings. Then the two main elements enter: first, 'a quick motive, strong and passionate, played by the trumpets' and answered by the strings. It draws some of its shape from the (much slower) 'statue theme'. It is followed immediately by the second element, 'slow, soft and tender' over a sustained, sweet harmony, played by ondes Martenot and strings. Its descending intervals are the first appearance of Messiaen's 'love theme'. After another alternation of the two elements, there is a more playful episode, in which flute and bassoon take up the first element, with swooping glissando on the ondes Martenot. A refrain brings in two further appearances of the main elements. Then, in a longer episode, an oboe worries away at a lyrical little phrase, seemingly undistracted by energetic interventions from brass, piano, and percussion. Another refrain follows, but this time the passionate first element is much extended, building to an enormous (indeed, orgasmic) climax. Here the second, tender element joins it ecstatically. In a coda, the first element is followed by its playful version, and a final joyful shriek from the ondes Martenot gives way to a last burst of energy.

3. Turangalîla 1

'A nostalgic theme on the ondes Martenot; a weightier theme on the trombones; slow, song-like melody for the oboe. Rhythmic play on three planes for the maracas, wood block, and bass drum.'

Clarinet and ondes Martenot alternate, playing a sultry line (evocative of Debussy's *Syrinx* for solo flute), accompanied only by light touches of percussion and a diffident pizzicato bass line. The clarinet falls silent. Beneath a gamelan-like complex of percussion and the swooping of the ondes Martenot, a mighty second theme is played by trombones, bassoons, and basses. The first theme is transformed into a passionate outpouring, alternating between strings and trumpets. Then an oboe unfolds a third theme, a long melody, free and complex in its rhythms, against a counterpoint of percussion and a subsidiary melody. Suddenly, trumpets enter with the first theme, which is joined by the second theme in the bass with a welter of percussion above. There is another sudden silence, and fragments of the third and first themes bring the movement to a close.

4. Chant d'amour 2

Messiaen describes it as 'A scherzo with two trios. In the restatement, the scherzo and two trios appear simultaneously, making a musical scaffolding in three tiers.' That sounds complex enough, but the movement is even more subtle and intricate than the description suggests. It opens with piccolo and bassoon playing a jaunty little tune that brings in references to the first theme of 'Chant d'amour 1' (and, through it, to elements of the 'flower theme' and the 'statue theme'). They are joined by an increasingly agitated piano, and the pace increases until the music bursts into the first trio. This is a glorious renewal of the ecstatic love music from 'Chant d'amour 1', with the strings surmounted by ondes Martenot, and rich harmonies over a sustained bass. Between the four statements of this theme comes a calmer, chant-like element on woodwind. Then the strings quietly play a new, chant-like element that becomes hypnotic in its iterations (this is what Messiaen means by a second trio). Then the first trio returns, and soon collides with the second trio, while elements of the scherzo are superimposed by piano and trumpet, with the piano also contributing birdsong, and yet other rhythms on percussion. A more agitated passage leads eventually into a reprise of the scherzo, almost submerged by other elements from the two trios. Into this dense texture steps the forbidding 'statue theme' on trombones. At a climactic moment the music suddenly cuts off, and the tension is dissipated in a flamboyant piano cadenza. From the silence that follows, the 'flower theme' and the 'statue theme' reappear briefly in their original form, before the love music of the first trio quietly brings the movement to a close.

5. Joie du sang des étoiles (Joy of the blood of the stars)

This is a giant scherzo and trio, 'the climax of sensual passion expressed in a long and frenzied dance of joy'. The joy is expressed in a swinging theme that could have come out of a Broadway musical, but is partly derived from the 'love theme'. It alternates with more frenzied elements, whoops and crashes, before coming to a recognizable close. The middle section of the movement is much more complex. While the rest of the orchestra continues its joyful celebration, the trombones and horns subject the 'statue theme' to rhythmic fragmentation. Then the trumpets take over the 'statue' fragments, while the trombones and horns play a reverse version of them. The effect is of cosmic chaos, until the scherzo theme returns with renewed energy. Out of the tumult comes a brief, cataclysmic piano cadenza, which leads into a final, massive statement of the 'statue theme', and a final crescendo worthy (once again) of a Broadway musical. Messiaen writes, 'In order to understand the extravagance of this piece, it must be understood that the union of true lovers is for them a transformation, and a transformation on a cosmic scale.'

6. Jardin du sommeil d'amour (Garden of love's sleep)

'This piece provides an utter contrast with the last one. The two lovers are immersed in the sleep of love. A landscape has emanated from them. The garden which surrounds them is called "Tristan", the garden which surrounds them is called "Isolde". This garden is full of light and shade, of plants and new flowers, of brightly coloured, melodious birds. "All the birds of the stars ...", says Harawi [a quotation from the first of Messiaen's 'Tristan' works, *Harawi*]. Time flows on, forgotten, the lovers are outside of time, let us not wake them.'[8]

We can glimpse in this description Messiaen's links to the surrealists. Around the time he was working on the symphony, he wrote, 'if you define Surrealism as a spiritual vantage-point where visible natural realities and invisible supernatural realities are no longer in opposition to each other and where they cease to be perceived as contradictions, then I am a Surrealist composer'.[9] This is the longest movement in the symphony (about 12 minutes), and it brings together for the first time the complete 'love theme'. It consists of an extremely slow melody on ondes Martenot with muted strings, which proceeds in simple block chords. Most of these are based on major chords with added sixths or sevenths, sometimes spiced with gentle dissonance, and often without their bass note, so that they seem to hang in the air. This is Messiaen at his most sweetly sensuous. The melody is formed of long phrases, and at the end of each a flute or a clarinet adds a gentle embellishment. The flute plays shapes derived from the 'flower theme', the clarinet a more angular line that has affinities with the 'statue theme', and these develop and take on a life of their own as the movement proceeds. Over the 'love theme', the piano plays birdsong. In the percussion (temple block, cymbal, celesta, glockenspiel, vibraphone) there are delicate touches that add to the magical atmosphere. Some of these form patterns derived from Indian rhythms. In the middle of the movement there are two large-scale rhythmic patterns, one in which the durations gradually increase, the other in which they gradually decrease. According to Messiaen, the first moves 'from the present to the future', while the second 'converts the future into the past'. The two together 'represent the flow of time'.

7. Turangalîla 2

The piano opens the movement with a cadenza of birdsong. Then follows a pointilliste theme in which staccato notes are passed from instrument to instrument, over a threatening bass line with ondes Martenot high above. Two episodes follow, the first on percussion alone, the second on woodwind, with tuba below and birdsong on the piano above. The pointilliste first theme returns briefly. Then follows a violent episode, which Messiaen described as 'a terrifying rhythm, using the "chord theme" and the metal percussion instruments, giving a double sense of enlargement and contraction, of height and depth, each rhythmic group ending in a tremendous stroke of the tam-tam. This recalls the double horror of the knife-shaped pendulum gradually approaching the heart of the prisoner, while the wall of red-hot iron closes in, together with the unnameable, unfathomable depths of the torture pit, in Edgar Allan Poe's celebrated story *The Pit and the Pendulum*.' More birdsong cadenza in the piano leads to an appearance of the 'statue theme', and then to a reprise of the pointilliste first theme. A final bird shriek and drum stroke bring the movement to an end.

8. Développement de l'amour (Development of love)

This is the ultimate consummation of the love of Tristan and Isolde. Messiaen writes, 'The love potion has united them for ever. Their passion increases steadily into infinity, but this is not the only significance of the title. It also refers to the musical development.' The four themes – 'Statue', 'Flower', 'Love', and 'Chord' – all appear several times in this movement, which is almost as long as the 'Jardin du sommeil de l'amour'. Whereas that movement was the quiet centre of the symphony, this 'development' is the passionate climax. As the other themes jostle for attention, the 'Love theme' breaks through three times, and is developed further at each repetition until the final, overwhelming statement. Messiaen describes these as 'explosions of the love theme' which 'symbolize Tristan and Isolde transcended by Tristan-Isolde, and the climax of the whole symphony'.

9. Turangalîla 3

This movement combines two sets of variations that evoke vividly the idea of the 'play' of time in the cosmos. The first is based on the melody that opens the movement, played by a clarinet. The second is a complex set of variations on a rhythmic pattern played by the gamelan-like percussion group of wood block, tam-tam, suspended cymbal, deep field drum, and maracas. The two sets of variations take place simultaneously. In this fairly short movement (about 5 minutes) one can hear particularly clearly the complex interaction of the percussion as they superimpose patterns on each other. Similar layered patterns occur throughout the symphony in many different ways. Here, each instrument plays rhythmic patterns derived from seventeen different durations, ranging from one semiquaver to seventeen semiquavers in length. For example, when the wood block first enters (about a minute from the beginning), it plays a sequence of the following durations (reckoned as numbers of semiquavers): 4–5–7–3–2–1–6–17–14. When the drum enters (after the wood block's third tap), it plays that same sequence in reverse. It is impossible for the listener to keep track of such rhythmic relationships, but this is an illustration of the complex strata of thinking that underlie the seemingly random effects that Messiaen creates.

10. Final

The joyful fanfare that opens this movement is related to the swinging theme of the fifth movement, 'Joie du sang des étoiles'. A second idea is more explicitly related to the 'Love theme'. Both are driven forward with unstoppable energy, until a final, climactic appearance of the 'Love theme' itself. There is a last burst of joyful energy, and the symphony ends on a great crescendo of a major chord. So this work of immense complexity ends with the simplest and most naive of conclusions.

DARIUS MILHAUD
(1892–1974)

Milhaud was one of the group of French composers known as Les Six – Georges Auric, Louis Durey, Arthur Honegger, Milhaud, Francis Poulenc, and Germaine Tailleferre (the only woman in the group). Students from the Paris Conservatoire, they had first been brought together by Erik Satie, the droll father figure of 'alternative' French music, in 1917 under the name 'Les nouveaux jeunes'. Under the influence of Jean Cocteau, a leading figure of the artistic avant garde, this metamorphosed into Les Six. Cocteau saw the group as a musical equivalent of movements in the visual arts and literature – surrealism, cubism, futurism, Dadaism – which in different ways turned their backs on the artistic establishment. In music, this meant reaction against Wagner and Richard Strauss and their influence, and the development of a specifically French point of view (for Cocteau, chauvinistically so). This was achieved by embracing popular entertainment – cabaret, circus, jazz, café culture – and by using satire and parody to distance themselves from the great figures of the establishment, which to an extent included even Debussy and Stravinsky (who was based in France). Such convenient groupings are never straightforward. Each of Les Six inevitably had a different character and outlook, and by the mid–1920s the group, which was always loose, ceased to have much meaning.

Of the six composers, Auric, Poulenc, and Milhaud had most in common, combining humour and satire with a vein of lyricism that owed as much to cabaret singing as it did to classical song traditions. Milhaud had been brought up in Aix-en-Provence, and described his own style as 'Mediterranean lyricism'. But, as his most famous works, *Le boeuf sur le toit* and *La création du monde*, demonstrate, his sources of inspiration extended far beyond the Mediterranean.

LE BOEUF SUR LE TOIT
Duration: approx. 15 minutes

During the First World War, Milhaud spent two years in Brazil. He had formed a close collaboration with the playright and diplomat Paul Claudel, and when Claudel was appointed as French Minister to Brazil, he invited Milhaud to accompany him as an attaché. In Brazil, Milhaud came under the spell of two quite new musical influences. The first was the sound of the rainforest: 'No sooner had the sun set than, as if operated by an invisible switch, all kinds of crickets, cooper-toads, which imitate the sound of a hammer banging on a plank of wood, and birds with dull, sharp, or staccato cries peopled the forest night with their different noises, which sometimes rose swiftly to a pitch of paroxysm'.[1] The second influence was the popular music of Brazil, which Milhaud first encountered during the Rio Carnival. He became fascinated by it, and when he returned to Paris, he began to incorporate dance tunes into his music: 'Still haunted by my memories of Brazil, I assembled a few popular melodies, tangos, maxixes, sambas, and even a Portuguese fado, and transcribed them with a rondo-like theme recurring between each successive pair. I called this fantasia *Le boeuf sur le toit*, the title of a Brazilian popular song.'[2]

Milhaud thought this fifteen-minute piece would be suitable to accompany one of Charlie Chaplin's silent films. But Jean Cocteau saw in it an opportunity for a show, and devised a humorous scene in a bar in America during prohibition. Various characters, including a boxer, a dwarf, and a red-haired woman dressed as a man, are offered cocktails by the barman. Milhaud continues, 'After a few incidents and various dances, a Policeman enters, whereupon the scene is immediately transformed into a milk-bar. The clients play a rustic scene and dance a pastorale as they sip glasses of milk. The Barman switches on a big fan that decapitates the Policeman. The Red-haired Woman executes a dance with the Policeman's head ... One by one the customers drift away, and the Barman presents an enormous bill to the resuscitated Policeman.' For the first production at the Théâtre des Champs-Élysées, in February 1920, Cocteau engaged a troupe of clowns and acrobats. 'In contrast with the lively tempo of the music, Jean made all the movements slow, as in a slow-motion film. This conferred an unreal, almost dream-like atmosphere on the show. The huge masks lent peculiar distinction to all the gestures, and made the movements of hands and feet pass almost unperceived.'[3] In July the production transferred to the London Coliseum for a fortnight, as *The Nothing-Doing Bar*. Although Milhaud collaborated with Cocteau, he was not altogether pleased with the effect on his reputation: 'Both public and critics agreed that I was a figure of fun and a showground musician – I, who hated anything comic and, in composing *Le boeuf sur le toit* had only aspired to create a merry, unpretentious *divertissement* in memory of the Brazilian rhythms that had so captured my imagination but had certainly never made me laugh ...'[4] Nevertheless, it was this collaboration that made Milhaud's score famous, and it gave its name to the bar in which Cocteau and Les Six used to meet.

The recurring theme, with which the piece begins, was composed by Milhaud himself. But most of the other tunes in the score, about thirty in all, are popular Brazilian melodies that he collected. Milhaud never listed these melodies, but many of them have been tracked down by Daniella Thompson.[5] Milhaud himself gave an important lead in an article on Brazilian music that he published in 1920. In it, he stresses the importance of popular composers 'such as [Marcelo] Tupynambá or the genius [Ernesto] Nazareth. The rhythmic richness, the everrenewed fantasy, the verve, the liveliness, the melodic invention of a prodigious imagination that are found in each work of these two masters make them the glory and the jewel of Brazilian art.'[6] Tupynambá was one of the most celebrated composers of popular songs and dances. As the opening rondo theme relaxes for the first time, we hear one of Tupynambá's melodies, a song in maxixe style called 'São Paolo futuro'. The tune from which the work takes its title is 'O Boi no Telhado' ('The Bull on the Roof'), a tango by José Monteiro, which featured at the annual Carnival in Rio in 1918. This is played on the trumpet about two and a half minutes into the piece while the strings play another of Tupynambá's tunes in counterpoint.

The basic structure of the piece is straightforward, and easy to grasp: Milhaud's jaunty opening theme occurs thirteen times (with a brief fourteenth echo). Its rhythm is made even more delightful by the sound of a guiro (a gourd with notches cut into it, over which a stick is scraped). Between each occurrence, there are pairs of Brazilian tunes, almost always one in a minor key and one in a major key. The major-key tunes are mostly jolly, sometimes bursting with energy, the minor-key tunes are often tinged with melancholy. Over the whole piece, Milhaud casts his characteristically spicy harmonies. Sometimes he clashes two keys against each other, giving an impression of bustling independent activity (like the insects and birds of the rainforest, or a carnival scene), or creating a ghostly or surreal effect.

All of this is clearly audible. What is not so obvious to the listener without the score is that Milhaud uses a carefully worked-out pattern of keys to structure the piece. He begins and ends with the rondo tune in C major. Every other occurrence of the rondo tune is in a different key, covering each of the twelve possible major keys in the following order: C, E flat, G flat, A, G, B flat, D flat, E, D, F, A flat, B, and back to C. This is not a random assortment of keys. They are arranged in three groups of four. Within each group, each key change is a rise of a minor third. So in the first group, the key rises as follows: C to E flat, E flat to G flat, G flat to A. Then the key shunts down a tone to G and starts the succession of rising thirds again: G to B flat, B flat to D flat, D flat to E. There is another shunt down a tone, to D, and the rising thirds continue: D to F, F to A flat, A flat to B. And finally there is a shunt up a semitone to arrive back at the starting key of C.

This might seem all very academic, but it does have an effect. It gives the piece a very unusual sense of exploratory freedom that is rooted in some sort of logic. Milhaud, with a characteristically French sense of fun, demonstrates that a composer does not have to declare his intellectual prowess to the listener in order to do something very clever.

LA CRÉATION DU MONDE
Duration: 15–19 minutes

Ouverture
Le chaos avant la création (Chaos before the creation)
La naissance de la flore et de la faune (The birth of flora and fauna)
La naissance de l'homme et de la femme (The birth of man and woman)
Le désir (Desire)
Le printemps ou l'apaisement (Spring, or the calming)

In 1922, Milhaud undertook his first visit to the United States. Here he conducted, played the piano, and lectured. But what made the greatest impact on Milhaud was his encounter with jazz. Like all French composers, he already knew about jazz from sheet music, and he had been fascinated by Billy Arnold's Novelty Jazz Band when he heard it in London. When he arrived in New York, Milhaud encountered Paul Whiteman's Band, which he considered 'a sort of Rolls Royce of dance music, but whose atmosphere remained entirely of this world and without inspiration.' Then he was taken to hear the jazz of black musicians in Harlem. Milhaud describes its profound effect in his autobiography:

> Harlem had not yet been discovered by the snobs and the aesthetes: we were the only white folk there. The music I heard was absolutely different from anything I had ever

heard before, and was a revelation to me. Against the beat of the drums, the melodic lines criss-crossed in a breathless pattern of broken and twisted rhythms. A Negress whose grating voice seemed to come from the depths of the centuries, sang in front of the various tables. With despairing pathos and dramatic feeling, she sang over and over again, to the point of exhaustion, the same refrain to which the constantly changing melodic pattern of the orchestra wove a kaleidoscopic background. This authentic music had its roots in the darkest corners of the Negro soul, the vestigial traces of Africa, no doubt. Its effect on me was so overwhelming that I could not tear myself away ... When I went back to France, I never wearied of playing over and over, on a little portable gramophone shaped like a camera, 'Black Swan' records I had purchased in a little shop in Harlem.[7]

When Milhaud returned from the United States, he was asked to collaborate with the writer Blaise Cendrars and the artist Fernand Léger on a new ballet, and the result was *La création du monde*, a jazz-inspired work that was first performed in October 1923, four months before the premiere in New York of Gershwin's *Rhapsody in Blue*.

Cendrars had recently published *Anthologie Nègre* based on his research into African myths and legends.[8] From this, he developed a ballet scenario, in which three gods create order out of chaos, including plants, animals, man, and woman. All the creatures surround the human couple in a dance. The couple contemplate each other, and kiss. The spring of life begins. Léger threw himself into the spirit of Cendrars' African-inspired scenario. Milhaud writes that Léger wanted to 'paint the drop curtain and the scenery with African divinities expressive of power and darkness. He was never satisfied that his sketches were terrifying enough.' He based his costume designs on 'the animal costumes worn by African dancers during their religious rites ... At last in *La Création du monde*, I had the opportunity I had been waiting for to use those elements of jazz to which I had devoted so much study. I adopted the same orchestra as was used in Harlem, seventeen instruments, and I made wholesale use of the jazz style to convey a purely classical feeling.'[9]

When the ballet was first performed, 'Léger's contribution helped to make it an unforgettable spectacle. The critics decreed that my music was frivolous and more suitable for a restaurant or a dance-hall than for the concert-hall. Ten years later the self-same critics were discussing the philosophy of jazz and learnedly demonstrating that *La Création* was the best of my works.'[10]

The work is scored for sixteen instruments plus percussion: saxophone, two flutes, oboe, two clarinets, bassoon, horn, two trumpets, trombone, piano, two violins, cello, and double bass. There is a large battery of percussion, including tambourine, metal block, wood block, cymbals, five sizes of timpani, and four other drums ranging from side drum to bass drum. Interestingly, in the score, the saxophone part is not placed with the other woodwind, but among the string parts, where a viola part would usually go.

Ouverture

The saxophone plays a slow, singing melody. The accompaniment is dark and evocative: gently flowing strings over deep piano octaves, with the slow beat of the bass drum, tapping and rolling of other drums, little swinging riffs from the trumpets. The music rises to a climax and falls back.

Le chaos avant la création (Chaos before the creation)

Piano and percussion break into the peaceful scene, and the double bass begins a fugue. The theme has a very jazzy character, with its insistent little phrases, bluesy major-minor harmonies, and touches of syncopation. The double bass is answered by trombone, saxophone, and trumpet, and the piece quickly rises to a jazz-like pitch of energy. Suddenly it breaks off.

La naissance de la flore et de la faune (The birth of flora and fauna)

The music returns to the mood of the overture, with the saxophone melody taken by the flute, combined with a half-speed version of the fugue subject on cello. Then an oboe develops the fugue subject into a blues melody. This has a very Gershwin-like character – it is very similar to one of Gershwin's Preludes for piano composed three years later. Disruptive elements begin to emerge, and eventually flutter-tonguing flutes lead into:

La naissance de l'homme et de la femme (The birth of man and woman)

The violins play a cheeky little dance derived from the fugue subject. With its insistent rhythms and percussion, it is reminiscent of parts of Stravinsky's *The Soldier's Tale*, but with more abandon, and more explicit jazz elements. The joyful emotion gives way to a reprise of the blues, as the couple contemplate each other.

Le désir (Desire)

This dance combines a jazzy clarinet solo with unmistakeably Latin American rhythms, recalling Milhaud's years in Brazil. As an oboe plays a plaintive line, elements of the overture creep in below. The dance begins again and becomes wilder, before fading away into:

Le printemps ou l'apaisement (Spring, or the calming)

The blues is renewed on oboe, horn, and bassoon. The music sinks into a reverie, ending with a delicate, flutter-tongued ghost of the Latin American dance, and a last look back from the saxophone. 'The couple, set apart, are united in a kiss which bears them away like a wave. It is spring.'

WOLFGANG AMADEUS MOZART
(1756–91)

Mozart was a prodigy, whose tours around Europe as a young child with his father (Leopold) and sister (Maria Anna or 'Nannerl') caused a sensation wherever they went. While he was in London he composed his first symphony at the age of nine, and in Milan at the age of fourteen he directed from the harpsichord his own opera *Mitridate, Ré di Ponto* to great acclaim.

There have been other musical child prodigies before and after Mozart, and, remarkable though the child Mozart undoubtedly was, this is not what makes him one of the greatest figures in the history of music. Mendelssohn was a prodigy at least as impressive as Mozart, and Mozart at the age of sixteen had composed nothing to equal Mendelssohn's Octet, written at that age. On the other hand, fine though many of Mendelssohn's later works are, none of them is greater than that teenage Octet. Mozart, starting out as a child prodigy, matured and developed at every stage of his short career, adding new depths to the expressive powers of his music. If you compare the music of his mid-teens with the symphonies and violin concertos of his late teens and early twenties, the later works inhabit an entirely new emotional and intellectual world. And if in turn you compare these with the music of his last years, you realize that Mozart had, by his thirties, created a subtle and powerful musical style unlike any other.

Mozart's greatest contemporary was Joseph Haydn, who was twenty-four years older than him. By the time Mozart reached musical maturity, Haydn was already long established as one of the most important living composers, particularly of symphonies and string quartets. The two composers became great friends, and Mozart undoubtedly learned a great deal from Haydn. The great leap in maturity that Mozart showed in his late teens was partly sparked by getting to know the music that Haydn had recently composed, and using it as a springboard for his own ideas.

Often, the music of Haydn and Mozart can sound very similar; they greatly admired each other's music, and influenced each other. But it is generally the case that when Haydn is jolly, he is jolly, and when he is sad he is sad. With Mozart you are not always sure. The most easy-going and cheerful movement can suddenly hint that all is not as it seems, with a sudden twist of harmony or a darkening of mood. Mozart's sister-in-law, Sophie Haibel (Weber), once described a trait of his character: 'he was always in a good mood, but even in the best of moods, he remained very pensive, always looking you keenly in the eye, replying in a considered way to everything, whether it be happy or sad, and yet he always seemed deep in thought and appeared to be working on something quite different.'[1] Often his music gives that impression too, suggesting that there are layers beneath the most serene of surfaces. It is partly this that gives the impression there is something unique in Mozart's command of the emotional landscape. He seems like a man who understands every aspect of the human condition.

Mozart's greatest work is probably an opera, *The Marriage of Figaro*. It is a comedy, and, in Beaumarchais's original play, a subversive one, in which the servant outwits the master, and the master is seen as ridiculous. In Mozart's opera, the emotions take centre stage. It is still a comedy, and the count is still outwitted. But what makes it a great work is the way that the witty plot is inhabited by real human beings who experience a full range of emotions, from sorrow and anger to bewilderment and delight. Mozart can turn in an instant from farce to profundity. There is a scene in which the servant Figaro is revealed to be the son of Dr Bartolo and his housekeeper, who, up to this point, have been absurd characters in the drama. The scene begins as pure farce, turns to anger as Figaro's fiancée, Susanna, enters the room and misunderstands what is going on, and ends in profound tenderness. No other composer in the history of music could have achieved quite what Mozart does in this short scene, juxtaposing the comic and the sublime to create a moment of deep human insight.

Despite the fact that Mozart's orchestral music has no singers to represent human characters, the music seems full of such moments. Light and energetic music is touched with moments of doubt and melancholy, and sad music is coloured with hints of consolation and hope. The development of orchestral music in the eighteenth century relied on the adoption in purely instrumental music of dramatic gestures and situations drawn from opera. Haydn was the composer who developed the potential of this new way of working. But Mozart had a unique way of creating a subtle integration of such drama with emotional depth, intellectual logic, and instrumental brilliance.

While Haydn was in London in 1791–2, he heard of the death of Mozart: 'For some time I was beside myself about his death, and I could not believe that Providence would so soon claim the life of such an indispensable man ... I have been often flattered by my friends with having some genius; but he was much my superior ... Posterity will not see such a talent again in a hundred years.'[2] Despite the wealth of great music that has been composed in the two centuries since Mozart's death, it is tempting to say that we are still waiting.

Concertos

CLARINET CONCERTO IN A MAJOR, K. 622
Duration: approx. 29 minutes

Allegro
Adagio
Rondo: Allegro

Apart from his famous series of piano concertos and his violin concertos, Mozart also wrote various concertos for wind instruments, all commissioned by (or for) particular players. There are fine concertos for horn, oboe, flute, flute and harp together, and a Sinfonia Concertante for four wind instruments. But the supreme wind concerto is the Clarinet Concerto, written in the final months of Mozart's life.

The premiere of *The Magic Flute* took place in Vienna on 30 September 1791, with Mozart directing from the keyboard. A week later, he wrote to his wife, Constanze, who was once again undergoing treatment at the spa of Baden, 'I've just come back from the opera; – it was full as ever. – The Duetto *Man and Wife* and the Glockenspiel in the first act had to be repeated as usual – the same was true of the boys' trio in the 2nd act, but what really makes me happy is the *Silent applause!* – one can feel how this opera is rising and rising.' Then, after a light-hearted account of playing billiards 'with Herr von Mozart ... the fellow who wrote the opera', of drinking coffee and smoking a pipe, he adds, 'Then I orchestrated almost the entire Rondo of the Stadler concerto.'[3] This is a reference to the Clarinet Concerto, composed for the clarinettist Anton Stadler.

The clarinet was a relatively recent instrument in Mozart's day, having been developed around 1700, and Stadler was one of those who was continually trying out various improvements. He played several forms of clarinet and basset horn (a closely related instrument at lower pitch), and the only autograph manuscript of this concerto by Mozart, which consists of most of the first movement, is written in G major for basset horn. Mozart then rewrote and completed that movement, transposed up a tone into A major for clarinet, and added two more. But it is not as straightforward as that. Scholars have established that Stadler played (and possibly co-devised) a clarinet in A with an extension, enabling it to play notes a major third lower than the standard instrument. They have also deduced that certain passages of Mozart's concerto would originally have included these lower notes, and that these passages were transposed up an octave for the published score, so that it was playable on the clarinet in A. Nowadays, many clarinettists use such an extended clarinet in A – known as a 'basset clarinet' – to play the concerto in what is thought to be its original form, complete with the low notes that are transposed in the original published score.[4]

Like Mozart's last piano concerto, in B flat, K. 595, the Clarinet Concerto inhabits that extraordinary world that sounds as if it has come from the mind of an old and wise man, even though Mozart was in his mid-thirties when he composed both works. This impression is created, as in the piano concerto, by a sense that the music has been distilled down to its essence. There is little display, none for its own sake, and there is a predominance of lyrical ideas. This is particularly striking in the Clarinet Concerto, which exploits the naturally 'liquid' sound of the clarinet to the utmost (as does Mozart's Clarinet Quintet, also written for Stadler). There is a sense of connection with *The Magic Flute*. In the opera, Mozart, and the librettist Emanuel Schikaneder, take simple, almost pantomime-like, ideas, which develop surprising profundity without ever losing a sense of simplicity. In the Clarinet Concerto, Mozart continually surprises by the way he adds nuance to simple ideas, often slipping from major to minor, so that simplicity seems to evolve without effort into profundity. It was his last completed instrumental work.

The first of many lyrical ideas opens the orchestral introduction, with gentle, perfectly balanced phrases. This leads on to an energetic forte passage, and from here lyrical and energetic passages alternate. The sound of the full orchestra is particularly bright and transparent, with pairs of flutes, bassoons, and horns, but no oboes. The clarinet enters with the first theme, which it immediately decorates and extends. But then, rather than revisiting the energetic ideas from the introduction, the music turns towards A minor, and the clarinet introduces a new, thoughtful theme. This thoughtfulness extends over a long span, moving through different keys, and only occasionally breaking into rippling arpeggios and scales. After a brief burst of orchestral tutti, the clarinet does at last revisit one of the cheerful running figures from the introduction. But a few bars later, the music darkens into yet another minor key, and the clarinet continues its ruminations. An arpeggio leads to a pause (where the soloist might play a few notes of cadenza). And then, finally, we do return to a passage from the introduction, with the first theme played briefly in canon between violins and cellos, and the clarinet adding a third voice. Rippling semiquavers in the clarinet are at first an accompaniment, but flower into a brief moment of exuberance to round off the first section of the movement.

An orchestral tutti brings us into the development. The clarinet begins by combining the opening of the first theme with a phrase drawn from its thoughtful second theme. Running scales then rise to a high note, and plunge down dramatically in yet another minor key (this is one prominent point where the 'basset clarinet' descends lower than the clarinet in A). After a brief burst of tutti, the clarinet turns again to a major key, and remembers part of its first solo. But soon this too turns towards the minor, and becomes agitated. It leads into a substantial orchestral tutti, at first serious and in the minor, later turning towards the major, and to the continuation of the opening theme. The clarinet emerges, and soon we find ourselves at the reprise of the opening. This proceeds much as before, but with some ideas extended, others shortened or omitted, until a final tutti brings the movement to a confident conclusion.

The clarinet opens the slow movement with the main theme in D major. The first strain of the melody begins simply – a rise and fall, a higher rise and a gentler fall. It seems as if it might be derived from part of the clarinet's thoughtful new theme in the first movement (in his Clarinet Quintet, Mozart even more obviously derives the theme of the slow movement from the second theme of the first movement). The strings, enriched by woodwind and horns, repeat the first strain. The melody of the second strain is equally simple: three phrases gently fall, starting from a higher note each time. But it is the harmonies underneath that turn this simple melody into something sublime, as the music is twice pulled towards a minor key before resolving back into D major. Again the orchestra repeats the strain.

The clarinet leads off the middle section of the movement with a new theme, which becomes increasingly elaborate. The latter part of it moves to the lower register of the clarinet, before rising through a series of flourishes to a pause (an invitation for a few notes of cadenza). This whole passage is like the middle section of an operatic aria. And, as in an aria, the opening now returns da capo. This time, the clarinet plays the whole of the theme before the orchestra repeats the second strain. And then the clarinet finishes off the movement with a tailpiece that is both thoughtful and decorative.

In the finale, Mozart once again takes simple ingredients and stretches them to express more than expected. This is a rondo, and the first part of the recurring theme, with its dancing lilt, consists of two charming, perfectly balanced four-bar phrases. The orchestra repeats them, but with the melody simplified (this is unusual: responses are usually the same or more elaborate). There is a six-bar middle section, in which the clarinet breaks into running scales. Then the first pair of phrases return. But instead of leaving it at that, Mozart extends the theme, broadening it out with lyrical elements (as in the first movement). The orchestra begins the process, sustaining rising chords in the woodwind while the violins continue the clarinet's scales. The clarinet plays a new, flowing phrase; the orchestra responds, as if rounding off the theme. But again the clarinet extends it, twice rising to a sustained high note. Only then does a trill signal the final cadence of the theme, and the orchestra is now able to round it off.

The clarinet begins the first episode with another charming theme that alternates simple phrases with playful arpeggios. The orchestra extends it poignantly in E minor, with harmonies slipping down semitone by semitone. The clarinet joins in the sombre mood for a moment, but then diverts the music to the major with an exuberant display of arpeggios and scales. The orchestra again tugs at minor harmonies, but the moment of anxiety is short-lived, and the clarinet turns a corner to a reprise of the rondo theme. After the first pair of phrases, the orchestra cuts straight to the conclusion, from which it moves on with new urgency into another minor key. This turns out to be the most extensive episode in the movement. The clarinet plays a broad, thoughtful new theme. Then, in another sudden shift of mood, it moves into a major key for a theme that shows off the clarinet's range, with leaps from low to high notes. There is a wistful little moment in which Mozart quietly touches on a phrase of the rondo theme, as if starting another passage in the minor. But once more the clarinet brushes the doubt aside, and instead reprises the charming theme from the first episode. The orchestra again becomes wistful, with echoes of the theme passing between pairs of instruments. The clarinet reasserts the cheerful mood with running scales, but then remembers the poignant extension to the theme, and the orchestra's response is to hesitate with two pauses. From here, the music soon finds its way back to a reprise of the rondo theme. This time, the whole of the opening is revisited, with its middle passage and extensions. The concluding bars of orchestral tutti lead straight into more exuberant clarinet arpeggios, and we sense that the end is near. One moment of shy hesitation leads to a last reminder of the theme, the clarinet plays final leaps down and up, and the orchestra brings the concerto to a joyful conclusion.

Horn Concertos

The numbering of Mozart's horn concertos is confusing. No. 1 in D major (now referred to as K. 386b), which Mozart never finished, turns out to be from his last year, 1791. No. 2 in E flat major dates from 1783, No. 3 in E flat major from 1787, and No. 4 in E flat major from 1786. There is also a Rondo in E flat major, K. 371, dating from 1781, which is now thought to go with the incomplete draft of a first movement, K. 370b, to create a two-movement concerto.

With the possible exception of the 1781 movements, all of Mozart's works featuring the horn – the four concertos and the Horn Quintet – were written for Joseph Leutgeb (or 'Leitgeb' in the Salzburg spelling that appears in Mozart's letters). Leutgeb had got to know the seven-year-old Mozart and his family when he played the horn in the court orchestra at Salzburg (Leutgeb was twenty-three years older than Mozart). He moved to Vienna in 1777, where he continued his career, and owned a cheesemonger's shop inherited from his wife's family. Mozart, who followed to Vienna four years later, took delight in playing jokes on Leutgeb, and the autograph scores of the concertos contain addresses to him as, among other things, a 'donkey'. But these are serious works, and Leutgeb was a seriously gifted player. A Paris critic in 1770 wrote of his ability to 'sing an adagio as perfectly as the most mellow, interesting and accurate voice'.[5] Part of the secret of this ability must certainly have been Leutgeb's mastery of hand-stopping technique, in which the insertion of the hand into the bell of the horn enables the player to change the pitch (mostly down, but sometimes up) so as to produce notes otherwise unavailable in the days before the invention of valves. Discussions of hand-stopping often stress the difference between the bright open notes and the more muffled, nasal stopped notes, and Mozart undoubtedly sometimes exploited these tone colours. But it was an important part of the skill of the horn player to even out the differences in tone as much as possible when a singing line demanded it, and that surely applied in Leutgeb's performance of these concertos.

The three complete concertos (Nos 2–4) are discussed in detail below. The work long known as No. 1, but actually the last of the four, is in two movements: a complete first movement, and an unfinished draft of the second movement. The first movement is in that transparent, innocent style familiar in certain of Mozart's late works, such as *Eine kleine Nachtmusik*. Its second movement is a charming little jig, a simpler example of the hunting-style rondos that conclude the other concertos, with the occasional diversion into minor keys that scarcely unsettles the cheerful mood. This finale was left unfinished and, apart from the opening section, Mozart's autograph consists of little more than a single melodic line. It has long been performed in a completion made after Mozart's death by Franz Xaver Süssmayr (who also completed the Requiem). Süssmayr ignores much of Mozart's sketch (or perhaps had not seen the complete manuscript), introducing new material including a clumsy little moment of fugue, and a passage based on a Gregorian chant that has nothing to do with Mozart. There have been several reconstructions in recent decades that adhere more closely to Mozart's draft.[6]

The horn part of 'No. 1' is technically less demanding than in the earlier concertos, and made still simpler in Süssmayr's edition. It is thought likely that Mozart (and Süssmayr) took account of Leutgeb's diminishing stamina (he was then in his late fifties). This might also help to explain the Italian monologue that Mozart wrote along the top of the score of the rondo, continuing it right to the end when he hadn't even written out the rest of the music. It takes his long-standing ribbing of Leutgeb as a 'donkey' to new lengths, encouraging him in his struggle to mate: 'For you, Mr Donkey – Come on – quick – get on with it – like a good fellow – be brave – Are you finished yet?' and so on.[7] The humour, at times obscene, may strike us as crude, but if there is anything linking it to the music, it is the thought that Mozart might have imagined Leutgeb as a sort of Papageno-like figure, for whom the artless style of this concerto, and the humour of the commentary, would be appropriate.

Allegro maestoso
Andante
Rondo: Più allegro

This is the earliest of the four horn concertos, dated by Mozart himself on the autograph score with a 'dedication' to his old friend: 'Wolfgang Amadé Mozart has taken pity on Leitgeb [*sic*], donkey, ox and fool, at Vienna, 27 March 1783'. The donkey motif will be taken up at greater length in the later concerto 'No. 1'. This foolery should not mislead us: Mozart took great care over the concerto, and its first movement in particular bears comparison with the piano concertos in its richness of themes (as does the first movement of No. 4).

The orchestral introduction is short, but it presents two themes, both with an eloquent dignity in accordance with the 'maestoso' (majestic) heading. The two themes both begin with two bars of long notes over an unchanging bass, followed by quicker notes as the bass changes – a simple and subtle link that makes them sound like cousins. The phrases of the second theme are charmingly echoed by oboes and horns.

The soloist enters with a third theme. It too begins with two bars of long notes followed by an animated run up in the third bar, so that it seems thoroughly at home in the company of the earlier themes. It is developed and extended, with several more ascending runs (Leutgeb seems to have been a more agile player in 1783 than he was a few years later). Then the soloist plays the eloquent second theme from the introduction. The violins join the horn an octave above for the second phrase, which is now varied to rise smoothly to its climax – a tiny example of Mozart's genius for detail. The horn develops the theme further, and the violins introduce yet another new theme. This has a tiptoeing elegance almost like a gavotte, and it too is lovingly extended. A return to exuberant scales brings in the orchestral tutti to round off the first section.

The development is simple and, again, eloquent. The horn begins with sorrowful descending phrases in B flat minor – these seem like another new idea. Once more the violins enhance the eloquence by joining the horn an octave above for a moment. Then a corner is turned into D flat major, and the horn plays a sequence of noble phrases that relate to its first entry (and to the orchestra's opening bars), but with a leap up instead of a fall, rising higher each time. From here, Mozart turns another corner to arrive back in E flat major for the reprise.

After the orchestra's opening theme, the horn comes straight in with its third theme (its relationship with the first theme is clear when the two are placed side by side like this). From this point on, the music proceeds much as before, with the violins playfully echoing the horn's running scales and then continuing to their second theme. This time, the violins play it first, and then the horn joins them for the second phrase – in unison, rather than an octave below, with the horn ascending to a high E flat. Then the music proceeds through the gavotte-like theme to a final tutti, without a cadenza.

The Andante in B flat major is a sort of rondo in which two ideas alternate, but with such subtlety that the movement seems to be one continuous flow of melody from beginning to end. The orchestra introduces the first theme. It has a particularly striking change of register after four bars, leaping from high violins with oboes down to violins alone on their lowest string, bringing out a depth of feeling in the gentle tune. The soloist enters and develops the melody further, up to a poignant chromatic rise that is echoed by the violins.

After a cadence in F major, the horn plays the second theme which, in its opening shape, is very closely related to the first. When the first theme returns, it begins as before, but its second phrase goes, with a tug of the harmony, in a different direction for a moment, before finding its way to the familiar cadence.

The music continues through the second theme to the final reprise of the first. Again the harmony tugs away for a moment. This time, the final cadence is diverted, to give way to the poignant chromatic rise that has not been heard since the first solo. It is played by the violins, and as they repeat it, the horn joins in a simple, descending counterpoint to bring this sublimely simple movement to a close.

Like the slow movement, the finale combines simplicity with subtlety, in a seemingly straightforward hunting jig. The soloist plays the rondo theme, whose opening is built from a simple arpeggio as in a classic horn call. The orchestra repeats it. Then the soloist begins the first episode with a new idea, similarly starting with a simple arpeggio. The elegant succeeding phrases acquire a delicate little galloping rhythm.

We arrive at a trill and a pause (and perhaps a little cadenza). The rondo theme returns, with the horn echoed by the orchestra. The next episode opens with a witty return to the little galloping figure. The harmonies shift into C minor, and the horn plays a rather serious melody, the most expansive theme in the movement so far. But meanwhile the violins have been infected by the wit of the galloping rhythm, and peck away quietly at a reiterated figure while the horn is trying to be serious. One can almost imagine this as a musical representation of the relationship between Leutgeb and Mozart.

The rondo theme returns. In the next episode, the horn stays in E flat major and plays a new, confidently flowing melody. As the strings take it up, the horn responds cheekily with the gallop rhythm. Then, as the episode winds to a close, there is a charming moment when strings and horn break into a tune with trills over a drone bass, like rustic bagpipers. The horn returns to the rondo tune. But now it twice hesitates in mid-phrase. Finally it gets going at an even faster tempo, and the concerto gallops home like a gleeful boy Mozart on his hobby horse – an image that Leutgeb might easily have conjured up in his memory.

HORN CONCERTO NO. 3 IN E FLAT MAJOR, K. 447

Allegro
Romance: Larghetto
Allegro

This concerto is now thought to have been composed in 1787, a year after No. 4. Its scoring is unique among Mozart's horn concertos, with pairs of clarinets and bassoons instead of oboes and horns. The clarinets are not particularly prominent, but they give a mellowness to the blend of the orchestra. Although there are no orchestral horns, twice in the first movement Mozart gets the solo horn to play along with the orchestra to enrich the texture.

The orchestral introduction opens with an expansive phrase on the violins that immediately gives way to full orchestra, with dramatic harmonies and leaps (the soloist joins in this tutti). This is followed by an elegant second theme, whose repetitive little shapes provoke a build-up over an unchanging bass (a miniature 'Mannheim crescendo'), and a further burst of full orchestra. The introduction is rounded off with a poised little phrase, and the soloist enters.

The horn takes up the opening theme, which is now extended and developed. The violins pass the second theme to the horn, and this culminates in an orchestral tutti, marking the end of the first section. Again, the next tutti ends with the poised little tailpiece, but now it is repeated in the minor, and the development begins in D flat major. The horn plays a new melody, even calmer than the expansive first theme. Its phrases end with two-note sighs (related to a shape in the second theme), and these reach a moment of mysterious stillness. The horn quietly holds long notes while the strings tentatively remind themselves of an energetic passage from the introduction. The horn emerges from its trance into arpeggios, and a series of changing chords brings us back to E flat major, and to the reprise.

With minor changes, the reprise unfolds as before, until the rhythm breaks into triplets, and with bold arpeggios and a trill we arrive at the pause for the cadenza (which Mozart does not supply). The horn joins in at the end of the final tutti, bringing the movement to a decisive close.

The slow movement in A flat major is a song-like Romance. The marking is Larghetto, the diminutive of Largo (broad), and the metre is two beats per bar, not four, so it is not very slow. The melody, eloquent in its balanced phrases, is sung first by the horn, and then by the strings, richly supported by clarinets and horns. A middle strain of the theme becomes more vigorous, and then the first part returns. Its last phrase is repeated, taking the music into a new key, and into the middle section of the movement.

After a few bars of horn solo, the violins again take up the main theme, but now in E flat major. As its opening phrase comes round for the second time, the horn joins in with a descant, a touchingly simple moment. There is a moment of darkness, with dramatic harmonies, and then the music calms once more into the reprise of the opening. This time the violins add an extra tailpiece, against which the horn fits the end of the theme. After a further moment of lingering, the movement comes to a serene end.

The final rondo is a hunting jig in the same style as the finale of the earlier No. 4, with a wealth of delightful interplay between horn and orchestra. The soloist plays the main theme, with its repeated notes and runs, and the orchestra then takes it up and extends it. With the pattering runs and echo phrases, you could almost imagine this as an ensemble in a comic opera, particularly when the orchestra pauses, and the soloist finishes off the phrase for them.

The interplay becomes more delicate in the first episode. After a few bars, the orchestra introduces galloping rhythms, to which the horn responds with hunting calls, but still quiet and delicate. The main theme returns. As the orchestral tutti runs its course, the pattering runs move off to A flat major, and the soloist enters in this key for the next episode. The horn plays a sturdy new melody, to which the strings respond playfully – again, the contrast between the two 'characters' is almost operatic. The delicate gallop and hunting calls return. There is a moment of unexpected seriousness, with stabbing, dissonant chords, but this cannot puncture the mood for more than a moment, and we are soon back at the final reprise of the rondo theme.

This time, as the orchestra responds it soon reverts to the delicate galloping rhythms, against which the horn plays more fanfares. These culminate in a triumphant whoop up a scale, and a final exchange between horn and orchestra brings the movement to a close in high spirits.

HORN CONCERTO NO. 4 IN E FLAT MAJOR, K. 495

Allegro moderato
Romance: Andante cantabile
Rondo: Allegro vivace

What we know as Mozart's fourth concerto is the most satisfying of all the horn concertos, on a par with his piano concertos. It presents a curious mystery. The second and third movements survive in Mozart's autograph score, and in both of them the music is written in different coloured inks. The Romance has red, green, blue, and black, and the final Rondo has just red and black. This has long been assumed to be another of Mozart's jokes for Leutgeb. The editor of the New Mozart Edition of the horn concertos, Franz Giegling, put forward a theory that the different colours were a coded way of indicating subtle gradations of loud and soft in the different parts, but this idea has not attracted much support. Henrik Wiese, editor of a Breikopf and Härtel edition, countered with the charming idea that Leutgeb, who was always short of money, might have given Mozart a gift of paper, pen, and inks instead of paying him with money, and that Mozart was playfully using the gift when writing the score (it is true that the horn concertos are written on different paper from most of Mozart's compositions of this period).[8]

The first movement is particularly rich in themes – a feature that, as in the second concerto, invites comparison with Mozart's piano concertos. The orchestral introduction has at least three distinct themes with several subsidiary ideas. The first is vigorous, with the violins playing three-note chords on the main beats, energetic runs, and plunging leaps. The second theme is a gentle line that falls and rises. This leads on to a dramatic crescendo over a persistent bass (a 'Mannheim crescendo'), with the high oboes adding to the drama, and culminating in more plunging leaps. The introduction ends with a third theme, another lyrical little tailpiece in which the solo horn and oboe join as it repeats – an unexpected anticipation of the horn's first solo passage.

When the solo proper begins, it is with yet another idea (as often happens in the piano concertos). This is the most extended theme so far, beginning with a rising arpeggio of three sustained notes, and ending with an exuberant run to bring in a brief orchestral tutti. The soloist then develops the melody at greater length. None of this refers back to the themes that the orchestra presented. But then the violins gently bring in the second theme from the introduction, followed by the 'Mannheim crescendo', though delaying the actual crescendo until the final bar so as not to mask the solo horn. This announces the end of the first solo, and a tutti rounds off the section.

The strings quietly move into C minor to begin the development. The horn enters with a melody that, once again, seems new, though its rhythm and falling line give it a subtle relationship to the second theme from the introduction. It opens out and extends over a long paragraph, accompanied just by the strings. At first it is like a sorrowful aria, remaining in C minor. Then, with bolder leaps, it moves into A flat major, and the mood lightens.

A moment of anticipation, with running semiquavers, brings in the reprise. Yet this does not, as one might expect, return to the opening theme of the introduction, but to the horn's first entry. A little later, new figurations lead on to the second theme, played by the violins and, with a charming touch, joined by the horn and oboe. The next build-up leads to a pause and a cadenza (which Mozart does not supply). The final tutti quietens for a moment to the third theme, which, as before, the horn also plays. Apart from the earlier brief phrase of the second theme, this is the only one of the orchestra's original themes that the horn plays in the entire movement, and its recurrence here gives a lovely sense of the movement being gently rounded off before the final burst of orchestral forte.

The slow movement in B flat major has the simple three-part structure of a song. Its opening theme begins with a phrase that undulates in fluid rhythm over a sustained bass note in a manner that seems to refer back to baroque pastoral movements (such as the 'Pastoral Symphony' from Handel's *Messiah*). Mozart was to use the beginning of this theme as the basis of a much more elaborate movement in his Sonata in F major for Piano Duet, K. 497, finished a month after the completion of this concerto. The horn and the violins sing the opening phrase together, a third apart, and then the horn rounds off the strain on its own. When the orchestra repeats the melody, its second half rises higher, with increased eloquence. The horn then continues with a middle part of the theme. This too rises to an eloquent high point, at which a turn of melody is played three times before slipping back seamlessly into the opening of the theme.

The middle section, as in many a song, moves sadly into a minor key, G minor. With a typically subtle sequence of harmonies, Mozart moves back to B flat major for a moment, but then slips through different keys in an effortless manner that only adds to the poignancy. Soon, we find ourselves at the reprise of the opening. This is now shortened, and a little coda provides a tender valediction.

The final Rondo is the most famous movement in the horn concertos, a cheerful hunting-style jig. The main rondo theme is a delightful regularly phrased tune, with the same scurrying semiquavers in the bass as in the finale of the second concerto. It is echoed by the orchestra, then interleaved with three episodes. The first stays more or less in the character of the main theme, introducing more fanfare-like shapes and arpeggios. After the next reprise, the second episode moves into C minor, and is anxiously thoughtful. There is more dialogue with the orchestra, and there are touches of counterpoint in the inner strings.

The next reprise is followed by a repeat of the first episode, though with new harmonic twists. The last of these culminates in a pause (possibly with a little cadenza). Then, after an orchestral climax, the soloist goes round a phrase of the theme again, with wistfully tugging harmonies below. This last moment of poignancy enhances the sense of arrival at the final cadence.

Piano Concertos

Mozart's mature piano concertos have a particular quality that has never been repeated in later music history. Over the two centuries since Mozart's death, from Beethoven to Prokofiev and beyond, we have come to think of the concerto, and particularly the piano concerto, as a vehicle for virtuoso display, a medium in which the soloist is supreme, riding powerfully over the orchestra or doing battle with it. But Mozart's piano concertos are not like that. They are works of subtle conversation, like large-scale chamber music, or sometimes more like an opera ensemble, with the piano and orchestra in dialogue, not opposition. This partly arises naturally, because the piano of Mozart's day was, by comparison with the concert giant we know today, a small and quiet instrument, a more expressive cousin of the harpsichord. And the orchestra with which Mozart pairs the piano would have been small to match. Mozart's senior contemporary Haydn also wrote a few charming concertos, playable on either piano or harpsichord. But it was Mozart who demonstrated the expressive potential of the new pianos and who, in his concertos, constructed works of extraordinary subtlety and depth. He himself was renowned as one of the first great pianists A biography published after his death described his exceptional 'quickness, neatness and delicacy', and went on to praise 'the most beautiful, most eloquent expression, and a sensitivity that went straight to the heart'.[9] And this will do equally well as a description of the piano concertos that Mozart wrote for himself and his pupils to play.

Between the ages of nine and eleven, Mozart arranged sonatas by other composers for keyboard and orchestra, to provide concertos for himself to play on his tours with his sister and father. His first original piano concerto dates from 1773, when he was seventeen, and three more followed in 1776. These contain attractive music, and some fine writing in the slow movements. But there is nothing in them to prepare us for his first masterpiece in this genre, the 'Jeunehomme' Concerto of 1777.

PIANO CONCERTO NO. 9 IN E FLAT MAJOR, K. 271, 'JEUNEHOMME'
Duration: approx. 32 minutes

Allegro
Andantino
Rondo: Presto – Menuetto cantabile – Presto

Written in 1777, around Mozart's twenty-first birthday, this is the earliest of his piano concertos that is widely performed, the first that has the stamp of mature Mozart from first note to last. The name 'Jeunehomme' has been attached to this concerto for nearly a century, in the mistaken belief that this was the name of the pianist for whom Mozart wrote it. In letters to his father, Mozart refers to her variously as 'Jenomy' and 'Jenomè', and his father spells her 'Genomai'. Recent scholarship has established that she was Victoire Jenamy, the daughter of Mozart's friend, the celebrated ballet-master, Jean Georges Noverre.[10]

The Allegro begins with bold octaves from the orchestra (strings, horns, oboes), which are answered by a more ornate phrase from the piano. This sounds rather like an exchange between two characters in an opera: an assertive statement, a confident, maybe even defiant, reply. At the age of twenty-one, Mozart was thoroughly experienced in the ways of Italian opera, and had written both comic opera and the more formal opera seria himself. Here, we can already sense how this opera background was crucial to the way he wrote for piano and orchestra.

After the brief opening exchanges, the orchestra sets out the principal themes of the movement. As often in Mozart, there are several of them, mostly delicate and lyrical, interspersed with bursts of vigorous material for full orchestra. It is just as the violins are presenting yet another delicate little idea that the piano nonchalantly sidles in with a trill, and a new thought of its own, as if it hasn't really been paying attention to what is going on – such 'absent-minded' moments occur frequently in Mozart's later concertos. The orchestra restates its opening octaves, the piano replies as before, and then takes off on a flamboyant passage, bypassing the original second theme, and eventually arriving at the gentle third theme. This too is characteristic of Mozart's concertos: the piano takes some of the material from the orchestral introduction, reordering themes or leaving some out altogether, and interspersing new material among them, sometimes taking off in passages of virtuoso fantasy. This unpredictability gives Mozart's concertos a sense of almost improvised dialogue between piano and orchestra, which is one of the delights of these works.

After the piano's exploration of several of the themes, a trill leads into the orchestral tutti that signals the end of the first section of the movement. As we enter the development, almost the first thing the piano does is to play the second theme that it bypassed earlier, as if it has suddenly remembered it. But much of the development is based on the opening exchange between the orchestra's octaves and the piano response, with the piano meditating on its response and taking it into new keys. When the reprise of the opening exchange arrives, it too soon develops unpredictably, with the piano meditating further on its response, once again omitting the second theme, and arriving at the gentle third theme. It is only after further passages of fantasy that the second theme comes sidling in (rather as the first piano entry did). One more statement of the opening exchange leads to a pause and the cadenza. In several of the later concertos, Mozart supplied one or more possible cadenzas (though certainly not insisting that they should always be played), but here he leaves the pianist to improvise one, or at least compose it in advance, as Mozart would have done himself.

If the first movement has something of the character of comic opera, the second movement takes us into the world of tragic opera seria. The marking Andantino is potentially puzzling to modern musicians. Nowadays this is taken to mean a pace faster than Andante, applied to music of grace but rarely profundity. In Mozart's day it generally meant a slower tempo than Andante. But even if we didn't know that, it would be impossible to mistake the deeply tragic character of this movement. It is an immense aria in C minor, which one could easily imagine being sung by the doomed heroine as she contemplates her fate. There is nothing like it in all of Mozart's other piano concertos. The only slow movement that resembles it is the equally beautiful and tragic slow movement (also in C minor) of the Sinfonia Concertante for violin and viola, written two years later. In this piano concerto movement, the strings are muted, to increase the sombre effect.

As the orchestra begins, the first violins play a low, dark line, with unsettling accents on the offbeats. The second violins echo them, playing exactly the same line a beat later (in canon), so that the offbeat accents tug against each other. As the melody reaches its first climax, oboes and horns solemnly intone an octave G, like funereal trumpeters. This introduction reaches an end with sighing phrases, and a stark cadence, just as if a singer is about to begin. The piano enters, and the violins repeat their opening dirge. At first, the piano seems to be improvising an expressively decorated line above it, but gradually it takes over the main role of melody-singer. A few orchestral bars take the music into E flat major, and in this warm key the piano's continuation takes on a more consoling tone. The melody weaves its way, with occasional reminders of the opening – the oboes and horns intone an E flat, with the same air of ceremony as before, and the piano ends this section with the sighs that concluded the violins' first paragraph.

There is a brief orchestral interlude, after which the piano muses on phrases from this interlude. The mood is still consoling, but eventually it turns darker, the music modulates back to C minor, with forceful emphasis, and with the oboes plaintively high in the chords. All this prepares us for the return of the opening, with the piano beginning, then the strings taking over and the piano decorating above. As before, the piano continues more consolingly in E flat major. But this time, it soon works back to the darker C minor, and it is in this key that the movement continues, until it reaches a pause for a cadenza. Mozart did not supply one but, remarkably, he did supply the ending for it. Instead of concluding with the conventional trill, to alert the orchestra to come in, the piano continues with bleak, sighing fragments. The orchestra interrupts with one of its most poignant phrases, the strings now suddenly without their mutes. The piano has one more attempt to carry on, with the sighing that concluded the introduction, and the tragic scene is finally brought to an end with another stark cadence in C minor, the piano this time joining in with the orchestra.

What could possibly follow this startlingly tragic slow movement? The answer is a bubbling Presto so unstoppable that it is as if the slow movement had never happened. This impression is emphasized by the fact that it is the piano that starts it, pouring out more and more paragraphs, several times seeming about to give way to the orchestra, but carrying on until it really has finished what it wanted to say. The orchestra takes up the bubbling, and introduces a new, cheeky element. The piano responds to this, but is not to be deterred from its patter of continuous quavers. Eventually, the piano comes to a halt. What follows, the central section of the movement, is a graceful dance in three-time, a minuet. The piano decorates this melody, while the orchestra accompanies with a beautiful mixture of delicate textures – pizzicato, bowed strings, and woodwind. After this oasis in the middle of the movement, the bubbling Presto returns, but with new dramatic turns. The ending is particularly delightful, the opening phrase repeated again and again obsessively, until two chords bring the work to an abrupt stop.

CONCERTO FOR TWO PIANOS IN E FLAT MAJOR, K. 365 (PIANO CONCERTO NO. 10)
Duration: approx. 27 minutes

Allegro
Andante
Rondo: Allegro

Mozart wrote this concerto in 1779, two years after the 'Jeunehomme' Concerto, for himself and his sister Maria Anna ('Nannerl') to play. Nannerl, five years older than her brother, was a highly accomplished musician in her own right, prevented only by the conventions of the day from developing a successful career of her own. Later, Mozart played the concerto with one of his best pupils, Josepha Auernhammer. This is not as deep a work as the 'Jeunehomme' Concerto, and has nothing like its dark slow movement, but it is a brilliant and delightful piece of music, with many witty and expressive touches. Mozart's solo concertos are characterized by conversational dialogue between piano and orchestra, almost like chamber music. Here, much of the dialogue is between the two pianos, which gives a different sort of conversation, and somewhat reduces the role of the orchestra.

As in the 'Jeunehomme' Concerto, the orchestral introduction begins with a theme in bold octaves. Here, however, the pianos do not immediately answer. This is a more conventional introduction, in which the orchestra sets out thematic material without interruption. As usual in Mozart, this contains several ideas, including moments of hesitancy, and lyrical melodies that give relief to the predominantly sunny and vivacious character. The pianos enter in turn, revisiting the opening two ideas, and adding brilliant trills and other elaboration. But then they come up with no less than four new ideas, to add to the store already set out by the orchestra. This exposition comes to an end with the conventional trill from both pianists, and a few bars of orchestra.

We are then into the development section of the movement. The pianists begin to pass between them an idea that they had previously ignored from the introduction; but after a few bars, they launch out into a forceful passage with dotted rhythms in C minor, which derives from an incidental little figure of dotted rhythms in the introduction. This is followed by a falling, lyrical phrase that seems to be entirely new. The orchestra quotes an idea that first occurred as they approached the soloists' first entry, but this time it signals the end of the development, and the arrival of the reprise. The orchestra reiterates its opening octave theme. This time, the pianos intervene and take this idea surprisingly into E flat minor. They then revisit the themes from their first entry, but now in a different order. This is such a characteristic procedure of Mozart's in the latter stages of a concerto movement, and gives the music a sense of semi-improvised conversation. Mozart provided his own brief but dramatic cadenza for the two pianos.

The opening of the Andante immediately presents two layers: below, delicate phrases played by the violins, above, a long oboe note, which eventually blossoms to round off the strings' phrases. This sets up the dialogue that the pianos continue as they enter, a dialogue full of the sort of expressive decoration that suggests opera singers freed from the limitations of their voices. The orchestra changes key, and the pianos begin the middle section of the movement with a grand flourish. But then, as the first piano moves into the minor, the oboe again holds a high note, the second oboe enters, and the decorative phrases in the piano create poignant clashes against the oboes. This is the quiet expressive climax of the movement.

The finale has a playful main theme, which, as always in a rondo, recurs throughout the movement. During the various episodes, the two pianos explore different moods, often dashing, occasionally more determined and serious. As in the first movement, Mozart provides a cadenza, in which the two pianists wittily exchange fragments of counterpoint and combine together in fast runs, before the movement is brought to an emphatic close.

Piano Concertos, K. 413–415

These three concertos formed an important milestone in Mozart's career, being the first in the series of great concertos that he wrote after moving to Vienna, and the first to be published in a printed edition. Initially, however, he followed the usual practice of making them available in manuscript copies. Mozart advertised for subscribers in January 1783: 'These three concertos, which can be performed with full orchestra including wind instruments, or only a quattro, that is with 2 violins, 1 viola and violoncello, will be available at the beginning of April to those who have subscribed for them (beautifully copied, and supervised by the composer himself).'

By offering concertos that could be played either with orchestra or with a chamber group, Mozart was trying out the Viennese audience and hoping to attract as wide a circle of music lovers as possible. And in the style of writing he was also aiming for a broad appeal, as he made clear when describing the concertos in a letter to his father: 'These concertos are a happy medium between what's too difficult and too easy – they are Brilliant – pleasing to the ear – Natural without becoming vacuous; – there are passages here and there that only connoisseurs can fully appreciate – yet the common listener will find them satisfying as well, although without knowing why.'[11] Compared with some of his later concertos – the dramatic D minor (No. 20), or the tragic C minor (No. 24), or even the earlier 'Jeunehomme' Concerto – these three concertos are, on the surface at least, easy-going. But they are easy-going in the most elegant and beautifully poised manner. The optional nature of their wind parts means that the important elements of the orchestral parts are focused on the strings (whether as an orchestra or as a quartet), the wind instruments doing little more than fill out chords and provide occasional punctuation. But the details of Mozart's orchestration, and the dialogue between orchestra and piano, are as satisfying as in his more grandly scored concertos. This is partly because Mozart had recently been honing his skill in writing counterpoint. He mentions in a letter of 20 April 1782 that he visits Baron von Swieten's house every Sunday.[12] Von Swieten was the librarian at the Viennese court, and an enthusiast for the great classical pieces of the past. He gathered musicians together to play the music of Handel and J. S. Bach, and Mozart used to borrow the scores and take them home. Mozart composed a number of works in homage to Bach and Handel around this time, including a fugue that he later elaborated into the magnificent Adagio and Fugue for Strings, K. 546. We can hear echoes of this study of counterpoint in these three piano concertos: there are few moments of formal counterpoint, but the relationship between simultaneous parts is subtle and satisfying.

PIANO CONCERTO NO. 11 IN F MAJOR, K. 413
Duration: approx. 23 minutes

Allegro
Larghetto
Tempo di Menuetto

This concerto opens with a movement of easy grace, in a gently swinging three-time. The special qualities of the strings-based writing are clear right from the opening bars. Little fragments of themes that in other concertos might have passed between violins and woodwind here pass instead between first violins, second violins, and violas. This gives a satisfying depth to the orchestration of the opening pages. The first entry of the piano is highly characteristic of Mozart. The orchestra has just begun what seems like yet another gently falling theme, when the piano takes it up, and sidetracks to a different thought altogether, as if half-remembering the opening themes of the concerto. After this delightfully absent-minded entry, the orchestra restates the opening theme, and the piano continues with the response and develops it into an exploratory passage. This includes more new material, though again with passing allusions to previous themes.

The development moves into minor keys, casting a cloud over the centre of this predominantly sunny movement. The move back to the reprise is subtle and masterly. The piano plays its 'absent-minded' first entry, but because it emerges out of the end of the development it disguises the reprise, so that it is only when the orchestra joins in with its forte opening bars that we realize we are back at the beginning.

The slow movement is a serenade, perfectly poised between tranquillity and melancholy, and beginning over a pizzicato bass. To the oboes and horns of the first movement are added bassoons, giving further mellowness to the wind chording. From time to time, falling phrases from the piano are echoed in the violins, and we learn to look forward to these moments. And there are times where the mood darkens, only to emerge again into the light. The music's subtle blend of operatic decoration with delicate emotional nuances gives the movement an extraordinarily satisfying sense of flow.

The finale, too, achieves a subtle balance, between the elegance of a minuet and the traditional dash of a rondo. This 'minuet-rondo' was a favourite form of Mozart's friend J. C. Bach, who had died shortly before Mozart wrote this trio of concertos. (Mozart quotes Bach more explicitly in the slow movement of the next concerto.) The movement starts almost like a piece of ecclesiastical counterpoint, only beginning to resemble a minuet after a few bars. Like the whole of the concerto, it has an unassuming grace. Despite episodes of virtuoso piano writing, it keeps returning to the subtle simplicity of the church-counterpoint opening. And, after a burst of brilliance towards the end, it finishes with two unassuming, quiet chords.

PIANO CONCERTO NO. 12 IN A MAJOR, K. 414
Duration: approx. 25 minutes

Allegro
Andante
Allegretto

Like the outer movements of the preceding concerto, this is scored for strings with oboes and horns (no bassoons this time). Gentle themes predominate in the opening Allegro. The first begins with a smooth rise followed by a tripping descent, a charming contrast within a single theme. Then there is a forte followed by another gentle theme. In both of these passages the violins are in dialogue with the violas, first vigorously, and then with sighing phrases. This is an example of the way in which Mozart passes material freely among the strings in these three concertos, rather than to the (optional) wind instruments. The piano enters with the first theme, with only the lightest of decoration. Mozart's first piano entry often begins with something entirely new, but here it is only once the first theme has been restated that the piano launches into an extensive passage of fresh material, eventually reaching the gentle second theme with the sighing answers from the violas.

The middle part of the movement, the development, begins with one of those passage from the piano that on the one hand seems new but on the other hand seems to grow naturally out of what has gone before. At first, the music remains firmly in one key (E major by now), but eventually it cuts loose into a passage of free fantasia, passing from one key to another until arriving back, with a flourish and a pause, into A major for the reprise of the first theme. Pianists sometimes add a little cadenza at this pause, as Mozart himself probably would have done. For the main cadenza near the end of the movement Mozart provided two written-out suggestions.

The opening theme of the slow movement begins with a quote from an overture by the Mozarts' old friend, J. C. Bach, who had died in January 1782. At the age of eight, Mozart had sat on Bach's lap, improvising piano duets with him before King George III of England, and this quote was surely intended as an affectionate tribute. Then the second half of the theme is a slowed-down version of the theme that opened the concerto, which takes on the character of a stately dance (the 'connoisseurs' mentioned by Mozart in the letter to his father would have spotted both of these subtleties). When the piano enters, it intersperses yet another new thought between these two elements, and delicately ornaments the line as it goes. In the middle of the movement, the piano picks up a little phrase with which the strings concluded, and develops an expressive passage of fantasia from it, moving into darker minor keys. This arrives at a pause, which invites the pianist to play a little cadenza, before launching into the reprise of the first theme, then on through another cadenza to the end of the movement. As in the first movement, Mozart supplied two alternative cadenzas for these points.

The finale is a kind of rondo, in which the main theme recurs from time to time with episodes in between, but it has a subtly adventurous form. The orchestra's opening ritornello has three distinct thematic elements (it is often difficult in Mozart to know whether to call each element a 'theme' or not). The first is jaunty, with little trills on the offbeats. The second is in smooth octaves, the third a bold forte, with a snappy rhythm that perhaps refers back to the 'tripping' rhythm of the very opening theme of the concerto. The piano's first episode begins with new material but soon revisits the smooth second element from the orchestra's opening. The piano develops it at length, contrasting it with another jaunty element. After a pause (suggesting a little cadenza, though Mozart only supplies a final run-up), the first theme returns. This time, the smooth second element leads on to a new theme from the piano, in a new key. After a time, the smooth second element again reasserts itself. This leads to another pause for the main cadenza of the movement (once again, Mozart supplies two examples). The piano emerges, not into the first theme, but into the new material that it played at its first entry. Twice there is a pause and a change of key, as if Mozart is searching for a way back. It is only after a passage of assertive arpeggios, and another pause, that the piano arrives back at the opening theme, and the orchestra cheerfully reprises the snappy rhythms from its opening tutti to bring the concerto to a close.

PIANO CONCERTO NO. 13 IN C MAJOR, K. 415
Duration: approx. 26 minutes

Allegro
Andante
Allegro – Adagio – Tempo primo – Adagio – Tempo primo

This is the grandest of the three concertos K. 413–415, with an orchestra that includes (optional) trumpets and drums as well as oboes and horns. It was performed by Mozart at a concert in Vienna that marked the first climax of his success in the city. His opera *Die Entführung aus dem Serail* had scored a triumph, and now, in March 1783, he held his own benefit concert at the Burgtheater. In a long programme, including the recently composed 'Haffner' Symphony (No. 35), he played this new concerto. The theatre was full, the emperor was present, he applauded enthusiastically and, 'against his habit', stayed for the whole of the concert.

The first movement opens in march rhythm, but quietly, on violins alone. The other strings enter in turn, and only then is there a burst of forte, with trumpets and drums. This is a subtly dramatic way in which to start the concerto. After the bold tutti there is another unexpected moment. There is a sudden hush, with a long, held G in the bass, over which the three upper string lines weave around each other with dark harmonies. The 'connoisseurs' to whom Mozart referred in his letter would have appreciated this demonstration of his mastery of counterpoint. In this orchestral introduction there is more than enough material for the building of a whole movement. But, as often in Mozart's concertos, the soloist enters almost absent-mindedly with a completely new thought. Indeed, most of this first entry of the soloist is new material. Even the second main theme, which is usually drawn from the orchestral introduction, is here a new idea, though it does incorporate touches of the march theme. The piano rounds off this first entry with a reminder of the way the orchestra finished its introduction. And so Mozart, with characteristic ease, ties what is almost a free fantasia to material that was stated early in the movement.

This combination of freedom and rigour continues into the central development section of the movement. Again, the piano seems almost to be improvising on material of its own. But in the midst of it, the orchestra quietly returns to the opening march theme, now in minor keys, while the piano elaborates above. A pause, with a moment of meditative decoration, signals the end of this section of the movement, and the piano begins the reprise, starting with the theme with which it first entered. Mozart supplied a cadenza to be played near the end of the movement.

The Andante is one of the most easy-going movements in this easy-going set of concertos. The melody pours out like an operatic aria, first in the violins and then in the piano. After a middle section, it is repeated. At the repetitions, Mozart introduces decoration just as a soprano of his day would have done, though as the movement proceeds the elaborations go beyond what would have been possible for a singer. Mozart supplies a little cadenza to lead into the reprise, and a main cadenza near the end – again, it is easy to imagine a singer doing something similar in an aria.

The finale has a charming, rustic quality, like an anticipation of Papageno's panpipes in *The Magic Flute*. The piano begins, the orchestra answers at greater length. The scene is set for a genial exchange, as in a conventional rondo. But the orchestra comes to a halt, and into this pastoral scene Mozart inserts the first of two episodes of tragic rhetoric, in which the piano takes the decorative style of the slow movement to higher, and emotionally deeper, regions. These episodes prove to be no more than dark clouds passing in an otherwise bright sky, and the concerto ends with an air of gentle contentment, as if Papageno and his mate Papagena are skipping off into the distance.

PIANO CONCERTO NO. 14 IN E FLAT MAJOR, K. 449
Duration: approx. 22 minutes

Allegro vivace
Andantino
Allegro ma non troppo

Like the first group of Viennese concertos, K. 413–415, this concerto was written so that it could be played as a chamber work, with or without its wind instruments. Mozart composed it for his pupil Barbara von Ployer, daughter of a councillor at the Viennese court. She was described as a very fine pianist, and that is borne out by the fact that Mozart later wrote a grander second concerto, in G major, for her. We can imagine Babette (as she was known) playing this Piano Concerto in E flat just with a string quartet. But Mozart himself also performed it in concerts in Vienna in 1784. He was constantly in demand as a pianist during this period, and boasted to his father that, when a series of Saturday subscription concerts was announced, 'the nobility let it be known that they were not interested unless I played in them'. He sent his father a list of more than 170 aristocratic subscribers to the concerts that he gave in March 1784, and in that year he wrote no fewer than six piano concertos. On 20 March he reported the success of this Piano Concerto in E flat: 'the new concerto that I performed won extraordinary applause, and now wherever I go I hear people speaking in praise of that concert'.[13]

The opening orchestral tutti sets out no fewer than six different ideas, by turns boldly assertive, fiercely in the minor, then lyrical and dancing. A more economical composer (such as Haydn) would have built this exposition out of two themes at the most, but Mozart's fertile imagination simply pours out ideas. The piano then enters with the first theme, and decorates and develops it. But the piano's second theme is yet another new idea, and only after that does it turn to the lyrical melody we heard in the introduction. In the central section of the movement, piano and orchestra spend most of their time exploring a tiny little motif with a trill from the end of the introduction, rather than one of the fully fledged 'themes'.

The second movement opens with a broad melody of heart-easing beauty, in which touches of chromatic harmony add a characteristic poignancy. Any danger of sentimentality is countered by Mozart's tempo marking – Andantino, not Adagio (Andantino in Mozart's day indicated a tempo a little slower than Andante). The melody itself is so satisfying that Mozart is able to develop the whole movement from it. After the orchestra's exposition the piano begins to repeat it, exploring its possibilities further, and adding on a tailpiece that takes the music into a new key. Then the theme is reconsidered, until it gradually winds back to the home key. Now there is a more complete reprise of the melody, with orchestra and piano alternating, and the piano adding more and more elaboration until the movement reaches a gentle conclusion.

The finale begins in jaunty mock-baroque style, like the entry of a liveried servant in a comic opera. This theme recurs from time to time through the movement, each time varied and treated to new versions of Mozart's contrapuntal wit, and the episodes and developments in between each reprise vary from the charming to the forceful. At the end, the baroque theme is transformed into jig rhythm, bringing the concerto to a close with that unassuming brilliance that so entranced Mozart's own audiences.

PIANO CONCERTO NO. 15 IN B FLAT MAJOR, K. 450
Duration: approx. 25 minutes

Allegro
Andante
Allegro

Mozart himself first played this concerto at a concert in Vienna in March 1784. After four concertos in which the wind instruments are optional, the oboes and bassoons begin this concerto with a genial theme that is given piquancy by its accents on chromatic notes. As so often, there are half a dozen thematic ideas in the orchestral introduction. They include, after the first forte, a beautifully simple theme of falling phrases, first in the violins over a simple bass line and then taken up by oboe and bassoon with the violins weaving a countermelody. The piano enters with an extended flourish, almost like a mini-cadenza, before playing the opening theme that, again, it elaborates. This leads on through a lyrical new idea in a minor key to yet another new theme in the major that has, in its shape and character, much in common with the very opening theme of the concerto.

After the next orchestral tutti, the piano launches into a passage of fantasia, beginning by elaborating the little reiterated phrase with which the orchestra finished, and continuing with runs, arpeggios, and explorations through various keys. As the piano trills, the orchestra returns to the opening phrases of the concerto, and this brings us to the reprise of the opening theme itself. What follows is a revisiting of earlier themes, but varied in subtle ways. And towards the end of this section, under a piano trill, the theme of simple falling phrases reappears, for the first time since the orchestral introduction. This is an example of Mozart's marvellously natural, conversational way of ordering his thoughts, quite unrestrained by conventional ideas of when things might be expected to occur. Mozart himself supplied a cadenza for this movement.

The slow movement is a set of two variations on a solemnly contemplative theme that could have stepped out of one of Handel's operas or oratorios. The theme is in two strains, each of which is repeated. In the theme itself, the strings play first, and then the piano elaborates. In the first variation, the piano accompanies the strings with gentle arpeggios, and then plays the theme solo, rather grandly, with arpeggios below. In the second variation, the relationship between piano and orchestra becomes more complex. The piano begins, with further decoration, the strings joining in halfway through the first strain. Then the wind enter for the first time in the movement, taking over the theme while the piano plays rippling arpeggios and the strings play pizzicato – a delightful combination of effects. The second half of the variation, with its florid decoration and touches of chromatic harmony, attains an almost ecstatic effect, of the kind that Beethoven was to develop in his piano writing. A final few bars bring the movement to a calm resolution.

The finale is a rondo in the popular jig rhythm, with a theme that incorporates hunting calls. The bright, open-air character is subtly emphasized by the addition of a flute to the orchestra. Between the appearances of the hunting theme the solo writing is very brilliant, with leaps, runs, and crossing of hands in complex rhythms. At one point the theme itself is drawn into these complexities, passing between piano, wind, and strings in delightful conversation. The end of the movement is charmingly naive, both piano and orchestra seemingly stuck in the hunting rhythm, until a sudden forte brings the movement to a close.

PIANO CONCERTO NO. 16 IN D MAJOR, K. 451
Duration: approx. 25 minutes

Allegro assai
Andante
Allegro di molto

The first movement of this concerto has an unusually ceremonial character. The orchestra includes trumpets and drums, and the movement sets off with full orchestra in splendid march rhythm. The rising phrases build up over a rock-solid, sustained bass note – this could as easily be the opening of a symphony. The substantial opening tutti is full of dramatic gestures and strong contrasts. Just as striking as the trumpets and drums is the role of the flute, which adds a note of sweetness to the gentle passages. And the most memorable moment is quiet and uncertain, with pulsating offbeats in the strings, and shifting chromatic harmonies – a typically Mozartian touch amid all the splendour. The introduction ends as it began, with powerful march rhythms. The piano takes up the march rhythm, decorating it with elaborate scales and arpeggios. The sense of military order, suggested by the character of the music, also applies more subtly to the construction of this movement. Often, Mozart introduces new themes in the piano's first entry, rather than just revisiting the themes stated by the orchestra. But here, the piano bases itself on the themes that have already appeared, in the same order that they occurred in the orchestral introduction. As you would expect, there is much elaboration, and the themes are shared out in new ways between orchestra and piano, and interspersed with passages of exploration and display. But the overriding sense, both in the piano's first entry, and at the reprise, is of a movement kept tightly under control and in order. Again, one of the most striking moments is the quiet, pulsating theme, which is now joined by muttering figurations in the piano. The central development section is in contrast to the military character of much of the movement. A questioning phrase in the woodwind is taken up by the piano, and sets the mood for an exploratory passage of fantasia, which carries through to the reprise of the first march theme on full orchestra.

The strings begin the slow movement with a theme in G major whose chromatic line undulates gently over a sustained bass note. This very still phrase is answered by a phrase with a leap upwards – a beautiful Mozartian touch. The movement is a rondo, in which this theme occurs three times. At the end of the first statement of the theme, the piano moves off into an episode in a new key, with a melody of short, sighing phrases, with the woodwind in constant dialogue. The mood becomes more like an opera aria, with the woodwind responses becoming more poignant, until they coax the music back to the home key for the first reprise of the main theme. The piano follows this with another new theme in a minor key. The mood is a little more agitated. But then, in a turn of events that could have come from no other composer, the woodwind guide the music into yet another major key, and the piano plays a new theme of great calm, over a gently pulsating accompaniment. Mozart's sister, Nannerl, herself a fine pianist, told Mozart that she found this passage a little plain as he had written it. Mozart replied that she was 'quite right that there is something missing', and sent her a more elaborate version that preserves the calm while enhancing the expressive power (it also gives us an example of the sort of elaboration that he was probably in the habit of adding in concert to the simpler passages of his piano music).[14] Now it is the turn of the strings to guide the music back to the main theme, which they do in a beautiful passage over a sustained bass note, the undulations circling round, the woodwind joining in, and settling gently to a chord of G major. The final statement of the main theme extends into a lovely coda, in which the woodwind, in yet another poetical intervention, bring in poignant phrases from the piano's first episode.

The finale is also a rondo, with extended episodes between each recurrence of the main theme. Writers have commented that it sounds more like Haydn than Mozart, and indeed its main theme is made up of four-square phrases of the kind that Haydn loved to deploy in his finales, giving them a simple 'folk-ish' character. The flute added to the violin line in the theme is pure Haydn too. It is perhaps this finale that accounts for this concerto being one of the least often played of Mozart's piano concertos. And yet it is delightful in its straightforwardly cheerful way, and the episodes have touches of Mozartian subtlety that, after all, make it clear who is the composer.

PIANO CONCERTO NO. 17 IN G MAJOR, K. 453
Duration: approx. 31 minutes

Allegro
Andante
Allegretto

The Piano Concerto in G major, like the Concerto in E flat, K. 449, was written for Mozart's pupil Barbara von Ployer, daughter of a councillor at the Viennese Court. This concerto, on a larger scale than the one in E flat, shows what a fine pianist she must have been. Its first performance was not at one of the grand venues in Vienna, but at the Ployers' house (no doubt very grand in itself) outside the city in the village of Döbling. Here, Mozart reports, on 10 June 1784 there was to be a concert at which 'Fräulein Babette will play her New Concerto in G; – I will play in the Quintet – and together we'll perform my grand sonata for 2 Claviers.'[15] It had been an astonishing six months, during which Mozart composed, as well as this concerto and quintet, three more magnificent piano concertos. He was by now constantly in demand as a pianist and teacher. In March he wrote to his father, 'I am obliged to play new things, hence I must compose. The whole of the morning is devoted to pupils. And in the evening I have to play almost every day.'[16]

The opening theme begins with exactly the same march rhythm as the preceding Piano Concerto in D major, and the next two concertos too, as if Mozart is trying out all the possibilities of this rhythm. Here it starts quietly, on violins alone, with the dotted rhythm made elegant by a little trill. As with so many of Mozart's mature concertos, this orchestral exposition overflows with themes, almost like the first section of a symphony. Half a dozen different ideas follow each other. Most of them are cheerful, but at the centre is a melancholy little theme, with sighing phrases echoed by the woodwind. Right from the start of the concerto, it is clear that the woodwind are going to play a major part, continually in dialogue with the strings, and later with the piano.

When the piano enters, it begins by revisiting and elaborating the same themes in turn. But suddenly there is yet another, new idea on solo piano, leading on through various keys, with more fresh ideas on the woodwind and rippling arpeggios on the piano, before Mozart works back to the sighing theme. The middle section of the movement is more of a free fantasia than a conventional 'development', beginning with piano arpeggios accompanied by woodwind that travel through unexpected keys. When the music finally settles, it is in a minor key, not with one of the main themes, but with a meditation on a little turn of phrase drawn from the extra theme that the piano introduced earlier.

This is a concerto in which, despite the easy flow of the music, ideas do not recur quite as you might expect. But as if to compensate, Mozart makes subtle links between one movement and another. The opening bars of the slow movement quote the melancholy sighing theme from the first movement. But this turns out to be just an introduction that punctuates the movement at important points. What follows is a lovely dialogue between oboe, flute, and bassoon, which sets a serene mood. The piano later takes the music into darker regions, with an almost operatic line of melody, in a manner that he was to explore more fully in his C minor Piano Concerto, No. 24.

The finale is a set of variations on a delightfully jaunty theme, whose opening bars sound almost like a rustic version of the theme that began the first movement. The prominence of the flute, oboes, and bassoons in the succeeding variations gives an even richer sense of dialogue than in the earlier movements, almost like chamber music – as if Mozart is revisiting the quintet for piano and wind that he had recently composed. The fourth variation, in the minor, plunges further into the dark regions touched on in the slow movement, but the fourth variation rebuffs these melancholy thoughts briskly. Then, after a pause, the orchestra sets off at a gallop for the final race to the finish. This sounds almost like the finale of a comic opera, with all the characters rushing about, whispered asides, sudden revelations and outbursts. In the middle of all this there are touches of the sighing theme from the first movement. But cheerfulness and wit finally prevail, as, in a last exchange, piano and chattering woodwind bring the concerto to a close.

PIANO CONCERTO NO. 18 IN B FLAT MAJOR, K. 456
Duration: approx. 29 minutes

Allegro vivace
Andante un poco sostenuto
Allegro vivace

This concerto was written not for Mozart himself to play (though he did perform it), nor for one of his pupils, but for a brilliant blind pianist, Maria Theresa von Paradies, who was the pupil of one of Mozart's rivals, the pianist and composer, Leopold Kozeluch. It is the third of Mozart's concertos in a row to begin with the same march rhythm. Like the G major Concerto, it starts quietly, but here the effect is almost like a distant band – offstage, perhaps. The wood-wind (flute, oboes, horns, and bassoons) answer the strings, also quietly. After a forte passage for the full orchestra, there is a sudden tug on a discord, and plaintive woodwind phrases descend to a held horn note. Oboes play chirruping pastoral phrases, answered by flute and bassoon. Then there is a tutti, followed by a lyrical passage, another delicate march element, and a final tutti. This is one of the richest and most varied of Mozart's introductions, all accomplished within a contained and intimate setting.

The piano enters with the first theme (not, as so often, with new material), and revisits and elaborates the events from the introduction. It does, however, insert one new element after the orchestra's first forte, yet another delicate idea with little touches of march rhythm. Then the piano opens the development with a theme that again seems new, but contains elements from earlier ideas. Delicate march rhythms in the woodwind accompany running scales, and then the piano draws on the 'tugging' harmonies to darken the mood, before a corner is turned to arrive back at the first theme. The reprise proceeds much as the first time, but with such a delicately balanced collection of elements that Mozart has little need to ring the changes.

The slow movement is a set of variations on a plaintive tune in G minor, with each half repeated. It is made all the more touching by its delicate poise, and by the way that the final phrase is extended, with melancholy chromatic harmonies. In the first variation, the piano, mostly unaccompanied, muses on the theme. In Variation 2, the theme becomes a wind ensemble, like a movement from one of Mozart's serenades. At the repeats, it moves to the strings, and the piano delicately accompanies with arpeggios – a decoration that only deepens the melancholy. In Variation 3, the bold full orchestra, suggesting defiance or even outrage, alternates with the piano continuing in a vein of sad contemplation. Variation 4 moves into the major, the theme transformed by the wind ensemble into a benediction. Despite the calm that settles on the piano, the end of the variation reaches a moment of poignant hesitation, before the wind round off the theme. Variation 5, the final variation, is back in the minor, with the piano again delicately playing arpeggios over the theme in the strings. This time the two halves of the theme are not repeated. Instead, it is prolonged in a series of poignantly extended phrases. This movement is one of the most beautiful of all Mozart's slow movements. The mood is tragic, and one could easily imagine a developing scene from an opera – the deserted heroine, the outraged father, the consoling mother, and so on. There is no reason to suppose Mozart had such a scene in mind, but it was one of his great achievements to be able to construct an emotional drama that has the power of such a scene while remaining 'abstract' (one might say 'universal').

The finale, like the finale of K. 450, has the swing of a hunting song. The piano begins with a theme that, with its repeated phrases, has a popular, naive feel. But the movement has far more scope than this simple tune might lead one to expect. The orchestral tutti that follows includes an element with thrusting leaps and scrubbing accompaniment that could have come out of the finale of a symphony. And this is followed immediately by an elegant line in the woodwind that rounds off the tutti with great poise. The piano's first episode is lengthy. It begins with a new theme, simple but shapely. This develops brilliance, and then gives way to another new theme, with witty syncopations. More brilliance follows, until the woodwind reprise their elegant line to bring the music to a brief pause, where the pianist usually inserts a little cadenza before returning to the opening hunting theme.

This leads on to an extraordinary episode, in which the music arrives in B minor, very remote from the home key of B flat major. There is a stormy outburst from the piano. The music is split simultaneously into two time signatures: the swinging 6/8 and a 'straight' 2/4. The piano, in the new rhythm, plays a snatch of a dramatic aria that seems to hark back to the mood of the slow movement. But it is over in a moment, and never recurs. Some more storming brings the music back, not to the first theme, but to the theme that began the piano's first episode. This leads on to the syncopated theme, and eventually to a pause, a cadenza, and a final reprise of the first theme. But it is the woodwind's elegant line that, for the last time, rounds off the final tutti of this fascinating concerto.

PIANO CONCERTO NO. 19 IN F MAJOR, K. 459
Duration: approx. 28 minutes

Allegro
Allegretto
Allegro assai

This is the fourth of the run of piano concertos from 1784 that all begin with the same march rhythm. Here the melody is played airily on violins with flute (Haydn's favourite combination), and with a trotting accompaniment in the middle strings, before being taken up by the full orchestra. The effect is more of a brisk stroll on a sunny day than anything with military associations. However, Mozart's own Thematic Catalogue of his works lists trumpets and drums in the orchestra for this concerto, parts that have not survived, so the impression we get of the tutti today (with flute, oboes, bassoons, and horns) is more intimate than he intended. As so often in the opening of Mozart's piano concertos, one idea succeeds another in quick succession, so that it is difficult to say how many 'themes' there are. Here, the character of these ideas ranges from lyrical through perky to surprisingly dramatic, but the overall mood is cheerful, with no trace of the melancholy that permeated the preceding concerto.

The piano enters, picking up the first theme, alternating with woodwind. Mozart develops his material straight away, taking the theme through a delightful series of transitions and harmonic changes, until he arrives at yet another new idea. Various other elements reappear, though the original march rhythm is never far away, and a tutti rounds off this section of the movement. The development (more like a fantasia) consists entirely of a network of arpeggios from the piano, passing through various keys and punctuated by the march rhythm from the woodwind. The reprise revisits the same sequence of events as the first time round, but there are extra touches – new counterpoints, yet another little twist of harmony – that show Mozart's

inexhaustible fund of thoughts about the simple march idea with which he started. The movement ends as the first orchestral tutti ended, with charming, perhaps tongue-in-cheek, elegance.

The slow movement (which is not very slow) is like a languid serenade tinged with a
wistful quality, the strings and wind combining in a rich texture. When the piano takes up the
theme it explores it further, leading it on to a more melancholy theme in the minor, which is
answered with a curious touch of bluntness by the wind. The same sequence of ideas is revisited, with new decoration. From time to time, developments of the first theme lead to passages
in which running staccato scales pass lightly between the wind instruments and the piano.
These sound very much like a premonition of Susanna's aria in the garden in the last act of
Figaro.

The finale is a splendid example of Mozart's ability to write music that is both effortless
and complex at the same time. The opening theme is as light as a feather, with a witty suggestion of offbeat syncopations in its phrasing. But after an exchange between piano and wind,
the full orchestra starts a passage of determined counterpoint, as if they are beginning a fugue.
They soon think better of it and alternate bustling and delicate passages, throwing the opening
rhythm of the theme between bass and treble. There is a rather elegant tailpiece, over a
sustained bass note, and they clear the way for the piano's next entry. The piano plays a new,
more flowing idea, but soon the wind remind it of the opening theme, and from this point on
its rhythm is never far away. Then the strings introduce yet another witty theme. This is very
firmly on the beat, in contrast to the offbeat syncopations of the first theme.

In the middle of the brilliant passage that follows, the fugue theme from the introduction
is suddenly brought in as a counterpoint. This is just a passing reference at this point. We
reach a pause (an invitation to a little cadenza), which is followed by a reprise of the opening
theme. As before, piano and wind share it, and then the orchestra embarks on its passage of
counterpoint. But this time it is extended into a much more elaborate fugal passage, with the
fugue theme and the first theme brought together simultaneously. This demonstration of
Mozart's contrapuntal skill is anything but dry. It builds up tremendous excitement, from
which the piano bursts out with rattling broken octaves and arpeggios. There soon follows the
strings' third witty theme, another pause, and a final reprise of the opening theme. Now the
woodwind return to their elegant tailpiece from the introduction, and this tone of elegant wit
persists right until the emphatic final chords.

PIANO CONCERTO NO. 20 IN D MINOR, K. 466
Duration: approx. 31 minutes

Allegro
Romanze
Allegro assai

On 11 February 1785, Mozart's father Leopold arrived in Vienna on a visit from Salzburg, and
that same evening Mozart performed this concerto for the first time. Leopold reported in a
letter to Mozart's sister, Nannerl, that 'the concert was incomparable, the orchestra excellent',
and that the following day Joseph Haydn had said to him, 'I tell you before God, and as an
honest man, that your son is the greatest composer I know, either in person or by reputation.'[17]

This concerto is one of the few works of Mozart that continued to be played all the way
through the nineteenth century. Beethoven admired and performed it, and wrote cadenzas

for his own use. It is easy to understand why this particular concerto should have been singled out by the Romantics. It has a ferocity and dramatic intensity that mark it out from all Mozart's other concertos. The orchestra unleashes an emotional turmoil, in which the piano seems caught. A sense of drama being played out is very common in Mozart's piano concertos, but nowhere else does it take on this confrontational character. It is exactly this aspect that Beethoven and later composers – Liszt, Tchaikovsky, Brahms, Rachmaninoff, Prokofiev – were to develop in their own piano concertos.

The key of D minor seems to have inspired in Mozart a particular quality of dark foreboding (or at least he chose that key for this quality). The opening bars have something in common with the first movement of his String Quartet in D minor, K. 421, and seem to look forward to the music that accompanies the terrifying appearance of the statue of the Commendatore in *Don Giovanni*, also in D minor. Quiet, pulsating syncopations begin in the strings, and menacing little thrusts in the bass gradually mount up until the tension bursts out on full orchestra (including trumpets and drums). A second theme on the woodwind has a plaintive character (even though it begins in a major key), but is soon pushed aside by another fierce tutti.

The piano enters with a lament, an entirely new theme that one could imagine being sung by an operatic heroine. The piano is swept up into the orchestra's menacing opening theme, and then into the woodwind's plaintive second theme, which it leads on to another entirely new theme with a consoling quality – the first that is wholeheartedly in a major key. From here until the next tutti, the dialogue between piano and orchestra seems almost as convivial as in other Mozart concertos. But, as we enter the middle section of the movement, the sense of unease returns. Three times the piano revisits its opening lament, in different keys, and each time the orchestra responds with the syncopations and menacing bass phrases from the introduction. These persist as the piano develops a brilliant passage.

A corner is turned, and we arrive at the reprise of the opening, the piano playing along this time, as if recognizing that there is no escape. When the piano reaches the reprise of its consoling theme, it is now in the home key of D minor, which entirely robs it of its sense of consolation; now it takes on a poignancy more akin to its opening lament. Mozart did not supply a cadenza for this movement. Pianists often play the cadenza by Beethoven, which is magnificent, but has the effect of seeming to break through into a thoroughly nineteenth-century glimpse of the sublime. The movement ends quietly and ominously, as it began.

The slow movement is a Romanze, that is, a movement in lyrical, serenade-like style (the slow movement of Mozart's *Eine kleine Nachtmusik* is his most famous example of the genre). Like several of Mozart's slow movements, it is a rondo, in which the first theme returns several times, with different episodes between each occurrence. But, like the first movement, it has elements that are very surprising in a Mozart concerto. The piano begins with a gentle theme in B flat major, with poised rhythms. The orchestra answers each strain, and finishes off the theme with an eloquent few bars, including beautifully rich wind chords. After this, the piano's first episode is more elaborate, a continuous outpouring like an operatic aria. This is followed by a brief reprise of the opening theme.

What follows is a second episode, as one might expect, but here Mozart does something very unusual. He moves into G minor, and, while the beat remains the same, the rate of activity increases, so that it sounds as if the pace has doubled. The piano keeps up a pattern of rapid triplets, while agitated fragments of a melody pass from bass to treble and back again, against a background of wind chords. This persists through two repeated sections, and then gradually ebbs away, until we reach B flat major for the final reprise of the first theme. The ending is beautifully extended, bringing a satisfying conclusion to one of Mozart's most remarkable movements.

The surprises continue into the finale. This begins with the piano throwing up a defiant gesture. The orchestra responds with an extraordinarily ferocious tutti. It is as if the furies from Gluck's *Orpheus and Eurydice*, which threatened in the first movement, have been unleashed (it is probably no coincidence that Gluck's 'Dance of the Furies' is also in D minor). But it turns out that their power is limited. The most intense passage in this introduction, in which first violins and then lower strings scrub obsessively at a repeated pattern, never occurs again in the movement, except in fragments. It is as if the piano spends the rest of the movement confronting, and ultimately defusing, the consequences of this event.

After the mighty opening tutti, the piano's response is a simple theme, rather like a pared-down version of the first entry in the first movement. It has a similar quality of lament, but proceeds in short, nervous phrases. Reminiscences of the opening defiant gesture lead on via changes of key to a new theme. This too has a rather nervous air, with its rhythmically insistent phrases. But soon the piano breaks into running quavers, and eases for the first time into a major key. The woodwind respond to this change of mood with a delightfully relaxed, even jaunty melody, which seems far from the turmoil with which the movement began. This turns out to mark the end of this episode, and the piano reprises its opening defiant theme. The orchestra answers as if it is going to renew its ferocious attack, but soon comes to a halt, leaving the piano to repeat its first entry, with its nervous phrases. This is the beginning of an extended passage of development, in which the piano and the woodwind are in dialogue. Despite the predominance of minor keys, the mood of this passage is conversational, even chattering – an example of Mozart's subtle command of ambivalent moods. This leads on to another reprise in the home key, starting not with the opening theme but with the piano's rhythmically insistent third theme. Then the music eases, as before, into the woodwind's jaunty melody, and leads on to a cadenza (as in the first movement, Beethoven's is often played). After this, the defusing of the furies' threat is complete; the music emerges into a sunny D major, with the woodwind's jaunty theme leading the way. There are moments of the original scrubbing from the strings, but now it is merely energetic rather than threatening. By the time the trumpets and horns add a genial little fanfare to the mixture, it is as if we are in the final ensemble of an opera, and we are being assured that all is well. This, like the ferocious elements of the concerto, is another idea that Mozart was to take up in *Don Giovanni* three years later.

PIANO CONCERTO NO. 21 IN C MAJOR, K. 467
Duration: approx. 28 minutes

Allegro maestoso
Andante
Allegro vivace assai

Mozart played this concerto for the first time on 10 March 1785, at a concert in Vienna at which he also improvised on a piano fitted with a pedal keyboard, which he had had specially constructed. If Mozart tended to use D minor for a particularly dark mood (as in the preceding concerto), C major was for him often the key of music with a majestic air (as in his 'Linz' and 'Jupiter' symphonies, Nos 36 and 41, and the finale of Act I of *The Magic Flute*). The first movement of this concerto has a march rhythm (like several earlier piano concertos), and this time Mozart specifies that the Allegro should be majestic. This is not heavy majesty, but majesty worn with ease. The march begins quietly, with the short notes of the strings' theme like drumbeats, and delicate touches of real drums and trumpets answering in the wind chorus. The tutti emphasizes that this is not a military march, more an expression of the joy of walking with a spring in one's step. The quiet second theme underlines this quality – it is a simple, even naive tune, with quiet trumpets and horns answered by the woodwind. The next tutti builds up the march motif with counterpoint, and we expect the entry of the piano. But Mozart cannot let go of this mood he has found, so he adds yet more ideas. Just as we are beginning to wonder when the piano is going to enter, it sidles in as if warming up. There is a pause (some pianists add a little cadenza), followed by a trill as the strings begin the first theme again, the piano taking up the second half of it. Of all the piano entries in Mozart's concertos, this is one of the most delightful, unassuming but masterly.

The piano extends the theme into a passage of brilliant fantasia. This is interrupted by a moment of anxiety in a minor key. But the cloud soon passes, and chromatic scales lead to a gloriously sunny and flowing third theme in the major. The return of the march motif underpins the start of a another brilliant passage of fantasia, which, like the end of the introduction, goes on far longer than we expect, Mozart pouring out one idea after another, until the first section of the movement reaches its final tutti.

After all this richness of ideas, the development begins with what seems like yet another new theme. This is a melancholy, aria-like melody in E minor, and even if it seems new, it contains a falling motif that is drawn from the first theme. It is then simplified into woodwind chords, as the piano embarks on a florid but meditative passage, staying in minor keys. It reaches a climax, softens into C major, and the march is back for the reprise. This time, the piano encounters no moment of anxiety on its way to the sunny, flowing third theme. After another brilliant passage, the sunny mood is emphasized by the recurrence of the naive second tune, played by trumpets and horns and answered by woodwind, for the first time since the orchestral introduction. The piano, which has never played this tune before, takes it up too. More brilliant semiquavers lead to a cadenza. And the final tutti, which begins splendidly, exits on tiptoe, as it entered at the beginning of the movement.

The slow movement in F major is one of the glories of Mozart's output. Its fame was suddenly widened when it was used in the soundtrack of the 1967 Swedish film, *Elvira Madigan*, and its association with the tragic love affair of the film has haunted it ever since. Purists might think this unfortunate. But there are elements of the dramatic and the tragic in the music, even within the context of the eighteenth century. As often in the slow movements of Mozart's piano concertos, there is an operatic feel to the music, and no other example more powerfully suggests what Alfred Einstein called 'an ideal aria freed of all limitations of the human voice'.[18] The orchestra sets the scene. The strings are muted, the middle instruments gently pulsating, the bass delicately touched in, the first violins floating a line full of aspiring leaps upwards and dramatic falls downwards. After the first two phrases, the wind join in, providing far more than just chords. In counterpoint with the falling violin melody, a bassoon plays a rising line, creating a series of dissonances, each of which resolves only to become a dissonance again as the chord shifts. This gives the melody a sense of increasing tragic intensity, until it reaches the keynote, and the tension is finally able to resolve in a serene descending line.

The piano enters, and takes up the theme. It introduces a second idea in a minor key, before reaching the series of dissonances that once again resolve. Now it moves on to yet more new material, reaching further away from the home key. The reprise is accomplished with great subtlety. For a brief moment the pulsating accompaniment comes to a halt, and the piano leads us into the remote key of A flat to begin the main theme again. But soon it moves away, and by a series of searching key shifts, arrives back in F major for the series of poignant dissonances, and the resolution. A few bars of farewell, and one of Mozart's most beautiful movements is over. Through all of this, the pulsating accompanying rhythm, which only once ceases throughout the movement, has three notes per beat, but the melody usually breaks into twos and fours per beat, rarely threes. So there is a subtle rhythmic disjunction between melody and accompaniment, which makes the melody seem to be floating in the air.

After the great aria of the slow movement, the finale is pure comic opera. The orchestra begins with a staccato theme on tiptoe, the trumpets and drums, as at the beginning of the first movement, adding delicate touches of emphasis. Instead of reaching a conclusion, the theme is rudely cut off, and a pause announces the entry of the piano (often a little introductory flourish is added here, as Mozart probably intended). Like many finales, this is a rondo. The main theme recurs, interspersed with other ideas and excursions in new directions. As so often in Mozart, there are little chromatic twists in the harmonies, but these never take on a poignant character, never inject an element of doubt, but only add piquancy to the wit. Likewise, there are no moments of complex counterpoint. There is much interplay between the piano and the wind, but in the spirit of playful banter. This simplicity, of the subtlest kind, gives the whole movement a character of pure delight.

PIANO CONCERTO NO. 22 IN E FLAT MAJOR, K. 482
Duration: approx. 36 minutes

Allegro
Andante
Allegro – Andantino cantabile – Tempo primo

Mozart first played this concerto in Vienna on 23 December 1785, and the audience demanded an encore of the slow movement – 'a rare occurrence', as he reported. The opening of the first movement has a grand, ceremonial feel, rather like the beginning of one of Mozart's wind serenades. And this comparison is reinforced by the sound of the wind ensemble, which is different from that of earlier concertos. The two oboes have been replaced by two clarinets, which are not only prominent in solos, but also add a distinct mellowness to the ensemble. The emphasis on the wind is strong straight away: after the opening bars, flute (single), clarinets, bassoons, and horns (all in pairs) each in turn lead the melody on with a new phrase. This opening tutti is rich in ideas, as so often in Mozart's concertos. When the piano eventually enters it is with a new idea. The orchestra then returns to the opening theme, and the piano elaborates on top of it, and develops it further. Two further ideas follow: a sudden dark, forceful outburst in a minor key; and then, after a melancholy passage, a lightening into a delicate, lyrical melody in the major.

After the next tutti there follows an extended passage of fantasia. Convention might call this the development section, but the piano is really letting itself move freely from arpeggio to arpeggio and from key to key, until it finds a new theme, rather like the piano's earlier lyrical melody, and then a few bars later it arrives back at the opening theme. This time round, there are some delightful changes to the sequence of events. Twice the piano takes over elements that previously only appeared in the orchestral introduction, and since these are two of the most memorable ideas, they make us feel that we have come full circle, rounding off the movement, and tying the roles of piano and orchestra more closely together.

The slow movement is one of the most beautiful in all Mozart's piano concertos, and it is easy to understand why the first audience insisted on hearing it again. It is also in a most unusual form. It is a set of three variations on a theme in C minor. But between the variations there are two episodes in major keys that once again feature the wind instruments. The theme itself is deeply tragic, with the melody on muted violins, giving it a veiled quality. In the first variation, the piano elaborates the melody with that highly expressive decoration that makes one think of a singer rather than an instrumentalist. Then follows the first episode, which is a passage for woodwind and horns in E flat major. This, even more than the opening of the first movement, calls to mind Mozart's great serenades for wind. Variation 2 follows, with rapid figuration in the bass giving the piano writing an agitated character. The second episode, in C major, is a charming duet for flute and bassoon accompanied by strings. The relaxed mood of this passage is cut off by Variation 3, in which the theme has become a confrontation. The orchestra plays forcefully, and the piano answers pleadingly. Rather like the confrontational Concerto in D minor, K. 466, this sounds like a premonition of Beethoven in his Fourth Piano Concerto. After this final variation, the mood becomes calmer, and in the final bars the wood-wind and the piano exchange sorrowful expressions of consolation.

After the tragic slow movement, the opening of the finale comes as a breath of fresh air. The first theme is a naive tune with the simplest of harmonies and the rhythmic bounce of a hunting song. Piano and orchestra answer each other, and then the orchestra embarks on a substantial tutti that adds three more delightful elements, all of them with an outdoor quality. When the piano next enters, it muses on some of these new elements, before dashing off on a brilliant chase. It then introduces yet another charming tune, after which a skittering flute sets off the chase again. This leads the music back to the opening theme, another tutti, and a pause.

What follows comes as a complete surprise (though it is also reminiscent of similar inter-ruptions in the finales of the E flat Piano Concerto, K. 271, and the C major Piano Concerto, K. 415). A gentle wind serenade begins, this time with a rather operatic air, like the introduc-tion to an ensemble in *Così fan tutte*. Wind and piano alternate, the piano, according to the score, simply repeating the melody in unison with the violins. An older generation of pianists used to play this as written, often to beautiful effect. But (as with some rather simple-looking bars in the first movement) it is increasingly understood that Mozart would have embellished the line, and would have expected other pianists to do so.

After this lyrical episode, the genial hunting rondo resumes. There are many subtle changes along the way, through two more of the earlier themes to a cadenza (not supplied by Mozart). In many concertos, the tailpiece after the cadenza is brief. But here Mozart lingers lovingly over several of his ideas, introducing more delightful interplay between piano and woodwind, before bringing the concerto to a close.

PIANO CONCERTO NO. 23 IN A MAJOR, K. 488
Duration: approx. 28 minutes

Allegro
Adagio
Allegro assai

Mozart completed this Concerto in A major on 2 March 1786, when he was finishing *The Marriage of Figaro*. Of all his concertos, it is closest to the spirit of *Figaro*, sparkling and buoyant in the outer movements, but with a slow movement of lyrical poignancy. As in most of Mozart's mature piano concertos, the wind instruments play a vital role, contributing to the sense of chamber music on a large scale. The opening movement has an easy flow, reminiscent of the earlier Concerto in A major, K. 414. But now, as in the preceding Concerto in E flat, K. 482, there are two clarinets, helping to create a mood of mellow cheerfulness that permeates the movement. Even the structure of the movement contributes to this character. In many of Mozart's first movements there is a lot of 'redundant' material. The orchestra pours out more than enough ideas for a whole movement, and then the soloist enters with yet more new themes. But in this movement, the piano elaborates on the orchestra's themes without adding any new ones, as if to imply that it is content with the world in which it finds itself.

The strings begin with a quiet, singing theme, which is answered by the wind chorus. A vigorous tutti leads to a second lyrical theme that contains a series of falling phrases, with beautiful touches of chromatic harmony. In the tutti that follows, there are thoughtful moments amid the cheerfulness – thoughtfulness is another ingredient that permeates this movement. The soloist enters with the first theme, then elaborates and extends it into a brilliant passage. When it comes to the second theme, the soloist first plays it then comments as the orchestra takes it up. All this follows naturally until the next tutti.

Here there is something unexpected. The orchestra suddenly comes to a halt, and after a moment of silence, plays a new, quiet idea. In it there is a characteristic little dotted rhythm that passes from melody to bass and back again in answering counterpoint (this refers subtly to the persistent dotted rhythm in the descending second theme). The piano responds with an elaboration of this new idea, and without realizing it, we have already moved on to the central development of the movement. The new idea predominates, piano and wind alternating and then combining. Minor keys and touches of chromatic harmony introduce a more serious note that persists all the way until the piano breaks into arpeggios, draws us back to A major, and leads into the reprise of the first theme.

All proceeds as expected until, after the second theme, the piano suddenly halts, and, following a silence, revisits the new idea that suddenly appeared in the middle of the movement. This leads on to the next tutti, where the orchestra again pauses for another quiet reminder of this idea. These moments are most striking in this predominantly fluent and cheerful movement, as if there are thoughts running below the surface. Mozart himself supplied a cadenza for this movement which, though shorter than most, alternates brilliance and questioning thoughtfulness in a manner that highlights the contrasts of the movement.

The thoughts lying below the cheerfulness of the first movement seem to come to the surface in the slow movement in F sharp minor (Adagio in Mozart's autograph, but Andante in most editions until recently). The piano begins alone. The opening bar has the poised rhythm of a slow dance (a siciliano), but this poise is subverted and fragmented at every turn. By the second half of the phrase, an unexpected bass note has interrupted, and the melody is syncopated. Then the harmonies become more chromatic, and the theme ends on an arpeggio that rises high before settling back to a final cadence. No theme by Mozart more subtly suggests the emotional effort of maintaining an appearance of calm while things threaten to fall apart. The strings enter with a sorrowful descending line made more poignant by a high clarinet and bassoon in counterpoint. The piano develops the opening theme further, turning it towards A major.

Flute and clarinet introduce a new theme, gently consoling, with second clarinet accompanying with rippling arpeggios. This too is developed and extended by the piano, with charming interplay with the wind instruments. The opening theme returns, but with its last phrase interrupted and repeated before the orchestra's descending line takes over. This time, the piano also takes up this melody, elaborating it sorrowfully. There then follows a concluding passage with pizzicato accompaniment. The piano part is notated as simple notes, high and low alternating. This is the way that pianists used to play it, and it produces a starkly beautiful effect. Now it is widely assumed that Mozart wrote this as a skeleton to be filled out with appropriate elaboration. The movement ends with further reminiscence of the descending line in the woodwind, with the piano touching in a response that sums up the poignant delicacy of the whole movement.

Nothing could be more refreshing and releasing than the opening of the final rondo. The piano launches into a theme of unstoppable energy and high spirits, which is enthusiastically taken up and extended by the orchestra. After this, the piano's first episode introduces a second theme that is hardly less cheerful. But after a while, the flute and bassoon introduce a note of doubt, with a new theme in a minor key. The piano takes this up and decorates it, sidesteps back into major keys, and develops a passage of great brilliance, rounding it off with a naive little tune that seems to say that all is settled. This takes us back to the first reprise of the opening theme, first on the piano and then on the orchestra.

Next the piano enters forcefully in F sharp minor (the key of the slow movement), and although there is still great energy in the runs, the woodwind soon inject a moment of quiet questioning. But when they do this for a second time, it leads on to one of those heart-easing moments that are unique to Mozart. The clarinets play a simple, singing tune in D major, the piano accompanies gently and then answers. Eventually this leads back to the home key of A major, and to a reprise of the theme that began the first episode. This time, doubts are thrown in its way almost immediately, the woodwind answering in the minor and the theme becoming fragmented. Then minor and major alternate, like the sun passing rapidly in and out of the clouds, and soon we are safely back into A major for a reprise of the brilliant passage familiar from the first time round. Via the naive tune we arrive back at the opening theme for the last time. It is typical of Mozart that, just as we seem to be heading for a conclusion, he introduces for one last time the comforting naive little tune. Then there is a final burst of joyful energy from orchestra and piano, and the movement comes to an end.

PIANO CONCERTO NO. 24 IN C MINOR, K. 491
Duration: approx. 31 minutes

Allegro
Larghetto
Allegretto

This concerto has an unusually brooding, troubled atmosphere. The orchestra includes trumpets and timpani, but rather than introducing any brilliance, they concentrate the uneasy atmosphere with moments of emphasis and determination. Mozart's music in C minor tends to have a particularly dark character (the Fantasia and Sonata for Piano, the Wind Serenade, the Mass in C minor). In this concerto, Mozart adds extra dimensions to the darkness. The sense of conversation, as so often in his concertos, is heightened by the writing for woodwind instruments, as if the stage is populated by a rich assortment of characters – it includes both oboes and clarinets, giving a particularly rich orchestral palette. The harmonies are complex and chromatic, often avoiding the obvious. The very opening seems particularly enigmatic.

The concerto begins quietly, with strings and bassoons in octaves, the sliding chromatic harmonies searching around for the key. After a forceful tutti, the woodwind on their own meditate on the opening theme in a rising pattern, which then overflows into descending scales that pass between flute and bassoon. This all seems so utterly natural and simple; but there seems no easy way to find a resolution, and there are several more turns along the way before Mozart brings this orchestral passage to a close. When the piano enters, it refers back to the woodwind's descending scales to create what seems like a new theme. There is a sense that the piano is searching for something, an impression partly created by the way in which Mozart avoids the keynote, C, in the bass, until the cadence that ends the theme.

The piano breaks into energetic semiquavers, from which emerges a new theme in E flat major, a moment of consolation in this dark movement. Although it is new, the theme is connected in its melodic shape with the piano's very first entry – this concerto is full of subtle connections of this kind. Soon, the piano breaks into a more extended passage of semiquavers, under which Mozart brings the dotted rhythms from the orchestral introduction. A trill seems to announce that this first section is drawing to a close. But unexpectedly the oboe brings in yet another new theme in E flat major. Soon, the flute reminds us of the dark opening theme, and the piano's semiquavers venture off into distant keys. After a while, the piano finds its way back to E flat major, and another trill is finally able to announce the end of the first section of the movement.

An orchestral tutti returns to the opening theme, now sounding more comfortable in the key of E flat major, and this leads in to the development section. One feature of this movement is that, after such an extended and searching first section, with so many different elements, this central development seems more straightforward. After an anxious exchange between piano and woodwind, the piano sets off on another journey of semiquavers, with the rhythm of the opening theme passing between strings and woodwind. The piano tumbles down to a forceful passage that, for a few bars, seems to have come from the ferocious world of the Piano Concerto in D minor, K. 466. Gradually, the music finds its way back to C minor, to bring in the reprise.

It is no surprise to find new touches as Mozart revisits his themes. But there is one partic-ularly telling change compared with the first section of the movement. As usual, the entire reprise stays close to the home key. This means that the subsidiary themes, which were origi-nally in a warm E flat major, are now in the darker C minor. And to add to this effect, Mozart reverses the order of two of the themes. The oboe theme that appeared as an unexpected extra the first time round now comes first, the smile taken from it by the minor key. For a moment, the piano takes it into F minor and decorates it wistfully. Then it returns to C minor for the other theme that was originally in E flat major. This is the theme that came as a welcome moment of consolation in the darkness. Here, in C minor, there is no consolation, and its memory in this dark key has wonderful poignancy.

From this point on, the piano renews its semiquaver explorations, but these too have a new urgency in the minor key. The orchestra returns for a moment to the opening theme, and a pause brings in the piano's cadenza (which Mozart did not supply). Then a final tutti reprises the end of the introduction. This time, the piano joins in quietly with accompanying arpeg-gios, and over a sustained bass oboes and bassoons exchange anxious memories of the opening theme, to bring the movement to a pianissimo end.

After the subtle complexities of the first movement, the second movement is simpler, with a theme in E flat major that alternates with two episodes in which the woodwind take the stage. The piano begins alone, with the first strain of the lyrical theme. The orchestra repeats it. The piano plays an even simpler middle strain, accompanied by the strings. There is a pause, perhaps with a little decoration, and the theme ends by returning to its opening, with piano and woodwind joining together.

The first of the two episodes is in C minor, and returns to the chromatic harmonies of the first movement. It begins like a wind serenade, with two oboes and bassoon joined by the flute. The piano takes up the theme and elaborates it poignantly. The wind ensemble plays the second half of the theme, and the piano answers with more elaborate decoration. A moment of cadenza leads in the first reprise of the opening theme.

The second episode also begins like a wind serenade, but this time the pair of clarinets replaces the oboes, with horns and flute adding to a rich ensemble. As this episode is also in a major key (A flat major), the effect is warm rather than plangent. As before, the piano answers and decorates each half of the theme.

The opening theme returns for the last time. The piano plays it throughout, and pianists often add a little decoration (as Mozart probably would have done). Then all the wind, including oboes and clarinets, combine for a last moment of serenading, and the piano deli-cately leads the theme on to a touching conclusion.

After the song-like slow movement, the finale returns to C minor, and to the troubled atmosphere of the first movement. It is a set of variations on a theme with a quietly agitated character, with timpani giving it a march-like emphasis. As in the first movement, its harmo-nies continually pull away from the home key (the way the bass pushes up to A flat, in both halves of the theme, is the principal cause of this sense of unease, as it often is in the first movement). The variations that follow retain the shape of the theme, but subject it to distinct changes of mood. At first the piano decorates the theme with nervous, chromatic elaboration. In the second variation, the woodwind ensemble alternates with running figuration in the piano. In the third variation the piano plays forceful dotted rhythms, alternating with the full orchestra. The fourth variation moves to A flat major, with a jaunty version of the theme played by clarinets and bassoons. This shift of key, and change of character, is reminiscent of the A flat episode with clarinets in the slow movement. The fifth variation, for solo piano, alternates between chromatic passages that sound almost improvised and the forceful dotted rhythms from the third variation.

After this, the sixth variation is like another 'episode', with the oboe weaving a melodic line in C major, and the piano responding with further decoration. This is the last moment of relief in the concerto. A seventh variation returns to the original theme, interspersed with agitated figuration from the piano. And then, after a pause (and usually a little cadenza), the piano launches into the final variation. This is one of the most original and subtle moments in the whole of Mozart's music. The shape of the theme is still recognizable, but Mozart has transformed it into the 6/8 rhythm of a jig. You might expect this to lighten the atmosphere. But the combination of the dance rhythm with the uneasy chromatic harmonies produces a sense of extraordinary poignancy, as if tragedy lurks beneath a cheerful surface. There is a reminiscence of Beethoven, listening with fellow composer and pianist Johann Baptist Cramer to a performance of this concerto. As the pianist began this final variation, Beethoven is said to have exclaimed, 'Cramer! Cramer! We shall never be able to do anything like that!'[19]

PIANO CONCERTO NO. 25 IN C MAJOR, K. 503
Duration: approx. 32 minutes

Allegro maestoso
Andante
Allegretto

In December 1786, Mozart presented two magnificent new works at concerts in Vienna, the 'Prague' Symphony (No. 38), and this piano concerto. From the brightness of No. 23 in A major and the darkness of No. 24 in C minor, Mozart returns to C major, a key that he often uses for a somewhat grand, ceremonial character (as in the Concerto No. 21 in C major). The orchestra includes oboes, trumpets, and timpani, but not the mellow clarinets of the three preceding concertos.

The opening of this concerto and that of its predecessor in C minor could not be more contrasted. The C minor Concerto opens tentatively, darkly. This Concerto in C major opens with a series of magnificent chords of C major for full orchestra, like the entry of an emperor. Indeed, the whole of this Allegro is the opposite of the first movement of the C minor. There, the darkness was sometimes alleviated by shafts of consolation, but was ultimately not to be conquered. Here the ceremonial splendour is sometimes darkened by questioning, but the triumph is never really thrown into doubt. However, the element that dominates this first movement is not the triumphal opening gesture, but the quiet, persistent rhythmic figure that gets going a few bars later. The first violins, echoed by the seconds, play in a rising sequence a little motif with an upbeat of three short notes (a bit like the motif that dominates the first movement of Beethoven's Fifth Symphony). Once this has entered the music, it is rarely absent for long. It is there throughout the next tutti, at the end of which it is hammered out (here it really does sound like a premonition of Beethoven's Fifth). Then there is a quiet second theme in C minor, built from the same rhythm, with a march-like tread.

Soon we are back in bright C major again, and we expect the entry of the piano. As in the earlier C major Concerto (No. 21), the piano sidles in, like someone entering a room hoping not to be noticed. Soon the orchestra returns to the opening grand flourish, the piano answering and elaborating. The piano goes on to present two new themes, the first melting out of the motif into a melody in E flat, with gently falling phrases. The second is a melody in G major, with rising phrases. This has a bright, sunny quality, but Mozart characteristically darkens its second strain with a touch of minor harmony, before cheerfully breaking into running semiquavers and handing the theme over to the woodwind.

The central part of the movement is once again dominated by the rhythmic motif, as it first occurred in the second theme of the opening tutti. The piano and woodwind exchange it in different keys. Then it is developed into a complex passage of counterpoint, which eventually works back to C major for the reprise of the grand opening tutti gesture.

The slow movement begins with an extraordinarily varied orchestral passage. Part of the variety is in the choice of instruments. The melody, in a slow three-time, opens with flute and bassoon two octaves apart. Then oboes and bassoons take over, the flute answering with silvery arpeggios and runs. And then, surprisingly, the strings break out of the slow rhythm, into a sort of double-tempo, tiptoeing dance, which is reminiscent of a similar moment in the slow movement of the 'Haffner' Symphony (No. 35). After this moment of unexpected energy, the tutti ends as serenely as it began.

The piano enters with the first theme, incorporating the flute's runs and arpeggios – there is something particularly delightful about this flute-to-piano transformation. The piano leads on to a second theme, but then, as if remembering something it had forgotten, breaks into the double-tempo dance. This is followed by more new material, with large leaps, echoed in the woodwind. Some of the piano writing in this opening section is quite spare, and many pianists fill the skeleton out with elaboration, as Mozart would probably have done. Eventually, the music winds round to a reprise of the opening, but not before there has been a long moment of beautiful suspense over a held C in the bass. The reprise incorporates increasingly elaborate decoration in the piano part, creating a kind of ecstatic effect that Beethoven was to develop in his piano writing.

The finale is an Allegretto with a gently dancing character. The mood of the opening theme is genial, but, as so often in Mozart, it incorporates towards the end a moment of darkness, as the theme moves to the bass and the harmonies turn minor and chromatic. After the gentle character of this main theme, the piano's first episode is brilliant and virtuosic. Soon it brings in a more lyrical theme, but, as it hands it over to the woodwind, the cascading arpeggios and runs resume. After the next reprise of the main theme, the piano launches into a more agitated, brittle, idea in a minor key. But after a while this gives way to the most extraordinary passage in this movement. The piano plays a singing melody, built from simple, repeating phrases. In dialogue with oboe, flute, and bassoon, this is built up into the most beautiful, spacious episode, passing through various keys before turning once again towards C major for another reprise of the main theme and the brilliant piano writing from the first episode of the movement. A final return of the main theme becomes playful, extending into a brilliant peroration to bring this most flamboyant of Mozart's concertos to an end.

PIANO CONCERTO NO. 26 IN D MAJOR, K. 537, 'CORONATION'
Duration: approx. 32 minutes

Allegro
Larghetto
Allegretto

This concerto is known as the 'Coronation' because Mozart played it at a concert in Frankurt during the celebrations for the coronation of Leopold II, Emperor of Austria, in October 1790. Mozart had travelled to Frankfurt from Vienna, even though he had not been invited to participate in the official wedding performances. He had composed the concerto two years earlier, and had already performed it in April 1789 at the court in Dresden. After that concert, the Elector of Saxony presented him with 'a very pretty snuffbox' containing a hundred ducats.

The first movement, as in several earlier concertos including the famous No. 21, opens with a quiet march, which after a few bars breaks into a splendid tutti, including trumpets and drums. But the movement is not dominated by march character. There is a second, delicate theme, which the violins introduce with an eloquent few bars of unaccompanied melody. And a third idea, a sort of tailpiece to the orchestral introduction, is simple and lyrical, and, again, highlighted by an introductory two unaccompanied bars. The soloist enters with a decorated version of the first theme, though now without its march-like accompanying rhythm. After a running passage, the orchestra seems to be leading into the lyrical third theme. But instead the piano launches into more running semiquavers, arriving at yet another new idea. This is a mixture of simple and poignant: simple arpeggio patterns in a dotted rhythm alternate with poignant touches of chromatic harmonies, giving a tinge of melancholy. After exploring the implications of this for a little, the piano arrives at the second, delicate theme. Again the music takes an unexpectedly serious turn for a few bars, before finding its way back to more brilliant semiquaver passages to bring the first section of the movement to a close.

As Mozart often does, he begins the development by concentrating on something seem-ingly incidental – the flourish with which the orchestra finished the linking tutti – and subjects it to serious discussion. It continues to be reiterated quietly in the orchestra as the piano begins a passage of free fantasia. This goes on a journey through different keys, before arriving at the reprise of the opening march theme. The reprise revisits the material of the piano's opening section. But at a late stage, Mozart suddenly remembers the simple and lyrical idea that had occurred towards the end of the orchestra's introduction – a lovely moment. A few more brilliant bars bring us to the cadenza (not supplied by Mozart), and then a brief conclusion on full orchestra.

The slow movement begins on solo piano with a melody of serene simplicity – music pared down to its essence (Mozart was to do something similar in the slow movement of his final piano concerto). Some pianists have been tempted to stress its profundity by taking it very slowly, but the time signature indicates two slow beats in a bar, not four. The form of the movement is simple. Between the opening and closing sections, based on the first theme, there is a middle section. This continues the mood of simplicity, with a spare melody in the piano over a straightforward bass, with little more than accompanying chords in the orchestra. This looks so skeletal on the page that it is now generally assumed that this is one of those passages that Mozart, who wrote it for himself to play, would have elaborated and filled out in performance.

The opening of the rondo finale sounds as if it was inspired by the opening of the slow movement. The melody that the piano plays starts with a similar shape, over simple harmonies. There is also an elegant simplicity about the form of this movement. Sections based on the opening rondo theme alternate with two episodes with new material. But, unusually for Mozart, the second episode revisits the same material as the first episode. The difference is that the first episode begins in the home key of D major, venturing only to closely related keys. But the second episode begins, after a surprising shift of harmonies, in B flat, and ventures far and wide through a succession of different keys, major and minor. Even when Mozart is back safely in D major, he launches out again into further modulations before finally returning. All this gives the movement a very satisfying shape. The sequence of ideas is, on one level, predictable, because of the repetition of material; but the variety of mood with which Mozart inflects his ideas is masterly.

PIANO CONCERTO NO. 27 IN B FLAT MAJOR, K. 595
Duration: approx. 30 minutes

Allegro
Larghetto
Allegro

According to Mozart's own Thematic Catalogue, this final piano concerto was finished on 5 January 1791, though studies of his autograph score suggest that he drafted it in 1788, the same year as the 'Coronation' Concerto. Mozart certainly performed it himself in March 1791, and this was his last appearance at a public concert in Vienna. The concerto has such a serene, simple, and unhurried character that one could easily imagine it as the work of an old man. But although Mozart was to survive only until December 1791, he was a man in his mid-thirties when he wrote it. It is one of the great mysteries of Mozart that he could produce music of such qualities at such a young age. If music can be wise, this music is full of wisdom.

Several of Mozart's piano concertos begin with a movement in march rhythm, softened by lyrical elements. The first movement of this concerto reverses the process. The opening theme is a lyrical outpouring from the violins. Three times the melody rises and then falls. It is twice punctuated by a little fanfare motif from the wind in march rhythm, and culminates in a moment of energy from the whole orchestra (there are no trumpets or drums in this concerto). A second idea continues this process, the melody in the violins rising higher at each phrase, the wind punctuating more gently this time, the whole orchestra rounding it off with a vigorous passage. Another lyrical theme follows in the violins, then another vigorous passage, and still another lyrical element. It is as if, even so early in the concerto, Mozart is reluctant to tear himself away from the vein of melody that he has discovered. Finally the tutti reaches a conclusion, and the piano enters with the first theme, punctuated by an echo in the strings of the wind fanfare. At the end of the theme, the piano takes the vigorous tailpiece and runs with it. From here, it arrives at a new theme, which suddenly darkens into a minor key, with plangent chromatic harmonies. But this soon passes, and a further passage of delicately running semiquavers leads on to the second and third themes from the introduction. An orchestral tutti winds up the first section of the movement.

The tutti ends quietly with a sudden change of key, and the piano begins the development with the first theme, now in the remote key of B minor. There is a series of unusual modulations from key to key, as the piano and woodwind weave the first theme in counterpoint. This passage has a mysterious and searching quality, with the lyrical and fanfare elements of the theme intertwining, and the music moving restlessly from key to key until it arrives back in B flat for the reprise of the first theme. The sequence of themes proceeds as before, with further elaboration from the piano. But, in a characteristic touch, Mozart adds on to this sequence of themes the beautiful idea with which the orchestra finished its introduction, which the piano now plays for the first time. After a cadenza (Mozart supplied one), the movement ends quietly.

The slow movement, in E flat major, even more than the slow movement of the 'Coronation' Concerto, seems to pare expression down its essence. Once again the movement has a simple, three-part form. Writers have compared it with some of the hymn-like sections of *The Magic Flute*, which Mozart composed shortly after he first performed this concerto early in 1791. If the concerto was drafted three years earlier, as scholars now suggest, the association with *The Magic Flute* does not have such relevance. But this does not take away from the extraordinary, serene character of this movement. Its opening theme, on solo piano, seems so simple, almost childlike. And yet it is not as simple as it appears. The way Mozart balances the phrases of the melody against each other is very subtle. The first strain of the theme is eight bars long, but the phrases are divided asymmetrically: 1½ bars, 1½ bars, 1 bar, 1½ bars, 1½ bars, 1 bar. This gives the melody an unusual fluidity which, with its simple harmonies, makes it sound ethereal rather than merely simple. After the orchestra repeats this strain, the piano plays the middle section of the theme, which has regular pairs of 2-bar phrases, before repeating the first part of the theme. The orchestra then rounds it off. In the middle part of the movement, the piano expands on these thoughts, developing an almost operatic, aria-like line, flowing freely through various keys. This section is very similar to the equivalent section of the 'Coronation' Concerto, and it too is spare in its writing, warranting some tasteful elaboration from the pianist. Eventually the piano winds back to E flat for the reprise of the opening section.

The finale, like that of several earlier concertos, has the swinging rhythm of a hunting song. Its main theme has a delightful, naive character – Mozart went on to use its tune as the basis for a spring song, 'Komm, lieber Mai' ('Come, lovely May'), which is often sung by children's choirs in German-speaking countries. The movement is a rondo, in which the theme occurs three times, interleaved with episodes. After piano and orchestra have completed their first statement of the theme, the piano launches into the first episode. This introduces two new ideas, both of which are bright and cheerful, interspersed with energetic running passages including a particularly delightful exchange between piano and flute. After a pause, during which pianists often play a short cadenza, the first theme returns. But soon the piano diverts it into new keys, with more running passages, and we find ourselves in the second episode.

In contrast to the first episode, this is more like a passage of development, in which elements of the first theme are combined with fantasia-like piano writing. At one point, there is a 'false reprise', when the first theme returns, but in the wrong key (E flat), and the piano continues on its journey of exploration. Eventually, the music arrives back in the home key of B flat, and a large portion of the first episode is revisited, including the two new themes that first occurred there. This culminates in a pause for a cadenza (which Mozart supplied), and then the movement is rounded off with a final appearance of the first theme, another burst of energy, a last exchange between piano and woodwind, and an emphatic final flourish from the full orchestra.

Violin Concertos

Mozart's father, Leopold, was a distinguished violinist, who published an important treatise on violin-playing in the year that his famous son was born, 1756. Wolfgang was brought up playing the violin, and he became very accomplished at it. During a visit to Munich in 1777, he played the violin in two of his Cassations at a private concert. Afterwards he wrote to his father, 'I played as though I were the greatest fiddler in all Europe!' To which Leopold replied, 'You yourself do no know how well you play the violin, if you will only do yourself credit and play with energy, with your whole heart and mind, yes, just as if you were the first violinist in Europe.'[20] It is therefore not surprising that Mozart should have written violin concertos. Indeed, since he was a first-rate violinist, why did he not write dozens of them, as he did piano concertos? It seems that playing the violin was too much associated with the routine of the court of the Archbishop of Salzburg, where the Mozarts were employed. After his travels to Munich and Paris, where he had vainly tried to get work, Mozart in 1778 agreed to return to his post in Salzburg. But he wrote to his father, 'I don't want to be only a violinist as I was before – I'm not a fiddler any more – I want to conduct from the piano.'[21] The piano was to be the instrument that made Mozart famous, and when that side of his career began to take off, he put the violin behind him.

Of the five violin concertos by Mozart that survive, No. 1 in B flat major, K. 207, and No. 2 in D major, K. 211, very much follow the style of Italian composers such as Tartini and Geminiani. They are charming and expressive, but there are only occasional moments that suggest the mature Mozart. But No. 3 in G major, K. 216, is a much more striking and original work, even though it was composed only a few months after No. 2. Nos 3–5 followed in the same year, 1775.

VIOLIN CONCERTO NO. 3 IN G MAJOR, K. 216

Duration: approx. 23 minutes

Allegro

Adagio

Rondeau: Allegro – Andante – Allegretto – Tempo I

This concerto was composed in September 1775, when Mozart was nineteen, and it is one of the works in which Mozart first achieved a truly personal way of writing a concerto. This was partly by injecting into the music dramatic elements drawn from opera – indeed, Mozart took the vigorous opening theme from an aria in his opera *Il Re Pastore*, written earlier the same year.

The orchestra introduces this theme and two others, one more sustained, the other on tiptoe. The soloist enters with the first theme, then adds more elements – in turn lyrical, energetic, pointed – on its way to the second theme. Already there is an unusually conversational character to the writing. After the next orchestral tutti, the middle section, the development, follows. This is where the dramatic element of Mozart's concerto style comes to the fore. The soloist enters in a minor key, with a serious tone, and with a theme that seems new and yet also seems to have grown out of earlier material. Phrases are exchanged between soloist and orchestra. Then, all of a sudden, an oboe steps out and sings the new theme, entering into dialogue with the soloist as the music moves from key to key. This culminates in a passage where the whole orchestra engages in dialogue with the soloist, as if, just for a moment, we find ourselves in an operatic recitative. There is a pause, where the soloist will probably play a short cadenza, and the two oboes lead in to the reprise of the opening theme.

The slow movement is the glory of this concerto. Mozart changes the instrumentation to create a soft, pastoral effect. The two oboes of the first movement have been replaced by two flutes, the strings are muted, and the bass is pizzicato. With the gently soaring melody and murmuring accompaniment we could be in the Elysian Fields of Gluck's *Orpheus and Eurydice*. The soloist takes this theme on a journey that seems like an ecstatic aria, freed from the constraints of the human voice.

As in the first movement, it is the transition from the middle section to the reprise that most clearly shows the new subtlety of Mozart's musical language. The repeated murmuring figure in the accompaniment is suddenly taken up for a moment by the solo violin, and from there it migrates to the bass, while the harmonies move to prepare for the reprise. The end of the movement is beautiful and unexpected. After a pause and a cadenza, the orchestra enters for the last time. Just as it is playing what seems to be the final cadence, the soloist enters again, and plays one last time the soaring opening phrase of the theme.

In October 1777, Mozart reported to his father that he played this concerto during a visit to Augsburg: 'In the evening at supper I played my Strasbourg concerto. It went like oil. Everyone praised my beautiful, pure tone.'[22] Mozart's pride in his beautiful tone, rather than technical brilliance, is all of a piece with the sublime lyricism of the slow movement. As for the 'Strasbourg concerto', this refers to a popular tune, 'The Strassburger', which Mozart incorporated into the finale. The movement begins as a conventional rondo (or rondeau, the French term), with a lively theme in a dancing three-time. The theme is first played by the orchestra. The soloist responds with a second theme, to launch an episode that develops into brilliant running semiquavers. The main theme returns, introduced this time by the soloist. Then there is a second episode, in which the soloist repeats the theme from the first episode, but now in the minor, with little plangent turns of harmony. The first theme returns again, and comes energetically to a cadence and a pause.

Now there is an unexpected turn of events. Over a pizzicato accompaniment, the soloist plays a gentle, courtly dance in G minor. This leads straight into a slightly faster, more 'peasanty' tune in G major, which the soloist elaborates: this is 'The Strassburger'. After this surprising excursion, the original three-time rhythm is nonchalantly picked up again, and a link passage takes us back to the principal theme. Much of the first episode is reprised, there is a pause, at which a little cadenza is usually played, and the orchestra rounds off the movement. Even at the last moment, Mozart surprises. The end is not an emphatic flourish, but the quiet little fanfare-like phrase with which oboes and horns originally announced the soloist. Mozart shows himself a master of making an effect with the most unassuming gesture.

VIOLIN CONCERTO NO. 4 IN D MAJOR, K. 218
Duration: approx. 22 minutes

Allegro
Andante cantabile
Rondeau: Andante grazioso – Allegro ma non troppo (alternating)

Early in the twentieth century a Violin Concerto in D major by Luigi Boccherini was 'discovered', which bore several striking resemblances to this concerto in the same key by Mozart.

Writers took this to mean that Mozart had based his concerto on the earlier work, until it was revealed that the Boccherini was a clever forgery, which had taken the Mozart as its model.

The first movement opens with a theme in march rhythm, though with courtly rather than military character – a style that was to become a favourite ingredient of Mozart's piano concertos. As so often in those, delicate and vigorous elements here alternate, and are succeeded by a more lyrical second theme. The solo violin takes up the march theme, but now high and delicate, like the entry of a coloratura soprano. Making this demanding first solo sound pure and natural is a great challenge for the violinist. As so often in Mozart's concertos, the soloist follows this with new material. The next idea begins sonorously, low on the instrument, but soon breaks into flowing semiquavers, with bold leaps and arpeggios. These are given added depth by touches of poignant harmony in the orchestra. A return to the high register of the violin leads on to the next orchestral tutti.

The soloist begins the middle section of the movement by picking up the little phrase with which the orchestra concludes, so that one is hardly aware of the transition. And, after some brilliant passages that move through a variety of keys and refer to some earlier turns of phrase, we suddenly find that we have reached the reprise of the soloist's sonorous theme – there is no conventional orchestral tutti to mark the end of the development. As before, this leads on eventually to the original second theme, and to a pause for a cadenza, after which the orchestra concludes energetically.

The slow movement in A major is simple in outline: a long melody, a middle section that ventures into other keys, and a return to the first melody in the home key. But Mozart enriches this straightforward scheme with great subtlety. The orchestra introduces the melody, which has three elements. The first consists of two slowly descending phrases over a static bass note. The second moves on, with the flowing melody rising to a climax. And the third is a little tailpiece, with a playful trill introducing a suggestion of dance. The soloist repeats the melody, in partnership with the orchestra. This time the little tailpiece leads seamlessly on into the middle section of the movement. The solo violin begins with another flowing idea, which it repeats an octave lower. Then a dance element again enters, with more playful rhythms in the melody and a gently tripping staccato accompaniment in the strings, and a conversation is struck up between soloist and oboe. This charming moment leads into the reprise of the opening melody, after which there is the usual cadenza. Then, as in the slow movement of the Third Violin Concerto, Mozart seems reluctant to tear himself away. Rather than finish with the conventional orchestral few bars, he has the soloist play a concluding, meditative pair of phrases, after which the orchestra rounds off the movement with a reminiscence of the most flowing part of the first melody.

In the finale two dancing themes alternate, the first poised and elegant like a gavotte, the second in a lively three-time. In the finale of the Third Violin Concerto, it was the first theme that provided material for the bulk of the movement, with the dance tunes as brief interruptions. Here Mozart reverses that procedure. The elegant first section is brief, like an introduction, and it returns to form interludes. The lively sections are developed at greater length. In the middle of the movement, after one of the lively passages, there is a slower section with the character of a solemn rustic dance, complete with the drone of a bagpipe or hurdy-gurdy. The whole movement has almost the feel of a little pastoral scene from an opera. It concludes with a reprise of the lively music that ends fading to pianissimo, as if the characters are disappearing into the distance, still dancing.

VIOLIN CONCERTO NO. 5 IN A MAJOR, K. 219, 'TURKISH'
Duration: approx. 25 minutes

Allegro aperto – Adagio – Allegro aperto
Adagio
Tempo di menuetto – Allegro – Tempo di menuetto

'Allegro aperto' is an instruction that Mozart occasionally used for concerto movements, and there are various opinions as to its exact meaning. Aperto literally means 'open', and he probably meant 'bright' or 'straightforward'.

The opening of this concerto could be the beginning of a symphony – it has the busy accompaniment, pointed arpeggios, and sudden contrasts of the symphonies by Mannheim composers that were then fashionable. High horns in A give it a particularly brilliant character (as they do in Mozart's Symphony No. 29 in A major, composed the previous year). Mozart, of course, has his own inimitable way of making something unique out of these ingredients. After the orchestra completes the introduction, we expect the soloist to enter with the first theme, or at least something in the same spirit. But instead, the violinist plays three long notes in a rising phrase (perhaps inspired by the orchestra's last phrase), and goes on to meditate for a few bars over a murmuring accompaniment. This ends with a pause, followed by a moment of genius. The orchestra starts its opening section again, and above it the violin adds a descant, beginning with a variant of that same pattern of three rising notes. This forms a new theme over the original. The soloist then extends this into a paragraph with brilliant figuration and leaps. When the orchestra ties this up with the same bars that ended the introduction, the soloist again takes the last phrase and builds a new theme out of it. The passage that follows also incorporates the second theme from the introduction. All of this seems so natural, so 'organic', that it is easy to miss the sheer cleverness of the construction. After a brief orchestral tutti, the music moves suddenly into a minor key, acquiring a plaintive mood. This intensifies as the harmonies shift, with the bass gradually side-stepping downwards, until regaining the home key of A major ready for the reprise.

This concerto was presumably written for Mozart himself to play, but among other violinists who performed it was an Italian who joined the Salzburg Court Orchestra, Antonio Brunetti. According to Mozart's father, Brunetti found the slow movement 'too elaborate', so Mozart supplied him with a replacement. This is the Adagio in E major, K. 261, which is indeed a much simpler piece. It is beautiful, but it is now difficult to imagine a violinist preferring it to the sublime achievement of the original movement.

This is certainly 'elaborate', like a complicated spell that takes time to weave. The theme is first played by the orchestra, and has several parts. At first it is built from a series of sighing pairs of notes. Then accented flurries of notes join the melody, becoming more dominant. And the theme ends with a return to pairs of notes, now poised and delicate. The soloist takes up the theme, not just repeating it, but exploring its possibilities, and soon moving into a different key. The delicate pairs of notes migrate, tiptoeing, to the accompaniment. After an orchestral tutti the soloist begins the theme again, but now takes it into more distant keys. Plaintive shifts of harmony create a sublime sense of tragic suspense. The bass moves gradually downwards, a semitone at a time.

After this passage of harmonic uncertainty, we arrive back in the home key without realizing it. The reprise of the theme is introduced with a beautiful counterpoint between the two violin parts of the orchestra before the soloist enters. At the second strain of the melody, there is yet another unexpected moment, as the bass once again descends step by step, creating a poignant series of harmonies, before the soloist regains the original direction of the melody.

The finale has the character of a minuet, but extended into a rondo with several episodes. This was a favourite form of J. C. Bach, who had formed a friendship with the eight-year-old Mozart when he visited London. The theme of the minuet starts with a repeated strain that is elegant and poised, but then it breaks into vigorous semiquavers, and ends with chirruping pairs of notes in an upward arpeggio, a pattern reminiscent of the very first theme of the concerto. The first episode continues elegantly, becomes more brilliant, and then regains its poise for the reprise of the main rondo theme. This time the theme, instead of ending, modulates into a minor key for a second episode with a bolder, more sonorous character than the first.

Again the first theme returns. This is followed by such a complete contrast of mood that it seems more like an interruption than an episode. This is the 'Turkish' music that gives the concerto its nickname. Throughout the eighteenth century, oriental elements were fashionable in operas and instrumental music. Music with bass drum and cymbals, and aggressive march rhythms, evoked the Turkish bands of Janissaries. The Turkish episode here begins with violin figurations that could as easily be Hungarian gypsy as Turkish. These alternate with fiery orchestral passages with pounding rhythms and threatening chromatic swirls. After this tempestuous interruption the minuet returns, with a charming new accompaniment, followed by its first episode refreshed with new harmonies and melodic details. The main theme recurs for the last time, delicately ornamented, and the soloist concludes quietly and unassumingly. The last notes are the familiar chirruping pairs of notes in an upward arpeggio. This is a charmingly unassuming ending, but it also takes us right back to the arpeggios with which the concerto began.

SINFONIA CONCERTANTE IN E FLAT MAJOR FOR VIOLIN AND VIOLA, K. 364
Duration: approx. 30 minutes

Allegro maestoso
Andante
Presto

Mozart composed this double concerto in 1779–80, towards the end of his years as a court musician with the Archbishop of Salzburg. He had recently travelled to the courts of Munich and Mannheim, hoping for a post there, but without success. Soon he was to make a final break from Salzburg, and from his father Leopold, and embark on a freelance career in Vienna. For now, his main duties were to compose church music. But his chief love was, as it had always been, instrumental music and opera, and this is the finest of the works that he wrote during this frustrating period of his career, in the months before receiving the commission to write his first great opera, *Idomeneo*.

The 'symphonie concertante' or 'sinfonia concertante' was a popular musical genre in the late eighteenth century, meaning a work on a large scale, like a symphony, with two or more soloists. Composers in Paris and Mannheim wrote large numbers of these pieces for performance in public concerts, and it was during and after visiting those cities that Mozart composed several examples. These include not only this famous Sinfonia Concertante and another for four wind soloists (though the authenticity of what has come down to us is in doubt), but also the Concerto for Two Pianos, and the Concerto for Flute and Harp, which are in effect examples of the same genre.

In this Sinfonia Concertante for Violin and Viola the strings of the viola are tuned a semitone sharp. This has the effect of brightening the tone of the instrument, and, with the highest two strings tuned to E flat and B flat, makes two of the most important notes in the scale of E flat available as open strings. In the generations after Mozart's death, as the prominent use of open strings went out of fashion, performers took to playing the part with the viola in its normal tuning. But with the rise of interest in historical performance practice in recent years, the use of the retuned viola has been revived. Mozart probably wrote this part for himself to play.

The opening orchestral tutti is full of the dramatic effects in which the orchestras and composers of Paris and Mannheim specialized. Sharply attacked chords, contrasted with delicate falling arpeggios, open the movement. A succession of little thematic elements follows, until, at a sudden hush, a series of trills gradually builds up in a sustained crescendo. Here Mozart has written a classic 'Mannheim crescendo', a dramatic effect made famous by the Mannheim orchestra and its composers. Mozart, with a stroke of genius, creates not just an effect, but a gloriously sustained emotional climax, enriched at its height by the middle voices of the orchestra. As this gently fades away in a series of falling scales, the two soloists do not so much enter as emerge, echoing these falling phrases as if they are fellow members of the orchestra. This subtlety is typical of the whole work – the interplay between soloists and orchestra, and between each other, is as much like chamber music as like a conventional concerto. The soloists answer each other, vie with each other, play together.

Amid a wealth of melodic invention, one moment stands out. After the soloists' exposition, and a second orchestral tutti, the development section begins with a sudden shift to a minor key, and a darkening of tone. First the violin and then the viola play a plaintive phrase, musing on a fragment of a theme they played early on. This reaches a pause, stopping them in their tracks for a moment. It is as if the soloists have become characters in an opera, hesitating before setting off again with determination. When, near the end of the movement, Mozart writes a cadenza for the two soloists, this too ends with a moment of poignant reflection, before a trill releases them back into the final orchestral passage.

These moments of reflection reach a culmination in the slow movement in C minor, which is the emotional heart of the work. Here, the sense of drama is unmistakable, as in the pioneering movement in the same key that Mozart wrote for his earlier Piano Concerto in E flat, K. 271. Like two operatic lovers who are destined to part, each instrument in turn sings plaintive melodies to the other – the first beginning with the very phrase that halted the first movement in its tracks. And, as in the opening Allegro, it is in the centre of the movement that the dialogue reaches its greatest intensity, with the melodic lines being condensed into gradually shorter, and more poignant, utterances. Mozart writes a beautiful cadenza, before the movement draws to a quiet close.

After the intensity of the slow movement, the finale comes as a delightful relief. The chirruping trills of the opening theme are related to the great crescendo of trills from the first movement, but now defused of all tension. This relaxed atmosphere is confirmed by the springing rhythms of the theme that the soloists play. The whole movement is orderly and its progress seems inevitable. After the rich unpredictability of the first movement, and the dramatic intensity of the second, Mozart has the genius to resolve the work in a rondo of the sunniest simplicity.

Divertimenti and Serenades

Divertimenti, K. 136–138

Mozart was only six when he and his sister were first taken by their father on tour around the cultural centres of Europe, creating a sensation wherever they played. At the same time, Leopold made sure that Wolfgang had a thorough grounding in the skills of musicianship, and, when the boy grew from child prodigy to a serious composer and performer, his father used his connections to obtain the best possible platform for Wolfgang's music. Three times while Wolfgang was still a teenager, Leopold took him on extended visits to Italy, the principal centre of opera, the genre in which any aspiring composer needed to shine. At the age of fourteen, Mozart's opera *Mitridate* was produced in Milan, with Wolfgang himself directing from the keyboard. This was such a success that he was invited to write a second opera for Milan, *Lucio Silla*, and he returned there to direct it two years later.

Between trips to Italy, Mozart was at home in Salzburg early in 1772. Far from taking things easy, he wrote eight symphonies and a number of church works in the space of only ten months. And he also composed a set of three smaller works for strings, which were published as Divertimenti. Mozart himself did not give them that title, nor did he specify whether they were to be played by a string orchestra or just by a quartet, and the bass line is labelled simply 'basso', not specifically 'cello'. Scholars continue to argue about which he might have meant, but the works are most often played by string orchestra, and they sound very much at home in that form, sometimes being referred to as his 'Salzburg Symphonies'.

DIVERTIMENTO IN D MAJOR, K. 136
Duration: approx. 12 minutes

Allegro
Andante
Presto

This Divertimento opens with one of Mozart's most joyful movements, full of gestures suggesting great confidence and bounding energy. One feature that gives a particular sense of communal *joie de vivre* is the interplay between first and second violins – a feature that Mozart might have learned from Haydn's string quartets. In the second section, there is an extraordinary moment. At first, the exploration of new keys is unsurprising. But then the mood suddenly clouds over, and the first violins play a sad, sustained line over a gently agitated accompaniment. This is an almost operatic moment, like a melancholy reminiscence in the middle of an aria, before the reprise restores the confidence of the opening.

The Andante in G major opens with first and second violins in lyrical duet. The metre is a gentle three-time, which gives an elegant suggestion of dance. As in the first movement, the interplay between the different instruments is striking. What begins as a duet for the violins becomes, after eight bars, a duet between second violin and viola, with first violins sustained above. Later, first and second violins play in quiet octaves together, until a rich forte brings the first section to a close. The second section opens as if embarking on new exploration. But within a few bars, it returns to the home key, and to a reprise that proceeds much as before – no disappointment, given the richness of ideas the first time round.

Four bars of cheeky chords introduce the theme of the finale, which is a simplified version of the first movement's principal theme. This has an even more straightforward sense of joy than the first movement. There are no clouds in sight, and the only moment of seriousness occurs (once again) at the start of the second section. Here Mozart introduces a little moment of fugue, which is soon brushed aside for a return to the wit of the opening.

DIVERTIMENTO IN B FLAT MAJOR, K. 137
Duration: approx. 11 minutes

Andante
Allegro di molto
Allegro assai

The first movement opens with a melody that could have come from the mature Mozart fifteen years later. Two phrases fall gently, coming to rest not in the home key of B flat, but first in C minor and then in D minor. Immediately we have that characteristic Mozartian sense of the poignant lurking behind the serene surface. Then, equally characteristically, the melody returns to B flat major and rises confidently and, at last, serenely – all this within the space of half a minute. The beginning of the second section is particularly subtle. It opens with something new that seems derived from what has gone before, as in a classic development section. After four bars it returns to the opening of the first theme in its original key, as if this is already the reprise. But then the opening phrases receive new answers and a new continuation, so that the development seems to be continuing. A few bars later, there is a real reprise, not of the beginning, but of the second idea. All this uncertainty – 'Is this a development?', 'Is this a reprise?' – is not just of academic interest. It is just this sort of subtle playing with expectations that makes Mozart a master of the emotional landscape, even in this work written at the age of sixteen.

The second movement is brisk and breezy. As in the first Divertimento, a particularly delightful feature is the interplay between first and second violins. And, as in the first movement, there is a particularly telling moment at the beginning of the second section, where the melody becomes simple and lyrical for six bars, before regaining its brisk character.

The third movement is a charming dance in three-time. At first it could almost have stepped out of a *concerto grosso* by Handel, with its balanced four-bar phrases. Then the harmonies become less predictable for twelve bars, and the first section ends by returning to balanced phrases, but now with the harmonies simplified and the melody in octaves, suggesting a rustic dance. The second section opens with playful scales, continues with a hint of poignancy, and concludes with a reprise of the opening.

DIVERTIMENTO IN F MAJOR, K. 138
Duration: approx. 10 minutes

Allegro
Andante
Presto

The third of the set of Divertimenti is as remarkable as the other two. It opens with a simple call to attention – two pairs of phrases that answer each other. Mozart's senior colleagues Joseph Haydn and J. C. Bach might have written the same. What follows is sheer genius: the first violins take wing with a soaring melody, while the second violins play a conversational counterpoint as if their minds are on something completely different. This complex conversation continues to unfold, until all the voices come together sweetly to round off the first section. The second section opens with a touch of anxiety, as Mozart takes elements from the earlier themes and makes something new from them.

The Andante could almost be an operatic aria. The first violin floats a vocal line, while the lower instruments supply an accompaniment that both enriches and comments on the melody. The beginning of the second section, so often eventful in Mozart, forms the emotional heart of the movement, as the music moves into minor keys and the mood darkens. And when the reprise comes, it jumps straight to the second strain of the melody, which is then extended for longer than before – an extraordinarily touching and unexpected moment.

The Presto is a rondo, with a wide range of mood between each appearance of its principal theme. The first episode introduces some playful counterpoint, the second turns wistful and, for a moment, seriously contrapuntal, and the third is delicate and tongue-in-cheek, like a premonition of Papageno in *The Magic Flute*.

EINE KLEINE NACHTMUSIK IN G MAJOR, K. 525

Duration: approx. 18 minutes

Allegro
Romance: Andante
Menuetto: Allegretto
Rondo: Allegro

Mozart composed this famous piece in the summer of 1787 while he was working on *Don Giovanni*. He listed it in his Thematic Catalogue as 'Eine kleine Nachtmusik, consisting of an Allegro, Minuet and Trio, Romance, Minuet and Trio, and Finale – 2 violins, viola, and bassi'. The page containing the first minuet and trio has been torn out of the autograph score and never found. Alfred Einstein suggested that the minuet of the Piano Sonata in B flat, K. 498a, might be the missing movement, arranged for piano.[23] But this theory is based on little more than a hunch, and we are left with the familiar four-movement work. It was not published until more than thirty years after Mozart's death.

The title, 'Nachtmusik' (which is not in the autograph score), is the German equivalent of the French 'nocturne'. Mozart in his letters referred to his serenades for wind as 'Nachtmusick' or 'Nachtmusique'. This is, therefore, a serenade, which we can imagine being played in an aristocratic household late in the evening. Mozart's Serenata Notturna, K. 239, must have been written for a similar purpose in 1776 but, as with that work, nothing is known about the circumstances of the composition of *Eine kleine Nachtmusik*. Mozart was a pragmatic composer who usually wrote to commission or for his own performance, so someone undoubtedly asked him to write it. Depending on the household, it could have been played by single strings or by a small string orchestra: 'bassi' suggests that he intended it for more than just a string quartet, probably with cellos and double basses.

This was the last of Mozart's serenades, following on from the dark and powerful Serenade in C minor for Wind Instruments composed four years earlier. Just two months before *Eine kleine Nachtmusik*, Mozart had written *Ein musikalischer Spass* ('A Musical Joke'), which pokes fun at the conventions of the serenade and the musical language of the time. *Eine kleine*

Nachtmusik is neither dark nor jokey. It is one of the least troubled of Mozart's mature works, in a sunny G major. It is, in a way, a throwback to the Divertimenti for strings that he composed as a teenager. But the lightness and charm are carried off with all the subtle craftsmanship of his maturity.

It opens with a simple call in octaves based on an arpeggio of G major – just the sort of cheerful, direct opening to command attention. Different elements follow in quick succession: energetic, then demure (with a touch of imitation between treble and bass), and energetic again, with a crescendo to the climax. Then follows the second real theme. Its interest lies not just in its poise, but in its subtle use of the four instrumental lines. First the melody tiptoes in octaves in the two violins, with chords and bass touched in delicately below. Then the melody moves to the second violin, with, above it, a counterpoint of repeated notes that eventually rises. The continuation of the theme in first violin has elegantly balanced phrases with, below, continuous quavers in the middle parts, and just one bass note per bar. Soon all parts come together in octaves (as at the opening), and the first section ends with a quiet little conclusion.

The second section opens with a miniature development, starting with a return to the opening call to attention, and continuing with the second part of the second theme that moves through different keys until we find ourselves at the reprise. This follows without surprises, until the quiet little conclusion extends charmingly, and the movement ends in high spirits.

The Romance is almost without the dark hints of so many of Mozart's slow movements, but its beauty is nevertheless underpinned by subtleties. As in the first movement, the relationship between the four instrumental lines is crucial to the effect. The movement begins with the two violins singing their melody an octave and a third apart, with the simplest of bass lines and no viola. As the melody swells to forte for its second strain, the viola enters with a trilling counterpoint between the two violin lines. In the second half of the theme, the first violins alone elaborate the melody. As they return to the simplicity of the opening, the second violins move up from C to C sharp, momentarily hinting at a new key, but the melody continues unaffected. A new section takes the opening of the melody and quickens its repeated notes. From here it flows more freely, moving into new keys, and introducing just a touch of poignancy before arriving at a brief reprise of the opening theme.

Now we enter an episode in a minor key. The pace, in effect, doubles, as the middle parts break into a pattern of gently agitated semiquavers (quavers have previously dominated the accompanying parts). A pointed little motif passes between first violins and bass, becoming more insistent in the second half of the episode. Seamlessly, the music suddenly returns to the calm of the opening, and the movement concludes with a reprise of the first theme.

The minuet is sturdy. The trio gives the first violins one of Mozart's most effortlessly flowing melodies, which is supported by the simplest of accompaniments.

The principal theme of the finale, with its upbeat of a rising arpeggio, refers directly back to the opening call of the first movement. Here, Mozart's subtlety extends to the overall structure of the movement. This opening theme behaves as in a conventional rondo, in which recurrences of the principal theme are interspersed with other episodes. But Mozart extends and develops his theme, so that the movement takes on something of the character of a symphonic movement. The exuberant theme is supported by the middle parts playing a pattern of bubbly repeated notes. A second theme is elegant and pointed (similar in character to the second theme of the first movement). After it, Mozart soon returns to further consideration of his opening theme, to round off the first section of the movement. Following the repeat of the first section, the theme undergoes a surprise shift of key up a semitone, and is developed with a new surge of power (this is the part of the movement that seems most 'symphonic'). Suddenly, we are into a reprise of the elegant second theme, followed, as before, by renewed exploration of the principal theme. After the repeat of this section, Mozart rounds off the movement with a coda. It begins with a simple return to the opening theme. But soon the theme moves to the bass, with a running counterpoint above, and then is passed playfully between first violins and violas, and finally between first violins and bass. This sudden burst of complexity brings the work to an exuberant conclusion.

SERENADE IN D MAJOR, K. 250, 'HAFFNER'
Duration: approx. 60 minutes

Allegro maestoso – Allegro molto
Andante
Menuetto – Trio
Rondeau: Allegro
Menuetto galante – Trio
Andante
Menuetto – Trio I – Trio II
Adagio – Allegro assai

In Austria in the 1770s many aristocratic and other wealthy families retained private orchestras, and commissioned music for special occasions. Mozart was employed at this time by the Archbishop of Salzburg as a court composer, and he was expected to write works ranging from church music to divertimenti, serenades, and other pieces for evening entertainment. But the most substantial of his serenades from this period was composed for a wedding. On 22 July 1776, Elisabeth (Elise) Haffner, daughter of the former Mayor of Salzburg, married Franz Xaver Späth. Elise's brother, Sigmund, commissioned Mozart to write a serenade for the occasion. It was performed for the guests the day before the wedding, in a summer house in the garden of Sigmund's residence in Salzburg. As well as the eight-movement serenade itself, there is also a March in D major, K. 249, which is presumed to have been used for a ceremonial entrance.

Three movements include a prominent solo violin part, which Mozart himself would have played – Mozart was a fine violinist, and this 'concertante' style was very fashionable in the 1770s.

The introduction of the first movement immediately sets a festive tone, with its stately rhythms and full scoring with trumpets and horns. It is assumed that timpani would also have been included, though there is no part for them. The energy level increases at the Allegro molto. After the bustling opening bars, the oboes resume their theme from the introduction, now at a faster pace. A second theme on strings begins gracefully, and continues with running staccato quavers. These then alternate between treble and bass, combined with assertive rhythms, to bring the first section to a close.

The development moves into new keys, with a series of dramatic chords – this could be the overture to an opera rather than a serenade. Soon, however, there is a quiet moment, and the music turns back to the home key for the reprise.

After the brightness of the first movement, the Andante immediately has a warmer sound, with richly scored chords in the strings, horns but not trumpets, and the silvery sheen of flutes above. The melody begins as descending arpeggios in the violins, then quietens to a simple rising line that takes longer than we expect to resolve – a lovely moment of extended concentration that looks forward to the mature Mozart. This is the first of the 'concertante' movements, with extended solo passages making it like a movement of a violin concerto. The soloist enters with the theme, decorating the ending, and then continues on to a second strain. This moves seamlessly into D major, to form the beginning of an expansive middle section. The solo line becomes higher and more elaborate, and a trill culminates in an orchestral tutti. We expect a reprise of the opening. But instead, Mozart returns to the beginning of the middle section, bringing in the lovely, simple rising line from the first theme. Once again this takes longer than we expect to settle, winding through poignant touches of harmony back to G major.

When the reprise does appear, Mozart starts not at the beginning, but with the flowing phrases that first introduced the soloist. Again the soloist moves on to the second strain. But this time it stays close to G major, so that it forms an extended coda to the theme. Once more, the simple rising line forms the emotional climax of the passage. As in a concerto, there is a cadenza (not supplied by Mozart), before the movement winds to a peaceful end.

The minuet is a surprising movement to include in a wedding serenade. It is in G minor, with urgent chromatic harmonies. The loud opening phrase is answered anxiously, with a bassoon an octave below second violins. The trio in G major is in complete contrast, with a cheerful solo violin accompanied by the wind: high horns, flutes, and oboes.

The rondeau returns to G major, rather than to the home key of D major. The rondo theme is a playful perpetuum mobile of staccato semiquavers on solo violin, answered by the orchestral violins. A tutti moves into D major to take us into the first episode. At first the running semiquavers continue. But soon a new theme emerges, with little rising shapes that relate to the second theme in the Andante. There is a poised tailpiece to the theme before it winds down to a pause (often filled in with a moment of cadenza), and on to the reprise of the rondo theme.

In the second episode, the soloist moves into E minor, and calms the semiquavers into more relaxed triplet quavers. The second half of this episode is particularly charming, with the soloist trying out a return to semiquavers, then easing for a moment into sighing. There is another pause (and cadenza), and the next reprise follows, back in G major. The next episode moves into C major, with a touch of stateliness in the rhythm. Soon, the running semiquavers return in the orchestral violins, while the soloist rises above with a more lyrical idea. Then the semiquavers return to the solo part, and lead on naturally to another reprise. Mozart spins out the ideas delightfully before returning for the last time to the theme, and allowing the movement to reach a conclusion.

The Menuetto galante returns to D major, with trumpets (and timpani), for the first time since the opening movement. The stately dotted rhythms add to the impression of a quasi-military courtliness. By contrast, the trio in D minor is for strings alone, and marked 'piano sempre'. It has a delicate, slightly anxious poise, with a pattern of accompanying triplets in the second violins. Poignant sighing harmonies add to the anxiety in the second half.

The sixth movement, an Andante in A major, is a loose kind of rondo, in which the opening material returns from time to time, but unpredictably, and with variations as it recurs. This is a form of rondo that Mozart was to develop a decade later in one of his greatest works, the Rondo in A minor for Piano. Here, in a prototype suitable for a wedding, it has an air of slightly ramshackle charm. The theme has three principal elements. The first is made of offbeat pairs of notes echoed in the bass, first on strings and bassoons, then tutti. A livelier second element has delicate runs, punctuated by horns, followed by a melancholy falling line. And the third is a tune of naive simplicity. This last element rambles on a little until, with a change of key, we find ourselves in the first episode. A sprightlier tune begins in the first violins, with running scales in the second violins below. The oboe responds with a memory of the third element, over gently descending harmonies, and the full orchestra elaborates the idea – an extraordinarily Schubertian moment. The episode winds to an end and leads to a reprise – not of the beginning of the theme, but of the second element with its delicate runs.

There is a hesitation, and change of key, and we enter the second episode. This is a sustained, singing melody on violins in F sharp minor, with a reiterated little accompanying figure in the second violins. The melody reaches a cadence, and perhaps we expect it to repeat its first strain. But instead, the music turns back to A major for a reprise of the rondo theme. It is disguised, first with gently syncopated dotted rhythms, and then smoothed out into triplets on full strings and wind. This leads on to the second element, with the delicate runs. Then, the oboe sidesteps back to the earlier 'Schubertian' moment, to which the full orchestra again responds, extending it further than before.

A further reprise of the second and third elements follows. The sprightly tune that opened the first episode returns, but only briefly. Soon, the music turns back to the rondo theme, disguised in a new way. A simplified outline of the melody is played by the first violins, while second violins and violas accompany with walking pizzicato. Then the theme breaks into vigorous dotted rhythms, while the second violins play running scales. For the very last time, the second and third elements are reprised, and the movement comes to a gentle close.

Trumpets (and timpani) enter once more for the next minuet in D major. This is grand, but its confidence is tempered in the second half with a touch of plangent harmony, followed by a hesitation in the Lydian mode (a Haydn-like rustic moment). The minuet alternates with two trios. The first is in G major, with a warm combination of violins doubled by bassoon an octave below, and a flute joining an octave above. In the second half, flute and bassoon are liberated from the strings for a brief moment. The second trio has a striking combination of wind instruments, with flutes in duet, and a quiet trumpet call below.

The opening melody of the Adagio begins with a simple rise, and then falls in a curling arabesque. The second half of the phrase is even simpler. This is an early example of Mozart's genius at creating perfect balance through a subtle kind of asymmetry. After this gentle opening, a full chord, with horns and trumpets in the middle of the chord, and timpani, has an effect of extraordinary nobility. This is enhanced by the poignant touches of harmony as the introduction winds its way, alternating between grandeur and delicacy.

Ticking repeated notes break into a jig rhythm to announce the Allegro. This has a feeling of great excitement, with its short-breathed phrases made up of repeated elements. The quieter second theme scarcely breaks the pattern, simply extending the principal shape from the first theme. A renewal of the ticking brings the repeat of the opening section, and, the second time round, takes us into the development. From a moment of drama emerges a new theme in G major, a charming, almost cheeky tune on violins, which turns out to be the most extended melody in the movement. The music returns to D major for the reprise, and the excitement is renewed. A repeat of the second half is marked, but is rarely played, and the serenade comes to an end in the highest of spirits.

Symphonies

Mozart started writing symphonies when he was very young. In reminiscences written after his death, his sister remembered the winter of 1764–5, when Wolfgang was nine: 'In London, when our father lay ill and close to death, we were not allowed to touch the clavier. So, to occupy himself, Mozart composed his first symphony with all the instruments, above all with trumpets and drums. I had to sit by him and copy it out. As he composed, and I copied, he said to me: "Remind me to give the horn something worthwhile to do".'[24] This was Symphony No. 1 in E flat, K. 16. Over the next few years, Mozart wrote a large number of symphonies, though it is impossible to establish exactly how many. Some that are in the standard list of forty-one have been shown to be by other composers, additional symphonies that really are by Mozart have come to light since the original numbering was established, and some that we know he composed are lost. What is certain is that, by the age of eighteen, Mozart had composed more than two dozen symphonies.

Like Haydn, Mozart in his early symphonies took the Italian opera overture, or sinfonia, as his starting point – indeed, some of these works that acquired the label of 'symphony' are reworkings of actual opera overtures. Mozart achieved some of his greatest early successes writing operas that were performed during his tours of Italy, so he was thoroughly familiar with the genre – both the ceremonial conventions of opera seria and the wit and melodic charm of opera buffa. Over his short career, Mozart, like Haydn and other German and Austrian composers, took the symphony and greatly enlarged it. To compare one of Mozart's early symphonies with one of his mature symphonies is to encounter one of the miracles of musical history. The early symphonies are witty, charming, and fizzing with energy. They have the buzz of a theatre waiting for the curtain to go up. But Mozart's mature symphonies (like Haydn's) have enlarged, emotionally as well as in scale, to become not just a prelude to drama, but the drama itself. It was this emotional development that created the genre of symphony that was to become the centrepiece of concerts right through the late eighteenth and nineteenth centuries.

It is in the symphonies of 1772–3, when Mozart was aged sixteen to seventeen, that we can hear him firmly stepping beyond the elegant conventions of the Italian theatre. In the serenade-like slow movement of Symphony No. 17 in G major, K. 129 (1772), the second half begins with a moment of serene counterpoint, introducing new emotional depth into the music. No. 18 in F major, K. 130 (1772), has two flutes instead of the usual oboes, and Mozart creates beautiful, transparent textures with strings, flutes, horns and, sometimes, a pizzicato bass. The first movement is all bustling energy, the slow movement like a pastoral landscape. The Andante of No. 19 in E flat major, K. 132 (1772), has chromatic harmonies and sudden changes of mood that give the music a sense of searching. No. 21 in A major, K. 134 (1772), has another fine Andante, with flutes enhancing a long-spun melody, and a living independence in the inner string parts that was to become a hallmark of Mozart's later orchestral writing. The playful outer movements are given a particularly bright character by the high horns in A (a Haydnesque effect more familiar from Mozart's Symphony No. 29 in A major, written two years later).

A significant breakthrough was encouraged by Mozart's stay in Vienna with his father during July–September 1773. It was in this period that Mozart widened his knowledge of symphonies by other composers, particularly the great Joseph Haydn. This encouraged him to step well beyond the spirit of the Italian opera overture. Of the symphonies he wrote in this period, the most remarkable, and most often played, are No. 25 in G minor (his first in a minor key), and No. 29 in A major.

Durations are not given in the following descriptions. As with Haydn's symphonies, the situation is complicated not only by great variation in tempo but by differing approaches to the marked repeats. Mozart's grandest symphony, No. 41 ('Jupiter'), can take less than 30 minutes or more than 40, depending on both of these factors.

SYMPHONY NO. 25 IN G MINOR, K. 183

Allegro con brio
Andante
Menuetto e trio
Allegro

Mozart finished this symphony in October 1773, immediately after his stay in Vienna when he got to know symphonies by Haydn. This is Mozart's first symphony in a minor key, and is far removed from the Italian comic opera influence of his earlier symphonies. It is in the spirit of the minor-key symphonies that Haydn composed in the years around 1770, particularly his Symphony No. 39 in the same key, which is similarly scored with two oboes and four horns. The term *Sturm und Drang* is often used to describe these turbulent Haydn symphonies, but their character has more to do with tragic opera than with literature (see note for Haydn's Symphony No. 26). Similarly, the opening of this symphony by Mozart evokes Gluck's 'Dance of the Furies' from *Orpheus and Eurydice*, which the Viennese had first encountered in its earlier incarnation at the end of Gluck's ballet *Don Juan* in 1761.

The echo of Gluck's furies is particularly strong at the opening of the symphony. The first theme is in stark octaves, its long notes descending like a baroque fugue subject, with agitated syncopations in the strings, followed by a pattern of fast rising arpeggios, each rounded off with a flourish. This is a movement of strong contrasts. Almost immediately the opening 'baroque' long notes are echoed plangently by the oboe. And a second theme has a delicate, tiptoeing character, though it never loses an underlying sense of agitation. The development in the centre of the movement concentrates the drama, with, again, contrasts between agitated passages and the plangent oboe.

In the second movement in E flat major, the violins are muted. They play a theme of sighing phrases echoed by a pair of bassoons (period instruments give this a particularly haunting quality). At the end of the theme the mood suddenly lightens for four bars, with more rapid figurations rounding it off.

The minuet in G minor has a dark, earnest quality, beginning in stark octaves like the first movement, and with some troubled chromatic harmonies and prominent inner voices. The trio is lighter and more serenade-like, with oboes and horns predominating.

The finale also opens with bare octaves, and the shape of the theme is like a pared-down version of the arpeggios from the first movement's opening theme. It begins quietly, then continues forte, with syncopations in the strings (again echoing the first movement). There is a gentler second theme in swinging dotted rhythms, and a development section with nervous chromatic harmonies. The symphony ends in the same spirit of agitation with which it began.

SYMPHONY NO. 29 IN A MAJOR, K. 201

Allegro moderato
Andante
Menuetto e trio: Allegretto
Allegro con spirito

If No. 25 in G minor shows Mozart using the influences of Gluck and Haydn to good effect, this symphony in A major represents another substantial leap towards the mature Mozart. He wrote it at the beginning of 1774 and, like No. 25, it would first have been played by the Archbishop of Salzburg's court orchestra, of which Mozart had been the concertmaster for two years. The orchestra must have had good horn players – the parts in this symphony are high, as in several of Haydn's symphonies of this period, giving the full orchestra an excitingly bright sound.

The quiet opening theme is an inspiration of genius. The melody itself is unremarkable: a simple sequence of phrases, each consisting of an octave leap, followed by a pattern mostly of repeated notes. What turns it into unmistakable Mozart is the way he combines it with shifting harmonies, and an inner voice (in the second violins) that swoops up and down in counterpoint. This gives the theme marvellous warmth and depth. When the melody is repeated forte, the lower strings imitate the upper strings at half a bar's distance, giving it great energy. The gentle second theme also has a touch of subtle counterpoint. The first four bars of the theme are accompanied by simple chords, but as the first violins continue the melody, the second violins play a variant of the first four bars below. A little later, after a forte, the second violins again imitate the firsts, one bar later.

The central development section opens with further imitation, staccato scales pursuing each other through all four of the string lines. And after the reprise, there is a little coda in which imitation is taken further still. The opening theme is pursued at half-bar intervals through four lines – first violins, cellos and bass, horns, and violas. All of these touches of counterpoint give a feeling of chamber music on a large scale, a characteristic that becomes more pronounced in Mozart's later years.

The independence of lines continues into the slow movement. The two violins are muted, and the elegant theme begins in the first violins. Then it migrates to the second violins, with the first violins playing a charming descant above. The music continues in this two-part counterpoint, with the violas also adding their voices in harmony with the second violins. A second theme begins on first violins, and then becomes a duet with the seconds, ending with a tiptoeing pianissimo tailpiece, the oboes joining in an octave above. This hushed mood continues into the middle section of the movement, where running triplets move to the second violins, while the first violins play a little figuration of trills above it. After the reprise, there is a thoughtful coda. Suddenly, an oboe enters, high and forte, bringing us back to the first theme. The first violins respond, the seconds turning what was a descant into an accompaniment, and the movement comes to an emphatic close.

The minuet has an almost military character, with sharp dotted rhythms, and clear-cut alternations of quiet and loud passages throughout. By contrast, the trio is lyrical, with touches of chromatic harmony giving a wistful tone.

Like the minuet, the finale is full of contrasts between loud and soft, with bold rhythms, assertive trills, and decisive runs, beginning with the same octave leap that opens the first movement. The end of each section is marked by a particularly forceful upward run in the violins. This is just the sort of effect that had become popular in Mannheim and Paris, though Mozart had not yet visited either city as an adult (see note for Symphony No. 31). Perhaps he had encountered these effects, or at least been told of them, during his visit to Vienna the previous year. Although the overriding spirit in this finale is exuberance, once again Mozart explores the possibilities of dialogue between the different instruments. The gentle second theme is introduced with a pecking little figure in the first violins, but the theme itself is played by the second violins, with the firsts continuing to peck wittily above.

The middle section of the movement develops the first theme, moving into different keys. First and second violins play the theme in counterpoint, and a dialogue develops between violins and bass. The bold upward run announces the arrival of the reprise. At the end of the movement, another run announces a coda. The theme is played by everyone in octaves, and capped by high horns. One last joyful run, and this exhilarating symphony is over. Mozart was just eighteen when he wrote it, and it is one of the great landmarks of his career.

SYMPHONY NO. 31 IN D MAJOR, K. 297 (K. 300A), 'PARIS'

Allegro assai
Andantino
Allegro

Four months after the astonishing Symphony No. 29, Mozart wrote a Symphony in D major (No. 30) that is less characteristic, and is not often played. Then there was a gap of four years before he wrote another symphony, No. 31 in D major. The occasion was a visit to Paris in 1778. Mozart had wanted to tour Italy with Aloysia Weber, the singer with whom he was in love (the sister of Constanze whom he eventually married). But his father put enormous pressure on him to abandon that idea and go to Paris instead, where he would have a better opportunity to further his reputation as a composer. Mozart arrived in Paris with his mother on 23 March 1778. Fifteen years earlier, when Mozart was seven and his sister was twelve, their father had taken them to Paris, where they had caused a sensation and been entertained at court. This second visit turned into a tragedy, with the death of Mozart's mother in July, probably from typhus. But from the start Mozart was ill-disposed towards Parisians, most of whom he found conceited, of poor taste, and ready to plot against him. However, very early in the visit he did gain a commission for this symphony. It was composed for the Concert Spirituel, an important series of public concerts.

Paris was one of the great centres for orchestral music, much influenced by musicians from Mannheim, notably Johann and Karl Stamitz. A style of symphony full of dramatic effects, coupled with a new level of orchestral discipline, had made the orchestra of Mannheim famous, and the musicians of Paris sought to emulate it. Mozart was well equipped to rise to the challenge of writing for Paris, because he had recently spent some time in Mannheim, absorbing the latest in orchestral developments. He had been most impressed by the Mannheim orchestra, under the concertmaster Christian Cannabich. 'What discipline they have in that orchestra! – and what authority Cannabich has – everything they do is done with real dedication.'[25] Mozart's father observed that, to judge by the symphonies that Stamitz father and son had published in Paris, 'the Parisians must be fond of noisy music'.[26] Mozart's 'Paris' Symphony is indeed his 'noisiest' so far. It has the biggest orchestra, including pairs of flutes, oboes, clarinets (for the first time), horns, and trumpets, with timpani and strings. And the first movement has an unusually high proportion of tutti passages in which all instruments are playing loudly, creating a grand, ceremonial impression.

Mozart's new symphony opened the concert on 18 June 1778 at the Palais des Tuileries. For once, we have Mozart's own detailed report on the performance in dutiful letters to his father. Before the concert, he wrote that he was very happy with the symphony, 'but whether others like it, I don't know ... but I do hope that even the stupid asses will find something they can like; after all, I made sure to include the premier coup d'archet, and that's enough to please them.' The *premier coup d'archet* (first attack of the bow) was a speciality of the Paris orchestra, and Mozart begins with a classic example: bold, sustained notes and a rushing upward scale. This upward scale recurs throughout the movement, forming landmarks (as a similar upward scale did in the finale of Symphony No. 29). At first, it is interleaved with a more delicate idea, which eventually gives way to a sustained, grand tutti. Another delicate idea, with pointed little flourishes in the melody and running triplets below, gives way to a further loud tutti, in which the little flourishes are incorporated. The recurrence of the bold opening with its rushing scale indicates that we have reached the arrival of the second main theme. This turns out to be based on the little pointed flourish we heard earlier, now in a new pattern, and alternating with woodwind phrases. Another delicate idea, with a charming pizzicato bass, leads to a further grand tutti, in which the rushing scale adds splendid urgency to the bass. Eventually, the first, bold theme, with its scale, announces that we have arrived at the end of the first section of the movement. There is no repeat of the opening section, and the music goes straight on into the development. At first, this continues just like the opening (though now in a different key). But the second rushing scale overshoots to a dissonant note, pulling the music through sliding harmonies to new keys. The pointed flourish of the second theme recurs, and now forms a beautiful counterpoint between the first and second violins. After a very poised moment, with lovely textures, we arrive back at the opening theme. At first this proceeds as expected, but, as so often in Mozart's later works, there is soon a surprise. At the second occurrence of the first theme, with its scale, the bass wrenches the harmony downwards, and the music is pulled through new keys – a powerfully dramatic moment. The sequence of events from then on is much as before, but with subtle changes to the instrumentation – oboes are more prominent than clarinets this time round. The final pages of the movement develop a joyful momentum, the ending punched home with a last statement of the bold opening idea.

Trumpets and drums are silent in the slow movement, and so, more surprisingly, are the clarinets. The remaining wind instruments (horns, bassoons, oboes, and a single flute) are particularly prominent. They have little passages of their own, in dialogue with the strings, but they also provide a beautifully warm sonority as a backdrop for the strings, with the flute often doubling the violins, sometimes an octave above (one of Haydn's favourite effects) The gently swinging rhythm of the movement gives it a pastoral feel. After the first performance, the director of the Concert Spirituel, Joseph Legros, told Mozart that the movement was too long and elaborate, so he supplied him with a shorter, simpler movement. Mozart had no doubts about the original movement: 'the andante has the greatest applause *from me*, from all experts and connoisseurs ... for it is natural – and short'. Posterity has agreed with him, not with Legros.

At the start of the finale Mozart once again plays to the tastes of the Parisians, but this time with a surprise. Finales in Paris usually began strongly. But Mozart begins with just the violins, quietly chattering for eight bars, followed by four bars of bustling forte from the full orchestra, and a return to the quiet violins. Mozart reported, 'the audience had, because of the quiet beginning, shushed each other, as I expected they would, and then came the forte – well, hearing it and clapping was one and the same'. But this is not just a movement of surprising tricks. Alfred Einstein rightly commented that it 'hovers continually between brilliant tumult and graceful seriousness'. After the chattering first theme, which culminates in a brilliant tutti, the second theme is a quiet moment of fugue. This continues delicately, then with a surprising serious and forceful moment in a minor key. After an emphatic conclusion to the first part of the movement, Mozart returns to his fugal second theme. This he develops at greater length, giving the centre of the movement a mood of serious concentration (his use of fugue in this way was to reach a climax in his last symphony, the 'Jupiter'). The chattering opening returns, but the fugal second theme does not. It has done its work of anchoring the centre of the movement, and it is as if this has had the effect of setting the music free, so that it can build cumulatively to a joyous ending.

SYMPHONY NO. 32 IN G MAJOR, K. 318
Allegro spiritoso – Andante – Tempo 1

This has traditionally been listed as Symphony No. 32, though it is more appropriate to think of it as an overture. It is very short (less than ten minutes), and the three movements are played without a break. In other words, like several of Mozart's earlier symphonies, it is modelled on the Italian opera overture. Mozart wrote it after returning to Salzburg in the spring of 1779, having failed to find a post elsewhere. It is not known whether he intended it to form an overture to an opera (some scholars suggest it was intended as the overture to *Zaide*), but in any case overtures were often played at concerts. Like the symphony-overtures of Mozart's earlier years, it is full of the spirit of Italian comic opera, though with a slow movement whose tenderness owes as much to Mozart's old friend J. C. Bach as to any Italian influence.

The symphony begins with an arresting *coup d'archet*, like the preceding 'Paris' Symphony. The first movement is, in effect, two-thirds of a symphony movement, which breaks off before the reprise. The first section includes brilliant tutti passages, with the opening flourish often recurring in the bass. A contrasting, delicate second theme is followed by a gradual crescendo (another speciality of Mannheim and Paris) culminating in another tutti to bring the first section to a close. The development section begins with a new delicate theme, followed by a dramatic passage in which the opening flourish passes between the middle voices, and takes the music into new keys. This reaches a climax, ready to return to the home key of G major.

Just at this moment the music breaks off, and the Andante movement follows. This has a gentle, lyrical character. The wind instruments (flutes, oboes, bassoons, horns) come into their own. They have passages as an ensemble, but also colour the violin lines in subtle ways – the bassoons add mellowness an octave below, the flutes add a silvery sheen an octave above. The Andante draws to a close, and leads straight in to a return to the Allegro spiritoso. This soon reaches a reprise of the first movement's delicate second theme. As before, this is followed by a 'Mannheim crescendo', now with chromatic harmonies adding an extra edge of expectancy. A final tutti, with repetitions of the opening flourish, brings the overture to a brilliant close.

SYMPHONY NO. 33 IN B FLAT MAJOR, K. 319

Allegro assai
Andante moderato
Menuetto and Trio
Finale: Allegro assai

After the extrovert brilliance of the 'Paris' Symphony (No. 31) and the overture (No. 32), this symphony returns to the more intimate style of No. 29, without trumpets or drums. As in that symphony, there is a pair of oboes and a pair of high horns, and now there are also bassoons. This wind ensemble and its individual members have a more independent life than in No. 29, a feature that gives Mozart's mature symphonies such a spirit of chamber music. When Mozart first wrote No. 33 in Salzburg in July 1779, it was in three movements. He added the minuet when he revived it five years later in Vienna.

The first movement is in a lively three-time, which gives it a dancing character. But there is a lot of elegant detail within the basic rhythm, so it is a tricky matter to allow room for everything to tell without labouring the dance. As usual by this stage of Mozart's career, there is a wealth of material, with incisive, delicate, and lyrical ideas following in quick succession. After a firm cadence we arrive at the second main theme, in which calm falling phrases from the violins alternate with comment from the woodwind. Even after this point there are several new ideas and a fortissimo climax, before emphatically repeated chords of F major announce the end of the first section (which is not repeated).

The development that follows begins by picking up delicate trills that featured earlier in the movement. But these soon give way to a new and surprising element: a four-note motif, like a fugue subject, the very motif that Mozart was to use nine years later in the finale of the 'Jupiter' Symphony. This forms the basis of a passage of counterpoint, giving a mood of concentrated seriousness to this part of the movement, until a brilliant tutti, with the trills in the bass, leads on to the reprise.

Andante moderato is an unusual marking in Mozart, presumably meaning a little slower than a plain Andante. Certainly this movement has great expressive richness. Like the first movement, it has a moment of counterpoint, as the beginning of a fugue starts in the strings and is taken up in the woodwind. The moment is short-lived, and soon the music returns to the home key. But it does not return to the beginning, instead going straight to the end of the first theme and the beginning of the second. The rich chording of the opening is saved until the final page of the movement, which gives a satisfying sense of symmetry to the movement as a whole, like the shape of an arch.

The minuet (composed later than the other movements) has an urgent character from its very first falling octave, which creates a syncopation against the main beat. The beginning of the second section injects yet more urgency, with a wrenching shift to G minor. By contrast, the central trio is relaxed, with the easy dancing character of an Austrian *Ländler*, enhanced by a pair of oboes in the first half, and a pair of bassoons in the second.

The finale is a movement of Haydn-like wit. Both halves are repeated in the score, though the second repeat is often omitted in performance. A rapid pattern of triplets forms the first phrase of the theme, and then migrates to the accompaniment. Later it is joined by a pizzicato bass, creating an almost Mendelssohn-like airy texture. Meanwhile, the melody above is full of pointed and delicate phrases. As in the first movement, there is a surprising moment of counterpoint at the beginning of the second half. This injects a mood of seriousness, but soon the chattering triplets return under the counterpoint, and pull the music back to a reprise. The ending is particularly Haydnesque. The opening theme is stated in octaves by the whole orchestra, and breaks off without the conventional final emphasis.

SYMPHONY NO. 34 IN C MAJOR, K. 338

Allegro vivace
Andante di molto
Finale: Allegro vivace

This symphony, composed in the summer of 1780, returns to the grand scale of the 'Paris' Symphony, with oboes, bassoons, horns, trumpets, and drums. It has all the devices associated with Mannheim and Paris – an assertive opening, strong contrasts, dramatic crescendos – but it also has a new spirit of concentrated energy and purpose. The first movement is in a vigorous march rhythm that Mozart uses to create a spirit of ceremonial excitement, rather than anything military. This was to become a favourite type of opening movement for Mozart in his piano concertos. The sustained brilliance of the opening tutti gives way to a gentle second theme. This alternates a melancholy falling line with a persistent little pointed figure. The falling line is echoed in counterpoint, first by a bassoon and then by an oboe. One of the features that most distinguishes this work from the earlier 'Paris' Symphony is this sort of informal counterpoint, used to deepen the expressive effect of the music. There is another example at the end of this theme. The first violins begin pianissimo, with a shimmering figure that gradually builds – a classic 'Mannheim crescendo'. But Mozart enhances the tension by counterpoint, the second violins entering two bars later with the shimmering figure, as if beginning a fugue. After a further tutti, the first section reaches a conclusion.

As in symphonies Nos 31 and 33, there is no repeat of this section, and the music moves straight on into the central section. Although this is conventionally called the 'development', here (as often in Mozart) most of the music seems entirely new. First a falling figure in the strings is reiterated under sustained wind chords – a rather ominous passage. The mood lightens, with oboes and violins in a dialogue of single notes and trills, dropped as if into water. Only the little trills seem to connect obviously to the early part of the symphony. There is a moment of hush, and the grand reprise bursts in. After the first two phrases, the tension is heightened, the theme moving into the bass with rapid tremolo above. The music proceeds through the gentle second theme, then leaves out the 'Mannheim crescendo' (Mozart no doubt thinking that such a striking effect would be weakened by repetition). And at the end of the reprise, the opening theme bursts in once again, and a sustained final tutti brings the movement to a splendid close.

The slow movement is remarkable both for its apparent simplicity and for its sophistication. The simplicity is in its scoring, which is for strings with the bassoons doubling the bass line, but no other wind instruments. This is not quite as simple as it appears: the violas are divided into two parts, creating the opportunity for rich textures. The sophistication is in the sustained intensity of expression and, again, its enhancement with counterpoint. The elegant rising line in the first violins is immediately echoed below by the second violins. The first phrase ends by modulating to a minor key, creating a moment of poignancy when the music has only just begun. The answering phrase relaxes back into the major. At the second strain of the theme, the pair of violin lines migrates down to second violin and first violas, while a falling descant accompanies it – not only above, in first violins, but below, in second violas. This is not just a counterpoint, but a gesture of the utmost tenderness, like a dancer gently holding his partner's face in two hands. Indeed, the whole movement seems like a love song. Passages of rich lyricism are interlaced with delicate, dancing episodes, which in turn melt back into lyricism. At the end, the opening strain of the theme returns for one more time. But now, the modulation into the minor has gone, all tension has disappeared, and the movement ends in complete simplicity and peace.

Mozart's autograph includes the first few bars of a minuet. But if he ever completed it, it does not survive. Alfred Einstein put forward the theory that a later minuet (K. 409) was composed for inclusion in a performance of this symphony, but this idea is no longer in favour and the three-movement form is accepted as being complete.

The finale, like that of Symphony No. 33, is in two halves, both marked to be repeated, but the second repeat is often omitted. The movement is full of wit and energy, and at times it takes on the character of an exuberant perpetuum mobile. The dance is dominated by the violins, but from time to time the pair of oboes joins in, like virtuoso shepherds' pipes. The second half introduces some surprisingly urgent changes of key, darkening the mood, but, just as simplicity ended the slow movement, straightforward exuberance brings this finale to a satisfying close.

SYMPHONY NO. 35 IN D MAJOR, K. 385, 'HAFFNER'

Allegro con spirito
Andante
Menuetto and Trio
Finale: Presto

This is the first symphony that Mozart wrote after settling permanently in Vienna. In July 1782 his father wrote to him with a commission from Sigmund Haffner of Salzburg, for a work to celebrate his ennoblement. Mozart had earlier composed the 'Haffner' Serenade for a Haffner family wedding, and he reluctantly agreed to write this new work. He was very busy with other composition, and the preparations for his own wedding. He replied to his father, 'Now you want me to write a new symphony! How can I do that! . . . Well, that's the way it is, I'll just have to work at night, I cannot do it any other way.'[27] He sent the symphony to his father as he completed it, movement by movement, and then forgot about it for six months. Then, needing a new symphony for a concert in Vienna, he asked for it back. When it arrived, he said that he remembered nothing about it, 'but I'm sure it is very effective.'[28] The original version was more of a serenade than a symphony, with six movements including an introductory march and two minuets. Mozart removed the march and one of the minuets to form a four-movement symphony, and added flutes and clarinets to the oboes, bassoons, horns, trumpets, and drums, creating an orchestra as large as for the 'Paris' Symphony. This revised work, which we know as the 'Haffner' Symphony, was first performed at the Burgtheater in

Vienna on 23 March 1783. The theatre was packed, and the emperor applauded enthusiastically. Mozart was at last enjoying a sustained period of success.

The opening of the symphony is another of those arresting effects beloved of Mannheim
and Paris. The violins leap up and down over two octaves, with dotted march rhythms and a
trill adding to the impact. But this is not just an effective opening. It is the germ for the whole
of the first movement. There are other ideas, but they come and go fleetingly, and none of
them really amounts to a second theme. In this, Mozart is following the example of Haydn,
who often writes first movements based on only one theme. Mozart's insistence on this
opening idea creates an effect of cumulative exhilaration. Within a few bars, the theme moves
to the bass, chased two bars later by the violins, and then breaks into rapid scales (this
symphony demands an orchestra with virtuoso violinists). When this tutti reaches a resolution, we expect a second theme. But instead, the main theme is played quietly in the violins
over a running bass, before moving again to the bass line, with dashing figurations in the
violins above. A few bars later there is a genuinely new idea in the violins, but still the main
theme forms a counterpoint below in the violas.

The first section of the Allegro reaches a close (this section is sometimes repeated, though
Mozart's revised score did not include a repeat). Then the development begins with the main
theme again in counterpoint, first exchanged quietly between the two violins, then loudly
between violins and bass. There is a quiet moment, in which counterpoint between the violins
is accompanied by mournful phrases in oboe and bassoon. These pensive moments are brief,
but Mozart uses them as vital points that balance the otherwise unstoppable vigour of the
movement. He wrote that this movement 'must be played with great fire'.[29]

The second movement is in keeping with the serenade-like original work. Its elegant
melodies are accompanied throughout by delicate tick-tock patterns that give the whole
movement a gently dancing character. Much of the beauty of this movement is created by the
effect of this accompaniment, which continues insistently while the melody above changes in
a moment from singing and lyrical to playful and balletic.

The minuet alternates loud, stately phrases with quiet, charming replies. The trio combines
the dance of the minuet with a singing melody – one could imagine it as a chorus of shepherds and shepherdesses.

The dashing finale has a theme that more or less quotes an aria from Mozart's recently
completed opera *Die Entführung aus dem Serail* (*The Abduction from the Seraglio*). There, the
comically bad-tempered overseer of the harem, Osmin, has recaptured the hero and heroine,
and sings 'Ha! How I shall triumph.' 'Triumphant' is a good word to describe this finale, which
Mozart said should be played 'as fast as possible'.[30] It is a rondo, in which the main theme
makes four appearances. The first time, its continuation leads to a poised second theme. The
second time, it quickly moves into new keys, and is followed by the second theme in the
minor. This has rather the character of a development section, after which the third occurrence of the main theme feels like a reprise. Again the second theme follows, rounded off by
another tutti. What follows is a coda, beginning with an almost comically simple idea, like
Osmin stamping his foot, and leading to the final appearance of the main theme. This time,
the leap in the melody overshoots delightfully, and a final vivacious tutti brings the symphony
to a close.

SYMPHONY NO. 36 IN C MAJOR, K. 425, 'LINZ'

Adagio – Allegro spiritoso
Andante
Menuetto and trio
Presto

On the way back to Vienna from visiting his father in Salzburg, Mozart and his wife stayed for three weeks in Linz. From there, he wrote to his father on 31 October 1783, 'On Tuesday, that's November 4th, I will give a concert at the theatre here. – and as I didn't bring one single Simphonie with me, I'll have to write a New one in a hurry, for it has to be finished by that time.'[31] Even allowing for the possibility that he already had it worked out in his head, it is scarcely believable that he should have been able to compose such a fine work, and have all the orchestral parts copied, in time for the concert. It is scored for pairs of oboes, bassoons, horns, trumpets, and drums (not flutes or clarinets).

For the first time, Mozart begins his symphony with a slow introduction (he was to do this again in Nos 38 and 39). Mozart's great mentor, Haydn, had rarely begun a symphony with a slow introduction at this date, though he was to do so from 1785 onwards. Perhaps Mozart had in mind the slow introductions of Handel and J. S. Bach, which he came to know at the Sunday baroque music gatherings at the house of the court librarian, Baron von Swieten. Like a baroque overture, the introduction begins with stately double-dotted rhythms. But the continuation is unlike anything in a baroque overture. With the harmonies continually pulling away from C major, melancholy lines interweave between the two violins, and then pass from oboe and bassoon to the bass, and back to the violins, before coming to rest. Something tragic seems to have been set up.

But the Allegro begins calmly and quietly, with interweaving lines, as in the introduction. Soon they give way to a vigorous and sustained tutti. Then there are quiet moments in which oboe and bassoon feature, contrasted with the full orchestra. But the new ideas do not really coalesce into a separate theme. After this first section (which is marked to be repeated), it is these subsidiary ideas that are explored further in the development, with more melancholy turns of harmony, before an outburst of tutti leads to the reprise.

The main theme of the slow movement has the lilting rhythm of a siciliano. But its textures are not always light – the trumpets and drums add emphasis from time to time. After the first section (which is marked to be repeated), the second part begins with the melody fragmenting, and the harmonies developing a dark edge. A tiptoeing scale rises in the bass, and comes to dominate until the reprise of the first theme enters with new decoration.

The minuet is vigorous, punctuated by military dotted rhythms. The elegant trio begins with the oboe an octave above the violins, continues with the bassoon an octave below the violins, and concludes with the bassoon playfully echoing the oboe in counterpoint.

The rapid finale begins quietly. Brief loud passages punctuate the progress of the music. Eventually a new theme is reached, but its opening phrase is almost a quote from the first theme, creating a close family resemblance. This theme ends by reiterating a little offbeat three-note motif, with sustained notes in counterpoint against it. It moves from violins to violas and on to the bass; there is a brief tutti, and then a haunting quiet passage in which the three-note motif persists against poignant harmonies in the woodwind. After this moment of anxiety, a crescendo leads to a vigorous tutti to finish the first section (which is repeated). A development follows, in which a brisk arpeggio figure from the first part of the movement is thrown playfully from instrument to instrument. The reprise revisits the events of the first section of the movement.

SYMPHONY NO. 38 IN D MAJOR, K. 504, 'PRAGUE'

Adagio – Allegro
Andante
Presto

The absence of No. 37 from the sequence of symphonies is explained by the fact that the work originally numbered as No. 37 turns out to be mostly by Michael Haydn (brother of Joseph). Only the slow introduction is by Mozart. Three years elapsed between symphonies Nos 36 and 38. This was the period of Mozart's greatest success in Vienna, but it was based on his reputation as a pianist and as an opera composer. He wrote and performed twelve of his finest piano concertos between the 'Linz' and 'Prague' Symphonies, and in May 1786 his career reached a climax with the premiere of his great comic opera, *The Marriage of Figaro*. There was not time or occasion to write symphonies, until he was invited to visit Prague in January 1787, where *Figaro* was enjoying a spectacularly successful run. He brought with him a newly composed symphony, which was first performed at a concert in Prague on 19 January.

If the preceding two symphonies show what Mozart could do in a hurry, this shows what he could achieve when he had time to work everything out. The first movement is of an emotional richness and complexity that is unprecedented in the symphonies of Mozart or Haydn. As in No. 36, Mozart begins with a slow introduction, but this is on a new scale, and with a new seriousness of purpose. The opening grand gesture, insistently repeated, is imme-diately thrown into doubt by an unexpected chord. What follows is a succession of attempts at a consoling melody, which is continually being questioned and thwarted. There is a series of full chords, between which the violins play delicate turns in a rising pattern, while the bassoons hold the bass note. The mood is ominous, suggesting not the recently completed *Marriage of Figaro* but an anticipation of *Don Giovanni*.

The mood remains unsettled as the Allegro begins, with syncopated repeated notes in the first violins, and a germ of a theme below (this is reminiscent of the even more unsettled opening of the Piano Concerto in D minor, written the previous year). The unsettled char-acter is contradicted by a march-like intervention from the wind, and the opening bars of the Allegro are repeated with an oboe descant above. Two of the features of the symphony are already heard in these few bars: the role of the woodwind (flutes, oboes, and bassoons) is prominent and independent (as it is in the piano concertos Mozart had recently composed), and there are often several things happening simultaneously. After two passages of bustling tutti, the music quietens to a second theme. This is in a major key, but at its second strain it turns to the minor, with bassoons mournfully echoing the violins. When it turns back to the major, the bassoons take up the theme, while the violins sing a consoling descant above it. After the first section of the Allegro (which is repeated), the development follows. This takes a descending scale from the wind section's first march-like intervention, and builds a passage of counterpoint out of it. First and second violins pursue each other at an interval of a bar, in canon. The bass instruments take up the scale, in canon with the violas, then this is combined with a phrase from the first theme, and then another phrase from the first tutti. Mozart uses his command of counterpoint (honed from his study of Bach and Handel) to create an urgent, concentrated passage, building to an extended tutti. The pulsating syncopations of the first theme return, but not yet in the home key, and a further, melancholy passage of counterpoint follows over a long, held bass note. At last we arrive back in D major, to find the full reprise of the opening theme. This whole movement is a tour de force, an achievement of dramatic complexity that is not to be equalled until Mozart's last symphony, the 'Jupiter'.

The second movement, Andante, moves with a gently swinging metre. It is elegant, and at times dancing. But it is continually assailed by complex turns of melody, poignant chromatic harmonies, and shifts of key. It is like a ballet dancer trying to perform while anguished by memories. The movement is as complex as the Allegro of the first movement. Its first section contains several themes and changes of key. It begins simply, but within three bars is already breaking into a sinuously chromatic line. A pointed staccato idea follows, which is soon echoed in the bass. A varied succession of other ideas follows, some simple, others complex, with woodwind and strings interacting and blending together like participants in chamber music. Each idea seems to lead naturally to the next, until a cadence signals the end of the first section.

At the repeat, the cadence is omitted, and the music passes straight on to the development. At first this is peaceful, even pastoral – indeed, Beethoven might well have had this passage at the back of his mind when writing the slow movement of his 'Pastoral' Symphony. But soon a staccato phrase enters abruptly, and the mood becomes more agitated, passing through minor keys, and culminating in a forceful tutti in which the treble and bass lines again pursue each other. Soon this calms, and leads on to the reprise.

There is no minuet (uniquely among Mozart's mature symphonies). The finale, like the slow movement, is more complex than it might at first appear. It begins lightly and genially, and there is a brief tutti. The woodwind take the music into a minor key, then there is another assertive tutti. A gentle second theme is also answered by the woodwind. The whole movement is made up from these strong contrasts – delicate string passages, woodwind ensemble, loud tutti – following each other in an almost mosaic-like pattern. But the force of this pattern changes as the movement proceeds. After the first section (which is repeated) the development begins with a succession of contrasting tutti and delicate woodwind, and then embarks on a more extended tutti in which (as at the equivalent point of the slow movement) upper and lower parts chase each other, with syncopated rhythms adding to the urgency. The reprise of the opening is quite quickly reached, but then there are more sudden eruptions of tutti, which seem to threaten the gentle woodwind answers. The movement comes to an abrupt end. The second section is marked in the score to be repeated. Increasingly, conductors observe this repeat, and the shock of being thrust back to the outburst that opened the second section adds to the sense of cumulative force in this movement, which began so innocently.

SYMPHONY NO. 39 IN E FLAT MAJOR, K. 543

Adagio – Allegro
Andante con moto
Menuetto: Allegretto – Trio – Menuetto
Finale: Allegro

This is the first of the group of three symphonies (Nos 39–41) that Mozart wrote in the summer of 1788. There is no record of them being performed in concerts that year, and, particularly as they are Mozart's last symphonies, this has led to a tradition of regarding them as works that he wrote simply out of inspiration, or 'for posterity'. But Mozart was an entirely pragmatic composer, who wrote when he was commissioned, or when he could gain money or prestige from concerts. So (as H. C. Robbins Landon argues), it is likely that they were performed in Vienna, perhaps in the autumn of 1788, though there is no conclusive evidence for this.[32] Austria was by now at war with Turkey, and one of the effects of the war was to restrict the cultural life of Vienna. Many aristocratic families left Vienna, and there were fewer resources or opportunities for concerts, particularly with large orchestras. It was probably for this reason that Mozart stopped composing symphonies.

The Symphony in E flat major is very different in character from the preceding symphonies (and from Nos 40 and 41). Its orchestra has a particularly mellow sound, because it includes prominent clarinets (as well as flute, bassoons, horns, trumpets, and drums), but no oboes. This immediately gives its opening chords a rich grandeur. The persistent dotted rhythms of the slow introduction suggest homage to the baroque overtures of Handel more strongly than the introductions to Nos 36 and 38. But there is a building sense of tension and conflict that takes it far beyond the conventions of the baroque. Quite how far from the baroque it seems depends partly on the tempo. It used to be usual to take this introduction at a very stately pace, giving it portentous weight. But Mozart's autograph has a time signature of two beats to the bar, not four, as in nineteenth-century editions. In recent decades, conductors have tended to take account of this, and the result is more galvanizing (and more baroque). After a mighty build-up, the introduction ends darky and mysteriously. When the Allegro arrives, it is with a complete sense of relief. The melody rises and falls in a relaxed three-time, with orderly and balanced phrases. There are elegant answers from horns and woodwind, and when the theme moves to the bass, the violins elaborate a counterpoint above. The tutti, when it comes, has great energy without any sense of stress. The gentle second theme features answers from the woodwind, from which the clarinets emerge as the leaders. It is only in the tutti that finishes the first section that Mozart introduces his characteristic chromatic tugs in the harmony, which here have the effect of underlining how confident and untroubled the Allegro has been so far.

After the (repeated) first section, the development picks up on an energetic little motif that, after a brief reminder of the second theme, drives forward a vigorous tutti, alternating between bass and violins. This comes to an abrupt halt, and three bars of woodwind introduce a moment of melancholy. But this is the end of such doubts, and the genial opening theme ushers in the reprise. The movement ends with redoubled energy, and a trumpet fanfare. The contrast between this energy and the lyricism of the opening theme may well have been in Beethoven's mind when he was writing the first movement of his 'Eroica' Symphony, which is in the same key, with the same time signature, and shares some of the same motifs.

The second movement is a dance in A flat major of the utmost charm, with persistent dotted rhythms, and at first scored for strings alone. This unruffled elegance is challenged by two extended episodes. The first begins in a turbulent F minor, the dotted rhythms now thrown up assertively. Clarinets and bassoons try to bring the music back to the first theme, but it is drawn into a further outburst, with fragments of the theme in the bass. Soon, bassoons and clarinets sing in a smoother rhythm, and the mood melts, ready for the first reprise. Here, the theme is accompanied by delicate counterpoints, first in the violins and then in the woodwind. Toward the end of the theme, the music wanders away from the home key, and there is a second stormy episode. This begins in B minor (very remote from A flat major), and struggles with greater intensity, and at greater length, than before. Again it is the bassoons and clarinets that calm the storm, leading to the final reprise. But this is not straightforward. After a few bars, the theme is beset by poignant harmonies, its elegant equilibrium is thrown into doubt, and the movement ends with a sense that the dance has been damaged by the challenges that it has faced.

The minuet returns to an unclouded courtliness. The marking 'Allegretto' perhaps cautions against too rapid a tempo. The repeated chords of the entire wind section, with timpani, help to give the minuet itself its firm and stately character. The trio is dominated by a charming clarinet solo (the first extended solo for this instrument in any Mozart symphony), with the second clarinet burbling an accompaniment, and the flute answering.

The finale is one of Mozart's most Haydnesque, full of wit and surprise, and all built out of one theme. It is, however an Allegro, not a Presto, and is a movement of serious substance as well as wit. The quiet energy and point of the opening theme develop, in the first tutti, into a virtual perpetuum mobile of running semiquavers. The key of this passage shifts to B flat, leading us to expect a second theme. But instead, what we get is a charming deconstruction of the first (and only) theme. Violins and woodwind banter with each other, and then the music slides weirdly to F sharp major, and bassoon and flute throw the opening phrase back and forth, as if lost in some private conversation, until the tutti pulls the music back to B flat. The conversation is rounded off with another outburst of banter between the three woodwind soloists, before the first section come to a close.

After the repeat, the development follows. This begins with another abrupt change of key, and a sudden halt – a particularly Haydnesque moment. The violins pick up the theme, and in an energetic tutti the opening phrase is thrown to and fro from violins to the bass, first a bar apart, and then half a bar apart, changing key as it goes. Again, there is an abrupt stop. Out of the silence emerges a solemn chorale, on clarinets and bassoons, while the opening phrase of the theme mutters an accompaniment. To anyone who knows *The Magic Flute* (1791), with its masonic brotherhood and its woodwind chorales led by clarinets, this little fragment has a distinctly masonic feeling (Mozart had joined the Freemasons in 1784, and composed a number of works for their ceremonies). The chorale gradually finds its way back to the home key of E flat, and the reprise follows.

The end of the symphony is another Haydnesque shock. The final tutti reaches an emphatic cadence, then tags on, as an afterthought, the opening phrase of the theme, twice. If the second half of the movement is repeated (as Mozart indicates), there is then a gap of a bar, and we are jolted back to the 'wrong key' of the development. When we reach the end of the movement for a second time, the opening phrase of the theme is left hanging in mid-air.

SYMPHONY NO. 40 IN G MINOR, K. 550

Molto Allegro
Andante
Menuetto: Allegretto – Trio – Menuetto
Allegro assai

This is the second of the final trio of great symphonies that Mozart wrote in 1788, probably for concerts in the autumn. If one wants to appreciate how Mozart had developed over the last fifteen years, one has only to compare this symphony with No. 25 in the same key, composed in 1773, with which this survey of his mature symphonies began. That earlier work was full of urgent theatrical gestures, inspired by Haydn's minor-key symphonies and Gluck's operas. In this later G minor symphony the emotional scale and subtlety is of a completely different order. It seems less theatrical, and more concerned with inner conflict. The original scoring has flute, oboes, and horns, but no clarinets, trumpets or drums. For a later performance (presumably), Mozart added a pair of clarinets, giving most of the prominent oboe moments to the first clarinet.

Over an agitated accompaniment in the violas, the violins worry away at a little three-note motif that is to dominate the movement. It forms a terse theme that eventually bursts out into an energetic tutti. The quiet second theme, in B flat major, is somewhat consoling. But the way that it passes rather awkwardly from strings to wind and back again, without ever developing a sustained line, gives it a somewhat nervous character. After the repeat of the first section, the development begins with a return to the opening theme, but now moving into remote keys, passing anxiously through F sharp minor, and then to a loud tutti in E minor, in which the theme alternates between bass and violins, with urgent running patterns in counterpoint. The passage eventually settles into a reiteration of the opening three-note motif, as if the first phrase of the theme has become frozen. It is passed quietly from violins to woodwind and back, over mournful held notes on bassoon, and harmonies that shift sorrowfully. The woodwind turn the three-note motif upside down, so that it rises, and this releases an outburst from the strings, followed by more sorrowful harmonies in the woodwind that prepare the reprise of the first theme.

The most striking feature if this reprise is what happens to the quiet second theme. The first time, it was in a major key. Now (as is usual) it reappears in the home key, G minor. This has a darkening effect on the latter part of the movement. After this melancholy version of the second theme, there is, as before, another tutti, but now much more agitated than before, with chromatic harmonies over a bass that rises step by step. The melancholy tone persists. Right at the end, there is another quiet return to the opening theme, in counterpoint, before a final brief tutti brings the movement to an abrupt conclusion.

No other movement in a Mozart symphony has provoked quite such a wide range of approaches as this first movement. The marking is Molto Allegro, with a time signature of two beats in a bar, not four (some early editions wrongly give it four beats in a bar). Recorded performances have varied in pace to an astonishing extent – the fastest are literally twice the speed of the slowest. The consensus today is that Mozart really must have meant quite a fast two-beat pulse. Even at a quick tempo, some conductors seem anxious to soften or beautify the opening theme. But the unsoftened terseness is surely the point.

The slow movement has also provoked widely differing interpretations. At a flowing pace, it has a gently swinging two-beat pulse. At a slower tempo, the subdivisions become more dominant. Mozart marks both halves to be repeated, which creates a movement about twelve minutes long even at a flowing tempo. A slower tempo makes the second repeat unsustainable (and it is not always observed even at faster tempi).

The opening theme, like that of the first movement, has an obsessive element. Violas, second violins, and first violins in turn play a rising interval and a succession of repeated notes. This is followed by drooping phrases, and little flicks upwards. The repeated notes start again in the bass, with a poignantly sustained counterpoint in the violins. The little flicking pairs of notes form a pattern, which accompanies woodwind phrases to round off the theme. The flicks then become a motif, passing between violins and woodwind, beneath which the opening repeated-note phrase is explored further. A second theme follows, with plaintive falling sighs.

The second section of the movement opens with a development that is dominated by two elements from the first theme – the repeated notes, and the flicked pairs of notes, both of which become menacing, with abrupt contrasts between loud and soft. The bassoons return to the opening theme, but at first it cannot settle, and is accompanied by mournful chromatic lines (derived from the original bass line) and the persistent flicks. Eventually this winds round to the reprise in the strings.

The minuet is no more conventional than the first two movements. Its rhythms cut across the metre of the bar, and its insistent rhythmic repetitions, in the minor key, give it a down-right character. This quality is exaggerated in the second half of the minuet, where the theme moves to the bass, with a counterpoint that leaps and tumbles above it in the violins. This turns into a canon, with the theme pursuing itself at the interval of a bar. After this crisis, the tailpiece of the minuet is most touching: over a poignantly falling chromatic line in the bassoon, flute and clarinets quietly round off the theme.

The trio is an oasis of peace in this unusually turbulent minuet. Like the theme of the minuet, its melody rises and falls, but with all the tension taken out of it. Oboes, flutes, and bassoons respond with a phrase that rises further, giving a beautiful sense of liberation. The rising phrase is developed further in the second half. And it has wider implications: it provides the idea from which Mozart will build his finale.

The principal theme of the finale begins with a rising arpeggio, like the serene idea in the trio of the minuet. But there is nothing serene about its transformation here. This finale is like the first movement, but with the terseness and the tension screwed up almost to breaking point. If you look at the score of the opening, it seems one of the most regular, orderly pieces of music: eight bars repeated, then another eight bars repeated. The first eight bars have an internal pattern of two bars soft, two bars loud, repeated. The second eight bars have an internal pattern of one bar soft, one bar loud, repeated, then two bars soft, two bars loud. It is like a mathematical mosaic. But the emotional effect is far from just orderly. The pattern is like a prison, not a source of comfort, and when the music succeeds in breaking out into a furious tutti, it seems inevitable: scales and arpeggios rush out unceasingly, as if trying to get as far as possible from the constrictions of the opening theme. Eventually, a gentle second theme is reached, like a sort of oasis in B flat major. This has something in common with the second theme of the slow movement, with little flicking rhythms enlivening a lyrical melody. Another tutti brings the first section to a close.

After the repeat, the second section begins (as in the first movement) with a lurch into an unexpected key. The principal theme passes between violins, flute, bassoon, and oboe, quietly at first. But then a ferocious passage of counterpoint develops, in which the theme is combined with the rushing scales from the first tutti. Sustained notes in the wind underpin it, like an organ. The counterpoint comes abruptly to a halt, and the reprise begins. This time each half of the theme is played only once, without its repeat, so that we are into the headlong tutti sooner than the first time. When the quiet second theme arrives, its effect is changed, as at the equivalent moment in the first movement. The sense of an oasis, which the theme evoked the first time, is darkened because it is now in a minor key (the home key, G minor). Mozart increases the sombreness, smoothing out the flicking rhythm, and introducing an anxious, undulating variation in the second half of the theme. And so on to the final tutti. This has the effect of an inevitable arrival, but not a release. The music goes hurtling to its end, without any softening or comfort.

Mozart indicates that the second half of this finale should be repeated. Until recent years, this was hardly ever done, because the effect of the ending is so decisive without the repeat. Modern conductors, encouraged by 'historical awareness', now often play the repeat. Sometimes this sounds like a pedantic miscalculation, which takes away from the effect of the ending. But if it is done with real emotional purpose, it can produce an even greater accumulation of power the second time round.

SYMPHONY NO. 41 IN C MAJOR, 'JUPITER', K. 551

Allegro vivace
Andante cantabile
Menuetto: Allegretto
Molto Allegro

For his final symphony, the last of the three composed in the summer of 1788, Mozart returns to the grand orchestra with flute, oboes, bassoons, horns, trumpets, and drums (but not clarinets). And in some ways he returns to the brilliant effects he first displayed in the 'Paris' Symphony (No. 31) ten years earlier, beginning with just the sort of arresting gesture from the whole orchestra that was first popularized by the Mannheim orchestra and its composers. This is a symphony on a majestic scale, culminating in a tour de force of counterpoint. The nickname 'Jupiter' was attached to it early in the nineteenth century.

From the opening bars, we can sense immediately the influence of comic opera. This might seem a throwback to the symphonies of a younger Mozart (or Haydn). But this is no longer the comic opera of the old Italian opera house, but the subtle and humane world of Mozart's *The Marriage of Figaro*. The opening theme consists of assertive gestures, answered by quiet rising phrases. One could almost imagine it as an exchange between the domineering count and the pleading countess in *Figaro*. But the way Mozart deploys these two elements is wonderfully subtle and effective. The opening becomes a sustained tutti, with trumpets and drums, dotted rhythms, and flurries in the violins combining to suggest ceremonial splendour. After a pause, the assertive opening phrase and its gentle reply are repeated quietly in the violins, with a counterpoint of chattering scales in the woodwind. Then the gentle answering phrase itself becomes assertive, combining with the dotted rhythms to lead the next tutti. This is followed by the second theme, in which another gently rising phrase is answered in the bass while the violins provide another charming counterpoint. After these ideas have been extended for a few bars, the 'pleading' answer from the first theme gently insinuates itself into the bass. Delicate phrases reach a silence. Then there is another splendid tutti, announced by a startling minor chord.

We seem to be heading for the conclusion of the first section. But there is another halt, and one more delicate, tripping theme. If the associations with opera have been indirect up to this point, here there can be no doubt. This little afterthought is a quotation from an aria, 'Un bacio di mano', which Mozart had composed the previous May as an 'insert' to be sung by a bass in an opera by Pasquale Anfossi. The aria warns of the dangers of kissing the hand of a beautiful woman, and the extract Mozart quotes has the words: 'You are a bit naive, my dear Pompeo. Go and study the ways of the world.' How many of Mozart's first audience would have recognized the quotation is unknown – perhaps Mozart put it in as a charming joke for himself. But it proves to be far more than a joke. The middle section, the development, begins with this quotation, in a new key, and it is built up into an urgent exchange between treble and bass. This gives way to a quiet reminiscence of the opening theme, with its pleading answer and chattering woodwind. But it is in the wrong key for the reprise, and is soon interrupted by another tutti, built from reiterations of the opening gesture of the theme, with its brusque flurries of notes. Another reminder of the aria quotation leads in to the reprise. This proceeds more or less as expected, but with the important difference that ideas are stretched out, with new counterpoint, and with a sense of searching through new keys to find the home of C major.

The Andante is one of the most elaborate and expansive of all Mozart's slow movements. The melody weaves a complicated pattern rather like a baroque keyboard piece, such as one of Bach's sarabandes. The melody is at first in the violins, and then moves to the bass, with the violins responding with further elaboration. All this has a delicate sheen, because the upper strings are muted. Then the key changes to the minor, and the mood darkens. There are stabbing accents, and agitated rhythmic patterns in the accompaniment. The harmonies are uneasy, with woodwind chords sliding upwards chromatically. This tension resolves to a hymn-like melody. But after two phrases, it breaks into fragments, with chromatic harmonies sliding downwards in the bassoons. Again there is a resolution, and the first section ends with strings and woodwind exchanging phrases with an almost curtsey-like charm.

After the repeat of the first section, the middle of the movement is dominated by the darker, second element, with its stabbing accents and unsettled harmonies. They develop greater tension than before, rising higher, before dissolving into reiterations of the 'curtseying' phrase. This leads, surprisingly soon, to the reprise of the first theme. But Mozart has not finished with his development. The theme begins in the bass, and is answered by the violins. This sets off a passage of swirling agitation, which climaxes in a return to the stabbing accents. Eventually the music settles, and we reach the second, hymn-like element, the fragmented phrases, and the 'curtsies'. On to the end, Mozart adds a final reminiscence of the first theme, and rounds it off with cadences decorated with a final pair of curtsies. The movement has ended as it began, in calm and formality. It has been a journey fraught with melancholy agitation that at times threatens to break the thread irrevocably. But throughout, the upper strings are muted. It is this conflict between the quality of the sound and the quality of the emotions that makes the satisfaction of this movement unique.

The minuet is unusually subtle. At first, the descending melody seems to float in the air, because it begins without a bass line. Then trumpets and timpani delicately touch in the bass of two chords at the end of the first phrase. The same happens at the end of the second phrase, before the whole orchestra rounds off the first strain. In the second half, the descending melody and an ascending bass line form a passage of counterpoint, the two lines taking it in turns to be the melody or the bass. In the trio, Mozart playfully reverses the shape that began the minuet: the woodwind play a cadence of two chords, and violins and oboe answer shyly. The second half of the trio begins with full orchestra. The first four notes played by the violins are a new idea. They will provide the seed from which the finale is built.

The finale of Mozart's last symphony is a tour de force. The whole movement is based on five little melodic elements, which are combined and developed in a brilliant display of symphonic drama and counterpoint. It begins innocently, with violins playing the four-note shape that first appeared in the trio of the minuet (the first element), to which is added a second element with repeated notes. A tutti introduces a third element played in unison, with a dotted rhythm and rapid downward scale. At the end of the tutti, the four-note motif of the first element quietly builds up a delicate web of counterpoint (a portent of things to come). Another tutti breaks in, introducing a fourth element, a rising staccato phrase with a trill. This little tutti ends with the third element (dotted rhythm and descending scale) chasing itself at an interval of half a bar. Then comes a fifth element, a graceful melody in the violins. The woodwind comment on it with cheeky counterpoint, combining the third element (flute) with the fourth element (bassoons). It is then the turn of the fourth element to chase itself, at an interval of a bar, over chattering violins. At the next tutti, the graceful fifth element has become another subject for counterpoint, building up great energy. Into this cauldron is thrown the second element (with its repeated notes), and then the third element (dotted rhythm and descending scale). Again this chases itself at a half-bar interval, but now both the right way up and inverted. The first section of the movement ends with flute and bassoon quietly playing the third element, as if nothing has happened.

After the repeat of the first section, the second section continues quietly, with the four-note first element in the strings, the third element in oboe and bassoon, both ways up. A tutti breaks in with a fierce passage of counterpoint, in which the third element again chases itself, now in four separate voices at half-bar intervals. The woodwind quietly intone the first element in almost ecclesiastical-style counterpoint, now in a minor key. The strings fiercely oppose it with their continued battle over the third element, punctuated emphatically by trumpets and drums. The contrast between these two sets of voices, and the minor harmonies with their chromatic twists, give a sense of things almost falling apart. But the music stabilizes, and we turn a corner to find ourselves back at the reprise.

As in the first movement, Mozart has not finished developing his material. No sooner have we started revisiting the first two elements than renewed conflict breaks out. The four-note first element is subjected to wrenching chromatic harmonies, with harsh dissonances created by the woodwind counterpoint, and brusque swirls in the bass. Eventually, the music wins through to the third element, and the reprise is able to come to a conclusion. This second section of the movement is marked to be repeated.

On to the end of this already virtuosic piece of writing, Mozart adds a brilliantly climactic coda. It begins quietly, with the first element (upside down to begin with) made poignant by a chromatic counterpoint in the woodwind, as in the early part of the reprise. Into this bursts a passage of 'double fugue': that is, Mozart combines the first and fifth elements, developing a web of counterpoint using both of them simultaneously. He also throws the fourth element into this, so that the texture becomes unbelievably complex. Eventually, the music coalesces in a triumphant reassertion of the dotted rhythms and rapid scales of the third element, and the symphony reaches a glorious ending.

MODEST MUSORGSKY
(1839–81)

Although he showed talent as a pianist from an early age, Musorgsky followed the family tradition and trained as a soldier, serving as a guard for two years. It was while on duty at a military hospital in St Petersburg that Musorgsky met Borodin, and through him got to move in a circle of musicians. Balakirev took Musorgsky's musical education in hand. His instruction consisted not of formal lessons, but of playing the classics in piano duet arrangements with Musorgsky, analysing them as they went. Balakirev, though the leader of the group of composers that gathered round him, had had no formal training in composition, and he recalled in 1881, 'Because I am not a theorist, I could not teach him harmony (as, for instance, Rimsky-Korsakov now teaches it) ... [but] I explained to him the form of compositions, and to do this we played through Beethoven symphonies and much else (Schumann, Schubert, Glinka, and others), analysing the form.' He introduced Musorgsky to the music of modern composers, such as Berlioz and Liszt.[1] Although Musorgsky had shown no evidence that he could earn a living as a composer, the financial backing of his family meant that he could afford to resign his commission and devote himself to music. He was only nineteen, and from this point on he began a career in which periods of feverish activity alternated with others in which he achieved little, suffered mental crises of an unexplained kind, and took to heavy drinking. His problems were exacerbated in 1861 when the emancipation of the serfs led to a severe reduction of his family's fortune, and he was forced to take work as a civil servant to give himself enough money to live on. He was forty-two when he died, a destitute alcoholic, in a military hospital.

Despite – and maybe partly because of – his mental and physical troubles, Musorgsky became one of the most striking figures in Russian music. He was a member of the group of composers known as 'The Five' or 'The Mighty Handful' (Balakirev, Borodin, Rimsky-Korsakov, Musorgsky, and Cui), whose aim was to build on the pioneering work of Glinka to forge a national school of Russian music. In his two greatest operas, *Boris Godunov* and *Khovanshchina*, Musorgsky went further than his contemporaries in the development of word-setting closely modelled on the rhythms of the Russian language, with harmony and orchestration that are unusually stark and direct. The result is a style that seems to cut through convention to reveal a potent musical world. This is also evident in his one major orchestral piece, *Night on the Bare Mountain*, and in a work for piano that has become famous in an orchestral version by Ravel, *Pictures at an Exhibition*.

NIGHT ON THE BARE MOUNTAIN (ST JOHN'S NIGHT ON THE BARE MOUNTAIN)
Duration (Rimsky-Korsakov's edition): approx. 12 minutes

As early as 1860, Musorgsky was commissioned to write an act of an opera based on a play, *The Witch*, by Georgy Mengden. As Musorgsky wrote to Balakirev, this was set on the Bare Mountain, and included 'a witches' sabbath, different episodes for sorcerers, a triumphal march for the entire obsene rabble, a finale: glorification of the sabbath.[2] Nothing came of this, but six years later the idea resurfaced when Musorgsky heard Liszt's *Totentanz* performed for the first time in Russia in 1866. This consists of a set of variations on the *Dies Irae*, full of wild and brilliant effects sometimes verging on the brutal – particularly the savage, low chords at the opening, which suggest an enormous bell. Liszt in turn had been inspired by Berlioz – in 1830 he attended the premiere of the *Symphonie fantastique*, which ends with a 'Witches' Sabbath' quoting the *Dies Irae*.

The original version of *St John's Night on the Bare Mountain* (as Musorgsky called it) was written in 1867. He twice revised it in later years, incorporating it into operas, but it was never performed in his lifetime. After Musorgsky's death, Rimsky-Korsakov heavily revised it, and this is the piece well known in the concert hall. The original 1867 version was not published until 1967.

The first third of the piece survived more or less intact in later revisions, and in Rimsky-Korsakov's version. It opens with the sort of elemental, impressionistic effect pioneered by Beethoven in the storm of his 'Pastoral' Symphony, updated via Liszt, and with a particular rawness of Musorgsky's own. Rapid swirling patterns in the strings, shrieks in the woodwind, and heavy treading in the bass, evoke an infernal scene. The first real theme is a stark chant on trombones and tuba, which suggests the sombre downward shape of the first phrase of the *Dies Irae* without actually quoting it. This is followed by cackling fanfares and urgent violins that again refer obliquely to the *Dies Irae*. All this passage is repeated a semitone up. Now a new element enters, a tune like a vigorous Russian dance. Its pair of phrases is repeated again and again, at first exchanged between woodwind and strings, and then more obsessively in the wind, with each phrase violently punctuated, culminating in ominous brass chords and swirling string patterns.

This is the point at which later versions diverge from Musorgsky's original. The first version enters into a wildly impressionistic, virtually themeless, passage, with climaxes ebbing and flowing on unstoppable waves. Another obsessively repeating shape starts up in the woodwind and the pace accelerates. After more waves, there is a sudden silence. The first dance tune reappears, answered by the shrieks from the opening and chattering chords of woodwind. From this point, the piece proceeds through a series of climaxes, culminating in a frenzied dance whose strangeness is heightened by the whole-tone scale, as in Glinka's *Russlan and Ludmilla* (Musorgsky referred to it as the 'chemical scale'). At the end, there is no dawn, no redemption. With a final burst of speed, the music breaks into fragments of rhythm answered by violent swirling, and abruptly, the piece is over.

That original 1867 score is uncompromisingly wild, clumsily constructed, with a number of clunky stops and starts and a rather exhausting lack of relief. It is perhaps all too realistic as a portrayal of a witches' sabbath, and it is easy to understand why Musorgsky was so proud of it, and why Balakirev considered it unfit for performance without revision. Musorgsky's response to Balakirev's judgement was defiant: 'I considered, do consider, and shall not cease to consider that this piece is worthy ... I have for the first time stood on my own feet in a large-scale piece.'[3] But Musorgsky himself obviously came to realize that it could be made more coherent. In 1872 he drastically revised it for a witches' sabbath in an opera, *Mlada*, which he started composing in collaboration with other composers.

This was never completed, but Musorgsky took his revised *Night*, complete with witches' chorus and baritone solo (Satan), and reused it as an intermezzo in his opera *Sorochintsy Fair*, which he worked on from 1877 but never finished. Here it takes the form (rather implausibly) of a dream intermezzo. A young peasant, Gritsko, is in love with a girl, but his mother refuses to allow the marriage. He falls asleep and is visited by a nightmare vision of a witches' sabbath. Musorgsky's sketch of the dream is as follows (in abbreviated form): The subterranean kingdom of darkness mocks Gritsko; Satan arrives and is glorified in a black mass; the sabbath, at the height of which a church bell sounds and Satan and his rabble vanish; the voices of priests are heard, the devils disappear, and Gritsko awakes. Daybreak.

This is the version of *Night on the Bare Mountain* that Rimsky-Korsakov used as the basis of his purely orchestral version. As well as adding the chorus, Musorgsky had radically changed the original piece. There are fewer stops and starts, there is greater variety of pace and mood, and he adds new material. The most important new idea comes at the end of the powerful opening section. After a long stretch of turbulence (most of it much as in the 1867 original), there is the first sustained easing of tempo and mood. Rising phrases are answered by an agitated little rising and falling pattern in the woodwind. This turns out to be an important element in the rest of the piece, its repetitive pattern becoming obsessive, and helping to build the tension. At the end, when the sabbath is interrupted by the church bell and the terrible vision fades, this same little figure takes on a melancholy, dream-like quality. Then clarinet and flute play a meditative melody. This links back into the action of *Sorochintsy Fair*, as the young man, Gritsko, wakes up and remembers his earlier lament for his love.

Rimsky-Korsakov's adaptation of this revision is the version of the score that has become familiar, and is still most often played. Rimsky has often been criticized for the extent of his interventions. But there is little in his version that is not at least based on material in Musorgsky. The overall effect, however, is a great deal more orthodox than Musorgsky's piece, less wild and dissolute. Instead of the orgiastic sabbath that occupies the middle of Musorgsky's revised version, Rimsky constructs a much more coherent sequence of events. It could comfortably have formed a movement of his own *Scheherazade*. The ending, however, is much as Musorgsky wrote it, and is the most haunting passage in the work.

PICTURES AT AN EXHIBITION (ORCHESTRATED BY RAVEL)
Duration: approx. 34 minutes

Promenade: Allegro giusto, nel modo russico, senza allegrezza, ma poco sostenuto
1. Gnomus (Gnome): Sempre vivo
(Promenade): Moderato comodo assai e con delicatezza
2. Il Vecchio Castello (The Old Castle): Andantino molto cantabile a con dolore
(Promenade): Moderato non tanto, pesamente
3. Tuileries (Children arguing after play): Allegretto non troppo, capriccioso
4. Bydlo: Sempre moderato, pesante
(Promenade): Tranquillo
5. Ballet of the Chicks in their Shells: Scherzino, vivo, leggiero
6. Two Jews, One Rich and the Other Poor ('Samuel' Goldenberg and 'Schmuÿle'):
   Andante. Grave-energico
(Promenade): Allegro giusto, nel modo russico, poco sostenuto (omitted by Ravel)
7. Limoges. The Market (The Big News): Allegretto vivo, sempre scherzando –
8. Catacombae (Sepulchrum Romanum): Largo – Con Mortuis in Lingua Mortua:
   Andante non troppo, con lamento
9. The Hut on Chicken's Legs (Baba-Yaga): Allegro con brio, feroce – Andante mosso – Allegro
   molto –
10. The Bogatyrs' Gate (in the ancient capital Kiev) (The Great Gate of Kiev): Allegro alla
   breve. Maestoso. Con grandezza

In August 1873, Musorgsky's friend, the architect and artist Viktor Hartmann, died suddenly of an aneurysm at the age of thirty-nine. Six months later, the prominent critic Vladimir Stasov organized an exhibition of Hartmann's work in St Petersburg. It was this that prompted Musorgsky to compose his own memorial to his friend: a set of ten piano pieces inspired by

Hartmann's works. Hartmann, like Musorgsky and the other composers that made up the Russian 'Five', was part of the movement to create distinctly Russian work, deriving inspiration from Russian history and myth, and from the art, literature, and music of the Russian people. He worked with extraordinary energy in many different artistic fields (the catalogue of the exhibition lists four hundred items), and his death was a great shock to Musorgsky. He had been walking with Hartmann shortly before his death, when Hartmann had had an attack of breathlessness, and Musorgsky reproached himself for having ignored these warning signs. He wrote a passionate letter to Stasov after Hartmann's death, quoting *King Lear*: '... what a terrible blow! "Why should a horse, a dog, a rat have life" and creatures like Hartmann die! ... No, one cannot and must not be comforted, there can be and must be no consolation – it is a rotten mortality!'[4]

Pictures at an Exhibition, as Musorgsky originally conceived it for piano, was not published until five years after his death, and was rarely performed until the mid-twentieth century. It was its transformation into an orchestral work that made it famous. The vividness of the pieces made them obviously suitable for orchestration. The first orchestral arrangement, by Mikhail Tushmalov (a pupil of Rimsky-Korsakov), was performed as early as 1891, and another by Sir Henry Wood appeared in 1915. Many others have followed, but none have had the success of the version by Ravel. This was commissioned by Serge Koussevitzky, who conducted the premiere in his concert series at the Paris Opéra in 1922. Ravel was not only a wonderful orchestrator, who was used to arranging his own piano pieces for orchestra, but was also a great admirer of Musorgsky. In 1913 the impresario Sergei Diaghilev had asked Ravel to collaborate with Stravinsky on a version of Musorgsky's incomplete opera, *Khovanshchina*, for performance by his Ballets Russes. Ravel's orchestration of *Pictures at an Exhibition* was published by Koussevitzky's own *Edition Russe de Musique* in 1929. The Musorgsky–Ravel version of *Pictures* rapidly became a popular concert piece, and this in turn sparked interest in the original piano version.

As for the quality of Ravel's orchestration, an obvious point of comparison is Rimsky-Korsakov's editions of Musorgsky – *Boris Godunov*, *Khovanshchina*, and *Night on the Bare Mountain*. Rimsky-Korsakov took quite a free hand in 'civilizing' not only Musorgsky's orchestration but even his harmonies, making them seem less stark and more conventional (his edition of the piano original of *Pictures at an Exhibition* is comparatively free of such liberties). Ravel thoroughly disapproved of such 'improvements', as he stated in an interview published during a visit to London in 1929: 'You cannot alter a composer's harmonies without altering the trend of his music. Rimsky-Korsakov, for instance, when he imagined himself to be correcting Mussorgsky's [*sic*] harmonies, was really substituting music according to his own conception for music according to Mussorgsky's conception. Mussorgsky's alleged incorrections are sheer strokes of genius, very different from the blunders of a writer lacking linguistic sense or of a composer lacking harmonic sense.'[5]

The first edition of Musorgsky's original piano pieces includes brief descriptions by Stasov of the relevant pictures. Stasov later augmented these in his biography of Musorgsky, and in letters.[6]

One of the most strikingly original features of the work is the way in which Musorgsky links the movements by returning to the 'Promenade'. As Stasov observed, it varies in character during the piece: 'The composer has shown himself pacing here and there; sometimes lingering, sometimes hastening to get near a picture; sometimes the joyful gait slackens –

Musorgsky thinking of his dead friend.' Musorgsky himself stated in a letter to Stasov, 'My physiognomy is evident in the interludes.' For most of the work the recurrences of the Promenade appear as separate interludes, but eventually it merges with the pieces themselves, to give a strong sense of coherence to the work.

The opening Promenade sets off at a confident stride, but the effect is subtle. 'In modo russico' suggests a relationship with Russian folk song, and indeed Musorgsky alludes to, but does not exactly quote, the well-known folk song 'Glory to the Sun', that he had already used in the coronation scene in *Boris Godunov*. The opening alternates between solo line and harmonized response, another allusion to tradition both in folk music and in orthodox chant. But the music is also metrically irregular: bars of five-time and six-time alternate, creating phrases eleven beats long. Even when the music settles into a regular six-time, the internal phrases and repetitions continually cut across the metre in a manner that sounds almost like proto-Stravinsky. Ravel's version begins with solo trumpet answered by brass chorus, continues with strings and woodwind, and concludes by returning to the brass chorus joined by strings and woodwind. This makes the overall structure of the Promenade more explicit than in Musorgsky's piano original.

'Gnomus' follows without a break. According to Stasov, Hartmann's drawing represented 'a little gnome walking awkwardly on deformed legs'. It was a design for a grotesque toy nutcracker made in 1869 for the Christmas tree at the St Petersburg Artists' Club. Musorgsky's music comes as a shock, not only grotesque but also threatening. It has three elements: fast, stumbling phrases, like a creature grabbing wildly; sinister, jerky, descending chords; and ominous, bare octaves, which form strange harmonies. At the end, the jerky chords in the treble are joined by muttering trills and swirls below (in the same weird pattern as the shrieks of the woodwind at the opening of *Night on the Bare Mountain*), and there is one final, wild grab. Ravel's re-imagining of the jerky, descending chords is particularly striking. At first, high woodwind are over a low, muted tuba; then celesta and harp are joined by ghostly string glissandi. The bare octaves, on wind, are made more ominous by touches of bass drum and low harp, and then by a cymbal roll and drooping glissandi on low strings.

Musorgsky's linking Promenade has the melody below the answering chords. Ravel gives this to a horn, answered by bassoon below higher woodwind. Hartmann's 'Il vecchio castello' was, according to Stasov, 'A medieval castle in front of which stands a singing troubadour.' This was presumably one of the watercolours painted by Hartmann in Italy, though it has not been traced. Musorgsky's piece is the least complicated, and most lyrical, of the whole set. Predominantly pianissimo, it is a lament, over an unchanging bass note (as in a bagpipe drone), with the lilting rhythm of a siciliano or barcarolle – this and the title hint at the Italian setting of the painting. The opening of the melody, decorated with little grace notes, has quite a rustic air. It recurs several times, giving a rondo-like shape to the movement. Between each recurrence, the melody and the harmonies pull away, while never escaping the persistent bass, creating a poignant tension. Ravel famously gives the solo to a saxophone, following the example set by Bizet in *L'Arlésienne*. The modern sophistication of this choice can seem at odds with the rustic simplicity of Musorgsky's original. But the tone of a French saxophonist in the 1920s, with French bassoons below, would have been rather reedier and less urbane than we are used to in modern performances.

A brief reminder of the Promenade returns to the boldness of the opening, with solo trumpet, but peters out after a few phrases.

'Tuileries (Children arguing after play)': Hartmann had spent three years in France after graduating, and this is the first of three of Musorgsky's *Pictures* inspired by work from those years. The painting is listed in the exhibition catalogue simply as *Jardin des Tuileries*, but Stasov confirms that there were children in the picture: 'A walk in the garden of the Tuileries with children and nurses.' Stasov's niece, Varvara, remembered how Musorgsky used to come to her family's house when she was seven, and how exceptional he was in his ability to behave naturally and seriously with children: '... because he did not "pretend" with us, did not talk in that unnatural way in which grown-ups usually talk with children at home when they are friends of their parents, we not only quickly became attached to him but began to consider him *one of us*'.[7] Musorgsky had already demonstrated his insight into a child's way of thinking in his set of songs, *The Nursery*. There is an echo of it in 'Tuileries', the first of two pieces relating to children in *Pictures*. Musorgsky's music is charmingly delicate and mercurial. In little more than a minute, it encapsulates not only the light energy of children in the park, but, in its centre, a moment of wistfulness, like a child in tears who is soon cajoled into rejoining the merriment.

'Bydlo' is the Polish and Russian for 'cattle', but in a letter to Stasov, Musorgsky specified 'Sandomirzsko bydlo (le télègue)'. 'Telega' is the Russian for a heavy cart. Sandomierz is a town in Poland where Hartmann spent a month painting (his two pictures of Jews, the subject of another movement, were painted there). And Stasov himself described the picture that inspired this movement as, 'A Polish wagon on enormous wheels drawn by oxen'. There is no Promenade separating 'Tuileries' from 'Bydlo'. Musorgky's intention was to hit the listener 'right between the eyes' with the ox-cart, fortissimo. But Ravel did not know this, having had to rely on Rimsky-Korsakov's edition (the first to be published), which begins 'Bydlo' quietly, as if the cart is approaching from the distance.

Ravel conveys the effect of the heavy cart by giving the melody to a tuba, with trudging accompaniment underpinned by contrabassoon. From the quiet opening, the middle section builds to an enormous climax on full orchestra, fades to a return of the tuba solo, and then just the accompaniment, and then silence. The effect of the melody over the inexorable rhythm of the accompaniment is not just that of a heavy cart; it also evokes the effortful Russian work song represented by the famous 'Song of the Volga Boatmen' – a song of barge-haulers that Musorgsky's mentor, Balakirev, had published in his 1866 collection of Russian popular songs.

The heavy 'Bydlo' is followed by the most pensive reappearance of the Promenade, first in the treble (high woodwind), then in the bass. Just as it is developing new thoughts, it is interrupted by a chirrup. 'Ballet of the Chicks in their Shells' was inspired by one of Hartmann's costume designs for a ballet, *Trilby, or the Demon of the Hearth*, choreographed by Marius Petipa, which he sketched in 1870. It shows, in the words of the catalogue, 'Canary-chicks, enclosed in eggs as in suits of armour. Instead of a head-dress, canary heads, put on like helmets, down to the neck.' This costume was for a divertissement danced by children of the Imperial Russian Ballet School. Musorgsky's music is cast as a chirruping little scherzo and trio, most of it pianissimo. Ravel gives the chirrups to high woodwind, with the bass enlivened by harp and pizzicato strings. The trio has high trills on violins, like the flapping of tiny wings.

Musorgsky moves straight on, without a Promenade, to a piece in complete contrast to the chicks: '"Samuel" Goldenberg and "Schmuÿle"'. This was published under Stasov's preferred title: 'Two Jews: rich and poor.' It was inspired by two drawings of Jews that Hartmann had given to Musorgsky, and which he lent for the exhibition. 'Schmuÿle' is the Yiddish version of 'Samuel'.

Much has been made of the possible anti-Semitic message of Musorgsky's title. The contemptuous caricaturing of Jews was commonplace in Russia in the nineteenth century, and Musorgsky was certainly not above it. But two surviving watercolour portraits of rich and poor Jews by Hartmann have great dignity. One shows the half-profile head and shoulders of a distinguished bearded man. The other shows an exhausted old man sitting at the edge of the road, his hands resting on a stick, his hat next to him on a stone. If the drawings that Musorgsky possessed were anything like these paintings, they could hardly have inspired an intentional gesture of anti-Semitism. However, Musorgsky brings Hartmann's two characters face to face, so we are given the impression of the poor Jew begging from the rich man – or, it has even been suggested, the two-faced character of a single Jew (again, Musorgsky would certainly have been capable of such an anti-Semitic characterization).[8]

The piece opens with bold octaves in an assertive rhythm, the Jewish character strongly suggested by the choice of scale and by the embellishments, both of which are characteristic of Jewish chant and Klezmer, giving an immediately 'exotic' effect. This assertive opening conveys the arrogant confidence of the rich man. The pleading of the poor man is suggested by a persistent little figure of repeated notes and a twiddle played by muted trumpet over a slow-moving chant, with an end-piece of further 'exotic' intervals. The pattern of repeated notes becomes more insistent, and is joined by the rich man's bold octaves below. There is a moment of quiet pleading, but it is brusquely dismissed. Deliberately anti-Semitic or not, it is an uncomfortable piece.

Musorgky's original version here repeats the whole of the opening Promenade, but Ravel omits it, moving straight on to 'Limoges. The Market'. This is the third of the pictures from Hartmann's years in France, and according to Stasov it showed 'French women furiously arguing in the market-place'. In the margin of his manuscript Musorgsky jotted down some specific imaginings. One of them reads (in French), 'Great news: M. de Puissangeout has recovered his cow, "The Fugitive". But the good women of Limoges are not altogether in agreement on this subject, because Mme. de Remboursac has acquired a beautiful set of porcelain dentures, while M. de Panta-Pantaléon still has his enormous nose – the colour of a peony.'[9]

Musorgsky's piece conveys a vivid impression of bustle and banter. The string of rapid notes is unflagging, beginning with two-bar phrases and then breaking into smaller units, with accents sometimes on the beat, sometimes offbeat. The harmonies start firmly in B flat major, but then change rapidly through other keys before returning. All of this gives a sense of many different voices and perspectives passing rapidly before us. In the original piano version the level of energy does not diminish for a second. Ravel's orchestration adds great subtlety of texture and colour. There are many instruments playing all the time, but the balance between them is constantly shifting, so that one moment we are most aware of horns, then violins, woodwind, trumpets, with touches of tambourine, triangle, cymbals, and celesta adding punctuation and sparkle. The bustle halts suddenly. Then the theme breaks into fast note values, and with an accelerating rush the music bursts into:

'Catacombae (Sepulchrum Romanum)'. The exhibition catalogue states: 'Interior of the Paris catacombs with figures of Hartmann, the architect Kenel, and the guide holding a lamp.' The light of the lamp gives a ghostly atmosphere to Hartmann's drawing, and Musorgsky has added further mystery by imagining the eighteenth-century catacombs as ancient Roman.

Nothing could be starker than the contrast between the animated bustle of the marketplace and this dead, awesome music. It starts as a succession of dissonant chords, alternating between fortissimo and piano, as if mysterious echoes are returning from the depths. A second phrase rises, alluding to Siegfried's Funeral March from Wagner's *Götterdämmerung*; but the nobility of this moment is denied by a persistent dissonance in the bass, and the passage ends in unresolved darkness. Ravel scores this section with full brass. Now follows the second part of the piece: 'Con Mortuis in Lingua Mortua'. Musorgsky noted in the margin of his manuscript, 'A Latin text: with the dead in a dead language … The creative spirit of the departed Hartmann leads me towards the skulls and calls out them – the skulls silently begin to glow.' In one of the most touching moments of the work, Musorgsky himself is represented by the reappearance of the Promenade (oboes and cor anglais), now sadly in a minor key, accompanied by mysterious tremolo above. As if Musorgsky is consoled by his encounter with the ghostly Hartmann, the piece ends by dying away to a soft resolution.

'The Hut on Chicken's Legs (Baba-Yaga)'. The starting point for this movement was a clock made of bronze and enamel designed by Hartmann in the shape of Baba Yaga's hut on chicken's legs. This is an elaborate, architectural object, but Musorgsky's piece strongly suggests the grotesque witch herself, who rides through the air in a mortar in search of children to devour. Stasov recalled that he had once seen Hartmann at an artists' fancy-dress ball. All the other guests were dressed as familiar characters – queens, harlequins, and so on – but Hartmann was dressed as the witch, Baba-Yaga: 'A big, felt hat was pulled down over her eyes, her feet were wrapped in cloth, bony arms stuck out of the sleeves of her dress, a sparse beard sprouted from her chin, her horrible eyes gleamed maliciously on her painted face, tusks stuck out of her half-open mouth.' The shock of this music, coming after the stillness of the catacombs, is like the shock of 'Gnomus' after the opening Promenade. The alternation of abrupt phrases and silences links the two pieces musically, too. Once the witch's ride gets going, the shrieks in the high woodwind are like the chirrups of the chicks in their shells – perhaps Musorgsky imagined those children as Baba-Yaga's prey. These cries are followed by trumpet fanfares, like a triumphant cackling. Ravel, true to Musorgsky's directness of style, emphasizes all this with incisive percussion – drums, cymbals, and triangle. A middle section become eerily quiet, with rapid tremolo on flutes and clarinets, and a stealthy version of the opening phrases on bassoon and pizzicato basses below. Touches of xylophone add a skeletal effect. The witch's flight resumes at full speed. It reaches a new height of frenzy, at which it bursts straight into:

'The Bogatyrs' Gate (in the ancient capital of Kiev)', usually abbreviated to 'The Great Gate of Kiev'. Bogatyrs were mythical warrior-heroes of Slavic legend. In 1869 there was a competition to design a gateway to be erected in Kiev (the ancient capital of Rus), to commemorate the escape of Tsar Alexander II from an assassination attempt three years earlier. Hartmann considered his design his finest work, but the project was abandoned and the gate was never built. Hartmann's magnificent design was described by Stasov: 'Its style is that of the old, heroic Russia. Columns, which support the elegant arch crowned by a huge, carved headpiece, seem sunk into the earth as though weighted down by old age, and as though they had been built God knows how many centuries ago. Above, instead of a cupola, is a Slavic war helmet with pointed peak.' Three great bells hang in the tower, and through the gateway a horseman is urging on the three horses of a troika.

Musorgsky's piece is a great culmination to the series of pictures. It consists of a massive chorale, which alternates with a chant. The chorale is clearly related to the Promenade that began the work – you might say that it is a distillation of it. This gives a powerful sense of having come full circle. Between the three statements of the chorale there is a solemn orthodox chant, taken from the baptism service, 'You who are baptized in Christ'. It is as if Musorgsky has imagined a choir at the solemn dedication of the great gate. In Ravel's version, the chorale begins on full brass, later joined by woodwind and strings. Sombre clarinets and bassoons play the orthodox chant. Then the chorale moves to the bass, with running scales on strings and woodwind evoking the pealing of bells. Again, clarinets and bassoons take up the solemn chant. Now a real bell begins to toll, and the forces of the orchestra gradually assemble around it. Ravel builds this crescendo with immense skill, creating a sense of an enormous crowd gathering for the great ceremony (Ravel was a master of the orchestral crescendo, as in the great dawn in *Daphnis et Chloé*). The piece ends in a great blaze of full orchestra declaiming the chorale for the last time, the bell, reinforced by the crashes of a gong, resounding to the end.

CARL NIELSEN
(1865–1931)

Nielsen, the most famous Danish composer, was born the same year as the great Finn, Sibelius. His father was a farm labourer and house painter, an amateur musician who played violin and cornet at local festivities. His mother sang traditional songs 'as if she were longing for something far away beyond the farthest trees of the land', as Nielsen wrote in *My Childhood*.[1] One of twelve children, Nielsen was brought up at a time when Denmark was going through a period of resurgent national pride and determination following its defeat in war against Prussia in 1863–4. Nielsen benefited from the rising interest in national music, and the drive to foster native talent. The family was, like most rural families, poor, but Nielsen's musical talent won him a place at the Copenhagen Conservatoire of Music at age eighteen, supported by sponsors. The director was Niels Gade, a composer whose music had been admired by Schumann. This was exactly the sort of Germanic conservatism that Nielsen was to react against.

It was many years before Nielsen established a reputation as a composer. He played the violin in the Royal Theatre Orchestra in Copenhagen for sixteen years. He won a scholarship to travel to Germany, where he met Sibelius and the influential violinist–conductor Joseph Joachim. In Paris he met a Danish sculptor, Anne Marie Brodersen, and they were married in 1891. She was a determined and independent-minded artist and woman, and the troubles and crises in their relationship undoubtedly contributed to Nielsen's own musical outlook.

Nielsen's First Symphony of 1894 had some success both in Denmark and in Germany. From 1901, a small state pension enabled him to devote more time to composition, and one of the earliest results was his Second Symphony ('The Four Temperaments'). He also developed a career as a conductor, becoming second conductor of the Royal Theatre in 1906. Six years later, his Third Symphony finally established his name internationally. In 1914 the post of first conductor at the Royal Theatre fell vacant, but when Nielsen was not appointed, he resigned from the Theatre and embarked on a freelance career as a composer. This coincided with a crisis in his marriage. His wife's work as a sculptor had often taken her away from home for long periods, and Nielsen had had several extra-marital affairs, which had produced at least two children. After the latest affair, the couple lived apart. Links between life and music are not straightforward, but it seems clear that this domestic crisis helped to precipitate a crisis in Nielsen's music, from which he emerged with new force and character with Symphonies Nos 4 and 5.

Like Sibelius, Nielsen retained strong links to the music of the past but forged a highly personal way of composing that was not tied to any particular school or fashion. His refusal to conform did not always advance his cause. Interviewed about his Third Symphony, he admitted that he had been 'a bone of contention ... because I wanted to protest against the typical Danish smoothing over [exemplified by Gade]. I wanted stronger rhythms and more advanced harmonies.'[2] At the same time, he was not attracted to the sort of complex atonality developed by Schoenberg and his pupils: 'I am surprised by the technical skills of the Germans nowadays, and I cannot help thinking that all this delight in complication must exhaust itself. I foresee a completely new art of pure archaic virtue.'[3] His mature works are often described as 'neo-classical', but this is an inadequate label for a composer who carved out a very personal style. Like Sibelius, Nielsen drew on classical methods of construction, but bent them to his will. The sense of struggling against orthodoxy, and particularly against traditional notions of harmony and keys, often gives his music a truculent quality that anticipates Shostakovich (though Shostakovich, born forty-one years later than Nielsen, knew nothing about him).

After a run of six symphonies, Nielsen's last orchestral project was a series of concertos for each of the members of the Danish Wind Quintet, for whom he had composed his Wind Quintet in 1922. He died after completing only two of the series – typically quirky concertos for flute and for clarinet.

SYMPHONY NO. 3, OP. 27, 'SINFONIA ESPANSIVA'
Duration: approx. 35 minutes

Allegro espansivo
Andante pastorale
Allegretto un poco
Allegro

This is the work that established Nielsen's international reputation, and the composer himself conducted the successful premiere in Copenhagen in February 1912. Nielsen wrote a programme note for a performance in Stockholm in 1931: 'The symphony is a result of many kinds of forces. The first movement is intended to be a burst of energy and acceptance of life out into the wider world, which we humans not only want to know in its diverse activity, but also wish to conquer and appropriate.' The finale 'is a hymn to work and to the healthy unfolding of everyday life'.[4]

The symphony is launched by a series of assertive, Beethoven-like octaves reinforced by timpani, increasing in frequency and with determined cross-rhythms, like a javelin released by an athlete. The momentum passes to the woodwind and horns, and with increasing energy to the strings and the rest of the brass, until it coalesces in a rolling melody in G minor. This being Nielsen, it does not remain in G minor for long, but searches far and wide as it unfolds in a mighty paragraph, until it reaches a chord of E flat major and subsides. The second theme is in complete contrast: flute then cor anglais play a gentle melody that rises and drops, accompanied by bittersweet harmonies. As it continues, it characteristically acquires a little phrase with staccato repeated notes. The staccato element passes to the bass as the violins develop the melody. This culminates in quirky, flicking grace notes that will feature in the main theme of the finale. After a brief passage of counterpoint, the confident roll of the opening reasserts itself, to bring the first section of the movement to a clear and decisive C major, with a tamed version of the succession of assertive chords that opened the symphony.

Nielsen now develops his various ideas, beginning by alternating the flicking grace notes in flute and clarinet with the rolling first theme on the strings. In a passage of charming delicacy, the music acquires the character of a Viennese waltz, and then starts to build again. It bursts into a full reprise of the opening theme, with a splendid swagger combining the original energy with the new dance element. As often with Nielsen, this reprise is not in the original key (G minor), but in E flat minor. As before, the continuation of the theme reaches a sustained chord, this time C sharp minor, and subsides. There is a moment of uncertainty before the gentle second theme is reached, now on clarinet. From here the music proceeds as before, though with new touches along the way, until the final paragraph extends to bring the movement to a close on a blazing chord of A major (harmonically very remote from the starting point of G minor).

The slow movement opens with a long, winding melody on strings in octaves, over a drone bass in the horns. It is in C major with a flattened seventh, giving something of the feel of traditional 'folk' music – a vision of shepherd bagpipes on a grand scale. There is a sudden timpani stroke and roll, over which flute, oboe, clarinet, and bassoon unfold a rustic counterpoint. The strings interrupt with a solemn hymn, fortissimo. More woodwind counterpoint over a drum roll is again interrupted by strings, now *fff*, high and impassioned. The woodwind counterpoint is more troubled in its harmonies, and the drum roll more agitated. This time the strings, together with the horns, interrupt with a reminiscence of their opening melody, now in determined counterpoint. The woodwind take up the opening melody, while the violins play the woodwind's line as a counterpoint. This unfolds over a held, deep chord of E flat major in the brass, evoking memories of the Prelude to Wagner's *Das Rheingold*. Into this spacious landscape emerge a wordless baritone and soprano, 'far in the background', adding a tone of ecstasy to the scene. For a moment, a solemn brass chorale interrupts, before the chord of E flat and the singers resume. As the chord fades, low, sinuous flutes bring the movement to a close.

The third movement is by turns lyrical and heftily energetic: you might think of it as Nielsen's take on the ambiguously toned third movements that Brahms favoured. A solemn horn call ushers in a melancholy oboe melody over bassoons. Piccolo and clarinets lighten the mood with a playful idea made of staccato runs, trills, and repeated notes. This is taken up enthusiastically by the strings. The oboe resumes a version of its melody, now in a major key and more wistful than melancholy, and accompanied more pointedly by two more oboes. This too is taken up by the strings. It develops a more powerful rhythm, and then breaks into a renewal of the trilling and staccato idea that is worked up in counterpoint to a climax. A little later, flutes and bassoons propose an interplay of the repeated-note element. But it is swept away by a new assault on the trilling and staccato idea, in more urgent counterpoint. As this develops momentum, the wind combine it with the oboe's original melody. Gradually the music calms, and the oboe's melody reacquires its melancholy. The movement ends, like the second movement, with low flutes, giving a final bittersweet touch of major-to-minor.

The finale starts straight in with the grandest of melodies in D major, somewhere between Brahms's First Symphony and Elgar's *Pomp and Circumstance* March No. 1 – if it had been composed by Elgar, he might have marked it 'nobilmente'. Its insistent, flicking grace notes refer back to an element in the first movement. After the tune has wound round twice, it strides off into a passage of sturdy counterpoint. This is turn softens, giving way to a wistful little melody that recalls the tone of the third movement. At first it is on oboe, then with pointed continuation on piccolo. Both have clarinets and bassoon two octaves below, which gives a particularly rustic effect. The violins join the melody, and it is taken to a climax.

Then there is a relaxed and amiable discussion of a phrase from the first theme. This too builds, first to an almost-reprise of the theme in C minor, and then to a splendid arrival in E major, at which the brass play the theme at half tempo, while the violins whip it along with the flicking grace notes. This grand climax subsides, and a brief moment of counterpoint leads into a more meditative passage. Strings and horns create a murmuring texture from a long, held chord of B flat major, over which an oboe reconsiders its wistful melody and then the main theme. This musing recalls the pastoral ecstasy of the slow movement. The mood is broken by a reassertion of the sturdy counterpoint from early in the movement. It quickly builds, fades for a moment, and then launches a final assault on the grand main theme. A splendid climax brings the symphony to a conclusion, brimming with self-confidence.

SYMPHONY NO. 4, OP. 29, 'THE INEXTINGUISHABLE'
Duration: approx. 36 minutes

Allegro –
Poco allegretto –
Poco adagio quasi andante –
Allegro

In the summer of 1914, Nielsen resigned from his conducting post at the Royal Theatre, and had more time to compose. Already in May, he had told his wife of an idea for a symphony 'which has no programme, but which is to express what we understand by Life Urge or Life Expression'. He imagined the work 'in one great movement in one flow'.[5] By the outbreak of the First World War in July, he had begun work. Despite Nielsen's powerful sense of what he wanted to do, the writing of the symphony was not straightforward, and it took him until January 1916 to complete it – he was still making changes a few days before the first performance on 1 February. Nielsen himself conducted the premiere, and provided a note, which later appeared in abbreviated form in the published score, explaining the significance of the title, 'The Inextinguishable':

'The composer, in using the title *The Inextinguishable*, has attempted to suggest in a single word what only the music has the power to express fully: the elementary will to life ... music is life and, like it, inextinguishable.' And in a letter he wrote, 'in case all the world were to be devastated by fire, flood, volcanoes, etc., and all things were destroyed and dead, then nature would still begin to breed new life again, begin to push forward again with all the fine and strong forces inherent in matter. Soon the plants would begin to multiply, the breeding and screaming of birds would be seen and heard, the aspiration and yearning of human beings would be felt. These forces, which are "inextinguishable", are what I have tried to represent.'[6]

The symphony is scored for a mostly conventional large orchestra. Nielsen's only extravagance is dramatic: there are two timpanists, each with their own set of drums, who are to be placed on opposite sides of the platform nearest to the audience. The battle between the two timpanists forms the climax of the last movement. The four movements are played without a break.

The opening of the first movement is turbulently energetic, with agitated flurries of notes and emphatic gestures exchanged between woodwind and strings, and vigorous punctuation from the timpani. The key is uncertain: at first we seem to be in mid-ocean, then in C major, then perhaps D minor or, for a moment, E minor. What is certain is that there is a determined search on. Even when the music begins to calm, and there is a sustained E in the bass, Nielsen takes time to settle into a specific key. It is only when a pair of clarinets sing a duet that we are at last in A major for a new theme. From a demure opening, the duet rises passionately, joined by full woodwind, with the strings tugging at a grace note in the bass, like a rustic hurdy-gurdy. As the melody attempts to move on, it seems to get lost, in a manner characteristic of Nielsen. At first the strings build and fade to tentative rising scales, once more uncertain in key. The violas interrupt with *ff* repeated notes, and the clarinets mournfully attempt a phrase of their duet. This is swept aside as their phrase is transformed into a vigorous dance. After this has developed for a few bars, passing through various keys, the trombones enter with the original clarinet duet, which is now transformed into a grand brass chorale. The whole orchestra joins in, now back firmly in A major, and in this key the music expands and settles, until all that is left is a sustained string chord of A major, to mark an end to the first section of the movement.

As the chord is held, a flute and a low horn quietly introduce doubt, exchanging an abrupt gesture from the opening of the movement. In another of Nielsen's characteristic 'Where are we?' passages, he works away at the little phrase, first in flute then in strings, over an enigmatic timpani roll, interrupted by *ff* repeated notes in the violas. A phrase from the opening bars of the symphony creeps in below on cellos and double basses. Suddenly, the whole orchestra breaks in at a faster tempo. Amid a welter of sound, motifs from early in the movement are audible. In sudden gaps, the clarinet duet is heard trying to re-establish itself. Gradually, this has a calming effect, and the music slows to a new version of the clarinet duet on flutes. Once more the music settles, this time to a long held bass note of C. Over it, duets of flutes, bassoons, and clarinets combine in sonorous counterpoint. This builds to a climax, at which, with a change of gear, we are into the reprise of the opening.

This is more impatient than before, the gestures even more emphatic. Fragments of what was the clarinet duet now enter on four horns, without any slowing or diminution of energy, and soon build to crown the last climax of the movement. Like the ending of the first section of the movement, this settles over a sustained bass note, now E, and the movement comes to a calm conclusion firmly in E major.

A hesitant duet of violins and timpani links to the second movement. After the surging complexity of the first movement, this comes as a relief. Clarinets and bassoons, later joined by flutes and oboes, play in chorus a charming melody like a folk tune, with elegant grace notes that remind us of the clarinet duet from the first movement. But the naivety of the tune is subverted by characteristic quirky touches of harmony and surprising turns of melody. The sonorities and style look forward to Nielsen's Wind Quintet. The movement has a simple three-part structure. The middle section has tiptoeing pizzicato strings, with interventions from oboe and bassoon that seem to be searching for a melody. The sense of losing one's way culminates in a return to the woodwind folk tune, which peters out and runs straight into the slow movement.

The Poco adagio is the most intense movement of the symphony, its emotional core. After the final, drooping phrases of the preceding movement, all the violins bursts in with an impassioned melody, the most sustained in the entire symphony. From a high fortissimo start it falls to pianissimo, rises, and falls again, its freedom of phrasing giving it a feel of a recitative. The passion of the music is underlined by the timpani, which add force to each note of the bass line as it falls chromatically (Nielsen was one of the first composers to exploit the relatively new pedal timpani, which can be quickly retuned). At first the melody seems to be in B major, but the key constantly swerves unexpectedly, and once again there is a strong sense of searching. The cellos and violas take over the theme, with the violins in counterpoint. With a series of three-note falling phrases, the melody comes to rest for a moment in E major. A solo violin plays a consoling new theme, with flute, clarinet, and bassoon interjecting the three-note falling phrase as a wistful comment. The full strings quietly take it up. As it falters, oboes, clarinets, and bassoons in unison interrupt with agitated *ff* repeated notes, as the violas did in the first movement, but now using shapes from the first theme of the slow movement to extend them into a chant. Trombones try to reassert the consoling theme, and the woodwind chant again interrupts. In this battle of wills, the agitated chant prevails, and is worked by the strings into a stern passage of fugue.

Now a great battle develops, with the chant in the strings, the consoling second theme declaimed by horns and, a bar later and at half speed, by trombones, the three-note falling phrase in the woodwind taking on an urgent character. The chant and the falling phrase become gradually more insistent, building to a great climax, at which the music, which has been searching for a key, finally breaks for a glorious moment into E major and can relax. As it falls away, fragments of the consoling second theme, the falling phrase, and the violins' opening theme, are all recalled, now drained of their tension. An oboe plays the chant for the last time, as high violins trill. Suddenly, the violins break into rapid scales, pursued by the lower strings (this passage strongly recalls Beethoven's third *Leonore* Overture). We are propelled into the final Allegro.

The opening theme seems to be in a sturdy two-time at first, but soon opens out into a swinging three-time. The tune has a grand sweep and is in a bold A major, apart from an insistent flattened seventh at the top of the phrase, giving the effect of a 'blue' note (not that such a term would yet have reached Denmark in 1914). The theme breaks into more acerbic harmonies and combative rhythms. Then, with an extraordinary stroke of originality, the music becomes a real combat, between the two timpanists at either side of the stage. Taking the rhythmic confusion of the opening theme as their cue, they challenge each other for predominance, the second timpanist following behind the first. This has the effect of galvanizing the orchestra to even greater striving, until it reaches a splendid, sustained A major (marked 'glorioso'), from which it falls away to a moment of calm. An oboe plays gentle, staccato repeated notes that open into an oscillating melody – this is a tamed version of the *ff* viola interventions from the first movement and the chant that grew out of them in the slow movement. It passes quietly around the orchestra over a timpani roll, then leads on to a whispered version of the sweeping first theme of the movement, played in counterpoint between violins and lower strings. Over this, the woodwind begin to join in, and flutes and clarinets remember the duet second theme from the first movement.

The music reaches a quiet close. Suddenly, the tempo increases, and over tapping drums the first theme continues in counterpoint, only to be overridden by a renewal of the battle between the timpani. This time the orchestra is reduced to alarmed shrieks, and attempts to renew the duet theme. The timpani battle comes to an impressive end with a rolling upward glissando (the first use of this effect in a major work). Once more the orchestra is galvanized into greater energy. From the feverish activity emerges the duet theme, now *ff* on horns, trumpets, and trombones. The music turns a corner, and, in a broader three-time, the duet theme has become a brass chorale. For the last time, the music gathers strength, the chorale shines out in a splendid E major, with violin figurations adding brilliance, and the timpani finally co-ordinating to lend it weight. The triumph of this conclusion would be at home in a Sibelius symphony; but the struggle through which Nielsen has achieved it is entirely his own.

SYMPHONY NO. 5, OP. 50
Duration: 33–38 minutes

Tempo giusto – Adagio non troppo
Allegro – Presto – Andante un poco tranquillo – Allegro (tempo I)

Nielsen began work on his Fifth Symphony in the autumn of 1920. As with No. 4, he took a long time to complete it. Having finished the first movement by the following March, he was afflicted by a feeling that 'my old abilities are failing me', as he wrote to his wife.[7] It was not until September that he resumed work. Finally, he managed to complete it in January 1922. Nielsen himself conducted the premiere, on 24 January 1922. On the day of the concert an interview with the composer appeared in a Copenhagen newspaper in which he tried to explain his approach in the new symphony. His remarks are, as usual, both revealing and enigmatic. He states that all his symphonies basically express the same thing: 'the only thing that music can express when all is said and done: the resting powers as opposed to the active ones . . . how should I explain it? I roll a stone up a hill, use the energy I have in me to get the stone up to a high point. And there the stone lies still. The energy is tied up in it – until I give it a kick, and the same energy is released and the stone rolls down again.' He also explains why he opted to have only two movements in this symphony. He sees the traditional four-movement structure as inherently problematic: 'in the old symphonic form you usually said most of what you had on your mind in the first allegro'. And in the finale, 'the ideas have all too often run out'.[8] This is perceptive: there are few symphonies by any composer in which the finale is as compelling in musical argument as the first movement.

Nielsen's No. 5 is much the same length as No. 4, but divided into two roughly equal sections (nearly twenty minutes each). The main difference in instrumentation between this symphony and No. 4 is the greater range of percussion instruments. No. 4 featured two timpanists; No. 5 has one timpanist, but also cymbals, triangle, tambourine, side drum, and celesta. It is the side drum that takes a leading role, building on the effect of the timpani battle in the Fourth Symphony in an improvised attempt to provoke chaos. Indeed, the idea of an ongoing battle between order and chaos informs the whole symphony. But there were limits to the destructive forces that Nielsen was attempting to unleash. This is still a symphony, with many of the conventions stretching back over more than two centuries. As he said in that same interview, compared with his earlier symphonies, 'I do know that it isn't all that easy to grasp, not all that easy to play. We've had many rehearsals of it. Some people have even thought that now Arnold Schönberg can pack his bags and take a walk with his disharmonies. Mine were worse. I don't think so.'[9] (Schoenberg's atonal *Pierrot Lunaire* had recently been performed in Copenhagen.)

The opening section has an almost continuous murmur of oscillating notes that persist without change while varieties of clashing harmonies and keys move around them. It opens with the violas oscillating between C and A. Two bassoons sing a gentle duet that might be in A minor, but the key is immediately subverted by E flat (a 'blue' note, as in Symphony No. 4). As other wind instruments join in, a pastoral landscape opens out, but with layer of different keys, as if we are seeing several perspectives at once. Horns call in D major, flutes answer in C major, then they combine, with the C major acquiring a 'blue' B flat. It is this bluesy C major that the strings take up, extending the ideas into a flowing theme, while the oscillating murmur continues, and, at the bottom, the cellos tug in a completely different direction. Nervous staccato repeated notes appear, as if we are to move on. But this comes to nothing, and there is an unexpected intrusion: a side drum enters quietly with a military pattern, and a triangle, loud woodwind, and timpani join in over a marching bass, as if a village band has appeared. This precipitates a darkening of mood. The melody, though still derived from its pastoral opening, becomes more disturbed. A raucous clarinet makes it even more agitated and acerbic. A flute brings in the repeated-note element, which earlier went nowhere, and this is developed by the strings into a bold new melody. All the while the side-drum pattern and the marching bass persist, and it is as if all these different elements are fighting against it without any resolution. Eventually, the violin melody peters out, and the accompanying march fades away, leaving only rapid woodwind figuration behind.

As this continues, the cellos play a low C, and over it, horns and bassoons revisit their opening theme. It develops in new ways, with richer harmonies, until the side drum re-enters with its familiar pattern, and the violins take up once more their abandoned, bold melody. It rises and, once again, peters out. Oboe and raucous clarinet develop the melody in yet freer ways, and the music fragments. Over a quiet timpani roll, the different thematic elements gradually fade, until the only things left are the delicate repeated notes on violins, and a final touch of the side-drum pattern.

The tempo changes to Adagio, and the lower strings sing a broad chorale, with the harmonies enriched by horns and bassoons and the melody on violas. This is essentially a new theme in G major, over a sustained G in the bass. Soon the melody rises to a B flat, yet another 'blue' note, and the key drifts until settling back in G major. Now the violins enter, and the theme interweaves in counterpoint, rises nobly and falls back. As the melody begins again, a new disruptive element appears: flutes and clarinets interject a rapid flurry of notes, remembering a phrase played in the first half of the movement by the oboe. The chorale theme continues to develop and build in solemn counterpoint, moving through different keys, while the woodwind obsessively repeat their rapid flurry, always in the same key. The strings are infected with the flurry, leaving only the brass playing the chorale. As the music builds, it comes as no surprise to find the side drum entering with the familiar military pattern. But the drummer is instructed to play in an Allegro tempo unrelated to the Adagio of the rest of the orchestra, 'as though determined at all costs to disrupt the orchestra'. The chorale continues to build, and the side drummer is instructed to improvise 'with all possible fantasy'. The sense of conflicting forces is worthy of Charles Ives (a composer unknown to Nielsen). Eventually, with a tremendous struggle, the forces are pulled together for a grand peroration of the chorale, in a glorious G major. The music fades, and over a long, held chord of G major, the clarinet quietly meditates on the repeated woodwind flurry, slowed to an expressive recitative. Meanwhile, the side drum, now in the distance, starts to play its military pattern again, fading until it becomes inaudible.

In the first movement of the symphony, potentially stable elements faced disruption. The beginning of the second movement presents a new version of this conflict. The theme itself seems to be struggling for control. It is in a vigorous three-time, but with continual cross-rhythms and unpredictable leaps. It is tethered to the ground by a bass that alternates between B and F sharp, giving the impression of a sort of B major. Once again there are 'blue' elements, not only in the melody itself but in the insistent horns. After a few bars, a familiar disruptive element enters – hammered repeated notes. The theme eventually quietens, and an oboe leads into a new violin melody, similar in mood to the more pastoral elements of the first movement, from time to time in a warm A major, but with the usual harmonic darkenings. This builds, but is interrupted. Now (as in the first movement) the repeated notes are transformed into a bold new idea.

For a moment, forces seem completely under control – this could almost be Brahms. But snarling horns and trumpets show that this cannot last. The strings break into chattering staccato octaves that quieten to a muttering. Over these, the woodwind play a series of calls taken from the earlier oboe lead-in. These build, in volume and tension, until once again the orchestra is full of elements pulling in different directions. The strings' chattering breaks into fierce scrubbing, and a point of high tension is reached. Gradually it ebbs away, until we are left in a strange landscape of repeated notes, like the calls of birds, over a murmuring accompaniment. What kind of world are we about to enter? The tempo accelerates to Presto, and we find ourselves in the last thing we expected – a whispered, rapid fugue.

For a moment, everything is once again strangely under control, with the leaps and repeated notes formed into an orderly fugue subject. The fugue progresses delicately, until the timpani rudely interrupt, and squalling clarinets play a rapid, discordant flurry of scales. This precipitates a forceful renewal of the fugue, led by the horns, and a passage of tremendous momentum develops. The clarinets renew their squalling, and are rebuffed. Finally, the energy is spent, and over a long, held bass note, plaintive flutes wind down to a moment of quiet expectation.

The tempo slows to Andante, and muted strings calmly embark on another fugue, whose subject is the first theme of the opening Allegro, slowed down. The mood is serene, but with tugs on the harmony that give it an edge of melancholy. Gradually it builds. Three flutes gently meditate on the theme for a moment. Then the strings re-enter with force, taking the symphony, in a few brief bars, to its emotional climax (Nielsen is closest to Sibelius at such a moment). Suddenly, the music breaks back into the Allegro with which the movement began. In a terse restatement, Nielsen revisits each element of that section. This time, the chattering strings and the calls of the wind instead of fading build to a final climax, and a long-awaited resolution on a chord of E flat major.

SYMPHONY NO. 6 (NO OP. NUMBER), 'SINFONIA SEMPLICE'
Duration: approx. 34 minutes

Tempo giusto
Humoreske: Allegretto
Proposta seria: Adagio
Tema con variazioni: Allegro

Nielsen started composing his Sixth Symphony during the summer of 1924. In August he wrote to his daughter that his idea was to write something 'quite idyllic in character: that is, quite beyond all time-bound taste and fashion'. In October, when composition of the first movement was well under way, he wrote to a friend, 'As far as I can see it will in the main be of a different character from my others; more amiable, flowing or what should I say – yet it is not good to say, since I do not know what currents may arise during the voyage.'[10] As usual, he experienced periods of doubt about the new work, and it was not until December 1925 that he finished it. Nielsen conducted the premiere on 11 December.

He gave it the title 'Sinfonia Semplice', but the 'currents' that Nielsen ran into while he composed it are anything but simple. In 1922, after the completion of his Fifth Symphony, he had suffered a series of heart attacks, and it is difficult to avoid an impression that the resultant sense of insecurity and disillusion found its way into this music. The audience and critics at the first performance were more puzzled than enthusiastic. Sibelius heard Nielsen conduct its premiere, and admitted that he was 'a genuine artist'. He described the symphony as 'a good work. But, as I see it, without compelling thematic material.'[11] It does, however, contain music of striking beauty and power, particularly in the substantial first movement, which is by far the longest of the four.

A glockenspiel, like a little clock, strikes four, the violins lift us gently into G major, with a phrase that seems introductory but will prove to be an important theme. Clarinet and bassoon flavour it with those familiar 'blue', or 'folkish' Nielsen touches of harmony. The second theme that follows immediately has high repeated notes on the violins over a ticking figure on woodwind. The reference to Haydn's 'Clock' Symphony (No. 101) is surely deliberate: like Prokofiev in his 'Classical' Symphony (No. 1), Nielsen begins with an affectionate backward glance. This 'amiable' opening very soon runs into the 'currents' that Nielsen anticipated. The meandering is punctuated by abrupt, chromatic gestures. Suddenly, there is an alarming, dissonant chord on the woodwind, echoed by the strings. The 'clock' theme is renewed for a time, but fades sadly away. Violins introduce a third theme in E minor, with spritely dotted rhythms that unwind into triplets. This too has a 'classical' feel, and is treated as a fugue subject. After three string entries, the woodwind add a phrase from the earlier meandering. Sonorous wind and energetic strings proceed together. The mood turns darker and the harmonies more acerbic, and the music develops a powerful sense of conflict. The lyricism of the opening theme returns in a rich, chorale-like passage. The strings emerge, by now in the remote key of F sharp major. There is a gentle touch of the glockenspiel, this time like a cuckoo clock, and, in one of the most vivid passages in the symphony, the strings, *ppp*, reiterate a simple phrase of repeated notes, while a pianissimo piccolo plays dotted rhythms, the glockenspiel continues to call, and the triangle gently rolls. It is like some vision from childhood.

A flute steps out to begin the development, quietly renewing the fugue. Clarinet, oboe, and bassoon join in. Their relationship is typically quirky: the flute starts in A minor, the clarinet answers in G sharp minor, the oboe in B flat minor, and the bassoon in C sharp minor – four different, unrelated keys, but which quickly begin to coalesce into harmonies that shift uncertainly from one key to another. Just as the fugue is in danger of beginning to sound academic, the violas enter with the lyrical opening phrase of the symphony, and the violins join above with the Haydn-like first theme. The contrast between them creates intricate counterpoint. But then the rhythm of the 'Haydn' theme moves to the timpani and to the bass instruments, with aggressive flourishes and trills above. This unleashes furious energy that develops into a major crisis. Everything that at first seemed amiable and elegant is transformed into something threatening and destructive: over rushing strings, the Haydnesque second theme is hammered out, first on horns then, more deliberately, on fortissimo trumpets, trombones, and tuba, and the gentle first theme becomes tortured counterpoint in horns and woodwind.

The savage climax leaves behind the bleakest of dissonances wailing in the woodwind, while violas and cellos try to salvage the lyrical elements, and a clarinet mocks with whooping dotted rhythms. The music subsides in a spirit of desolation, and muted violins renew their quest for lyricism with a pianissimo return to the opening theme, now in fragile counterpoint. Touches of glockenspiel, which used to be so charming, provide no comfort now. Violas and cellos, in a four-part chorus, respond compassionately. Then the music builds once again, with renewed energy. An acceleration leads into a reprise of the fugal third theme. This too has turned aggressive, with clashing keys, violent punctuation from the timpani, and raucous swirls from the clarinets. Another crisis builds. But this time some semblance of calm is more quickly restored. For the last time, the violins play their gentle first theme, pianissimo, muted and unaccompanied, as if exhausted. The music settles, and finally manages to unwind onto a chord of A flat major. The delicate bells of the glockenspiel seem to suggest that we have achieved a moment of calm.

Writers have suggested that the struggles and crises of this movement might have some autobiographical element. Later in the symphony, there are passages that Nielsen himself admitted were inspired by the thoughts of death. But if any part of the symphony expresses naked mortal terror, it is this first movement, with its trajectory from the sweet and amiable to the terrifyingly bleak, and its attempt to trace its steps back to that lost serenity. 'Semplice' it is not.

After a substantial first movement, both of the middle movements are short. The second, 'Humoreske', is widely regarded as the most problematic movement in all of Nielsen's symphonies. At first hearing, it seems like nothing more than a heavy-handed joke. On more than one occasion, Nielsen explained the Humoreske by means of a story. One version goes as follows: 'It's a little night-time tale, told by purely musical means. The instruments lie sound asleep in their sweetest dreams – now and then making small nocturnal sounds. Then gradually they wake up to a terrible row. But they seem to fall calm again, then the clarinet, supported by the bassoon, goes to work on a happy little tune. But *that* is too much for the trombone: it breaks out in "a contemptuous yawn" [a note in a draft of the movement], a big *glissando* meant to say "Oh, give all that baby food a rest." They all get terribly excited. But sleepiness prevails all the same. And soon they are again sleeping peacefully side by side.'[12]

This is all very well, but a nursery story hardly explains why Nielsen would think it appropriate to include this strange, quirky movement within a serious symphonic work. Perhaps we get nearer to the reason in an interview that he gave at the time of the premiere: 'In my new symphony I have a piece for small percussion instruments – triangle, glockenspiel, and drum – in which everyone proceeds according to their own tastes. Times change. Where is new music leading us? What will be left behind? We don't know! You will find this in my little Humoreske . . .'[13] Putting the two descriptions together, one could describe the Humoreske as a musical fairy tale that functions as a metaphor for the conflicts of modern music.

It begins with triangle and side drum playing disconnected bursts of rhythm, with chirrups from piccolo and clarinet, nervous touches of glockenspiel, and harrumphs from bassoon, culminating in a wild, atonal leaping melody on clarinet. This seems like a grotesque nightmare of Schoenbergian atonality. The clarinet's melody is subjected to dissonant counterpoint, culminating in a mocking clarinet duet. Then triangle, side drum, and glockenspiel manage to establish a regular rhythm. The clarinet falls in with this idea, and plays a fair-ground tune accompanied by bassoons, evoking memories of Stravinsky's *Petrushka*. This provokes ridicule from the trombone, who responds with a mocking glissando (this is the 'contemptuous yawn'), egged on by the percussion. The clarinet acquires supporters in the charmingly naive tune, which provokes further yawns. Another outbreak of Schoenbergian dissonance, competing with fragments of the fairground tune, leads to a bad-tempered climax. The fairground tune tries to re-establish itself, but is overcome by further banter, including a renewal of the mocking clarinet duet and more yawning. From here the music gradually frag-ments, and fades into sleep, with nothing resolved.

'Proposta' is the Italian for 'proposal', but also an old term for the subject (theme) of a fugue or canon. 'Proposta seria' could therefore mean a serious fugue subject, or a serious proposal. Why Nielsen should have used this archaic term for his title is a mystery (perhaps he was poking fun at Schoenberg's pretentiousness in calling a movement of his Five Orchestral Pieces, 'Peripetie'). The Proposta seria does indeed begin as a slow fugue, but did Nielsen mean more than that? The heavily accented 'ya-da' rhythm sounds rather Hungarian, and out of context one might mistake the opening of the movement for Bartók. Nielsen had visited Hungary in 1920, where he met both Bartók and Kodály. But there is no reason to suppose that the Hungarian feel to this theme is intentional.

The three opening entries of the fugue subject are marked 'molto intensivo', and Nielsen ensures their intensity by the way he pitches the instruments: the cellos begin high, then the first violins enter below them, on the powerful G string, and finally the violas enter above both violins and cellos. The tone is lamenting, and when the second violins enter, it is not with the fugue subject, but with a sustained high note, *ff* but muted, which then breaks up into disconsolate meandering made of half-remembered fragments of the fugue subject. As the violins' meandering forms itself into an uneasy pattern, the opening of the fugue subject appears over it as a horn duet, interleaved with a bassoon duet. Violas and cellos join in, and the violins' line becomes an intense, rapid murmuring, rising to a climax that breaks off.

Flute, clarinet, and bassoon embark on another round of fugue entries, with a new subject that soon breaks into dotted rhythms that remind us of the first movement. The violins cut through this with a renewed attack on the first fugue subject, but it too breaks up into heavy dotted rhythms, and then into the meandering pattern as the lower strings enter. This fades, as the second fugue subject, like the first, becomes a gentle duet of flute and clarinet. From this point the movement drifts into an atmosphere of quiet mystery. The meandering pattern is on muted violins, the 'Hungarian' rhythm of the first fugue subject becomes a quietly insis-tent motif that builds into strangely peaceful chords. The movement ends with what seems like a calm resolution, until, right at the end, the bass quietly drops by a semitone, leaving the silence unresolved after all.

If the Humoreske is Nielsen's most problematic movement, the finale runs it a close second. Ending a symphony with a set of variations is highly unusual. The obvious precedents are the finale of Beethoven's 'Eroica' Symphony and the passacaglia of Brahms's Fourth Symphony. Beethoven's variations are predominantly playful, Brahms's are powerfully cumu-lative. Nielsen's movement is much closer to Beethoven than to Brahms, though even more volatile in mood and ultimately enigmatic. It resembles the variations that conclude his recent Wind Quintet, by turns serious and quirky, and with a strong element of parody that looks back to the Humoreske.

High woodwind open the movement with a rapid, clattering introductory few bars that unwind into something like the meandering of the preceding movement. It turns out that the opening shape of this clattering contains the seeds of the theme that follows. The theme itself is played by an unaccompanied bassoon. The first half has the formality of a folk tune in B flat major, but the second half characteristically loses itself in harmonic byways before finishing with a return to the opening phrase. Variation 1 is a wistful woodwind ensemble, beginning dissonantly in two keys at once, and ending with a surprise return to B flat major. Variation 2 is a mock-battle, alternating between horn duet and rude interruptions, and ending with hammered repeated notes from the horns. The violins take up the repeated notes in Variation 3. Muted first violins play a rapid, nervous pianissimo jig. The second violins repeat it a tone lower, while the first violins accompany in tentative, agitated accompaniment. It is like the beginning of a fugue. But, after slowing for a moment, it leads straight into Variation 4. The lower strings ferociously take up the jig fortissimo, while the violins cut across the rhythm with a new, firmer counterpoint. Raucous clarinets and blaring horns intervene, and the strings respond with agitation.

Before we know it, we are into Variation 5. The agitation of the strings becomes a rapid running pattern, while the theme struggles to take shape in the woodwind and horns. The rapid string pattern quietens, and comes to a halt. Variation 6 is an ironic waltz played by muted strings. But the harmonies get stuck, and in the second half the tune struggles to retain its innocence in the face of quirky interruptions. These reach a head as we move straight into Variation 7. Trombones and bass drum mock the tune in a disruptive counter-rhythm, as if a brass band has invaded the ballet stage. The tune fights back with increasing desperation. There is no winner in this contest. Instead, trombone chords fade, and, as if the stage has emptied and darkened, the Variation ends quietly and sombrely.

Variation 8 begins slowly and tragically, with the theme enmeshed in a dense web of coun-terpoint. As a muted trombone plays a plangent solo, it seems that the music might build to the emotional climax of the movement. But instead, woodwind and glockenspiel use the opening phrase of the theme to set up a clock-like rhythm (once again nodding back to the opening of the symphony and the Humoreske). For a moment, the strings try to return to the tragic mood of the opening. But the glockenspiel continues ticking, until the variation ends inconclusively. Variation 9 begins by returning to the mood of the Humoreske. Side drum and bass drum beat out the rhythm of the theme, a xylophone clatters, and the tuba comments with low phrases similar in effect to the 'yawns' of the trombone. To this dry joke the brass respond with a celebratory fanfare. Now the violins convert the theme into a gallop. The side drum plays disruptive rhythms, as if trying to stop them. Brass interventions sound as if they are trying to find their way back to the theme. The music builds to a tense climactic chord, which relaxes into a moment of jolly marching that quickly fades, leaving a bassoon playing the last phrase of the theme. The strings rouse themselves to a final burst of energy, the brass manage a cheerful chord of B flat, piccolo and clarinet squeal the opening phrase of the theme, and the bassoons are left holding a loud, low B flat.

According to a violinist who played in the premiere, Nielsen said that the passage for percussion and tuba that opens the final Variation represented death knocking on the door, and that the fanfare was intended as a gesture of defiance.[14] This suggests that autobiograph-ical theories about the symphony might have some foundation. But the inconclusive way that Nielsen finishes the symphony leaves us with a curiously bitter and unsatisfying taste in the mouth. The first movement had struggled through terrifying bleakness to a moment of serenity. Now, at the end of the whole work, that struggle seems to have dissipated into a feeling of bitter irony, as if life, or at least mortality, is no more than a cruel joke.

SERGEI PROKOFIEV
(1891–1953)

Prokofiev was born in Ukraine, studied at the St Petersburg Conservatoire, and first made his name as a composer–pianist. At the time of the Russian Revolution, he travelled abroad, first to the United States in 1918. Then, after successful visits to Paris, he settled there in 1923. But, unlike Rachmaninoff, he did not break his ties to Russia. He returned in 1927 for a triumphant tour, and then in 1934 decided to return to live there. Despite the difficulties faced by composers in the Soviet Union, Prokofiev was tempted by the promise of commissions, and an assurance that he would remain free to travel. He was also homesick, as he revealed in conversation with a French critic in 1933: 'The air of foreign lands does not inspire me, because I am a Russian, and there is nothing more harmful to a man than to live in exile, to be in a climate incompatible with his race. I must again immerse myself in the atmosphere of my homeland – I must once again see real winter and spring, I must hear Russian speech and talk with the people dear to me. This will give me what I lack here, for their songs are my songs. Here I'm restive. I'm afraid of falling into academism. Yes, my friend, I am going home.'[1]

Life did not turn out quite as he had been led to expect. There were major successes, including his greatest work, the ballet *Romeo and Juliet*, and his Fifth Symphony. But, like other Soviet composers, he was eventually ground down by the Soviet machine, subjected to official disapproval and censorship, and, together with Shostakovich, condemned in the infamous Zhdanov Decree of 1948 for his 'formalist perversions and anti-democratic tendencies alien to the Soviet people and to their aesthetic requirements'. His last tour of Europe and the United States was in 1938. By the time the Second World War was over, he had suffered a collapse brought on by high blood pressure, and he spent his remaining years dogged by ill health.

In his 1941 *Autobiography*, Prokofiev, with characteristic neatness, sums up 'the basic lines along which my work had developed' in his early works (up to the Second Piano Concerto), and this is helpful in thinking about his later development. He identifies four lines: the classical, traceable back to the Beethoven sonatas his mother used to play; the 'modern trend', particularly the search for 'my own harmonic language'; 'the toccata, or "motor" line', which was first inspired by Schumann's Toccata; and the lyrical line, about which Prokofiev writes, 'For a long time I was given no credit for any lyrical gift whatever, and for want of encouragement it developed slowly. But as time went on I gave more and more attention to this aspect of my work.' The 'grotesque' element in his music, 'which some wish to ascribe to me', he refuses to regard as a fundamental aspect of his style: 'I strenuously object to the very word "grotesque" which has become hackneyed to the point of nausea. As a matter of fact the use of the French word "grotesque" in this sense is a distortion of the meaning. I would prefer my music to be described as "scherzo-ish" in quality, or else by three words describing various degrees of the scherzo – whimsicality, laughter, mockery.'[2]

There is another important ingredient in Prokofiev's make-up, and that is his devotion to the precepts of Christian Science, to which he and his wife became attached in the mid–1920s. The relationship between his religious belief and his music are complex and not possible to pin down. But the growing lyricism and accessibility of his later music certainly owes some-thing to Christian Science's use of the metaphors of discord and harmony to represent the contrasts between the human and the divine. Prokofiev used his own metaphor to express the importance of music as a source of uplifting strength: 'The more the sea rages, the more precious a hard rock among the waves becomes.'[3] This concept of music, already developed before Prokofiev's return to Russia, has much in common with Soviet ideas of 'music for the people'. In 1934, before his return to Russia had become permanent, Prokofiev wrote an article that included some thoughts about the future of Soviet music, which he quoted in his 1941 *Autobiography*:

> What we need is great music, i.e. music that will be in keeping both in conception and technical execution with the grandeur of the epoch. Such music would be a stimulus to our own musical development; and abroad too it would reveal our true selves. The danger of becoming provincial is unfortunately a very real one for modern Soviet composers. It is not so easy to find the right idiom for this music. To begin with it must be melodious; moreover the melody must be simple and comprehensible without being repet-itive or trivial. Many composers have difficulty in composing any sort of melody; all the harder is it to compose a melody that has a definite function. The same applies to the tech-nique and the idiom: it must be clear and simple, but not banal. We must seek a new simplicity.[4]

The composer had clearly travelled a long way from the complex and dissonant bravura of his Second Piano Concerto. This spiritually driven search for simplicity and accessibility made it easier for Prokofiev than other modernist composers to adapt to the official Soviet policies, at least for a time. But even he was eventually to be crushed. He died the same day as Stalin, 5 March 1953.

Concertos

PIANO CONCERTO NO. 1 IN D FLAT MAJOR, OP. 10
Duration: approx. 15 minutes

Allegro brioso –
Andante assai –
Allegro scherzando

As a student at the St Petersburg Conservatoire, Prokofiev began work on his First Piano Concerto in the autumn of 1910, soon after the death of his father. The following June, he wrote in his diary that, as summer approached, he was planning 'the famous "big concerto" for piano, which I had already started, but which I could not get around to continuing'. Even before it was finished, Nikolai Myaskowsky (ten years older than Prokofiev and his closest friend at the Conservatoire) managed to secure the promise of a performance of the concerto in Moscow the following year. It was finished by early 1912, and Prokofiev himself played it with the conductor Konstantin Saradzhev on 25 July that year.

This was the first time Prokofiev had ever played in public with an orchestra. At twenty-one he was astonishingly confident, as his letters reveal: 'Saradzhev knew all the tempos perfectly.

The music was right in my fingers. The orchestra was faking it at times and was on a slightly lower level. I was told that the concerto sounds good from an instrumental point of view, and that the orchestra didn't once obscure the piano part. The audience responded with considerable enthusiasm ... I am satisfied. It was not difficult to play with an orchestra – it was even extremely pleasant.'⁵ Two years later, Prokofiev had the temerity to play this concerto at the Conservatoire in the final piano competition for the Anton Rubinstein prize, the only pianist in the history of the competition to play his own music. Even though he had wisely chosen to perform this concerto rather than the even more outrageous No. 2, he was aware of the risk he was taking: 'Will my Concerto be my salvation or my doom? Will the judges be repelled by its dissonant harmonies or will they, on the contrary, be stunned by its brilliance and ardour?' Much to the disgust of the conservative Alexander Glazunov, Prokofiev was voted the winner, and left the Conservatoire with exactly the aura of defiant brilliance that he had intended. Within a few years the concerto had established itself as one of his most popular works, though in later years it has come to be outshone by No. 3.

The concerto is played without a break and is constructed as a great arch. The first block of the arch is a massive introduction, which recurs at the very end. After the introduction comes the longest section (the second part of the Allegro brioso), in which Prokofiev presents three themes, rounding them off with a return to the introduction. These themes are later developed in the penultimate section of the work (the first part of the Allegro scherzando). And in the middle of the arch is a slow section, with a new theme, marked 'Andante assai'. As Prokofiev himself wrote in his diary of 1912, this scheme draws on the conventional form of a large symphonic movement, with its exposition of themes, development, and reprise, but departs from it. 'It is the threefold repetition – at the beginning, middle and end – of this powerful thematic material [i.e. the introduction] that assures the unity of the work.' He follows this assertion with a comment that reveals his extreme self-confidence at the age of twenty-one: 'Leonid Nikolayev [piano teacher and composer], however, says that the Concerto is not an integrated whole but a series of fragments that relate well to one another and have been skilfully stitched together. Oh, really?'⁶

With enormous panache, orchestra and piano together launch into a grand introduction in D flat major, which the orchestra alone then takes to a climax. This has something of the effect of the opening of Tchaikovsky's First Piano Concerto, and similarly teeters on the edge of banality. It is saved from it by the way in which Prokofiev spices the repetitive phrases with quirky twists of harmony (and it helps if pianist and conductor observe the 'brioso' and the fast metronome marking). The piano then bursts into a rapid toccata full of brilliant display. This eventually calms to a playful theme with tarantella-like rhythms (this began life as a piano piece Prokofiev wrote in 1907). Elements of this theme and of the toccata passage combine and build up to a climax and a halt. With a sudden change of mood, trombone chords announce a sombre second theme in E minor, like a slow march. The piano decorates this with gradually more elaborate figurations and glissandi, which eventually break into a moment of free cadenza. Out of this emerges a third theme with an almost jazzy character, at a slightly faster tempo. The piano's elaboration of this theme sounds rather like Rachmaninoff at his most playful. An acceleration leads to a fourth thematic element, with the piano playing rapid bursts of descending chromatic scales in octaves. This culminates in a return to D flat major and the music of the introduction, to round off this section of the concerto.

'Andante assai' ('very going') would mean faster than plain Andante to an Italian-speaker, but Prokofiev clearly meant it as a slow Andante. This is the lyrical heart of this otherwise hyper-energetic concerto, with a melody full of sighing downward phrases and poignant harmonies. The orchestra begins, taking us into a dreamy realm, a portent of the love music to come in the ballets. The piano takes up the theme with a dash of delicate fantasy that builds to a great outpouring before falling away. The ending is the most beautiful passage in the whole of the concerto, as the orchestra steps delicately from one enchanting chord to another, until the music is suspended on an agonizingly delicious discord.

The Allegro scherzando does indeed sound at first like a scherzo to the listener. But it is built from references back to the themes of the first Allegro, justifying Prokofiev's statement that this acts as the development section in his grand scheme. It begins with the piano playing the fourth of the themes, the rapid descending chromatic scales, now incorporating bits of the toccata that followed the introduction. Then trumpets and horns remember the tarantella-like theme. We expect the piano to take it up, but instead the orchestra comes to a portentous halt, and the piano launches into a cadenza. This begins delicately, but it soon explodes into a massive display. Trombones and tuba quietly enter with the sombre second theme, with a new counterpoint in the piano above it. As the piano's figurations become more complex, the jazzy third theme creeps in below. The pace gradually increases, the rapid descending chromatic scales, in orchestra and piano, build up. With double octaves thundering in the piano, the orchestra ushers in the grand theme in D flat from the introduction. This brings the concerto to a massively confident conclusion, and Prokovief's arch is complete.

Despite the extravagant writing of some of this concerto, there is a strong intellectual musical mind at work. While he was waiting for the opportunity to perform it, Prokofiev wrote in his diary (10 December 1912), 'Tcherepnin has formed the conclusion that my musical *Weltanschauung* [philosophy of life] is not decadent at all but classical: I am attracted by precision in thematic material, clarity of exposition and integration of form. This is true.'[7]

PIANO CONCERTO NO. 2 IN G MINOR, OP. 16
Duration: approx. 30 minutes

Andantino – Allegretto
Scherzo: Vivace
Intermezzo: Allegro moderato
Finale: Allegro tempestoso

Prokofiev played the premiere of the original version of this concerto in the summer season at Pavlovsk in August 1913, while still a student at the St Petersburg Conservatoire. In his diary he wrote, 'Following the violent concluding chords there was silence in the hall for a few moments. Then, boos and catcalls were answered with loud applause, thumping of sticks and calls for "encore" ... I was pleased that the Concerto provoked such strong feelings in the audience.'[8] His pleasure in having provoked such reactions stayed with him. In his brief *Autobiography* of 1941 he quotes at some length a description of the concert that appeared in the *Petersburg Gazette*:

On the platform appeared a youth looking like a Peterschule [high school] student. This was Sergey Prokofiev. He sat down at the piano and appeared to be either dusting the keyboard or tapping it at random with a sharp, dry touch. The public did not know what to make of it. Some indignant murmurs were heard. One couple got up and hurried for the exit: 'Such music can drive you mad!' The hall emptied. The young artist ended his concerto with a relentlessly dissonant combination of brass. The audience was scandalized. The majority hissed. With a mocking bow Prokofiev sat down again and played an encore. 'To hell with this futurist music!' people were heard to exclaim. 'We came here for pleasure. The cats on the roof make better music!' The modernist critics were in raptures. 'Brilliant!' they cried. 'What freshness!' 'What temperament and originality!' Even sympathetic critics found the concerto at times excessively harsh. But one predicted, 'Ten years from now the audience will atone for yesterday's hissing with unanimous applause for the now famous composer with a European reputation.[9]

The concerto we know today is not quite the one that Prokofiev played at Pavlovsk. He left the score in his apartment in Petrograd when he emigrated to the United States in 1918, and received a letter from his friend Boris Asafyev to say that, in the upheaval of the revolution, the score had been destroyed: the new occupants of the apartment had used it 'to cook an omelette'. Prokofiev wrote a new version of the concerto in 1923, which he claimed 'was so completely rewritten that it might almost be considered No. 4'.[10] This revised version was premiered in Paris by Prokofiev in 1924, with Koussevitzky conducting. We can never know how radically Prokofiev revised the concerto. He himself wrote that he had not introduced any new thematic material, but had improved the orchestration and the piano writing, and had made 'the form more graceful – less square'.[11] If the result is a more refined version of what the Russian audience heard in 1913, it is easy to understand why the first premiere provoked such a storm of contrasting reactions.

The opening Andantino is deceptively simple. Pizzicato strings and clarinets play a hesitant two bars of introduction. The piano plays a theme that seems both demure and strange. 'Narrante' is Prokofiev's instruction to the pianist, and it is as if he has deconstructed the opening of a Chopin Ballade. The sense of strangeness is heightened by wonderfully weird chords in the strings. A bolder melody rises from the middle of the piano. As it quietens, clarinet and flute delicately steer the piano back to the opening theme. The bold rising melody returns, with new flourishes and chords. As it fades, the weird chords in the orchestra drift upward in a dreamlike state, and lead into the Allegretto.

The orchestra sets up a relentless march rhythm, and the piano enters with a strutting, spiky theme. This is the sardonic, cheeky young Prokofiev. As it advances, the theme develops power, with bravura flourishes. Suddenly the tempo eases, and a moment of dreamy reflection leads in a return to the piano's opening Andantino theme. It seems that the movement is to be rounded off with a classical reprise. But Prokofiev has a surprise in store. This is just the beginning of a mighty cadenza lasting four minutes or more, seeming to improvise wildly on the main themes. It develops immense power, with huge chords, rapid arpeggios, and at its height the instruction, 'colossale'. It is what Liszt might have dreamed of if he had been transported to the early twentieth century. The full orchestra brings the cadenza to a grandiose conclusion. This orchestral passage is not just a rhetorical gesture: the portentous brass entry is a transformation of the hesitant opening bars of the concerto, bringing the movement full circle. Out of the orchestra's final crashing chord the piano emerges with the demure first theme, accompanied by the clarinets with their opening bars, now restored to their hesitant rhythm. And so this extravagant movement draws to a quiet close.

The scherzo in D minor is a brief and relentless perpetuum mobile, in which the two hands of the pianist play an unceasing torrent of semiquavers an octave apart. It is like the monstrous offspring of the 'Wild Asses' from Saint-Saëns's *Carnival of the Animals* (the pianist Sviatoslav Richter famously said that it evoked an image of a dragon devouring its young). Hidden inside this outpouring is the ghost of a conventional scherzo-trio-scherzo form. This is detectable in the recurrences of the figure that opens the scherzo, with its violent trilling in the piano and insistently repeated chords in the orchestra. It occurs three times in the opening part of the movement, first in D minor, then in C sharp minor, and the third time returning to D minor. The middle part of the movement moves into other keys, new shapes predominate in the piano (still in unceasing semiquavers), and the orchestra's repeated chords give way to disjointed fragments. The final section is marked by a return to the opening trilling figure with repeated chords accompanying.

Intermezzo might imply some relief after the first two movements, but this is no conventional intermezzo. It is a grotesque (despite Prokofiev's objection to this adjective), clumsy dance in G minor, as if the bear out of Stravinsky's *Petrushka* or the oxen from Musorgsky's *Pictures at an Exhibition* had broken loose. It is more than twice the length of the scherzo (about six minutes), but the characters of the two movements have much in common. The scherzo is a relentless chase, the intermezzo is a relentless trudge. In the opening two bars the bass instruments, including tuba, timpani, and bass drum, mark out a pattern of eight heavy beats. This sets the character, and the basic musical cell, for the whole movement. The first bar begins on G, the keynote of G minor, but the third beat is D flat, a note completely foreign to G minor. This gives a characteristic lurching effect, which colours the whole movement. The intermezzo has something of the character of a passacaglia: for much of the movement the bass repeats a version of the pattern set in the opening bars. Sometimes the two-bar pattern persists, sometimes it breaks into repetitions of a single bar. There are passages where the pattern breaks down entirely, and the return of the bass pattern has the effect of a reprise.

Over this trudging bass, Prokofiev produces an array of striking variations. He begins simply, with trombones and trumpets blaring a single note. Clarinets chatter in descending triplet scales. The piano enters with cascades of notes sweeping in opposite directions, and builds through assertive rhythms to massive chords. There is a moment of relief, as the piano plays solo and quietly. The trudging bass returns (now in B minor), quietly at first, with the clarinets' triplet scales above. The piano takes up the triplet pattern, and again proceeds through increasingly powerful rhythms to massive chords. A little later, there is a magical passage in which oboe and bassoon play a plangent melody, while the piano plays rapid pianissimo runs, like the delicate brush of a cymbal, and underneath the one-bar version of the bass repeats pizzicato (now in D minor). The piano emerges from the dream to resume chattering triplet patterns, at first solo then joined by the orchestra. Soon there is a return to the powerful rhythms from the early part of the movement, and these build to a climax of terrifying force, at which the original two-bar pattern returns in the bass (back in G minor), and the trombones and trumpets blare. This disperses into a chattering descent of triplets in the woodwind, and a last flourish from the piano. The cellos and basses play a reminder of the bass pattern, pizzicato and now cleansed of its strangeness, and the movement ends quietly and demurely.

As the finale opens in outright panic, listeners are entitled to ask, like their predecessors at the premiere, whether they have not been battered enough in the previous three movements. Wisely, Prokofiev does not sustain this level of hyperactivity through the movement, but restricts it to the beginning and end. The panic of the opening settles into a pattern of rapid octaves leaping in dissonant intervals from top to bottom of the keyboard. Powerful dotted-rhythm chords appear, as if borrowed from the preceding movement. Fearsome low tuba and trombone blare, like some primitive signal, and the panic begins to recede. The piano plays mysterious chords, and violas, clarinets, and bassoon enter with a gentle rocking figure, which the piano develops into a sombre melody and then elaborates together with the orchestra. Even the most perplexed members of the first Moscow audience might have recognized this as being a traditional treatment of a theme in Russian 'folk style', evoking memories stretching back through Tchaikovsky and Musorgsky to Glinka.

The pace increases, as if this is a faster variation on the theme. Fragments of the melody alternate with nervous chattering chords, which the piano dismembers as if remembering the leaping octaves from the beginning of the movement. A bassoon wistfully plays the theme but is brusquely swept aside by violent chords, and the piano embarks on a cadenza. It begins with a reminder of the mysterious chords that introduced the 'Russian' theme, and then builds up as if we are embarking on another mighty cadenza to match that in the first movement. But suddenly the torrent quietens, and the Russian theme reappears in the bassoons. The orchestra and piano proceed together with further elaboration of the theme, the piano writing becoming more and more flamboyant as the music builds to a great climax. It fades to a moment of calm. A clarinet quietly trills, the piano tries to remember the Russian theme, but can manage only a vague chant-like shape, which evaporates into repeated notes. Into this reverie burst chattering chords from the 'Russian' variations, and all at once we are back in the panic from the start of the movement. In a mood of reckless daredevilry, the concerto ends with a final crash.

PIANO CONCERTO NO. 3 IN C MAJOR, OP. 26
Duration: 25–30 minutes

Andante – Allegro
Tema con variazioni (Andantino)
Allegro ma non tanto

As early as 1913 (the year of the Second Piano Concerto), Prokofiev had written a theme for variations, but it was not until three years later that he returned to it, composing over 1916–17 two variations that were to be developed into the second movement of the Third Piano Concerto. He completed the work during the summer of 1921 in Brittany. While he was there, he struck up a friendship with another Russian emigré who was living nearby, the poet Konstantin Balmont. Prokofiev set some of Balmont's poems to music (Opus 36), and dedicated his new concerto to him. When Prokofiev played some of the concerto to Balmont, the poet wrote a sonnet that concludes with the line: 'And the invincible Scythian beats on the tambourine of the sun.'[12]

Prokofiev played the concerto in Chicago in December 1921, and New York the following January. His opera The Love of Three Oranges had recently been staged in both cities, and had been received warmly by audiences. But the New York press savaged it: 'It was as if a pack of dogs had been suddenly unleashed at me and were tearing my trousers to bits.' As for the concerto, Prokofiev writes in his *Autobiography*, 'In Chicago there was less understanding than support ("the composer whose opera we produced"); in New York there was neither understanding nor support. I had to face the truth: the American season, which had begun so promisingly, fizzled out completely for me ... I was left with a thousand dollars in my pocket and an aching head, to say nothing of a fervent desire to get away to some quiet place where I could work in peace.'[13]

Despite this unpromising start, the work later became his most frequently played concerto. Like Nos 1 and 2 it is technically very challenging, but compared with the earlier concertos, which are filled to excess with the swagger of the young virtuoso, No. 3 has a much better balance between piano and orchestra, and between power and lyricism. The piano and orchestra are frequently woven together in complex textures, like giant chamber music. Because of its challenges, it is a favourite choice for competition finalists. But this is generally a mistake. The subtleties of this concerto demand meticulous rehearsal and attention to detail if everything is to tell. This is the only one of his concertos that Prokofiev recorded himself, in 1932 with the London Symphony Orchestra conducted by Piero Coppola. His performance is full of dash, and unsentimental to the point of dryness.

The concerto opens with a haunting melody on clarinet. This is the descendant of all those 'Russian' themes that evoke folk music, with a modal scale that hovers between major and minor (Borodin's *On the Steppes of Central Asia* is an obvious antecedent). The opening phrase reaches up to A. When the violins take up the melody, they reach up to C, and the home key of the concerto is established. This gentle introduction is brief, but it contains seeds that recur throughout. With a bustle of anticipation, running scales rise up in the strings, and the piano enters with a breezy theme built from little fanfare-like phrases that derive from the shape of the opening clarinet melody. This being Prokofiev, it is not long before the music builds to big chords, at first rapid, and then massive. Out of these steps a cheeky, gavotte-like second theme in A minor on oboe and then clarinet, its cheekiness underlined by castanets (it too shares some of its shape with the opening idea). The piano decorates the theme with insouciant flourishes. There is an increase in tempo, the piano breaks into triplets (another of Prokofiev's favourite toccata-like patterns), which combine with nervous falling phrases to create a third theme. The energy increases, and there is a climax at which the music bursts into a glorious fortissimo reprise of the 'Russian' theme from the introduction. The piano takes up this theme for the first time and extends it, with bassoon and clarinet in counterpoint. This culminates in a moment of reverie, with the piano playing rippling pianissimo patterns, over a sustained B flat in the bass. As these subside, there is a quiet change of pace and key. Suddenly we are back at the running scales of the opening of the Allegro, introduced this time by the piano, and, with a longer build-up than before, they culminate in the piano's breezy first theme. The second and third themes are then reversed. The triplet patterns of the third theme come next, now high up in the piano with a piccolo, and sounding like the chattering of birds. This combines with fragments of the first theme, and new virtuoso elements increase the energy.

Suddenly there bursts onto the scene the cheeky, gavotte-like second theme, now transformed into a strutting march as if mocking all these virtuoso pretensions, with the strings tapping the rhythm with the wood of their bows. But the piano defuses the mockery with its witty commentary, and to the doleful sound of trombones the gavotte-march is bundled away (this passage has the vividness of a ballet score). The piano resumes the running scales of the first theme, and with a final dash the movement comes to a brilliant conclusion.

The balletic character that was hinted at in the first movement becomes overt in the second. This is a set of variations on a shy and delicate gavotte in E minor, given piquancy by Prokofiev's characteristic bittersweet harmonies. It could have stepped out of the ballet score that he was to write for *Romeo and Juliet* in 1935, but this is the theme that he composed as early as 1913. After the orchestra has played it, the piano enters for Variation 1 with a trill and a rushing upward scale, and brings expressive grandeur to the theme by expanding its harmonies and opening it out with bold arpeggios. Variation 2 is an urgent chase in two clashing keys, with the piano dashing around the keyboard while a trumpet plays the theme. It reaches a forceful climax, but, like the theme and Variation 1, ends on a demure chord of E minor. Variation 3 pits offbeat accents and dissonances in the piano against fragments of the theme in the woodwind. Variation 4 is a slow meditation on the theme, almost like a Chopin nocturne, but suffused with Prokofiev's dark and mysterious harmonies. The final variation abruptly breaks into this atmosphere, with an energy and repetitiveness that become absurdly insistent, before bursting into the wildest of arpeggios. But at their height, the woodwind enter demurely with their gavotte, as the piano continues chattering in a delicate pianissimo. The delicious sense of two worlds colliding persists to the end of the theme. It is rounded off three times, ending with the darkest of deep chords in the piano.

The finale opens on tiptoe, with bassoon and pizzicato strings in teasing cross-rhythms. Although this sounds like an entirely new theme, it derives its elements from the clarinet melody that began the concerto, with its modal hovering between A minor and C major, and its opening turn of phrase. The piano enters, filling out the theme with challenging rapid chords. A new idea, with assertive dotted rhythms and plunging scales, takes hold of both piano and orchestra and rises to a high pitch of energy. Suddenly the pace increases, and the piano returns to the original theme. Again this becomes more and more forceful until it too subsides. Oboe and clarinet enter with a quiet, lyrical theme. This too seems new, but it takes the opening theme of the movement and smooths it out into a series of rises and falls. The strings take the melody higher, relishing the poignant harmonies. At first, the piano seems unable to accept this change of mood, and responds with a quirky, anxious little tune over a drone bass – a quasi-ritualistic moment that could have come out of *The Rite of Spring*. But eventually the cellos re-enter with the lyrical theme, and the piano accompanies it to a climax of Rachmaninoff-like splendour. This fades to a sustained moment of hush, as the piano decorates the melody with the most delicate of arabesques. For a second time the melody rises to a great climax, and falls away. The bassoons and pizzicato strings return for the last time to the opening theme. At a faster tempo than before, this develops huge energy and power, testing the pianist's virtuoso technique to the limit, and with hammering rhythms the concerto comes to a brilliant finish.

VIOLIN CONCERTO NO. 1 IN D MAJOR, OP. 19
Duration: approx. 22 minutes

Andantino
Scherzo: Vivacissimo
Moderato – Allegro moderato

Prokofiev began composing a 'concertino' for violin and orchestra in 1915, but put it to one side while working on his opera, *The Gambler*. By 1917 the concertino had grown into a three-movement concerto. It should have been premiered in November 1917, but the revolution made it impossible, and it was first performed five years later in Paris, with Koussevitzky conducting, and Marcel Darrieux playing the solo violin. At the same concert Stravinsky conducted his new Octet for Wind Instruments. Compared with the fashionably spiky and spare Octet, Prokofiev's Violin Concerto seemed rather traditional – the composer Georges Auric went so far as to describe it as 'Mendelssohnian'. But the great violinist Joseph Szigeti, who was in the audience, was attracted by the concerto's 'mixture of fairy-tale naiveté and daring savagery', and took it into his repertoire.[14]

The relationship between violin and orchestra is not like that of a conventional modern concerto. As the violinist Israel Yampolsky put it, 'the solo violin is not set against the orchestra, but rises from within to dominate it. This is a unique modern treatment of the *violino princi-pale* role found in the pre-classical violin concerto'.[15] This must have been one of the features of the concerto that appealed to Szigeti, a great Bach-player, whose performances of the unaccompanied sonatas were particularly admired.

The concerto reverses the usual fast-slow-fast pattern of movements, with a central scherzo surrounded by two lyrical movements.

The delicate interaction between violin and orchestra begins straight away. Over tremolando violas the violin sings the lyrical opening theme, marked 'sognando' (dreaming). As the melody unfurls, the violin is joined in turn by clarinet, flute, and oboe in counterpoint. Then the theme itself passes to violas and oboe, as the solo violin line begins to open out, becoming increasingly elaborate until it is festooned with energetic trills. There is a moment of calm, and the cellos take up a pointed little phrase, which they play repeatedly as the solo violin embarks on the second theme. This is a bold melody that is ornamented with grace notes, somewhat in the manner of a rural bagpiper – it could well have come from one of the folk-inspired works of Bartók (another feature that must have attracted Szigeti, who was closely associated with Bartók). The melody, too, develops energy until it breaks into brilliant running patterns, which the cellos and basses anchor with elements of the second theme (without its ornaments).

There is a sudden fade, and a pause. Flute and clarinet quietly meditate on the opening interval of the first theme. This proves to be the motif that will energize the centre of the movement. The soloist enters, and develops an unstoppable virtuoso momentum, underpinned by dogged rhythms in the bass. Eventually, this fades away, and there is a moment of peaceful unaccompanied violin, playing in two-part counterpoint (a skill in which Szigeti, the Bach-player, excelled). The opening tremolando violas return. The tempo slows, and the first theme appears, not in the solo violin, but on flute, and later piccolo. The soloist, now muted, accompanies it with soft, rapid, high, intricate patterns, together with harp. Again, this is reminiscent of Bartók in his 'night music', evoking darkness and the sound of nocturnal insects. In this shimmering, dream-like state the movement ends.

The central movement is a brief, rapid scherzo, in which the element of savagery is at its most relentless. The soloist's opening theme is constructed of fragments of rising chromatic scales, descending runs, quick alternations of bowed and plucked notes, giving a frantic impression as if pursued by Prokofiev's favourite 'motoric' rhythms in the orchestra. This gives way to the first of two episodes, in which the soloist plays fierce octaves, alternating two pitches. This simple idea is elaborated, as if the soloist is haunted by it and unable to escape. Now it is side drum, tambourine, and timpani that suggest pursuit. Eventually the violin breaks back into the opening theme. Abrupt, dissonant chords announce the second episode.

Again, the violin seems trapped. It works away at a repeating pattern 'sul ponticello' (bowing right next to the bridge, producing a scratchy sound), which alternates with swirling shapes (reminiscent of Rimsky-Korsakov's 'Flight of the Bumblebee'). At first these are fortissimo, but then eerily muted. It is the flute that rescues the violin from this nightmare, with a return to the opening theme, and the movement is suddenly over.

The finale opens with another of Prokofiev's persistent rhythms, this time more clock-like than motoric. Bassoons put forward an ironic suggestion, and at first the soloist's entry seems to echo this mood. But within a few bars the violin is singing lyrically. Then it is the soloist who takes over a persistent pattern, while fragments of melody continue in the orchestra, building twice to a climax. Now the violin becomes yet more lyrical, with passionate two-note chords rising to a greater climax (all of this seems to develop organically, rather than constituting a distinct second theme). The music gently descends to a moment of calm.

A tuba, a little pompously, proposes an attempt at an upside-down version of the concerto's opening theme, which the violin decorates with delicate runs. This becomes more and more brilliant, and the music builds to a virtuoso climax. As it fades away, Prokofiev brings together the opening theme of the finale, in flute and clarinet, and the lyrical first theme from the first movement, in the first violins, decorated with trills by the soloist. This clever combination is achieved with delicate and sensitive orchestration, producing an ecstatic sense of the music rising into the air as the concerto comes to a close.

VIOLIN CONCERTO NO. 2 IN G MINOR, OP. 63
Duration: approx. 26 minutes

Allegro moderato
Andante assai
Allegro, ben marcato

Early in 1935, Prokofiev was commissioned to write a violin concerto for the French violinist Robert Soëtens, who had played the Paris premiere of Prokofiev's Sonata for Two Violins with Samuel Dushkin in 1932. This turned out to be the last of Prokofiev's works to be commissioned in Western Europe before his return to Russia in 1936. He began it in Paris early in 1935, and completed it in Baku in August. Its composition overlapped with work on *Romeo and Juliet*, and the two scores share qualities of directness and (compared with Prokofiev's earlier works) simplicity – qualities that were to stand him in good stead in the Soviet Union, at least for a time.

In November and December 1935, Prokofiev toured Spain, Portugal, and North Africa playing solo piano recitals and duo concerts with Soëtens, and it was during the tour that the concerto was premiered in Madrid. The Spanish Republic was in a state of political turmoil, which was to explode into the violence of the Civil War in the summer of 1936. Prokofiev, seen as a prominent representative of the Soviet Union (though not yet permanently resident there), was greeted as a hero by the Republicans in Spain, and the premiere of the concerto in Madrid was a triumph.

Beginning on the lowest note of the violin (G), the soloist, unaccompanied, plays a plaintive melody. It has something of the character of a Russian folk song, with its repetition of phrases that are irregular in length – five beats at first, and then four. With an evocative shift to B minor, the muted basses and violas quietly take up the melody. Very soon this breaks into chattering figuration in the strings, with bold octaves in the solo violin, and then calms again.

But all the time the key is shifting uneasily between unrelated keys – back to G minor, C sharp minor, F major. The pace increases, and the soloist breaks into energetic running staccato. With another unexpected change of key the music eases into B flat major, and the soloist plays the lyrical second theme. With its long line and tender shifts of harmony, it could have come out of the love music in *Romeo and Juliet*. The pace increases, there is a climax, another moment of calm, and a pause, marking the end of the first section of the movement.

The development begins, not with one of the main themes, but by picking up a phrase with which the violinist had just finished (something that Mozart often does). The soloist once more breaks into running semiquavers, and the opening theme appears below, on pizzicato cello and bass with bassoons. Virtuoso elaboration develops over the theme in the bass, almost like an informal set of variations. At a climax, the falling line of the second theme appears in horns and woodwind. It quietly moves to the upper strings, and the soloist gently elaborates above it, as if starting another set of variations. After this gentle interlude, the first theme returns in pizzicato bass and bassoons, with the soloist elaborating above, but now delicately and playfully, with solo and orchestral violins muted.

The music builds to a climax, quickly fades, and we are back in G minor, at the opening tempo, for the reprise of the opening theme, first on cellos and basses, with the solo violin joining in tentatively at first. More quickly than before, the lyrical second theme arrives (now in G major). This time the melody is even more tender than before, singing high on the solo violin, and with warm two-part writing. There is a brief burst of energy, after which the opening theme returns for the last time on the solo violin. It builds rather menacingly, and then, with sudden hesitations, comes to an end with a final cadence of pizzicato chords.

The slow movement opens with a tiptoeing background of pizzicato strings and clarinets, over which the soloist sings an unfolding melody of classical simplicity. The way its 'straight' pairs of notes cut across the 'swung' triplets of the accompaniment evokes the slow movements of Mozart's Piano Concerto in C major, K. 467, and Rachmaninoff's second Piano Concerto, with a nod to the 'Prize Song' from Wagner's *Die Meistersinger* along the way. After all the acerbic and unsettled music that Prokofiev had written over his career, it comes as a deliberate harking back to unthreatening times – an effect that Shostakovich was to emulate in his Second Piano Concerto twenty years later. With a melting change of key (from E flat to B major, one of Schubert's favourite shifts), the theme moves to the muted violins of the orchestra, with the soloist rising in an impassioned descant. Now the soloist takes over the triplet rhythm of the accompaniment, in exploratory phrases that contain a memory of the first movement's opening theme. Breaking into smaller notes, it passes airily to the flute (another *Romeo and Juliet* moment). Just as this new idea is developing, it vanishes, and the violinist suddenly remembers the opening theme, with more passion than before.

There is yet another change of key, back to B major. Horns and muted trumpet intone a chant that circles round a small interval, while the violin decorates it with rapid pianissimo figures. This passes on to a new, flowing melody on clarinet, over running violas, which the violin embraces lyrically. Then there is a surprising moment, as the brass introduces a chunky little phrase, as if we have entered the world of Stravinsky's *Pulcinella*. A moment later, this recurs, and the music hesitates in a moment of strange irony. It finds its way back to the original tempo, and the pizzicato and clarinet accompaniment resumes.

The soloist plays a new idea, and it is only as the orchestral violins enter with the opening theme that we realize that the soloist is playing a descant – a beautiful moment of revelation.

The muted trumpet and horn chant reappears. The violin rises to a forceful climax, which resolves on a chord of E flat major. The final bars are not quite what one might expect. Slowly, cellos, horns, and low clarinets in unison (a rather Elgarian combination) play the opening phrase of the first theme, while the soloist plays the accompanying pizzicato. The last bar is a counterpoint of low clarinet and solo double bass, resolving the final chord to curiously ironic effect. It is as if, at the end of a movement full of unashamed sentiment, Prokofiev is anxious not to tip over into sentimentality.

The third movement is in the tradition of the rugged finale familiar from the violin concertos of Brahms and Bruch, with much virtuoso display of chords and octaves. And, like those movements (and the Beethoven finale before them), it is a rondo, in which the opening theme recurs with contrasted episodes between. As you would expect, Prokofiev puts his own quirky slant on the genre, with distinct hints of Saint-Saëns's *Danse macabre*. The soloist begins with a bold theme in a big, swinging three-time. At first this is in massive three- and four-part chords, then in octaves. A broader melody is played on the lowest (G) string of the violin. All of this has echoes of earlier violin concertos, but with a characteristically bitter-sweet, ironic twist.

The first episode becomes more complex, with leaping arpeggio patterns. This too is a traditional development, but again Prokofiev introduces new spice, by putting the patterns in seven-time. The rondo theme returns, and is elaborated. A second episode introduces a plaintive, chant-like theme, whose intervals and insistent repetitions evoke memories of the theme that opened the concerto. The violin plays this high on the G string, giving a strained, plangent effect. The next return of the rondo theme is enlivened by castanets. Perhaps Prokofiev thought of introducing them because the concerto was to be premiered in Madrid, but they too sound ironic, as if a flamenco dancer has joined the *Danse macabre*. It soon breaks off into the next episode.

This begins with ghostly, muted running passages, and continues with another plaintive, repetitive melody, in which the solo violin is accompanied first by double basses an octave below, a strangely mournful effect, and then by a running flute. A leaping passage from the previous episode leads in the final appearance of the rondo theme, again with castanets. The leaping passage keeps reappearing, and eventually becomes a continuous pattern in five-time, accompanied only by pizzicato double basses and bass drum. This cumulative passage has an effect between a cadenza and a jazz riff. It acquires unstoppable momentum, and hurtles to a conclusion.

ROMEO AND JULIET, OP. 64

It was in November 1934 that the idea of a ballet based on Shakespeare's *Romeo and Juliet* first arose. Prokofiev was in Leningrad to discuss current and future productions at the State Academic Theatre (soon to be renamed the Kirov, after the chairman of the Leningrad Communist Party who was assassinated in December that year). Various possibilities were raised, but at the mention of *Romeo and Juliet*, Prokofiev recalled, 'I blurted out, a better [subject] cannot be found.' A scenario was then developed, with several people throwing in suggestions and revisions, principally the theatre director Sergei Radlov. Then the State Academic Theatre cancelled the agreement to stage it, after Radlov's resignation from the theatre, and, the following year, the Bolshoi Theatre in Moscow agreed to take it on.

It was at this point, in the summer of 1935, that Prokofiev wrote the score while staying in a cottage on the banks of a river, part of an estate in the country reserved for staff of the Bolshoi Theatre: 'It's a marvellous little spot, a bit noisy when ¾ of the Bolshoi Theater troupe comes here on vacation, but it's actually fun, especially since I have a separate little cottage with a Blüthner [piano] and a terrace overlooking the Oka river, where it is very quiet and conducive to good work.'[16] He systematically worked his way through the fifty-eight numbers of the ballet scenario, finishing the piano score in September and the orchestral score a month later. The production was scheduled for the following season. But it was first delayed for a year, and then suspended indefinitely, following political upheavals at the theatre and the arrest and execution of the theatre director. The ballet was first staged in 1938 in Brno, and it was not until 1940 that the Russian premiere took place – at the Kirov, which had originally commissioned it six years before.

By this time, the scenario had undergone a fundamental change. The original version of the score, which Prokofiev completed in October 1935 for the Bolshoi, culminated in a rewriting of Shakespeare's ending. In the original, Romeo arrives at the tomb and finding Juliet (as he thinks) dead, takes poison. When Juliet awakes, she stabs herself with Romeo's dagger. But in the revision for the ballet, Friar Laurence struggles with Romeo to stop him killing himself, Juliet begins breathing again, and the couple are reunited for a happy ending. Different justifications for this rewriting were given by the various participants, some (including Prokofiev) arguing that it made the ending more suitable for choreography, others supporting it because it was more in line with the need for 'uplifting' drama in the Soviet Union.

By 1938, however, the decision had been made to revert to Shakespeare's narrative, and Prokofiev rewrote the ending in time for the Brno premiere. At the rehearsals for the first Russian production in 1940, the choreographer, Leonid Lavrovsky, insisted on further detailed changes to the score. The dancers found the music very difficult to dance to, partly because of its rhythmical complexity, partly because Prokofiev's delicate scoring was sometimes inaudible to them onstage. The ballet was also deemed lacking in the display 'variations' to which the company was accustomed. These changes were made in the teeth of Prokofiev's opposition, sometimes without even consulting him, though he was obliged to go along with them in order to get the production on the stage. The tension between cast, choreographer, and composer threatened the whole enterprise. But eventually the conflict reached an uneasy truce, and the successful premiere took place on 11 January 1940.

The original 1935 score was reconstructed in 2008 by Simon Morrison for a production choreographed by Mark Morris (complete with the happy ending). The version otherwise known today is the 1940 revision. Prokofiev extracted two orchestral suites from the score in 1936 (Opus 64bis and 64ter), and these were performed several years before the premieres of the ballet. He selected a third suite, Opus 101, in 1946, the year in which Lavrovsky revived the ballet in Moscow.

The following is a list of the movements of the three suites in the order in which they appear in the full ballet (totalling about half of the music of the ballet):

Romeo at the fountain (Suite No. III, 1) = opening of No. 1, and No. 2
The street awakens (Suite No. I, 2) = No. 3
Morning Dance (Suite No. III, 2) = No. 4

Juliet as a young girl (Suite No. II, 2) = No. 10
Minuet: the arrival of the guests (Suite No. I, 4) = No. 11
Masks (Suite No. I, 5) = No. 12
Montagues and Capulets (Suite No. II, 1) = No. 7 and No. 13
Juliet (Suite No. III, 3) = No. 14
Madrigal (Suite No. I, 3) = No. 16
Romeo and Juliet: Balcony Scene (Suite No. III, 6) = No. 19
Folk Dance (Suite No. I, 1) = No. 22
Dance (Suite No. II, 4) = No. 24
Friar Laurence (Suite No. II, 3) = No. 28
The Death of Tybalt (Suite No. I, 7) = No. 35
Dawn: Romeo and Juliet part (Suite No. II, 5) = No. 39
The Nurse (Suite No. III, 4) = No. 40
Aubade (Suite No. III, 5) = No. 48
Dance of the Girls with Lilies (Suite No. II, 6) = No. 49
Romeo at Juliet's Tomb (Suite No. II, 7) = No. 52 part 1
The Death of Juliet (Suite No. III, 6) = No. 52 part 2

The notes describe the revised ballet. The quotations under each number are from the original handwritten scenario from which Prokofiev worked in 1935, together with later revisions.[17]

Act I
Scene 1: The Street

1. Introduction (Opening bars introduce Suite No. III, 1)
This brief introduction presents three elements. The first is a sweeping string chorus tinged
with poignant harmonies, in anticipation of the tragedy to come. The second is an elegant,
innocent-sounding violin line, associated with Juliet. A brief reminder of the string chorus
brings in a livelier, delicate rhythm, over which a clarinet plays a sustained line that will be an
important element in 'Juliet's Variation' and the 'Love Dance' with which the act concludes.

2. Romeo (Suite No. III, 1)
'Early morning. Romeo passes by, very pensive. Perhaps some female passers-by seek to halt
him, but he pays no attention.'
     The opening – pizzicato strings and harp, with a staccato bassoon line – sounds carefree.
A clarinet plays a lyrical melody, which becomes impassioned as it passes to high violins, and
the number ends with a final cadence of dreamy chords. Within a minute and a half Prokofiev
has suggested the main elements of the young Romeo's character (the subject of his dreams is
not Juliet, whom he has not yet met, but Rosaline).

3. The Street Awakens (Suite No. I, 2)
'Entrances, meetings, disputes. The stragglers return home. The mood is inoffensive.' A
bassoon plays a droll little tune, with a comic twist. As this passes to solo violin, all the first
violins, and on, we sense the daily good humour of people going about their business.

4. Morning Dance (Suite No. III, 2)

Suddenly, the pace increases, and an energetic dance ensues. Under the insistent rhythm, the bassoon's tune from the preceding number has been transformed into something more urgent. In the middle of the dance there is a more lyrical melody, with violins quietly iterating a troubled little motif, as if anticipating the fight ahead.

5. The Quarrel

'Servants and citizens quarrel.' The quarrel is between the Montagues (Romeo's family) and the Capulets (Juliet's family), bitter rivals for generations. Aggressive rhythms culminate in tense high and low chords, and a quiet moment suggesting an attempt at dialogue. Renewed aggression leads to a resumption of the Morning Dance, but with a harder edge.

6. The Fight

'Knights with weapons, general mayhem'. In Shakespeare's play, even the heads of the families, old Capulet and old Montague, confront each other. Frantic running strings alternate with defiant horns. The middle section becomes more violent. At the end, a bell sounds: 'the Prince of Verona enters on a horse, and the brawl ceases'.

7. The Prince's Command (Suite No. II, 1, first part)

'The Prince's edict ... in response, the weapons are dropped'. The Prince declares that any further fighting between the families will be punishable by death. The anger and authority of the Prince are represented by two crescendos to terrifyingly dissonant chords, out of which a stunned pianissimo emerges. Leads straight into:

8. Interlude

'The Prince departs. Interlude between the scenes, expressing the Prince's power.'
The Interlude culminates in a blaze of brass. This leads straight into:

Scene 2: House of the Capulets

9. At the Capulets' (Preparation for the Ball)

Russian title in the score: Preparations for the ball (Juliet and the Nurse)
There is a mood of quiet anticipation, in which the bassoon tune from 'The Street Awakens' reappears, joined by sweet woodwind above (as Juliet and the Nurse appear) and pompous brass below.

10. The Young Juliet (Suite No. II, 2)

This is a portrait of Juliet: 'Just fourteen years old, she girlishly jokes and pranks, unwilling to dress for the ball. The nurse nevertheless gets her into a gown. Juliet stands before a mirror and sees a young woman. She briefly muses, and then dashes out.' Skittering violin scales and pizzicato chords spiced with woodwind and unexpected harmonies suggest the vivacious side of her character, and a clarinet melody (which we met in the Introduction) conveys beauty and elegance. There is a meditative middle section, with pairs of flutes and clarinets, and a cello solo, after which the clarinet melody returns (now on flute), followed by the skittering strings. The ending melts into another brief moment of meditation.

11. Arrival of the Guests (Suite No. I, 4)

The guests arrive to a stately minuet. Prokofiev characteristically subverts the straightforward three-time of the dance with irregular metre and phrase lengths, together with quirky harmonies. The main theme is interspersed with two episodes ('trios', if this were a conventional minuet). The first is a sentimental cornet solo that is handed to cellos and clarinet. The second is jauntier, with glockenspiel and piccolo at the top, and contrabassoon at the bottom. This second episode returns, to bring the minuet to a quiet close.

12. Masks (Suite No. I, 5)

The young Montagues, Romeo and Benvolio, with their friend Mercutio, enter wearing masks. The dance is 'a march', though with the poise of a gavotte, whose melody begins with a baroque flourish. Percussion quietly set the rhythm – triangle, tambourine, side drum, and cymbals, later enriched by harp and piano. The middle section of the dance has quirkier phrases ('Mercutio and Benvolio joke'), and then the baroque melody returns. At the end, 'Romeo is pensive': the dance recedes, giving way to Romeo's yearning theme (from No. 2), and its dreamy final cadence.

13. Dance of the Knights (Suite No. II, 1, second part)

'In the interior, a portière is opened. A ponderous dance for the knights, perhaps in armour.' This is the most famous number in the whole score. Underpinned by a march rhythm with bass trombone, tuba, contrabassoon, bass clarinet, and bass drum, the bold theme leaps up in the violins. It combines stateliness with menace, and the horns emphasize the menace by bringing in their defiant melody from The Fight (No. 6). This dance is interspersed with two gentler episodes in three-time. The first (marked in the score as 'Ladies' dance') has a smooth melody introduced by cornet. The second begins as a fragile three-time flute solo, as Juliet dances with Paris 'formally and indifferently'. The oboe enters, playing Juliet's theme. The march rhythm returns, at first on saxophone, and the dance builds up again to an aggressive final cadence.

14. Juliet's Variation (Suite No. III, 3)

This begins with a reprise of Juliet's dance with Paris, out of which emerges Juliet's theme, followed by a sweeping waltz. At first this seems like a new theme, but as it broadens into four-time over a gently agitated accompaniment, it is revealed as the haunting clarinet melody with which the Introduction concluded, now high on violins. A coy reference back to the dance with Paris brings the Variation to a close.

15. Mercutio

The music of this dance is full of energy and dashing leaps. The original scenario suggests the dance is 'somewhat buffoonish. He enlivens the gathering.' It is written in three-time, but that is only audible from time to time because of the cross-rhythms of the phrases. The dance slows briefly for a slower middle section.

16. Madrigal (Suite No. I, 3)

Romeo has spotted Juliet, and dances with her. 'Romeo dances amorously, and Juliet playfully. Romeo dances more ardently than before, Juliet remains playful. They dance together, tenderly. Juliet untangles herself from Romeo and teasingly dashes out.'

Two elements alternate. The first is a lyrical string chorus, whose melody is like a simplified version of Juliet's theme. The second is Juliet's theme itself.

17. Tybalt recognizes Romeo

'Capulet subdues Tybalt. He becomes enraged; Capulet subdues him once more. Mercutio and the Capulets escort him out.'

Tybalt's anger is expressed with elements from The Fight (No. 6) and the Dance of the Knights (No. 13), with the climactic chords from The Quarrel (No. 5). Gentle episodes allude to the conversation between Romeo and Juliet.

18. Gavotte

'The Guests disperse. The stage clears; the candles are extinguished.'

After the near confrontation of Tybalt and Romeo, prevented only by the intervention of Tybalt's father, order is restored and a gavotte rounds off the ball scene. This is an adaptation of the miniature gavotte from Prokofiev's Symphony No. 1 ('Classical'), doubled in length by repetition and extension. Its orchestration is also strengthened, perhaps to suit the grandeur of a ballroom scene.

19. Balcony Scene (Suite No. III, 6)

The original scenario envisaged this as a continuation of the ballroom scene, to which 'Juliet returns, perhaps in her nightclothes, looking for the kerchief or flower she dropped during her encounter with Romeo.' But it adds, 'If the theatre has the means to change the décor instantly, then these numbers could be offered as a balcony scene', as in Shakespeare's play.

Juliet is alone. Romeo's dreamy chords indicate her thoughts, followed by a trio of two solo violins and solo viola. A flute reminiscence of Juliet's theme marks the entrance of Romeo ('from behind a column. Juliet blushes'). Cellos and cor anglais, and then violins, sing a love theme full of yearning leaps. It leads straight into:

20. Romeo's Variation

The love theme is transformed into a passionate waltz. This in turn leads into:

21. Love Dance

Romeo and Juliet dance together. All the depth and intensity of their young love is expressed in this music, with its sweeping melodic line, full of yearning leaps and sudden surges. The orchestration spreads across a huge spectrum, with piccolo and tremolando violins at the top, tuba and bass drum at the bottom, a delicate filigree of harp and piano, and the theme carried by the horns and cornet and then moving up from cellos and violas to violins, until it soars above everything. As it subsides, a delicate rippling of clarinet and flute takes us back to the tender melody that concluded the Introduction and Juliet's Variation (No. 14), now on violins. Then Romeo's dreaming chords reappear, and the scene ends ecstatically, tinged with the 'sweet sorrow' of parting.

Act II

Scene 1: The Square. 'The entire scene represents a folk celebration, against which the separate episodes occur.'

22. Folk Dance (Suite No. I, 1)

This lively dance was originally, and appropriately, called 'Tarantella'. It begins with one of Prokofiev's characteristic fleeting, high melodies on violins – a simple, transparent effect, but extremely hard to play. The dance is, by turns, delicate, robust, and festive.

23. Romeo and Mercutio

'Romeo enters, thinking about Juliet, to the first theme of the Madrigal (No. 16). Mercutio greets and teases Romeo.' Mercutio's teasing is to the strains of 'Masks' (No. 12), with its baroque flourish. The number ends with a return to the melancholy Madrigal – Romeo is clearly not distracted by the teasing.

24. Dance of the Five Couples (Suite No. II, 4)

The scenario describes the first and third sections of the dance as being in a fast two-time with 'diminutive movements', the second section as a march, in which 'a cheerful procession passes by on the street'. The first theme, played by an oboe, has a curiously unsettled character, with irregular patterns adding up to an eleven-bar phrase. As it passes to other instruments, it becomes more regular in phrasing, and nervously playful. The central march is a little slower, played by an onstage brass band.

25. Dance with Mandolins

The mandolins are 'on the stage' with cornet and trombones. Their awkward dance is joined by strident clarinets and, at the end, tambourine and triangle.

26. The Nurse

'The Nurse seeks out Romeo on Juliet's instructions. Mercutio, concealing Romeo, exchanges bows with the Nurse and teases her.'

This number has a most unusual tempo instruction: Adagio scherzoso (playfully slow). The rather formal phrases, with offbeat accents, combine solemnity with a hint of traditional dance, suggesting a woman of simple dignity (this material, and the sweet phrase on the oboe that follows, briefly appeared in 'Preparations for the Ball', No. 9). Mercutio's teasing is at first playful (violins alternating with harp and piano), and then mockingly pompous (trombones and high cornet).

27. The Nurse gives Romeo a note from Juliet

Romeo's ecstatic reaction is conveyed by an excited reprise of the skittering scales from 'The Young Juliet' (No. 10). In the original scenario this was followed by a reprise of the Tarantella. The final version instead slows for the final bars, as if to convey the simple nurse's attempt to understand what is going on.

Scene 2: At Friar Laurence's

28. Romeo at Friar Laurence's (Suite No. II, 3)

The ballet combines Romeo's two visits to Friar Laurence's cell into one. A bassoon plays a chant-like melody with an accompaniment that is both emphatic and delicate – tuba, bass drum, cellos, and violas pizzicato, double basses bowed, harp, and clarinets (a combination typical of Prokofiev's subtlety.) The chant becomes more fervent as it is taken up by cellos divided into three parts and then violins. The entry of Romeo is signalled by a quietly impassioned rising violin line.

29. Juliet at Friar Laurence's

'Laurence opens the inner doors and admits Juliet. Dressed in pure white, she embodies virginity.'

Magic is cast over Juliet's entry by shimmering tremolando strings. A delicate flute solo begins with a drooping shape that occurred in 'Juliet's variation' and before that in the Introduction. Cellos sing a melody full of impassioned leaps. Friar Laurence's chant resumes as he conducts the marriage ceremony, and is raised to new heights of fervour by a quartet of horns and soaring violins. This leads straight into:

Scene 3: The Square

30. The people continue to make merry

The scene changes back to the square as public festivities continue. The music resumes in the middle of the 'Dance of the Five Couples' (No. 24). Twice an anxious, falling violin line appears (the motif that first appears in the Juliet-related melody from the Introduction), unsettling the mood for a moment. But the dance ends with a rumbustious reprise of the march, now at the same tempo as the dance.

31. Further Public Festivities

This is a resumption of the 'Folk Dance' (Tarantella) that began Act II. 'Appearance of Mercutio and Benvolio with girls. The dance breaks off in dramatic fashion when Tybalt enters and bumps up against Mercutio.'

32. Meeting of Tybalt and Mercutio

'Tybalt and Mercutio stare at each other like bulls.' Several familiar elements are given a cruel twist: the droll bassoon tune from 'The Street Awakens' (No. 3), the anxious falling line, and the 'Dance of the Knights' (No. 13), now at urgent tempo. The tense high and low chords from 'The Quarrel' (No. 5) recur. 'Tybalt throws down a glove; Romeo returns it to him not accepting the challenge.' Fragments of Juliet's delicate theme pass by. 'Mercutio throws himself at Tybalt.' This leads straight into:

33. Tybalt and Mercutio fight

This fight is dominated by dashing music from the earlier dance of Mercutio (No. 15) together with forceful phrases from No. 17, where Tybalt recognizes Romeo at the ball. There is a new element, a pleading string phrase, which evokes fear of what might happen (it was this tragic phrase that began the Introduction). Suddenly the tension increases, and with a strident chord, Mercutio is wounded.

34. Death of Mercutio

Over agitated strings, muted horns slowly play the anxious falling phrase. As in Shakespeare, Mercutio 'jokes before his death'. The music conveys this by bitterly ironic references back to the bassoon tune from 'The Street Awakens' (No. 3), and to 'Masks' (No. 12). Mercutio's final struggle for breath is conveyed by cellos and basses scratching at chords, and he dies to the solemn sound of brass instruments.

35. Romeo decides to avenge Mercutio (Suite No. I, 7)
'Benvolio throws himself at the pensive Romeo with a wail. Romeo decides to avenge Mercutio's death … In contrast to Tybalt's duel with Mercutio, where the combatants fail to consider the seriousness of the situation and fight out of youthful ardour, Romeo and Tybalt battle fiercely, to the death.' Once the fight begins, it is relentless. Prokofiev takes the music of 'The Fight' from Act I (No. 6) and drives it in an unstoppable perpetuum mobile, until a succession of savage beats evokes the fatal blow and Tybalt's death throes. This leads straight into:

36. Finale
'The stage fills; Benvolio, suddenly energized, wraps Romeo in a cloak and pushes him out: "flee!" The Capulets grieve for Tybalt and promise vengeance. A procession with Tybalt's body.' Over a repeated pattern of savage chords, horns, trumpets, and violins weave a wailing counterpoint, which builds to a climax at which wrenching harmonies culminate in a final, abrupt chord.

Act III
Scene 1: Juliet's Bedchamber. 'Unlike the previous act, which occurs on the square, the third act unfolds in rooms. Accordingly, the orchestration is more chamber-like.'

37. Introduction
'Recalling the Prince's power over Romeo's destiny', this brief Introduction repeats the terrifying chords of 'the Prince's Command' (No. 7), reminding us of the threat that now hangs over Romeo. This leads straight into:

38. Romeo and Juliet
'Curtain. Predawn haziness. Romeo and Juliet behind the bed curtain. In order to avoid a misleading impression, the composer attempted to make the music clean and bright.' The music reprises that of 'Juliet at Friar Laurence's' (No. 29), with the delicate flute solo taken up by violins, and then the flute joined magically by a celesta (perhaps the reference back is supposed to remind us delicately that Romeo and Juliet are married).

39. Romeo bids Juliet farewell (Suite No. II, 5)
Reflective music rises to the melancholy yearning phrases with which the ballet opened. A viola d'amore (or normal viola) solo remembers another yearning melody from the 'Love Dance' (No. 21). As it passes from instrument to instrument, the accompanying texture become more complex, until the melody once more soars in the violins. A brief reprise of the opening music of the number leads to another appearance of the tender melody that concluded 'Juliet's Variation' (No. 14), at the end of which Romeo is gone.

40. Nurse (Suite No. III, 4)
'The nurse forewarns Juliet that her parents and Paris are coming. Juliet goes behind the bed curtain to change. They enter and report to Juliet that Paris is her suitor (he presents her with

a bouquet).' The nurse's music from No. 26 is remembered. Then the rather grand minuet from 'The Arrival of the Guests' (No. 11) is played on solo strings, sounding rather pompous and out of place in the bedchamber. A clarinet takes up the smooth middle section of the minuet. This leads straight into:

41. Juliet refuses to marry Paris

'Juliet's hysteria. Juliet does not want to marry Paris; she weeps; she becomes angry. She is small, powerless and despondent. During this scene her parents gingerly move Paris away. Juliet's father orders her to marry Paris, "or you are not my daughter." Her parents exit.' Juliet's skittering scales (from 'The Young Juliet', No. 10) take on an air of desperation, punctuated by a peremptory trombone. The calm middle theme from 'The Young Juliet' turns to the minor as Juliet weeps. Her father exerts his authority to the harsh sound of 'The Dance of the Knights' (No. 13).

42. Juliet alone. 'She decides to go to Laurence. Curtain.' Juliet contemplates her situation to the familiar tragic yearning phrases. Music from the 'Love Dance' (No. 21), which was so recently remembered with happiness, is newly tinged with melancholy by subtle shifts of harmony. This leads without a break into:

43. Interlude
This brief interlude conjures up the immensity of what Juliet is about to contemplate, with the tragic theme played by six horns in the midst of a tumultuous accompaniment, giving it a sense of heroic grandeur. This leads straight into:

Scene 2: At Friar Laurence's

44. At Friar Laurence's Cell
'Laurence suggests the sleeping potion. Juliet's preparedness, calmness, even elation. Juliet leaves, having become a tragic figure.' Cellos divided in three parts reprise their calm chorale from the earlier scene in Friar Laurence's cell (No. 28). A clarinet plays the passionate, leaping melody from the 'Love Dance' (No. 21) as Juliet enters, and the two themes alternate, becoming more serious as they do so. There is a moment of mystery, with tremolando violas and a flute, and Laurence gives Juliet the potion (deep rising phrase on basses, contrabassoon, and tuba, a newly darkened version of an aspirational motif, which Prokofiev called 'the death theme'). The mood lightens, and cellos sing a melody full of optimistic yearning. A tender theme from the 'Balcony Scene' (No. 19) returns, at first on violas and clarinet, then taken up with renewed confidence and fervour by violins. This leads into:

45. Interlude
As the scene returns to Juliet's bedchamber, we hear first a reminder of the tragic theme, then an abrupt snatch of the 'Dance of the Knights' (No. 13), associated with the anger of Juliet's father. The music quietens as the curtain rises. This leads straight into:

Scene 3: Juliet's Bedchamber Again

46. Juliet
'Juliet informs her parents of her preparedness to marry Paris. Juliet, her mother, and her girlfriends fit the wedding dress. Juliet dispatches everyone, respectfully kissing her mother's hands.' The scene opens with the cool flute solo to which Juliet and Paris danced during the 'Dance of the Knights' (No. 13). The theme becomes animated as everyone bustles round to clothe Juliet in her wedding dress, but there is a tone of desperate urgency in the music. Once again the mood calms, and the flute melody resumes, now accompanied by a ghostly descant, first on violins, then on celesta (a masterly touch in a score full of delicate orchestral blending). Juliet is left alone.

47. Juliet alone
'Juliet alone with her hourglass: the death theme. Dance with the poison: "I drink for you, Romeo!" She drinks, becomes drowsy, drinks twice more, weakens and falls onto her bed (or just short of it), pulling down the bed curtain.' The strings play rasping, scratchy chords, as in the 'Death of Mercutio' (No. 34). The 'death theme' rises from the depths, as Juliet contemplates with horror what she is about to do. But this is followed by the leaping theme from the 'Love Dance' (No. 21), first on oboe and solo viola (d'amore), then more passionately on violins as her courage returns. As she takes the potion, the music becomes still (as at the moment when Friar Laurence gave her the poison), and the scene ends in deep mystery.

48. Aubade (Suite No. III, 5)
'The quiet, happy sound of a mandolin orchestra is heard from the wings. Entrance of Paris and others to (and with) an orchestra of mandolins and trumpets ... According to custom, Paris comes with a gift-bearing retinue to rouse his bride on the day of their wedding.' The mandolins come with piccolo, clarinets, and a solo violin playing showy scales and arpeggios. A cornet and two trumpets play a little chorale. Despite the carefree manner, there are little twists in the music that make it sound not quite right.

49. Dance of the Girls with Lilies (Suite No. II, 6)
This replaces three exotic dances in the original scenario (Dance of the four Antilles Girls, Dance of the three Moors, and Dance of the two Pirates). The dance has a solemn tread, marked by tambourine, maracas, and bass drum, and a quirky, oriental-style melody.

50. At Juliet's Bedside
'Worry that Juliet has not reacted. Juliet's mother and nurse attempt to rouse Juliet; she is dead.' After a moment of anxiety, there are cheerful, cajoling references back to 'The Nurse' (No. 26). High pianissimo violins and a solemn brass chord mark the moment when they realize that she is (apparently) dead.

Act IV
51. Juliet's Funeral
In the original 1935 scenario Friar Laurence intervenes, preventing Romeo from stabbing himself before Juliet revives. The revision for the 1940 production reverted to Shakespeare's ending, in which Romeo, thinking Juliet is dead, takes poison. Juliet, reviving, finds him dead beside her, and takes the remaining poison to kill herself.

The 'death theme' is developed into a powerful threnody. First it appears as a string chorale, with the melody high in the violins, then in the horns, and then with the full weight of the brass in a tragic slow march. It returns to the horns, the music becomes more frenzied, and, as Romeo enters to find Juliet, their tragic theme and the leaping melody from their 'Love Dance' (No. 21) appear. The music builds to a final, massive statement of the 'death theme' as slow march. This is followed by an outburst of grief that dissolves into mysterious tremolo as the poison takes hold. The music descends into darkness, leading straight into:

52. Juliet's Death (Suite No. II, 7, and Suite No. III, 6)
Juliet slowly wakes to find the dead Romeo by her side. The first music we hear, high and soft in the violins, is a chaste melody from Juliet's first appearance, 'The Young Juliet' (No. 10). There are deep brass chords as she sees Romeo. Then the young Juliet's melody flowers into a sweet and regretful outpouring, suffused with a sense of what might have been (as in Shakespeare, the deep emotional reactions of Juliet are very different from the violent passions of Romeo). There is a sharp tug of harmony in the woodwind as she takes Romeo's dagger and stabs herself. The regretful melody rises to a tragic climax, and falls away, lingering as the families come to find the two lovers lying dead.

Symphonies

SYMPHONY NO. 1 IN D MAJOR, 'CLASSICAL'
Duration: approx. 15 minutes

Allegro
Larghetto
Gavotta: Non troppo allegro
Molto vivace

Prokofiev wrote a symphony in E minor in 1908, while he was still a student at the St Petersburg Conservatoire. Although it received a private rehearsal it was never performed publicly, and Prokofiev eventually recycled some of its material in his Fourth Piano Sonata. The work that he eventually called his First Symphony was written nine years later, in the year of Russian revolutions, 1917. Far from being in any way 'revolutionary', this was a deliberate look back to the classical methods of Haydn and Mozart. Prokofiev revealed in his *Autobiography* that this came about because he wanted to try composing away from the piano. Naturally, as a virtuoso pianist, he had the habit of writing at the piano:

> but I had noticed that thematic material composed without the piano was often better in quality. When transferred to the piano, it sounds strange for a moment, but after a few repetitions it seems that this is exactly the way it should have been written. I was intrigued with the idea of writing an entire symphonic piece without the piano. A composition written this way would probably have more orchestral colours ... Haydn's technique had become particularly clear to me after working with Tcherepnin and it seemed it would be easier to dive into the deep waters of writing without the piano if I worked in a familiar setting. If Haydn had lived to our era, I thought, he would have retained his compositional style but would also have absorbed something from what was new. That's the kind of symphony I wanted to compose: a symphony in the classical style.[18]

He dedicated the symphony to a fellow student, the composer Boris Asafyev. But in 1925, Prokofiev admitted to Asafyev that Stravinsky's 'neoclassical' works had led him to have doubts about the premise of the symphony: 'In general, I don't think very highly of things like *Pulcinella* or even my own "Classical" Symphony (sorry, I wasn't thinking of this when I dedicated it to you), which are written "under the influence" of something else.'[19] Two things are worth remembering as the context for this remark. The first is that Prokofiev's 'Classical' Symphony was written two years before Stravinsky's *Pulcinella*, and was truly a pioneer of 'neoclassical' composition. The second point is that, just as Stravinsky always sounds like Stravinsky, so Prokofiev's symphony sounds thoroughly like Prokofiev. It is Prokofiev adopting unusually refined manners – Myaskovsky called it his 'boulevard music' – but it is not a pastiche. And in its clarity and lyricism it gives us a foretaste of the style that Prokofiev was later to develop in his search for 'a new simplicity'.

Prokofiev's instrumentation is that of Haydn and Mozart's orchestra: two each of flutes, oboes, clarinets, bassoons, horns, trumpets, plus timpani and strings. With these modest forces, Prokofiev succeeds brilliantly in suggesting the sort of symphony Haydn might have written if he were alive in the early twentieth century. It has the fizzing energy and liveliness that, in Haydn's day, went hand in hand with the composing of comic opera. The first theme begins with an emphatic flourish based on the notes of a simple arpeggio of D major. From the first fortissimo chord, it rushes upwards in a rapid crescendo from piano to fortissimo – Prokofiev's updating of the famous 'Mannheim Rocket' that became popular in Haydn and Mozart's day. There are several delicate elements to the first group of ideas, and then, as in most Haydn symphonies, we arrive a fifth above the home key, in A major. The second theme is a delicate little tune with comically enormous leaps, accompanied by a staccato bassoon – a delightful reference to Haydn's 'Clock' Symphony (No. 101).

Unlike Haydn, Prokofiev does not repeat the first section, but, with an abrupt change of key, goes straight into the development. The different elements are thrown around and discussed in truly classical fashion, and the energy builds. The delicate second theme moves into the bass and becomes strongly assertive, and then it slips a beat. The onbeat and offbeat versions fight each other, and reach a climax at which the music bursts into the reprise of the opening theme. This is at first in the 'wrong' key (C major instead of D major), a new twist on a classical procedure – Haydn and Mozart sometimes began their reprise in a key other than the home key, but never like this. By the time the delicate second theme arrives, we are back in D major, and the movement continues more or less as expected to an energetic finish.

The gentle introductory bars of the slow movement in A major could almost be Schubert. But then the violins enter on a high A, and as they descend, they unfurl a melody of delicate serenity. This is pure Prokofiev – the sort of memorable lyricism that gives the heart to his ballet scores. On the other hand, its playful decoration is also a further nod to the Haydn of the 'Clock' Symphony. The melody comes to an elegant conclusion. Bassoon and pizzicato strings enter pianissimo, more like the tripping of cygnets in a ballet than an identifiable theme. The music builds to a moment of grandeur in C major, from which wistful little phrases lead down to a resolution in F major. This is not the home key, but the violins nevertheless enter, as at the beginning, on a high A, and unfurl their melody in A major. This is a touch of magic as the two keys, A major and F major, melt into each other until pure A major is left. Elements of the tripping second idea persist, accompanying the melody to its end, and the movement finishes as it began.

For the third movement, Prokofiev replaces the classical minuet with a gavotte. This is very short, only a minute and a half long. It begins pesante (heavily), with the sort of rugged charm that Prokofiev was to deploy in ballet music (indeed, he reused this gavotte in *Romeo and Juliet*). The middle section is like a moment of Tchaikovsky: eight bars of a miniature procession over a drone bass, repeated with charming decoration. Instead of returning to the ruggedness of the opening, the reprise is played quietly by the flutes, and fades out on a pizzicato cadence.

The fourth movement has the sort of non-stop, sparkling energy that Haydn loved in his finales, but with an additional demand for virtuoso playing through rapidly changing keys – challenging even for modern orchestras. The first theme, like that of the opening movement, plays with a simple arpeggio of D major (themes in classical symphonies are often subtly related). A second idea emerges wittily from rapidly repeated notes, and the first section of the movement concludes with a third idea, a demure little folk-like tune on the flutes. Here (unlike in the first movement) Prokofiev repeats this first section. The development begins by throwing the third idea around, and then interleaving it with the repeated-note second idea. The reprise of the first theme slips in quietly in the flutes, with the violins playing a rapid broken scale *ppp*. The theme goes through new developments (a very classical procedure), and when the second idea appears, its rising shape has been turned upside down. There are further playful touches to the third idea, before the symphony ends in a mood of truly Haydnesque confidence.

SYMPHONY NO. 5 IN B FLAT MAJOR, OP. 100
Duration: 38–45 minutes

Andante
Allegro marcato
Adagio
Allegro giocoso

In 1925, Prokofiev composed a Second Symphony that even he described as 'chromatic and ponderous'. His Third Symphony (1928) was based on music from Prokofiev's opera *The Fiery Angel*, almost like a suite, and a Fourth Symphony (1929–30) shared material with his ballet *The Prodigal Son*. But the symphony that has held its place in the repertoire, together with the first, is his fifth and last, which echoes the clarity and 'new simplicity' of *Romeo and Juliet*.

Prokofiev composed the Fifth Symphony in the summer of 1944, breaking off from his work on Sergei Eisenstein's film, *Ivan the Terrible*, in order to complete it. He was staying at a retreat for Soviet artists, a former imperial estate near Ivanovo, and the peaceful surroundings enabled him to concentrate on the symphony without interruption. The composer Dmitry Kabalevsky remembered the occasion when Prokofiev first played the symphony on the piano:

> On August 26, I remember, a group of us, Myaskovsky, Shostakovich, Muradeli [a Georgian composer] and I gathered in the little peasant hut where Prokofiev worked to hear the symphony. For some reason Prokofiev was extremely nervous; he talked a great deal about irrelevant matters and seemed anxious to put off as long as possible the moment when he would have to sit down and play for us. When he did, however, he played very well,

contriving to convey the orchestral timbres on the piano. He was very pleased, for he always (and rightly) considered the Fifth Symphony one of his best compositions.

Strangely enough, in spite of his unbounded self-confidence and faith in his own talent, Prokofiev deeply appreciated a sympathetic understanding attitude to his music on the part of others. The need to associate with people, and especially the need for warm, friendly contact with his fellow musicians, became more marked in him during the war years. He himself seemed to become gentler, more responsive, simpler and more sociable during that period. Everyone who knew him more or less intimately noticed this change in him.[20]

It was fourteen years since Prokofiev had composed a symphony, and he wrote, 'I regard the Fifth Symphony as the culmination of a long period of my creative life. I conceived it as a symphony of the grandeur of the human spirit ... praising the free and happy man – his strength, his generosity, and the purity of his soul.'[21] It was first performed in Moscow on 13 January 1945, at the time when Russian troops were advancing into Germany over the river Vistula. This was Prokofiev's last appearance as a conductor. Shortly afterwards, he had a dizzy spell, fell downstairs, and suffered concussion. From then on, he suffered from high blood pressure and severe headaches, and never fully recovered, though he was able to compose two more symphonies.

The symphony opens with a gently rising line on flute and bassoon, in a simple B flat major. As the violins take up the melody, it shifts sideways for a moment to A major, in a characteristic bittersweet twist. Power begins to build, and the brass inject an element of threat, underpinned by a low tuba (one of Prokofiev's favourite effects). If this were Shostakovich, it would lead immediately to a climax. But Prokofiev instead keeps his forces in check. The threat comes and goes, and eventually gives way to a second theme. Played by flute and oboe, this too is at first gentle, though a little faster and uncertain in key. Again the violins take it up, and it becomes more assertive. As it builds, it breaks back to the original tempo, and to the simplicity of a clear key (F major). Forceful dotted rhythms and a trumpet solo rise to a first climax. It fades away, pursued by a quirky, repeated chattering figure. Back in B flat, the opening theme returns in the bass. As it is explored further, the chattering figure joins it. This generates new energy, and a struggle between lyrical and disruptive elements develops. Eventually, the opening theme returns, now as a fortissimo brass chorale, back in its original B flat. This quietens, without ever quite regaining the serenity of the opening. After a forceful climax, it does find its way to the gentle second theme. But this is a brief moment of calm. Soon the power builds again, and at the end of the movement the first theme finds itself transformed into a mighty declaration of force.

The second movement is a scherzo in D minor. The tempo is fast, the mood ironic, building to moments of violence. There are similarities to Shostakovich, but the irony is subtler and less brutal, more in the older Russian tradition of Musorgsky and Rimsky-Korsakov. It is basically in the classical form of scherzo–trio–scherzo, but with many twists and complexities along the way. The violins set up a ticking staccato that persists throughout the outer sections of the movement. The little theme, on clarinet, consists of an earnest first phrase, but a second phrase that turns cheeky as it swerves into F major. Oboe and violas finish it off with a nervy little descending conclusion. This theme is thrown around the orchestra in various keys, punctuated with bursts of force from brass and percussion (including wood block, which heightens the sense of irony). Over the persistent ticking, a swirling second element is quietly slipped in by muted violins. After this, the first theme acquires wider intervals and accented offbeats, and is played half-speed by a bassoon.

The first section of the movement fades away, the tempo slows, and oboe and clarinet introduce the middle section with a new theme whose contours seem derived from the swirling second element of the scherzo. This has the character of an incantation, as if a magician has stepped from the pages of a Rimsky-Korsakov opera. The sense of mystery continues, as violas and clarinet quietly play another version of the swirling element, now in three-time, with the rhythm marked by pianissimo side drum and tambourine. This soon builds up, with playful gestures thrown in first by woodwind and then by violins. A trumpet cuts across the three-time with a reminder of the incantatory theme, setting off an outburst of wild energy. This is short-lived, and soon we are back in a slower four-time for a reprise of the incantation. This time the continuation is in the same metre and tempo, as staccato trumpets play a repeated chromatic pattern, with fragments of the first theme, as if something sinister has been lurking behind the ticking pattern. The pace gradually increases, the sinister becomes violent, and breaks into a reprise of the scherzo, with heightened tension and fiercer accents. The power builds relentlessly to a final crash.

The Adagio has the intense lyricism of the tragic love music in Prokofiev's *Romeo and Juliet*, and if the mood seems remarkably close, this is not surprising: having rewritten the happy ending of his original 1935 ballet score, Prokofiev reused some of the material in the opening of this movement. Over a rocking accompaniment, clarinet and bass clarinet play a calm melody in F major. The first phrase could be Rachmaninoff. But then the intervals become wider and more unlikely, and the violins enter, swooping up to a poignant dissonance. The combination of the very high violins with the low bass line reinforced by tuba is one of Prokofiev's most characteristic touches. Soon the melody slips sideways and is repeated down in E major. Briefly, the mood becomes more severe, with the beats marked by a side drum, then the violins round off the first section with the end of the great melody. From the depths (tuba, contrabassoon, double basses) arises a new idea in E minor that draws on elements of the first theme, and it is answered with urgent dotted rhythms and upward swirls. Soon the mood darkens, and the key shifts to C minor (Prokofiev loves swerves into unrelated keys). Woodwind and low trumpet introduce a theme with a sombre tread. The tempo increases, and all the new elements combine, building up to a huge climax with blaring dissonances. It soon dissipates, the ghost of the rocking figure reappears, the key returns to F major, and the violins very softly begin the reprise of the opening melody. The ending is Prokofiev at his most magical, with a high piccolo over a shimmering accompaniment, the violins tenderly taking up the melody for the last time, and the rocking figure tentatively finding its way to a final, delicate chord of F major.

The finale opens with a gentle, pastoral introduction. Over a drone, flute and bassoon seem to be trying to find their way back to the melody with which they opened the symphony. But it is the cellos that succeed, divided into four parts and playing the theme as a beautiful chorale. After this brief reminiscence, the violas set up another of Prokofiev's insistent rhythms, over which a clarinet plays a cheeky little tune, as if reprising its role in the scherzo. Violins answer with vivacious cascading phrases. What follows is a rondo, in which this theme recurs. More than anywhere in the symphony, the finale is where Prokofiev and Shostakovich meet. The mood is ironic and vivacious, barely able to contain its nervous energy. Shostakovich would have led it through a series of increasingly violent climaxes. Prokofiev, as in the first movement, harbours his resources, saving the outburst for the end. The opening theme plays out and fades gently away. The key shifts to F major, and a flute enters with the poise of a ballerina, playing yet another of Prokofiev's themes full of wide intervals (its opening phrase has the same shape as the sombre C minor theme from the slow movement). As the theme is developed, the strings introduce a skittering little figure, to remind us of the energy bubbling beneath the surface.

The music returns to B flat and the insistent rhythm, and the clarinet reprises the first theme. This goes in new directions, the opening pastoral melody returns, and the mood calms. Now Prokofiev embarks on a passage of smooth counterpoint. It evokes two further reminiscences: the middle of the slow movement, and a turn of phrase associated with Juliet in Prokofiev's *Romeo and Juliet*. It is not long before the ebullience begins to break through, and the clarinet tune in B flat returns, followed by the balletic second theme. The skittering violins become more and more frenetic, and beneath them horns and tuba ponderously take on the clarinet tune. Timpani, side drum, bass drum, and wood block join in, accompanied by woodwind shrieks. The momentum becomes unstoppable, as other fragments of themes appear. As if to remind us that this is Prokofiev, not Shostakovich, the mayhem quietens for a moment to reveal a delicious combination of solo violins and violas with piano, harp, and percussion, before a swift crescendo and the final crash.

SERGEI RACHMANINOFF
(1873–1943)

Rachmaninoff was born on an estate near Novgorod in Russia, into an aristocratic family that had been impoverished by his father's recklessness. Having lost most of their estates, the family moved to St Petersburg, where, at the age of ten, Sergei entered the Conservatoire. The death of his sister from diphtheria, and the separation of his parents, contributed to the young boy's lack of concentration, and he failed his exams in 1885. It was Alexander Ziloti, a cousin of his mother and a pupil of Liszt, who suggested that he should be sent to his old teacher at Moscow, Nikolai Zverev, a strict disciplinarian. Under his tuition, and with Sergei Taneyev and Anton Arensky teaching him harmony and counterpoint, Rachmaninoff thrived. In 1888 he transferred to Ziloti himself, and in 1891 he graduated from the Moscow Conservatoire, having already begun composing his First Piano Concerto. He was to become one of the most admired pianists of the early twentieth century. But he really wanted to devote himself to composition, and this led to a serious rift with Zverev.

Rachmaninoff's graduation exercise in 1892 was a one-act opera, *Aleko*. It won him the rare accolade of a gold medal. Its performance the following year was so successful that it was taken up by the Bolshoi Theatre, and earned the praise of Tchaikovsky. This launched a poten-tially successful career as a composer. However, the premiere of his First Symphony was a failure, because according to Rachmaninoff the conductor, Alexander Glazunov, 'wrecked it'.[1] This disaster crushed Rachmaninoff's self-confidence, and for three years he composed almost nothing. A visit with the bass Feodor Chaliapin to the great Leo Tolstoy in 1900 can hardly have improved his spirits. The elderly Tolstoy, whose ideas by then centred on personal asceticism and the fight against social injustice, declared that Beethoven was nonsense, and, in response to Rachmaninoff's own music, said, 'Tell me, does anyone need music like that?'[2]

Soon after that encounter, Rachmaninoff met the therapist Nikolay Dahl, who helped him over a period of three months. Rachmaninoff began to recover, and in 1901 he composed the Piano Concerto No. 2, which he dedicated to Dahl.

Marriage to his cousin, Natalia Satina, followed in 1902, despite the opposition of the Orthodox Church, and they settled in a house on the surviving family estate, Ivanovka, near Tambov some 300 miles south-east of Moscow. It was here that he composed his Second Symphony, *The Isle of the Dead*, and the Third Piano Concerto. The concerto was written for performance on Rachmaninoff's first tour of the United States in 1909. Although he hated the experience, and refused several offers of return visits, his popularity there was to stand him in good stead. At the Revolution in 1917, he lost what was left of his family's land, and emigrated, first to Stockholm and Copenhagen, and then, the following year, to the USA, where, despite his hatred of touring, he realized that there was a ready audience for his piano-playing. He began his exile by playing forty concerts in an exhausting four-month tour, and then signed a record contract, making his first recordings in 1919.

The following year the Rachmaninoffs bought a house in New York, where they attempted to recreate something of the atmosphere of their lost Russian estate. The need to keep his performing career going, together with his overwhelming homesickness, meant that Rachmaninoff composed only half a dozen works in his remaining years. He never returned to Russia, but he did regain a base in Europe. In 1932 he built a house on Lake Lucerne, Switzerland, where he spent the summers of 1932–9. It was there that he found the time and peace of mind to compose his Rhapsody on a Theme of Paganini, the Third Symphony, and the Symphonic Dances. His profile during his American years was enhanced by his friendship with the brilliant young Russian pianist Vladimir Horowitz. Horowitz became a great champion of Rachmaninoff's music, particularly of his Third Piano Concerto. Rachmaninoff's own recordings reveal him to have been not only one of the most brilliant but also one of the most eloquent of pianists. His performances of other composers' works – Beethoven, Schubert, Schumann, Chopin, and others – are full of telling insights, though also incorporating a degree of freedom that is very much of its time. In his own music, Rachmaninoff as a performer is supreme. His recordings are not only impressive in themselves, but are also a valuable antidote to the overblown, super-Romantic interpretations that became fashionable in the later twentieth century. Rachmaninoff (like Elgar) cuts directly to the heart of his music in his performances, using subtle nuance and delicate emphasis where later pianists often lay on 'expression' with a trowel. A new generation of pianists has rediscovered Rachmaninoff's own recordings and his subtle and direct approach. The result is as if his music has been 'restored', revealing it as a unique mixture of the mercurial, nostalgic, intellectually satisfying, and heartfelt, complex in its detail, simple in its overall impulse.

His reputation as a composer had to weather the contempt of the modernists for much of the twentieth century, for whom music so deeply rooted in nineteenth-century Russia could scarcely be tolerated in the fashionable new world of atonality and harsh asceticism. Rachmaninoff himself gave poignant expression to his dilemma in an interview in 1939: 'I feel like a ghost wandering in a world grown alien. I cannot cast out the old way of writing, and I cannot acquire the new. I have made an intense effort to acquire the manner of today, but it will not come to me.'[3] But despite this, his status as one of the most intensely lyrical of early twentieth-century composers is now secure.

THE ISLE OF THE DEAD, OP. 29
Duration: approx. 21 minutes

The Swiss painter Arnold Böcklin (1827–1901) painted a series of five paintings with the title *The Isle of the Dead*. Rachmaninoff first came across a black-and-white reproduction of one of them, and only later saw the original, in either Leipzig or Berlin. In an interview published in 1927, he confessed that the reproduction had impressed him more than the painting itself: 'The massive architecture and the mystic message of the painting made a marked impression on me, and the tone poem was the outcome . . . If I had seen the original first, I might not have composed [the work].'[4]

The five versions of the painting differ in colour and lighting, but all show a very similar scene. A rocky island fills most of the canvas. In the centre are tall cypress trees, and either side towering cliffs, in which there are imposing galleries and doorways. This is an island cemetery. Approaching the shore of the island on the still, dark water, is a boat, rowed by an oarsman. In the prow is a coffin, behind which stands a tall figure clad from head to foot in white. Part of the effect of the painting arises because we see these figures from the back, so their faces are a mystery to us. Inevitably, the painting powerfully suggests a reference to Charon, the ferryman of Hades, who conveyed souls across the river to the Underworld.

Rachmaninoff composed *The Isle of the Dead* early in 1909, and conducted the first performance in Moscow on 18 April. It is perhaps his finest orchestral work, powerfully conjuring up a musical landscape, and sustaining it through a huge emotional range. It shows Rachmaninoff's command of orchestration, in the way that he calculates the combination of strings, brass, and woodwind and the voicing of chords so as to create a sense of dark inevitability.

The long first section of the work consists of a series of great waves beginning in A minor, and resting on a deep foundation of the bass note A, which is held for long stretches at a time. The whole of the first and last sections is in five-time. This enables Rachmaninoff to set up a hypnotic rocking rhythm, predominantly in a 3 + 2 pattern, but sometimes changing briefly to 2 + 3. This creates a wonderfully natural, sea-like effect, with waves coming and going in a rhythm that has inevitability without mathematical predictability – there is a chaotic element. As the waves continue inexorably, a persistent mournful call is heard passing from horn to woodwind to trumpet to violins. From time to time more rapid movement is heard, as of sudden gusts of wind, or flocks of birds. Rachmaninoff himself cut some of these passages, both in his recording and in concert performance, and other conductors have followed his example. This has the effect of tightening up the thrust of the first section of the work, but it also removes some of the most imaginative and effective passages of orchestration.

For a moment the sombre A minor warms into C major, and the violins play a high, yearning melody, which passes to an oboe. Then the texture becomes more complex, and the intensity increases. A mighty chord of C minor is reached, and the wave motion recommences, building, with dark brass chords and emphatic timpani, to the first great climax. The climax evaporates, unresolved, leaving a lone flute, and the music falls away to silence. Then the brass, low and sombre, play a fragment of chorale derived from the first four notes of the *Dies Irae* (the medieval chant evoking the Day of Judgment). This powerful reference hints at the possibility that this chant might also be the origin of the mournful cries that have haunted the music to this point.

With a surge of energy the violins lead into a central section in a warm E flat major (utterly remote from the A minor of the opening). In a letter to the conductor, Leopold Stokowski, Rachmaninoff characterized the contrast between the outer sections of the work with this middle section: 'In the former is death – in the latter life.'[5] The effect is perhaps of clinging on to a memory of life, at first nervously and hesitantly, and then increasingly passionately and ecstatically. But this cannot be sustained. The music moves further away from the comfort of E flat major, becoming gradually more and more desperate and agitated, arriving at a climax. As it falls away, cellos and violin sing fragments of the 'life' melody. But this only serves to stoke a yet more terrible climax, at which violent chords seem to thrust any hope away.

Quietly, clarinet and tremolando strings set up a repeating pattern from the *Dies Irae* motif. An oboe sadly recalls the 'life' melody, now in a minor key. The dark brass chorale returns, and the strings start up their sombre five-time pattern again. The yearning phrases from the first section are briefly reprised, and the music retreats to the darkness from which it first emerged. Just before the end, the cellos extend the *Dies Irae* quotation, making the reference unmistakable for the first and only time in the piece.

PIANO CONCERTO NO. 1 IN F SHARP MINOR, OP. 1
Duration: 25–29 minutes

Vivace
Andante
Allegro vivace

In the spring of 1891, Rachmaninoff's piano professor, Alexander Ziloti, resigned from the Moscow Conservatoire after continual disagreements with the director, Vasily Safonov. Rather than transfer to another teacher, Rachmaninoff was allowed to take his final exams a year early, and graduated with honours and a gold medal. That summer, at the age of eighteen, he completed this concerto, which he dedicated to Ziloti, and played the premiere of its first movement at the Conservatoire.

Rachmaninoff had begun work on the concerto the previous summer on his family estate, Ivanovka. Ziloti was a guest there and was practising Grieg's Piano Concerto for future concerts. It would be an exaggeration to say that Rachmaninoff modelled his concerto on Grieg's, but there are many unashamed touches of homage scattered through his score. In 1917, shortly before leaving Russia with his family, Rachmaninoff revised the concerto, tightening it up and making its textures more transparent. By this time, his Second and Third Piano Concertos were already well known, and the first never became as popular as those, to Rachmaninoff's regret: 'All the youthful freshness is there, and yet it plays itself so much more easily [after revision]. And nobody pays any attention. When I tell them in America that I will play the First Concerto, they do not protest, but I can see by their faces that they would prefer the Second or the Third.'[6] The description that follows is of the revised version of the concerto.

After a horn call and an arresting chord on full orchestra, the piano enters with a cascade of descending double octaves, as in Grieg's Piano Concerto. But the essential differences between the two works immediately begin to open out. Grieg's first theme is an unassuming folk dance, whose second half develops into a sweeping melody of rising phrases. Rachmaninoff launches immediately into a melody on violins that is steeped in melancholy harmonies, with no trace of folk dance – though its rising phrases seem inspired by the second half of Grieg's theme. The piano takes up the melody, with the violas playing it in sorrowful counterpoint. As in the Grieg, this is followed by a brilliant passage at faster tempo. After a little moment of cadenza, piano and woodwind exchange melodic phrases in counterpoint over an unchanging bass note (Rachmaninoff is much fonder of this sort of complexity than Grieg), and then the piano quietly leads in to the second main theme. This is another melody of rising phrases in the violins, a cousin of the first theme, though it rises higher, and is accompanied by glittering figuration from the piano. The theme is taken up by the woodwind, but soon the piano figurations overwhelm it, and build to a climax.

An orchestral tutti bursts in vigorously, recalling the descending piano octaves from the opening, and this marks the transition from the first section of the movement into the development. The energy falls away, and mournful fragments of the second theme combine with the vigorous pattern of the octaves. This passage culminates in another horn call, and the piano enters. Phrases of the second theme continue in the orchestra while the piano plays glittering patterns. These give way to a meditative passage, bringing in reminiscences of the first theme, and a sorrowful little falling phrase (distilled from the pattern of the descending octaves). Soon the pace and the tension increase, the piano briefly recalls the opening octaves, and we are then at the reprise of the first theme on solo piano. As before, this leads through to the second theme, now on violas followed by solo violin, the piano accompanying with more delicate decoration than the first time. An energetic tutti leads to the cadenza. As in Grieg's cadenza at the equivalent point, this begins with Liszt-like fantasy, moving from powerful octaves to a meditative passage, and culminating in a grand reprise of the first theme. The orchestra enters, and a final burst of brilliance at the vivace tempo brings the movement to a close.

The second movement is short and intimate. It is as if the public melancholy of the first movement's themes has been exchanged for private regret. The first sound is a solo horn, playing a rising phrase that evokes the latter part of the theme in Grieg's Concerto. After a moment of musing, as if improvising, the piano launches into the main theme. At first this still has an improvisatory quality, with an elaborate line that hints at the piano's first entry in Grieg's slow movement, and with melancholy changes of harmony that are highly characteristic of Rachmaninoff. But the continuation of the theme proceeds firmly, in a series of rising phrases related to the opening horn solo. As the piano's phrases rise, a bassoon plays a falling counterpoint. The horn and the upper woodwind take over the rising phrases, while the piano decorates elaborately, bringing an ecstatic element to the rising line. This subsides to a moment of darkness. Then the violins and cellos play the theme, now simplified into a song-like melody, while the piano breaks into staccato chords and running semiquavers. This is another moment of pure Rachmaninoff, with singing melancholy combined with delicate figuration, like nostalgia for past delights. Soon the memory fades, and the movement is over.

Rachmaninoff revised the finale more radically than the other movements, giving it more impact and brilliance, and removing a rather bombastic reappearance of the second theme at the end (a device that works more successfully in Grieg's Concerto). The revised movement is a glittering, breathless display. The opening theme is in a very fast tempo, with alternating metres and cross-rhythms, giving an effect of bewildering playfulness (and it is very difficult to accompany accurately). A few seconds in, another element has a hint of Grieg-like folkishness, but it is gone in a flash. After a while, the music eases, as if to a more relaxed second theme. But Rachmaninoff plays with our expectations, continuing at almost the same tempo, now in a simple four-time metre. Beneath the skittish piano figuration, fragments of a lyrical line appear in the violins, evoking memories of the second theme in the first movement. But these too are soon gone, and the orchestra responds to the piano's rapid chords with an emphatic tutti.

There is a dramatic change of key, and at last the pace does ease for a lyrical second theme. This is a warm melody on violins, on which the piano comments tenderly with delicate arabesques (another Grieg-like element). The piano then extends the theme further in improvisatory style, and when it returns to the melody itself it is answered by flute and horn. The moment of tenderness lingers, coming to a quiet conclusion. Then, with a rush of strings, the first section of the movement returns. When we reach the deceptive moment of easing, the piano breaks into a pattern of triplets in the new four-time metre. This passage continues longer than the first time before the fragments of lyrical melody appear in the strings, and they are accompanied by delightful chirruping in the woodwind. The tempo accelerates, and with a final brilliant dash the concerto comes to an end.

PIANO CONCERTO NO. 2 IN C MINOR, OP. 18
Duration: approx. 34 minutes

Moderato
Adagio sostenuto – Più animato – Tempo 1
Allegro scherzando

Following the disastrous premiere of his First Symphony in 1897, Rachmaninoff suffered a prolonged period of writer's block. He continued to pursue a career as pianist and conductor, but composed almost nothing until 1900. It was the hypnotherapist Nikolay Dahl who helped him out of this over a period of three months, and Rachmaninoff gradually regained 'cheerfulness of spirit, energy, a desire to work, and confidence in his abilities', as his sister-in-law Sofiya Satina reported.[7] The Second Piano Concerto was the first fruit of this recovery. It is still a matter of debate whether Dahl actually treated Rachmaninoff or merely talked him into rising above his problems. But the encounter was clearly important, and the composer dedicated the concerto to Dahl. It was a great success at its first performance, and it remains (together with the Prelude in C sharp minor) Rachmaninoff's most popular work. It is a powerful example of a brooding, late-Romantic concerto. But it is also a supremely well-crafted work, written with the skill of a musician thoroughly steeped in the methods of the great classical composers.

The concerto opens with the piano playing a series of solemn chords that increase from pianissimo to fortissimo over eight bars. Each time, as the next chord sounds, one note changes by a semitone, upwards for four bars, then downwards for the next four. This builds up the tension, pulling against the bass note that remains a constant, deep C, like a huge bell tolling. Then the piano breaks into forceful arpeggios, and over them the violins and violas enter 'con passione'. The opening of the melody that they play circles around a narrow compass of notes like a chant. Rachmaninoff was brought up to love the music of the Orthodox Church from an early age, and many of his themes have an element of chanting. The upward sigh of the melody's opening pairs of notes is to become a recurrent motif throughout the concerto. Beginning with regular four-bar phrases, the theme becomes less predictable as it unfolds. After the first paragraph, it passes to the cellos, and becomes more fluid and irregular, as if undergoing a moment of searching. Then the full strings join in, regular phrases are restored, and the melody rises to a climax and falls gently away. The piano emerges, plays a brilliant linking passage that culminates in an orchestral climax, and continues with the second theme – another glorious melody, in E flat major.

A few days before the premiere, Rachmaninoff responded to the comments of a friend, Nikita Morozov, who had seen the score, with a sudden panic that he had made a serious mistake in leaving the piano's playing of a real theme until this point: 'You are right . . . in this form the first theme is no more than an introduction . . . when I begin the second theme no fool would believe it to be a second theme. Everybody will think this is the beginning of the concerto. I consider the whole movement ruined . . .'[8] But this ambiguity is just what makes this movement so original in its effect. Rachmaninoff does indeed evoke the tradition in which the orchestra introduces the most important material first, after which the soloist enters. But the fact that the piano does not play the sweeping first theme (and never plays the first part of it) sets up a powerful psychological situation, whose attempts at resolution later on prove extremely powerful.

The second theme consists of a series of strains that rise confidently and then fall away in sighing chromatic phrases, each sigh echoing the opening of the first theme. The first two strains are concluded by the cellos with a yearning phrase. The third time, the piano moves on, at first musing on the sighing phrases, and then returning to the confident first part of the theme and coming to rest with one of those simple turns of phrase that are so characteristic of Rachmaninoff. This new phrase is taken up by oboe and clarinet, echoed in counterpoint by the piano. After a calm conclusion, the piano dashes off delicate arpeggios as a horn plays the cellos' yearning phrase.

A moment of brass chorale marks the transition from the first part of the movement to the development, with a change of key. The melody of this chorale consists of five notes in a pattern that is to play a large part in the music from now on. After a glittering descent in the piano, the orchestra quietly muses on the opening phrase of the first theme. At the end of each phrase, the flutes play a delicate little curling phrase that is derived from the shape of the brass chorale. This shape is taken up and developed by the piano, through a passage of rapid inter-play between piano and orchestra. Below the piano figurations, the violas return to a phrase from the second theme. Against it, flutes and oboes play a lively counterpoint derived from the first theme. The viola line develops momentum, and is joined by the violins. Meanwhile, the piano has transformed the new curling shape into an energetic figure, which it plays in chords with increasing boldness as the strings' melody surges up from below. The greatest climax of the movement builds up. At its height, the string melody draws in the curling shape, and a final crescendo brings in the magnificent return of the first theme.

As before, it is the strings that play it, not the piano. Against it, the piano plays the energetic figure that has developed from the brass chorale, now marked 'alla marcia' ('like a march'). This is a moment of splendid synthesis. And the resolution is complete when, as the first paragraph of the theme falls away, the piano is finally allowed to take up its continuation as a solo. This time, the melancholy falling phrases of the ending lead straight into the second theme, now quietly on solo horn over shimmering strings. From the end of the theme emerge low clarinet and bassoon, playing the curling shape from the development. This moves up through the woodwind, and is taken up by the piano, and developed into a meditative passage with fragments of the second theme in the orchestra. At the end of this rhapsodic moment, a reiterated rhythmic pattern is set up in strings and piano. The cellos play yearning phrases, like those with which they punctuated the second theme when it first appeared. The rippling of the piano gradually becomes more assertive, the pace accelerates, and the energy builds up. Suddenly, with an emphatic final cadence, the movement is over.

The slow movement is in E major, very remote from the C minor of the first movement – Rachmaninoff was probably paying homage to Beethoven, whose Third Piano Concerto in C minor also has a slow movement in E major. Rachmaninoff, unlike Beethoven, softens the contrast by starting the slow movement with a linking introduction: muted strings begin with a chord of C minor, and by a series of harmonic shifts arrive in E major. In doing this, Rachmaninoff was orchestrating a custom that, in the early twentieth century, was still common in piano recitals. Pianists would often play an improvised passage moving from the key of one piece to the next (and it is quite possible that a pianist in Beethoven's day might have done the same thing in his C minor Concerto).

As the orchestra reaches E major, the piano enters with calm arpeggios over a sustained E in the bass. The arpeggios outline a series of chords within which a chromatic scale gently falls, semitone by semitone, over an unchanging bass note. This subtly refers back to the chords that opened the concerto. But, at least in order of composition, the reference is the other way round, because this introduction is lifted from an earlier Romance for piano, six hands. It was an inspired act of recycling.

There seem to be four notes per beat, creating a slow three-time. But as the piano repeats this four-bar passage, a solo flute enters with a melody over it. It is at this point that we realize the piano's pattern is syncopated: there are three notes per beat, not four. This creates a moment of beautiful, floating uncertainty, until the flute melody makes the rhythm clear. The theme seems a natural successor to the themes of the first movement, and is related to them in subtle ways. It begins with a rising phrase and incorporates a series of two-note sighs, like the second theme from the first movement, and continues with a more chant-like character. What starts as a flute melody soon passes, in mid-phrase, to clarinet, just before the melody becomes chant-like – an unexpected and evocative effect. Then the syncopated arpeggio accompaniment passes to clarinets and pizzicato violins, and the piano, with the utmost simplicity, plays the melody.

As it winds to an end, the melody takes a turn to a new key, B major, and the muted violins play the beginning of the melody. Then the piano develops a phrase from it into an extended, rhapsodic passage. Three times it builds to a climax, moving through new keys. At the third climax the piano bursts into arpeggios at a faster tempo, beneath which fragments of the opening theme from the first movement are heard in violins and oboe. Another climax is reached, and a moment of brilliant cadenza. The tolling of the opening bars of the concerto is evoked: over four bars, the bass descends by semitones, and then, with a leap, down to a deep, fortissimo B.

A flurry of notes condenses into a trill, and the piano reprises the syncopated arpeggio pattern. Muted violins play the whole of the theme (having previously been cut off after the first phrase). The ending is extended into a sublime farewell, the violins clinging on to their final phrases, the piano playing chords that contain a descending melodic shape (a version of the descending scale that first occurred in the opening chords of the concerto), and woodwind playing staccato, bell-like chords, drawn from the arpeggios that began the movement. So the Adagio ends with a satisfying sense of everything being drawn together.

The finale opens with another bridge, this time from the E major of the Adagio back to the home key of C minor. The movement has the character of a light-footed march. The melodic fragment, passing between upper and lower strings, is taken from the 'curling' shape that dominated the middle of the first movement. It begins quietly and expectantly, and builds up to a fortissimo complete with cymbals and bass drum. The piano enters with another moment of brilliant cadenza, and settles into the first real theme, still in the fast march tempo and deco-rated with elaborate triplet figuration. The latter part of the theme incorporates a three-note motif of rising sighs. The theme comes to an emphatic close with block chords, and the piano, in a grand linking passage, calms the mood to arrive at the second theme. This is a lyrical melody on violas and oboe, whose first half is formed of phrases that fall over an unchanging bass note – this makes it sound like a cousin of the second theme in the first movement. The second half rises to a climax, and falls away. The piano then takes up the theme, extending its second half on to a later and more emphatic climax, and a more lingering falling away.

This leads into a mysterious passage at a much slower tempo, over a sustained bass note, with a timpani roll and touches of cymbals, like the ghost of the march with which the move-ment began. This is the beginning of the development section. The piano weaves a persistent pattern in triplet rhythm – a slowed-down version of the figuration that decorated the piano's first theme in this movement. There is a sudden change back to the fast march tempo. The piano revisits the first theme, now with double octaves and emphatic chords in dotted rhythms. The pace increases, with the piano chords and octaves marked 'leggiero' ('lightly' – very difficult to achieve), and then there is a further increase to presto. The violins begin a moment of quiet, agitated fugue. But this soon loosens into a more brilliant passage, with the theme continually reappearing in different parts of the orchestra.

Eventually, this comes together in a climax, and we find ourselves back with the second theme, without having obviously reprised the first theme. The end of the second theme leads on, as before, to the mysterious slow march, with the piano's winding triplet pattern. Out of this emerges the beginning of the end. Clarinets and bassoons revisit the first theme, in quiet and urgent staccato, and with the offbeat sighing motif. The piano enters, and the tension begins to mount. Under the brilliant piano figurations, and continuing staccato phrases in the woodwind, the cellos begin to sing. At first their melody seems merely in character with the other lyrical melodies of the concerto, but soon a persistent phrase of three notes, falling chro-matically, links it directly to one of the main motifs. The music builds up to a great climax, at which the piano once more bursts out into an exuberant moment of brilliant cadenza. There is a silent pause, and the great second theme comes striding in fortissimo, on full strings, with the piano playing forceful patterns of chords. There is a final increase in pace, and a last dash incorporating the triplet figuration and the offbeat sighing motif of the first theme. With the clashing of cymbals and beating of the bass drum, the concerto comes to an exuberant close.

PIANO CONCERTO NO. 3 IN D MINOR, OP. 30
Duration (uncut): approx. 43 minutes

Allegro ma non tanto
Intermezzo: Adagio
Finale: Alla breve

By the time he started work on his Third Piano Concerto in the summer of 1909, Rachmaninoff was married to his cousin, Natalia Satina, and they had settled happily at Ivanovka, the one surviving Rachmaninoff estate. He composed it because he had agreed to tour the United

States for three months, and what he needed was a new work that would show off both his composing and his performing skills to the greatest effect. It was his most difficult and taxing concerto so far, and Rachmaninoff took a dummy keyboard with him on the transatlantic voyage, so that he could keep his fingers in training for it. The most important of his performances in America was with the New York Philharmonic under the great Gustav Mahler. The reception by public and critics was politely enthusiastic, though the concerto did not strike audiences as forcefully as No. 2 had. It was not until the young Vladimir Horowitz took up the work in the late 1920s that it was fully accepted as one of Rachmaninoff's finest works.

Muted strings, clarinet, and bassoon begin with two quiet bars, which have a similar effect to the opening bars of Mendelssohn's Violin Concerto. They seem like nothing more than a brief introduction, but their gently pulsating dotted rhythm, marked out by the timpani, will prove important throughout the concerto. The piano enters unassumingly, playing a chant-like melody that winds to a little climax and falls away. Pianists and conductors have often been reluctant to believe that Rachmaninoff meant this to sound quite as simple as it looks, and have attempted to increase its significance by drawing it out mournfully. But Rachmaninoff's own recording shows that he really did mean it to be simple and understated. Horn and violas (still muted) take up the theme, while the piano breaks into a counterpoint of semiquavers, increasing the pace a little. When the melody has wound to its conclusion, the piano's figurations come to dominate, the pace and the energy building until they arrive at a moment of brilliant cadenza. This soon collapses, and the strings and woodwind take up the opening theme with renewed warmth, the warmth emphasized by the fact that the strings have now removed their mutes. They build as if to introduce a lyrical second theme. But the second theme, when it comes, begins at first with nervous playfulness, the strings and piano answering each other (there has been a subtle anticipation of this opening phrase in the wind about a minute earlier, though it is easy to miss). The piano eventually continues with a lyrical version of the new theme, developing it at length. There are touching comments along the way from solo wind and violins, and the piano builds to a passionate climax. It falls gently away, and then once again turns playful. Brilliant figuration is momentarily interrupted by a reminder of the piano's recent lyrical solo (Rachmaninoff cuts this little passage in his recording), before bringing the first section of the movement to an end.

We are back at the opening, with the piano reverting to the simple chant-like first theme in D minor. But soon it takes a different direction with new keys. The piano embarks on more florid passages, beneath which cellos and bassoon play phrases with the dotted rhythm of the opening bars, and above which the woodwind chatter. As often in Rachmaninoff, these elements co-exist as equals, without any clear indication of who is accompanying whom. The piano breaks into cross-rhythms, and the music begins to build once again. This time piano and orchestra together rise to a frenetic climax, from which the energy gradually ebbs away. The piano emerges from this into a solo cadenza. (Rachmaninoff wrote two versions of this cadenza, one longer than the other. He played the shorter version, and most pianists have followed his example.) As it builds in power, the opening chant theme is elaborated with massive chords, and another huge climax is reached. This dissolves into rippling arpeggios, over which solo flute, oboe, clarinet, and horn play reminiscences of the opening theme. But the solo cadenza is not finished yet. It is the piano's turn to reminisce, quoting the lyrical second theme. This too dissolves, into rapid trills, and the opening dotted rhythms are recalled.

With a sudden change the piano turns to the home key of D minor, and we find ourselves back at the opening, with the two bars of dotted-note introduction, and the theme played simply by the piano. As the melody comes to an end, we expect the violas to take it up as before. But instead a trumpet plays the opening phrase of the second theme as a quiet fanfare. Over repetitions of this fanfare, the piano elaborates delicately. The music unwinds, as the fanfare combines with the opening dotted rhythm, and with a final quirky reminiscence of the second theme, the movement comes to an end.

Rachmaninoff calls the second movement an Intermezzo, perhaps because it leads into the finale without a break. But it is more substantial than that title might imply. The principal theme, played first by the orchestra, is deeply melancholy, full of falling phrases and sliding chromatic harmonies, and hovering between D minor (the key of the first movement) and A major. It evokes memories of Tchaikovsky's *Eugene Onegin*, particularly in its haunting wood-wind writing. The violin line is unable to settle to a consistent level of volume, continually surging to *mf* and then back to *p*, like someone trying to hold back tears as they speak. After a final outburst and descent, the piano enters, breaking passionately into F sharp minor, and then settling calmly to take up the principal theme in D flat major. This is remote from the key in which the movement started, and the harmonies have lost their melancholy uncertainty. It is as if Rachmaninoff has for a moment found peace in an unlikely place. But the moment is short-lived. The orchestra reintroduces the tinge of melancholy, and the piano breaks out into an impassioned continuation of the theme. This is the first of three outbursts.

Twice the melancholy orchestra intervenes, and the piano is calmed. During the second of these paragraphs, the orchestra remembers the opening theme from the first movement (Rachmaninoff cuts this passage in his recording, probably to allow the side-change to occur at a musically reasonable point). The third paragraph builds up and extends, searching through new keys, until it once again reaches the stability of D flat major, though now in a sonorous fortissimo. The music calms again, the pace increases, the piano texture lightens, and we enter a scherzo-like passage, with playful phrases exchanged between piano and woodwind. As the piano develops a virtuoso passage of rapid repeated notes and scales, the woodwind again remember the chant that opened the first movement. Eventually this leads in to a reprise of the opening theme on the oboe, and woodwind and strings return to the deep melancholy with which they began the movement (though not the original key). The music winds to a quiet conclusion. The piano abruptly enters, builds rapidly to a brief and forceful cadenza. With two chords, we enter the finale, back in D minor.

The finale is marked 'alla breve', which is a traditional way of indicating two large beats in a bar, rather than four small ones. In this movement, the result is music that is full of rapid, kaleidoscopic detail, but with harmonies that often move quite slowly. The opening theme has the clangour of church bells, and is reminiscent of Rimsky-Korsakov's *Russian Easter Festival Overture*. It also has a clear relationship to the opening of the first movement, both in its rhythms and in its stately procession of harmonies. After this theme has passed back and forth between piano and orchestra, it eventually gives way to a second theme. This at first has a brusque, dogged character, with very emphatic rhythms over an unchanging bass note. This is subtly related in its melodic shape to the second theme from the first movement. In the original score, this soon blossoms into a lyrical melody. But Rachmaninoff himself habitually cut this blossoming, in order to save it for later in the movement.

This is followed by a tutti in which the orchestra returns to the clangorous opening material. It quietens, with sombre dotted rhythms (as at the opening of the concerto). Into this moment of calm the piano leaps, like a dancer from the wings. The whole of the section that follows has a playful, balletic feel, but all the pirouettes and jumps are, at heart, elaborations of the rhythms and shapes from the two themes of the first movement, like a miniature set of variations (this is another passage that Rachmaninoff always shortened in performance). As the energy ebbs away, the first theme from the first movement enters in the violas. The piano is drawn into the mood of nostalgia, and it evokes the second theme from the first movement. On reaching a powerful climax, the piano breaks once again into rapid figurations, as the violins quietly continue nostalgically singing in the rhythm of the opening bars, creating, together with the piano, a sense of wistfully remembered joy that is utterly characteristic of Rachmaninoff.

Eventually the delicate piano figuration settles, and there is a moment of peace. The violins return to the original alla breve tempo, at first pianissimo and then building up to a clangorous reprise of the opening dialogue between piano and orchestra, with new changes of direction. As before, this is followed by the brusque second theme, and the piano develops a lyrical continuation (if Rachmaninoff's earlier cut has been observed, this is the first time this has happened). Just as it seems to be heading for a climax, it is interrupted by yet brusquer phrases from the strings. These too build up quickly, arriving at a fortissimo climax, and a brief but dramatic cadenza. The piano steps out with a march-like version of the brusque theme, from which orchestra and piano together build a splendid, lyrical peroration, accelerating in the final pages to a brilliant finish.

RHAPSODY ON A THEME OF PAGANINI, OP. 43
Duration: approx. 23 minutes

This is the most celebrated of the works from Rachmaninoff's years of self-imposed exile in the United States. He composed it over a period of six weeks during the summer of 1934, at his villa on the shore of Lake Lucerne. He himself performed the premiere, with the Philadelphia Orchestra conducted by Leopold Stokowski, on 7 November that year, and they recorded it together on 24 December.

The theme is taken from the twenty-fourth and last of Paganini's Caprices for solo violin. Paganini's piece itself consists of a set of variations on this theme, and many subsequent composers have written their own sets of variations on it, notably Liszt and Brahms. The theme is like a latter-day equivalent of *La Follia*, the traditional theme and chord sequence on which countless baroque composers wrote variations (Rachmaninoff himself wrote variations for solo piano on Corelli's version). Like *La Follia*, Paganini's theme is a simple formula with a clear chord sequence that provides endless possibilities.

Rachmaninoff's Rhapsody is a set of variations on the theme, scored for an orchestra that includes trombones and tuba, two harps, side drum, bass drum, and glockenspiel. But Rachmaninoff uses his forces delicately, with only occasional moments of a full tutti. It is a fascinating work, full of mercurial piano writing, darkened from time to time with a demonic edge. He had attempted such a balance of characteristics in the finale of his Fourth Piano Concerto in 1926, without being able to make much of them. But these elements must have lain dormant, maturing in his mind until they were ready to be transformed into this masterpiece.

The theme is short, consisting of two strains, each of which is repeated. Most of the twenty-four variations run into each other without a break, so the listener perceives the arrival of a new variation by the change of character. The theme itself is preceded by an introduction that wittily pays homage to the finale of Beethoven's 'Eroica' Symphony (and of the 'Eroica' variations, Opus 35, for solo piano). After a vigorous opening flourish, derived from a recurrent semiquaver turn of phrase in Paganini's theme, the orchestra quietly plays a skeleton of the theme, like the unadorned bass line that begins Beethoven's variations – Rachmaninoff labels this 'Var. 1 (Precedente)'. Side drum and glockenspiel add a touch of piquancy to the bare bones, and there is a hint of sinister mockery in the interjections of the low clarinets and bassoon. Paganini's theme itself is (appropriately) then played by the violins, the piano merely punctuating. The piano takes up Variation 2, at first adding cheeky grace notes to the theme, then breaking into delicate semiquaver arpeggios. The semiquaver pattern returns to the violins and flute in Variation 3, while the piano plays a counterpoint in longer notes that introduces a melancholy element – a typical Rachmaninoff combination of chattering and wistful.

Variation 4 increases the pace a little, with the semiquaver pattern returning to the piano. Once again, wistful touches enter the second half, with a counterpoint in the cor anglais, and sweeping intervals in the violins. The rhythm tightens for Variation 5, giving a hint of military briskness, with the cadences snappily marked. The piano attempts to continue this mood into Variation 6. But each strain dissolves, as if its mind is really on other things. There are touches of dark harmony, and the theme is slowed down in the cor anglais. It seems natural, therefore, that the next variation, Variation 7, should be altogether more solemn. The theme, at a slower pace, moves to the bass, in bassoon and pizzicato cellos. The piano plays over it a simple chorale, whose first phrase is that of the *Dies Irae*, the medieval chant evoking the Last Judgment. Fragments of this chant recur in Rachmaninoff's Rhapsody, providing an oblique reference to the myth that Paganini owed his virtuoso brilliance to demonic powers. The violins from time to time interject a memory of the semiquaver flourish from the theme.

Variation 8 returns to the original tempo, with a bold version of the theme that becomes more flamboyant in the second half. In Variation 9 the violins and violas tap the strings with the wood of the bow, and two-against-three patterns build energetically in the second half. Variation 10 begins as a march, with falling chromatic phrases in the clarinet that recall its interventions during the introduction that preceded the theme. In longer notes, the piano plays against this the *Dies Irae*, now in stark octaves. As the music builds up, the march metre is disrupted by bars of three-time, and the variation ends with delicate swirling patterns passing from piano and strings to woodwind, and touches of glockenspiel, while fragments of the *Dies Irae* are heard quietly in trumpet and trombone, and then horn and tuba. There is a brief silence after this variation (the first pause since the beginning).

Variation 11 is like a cadenza in which the piano meditates on each phrase of the theme. As flute and cor anglais take up a melancholy version of the melody, the piano erupts in a delicate shower of figurations. Variation 12 returns to a consistent pace, 'Tempo di minuetto'. This evokes a nostalgic image of a formal ballroom, the slowly sweeping lines of the orchestra contrasted with the piano's clipped rhythms (one could imagine a pre-revolutionary scene in which Russian men in military uniform dance with women in elegant long dresses). Variation 13 is still in three-time, but at a faster tempo, as if some dashing ballet dancer has entered the room. Each phrase played by the strings ends with a syncopated delay of the last note, as if timed for a dancer's leap. Variation 14 bursts into F major but with a surge of energy, as if the whole corps de ballet is dancing. The fanfare-like phrases in woodwind and violins are marked 'quasi tromba' ('like a trumpet'), and the strutting three-time has almost the feel of a fandango. The piano is silent for the first half of this variation, joining in (with the actual trumpets) in the second half. The pace increases for Variation 15, which is still in F major, and marked 'scherzando'. The piano plays a glittering perpetuum mobile, the orchestra entering delicately towards the end. After a final flourish, the solo piano ends with a pause on a simple chord.

There follows a series of three variations at a slower pace, and in keys that are remote from the home key of A minor. Some commentators liken this to the slow movement of a concerto. But it is more akin to the extended slow variation which, in the finale of Beethoven's 'Eroica' Symphony, creates the emotional climax (Elgar does much the same thing with 'Nimrod' in his 'Enigma' Variations). Variation 16 is delicate, with a tiptoeing rhythm on muted strings that slips into B flat minor – the variations are getting further and further away from the home key. The theme passes from oboe to cor anglais, then becomes a duet between solo violin and horn. The mystery deepens in Variation 17, which is still in B flat minor. The theme has almost vanished, reduced to simple, yearning leaps in woodwind and brass, while the piano maintains a dark, creeping pattern, as if searching. Eventually, the search results in another shift of key, and the music moves out of the darkness to the warmth of D flat major (harmonically, this is as far as one can get from the home key of D minor). What emerges in Variation 18 is one of Rachmaninoff's most sublime inspirations. As with so many great inspirations, it is based on the simplest of ideas: he turns the reiterated phrase of the theme upside down. The second half of the melody is allowed free rein, expanding upwards through a beautiful series of harmonies until it falls gently back. The whole of the varied theme is played first by the piano, unaccompanied. Rachmaninoff's own recorded performance is an object lesson in refined simplicity, creating a moment of relaxed and unforced eloquence, rather than the inflated, high-Romantic utterance that it often became in the hands of later pianists. The strings take up the theme, building to a climax while the piano plays rich chords. The melody is reluctant to finish, extending onwards until the solo piano draws it to a simple conclusion.

Variation 19 breaks the mood, and the key, with a pizzicato chord. This is the beginning of the final sequence, a scherzo-like variation back in the home key of A minor, with rapid arpeggios in triplet rhythm in the piano, marked 'quasi pizzicato' – in other words, very light and detached. In Variation 20 the triplet rhythm breaks into even more rapid semiquavers in the violins. Against them, the piano plays sharply defined dotted rhythms (rather as the piano added clipped rhythms to the minuet of Variation 12). Variation 21, even faster, has the piano playing a complex triplet pattern with syncopations. Variation 22, yet faster, is in a rapid march rhythm, beginning quietly and expectantly. There are drumbeats in the timpani, imitation drumbeats in the strings. In this context, even the familiar little flurry of semiquavers from the theme sounds like a flourish of drums. The music gradually builds, over an unchanging bass note (the key note, A). The piano begins to struggle against it, in an attempt to develop a melody and to break out of the restricted harmony. Eventually a climax is reached, and the music suddenly breaks away to a new key, a sweeping melody begins to develop in the strings, against swirling patterns in the piano. Energetic phrases from the theme build the tension, and at a great climax the piano breaks into thundering double octaves. We seem to be starting a mighty cadenza.

But, with a sudden change of mind, the piano turns cheeky, playing the opening phrase in a remote key. This is Variation 23. The orchestra fiercely brings the piano back to A minor. A further mighty build-up follows, culminating in another burst of cadenza. This ends quietly and delicately, at the top of the keyboard, and then the piano launches into Variation 24. This begins with a fearsomely challenging pattern of triplets with syncopations, and rapid leaps. Rachmaninoff himself was nervous of this passage, until his fellow pianist Benno Moiseiwitsch suggested, at a dinner party during which Rachmaninoff was to give the guests a preview of the variations, that he should take a small glass of crème de menthe to make the passage easier. This seemed to do the trick, and Rachmaninoff (otherwise a teetotaller) regularly followed this advice, and labelled this passage in Moiseiwitsch's copy of the score, 'The Crème De Menthe Variation'.[9] It builds to a final climax, at which the brass intone the *Dies Irae*. The piano cascades to an exciting finish. But its last word is a cheeky aside, like a playful farewell gesture to the audience as a brilliant dancer leaves the stage.

SYMPHONIC DANCES, OP. 45
Duration: approx. 34 minutes

Non allegro
Andante con moto (tempo di valse)
Lento assai – Allegro vivace – Lento assai – Allegro vivace

After the success of the Rhapsody on a Theme of Paganini, Rachmaninoff felt confident enough to attempt his Third Symphony, after a gap of nearly thirty years since the Second Symphony. But when No. 3 was premiered in Philadelphia in November 1936, it failed to repeat the success of the Rhapsody. Rachmaninoff himself had faith in it, and conducted a recording in 1939. It is most successful when Rachmaninoff is not trying to shed his naturally Romantic character. But elsewhere the 'harder edge', which he used so successfully in the Rhapsody, seems rather lost without the brilliance of the piano writing, and there is evidence of a struggle to construct a large-scale symphony somewhat against character.

Four years after the unsuccessful premiere of the Third Symphony, Rachmaninoff and his wife spent the summer of 1940 on a rented seventeen-acre estate on Long Island, having been prevented by war from undertaking their usual trip to Switzerland. It was here that Rachmaninoff had a sudden burst of creative energy, and composed his last work, the Symphonic Dances. It was the only major score that he composed entirely in the United States. Freed from the daunting task of constructing a massive symphonic structure, as in the Third Symphony, the Symphonic Dances achieve a balance between Rachmaninoff's traditional, Romantic style and a leaner, more 'modern' palette, much as the Rhapsody had done. The work has never achieved the popular success of the Rhapsody, but it is impressive nevertheless. Eugene Ormandy, who conducted the premiere with the Philadelphia Orchestra in January 1942, reported in a radio interview that, at the last rehearsal, Rachmaninoff addressed the orchestra. He said that, since the death of his great idol, the bass Feodor Chaliapin, who had always been in his mind when he composed, now 'everything I write is with the Philadelphia sound in my ears. Therefore may I be permitted to dedicate my latest, and I think my best, composition to my beloved Philadelphia Orchestra and my friend' (that is, Ormandy).[10]

Rachmaninoff originally called the work Fantastic Dances and gave the movements headings: 'Noon', 'Twilight', and 'Midnight'. But eventually he changed the title to Symphonic

Dances and abandoned the individual headings. He also discussed with the choreographer Mikhail Fokine the idea of a ballet to the Symphonic Dances (Fokine had earlier created a ballet on the Rhapsody), but Fokine died in 1942 before the project could be completed. There is no explicit evidence of any sort of extra-musical programme behind the work. But there are some clues in the music itself. There are quotes from a number of his earlier works scattered throughout. The *Dies Irae*, which featured prominently in the Rhapsody, here begins as a subtle allusion, becoming a powerful force in the finale, and eventually being transformed, and overcome. Near the end of the finale, Rachmaninoff writes in the score, 'Alliluyah', and at the end of the manuscript he writes, 'I thank Thee, Lord'. The allusion to Christian belief in Christ's triumph over death is inescapable.

The published score heads the first movement 'Non allegro', an instruction that might seem curiously at odds with the vigorous character of the music. Some have taken it to be a misprint for simple Allegro. But there exists a private, unpublished recording of excerpts from the Symphonic Dances played on the piano by Rachmaninoff, possibly made when he played them to Ormandy before the premiere (the recording is in the Ormandy Archive at the University of Pennsylvania). According to pianist Stephen Kovacevich, who has listened to the recording, in Rachmaninoff's performance 'the precautionary tempo marking "non-allegro" . . . is adhered to'.[11]

A few delicate bars introduce one of the main motifs, a three-note falling pattern. A series of savage chords breaks in, and over a fierce stamping rhythm in the strings the three-note fall becomes the first main theme, in trumpet and woodwind, then in the violins. This is developed at length, with a punchy persistence that was occasionally glimpsed in the Rhapsody on a Theme of Paganini, but is carried to a new level of boldness here. It sounds more like Prokofiev than the familiar Rachmaninoff, with even an occasional hint of Stravinsky's *Rite of Spring*. Particularly striking in Rachmaninoff is the use of his beloved piano as an orchestral percussion instrument.

Eventually, the fierce dance recedes and we enter the central section of the movement. Oboe and clarinet convert the three-note motif to a pastoral meditation. Beneath it enters a flowing, almost chant-like melody, full of the three-note motif gently rising and falling. It is played by an instrument one would not have expected in Rachmaninoff, the alto saxophone. The simple accompaniment of wind instruments adds to the impression of a pastoral episode. The melody is taken up by the violins, accompanied by piano and harp, developing a more passionate sweep. From time to time there are touches of the old, melancholy Rachmaninoff harmonies, made all the more poignant for their sparseness. The melody winds to its end, and there is a moment of darkness. Out of it the rhythms and shapes of the opening dance begin to emerge. This passage of transition is one of the most compelling in the movement. The melodic shape taken from the savage opening chords develops a life of its own. The music builds with great force (again sounding quite like Prokofiev), until, at the climax, the stamping dance resumes. At the end, the energy again ebbs away, and there is a moment of radiance. Glockenspiel, piano, and harp create a texture reminiscent of the musical clock from Kodály's *Háry János*, beneath which the strings sing the end of the melody from the middle section, now in a simple C major. The opening notes are the same shape as the *Dies Irae*, which Rachmaninoff quotes in earlier works (prominently in the Rhapsody). Here, the melody sounds unthreatening in C major, but it is to take on its familiar form in the finale.

The second movement is a valse triste. It begins with sinister muted trumpet calls that could have stepped out of Dukas's *The Sorcerer's Apprentice*, and continues with an anxious violin solo. Once the waltz gets under way, it too strongly evokes memories: Tchaikovsky in the 'Valse mélancholique' from his Third Suite, Ravel in *La Valse* and *Valses nobles et sentimentales*, as well as Sibelius in his *Valse Triste*. The overall effect is haunting and passionately nostalgic. Renewed trumpet calls mark the entry into the middle section. Here the phrases are more fragmented, the harmonies uncertain. The trumpet calls, more insistent and threatening, again mark the transition to the reprise. This soon rises to a more impassioned climax than before. The pace accelerates, and it seems that we might be heading for a catastrophe, as in Ravel's *La Valse*. But the headlong rush is pulled back, elegance is restored, and the dance ends almost flirtatiously.

Hints of the *Dies Irae* from the first movement, and suggestions of the demonic from the second, come into the open in the finale. Rachmaninoff had recently performed Liszt's *Totentanz* for piano and orchestra, a dazzling and wild set of variations on the *Dies Irae*. What Rachmaninoff achieves in this movement is far more subtle. There is a brief slow introduction, with mysterious, drooping chromatic harmonies which relate to harmonic patterns that have occurred in both the earlier movements. The music breaks into agitated scuffling (again like *The Sorcerer's Apprentice*), and a bell strikes midnight. The demonic dance gets going, its melody derived from the mysterious chords that began the movement. Hidden in this melody is the shape of the *Dies Irae*. Soon this becomes more obvious as it is marked out by high piccolo, flute, and xylophone, and, a little later, by the violas. By now, the whole dance seems infected by the *Dies Irae*.

This opening section of the dance comes to a climax. Then the mysterious opening chords return. This time they are developed further, with rushing swirls in the woodwind and glissandi in the strings, and fragments of the *Dies Irae* interwoven. There is a pause, and a moment of darkness, with low bass clarinet and tremolando strings. Out of this emerges an extended passage dominated by the strings, which is full of striving upward and sighing downward phrases. It ends with a moment of warm resolution, before the dance takes off again. This time it rises to a great climax of force and energy, in the middle of which the *Dies Irae* is heard intoned by the horns. As the climax falls away, there is a drum roll, and the music shifts to a steadier tempo. The dance melody derived from the *Dies Irae* takes on a more determined mood, with syncopated accents that seem to have thrown off the demonic elements. As the trumpets delicately join the dance, Rachmaninoff writes 'Alliluya' over the score. The trumpets are quoting the setting of the word 'Alliluya' from Rachmaninoff's All Night Vigil of 1915. The music builds to a huge climax. And with a last gesture, in which he seems to banish all the forces of darkness, Rachmaninoff utters his final word as a composer.

SYMPHONY NO. 2 IN E MINOR, OP. 27
Duration: approx. 54 minutes (without 1st movement repeat)

Largo – Allegro moderato
Allegro molto
Adagio
Allegro vivace

Rachmaninoff's First Symphony was a dismal failure at its premiere in St Petersburg in 1897. He left the score behind when he emigrated to the United States in 1917, and it was only after his death that it was reconstructed from a two-piano score and surviving parts. Rachmaninoff wrote, 'It has some good music, but it also has much that is weak, childish, strained and bombastic.'[12] On the other hand, the composer Robert Simpson went so far as to admire it for 'achieving a genuinely tragic and heroic expression that stands far above the pathos of his later music.'[13]

Of Rachmaninoff's three symphonies, it is the Second Symphony that has firmly established itself in the repertoire. Rachmaninoff spent three years from 1906 to 1909 living in Dresden, having resigned from his conducting post in Moscow in order to concentrate on composition. It was during this period that he completed his Second Symphony, finishing a rough draft in 1906, and then working on it over the summer of 1907 back at his estate, Ivanovka. Rachmaninoff himself conducted the premiere in St Petersburg in January 1908, and, unlike the First Symphony, it was enthusiastically received. It is very long, and was for many years shortened by making cuts. Today, it is usually performed complete, though the repeat of the first section is often (wisely) omitted. Rachmaninoff dedicated the symphony to the composer Sergei Taneyev, who had been one of his teachers in Moscow.

The symphony opens with a magnificently gloomy introduction that rises and falls in a great arch. In mood, it recalls the tragic opening of Tchaikovsky's *Francesca da Rimini*, though Rachmaninoff's characteristic harmonies supply an extra poignancy. A gently rising and falling line, beginning in the cellos and basses, provides material for the whole introduction, and, in various transformations, for the entire symphony. The cor anglais rounds off the introduction with a plaintive solo. Then the Allegro opens with an expansive theme on the violins, based on the same rising and falling shape as the opening of the introduction. An energetic passage leads on to the second theme. This begins as a demure exchange between woodwind and strings, but then, like the first theme, it blossoms into an extended melody that rises and then falls. A second time it rises higher and more intensely than before, and then falls away to conclude the first section of the movement.

Now (after the repeat, if it is observed), Rachmaninoff develops these rising and falling lines. First there is a duet between violin solo and cor anglais. Then the pace increases a little, and the rising and falling shape becomes agitated. The main melody moves from clarinet to violas, and a syncopated counterpoint increases the agitation. It seems that the music is building up. But instead, it retreats once more to the darkness of the introduction. Violas and timpani beat out an ominous rhythm. It is only then that the movement begins to move towards a climax, with an almost Brucknerian sense of slow inevitability.

Out of the aftermath of the climax, with trumpet calls still ringing, emerges the reprise of the first Allegro theme on the violins. But, instead of proceeding as before, the melody builds up quickly, soon arrives at the energetic continuation, and then on to a climax more intense than the preceding one. The music does not immediately recover from this turn of events. The climax recedes to deep gloom and we re-enter the mood of the introduction, with dark, threatening chords, and a reminiscence of the cor anglais solo. Finally, the darkness lifts, and we continue the reprise with the second theme, which rises more expansively than before and falls away. Suddenly, the faster tempo returns, and the violas again beat out their ominous rhythm. The movement, which has spent so much of its time in leisurely expansion, ends with a coda of intense agitation.

The second movement is a big-boned scherzo. The strings set up the rhythm of a gallop, over which the horns play the fanfare-like principal theme. The minor key gives the joyful mood an edge of determination, but the occasional intervention of the glockenspiel brings a touch of brightness. The pace eases for a second theme on the violins, another lyrical, rising and falling line related to those of the first movement. As it reaches its height, it gives way to a trotting rhythm in the woodwind, heard as if in the distance. After a time, this suddenly switches back to the gallop of the opening, and the horns repeat their call. This time the gallop ebbs away to a quiet conclusion.

The middle section begins with a crash, and continues, surprisingly, with a rapid fugue. The pattern of the fugue subject is taken from that of the horn call, speeded up and given a regular rhythm. This is not, of course, going to be an academic, worked-out fugue. Like Tchaikovsky, Rachmaninoff uses it to inject extra energy. Soon the combining of separate voices is abandoned, and it becomes more of a perpetuum mobile, rising to a fortissimo, then down to a scampering pianissimo. Against it, the brass quietly play a march derived from the horn call. Then there is a build-up, the pace accelerates, and breaks back into the opening gallop.

The reprise proceeds through the second theme, the trotting passage, and back to the gallop. As the gallop resumes, the trumpets and trombones quietly intone a slower version of the horn-call shape. This has an ominous effect, and the melodic line in this form shows a similarity to the medieval death chant, *Dies Irae*, which Rachmaninoff often quotes in other works. (Some writers suggest that Rachmaninoff derived not only this moment, but every occurrence of similar shapes in the symphony, from the *Dies Irae*. But if so, it is a private reference that has little impact on the listener.) As the energy ebbs away for the last time, the brass twice play a fragment of chorale, this time derived from the very opening of the symphony. The scherzo ends with the ghostly sound of the gallop disappearing into the distance.

The slow movement begins with a sequence of four rising phrases in A major in the violins that sound like an ending, not a beginning. This proves to be a refrain that recurs throughout the movement. A solo clarinet plays a slow, meandering melody, which at first hovers around a narrow compass of notes, only gradually rising higher, and then, even more gradually, falling back. Like many of Rachmaninoff's themes, it has a distinct echo of religious chant, or rather the nostalgic reminiscence of chant, and it is one of the longest themes he ever wrote (and one of the longest clarinet solos in the history of orchestral music). Its beauty is enhanced by the subtle counterpoint of murmuring, syncopated triplets in the violins, the bassoons that accompany it along part of the way, and the succession of harmonies, which several times seem about to come to rest, and instead move off again. The violins continue the melody as the clarinet finishes, and then round it off with the refrain from the beginning of the movement.

Dark brass chords and a surge of energy draw us into the central part of the movement. The murmuring triplets have broken up into semiquavers, in rising and falling patterns familiar from the opening of the symphony. Cor anglais and oboe reiterate hypnotically a melancholy little phrase. The strings develop this into a continuous line, which very slowly and inexorably builds to a climax, capped by the refrain from the beginning of the movement. This descends to a pause. The refrain passes from horn to solo violin, cor anglais, flute, oboe, seeking its way back to the home key. It is the clarinet that finds it, playing the refrain in A major as the violins originally did. Then the violins take up the long melody first played by the clarinet. This time it is accompanied throughout its journey, most touchingly, by fragments of the refrain, which originally took no part in it. As the theme winds to a conclusion, it reaches a quiet, high climax, almost Mahlerian in its ecstatic serenity, before coming gently to rest.

The opening of the finale has a brilliant, festive air, with a thrusting upbeat like that of Richard Strauss's *Don Juan*. The theme is full of rapid rising and falling phrases, the joyful outcome of the gloomy phrases with which the symphony began. After the first strain of the theme, the mood darkens as the music slips into a minor key, and a sombre march starts up. But the impetus of the opening theme cannot be restrained for long, and soon it is back. This time, the theme ends in an explosive chord, erupting into a new key. The strings are instantly transformed into singers, and we enter the second theme. The melody has features in common with the lyrical second theme in the first movement, but it is on a much bigger scale. It begins over an organ-like sustained bass note (as so often in Rachmaninoff), and then extends far and wide, both in the range of the melody and in its harmonies. By the time it comes to rest, a hundred bars have gone by. This is the greatest test of the conductor's grasp of the work. If the mighty theme is allowed to wallow, it can seem like one big tune too many. Rachmaninoff specifically marked it to be played as fast as the brilliant opening of the movement, and he knew what he was doing.

The theme gradually winds down to a point of rest. Here there is a moment of wistful reminiscence, as the violins remember the refrain from the slow movement, and the wood-wind play the rising and falling phrases from the beginning of the symphony. The moment is short-lived. The strings aggressively break in with renewed energy. Fragments of the first theme become an accompanying figure, while oboe and bassoon evoke the melancholy repeated phrase from the slow movement. The mood is fragile, at times sombre, the next moment lightening to sound almost like the tarantella from Mendelssohn's 'Italian' Symphony. Falling scales are heard in the texture.

Another quiet point is reached, and, over a held bass note, a bassoon plays another descending minor scale. Other instruments join in, playing the scale at different rates – half-speed, double speed, syncopated. As the whole orchestra joins in, with glockenspiel and cymbals, it is as if a whole city of church bells is pealing. From this bursts the reprise of the joyful first theme, into which the violins throw phrases from the second theme. After the first theme has run its course, there is a long, expectant build-up over another sustained bass note. And when the great second theme arrives, Rachmaninoff takes it to a greater height than before, with the bass striding magnificently downwards, and the melody reaching the climactic peak of the whole symphony. There is a final return to the jubilation of the first theme, and the symphony ends in unabashed Tchaikovskian splendour.

MAURICE RAVEL
(1875–1937)

As a student, Ravel already had the air of an aloof dandy, reserved and immaculately dressed. And yet his fellow student, the pianist Ricardo Viñes, wrote in his diary that, at a performance of the Prelude to Wagner's *Tristan* in 1896, 'he who looks so cold and cynical, Ravel the super-eccentric decadent, was trembling convulsively and crying like a child'.[1] Ravel's mother was Basque, his father Swiss. From his mother he acquired a fascination with Basque and Spanish music. From his father, who was an engineer, he inherited a love of machines, and a desire for precision. As a musician, he was complex and subtle. Like his senior contemporary, Claude Debussy, Ravel is often linked with the term 'Impressionism'. But he never spoke of his music in such terms. On the one hand, he said that 'sensitivity and emotion constitute the real content of a work of art'. On the other hand, he regarded sincerity as useless in art without the quest for perfection. 'My objective, therefore, is technical perfection. I can strive unceasingly to this end, since I am certain of never being able to achieve it. The important thing is to get nearer to it all the time. Art, no, doubt, has other *effects*, but the artist, in my opinion, should have no other aim.'[2]

As for his musical influences, these ranged from the Basque folk songs of his childhood to Chabrier, Debussy, and Satie via Mozart, whom he admired above all other composers. Unlike Debussy, he lived into the jazz age, and the influence of jazz, and specifically of Gershwin, is strong in his later works. The influences were reciprocal: the complex chords that colour Ravel's music, particularly the elaborations of seventh chords and other 'spicy' dissonances, are already there in Gershwin and found their way into jazz, remaining the stock in trade of many jazz-players to this day. But influences on Ravel were as often literary as musical. In a lecture delivered in the United States in 1928, Ravel said, 'The aesthetic of Edgar Allan Poe, your great American, has been of singular importance to me.'[3] He had been particularly struck by an essay by Poe, 'Philosophy of Composition', published in 1845 and translated into French by the poet Baudelaire (another great influence, and the original French dandy). Poe describes how he used his methods to construct his most famous poem, 'The Raven', and how emotional effect must be achieved by meticulous planning: 'no one point in its composition is referable either to accident or to intuition ... the work proceeded step by step, to its completion, with the precision and rigid consequence of a mathematical problem.'[4] Ravel's methods were similarly methodical and painstaking, but the result is music of wonderful expressive intensity and evocation.

BOLÉRO
Duration: approx. 16 minutes

In 1928 the dancer Ida Rubinstein commissioned Ravel to write a ballet score with a Spanish character, based on movements of Albéniz's piano suite, *Ibéria*. But when he discovered that Enrique Arbos had already orchestrated them, he decided first to arrange some of his own Spanish-inspired music, and eventually to write an original piece. Exotic Spanish flavours were nothing new in Ravel's music, but here he did something radical and daring. He took the basic rhythm of the bolero, and constructed a set of variations, leaving the melody and harmony unchanged and simply varying the orchestration. This was taking to extremes the Russian variation-technique pioneered by Glinka. To call the result repetitive is to state the obvious. What is more surprising is its cumulative power. Ravel described it in a statement published in 1931 as 'an experiment in a very special and limited direction ... a piece lasting seventeen minutes and consisting wholly of orchestral tissue without music – of one long, very gradual *crescendo*. There are no contrasts, and there is practically no invention except in the plan and the manner of the execution. The themes are impersonal – folk tunes of the usual Spanish-Arabian kind.'[5] Ravel had only envisaged it as a ballet score, and was surprised when the work became so popular as a concert piece. His original title was *Fandango*, but he eventually settled on *Boléro*, a dance that traditionally has a slower tempo.

The programme for the original 1928 production described the ballet scenario: 'Inside a tavern in Spain, people dance beneath the brass lamp hung from the ceiling. [In response] to the cheers to join in, the female dancer has leapt onto the long table and her steps become more and more animated.'[6] Just how animated the tempo should be was to become an issue of dispute between Ravel and Arturo Toscanini, who conducted the New York Philharmonic in the American premiere of *Boléro* in 1929. Toscanini took the piece faster than Ravel's metronome marking in the score, and when Ravel complained, stated that the music didn't work at Ravel's tempo.[7] Ravel's insistence on holding the tempo down is demonstrated in his own recording (the only recording that he made as a conductor).

The winding melody that dominates the entire piece is in two halves. The first half is played twice, then the second half is played twice, and that pattern is repeated again and again. The first half of the melody is like a relaxed and extended version of the Basque-style pipe-and-drum tunes that Ravel used elsewhere in his music (as in the opening of his Piano Concerto). The second half of the melody is like a jazz improvisation on the first half, with prominent 'blue' notes. Under these two quite different halves of the melody, the bolero rhythm continues unchanged from the first bar to the last, and it is the tension between these elements, together with the accumulation of orchestral effects, that gives the music its fascination.

A side drum sets up the bolero rhythm, a pattern that it plays 169 times during the course of the piece. Towards the end, after almost three hundred bars, a second side-drum player joins in. The effect has to be of a continuous crescendo over a quarter of an hour, and this is one of the great challenges for any percussionist. The rhythm begins pianissimo, with strings pizzicato, and a demure flute plays the first half of the tune. Other woodwind solos follow – clarinet, bassoon, high E-flat clarinet, oboe d'amore (an oboe midway between the standard oboe and the cor anglais). As these solos succeed each other, the accompanying rhythm is subtly reinforced, first by a flute, then by bassoon, with the pizzicato chords gradually thickening.

From this point on, the orchestration becomes more complex and more unorthodox. The tune is played by muted trumpet with flute, then tenor saxophone, and then sopranino saxophone. The saxophones make the jazz elements of the second half of the tune crystal clear, and to emphasize that he does not want 'straight' classical playing, Ravel marks the saxophone solos, 'espressivo, vibrato', and specifies some jazz glissandi. In the next variation, Ravel experiments with a clever piece of orchestral engineering. Horn and celesta play the tune at pitch (in C major), while one piccolo plays a fifth above (in G major), and the other piccolo an octave and a third above (in E major), both pianissimo. What Ravel is doing here is to create the effect of natural harmonics – a trick well known to organ-builders, with their 'mixtures' consisting of several ranks of pipes, but rarely used in the orchestra. If this is well balanced, the instruments blend to create a startlingly organ-like sonority (if the piccolos are too prominent, you just hear three different keys simultaneously). In the next variation, the oboe d'amore plays at the fifth, creating a slightly different 'organ stop'. A trombone now takes up the second half of the melody, which Ravel again marks with jazz glissandi.

Then the woodwind play parallel chords (rather than harmonics) – this almost suggests the medieval, but the saxophone has 'jazz-glissandi' marked. In the next variation, the first violins play the tune for the first time, with woodwind, and without any fancy chords or harmonic effects. All the violins join in, once again with parallel chords, the third and fifth of the chord shared out between violins and woodwind. The second half of the tune is played straight, with a trumpet joining, and, at the repeat, trombone and saxophone. Next, four trumpets join, and again parallel chords (with the third and the fifth) are played. For the first time in the sequence, the first tune is not repeated. The second tune comes next, with trombone 'as *ff* as possible', with parallel chords. Just as the tune is winding to its conclusion, it takes a new turn upwards, and suddenly bursts from C major to E major – a thrilling moment after the hypnotic persistence of C major. A few bars later, with another twist, the tune returns to the home key, trombones bray jazzy discords, and, after a final moment of suspense, the *Boléro* thunders to a close.

DAPHNIS ET CHLOÉ: SUITES NOS 1 AND 2

Sergei Diaghilev commissioned Ravel to compose a ballet score on the story of Daphnis and Chloe for his Ballets Russes in 1909, but there were many delays, negotiations, and disagreements before it reached the stage in 1912. The difficulties began in June 1909, when Ravel and Fokine worked on the scenario together. Ravel reported in a letter, 'I've just had an insane week of preparation of a ballet libretto for the next Russian season. Almost every night I've worked until 3 a.m . . . Fokine doesn't know a word of French, and I only know how to swear in Russian. Despite the interpreters, you can imagine the flavour of these discussions.'[8]

The scenario was loosely based on the romance by the second-century Greek writer Longus, in which two abandoned children, Daphnis and Chloe, are brought up by rural foster-parents, fall in love, are abducted by pirates, saved by the god Pan, and reunited in marriage. There are strong elements of eroticism and violence running through the original, and Ravel and Fokine had quite different ideas about what they wanted to achieve. Fokine declared that he wanted 'to recapture, and dynamically express, the form and image of the ancient dancing depicted in red and black on Attic vases'. But Ravel said that he wanted to create 'a vast musical fresco, less concerned with archaism than with fidelity to the Greece of my dreams, which is close to that imagined by the French artists of the late eighteenth century'.[9]

One specific disagreement was about the abduction of Chloé by the pirates. Fokine wrote, 'I planned to make an elaborate dramatic sequence out of the attack of the pirates. Ravel, however, wanted to produce a lightning attack. I yielded . . . unable to inspire him to create musically that violent, gruesome picture which was so vivid in my imagination. I later came to reproach myself for not having insisted on this point.'[10]

There were further arguments along the way. Ravel unwisely offered part of the score (which later became the first Suite) to the conductor Gabriel Pierné for a concert in April 1911, without consulting Diaghilev who had commissioned the music. Ravel was then unhappy with the contract Diaghilev offered him. And when, after long delay, the ballet went into production, Fokine found the rehearsal time squeezed because of the rival demands of Nijinsky's ballet to Debussy's *Prélude à l'après-midi d'un faune*: as the ballerina Tamara Karsavina remembered, 'nothing was really ready except the orchestra'.[11] Diaghilev had become exasperated by the whole project, and when *Daphis* finally reached the stage of the Théâtre du Châtelet in Paris, it was for two nights only instead of the planned four, at the end of the Ballets Russes season, following on from the scandalous success of the erotic *Prélude à l'après-midi d'un faune*. Although it attracted some favourable reviews, *Daphis* was not the success it should have been, despite the potentially winning team of Ravel as composer, Fokine as choreographer, Léon Bakst as designer, with Nijinsky as Daphnis and Karsavina as Chloé, and the brilliant and utterly reliable Pierre Monteux as conductor.

Daphnis et Chloé has, however, come to be acknowledged as one of Ravel's greatest scores. The music may not be overtly erotic, but it is wonderfully beautiful. And if one is looking for a sustained and overwhelming climax, there is none more impressive in music than the dawn that begins the final part of the ballet.

In the original Greek romance, Daphnis and Chloe, children from different noble families, were both abandoned at birth. Daphnis was found by a goatherd, Lammon, and Chloe by a shepherd, Dryas. Brought up by their foster-parents, the two herd their flocks together, and fall in love. Not knowing what is happening to them, they are told by an old cowherd, Philetas, that the only cure for their distress is kissing and lying together. Not understanding what this means, they are still unsatisfied, and it is not until a woman from the city, Lycaenion, initiates Daphnis into love-making that he fully understands what is involved. But warned that Chloe will cry out from pain, and will bleed, Daphnis is reluctant to put his new knowledge into action. Meanwhile, Chloe receives several suitors, and is abducted by pirates. She is saved by the intervention of the god Pan. Daphnis too is kidnapped and beaten up. Finally, the noble birth parents of Daphnis and Chloe appear and are united with them. The two get married, and their love finally achieves its long-delayed consummation.

The erotic elements of the story are a prominent thread of the original romance, but the eventual scenario for the ballet downplays the erotic and elevates the mystical. Ravel's fastidiousness and his preference for allusion rather than directness certainly contributed to this, and no doubt stoked the arguments between him and Fokine. The scenario maintains the outline of the story. One of Chloé's suitors, Dorcon, competes with Daphnis in dancing, and the reward is to be a kiss from Chloé. It is this reward, offered to Daphnis, that awakens his painful ecstasy. Lyceion (originally Lycaenion) is, in the ballet, a temptress who taunts Daphnis with her dancing, shedding her veils and then running off. Chloé is kidnapped, but Daphnis is not, and he waits anxiously until, with the help of Pan, she reappears. Learning that Pan has saved Chloé in memory of his love for the nymph Syrinx, Daphnis and Chloé mime the story. Chloé, as Syrinx, hides in the reeds, and Daphnis, as Pan, cuts the reeds to make a flute and plays it. Chloé dances to the music of the flute, and, as the dance becomes more and more animated, she falls into Daphnis's arms. The ballet ends with a dance of rejoicing.

Ravel called his score for *Daphnis et Chloé* a 'Symphonie choréographique'. Like the major works of Debussy, it might at first seem merely fluid and 'impressionist', but it is constructed from a number of little themes or motifs, and their variation and development are carefully structured to create a coherent form, in sections, and across the whole span of nearly an hour. The three most important motifs are heard right at the beginning of the ballet. Three horns play quiet chords that rock gently down and up. A flute plays a florid line, like a recitative or (in the context) an elegant series of balletic gestures. A horn answers with a solemn line that falls, rises, and falls again. These are the three most important elements that knit the whole score together.

Ravel extracted from the score two Suites for concert use, which he called 'fragments symphoniques'. These consist of continuous sections of the score, each comprising three parts that run into each other. The first Suite is taken from the end of Part 1 and the beginning of Part 2. The second Suite, which is much more often performed than the first, consists of the end of the whole ballet. In most performances, the suites are played with the offstage chorus replaced by instrumental parts that Ravel supplied.

SUITE NO. 1
Duration: approx. 13 minutes

Nocturne
Interlude
Danse guerrière (War dance)

Suite No. 1 is a continuous section from Part 1 and the beginning of Part 2. The following description is based on the scenario as printed in the ballet score, interleaved with brief notes on the music.

Nocturne

Chloé, seeking protection at the altar of the Nymphs, has been captured by pirates and taken away. Daphnis enters, finds her abandoned sandal, and, mad with despair, curses the divinities who were unable to protect her, and falls to the ground at the entrance to the cave. This is the point at which the Nocturne starts. An unreal light illuminates the scene (shimmering, strange string chords). A flame suddenly appears on the head of one of the statues, and the nymph comes alive, and descends from her pedestal (florid flute line, one of the main motifs). A second and then a third nymph descend (muted first horn and then a clarinet develop the flute line). They come together (rocking chords on woodwind and horns, another of the main motifs, with wind-machine), and begin a slow and mysterious dance. (Rocking chords on flutes and alto flute are elaborated. The flute motif is further elaborated by oboe and clarinets.) They see Daphnis, revive him, and lead him to the rock (the falling and rising motif, on violas and clarinet). They invoke the name of Pan (rocking chords on horns and woodwind, over shimmering strings), and slowly the form of the god becomes visible (the shimmering strings begin *ppp* over low brass chords, and build higher). Daphnis prostrates himself.

Interlude

Behind the scene, voices are heard, very distant at first. (Mysterious chords are sung by offstage chorus in the ballet, replaced by woodwind and muted horns in the suite. The rocking motif is present throughout this passage, and the creeping, descending melodic line is another important motif.) After a while, there is the sound of distant trumpets (actually horn and trumpet), and the voices come nearer. The scene changes to a rocky shore, with dim, glimmering light. This is the pirate camp. The pirates bring torches that break violently through the gloom. Swirling string patterns build up from the bass and lead straight into:

Danse guerrière (War dance)

The pirates dance their savage war dance, which becomes wilder and wilder until they fall, drunk. (Although the rhythm is a straightforward stamping two-time, the swirling figures and some of the harmonies are the same as in the five-time dance that concludes the ballet and the second suite. At a quiet moment halfway through, an alto flute takes the melody – a strikingly sultry sound.)

SUITE NO. 2
Duration: approx. 16 minutes

Lever du jour (Daybreak)
Pantomime
Danse générale

The second Suite is more often played than the first, no doubt because it contains Ravel's single most complex and satisfying piece of orchestration, the magnificent daybreak with which the final part of the ballet begins. This is writing of extraordinary subtlety, multi-layered, with the different voices of the orchestra skilfully balanced against each other to give an effect that is both rich and transparent, from the pianissimo with which it opens, to the mighty fortissimo that it reaches at the climax, four minutes later.

Lever du jour (Daybreak)
The scene dissolves to the landscape at the beginning of the ballet, a meadow at the edge of the sacred wood, at the end of the night. No sound but the murmur of rivulets produced from the dew that trickles from the rocks. Daphnis is stretched out before the grotto of the nymphs (Rippling flutes alternating with clarinets, with harp and celesta. The creeping bass below is one of the important motifs in the ballet). Gradually the day breaks. The songs of birds are heard (gradual crescendo, with the falling-and-rising motif passing from instrument to instrument. Bird calls in piccolo and violin harmonics). Far off, a shepherd passes with his flock (piccolo flourish, related to the flute motif). Another shepherd crosses in the background (high clarinet takes up the piccolo flourish. Soon, the offstage chorus is heard, as the falling-and-rising motif reaches the violins). A group of herdsmen enters looking for Daphnis and Chloé. They discover Daphnis and wake him (rocking motif in the offstage chorus). Anxiously he looks around for Chloé (agitated figure in violas and then violins). She appears at last, surrounded by shepherdesses. They throw themselves into each other's arms (climax as high strings play the falling-and-rising motif). Daphnis notices Chloé's wreath. His dream was a prophetic vision. The intervention of Pan is manifest (massive crescendo to a great climax, which then fades away). The old shepherd Lammon explains that, if Pan has saved Chloé, it is in memory of the nymph Syrinx whom the god once loved.

Pantomime
Daphnis and Chloé mime the tale of Pan and Syrinx (all of this passage has a narrative-style accompaniment, with little motifs moving from instrument to instrument, and little changes of pace). Chloé plays the young nymph wandering in the meadow. Daphnis, acting as Pan, appears and declares his love. The nymph rebuffs him. The god becomes more insistent. She disappears into the reeds. In despair, he picks several stalks to form a flute and plays a melancholy air. Chloé reappears and interprets in her dance the accents of the flute (the music settles into a slow dance rhythm, and the flute plays an extended, elaborate solo, based on the flute motif from the very beginning of the ballet). The dance becomes more and more animated and, in a mad whirling, Chloé falls into Daphnis's arms (climax, at which a rapid descent passes from piccolo to flute to alto flute, which plays the falling-and-rising motif. This is taken up ecstatically by the strings. The section ends with a final reminder of the rippling streams in the woodwind). Before the altar of the nymphs, he pledges his love, over an offering of two ewes (rocking motif in woodwind, against the flute motif in trumpets).

Danse générale
A group of girls enters, dressed as bacchantes, shaking tambourines (the music suddenly breaks into a five-time dance, with a melody that distinctly echoes Rimsky-Korsakov's *Scheherazade*, gradually increasing in energy and power to the end). Daphnis and Chloé embrace tenderly. A group of youths rushes onstage. Joyful commotion. General dance.

MA MÈRE L'OYE (MOTHER GOOSE)

Pavane de la Belle au bois dormant (Pavane of Sleeping Beauty): Lent

Petit poucet (Hop o' my Thumb): Très modéré

Laideronette, impératrice des pagodes (Laideronette, Empress of the Pagodes): Mouvement de marche

Les entretiens de la Belle et de la Bête (The Conversation of Beauty and the Beast): Mouvement de valse très modéré

Le jardin féerique (The Fairy Garden): Lent et grave

Ma mère l'Oye is the popular name of a collection of fairy tales published by Charles Perrault in 1697 as *Histoires ou contes du temps passé, avec des moralités*. In 1908, Ravel wrote a suite for piano duet inspired by some of Perrault's tales, together with others. 'La Belle au bois dormant' and 'Petit poucet' are from Perrault, the others from different collections, with the final 'Le jardin féerique' evoking the magical garden of fairy tales rather than a particular story.

Ravel wrote the suite for Mimi and Jean Godebski, children (aged six and seven) of his friends Cipa and Ida Godebski, to whom he had earlier dedicated his Sonatine. Mimi remembered that he used to tell them fairy stories: 'There was a childish side to Ravel and a warmth of feeling which remained almost invisible beneath his *pudeur* [reserve].' As for *Ma mère l'Oye*, 'Ravel wanted us to give the first public performance but the idea filled me with a cold terror. My brother, being less timid and more gifted on the piano, coped quite well. But despite lessons from Ravel I used to freeze to such an extent that the idea had to be abandoned.'[12] In 1911, Ravel orchestrated the suite, and enlarged it to create a ballet score for Jacques Rouché's Théâtre des Arts, and it was premiered in Paris in January 1912. The five original pieces, in their orchestrated form, are often played as a concert suite. For the full ballet, Ravel added a beautiful prelude and interludes. Ravel's orchestra has no trumpets or trombones, and only pairs of woodwind instruments, with the second players doubling piccolo, cor anglais, bass clarinet, and contrabassoon. But the percussion is very varied, with gong, xylophone, celesta, and glockenspiel. These, together with a harp, enable Ravel to paint a wonderfully rich evocation of magical landscapes and events.

Pavane: The scenario for the ballet instructs, 'While attendants dress the sleeping beauty for her night of a hundred years, lords and ladies dance a slow and melancholy pavane.' This is the briefest of solemn dances, with the melody passing from low flute to high flute, to clarinet, back to flute, and ending on high pianissimo violins. The accompaniment is delicate pizzicato, with at first a distant counterpoint of muted horn.

'Petit poucet': Hop o' my thumb is the youngest and cleverest of the seven children of a poor woodcutter. Unable to feed the children any more, the parents have abandoned them in the middle of the forest. Petit poucet has scattered breadcrumbs during the journey, so that the children can find their way back. But as they sleep, the birds come and eat the bread, and when the children wake, it has all gone. Over a mournful accompaniment of muted violins, a melody passes from oboe to cor anglais, then clarinet and flute. With its simple phrases and modal harmonies, it has something of the character of a folk song. But its phrases flow into each other, with changes of metre and phrase length that evoke the wandering of the children. As a bassoon takes up the melody, solo violins play swooping harmonics and trills to suggest the arrival of the birds.

'Laideronette, impératrice des pagodes': Laideronette is a princess who has been turned into an ugly woman by a wicked fairy ('laid' is the French for 'ugly'). She finds herself in the kingdom of the Green Serpent, a prince who has similarly had a curse put on him. The kingdom is populated by 'pagodes', the name given to toys in the form of Chinese mandarins with nodding heads. At the head of the score is a quote from the story published in the seventeenth century, Madame d'Aulnoy's *Serpentin vert*: 'She undressed and got into the bath. Immediately pagodes and pagodesses began to sing and to play instruments. Some had theorbos [lutes] made from walnut shells; some had viols made from almond shells; for the instruments had to be appropriate to their size.' Ravel stated in an interview in 1931 that this movement, 'with the tolling of its temple bells, was derived from Java, both harmonically and melodically'. Ravel had heard a Javanese gamelan for the first time at the Paris World Exhibition in 1889, when he was a teenager, and, like Debussy, had been captivated by its complex patterns.

'Laideronette' begins with an accompaniment of muted strings, harp, and celesta, over which oboe, flute, and piccolo play a tune with rapid repeating patterns, its pentatonic (five-note) scale, and touches of cymbals, glockenspiel, and xylophone creating the Javanese evocation. The oboe takes up a new melodic pattern, and the buzz of activity reaches a climax. This is followed by a grand, processional theme, with strokes of a gong (the 'tolling of the temple bells') and low notes on the celesta adding to the evocation of a gamelan orchestra. A flute solo over poignant harmonies suggests the anxiety of Laideronette. As the processional music returns, the celesta plays the rapid pattern from the opening, and this leads to a reprise.

'Les entretiens de la Belle et de la Bête': This movement is headed by extracts from the story, in the version by Mme Leprince de Beaumont. Beauty overcomes her fear of the monster, and discovers that he has a kind heart. But when he asks her to be his wife, she refuses. Left on his own, the Beast is dying, and when Beauty returns to him he says, 'I die happy because I have the pleasure of seeing you one more time.' 'No, my dear Beast, you shall not die: you shall live to become my husband!' As she says these words, the spell is broken, and the Beast is transformed back into a handsome prince. Ravel's music is in slow waltz time, reminiscent of Satie's *Gymnopédies*. A shy, chaste melody on clarinet evokes Beauty, accompanied by harp and muted strings with pizzicato bass. The Beast quietly enters, represented by a low contrabassoon playing a creeping figure. Beauty's theme is combined with the contrabassoon of the Beast, but with anxious harmonies. The music builds to a climax (the Beast imploring Beauty), and then, as she is reassured, her theme returns to more comfortable harmonies, still accompanied by the contrabassoon. This time the music builds to a passionate climax, and a cymbal crash. There is a harp glissando, followed by high harmonics on a solo violin, and, as the Beast is transformed into the prince, the movement ends with delicate final chords. The piece is highly evocative, but it is also classically formal – like a minuet and trio.

'Le jardin féerique': The final movement of the suite is simply called 'The Fairy Garden'. But in the ballet it is also headed 'Apotheosis', and is set to the scene in which a prince awakens Sleeping Beauty while dawn is breaking. As she awakes, 'All the characters from the earlier *tableaux* return to the stage, and group themselves around the Prince and Princess, united by love.' The opening is almost like a hymn, for strings only. This is the first time in the entire suite that the strings have played a theme on their own, without woodwind, harp, or other instruments. This has a simple and touching effect, cleansed of all spells and evils. The hymn builds up, and from its beautiful climax (with rather Fauré-like, modal harmonies) emerges a solo violin, accompanied in unison by celesta. Eventually, the mood of the opening hymn returns. The music builds to a final climax for full orchestra, with glissandi in harp and celesta, and a peal of bells on the glockenspiel.

PIANO CONCERTO IN G MAJOR
Duration: approx. 21 minutes

Allegramente
Adagio assai
Presto

In 1928, Ravel toured the United States and Canada for four months, to the sort of acclaim that had eluded him in Europe. One of the works that he played during the tour was his Sonata for Violin and Piano, whose second movement has the title 'Blues'. The influence of ragtime, blues, and jazz was already well established in France, and Ravel was one of several composers working there who had incorporated elements of its style into their music (Milhaud and Stravinsky were two others). Ravel's interest in jazz was deepened by the music he heard in New York and Philadelphia, and by meeting George Gershwin. In an interview during his American tour, he was quoted as saying, 'Jazz is a very rich and vital source of inspiration for a modern composer, and I am astonished that so few Americans are influenced by it.'[13]

On his return from America, he wrote three works strongly influenced by jazz: *Boléro* and two piano concertos (the other is for left hand only). He began working on this Piano Concerto in G major in 1929, was then interrupted by the commission for the Piano Concerto for the Left Hand, and finally completed this work in 1931. He had originally intended it as a vehicle for his own playing. But Ravel, never a virtuoso of the first rank, in the end gave the premiere to Marguerite Long, one of his most loyal champions. In 1932 they toured the concerto around twenty cities of Europe together, with Long playing and Ravel conducting, and the same year they made a recording of it together. However, although Ravel's name appeared on the label as conductor, it was later revealed that he had supervised the recording while a young Portuguese conductor, Pedro de Freitas-Branco, took the baton (he had shared the programme at which the concerto was premiered). Marguerite Long was quoted as saying that Ravel had insisted on take after take late into the night: 'I could have killed him, but I did it all the same.'[14] Ravel said that he had written the work in the spirit of the concertos of Mozart and Saint-Saëns: 'The music of a concerto, in my opinion, should be light-hearted and brilliant, and not aim at profundity or at dramatic effects.'[15]

The crack of a whip announces the opening of the concerto, like a ring-master opening the circus. A piccolo plays a lively dance tune, accompanied by rippling patterns and glissandi on the piano, with pizzicato chords on the strings, and a roll on the side drum. This evokes the Basque pipe-and-drum tunes that Ravel would have known as a child. But it also resembles the opening of Stravinsky's *Petrushka*, with its fairground scene and sense of gathering activity. At first the piano is treated as one of the orchestra (again as in *Petrushka*). The tune builds up, moving from piccolo to trumpet, and then to the strings, before ebbing away on cor anglais. It is only as the music calms that the piano comes to the fore, with a second theme. This has a quirky, jazzy character with blues harmonies, the clarinet answering with a phrase that could have come straight out of Gershwin's *Rhapsody in Blue* (composed in 1924). Rhythmic wood blocks and muted trumpet add to the blues-jazz impression. This leads on to a more lyrical melody, at first on the piano, then on bassoon, high in its most saxophone-like register. All of this passage is marked 'Meno vivo'. The recording by Marguerite Long, which Ravel supervised, makes it clear that he meant the tempo to ease without completely losing momentum – which it does in many modern performances.

A sudden return to the original tempo signals that we are entering the central, development section of the movement. This consists of a continuous toccata for piano, based on the material from the first theme, but with the blues elements of the second theme thrown in from time to time. It develops an unstoppable momentum, which culminates in a brief solo cadenza, finally breaking into the reprise of the opening. As before, the tempo eases to the second theme. This is extended by an episode for harp, with sweeping glissandi and harmonics, which leads on to a very high horn solo, accompanied by rapid woodwind flourishes. The whole passage has an exotic, dream-like character. The piano takes up the lyrical extension of the theme, now decorated with trills as if it has been transformed into a cadenza. A return to the fast tempo takes us back for the last time to the opening material, which builds to a joyful climax, and the curtain abruptly falls.

The complexities of the first movement sometimes suggest Stravinsky, but the simplicity of the slow movement evokes Satie. And, as in Satie, the music is not quite as simple as it sounds. The movement opens with a long piano solo. The right hand plays a melody, the left hand plays a bass and chords. The music has a rhythmically floating quality that results from an ambiguity in the relationship between melody and accompaniment. The time signature is 3/4 – three crotchets per bar. But most bars of the left-hand accompaniment have two groups of three quavers, as if the time signature were 6/8. So the accompaniment subtly pulls against the melody. A succession of woodwind solos joins this reverie. Then the piano introduces a new idea into the melody, with a frisson of blues as notes clash against the prevailing harmonies. As the piano line becomes more highly decorated, the harmonies and colours become darker, with clashes not just between individual notes but between one key and another. This reaches a climax, and then the tension dissolves to a reprise of the long opening theme. The cor anglais plays the melody, while the piano's left hand reverts to its regular, ambiguity-creating pattern, and the right hand decorates above, almost like Beethoven. As the melody winds to a conclusion, other woodwind join in as before, and the strings bring the movement to a close while the piano continues quietly trilling to the very end.

If the opening of the first movement suggests a fairground or circus, the finale is like a race. Four chords over a drum roll, a thwack of the bass drum, and they are off. The piano sets a rapid toccata going, like a twentieth-century update of a virtuoso harpsichord piece, and this creates a perpetuum mobile that continues almost without ceasing to the end of the movement. Over this toccata, high E flat clarinet, trombone, and piccolo throw wild gestures like the crowd shouting encouragement from the sidelines (Stravinsky via jazz again). The piano responds with more ideas – one with chunkier chords that seem to have come out of the first movement, and another with a pattern of rapid repeated notes. The woodwind take up a version of the opening toccata pattern, then the horns play a fanfare. This develops a brittle, almost comic edge, and then the piano embarks on more virtuoso passages.

There is a sudden hush, and bassoons restart the toccata pattern. This reprise prompts the return of all the main elements of the movement, sometimes combined together, while the perpetuum mobile continues persistently. The violins take over the toccata pattern, while the piano plays the clarinet's shouts (they sound even more like Stravinsky on the piano). The movement races headlong to a conclusion, and it ends as it began, with four chords and a thwack of the bass drum.

PIANO CONCERTO FOR THE LEFT HAND IN D MAJOR
Duration: approx. 19 minutes
Lento – Allegro – Tempo primo

While he was working on his piano concerto, Ravel was interrupted by a commission to write a concerto for left hand by the pianist Paul Wittgenstein, who had lost his right arm during the First War. It is a more difficult work to grasp than the concerto for two hands, partly because it is played without a break, and has a very fluid construction including long passages of cadenza. Wittgenstein himself was not at first impressed by it: 'It always takes me a while to grow into a difficult work. I suppose Ravel was disappointed, and I was sorry, but I have never learned to pretend . . . Only much later, when I'd studied the concerto for months, did I become fascinated by it and realized what a great work it was.'[16]

The two concertos each have a distinct character. They share the influence of jazz, and a masterly use of a large orchestra. But their spirit is rather different. The two-hand concerto is bubbly and transparent, light on its feet, and overflowing with good humour. The concerto for left hand is much darker, with a sense of violent forces that are at times barely under control. It has extensive slow movements either side of the central Allegro, in contrast to the two-hand concerto that has two rapid movements framing a central Adagio. And the music that Ravel manages to write so that it can be played with only the left hand is extraordinary. As he himself explained, 'In a work of this kind, it is essential to give the impression of a texture no thinner than that of a part written for both hands.'[17]

The concerto begins with a swirling of double basses. Out of the darkness a deep contra-bassoon emerges, like the Beast in Ravel's *Mother Goose*, with the first theme, whose stately dotted rhythms almost suggest a ghostly memory of a baroque French Overture. Horns respond with a more chant-like second theme. Gradually, these two elements build up, in a web of orchestral textures, to create Ravel's greatest crescendo since the dawn scene that begins the final part of *Daphnis et Chloé*. The climax breaks off, and the piano thunders in, with a huge bass octave and clattering fifths. In a long solo cadenza, it develops the contrabassoon's theme, building it in enormous steps to reach another climax. Then the full orchestra takes up the theme. The massive sonorities are sustained, and when they fade away, the piano introduces a gentle second theme, related to the chant-like horn melody from the opening. At the end of this theme, the tempo increases a little, and the flute reintroduces the dotted rhythms of the first theme. This passes to clarinets, bassoons, and horns, as the piano plays elaborate decoration. Eventually, this leads to another build-up and an acceleration, and the music bursts into the central Allegro.

With its fast, dancing metre (6/8), you might think of this as a massive scherzo. But it has much more power than that suggests, and as its relentless beat persists, it takes on an air of menace reminiscent of processional passages in Stravinsky's *The Rite of Spring* (though Ravel had his own example of relentless beat nearer at hand in *Boléro*). Over the continuing beat, the music is at first fragmentary. A falling scale of chords, like a demonic cackle, alternates with jazz-like stabbing chord shifts. Then the piano part becomes more like a toccata which, over the persistent beat, develops a momentum of its own.

Suddenly, with a trill and a harp glissando, this is swept away to reveal an enchanting scene, with flutes, piccolo, and harp playing a delicate melody. Once again we seem to be back in the fairy land of *Mother Goose*, with the Empress of the Pagodes. But the moment is short-lived. The beat is soon back, quiet but still insistent. Over it, a bassoon plays the chant-like melody that horns introduced right at the beginning of the concerto, now rendered a little jazzy by syncopations (and by the saxophone-like quality of a high bassoon). The piano delicately responds with its toccata, while the strings sweep up and down on eerie harmonics, as at the beginning of Stravinsky's *The Firebird*. A trombone takes up the chant, now sounding more jazzy, with touches of blues harmonies and accompanied by a side drum. This begins to build up, with the whole orchestra joining in. For a moment we seem to be back in *Boléro*. Out of the climax, a solo bassoon reprises the piano's toccata theme, and the piano responds with its cackling line of falling chords. This leads on to a reprise of the 'Empress of the Pagodes' episode.

Then the piano begins an accelerating pattern of leaping chords, which culminates, with an *fff* glissando, in a return to the stately French-Overture-style dotted rhythms of the opening theme, on full orchestra. Once again it builds in a series of huge steps to a climax, which collapses in swirls to leave the piano alone. This is the main cadenza, which begins low in the keyboard, musing on the chant theme, and builds to a mighty fantasia. As the orchestra begins to enter, blues harmonies reappear, and finally the music erupts in a final burst of the Allegro, bringing the concerto to a startlingly abrupt end.

RAPSODIE ESPAGNOLE
Duration: approx. 14 minutes
Prélude à la nuit (Prelude to the Night): très modéré
Malagueña: assez vif
Habanera: assez lent et d'un rhythme las
Feria (Festival): assez animé

The history of *Rapsodie espagnole* goes back to 1895, when Ravel composed a Habanera for two pianos as the first movement of a two-movement work with the Satie-like title, *Sites auriculaires* ('aural sites', or perhaps 'acoustic locations'). It was performed at a concert of the Société Nationale de Musique in 1898, the first time Ravel's work had been included by the Société. The Habanera was Ravel's first piece to have been inspired by Spain, in the French tradition stretching back to Saint-Saëns's friendship with the Spanish violinist Pablo de Sarasate, Bizet's *Carmen*, and Chabrier's *España* (and, of course, *Carmen* contains the most famous of all Habaneras). Ravel placed at the top of the score a quote from Baudelaire: 'Au pays parfumé que le soleil caresse' ('To the perfumed country caressed by the sun'). Debussy, Ravel's senior by twelve years, was in the audience and, despite the generally cool reception, asked to borrow the score. Five years later, Debussy published his piano piece, 'La soirée dans Grenade' ('Evening in Grenada'), which is also a Habanera, and contains some details obviously inspired by Ravel's piece. Perhaps this is why, when Ravel orchestrated his Habanera in 1908 for use in the *Rapsodie espagnole*, he took care to include under the title the date of its original composition, 1895.

The relationship between Debussy and Ravel was never simple, and although their friendship cooled as Ravel's fame increased and they found themselves pitted against each other by public factions, their influence continued to be mutual. Ravel's music was steeped in the influence of Debussy, in his harmonies and orchestration, and in his ways of developing a musical narrative and structure. But Debussy also gained from Ravel's ideas, not just in the simple matter of echoing a Habanera, but in more important and subtle ways.

Ravel added three more pieces to his Habanera to form his *Rapsodie espagnole* in 1907. This too began as a work for two pianos, and was orchestrated the following year. It was the third work inspired by Spain that Ravel had composed in 1907, following on from his one-act opera *L'Heure espagnole* and the wordless song, 'Vocalise-étude en forme de habanera', which became better known in Ravel's arrangement for violin and piano as 'Pièce en forme de habanera'. The *Rapsodie* was Ravel's first major orchestral work, and its virtuoso writing shows how much he had learned from Debussy, as well as from the great master of Russian orchestration, Rimsky-Korsakov, whose *Spanish Capriccio* must have been a direct inspiration for Ravel's *Rapsodie*. Debussy, in turn, was to show the direct influence of Ravel's *Rapsodie* when he came to write *Ibéria*, the second of his orchestral *Images*, in 1908. But despite the borrowings, it was Ravel who most passionately defended Debussy against the critics, finding *Ibéria* 'profoundly affecting' and praising its 'intense musicality' (see entry for Debussy's *Images*).

'Prélude à la nuit' is slow, quiet, and sultry. Muted violins and violas, *ppp*, reiterate a falling four-note motif. Then woodwind with harp and pizzicato bass play chords that might be the tentative start of a slow dance. They do it again, and fall silent. Nothing is certain: the key seems as if it might be D minor, but the chords are strange. The falling motif is in patterns of four notes, suggesting two beats, but the brief woodwind entry cuts against it in a slow metre of three beats. At first, the falling pattern is played four times, then after the woodwind chords it is played three times. After the second appearance of the woodwind chords, the falling pattern is played six times as it fades. Within forty seconds, Ravel has created a scene of shifting uncertainty. Clarinets enter with the slow dance, elaborating it into the first fragment of melody, in a scale suggestive of 'Moorish' Spain. There are sudden, delicate bursts of string tremolo, like a breeze in the night. All the while, the falling pattern continues hypnotically, changing subtly in sound as it passes from high violins to cellos and cor anglais, to violas and flute, to low violins and clarinet. The pattern fades once again on solo clarinet.

But the scene is not as peaceful as it seems: the strings suddenly break out with a passionate fragment of melody (derived from the earlier fragments on clarinet). It is an indication of how deeply Ravel has lulled us into this dreamy atmosphere that this seems like such an outburst, though the muted strings rise only to *mf*. As the outburst calms, the falling motif changes from a four-note to a three-note pattern, subtly enhancing the feeling of increased passion. As peace descends, the music settles for a moment in a warm major key (F major). Suddenly two clarinets erupt in a cadenza, like arguing voices heard in the distance (this too has 'Moorish' intervals, though the idea of the clarinet cadenza probably comes from Rimsky-Korsakov's *Spanish Capriccio*). Peace is restored, and, in a new key, the fragmentary theme returns on solo violin and cello, with the four-note pattern on delicate celesta with shimmering tremolo below. Again the peace is interrupted, this time by a duet of bassoons in cadenza echoing the clarinets. Finally, the music returns to its opening, back in its original key, and comes to an end on the first simple chord in the whole piece – a chord of A major.

Ravel takes the three-beat metre and repeating bass of a traditional Malagueña, but does something highly personal with it. The phrases are three bars long instead of the usual four, giving it a gently urgent character right from the start. The repeating bass begins quietly in double basses and bass clarinet, and builds up. As the upper strings and flutes introduce a delicate flourish on the second beat, it sounds very much like the Fandango from Rimsky-Korsakov's *Spanish Capriccio* (there is considerable overlap in style between the Malagueña and the Fandango). Swirling woodwind give way to shimmering strings. Then there is a sudden change of key and the dance turns bolder, with a five-bar tune on muted trumpet. The violins echo it sentimentally with swooning glissandi. The dance builds to a climax, and cuts off. The cor anglais sings a plaintive recitative, and into it creeps a memory of the descending motif from the 'Prélude à la nuit'. Very soon a playful run on flute and piccolo pulls the music back to the dance. But the moment of reprise is fleeting, and the movement evaporates in a final flick of an arpeggio.

The Habanera, like the Malagueña, is the briefest of evocations. The 'rhythme las' ('weary rhythm') is set up by the woodwind, and repeats hypnotically all the way through the piece. The strings are muted, and the range of tone colours is subdued. But there are subtleties throughout as Ravel balances and blends woodwind, muted strings, and muted horns and trumpets, with touches from the two harps, celesta, and low drums. For a moment, it seems to be gathering strength, with the arrival of a tambourine. But the music soon lapses into sleepiness, with the rhythm fading out on celesta.

After three short movements of subtle and muted colours that rarely rise beyond *mf*, Ravel finally lets his hair down in 'Feria' ('Festival'). It returns to a three-time dance rhythm, as in the Malagueña/Fandango, now using it to build up a dance of joyful celebration. The piece begins as if on tiptoe, with the rhythm set by piccolo and harp, and the brief, inviting arabesque of a tune played on flute. A harp glissando and string harmonics whizz into the air like a firework. Then deeper sounds suggest sleeping energies ready to spring to life. The invitation is renewed by a clarinet. This time the awakening brings in muted trumpets, playing a variant of the dancing phrase they played in the Malagueña. It sparks off answering phrases from woodwind and xylophone, and a muted horn – all this muted brass suggests exciting potential. The crowd gathers, until all the trumpets and horns (no longer muted) take up the dance, and a new, sweeping melody comes in on the strings. Again the excitement builds, from solo flute and muted trumpet to the whole orchestra, with the sweeping melody on the horns. A climax fades away back into the depths.

The pace eases, and over a lazy, repeated phrase, first cor anglais and then low clarinet play a melancholy, flamenco-inspired recitative. The strings burst out in a passionate answer. This is very like their outburst in the Prélude, and it is followed by a ghostly reminder of the falling motif. This alerts us to the fact that this whole slow section of Feria is a variation of what happened in the Prélude, the fragments of melody extended into the recitatives, and followed by the string outburst and falling motif.

As the falling motif sleepily continues, a muted trumpet reminds us that the Fiesta is in progress. The energy builds again, urged on by castanets, until the full orchestra has joined in. The force is held back for a moment of sentiment, with another echo of the falling motif. Then the pace accelerates, until a flourish culminates in an emphatic final chord, like a rocket exploding in the air.

LE TOMBEAU DE COUPERIN
Duration: approx. 18 minutes

Prélude: Vif
Forlane: Allegretto
Minuet: Allegro moderato
Rigaudon: Assez vif

In April 1914, Ravel transcribed for piano a 'Forlane' (a dance originally from northern Italy) from the fourth of François Couperin's *Concerts royaux*, music that Couperin had written for himself to play with other instruments for Louis XIV's regular Sunday chamber-music concerts in the early eighteenth century. By September, while Ravel was attempting to enlist in the army despite his physical delicacy, he had begun work on a *Suite française* by writing his own 'Forlane'. But it was not until 1917 that he returned to the project. By then, everything had changed. Ravel had been working as a lorry driver at Verdun, but had been discharged, suffering from a heart condition and exhaustion. The death of his mother was a terrible shock. Worst of all, many of his friends had been killed in the war. Ravel decided to take his suite and convert it into a memorial on two levels. The immediate level was a tribute to fallen friends, named in the dedication of each movement. The second memorial was to François Couperin, the greatest of the eighteenth-century composers of keyboard music, though Ravel added, 'The tribute is directed not so much toward the individual figure of Couperin as to the whole of French music of the eighteenth century.'[18] As in other works, such as his recent piano trio, Ravel took the inspiration of the distant past and used it to create music of unique character, a sort of elegant poignancy that seems both ancient and modern. His contemporaries had some difficulty coming to terms with the airy, and at times vivacious, character of this music, which seems scarcely like a memorial. The composer Jean Roger-Ducasse confided to a friend after hearing Marguerite Long perform the suite, 'Not a trace of emotion, and, after all, the memory of these soldiers requires it.' Long, who was closely associated with Ravel's piano music, and whose dead husband, Joseph de Marliave, was the dedicatee of the lively Toccata that ends the piano suite, defended Ravel against such criticisms. It was precisely the lightest and most brilliant style in which she excelled, and she saw no reason why a memory of a friend should express itself only in lamentation.[19] Ravel himself drew the design for the title page, with a classical urn above a draped tomb-like inscription giving the title of the work. In 1919 he wrote a version of four of the pieces for a modest-sized orchestra: pairs of flutes, clarinets, bassoons, and horns, oboe, cor anglais, trumpet, harp, and strings.

Prélude: in memory of Lieutenant Jacques Charlot (cousin of Ravel's publisher, who died March 1915, aged thirty; he had transcribed *Ma mère l'Oye* for solo piano)
The Prélude has running triplets, like many a prelude in eighteenth-century harpsichord suites, with little ornaments and subtle cross-rhythms. The orchestral version gives it a more rustic feel than the original for piano, particularly because of the oboe. It rises to a climax in the second half.

Forlane: in memory of Lieutenant Gabriel Deluc (Basque painter from St Jean de Luz, died September 1916, aged thirty-four)

Ravel's Forlane is rhythmically similar to Couperin's harpsichord Forlane, which Ravel transcribed, with a dancing dotted rhythm within a triplet (like the more familiar siciliano). Pungent dissonances give it a sweet-sour character. Couperin's piece is a 'Forlane-Rondeau', in which the opening strain returns as a recurrent refrain. Ravel does the same, with episodes that are by turns playful and lyrical.

Minuet: in memory of Jean Dreyfus (died late 1916; Ravel recuperated at the Dreyfus family home near Rouen after he was demobilized)

Ravel had composed several minuets before this one (including the second movement of his Sonatine), and they all share a quality of gentle intimacy. One ingredient that contributes is its harmonic language, which shifts ambiguously from major to modal and back again. The sombre middle section is a 'musette', the name not only of this kind of music, with a drone bass, but of a kind of bagpipe that might play it. The drifting chords rise to a climax in the second half. Couperin's suites include several 'musettes'.

Rigaudon: in memory of Pierre et Pascal Gaudin (brothers, aged twenty-six and thirty respectively, killed by a single shell on their first day at the front in November 1914, lifelong friends of Ravel, whose home was in St Jean de Luz)

The Rigaudon was a vigorous dance popular in France in the seventeenth and eighteenth centuries, both among ordinary people and at court. As in the Forlane, the opening fanfare-like flourish acts as a recurrent refrain, framing a simple three-part structure. The slower middle section has a gently processional character, with an oboe solo in Ravel's orchestration.

LA VALSE
Duration: approx. 13 minutes

On 28 January 1905, Ravel was invited to the Paris Opéra with, among other guests, his close friend the pianist Ricardo Viñes. Viñes wrote in his diary, 'It was the first time I have been to the Opéra ball, and as always when I see young, beautiful women, lights, music and all this activity, I thought of death, of the ephemeral nature of everything, I imagined balls from past generations who are now nothing but dust, as will be all the masks I saw, and all too soon! What horror, Oblivion!'[20] A year later, Ravel wrote to the critic Jean Marnold about the waltz, 'You know my intense feeling for these marvellous rhythms' and their deep 'expression of joie de vivre'. By July 1906, Ravel was planning to write a piece he referred to as 'Vienne' (the French for 'Vienna').[21] But this came to nothing, and it was not until 1914 that Ravel revealed he was working on a symphonic poem, now called 'Wien' (the German for 'Vienna').[22] By now, Ravel had composed another set of waltzes, the *Valses nobles et sentimentales*, which had been performed in 1911 and orchestrated the following year. In December 1919, Ravel reported in a letter, 'Back to *Wien*. It's going well. I've got started at last and in top gear.'[23] He finished orchestrating the work in April 1920, and by now was calling it *La Valse*.

As Roger Nichols observes, it is 'more than tempting' to think that the idea for this slowly gestating work could be traced back to Viñes's diary entry in January 1905. He and Ravel had been close friends since they were fellow students at the Paris Conservatoire, and it seems altogether likely that Viñes would have shared these thoughts with Ravel after the ball. *La*

Valse has always been the subject of speculation about its symbolism, or even programme. By the time Ravel had completed it, he described it as a 'choreographic poem', and was hoping that Diaghilev would create a ballet to it for his Ballets Russes. Ravel and Marcelle Meyer played the version for two pianos to Diaghilev, in a gathering that included Stravinsky and Poulenc. Poulenc remembered, 'I knew Diaghilev very well at this time, and I saw his false teeth and his monocle begin to twitch. I saw that he was embarrassed, that he didn't like it and that he was going to say "No". When Ravel had finished, Diaghilev said something which I think is absolutely right. He said, "Ravel, it's a masterpiece ... but it's not a ballet ... It's the portrait of a ballet ... the painting of a ballet." '[24] This initiated a permanent rift between Ravel and Diaghilev. Diaghilev never set a ballet to *La Valse*, though Ida Rubinstein did in 1929, with choreography by Bronislava Nijinska, followed by Georges Balanchine in 1951 and Frederick Ashton in 1958.

The principal life of this 'choreographic poem', however, has been as a much-loved concert piece. Ravel provided a brief programme to the music, printed at the beginning of the score: 'Through swirling clouds we catch intermittent glimpses of waltzing couples. The clouds gradually disperse: we make out an immense ballroom filled with a circling crowd. The scene becomes progressively clearer. The chandeliers burst into light at the *fortissimo*. An imperial court, around 1855.'

Despite the date in which Ravel locates this synopsis, many writers have found in the music echoes of the time through which he conceived and composed the piece. Ravel himself rejected any such interpretation. In a newspaper interview in 1922 he was reported as saying, 'It doesn't have anything to do with the present situation in Vienna, and it also doesn't have any symbolic meaning in that regard. In the course of *La Valse*, I did not envision a dance of death or a struggle between life and death (the year of the choreographic setting, 1855, repudiates such an assumption).'[25] And in a letter around the same time he wrote, 'Some people ... definitely see a tragic allusion – the end of the second Empire, the state of Vienna after the war ... Tragic this dance may seem, as with all feeling – desire, joy – pushed to the extreme. One should see in it only what the music expresses: an ascending progression of sonority, to which the stage will add those of lighting and movement.'[26] This sounds almost Stravinskian in its bald dismissal of any outside symbolism, and, as with many of Stravinsky's statements, need not be taken at face value. It is certainly more than a dance, more than a 'portrait' of a dance, and the idea that the end represents some kind of destruction or death, whether or not the idea was sparked by Viñes, is irresistible – though perhaps best left unspecific. Ravel himself issued contradictory statements at different times, including the following, in his *Autobiographical Sketch* of 1928: 'I conceived this work as a kind of apotheosis of the Viennese waltz, mixed, in my mind, with the impression of a fantastic and fatal whirling.'[27]

Ravel's earlier *Valses nobles et sentimentales* were inspired by Schubert's waltzes for piano, and consisted of a string of separate dances. *La Valse*, in one continuous movement, and set in about 1855, is more evocative of the heyday of the Viennese (and pan-European) craze for the waltz associated with the Strauss family. By that date, Johann Strauss II had succeeded his father as the undisputed king of the waltz, and his waltzes (unlike Schubert's) were built into a continuous sequence, lasting up to ten minutes. While the metre of the waltz was maintained, the character and emphasis of the music was varied from waltz to waltz, and a loose sense of structure was created by occasional simple repetitions of sections, and by a return at the end to the first waltz of the sequence. Ravel takes this informal sequence of dances and transforms and extends it into a dance-drama lasting nearly a quarter of an hour. The music begins in darkness, twice rises to a climax, the second increasingly wild, and then seems to disintegrate. It is as if the joyful forces that created the energy of *Rapsodie espagnole* have unleashed destructive power. *La Valse* is scored for a large orchestra with two harps and an array of percussion including several types of drum, glockenspiel, and antique (i.e. miniature) cymbals.

The opening suggests the 'swirling clouds' with occasional glimpses of dancers – it could almost be a 'representation of chaos' (à la Haydn) before the creation of the universe. From low shuddering strings, fragments of waltz rhythm and melody begin to appear: first pizzicato basses and bassoons, then low clarinets and violas. These fragments start to coalesce, until the music settles into a coherent waltz, in a definite key (D major). This is the point where Ravel specifies that we make out the immense hall full of waltzing couples. The music is full of atmospheric detail: flurries of woodwind, harp glissandi, shimmering tremolando strings, sentimental slides. Gradually the different elements come together, until they reach a grand fortissimo ('the chandeliers burst into light'), and for a moment there is the elegant rhythmic snap of a traditional waltz. As soon as this point has been reached, the music quietens to a second waltz, a sweetly rocking melody, first on oboe, and then on high violins and violas. A second strain of this waltz becomes more playful, the phrases ending with a staccato bounce. The brass and percussion enter with a vigorous new theme and a change of key (to B flat major), and we are into Waltz 3. Then, with another change of key, violins play a sonorous new melody, with swirling cellos below (Waltz 4). There is a playful little tailpiece, on oboe and clarinet (which some writers identify as a separate waltz, though it is brief).

A rhythmic burst of full orchestra fortissimo propels us into Waltz 5 (F major), in which snappy waltz rhythms alternate with swirling figures. The music quietens again to Waltz 6 (back in D major). This is low on cellos and clarinets in a duet of thirds, its intimate sound suggesting a smaller group of dancers separate from the throng. But soon other instruments join in, and the waltz builds to a splendid climax. Now there is a moment of real intimacy (Waltz 7). The tempo slows, and two solo violas and solo cello play sustained, swooning phrases ending in a coquettish flick – a moment of true Viennese Schmalz – accompanied by decorative arpeggios on clarinet and harp. Again, other instruments join in, until the momentum is regained, and sweeps us into Waltz 8. This is pointilliste, with the staccato melody on flutes and clarinets, and delicate harmonics, trills, harp glissandi, and touches of glockenspiel creating an intricate accompanying texture.

Once more the orchestration builds up, and the music accelerates. But instead of reaching a climax, it breaks up, and we suddenly find ourselves back at the dark opening, with the tremolo in the bass and fragments of a waltz on bassoons. This echoes the moment of the traditional Viennese reprise, and in a waltz of the Strauss era it would signal that the end was approaching. But Ravel draws this process out, creating an extraordinarily powerful build to the final cataclysm (Ravel was a master of the extended emotional crescendo). He does this by revisiting the more energetic of the elements, and omitting the more lyrical and sustained ones. As before, fragments of waltz begin to appear, and build up. But as they reach the first of a series of climaxes, each bar of waltz rhythm is broken up by bars of wildness, as if the effort to hold the music together is beginning to crack.

The tension dissipates, and a playful melody, formerly on oboe, is now on trumpet (the sonorous melody that originally preceded it is omitted, tightening the momentum). The music builds to another climax, which then dissipates to the last low point before the final crisis. Low clarinet and cellos reprise their intimate dance, over a persistent rhythm that has become ominous. There is another build-up, longer than the first time, which gradually accelerates until it is suddenly held back. What was an intimate, swooning phrase with a coquettish flick now becomes a threatening *fff* gesture, as if the elegant waltz has revealed its destructive potential. The tempo and rhythm recover. As the waltz begins to accelerate again, the rhythm is punctuated by fearsome, thundering bars, like some gigantic javelin-thrower running up before hurling. The waltz rhythm begins to struggle, until the momentum breaks, and a phrase of melody cries out, as if pleading. But it is too late. The hurling becomes violent thrashing, and with an immense gesture, reminiscent of the end of *The Rite of Spring*, the music crashes to the ground, breaking from its waltz rhythm into a brutal four-beat final bar of hammer blows.

NIKOLAI RIMSKY-KORSAKOV
(1844–1908)

Rimsky-Korsakov is a fascinating figure in the history of Russian music. Together with Balakirev, Musorgsky, Borodin, and Cui, he was one of the group of composers known as 'The Five' or 'The Mighty Handful', who were part of an artistic movement aimed at developing a Russian school of composition, founded on the work of Glinka and traditional Russian music, and distinct from the Austro-German approach that had dominated Russia. At first, like most of his fellow composers, he developed his musical interests while pursuing a conventional career, in his case as a naval officer. With the encouragement of Balakirev, he completed a symphony by the age of twenty-one, and only six years later took up a post of professor of composition at St Petersburg Conservatoire while still pursuing his naval career – a move that Balakirev viewed as selling out to the conservative establishment.

Rimsky-Korsakov was first and foremost a composer of fifteen operas. He did more than any other composer to establish Russian opera as a regular feature of the culture of the time. But this was not just through his own compositions: he was also a vigorous promoter of the music of his fellow Russians. After Musorgsky's death he edited his works for publication, and he did the same (with Glazunov) for Borodin's opera *Prince Igor*, which had been left incomplete at the composer's death. Rimsky's edition of Musorgsky's *Boris Godunov* was the only version known on the stage for many years. But his approach to orchestration was rather different from Musorgsky's. He very skilfully 'improved' Musorgsky's original, smoothing out what he perceived as its crudities and adding brilliant touches to give it a more sophisticated sound. The result is undoubtedly grand and effective, but revivals of Musorgsky's original score in recent decades have demonstrated the direct power of the 'crude' original.

Rimsky-Korsakov's own compositions reveal him as a master of the orchestra. His virtuoso flair for creating variety of colour and effect influenced later composers, most obviously his pupil Stravinsky, but also, more subtly, Debussy and Ravel. Rimsky wrote a treatise, *Principles of Orchestration*, which remains one of the classic texts for composers and conductors. In the concert hall he is best known for the three spectacular orchestral pieces that he wrote in 1887–8: *Spanish Capriccio*, *Russian Easter Festival Overture*, and *Scheherazade*.

SPANISH CAPRICCIO, OP. 34
Duration: approx. 16 minutes

Alborada –
Variazioni –
Alborada –
Scena e canto gitano –
Fandango asturiano

During the summer of 1887, Rimsky was at work completing Borodin's opera *Prince Igor*, which the composer had left unfinished at his death. He broke off from this work to look again at some sketches he had written for a Fantasia for Violin and Orchestra on Spanish themes. It was these sketches that became the *Spanish Capriccio* (*Capriccio espagnole*, or, from the original Russian, *Capriccio on Spanish Themes*). Russian musicians' fascination with Spain stems back to Glinka, who spent two years there from 1845 to 1847 and composed a pair of lively 'Spanish Overtures'. Later Russian composers wrote works with a Spanish flavour, but Rimsky-Korsakov's *Spanish Capriccio* is by far the best known, drawing not only on Glinka but also on Chabrier's *España*. It explores the emotional range of traditional Spanish music more widely than Glinka's overtures, including not only vigorous dances but at least a touch of Spanish melancholy. This in turn inspired Ravel and Debussy, whose *Rapsodie espagnole* and *Ibéria* respectively are the most brilliant of twentieth-century Spanish evocations.

The *Spanish Capriccio* was first performed at the Russian Symphony Concerts in St Petersburg, with Rimsky himself conducting. He wrote about this premiere in his autobiography: 'At the first rehearsal the first movement had hardly been finished when the whole orchestra began to applaud. At the concert itself the composition called forth an insistent encore, despite its length. But the opinion formed by both critics and the public, that the Capriccio is a "magnificently orchestrated piece" is wrong. The Capriccio is a brilliant composition for the orchestra. The changes of timbre, the felicitous choice of melodic patterns to suit each instrument, the brief virtuoso cadenzas, the rhythm of the percussion instruments, constitute the very essence of the composition, not just its garb or orchestration'.[1] In this 'variation by orchestration', Rimsky was following the example set by Glinka, not only in his Spanish-inspired pieces but, more famously, in his *Kamarinskaya*.

Alborada is the Spanish equivalent of the French, *Aubade* (dawn song), and the first movement is based on a traditional tune from Asturias (north-western Spain). 'Strepitoso' means 'clamorous', and Rimsky's music suggests a joyful procession, with the full orchestra including tambourine, triangle, cymbals, and bass drum. The whole piece lasts scarcely more than a minute, with its bass never straying from the note A – this is a tune traditionally played by groups including bagpipes. Two figures stand out from the crowd: a clarinet that plays a virtuoso variation of the tune, and a solo violin, which flings arpeggios into the air as the procession disappears into the distance.

The second movement is the slowest and longest, a meditative set of variations – perhaps recovering from being awoken at dawn by the procession. A quartet of horns plays the theme. The tone is mellow and peaceful, but there is just a hint of melancholy in the melody that curls around itself in five-bar phrases. In the first variation the melody moves to high cellos. The second variation is played by cor anglais, whose plangency was particularly favoured by both Russian and Spanish composers. Tremolando accompanying strings and chromatic harmonies bring an element of mystery, which is heightened when each phrase is answered by horn calls, first in normal 'open' sounds, and then hand-stopped to create an echo. For the third variation, there is a change of key, and the strings take up the theme in a grand chorus of widely spread chords. Then the fourth variation moves on again in key and passes to the woodwind, horns, and cellos, with delicate pizzicato accompanying. But after the first strain of the melody, there is another dramatic shift back to the home key, and high violins join the woodwind to take the variations to a climax. As the music calms for the final part of the theme, a flute plays a delicate counterpoint of chromatic scales.

At the end, a flute trill leads straight into the reprise of the *Alborada*. This too is a variation of the original. It is in the key of B flat, a semitone higher than the first time, and the predominant instruments are the wind, with the strings accompanying pizzicato. The soloists appear in reverse order, and seem to have been emboldened. First the solo violin plays the theme, elaborating it flamboyantly with double notes and arpeggios. As the violin continues, the clarinet joins in with even flashier arpeggios, as if trying to steal the show.

A side drum rolls, and trumpets and horns break in with a sort of fanfare to announce the start of the *Scena e canto gitano*. The 'scene' consists of a series of cadenzas that contain the seeds of the 'gypsy song' to follow. It is already there in the opening fanfare, and continues in a violin cadenza. Quietly, percussion and strings start up a rhythm over which flute and clarinet try out the beginning of the song. Further brief cadenzas follow, first from flute then from clarinet, and an oboe plays a fragment of the song. There is a final cadenza from the harp, ending with a sweeping arpeggio. Then, with two incisive brass chords we are off. Ferocious swirls in the violins bring in the rhythm. The gypsy song enters passionately on violins. From here, the song alternates with the swirls, sometimes ferocious, sometimes delicately staccato.

The song builds to a climax, and seamlessly moves into a bold new theme in a swinging three-time, announced by the trombones. This is the *Fandango asturiano*, and as in the *Alborada*, the florid melody and the persistent bass note evoke traditional Asturian bagpipers, in giant orchestral form. Here, unlike in the *Alborada*, Rimsky soon moves away to other keys, clothing the melody in new orchestrations. There is delightful interaction between solo violin, flutes, and piccolo. Then, over a dreamy cello line, a clarinet resumes the assertive role it played in the *Alborada*. The mixture of instruments changes continually, and first castanets then other percussion add to the rhythmic energy. The excitement builds, until suddenly the music breaks back into the *Alborada*, faster than before, and accelerates to an exhilarating conclusion.

SCHEHERAZADE, OP. 35
Duration: approx. 46 minutes

Largo e maestoso – Allegro non troppo (The sea and Sinbad's ship)
Lento – andantino – vivace scherzando – allegro molto ed animato (The Kalendar prince)
Andantino quasi allegretto (The young prince and princess)
Allegro molto – vivo – allegro non troppo maestoso (The Baghdad festival, the ship dashing against the rock)

Rimsky-Korsakov wrote *Scheherazade* in the summer of 1888, soon after working on his completion of Borodin's *Prince Igor*. Rimsky himself identified specific episodes from *The Thousand and One Nights* that had inspired him: the sea and Sinbad's ship, the prince disguised as a Kalendar (a dervish beggar), the young prince and princess, the Baghdad festival, and the ship dashing against the rock surmounted by a bronze horseman. The movements were originally given these titles, but Rimsky-Korsakov later insisted that there was no simple relationship between the stories and the movements, and withdrew them. He wrote in his autobiography, 'I had intended these hints merely to direct the hearer's fancy along the path which my own fancy had travelled and to leave more minute and particular conceptions to the individual will and mood.'² And he stated that musical ideas drawn from these episodes are to be found in all four movements. The tempo markings given above are only the most important – frequent changes of pace and mood are characteristic of the piece.

The inspiration for the opening two elements is unmistakable, and both recur in later movements. A stern unison theme, dominated by trombones, suggests the implacable Sultan Shakriar. The delicate and fantastic violin solo, accompanied by harp, suggests Scheherazade, whose stories prevented the Sultan carrying out his plan to put her to death after her wedding night, like her predecessors. And the swell of the sea is unmistakable in this first movement, with its great repeating paragraphs, and its gradual crescendos to mighty climaxes. The sense of narrative is enhanced by the solo violin, which is heard at the low point of each wave.

The violin again introduces the second movement, which is associated with a Kalendar prince. Since there are three in *The Thousand and One Nights*, it is not possible to associate the music with specific episodes. But the plaintive solo bassoon, which first plays the principal theme, certainly gives a monk-like impression, over a drone on double basses (Richard Strauss was to associate bassoons with monks in his *Don Quixote*). Oboe, and then violins, take up the theme, and then it becomes a dance. But this is interrupted, and after a moment's hesitation, fierce and strange fanfares ring out (strange, because they are chromatic, unlike conventional fanfares), and these are linked to the stern voice of the Sultan from the start of the work. There is an oriental cadenza from the clarinet, based on a phrase from the bassoon solo. Then a wild scherzo gets going, until, at another interruption, the bassoon takes up the clarinet's oriental cadenza. Now the bassoon's original tune, played by violins and woodwind, takes on a dancing rhythm, and this drives the rest of the movement, with episodes by turns vigorous and wistful, ending with an accelerating climax.

The third movement begins with a beautiful, rich melody played by all the violins. It has just the suggestion of oriental voluptuousness that Borodin had conveyed in his Polovtsian Dances, and elaborate swirls punctuate the melody from time to time. In a central episode, a tambourine introduces a dance, whose tune is based on the opening phrase of the first melody. When the original melody returns, the violins are in octaves, and, after a reminder of Scheherazade's solo, the tune reaches a climax. A renewal of the dance rhythm brings the movement to a close.

The finale opens with the stern Sultan's motto, but now very fast. There is a brief violin cadenza, the Sultan's theme returns more insistently, and is followed by another little cadenza. Finally the movement is off, with the flutes leading a hypnotically repeating dance tune that develops unstoppable energy. Into the dance are thrown various elements from earlier movements: a phrase from the monkish bassoon solo, the dance from the middle of the third movement, which is then fragmented into calls on the brass, and later a rhythmically transformed version of the Sultan's theme. A series of climaxes and restarts, with ever increasing energy and complexity, culminates in a great final outpouring, like an enormous wave, as the first theme of the sea returns, scored with the utmost magnificence, with harp and chromatic woodwind runs enhancing the effect. Gradually this subsides, leaving Scheherazade's solo violin and the mysterious chords from the opening, and this most tumultuous work comes to an end on a high, serene pianissimo.

GIOACHINO ROSSINI
(1792–1868)

Rossini was the most successful composer of opera in the early nineteenth century, principally because he had an exceptional gift for melodic invention. This shines through in his earliest instrumental music, the delightful sonatas for strings, composed when he was only twelve. Scored for two violins, cello, and double bass, they are often played by string orchestras. The music seems effortless, and is recognizably the work of the composer who was to dominate the opera stage.

His operas covered a wide range from the comic to the serious and tragic. But as a composer of comedy, he was universally acknowledged as a master. He had a reputation for writing in a great hurry. The best-known aria from his opera *Tancredi*, 'Di tanti palpiti', came to be known as the 'Rice Aria', because, according to his biographer, Stendhal, he claimed to have written it in the time that it took to boil rice. Rossini's advice about writing overtures reveals much of his wit: 'Wait until the evening before opening night. Nothing primes inspiration more than necessity, whether it be the presence of a copyist waiting for your work or the prodding of an impresario tearing his hair. In my time all the impresarios in Italy were bald at thirty.'[1]

Rossini's overtures are often played in concert. Most of them do have a certain feeling of having been written to a formula: slow introduction, witty fast theme, loud outburst, charming second theme, long crescendo, back to the first theme and repeat the sequence, end with a breathless acceleration. They would not still be played in concert halls if it were not for Rossini's genuine dramatic wit. Even in the overtures you can virtually see the cast of comic characters and young lovers walking about the stage. In recent years his serious grand operas, long neglected, have been revived.

The two overtures described here show Rossini's range. *The Barber of Seville* is the most celebrated of his comic operas, and *William Tell* is an adaptation of Schiller's drama. Rossini's overture to *William Tell* is far more serious and extensive than anyone who only knows the concluding gallop would suspect.

IL BARBIERE DI SIVIGLIA (THE BARBER OF SEVILLE), OVERTURE
Duration: approx. 8 minutes
Andante maestoso – Allegro vivo

The most enduring of Rossini's operas is based on the first of a trilogy of plays by Beaumarchais, *Le barbier de Séville*. The second of the trilogy, *Le mariage de Figaro*, had already been made into an immensely successful opera by Mozart. In *The Barber of Seville*, a young count, Almaviva, has fallen in love with Rosina, the young ward of Dr Bartolo, who guards her jealously and intends to marry her himself. Figaro, a former servant of the count, working as a barber, has access to Bartolo's house. Figaro arranges for the count to meet Rosina, in disguise, and the opera ends with Bartolo foiled, and the count and Rosina married.

The overture is an example not only of Rossini at his wittiest, but also of his pragmatism in reusing material. It began life as the Overture to *Aureliano in Palmira* (1813), then reappeared as the Overture to *Elisabetta, regina d'Inghilterra* (1815), before finding its final destination as the Overture to *Il barbiere di Siviglia* (1816). It is altogether better suited to *The Barber* than to the earlier two operas, neither of which is a comedy.

The slow introduction opens with an arresting pair of chords, followed by a quiet, rising line with staccato repeated notes. This has such potential to suggest a comic figure like Dr Bartolo that it is difficult to imagine that this was ever the overture to a serious opera. A little later, over pizzicato, violins play an elegant pair of phrases, and are then joined by a flute as the melody continues – an example of Rossini's fine ear for instrumental detail.

The introduction is followed by the Allegro vivo. After the major key of the introduction, this is in the minor, and its breathless little phrases have a sense of urgency. They quickly build up to a fierce passage for full orchestra. This part of the overture could equally well be for a tragedy. But then an oboe brings in the second theme, alternating charming phrases with a cheeky reply, and ending with a rapid descending pattern like laughter. The repeat of the theme (on horn) is followed by a classic 'Rossini crescendo', which, over a pattering bass, builds and builds to an exhilarating climax. Then, with the simplest of steps back to the home key, we return to the first theme for the reprise. This time, there is no fierce tutti: instead, Rossini jumps seamlessly to the second theme (on clarinet and bassoon), and then on to a repeat of the long crescendo. At its climax, it breaks into a faster tempo, and the overture ends in exuberant spirits. In the opera house, this guarantees that the audience is in just the right mood for the opening of a comedy – but perhaps not for a tragedy.

GUILLAUME TELL (WILLIAM TELL), OVERTURE
Duration: approx. 12 minutes

William Tell was the last of Rossini's thirty-nine operas, staged in Paris in 1829. It is an opera on the grandest scale, based on Schiller's play, and lasting more than four hours (though rarely performed complete, even in Rossini's day). After *William Tell*, Rossini retired from his triumphant career as an opera composer. He was in poor health, but he lived for another forty years.

Berlioz wrote admiringly of the opera in a Paris journal: 'Tired of hearing his operas endlessly criticized for violating the norms of dramatic expression and still more tired, perhaps, of his fanatics' blind admiration, Rossini found a simple means of silencing the opposition and shaking off his partisans: he composed a work that was seriously conceived, pondered at leisure, and executed from beginning to end according to the time-honoured principles of reason and taste. He wrote *William Tell*.' As for the overture, 'For the first time, Rossini decided to compose his overture in the dramatic manner accepted by everyone in Europe, save the Italians.' In doing so, 'he enlarged the form and turned the ordinary two-movement piece into a veritable symphony in four distinct parts'.[2] The most admired example of the model to which Berlioz refers was Weber's Overture to *Der Freischütz*, composed eight years earlier, and it is easy to hear how much Rossini is indebted to it, and the extent to which (as Berlioz says) he enlarges it.

Schiller's play is based on the legend of a Swiss huntsman and master of the crossbow, William Tell, who rises from obscurity to lead a peasants' revolt against the tyranny of the cruel Austrian governor. Tell's flaunting of the governor's orders leads to the famous scene in which he is required to place an apple on the head of his son, and shoot it with an arrow from his crossbow. But it is the governor who is, at the end of the play and the opera, killed by Tell's arrow.

The overture opens with an introduction for five solo cellos. This is one of the most beautiful passages in all of Rossini. Berlioz admired its evocation of 'the solemn silence of nature when the elements – and human passions – are at rest'. But there is also yearning as the cello line reaches upwards, and it is this element that inspired similar choruses of solo cellos in later Italian operas, notably the introduction to the love duet in Verdi's *Otello*. Twice a soft timpani roll warns of the storm to come. The cellos reach a quiet conclusion, and the violins suggest the beginnings of a swirling wind, with the first raindrops touched in by the woodwind.

The storm breaks fiercely. As Berlioz points out, its four-square phrases are too 'orderly' to have quite the overwhelming force of the storm in Beethoven's 'Pastoral' Symphony, but perhaps that is not what one needs in an overture. The storm fades, and is followed by 'a pastoral scene of great freshness'. This is a *ranz des vaches*, mimicking the traditional melodies played on the Alpenhorn by Swiss cowherds. The way it emerges from the storm certainly has echoes of Beethoven's 'Pastoral' Symphony, but here Rossini chooses cor anglais echoed by flute, rather than Beethoven's French horn. (Berlioz himself had a cor anglais echoed by offstage oboe play a *ranz des vaches* in his *Symphonie fantastique*, composed the year after the premiere of *William Tell*.) As the melody continues, the flute adds elaborate decoration evoking birdsong, and there is the delicate sound of a triangle, which Berlioz takes to be 'the bell of the herds peacefully feeding'.

Trumpets break into this peaceful scene with a call to arms. The overture ends with the famous gallop, a rallying call for the struggle against tyranny.

CAMILLE SAINT-SAËNS
(1835–1921)

Like Mozart and Mendelssohn before him, Camille Saint-Saëns was an immensely gifted child prodigy, both as a composer and as a performer. He began composing at three, and was playing concertos in public from memory by the age of ten. Wagner, who first met Saint-Saëns in 1859, later wrote that he could play his operas, including *Tristan*, from memory 'with such precision that one might easily have thought that he had the actual music before his eyes'.[1] Saint-Saëns was the organist at the church of La Madeleine in Paris for several years, and Liszt, who heard him improvise there, declared that he was the greatest organist in the world. He had very wide musical sympathies. He revived the music of J. S. Bach and Handel, and French composers such as Rameau, Lully, and Charpentier, while at the same time promoting the work of living composers. During a long life he wrote huge quantities of music, including twelve operas.

But, for a composer of such extraordinary abilities, Saint-Saëns has had a patchy reception from posterity. Only a handful of his works are still played regularly, the most popular being one that he dashed off for fun, and did not allow to be published in his lifetime, *The Carnival of the Animals*. Many writers have suggested that he wrote almost too fluently, and he himself said that he spent his career 'fulfilling the function of my nature, as an apple-tree grows apples'.[2] He also had the misfortune, over his long life, to grow out of fashion.

In 1871, Saint-Saëns co-founded the Société Nationale de Musique, devoted to the performance of works by young French composers. In 1886 he resigned from it, ostensibly because of a proposal to include non-French works in the society's concerts, but largely because of the dominance of César Franck and his pupils, from whom he had become ever more distant. Much of Saint-Saëns's isolation arose from his opposition to the 'Wagner-mania', which had engulfed the musical life of Paris like an epidemic. Saint-Saëns wrote, 'People who are unable to play the simplest thing on the piano, and who don't know a word of German, spend whole evenings deciphering the most difficult scores in the world … Wagner was the inventor of everything; there was no music before him and there can be none after.'[3] Although Saint-Saëns admired much of Wagner's music, he regretted that he found himself surrounded by a generation of young composers for whom Wagner had made the old classical values of Mozart and Beethoven irrelevant.

As the musical world advanced through its Wagner craze to the tumult of the early twentieth century, Saint-Saëns proceeded steadily on his way, sticking to his own values. Romain Rolland wrote in 1908, 'Compared with the restless and troubled art of today, his music strikes us by its calm, its tranquil harmonies, its velvety modulations, its crystal clearness, its smooth and flowing style, and an elegance that cannot be put into words. Even his classic coldness does us good by its reaction against the exaggerations, sincere as they are, of the new school. At times one feels oneself carried back to Mendelssohn, even to Spontini and the school of Gluck.'[4] This very cleanness and transparency of approach, which often led Saint-Saëns to be labelled as lacking in passion, gives the best of his music a distinctive appeal. Perhaps, in the twenty-first century, we have learned enough about musical fashions and their sometimes dire consequences to relish anew a composer who (like his pupil Fauré) had his own way of doing things, and paid little attention to current fads.

Concertos

CELLO CONCERTO NO. 1 IN A MINOR, OP. 33
Duration: approx. 19 minutes
Allegro non troppo – Allegretto con moto – Tempo primo

Saint-Saëns composed this concerto in 1872 for a Belgian cellist, Auguste Tolbecque, who played its premiere in Paris in January 1893. The concerto demonstrated how it was possible to write for cello and nineteenth-century orchestra in such a way as to exploit the singing, tenor character of the cello and give it an opportunity for brilliant virtuoso display. Saint-Saëns's subtlety and delicacy of orchestration seems so natural that it is easy to take it for granted. One can hear echoes of his methods and style in Tchaikovsky's Variations on a Rococo Theme (five years later) and Dvořák's Cello Concerto (twenty-two years later).

The concerto plays without a break. Material from the first section returns and is developed further in the third section. This gives the work a satisfyingly rounded, 'organic' feel, reminiscent of some works by Schumann, particularly his Fourth Symphony and the Cello Concerto. Saint-Saëns was a great admirer of Schumann, and knew his symphonies intimately. Schumann's Cello Concerto was rarely played during Saint-Saëns's lifetime, though he probably knew it.

One reason for the popularity of Saint-Saëns's concerto is the power of its opening. After an arresting chord from the orchestra, the soloist comes straight in with the principal theme: a tumbling whirl of notes, ending with a defiant gesture echoed on the lowest string. Four times the phrase is repeated, ratcheted up in pitch each time. The theme is taken over by the woodwind and then the violins, while the soloist tugs at the harmonies that help create the tension. A little later, the soloist eases into a second theme. For a brief moment, all the urgency falls away as the cellist plays a yearning melody that (like the first theme) rises phrase by phrase. As the cellist reaches a high harmonic, flute and clarinet enter with the tumbling first theme again. The cello responds with increasing power and virtuosity, until a final ascent brings in an orchestral tutti. After all the lyrical freedom of the movement so far, this passage has a slightly formal, old-fashioned air.

A woodwind chord, and a shift of key, takes us into the centre of the movement. The first theme returns, now in a major key, which makes it more playfully energetic. The soloist passes it to the woodwind, which alternate with the strings in rapid dialogue while the cello plays fragments in counter-rhythm against them (the rich interaction between soloist and orchestra is one of the delights of this concerto). The tension builds, until it breaks into a brief orchestral tutti. The soloist emerges, and launches into a reprise of the lyrical second theme (having bypassed the first theme). This extends into a lingering meditation, and a pause.

What do we expect? Perhaps a return to the first theme, as before. But instead, muted strings quietly begin a demure minuet. It is as if a curtain has been raised to reveal a scene in an eighteenth-century drawing room. Shortly before Saint-Saëns composed this concerto, his great-aunt Charlotte had died at the age of ninety-one. She was the woman who, when Camille was a two-year-old child, had introduced him to her piano, and had nurtured his musical talent. She was as important as his own mother to him, 'a woman of keen intellect and brilliant attainments' who 'remembered perfectly the customs of the *ancien regime*, which she enjoyed talking about'.[5] Saint-Saëns seems here to be evoking the pre-revolutionary days that Charlotte would have known as a child. The strings repeat the minuet, and over it the cello floats a tender countermelody. The continuation leads to a moment of cadenza and a trill. The woodwind repeat the minuet, then the cello takes it to a heartfelt climax. As it falls away, it is as if the soloist is reluctant to leave these memories.

Eventually, the first theme steals quietly in on oboe, and we return to the material of the opening section. It quickly builds in ferocity, but soon gives way to an eloquent theme on the cello. This might seem quite new, but there are shapes in it that are drawn from the cello's countermelody to the minuet. Unlike the lyrical second theme in the first section, this one is in the minor, and has more the character of a lament. It climaxes in a fierce tutti, which sparks off virtuoso cello runs. There is a moment of cadenza, another tutti, and the music calms to yet another theme. This is warm and sonorous, without the lamenting character of the previous melody. It ascends to a high note, the energy returns, and with it more virtuoso fireworks. But soon the music again draws back. Saint-Saëns returns to the lament, and we get a sense that this melody is the emotional heart of the work (and one can hear an echo of it in Tchaikovsky's Variations on a Rococo Theme). At the end of the melody the orchestra breaks in fiercely with the first theme. There is a sudden increase in tempo, and a return to the tutti that concluded the first section of the concerto. A powerful final solo brings the work to an end.

INTRODUCTION AND RONDO CAPRICCIOSO IN A MINOR, OP. 28
Duration: approx. 9 minutes
Andante (malinconico) – Allegro ma non troppo

This is the best known of Saint-Saëns's works for violin and orchestra, which he composed for the Spanish violinist Pablo de Sarasate in 1863. Saint-Saëns had first met Sarasate in 1858, when the violinist was only fifteen but already a celebrity. Sarasate awakened in him a fascination with Spain and the Spanish character. In later years, there was to be a lasting love affair between French composers and Spain, sparked off by Chabrier's *España* and Bizet's *Carmen* (both 1874), and continuing through to Debussy and Ravel in the twentieth century. Saint-Saëns described his Introduction and Rondo Capriccioso as being 'in the Spanish style'. The flavour may be mild compared to those later works, but there is no mistaking the sincerity with which Saint-Saëns evokes a spirit of passionate volatility, an evocation as much to do with Sarasate himself as with Spanish character in general. Sarasate was ten years younger than Saint-Saëns, but they became friends, and Sarasate regularly attended Saint-Saëns's Monday musical soirées. Saint-Saëns later recalled, 'for several years afterwards no violinists could be prevailed upon to perform at my house, so terrified were they at the idea of inviting comparison. Not only did he shine by reason of his talent alone, but also because of his brilliant intellect and the inexhaustible animation of his conversation which was invariably interesting and suggestive'.[6]

The Introduction, with its falling sighs and rising arpeggios, is accompanied by strummed pizzicato, like a guitar. Saint-Saëns has certainly caught the 'melancholy' mood, and the moments of sudden animation and virtuoso flourishes add an element of volatility. A series of fierce trills bring in the Allegro. Apart from 'The Swan' from the *Carnival of the Animals*, this is probably Saint-Saëns's most famous melody, but its popularity cannot take away from its spirit of proud elegance and determination. Part of the effect is created by the strutting chords underneath the melody, with shifting harmonies over a fixed bass. It would fit perfectly well as an aria for the toreador in Bizet's *Carmen*. This opening theme recurs, to create a rondo. The first episode moves into a major key and becomes more playful. Again, the accompaniment is crucial to the effect, with rapid little clusters of notes that one could imagine as the clapping of flamenco musicians. The violin line evolves into a virtuoso display, ending with a trill and a run.

The rondo theme returns with a bang on the upbeat rather than the downbeat – a strikingly bold effect. The theme ends with another virtuoso run-up, and the orchestra brings in the next episode. This is fiercer and more energetic, and one can imagine the stamping of heels as well as the clapping of hands. From here, the soloist brings in a soulful, sultry melody (Saint-Saëns marks this 'con mordibezza', with tenderness). There is another burst of virtuoso runs, and the main theme is back, this time with a new, chattering element to the accompanying rhythm, drawn from the earlier fierce dance. This leads on to a return to the fierce dance itself, then to a new key, and a new melody. It has an amorous, nostalgic character, with phrases that remind us of the Introduction. That takes us back to the playful first episode, and then more fireworks ending with an arpeggio pattern over which an oboe brings in the rondo tune. The arpeggios become more and more extravagant, until they burst out into a little cadenza of forceful chords. There is a pause, the tempo increases, and with a display of the utmost brilliance the piece comes to a breathless end.

PIANO CONCERTO NO. 2 IN G MINOR, OP. 22
Duration: approx. 23 minutes

Andante sostenuto
Allegro scherzando
Presto

When we think of the great composers who wrote piano concertos in the first half of the nineteenth century, none of them was French. Chopin (a Pole) and Liszt (a Hungarian) were the darlings of the French salons in the 1830s, but little of the music they played was French. Saint-Saëns, a generation later, was the composer who put the French piano concerto on the map. His Second Piano Concerto had some success during his lifetime, and has remained the most popular of his five.

He composed it in 1868. The great Russian pianist Anton Rubinstein was in Paris, where he gave a series of eight concerts that Saint-Saëns conducted. When Rubinstein proposed that he should make his Parisian debut as a conductor, with Saint-Saëns as soloist, Saint-Saëns composed this concerto in less than three weeks. Despite an inadequately prepared premiere, it went on to become the most successful of his five piano concertos. It has a most unusual shape, consisting of a slow movement, which occupies half the total length of the concerto, followed by a scherzo and a finale.

The concerto begins with an introduction played by the piano alone. It is often said that this is a homage to J. S. Bach, and Saint-Saëns himself later revealed that it was based on an idea he had while improvising on the organ (he was famous for his improvisations). What is most impressive is not the fact that Saint-Saëns could improvise a Bach prelude, but the journey that this homage then takes. The solemn opening, with two voices answering each other in counterpoint, rises, accelerating as it goes, until it bursts into a brilliant cascade that could have come out of a study by Liszt (another composer who revered Bach). It is as if Saint-Saëns is leaping the centuries. Glittering arpeggios culminate in a series of massive chords, over a bass that rises, a semitone at a time, in a chromatic scale. This powerful harmonic progression cuts off, the bass falls downwards, and the orchestra enters with massive chords, and the assertive 'double-dotted' rhythms associated with the French Overture of Bach's time.

The introduction comes to a quiet conclusion, and the piano launches into the first fully fledged theme. This is a sombre melody, borrowed by Saint-Saëns from his pupil at the École Niedermeyer, Gabriel Fauré, who had written it for a choral work and then discarded it. Its passionate undertones gradually assert themselves, building to powerful exchanges with the orchestra. These calm to a second, lyrical theme, which reaches delicate trills and is then handed to a clarinet and the violins for its final phrase – a beautiful touch. A passage of charming, Chopin-like running thirds follows. The music accelerates and develops a Lisztian power, until massive double octaves climax in the return of the first theme on orchestra. As the piano continues, its meditation takes on the character of a cadenza, until the orchestra joins it for a final musing on the first theme. From here, we find ourselves back at the beginning, with the Bach-like fantasia recalled in a serene spirit. The movement ends with an assertive restatement of the first orchestral entry.

The second movement impressed even at the roughly performed premiere. It is in effect a scherzo, light as a feather, in the tradition of Mendelssohn, but with touches of wit and harmonic spice that are entirely Saint-Saëns's own. These are evident right from the opening bars, which begin with the timpani tapping out the rhythm. The piano enters with the first theme, a tune with delicate, dancing chords, ending with a laughing flourish of semiquavers like a balletic gesture. As the theme is developed, the interplay between piano, strings, and woodwind is delightful, with subtle turns of harmony, and even a fleeting moment of wistfulness.

Then a cascade of arpeggios brings in a second theme. This has the easy charm of a popular song. Many pianists slow it considerably, so that its opening acquires a rather gallumphing character. But there is nothing in the score to suggest it, and it is more charming if the rhythm is kept light. This theme, too, is full of subtleties of harmony. Scintillating runs over string tremolo bring the first section of the movement to a close. The opening theme returns, and the piano takes it into a minor key. Elements from the second theme take a new turn, building up a head of steam. A wistful reminder of the second theme itself leads, with coy changes of mind, through to the reprise of the opening. There are new little touches throughout, and at the end, the ballet dancer exits with the sweetest and most weightless of gestures.

After the scherzo, one might expect a more solid, serious finale. But Saint-Saëns boldly takes the opposite course, with a wild tarantella. The piano hurls us straight in, and the pace does not let up during the first paragraph. Various elements are drawn in as the music races by: a falling chromatic phrase that maybe harks back to the chromatic scales in the first movement, perky trills that will take on more significance later, frenetic repeated chords exchanged with the orchestra. We return to the beginning, and the music quietens, moving into new keys and alternating the main theme with the trill motif. Then the piano picks away at the trills obsessively, and wind chords develop into a sort of chorale. The piano breaks out of its obsession with the trills, and thundering octaves bring us back to a repeat of the main theme.

The different elements pass by as before, with subtle changes. The momentum builds, and at its climax the piano interrupts with commanding and unexpected bass octaves, over which it places chords like massive chunks of rock. It is as if the power of the first movement has been reawakened. This is twice repeated, majestically shifting up in pitch each time (this is another of those moments when Saint-Saëns demonstrates his sure-footed control of harmony). Then the theme continues as if nothing has happened, hurtling unstoppably to the concluding chords.

VIOLIN CONCERTO NO. 3 IN B MINOR, OP. 61
Duration: approx. 29 minutes

Allegro non troppo
Andantino quasi allegretto
Molto moderato e maestoso – Allegro non troppo

This is the most successful of Saint-Saëns's three violin concertos, and the third work that he composed for the Spanish violinist, Pablo de Sarasate. Sarasate was only fifteen when he first approached Saint-Saëns in 1858 and asked him for a concerto. Saint-Saëns late recalled, 'Years have now passed since there once called upon me Pablo de Sarasate, youthful and fresh-looking as the spring and already a celebrity, though a dawning moustache had only just begun to appear. He had been good enough to ask me, in the most casual way imaginable, to write a concerto for him. Greatly flattered and delighted at the request I gave him my promise and kept my word with the *Concerto in A major* to which – I do not know why – the German title of *Conzertstück* has been given.'[7] The reason for the title of 'Concert Piece' was that, though it is a charming work, it lasts only about twelve minutes, playing without a break. It was published as Concerto No. 1, though Saint-Saëns had already composed a Violin Concerto in C major, which was not performed for another twenty years. Saint-Saëns also wrote for Sarasate the Introduction and Rondo Capriccioso 'in the Spanish style' (see Introduction and Rondo Capriccioso), and this Concerto No. 3 in B minor: 'During the composition of this Concerto he gave me valuable advice to which is certainly due the considerable degree of favour it has met with on the part of violinists themselves.'[8] Saint-Saëns completed this concerto in 1880.

Over shuddering *pp* tremolando strings and a timpani roll, the soloist enters straight away with the first theme. This is bold and forte in the most sonorous register of the violin, with big, square phrases and leaps that convey a sense of striving. Its continuation is more complex, with runs and heavy chords giving way to more lyrical moments. After an orchestral tutti, the next solo becomes calmer, until it reaches a quiet, tense chord. This resolves into a second theme, serene and tender, which culminates in a rise to a high note. The opening tremolo returns, and the first theme moves into new keys, alternating playfully with virtuoso runs, arpeggios, and chords. The power builds until, unexpectedly, we find ourselves in the approach to the reprise of the second theme. The serene melody unfolds, and as it does so it is beautifully enhanced by harp-like patterns of pizzicato in the accompanying strings. Once more the opening tremolo returns, signalling that the end is near. The soloist's first theme gives way to increasingly virtuoso passages, and the tension builds to a powerful finish.

The slow movement opens with the solo violin singing a pastoral melody in a gently lilting rhythm that goes back to the baroque siciliano. The last bar of each phrase is sweetly echoed by violins and oboe, with a delicate arpeggio from the flute. Saint-Saëns skilfully extends and varies the melody and its interactions to create the first paragraph of the movement. Then with an increase in volume and energy, the violin embarks on a bolder, broader theme for the middle of the movement, accompanied by little flourishes like the decorations of a bagpiper. These flourishes are taken over by the violin solo, to bring the music to a reprise of the opening, first on the orchestral violins, then played by the soloist. A moment of cadenza leads into the theme high on the solo violin, in a new key. It eases its way home, with a sweet oboe solo, and the movement ends with the soloist playing arpeggios in harmonics, together with a clarinet – an ethereal effect.

The finale opens with a passage of cadenza, in which the soloist takes the flourishes from the slow movement and turns them into a forceful gesture, with a leap at the end of the phrase that hints at the theme to come, and with dramatic tremolo interventions from the orchestra. The Allegro begins as a tarantella, like the successful finale of Saint-Saëns's Second Piano Concerto. But here the dance is not so relentless, and contrasted elements are drawn in. The first solo is full of leaps and runs. But then a sweeping, lyrical melody intervenes, while the orchestra quietly keeps the tarantella rhythm going. The soloist breaks into virtuoso passages, alternating with the leaps of the tarantella theme.

Then a second lyrical theme comes in, rather Mendelssohn-like in its straightforward phrasing. Further alternations between the tarantella rhythm and virtuoso passages follow. Then an expectant orchestral tutti leads to a hushed chorale on muted strings. Each line of the chorale is repeated by the soloist, with counterpoint in the woodwind. The second part of the chorale has touches of melancholy harmony that make this moment sound almost operatic. From the end of the chorale, the soloist begins gently to reintroduce the tarantella. The energy builds, until suddenly we are back at the opening cadenza. The soloist's dramatic flourishes alternate with longer interventions from the orchestra. From here the energy builds again, to the reprise of the tarantella theme. The orchestra reminds us of the first of the lyrical elements, then the soloist returns to the Mendelssohn-like melody. There is a moment of expectation, the music builds, and culminates in a reprise of the chorale, now fortissimo and majestic on the brass (this too is very Mendelssohnian). The soloist takes it up, high over tremolando strings, then breaks into arpeggios, and into more rapid figuration. The excitement grows, the orchestra breaks into the Mendelssohn-like theme at a faster tempo, and with a final virtuoso dash the concerto comes to an end.

SYMPHONY NO. 3 IN C MINOR, OP. 78, 'ORGAN SYMPHONY'
Duration: approx. 37 minutes

I
Adagio – Allegro moderato –
Poco adagio

II
Allegro moderato – Presto – Allegro moderato –
Maestoso – Allegro

When Saint-Saëns published this grand symphony, he dedicated it to the memory of Franz Liszt, who had died soon after its first performance in 1886. Liszt had been one of Saint-Saëns's most ardent champions. It was he who used his influence to press for the premiere of Saint-Saëns's opera *Samson et Dalila* in Weimar many years before it was performed in France. It was also Liszt who described Saint-Saëns as the greatest organist in the world. This was a most suitable work to dedicate to Liszt's memory. Of all Saint-Saëns's works, it is the one that most demonstrates the influence of Liszt – flamboyant Romantic gestures, vivid orchestration, and a subtle unity of form achieved by the transformation of themes. This is Saint-Saëns at his best, combining virtuoso subtlety in his command of the orchestra with a sort of gothic magnificence to create an overwhelming effect. It is the only one of his three symphonies to be played regularly. The large orchestra includes not only an organ, but also a piano with two players.

Unusually for a symphony the score is divided into two large sections. But within this two-part structure there are the conventional four movements of a nineteenth-century symphony. The first movement (Allegro moderato preceded by a brief Adagio introduction) leads without a break into the slow movement (Poco adagio). The second half of the symphony begins with a scherzo and trio (Allegro moderato – Presto – Allegro moderato), which leads without a break into the finale (Maestoso – Allegro).

The symphony is perfectly judged so that not only the grand gestures but also the fascinating details are effective in the acoustic of a large church. The fast themes in the first Allegro and the scherzo have agitated articulations within them, and are brilliantly orchestrated; but the harmonies move quite slowly, so that the texture shimmers and catches the ear without the overall effect becoming blurred.

The symphony opens with a brief and mysterious Adagio introduction. With its uncertain harmonies, interleaved falling and rising phrases, and dramatic pauses, it pays homage to the Prelude to Wagner's *Tristan* (Wagner was, apart from Liszt, the greatest influence on French music at this period). This soon gives way to the Allegro moderato. A quietly agitated, pulsating figure in the strings, reminiscent of Schubert's 'Unfinished' Symphony, forms a meandering pattern that is to play an important part throughout the work. Above it, woodwind play the rising phrase from the introduction. Much of this movement is developed from these two ideas, whose relationship shifts subtly – between strings and woodwind, and between a prominent and an accompanying role – and climaxes are built up. The last of these dies down, and the Adagio follows without a break.

The organ enters softly, and over its sustained chords the strings quietly intone a hymn-like melody built (again) from rising phrases. The repetition of this melody is played by clarinet, horn, and trombone in octaves – a most unusual combination, which sounds strikingly organ-like. The theme is then softly elaborated in counterpoint by the strings, with the organ again joining with soft chords. The meandering pattern from the beginning of the Allegro is quietly touched in pizzicato, in cellos and bass. This gradually builds up through the strings, until the theme re-enters pianissimo high in the violins, with viola and cello below, and the organ accompanying. The movement reaches a quiet conclusion, and the only full break in the symphony.

After the gentle drifting of the slow movement, the scherzo is splendidly incisive. As in the first movement, the theme features rapidly repeated notes, and the original meandering pattern has been simplified to an assertively rhythmic figure, punctuated by the timpani. A second motif, first heard on the woodwind, is closer to the original meandering pattern, but now rhythmically disjointed.

For the middle section of the movement (the trio of a conventional scherzo), the pace increases to Presto. Here the delicate woodwind are joined by brilliant arpeggios from the piano, entering for the first time. Touches of the meandering pattern, and the rising phrases, predominate, and they eventually form themselves into a new melody rising in the strings. At the climax, the music comes to an abrupt halt with a cymbal crash, and the scherzo is repeated. Then once more the faster Presto returns, as if we are to go round the loop again. But this time it peters out, leaving the strings quietly exchanging rising phrases, as if remembering the slow movement. There is another pizzicato reminder of the meandering phrases in the bass, with soft chords, and then a moment of silence. This is broken by a great chord of C major on the organ, announcing the beginning of the finale.

The organ chords are answered by counterpoint from the orchestra, built from rising phrases. This gives this opening a very ecclesiastical feel, as if Saint-Saëns wishes to root the movement in the great tradition of church music stretching back over the centuries. But this formal gesture is followed immediately by one of Saint-Saëns's most magical effects. The strings, in quiet chords spread over four octaves, intone a chant-like theme distilled from the original meandering shape, while the piano duet enlivens the texture with sparkling arpeggios. Then the chant is taken up by the organ, fortissimo, answered by cymbal crashes and brass fanfares. More counterpoint intervenes, and a new version of the rising phrase is developed and passed quietly from instrument to instrument. A climax builds up, led by the trombones, but is inconclusive.

The quiet rising melody returns, and is again passed around. Once more the trombones lead a build-up, and this time there is no stopping it. More contrapuntal treatment of the chant leads to an acceleration, and the pace increases steadily to the final pages of the symphony. The ending is magnificent, with rushing upward scales against a descending bass underpinned by the low notes of the organ, and a final blaze of trumpet fanfares and thundering of timpani.

ERIK SATIE
(1866–1925)

S atie is one of those figures whose perceived importance seems out of proportion to the music that he wrote. Most of the music for which he is known consists of tiny piano pieces, some of them austere and elegant, such as the *Gymnopédies*, most of them droll and enigmatic, with titles such as 'Choral inappetisant', *Embryons desséchés* ('Dessicated Embryos'), and *Préludes flasques (pour un chien)* ('Flabby Preludes for a Dog'). He took to adding little descriptive phrases and instructions in the scores. For example, the first of the *Embryons desséchés*, the 'Holothurian' (Sea cucumber), includes the following: 'It is raining', 'What a pretty rock!', 'Like a nightingale with toothache', and 'I have run out of tobacco. Fortunately I don't smoke.' He issued a fierce prohibition against reading these commentaries out in performance, but, as with the music, it is not clear how seriously this is to be taken.

Satie began his musical studies in an orthodox way, by attending the Paris Conservatoire, but he was ill-suited to formal study and was regarded by his teachers as lazy and untalented. His musical gifts really began to show themselves when, at the age of twenty-one, he left home and took a room in Montmartre. He played the piano and conducted the orchestra at the famous Chat Noir cabaret, a meeting place for radical writers and artists. Here he developed a friendship with Debussy. Debussy understood that something serious lay behind Satie's enigmatic facade, with his affectation of bohemianism and his musical aphorisms that seemed to exist solely on their own terms. Debussy admired the static simplicity of Satie's music, which seemed to evoke an aura of antiquity. He later orchestrated two of Satie's *Gymnopédies*, a set of hauntingly static piano sarabandes inspired by evocations of ancient Greece, published in 1888 (the previous year, Satie had introduced himself to the director of the Chat Noir as a 'gymnopédiste').

Satie for a time associated himself with a mystical Rosicrucian sect, and in 1892 wrote *Uspud*, a 'Christian ballet'. Uspud, a figure in Persian clothing, is a persecutor of Christians who is visited by a vision of Mother Church. He attempts to destroy her, but this provokes 'a great convulsion of nature'. Christ reaches down from the Cross to bless him, Uspud is martyred by being torn to pieces, and his soul is born up to Christ in heaven. The score, slow and halting throughout, consists of simple motifs with strange harmonies in a hypnotic pattern of repetitions that seem to anticipate by more than a century the ideas of the minimalists. It was taken to be a parody of Flaubert's *The Temptation of Saint Anthony*, and provoked laughter and outrage when Satie played it on the piano, reading out the stage directions. But Debussy saw behind the parody. He described Satie at this period as 'a gentle medieval musician lost in this century'.[1]

Satie reinvented himself over the course of his life, swapping his bohemian dress for grey velvet suits, and contradictions remained at the heart of his music and his public persona: a shy wit, who hid seriousness behind jokes and punctured pretension with mockery. The climax of his public career came in 1916–17, when he composed his two most successful major works, *Socrate* and *Parade*. *Socrate* was the result of a commission from the Princesse de Polignac to write a work for female voices based on ancient Greek texts. The music that Satie composed is the culmination of the ancient, mystical side of his personality. It sets extracts from Plato's dialogues in French translation, culminating in the death of Socrates. It is scored for a single female voice (or several in succession taking each role), with piano or small orchestra. As in *Uspud* two decades earlier, Satie constructs his score from repetitions of a small number of motifs, deliberately avoiding any sense of conventional musical development. His intention was to create a work 'as white and pure as Antiquity', and the effect is peculiarly touching (though this did not stop some members of the audience at the premiere of the orchestral version from assuming it was another of Satie's jokes).

By this time, Satie's piano pieces had acquired a following, and the famous pianist Ricardo Viñes had begun to play some of them. Satie's deadpan, enigmatic style, which had seemed merely eccentric in the 1880s, was now in tune with the brittle, satirical Parisian scene. Jean Cocteau had heard Satie and Viñes play his *Trois pièces en forme de poire* ('Three Pear-shaped Pieces', for piano duet), and suggested that he should create a ballet on them. Satie was unwilling to allow them to be used, but offered to write a new score. *Parade* was staged for Diaghilev's Ballets Russes in 1917, with set and costume designed by Picasso and choreography by Massine. This was the breakthrough that enabled Satie to give up his work in cabaret, and to survive from now on through commissions for theatre works. His collaborations with Diaghilev, Cocteau, and Picasso brought him to prominence in the avant garde, and he became associated with the latest developments in the arts – cubism, surrealism, Dadaism. And, once more with the involvement of Cocteau, Satie became the father figure of the group of iconoclastic young French composers known as Les Six.

The influence of his approach to music, by turns mystical and ironic, and sometimes both, extended far and wide, from Debussy and Ravel through the members of Les Six (including Milhaud and Poulenc) to Messiaen, John Cage, and the minimalists.

PARADE (A REALISTIC BALLET IN ONE SCENE)
Duration: approx. 10 minutes

Choral
Prélude du rideau rouge (Prelude of the red curtain)
Prestidigitateur chinois (Chinese conjuror)
Petite fille américaine (Little American girl)
Rag-time du paquebot (Ragtime of the packet steamer)
Acrobates
Final
Suite au Prélude du rideau rouge (Continuation of the Prelude of the red curtain)

The ballet *Parade* was first staged by Diaghilev's Ballets Russes in May 1917 at the Théâtre du Châtelet in Paris. For the second time within three years, Satie inherited a commission that had been offered to Stravinsky (the first being the illustrated volume of piano pieces, *Sports et Divertissements*). Jean Cocteau had devised a ballet scenario set in a French street fair, whose popular mixture of circus and music-hall attractions provided rich material for artists and writers of the time. Satie, with his attachment to cabaret and his anti-establishment wit, was Cocteau's ideal partner in this project (really much more suited than Stravinsky). The choreographer was Léonide Massine. In Cocteau's scenario, a series of performers at the fair try to persuade the theatre audience to come in to see the show. These include a Chinese conjuror, an American girl, and an acrobat. Each performer is accompanied by a manager. For the managers, Picasso had designed cumbersome cardboard costumes that restricted the dancers' movements, an encumbrance that Massine used to witty advantage. *Parade* was described ironically as a *Ballet réaliste*, but the reality had little to do with the conventional meaning of the word, and the ironical character of the ballet, staged in the middle of the First World War, was clearly meant as a provocative gesture. Guillaume Apollinaire, in an article that was reprinted in the programme for the premiere, wrote about the close collaboration between Picasso and Massine, coining a new term to describe it: 'This new union – for up until now stage sets and costumes on the one hand and choreography on the other were only superfi-cially linked – has given rise in *Parade* to a kind of sur-realism.'[2]

Satie entered enthusiastically into this new collaboration. His score deliberately lacks most aspects of conventional structure and development, instead simply repeating and juxtaposing elements in a collage-like manner that has echoes of cubism. But Satie was also fascinated by mathematical proportions, and scholars have shown that he took great care to employ them in *Parade* (as in much of his music). These include use of the Golden Section, numbers related to the Fibonacci series, and allusions to cubes and cylinders. None of this is apparent to the listener, but, as with Debussy, who was similarly fascinated by mathematical proportions, it indicates an unexpected level of intellectual seriousness behind music that sounds formally relaxed.[3]

Cocteau asked Satie to include sound effects in his score including typewriters, gunshots, 'flaques sonores' ('sound puddles', undefined), sirens, and a lottery wheel. Cocteau described the effect of these sounds: 'These imitated noises of waves, typewriters, revolvers, sirens or aeroplanes, are, in music, of the same character as the bits of newspaper, painted wood-grain, and other everyday objects that the cubist painters employ frequently in their pictures, in order to localise objects and masses in nature.'[4] Satie accepted the insertion of these effects by Cocteau into his score with reluctance. He wrote to Diaghilev, 'I don't much like the "noises" made by Jean. But there's nothing we can do here: we have before us a likeable maniac' (a description of Cocteau that suggests why he and Satie were well suited to each other).[5]

The audience reaction to *Parade* was almost as noisy as at the premiere of Stravinsky's *The Rite of Spring*, staged by the Ballets Russes in 1913, though in both cases the outrage was directed as much at the visual effect of the choreography and costumes as at the music. *Parade* was highly experimental for all concerned: it was Massine's first choreography, Cocteau's first ballet scenario, Satie's first ballet score, and the first time that Picasso had designed sets and costumes for a ballet. Together, they created something deliberately anti-traditional and anti-establishment. Satie's music certainly joined in the fun of mocking people's expectations of a ballet score, echoing the cardboard costumes and stiff movements of the dancers with stolid repetitions and lumpen rhythms that seem both simple and bizarre, though this impression is often achieved by subtle and carefully calculated means. When *Parade* was staged in London in 1919, a critic commented, 'Satie has been termed a cubist composer, though what the term exactly signifies in this connection, I am unable to say. If it means that his music is mordantly witty, perverse and unlike anything else, then by all means, let him be cubist. In any case it is said that he is the preferred composer of the cubists.'[6]

Satie's score opens with a somewhat portentous chorale intoned by sonorous trumpets and trombones. It gives way to timid phrases on high violins and flute.

This leads straight into the 'Prelude of the Red Curtain'. The 'Red Curtain' by Picasso was a beautiful, lavish design incorporating traditional figures from the circus, *commedia dell'arte*, and Eastern mythological stories: a winged horse and its foal, a winged ballerina, Pierrot and Harlequin, a black man wearing a turban, and a trapeze artist ascending a multi-coloured ladder, all enveloped in opulently draped curtains. It must have lulled the audience into expecting the sort of lavish, evocative evening for which the Ballets Russes was famous. Satie at first does not upset the mood, proceeding with an apparently serious little passage of fugue. Soon, however, it breaks off, first delicately, and then with a sudden swagger.

The Red Curtain rises to reveal the French manager, whose cardboard costume was like a cubist portrait constructed from fragments of buildings, with a moustache. Satie's music is at first mysterious, with repeating patterns that shift uneasily over a persistent, quiet drumbeat. Suddenly, it bursts out with a crash of cymbals and the shriek of a high siren. The rattling of the lottery wheel introduces the Chinese conjuror.

Massine described his movements in this role: 'I marched stiffly round the stage, jerking my head at each step ... With an elaborate flourish I pretended to produce an egg from my sleeve and put it in my mouth. When I had mimed the action of swallowing it, I ... pretended to pull the egg from the toe of my shoe ... When I had retrieved the egg I leaped around the stage again, then paused, puckered up my lips and pretended to breathe out fire.'[7] This was the point for the 'sound puddles', as the spectators try to put out the sparks. Satie's music begins and ends with strutting trombones. In between, there is a collage of little sections made from repeating motifs, scored with Debussyan subtlety, over a continuing drum pattern. Horn and flute play the only extended melodies. The lottery wheel and the cheeky trombones return to round off the conjuring act, which gives way to the Little American Girl and her manager.

The American manager was costumed with an assembly of cardboard skyscrapers. The Little American Girl was dressed to look like Pearl White, the American actress who starred in the silent film series, *The Perils of Pauline*. According to Massine, she 'did an imitation of the shuffling walk of Charlie Chaplin, followed by a sequence of mimed actions reminiscent of *The Perils of Pauline*, jumping on to a moving train, swimming across a river, having a running fight at pistol-point, and finally finding herself lost at sea in the tragic sinking of the *Titanic*'.[8] Satie's music begins with an urgent entry and then acquires a strutting character with touches of ragtime syncopation, though with unsettled whole-tone harmonies. A quiet moment introduces the typewriter(s). After a series of gunshots, the violins take up a real ragtime song, Irving Berlin and Ted Snyder's 'The Mysterious Rag', in a parody that is close enough to be familiar to aficionados of the latest American trends, but no doubt distant enough to avoid a copyright dispute.[9] Here it is labelled 'Ragtime of the packet-steamer'. This refers to the band of the *Titanic*, playing as disaster approaches (in 1912, the same years as 'The Mysterious Rag'). Over a threatening roll of timpani the ship's hooter sounds, and there is a great wave in the orchestra (an early version of this passage was even more tasteless, incorporating sung words, 'Tic, tic, tic, the Titanic sinks into the sea'). After a few nervous bars of pizzicato, the urgent music from the beginning of the section returns, and propels us into the third of the acts.

The manager who introduces the Acrobats was the figure of a jockey mounted on a pantomime-horse (the premiere had to do without the jockey-manager, which had become detached). The absurdity is highlighted by a xylophone and a trombone glissando as the music settles into a waltz rhythm. Any sense of normal elegance is disturbed once again by whole-tone harmonies. In the middle of this section is a strange episode. A low note of an organ is heard (an organ with two pipes had been specially constructed for the premiere), over which violins and violas play an insistent pattern of fourths, while a flute plays a simple solo above. After this static moment, the waltz returns, with its xylophone. There is a brief silence, followed by a moment of mayhem, as the outburst from the Prelude of the Red Curtain returns, accompanied by the shrieking of the high siren. This is the 'supreme effort and downfall of the managers', as they fail to entice any of the audience into the main show.

Another silence brings us to the finale. This consists of a series of allusions back to earlier moments in the ballet, in a spirit of reprise rare in Satie's music. It concludes with a return to the outburst from the Prelude, which seems to be heading towards a final climax when it is cut off by a silence.

Instead of a climax, the last bars of the ballet return to the fugue subject that opened the Prelude of the Red Curtain. It is now sorrowfully recalled with mournful harmonies, as if the performers and their managers sadly realize that, if they are to attract any audience to their show, they will have to do the whole thing again.

ARNOLD SCHOENBERG
(1874–1951)

Schoenberg (or Schönberg, as he spelled his name before his emigration to the United States) began his career in the last years of the nineteenth century, writing music in a highly charged late-Romantic style, on a grand scale. His *Gurre-Lieder* for massive orchestral and vocal forces suggests that he was well on the way to establishing himself as the successor to his older contemporary Gustav Mahler, writing works of ever greater length and extravagance. But by the time he had finished *Gurre-Lieder* in 1911, Schoenberg had come to feel that musical language had reached a crisis.

Ever since Wagner, and particularly *Tristan und Isolde*, music had tended to become more and more chromatic, its harmonies further and further removed from a sense of key. By the early twentieth century, Schoenberg arrived at a point where traditional methods of structuring music were ceasing to have any meaning. For a time he wrote music that was simply atonal – that is, it avoided any sense of keys or traditional harmonies. But Schoenberg found it difficult to write music with a sense of structure in so free-floating a style, unless he was setting words (as in the cabaret song-cycle, *Pierrot Lunaire*, and the monodrama, *Erwartung*), and he sought a method to bring order to it.

All composers of the time faced the challenge of post-Wagnerian harmony, and reacted in different ways, some breaking away from the traditions of European classical music. But Schoenberg was passionately devoted to the great line of Austro-German music, which stretched back through Brahms and Beethoven to J. S. Bach, and was anxious to find a way of renewing it while preserving it.

His solution was to take atonality and to rationalize it. The result was his famous 'twelve-note' or 'serial' technique ('twelve-note' is a less ambiguous translation than 'twelve-tone'). The twelve notes of the chromatic scale were to be treated equally, and composition was to be based on a 'row' of all twelve in a chosen order. When he first developed this idea in 1922, Schoenberg said to a pupil (with a turn of phrase that sounds more unfortunate now than it did then), 'I have discovered something which will guarantee the supremacy of German music for the next hundred years.'[1] Schoenberg devised subtle and complex ways of organizing his material: dividing the row into smaller groups, playing them not only at different pitches, but backwards and inverted, and combining them to form chords.

The basis of this manipulation of material was already to be found in traditional counterpoint (J. S. Bach's fugues, for example). But Schoenberg's logical development of it, together with his abandonment of traditional tonality, marked one of the most radical departures in the history of music, and its impact continues to reverberate to this day.

Schoenberg's instrumental music extends from lush, Romantic early works (such as *Verklärte Nacht*), through increasingly atonal and acerbic works (two Chamber Symphonies for large chamber group, Five Pieces for Orchestra), to the twelve-note works (Variations for Orchestra). Even though the later works are very difficult to follow, let alone understand, they do inhabit an extraordinary sound-world. Through the arcane constructions of his highly dissonant language speaks a mind of strange intensity. Fevered intensity is already there in *Verklärte Nacht* and *Gurre-Lieder*. In later works, this quality becomes nightmarish, partly because of the perpetual dissonance, but also because of a sense of nervous instability, like the writing of a man undergoing a mental breakdown. Their dissonance and fragmentation have resonance beyond the field of music. As with much of the 'expressionist' visual art of the first half of the twentieth century, the strange, neurotic music of Schoenberg seems to inhabit, all too starkly, the time in which it was written (and Schoenberg himself painted nightmarish paintings too). One can almost feel that he needed his system in order to keep sane.

This unfamiliar musical language required painstaking determination for it to be performed adequately, and musicians with the dedication to achieve it were rare in Schoenberg's lifetime. Among the most remarkable was the string quartet led by Schoenberg's brother-in-law, Rudolf Kolisch, who played Schoenberg's string quartets from memory, including the twelve-note Nos 3 and 4. Even the most conscientious of musicians faced enormous difficulties with his music. Adrian Boult, who conducted the British premiere of Schoenberg's Variations for Orchestra, to Schoenberg's satisfaction, admitted that even the most careful preparation soon evaporated. Following the premiere, 'Three years later the Variations again came into rehearsal for a performance in Vienna (the first ever heard in public there) and when I opened the score I found nothing in it to remind me of the previous performance, and actually said to myself that if someone had told me it was an entirely new set of variations on a different theme, I could have believed him.'[2]

Schoenberg was a controversial and often lonely figure in his lifetime, and his effect on the music of the twentieth century was as profound and as divisive as Wagner's had been in the previous century. As with Wagner, the heat generated by supporters and detractors made it difficult for questions of musical value to be debated dispassionately, and the arguments are not over yet. On the one hand, music historians regard him as one of the pivotal figures of modern music, and on the other, the great majority of music lovers – and even many musicians – still find his twelve-note music incomprehensible a century after he first developed his method.

Although Schoenberg throughout his life struggled for the recognition that he thought he deserved, many pupils and other young composers took up and adapted his method in different ways. There was a long period in the latter part of the twentieth century when much of the musical establishment in Europe and the United States regarded Schoenberg as the founding father of modern classical music, and his methods as the way to the music of the future. This view was bolstered by the fact that Schoenberg and his colleagues were condemned by the regimes of Stalin and Hitler. This made Schoenberg seem, in the 'West', to be a symbol of fearless intellectual freedom.[3]

Many composers refined and extended his methods. Pierre Boulez and Karlheinz Stockhausen in the 1950s adopted a method of 'total (or integral) serialism', whereby not just pitch, but all other aspects of a composition – duration, tone colour, loudness, mode of attack – were subjected to organization in ways analogous to Schoenberg's use of the row of twelve notes.

But by the beginning of the twenty-first century, the basic problem of understanding atonal music with a complex structure remains as intractable as ever, and composers who wish to make themselves comprehensible to a wider audience have been moving away from

Schoenberg's influence. It is telling that, of his original group of pupils, the only one to have achieved some measure of general public esteem is the one who developed a 'compromise' language, using elements of twelve-note technique, but retaining a strong ingredient of traditional tonality – Alban Berg.

There is something of a paradox in Schoenberg's position. With his focus on the great line of German music, he showed himself to be far more traditional than all those composers pursuing a broader range of new ideas. How far removed Schoenberg was from the wider musical world of his time is illustrated by his famous books on harmony, which contain only fleeting references to the other giants of modern music. In *Structural Functions of Harmony* (1948), the index does not include the names of Bartók, Stravinsky, or Ravel. Debussy is mentioned twice only, once in a list of composers who 'cast new obstacles in the way of the comprehensibility of music'. So perhaps one might say that Schoenberg's problem was that, tied to a traditional, Germanic view of what music should be, he was not revolutionary enough.

FIVE PIECES FOR ORCHESTRA, OP. 16
Duration: approx. 18 minutes

Vorgefühle (Premonitions): Sehr rasch (very fast)
Vergangenes (The Past): Mässige Viertel (moderate crotchet/quarter note)
Farben (Colours): Mässige Viertel (moderate crotchet/quarter note)
Peripetie (Peripeteia): Sehr rasch (very fast)
Das obligate Rezitativ (The Obbligato Recitative): Bewegte Achtel (moderate quaver/eighth note)

The year 1909 was crucial in Schoenberg's development of a new musical language. He had experimented in small-scale works with music that has no sense of key or conventional harmony – 'atonal' music. Now he brought this to fruition in two major large-scale works: the Five Pieces for Orchestra, and *Erwartung* ('Expectation'), a one-act monodrama for soprano and orchestra. *Erwartung* provides a useful way in to the Five Orchestral Pieces, even though it was composed after them. It is a nightmarish monologue, in which a distraught woman searches through a wood at night for her lover, and finds him dead. There is no such programme for the Five Pieces, but the similarity of the musical language, with its continuous dissonance, inevitably creates a nightmarish effect. In this the two works parallel developments in drama and the visual arts in Vienna and Berlin at the time, to which Schoenberg himself contributed haunting paintings. And he had real nightmares on which to draw. The previous year, Schoenberg's wife, Mathilde, had eloped with the young painter Richard Gerstl. When Schoenberg persuaded her to return to him shortly afterwards, Gerstl committed suicide, hanging himself naked in front of his studio mirror.

Although it is often naive to assume direct connections between life and art, it is difficult to escape the impression that real events fed into Schoenberg's music at this period. Although there is no programme for the Five Pieces, Schoenberg was persuaded by his publisher to add titles in 1912, so as to give audiences something to grasp. Schoenberg's reluctance can be judged from the following entry in his diary:

> The wonderful thing about music is that it allows you to express everything so the initiates will understand, but without betraying your innermost secrets – the secrets you don't

confess even to yourself. But titles betray you after all: Moreover, the music already
expresses the ideas that are important – so why use words? If words were necessary you
would use them in the first place, whereas in art you can express more than in words.
Anyway, the titles I might use betray no secrets, because they are either very cryptic or very
technical. Thus: I. Premonitions (everyone has them) II. The Past (everyone has one of
those too) III. Chord-colours (just technical) IV. Peripeteia (vague enough, I suppose) V.
The Obbligato (or perhaps 'fully-developed' or 'endless') Recitative. But there should be a
note to say that these titles were added as a necessity of publication and not to provide
'poetic' atmosphere.[4]

In a letter to Richard Strauss, whom he hoped to interest in conducting the Five Pieces,
Schoenberg wrote that they were 'without architecture, without structure. Only an ever-
changing, unbroken succession of colours, rhythms and moods.'[5] Strauss replied, 'your pieces
are such daring experiments in colour and sound that for the moment I dare not introduce
them to the more than conservative Berlin public.'[6] Strauss never did conduct the work, and
two years later wrote in a letter to Alma Mahler, 'The only person who can help poor
Schoenberg now is a psychiatrist . . . I think he'd do better to shovel snow instead of scribbling
on music-paper.'[7] This quote from Strauss is as reported by Schoenberg himself: Alma, characteristically, had passed these remarks to him, and that was the end of the relationship
between the two composers.

The 1909 score is for a huge orchestra. Schoenberg made a reduced version for a more
normal-size orchestra in 1949, and also a version for chamber orchestra in 1925. The premiere
was given – astonishingly – at a Promenade Concert in London in September 1912, conducted
by Sir Henry Wood. Wood was a fearless champion of new music, and he encouraged the
reluctant orchestra with the prophetic words, 'Stick to it, gentlemen. This is nothing to what
you'll have to play in 25 years' time.'[8] Schoenberg was invited to London to conduct a repeat
performance in January 1914. The reaction of audience and critics was almost universally
hostile: there was hissing and laughter at the premiere, silence and polite applause when the
composer himself conducted the second performance. For modern audiences, the music's
sound-world is still very strange – as it surely always will be – but it is a strangeness that has
become more familiar, if only as the sort of music that is widely used to evoke horrors and
nightmares in film and television scores.

The first piece, 'Premonitions', is the shortest, with a brooding, ominous character, full of
explosions. There are nothing like consistent themes to grasp on to, but the listener nevertheless gets a strong sense of some sort of narrative or drama being played out. There are hesitant, anxious phrases, painful cries, suggestions of fanfares. Turbulent undercurrents coalesce
into a strong rhythmic drive.

The nightmarish effect is achieved partly by the choice of chords. Everything is dissonant,
but in varying ways. Sometimes the harmonies, and the fragments of melody, have a strong
feel of the whole-tone scale. The cello melody that opens the piece is the prime example: its
rising shape moves from F to A to C sharp. Sometimes the chords seem like conventional
chords to which dissonant notes have been added. The most important of these is sustained,
like a drone, through much of the piece: about half a minute in, three bassoons hold a three-
note, low chord, D, A, and C sharp. D and A are a fifth apart, as in traditional drones, C sharp
creates a dissonance. This drone persists all through the following tumult, sometimes

becoming inaudible and resurfacing. At the end, three trombones take over the chord, which climaxes in a rasping flutter-tonguing.

The second movement is the longest of the five, and most strongly evokes traditional ways of composing – which is probably why Schoenberg thought of its title, 'The Past'. A solo cello plays a slow, yearning phrase, which proves to be the main theme of the entire piece. The woodwind answer with a chord that refuses to resolve and lines that rise further and fall again. In a more flowing passage, woodwind and muted trumpets weave in counterpoint, some of whose threads are closely related to the opening cello solo. The music becomes still again, and the unresolving chord returns. This is followed by another flowing passage of counterpoint, again based on variants of the opening cello solo. This section develops a haunting quality as faster and slower lines interweave, strings enter first low then high, and the celesta glitters mysteriously. The texture is complex and transparent, joined by staccato bassoon, solo violin, and harp.

Over the continuing staccato patterns a slower version of the theme emerges in counter-point, first on oboe and solo viola, then inverted on clarinet and horn. The intricate web rises to a passionate climax and fades, with contrabassoon low in the bass and a violin harmonic high above. The remainder of the piece returns to the eerie stillness of the opening, evoking a conventional reprise. Slower and faster variants of the theme combine, with frag-ments formed into a running pattern in the celesta. The music unwinds, like a tapestry unrav-elling, to a final chord of extreme density, with (once again) contrabassoon at the bottom and violin harmonics at the top. The last phrase on clarinets, consisting of three falling notes, is taken from the melody of the fugue-like middle section of the piece. But these same three notes (as Robert Craft points out) are also the first notes of 'Premonitions', played backwards.[9] So this piece in particular is far from 'without structure', as Schoenberg claimed in his letter to Strauss.

The third piece is called 'Colours'. Schoenberg renamed it 'Morning by a lake' in 1949, though, according to his pupil Egon Wellesz, who had known Schoenberg since 1905, he had always called it that in private. In her memoirs of Mahler, Alma Mahler writes, 'I remember a discussion Mahler once had with Schönberg about the possibility of producing a melody from the variations of a single note played successively on different instruments. Mahler denied that it could be done.'[10] In his treatise on harmony of 1911, Schoenberg returned to the idea of 'melodies that are built of colours [Klangfarbenmelodien]. But who dares to develop such theories?'[11] Already in this piece, he had gone some way towards experimenting with the idea.

'Colours' consists of a succession of sustained chords. The starting chord consists of the notes (from bottom to top) C, G sharp, B, E, and A. The notes C, E, and A on their own are a chord of A minor; the notes G sharp and B add a contradictory, pulling dissonance. So the effect is of conventional harmony that has been distorted (or perhaps poisoned) by disso-nance, and floats uncertainly. The entire piece consists of chords like this that slowly shift, with groups of instruments overlapping to create a slow, pulsating breath, while the top notes of the chords form an equally slow-moving melody. In the first section, the chords and melody pull only minimally away from the starting chord. There is just one other sign of life, a two-note stirring, first in bass clarinet, then in clarinet, bassoon, and trombone, echoed in the double basses.

The music comes to a standstill, then moves on into a middle section. Here, the activity increases. The range of the chords widens, the texture of the orchestration becomes more open and bright. And there are interjections, notably a sudden, brief flash of notes upwards and downwards (Schoenberg referred to these as 'leaping fish'). Eventually, the music settles again, arriving back at the 'poisoned' A minor chord with which it began.

'Peripeteia' is a word derived from Greek tragedy, meaning a turning point, a sudden reversal of fortune, characteristically arising from a shocking discovery (such as the moment when King Oedipus discovers that he has killed his father and married his mother). Schoenberg had certainly experienced his own Peripeteia the previous year, on the discovery of his wife's affair with Richard Gerstl, and Gerstl's suicide shortly thereafter. Schoenberg considered this title 'vague enough', but it is tempting to imagine that the piece has some connections with Schoenberg's experience, and his 'inner secrets'. What is certain is that the music alternates between violent shock and a sort of paralyzed horror. It represents, perhaps, the terrible event of which the first piece was a premonition.

'Peripeteia' opens with a violently leaping phrase in clarinets and bassoons, which sets not only the tone of the whole piece but also its main melodic shape. Trumpets and trombones answer with a rushing slide of chords, high woodwind with more leaping. It is like a nightmarish perversion of the opening of Richard Strauss's *Don Juan* (a suitable reference if there is any truth to the autobiographical theory). From dismal, quiet chords emerges a clarinet, with a slower version of the leaping figure. From this point on, the music becomes more complicated. Various versions of the leaping motif, together with more sustained phrases, collide with each other in counterpoint. A climax is reached, with the horns in unison – in Richard Strauss they would sound heroic, but here they sound desperate. Strange, quiet horn chords follow. This time they give way to a desolate counterpoint of bassoon, muted trumpet, tuba, and solo cello. This is interrupted by increasingly violent gestures, until there is one final, brief climax, in which the leaping figure engages the whole orchestra in multi-voice counterpoint. There is a last, savage *fff* chord, followed by a muttered reiteration of the leaping gesture from the clarinets, like the twitching of a corpse. And the piece ends with a ghostly, rasping chord on low, hand-stopped horns and tremolando double basses.

'Obbligato' is a word traditionally used in music to indicate an important melody, such as a solo instrumental line accompanying a singer. In 'The Obbligato Recitative', Schoenberg indicates in the score a thread of melody that runs through the whole piece, moving from instrument to instrument. Within the first few bars, for example, the highlighted melody consists of a sigh of two falling notes on oboe, a rising phrase on clarinet, a single note on violin, a single note on viola, and a staccato leaping phrase on violins. These principal melodic elements are enmeshed in a web of counterpoint on other instruments. There is little sense of traditional structure or development. From time to time there are recognizable recurrences of some of the melodic shapes, but the main impression is of a free, improvisatory flow of melodic counterpoint, with some unspecified, strong emotional drive. It has a sort of purposeful chaos, like the patterns of the weather, or a ballet representing the movements of a crowd. From time to time elements coalesce to start building a climax, but fall back. Eventually, a huge *fff* climax is reached, with desperate, leaping phrases, and the music collapses to a final enigmatic, dissonant chord. Like so many dissonances in the work, this sounds as if it is formed from a collision of different consonances fighting for resolution. But resolution never comes, and we are left haunted by the nightmarish intensity of this extraordinary music.

VARIATIONS FOR ORCHESTRA, OP. 31
Duration: approx. 21 minutes

In October 1925, Schoenberg was appointed to chair a masterclass in composition at the Academy of Arts in Berlin, in succession to Ferruccio Busoni who had died the previous year. He took it up in January 1926, and enjoyed for the first time in his life a prestigious, regular post that was to last for seven years, until the Nazi government's purge of the Jews from the Academy forced him to leave in 1933. Soon after settling in Berlin, he began to write the Variations for Orchestra.

Since developing his twelve-note method of composition in 1922, Schoenberg had tried it out in piano pieces, a serenade for chamber ensemble, and a wind quintet. Now he was ready to tackle an orchestral work, and embarked on his first music for full orchestra since the Five Orchestral Pieces of 1909. It took him two years to write it, and the spur to complete the score was provided by Wilhelm Furtwängler, conductor of the Berlin Philharmonic Orchestra, who offered to undertake the premiere. Schoenberg wrote to Furtwängler in September 1928 to say that he had finished it: 'I do not think the work excessively difficult from the ensemble point of view. Easier indeed than e.g. "Pierrot Lunaire" or "Erwartung". On the other hand, the individual parts are for the most part *very* difficult, so that in this case the quality of the performance depends on the *musicianship* of the players . . . in such cases I have found it very useful to read the piece through once with the players a fair time beforehand. Then they see which bits they must practise, and they do so.'[12] Furtwängler scheduled three rehearsals, which was scarcely sufficient for the musicians to get to grips with music in such an unfamiliar and bewildering style. The equally bewildered audience gave the work a hostile reception.

Schoenberg later wrote to Furtwängler expressing his disappointment that he had not repeated the work at a subsequent concert: 'considering, after all, that the hissing was at least as much of an oafish impertinence towards you as towards me. Frankly, I expected that you would repeat the work at the next concert, showing the rabble that *you only do what you consider right!*'[13]

The British premiere, performed by the BBC Symphony Orchestra under Adrian Boult in November 1931, was much more carefully prepared. Schoenberg heard the performance on the radio, and wrote in a letter to Boult that it was 'remarkably beautiful, clear and vital' (see introduction to Schoenberg for Boult's reminiscence).[14]

The same year as the British premiere, 1931, the Variations for Orchestra were performed in Frankfurt, and Schoenberg gave a radio talk about the work. In it, he fiercely defended his role as a pioneer, insisting that he deserved as much respect as the great explorers: 'It is unthinkable to show hostility towards those heroes who dared fly over the ocean or to the North Pole; their achievement is immediately obvious to everyone. But even though experience has shown that many path-finders have been on a clear, well-conceived course while others took them for half-crazed wanderers, thus the hostility of the majority always turns against those who forge ahead into the unknown regions of the intellectual realm.'[15]

The work consists of an introduction, a theme built from the twelve-note row, nine variations, and a finale. Most of these sections have a clearly defined beginning and end, apart from Variation 8, which leads straight into Variation 9 without a gap. To help orientation in this difficult landscape, durations are given for each section in the description that follows. The timings are those of the recording by the Philharmonia Orchestra conducted by Robert Craft.[16] The durations of each variation in other recordings are within a few seconds of these figures.

Introduction (1'36"): As soon as the first notes sound, it is clear that this is no mere academic exercise, but a study in subtle orchestral combinations. Over a *ppp* violin tremolo the harp plays pianissimo harmonics, answered by double-bass harmonics, then a clarinet joins the harp in a rocking figure, B flat to E. Already Schoenberg has highlighted one of the intervals that will characterize his row – B flat to E is a tritone, an interval much used to evoke mystery because of its floating, key-less sound. From this web of sound start to emerge fragments of the twelve-note row, which build to a climax and fall away again. The tempo eases to a harp note (1'00"), and a trombone quietly intones the notes B flat, A, C, B natural. In German notation, these spell out the name BACH. This is Schoenberg's homage to J. S. Bach, the great contrapuntalist who was a major inspiration for his methods. The introduction fades away with the rocking tritones with which it began.

Thema (0'56"): The theme is played by the cellos. It consists of the row of twelve pitches played three times. The second time it is played retrograde (backwards) and inverted (upside down) and at a different pitch, and the third time it is played backwards at the original pitch. As the cellos finish, the violins round off the theme with another inverted version of the row. This gives some idea of the intellectual complexities that underlie the whole piece. But for the listener, the effect is of a theme full of a nightmarish yearning, reinforced by the quietly dissonant chords that accompany it.

Variation 1 (1'06"): The theme is played by pizzicato double basses, with bass clarinet, bassoons, and contrabassoon. It is divided into little fragments, while a rapid fluttering of other fragments, all derived in some way from the row, pass among the upper instruments. The variation includes almost every member of the orchestra, but they never play all together. Instead, Schoenberg uses his resources to create an ever-changing landscape of pitches and tone colours.

Variation 2 (1'44"): This slow variation follows without a break. It is constructed from overlapping canons played by a small group of soloists. A solo cello is echoed by a bassoon, and a bass clarinet is echoed by a flute. In both of these canons, the second instrument plays an inversion of what the first instrument plays. The most prominent canon is between solo violin and oboe, which both play an inversion of the row. Other instruments join them to create a complex web of counterpoint.

Variation 3 (0'42"): In this faster variation, the original theme is played by horns, while aggressive figures of rapidly repeated notes and dotted rhythms in the rest of the orchestra seem to be trying to drown them out.

Variation 4 (1'19"): This variation is in waltz tempo, and, like Variation 2, begins with a small group of soloists. The rapid repeated notes of Variation 3 are here taken over by harp and mandolin, which, with the celesta, outline the theme. They are, however, submerged in a more prominent network of dancing shapes, led first by a flute and then by a clarinet. Halfway through, muted strings, trombones, and horns enter, bringing a more threatening character to the music. At the end, a high solo violin is left hanging in mid-air.

Variation 5 (2'01"): This is the emotional climax of the Variations. High violins play a passionate melodic line derived from the second half of the row, accompanied (or rather challenged) by jagged rhythms in the trombones and trumpets, over a syncopated bass line. Half a minute in, a trombone reminds us of the BACH motif, a moment of solidity amid this disturbed scene. Touches of delicacy alternate with passionate outbursts, until a solo violin leads to a cataclysmic final bar.

Variation 6 (1'27"): This variation is scored for a small group of solo instruments in which none is dominant. The mood is delicate and cool until, near the end, the violins enter, bringing the familiar note of haunting anxiety.

Variation 7 (2'15"): This is the longest of the variations, with a high level of activity that disguises the slow beat. The main melodic material derived from the row is carried by a high solo bassoon, followed in turn by clarinet, oboe, and flute. These are embedded in a scintillating combination of piccolo, celesta, glockenspiel, and solo violin, with brief contributions from other instruments. Eventually the solo violin takes over the melody, which then passes to cellos, violas, and horn. The music becomes more fragmented towards the end.

Variation 8 (0'37"): This is a very fast variation. Oboes and horns, both in unison, throw fragments of the row at each other, the bassoon mirroring each oboe shape upside down. The cellos keep up a frantic running bass. The music becomes gradually more frenzied, reaching a climax on full orchestra. This leads without a break into the next variation.

Variation 9 (0'59"): From the climax of the preceding variation emerges a piccolo, playing the row in its original form as a falling arabesque, with trumpet and viola touching in the inverted version below. A clarinet answers with a rising, inverted version, with bassoon and violin playing the original version below. Low brass and a gong stroke pull the music back for a moment, and it then continues in a fragmentary, jigsaw-like manner.

Finale (5'55"): By far the longest section of the work, the finale develops elements from the Variations into an extended climax. The first section, lasting about 1 minute, reintroduces the BACH motif. At the beginning, violins play it as a mysterious tremolo. The double basses play a retrograde version of the row in the manner of a truculent recitative – perhaps a reference to the opening of the finale in Beethoven's Ninth Symphony. Over it, violins play BACH as abrupt chords. As the truculence continues in other instruments, the BACH motif is sounded by the horns, and then passes to violas and cellos, and to a trumpet. Fragments coalesce as the BACH motif is repeated again and again in the bass, and the music accelerates to a climax.

Suddenly the mood changes, and in a passage marked 'grazioso' (graceful), oboe and horn play a delicate duet, which later becomes a duet between solo violin and trumpet. The music becomes more insistent as other instruments join in. The texture thickens and then clarifies again to another grazioso passage. The first two notes of BACH occur from time to time, then the whole motto is stated by violas and horns. A fierce entry of trombones and timpani changes the mood again, with high violins and insistent patterns in the other instruments creating an atmosphere of strident urgency. There is an acceleration leading to an abrupt silence.

The pace increases to Presto, and BACH is heard on the cor anglais under an oboe playing energetic dotted rhythms. The dotted rhythms, sometimes themselves formed into BACH, reach a frantic climax and a brief pause. The tempo increases again, and scurrying figures build up to another climax, at which trumpets play BACH, and another pause is reached on a hideously dissonant chord. There is a last hush, during which a solo violin plays the end of the original theme (the inverted version of the row), in a moment that is as close to serenity as anything in this nightmare vision. A final, brutal Presto brings the Variations to a close.

VERKLÄRTE NACHT (TRANSFIGURED NIGHT), OP. 4

Duration: approx. 29 minutes

The German poet Richard Dehmel (1863–1920) published a volume of poetry, *Weib und Welt* (*Woman and World*), in 1896. Its publication caused a scandal, and Dehmel was charged with blasphemy and immorality. Defending himself in an open letter, he wrote, 'I believe that anyone who helps the human soul open its eyes to its animal urges serves true morality better than many a moralistic accuser.'[17] If this has a Freudian ring, that is no coincidence. Ideas about the powerful forces of sexual feeling and the functioning of the unconscious mind were in the air, and Freud was to publish his *Interpretation of Dreams* in late 1899. Schoenberg had already set some of Dehmel's poetry to music. Now in 1899 he embarked on an attempt to convey the full emotional scope and power of a section of *Weib und Welt*. Coincidentally or not, this was just as Schoenberg began a relationship with Mathilde Zemlinsky, whom he was to marry in 1901.

The original score of *Verklärte Nacht* is for string sextet. In 1917 Schoenberg arranged it for string orchestra, revising this version in 1943. Unlike Schoenberg's later works, with their full-blown atonality and 'twelve-note' technique, *Verklärte Nacht* has come to seem as accessible as Wagner's *Tristan* or the tone poems of Liszt and Richard Strauss. It shares with *Tristan* a passionately charged chromatic language, which Schoenberg uses to build a series of powerful climaxes covering an enormous span. It shares with Strauss the attempt to use literary narrative as the basis of a musical structure, or at least to provide its background. At the same time, it is, in its original version for string sextet, firmly in the great tradition of Austro-German chamber music, represented by Brahms. *Verklärte Nacht* is therefore a work of reconciliation, bringing together conflicting strands of contemporary music into a marvellous synthesis. For anyone who regrets the coming destruction of the old musical world, generated as much by Schoenberg as by anyone, this is a poignant moment in musical history.

In Dehmel's poem, a man and a woman walk through a wood on a cold, moonlit night. The woman confesses that, before she met the man, in a desperate longing to be a mother she gave herself to a stranger and became pregnant. Now, meeting this man seems like life's revenge for her sin. As the moonlight streams onto the woman's anguished face, the man reassures her. Just as they are transfigured by the moonlight, so the child will be transfigured. It will become their child. The man and woman embrace, and walk on through the moonlit night.

Schoenberg's *Verklärte Nacht* does not 'tell the story' of the poem, any more than Strauss's tone poems tell stories. What Schoenberg does is take the emotional core of the poem, its trajectory from darkness to light, from despair through anguish to ecstatic serenity, and build an equivalent musical structure. It is a continuous movement lasting about thirty minutes.

The first half begins with a dark and sombre introduction. The anguished confession of the woman is carried in a series of climaxes, becoming more and more agitated, and culminating in a mood of tragic desperation. The music subsides to a quiet midpoint. Then, a warm chord of D major introduces a noble cello solo – clearly, the moment at which the man speaks to reassure her. The transfiguration begins with a pattern suggesting rustling leaves, with plucked chords, a beautiful high violin solo, and all the instruments muted (a passage reminiscent of Wagner's 'forest murmurs'). A long series of climaxes follows, mirroring the series in the first half of the piece, but now increasingly impassioned and ecstatic. The music finally reaches a serene resolution, and ends with a reprise of the transfiguration pattern, as the couple walk on through the moonlight.[18]

FRANZ SCHUBERT
(1797–1828)

When Schubert died at the age of thirty-one (four years younger than Mozart at his death), most of his music was virtually unknown except to a circle of friends and connoisseurs in and around Vienna. The dominant musical figure in Vienna during Schubert's lifetime was Beethoven, who died in 1827, just one year before him. Schubert greatly admired Beethoven, but probably never even met him (despite a plausible anecdote), and was merely one of many young composers struggling to earn a living in his shadow. When he was a teenager, Schubert's early symphonies were tried out by the amateur orchestra in which he played violin and viola. But many of his large-scale works – symphonies, piano sonatas, string quartets, and other chamber music – remained unplayed and unpublished until several decades after Schubert's death.

The only field in which he achieved limited success was as a writer of songs and dances. Schubert himself used to sing and play them at private gatherings of artistic friends that came to be known as Schubertiads. There is a touching watercolour from 1821 that shows Schubert at such a soirée while charades are being played. The composer is sitting at the piano, with a dog by his side. We know from reports that later in the evening, after food and drink, he would have played music for dancing, improvising some of it on the spot. There was a ready market for published dance music, and Schubert wrote more than four hundred dances for piano, as well as many for chamber groups. A handful of his songs (of which he wrote more than six hundred) became well known in Vienna during his lifetime, and some of them were modestly successful when published, selling about five hundred copies each while he was alive. These include his first masterpiece, 'Gretchen am Spinnrade' ('Gretchen at the Spinning-Wheel') from Goethe's *Faust*, composed when he was seventeen. But this local reputation hardly amounts to 'success' for a composer who has since come to be regarded as one of the major figures in the history of music.

In January 1839, ten years after Schubert's death, Robert Schumann paid a visit to Schubert's brother, Ferdinand. Ferdinand showed him a trunk full of unpublished manuscripts, including the 'Great' Symphony in C major. Mendelssohn conducted its first performance in Leipzig later that year. The equally great String Quintet in C, which Schubert's publisher had refused shortly before the composer died, had to wait until 1850 for its premiere. These are enormous works, each lasting nearly an hour. They have come to epitomize the greatness of Schubert, a composer with a vision of music that stretched its possibilities beyond even what Beethoven had imagined.

At the opposite extreme, Schubert was also the master of the song lasting a few minutes. He could encapsulate within a few bars (as in 'Gretchen') a mood, a situation, emotional conflict, despair, hope, joy, and the swift changes from one to another. But Schubert the songwriter and Schubert the composer of enormous instrumental works are not two musical personalities. Song-writing clearly came easily to him. He struggled all his life to create longer musical structures that satisfied him, often leaving works incomplete (the 'Unfinished' Symphony is only the most famous example). But in his mature instrumental works he learned that he did not have to abandon song in order to construct long instrumental pieces. Song is at the heart of his music, sometimes in the form of seemingly endless melody, sometimes giving the impression that a song is struggling to surface from a tangle of conflicting ideas. His ability to switch in an instant between one mood and another, and to create ambiguity so that the listener does not know quite what the mood is, is essential to his command of long structures, in which our intense involvement is kept engaged by this precisely calibrated command of mood and tension.

ROSAMUNDE: INCIDENTAL MUSIC, D. 797

In 1823, Schubert supplied incidental music for a play by Wilhelmina von Chézy, *Rosamunde, Princess of Cyprus*. Like her libretto for Weber's *Euryanthe*, *Rosamunde* was nothing more than a conventional Romantic tale, and the play, staged a few weeks after the premiere of *Euryanthe*, was a failure, performed only twice. Schubert, however, supplied for it a score containing some of his most beautiful music. He assembled his material very quickly for the first production, making use of some existing works. The eleven numbers associated with *Rosamunde* include choruses and a song, and there are six orchestral items of which the following four are often played.

Overture (approx. 10 minutes)
For the two performances of *Rosamunde*, Schubert used his overture to *Alfonso und Estrella*. But later he renamed another overture, originally written for the play *Die Zauberharfe* (*The Magic Harp*), as the overture to *Rosamunde*, and this is the overture commonly known by that name. The full orchestra, including trombones, begins with Beethoven-like weight and seriousness. But once the slow introduction gets under way, the mood lightens, becoming lyrical. The Allegro that follows is Schubert at his sunniest and most effervescent.

Entr'acte in B minor (approx. 8 minutes)
This is a substantial movement. It has been suggested that it is the missing fourth movement of Schubert's 'Unfinished' Symphony, and the key and the length make that possible. As in the first two movements of the symphony, confident and insistent music alternates with passages that are hesitant and tinged with melancholy. But the pace seems too deliberate for a finale, and there is no real sense of accumulation – on the other hand, maybe that is why Schubert decided to remove it from the symphony, and redeploy it as stage music.

Entr'acte in B flat major (approx. 7 minutes)
This is one of Schubert's best-loved pieces, which shares its opening melody with a movement of his String Quartet in A minor, composed around the same time. It is constructed like a dance with two trios. But the opening section is pure song, without any sense of dance rhythm. It culminates in a pause, followed by one of those heart-stopping shifts of harmony that became so much a feature of Schubert's late works. The two interleaved trios have a dance tread, but are in the minor, with gently winding triplet figures in the woodwind melody, giving the music a wistful air.

Ballet in G major (approx. 7 minutes)
The dance rhythm is more pointed in this ballet. The short-phrased melodies suggest rustic celebration, with, at one point, a 'yodelling' figure in the clarinet.

Symphonies

SYMPHONY NO. 1 IN D MAJOR, D. 82
Duration: approx. 27 minutes

Adagio – Allegro vivace
Andante
Allegro
Allegro vivace

Schubert composed his First Symphony at the age of sixteen, in October 1813, shortly before leaving the imperial boarding school at which he had been a pupil for seven years. It would certainly have been performed by the excellent school orchestra, in which Schubert played violin.

The symphony begins with an Adagio introduction. This looks back not just to Mozart and Haydn, but further back to the baroque overture, with its very sharp, double-dotted rhythms and its stately harmonic progression. The pace is majestic rather than slow – two beats in a bar, not four – so that the tempo of the Allegro can (more or less) be achieved by doubling the speed of the beat of the Adagio. This is a technique of seamless transition that Schubert was to reuse in his 'Great' C major Symphony, No. 9.

The first theme of the Allegro, with its running upward scale answered by drooping wood-wind phrases, is very like Haydn. This Allegro is on a grand scale. A substantial tutti gives way to a charming, rather four-square second theme, and then this is developed into a long, discursive passage to round off the first section. It is probably too long, but there are many Schubertian moments to sustain interest along the way, particularly little poignant touches of harmony. After the repeat (if played) the development continues to be dominated by the second theme, at first in the major in the woodwind, and then in the minor and venturing into new keys. It develops quite a sweep, despite relying on much repetition of the same idea.

A quiet woodwind passage leads, unexpectedly, to an abbreviated reprise of the Adagio introduction, incorporated into the metre of the Allegro by simply doubling the note values. This is a most striking moment, highly unusual in a symphony, but again recalling the baroque overture with its reprise of the slow opening. The Allegro's first theme then leads on to a full reprise. By the end, we certainly get a sense of a young composer of immense ambition, even if not everything quite comes off.

The Andante is less ambitious but more consistently successful. Schubert's fellow musicians would certainly have realized that its model is Mozart, with references to the slow movements of the 'Linz' Symphony (No. 36) and the 'Prague' Symphony (No. 38). It shares its key (G major) and its metre (6/8) with both. The lilting siciliano rhythm recalls the 'Linz', and the overall form is more like that of the 'Prague'. Schubert's melody on the strings is more straightforward than those in either of Mozart's slow movements. The second strain seems to end prematurely, after three bars instead of four, but is then delightfully extended by the woodwind, before the melody is repeated with subtle variations in instrumentation and harmony.

As in the 'Prague' Symphony, there is now an episode in a minor key, beginning with forthright accents, and then developing a truly Mozartean poignancy. The return of the main theme is beautifully varied with new woodwind parts and twists of harmony. After this reprise, the music turns again to the minor. But this is not a clear-cut 'episode' so much as a development, with the main theme going in unexpected directions, and seeming to lose itself – this is an early glimpse of the mature Schubert. The final reprise of the theme ends with a delightful touch: first the violins and then the oboe round off the movement with a rising chromatic scale. This is a direct quote from Mozart's 'Prague' Symphony, giving the impression of Schubert embracing the master.

The third movement is a fast minuet (or scherzo). With its punctuating trumpets and timpani and its brusqueness it is less like Mozart or Haydn and more like Beethoven, with nods towards the scherzo of his Second Symphony. But the harmonies are quirky, and the extensive second half of the minuet has moments of intimate geniality that Beethoven would surely have scowled at. In the trio, Schubert puts a bassoon solo an octave below the violins, as Haydn liked to do. In the second half, the melody rises higher, phrase by phrase, in a lingering moment that is pure Schubert.

The finale is a movement of exhilarating energy. Like the finales of Mozart's 'Paris' and 'Haffner' Symphonies and Haydn's last 'London' Symphony, which are all in the same key, it begins quietly and then bursts out into a vigorous tutti. Like the Haydn symphony, there's a suggestion of popular song in its melodies. The second theme is particularly charming, and is scored, like the trio of the minuet, for violins with bassoon an octave below. Throughout the movement, the recurrent little upbeat figure from the first theme is ever-present, and gives a Haydnesque tongue-in-cheek edge to the music. It provides witty dialogue between woodwind and strings, and, in the next big tutti, moves to the bass. A mock-mysterious moment leads on through an exploration of new keys to a pause. The reprise is capped by a rousing coda to bring this remarkable student work to a close.

SYMPHONY NO. 2 IN B FLAT MAJOR, D. 125
Duration: approx. 33 minutes

Largo – Allegro vivace
Andante
Allegro vivace
Presto

Schubert began this symphony in December 1814, two months after composing the astonishing song, 'Gretchen am Spinnrade' ('Gretchen at the Spinning-Wheel'), and finished it the following March. It would first have been played at the orchestral gatherings that had grown out of chamber music at the Schubert family house.

The first movement of Schubert's First Symphony was already ambitious, but the first movement of his Second Symphony is more so. It is even longer – about fourteen minutes, if the repeat is observed. Of the eight symphonies Beethoven had composed so far, only No. 3, the 'Eroica', had a longer first movement. Schubert probably knew Beethoven's first six symphonies, which had already been published, and he had attended the premiere of the revised *Fidelio* in May 1814 (selling his schoolbooks to afford the ticket, according to his friend Moritz von Schwind).

The first movement of this symphony suggests that Beethoven was much on Schubert's mind, and gives the impression that he is unashamedly attempting to tackle Beethoven on his own ground. But he begins by paying homage, once again, to Mozart. The Largo introduction is based on that of Mozart's Symphony No. 39 in E flat, with its grand chords for full orchestra, including trumpets and timpani, alternating with a falling pattern in the strings. The first theme of the Allegro, by contrast, is modelled directly on Beethoven's Overture to *Die Geschöpfe des Prometheus* (*The Creatures of Prometheus*). Schubert, indeed, manages to sound very like Beethoven, with the scurrying strings creating real energy in both loud and soft passages. These string figures continue under the broad second theme, and then reassert themselves in a bold tutti. The violins take up the first theme again. This is decorated by wind chords and a fragment of a countermelody in the cellos, touched in with Mendelssohnian delicacy. It is as if Schubert has abandoned the traditional repeat, and is moving on to his development section in new keys. But no: this is all part of the first section of the movement, and after another burst of energetic tutti the repeat is marked (though the movement arguably works better without it).

The 'official' development is a passage of informal counterpoint. A three-note phrase is pitted against the scurrying quavers, moving from upper to lower strings, and then to the woodwind, where it makes elegant patterns over a sustained passage. After a moment of calm, the reprise of the first theme arrives. This begins, as it sometimes does in Mozart, in the 'wrong' key (E flat), a fifth below the home key, and it is only when we reach the second theme that we are at last in B flat. The reprise continues energetically on its way. The sense of this being rather like Beethoven has perhaps faded somewhat by the time we reach the end. Schubert at seventeen unsurprisingly does not have Beethoven's genius for powerful inevitability. But the journey contains many delights that are not to be found in Beethoven's world.

The second movement is a set of variations in E flat major on a theme with a charming, serenade-like quality. The charm lies not just in the melody, but in the beautifully written inner voices on which the melody floats. The naive straightforwardness of the theme is given a subtle twist at the end, where the last phrase is elongated from two bars to three. The variations, like the theme itself, are straightforward, but beautifully judged. In Variation 1, the melody moves to the oboe, with the other wind instruments joining in. The bass instruments are silent, and the bass line is supplied by the second violins. In Variation 2, cello and bass have the theme in the first half, and in the second half it moves to the flute and back to the bass. Variation 3 simplifies the melody to a horn call, with a counterpoint of running arpeggios in the violins.

Variation 4 is in C minor, with a running pattern of triplet arpeggios in the violins, accompanied by brusque chords. In the second half, the arpeggios move to the bass. The final variation, No. 5, returns to E flat major and the melody begins in the clarinet, with the triplets from the preceding variation persisting as a delicate counterpoint in the violins. A gentle coda rounds off the movement, with the harmonies coming to rest over a held bass note.

The third movement is a minuet in C minor, bold and vigorous. The trio is in E flat major, with an easy-going melody on oboe, joined in the second half by clarinet and flute. This minuet and trio seems almost like a reversal of the Andante, in which charming variations in E flat were interrupted by a brusque variation in C minor.

The finale is an early example of the delightful, tripping style that was to become a feature of Schubert at his most relaxed, as in the Sixth Symphony and (later still) the overture to *Rosamunde*. Those were written after the staging of Rossini's operas in Vienna from 1816 onwards, bringing his style of witty melodiousness into fashion. But here is Schubert in 1814, already writing music that sounds almost Rossinian.

Like the first movement, the finale plays us something of a trick. It opens with a tiptoeing theme on strings, with playful interventions from the woodwind. This bursts into a high-spirited tutti, which arrives at a pause. Now there is a second theme, in E flat, which has such an air of debonair innocence that it really could have been written by Rossini. This leads on to another tutti, and then to a reprise of the first theme, now in C major. It seems as if the movement must be a rondo, in which appearances of the first theme alternate with episodes. But no: after another tutti, Schubert reaches a double bar, and indicates that the whole of this section is to be repeated.

As in the first movement, this is followed by a development section. Here, Schubert takes the rhythm of the first bar of the movement and gives it a driving force. After a time it relaxes, and leads to a reprise of the opening. Although this follows the sequence of events as before, there are striking and imaginative variations and new turns of harmony along the way. The Rossinian second theme is now in G minor, which gives it a melancholy tone, and as we approach it we get a momentary glimpse of the opening bars of Mozart's Symphony No. 40 in G minor. But, as the movement comes to a joyful close, the overriding impression is of a composer who can take his models as he pleases, and has more than enough confidence to forge ahead on his own.

SYMPHONY NO. 3 IN D MAJOR, D. 200

Duration: approx. 23 minutes

Adagio maestoso – Allegro con brio
Allegretto
Menuetto: Vivace
Presto vivace

Schubert's Third Symphony followed on soon after his Second Symphony, and was composed between May and July of 1815. It would first have been performed by the amateur orchestra led by professional violinist Otto Hatwig, first at the Schubert family house, and later at his own, where there was more room. Having tried out rather extravagant structures in his first two symphonies, Schubert now writes a tighter first movement, two-thirds the length of the equivalent movement in the Second Symphony, and achieves a more Beethoven-like concentration of power and structure.

The slow introduction begins with the keynote, D, sustained by full orchestra. If this seems reminiscent of the opening of Beethoven's Second Symphony, the reference is confirmed by rushing upward scales against pulsating woodwind chords. Later, when the scales move to clarinet and flute, and the harmonies shift uneasily, there is a hint of the 'Representation of Chaos' from Haydn's *The Creation*. This brooding atmosphere gives way at the Allegro to a rather jaunty clarinet, playing dotted-rhythm arpeggios in almost yodelling style. This is like a foretaste of the theme that opens the Allegro in Schubert's 'Great' C major Symphony (No. 9). But here the effect is entirely relaxed, until a dramatic crescendo culminates in a forceful tutti. This is a truly Beethovenian moment, at which the rushing upward scales from the introduction are deployed to powerful effect. The second theme is another rather playful tune, on oboe, in which dotted rhythms are again prominent. The dotted rhythms suddenly acquire force at the next tutti, as the music moves decisively on to the end of the section. These same dotted rhythms provide the driving force through the development, against which the woodwind play fragments from the second theme in smoothed-out rhythm. After an excursion through different keys, we arrive back at D major and the yodelling clarinet melody for the start of the reprise. The final bars again evoke Beethoven's Second Symphony as they culminate in forceful chords, ending, as the movement began, with the full orchestra playing the keynote, D.

The young Schubert sometimes most clearly demonstrates his confidence by doing something utterly simple. The Allegretto has been compared to the second movement of Beethoven's First Symphony. But this is something far more naive: a delicate little tune which, in other hands, would seem banal. Schubert has a sure touch with everything – the melodic shape, the harmonic progression, the relationship between the melody, the middle parts, and the bass, and the right moment to add an oboe or a flute – and the result is something utterly natural and disarming. In the middle section, the clarinet plays a mountain song over a pizzicato bass, recalling the yodelling of the first movement. As other instruments join in, the delicate texture of the orchestra seems to have been built out of fresh air, culminating in a moment with violins high above, and the lower strings far below. The first melody returns, and winds to a conclusion as naturally as it began.

The minuet has a repeated accent on the upbeat, which in Beethoven would have seemed fierce, but in Schubert seems merely high-spirited. In the second half, there is a quiet moment like a distant view of peasants dancing a *Ländler*. This pastoral impression comes to the fore in the trio, in which oboe and bassoon step forward to play a charming duet.

The fourth movement shares its lively jig metre (6/8) with the finales of several symphonies and string quartets by Haydn, and its spirit owes something to Italian comic opera. But Schubert gives it a joyful fleetness that is entirely his own. It is a tarantella, danced with the feet hardly touching the ground – a sunny prototype of the fearsome tarantella that concludes Schubert's 'Death and the Maiden' Quartet. Emotionally as well as rhythmically it looks forward to Mendelssohn at his most exuberant (as in his 'Italian' Symphony, No. 4), though Mendelssohn never knew this symphony by Schubert (it was not premiered in its entirety until 1881).

The opening theme is a delicate pianissimo on strings, but each phrase ends with an offbeat kick from the wind and timpani. This sets the mood for the whole movement, which is full of surprises: abrupt changes from quiet to loud, often together with unexpected shifts of harmony, sudden crescendos, and everywhere accents on the offbeats. The rhythm of the first theme predominates until the arrival of the second theme. This consists of little chattering cells of one bar each, wittily distributed between woodwind and strings, still with an offbeat accent on the end of each phrase. The insistent rhythm of this theme carries the music all the way to the end of the first section, which is repeated.

The same rhythm continues to drive on through the development until, after a moment of calm, the first theme reappears. This is not in the home key of D, but in A major. It is only when we reach the second theme that we reach D major (Schubert has developed something of a habit of starting the reprise in an unexpected key, as Mozart sometimes did). As before, the rhythm of the second theme carries the music on, this time developing a powerful momentum that foreshadows the driving rhythms of Schubert's 'Great' C major Symphony. The symphony ends triumphantly, with a feeling that Schubert, at the age of eighteen, has truly found himself.

SYMPHONY NO. 4 IN C MINOR, D. 417, 'TRAGIC'
Duration: approx. 31 minutes

Adagio molto – Allegro vivace
Andante
Menuetto: Allegro vivace
Allegro

Of Schubert's symphonies, No. 4 in C minor, composed in April 1816 when he was nineteen, is the last of the 'apprentice' works in which the listener can clearly sense him responding to models, and trying things out for himself. It would certainly have been played by the mostly amateur orchestra run by violinist Otto Hatwig at his house, though there is no record of its performance. The symphony is full of beautiful things (particularly the slow movement), but there are also passages that sound clumsy or laborious. It is not that he had taken a step back after the supremely accomplished No. 3: more that he was attempting something that was not yet quite in his nature. At some point, Schubert decided to give it the title 'Tragic'. This was probably a mistake. It has led writers to expect more from it than Schubert was capable of supplying. He was already a fine composer, and in *Lieder* a great one. But an assault on the tragic mountain in C minor inhabited by Beethoven was not yet within his capabilities. That had to wait for greater maturity and (genuinely tragic) life experience.

If the opening of Schubert's Third Symphony hinted at the 'Representation of Chaos' from Haydn's *The Creation*, the Adagio introduction to No. 4 is steeped in it, from the stark opening octaves, through the searching, quiet passages that follow, to the little runs in the clarinet and the sudden accents with clashing harmonies. But it is not an imitation: this is an orderly, sombre introduction.

The Allegro, on the other hand, pays direct homage to Beethoven, drawing its agitated, quiet opening phrases and its insistent rising intervals from the first theme of his String Quartet in C minor, Opus 18, No. 4. A forthright tutti follows, and then a more lyrical second theme that seems to nod towards Beethoven's *Coriolan* Overture. The bald repetitions of the next tutti begin by sounding like pseudo-Beethoven, but mysteriously metamorphose into unmistakable Schubert as the mood softens a little. The development begins with arresting brusqueness, as if we are venturing somewhere quite new. But then Schubert simply repeats his opening theme, first on violins and then on cellos. The theme is then played in counterpoint between treble and bass, and after an agitated passage the music arrives in G minor. Here the first theme is played again, and leads on to a full reprise.

The slow movement is the best and most Schubertian part of the symphony. It is a foretaste of the sweet melancholy of Schubert's *Rosamunde*, a mood that derives less from Beethoven than from Mozart (for example, the slow movement of the Piano Concerto No. 14 in E flat, K. 449). The tender melody is played first on strings alone, and then with a touching descant on the oboe. This is interleaved with an episode that occurs twice. It begins with assertive phrases taken from the very beginning of the first movement Allegro. After a time, a sighing phrase (which occurs in the opening themes of both the first and the second movement) comes to predominate, developing into a plangent melody which, the second time round, is echoed in the bass. The sequence of harmonies that take it back to the first theme is particularly poignant. And after the final reprise, the coda, seemingly reluctant to come to an end, strongly looks forward to mature Schubert.

The minuet returns to the world of Beethoven, with its insistent syncopations. But these prove to be as much playful as forceful, as Schubert's characteristic shifts of harmony soften any threat. In the trio, the opening theme of the first movement Allegro once again supplies the material for the melody, a charming pastoral song with a gentle swing.

The finale is rather more successful at evoking Beethovenian anxiety than the first movement. Its opening theme has a similar insistence, but with the agitation at the end of the bar instead of the beginning, and with a little push from the accompanying strings at the conclusion of each phrase. With this simple idea, Schubert builds up considerable tension. At first this is mostly quiet, but as the pattern breaks into continuous quavers (again reminiscent of Beethoven's *Coriolan* Overture) the tension bursts into a forte. The quiet second theme of sighing phrases would be a moment of calm, except that the agitated quavers continue under it. The tension bursts again in a fierce tutti that continues to the end of the first section. After the repeat, the development begins pianissimo, with the murmuring suggesting distant thunder (more a premonition of Rossini's *William Tell* than a memory of Beethoven's 'Pastoral' Symphony). But instead of a storm, out of this comes a mountain song in which the woodwind extend the first theme with yodelling phrases. Soon there is a forceful tutti in which the theme moves to the bass. This leads into the reprise, not in C minor, but in C major. It seems for a moment as if Schubert is planning to defuse the tension entirely with a cheerful conclusion. But soon the music gets diverted to A minor, and from here he reprises the fierce tutti that ended the first section. This is not the concentrated power of a Beethoven. But Schubert's unpredictable switching of harmony from major to minor, and abruptly sidestepping from one key to another and back again, create ambiguities and anxieties that build up a substantial momentum of their own, in a manner that is unmistakably Schubert and nobody else.

SYMPHONY NO. 5 IN B FLAT MAJOR, D. 485
Duration: approx. 28 minutes

Allegro
Andante con moto
Menuetto: Allegro molto
Allegro vivace

On 16 June 1816, between writing his Fourth and Fifth Symphonies, the nineteen-year-old Schubert attended a celebration of Antonio Salieri's fiftieth year in Vienna, at which his pupils (including Schubert himself) contributed their own compositions. Schubert found in the music of Salieri's pupils 'the expression of pure nature, free from all the eccentricity that is common among most composers nowadays, and which is due almost wholly to one of our great German artists; that eccentricity which combines and confuses the tragic with the comic, the agreeable with the repulsive.'[1] In other words, Schubert had come to think that Beethoven, the great genius of the age, was a bad influence on younger composers. Two days earlier, he had heard one of Mozart's string quintets at a musical gathering, and wrote in his diary, 'As if from afar, the magic notes of Mozart's music still gently haunt me ... Thus does our soul retain these fair impressions, which no time, no circumstance can efface, and they lighten our existence.'[2] Despite the fact that his earlier symphonies, Nos 1–4, are steeped in the influence of Beethoven, Schubert's greater model as he wrote the Fifth Symphony was Mozart. It is scored for a modest orchestra, with one flute, pairs of oboes, bassoons, and horns, and no timpani or trumpets. It was composed in September–October 1816, and performed soon after by the private orchestra led by violinist Otto Hatwig, in which Schubert played viola. There is no record of the symphony having been performed again in Schubert's lifetime.

The first movement begins with the tiniest of introductions: four bars of woodwind chords, and a delicate running scale on violins to lead into the first theme. Like many moments in Mozart's symphonies and concertos, this sounds almost like an operatic character running onto the stage, and the theme that follows has all the charm of Susanna from *The Marriage of Figaro*. At first the little phrases rise pertly, then the rise is matched by a gentle fall. Also Mozartian is the informal counterpoint, as each phrase of the theme is echoed in the bass, followed by poignant touches of harmony as the melody swings round for its second strain. This time, over the echoes of each phrase in the bass, the flute plays the gentle fall. Already, in less than a minute, Schubert shows how he really is the heir to Mozart in the unassuming subtlety of his thinking.

After a vigorous tutti, in which the bass continues to echo the melody, the violins play an equally charming second theme. Schubert achieves a contrast with the first theme by lengthening the phrases and reversing their contour: they first fall and then rise. As the woodwind take over the melody, the strings answer each phrase (again, a reversal of what happened in the first theme). A twist of key takes us to another tutti, and, as the first section of the movement reaches its conclusion, the general spirit of energy is from time to time coloured by darker harmonies.

After the repeat, the development begins. As Mozart often does (again), Schubert concentrates not on the main themes, but an incidental little rising motif that finished the first section. This alternates with the delicate running scales, in a beautiful sequence of harmonies that fall step by step. A vigorous passage follows, interleaved with thoughtful moments. Eventually the reprise of the opening theme arrives – though not at first in the home key. It is in E flat, instead of B flat (another Mozartian tactic), and it is only after a tutti and a series of key shifts that the music finally reaches the home key in time for the second theme.

The Andante has a clear and simple structure: the principal theme in E flat occurs three times, alternating with an episode that ventures into other keys. The theme itself is a melody that, like Mozart's best melodies, seems to achieve perfect balance without any effort. But balance is not the same as symmetry. The first half of the melody is indeed symmetrical, with a phrase of two bars answered by another, the whole four bars repeated (with woodwind joining the strings), and the rise and fall of the phrases repeated with tiny variations. This is charming, but it is the second half of the theme that shows that Schubert at nineteen was a great melodist. He moves away from the home key, then back again, in two-bar phrases, with the violas echoing the melody in counterpoint. Then the pattern is broken. The melody rises up, over a held bass note, with plangent chromatic harmonies, and stretches to a three-bar phrase, with a two-bar echo from the woodwind. The opening of the melody returns, now broken into one-bar phrases, and the woodwind answer with a subtly new shape. The turn of phrase that ends the theme is played three times, linked by a little rising arpeggio passing from flute and bassoon to oboe. Then the whole of this second strain is repeated. This all seems natural and organic, and achieves a sense of perfect balance.

The first episode moves down a major third, one of Schubert's favourite moves. Oboe and bassoon sing a new theme, with a violin counterpoint drawn from the little rising arpeggio. This new theme moves into the minor, on violins with bassoon an octave below, emphasizing the mournful fall of the phrases. Sudden, urgent chords lead to an extended tutti, which eventually winds back to E flat and the reprise of the first theme, with some charming elaboration of the melody, and an unexpected turn to the minor in its second half. This is followed by the second episode, which follows the same course as the first episode, but with a shorter tutti ushering in the final reprise of the first theme. Rather than play the whole theme again, Schubert cuts seamlessly from the first strain to the ending. But then he adds on a haunting coda. Twice the bass shifts sideways, as if we are about to venture off into another episode, and twice the music is pulled gently back to the home key. The movement ends with a sense that everything has been perfectly resolved.

The minuet is not in the home key, B flat, but in G minor, the key of Mozart's Symphony No. 40. The homage to Mozart in Schubert's minuet is obvious, but the effect of the two movements is very different. Mozart's minuet is seriously disturbed by cross-rhythms, sharp accents, harmonic clashes, and combative counterpoint. Schubert was, by the end of his life, to surpass Mozart in this sense of tragic internal conflict. But at the age of nineteen, he had more modest aims. The opening strain of the minuet echoes specific features of Mozart's. Its melody begins with the same three notes, and the chromatic descent of the latter part is virtually a quote from Mozart's minuet. But the punch of Schubert's minuet is more of a dramatic gesture than a serious threat, in balance with the genial quality of the rest of the symphony. The trio, in the major, has the flowing sweetness of a lullaby, with a bassoon adding comforting warmth to the violin melody.

The opening of the fourth movement might almost be the finale of a Haydn symphony. The dancing first theme, and its sudden outburst into a tutti in the minor, are thoroughly Haydnesque. There is a sudden silence, where, in Haydn, we would expect a witty surprise. But at this point we realize that Schubert's genius is attuned to charm, not wit. The second theme that follows is a melody of great elegance, first on violins alone, then joined by flute an octave above (one of Haydn's favourite combinations). The tone darkens for a moment as chords turn to the minor; but the first section ends with a return to Haydn's style, with a gentle cascade of triplet broken scales.

After the repeat, the development takes the opening phrase of the first theme and treats it to counterpoint between bass and oboe. After a sudden tutti in the minor, the rising scale of the theme metamorphoses into a chromatic scale. This passes from instrument to instrument, and from key to key, until it reaches a pause, and the reprise of the opening. This time the outburst in the minor is more prolonged. But still the outcome is the elegant second theme, now in the home key, and, without further elaboration, Schubert continues on to bring the movement to a close.

SYMPHONY NO. 6 IN C MAJOR, D. 589
Duration: approx. 32 minutes

Adagio – Allegro
Andante
Scherzo: Presto – Più lento
Allegro moderato

This symphony was written in late 1817 and early 1818, and is, like the Fifth Symphony, a genial work, but with the addition of clarinets, trumpets, and timpani, and an extra element of comic opera. The operas of Rossini had recently swept Vienna, and his influence in this symphony is very clear (as it is in his two 'Overtures in the Italian Style' from the same period). It is sometimes referred to as 'The Little C major' to distinguish it from 'The Great' C major Symphony (No. 9).

The opening chords of the slow introduction could be Beethoven, the woodwind continuation could be Haydn, but a singing clarinet shortly before the Allegro could only be Schubert. The Allegro itself starts with woodwind in playful mode, almost like Rossini. The mood is cheerful, the occasional offbeat accents teasing rather than earnest in a Beethoven-like way. The second theme has, again, a suggestion of Rossinian cheek, and an irresistible dance element as so often in Schubert's most charming melodies, with woodwind chasing each other like dancers around a circle. Woodwind continue to lead the development section that follows, so that the reprise seems to grow naturally out of it. Only the coda that completes the movement strikes a more serious note, but this is quickly swept aside.

The slow movement is also light-footed, beginning with a melody of easy charm like a serenade sung at a window (once more, one can almost imagine a scene in a Rossini opera). A little figure of triplets from the melody gives the cue for an extended central episode, which occasionally develops some power, but without losing the light touch. When the opening melody returns, it too has been infected with the insistent triplets, and it is they that sustain the movement almost to the end, where a brief reminiscence of the opening melody brings it to a close.

The rhythm of the scherzo seems to grow naturally out of the triplets of the slow movement. As in the first movement there are playful offbeat accents. The trio is slower, with an insistent emphasis at the beginning of each two bars, giving the music the feel of a procession (or at least a processional dance).

'Playful' is once more the obvious word to describe the finale, and the gentle, naive humour of its quiet opening theme seems to have come from Haydn via Rossini. A sense of operatic wit pervades the whole movement, the moments of weight soon forgotten in the accumulating charm.

SYMPHONY NO. 8 IN B MINOR, D. 759, 'UNFINISHED'
Duration: approx. 25 minutes

Allegro moderato
Andante con moto

Schubert left behind dozens of substantial fragments. A 'Symphony No. 7' consists mostly of a single melodic line. A 'Symphony No. 10' consists of a patchwork of sections, some complete, others fragmentary. Both works have been filled out to create performing versions by Brian Newbould. But by far the most remarkable of Schubert's incomplete works is this 'Unfinished' Symphony. It was certainly intended to be a symphony in the usual four movements, but he completed only the first two, and a few bars of the scherzo. Scholars have yet to unearth any conclusive reason why it was never finished. Some have conjectured unconvincingly that the Entr'acte in B minor from the music for *Rosamunde* might have been intended as the finale. What is known is that Schubert wrote the two completed movements in 1822, and two years later sent the manuscript to his friend Anselm Hüttenbrenner, who, for reasons that remain mysterious, kept it concealed until 1860. A conductor visited him, and came across it in a drawer. Hüttenbrenner was persuaded to part with it in exchange for a promise to perform one of his own compositions. The 'Unfinished' Symphony was finally premiered in 1865, thirty-seven years after Schubert's death.

The symphony's melancholy atmosphere, its status as a great fragment, and Schubert's early death, have combined to lead some conductors to treat the work with ponderous significance, so that the listener sometimes gets the impression of two substantial slow movements. But they are marked 'Allegro moderato' and 'Andante con moto', not 'slow' and 'slower'. Schubert was beginning to achieve modest success as a composer, at least of *Lieder*, he was writing large-scale works with increasing boldness, and he was still in good health. The 'Unfinished' Symphony certainly contains dark and powerful elements, which are even more striking because there is nothing like them in his earlier orchestral works. But these elements are the product of Schubert's imagination, rather than portents of terrible things to come, and need to be treated in the context of two movements that he intended to form part of a four-movement symphony.

Nothing in Schubert's earlier orchestral music could have prepared us for the opening of this symphony. It begins quietly, with eight unaccompanied bars rising and falling on cellos and basses. This sombre phrase seems at first more like an introduction than a fully fledged theme, but it proves to be more important than the obvious 'theme' that follows. The violins begin a rippling pattern of repeated notes, with pizzicato below, bringing an element of anxiety to the sombreness of the opening. A plaintive melody, on oboe and clarinet, is punctuated by sudden accented chords, adding urgency to the anxious mood. This builds to a first climax, leading to the second theme. Now the anxiety has subsided, and over pulsating chords cellos, and then violins, sing a warm, consoling melody, in G major. Its first four bars fold round on themselves with perfect symmetry. It is the sort of melody that might be expected to be extended and developed at length. But instead it breaks off unexpectedly, and after a bar of silence, powerful chords bring the mood back to a minor key and the anxieties of the opening. Now fragments of the second theme do develop, but drawn into the prevailingly unsettled atmosphere.

The first section comes to a close, and is (usually) repeated. The middle section of the movement returns again to the sombre cello and bass opening, which is greatly enlarged with an expansive crescendo and sudden contrasts. A fortissimo statement of the opening is taken up by the trombones, and developed with rushing string scales and fierce rhythms. This is the only extended loud passage of the movement, the point at which the brooding anxieties of the first part are given full rein. After this development, which has concentrated exclusively on the opening cello and bass phrase, the reprise goes straight into the clarinet and oboe theme. The material of the first section is played in the same sequence as before. At the end, Schubert returns to the sombre opening, and a crescendo suggests that he may be working up to more development. But the climax is quickly over, the opening phrase is reiterated plangently, and four chords bring the movement to a close.

The second movement is in E major, which, after the B minor of the first movement, immediately brings a sense of serenity. Like the first movement, it opens with bars that sound introductory, but prove to be important: three shifting chords on horns and bassoons, and below them a descending pizzicato bass line. Cellos answer the basses with a lyrical four-bar phrase, with yearning upward intervals, while, above, violins answer the simple line of the horns. This pattern then repeats, culminating in an accented chord like a sudden pang of pain, which is immediately calmed by a rising arpeggio figure. All of these elements are brief, and they give much of the movement a sense of searching for lyrical expression without quite finding it. A few bars later there is a sudden forte, with the opening horn figure proclaimed on all the wind, including trombones, with the bass line striding below.

There is a hush, with quiet held notes on the violins, and then a gentle syncopated pattern in the strings. This is the moment at which the music has found the lyrical heart for which it was searching. Over the syncopated string pattern rises a sustained clarinet melody of sublime poignancy. As the clarinet holds the highest note of the melody, A, the harmony shifts under-neath – from C sharp minor to D major, D minor, F major, and slipping back to C sharp minor – and the clarinet continues serenely to the end of the melody. This is exactly the kind of harmonic subtlety in which Schubert was to excel in his late works, a moment in which time and space seem momentarily suspended, as the music loses its way and then finds it. The oboe answers the clarinet, with a final phrase echoed by the flute.

There is a fortissimo outburst on the whole orchestra, with the opening notes of the clar-inet melody now forming a rock-like bass line. The clarinet theme is then quietly explored by cellos and violins in counterpoint with one another. This quietens yet further, reduced to a single repeated phrase, and then a simple octave fall reiterated very quietly by a horn, leading into the reprise of the opening.

The whole of the movement so far is then worked through again, though with variations. The long lyrical clarinet melody is taken first by the oboe, with clarinet answering. At the fortissimo outburst, the clarinet/oboe melody, previously in the bass, is now in the violins. The music winds down to *pp* and then *ppp*, as before, and quiet sustained notes on the violins seem to be introducing the sustained clarinet melody yet again. But instead, the woodwind quietly repeat their little theme from the opening of the movement, now surprisingly in the remote key of A flat. Violins, with another poignant turn of the harmony, bring the music back to E major, and the movement ends gently with the reiterated arpeggio, and the pizzicato bass line.

With hindsight, it is easy to understand how Schubert found it impossible to continue. This pair of movements seems so complete in itself, the lyrical anxiety of the first balanced perfectly by the poignant lyricism of the second.

SYMPHONY NO. 9 IN C MAJOR, D. 944, 'THE GREAT'
Duration: 45–60 minutes

Andante – Allegro ma non troppo
Andante con moto
Scherzo: Allegro vivace
Finale: Allegro vivace

This symphony is known as 'The Great' not just as a mark of esteem, but to distinguish it from 'The Little' C major Symphony (No. 6). Schubert worked on it during the summer of 1825, while he was spending an idyllic four months touring the countryside of Upper Austria with his singer friend Johann Michael Vogl. He offered the symphony to the Vienna Gesellschaft der Musikfreunde in October 1826, but they deemed it too long and difficult, and it was not performed during his lifetime. It lay, together with many other Schubert manuscripts, in a trunk in the house of his brother Ferdinand, until New Year's Day 1839, when Schumann visited. He rescued it and sent it to Mendelssohn, who conducted the first performance with the Gewandhaus Orchestra in Leipzig the following year. But orchestras in London and Paris abandoned it during rehearsal. At the Philharmonic Society in London even Mendelssohn could not persuade the players to persevere – they laughed at the violin writing in the finale, and declared it unplayable.

It is indeed a long and exceptionally demanding work. It can last an hour if all repeats are observed – almost as long as Beethoven's Ninth. Schubert's way of filling this length is, however, quite different from Beethoven's. Even when writing massive works, Beethoven always seems to be searching to bind everything together. He is, you might say, seeking 'closure'. Schubert enters a world of the imagination and roams around it. You feel that he could go on for ever. There is logic and structure – themes repeat, develop, return, and reach satisfactory resolutions – but he seems ready to spend as much time as it takes to understand every aspect of the world he has created. It is as if the great structure emerges from the accumulation of events, rather than being preordained. This makes this symphony (like his late chamber works) immensely challenging to play. It is full of endlessly repeated details that demand unblinking concentration from the players if the great rolling waves of events are to make sense.

The introduction is Andante, with two beats to the bar (not the heavily portentous slow four beats adopted by some conductors, encouraged by corrupt editions). It begins with a quiet melody on the horns in unison. If it were loud, it might sound fanfare-like, but this is more like a moment of gathering as one sets off on a long journey. The melody itself is not straightforward. Not only is it quiet, but the phrasing is irregular: it consists of two three-bar phrases, then an extended echo of the last bar. The overall effect is wonderfully mysterious. The oboe takes up the melody, and is answered by a rich four-part texture of violas and cellos playing a warm (and regularly phrased) melody. Further variations on the opening horn melody follow: full orchestra with trombones, with the oboe rising plaintively above, and then a quiet chorus of woodwind, with violins decorating it with a rising pattern of triplets. Schubert wrote this only a year after the premiere of Beethoven's Ninth, and yet it is utterly different from Beethoven, in its richness of textures, with trombones an integral part of the orchestral tutti rather than 'extras', and in the unhurried sequence of events unfolding.

A long crescendo leads straight into the Allegro. Conductors of the past, with their four-in-a-bar introduction, had to accelerate mightily to make this work, but a more flowing pace for the introduction makes it possible to accomplish this join seamlessly. The Allegro greets us with not so much a theme as a series of fragments – sturdy dotted rhythms in the strings, answered by reiterated crescendos of triplets in the woodwind. Schubert's technique of building by accumulation is very clear here. Gradually, these fragments coalesce into a coherent sequence of phrases, gathering power. This subsides to the delicate second theme in the woodwind. This too builds up, with accented rhythms repeated again and again, and when it subsides trombones quietly enter, reiterating a phrase from the opening horn call, at first solemnly, and then more urgently with the phrase doubled in speed. It culminates in the end of the first section (the repeat of this long section was rarely taken in the past, but is increasingly played in modern performances).

The development begins with the delicate second theme in the woodwind, now countered by the dotted rhythms of the opening theme in the strings. Another long crescendo begins, with three elements combining to increase the tension – dotted rhythms in the woodwind, the tripping, even rhythms of the second theme, now in the strings, and triplets cutting across in the horns and trombones. At a climax, the trombones again enter with the phrase from the introduction, now with the dotted rhythm made even snappier by 'double-dotting'. Up to this point, the development has centred on the key of A flat, and as the energy ebbs away, phrases exchanged between woodwind and strings seem to be trying to pull the music back to C major. Eventually, at the lowest point of the diminuendo, they succeed, and the opening of the Allegro reappears pianissimo. This seems like the conventional return of the opening theme, though now whispered. But it continues on into new keys, and there is another build-up. Perhaps this is not yet the reprise. Then Schubert turns a corner, and we find that we are back at the woodwind's second theme. So that was the reprise after all – a characteristically Schubertian sequence of seeming progress, doubt, and then confirmation. The reprise continues to its conclusion, and then the pace suddenly increases for a substantial coda, in which there are three further climaxes. At the end, the horn call from the introduction returns in splendour.

The second movement has a very poised, somewhat dancing tread, set up by cellos and basses before the oboe enters with the theme. This melody has so many pointed dotted rhythms in it that it seems related to much of the first movement – as if the same dancers have relaxed into a slower tempo. The theme is in the minor, but there is a lovely tailpiece in which it warms into the major with a rising phrase. After several reiterations and contrasts, the music quietens to a moment of calm. A theme with a beautiful falling line is played by violins, and answered by clarinet, with a lovely counterpoint running under it on the cellos. This theme is discussed and developed, until another moment of calm, more profound than before, at which pianissimo horns intone a single note while the harmony changes round them – a moment that Schumann described: 'It seems to come from another sphere. Here everything listens, as if a heavenly spirit were wandering through the orchestra.'[3]

Now the poised oboe theme returns. But this time the loud responses of the strings, which were passing comments the first time round, get the upper hand. A climax develops, with the rhythms becoming more and more insistent, the harmonies developing tremendous urgency, until a great crisis is reached, and the music breaks off. After a silence, cellos tentatively try to re-establish the theme, and eventually it is the second theme in the major that sounds in the woodwind, with an anxious pattern of interjections in the violins. Finally, the first theme returns, and the movement winds quietly to a close.

The scherzo is extremely vigorous, and, like the first two movements, has rhythmic figures that are repeated again and again, interspersed with a rising, song-like second theme. The second half of the scherzo shifts up surprisingly from G to A flat, just as the first movement had done at the end of its first section. There is such a full development before the reprise of the opening that this is almost like a first-movement form rather than a conventional scherzo. The middle section, the trio, has an expansive melody with a broad swing, sung by all the woodwind, giving it a chorale-like quality. The scherzo returns at the end of the trio.

Repetition of rhythmic 'cells' has been a feature throughout the symphony, and this culminates in the finale. As in the first two movements, patterns of dotted rhythms are established straight away and persist, together with triplets, sometimes in swirling figures on the violins (it was these relentless patterns that made early orchestras deem this symphony unplayable). The overall effect is of an unstoppable jig on an enormous scale, insistent to the point of obsession. A second theme again has a suggestion of a chorale, with four sustained repeated notes as a recurrent feature. As in the first movement, there is quite a long repeat of the opening section, which is more often played today than in earlier years.

A central section develops a falling phrase from the end of the chorale-like second theme, led by clarinets. As a crescendo builds, trombones intone the four repeated notes from the chorale, and this becomes a dominant feature as the tension mounts and then falls away again. The four-note pattern persists through the quiet link to the reprise of the opening theme, with its dotted rhythms. This is in the 'wrong' key of E flat, and it moves through various keys as if searching for C major. But it only finds that key when it reaches the second theme (the wood-wind chorale).

The reprise continues on, and reaches a climax followed by a quiet conclusion, as it did the first time round. But this is not the end. With one more surprising key change, Schubert begins another, yet longer and yet more intense build-up, and at its climax the repeated four notes are hammered out. This seems, emotionally and in its insistent rhythmic repetitions, like a return to the great crisis of the slow movement. Such cataclysmic climaxes in this predominantly energetic and sunny work have shocking impact. They give a sense of dark fears kept at bay, but finally glimpsed just for a moment. So much of the music of Schubert's last years contains this kind of conflict, between the serene and the troubled, the joyfully energetic and the desperately struggling. No other composer has brought together such contrasting elements in such a personal way.

ROBERT SCHUMANN
(1810–56)

In an undated diary entry from 1829 or 1830, Schumann assesses his own character: 'I would not rank him among ordinary men ... His temperament is the melancholy, which is to say, he is given to emotion rather than to contemplation, tends to the subjective rather than to the objective ... Distinguished equally in literature and music, but no musical genius.'[1] That same year, he obtained his mother's permission to give up his law studies, and pursue a career as a concert pianist. His teacher, Friedrich Wieck, had unwisely assured Schumann's mother: 'I pledge within three years, by means of his talent and imagination, to make your son Robert into one of the greatest pianists now living ... Proof of this I present to you my eleven-year-old daughter.'[2] The daughter was Clara Wieck, destined to become one of the leading pianists of her generation, who, in the teeth of her father's opposition, married Robert Schumann in 1840.

It was in the years of frustration and separation before their marriage that Schumann poured out the piano works for which he is most famous, drawing for inspiration on the fantastic literature to which he was drawn – Jean Paul, E. T. A. Hoffmann – and driven by his thwarted passion for Clara. This torrent of piano music was followed, after their marriage, by a spate of orchestral works – in quick succession, two symphonies, a virtual symphony (the Overture, Scherzo, and Finale), and a movement of a piano concerto. The completed piano concerto, two more symphonies, and concertos for cello and violin followed.

For later generations, Robert Schumann was one of the central figures in German music of his time. But his personal success was limited by his introverted and moody character and by his health, physical and mental. With some success as a writer of orchestral music, he attempted a career as a conductor, becoming music director at Düsseldorf where he conducted orchestral and choral concerts for a season. But, despite his musical expertise, Schumann did not really have the right personality to be a successful conductor. He was withdrawn, conducting with his head in the score, and undiplomatic in his dealings with musicians and administrators. The opening season had its successes, including the premiere of his Third Symphony. But his relationship with the musicians deteriorated, his third season in 1853 was a disaster, and his conducting career came to an end. Within a few months Schumann's mental health had collapsed. He attempted suicide and was admitted to an asylum, where he remained until his death in 1856.

Schumann's orchestral music has received a mixed reception over the years. His tumbling thought processes tend toward density, often with obsessively repeating rhythmic patterns. It is as if the delight in the fantastic, which is evident in his favourite literature and in his own delightful critical writings, is struggling to be expressed within conventional musical means. His orchestration has often been considered rather thick. It is certainly inclined to be organ-like, with layers of sound added and subtracted. For many years the re-orchestrations by Mahler were favoured. Since the rise of the period instrument movement, Schumann's orchestration has been reassessed. The use of nineteenth-century brass instruments, with their narrower bore and less massive tone, rebalances the relationship between strings and wind, so that textures that once seemed dense are now revealed as satisfyingly rich. Conductors with a sensitive ear for balance always understood this: it is not necessary to have period instruments in order to make Schumann's orchestra both rich and transparent.

Concertos

CELLO CONCERTO IN A MINOR, OP. 129
Duration: approx. 24 minutes

Nicht zu schnell (Not too fast)
Langsam (Slow)
Sehr lebhaft (Very lively)

The Cello Concerto dates from 1850, when Schumann had just taken up his post as music director in Düsseldorf. He wrote it shortly before his Third Symphony. It took him three attempts to find a publisher, and Schumann was also unsuccessful in persuading cellists to play the concerto. So he made an arrangement for violin, and sent it to Joseph Joachim. This version suffered the same fate as the later Violin Concerto: Joachim never played it, and it was only rediscovered in the 1980s. It was during Schumann's mental decline in 1854 that he finished correcting the proofs of the Cello Concerto, and sent it off to the publisher. Even then it was not performed in public until 1860, after Schumann's death, and thereafter it received only sporadic performances through the rest of the nineteenth century. It was not until the twentieth century, with the championing of Gregor Piatigorsky and Pablo Casals, that the work finally found its place in the classical repertoire.

Schumann called his concerto a *Konzertstück* (concert piece), and the unconventional style is revealed straight away. It dispenses altogether with the usual orchestral introduction, launching the soloist into the main theme of the first movement, perhaps inspired by the famous example of Mendelssohn's Violin Concerto. This opening melody in A minor is typical of Schumann, combining lyrical flow with aspirational leaps and arpeggios. It expands at length, culminating in a brief orchestral tutti that further develops the energetic elements of the theme. The cello continues in a predominantly meditative mood, moving into C major for a second theme, which is more serene than the first. The woodwind then introduce a playful element, and the cello part becomes more elaborate. But, this being Schumann, the music never becomes whole-heartedly virtuoso, and the interplay of the playful, the lyrical, and the elaborate continues through to the next orchestral tutti.

The mixture of elements persists through the substantial development section, with the cello line alternating between lyrical and determined, and continually accompanied by pointed little comments in the lower strings of the orchestra. There are several attempts to regain the opening theme in different keys, before the cello finally finds its way back to A minor for the reprise.

The movement culminates in the expected orchestral tutti. But, instead of rounding it off, with or without a cadenza, the cello emerges from the chorus of woodwind, and gently descends without a break into the main theme of the slow movement. This consists of a solemn melody that could almost be an operatic aria. It is delicately accompanied by pizzicato, with touches of bowed counterpoint in the orchestral cellos. A middle passage of the melody becomes more hymn-like, with the cello playing sonorous two-part chords. Suddenly, a reminiscence of the first movement provokes a passionate outpouring from the cello, like a moment of operatic recitative. From here, an acceleration leads straight into the finale. Marked 'very lively', this is a robust dance, reminiscent of the finale of Schumann's Fourth Symphony, with insistent rhythms and a cello part containing ferociously difficult arpeggios and high passages. But it is far from a display piece: the element of yearning persists, particularly in the sighing phrases of the brief second theme. The movement ends with an unusual feature, a dramatic cadenza that is accompanied by the orchestra, leading seamlessly into the final dash.

PIANO CONCERTO IN A MINOR, OP. 54
Duration: approx. 30 minutes

Allegro affetuoso
Intermezzo: Andante grazioso –
Allegro vivace

Schumann wrote all of his best-known solo piano music in the 1830s, when he was in his twenties, much of it directly related to his passion for Clara Wieck, whom he married in 1840. But, despite the inspiration of a fine concert pianist at his side, he had not managed to compose a piano concerto. After three abandoned attempts, he completed a one-movement Phantasie in 1841, around the time that he was starting work on his D minor Symphony (published as No. 4). Clara tried out the Phantasie with orchestra at the Leipzig Gewandhaus in August 1841, when she was eight months pregnant, commenting, 'The piano is interwoven with the orchestra in the most subtle way – one cannot imagine the one without the other.'[3] But it was an awkward work to programme, and Schumann failed to find a publisher for it. Four years later, recovering from a period of illness and depression, he returned to it with vigour, and quickly added two more movements and revised the Phantasie itself to create a concerto.

In the years when Clara had a regular career as a concert pianist, this would have been a major addition to her repertoire. But, although she was still playing concerts, by now she was the mother of three children, and was pregnant with a fourth. It came too late for her to make much use of it. She nevertheless began to learn the concerto in September 1845, and wrote in their diary, 'How rich in invention, how interesting from beginning to end it is; how fresh, and what a beautifully connected whole!'[4] Clara performed it in December in Dresden, conducted by its dedicatee Ferdinand Hiller, and then in Leipzig on New Year's Day 1846, with Mendelssohn conducting. A year later she played it in Vienna, with little impact, and in Prague, with more success. Although in later years it was to become one of the most loved of piano concertos, in Schumann's lifetime it was rarely performed. It uses a classical orchestra, with two each of flutes, oboes, clarinets, horns, and trumpets, but is in other ways unconventional. Its character is meditative and unshowy, and neither critics nor public were used to such characteristics in a concerto.

It announces its unconventional character straight away. There is one abrupt chord from full orchestra, and the piano tumbles down to a cadence in A minor. This seems to echo Beethoven's 'Emperor' Concerto, with its dramatic opening cadenza. But Schumann is not a dramatic composer by nature, and this forceful opening immediately melts away, to leave an oboe singing the beautiful first theme ('affetuoso' means 'affectionate'). Again, Schumann contradicts convention, which would expect the orchestra to continue with an exposition of the main themes before the next piano entry. Instead, the piano enters straight away, echoing what the oboe has just played. And then it continues with rippling arpeggios and a melody that is constantly developing, reminding us that this is the movement that began life as a Phantasie. Piano and orchestra have a subtle relationship with each other, first one and then the other leading in the singing of the melody. Eventually, bold piano octaves emerge from this texture, there is a brief orchestral tutti (the first of the concerto), and further meditation takes the piano to a reminiscence of the first theme, now in a major key. This leads to what is, in effect, the second main theme, on clarinet – 'in effect', because it begins with the same melodic shape as the first theme, but now extended and developed. The melody passes from clarinet to piano and on to oboe, with the piano keeping up a continuous ripple of arpeggios. After a time these build up, and bold octaves once again lead into an orchestral tutti.

This is the first moment in the concerto where Schumann follows convention, the tutti announcing the join from the first section of the concerto to the central, development section. There is a warm change of key, down to A flat major. The development begins as a continuation of the dialogue between piano and clarinet, with further musing on the first theme, but at a slower tempo. Suddenly, a full orchestral chord brings the piano back to the beginning of the concerto, at the original Allegro tempo (though still in A flat major). The opening flourish of chords becomes an impassioned dialogue between piano octaves and the orchestra. This leads on to a revisiting of the second theme (which was already a development of the first), now given a new surge of energy that carries it on and on, passing through various keys until it gently relaxes back into A minor, and we are at the reprise of the first theme on the oboe.

The sequence of events proceeds much as before, with occasional abbreviation and surprising turns of harmony. This time, the rippling arpeggios build up to a high level of tension, with an increase in pace, and piano and orchestra together reach a climax. The orchestra breaks off, leaving the piano to play a cadenza. Without directly quoting any theme, Schumann takes a little turn of phrase that seems to have emerged from earlier material, and builds a moment of reflective counterpoint out of it. This gradually becomes stronger and more purposeful, until the first theme is recalled under a flourish of dramatic trills. A final trill signals the end of the cadenza, and the woodwind enter with a new, faster, dancing version of the first theme. Piano and orchestra together bring this predominantly meditative movement to a surprisingly exuberant close.

The second movement is a five-minute Intermezzo with a delicate, tiptoeing first theme. This has a sense of naive narrative, as if it had stepped out of Schumann's *Kinderszenen* (*Scenes of Childhood*). In the middle of the movement is a glorious cello melody, built from yearning upward leaps. This is made even more touching by the way the piano responds, finishing off each phrase with a heartfelt arabesque drawn from the earlier part of the movement. After the melody has passed to violins, clarinet, and bassoon, and back to cello and violin, the piano returns to the tiptoeing first theme. This time, just as it is coming to a close, it changes key, wanders off, and reaches a moment of hesitation. Clarinets and bassoons quietly recall the first theme from the first movement, and the piano replies with delicate falling chords, like a distant echo of its dramatic opening. The tempo accelerates, there is a surge of energy from the piano, urged on by the orchestra, and we are into the finale.

The principal theme has a joyful rhythmic lift, in a moderately paced three-time. Its character is new, but its shape is distilled from the melody of the concerto's first theme (this is an example of what Clara meant by 'the beautifully connected whole'). The finale is a sort of rondo, in which the principal theme recurs, with episodes in between. The first occurrence of the theme is followed by a passage of sprightly running patterns and arpeggios. This comes to a conclusion as the orchestra starts up a rhythm that cuts across the metre, creating a longer three-time pattern. Schumann plays with the confusion between the old and the new metres, continually settling into a regular rhythm and then contradicting it. This passage must surely have caused havoc at early performances, and is still a minefield for inexperienced conductors and orchestras.

There is twice a brief reprise of the opening theme, and then the music moves on into another extended episode. The orchestra treats the main theme to a brief passage of counter-point that leads the music into new keys, and to a wide-arching melody in the oboe. The piano takes this up, and then introduces a robust element that derives from the opening bars of the finale and alternates with delicate rippling passages. The next occurrence of the main theme leads to a reprise of the episode with conflicting metres, and on through its continuation to the main theme, now back in the home key. The rest of the movement is an extensive coda, dominated by almost continuous running passages and arpeggios in the piano, which bring the work to an emphatic close.

This finale is not easy to bring off convincingly. Schumann's tempo (seventy-two bars per minute) is quite easy-going for a finale, there are few displays of bravura, and there are long ruminative passages with a lot of repetition. It was characteristic of Schumann to work away at ideas in an almost obsessive manner, and this can become tiring. Pianists who try to make this finale too brilliant can seem as if they are skimming over it; those who take it at his metronome marking can seem dogged. It needs subtlety, a sense of direction, and a certain tenderness. The instruction for the first movement, affetuoso, might well apply to the whole concerto.

VIOLIN CONCERTO IN D MINOR, WOO 23
Duration: approx. 30 minutes
Im kräftigem, nicht zu schnellem Tempo (In energetic tempo, but not too fast)
Langsam (Slow)
Lebhaft, doch nicht schnell (Lively, but not fast)

In 1853, Robert Schumann was in his third season as music director in Düsseldorf. He was becoming physically and mentally weak, and he had increasing difficulty in conducting clearly and engaging with his musicians. In May he conducted concerts at the Düsseldorf Festival, in which near-disasters were only averted by the leader of the orchestra. But one great success at the Festival was the visit of the young Joseph Joachim, who was to dominate violin-playing in Germany for the next half-century. He played Beethoven's Violin Concerto, with Schumann conducting, and afterwards asked the composer to write him a concerto. This Schumann did in October and November of that year, during what was to be his last period of creative energy. In declining health, and facing problems with the musical establishment of Düsseldorf, these were rare days of happiness for Schumann.

It was while Schumann was writing the concerto that Joachim for the first time brought the young Johannes Brahms to visit Robert and Clara, and Robert immediately recognized in him 'the true apostle'.[5] Once the Violin Concerto was completed, there were plans for Joachim to perform it in Düsseldorf, but these had to be abandoned when Schumann resigned from his post in November 1853 following rows with the music committee about his conducting. When, after Schumann's death three years later, Clara Schumann and Brahms were preparing a complete edition of Schumann's music, they decided not to include the Violin Concerto. Clara's painful experience of Schumann's decline into mental collapse led her to feel a sense of weakness in his late works, and Joachim agreed that the concerto betrayed 'unmistakable signs of a certain weariness'.[6] It lay unplayed and unpublished for more than eighty years, until Georg Schünemann prepared an edition. Georg Kulenkampff gave the premiere in Berlin in November 1937, followed a month later by the first recording.

As with Schumann's late chamber music, so with this concerto, the characteristics that Clara saw as 'weak' have come to be appreciated in their own terms by later generations. And the mood of the music reflects the fact that it was written during a period that for Schumann, despite his difficulties, was basically a happy one. He himself wrote to Joachim that it 'reflected a certain seriousness, relieved by gleams of a lighter mood'.[7] The concerto is technically diffi-cult but not at all flamboyant; there is no cadenza, and the violin and orchestra work in part-nership throughout – the solo violin line is almost continuous.

The orchestra opens with a sturdy theme full of Schumann's characteristic bold leaps and insistent dotted rhythms. Soon, this yields to a meltingly warm second theme. A return to the opening dotted rhythms soon retreats to give way to the soloist, who meditates on both themes in a manner both vigorous and lyrical. This is reminiscent of Beethoven in his Violin Concerto, and the comparison becomes even more striking as the meditation deepens in the central section of the movement.

The second movement begins with an achingly beautiful cello solo, full of yearning upward leaps, and syncopated against the bass – a very Schumannesque mixture of serene and unsettled. The solo violin answers with a melody whose poignancy is underlined by a sad story associated with it. Six months after he wrote the concerto, Schumann was suffering from hallucinations. One night he imagined that angels were singing to him, and got out of bed to write down their song. Later he composed a set of variations for piano on this theme. It turned out to be the violin's melody from the slow movement of the concerto, half-remembered but not recognized by Schumann as his own music.

The finale follows the slow movement without a break. It is a rondo whose main theme is a stately polonaise, perhaps inspired by the finale of Beethoven's Triple Concerto, Opus 56. The shape of the main theme is clearly derived from the lyrical second theme of the first movement, though its rhythmic character is completely transformed. Episodes include moments of tenderness, brilliant passages, and delicate woodwind calls, and there is a touching moment when the cello theme from the slow movement is remembered in the accompaniment. The tempo remains stately throughout, and, as in the finale of Schumann's Piano Concerto, the music proceeds steadfastly on its way, determined to complete the narrative as thoughtfully as it began it.

Symphonies

SYMPHONY NO. 1 IN B FLAT, OP. 38, 'SPRING'
Duration: approx. 32 minutes
Andante un poco maestoso – Allegro molto vivace
Larghetto –
Scherzo: molto vivace –
Allegro animato e grazioso

This was not Schumann's first attempt at a symphony. In 1832 he had completed the first movement of a symphony in G minor, which was performed at Zwickau in a concert featuring Schumann's wife-to-be Clara Wieck, then aged thirteen and already a well-known pianist. However, Schumann's focus of attention in the 1830s was his solo piano music, and he never managed to complete the 'Zwickau' Symphony. It was not until the 1840s that he took seriously to orchestral music again, and when he did, he produced (as was his habit) a string of compositions in a rush. In 1841, during the first months of his marriage to Clara, he completed two symphonies together with his Overture, Scherzo, and Finale (which is, in effect, a three-movement symphony). He wrote in their joint diary on 23 January, 'Spring symphony started', and three days later on 26 January, 'Hurrah! Symphony finished.'[8] Clara had to suffer during this intense period of work, unable to play the piano while Robert was composing, and feeling ignored, as she admitted openly in the diary: 'When a man composes a symphony, one supposedly cannot ask him to concern himself with other things – even the wife must see herself sent to the back of the queue!'[9] After the initial burst of composition, Schumann took another month to orchestrate the symphony, completing it on 20 February.

He called it his 'Spring Symphony', after a poem by Adolph Böttger, to whom he dedicated the work. The poem is addressed to the Cloud Spirit, urging it to depart and reveal the spring. Schumann was particularly struck by its final two lines:

O wende, wende deinen Lauf   Oh turn, turn aside your course,
Im Thale blüht der Frühling auf!   In the valley spring is coming into bloom.

When Schumann eventually played some of the new symphony on the piano to Clara and others on 11 February, Clara wrote that she heard 'the little buds, the scent of the violets, the fresh green leaves, the birds in the air'.[10] Robert originally planned to give titles to the movements: 1. The beginning of spring 2. Evening 3. Merry playmates 4. Full spring (or, as he later decribed it, 'Farewell to spring'). But he did not want it to seem like a work of 'programme music', and dropped the titles for publication. The symphony was performed at the Leipzig Gewandhaus on 31 March 1841, with Mendelssohn conducting. And by the end of May, Schumann was already working on his next symphony (published as No. 4).

The 'Spring' Symphony, and the Symphony in D minor that followed it (No. 4), often recall Schubert's 'Great' C major Symphony. This is no coincidence. Two years earlier, Schumann had discovered the manuscript of Schubert's symphony among a collection of unpublished works at the house of Schubert's brother, Ferdinand, in Vienna. It was the experience of hearing it performed under Mendelssohn in Leipzig in 1840 that, more than any other stimulus, turned Schumann's mind towards trying again to compose his own symphony.

The 'Spring' Symphony begins with a call of trumpets and horns that matches the rhythm of Böttger's line: 'O wende, wende deinen Lauf'. Schumann said he wanted it 'to sound as if from on high, a call of awakening'.[11] The call is taken up by full orchestra. Out of this rather grand opening a flute comes tripping down a scale. Over a gentle murmuring, flute and clarinet play bird-like flourishes. The murmuring gradually gathers energy and pace, and we enter the Allegro with a bound.

Its opening theme begins with the trumpet call speeded up: the snappy dotted rhythm is to dominate the whole movement. To complete the theme, Schumann extends the trumpet call, and adds a response of energetic semiquavers. The persistent vigour of these two elements throughout the movement vividly recalls Schubert's 'Great' C major Symphony. Even the second theme is little more than a momentary lull in the onward drive: its demure little phrases are soon joined by running semiquavers.

After the repeat of the first section of the Allegro, the development is delightfully light and transparent, with the woodwind coming to the fore in Schumann's characteristic orchestral mixture. The dotted-rhythm motif of the trumpet call is always present, moving through new keys, and with varying orchestration. Against it there is a new, singing descant, first in woodwind then in the strings with flute. The persistent rhythm of the theme goes in waves, twice building up to a climax at which the main theme is reprised. The first time proves to be just a passing recall, with more development to go. The second time the build-up is longer and stronger. It culminates not in the Allegro theme, but, splendidly, in a return to the half-tempo grand opening trumpet call, on full orchestra. There is a pause, and then we are straight back into the bustle of the Allegro, continuing on from the end of the theme itself. The reprise continues as expected, and then the pace accelerates, as if approaching a straightforwardly spirited conclusion. But there is one more surprise. In the middle of all this excitement, the violins quietly sing a hymn-like melody (derived from the rising intervals of the second theme), as if the beauty of the spring has imparted a sense of holiness. A delicate flute scale leads the music out of this reverie (as the flute had led out of the opening trumpet call), and the movement ends in splendour.

In retrospect, the hymn-like passage near the end of the first movement seems like a portent of the slow movement ('Evening'). This develops the sense of tenderness and reverence, and its melody is similarly full of yearning upward intervals. It is a movement of simple beauty – the sort of music in which you can feel Schumann doing what comes most naturally to him. The first strain of the melody is on violins. A change of key takes it to the woodwind for a few bars, in which the intervals are downwards and the mood is exploratory. Twice a phrase is rounded off with a beautiful turn that comes straight out of Schubert's 'Great' C major Symphony. Then the cellos reprise the opening melody.

This leads on to the middle part of the movement, which takes the downward intervals from earlier, and leads them on to a little climax. Here, the intervals fall in a rhythmic pattern that might evoke memories of the opening of Brahms's Third Symphony (this idea will crop up again in Schumann's own Third Symphony). With a gentle modulation back to the home key, the opening melody is taken up again by oboe and horn – the rather high placing of the horn gives the upward intervals a particularly poignant 'pull'. The overall shape of this movement might be simple, but its orchestration is remarkable. Strings and wind interact and combine in beautiful and shifting combinations, and melodies are supported by a delicate web of figurations, above and below. Schumann's orchestration, which used to be described as 'thick', is revealed as wonderfully subtle in a movement like this – and it is a subtlety from which Brahms was to learn.

Just before the end of the Larghetto, the trombones enter for the first time in this movement. They solemnly intone a phrase that falls chromatically, and mysteriously. The movement comes to a half-close, and, without a break, the scherzo follows. The trombones' mysterious falling phrase is revealed as the theme of the scherzo. Schumann's original title for this, 'Merry playfellows', was no doubt inspired by Beethoven's 'Merry gathering of peasants' in the 'Pastoral' Symphony. Indeed it would be a straightforward rustic dance, a *Ländler*; but it is in a minor key, and this, combined with the chromatic notes in its falling phrases, gives it a serious air. This quasi-*Ländler* is interleaved with two trios. The first is faster, in the major, and built out of almost nothing – a simple rhythmic pattern that repeats again and again, evolving with changing harmonies and accompaniments (once again the inspiration of Schubert is clear). The second trio, in another major key, stays at the same pace as the scherzo and has a relaxed, genial character. After the final return to the scherzo, there is a coda. This begins with a reminiscence of the second half of the scherzo. After a pause, woodwind and strings wistfully remember the first trio, and then, with a strange final exhalation, the music reaches an expectant pause.

The finale, a 'farewell to spring', bursts in with a rapid ascent in the violins (this is very like a moment near the end of Weber's overture to *Der Freischütz*), and a confident stride upwards, on full orchestra. This seems like just an opening flourish, but it will prove an important motif later. It is followed by a delicate little theme on violins, with a characteristically persistent rhythm. A simpler, tiptoeing second theme in the woodwind is answered by the opening stride on violins, now taking on a stern character, in a minor key. After a hesitation, the delicate little opening theme tries to resume, but it culminates again in the rhythm of the striding motif, now in the major, and with a melodic shape that is more like the trumpet call from the first movement. This new version is taken up by woodwind, and then full orchestra, so that the first section of the movement ends in a spirit of high optimism.

The middle of the movement is a development of this striding motif in various forms. It begins simply on woodwind, and is interrupted by a sudden call of the trombones. The striding motif continues in tremolando strings, while wind chords gradually build up. At a sudden pianissimo, the striding rhythm expands to an arpeggio in the woodwind, and there is another build-up to a pause, and a moment of calm. Horns quietly call in rising arpeggios (an effect that seems to look forward to Wagner, whose *The Flying Dutchman* was just round the corner), and a flute relaxes bird-like into a cadenza. At the end of it, a bassoon joins the flute to reprise the delicate opening theme. From here, the music unfolds as it did at the beginning of the movement, though with a different sequence of keys. Back in the home key, the final pages of the symphony are dominated by the striding rhythm in its arpeggio form, and, with the tempo gradually increasing, it takes on a joyfully triumphant character, as of spring in full flower.

SYMPHONY NO. 2 IN C MAJOR, OP. 61
Duration: approx. 35 minutes

Sostenuto assai – Allegro, ma non troppo
Scherzo: Allegro vivace
Adagio espressivo
Allegro molto vivace

On 20 September 1845, two months after completing his Piano Concerto, Schumann wrote to Mendelssohn, 'for days my head has been a whirl of drums and trumpets . . . I don't know what will come of it.'[12] As with his first two symphonies (published as Nos 1 and 4), Schubert's 'Great' C major Symphony was an inspiration – he heard it performed again in December 1845 in Dresden. Despite persistent illness, Schumann managed to complete the piano score of his new symphony by the end of December. He began orchestrating it in February 1846 but was again interrupted by ill health. As well as his generally weak and nervous state, which had never been fully diagnosed, he now started suffering from what he described as 'strange distortion of the hearing.'[13] He had to take extended periods of rest, and it was not until October that the score was finished. Mendelssohn conducted the premiere in the Leipzig Gewandhaus on 5 November 1846, but it was not a great success. Schumann made further revisions, and conducted the revised version himself at a little festival in his honour at his birthplace, Zwickau, in July 1847. Clara reported, 'Robert conducted with greater energy than I have ever witnessed in him before, and so the symphony went very well.'[14]

The long time that Schumann took to write this symphony was not just the result of illness. He had habitually composed very quickly, in the heat of inspiration. But, as he himself observed, 'Only from the year 1845 on, when I began to invent and work out everything in my head, did a completely different way of composing start to develop.'[15] This partly arose from his renewed interest in counterpoint, based on his study of the fugues of J. S. Bach. Schumann had written fugues of his own earlier in 1845, and from now on a more sophisticated use of counterpoint became a feature of his major compositions. His Second Symphony shows the result of this change, with its richness of textures and artful interweaving of lines.

The symphony opens with a spacious introduction. The brass quietly intone a chorale, while the strings play a smoothly winding line in counterpoint. The atmosphere is distinctly religious, like the impression of entering a great cathedral (an effect Schumann was to develop in his next symphony). A moment of agitation leads to a build-up, with the chorale capping its climax. After some abrupt, Beethoven-like chords, the music subsides and, with another acceleration, quietly enters the Allegro.

The theme, like several in his first two symphonies, is one of Schumann's nervy inventions, full of jumpy dotted rhythms. It is extended and developed, giving way to smoother elements, but there is no distinct second theme. After the repeat, the middle section begins with the dotted rhythms, but soon calms, and develops the smooth elements. The woodwind chorus is dominant, exchanging phrases with the strings. Throughout, agitated elements continue under the smooth lines, and eventually these rise to the surface to build up an energetic contrapuntal web of sound. Twice there is a climax, at the second of which the first theme returns, now on full orchestra. All the opening material of the Allegro is reprised. After a moment of calm, the intensity increases, and the trumpets sound the chorale from the opening of the symphony. The movement drives to a conclusion in a triumphant spirit that shows no sign of the troubles Schumann was experiencing as he wrote it.

The second movement is the scherzo. Once again it has a characteristic nervous alertness and relentlessness. But it is also delightful, with subtle shifts of harmony, playful interaction between strings and wind, and an exhilarating virtuosity tempered with delicacy and humour. In between the three statements of the scherzo there are two trios. The first breaks from the rapid four-notes-per-beat to a more relaxed three notes, with chattering woodwind contrasted with urbane strings.

In the second trio, the running and chattering cease, and a hymn-like melody is sung first by strings and then by woodwind. As the woodwind take over, violas play a counterpoint of a trotting bass, and this sparks off a contrapuntal working of the hymn tune, in which the trotting bass is also incorporated. Within this counterpoint, Schumann has planted references to J. S. Bach, which are not obvious unless one is looking for them. The notes B flat, A, C, and B natural spell, in German notation, BACH. Schumann incorporates this turn of phrase several times, referring both to his study with Clara of Bach's works, and to his own fugues for organ on BACH which he had composed a few months before starting work on the symphony.

As the hymn winds to a conclusion, a hesitant, double-speed few notes of the trotting bass start up in the violins. This (we suddenly realize) is the same as the opening notes of the scherzo theme, and after a few attempts, the scherzo itself gets going again. As it races to a conclusion, the trumpets and horns call out with the first phrase of the chorale from the first movement, elevating the end of the scherzo to a note of triumph.

The slow movement begins with a melody of heart-easing poignancy. Its effect is achieved partly by Schumann's new care over counterpoint and the relationship between simultaneous parts. Under the melody, the bass is a beautiful independent line. When the oboe takes up the melody, the bassoon plays a new counterpoint. There is a gentle horn call before the melody continues, developing as it goes. It reaches a beautiful climax, high on the violins, with new decoration and trills enhancing the magical effect of the harmonies.

What follows is a passage of more formal counterpoint, with tiptoeing staccato against a smooth line that descends chromatically – rather than J. S. Bach, this evokes memories of the chorale sung by the two armed men in Mozart's *The Magic Flute*. For a time, Schumann proceeds formally, even drily, but soon the beautiful theme returns in the woodwind, while the staccato counterpoint continues in the strings. The music changes key, moving away from E flat to the C major of the first movement. Again the strings rise to their lovely climax, and the movement comes gently to a close. This is perhaps the most beautiful movement in all Schumann's symphonies, perfectly balanced between tragedy and serenity.

The finale opens with a rush upwards, and an almost fanfare-like theme of bold dotted rhythms. This is like a more confident cousin of the nervy dotted rhythms that opened the first movement Allegro, and it proceeds like a joyful procession, once again recalling *The Magic Flute* (the grand entry of Sarastro). The violins break into rapid scale passages, against which woodwind and horns play a triplet figure that is perhaps drawn from the horn call in the slow movement. Beneath this energetic activity, cellos and violas remember the opening theme of the slow movement, and its falling interval is reiterated in the violins.

A return to the opening fanfare leads on to an extended passage in which the processional theme, the rushing scales, and the persistent triplet rhythms combine. Out of this emerges a clarinet playing the theme from the slow movement upside down. As this moves to the other woodwind, horns and trumpets quietly remind us of the opening chorale. Eventually the music comes to a moment of quiet. Perhaps we expect a reprise of the opening theme. But instead, the woodwind play a gentle theme of rising phrases that seems to have come out of nowhere. It is drawn into the ongoing dialogue, and extended into a longer line. The opening rushing scale returns, and a climax brings us to another pause.

At this point the nature of the new theme becomes clear. The rising phrase becomes a rising and falling phrase, and reveals itself as a quote from the last song of Beethoven's *An die ferne Geliebte* (*To the Distant Beloved*). This was a phrase of deep significance for Robert and Clara. In the summer of 1836, when he had been separated from Clara by her father, this same phrase formed the sorrowful climax of the first movement of his Fantasie for piano, reminding them both of the poignant words of the song, 'Take these songs which I used to sing to you, and sing them to yourself in the evening.' A trotting bass joins the song, recalling a similar moment in the second trio of the scherzo. Quietly, trumpets and trombones play the first phrase of the opening chorale, and this encourages the song to expand into a chorale itself. With a hint of Beethoven's 'Ode to Joy' from the Ninth Symphony, the music builds to a grand final climax.

SYMPHONY NO. 3 IN E FLAT MAJOR, OP. 97, 'RHENISH'
Duration: approx. 32 minutes

Lebhaft (Lively)
Scherzo; sehr mässig (Very moderate in speed)
Nicht schnell (Not fast)
Feierlich (Ceremonial)
Lebhaft (Lively)

In September 1850, Robert and Clara Schumann moved to the Rhineland. Robert had been appointed as music director in Düsseldorf with responsibility for the city's orchestra and chorus, a job that had recently been vacated by his friend, the composer Ferdinand Hiller. The Symphony No. 3 was the first major new work that Schumann conducted in Düsseldorf, on 6 February 1851, and it was well enough received to be repeated a month later. Within two years, things were to go seriously wrong, but for now, Schumann's reputation as a composer was able to carry him through and create a period of comparative success.

Soon after this new appointment the Schumanns paid a visit to Hiller, who had moved to Cologne, and it was on this occasion that they visited its cathedral. Robert had first seen it from a distance twenty years earlier, as he travelled on a boat down the Rhine. Now, in 1850, six hundred years after its foundation, the cathedral was being completed to its original design, though its famous spires were not yet built. As soon as he returned to Düsseldorf, Schumann began work on his Symphony No. 3 (the fourth to be written). Although he did not give it the nickname, 'Rhenish', he did admit that it was partly inspired by his travels through the Rhineland. As well as the usual four movements, it has an extra movement before the finale that is clearly linked to the impression made on Schumann by Cologne Cathedral.

The character of the first movement suggests homage to the first movement of Beethoven's 'Eroica' Symphony, in the same key. It is similarly full of driving rhythmic energy. Strong cross-rhythms, which Beethoven uses to powerful effect, are a striking feature of Schumann's movement right from the start. An exuberant, leaping melody creates an emphatic three-time metre. It is only as it breaks into a faster three-time after a few bars that we realize that the opening was a cross-rhythm straddling the bar line. This deliberate confusion creates a splendid release of energy (Schumann had played a similar rhythmic trick, though to different effect, in the finale of his Piano Concerto five years earlier). The tension between these two rhythms informs the character of the whole movement.

A quieter second idea follows the opening passage. As in the Beethoven, this is a gentle theme on woodwind, with oboe leading, though it has an unmistakably Schumannesque poignancy. The first section of the movement ends with Beethoven-like emphasis before moving on (without a repeat) into the development. More Beethovenian passages of energy give way to musings on the quiet second theme, now in counterpoint between treble and bass. Later, this theme is combined with running scales from the first part of the movement. The cross-rhythm opening begins to reappear as the music moves on from key to key. Eventually, it arrives back in the home key of E flat, and the four horns announce the approach to the reprise, sounding the first notes of the opening theme, at first with a broader rhythm, then reverting to the cross-rhythms. But it takes some time for the music to build up the energy for the full reprise, which finally strides out of the climax.

The music works its way to a moment of reflection, where it falls in a descending arpeggio, like the opening of Brahms's Third Symphony (a work that owes a great deal to this movement). The first falling interval is repeated, and then becomes the opening of the gentle second theme – a link between first and second themes that we might not otherwise have noticed. The movement proceeds onwards to a confident close. Of all Schumann's strongly rhythmic movements, this is perhaps the finest. Sometimes his repetitive rhythms can begin to seem laborious, but here the energy and invention are maintained from beginning to end.

Schumann originally gave the second movement the title 'Morning on the Rhine'. Despite its scherzo heading, its moderate tempo and gently swinging rhythm, punctuated by timpani, make it sound as much like a rumination as a dance (this sort of ambiguity is again something from which Brahms learned). The second strain has phrases that cut across the three-time bar, so that any sense of dance is further softened. After the first statement of the scherzo, the music breaks into delicate semiquavers, which really do dance. These maintain the shape of the scherzo, like a variation, and towards the end of the second strain the original melody comes creeping in below the semiquavers.

This is followed by a new idea in a minor key, with the four horns in chorus, muttered semiquavers below, and a long held bass note. The haunting, slightly ominous quality of this passage must surely have inspired Tchaikovsky to create a similar effect (with similar harmonies) in the middle of his five-time movement in the 'Pathétique' Symphony. The scherzo theme returns briefly, though not yet in its original key, leads on to a sturdier passage, then a brief recall of the horn theme. The reprise of the scherzo follows.

The slow movement opens with a beautiful clarinet melody, whose leaping intervals give it a sense of connection with the opening theme of the first movement. From this melody the violins emerge with an idea that alternates tiptoeing with sighing phrases (reminiscent of the slow movement of the Piano Concerto). At the end of the opening paragraph these two elements are briefly combined. The middle part of the movement begins with violas and bassoons introducing a third element, a gently falling line, richly scored with divided cellos below, which moves on to new keys. The tiptoeing idea resumes and is developed, and the violas' falling line rounds off the middle section. As the clarinet melody returns, the tiptoeing strings continue with a tender counterpoint, and the movement ends with a beautiful coda that brings all three elements together.

Schumann had already begun writing the symphony when, in November 1850, he and Clara returned to Cologne and attended the ceremony in the cathedral elevating Archbishop Johannes von Geissel to cardinal. Schumann originally gave this movement the title, 'In the style of a solemn procession', but later replaced it with the single word 'feierlich' ('solemn' or 'ceremonial'). This is perhaps the single most impressive movement in all of Schumann's symphonies. It combines the ancient and the modern, evoking the counterpoint of German Renaissance masters and the traditional religious use of trombones, and making it vivid through the subtle use of modern orchestral resources. Taking a leaf out of Beethoven's fifth and sixth symphonies, Schumann has saved his three trombones to create a dramatic effect as they enter at this late point.

Trombones and horns intone a chorale, in five-part counterpoint. The alto trombone and the first horn in unison play the top line, soaring higher at each turn of phrase, as if the wide intervals of the opening theme of the symphony have been distilled into their essence. This is the theme from which the whole movement is constructed. The strings take up the web of counterpoint, with violins soaring higher, and the contrapuntal web gradually grows in strength. A double-speed version of the theme is introduced into the counterpoint. Then this becomes quadruple-speed, and is combined with the original version (this seems like a moment of homage to Beethoven's Piano Sonata, Opus 110, whose final fugue does the same with a rather similar theme). Again the great structure gradually builds up, with the choruses of strings, brass, and woodwind combining while remaining distinct.

There is a sudden hush, and the opening chorale quietly and majestically reappears, moving forward and coming to rest. As if announcing the great moment, trumpets (which have played almost no part in the counterpoint) join the other brass in twice playing a solemn fanfare. Hushed strings respond, as if conveying the reverberation of the great building, and the movement comes to a close.

Schumann marks the finale Lebhaft (lively), and the first theme Dolce (sweetly), so he clearly did not intend it to sound frenetic. But his very fast metronome marking (two beats per second) makes it very difficult to achieve lightness once one gets beyond the easy-going rhythms of the opening. The movement is full of little touches of syncopation and awkward corners that need time to achieve their effect, and it takes great skill by both orchestra and conductor to make it all fall naturally into place (even if the metronome marking is taken with a pinch of salt).

The movement opens with the most straightforwardly outgoing theme in the symphony so far, at first four-square, and then breaking into livelier rhythms. A graceful second idea alternates little sighs with staccato phrases. None of this has obvious links to earlier themes but, this being Schumann, the movement is full of subtle allusions. The opening theme is like a straightened and energized version of the tiptoeing second theme from the third movement. As the graceful second theme finishes, the horns introduce a vigorous offbeat fanfare that takes us back to the leaping first movement. When the first section of the movement has come to a close, a rapid version of the theme from the fourth movement is muttered by the violins, and this becomes a running commentary underneath the woodwind, as they pass a phrase from the first theme back and forth with the violins.

In the middle of this development, the horns play a joyful rising arpeggio. This seems quite new, but it is like an outgoing version of the scherzo's first theme. This same arpeggio launches the music into a reprise of the opening section. When the themes have run their course, there is a climactic, grand fanfare with rushing strings (Mahler quotes this splendid passage in the finale of his First Symphony). There is a moment in which a rising interval is played in counterpoint, reminding us of the processional fourth movement, and then another horn call launches the music into a final burst of energy.

SYMPHONY NO. 4 IN D MINOR, OP. 120
Duration: approx. 30 minutes

1841 original	1851 revision
Andante con moto – Allegro di molto	Ziemlich langsam – Lebhaft (Quite slow – Lively)
Romanza: Andante	Romanze: Ziemlich langsam (Quite slow)
Scherzo: Presto	Scherzo: Lebhaft (Lively)
Finale: Largo – Allegro vivace	Langsam – Lebhaft (Slow – Lively)

Towards the end of May 1841, Clara Schumann wrote in their joint diary that she hears Robert at work, with 'D minor sounding wildly in the distance, so I already know in advance that it is again a work created out of the deepest soul'.[16] Only three months after completing his First Symphony, Robert was composing his second. This is the symphony that was ten years later to be published as No. 4, after Schumann had revised it. Like No. 1, it is a work that is deeply influenced by Schubert's 'Great' C major Symphony, which Schumann had recently discovered in Vienna (see Symphony No. 1, above). It has similar rhythmic drive, generated by insistent repetition of little rhythmic cells. The key of D minor gives it a darker, more earnest character, but there is also, as in No. 1, much *joie de vivre*.

The premiere in Leipzig of the first version of the symphony took place in December 1841, and was not a success. It was conducted by Ferdinand David, who made much less of an impression with it than Mendelssohn had done with the First Symphony the previous May. Schumann withdrew this first version, and left it untouched for ten years. In 1851 he looked at the score again, and revised it for a performance in Düsseldorf. He bolstered the orchestration, adding an extra pair of horns, and having the woodwind and strings support each other more of the time. Clara Schumann declared that the revised version was much superior to the original, perhaps because she had vivid memories of the failure of the first version. But Brahms disagreed, and despite Clara's protests, had the original score published in the 1880s. The revised version is 'safer', but requires very careful balancing if it is not to sound thick and relentless. The original version is more transparent and varied in its textures, and has come back into favour in recent years, particularly in period-instrument performances.

The symphony begins with a brief but spacious introduction, whose flowing down-and-up melody recurs in various forms later. In the original version, the link into the Allegro is a Beethoven-like series of abrupt chords. But in the revision, Schumann introduces a new rising shape in the violins, which, speeded up, becomes the theme of the Allegro (Lebhaft). The Allegro itself is a highly unconventional movement, with more the character of a free fantasia than the first movement of a symphony. The first section is dominated by the vigorous opening theme which, with its relentless semiquavers, becomes almost a perpetuum mobile. It changes in character as the music moves from key to key, but there is no real second theme.

The first section is repeated in the revision (not in the original version). Then the movement continues, as expected, with a development. The vigorous semiquavers are still dominant, but interleaved with them appears a solemn call from the trombones (one of the passages that evokes memories of Schubert's 'Great' C major Symphony). This builds up until the wind introduce a triumphant, march-like idea, which twice reaches a pause.

The second time, a new theme follows, the first lyrical melody in this movement – the sort of idea you might have expected to form the second theme much earlier. Its shape, with a falling interval at the start of each phrase, is rather like an elaboration of the trombone call. It too alternates with the persistent semiquavers, and soon these are dominant again. Once more the trombone call appears, and again it builds up to the march idea, culminating in two pauses. The lyrical melody returns, giving way to the persistent semiquavers. Yet again the lyrical melody reappears, this time leading higher. The music breaks into D major, and the lyrical melody takes on a march rhythm, on full orchestra. It gives the music the impetus to draw this exhaustingly energetic movement to a close.

After a brief pause, the Romanze follows. Oboe and solo cello play a brief, folk-song-like melody, and then the strings reprise the introduction from the beginning of the symphony. The music breaks into a sunny D major, and the strings develop this introduction into a flowing melody, over which a solo violin weaves a charming elaboration. The movement ends with a reprise of the oboe and cello's melody.

The scherzo is fast and energetic, built from a phrase that reverses the down-and-up shape of the introduction. The trio simply takes the melody from the middle of the Romanze, now in three-time, with all the first violins playing the solo violin line. This trio comes round twice. The second time, instead of reaching a conclusion, it gradually fragments, weakens, and slows. Very quietly, as at the end of the opening introduction, the violins play their familiar rising figure, while trombones slowly intone the march-like idea from the middle of the first movement. This rises grandly, with trumpets and horns joining in.

The rising figure accelerates, and it seems as if we are about to reprise the opening Allegro. But, instead, after a pause, the music breaks in to the march idea, with (in the revised version) the bustling semiquavers in the bass. This is now rounded off to a complete theme and followed by a new continuation, with short lyrical phrases that then develop dancing dotted rhythms.

After a climax this opening section is repeated in the revised version (not in the original). Stern trombones announce a new section, just as they did in the first movement. The dancing dotted rhythms take over, played in simple counterpoint, and developing momentum. Once again trombones and horns build up. Eventually the music arrives at a reprise, not of the first theme, but of its lyrical continuation. The music proceeds as before to a climax, and again the stern trombones interrupt. The remainder of the movement is a coda of gathering energy. After one more pause, there is a final Presto, which brings the work to an exhilarating close.

ALEXANDER SCRIABIN (ALEKSANDR NIKOLAYEVICH SKRYABIN)
(1872–1915)

At the time of his death from blood poisoning, the Russian composer Scriabin had been working for more than a decade on a grand project more final than any conceived in the history of music, a multimedia event for performance in India that would make Wagner's notions of a *Gesamtkunstwerk* (complete artwork) seem modest. In the words of his brother-in-law and biographer, Boris de Schloezer, this *Mysterium* 'was to encompass the vision of an apocalyptic ecstasy and the end of the world. Scriabin firmly believed that the production of this work would actually lead to cosmic collapse and universal death.'[1] It was, of course, an unattainable project, which resulted in nothing more than a pile of sketches, but its vision dominated Scriabin's thinking: 'As the *Mysterium* receded into the misty distance of remote temporal and spatial categories untainted by earthly impurities, dwelling entirely on the idealistic plane and absolved of reality, it became a peculiarly powerful vehicle for the ancient dream of a universal reunion of humanity with divinity, whose agent Scriabin believed himself to be.'[2]

It is easy to ridicule Scriabin's ambitions, and many have done so. The Russian conductor Serge Koussevitzky, who first met Scriabin in 1908 and championed his music, was reported as saying, 'Alexander Nikolaevich (Scriabin) is so naive about his "Mystery" that he thinks the whole world will burn up with his music. But what actually happens is that we play the "Mystery" and then go to a good restaurant and have a delicious supper.'[3] Even his closest friends and collaborators recognized that Scriabin, a highly neurotic man, occupied the uncomfortable borderline between madness and genius. His thought processes are vividly revealed in a series of notebooks written in Switzerland over 1904–6. These include rambling passages of prose-poem, exalted, mystical, and egocentric, influenced by Russian mysticism, the Theosophists, and the *Übermensch* (Super-human) of Friedrich Nietzsche. Here is a representative extract from November 1905:

> I am desire, I am light, I am creative ascent that tenderly caresses, that captivates, that sears, destroying, reviving. I am raving torrents of unknown feelings. I am the boundary, I am the summit. I am nothing.
>   I am God!
>   I am nothing, I am play, I am freedom, I am life.
>   I am the boundary, I am the peak.
>   I am God![4]

All this would be no more than a footnote in the history of mysticism, if it were not for Scriabin's music. He was an outstanding pianist, a contemporary of Rachmaninoff at the Moscow Conservatoire, and composer of a substantial body of piano music. His early works were inspired by Chopin, but in a series of ten sonatas Scriabin developed a fusion of high Romanticism with his own take on modern harmony to create music of exceptional power and nervous intensity. As with Liszt, it is his piano music that has most firmly stood the test of time, despite all the limitations of the instrument (or even because of them). However, the orchestra gave Scriabin the opportunity to explore these ideas on a massive canvas. The *Poem of Ecstasy* is the most frequently performed of his orchestral works.

THE POEM OF ECSTASY, OP. 54
Duration: approx. 22 minutes

Scriabin composed *The Poem of Ecstasy* in 1905–8, often referring to it as his Fourth Symphony. It is the second of three symphonic poems, composed between *The Divine Poem* (Symphony No. 3) and *Prometheus: The Poem of Fire* (Symphony No. 5). *The Poem of Ecstasy* was premiered in New York in December 1908 by the Russian Symphony Orchestra of New

York, conducted by Modest Altschuler. There were plans for a Russian premiere in Moscow the same year, but the complexity of the work defeated the conductor, Felix Blumenfeld, and it was cancelled during rehearsals. It was finally performed in St Petersburg in 1909 under Vassily Safonoff. Scriabin travelled from the United States to Moscow for the occasion, and performed its companion piece, the fifth piano sonata.

Before composing the music, Scriabin wrote a poem, which he first called *Poème orgiaque* ('Orgiastic Poem'), later changing the title to *Le Poème de l'Extase* ('The Poem of Ecstasy'). The poem formed the basis not only of the musical *Poem of Ecstasy*, but also of his fifth piano sonata, composed in a few days after finishing the orchestral work. He had the poem printed in Russian, intending that it should be available to the audience for the (cancelled) premiere in St Petersburg. But he drew back from the idea of having it printed in the score, saying, 'Conductors who want to perform the Poem of Ecstasy can always be apprised that it has such a thing, but in general I would prefer for them to approach it first as pure music.'[5]

The poem, of more than three hundred lines, is difficult to read, with its combination of mystical aspiration with imagery that ranges from the cataclysmic through orgasmic eroticism and elements of sado-masochism to the sensually voluptuous, culminating in the world's joyful cry, 'I am!' (a modification of the cries of 'I am God!' that peppered his earlier notebooks.) It is, however, useful in giving us some idea of the symbolism that lay behind the music, and of its links to the thinking that lay behind Scriabin's project for the unattainable final *Mysterium*. Two extracts from his notebooks help to focus these ideas:

> Absolute being, as opposed to absolute non-being, is being in All, and as such it is realized at a moment that must illumine the past; it will recreate the past at the moment of divine creativity, at the moment of ecstasy. Time and space and all that they contain will be consumed at that supreme moment of great efflorescence and divine synthesis.
>
> Ecstasy is the highest exaltation of action; ecstasy is a summit ... Intellectually, ecstasy is the highest synthesis; emotionally, it is the greatest happiness.[6]

When he came to compose the music, Scriabin did not set out to follow the poem in detail, wanting the two works to remain independent. Nevertheless, the musical and poetic versions of *The Poem of Ecstasy* are closely related. Soon after the completion of the score, Boris Schloezer reported, 'Scriabin and I worked together comparing text and music. I remember the pleasure and surprise he felt when the music was fully free yet followed the development of the text.'[7] The extracts from the poem that follow are from the translation by Hugh McDonald.[8]

The work unfolds in one continuous movement. It opens quietly, with Scriabin's characteristically mysterious, floating harmonies hanging in the air. The first theme, gently folding downwards and upwards, represents 'longing':

> The spirit
> Pinioned on its thirst for life
> Soars in flight
> To heights of negation.
> There in the rays of its fantasy
> Is born a magic world

Of wondrous images and feelings.
  The playing spirit,
  The longing spirit,
The spirit that creates all things in fantasy
Gives itself to the bliss of love.

The music alternates between voluptuous passages, marked 'languido', 'soavamente', featuring a pleading solo violin, and glittering, fleeting passages. The musical language is rooted in the magical-fantastic world of Rimsky-Korsakov, but with an extra twist in the harmonies. One of the first things that will strike many listeners is the similarity to parts of Stravinsky's *The Firebird*, composed shortly after the St Petersburg performance of *The Poem of Ecstasy*. Stravinsky later liked to claim that he had never thought much of Scriabin, but his influence on *The Firebird* is unmistakable.

The enchanted, erotic atmosphere is threatened for a moment:

  But suddenly . . .
The terrible rhythms
Of dark presentiment
Break roughly upon
An enraptured world,
  But only for an instant.
With a light exertion
Of the divine will
It drives away
The fearsome illusions.

There are two contrasted trumpet calls: the first agitated (representing the 'dark presentiment'), the second rising in confident leaps. This is the 'victory' theme, marked 'avec noble et douce majesté' ('with noble and soft majesty'). It contains echoes of a number of 'heroic' themes: Siegfried's motif from Wagner's *Ring*, and themes from Richard Strauss's *Ein Heldenleben* and *Don Juan*.

Now the spirit gives itself to the bliss of love:

Amid the flowers of its creations
It abides in kisses,
In a plenitude of delight
It calls them to ecstasy.

From a sensuous delicacy, marked 'très parfumé', the music gradually increases in power, 'avec une ivresse toujours croissante' ('with ever-increasing intoxication') and 'presque en delire' ('almost delirious'). But this is too soon for a climax, and the music dies again, giving way to another Allegro passage, with the trumpet call renewed. This is the beginning of a much longer paragraph, which develops the musical material, like the middle of a conventional symphonic movement, and at the same time it relates to the section of the poem that depicts the struggle between the spirit and the forces assailing it:

With burning gaze
It pierces
The darkest chasms;
Filled with anger
And indignation
It throws down the audacious challenge –
The battle begins to rage.
The gaping jaws
Of monsters yawn . . .

Twice, enormous climaxes develop and subside. The second time, the music calms and slows to Lento, and clarinet and violin solos return to the mysterious atmosphere of the opening. The elements from the beginning of the work shyly begin to return. This corresponds to the moment in the poem at which the great struggles are over, and the spirit regains its determination:

. . . pinioned once more
On its thirst for life
It soars in flight
To heights of negation.

After a while, the music breaks once more into a glittering Allegro (the rapidly leaping figure alternating between flute and oboe is a transformation of the trumpet call). Once more this is cut short, and the music returns to a languorous Lento. Soon it accelerates to another Allegro, with a renewal of the trumpet call. Again a climax develops, subsides, begins to develop again, and is once more denied. There is a moment of playfully trilling flutes with silvery touches of celesta. A horn call signals a revival of energy, and the playfulness develops into a great series of waves leading to a huge climax, all rooted in a sustained low C in the bass (in contrast to most of the piece that has been harmonically restless). There is a sudden silence, from which emerges a long crescendo, culminating in a final, massive chord of C major:

The world is consumed
In universal flame.
The spirit is on the summit of being.
And it feels
The endless coursing
Of divine strength,
Of free will.
It is total audacity;
What once threatened
Is now excitation,
What once terrified
Is now delight,
And the bites of panthers and hyenas
Have become but a new embrace,
A new torment,

> The snake's bite
> Is but a burning kiss.
> And the world resounds
>   With the joyful cry:
>   I am!

DMITRI SHOSTAKOVICH
(1906–75)

Of all the major classical composers, Shostakovich is the one whose music is most closely tied to actual events. He lived in Russia through the Revolutions, the rise of Stalin, the Second World War, and most of the Soviet era. His orchestral music extends from a brilliant First Symphony composed when he was a student at the age of eighteen, through massive war symphonies to the bleak song-cycles and eerie landscapes of the works written in his sixties. He narrowly survived the repression of artists who did not toe the party line, which required that music should be optimistic and uplifting for the people. There was a time when, because of his status in Soviet Russia, Shostakovich was regarded with hostility in some parts of the West. In America during the Cold War, his massive, accessible works were officially regarded as propaganda for the communists, and treated with deep suspicion.[1] Now, in the twenty-first century, we can view his position with a little more perspective.

The Russian conductor Yevgeny Mravinsky, one of the greatest champions of Shostakovich, described his first meetings with him, when he was to conduct the premiere of his Fifth Symphony in 1937. The conductor and composer were to develop a close understanding of each other, but at first Mravinsky was disconcerted not only by Shostakovich's reluctance to say anything about his music, but also by their divergent approaches to music: 'In truth, the character of our perception of music differed greatly. I do not like to search for subjective, literary and concrete images in music which is not by nature programmatic, whereas Shostakovich very often explained his intentions with very specific images and associations.'[2]

Shostakovich certainly wears his experiences on his sleeve. He declares to the world, 'I am a Russian living through terrible times, and this is what it is like.' This is not to say that everything in his music derives from personal experience. If you want to know how it was to live through the siege of Leningrad, in which 600,000 died, or the battle of Stalingrad, which lasted for six months, you will not get it directly from his music: Shostakovich escaped from the former, and did not experience the latter. In any case, it would be naive to expect music to convey such horrors. The relationship between life and music is never that straightforward. But Shostakovich's music comes closer than any to expressing the raw despair, the pointless waste of life, and the cruel destructive force of terrible events.

One of the essential ingredients of Shostakovich is his use of irony. This is not like French irony, with its wit and lightness, nor quite like the irony of Mahler, with its strong element of nostalgia. Shostakovich certainly admired Mahler and learned a lot from his music, but his is the mirthless irony of one who wishes to express the bitterness of being crushed by the banal. It is the offspring of Stravinsky, Prokofiev, and Hindemith, filtered through Mahler and through Shostakovich's own experience. The links with his experience of war and of the repressive obsessions of the Soviet regime are obvious. Just as ridiculous rules and prohibitions become menacing in such a society, so Shostakovich uses insistent motifs of marches, warlike fanfares, and the like to build up climaxes of destructive force. When it works, it is terrifying. If you are not in the mood, or not attuned to the irony, it can seem indeed banal. Bartók hated the endless pounding of Shostakovich's 'Leningrad' Symphony so much that he parodied it in his own Concerto for Orchestra. It is not always easy to know when Shostakovich is being ironic and when he is not. He wrote his Fifth Symphony after Stalin had objected to the pessimism of his music, and a journalist dubbed it 'A Soviet composer's answer to just criticism'. The sweeping climaxes of the finale sound triumphant. But are they really triumphant or ironically triumphant?

If bitterness and irony were all there were to Shostakovich, he would not have become the popular composer that he has. There is, whatever the historical references, a deeply personal core to Shostakovich's music. Whether he accurately reflects a particular horror is less important than what he does do very powerfully – to express the human experience of bleakness, hopes raised and dashed, triumphs that might at any moment crumble away, strivings that seem to be getting somewhere painfully slowly, or nowhere. One does not need to have lived through the Soviet era to feel the truth in such things. Knowing about the circumstances and impulses behind Shostakovich's music helps us to appreciate the sources of its power. But, in the end, music cannot rely too much on its 'back story'. In a televised rehearsal of the Fifth Symphony, the conductor Valery Gergiev said, 'We can't restore the picture of 1937. We must find the music.'

Concertos

CONCERTO FOR PIANO, TRUMPET, AND STRINGS, OP. 35 (PIANO CONCERTO NO. 1)
Duration: approx. 21 minutes

Allegro moderato
Lento
Moderato –
Allegro con brio

Shostakovich composed this concerto at the age of twenty-eight, and performed the premiere himself in October 1933. He had married the previous year. He had already composed his opera *Lady Macbeth of the Mtsensk District*, which would be premiered to acclaim in 1934 and officially condemned in 1936. But he had been spending most of the last few years on music for theatre, ballet, and film. This concerto shows a vein of irony associated with Prokofiev, Stravinsky, and the French. Irony had, of course, been an important aspect of Shostakovich's character ever since his first symphony. Here, it is taken to extremes, with a peppering of quotations and parodies, some easily recognizable, others less so. These elements have led commentators to regard this concerto as light-hearted, even hilarious. But even at his most overtly ironic, Shostakovich almost never really relaxes, and if he smiles, it seems to be through gritted teeth or with a sneer. This is particularly the case in the recordings of his own nervous and brittle playing.

The first movement has an ambivalent air, as if not sure whether to take itself seriously or not. After an opening flourish, the first theme, with its hint of Beethoven's 'Appassionata' Sonata, is almost solemn. But soon the piano skitters off at a faster tempo, and much of the movement is like a game of catch, with the piano continually evading capture. The mood is mercurial, switching from light-hearted to frenzied and back again. The solo trumpet, on the few occasions when it intervenes, seems to want to simplify matters, with square-cut military calls. At the end of the movement a moment of lyricism suddenly wells up in the lower strings, and the piano finishes the movement in the sombre mood in which it began, with the trumpet holding a low, sustained note.

The principal theme of the slow movement is like the ghost of a waltz (did Shostakovich know Sibelius's *Valse Triste*?). The violins gently set it going, rising to a high, quiet climax that recalls Prokofiev at his most ecstatic. The piano enters with an almost classical-sounding trill. But as the melody moves on, Shostakovich characteristically interrupts it with a sardonic flourish, as if dismissing such lyricism as sentimental. The piano becomes more agitated, and reaches a mighty climax. Just as we think there can be no going back, the opening mood is restored. The frozen waltz is taken up by muted trumpet – a magical effect when well played – and the piano rounds off the movement with the mood of calm restored.

The third movement lasts less than two minutes, and is no more than an introduction to the finale. The piano plays a meditative fantasia, as if trying to find its way back to the mood of the first movement. The strings intervene with a passionate, forceful melody. When the piano enters again, it has caught some of this spirit. Gradually, this ebbs away, and after a moment of hesitation the piano propels us straight into the finale.

The finale is full of allusions and actual quotes. This has led writers to describe it as little more than a romp, though it is full of Shostakovich's characteristic jumpiness, and even the overt parodies have a nervous edge. After a few bars of piano introduction the strings set off. The impression, as in the first movement, is of a game of catch, now even more fleeting. The trumpet joins in, its second intervention being a quote from a Haydn piano sonata. This provokes a passage of grand rhetoric from the piano, answered by a fanfare from the trumpet. The level of frenzy increases, with piano and trumpet alternating in a chase suggestive of silent films such as the Keystone Cops (as a student, Shostakovich earned cash playing for silent films).

After an abrupt crash the music goes quiet, as if the chase has vanished out of sight, and slows in tempo. Like a strutting circus figure, the trumpet plays a naive tune. To English-speakers, this is familiar as the children's game, 'Poor Jenny', though it is also rather like the Viennese song, 'O du lieber Augustin' (which Shostakovich is presumably more likely to have known). The trumpet persists, like a tiresome drunk, but eventually the tempo increases and brings in a reprise of the opening theme in the violins. This reaches a climax and a pause. A trill from the piano turns once again serious and classical-sounding for a moment, and then it launches into a romping cadenza, starting with a quote from Beethoven's *Rondo a capriccio*, 'Rage over a lost penny'. After the cadenza, the music becomes even faster and increasingly frenzied. Humorous fanfares collide with attempts to launch a gypsy dance, and the concerto ends in a spirit of hysterical mayhem.

PIANO CONCERTO NO. 2, OP. 102
Duration: approx. 20 minutes

Allegro
Andante
Allegro

After the death of Stalin in 1953, life for artists in the Soviet Union underwent a gradual thaw. Shostakovich's reputation was largely rehabilitated, with the award of the Order of Lenin in

1956. But there were limits: that same year his condemned opera *Lady Macbeth of the Mtsensk District* was reassessed, and its ban was upheld. During this period of limited warmth, Shostakovich wrote a number of works that were uncharacteristically relaxed in mood. The best known of them is his Second Piano Concerto, composed for his son Maxim, who performed it in Moscow on his nineteenth birthday, 10 May 1957. Shostakovich described it in a letter to the composer Edison Denisov as having 'no redeeming artistic-ideological merits', but Denisov would surely have understood this as a parody of the sort of opinion handed out by the Soviet artistic authorities.

The concerto opens with a fast march that is set going by bassoon, joined by other wood-wind. The piano enters coolly, playing in chaste octaves – a style that predominates even more in this concerto than it had in the first. A second idea is more agitated (conjuring up for English-speakers memories of 'What shall we do with the drunken sailor?'), and a third is more lyrical. There is an abrupt change of key, which signals the start of a stormy development, in which thundering octaves and rushing scales are pitted against the various thematic elements. This is pursued relentlessly for several minutes, until a glorious climax is reached. From this emerges the piano with the reprise of the opening theme, now in gritty two-part, Bach-like counterpoint. The woodwind pull the music back to the charming mood of the opening, but the piano is insistent on maintaining its brilliant passage work. The movement ends with a splendid swagger, which alerts us to the fact that the theme bears more than a passing resemblance to the march from Prokofiev's *The Love of Three Oranges*.

To anyone who knows the habitually acerbic harmonic language of Shostakovich, the slow movement comes as a gentle shock. The opening lament from the strings is in C minor, with touches of modal harmony that evoke Russian chant. It could have stepped out of Rachmaninoff or even Tchaikovsky. The piano enters in a melting C major, with a falling line that seems to pay homage to the equivalent moment in Beethoven's 'Emperor' Concerto. There is some-thing particularly touching about the way this music, written in the 1950s, inhabits both the Romantic and the Classical worlds. The harmonies are beautifully poignant, and the unfolding arabesques of the melody have a Beethovenian eloquence. As the opening of the melody returns, the harmonies darken, and the piano elaborates the elegiac chant from the beginning of the movement. Then it attempts to reprise the C major melody. But the sombreness of the elegy lingers, and the sunny melody is now in the minor, sounding more Rachmaninoff-like than it did before. Eventually the attempt at the reprise is abandoned, and further meditation on the elegy brings the movement to a dark close.

The finale follows without a pause, and brings a total change of mood. The piano works away again and again at an energetic little phrase. This is just the sort of obsessive behaviour that often becomes frenetic in a Shostakovich finale. But here it remains good-humoured, and the orchestra caps it with a second idea that burst with high spirits. This takes away one quaver from each bar to create a dance in seven-time that becomes increasingly energetic as the piano joins in. Just at the moment where it too is in danger of developing destructive force, the piano launches into scale passages. Like the pianists in Saint-Saëns's *The Carnival of the Animals*, this evokes student exercises – and indeed it is a quote from the second study in Hanon's *The Virtuoso-Pianist*, which no doubt both Dmitri and Maxim Shostakovich had to endure during their training as pianists. This leads on to an extended middle section in which the three elements – the opening theme, the seven-time dance, and the exercises – take it in turns, building up a head of steam. As it approaches a climax, the piano plays the opening phrase of the movement in a simpler, more military rhythm, and a side drum enters. This really is beginning to sound more like the Shostakovich we know and fear. But any sense of menace is diffused as the side drum joins in enthusiastically with a reprise of the seven-time dance. Another burst of scales, a return to the opening phrases of the movement, and the concerto comes triumphantly to an end.

VIOLIN CONCERTO NO. 1, OP. 99
Duration: approx. 35 minutes

Nocturne: Moderato
Scherzo: Allegro
Passacaglia: Andante
Burlesque: Allegro con brio

Shostakovich began composing this concerto for David Oistrakh in July 1947. It was while he was working on the third movement in February 1948 that the Zhdanov Decree was published, in which the Politburo denounced Shostakovich for his anti-Soviet 'formalism'. He was dismissed from his teaching post at the Leningrad Conservatoire, and his works were no longer played. At his last composition class at the Conservatoire in March he played the concerto on the piano to his students. He asked one of them, violinist Venyamin Basner, to sight-read the violin part, which he did, 'shaking like a leaf'.[3] Shostakovich and Oistrakh made further revisions, but the first public performance was delayed until 1955, after Stalin's death, by which time Shostakovich's official reputation had been somewhat restored. Oistrakh described the soloist as playing 'a Shakespearean role, which demands complete emotional and intellectual involvement'.[4] The concerto is scored for a large orchestra, with four horns and tuba, percussion including tam-tam, tambourine, xylophone, and celesta, and two harps. But there are no trumpets or trombones, and the woodwind ensemble is often used in combinations that create an unusual plangency and starkness.

Cellos and basses open the Nocturne, with a dark melancholy that sets the mood for the whole movement. The solo violin enters with a sorrowful fantasia, which continues almost without pausing for breath to the end. The woodwind in the outer parts of the movement have an organ-like solidity, underpinned by the contrabassoon, and with dark clarinets and no oboes. Only at the climax towards the end do the oboes enter, providing one moment of light in the darkness. The outer sections contrast with a more dream-like middle section, accompanied by soft strings, with harp harmonics and celesta. These return at the end as the darkness closes in, intensified by quiet timpani and gong. Oistrakh, in conversation with his son Igor, found in this movement not just 'melancholy hopelessness', but 'tragedy in the best sense of purification'.[5]

Oistrakh described the scherzo as 'evil, demonic, prickly'. It is strongly reminiscent of the scherzo in Shostakovich's second piano trio (1944), which was written partly in response to the suffering of Jews during the war. In the middle of the concerto's scherzo, a Jewish-style folk dance is treated to similar destructive force, and this returns at the end. The whole scherzo is hard-driven, as if desperately trying to escape. Even more than in the first movement, the woodwind are dominant. At first, flute and bass clarinet, three octaves apart, sound ironic. But soon the woodwind become the driving force of the scherzo, with strings in a supporting role. About a minute in, the woodwind declaim, like a chant, the four notes, D sharp, E, C sharp, B, and the violin soon echoes them in octaves. This is a version of the motto that Shostakovich was to use in the Tenth Symphony to represent his signature, 'D. Sch.' (see Symphony No. 10).

The third movement is a Passacaglia. The recurring bass line is first stated forcefully by cellos and basses, underlined by timpani, with the four horns pitting against it a fanfare of Mahlerian fatefulness. This is the first of nine statements of the bass. The second has the woodwind chorus in another striking combination, with cor anglais and clarinet on the top, giving a plaintive reediness to the ensemble, and tuba on the bottom, giving solidity. The violin enters for the third statement, meditating over the strings. For the fourth statement, it is joined in counterpoint by cor anglais and bassoons in unison, another variation on plaintive reediness.

Statement no. 5 has the passacaglia bass moved up to the horn, with cellos and basses in counterpoint with the soloist. In no. 6, the passacaglia moves back to the bass, and the soloist breaks into impassioned figuration. No. 7 has the soloist playing the passacaglia theme in fortissimo octaves, with counterpoint in the bass. In no. 8, the soloist returns to its opening meditative line, accompanied by a sombre wind ensemble of clarinets, bassoons, and tuba.

In the final variation, the soloist struggles to move from the reiteration of a single note, recalling the horns' opening fanfare, while the accompaniment is reduced to pizzicato chords and timpani. The movement ends with the violin rising over a sustained bass and timpani roll. This leads straight on to a long cadenza (nearly five minutes). It begins with the horn fanfare, whose insistent rhythm becomes a motif through the early part of the cadenza. The music becomes gradually more determined and powerful. As it approaches a climax, we hear again the 'D. Sch.' signature. The cadenza becomes more and more frenetic, culminating in glissandi in octaves and fifths, which burst into the opening of the finale.

The Burlesque is one of those characteristic Shostakovich movements that lives in the tension between exhilaration and nightmare, with much of the fierce, driven character of the scherzo of the Tenth Symphony. It begins with a savagely banal tune on woodwind and xylophone – according to Venyamin Basner, Oistrakh pleaded with Shostakovich for a few bars rest for the soloist, so that he could 'wipe the sweat from his brow'. The solo entry is almost playful, though pursued closely by a clarinet. A second theme is a fierce dance with offbeat accents, punctuated by a snarling ensemble of woodwind, with oboes and clarinets low and dissonant, and then clarinets high and shrieking.

After the soloist returns to the opening theme, the orchestra becomes more and more rhythmically insistent, with woodwind and strings alternating. During the next wild solo passage, the clarinets and xylophone play a savagely mocking version of the theme from the passacaglia. As the soloist continues unflinchingly, the forces of the orchestra muster menacingly, with timpani and tuba below and shrieks on the woodwind above. The pace increases to presto, the horns call out a final reminder of the passacaglia theme, and the soloist hurtles on to the end.

The title of this movement, 'Burlesque', did not satisfy Oistrakh: 'I would look for another name to convey the wildness and shining jubilation of its deeply Russian experience'[6] – though whether 'jubilation' quite evokes the danger of all this wildness is open to opinion. Perhaps one has to be Russian to understand what Oistrakh meant.

Symphonies

SYMPHONY NO. 1, OP. 10

Duration: approx. 32 minutes

Allegretto – Allegro non troppo
Allegro
Lento –
Lento – Allegro molto – Largo – Presto

In May 1926, Shostakovich's First Symphony was performed in Leningrad (St Petersburg), conducted by Nicolai Malko. A year later it was played in Berlin, under Bruno Walter, and the following year Stokowski conducted the symphony in Philadelphia. This might seem like a routine catalogue of events, until you realize that Shostakovich was only eighteen when he wrote it, and that it was his final composition assignment for graduation from the Conservatoire in Leningrad. It launched him on a brilliant career. It is not just an extraordinarily accomplished work. It also gives a powerful impression of Shostakovich's musical personality already fully formed. He was to compose far longer, more ambitious symphonies in later life, but there is almost nothing in them that is not already there in essence in this teenage work. Apart from Mendelssohn, it is difficult to think of another composer who seems so complete at this age. And, as with Mendelssohn, there are questions about how many of his later works lived up to the promise of his teenage years.

The symphony is written for a large orchestra including a prominent piano part, and covers an enormous stylistic and emotional range, from humour and irony through bitterness and violence to tragic lyricism. This reflects not only Shostakovich's precocious talent, but also the range of music he had studied at the Conservatoire, from the great classics through to modern scores by Prokofiev, Stravinsky, Hindemith, Milhaud, and Ernst Krenek. It was the irony and contradiction in modern music that most chimed with his own musical character, as is clear from the first bars of this symphony.

The opening might evoke memories of Stravinsky's *Petrushka*, or, more distantly, Strauss's *Till Eulenspiegel*, with its impression of 'Once upon a time . . .', but it has a deft, ironical sourness all its own. It could be music for the silent cinema, where Shostakovich had played the piano to supplement his family's meagre income. A muted trumpet announces the opening of the scene, a bassoon enters with a quirky expression. Fragmentary and seemingly disconnected events ensue, like the separate activities of people in a street. Eventually, a coherent theme emerges: a jaunty march (or perhaps strut) on the clarinet. With anxious undercurrents, this builds to a brief climax, and fades away to leave a flute playing a second theme, an uneasy waltz – uneasy because it is not clear until the last few bars of the melody where the main beat is. Others join in, until the waltz too fades away, as if the street is deserted for a moment. This is the end of the first section of the movement.

A solo violin enters, beginning a hesitant and fragmentary passage that refers back to the introduction and to the waltz. This is the beginning of the development. The clarinet's march starts up, now on the violins, with a more insistent accompaniment. It quickly builds to a tutti, with full brass and percussion, as if we have rounded a corner to be confronted by a marching band, or a riot, or both. At its climax, trumpets blare out the fanfare with which the movement began. As the mayhem suddenly disperses, pizzicato strings and a flute are left playing the waltz, and we realize that we are already into the reprise. The waltz tune passes to other instruments, including horn and trumpet (a very *Petrushka*-like moment). There is one more sudden climax, in which the march theme is combined with an element from the end of the waltz, at normal and half speed (powerfully in the horns). The movement ends as it began, with the fragments from the introduction revisited.

This is an extraordinarily clever movement. Although it gives a vivid, almost cinematic, impression of events unfolding unpredictably and fluidly, it is also tightly constructed, according to the conventions of classical symphonic form. It is Haydn out of Stravinsky, but with an unmistakable combination of irony and anxiety, force and delicacy, that is utterly characteristic of Shostakovich.

The second movement is a whirlwind of a scherzo. Like the first movement, it has a strong atmosphere of the silent cinema – it could be a chase scene. It begins in mid-chase, with basses and cellos, then clarinet, then (for the first time) piano. A coherent theme emerges, which starts on violins, passing again to the piano. There is a brief climax, and the theme passes in turn to bassoon, oboe, and clarinet, and is interrupted by the violins.

There is a sudden switch of mood and pace to what, in a conventional scherzo, would be the trio. Flutes, then clarinets, and later oboes and bassoons, play a strange, creeping duet, with the violins holding a reiterated note, and little taps on side drum and triangle. It is like a ghostly procession, with echoes of Stravinsky's *The Rite of Spring*. The return to the scherzo begins on bassoon at half speed – a moment of ironic pedantry typical of Shostakovich. An acceleration leads to the reprise of the scherzo's theme on piano. As before, there is a rapid build-up, but this time the brass cap the chase theme with a blazing recall of the processional theme from the middle of the movement. This is cut off at the climax. The piano plays three massive chords, and violas play the scherzo theme in slow motion. The strings play a chord on eerie harmonics, and, with a touch on percussion and a bass pizzicato, the movement ends in ominous disintegration.

The disintegration at the end of the scherzo has changed the mood utterly. All traces of irony have vanished, to be replaced by a tragic slow movement. It begins with a poignant oboe solo, whose opening phrase is derived from the first five notes of the clarinet's march in the first movement. This wide-ranging melody, full of yearning intervals, is taken up by solo cello, and then extended and developed by the violins with great passion. A little fanfare on trumpets and side drum, with military dotted rhythm, becomes menacing. As the climax fades away, the fanfare finds its way into the cellos and bass, and it is they who then take the lament in a new direction. The oboe, as if responding to the menacing fanfare, introduces a new element with anxious dotted rhythms. As the music builds up once more, dotted rhythms are drawn into the lament, giving it more urgency than before. The second climax, on brass alone, is cut off, leaving pianissimo strings, as if stranded in a bleak landscape.

Over their soft tremolo, a solo violin reprises the oboe lament. The other violins join in, menaced by the trumpet fanfare. Although the lament begins to build up, its earlier force is spent, and the music soon quietens again. A muted trumpet plays the oboe's dotted-rhythm melody, accompanied by two flutes and clarinet (a haunting and unusual combination). With further reminiscence of the lament, and of the fanfare, the movement comes to a close with quiet string chords. But as it does so, the side drum begins a roll, pianissimo at first, and increasing until we are suddenly launched straight into the finale.

The tragic mood of the slow movement takes time to clear. The finale begins with a slow introduction in which oboe, flute, and clarinet continue to brood over ominous tremolo. Cellos and basses lurch upward threateningly, answered each time by muted trumpets – a moment very reminiscent of Debussy's *La Mer*. The third time, the Allegro molto is launched. A solo clarinet plays a swirling theme, as if trying desperately to remember its march from the first movement, driven on by a rolled cymbal. The piano takes up the theme, and it develops into a huge climax, with *fff* chords. Panic ensues, followed by a sudden collapse.

A solo violin plays a lamenting melody, related to the lament from the slow movement, in mood if not in shape. Cellos join in, and a glockenspiel, and then horn and trumpet accompanied by piano trills. The melody bursts out on full violins, and the swirling Allegro molto is back, with the violent elements stronger than before, and the climax arriving sooner. Aggressive brass trills culminate in a sudden cut-off. The timpani play the rhythm of the menacing fanfare, but now in a rising shape, at first violently, then quieter, then quieter still. A solo cello takes up the lament. The rising fanfare punctuates, at first softly in the timpani, then in the woodwind, with rather *Scheherazade*-like chords. Eventually, a twist of harmony – more Scriabin than Rimsky-Korsakov – brings the lament to the strings, which take it with renewed passion to a final climax. At its height, the music breaks into a rapid Presto, and the menacing fanfare rhythm propels the symphony to a savage end.

SYMPHONY NO. 3, OP. 20, 'THE FIRST OF MAY'
Duration: approx. 27 minutes

Following the spectacular success of his First Symphony, Shostakovich composed two more when he was in his early twenties. The Second Symphony was in response to a commission from the State Publishing House in 1927 to write a work celebrating the tenth anniversary of the October Revolution. It is a continuous piece lasting twenty minutes, which Shostakovich originally called *To October, a Symphonic Dedication*. Factory whistles announce a choral finale in heroic declamatory style, a hymn to the struggles of the October Revolution, and to Lenin in particular, with words that Shostakovich found 'repulsive'.

Two years later, in 1929, Shostakovich composed his Third Symphony. This too concludes with a choral finale, and was written to celebrate International Workers' Day. Shostakovich wrote it as a submission to the Petrograd (St Petersburg) Conservatoire, in order to preserve his status as a postgraduate. He chose to evoke what he called 'the festive spirit of peaceful development', and the 'intense struggle' that inevitably goes into achieving it. Unlike in later symphonies, the heroic element is not obviously undermined by irony. Five years after the death of Lenin, the full horrors of Stalinist repression were still in the future. Like the Second Symphony, it is rarely performed, but it makes a fascinating contrast to the much more combative, and politically controversial, works that were to follow.

Played without a break, most of the symphony consists of a very loose, almost cinematic, sequence of events, which conclude with a four-minute burst of heroic chorus. It starts with an improvisatory passage for clarinet, at first solo, then in duet. After a trumpet call, the mood becomes determined and soon leads to a frantically busy Allegro – it could accompany a film of factory workers in zealous pursuit of their duties. Elements of struggle come to the fore, and the mood becomes yet more frenetic. After a climax, a side drum sets up a fast march rhythm, and trumpet and horn joyfully set out, followed by piccolo, bassoon, and oboe. There is a circus-like air to this passage.

The scene empties. Tentative violin phrases lead to a violent interruption by the brass, followed by a violin solo, joined by piccolo. In a long, fragmentary passage the violins seem to be searching for something meaningful. Eventually, another Allegro begins, with fast motor rhythms, building up to another frenetic pitch of relentless drive. The climax culminates in drum rolls, and a fiercely commanding declamation in octaves from the whole orchestra. After a long time, this fades away, to leave dark mutterings from the basses and tuba. Glissandi in the basses, gong strokes, brass fanfares, suggest some mighty thing awakening. Eventually, the chorus enters with its heroic hymn: 'Today on this shining May festival, let our songs resound ... The land belongs to the workers, the age is theirs ... Every May Day is a step nearer to our socialist goal. Solemnly through the cities millions of us surge.'

SYMPHONY NO. 4, OP. 43
Duration: approx. 65 minutes

Allegretto poco moderato – Presto
Moderato con moto
Largo – Allegro

In January 1934, Shostakovich had a resounding success with the first production of his opera, *Lady Macbeth of the Mtsensk District*. Full of confident plans, he was soon sketching ideas for a Fourth Symphony. It was in the autumn of 1935 that these began to take coherent shape, and by January of the following year he had composed a substantial proportion of the new work. It was then that an article, 'Muddle instead of Music', was published in *Pravda*. Stalin and officials had attended a performance of *Lady Macbeth*, and the article condemned Shostakovich as one of those responsible for ' "leftist" confusion, instead of natural, human music'. Shostakovich, with his interest in the newest developments in music, was an obvious target in the ongoing wave of repression of artists, writers, and now musicians. Despite this devastating attack, Shostakovich persevered with the symphony, completed it in May, and went ahead with plans for its performance in November. What the authorities would have thought of the Fourth Symphony is clear from the fact that Shostakovich was 'persuaded' to withdraw it while it was in rehearsal. It is a gigantic work, much influenced by Shostakovich's study of Mahler. It was not performed until 1961, when, under the Khrushchev regime, conditions were beginning to thaw a little (if unpredictably).

It is scored for an enormous orchestra: 4 flutes and 2 piccolos, 4 oboes (3rd doubling cor anglais), 5 clarinets and bass clarinet, 3 bassoons and contrabassoon, 8 horns, 4 trumpets, 3 trombones, 2 tubas, a large percussion section including two timpani-players, xylophone, glockenspiel, celesta, 2 harps, and strings.

From the very first bars, the tone is bitterly ironic. High woodwind and xylophone begin with a sort of parody of a Bach toccata. With a thwack of drums, this becomes a heavy march, played by brass over treading strings, with a mocking level of bombast, quickly rising to the first of many threatening climaxes. A quieter passage leads to a more lyrical idea, though the wayward harmonies and desultory moments of counterpoint ensure that the mood remains anxious. The tension rises again, and another big climax is reached and fades away. The woodwind break across the prevailing metre with triplet rhythms, ushering in a passage that, with different harmonies, might almost have seemed playful. This culminates in a sudden outburst from full orchestra. A solo bassoon, at a slower tempo, begins a desolate melody that is taken up by violas and cellos, then violins. This is the second main theme. This leads to a very delicate episode, with bass clarinet accompanied only by harps, then joined by piccolo and flute. A horn takes up the bassoon melody, and the music begins to build again. Another climax is reached, which then fragments. The bassoon melody continues in the bass, with abrupt octave leaps thrown at it from above.

After a grinding passage, the woodwind lighten the atmosphere, with a return to the first march theme of the movement, now at a more playful tempo. This develops momentum, with strings pizzicato. There are snarling interventions from flutter-tongued brass. Then, with no warning, the violins break into a manic Presto, with the other strings gradually joining in, like a nightmare memory of Beethoven's *Leonore* No. 3 Overture. But this is only the beginning of the nightmare: woodwind and brass join the mayhem, and then a battery of drums, leading to a climax of destructive force, with fragments of earlier themes completely submerged.

Out of this, with juddering aftershocks, emerge brutal fragments of the opening march. The atmosphere is gradually drained of its menace, and the strings return almost playfully to a transformation of the desolate second theme, developing a Mahlerian waltz-like swing. This moves to bass clarinet, then to cellos and basses, arriving at mysterious chords. The music comes to a stop. Timpani rolls and dissonant muted brass chords build insistently. The woodwind solemnly return to the opening tempo, and the first march theme is reprised. Its rhythms have been changed, however, elongated and rhythmically dislocated, with the metre uncertain whether it is subdivided in three or two. This leads into a melancholy cor anglais solo. Then, over the second theme in violas, a solo violin meditates. A quiet bass drumbeat starts up, and a bassoon quirkily returns to the march theme for the last time. There are dark chords, a final outburst from muted brass, and the music fades away in fragments, with a thoroughly Mahlerian sense of disintegration and an uncertain future.

The overtly Mahlerian references continue in the second movement. This is in the easy-going three-time of an Austrian *Ländler*, and it has a number of specific features drawn from such movements in Mahler's symphonies: the alternation of more lyrical and more robust passages, ornamental turns in the melody, and occasional glissandi. But any air of Viennese nostalgia is undermined by Shostakovich's persistently sour harmonies, which make the movement seem almost like a bitter parody of Mahler.

The opening material, for strings alone, alternates with other elements. After a passage of spiky woodwind, and a surprisingly aggressive climax, a central episode has a delicate, sustained line on the violins, with a very Mahlerian glissando up a large interval. This leads to the most charming passage in the movement, a duet between horn and piccolo. The return of the opening violin theme soon expands into a longer passage of uneasy counterpoint. Continued by high woodwind, this leads to a grand reprise of the delicate violin episode, now on four horns against widespread chords of woodwind – a combination which (despite the Mahlerian unison horns) sounds like pure Shostakovich. The music reaches a climax and winds down. Against a clock-like background of castanets, woodblock and side drum, the violins play a final ghostly version of the opening theme.

If the second movement has echoes of Mahler, the opening of the third and final movement could actually be Mahler, with a bassoon playing a funeral march accompanied by timpani and a pizzicato bass (very reminiscent of Mahler's 'Der Tamboursg'sell' ['The Drummer Boy'] from *Des Knaben Wunderhorn*, and a similar theme from the opening

movement of his Fifth Symphony). This impression is heightened as other wind instruments
join in the march, but the characteristically bitter harmonies soon drain any sense of imper-
sonation. The music rises surprisingly quickly to a huge climax, and then falls away, leaving
the violins playing a bleak melody over a quietly agitated accompaniment. Just as it begins to
become warmly lyrical (a rare moment in this symphony), the woodwind return with their
funeral procession. A reiterated call begins in the oboe and grows, until the music suddenly
breaks into an Allegro.

This is in a fast three-time, but any sense of dance is undermined by insistent, relentless
rhythms. On and on it goes, as if driven by a pursuing malignant force. As the intensity
increases, there are moments that sound almost exultant, but the descent from the climax
has thundering timpani and dissonant low tubas ensuring a continuing sense of threat.
Shostakovich defuses this with a switch to two-time, with mockingly playful clarinet
and piccolo. This immediately leads on to a puzzlingly serene moment, with an expressive
viola line in three-time, accompanied by a harp rhythm persisting in two-time. This is
soon joined (once more in Mahlerian style) by decorations and waltz elements. A pair of
flutes seems to have stepped out of the corps de ballet. They are thrown off course by sudden
chords and a low contrabassoon. The strings renew the waltz, which turns sweet for a
moment.

There is an acceleration, and a bassoon launches into another of Shostakovich's quirky
marches. A xylophone enters, and there are disruptive low tuba notes on offbeats. A trombone
solo, which might have seemed noble in other contexts, strikes an ironic note. The march
returns to bassoon, accompanied by cheeky piccolo. There is another switch back to waltz
time, with the melodies, on woodwind and trombone, becoming more banal, almost as if
Shostakovich is reverting to his days as a cinema pianist. The strings are left alone for a time,
not sure whether they are dancing or trying to escape. Still the trombone persists with
unwanted remarks that everyone ignores.

Eventually, oboe and bassoon calm the mood, and the strings are left alone for another
moment of anxious meditation. Again this switches into waltz time, dying away over a still-
agitated bass. This too falls away. Bass drum and timpani enter quietly, rapidly increasing to
lead in a Mahlerian chord of C major on full brass. This is the beginning of a long passage of
splendid brass writing, which comes back again and again to the simple chord of C major,
interspersed with moments of doubt and discord, all held together by a continuous drumming created by the two timpani-players playing overlapping patterns. The climax falls away
to dark chords on bassoons, contrabassoon, and bass clarinet, still with the note C persistently
reiterated in the bass. There are solos on horn and flute, with weird chords in violas and harp.
The music softens to *ppp*, and the violins play a mysterious, yearning melody. The symphony
fades on a chord of C minor, with little fragments of themes on muted trumpet and celesta.
The last note played by the celesta is an unresolved D, as the string chord of C minor dies
away to nothing.

One member of the audience at the first performance of the Fourth Symphony in 1961
was Shostakovich's old friend Flora Litvinova: 'It was the first time we heard it, and it made a
shattering impression on us. Why do Dmitri Dmitriyevich's later works lack those qualities of
impetuosity, dynamic drive, contrasts of rhythm and colour, tenderness and spikiness? One
involuntarily thinks what a different path he would have taken, how different his life would
have been, if it were not for the "historic" Decree which warped the living spirit in him'.[7] The

symphony is certainly full of drive and contrasts. But critics continue to debate whether it really forms a coherent whole, or is more of a gigantic improvisation, full of sudden effects that have little or no relationship with each other. Shostakovich's path would certainly have been very different if the symphony's first performance had gone ahead. It is scarcely conceivable that the authorities would have responded tolerantly to such an act of defiance after the official condemnation. Shostakovich might well have joined the ranks of purged artists, and nothing more would have been heard from him. And if there had been no condemnation in the first place – well, that would have been a different world, and Shostakovich would have been a different composer.

SYMPHONY NO. 5, OP. 47
Duration: approx. 50 minutes

Moderato
Allegretto
Largo
Allegro non troppo

Because of the withdrawal of the Fourth Symphony (see above), the fifth was the next of Shostakovich's symphonies to be performed after the official condemnation of his opera, *Lady Macbeth of the Mtsensk District*. The premiere in November 1937 was a spectacular success, but an ambivalent one. The symphony soon acquired a subtitle, 'A Soviet artist's creative reply to just criticism' (though this originated as a journalist's description, not from Shostakovich himself). At the early performances, there was not just enthusiasm, but an overwhelming feeling of relief that Shostakovich had ensured his survival with this work. The symphony culminates in a climax of blazing triumph. But the climax comes as a brief and unexpected outcome at the end of a symphony that covers a huge span, in time and in range of emotion, from bleakness through biting irony to intense yearning. What does this grand climax mean? Is it triumph of the spirit, or ironic triumph disguised as triumph of the system? Shostakovich himself provided no answers to this question, but the ending certainly fulfilled, at least superficially, the Soviet authorities' requirement that works of art should be optimistic and uplifting in tone. However, it fulfils it in the nick of time.

After Shostakovich's First Symphony, the fifth is the next one that has become truly popular. The comparisons with the first are fascinating. The scale is now so huge, the pace so expansive. The essential character of the musician is still much the same, but deepened and broadened. This is partly a matter of maturity (Shostakovich was thirty when he wrote the Fifth Symphony), but partly a result of Shostakovich's absorption of other music. In particular, he had got to know and love the music of Mahler, and his own writing was now steeped in it. It was from Mahler's example more than anyone's that Shostakovich dared to write on a hugely expanded scale. Shostakovich's most characteristic evocation of bleakness and empty landscapes – thin, pianissimo string lines, often with a flute above – is closely related to the textures of Mahler's 'Farewell' from *Das Lied von der Erde*. There are other touches that evoke Mahler – the playful but sinister violin solos in the second movement (akin to those in Mahler's Fourth Symphony), the characteristic combination of quiet strings with harp (as in the famous 'Adagietto' from Mahler's Fifth Symphony), the abrupt final climax, so insistent as to seem frantic (as in countless Mahler climaxes). But these are genuine absorptions, not just references. There is nothing more characteristic of Shostakovich than the way he has taken all these ideas and made of them something entirely his own.

The symphony opens with the strings throwing defiant, jagged dotted-rhythm fragments at each other, almost like a fierce parody of an eighteenth-century French Overture. These subside into the first of the symphony's sustained, yearning violin melodies, as if we are setting off across a great, empty landscape (an image that so often comes to mind in Shostakovich). Over a long paragraph (nearly five minutes), this theme extends and develops, with elements of the jagged opening reappearing from time to time. After a first string climax, the wood-wind take over the melody, led by a bassoon, with the strings interjecting the dotted rhythms from the opening below. Another, bigger climax subsides, and we reach the second main theme. Over a quiet, insistent tread, punctuated by harp chords, the violins play an even more sustained line consisting of long notes and leaps, as if their earlier melody has been distilled into the simplest of essences. The constantly shifting harmonies give it an anxious, searching quality. The melody gives way to solemn, low wind chords, a plaintive flute searches above, and a sombre clarinet descends. The treading theme returns on the violas. But after a moment it falters, reiterating a little rhythmic phrase.

The pace increases, the piano enters low, bringing a sinister, clanking element to the rhythm. Shostakovich has moved seamlessly into the central development section of the movement. Snarling low horns enter with the first violin melody, followed by trumpets in counterpoint, while the lumbering rhythm continues in the bass. The woodwind join in as the acceleration continues. The accumulating energy seems unstoppable. But as the acceleration reaches a climax, the tempo is suddenly held back, and the trumpets, urged on by a side drum, transform the theme into a sinister march. This too is drawn into the acceleration. The strings desperately try to regain control with the opening jagged theme. The full brass bring in the second theme, and the music builds to a huge climax.

Finally, the tempo is pulled back, and at a cymbal crash the jagged opening returns, *fff*. A declamatory passage, based on the first violin theme, rises to a yet greater climax ('con tutta forza'). Savage fragments of the jagged opening on trombones ebb away, and the music subsides to the gentle tread of the second theme, now peacefully in a major key, with flute answered by horn. The movement ends with a long, meditative coda. Clarinet and piccolo play in duet, then oboe, clarinet, and bassoon in three-part counterpoint. The ending is very delicate, with a characteristically vulnerable piccolo solo echoed by solo violin and celesta. Low trumpets interject a final echo of the jagged rhythm of the opening, suggesting that the sinister threat has not entirely gone away.

The second movement is an unsmiling scherzo. It begins in the bass, with cellos and double basses *ff*, evoking a memory of the scherzo of Beethoven's Fifth Symphony. Despite its moderate tempo, there is a manic element to the music, with a high clarinet sounding as if it is being made to play a *Ländler* against its will. The unsmiling dance is mostly in a straight-forward three-time, but throws in an extra beat from time to time, with fierce horns and side drum adding to the impression that the dance would prefer to be a march. There is a coy little episode in which an ingratiating violin solo is followed by flute in duet with bassoon, like puppets out of Stravinsky's *Petrushka* (Maxim Shostakovich chillingly describes the violin solo as 'a child's voice from beneath a soldier's boot').[8] This is followed by a more Mahlerian development, at the end of which bassoon and contrabassoon bring in a pizzicato reprise of the opening. Just before the end, there is a reminder of the coy violin solo on oboe, before a final fortissimo brings the movement to an abrupt close.

The slow movement opens with a long, expansive passage for strings. It begins like a memory of J. S. Bach, with three-part counterpoint of violins and violas over a bass. Eventually other strings enter, until they are playing rich, six-part chords, over which the violins sing a climactic phrase with impassioned repeated notes. The effect is spacious but anguished – haunting and almost like Sibelius. The strings give way to harp, over which a flute plays a spare melody derived from the violin melody from the opening of the symphony. A second flute joins in counterpoint, and cellos wind gradually down to bring back the string chorus. This builds to a climax, supported by woodwind. Cellos and basses play a moment of bold recitative reminiscent of the opening of the finale of Beethoven's Ninth Symphony.

Ghostly tremolando violins bring in a haunting new idea on oboe, which begins with plaintive falling phrases, and then ascends. After another moment of cello recitative, a clarinet rises up and adds to the oboe's thought. All the while, the ghostly violin tremolo continues in the background. For a fleeting moment, the rich, pianissimo string chords reappear – a desperately beautiful reminder in the midst of this empty landscape. A flute echoes the oboe's phrases. Then a low woodwind chorus take up part of the string chorale – two low clarinets, bassoon and contrabassoon, a sombre combination. The cellos enter, followed by the rest of the strings, and the music soon builds to an urgent tremolo. Over it, the fervent repeated-note phrase is sounded by strings, reinforced by xylophone.

The music cuts off, then the cellos enter fortissimo with the plaintive falling phrases, which develop into an anguished line. This rises to a fervent climax of strings and woodwind (there are no brass instruments in this movement, not even at this emotional crux of the symphony). The cello line falls away, and the lovely string chorus returns, muted and pianissimo, with the violins rising higher and higher to reach a new peak of longing. Now the harp returns, with the second violins playing the melody earlier played by the flute. Soon this becomes a consoling duet, and settles to a minor chord. Harp harmonics delicately touch in the oboe's falling phrases, and the movement ends on a rich, pianissimo major chord.

The finale begins with an extraordinarily sustained tour de force. Over thumping timpani the brass declaim a threatening, pompous march. As soon as the rest of the orchestra joins in, the march begins to accelerate. At first it seems as if it might become jolly. But soon we realize that we are on an unstoppable course, and are trapped. Over a long span, the march gradually becomes more and more frantic until, over the rapid scurrying of the strings and woodwind, a trumpet plays a heroic theme that seems related to the yearning melodies of the first and third movements. When the violins take it up, it does seem genuinely fervent and aspirational, like a glimmer of hope amid all the destructive forces. But it is soon cut off brutally by the re-entry of the march on *fff* brass, and the climax collapses. Quietly a horn remembers the heroic theme. But while it is doing so, the strings rise in tension, and finally they burst out with the impassioned repeated-note idea from the slow movement. This is the beginning of a long meditation on the various earlier themes, with a tone of sorrowful yearning.

From a quiet, and momentarily serene, chord, emerges the distant sound of a march rhythm on timpani and side drum. The march tune enters, slowly at first, on clarinets and bassoons and begins to build. This time there is no massive acceleration: the tempo reaches a conventional march tempo and sticks there. The march builds ominously, searching for resolution. Eventually, at a great climax of tension, there is a sudden Mahlerian twist in the harmonies, and the music bursts into D major. The rest is blazing fanfares, drum rolls, and scrubbing strings. Is this really a resolution? It declares a triumph of sorts, but whose?

SYMPHONY NO. 6, OP. 54
Duration: approx. 30 minutes

Largo
Allegro
Presto

The two years between the overwhelmingly successful premiere of the Fifth Symphony and the outbreak of the Second World War were for Shostakovich a period during which he kept himself out of trouble, writing generally undemanding works and film scores. He had been allowed to begin teaching composition at the Leningrad Conservatoire in 1937, and in June 1939 was made a full professor. It was the following October that he completed his Sixth Symphony, which was premiered in Leningrad during a festival of Soviet music in November. He had announced the previous year in a journal that he intended to write a choral symphony in honour of Lenin, but in the event he produced a purely instrumental work with no mention of an extra-musical programme. Before its premiere, Shostakovich was quoted in a Leningrad newspaper as saying, 'I wanted to convey in it the moods of spring, joy, youth.'[9] Critics and audiences, however, have found it a puzzling work. By the time the opening slow movement has finished, more than half of the time has gone. The second and third movements, both short and fast, are over in a flash.

The symphony opens with a declamation from cellos, violas, and woodwind in unison. You can hear Tchaikovsky and Mahler, but as the upper strings and woodwind join in, and then the horns, the twisting asperities of the harmony seem uniquely Shostakovich in their mood of nervous determination. The first part of the movement develops great passion. The middle of the movement is bleak, with characteristically isolated and meandering woodwind solos over the merest hint of accompanying strings. A momentarily comforting brass chorale, under a high violin trill, leads into the reprise. Here the earlier passion seems only half-remembered, and the movement dies away in a mood almost of serenity.

The scherzo is one of Shostakovich's characteristic virtuoso whirlwinds, with rushing woodwind and strings, and punchy climaxes. The mood might be joyful, if it were not for the asperity of the harmonies. The middle of the movement begins darkly, and rises to a climax of enormous power, with persistent hammered rhythms. The ending is almost like Sibelius in its sense of disintegration, and it ends with a woodwind flourish disappearing to *pppp*.

The finale is a rapid, cheeky frolic, at times like an opera ballet, often very delicate, exploding in sudden outbursts, then developing great momentum and culminating in massive climaxes. It has a more uncomplicated spirit of wit and *joie de vivre* than most of Shostakovich's music. In itself, it is irresistible – it was encored at the premiere – but quite how it relates to what has gone before is a conundrum that musicians and audiences have been contemplating ever since the first performance.

SYMPHONY NO. 7, OP. 60, 'LENINGRAD'
Duration: approx. 75 minutes

Allegretto
Moderato (poco allegretto)
Adagio
Allegro non troppo

The German army invaded Russia in June 1941. Soon, they were advancing on Leningrad, with the intention of besieging it. Shostakovich refused an offer of evacuation in August, and continued working on his Seventh Symphony and teaching at the Conservatoire. The siege began on 8 September. Finally, Shostakovich was flown out of the city in October to Kuybyshev in the Urals, having composed three movements of the new symphony. He completed it on 27 December, and it was first performed in Kuybyshev in March 1942. By this time the association between the symphony and the siege of Leningrad had become cemented.

Shostakovich had, however, begun working on it before the German invasion.[10] Although it is not certain quite when he started it, it seems clear that its depiction of destructive forces – particularly the famous onslaught of the first movement – was associated in Shostakovich's mind as much with Stalin as with Hitler, and more generally with the human struggle against forces of oppression. But the circumstances of its early performances made sure that it became irrevocably tied to the terrible siege of Leningrad, which was to last until January 1944, and resulted in the death of at least 600,000 people.

Microfilm of the score was flown to the West, where it was first performed at a Promenade Concert in London conducted by Sir Henry Wood in June 1942. Toscanini conducted the American premiere in July. And in August a performance was given back in Leningrad by an orchestra assembled from those musicians who were still alive and capable of playing. The symphony became familiar through radio broadcasts both in Russia and the West, and it gave Shostakovich international fame based as much on what the music was taken to stand for as for the quality of the music itself. Not all critics were enthusiastic, and it remains a work that divides opinion. Its overwhelming force guarantees a strong reaction among audiences. But there are those who find its crude and garish elements excessive. Shostakovich originally gave the four movements evocative titles, but later dropped them.[11]

Allegretto is a marking most often associated with delicate movements of modest proportions. But the first movement of the 'Leningrad' Symphony is huge and granite-like, lasting nearly half an hour, which Shostakovich originally planned to call 'War'. The metronome mark indicates a march tempo, and the opening theme, with its bold string octaves, sets out with utter determination. The military character becomes more pronounced as the wind join in, and the determination extends the theme with characteristically quirky and acerbic harmonies. Eventually the character of the music softens, and a solo flute plays a passage that would sound pastoral if it were not for its mournful tinge. This leads to the second main theme, which is a quiet melody on violins, over a rocking accompaniment that makes it sound almost like a lullaby – and yet its four-square phrases and simple harmonies (at first) make it sound as if it has grown out of the march theme. When the wind choir takes it up, they give it a melancholy slant. Then it moves into the bass, and the rocking motif (in the violins) develops onwards and upwards. It comes to rest, and a piccolo improvises on the melody, followed by a solo violin. The passage ends with a moment of serenity.

Almost inaudibly, a side drum starts up a pattern that repeats monotonously, at a tempo slightly faster than the opening march. Pizzicato strings begin a jaunty tune, such as soldiers might sing or whistle to keep their spirits up. Flute and piccolo join in, with fragmentary reminders of the march theme creeping into the bass. Then oboe and bassoon alternate, with another monotonously repeating rhythm added in the cellos. The piano joins, as if stepping out of a nightclub, and muted trumpet and trombones take over the tune, which is beginning to sound increasingly banal despite the edgy harmonies it has acquired. Clarinets and oboes play it in a simple canon, as if mocking it. The strings take over the tune, with strangely familiar parallel harmonies, making us aware that this is turning into some sort of parody of Ravel's *Bolero*. From this point on, as the increasingly unbearable tune passes to different groups, the rhythm of the side drum becomes more relentless, the whole of the orchestra is drawn in, and the music evokes a scene of relentless destruction. Eventually, there is a brutal change of key, as if the army has battered its way through, and the result is mayhem. The tune begins to break apart, though the relentless rhythm is intact. And sheer force drives us to a mighty climax at which, above the carnage, appears the opening march theme, now transformed into a terrible apotheosis.

At last exhaustion overcomes it, and flute and violins play their pastoral line over the devastation. A bassoon plays a long melancholy solo, in which occasional fragments of earlier themes occur, as if there is an occasionally familiar landmark amid the devastation. The strings take up the march tune, now transformed into a lament. It tries to regain some of its former energy, and falls back. Instead, it finds some comfort in a beautiful phrase from the quiet second theme. This winds gently down as if coming to a conclusion. But the movement is not yet finished. The side drum restarts its rhythm, pianissimo, a trumpet remembers for a last time a phrase or two of the dreadful tune, and with this ghastly apparition the exhausting movement is finally over.

Shostakovich originally called the second movement 'Memories'. The violin line is like a delicate eighteenth-century dance. The second violins begin, and the first violins join them, creating elegant counterpoint. But it is not a pastiche: the metre shifts uneasily, from four-time to five-time and three-time, and the harmonies of the simple string accompaniment are slightly 'wrong'. It might conjure up an image of an elegant ballroom, but the memory has a disturbing edge. After a time, the dance is reduced to an accompanying pattern, over which an oboe plays a long, plaintive, nostalgic melody, which is then taken up by the cor anglais. The emotions lurking under the surface elegance become more intense as the cor anglais finishes, with plangent bassoons underpinned by contrabassoon. The cellos intensify the emotion further, so that what began as a delicate dance has developed into a melody of deep yearning. There is a moment of peace, out of which comes a reprise of the dance, now very quiet and pizzicato.

Suddenly, there is a break into a lively three-time, and a raucous high clarinet leads a faster dance, which becomes increasingly wild. At first it is accompanied by clarinets and bassoons sounding remarkably like an accordion. The brass join in, and then the dreaded side drum, evoking all too recent memories of the first movement. This section begins like a memory of wild celebration, with a distinct suggestion of Jewish klezmer, but becomes gradually more acerbic and menacing (klezmer undergoing destruction was to form the climax of Shostakovich's second piano trio, written when the siege of Leningrad came to an end in 1944).

Eventually the violins emerge from this scene, to return once more to the delicate dance. Then a nervous little rhythmic pattern begins in the flutes, delicately punctuated by harp, beneath which the bass clarinet dolefully reprises the oboe melody from the early part of the movement. The first clarinet, two octaves higher, finishes off the melody, with a change to major harmonies that seems to melt through the bleakness to reveal a memory of happier times. The violins, now muted, return to the bleakness, ending the movement with one last return to the dance, by now utterly careworn.

The original title for the Adagio, 'Our country's vast spaces', suggests the scale of the movement (about twenty minutes). But there is also, once again, a strong suggestion of lament for something lost. It begins with a stark succession of wind chords, evoking a memory of Stravinsky's Symphonies of Wind Instruments. These alternate with declamatory passages on the violins, which almost seem as if they are half-remembering unaccompanied Bach. The violins settle into a more lyrical, melancholy melody that leads on to a solemn bassoon solo. All of this seems like a prelude to what follows. Over simple pizzicato, a solitary flute plays an innocent melody, joined after a time by a second flute. They could almost be shepherds in a field, or children. The violins take up the melody, making it more melancholy. At the end of it, they return for a moment to their Bach-like declamation. But a surge of intensity leads into the fierce middle section of the movement.

Against a heavily syncopated accompaniment, the violins play a jagged theme. Once again the music develops power and intensity, with even the side drum joining in, until it reaches a mighty climax. The trumpets transform the violins' Bach-like declamation into a fanfare. The power ebbs away, as the wind recall their opening chords. A melancholy peace descends. Out of it, the innocent flute melody is heard, now on violas, and taking on a quality of passionate longing. The melody gives way to the stark wind chords, now played by the strings, pianissimo, so that they too are drawn into the sense of longing. A burst of violin declamation leads to one last passionate climax. The music ebbs away, and dark wind chords, with the chilling stroke of a gong, bring the movement to a close.

The finale was originally called 'Victory'. As it opens, the world is still in darkness. A hint of a vigorous theme twice occurs in the bass. Then little pianissimo fanfares pass between oboe and muted horn. The theme that was hinted at emerges into the light, revealing its determination, and bearing more than a suggestion of the march theme that started the first movement. Moments of counterpoint help to generate energy, until yet another unstoppable force has been established. Once again strings, brass, and woodwind fight it out, and the side drum propels it on to ever greater frenzy. It recedes, leaving the violins working nervously away at a little repeated figure in seven-time.

There follows a string chorus which, like the violin declamations in the slow movement, have a distinctly baroque air, with the emphasis and dotted rhythms of a chaconne or sarabande. This too develops a passionate intensity, as if it is another memory that must be retained at all costs. The sarabande moves to the woodwind, then back to the cellos, darkened by a bass clarinet. Now the determined first theme of the movement is transformed into a lament, pianissimo on muted violins and then violas, with a vestige of the sarabande rhythm persisting in the background. The violas break into staccato patterns, and the little fanfare is heard on cor anglais.

The music is awaking again, preparing to build for one last time. Horns hark back to the opening march theme of the symphony. With relentless persistence and the marshalling of enormous forces, battering one step at a time, the music reaches a sustained conclusion of major harmonies. After more than an hour of tortured struggle to reach this point, clearly the symphony has won through to some sort of victory, if only the victory of hope.

SYMPHONY NO. 8, OP. 65
Duration: approx. 65 minutes

Adagio
Allegretto
Allegro non troppo –
Largo –
Allegretto

This is the second of the two symphonies that Shostakovich wrote during the struggle between Russia and Germany for supremacy in the Second World War. He composed it during the summer of 1943. The first movement lasts about 25 minutes, almost as long as the first movement of the 'Leningrad' Symphony. But the other four movements are much shorter, and movements three, four, and five run into each other. After the international triumph of No. 7, this symphony was received as rather a disappointment. In an interview before the premiere, Shostakovich said, 'The Eighth Symphony contains many inner conflicts, both tragic and dramatic. But, on the whole, it is an optimistic, life-affirming work.'[12] This is not how it was judged by audiences and critics. Indeed, its climaxes seem brutal and crushing, and if life emerges after them, it is not clear what sort of life this might be.

The sombre dotted rhythms of the opening theme are a recurring 'motto' through the movement. It recalls the opening of the Fifth Symphony, with its sombre, jagged dotted rhythms suggesting a modern version of a baroque French Overture, transformed into a gesture of defiance. But the mood in this symphony is much bleaker than in the fifth. The opening soon settles, and the violins sing a second theme, a lament, which rises high, intensified at its climax by flutes and trumpets. As it falls back, the dotted rhythms of the opening begin to find their way in. When the woodwind take over, these move to the bass (three bassoons and bass clarinet in unison). There is a slight increase in pace, and over a quiet, repeating rhythmic pattern, the violins sing a third melancholy theme. This is another lament, simpler than the second theme, with yearning intervals, and in an awkward five-time that gives it a very anxious quality.

The violins break into mournful rising scale patterns, in counterpoint with the cellos, while the melody moves to the violas, and, after a time, back to the violins. As this theme winds to a conclusion, the opening theme returns quietly in the flutes. Other instruments join in to create a moment of counterpoint, as if a fugue is beginning. Shostakovich uses this to build tension, and soon the crisis is upon us, with blaring brass fanfares, military side drum, shrieking woodwind, and tortured harmonies. It reaches a climax, and breaks into a faster tempo, the jagged dotted rhythms of the opening taking on ferocious energy, with fragments of the theme in the woodwind seeming to mock. Horns cut across the rhythm with the third theme, now transformed from a lament into a threatening fanfare. The music breaks into a brutal march. Soon its rhythm is distorted into irregular rhythms, and a devastating climax is reached. Five times a roll of drums crescendos to an outburst, as if we are witnessing a dreadful scene of mass execution.

Suddenly it is all over, and accompanied by pianissimo shuddering string tremolo, the cor anglais returns to the lamenting of the first part of the movement, drawing in elements of the first two themes in a long recitative. This culminates in a return to the third theme, still on cor anglais. As before, this moves to the violas, with mournful rising scales above, and then to the bass. Muted trumpets and horns interrupt with a sudden reminder of the jagged opening theme. Then the strings meditate on the second theme, bringing this immense movement to a quiet close.

The second movement is a grim mockery of a scherzo, in march time. Its four-square theme builds to a climax, and fades away. The strings keep up the march rhythm, imitating a side drum, through the middle section. The piccolo plays an elaborate, playful line, like a clowning mascot dancing in front of the marching army. It is joined in these antics by bassoon and contrabassoon lumbering to keep up, and a high clarinet full of cheeky squeals. Other wind instruments join in, then the strings, with the volume and tension gradually rising, until the original march theme returns, now blared out on trombones and tuba. The full orchestra enters, with squealing piccolo and crashing cymbals. At the end, a flute returns to the playful middle section for a moment, the music calms, and there is a final thwack from the full orchestra.

The third movement is another unrelenting piece, with an air of mockery. The violas set up a perpetuum mobile of rapid footsteps, as if running around in a confined space, unable to escape. There are sporadic grunts from the lower strings, and shrieks from the upper wood-wind. As more instruments enter, a sense of coercion develops. Patterns and instruments change, but the relentless rhythm does not. A trumpet plays a cheery fanfare, like a commanding officer looking on approvingly at all this pointlessly exhausting activity. The enthusiasm catches the strings (or is forced on them), and for a moment this spreads to the whole orchestra before fading away. The violas reprise their opening perpetuum mobile, with the sporadic shrieks now in the strings and brass. This time it builds up to full orchestra, with frenzied drumming from the timpani. A final impact leaves a ferocious side-drum roll carrying us straight into the fourth movement.

The fourth movement opens with the consequences of the preceding frenzy. There are two mighty crashes, and the brass intone a harsh version of the lamenting second theme from the first movement, as if some monstrous creature of war has been released from the depths. It recedes. Muted violins try to play that lament, but its melody has been crushed into a narrow range, and they painfully pick their way, as if half remembering it, with the other strings gradually joining in. Underneath, cellos and basses reiterate a solemn bass line – this is a passacaglia. A horn plays a line that seems like a similarly vague memory of the third theme from the first movement. A piccolo plays plangent arabesques, and the flutes flutter-tongue strange chords. A clarinet takes over the arabesques, but these too have been crushed, and they end up as ominous offbeat accents, like tolling bells. This is the musical equivalent of a wasteland. We have reached the border with the finale.

Without a break, the finale starts with an unexpectedly serene chord. A bassoon stirs, playing a tune that would be almost easy-going, if it were not for its irregular phrase lengths and its strange harmonies. The strings introduce some warmth into the tune. A flute and a triangle lighten the atmosphere, and the cellos play a long, yearning melody against staccato wind chords. From the oboes, the melody returns to the strings, and now the pace and the energy begin to increase. The staccato wind chords take on the familiar air of mockery as they move to the brass, and the violins become wilder.

There is a lull, with a passage of counterpoint, first on strings, then on woodwind. When it passes back to the strings, it quickly builds up to another passage for the wind, with raucous calls from horns and trumpets. The music accelerates to a final massive climax. We are back at the terrifying climax of the first movement, with its drum rolls and brutal chords. Out of this final act of violence there emerges a bass clarinet. Its low-pitched, elaborate line has an uneasy humour about it, as if it has not noticed what has been going on. A solo violin joins it, with almost carefree flourishes, then a solo cello recalls the yearning melody that the cellos played at the beginning of the movement, and a bassoon reprises its opening solo. It is accompanied by xylophone, flute, and clarinet, picking out the outline of the lament from the very beginning of the symphony. The strings bring a little warmth, like the weakest of sunlight, together with a plaintive piccolo. As the strings hold a high, pianissimo chord of C major, pizzicato violas quietly reiterate the opening notes of the bassoon solo, and the symphony draws to a close in an atmosphere of unexpected calm.

SYMPHONY NO. 9, OP. 70
Duration: approx. 25 minutes

Allegro

Moderato

Presto –

Largo –

Allegretto

After the massive wartime symphonies, No. 9, composed in 1945 after the end of the war, is a comparatively modest work. Less than half the length of its predecessors, it was not at all the victory symphony that Shostakovich had led the public, and the authorities, to expect. It fell so far short of what the state, and Stalin in particular, required, that it was banned from further performance until after Stalin's death. It consists of five short movements, of which the last three are linked (as in Symphony No. 7).

As the first movement begins, it is easy to imagine the outrage of those who were expecting a hymn to Russian endurance. After Russia's four years of terrible suffering, Shostakovich has come up with something that could be the overture to a comic opera – and, at five minutes, this opener is no longer than many overtures. There is an air of insouciance as the music trots briskly along. A trombone and a piccolo might be announcing the arrival of the circus. The build-up in the middle of the movement develops a certain manic energy, but it never becomes threatening, and the movement ends as it began. This seems like a reversion to the student irony of Shostakovich's First Symphony – and perhaps that was as appropriate a reaction to the ending of the slaughter as the 'victory symphony' that people were expecting.

The second movement opens with a clarinet solo, characteristically sweet and sour, with an almost pastoral feel but with shifting harmonies and metres. It culminates in a wind chorus with a touch of Stravinskyan stridency, and falls away as a flute solo. This gives way to an anxious, plodding string passage, over which oboe and clarinet in unison wail, leading to a climax that again falls away to anxiety. A solo flute resumes the earlier theme. The strings enter again, taking their anxious idea more lightly, and up to a beautiful high summit, from which they gently descend. The movement ends with the theme resumed by flute and, with sad emphasis, by the piccolo (it was from Mahler that Shostakovich learned the poignant potential of the piccolo).

If the first movement was like an operatic overture, the third movement, a snappy scherzo, could have been written for a Keystone Cops film (the young Shostakovich used to earn money as a pianist for the silent films). A clarinet starts the chase, with woodwind and strings following on enthusiastically. In the middle (where a scherzo would have a trio) a trumpet plays what sounds like a parody of a Neapolitan popular song. This is taken up, rather ridiculously, in the bass, before the opening theme returns to the woodwind. The ending is not what one might expect. The chase gradually fades away, as if it was just a dream. Solemn chords and a held note lead straight into the fourth movement.

All of a sudden, the fourth movement takes us back to the starkness of the Eighth Symphony. Trombones and tuba intone fierce dotted rhythms, and a solo bassoon meditates. It refers back to elements of the chase music from the third movement, as if remembering a darker context. But the mood suddenly changes.

With a little flourish, the bassoon embarks on the finale with a quaint little tune, as if shrugging off these memories (it is easy to see how this transition in particular could have shocked people in 1945). When the violins take it over, it begins to sound like ballet music. An oboe plays a more plaintive tune, with clarinets creating a drone like a hurdy-gurdy, and the ballet music returns. The strings play a sturdier tune, and the brass interpolate mock fanfares. The original tune moves to the bass, with the sturdy tune occasionally appearing in the woodwind. The energy builds, the pace increases, and a frantic edge develops. At the climax the trumpets reprise the little tune, defusing any sense of crisis. Then the tempo increases again, and the music hurtles to an exhilarating end.

This is Shostakovich in 'unbuttoned' mood, and the symphony is one of his most attractive compositions. But is this jollity straightforward? The mocking element, never far away in Shostakovich's lighter music, was seen, particularly in Russia, as containing a veiled attack on the forced cheerfulness of Soviet life. Politically, his timing for such a work could not have been worse.

SYMPHONY NO. 10, OP. 93
Duration: approx. 50 minutes

Moderato
Allegro
Allegretto
Andante – Allegro

This symphony was premiered in Leningrad in December 1953. Stalin, the figurehead of the brutal system that had been the bane of Shostakovich's life, had died in March that year. This was an immensely significant moment for Shostakovich. He had not composed a symphony for eight years. The official denouncement of his Ninth Symphony had been followed, in 1948, by a decree condemning composers who undermined the health of Soviet music with their 'formalism'. His music was no longer played, he was sacked from his teaching post in Moscow, and was forced to earn a living writing scores for patriotic films and heroic choral works, and to act as a mouthpiece for Soviet artistic principles at international conferences. These approved activities enabled him to claw his way back to some degree of official tolerance.

Accounts differ as to how much of the Tenth Symphony was already written before the death of Stalin, but it is clear that its final form was deeply influenced by this event. The posthumously published volume of supposed interviews with Shostakovich, *Testimony*, goes so far as to state that the symphony was essentially about the Stalinist years, and that the second movement was 'a portrait of Stalin, roughly speaking'.[13] This is widely considered likely to be an exaggeration, at the least. And it is known that Shostakovich also wove into the symphony autobiographical references. There are two 'mottos' that dominate the last two movements of the work. The first consists of the five notes E-A-E-D-A. This is an encoded version of the name 'Elmira', using a combination of the usual letters and the names of the notes in tonic sol-fa: E-La-Mi-Re-A. Elmira Nazirova was a musician who, aged nineteen, had studied with Shostakovich at the Moscow Conservatoire in the year 1947–8 before he was dismissed from his post. Shostakovich conducted an intense correspondence with her for the rest of his life, and she acted as a kind of muse for his Tenth Symphony, attending its premiere with him. The second motto is made up of the four notes D-E flat-C-B. In German terminology, these notes are D-Es-C-H. Shostakovich used this as an abbreviation for his own name: 'D. Sch.' The public face of Shostakovich's music can often seem all too clear. But the motivation lying behind it is not necessarily as it appears on the surface.

After the 'miniature' Symphony No. 9, the Tenth Symphony returns almost to the scale of No. 8, with a first movement that lasts nearly half of the total length. It opens with cellos and basses quietly repeating a rising three-note pattern that is to become significant. This develops into a calm but mournful string passage, in which this pattern also falls. A solo clarinet plays the first fully formed theme, in which the rising pattern features, with a violin counterpoint in which the pattern falls. This builds up to a first climax, in which the violins introduce a more agitated repeating pattern, and then falls back, leaving the clarinet reprising its earlier solo. There is a slightly faster flute solo, which takes the agitated pattern from the climax, and, through rather nervous repetition, develops it into a second theme. It too is taken up by the strings, and develops into a second build-up.

This leads into the central development of the movement. The first (clarinet) theme becomes a lament on bassoon, its dark mood emphasized by contrabassoon and drum rolls. The rest of the woodwind join in, and, with elements of the second theme adding agitation, the music builds up again to the first sustained fortissimo, in which the two themes combine. At the climax, the horns insistently repeat again and again the falling three-note pattern. From this climax the strings lead the struggle on to a further climax, from which the music is finally able to descend.

Two unaccompanied clarinets in counterpoint quietly reprise their first theme. But soon this drifts towards the second theme, and the duet becomes an anxious meditation. Eventually, the strings reprise the music with which they began the movement. Finally, two piccolos continue the clarinets' meditative duet over rolling timpani, and the movement ends in an atmosphere balanced between bleakness and serenity – a characteristically ambivalent way for Shostakovich to end a long movement.

The second movement is a ferocious gallop, based on the three-note up-and-down shape from the beginning of the symphony. It may or may not be 'a portrait of Stalin', but the overwhelming ferocity of the movement, with its relentless repeating rhythms and savage attack, and a tempo that is really prestissimo rather than allegro, suggest unstoppable destructive force (any doubts about the terrifying effect that Shostakovich intended are answered by the composer's own frenetic performance with Mosei Weinberg of the piano duet arrangement, recorded only two months after the premiere).[14] In the middle of the mayhem, the brass intone the up-and-down motif in doubled note lengths, like a contorted version of the *Dies Irae*.

The violins begin the third movement like an elegant gavotte (again beginning with the rising three notes), but with a confusing extra beat at the end of the first phrase. By the second phrase it becomes clear that it is really in three-time. Shostakovich continually subverts the metre, and cuts across it with counterpoint. This charming, though somewhat disturbed, tune is interrupted by what sounds like the village band, with a new idea and its own confused sense of rhythm. The strings throw this idea back at them, eventually returning to the opening theme, which is then played by a bassoon.

Suddenly, a horn bursts in with a sustained fanfare of five notes. This is the first occurrence of the 'Elmira' motto, and it is sounded repeatedly. At first, the strings respond by taking us back to the mournful opening of the symphony. Then flute and piccolo play a new, anxious shape, and the strings play hesitant pizzicato. After an ominous gong stroke, the first theme of the movement returns, on cor anglais. The brash 'village band' idea returns, now on unison strings, with trumpets. Into this the strings bring the first theme of the movement, now turned into something bold and threatening, with an urgent running bass underneath. The pace increases, and the strings insistently repeat a four-note pattern. This is the motto representing 'D. Sch.' himself. At the height of this passage, the 'D. Sch.' and 'Elmira' mottos alternate. The movement ends mysteriously, with the horn still calling the 'Elmira' motto, and the 'D. Sch.' motto having the last word.

The finale opens quietly with a slow introduction. First an oboe and then a bassoon meditate plaintively. Prominent in the melody is the anxious little shape that first occurred in the woodwind in the middle of the third movement. At the end of the introduction, this suddenly metamorphoses into a cheeky little theme, and we are into the final Allegro.

This is a gopak, a dance that is traditionally wild, but here elevated to a level of wildness that is either nightmarish or hysterically joyful. It is characteristic of Shostakovich that we can never be sure which emotion is predominant, or whether the two can even be separated. The first section of the dance reaches a climax that is cut off by the brass blaring out the 'D. Sch.' motto. The strings quietly recall the sombre introduction of the movement, the woodwind remember the anxious little shape from the third movement, and the 'D. Sch.' motto hovers quietly in trumpet and trombone.

The moment of darkness is broken by a bassoon, playing a simplified, staccato version of the gopak tune. This has rather the effect of the entry of the drunk in a Russian opera – comic in itself, but implying that the only response to tragedy is to keep on dancing and drinking. From here the music quickly builds up to a pitch of fury that threatens to break through to the destructive force of the second movement. The wildest of wild endings has Shostakovich's motto blasted out in triumph, defiance, or recklessness – or, very probably, a combination of all three.

JEAN SIBELIUS
(1865–1957)

Sibelius's last major work, *Tapiola*, was written in 1926. If you glance at Sibelius's dates, you might think this is a misprint. But he did indeed live for another thirty-one years, during which he wrote virtually nothing. Feeling overtaken by the musical developments of the time, and destructively self-critical, he lived in alcohol-fuelled retirement in Finland, supported by a government pension.

Perhaps a contributory factor in Sibelius's 'burnout' was that he suffered from the effects of excessive praise during his lifetime. There was a period during the 1920s and 1930s when certain writers, notably Constant Lambert and Cecil Gray, regarded Sibelius as the great hope for the future, in contrast to the 'official' revolutionaries Schoenberg and Stravinsky. According to Gray, works such as Schoenberg's *Pierrot Lunaire* or Stravinsky's *The Rite of Spring* 'are *tours de force*, exploits upon the tight-rope which is our present age, stretched across the gulf between past and future. Moreover, they are feats which can never be repeated, not even by their creators. Sibelius seems to belong to a different race, a different age even; whether to the past or to the unborn future it would be difficult to say.'[1]

Sibelius became, in his lifetime, a genuinely popular classical composer, like Beethoven or Brahms. But perhaps he was overpraised and overplayed. Certainly a reaction set in, and as the radical experiments of Schoenberg and Stravinsky looked as if they were here to stay, Sibelius began to seem rather faded. Now, in the twenty-first century, the pendulum has swung again. The influence of Sibelius seems stronger than ever on a new generation of composers – Henryk Górecki, Arvo Pärt, John Adams, Steve Reich, Philip Glass, and other 'minimalists' – while the composers of the Second Viennese School seem more and more like a brilliant but esoteric backwater.

Sibelius took time to find his distinctive voice. He began as a law student, simultaneously studying the violin and composition. It was while he was in Vienna in 1890–1 that he encountered two major sources of inspiration. After hearing a performance of Bruckner's Third Symphony, he declared him to be the greatest living composer, and the epic grandeur of Sibelius's own music owes much to his influence. Around this time Sibelius began studying the collection of Finnish traditional poetry, the *Kalevala*. The importance of the *Kalevala* in Sibelius's thinking was profound. This compilation of traditional sung poems, known as 'runes', was collected in Karelia by Elias Lönnrot, and published in the early nineteenth century. The poems are grouped in cycles, and acquired the status of the Finnish national epic, becoming a symbol of Finland's struggle against Russian domination.

The poems are in a distinctive 'Kalevala metre', a trochaic tetrameter, as in this extract from Rune 31, describing the infant Kullervo (the 1910 translation from the Finnish by William Forsell Kirby preserves the characteristic metre):

> When the boy began his kicking,
> And he kicked and pushed about him,
> Tore his swaddling clothes to pieces,
> Freed himself from all his clothing,
> Then he broke the lime-wood cradle,
> All his rags he tore from off him.[2]

If the rhythm seems familiar to English-speaking readers, it is because Henry Wadsworth Longfellow, having come across the *Kalevala* soon after its publication, used its metre for *The Song of Hiawatha* (1855). The solemn, incantatory effect of the metre, and its relation to the speech rhythms of Finnish, had a lasting effect on Sibelius's music, though in ways that were subtle rather than direct. Sibelius himself described his relationship with this and other traditional Finnish sources in an interview while he was visiting Italy in 1923: 'I do want to make one point clear: my music is not folkloric. I have on no occasion made use of Finnish folk melodies. I have admittedly composed melodies in a folk-like style, but they have all been created in my mind, or rather in my heart, as I am a devoted Finn.' Asked if he has therefore followed the example of Musorgsky or Grieg, Sibelius replied, 'Absolutely. I am completely steeped in the poetry and mythology of Finland and have set much of the former and found inspiration in the latter, and particularly in the *Kalevala* . . .'[3]

Sibelius began his career at a time when there was a powerful movement in Finland for the promotion of Finnish language and culture. Finland had been under the rule of Sweden until 1809, and then was part of the Russian Empire until its independence in 1917. Swedish was the language of the educated elite, and Finnish was spoken by the majority. Sibelius was brought up in a Swedish-speaking family, but he attended a Finnish secondary school, and was later engaged to a Finnish speaker. When he became fascinated by the *Kalevala*, he planned a grand choral symphony setting some of its texts. *Kullervo*, which was performed in 1892, established Sibelius as a powerful new voice in the Finnish movement. As Finland's first composer to establish an international reputation, Sibelius was awarded a state grant in 1897 that enabled him to devote his time to composition.

Sibelius forged a distinct musical identity, bringing together elements of Bruckner, Wagner, Liszt, Russian composers, Debussy, the 'folk' music and poetry of Finland with their characteristic modes and rhythms, and a particular cast of mind that tended to state things either bluntly or elusively, but rarely effusively or extravagantly. When climaxes occur, they are hard-won, and the route to resolution is pitted with stumbling blocks and things not entirely stated or understood. It was this approach that enabled Sibelius to create large-scale works in a rethinking of the traditional formal procedures of earlier symphonic music. From the immense *Kullervo* of 1992, Sibelius developed an increasingly economical, terse style that reached its extreme in the Fourth Symphony. His last works, the Seventh Symphony and *Tapiola*, developed this laconic style to its ultimate power, before Sibelius lapsed into silence.

FINLANDIA, OP. 26

Duration: approx. 9 minutes

Andante sostenuto – Allegro moderato – Allegro

Finlandia was written as part of celebrations in 1899 whose official purpose was to raise money for the pension funds of Finnish newspapers. At the same time, they acted as a demonstration against Russian censorship, which Tsar Nicholas II had imposed as part of a campaign to bring Finland under tighter Russian control. The celebrations culminated in a series of tableaux celebrating Finnish history, for which Sibelius wrote an overture and six pieces (the *Karelia Suite* had had a similar origin six years earlier).

What we now know as *Finlandia* was composed for the final tableau, 'Finland awakes', which followed on from a tableau symbolizing the brutality of the conquest of Finland by the Russian army in the early eighteenth century. In 1900, Sibelius converted 'Finland awakes' into a concert piece, and the following year retitled it *Finlandia*. In this form it became extremely popular, and its culminating theme, known as the Finlandia Hymn, acquired patriotic words. Its fate, therefore, was similar to that of Elgar's first *Pomp and Circumstance* March, though with the important difference that Sibelius's piece expressed the struggle against oppression, whereas 'Land of hope and glory' celebrated the glory of British supremacy (somewhat to Elgar's dismay).

Finlandia opens with defiant snarls from the brass. These begin to form themselves into a more continuous melody, which becomes chorale-like as woodwind and then strings take over – though still with a defiant and sombre quality. The pace increases (Allegro moderato). The brass play aggressive fanfares, alternating with the strings playing the original snarls, now faster, and with the addition of energetic swirling figures. The bass instruments, with tuba, set up a yet faster tempo (Allegro) in what for a moment sounds like five-time. The brass fanfares punctuate a new theme, for the first time in a major key, which is full of optimistic energy. The brass fanfares are incorporated into it, now given a determined drive by the strings.

After going twice round this section, the music calms, and the woodwind chorus sings a new theme (this is the Finlandia Hymn). As usual in Sibelius, it is not as new as it seems: the opening of the melody has the same shape as the snarling brass at the very beginning of the piece. The woodwind pass the hymn to the strings. At the end, the music returns to the opening of the Allegro, with the brass fanfares and optimistically rising theme. This climaxes with a reprise of the Finlandia Hymn, now on full orchestra, to bring the work to a stirring finish.

KARELIA SUITE, OP. 11
Duration: approx. 15 minutes

Intermezzo: moderato
Ballade: tempo di menuetto
Alla Marcia: moderato

In 1893, the year after the first performance of his *Kullervo*, Sibelius was invited to write the music for a series of tableaux based on episodes from the history of Karelia. Karelia, in the south-east of Finland, was an important source of Finnish traditional music and legend, including the *Kalevala* epic that inspired so much of Sibelius's music. He had spent his honeymoon in Karelia the previous year, and had collected folk songs in the region. The tableaux were part of an educational fund-raising event organized by the students' association of Vyborg (Viipuri), an ancient town in Karelia, which has at various times been ruled by Sweden, Russia, and independent Finland, before being incorporated into the Soviet Union. From the series of tableaux, Sibelius in 1906 selected three movements to form his well-known Karelia Suite. It is scored for a large orchestra, with full brass and percussion.

The Intermezzo is taken from a tableau evoking a fourteenth-century scene, in which Duke Larimont of Lithuania collects tribute from a procession of Karelian citizens. The movement begins with a gentle rustling of the strings, over which a quartet of horns calls softly. Alternate calls are 'stopped', with the hand inserted in the bell to muffle the tone. The effect is of two groups calling to each other across the forest. There is an agitated crescendo in the strings, and three trumpets take up the call, with percussion turning it into a stirring march. It reaches a climax on full orchestra, and dies away to leave the horns calling quietly as they began.

The Ballade is from a tableau of the fifteenth century, in which a bard sings to Karl Knutsson, military governor of Vyborg (and later King of Sweden), in his castle. The marking is tempo di menuetto, but the firmly reiterated phrases have an emphasis more like a sarabande. Stronger still is the influence of the Karelian folk tunes that Sibelius had collected, with their sombre, recitative-like structures and narrow compass. The movement is built from three rather similar melodies. The first begins on clarinets and bassoons, and is taken up and extended by the strings, rising to a climax and falling away. The second melody is more hymn-like, predominantly on strings, and again rising to a climax. This is followed not by a reprise of the opening, as one might expect, but by a third, rather similar melody, on cor anglais, accompanied by pizzicato strings. This section most clearly evokes the idea of a bard singing to a harp. The movement ends with a brief reminiscence of the first melody, now on oboes.

The third movement, Alla Marcia, accompanied a sixteenth-century tableau, in which Pontius de la Gardie, a brilliant French soldier who rose to high rank in Sweden and helped it conquer Karelia, stands with his army before the town of Kexholm (Kakiholma). It is a brisk, cheerful march, which begins on strings. The trumpets enter with a second theme, closely related to the horn calls from the first movement. Trombones and cymbals repeat it grandly. The first march returns, at first on high woodwind with the piccolo taking the melody. Alternations between these two themes take the movement to a grand conclusion.

KULLERVO, OP. 7
Duration: approx. 72 minutes

Introduction
Kullervo's Youth
Kullervo and his Sister
Kullervo Goes to Battle
Kullervo's Death

Kullervo was Sibelius's first substantial work to be inspired by the *Kalevala*, the collection of Finnish national myths (see introduction to Sibelius). It brought him to prominence, not just as a composer, but as an artistic spokesman for Finnish national culture. One cycle of poems in the *Kalevala* is devoted to the adventures of Kullervo. Kullervo is a man of magical powers from his birth, but as a character he is impulsive, destructive, and ultimately tragic. It is interesting that Sibelius, in his twenties and just embarking on his public career, should feel so drawn to this flawed hero. The dark side of human nature never seems far away in Sibelius's music, and it is powerfully present in this early work.

Sibelius described *Kullervo* in his autograph score and at the premiere as a 'symphonic poem', but often referred to it as a symphony. It is, in effect, a massive choral symphony in five movements, of which numbers three and five are choral, and the others are purely instrumental. The third movement also includes solo mezzo-soprano and baritone. Sibelius began working on it in 1891 when he was studying in Vienna. Engaged to a supporter of Finnish culture and national aspirations, Sibelius had become engrossed in reading the *Kalevala*. He was inspired not just by its epic narratives, but by the incantatory rhythms of its poetry. Its influence came together with that of Finnish traditional rune-singing and folk song in Sibelius's attempt to create a new way of composing, one that would draw on what he described as 'the deep melancholy and insistence on one mood or phrase which is at the heart of so many Finnish folk songs'.[4]

Kullervo takes a broad sweep through Kullervo's life and exploits as narrated in the *Kalevala*. For the choral movements Sibelius sets sections taken directly from the poems. The text of the third movement, 'Kullervo and his Sister', is the tragic climax of the story, in which Kullervo seduces a young woman only to discover that she is his sister. Kullervo's suicide is the subject of the final movement, 'Kullervo's Death'.

Sibelius himself conducted the premiere in April 1892, with the Helsinki Orchestral Society which had been founded that year. It was a great success, recognized as a milestone in Finnish music. But Sibelius became dissatisfied with *Kullervo*, and after four performances withdrew it. It was only at the end of his life that he agreed to release the score. It was performed complete in 1958, the year after his death, and published in 1961. But it was the premiere recording by the Bournemouth Symphony Orchestra and Helsinki University Male Voice Choir conducted by Paavo Berglund in 1971 that brought *Kullervo* to wider public attention, and established this sprawling, astonishingly original work as fully worthy to take its place beside Sibelius's more concise later works.

The Introduction is like the first movement of a conventional symphony: a succession of themes is put forward in the first part, developed in the middle of the movement, and reprised at the end. But Sibelius already has a particular way of characterizing his material and developing it to create a powerful sense of narrative. Over turbulent strings, the first theme rises in the wind, and then passes to the violins. It has a bold, resolute character, its modal harmonies giving it something of the character of a folk song. It builds to a climax, then falls away to the second theme. Solo horns rock between major and minor, rise up a scale, then rock again. Again, it is the harmonies that give this its distinctively brooding character, with a sustained, gently agitated seventh chord in the strings, and uneasy harmonic shifts in the melody itself. A sudden chord brings in a further element in a broad triplet rhythm, which soon breaks up into more playful figurations. For a moment, the music becomes fragmented, before a quiet wind chord takes us back to the opening theme and into the development section of the movement.

As the music moves into new keys and the theme forms a web of counterpoint, we have a sense of venturing deeper into the landscape. Two oboes alternate in rapid repeated notes as the theme moves to the horns. Forces gradually begin to build over a sustained bass note, with a Bruckner-like sense of potential power, and with the uneasy harmonies of the second theme continually introducing an ominous element. The climax fades over a long chord with timpani roll, the wind lead us back to the first theme, and the strings take it up forcefully. The quiet second theme on horns emerges from beneath the bird-like calls of woodwind. Gradually the music builds up again, underpinned by a persistent rhythm in the timpani. Before reaching a climax it breaks off – another very Brucknerian moment – and descends to a moment of uneasy stillness. With a sudden blast, the first theme enters as a wall of brass, but agitated strings undermine its certainty with tortured harmonies. The movement ends with the theme reduced to sombre fragmented phrases on the woodwind.

Sibelius described the second movement, 'Kullervo's Youth', as a lullaby 'whose intensity is increased by variation'.[5] It defies easy description, because Sibelius is already a master of the fluid, seemingly organic development that was to mark his approach throughout his career. Kullervo's youth, as described in the *Kalevala*, was tempestuous. His uncle, Untamo, had killed the clan of Kullervo's father. When Kullervo was born, he was a miraculous child who rocked his cradle to destruction, obviously destined to be a hero. Untamo saw him as a threat and attempted to kill him, first by drowning, then by burning, and finally by hanging. But he survived, and Untamo put him to work. When it became clear that Kullervo was bent on destruction, Untamo sold him as a slave to the blacksmith. But Kullervo later escaped, and was reunited with his family (who, after all, seem to have survived Untamo's slaughter).

The lullaby is sombre, its repetitive, short-breathed phrases in a trudging metre evocative of Finnish rune-singing, and the tug of dissonant harmonies adding an extra shade of darkness. A sustained bass note lingers not on the keynote but on the fifth of the chord, so that the melody seems to be hanging in mid-air. The second note of the melody is broken into repetitions that produce a subtle shuddering when first played by the strings. But later the brass will transform this into baleful hammering. The middle strain of the melody opens out more passionately, before the first strain returns. A third element returns to the repetitive rune style of the opening, but with nervous descending arpeggios above it and pizzicato below. The second strain returns briefly, then the first, now as an airy string chorus. A moment of relaxed counterpoint builds in energy with rushing string scales below. The first strain restores calm, and there is a moment of hesitation.

A chord announces a change of key to take us into new areas. Clarinet and cor anglais play flourishes, like shepherds on the hillside, and are echoed by others. A steady chugging rhythm starts up (the prototype of 'journeying' rhythms in later Sibelius), and flutes play a cheerful tune. For a moment the energy builds, but it soon drains away, until high woodwind are left holding an anxious chord (its 'tritone' has been a frequent ingredient of the harmony, ever since the horn theme in the Introduction). Now the opening theme returns forcefully, building to a mighty climax over another sustained bass note and with the brass hammering. The high strings are left pleading (another portent of later Sibelius) as the music gradually fades. The third element returns on cor anglais, and again the music builds to a huge climax, with more triumphant hammering in the brass.

Suddenly the pastoral clarinet episode returns, though over a dark background that has difficulty regaining a sense of calm. The chugging rhythm and the cheerful tune return. Over a persistent drumbeat the opening theme builds once more to a last climax and down again. But suddenly the hammering brass erupt, answered by a quiet wind chord in a remote key. The movement ends by returning to the sombre theme from which it started.

'Kullervo and his Sister' is the longest of the five movements. The orchestra is joined by solo mezzo-soprano and baritone, and a male chorus that sings the narrative sections of the *Kalevala* text. Most of this movement is in five-time, a metre that is often encountered in traditional Finnish runes. The effect is not regular, easily identifiable five beats, but rather a free, declamatory style.

The orchestral introduction is wild and energetic, its wildness heightened by the lack of an obvious metre. The male chorus enters. Through most of the movement they sing in unison or in simple octaves. Sibelius treats the metre of the poetry quite freely, but without distorting word stresses (he was much admired at the time of the premiere for this achievement). The music therefore does not have the regularity of the poem's metre, but it does preserve a powerful sense of incantation. As the narrative unfolds, in a ritualistically formal manner, the role of the chorus is like that in Greek tragedy. The closest resemblance to this effect is to be found in Stravinsky's *Oedipus Rex*, thirty-five years later. The Russian connection is perhaps significant: Musorgsky's *Boris Godunov* uses the chorus to represent the voice of the Russian people, and Sibelius's chorus evokes something of that power.

The chorus narrates the journey of Kullervo. The first English translation from the Finnish, by William Forsell Kirby (1907), preserves the characteristic metre of the original:[6]

Kullervo, Kalervo's offspring,
With the very bluest stockings,
And with yellow hair the finest,
And with shoes of finest leather,
Went his way to pay the taxes,
And he went to pay the land-dues.
When he now had paid the taxes,
And had also paid the land-dues,
In his sledge he quickly bounded,
And upon the sledge he mounted,
And began to journey homeward,
And to travel to his country.

The first section of chorus is emphatic, but from time to time more reflective, with a piccolo suggesting the glittering landscape through which Kullervo is travelling. The chorus's chant is in the Dorian mode, familiar from many folk songs, which adds a distinctly 'ancient' tone to the effect.

The harmonies take a more ominous turn as Kullervo encounters the first young woman. He invites her into the sledge, but she abruptly refuses, wishing death upon him (all three women are sung by the mezzo-soprano). The orchestra returns to the energetic opening of the movement, and the chorus enters for a second verse. Kullervo encounters a second woman, walking across the frozen lake. He invites her into the sledge, and she too rejects him, wishing the god of death upon him. The orchestra once more returns to the energetic opening, with darker power than before.

The chorus enters for a third verse. As they describe the appearance of the third young woman, singing as she walks, a trilling flute and high violin note add an air of mystery. Kullervo invites her in, offering her warmth and food. But she spits at him and at the darkness of his sledge. As the chorus describes how Kullervo drags the girl into the sledge, they break for the first time into harmony – an extraordinarily powerful moment after so much unrelenting unison chanting. The girl threatens to smash the sledge to pieces, the chorus overlapping with her cries. The chorus describes how Kullervo tempts her with fabrics embroidered with gold and silver, and the sombre chords of their chanting are joined by a poignant counterpoint in strings and horns.

As she succumbs, there is a moment of peace, with a tender oboe melody. This extends into an orchestral interlude that expands to a glorious, sustained climax. An agitated return to the opening music quickly develops into a second climax, which culminates in a terrifying shriek and a violent chord and drum roll.

Lamenting phrases lead into the girl's question: who is this stranger's family? An ominous drum pattern repeats as Kullervo replies that he is the son of Kalervo. A clarinet pattern suggestive of dread takes over as the girl replies that she too is the offspring of Kalervo. Poignantly, she describes how, when she was a little girl, she became lost in the woods while picking berries. On the sixth day, thinking she would never be found, she called out from the mountain top, but the woods replied that no one would hear her. Piccolos suggest birdsong in a moment that touchingly conveys the innocence of the young girl in the forest. She attempted to kill herself, but failed. In a lament of tragic simplicity, she regrets that she has lived to know this horror. Her lament ends bluntly – the point in the *Kalevala* at which she hurls herself into the river.

Kullervo now takes up his own lament, punctuated by savage chords. He sings of the shame he has brought on his aged parents, and regrets that he did not die in infancy. This lament too comes to an abrupt conclusion, and thunderous chords bring the movement to a close.

At this point in the *Kalevala*, Kullervo returns home, confesses his sin to his mother, and asks how he should kill himself. But the mother urges him not to die. Kullervo sets off to avenge his family by engaging in battle against Untamo, hoping that he will himself be killed. Fired by this new purpose in life, Kullervo 'went off piping to war, went rejoicing to the battle'. After the stark tragedy of the preceding movement, and without any intervening narrative, the opening of 'Kullervo Goes to Battle' seems almost indecent in its dancing cheerfulness. It is saved from banality by an underlying element of nervousness, as the confident energy of the music is continually subjected to trilling hesitations. There are passages of charming delicacy interspersed with others of sudden power. The recurrences of the opening theme hold the movement together as a sort of rondo, and the repetitions of the final chord seem to suggest the hollowness of Kullervo's victory in the light of what is to come.

Kullervo returns home to find that his entire family is dead. Only an old black dog survives, and Kullervo's mother, speaking from the grave, tells him to take it with him into the forest. This is the point at which 'Kullervo's Death' begins. The narrative is sung by the choir, alternating between the austere unison or octaves of most of their previous entries and warmer harmony for moments of compassion.

Under mysterious string tremolo the choir sings of Kullervo's search in the forest for the place where he seduced his sister. Their melody is based on the horn's second theme from the first movement. Throughout this final section there are reminiscences of earlier themes, giving a sense of Kullervo looking back over his life. He recognizes the spot, and the lamentation grows as he finds the grass weeping and the flowers grieving for the ruin of the young woman. The music rises to a moment of dissonant climax, the harmony dominated by the tritone that has appeared at many tense moments. Kullervo grasps his sword, and asks it if it would be pleased to kill him, to devour his guilty body and to drink his sinful blood. The sword replies: why would I not do so:

> I who guiltless flesh have eaten,
> Drank the blood of those who sinned not?

The music rises to a mighty climax. Kullervo throws himself on his sword, and a drumbeat treads out a funeral march. The orchestra bursts out with a final return to the first theme, and the chorus sings:

> Even so the young man perished,
> Thus died Kullervo the hero,
> Thus the hero's life was ended,
> Perished thus the hapless hero.

POHJOLA'S DAUGHTER, OP. 49
Duration: approx. 13 minutes

As often with Sibelius, *Pohjola's Daughter* went through a complicated evolution from various ideas before reaching its final form. In 1905 he was working on an orchestral tone poem called *Luonnotar* (the spirit of nature and creator of the world), inspired by the creation myth in the *Kalevala*. But the work that he completed the following year (which may or may not have been the same as *Luonnotar*) returned to the story from the *Kalevala* that he had planned as an opera more than a decade earlier, *The Building of the Boat*. It centres on the great hero Väinämöinen who, during his travels in Pohjola (the dark Northland), catches sight of the beautiful maiden of the rainbow ('Pohjola's daughter') as she sits in a bank of cloud weaving golden and silver thread. He falls in love with her, but she tells Väinämöinen that she will marry him only if he fulfils certain tasks, including turning the splinters from her spindle into a boat by his song. Väinämöinen travels to Tuonela, the land of the dead, to find the magic words that will enable him to do this.

Pohjola's Daughter does not tell the story in detail. Rather, it takes contrasting elements that suggest the great hero and the beautiful maiden, and builds a musical structure from them. Over a low chord, cellos begin a meditative recitative, like a bard introducing the subject of his story. Over a persistently repeated note in the cellos, the hero's melody begins to cohere in the woodwind. The tempo gradually increases, the rhythm becomes more insistent, and the music takes on an air of adventure, of the bold traveller setting forth. This culminates in a heroic climax on the brass. Suddenly, there is a complete change of atmosphere, key, and musical texture. A rippling harp, high strings, and curls of melody on oboe, cor anglais, and flute evoke a scene of delicate beauty (the 'maiden' element). No sooner has this vision come into focus than, with a flourish on the clarinet, it is gone. Mysterious tremolando strings lead to a moment of hesitation. Uncertain pizzicato coalesces into another repeating rhythmic pattern, and phrases derived from the 'hero's melody' burst out in the violins and loom up from the bass. This begins what, in formal terms, could be called a development section, but the effect is of a psychological battle, as fragments of the maidenly theme come and go, and the heroic elements struggle to prevail (not for the last time in this work, there is a distinct echo of Richard Strauss in this passage). Once more a moment of calm is reached, with high woodwind trills, and again it vanishes to leave uncertain pizzicato. This time, it is followed by a sudden increase in tempo. Above agitated strings the maiden's theme appears in the woodwind in rapid snatches. The heroic element becomes more determined, both in bass and in violins, and the insistent rhythmic pattern becomes an urgent cry in the woodwind. After further struggle, the music finds its way back to the first build-up of the piece. There is another moment of calm followed by a grand reprise of the heroic brass climax, now extended, and leading on to a very passionate melody on the violins that could have been written by Richard Strauss. This seems ready to sweep all before it to a great conclusion. But it evaporates, leaving a solitary line quietly working its way up through the strings, and a final phrase, *ppp* in cellos and basses, that seems to leave the story suspended rather than finished.

EN SAGA, OP. 9
Duration: approx. 18 minutes

'En' is the Finnish article, so the title simply means 'A Saga'. This was Sibelius's first major orchestral work after the early *Kullervo*, and was written at the prompting of the conductor Robert Kajanus in 1892. Ten years later, when Sibelius was invited by Busoni to conduct it in Berlin, he revised and shortened it. It is this revised version that has usually been performed, but in recent years the original score has also been revived.

It is described in the score as a 'tone poem', the term that Richard Strauss had adopted, and is in a single movement. Unlike Sibelius's later works, many of which are associated with particular episodes in the *Kalevala*, *En Saga* has no specific references beyond the music itself. Many years after its composition, Sibelius told his secretary, 'It is the expression of a state of mind. I had undergone a number of painful experiences at the time, and in no other work have I revealed myself so completely. It is for this reason that I find all literary explanations alien.'[7] But he also said in an interview, 'How could one think of anything but Finland while listening to it!'[8] He began *En Saga* soon after his wedding, and finished it after an expedition in Karelia during which he collected folk music and poetry, and heard a traditional singer of runes. Although there are no obvious quotations from traditional music in *En Saga*, already its musical language, with repetitive 'cells' – emphatic phrases that circle round a few notes – owes something to Sibelius's interest in tradition material. It is this, together with its mysterious, dark, brooding textures, that makes it sound 'Finnish'.

It begins mysteriously, with a delicate shimmering of arpeggios in the strings. The woodwind play awkward little fragments, with dissonant harmonies. It is from these fragments that one of the main themes of the piece will grow. Soon, from the middle of the wash of string arpeggios, we hear a second element on bassoons, like a sustained chant. There are several build-ups, the pace increases, and elements begin to coalesce into something like a theme. The music becomes more urgent, with wonderfully complex orchestration, and from another climax emerges a third element, beginning quietly on violas. This is the coherent outcome of the opening woodwind fragments, with characteristic dotted rhythms. There is a continuation of this theme, with a rapid rising and falling shape that is important in its own right. Then the strings burst out with a vigorous fourth element, with firm repeated notes followed by a flourish, a characteristically 'downright' Sibelius theme. This is taken up by the brass, over an insistent offbeat rhythm, and is then repeated and extended to reach a climax.

At this point Sibelius moves into what would, in a conventional symphonic movement, be the development, an extensive passage in which his various thematic elements are explored, juxtaposed, and moved on through new keys. The dotted rhythms of the viola theme are never far away, and its continuation, with its rise and fall, provides much of the material. The range of orchestral effects is very wide. At times the themes jostle together almost like the counterpoint in a symphony by Mozart or Beethoven.

At the centre of the development is a sinister passage in which the strings play pianissimo and *sul ponticello* – that is, bowing close to the bridge to produce an eerie, glassy effect. From this low point the music builds very gradually, arriving at a great *fff* climax. Then, after a long descent to *ppp*, the hypnotic dotted rhythms coalesce into the reprise of the violas' theme, back in its original key (C minor), with fragments of other themes in counterpoint. This is followed by the fourth element, with its insistent repeated notes, now quietly on oboe, again with little fragments of counterpoint decorating it. In contrast to the early part of the piece, where these elements gradually built up, here they become increasingly meditative, ending with a passage of quiet, mournful string chords and distant horn.

After a pause, the oboe and other woodwind enter, the pace increases, and there is a great surge of energy. Into this come the horns, with the chant-like second element. In the complex melée of the full orchestra, this now takes on the character of something in full pursuit (or perhaps being pursued), and there is a gradual build-up to another *fff* climax, the last and greatest climax of the work. Much of this build-up has continued in the home key of C minor. But by the time the climax has arrived, and abruptly collapsed, Sibelius has moved to a remote key, E flat minor, where he remains for the rest of the piece. Quiet, mysterious chords usher in the clarinet, which sings an extended meditation on the chant-like element, accompanied throughout by the strings, and the gentle brush of a cymbal. This is the most overtly bard-like passage in the whole of *En Saga*. The work ends with the cellos reminding us of the viola theme, whose hypnotic dotted rhythms have underpinned so much of the music.

THE SWAN OF TUONELA, OP. 22, NO. 2
Duration: approx. 9 minutes

In 1893, Sibelius began planning an opera on episodes from the *Kalevala*. He called it *The Building of the Boat*. This was to tell the story of the great hero Väinömöinen, who (in Sibelius's version) falls in love with the daughter of the moon as she sits on a bank of cloud weaving. She tells him that she will marry him only if he can turn the splinters from her spindle into a boat by his song. He travels to Tuonela, the land of the dead, to find the three magic words that he needs to accomplish this task.

The ideas of Wagner had inspired Sibelius to attempt to use Finnish mythology as the basis of an opera; but it was partly the experience of Wagner's *Parsifal* and *Tristan* that made him doubt his ability to complete it. After visiting Bayreuth in the summer of 1894, he wrote to his wife, 'I can't begin to tell you how *Parsifal* has transported me. Everything I do seems so cold and feeble by its side.'[9] He soon abandoned his opera, and by the autumn of 1895 was working on *Four Legends* (*Lemminkäinen Suite*). This was similarly inspired by episodes from the *Kalevala*, but now centring on the young hero *Lemminkäinen*. According to Sibelius, it was the overture to *The Building of the Boat* that he adapted to form the most famous of the four movements, 'The Swan of Tuonela', though he was not satisfied until he had twice revised it, publishing the final version in 1901.

Lemminkäinen asks Louhi, the sorceress of Pohjola (the dark Northland), for the hand of her fairest daughter. To win her, Lemminkäinen must travel to Tuonela (the Land of the Dead) and kill with a single shot of his crossbow the sacred swan that swims on the black waters of the river that surrounds Tuonela. But he is himself killed, and his dismembered body is thrown into the river. Lemminkäinen's mother gathers up the pieces of his body, and, with the help of a drop of sacred honey, restores him to life. (These events inspired the third and fourth of the *Legends*, 'Lemminkäinen in Tuonela' and 'Lemminkäinen's Return', as well as the later work, *Pohjola's Daughter*.) A note in the first edition of the score reads, 'Tuonela, the Kingdom of Death, the Hades of Finnish mythology, is surrounded by a broad river of black water and swift current. On it, the Swan of Tuonela glides majestically as it sings.'

The orchestration is unusual. The choice of wind is weighted towards the lower instruments: solo cor anglais, one oboe, one bass clarinet, two bassoons, four horns, three trombones, with harp, timpani, bass drum, and strings. Sibelius uses this orchestra to conjure a wonderful range of sonorities.

The music begins with a chord of A minor, which begins deep in the basses and cellos, and spreads upwards in an overlapping wave through the other strings, each divided in four parts, until it reaches the first violins. Out of this haze of muted strings emerges the solo cor anglais, singing its plaintive song. In its melancholy and almost improvised quality, it evokes memories of the mournful shepherd's pipe at the opening of Act III of Wagner's *Tristan*, which had so impressed Sibelius. But transposed to this dark landscape, the cor anglais takes on a uniquely haunting quality. Its opening phrase does not sound like a beginning – it is as if the singing has been going on for some time, and we have only just become aware of it. Solo cello and viola join with their own lament, in rising arpeggios, and a quiet roll on the bass drum deepens the darkness. The melody of the cor anglais rides not on top of the accompanying chords, but through them, and sometimes below them. At times it seems to fade from sight, almost swamped by the chords, and then re-emerges.

The quietest point is reached, with the cor anglais accompanied by high, tremolando violins. Gradually the music rises to a climax. Here, at the halfway point, the music begins to change. A pizzicato accompaniment starts up, the pace increases a little, and a moment of agitation is reached, with bass clarinet, bassoons, horns, and harp entering. Then sombre repeated chords, with a portentous rhythm, begin in horns, trombones, timpani, and bass drum. The strings take up the lament in unison, forming it into a sonorous, sweeping chant, like a vision of a ghostly funeral procession. As it fades, the cor anglais returns for the last time, against a background of shimmering strings and the continuing sombre rhythm of the drums. Finally, the dark music with which the piece began returns, a solo cello rises, and a chord of A minor remains suspended in the air as it fades away.

Symphonies

SYMPHONY NO. 1 IN E MINOR, OP. 39
Duration: approx. 38 minutes

Andante ma non troppo – Allegro energico
Andante (ma non troppo lento)
Scherzo: Allegro – Lento (ma non troppo) – Tempo 1
Finale (Quasi una Fantasia): Andante – Molto allegro

Sibelius wrote his First Symphony in 1899, and revised it a year later. It was this revised version that Sibelius's friend, the conductor Robert Kajanus, took on a European tour with the Helsinki Philharmonic Orchestra in 1900, when it was well received. It was Sibelius's first attempt since the early *Kullervo* to construct a work on a symphonic scale. In its struggle to build large structures from terse, somewhat 'folk'-inspired material, there is no mistaking the voice of Sibelius, despite some obvious debt to Liszt, Tchaikovsky, and Borodin. Politically, the timing of its appearance was fortunate for Sibelius. Russia was tightening its stranglehold on Finland, and this increased the Finnish public's willingness to see this stormy work as symbolic of their struggle, and Sibelius as a national hero.

Over a quiet timpani roll, a solo clarinet broods, as if improvising. Elements of the melody will be important later on: the opening notes that circle round, and later a succession of leaps upwards. Tremolando strings usher in the Allegro. It begins with a quirky phrase, of three notes ending with a flourish like an ornament on a rustic bagpipe. This passes between the violins, and on to the brass. Its continuation is more sustained, like the opening of the clarinet solo, and this builds up to a climax worthy of Liszt. It evaporates to reveal a complete change of scene: flutes play a spritely dance over harp chords, like elves in a forest glade. After a while, an oboe interrupts with a mournful phrase, returning to the mood of the clarinet solo. But this interruption is brief, and the dancing figure begins to accelerate and gather force. It seems as if it is going to lead to some sustained energy. But instead the music fragments, in a manner characteristic of Sibelius.

We enter the development. Tremolando strings alternate with decisive utterances from woodwind and brass (both these elements derive from the opening clarinet solo). This pattern repeats itself, acquiring a more coherent sense of direction. After a climax, the energy dissipates, leaving a solo violin playing the mournful oboe phrase from earlier. The dancing flute idea is taken up by pizzicato strings, and this too begins to develop momentum. Eventually, the violins find their way back to the more sustained continuation of the original Allegro theme, building up to a full-blown reprise of the first brass climax.

This time, the climax dissolves into poignant harmonies reminiscent of Tchaikovsky in his 'Pathétique' Symphony. The mournful oboe phrase returns, and passes to clarinet, trumpet, and horn. As before, this is followed by the dancing figure, which again gradually accelerates, developing great energy. It reaches a climax at which the brass intone blunt phrases, like pieces of a chorale, which seem to have been stripped down from their earlier climaxes. The end of the movement is particularly quirky: a final burst of string tremolo culminates in a powerfully sustained bass note and timpani roll, and the music is cut off abruptly by two pizzicato chords.

For the opening theme of the slow movement, Sibelius writes the first fully formed melody in the symphony so far. Although it is not overtly like a folk song, it has features that give it a distinct flavour of traditional music. The entire melody is over a sustained bass note, like a drone. Each phrase contains repeated, sighing pairs of notes and the insistent tug of a dotted rhythm, giving the melody the character of a lament. The overall effect is quite Russian, and the rich horn chords that accompany the melody specifically evoke Tchaikovsky. The woodwind increase the pace, and the tension develops to a climax. Then there is a more relaxed middle section, in which horns sing over Wagnerian murmuring strings.

It is the horns that also usher in the reprise of the principal theme. This is sonorously taken up by the violins and cellos, against agitated swirls in the woodwind. This too builds, reaching a fiercer climax than the first time. The pace increases dramatically until it has doubled, the rapid string figurations building up to a storm, into which the brass bring the theme again, at its original pace. The crisis quickly subsides, leaving the strings to bring the melody to a quiet conclusion.

The scherzo is vigorous. It begins with thrummed pizzicato chords, and the first phrase of the tune is punched out by the timpani (perhaps a moment of homage to Beethoven's Ninth). The first part of the scherzo is dominated by the woodwind, at first with a firm attack, and later skittering lightly – Sibelius loved to use his woodwind to create such contrasts. There are playful cross-rhythms, and an almost waltz-like swing develops. The energy of the opening returns, and just as it begins to seem unstoppable there is an abrupt change of gear and mood into the middle section (the 'trio' in a classical scherzo). The horns intervene at a slower pace, much as they did in the middle of the slow movement, and with a similarly shaped melody. The return of the first section culminates in a forceful ending.

The finale begins with a broad, passionate theme on the strings. This is the start of the clarinet meditation with which the symphony opened, now transformed into the grandest of utterances (this transformation is one of the most striking occasions when Sibelius shows his debt to Liszt). After a few bars of musing on this theme, the woodwind introduce a chattering motif. At first tentative, this develops tension and, with the introduction of a snappy dotted rhythm, a fierce energy. An acceleration ends in a sudden rapid descent in the violins, and an abrupt moment of silence.

Out of this comes a heart-easing second theme, which seems to share characteristics with both the opening clarinet solo and the main theme of the slow movement. Gradually the theme winds up to a climax. Then the main motif from the earlier part of the movement is developed, more rapidly and energetically than before, passing from instrument to instrument. It gathers great momentum, eventually harking back to the beginning of the Allegro, and reprising the approach to the lyrical second theme. At first this is played pianissimo and mysteriously on clarinet, but eventually the strings sweep it up, to create a great peroration, and a mighty climax. At this point, still at the grand tempo of the second theme, the main motif of the earlier Allegro is hammered out, and the movement reaches a conclusion with massive wind chords, followed, as if exhausted, by two pizzicato chords from the strings, in an echo of the end of the first movement.

SYMPHONY NO. 2 IN D MAJOR, OP. 43
Duration: approx. 45 minutes

Allegretto
Andante ma rubato
Vivacissimo –
Allegro moderato

Sibelius completed his Second Symphony in 1902, and, as with his First Symphony, revised it after its first performance (which he conducted himself). It cemented his reputation as the first Finnish composer of international stature, and inevitably became closely associated with the continuing struggle to preserve Finnish culture at a time of tightening Russian oppression. The conductor and composer Robert Kajanus made this link clear in an essay at the time of the premiere. In particular, he stated that the effect of the slow movement was 'the most broken-hearted protest against all the injustice that today threatens at the present time to deprive the sun of its light and our flowers of their scent'.[10]

As with all great music, there is danger in taking too simplistic a view of cause and effect. Sibelius declared himself unhappy with the idea that the symphony was symbolic of political struggle, and much later said that it was 'a confession of the soul'.[11] Two of the themes in the slow movement derived from sketches that he jotted down in 1901 in Italy, and which had nothing to do with Finland, the Kalevala, or the Russians. One was inspired by the death of Don Juan, and the other was labelled 'Christus'. There is certainly struggle in this symphony, and the ending is undoubtedly triumphant. But its power resides in the fact that Sibelius cuts a route through struggle to triumph with a lucidity that can be understood by anyone who has experienced and imagined ordinary human life. He does this through a network of terse, potent fragments, which at first seem disconnected, almost lost. But the principal fragments are all related thematically, and in the end everything comes together with an overwhelming sense of unity.

The symphony opens with gently pulsating string chords, in a pattern that rises over three notes of a scale. The oboes and clarinets answer with staccato phrases with a three-note fall. Then the horns enter with a rising three-note pattern. These rising and falling three-note patterns are the seeds from which the symphony is built. Soon there is a powerful recitative on the violins. Then, after more exchanges between woodwind and strings, there is a passage of pizzicato that accelerates. At the end of this, the pulsating opening figure returns, but with a new, forceful element in the woodwind over it – a long note, a rapid alternation like a trill, and a fall. The tension builds up to a reiteration of this new element, and the pulsating strings bring the first section of the movement to a close, with yet another terse counterpoint in the woodwind over it. The sense of the first section coming to an end is absolutely clear. And, despite the highly personal musical language, Sibelius's key structure in the movement is traditional. He began the movement in D major, and has now reached A major, just as you would expect in a symphony by Mozart (a composer Sibelius greatly admired).

The development begins with the oboe, in a new key, reiterating the long note-trill-fall element. The bassoon extends it with the rising three-note shape, while the three-note pattern also forms a quietly agitated accompaniment in the strings. These elements combine, build up, and subside. The clarinet quietly reiterates the long note-trill-fall, and this sets off a passage in which the different elements engage in terse counterpoint, gradually increasing in tension.

The violin line becomes more insistent, and begins to coalesce into a powerful melody. It reaches a climax with the long note-trill element, in which the final fall of the phrase is now widened to an enormous drop. This provokes the brass to a powerful intervention, which builds to a mighty climax. The sense of culmination is achieved by the spacious rhythms and sonorous scoring, more than by sheer volume. Again, Sibelius arrives at a clear landmark, with the oboes reprising the music with which they began the symphony, back in the home key of D major. And, in Mozartian fashion, Sibelius abbreviates the rest of the reprise, concentrating on the main elements, and ending with a simple reiteration of the pulsating strings with which the movement opened.

The slow movement begins with mysterious pizzicato passing between basses and cellos. Bassoons intone a chant-like melody (this is the theme associated in a sketch with the death of Don Juan). The chant begins with a rising scale, and the oboes answer with a falling scale, a pattern that echoes the opening of the first movement. The pace increases, urged on by horn calls and a new, agitated figure in the strings. This builds rapidly to a climax, with phrases abruptly alternating between strings and woodwind, like chunks of rock being hurled. It finally reaches the brass, still in savagely broken fragments, and the climax subsides. What follows is like a healing chorale, very quiet on the strings, and in a key (F sharp major) utterly remote from the key in which the movement started (D minor). This is the theme that origi-nated in the 'Christus' sketch. But it is also a slowed-down version of the agitated string figure that built to the preceding climax. It too seems to be moving toward a climax, but eventually it peters out. Solo trumpet and flute reprise the opening bassoon chorale (though not yet in the home key). As before, it develops urgency, taking longer than before to fight its way to another brass climax. This time, the silences between the fragmentary brass phrases are filled with woodwind chords, with oboes and clarinets low and snarling – a wonderful effect.

After a pause, the woodwind and lower strings take up the 'Christus' chorale, now sounding more ominous than consoling. There is further development, and another petering out. The end of the movement, far from reaching resolution, becomes incoherent. Shreds of the themes are interrupted by wildly agitated woodwind and strings, and eventually a brass chord of D minor, and pizzicato strings, bring the movement to an abrupt end.

The scherzo is very rapid, with extreme contrasts between forte and pianissimo phrases. Over the agitated strings the woodwind introduce a second idea, a new variant of the three-note rising shape. This highly volatile music eventually subsides, and reaches a pause. The middle section ('trio' in a conventional scherzo) is a complete contrast. Over quiet chords of horns and bassoons, an oboe sings a plaintive recitative. With its insistently repeated notes and its rising scale patterns, it echoes the very opening of the symphony. The phrases are repeated and developed with touching simplicity, until, with sudden force, the brass and timpani hammer out the rhythm of the scherzo, and the reprise is under way.

In the middle of this reprise, the horns briefly intone another chorale-like phrase. The moment is soon gone, but it is a portent of what is to come. This time, the scherzo does not reach a pause, but suddenly gives way to sustained chords, over which the oboe again takes up its mournful recitative. In the middle of this, an unexpected chord signals a sudden change of direction, and the strings begin another agitated figure with an offbeat pattern. We are being pulled towards something unknown, and in the middle of the texture there seems to be a new theme trying to get out (this is what the horns were hinting at in the middle of the final scherzo section). It gradually coalesces into a more coherent pattern as the music builds, and the pace steadies.

Without any change of gear, we arrive at the finale, as if emerging from a river into the open sea. But, this being Sibelius, the great melody that emerges majestically is not an easily flowing tune. It is built, once again, of fragments, passing from strings to brass. Underneath it, propelling the ship forward, trombones, tuba, and timpani keep up a relentless rhythm. The melody itself, inevitably, begins with the three-note rising phrase that has been the central motif of the symphony.

This movement has a strikingly simple structure, in which the grand melody alternates with sections that have a more brooding character. The melody comes to the end of its first statement, and there is a continuation that, after some passionate development, settles to a quiet, continuous muttering in the violas and cellos. Over this, phrases with an insistent rhythm are repeated again and again in the woodwind. They have a spirit of incantation that, for the first time in this symphony, evokes memories of the *Kalevala*. This culminates in a forceful call on trumpets and trombones, which quickly evaporates to a dreamy passage in which phrases of the incantation alternate with phrases of the first theme.

From this low point, the tempo very slowly increases, the first few notes of the first melody gradually develop a head of steam, and are combined with reiterations of the trumpet call. The music builds up and, as in the first entry into the finale, culminates in the grand, frag-mented melody of the first theme. It proceeds unstoppably as before, until, as it reaches its last note, there is a sudden lurch of harmony, propelling the music on to the most passionate part of its continuation.

As before, this settles to the muttering violas and cellos, and the hypnotically repetitive incantation in the woodwind. This time, the repetitions go on and on, building relentlessly as instruments join in. Eventually this culminates in the trombone and trumpet call, as before.

But now it does not fade away, but is carried over a sea of rapid string tremolo into a final peroration of the first theme. This is now transformed into a triumphant conclusion, and, for the first time in the symphony, all the fragments are allowed to find a coherent resolution.

SYMPHONY NO. 3 IN C MAJOR, OP. 52
Duration: approx. 30 minutes

Allegro moderato
Andantino con moto, quasi allegretto
Moderato – Allegro ma non tanto

Sibelius completed his Third Symphony in 1907, and dedicated it to the composer Granville Bantock, who was championing Sibelius's music in Britain. It caused some puzzlement at its early performances. It does not wear its heart on its sleeve as much as the first two symphonies. It is shorter and more condensed in its structures, leading many writers to describe it more 'classical' in style than Nos 1 and 2. Sibelius himself acknowledged his debt to classical composers, and his intention of forging a coherent method of creating structures in the tradition of Mozart, Haydn, and Beethoven. It was shortly after he had finished this symphony that Sibelius met Mahler in Helsinki, and discussed the symphony as a genre. According to Sibelius's recollection, he said to Mahler that he admired the symphony for its 'severity of style and the profound logic that created an inner connection between all the motifs'. Mahler (who knew little of Sibelius's music) famously replied, 'No! A symphony must be like the world. It must embrace everything.'[12]

The third (rivalled only by the sixth) is the least performed of Sibelius's symphonies. Sibelius's harmonic language is becoming more wayward, and his characteristic fragmentation of ideas makes large swathes of the symphony elusive until you get to know it – and even then, you have to accept that elusiveness is part of the point. It is also very difficult to play. Symphonies Nos 1 and 2 can be managed triumphantly by a good amateur orchestra. No. 3, particularly the finale, requires an orchestra of virtuosi in order to sound coherent. For these reasons, it has tended not just to be underplayed, but also underrated.

The symphony begins with absolute directness. Cellos and basses play a quiet, rhythmically repetitive tune in C major that, like traditional Finnish melodies, circles round just a few notes. It seems as if we can expect music firmly rooted in simple folk-like material. At first, Sibelius does indeed elaborate this idea, building it up over a persistent bass note of C, like a drone (one of Sibelius's favourite devices). This development of folk-like material is something that Sibelius does share with Mahler: there are moments where this music is reminiscent of the first of Mahler's *Lieder eines fahrenden Gesellen* (*Songs of a Wayfarer*), which Mahler quotes in his First Symphony.

Other ideas are thrown in, adding to the feeling of music of outdoor energy. There are strange notes and harmonies along the way: in particular, the frequent occurrence of F sharp in the melody gives it a flavour of the Lydian mode, and perhaps even a somewhat oriental tinge. None of this impedes the rapid build-up to a climax, still in C major. But just as the trumpets and trombones blaze their last note, the woodwind contradict them with a pungent F sharp, and the music abruptly changes key and mood.

The cellos sing a theme in B minor which, like the opening theme, circles around a few notes, but now smoothed out and sounding more like a lament (Sibelius once described

Finnish traditional music as possessing 'sonorous, strangely melancholic monotony').[13] This breaks up into chattering semiquavers derived from the continuation of the first theme, which move through different keys. More lamenting phrases emerge, on violins, and the music reaches a quiet passage of string chords. At first this seems to be in G major (as in a Mozart or Haydn symphony at this point). But the harmonies become strange and bare, with little reiterations of previous ideas on violins and flute. From the confident, no-nonsense, start, the music seems to have lost its way.

Eventually some energy is regained, and the chattering semiquavers quietly resume. This is the beginning of a long development, in which fragments of the first theme pass from instrument to instrument against a background of pattering semiquavers, with passages of counterpoint in the woodwind. There is the atmosphere of a restless search. The cello lament is taken up by bassoon, clarinet, and oboe in turn. The semiquavers, which have never ceased, begin to reassert themselves, and the fragments of the first theme come together as the bass moves back to C major, and a sturdy, optimistic reprise is under way.

As before, it builds to a brass climax in C major. This time it is not punctured by a change of harmony. The harmony does indeed shift, but in such a way as to heighten the tension. What was a cello lament becomes a forthright outpouring, with violins, violas, and cellos together in unison. As before, it breaks into chattering semiquavers, but maintaining power for longer before it recedes. A mysterious passage of pizzicato ends with a quiet, questioning chord. A woodwind chorus sings a forthright, hymn-like melody, derived from the lament. And this, passing to horns, and then to strings, and alternating with bursts of the opening theme, brings the movement to an end. The ending is neither climactic nor quietly resolving, but somewhat enigmatic and provisional – an ambiguity that was becoming typical of Sibelius.

Following the resounding final C major chord of the first movement, the slow movement is in a remote key, G sharp minor, and is not very slow. It opens with the flutes playing a mournfully swinging tune that, once again, shares something with Mahler's approach to folk-inspired melodies (specifically, the last of his *Lieder eines fahrenden Gesellen* – though the orchestral version was not yet published). The ebb and flow, up and down, of the melody, and the hypnotic repetition of its rhythms, have much in common with the two main themes of the first movement. This melody haunts the entire movement, but is interrupted twice. The first interruption is a hymn-like passage, beginning quietly in the strings then continuing strongly in the woodwind. It originated a year earlier, as an idea that Sibelius called a 'Prayer to God'. But it is also reminiscent of the hymn-like melody at the end of the first movement (which in turn derives from the earlier cello lament).

When the first theme returns, it is accompanied by busier, more anxious pizzicato and an ominous bass line. Eventually the pizzicato accelerates, leading to a second interruption. Here, swirls of woodwind end with pauses on questioning chords. After a while, the original tempo is restored, and the main theme returns in the violins, with wistful counterpoints in the woodwind. The movement ends with a reminiscence of the hymn-like interruption.

It might seem that there is no scherzo in this symphony, but the third movement combines a scherzo-like first half with a grand finale-like second half (Sibelius had already joined the scherzo to the finale in the Second Symphony). Sibelius described this finale as 'the crystallisation of ideas from chaos'.[14]

The opening could certainly be described as chaotic, as hesitant swirls of melody and brief glimpses of earlier themes pass rapidly by. Soon the music settles into a fast scherzo tempo and rhythm. This is rather like a swung (6/8) version of the chattering semiquavers from the first movement, and some of the striking harmonies are also familiar from there, particularly the Lydian/oriental F sharp intruding on C major. The music develops unstoppable energy, with endlessly repeated figurations building up great momentum.

There are hints of a chorale in the horns. Eventually this emerges from the middle of the strings, and takes over the rest of the movement, a statement of absolute determination and solidity. Rhythmically, it is doggedly repetitive, the logical outcome of the sturdy theme with which the symphony began. The rolling out of its mighty rhythm once again inevitably suggests the inspiration of the *Kalevala*, and it is also reminiscent of the hymn in Sibelius's *Finlandia*. Like so many of the principal themes in the symphony, it circles around a small range of notes, and it features the frequent recurrence of the 'foreign' F sharp. This has a striking effect, as if it is constantly trying to drag the harmonies off course, but is always being thwarted. The power and energy build steadily. The ending is magnificent but without bombast. Sibelius simply reaches a final blazing chord of C major and stops, there being nothing more to say.

SYMPHONY NO. 4 IN A MINOR, OP. 63

Duration: approx. 38 minutes

Tempo molto moderato, quasi adagio
Allegro molto vivace
Il tempo largo
Allegro

Sibelius completed this symphony in 1911. In the four years since the Third Symphony, he had travelled and had become acquainted with the latest developments in music. Britain, however, was the only country in the rest of Europe where he had developed a following. Elsewhere, and particularly in the musical heartlands of Germany and Austria, he found himself isolated, misunderstood, and regarded as an old-fashioned nationalist composer with little to contribute to the rising flood of modernism. In return, Sibelius cultivated his own sense of isolation, distancing himself from the music of Debussy, Richard Strauss, and Stravinsky. It was at the height of this crisis that he wrote the Fourth Symphony, which he said 'stands as a protest against present-day music. It has nothing, absolutely nothing of the circus about it.'[15]

The Fourth Symphony is the work of a man who realizes that he must set out on his path alone, with no one by his side. As well as his feelings of artistic isolation, Sibelius had serious personal problems. He drank heavily, was in serious debt, and had endured operations on a throat tumour (which forced him to abstain from alcohol for several years). The symphony that he wrote in these circumstances is bleak, uncompromising, and strange. But, once one gets to know it, it is compelling and powerful, and gradually reveals itself as one of the most touchingly personal works that Sibelius ever wrote.

At the heart of its strangeness is a musical interval, the tritone. Already in the Third Symphony this interval (C to F sharp) had featured as a somewhat 'oriental' colouring of melodies, derived from the Lydian mode. Here in the Fourth Symphony, right from the opening bars, it becomes one of its basic harmonies, haunting the entire work with an atmosphere of foreboding. (Five years later, Holst was to use the tritone in a similar, and more explicit, way in 'Saturn, the bringer of old age'.) The symphony begins, unusually, with a slow movement. Low bassoons, cellos, and basses begin fortissimo, with a low C over which two notes (E and F sharp) alternate in a slowly rocking figure. Over this, a solo cello begins a lament. Gradually, cellos, violas, and violins join in (all muted), and the music builds up to a climax at which the harmonies, already uneasy, are punctured by cruel dissonances. There are menacing phrases from the brass, desperate leaps upwards in the violins, after which, for the first time in the movement, the music settles on a harmonious chord of B major, with quiet horn calls. But this is a fleeting moment of peace.

There is a solemn fanfare on the brass that could almost have stepped out of Wagner's *Parsifal*, and the lamenting phrases resume. After a time, a plaintive, simplified version of this theme is played by the oboe, then clarinet, then violins, over a sparse accompaniment. This develops into a continuous, unaccompanied melody, beginning on solo cello, and moving up to high, fortissimo violins. The melody is continually shifting from key to key, never settling, as if the spirit of the strange tritone is pursuing it. The rhythm is consistently off the beat, though this is only noticeable where it occasionally brushes against phrases that are on the beat, creating moments of disorientation.

A variant of this line starts up in counterpoint in the cellos, with 'scrubbed' tremolo and a triplet rhythm, causing even more sense of disquiet. This too gradually invades the upper strings and builds up. A more elaborate variant of the lamenting theme is played against this by the woodwind, with an ominous version of it in the lower strings.

Finally we arrive at a climax, at which the brass reprise their menacing phrases, and there is one desperate leap upwards in the violins. Then the music, as before, settles just for a moment, with quiet horn calls, this time to a chord of A major. The Wagnerian brass fanfare follows, and the lamenting phrases resume. Once again they are distilled into the bleak calls of oboe and clarinet, over the distant thunder of timpani. The movement ends with this phrase rising in the strings, but now warped to include the strange interval of the tritone with which the movement began. Finally, this resolves uncertainly onto a quiet, high A.

Having started with a slow movement, Sibelius places a scherzo second. It retains some elements of a traditional scherzo – a fast three-time, and a principal theme that returns later – but there is no sense of certainty about the direction in which the music is heading at any moment. It sounds almost carefree at first. Over a rippling accompaniment, an oboe plays a supple line, which incorporates some of the melodic shapes from the first movement. The tritone appears, but fleetingly, and without disrupting the mood.

When the violins take over the melody, the easy-going atmosphere begins to colour with anxiety. The theme fragments into a series of leaping tritones, shared between oboe and violins. The original mood is briefly restored, and then the metre changes from three-time to two-time, and the violins begin a tiptoeing dance. This too soon darkens, the harmonies become sour, timpani and a low bassoon threaten. The passage culminates in ominous brass chords reminiscent of the climaxes in the first movement. Then the strange leaping tritones return in the lower strings.

Eventually, there is a brief return of the easy-going theme. This time it is interrupted by delicate flutes, which might have wandered in from Mendelssohn's *A Midsummer Night's Dream*. This onset of charm lasts for a few bars, and leads to a return of the opening theme and its continuation. Another moment of uncertainty culminates in a passage in which the tempo is halved. Oboe and clarinets intone a falling phrase (derived from part of the original theme), and the strings respond with a pungent falling tritone. The texture of the music becomes complex, with a persistent trill in the violins, snarls from muted horns, low bassoons, and then a shuddering bass that gradually moves upwards. This brooding passage reaches a climax. Where can it be heading? The answer is: nowhere. The music suddenly evaporates, and with three taps on the timpani, the movement is over.

The slow movement returns to the mood of the first movement, now intensified, as if set in a bleak, deeply frozen landscape. Over sombre, low chords, flutes play mournful phrases related to the cello lament with which the symphony began. The very first phrase curls around to outline the mysterious tritone again. This expands upwards in the flute, while bass and cello play the lament in counterpoint below. Four horns play a fragment of a chorale, and the cellos strive upwards. The music proceeds haltingly, rising hopefully, falling down, struggling through dissonances, as if in an anguished search. This culminates in a passage of high wood-wind above a quietly held chord.

The mood lightens a little. Mysterious string tremolo begins, and below it the cello line rises higher than before. From this point on, the music moves forward in a series of waves, slowly rising and falling. The upward, striving theme has no sooner begun to establish itself than the lamenting phrases freeze the atmosphere again. But eventually the struggle results in two climaxes. At the second of these, the harmonies clear, the brass blaze, and we are allowed to glimpse, just for a moment, a vision of how things might be, or perhaps how they once were.

Again, the progress of the movement to this point brings to mind Wagner's *Parsifal*, and its anguished striving for redemption. As a young man, Sibelius had been deeply moved by a performance of *Parsifal* at Bayreuth. And although he was by now well past the direct influence of Wagner, something of that experience seems to have surfaced in this movement, not just in its mood, but in its melodies and chords. The movement does not end in consolation or redemption. The moment is gone, the frozen darkness returns, and it ends with the same mournful phrases with which it began. The very last phrase, just like the first, outlines the mysterious tritone that has dominated the symphony.

The finale begins with a theme that immediately returns us to the volatile mood of the scherzo. The rising and falling melody does not seem to know where it is going, never settling, with little stabbing accents, sudden drops, clashing of harmonies, stops and starts. Many of its details can be traced to earlier themes, but the overall impression is of nervous energy and uncertainty. The bright tinkling of a glockenspiel does nothing to ease the tension. A solo viola starts a second idea, rapidly muttering away at a tune that circles around a few notes. This is taken up by the violins, and joined to elements from the first theme, becoming more forceful, with larger leaps. The muttering returns to the strings, developing into a quiet, persistent pattern. There are haunting woodwind calls (the haunting quality is caused by, once again, the interval of a tritone in relation to the bass). The clarinet plays a defiantly flamboyant flourish. The mood is heightened anxiety, like a room full of people waiting for a bomb to fall.

Suddenly all this hyperactivity stops, giving way to a gently rocking figure in the strings, with phrases of a mournful chorale in woodwind and horns. The chorale moves to the strings, which maintain it quietly and hypnotically, eventually arriving at a mysterious passage with menacing wind chords and rushing scales in the strings. This dissipates into pizzicato, over which fragments of the chorale in the oboe are answered by the horns. Once again the persistence becomes hypnotic, gradually building up.

Suddenly, without realizing it, we are into a reprise, with the flamboyant clarinet flourish, the quiet muttering figure, the haunting woodwind calls. This time, all the hyperactivity becomes more violent, eventually building painfully to a massive climax, but not the sort of climax that brings any sense of resolution. Instead, out of the climax the strings emerge with a syncopated, descending figure from the chorale-like passage, followed by a fierce falling figure in the brass, and the haunting calls in the woodwind. The music seems transfixed by this melancholy combination of elements, which carries through to the end of the movement. At the very end, the haunting phrase high in the flute, the falling phrase in the oboe, and the descending figure in the strings, evoke a landscape of utter bleakness, particularly so if one feels it as a landscape of the mind.

The symphony does manage to end with chords of the home key, A minor. But they are neither firmly resolving nor mysteriously vanishing. The marking is *mf*, neither loud nor soft. We are here, there is no way up or down, there is nothing to do but stop.

SYMPHONY NO. 5 IN E FLAT MAJOR, OP. 82

Duration: approx. 32 minutes

Tempo molto moderato – Allegro moderato (ma poco a poco stretto)
Andante mosso, quasi allegretto
Allegro molto

The origins of this symphony demonstrate the status that Sibelius had achieved in Finland. Sibelius's fiftieth birthday fell on 8 December 1915, and in honour of the occasion the Finnish government commissioned a symphony from him, and declared a national holiday. Sibelius himself conducted the premiere on the day, but then twice revised the work. It is the final version of 1919 that is usually performed, though the original version has been revived in recent years. The differences between the two versions are very striking. The symphony was originally in four separate movements. But in the revision, Sibelius joined the first two together, creating a wonderfully satisfying journey through to a triumphant conclusion. He also emphasized this celebratory outcome by altering the harmonies in some passages, making them less astringent, more straightforwardly concordant. It is the familiar revised version that is described in the notes that follow.

The symphony opens with a horn call that rises and falls. This sets an atmosphere that dominates the whole symphony – open-air, evocative of looking up into the distance. Flutes, oboes, and clarinets answer with musings on this call, sharpening the rhythm of its ascent, adding a decorative curl as it falls. This mutates into a new element, in which this curling becomes a continuous flow. The strings enter with a sudden shudder, the woodwind continue above, with simplified elements of the call. From time to time there is a quiet timpani roll, like distant thunder. With a sudden crescendo, the strings urge the wind on to a brief climax.

As it subsides, a trumpet, echoed by flute, plays the horn call, reduced to a simple fanfare. There is a change of key, and the main elements are revisited. This time, as the woodwind finish their continuously curling melody, over the quietly shuddering strings, flutes and bassoons give a more ominous twist to a phrase that passed almost unnoticed the first time, extending it into a shape that slides chromatically, curling around on itself like the earlier element. This is to become important later on. As before, there is a build-up, more energetic than before, to another climax.

As the climax dies away, instead of the trumpet call, this time horns play the ominous sliding chromatic line that flutes and bassoons introduced earlier. This is taken up quietly by the strings, which work away at it anxiously. It gradually metamorphoses, first with a gently syncopated rhythm, then breaking into a continuous, agitated pattern. Over it, a bassoon (at first with clarinet in unison) intones mournful fragments of the same chromatic element. This too becomes continuous, gradually rising, like a lone figure emerging out of the mist. There is a strange wind chord, and the strings enter boldly, combining elements of the horn call with the sliding chromatic shape. They are twice interrupted by savage trills in woodwind and horns. Gradually this builds up to a grand climax, at which the trumpets reprise the original horn call.

It was at this point that the original first movement of the symphony wound to a rather perfunctory conclusion, and was followed by a separate scherzo. In his masterly revision, Sibelius instead creates a seamless link from this climax to a scherzo-like section in a dancing three-time. There is no new thematic material. Sibelius simply takes the familiar elements that he has presented so far, and transforms them yet again. The almost waltz-like beginning of this section is based on the horn call, and this is immediately developed over the first few pages by strings and woodwind, until a trumpet sounds a new, extended version of the horn call. The rest of the movement is built from this, together with other familiar elements, building energy that becomes unstoppable, and reaching a blazing conclusion.

The marking at the beginning of this section is Allegro moderato (ma poco a poco stretto). Sibelius means by this that the pace should be gradually increased over the whole of the rest of the movement. He provides markers along the way: Vivace molto, then Presto, and Più presto. This takes place over four or five minutes, and metronome markings that Sibelius later published (but are not printed in the score) make it clear he wanted an even acceleration over the whole of the passage, to a frenetic ending that hurls itself against the final chord. Not all conductors have understood this, and many performances are far more restrained in acceleration than Sibelius intended. One of the greatest accelerations is in the first recording, conducted by Sibelius's friend Robert Kajanus in 1932, though even he does not go quite to the extremes that Sibelius suggests.[16]

The slow movement is a set of variations, though with a loose, improvisational character as if Sibelius wishes to evoke something of the traditional Karelian rune-singer. It begins with hymn-like chords in the woodwind, which prove to be an important element throughout the movement. The theme tiptoes on pizzicato strings alternating with flutes. The melody curls repetitively round and round, referring back to elements of the first movement, but also resembling many of Sibelius's melodies inspired by Karelian traditional music. The strings break into a faster pattern, which then combines with the pizzicato. For a moment a lyrical melody tries to emerge, before the earlier pattern resumes.

The music accelerates, with rasping horns, to a change of key. The tempo eases for another moment of broad melody, grander than before. But this too soon reverts to pizzicato, accompanied by a chaste series of chords in the flutes. The music returns to the original key. Again there is a gradual acceleration, another pull back, and a gentle halt. Then the pizzicato turns menacing, and the pastoral mood is threatened by brass chords. The moment soon passes, the pizzicato and the tripping woodwind return, but with touches of thunder in the timpani and shuddering tremolo in the strings. The oboes pause in melancholy reflection. For a third and final time, the theme broadens into a singing melody in the strings over sonorous brass chords. But once again it proves impossible to sustain. The woodwind complete the tune, and suddenly the movement is over.

The finale begins in an atmosphere of excited anticipation. More shimmering tremolo introduces the theme, at first in the violas, then moving to the violins. This is another version of the 'curling' element from the earlier movements, and it takes on the character of a perpetuum mobile, with the woodwind joining in. This gives way to pairs of horns, playing a repeating pattern that seems like a distillation of the horn call with which the symphony began. This ostinato will come to dominate the movement, and we know from Sibelius's diary what inspired the idea. At his home in the forests, on 21 April 1915, he wrote, 'Today at ten to eleven I saw 16 swans. One of my greatest experiences! Lord God, that beauty! They circled over me for a long time. Disappeared into the solar haze like a gleaming, silver ribbon.' And three days later: 'The swans are always in my thoughts and give splendour to [my] life. [It's] strange to learn that nothing in the whole world affects me – nothing in art, literature or music – in the same way as do these swans and cranes and wild geese. Their voices and being.'[17] Over this horn ostinato, the woodwind intone the curling motif, now expanded into a chant-like melody (a hymn to nature, perhaps). As the horns continue, the trombones fill out the chords, creating a texture of the utmost grandeur.

The vision evaporates, and the woodwind resume the chattering opening theme. This is passed through different keys and elaborated until it moves to the strings, with shimmering tremolo as at the opening, but now muted and *ppp*. Out of this mysterious texture the horn ostinato is quietly heard, followed by the woodwind curling melody. The shimmering tremolo settles into a calmer pattern. The pace eases, and, against the pattern of the horn ostinato in the woodwind, the strings take up the curling melody, now expanded further into a lyrical outpouring – the first time in the entire symphony that a melody has been allowed to do this. As this melody arrives back in the home key, the trumpets enter with the horn ostinato, now at a broader tempo, and marked 'nobile'. This is the beginning of the final peroration. But it is not to be accomplished easily. As the hypnotic ostinato continues and builds up, the harmonies turn dark and then tortured. It takes an enormous wrench to pull the music back to safety, before it is able to proceed to its home.

The final page consists of a series of isolated chords, with long gaps between them, before the final cadence is reached. In the original version of the symphony, these chords were accompanied by continuous tremolando strings and rolling timpani. The isolated chords of the revision are much starker, and much more difficult to perform convincingly. In a dry concert hall, and at too slow a tempo, it often seems like a mistake. Sibelius's instruction is to speed up the approach to these bars, delivering each chord *fff* – and some reverberation helps.

SYMPHONY NO. 6, OP. 104
Duration: approx. 27 minutes

Allegro molto moderato
Allegretto moderato
Poco vivace
Allegro molto

This symphony is one of those works that demonstrate how unreliable it is to draw analogies between music and life, and between the character of a composer and the music. After the success of the Fifth Symphony, and following a seven-year period of abstinence, Sibelius had taken to drink again. By November 1923, he had reached the point of writing in his diary, 'Alcohol, which I gave up, is now my most faithful companion. And the most understanding! Everything and everyone else has largely failed me.'[18] And yet the Sixth Symphony, which he first conducted in Helsinki in February 1923, contains some of the most serene music that he ever wrote. He once said that it 'always makes me remember the scent of the first snow', though he also said, 'Rage and passion ... are utterly essential in it, but it is supported by undercur-rents deep under the surface of the music.'[19] Some of the ideas that found their way into this symphony began life a few years earlier in a symphonic poem inspired by the Moon Goddess, which Sibelius never completed. The Sixth Symphony certainly does not sound like the work of a man going downhill towards the premature end of his composing life.

This symphony is often described as being 'in D minor', though Sibelius did not state a key on the score. It would be truer to say that it drifts between C major and D minor, tending to settle on the latter. As it drifts, Sibelius often introduces the note B natural into the scale and harmonies of D minor. This gives the music an evocatively 'ancient' or 'rural' feeling, because this scale is the Dorian mode, which is found in many folk tunes and chants. The effect is particularly striking as the symphony opens, with a chorus of strings playing slow-moving independent lines that float serenely. Many writers have suggested that these weaving lines specifically evoke the choral polyphony of Palestrina, though Sibelius refused to be drawn about such an association. This passage is dominated by gently falling lines. When the oboes enter, it is with a rising line, followed by the flutes with a new falling shape. These are the three main motifs that Sibelius uses to build his symphony. The web of string chords rises to a high climax. Below it enter the brass. The two chords clash for a moment, until the strings stop, to reveal a calm chord of C major.

At this point the music changes gear: there is no change of tempo, but the bars subdivide into faster notes. The mood lightens, harp and strings set up a gentle rhythm, over which flutes and oboes play a new, playful phrase. This is answered by a dancing variant of the descending line from the opening of the movement. A jogging, rather pastoral section gets under way. There are hints of a lyrical melody in the violins (the rising line), then further pastoral exchanges with the woodwind. Eventually, the music builds up to a new surge of energy, though with the jogging rhythm persisting below.

Another rising string climax leads to a collapse of this easy-going mood, and a threatening crescendo and a strike of the timpani bring the music to a stop. The rising line tries to get going again. There is another climax, this time to a sonorous chord of C major. But the strings return to the modal, 'sort of' D minor, and the movement ends in a mood of uncertainty.

The second movement is the slowest of the four, though not very slow, and, again, is vola-tile and ambivalent in mood. It opens with a succession of strange chords on oboes and bassoons. These are joined by little fragments of melody in the violins, which relate to one of the falling elements from the first movement. Then rising scales begin to release the spell of the strange chords, though they soon return. The rising shape returns to the strings, quietly at first, but soon building up to a typically threatening entry of the brass.

Again the mood lightens a little. The violins develop their melodic fragments, but soon these too falter, giving way to more rising lines in the woodwind, and another build-up. Once more this breaks off, leaving the strings quietly muttering a pattern based on the strange chords with which the movement began. The woodwind join in with almost playful phrases (like their first playful intervention in the first movement). This is just beginning to develop momentum, when it comes to a halt. The movement ends with rising woodwind phrases, and a final cadence in the strings that gives a further reminiscence of the modal harmonies from the first movement.

The third movement is like Sibelius's take on a Mendelssohn scherzo. It opens as a fairy march, with sharp dotted rhythms. Flurries of notes introduce a more dancing mood, but soon the dotted rhythms are back, keeping up a determined tread as other melodic fragments pass by. There is a build-up, and a savagely discordant intervention from the brass. But the scurrying dance and the dotted rhythms are soon restored, leading to another build-up, another savage discord. This time the savagery continues, as if ogres have taken over the stage. In this aggressive mood the movement comes abruptly to an end.

The finale, like the first movement, seems to hark back to the Renaissance. The opening has something of the formality of a courtly dance, with high and low answering each other, like consorts of instruments in opposite galleries. The high phrases fall, the low phrases rise, in an echo of the opening of the first movement. A timpani roll signals that this antique reminiscence cannot last, and the formal dance begins to unravel. The music breaks into a more agitated dancing figure. This soon develops urgency, with sudden crescendos, and snarls from the brass. At one point the whole thing seems likely to fall into chaos. But it manages to keep going, the harmonies becoming more astringent, the punching of the brass and timpani more intrusive, until there is a mighty crescendo, and the dance is over.

Out of it the strings emerge, trying to recapture the spirit of the opening courtly dance. But there remains an element of agitation, and even the woodwind have difficulty maintaining their poise. The situation resolves itself with an acceleration to a faster dancing rhythm that develops momentum. Soon this settles, and the strings play a chorale that seems like a simple reminiscence of the music with which they began the symphony. The woodwind answer, the chorale rises higher. The symphony ends with a simple falling phrase, and a sustained, quiet chord of D minor.

SYMPHONY NO. 7, OP. 105

Duration: 21–26 minutes

Adagio – (Poco a poco affretando il tempo al) Vivacissimo – (rallentando al) Adagio – (Poco a poco meno lento al) Allegro molto moderato – (Poco a poco rallentando al) Adagio

Ideas for Sibelius's last major works – the Symphonies Nos 6 and 7, and *Tapiola* – extend over several years. Just as the works themselves in performance seem to evolve like organic structures, the way that Sibelius composed them was a process of evolution. Themes that found their way into the Seventh Symphony can be found in earlier sketches for his fifth. Sibelius completed No. 7 only a year after No. 6. When it was first premiered in March 1924, he described it as a 'Symphonic Fantasia', only afterwards deciding to label it as Symphony No. 7. This is the culmination of everything that Sibelius had been working towards in his earlier symphonies. It is cast in a single, continuous movement. The list given above does not include all tempo instructions, but it outlines the tempi of the basic structure, which is as follows.

There is an Adagio introduction that culminates in a noble trombone call. The tempo increases, the mood lightens to an almost scherzo-like section (Vivacissimo). The tempo slows to a reprise of the Adagio trombone call (this occurs exactly at the halfway point of the symphony). Again the tempo increases and the mood lightens (Allegro molto moderato), becoming more and more frenetic. Finally, the tempo slows to the grandest of reprises of the trombone call. The whole work is like an enormous double arch, with the trombone call forming the three pillars. Sibelius himself acknowledged that the grandeur of ancient Greece informed the spirit of the symphony, saying that 'The trombones are handled like the musical instruments of antiquity.'[20]

Despite this sense of architectural grandeur, there is nothing rigid or clear-cut about the symphony, either as a whole or in detail. The music develops organically through the metamorphosis of little motifs, and the effect is extremely fluid. We get this sense from the very opening bars. The strings trudge slowly up a scale, with the basses half a beat behind everyone else, as if they are being pulled reluctantly. This simple scale culminates in a poignant chord, and a series of discords that have difficulty resolving (the spirit of Wagner's *Tristan* seems to be lurking behind these opening bars). Fragments of themes emerge: an undulating figure in flutes and clarinets, sighing phrases in oboes and clarinets, a falling scale in the woodwind answered by a rising line in the strings, an up-and-down shape in the woodwind. They seem like simple ideas passing by, but most of what happens later in the symphony can be related to them. These restless events fall silent, and the strings begin a chorale-like passage reminiscent of the opening of the Sixth Symphony, and similarly evoking a sense of ancient choral music. It builds slowly, and leads to the majestic entry of the trombone call, a glorious affirmation of C major, the key on which the symphony is based.

The falling away from the climax is sombre, with woodwind intoning falling lines over shuddering strings. Eventually, the mood lightens, the falling lines give way to rising and curling lines, and the pace gradually increases. A crisis is reached, but the gentler mood is re-established. This time, the gradual acceleration continues (affretando means 'speeding up'), reaching a frantic pace (Vivacissimo) like a rather desperate dance. Suddenly the rhythm smooths out, and the dance retreats to a sombre, swirling figure. Over this, the trombones take up their call again, echoed by trumpets and horns, as if we are surrounded by them in a great colosseum. This is not just a reprise of the trombone call. The key has darkened from the glorious C major of the first call to C minor, with the sombre swirling of the strings continuing below. The fanfares continue longer than before, building up a sense of dark powers, with the tortured harmonies from the opening of the symphony becoming menacing. This reaches a climax, the strings tear themselves back to the frantic energy that had brought them to this point, the mood relaxes, and the music becomes more delicate.

Eventually an almost pastoral mood takes over (Allegro molto moderato), with woodwind and strings exchanging elegant phrases, reminiscent of the 'courtly dance' that opens the finale of the Sixth Symphony. This rises to a crisis, and a moment of uncertainty. The dance is resumed, but over an agitated undercurrent. It develops further, and rises again to a crisis. This time the dance is unable to resume, and instead stuttering woodwind begin a passage of increasing tension.

A quiet, sustained bass note announces that we are on the brink of the home key of C major, and beneath an accompaniment full of quiet anticipation the trombones gradually awake from their sleep, playing a rising scale that takes us right back to the start of the symphony. The trombone call, back in glorious C major at last, returns, and the strings rise to a pitch of splendour. But now the build-up is long and troubled, with rolls of the timpani, swirling bass, and insistently plaintive violins. At the final climax, the strings break out into a great lament, based on the sombre falling lines that the woodwind intoned after the first trombone call. It reaches a resolution as the horns enter with a last farewell to the trombone call. Sighing woodwind phrases take us to the moment of the final cadence. There is a great crescendo from the brass in a final chord of C major. But the last word is left to the violins, rising from B to C – such a tiny and simple step, but it seems like the great resolution, the great reconciliation, that Sibelius had been striving for all his life.

TAPIOLA, OP. 112
Duration: approx. 18 minutes

This was Sibelius's last major composition, written in 1926 to a commission from Walter Damrosch, conductor of the New York Symphony Orchestra. It is a work of brooding and magnificent power. Tapio is the forest god of the *Kalevala*, and Tapiola is his realm.

At the head of the score, in three languages, stands a verse based on lines written by Sibelius to explain the inspiration for the work:

> Widespread they stand, the Northland's dusky forests,
> Ancient, mysterious, brooding savage dreams;
> Within them dwells the Forest's mighty God,
> And wood-sprites in the gloom weave magic secrets.

Cast in a single movement, *Tapiola* is almost as long as the Seventh Symphony, but there is no sense of division into distinct sections. At first hearing, the impression is of a gloomy, icy stream of consciousness, punctuated by occasional outbursts of violence that eventually become cataclysmic. It has much in common with Debussy's *La Mer* in its evocation of implacable natural forces, and particularly in the role of the brass section at the great climaxes. But as always with Sibelius (and with Debussy), there is an underlying logic tying everything together.

After a timpani stroke, the strings play a tiny theme that curls upwards, and descends. Virtually every melodic shape in *Tapiola* is derived from this motif, either in its original form, or extended, compressed, upside down, or combinations of these. Sibelius used this technique throughout his career, but in *Tapiola* he takes it further than ever before.

Another striking feature of this opening is the very first chord. It is arresting and disorientating – a seventh chord of E major, with the seventh, D, in the bass. This disorientation is also a characteristic that permeates *Tapiola*. Its harmonies are disturbing, wrenching, acerbic, and seem to hang in the air. From time to time there are plain chords, major or minor, but often we wait a long time for them, we glimpse them, and they are gone. Underlying these chords are harmonies that are very slow-moving, with long held bass notes and with patterns that repeat hypnotically.

After two statements of the opening motif, and a moment like pastoral improvisation from the woodwind, there is agitation (still based on the motif), a sudden climax, and then an abrupt return to the opening motif. A long passage ensues, in which the motif is repeated sorrowfully, again and again. In the background, there is a held bass note, and chords slowly rise and fall (like the rise and fall of the motif). Eventually the chords rise higher and higher in the strings. A new, more continuous melody of rising and falling begins in the woodwind, with eerie chords in the strings – Sibelius has the strings leap up and down an octave simultaneously, in opposite directions, giving a strange inner life to what is, in effect, a continuous chord. At one moment, flutes and piccolo burst out with a rapid scale up and down, the first indication of destructive forces lying below the ominously calm surface. Soon, the woodwind pattern becomes more agitated, rising higher. This is followed by deep, gloomy woodwind chords (still in the up-and-down shape of the motif), which then move to the lower strings.

There is a sudden change to a scherzo-like mood and pace. A delicately dancing pattern (related to the motif) passes rapidly between strings and woodwind. As in Mendelssohn's Overture to *A Midsummer Night's Dream*, it evokes fleeting glimpses of the supernatural, but set in a colder, bleaker landscape. As this continues, in the background the woodwind melody re-emerges, in clarinet and cor anglais. The energy builds and falls away, the dancing evaporates, leaving the flutes mournfully intoning the melody, now compressed to creeping up and down by semitones, and with yet stranger, Debussy-like harmonies. This leads to a beautiful passage for strings, divided into a chorus of twelve voices. It is an anxious, sorrowful meditation on the motif, which has become expanded into a hymn-like incantation. Suddenly the brass enter, with a crescendo to *fff*, at which they hammer out the shape of the incantation with savage force. This lasts only a moment, but its effect is profound. The music never regains the uneasy calm that preceded the outburst.

The pace increases, reiterations of the incantation continue with more urgency, as if searching for escape from the threat. Again the brass enter, twice building up to *fff*, and again vanishing, without reaching the final hammering rhythm of their first attack. They leave in their wake the woodwind, anxiously repeating their creeping line, now with the hammering rhythm added to it, as if they know it cannot have gone for long. This leads on to a reprise of an earlier version of the woodwind melody, against eerie string chords.

After a brief intervention from the brass, the music settles, reaching a moment at which the violins hover almost inaudibly, playing rapid tremolo. Gradually the other strings join in, and the music builds to a tremendous storm, like a reimagining of the climax of Beethoven's third *Leonore* Overture. As the music reaches its height, trapped in a swirling vortex, the brass enter. There are three assaults, and the third builds up to a reprise of the savage hammering. The storm subsides, leaving a scene of devastation. As the harmonies twist relentlessly, the strings rise to a reprise of their sorrowful incantation, now high and fortissimo, like a last cry of despair. This subsides to a series of solemn chords, rising to a final climax. The chord of this climax is the very chord with which *Tapiola* began, a chord with its seventh in the bass that seems to hang unresolved in mid-air. Finally, the release is found, in a simple, beautifully spread chord of B major. This is deeply poignant. Surely the great struggle to reach this point cannot resolve itself just with this one chord. But Sibelius ends his last major work, like so many others, with a refusal to soften the situation. That is all there is.

VIOLIN CONCERTO IN D MINOR, OP. 47
Duration: approx. 30 minutes

Allegro moderato
Adagio di molto
Allegro, ma non tanto

Sibelius began his musical career as a professional violinist, and taught the violin. His works for violin and orchestra include two serenades, two 'solemn melodies', and six humoresques, as well as this concerto, and there are also pieces for violin and piano.

The Violin Concerto was composed in 1903–4 and revised in 1905, between his second and third symphonies. When the first version was performed in Helsinki, it was heavily criticized by Karl Teodor Flodin, a writer whom Sibelius admired. According to Flodin, Sibelius had nothing new to say in a traditional virtuoso concerto, and he should instead have written a more symphonic work. Sibelius withdrew the concerto and rewrote it. But even in its final form it met with conflicting opinions. Some early critics thought that it lacked coherence, but Donald Tovey wrote, 'In the . . . looser concerto form invented by Mendelssohn and Schumann, I have not met with a more original, a more masterly, and a more exhilarating work.'[21] Its originality lies particularly in the dark sonorities of the orchestral writing, which are highly characteristic of Sibelius. And as for incoherence, it is true that the concerto can ramble in some performances. The first movement in particular can seem loosely rhapsodic unless tightly controlled by the soloist.

Its opening is very like that of Mendelssohn's Concerto in E minor, and was surely inspired by it. Introduced only by a shimmering tremolo on the muted violins, the soloist launches straight into a sweeping melody in the 'speaking' style that owes much to traditional Finnish music. As it becomes more elaborate, it breaks into ferociously athletic declamation, and culminates in a moment of cadenza, from which the orchestra launches into a second theme. This is one of Sibelius's characteristic melodies that develops as soon as it is born, its curling shape building up and then falling back. Bassoons and then clarinets give it what seems a final, nostalgic farewell. But then the soloist enters with a rising melody and rejuvenates the second theme passionately, first in bold chords and octaves, then eloquently singing it while the violas muse on the rising phrase from the soloist's last entry. Again the second theme seems to reach a resolution. But the soloist has still not finished with it: gingerly it tries out a high, meditative version, arrives at a trill, plays the curling shape one last time under the trill (a very tricky thing to accomplish), and only then lets the trill resolve itself.

The orchestra enters forcefully and, for the first time, at a fast pace, Allegro molto. The theme that the violins play seems new, but it is a version of the rising melody that the violas took over from the soloist at the beginning of its last entry. Flutes answer with a playful element. This orchestral tutti is a breath of fresh, bracing air after the rhapsodic comings and goings of the movement so far. It is in the conventional position between the soloist's exposition of themes and the development section; or perhaps it is already the beginning of the development – this sort of deliberate, organic ambiguity is typical of Sibelius. What follows is anything but conventional. The music builds to a climax, and fades away as bassoon and cellos remember the rising phrase one more time. Over a held bass note the soloist enters with an assertive leap up and tumble down, followed by arpeggios. This is the beginning of an extended cadenza that replaces the usual development section. It clearly owes its inspiration to Mendelssohn and Tchaikovsky, both of whom placed a cadenza at a similar point in their violin concertos. Virtuoso passages, with fast runs and chords, incorporate references to the first theme, sometimes played in canon.

As the cadenza winds down, a bassoon enters with the first theme. This is the beginning of the reprise – though it is not in the original key, D minor, but a fifth lower, in G minor (a procedure to be found in some of Mozart and Schubert's first movements). The soloist echoes the darkness of the bassoons, playing the theme on the lowest string of the violin, a complete contrast to its airiness at the start of the concerto. This reprise builds with far greater sense of effort than the first section of the movement. When the orchestra takes over from the soloist, it is not with the curling second theme, but with a continuation of the first theme, building up to a magnificent climax in a major key (B major – unusually distant from the home key of D minor at this stage of a movement). An oboe plays the familiar rising melody, the clarinets touch on the curling second theme (for the first time in the reprise), and then the soloist takes up these two elements. As before, this passage culminates in a trill, and the orchestra enters at a faster tempo, Allegro molto vivace (by now we are back in the home key, D minor). The violas play the forceful version of the rising melody, while the soloist plays rapid patterns and virtuoso octaves above. As the flutes introduce their playful element, the soloist breaks into a fast, delicate arpeggio pattern. With assertions of the first theme, in octaves, the soloist brings the movement to a powerful close.

The rhapsodic passages of the first movement need careful control if the piece is to hold together as a coherent whole. The second and third movements, by contrast, can scarcely fail if played strongly and competently. The slow movement is introduced by an elegant rising and falling duet, first on clarinets, then on oboes. The soloist plays a long, singing melody, supported by a rich carpet of four horns and bassoon. As the melody begins a gradual ascent, pizzicato cellos and violas help to move it forward. It rises to a climax, then has a sudden, and touching, moment of doubt, before reaching a resolution.

Over a persistent, syncopated bass rhythm, the strings enter with a forceful version of the elegant phrase with which the movement began, now in a minor key. Trumpets answer with a phrase echoing the syncopation of the bass. As the music builds up, it becomes clear that this phrase also echoes the magnificent climax from the reprise of the first movement. Against the persisting rhythm in the bass, the soloist enters with cross-rhythms in two parts. The writing becomes more and more complex, but just as it seems ready to rise to another climax, the main theme of the movement creeps in below the soloist, in the wind and violas. Very gradually, the theme moves on, dipping to pianissimo and then building, with the soloist's figurations providing a counterpoint above. The soloist plays powerful octaves to urge the melody on to its climax. Then the movement ends quietly and simply.

The third movement is an invigorating and relentless dance, a sort of Nordic polonaise (Donald Tovey famously called it 'a polonaise for polar bears').[22] Here the temptation is the opposite of that in first movement – to play the finale very fast in order to work up the excitement. But the exhilaration is in the inexorable rhythm, not in the speed, and Sibelius underlines this by marking the movement Allegro, ma non tanto. The theme in D major has a refreshing simplicity, with its emphatic dotted rhythms and repetitions over a bass anchored to the keynote, D, like the drone of a bagpipe. But it soon becomes clear that Sibelius is going to treat it to the wildest of virtuoso embellishments. As it continues, the soloist breaks into rapid triplets and arpeggios, scales in thirds, and octaves, before winding up the paragraph with a trill.

The orchestra plays the second theme in G minor, which alternates a syncopated rhythmic kick with emphatic stamping. The effect is both assertive and unsettled. This is because, like the first theme, it has an unchanging bass note, but this time it is not the keynote, G, but the third of the chord, B flat, so that it has a strangely unanchored quality. The soloist plays the theme in bold chords, and then moves away to a passage of staccato semiquavers. This drifts off into a memory of a phrase from the end of the first theme, which is echoed in the woodwind – the quiet low point of the movement.

As the soloist gradually rebuilds the energy, more fragments of the first theme begin to appear in the clarinets. The music rises to a great climax, with high octaves in the solo violin, and the orchestra bursts out into the reprise of the first theme. This has been transformed from its assertive dotted rhythms to powerful, tumultuous semiquavers. Suddenly the soloist takes it back to its original character. When the second theme reappears, it is played quietly by the clarinets, with the soloist weaving trills and a descant of harmonics over it. The end of the theme again breaks into continuous semiquavers, but this time they build up powerfully, until they reach a passage of wild octaves. The music flails for a moment as if ready to break apart. Dark, massive brass chords, and a final ascent from the soloist, bring the concerto to a close.

BEDŘICH SMETANA
(1824–84)

Smetana is to Czechs what Glinka is to Russians, and Chopin to Poles: the composer who pioneered a national school of composition. Until Smetana, earlier Bohemian composers, like those in other countries under the Austrian Habsburg Empire, wrote music in the international style of the day, with little or nothing to distinguish them from those in other countries. If they wrote opera, it was to Italian or German libretti, not Czech. Smetana himself began his career as a virtuoso pianist–composer, and, like many others, was inspired by Liszt, both as a pianist and as a composer. Smetana visited Liszt in Weimar, and, influenced by his music, composed three symphonic poems, *Richard III*, *Wallenstein's Camp*, and *Hakon Jarl*. The command of orchestral forces and of Lisztian-style dramatic narrative that Smetana showed in these works laid the foundation for the great orchestral work of his later years, *Má Vlast*.

Liszt encouraged Smetana's first steps towards creating a distinctly national music. This coincided with an important shift in perceptions of Czech culture in Bohemia. Smetana was working in Sweden, developing his reputation as conductor and composer, when the October Diploma of 1860 was declared, devolving limited powers to Bohemia and other countries within the Habsburg Empire. This new political development helped to boost an interest in Czech culture, which for centuries had survived only in the poorest and least educated layers of society. The Czech Provisional Theatre (the first permanent professional Czech Theatre) was being built, and would open in 1862. Smetana moved back to Prague in 1861, becoming an important figure in Czech cultural circles. Like all educated Bohemians, he had been brought up speaking German, but he learned Czech, and began composing operas to Czech texts. In 1866 he was appointed principal conductor of the Czech Provisional Theatre, where the young Dvořák was one of his viola players. That year, Smetana's first two Czech operas were staged: *The Brandenburgers in Bohemia*, and the most famous of all Czech operas, *The Bartered Bride*. Smetana's position as the founder of a Czech national school of music was assured.

But at the peak of his career, tragedy struck. For some years he had suffered from tinnitus. In July 1874 he noticed that his two ears were tuned to different pitches, and began to experience rushing noises. His hearing rapidly deteriorated, and one morning in October he reported that he 'awoke stone deaf, unable to hear anything in either left or right ear'.[1] He was forced to resign from his position at the Provisional Theatre. But, far from sinking into depressed inactivity, he immediately threw himself into composition, writing the only major orchestral work of his mature years, *Má Vlast* (*My Country*).

MÁ VLAST (MY COUNTRY)
Duration: 70–80 minutes

1. Vyšehrad
2. Vltava
3. Šárka
4. From Bohemia's Woods and Fields
5. Tábor
6. Blaník

The writing of *Má Vlast* was the second time in his life that Smetana had responded to tragedy with an intense bout of composition. Twenty years earlier, when his four-year-old daughter died from scarlet fever, he had poured his grief into his first great work, the Piano Trio. Now, in 1874, his diary reports that, within a few weeks of becoming deaf, he completed the first movement of *Má Vlast*, 'Vyšehrad', on 18 November, followed by 'Vltava' on 8 December. On 14 March 1875 he writes, '*Vyšehrad* was given its premiere today at the [Prague] Philharmonic. Although I was listening from the gallery, I did not hear a thing.' 'Šarka' was already finished, and 'From Bohemia's Woods and Fields' followed by October. That was intended to be the end of a four-movement cycle, but Smetana later added two more, 'Tábor' in 1878 and 'Blaník' in 1879. He dedicated the cycle to the city of Prague, and the first complete performance was given in 1882.

Smetana gave his publisher a detailed programme for the cycle, which is quoted from below.[2]

1. Vyšehrad
Vyšehrad is the castle that towers over the city of Prague, the seat of the earliest kings of Bohemia. It is here that Smetana's recently composed opera *Libuše* is set – Libuše was a legendary Queen of Bohemia – and several elements from the opera found their way into *Má Vlast*. Smetana summarizes the programme of 'Vyšehrad': 'The harps of the bards begin: one bard sings of the events that have taken place on Vyšehrad, of the glory, splendour, tournaments and battles, and finally of its downfall and ruin. The composition ends on an elegiac note.'

The piece opens with two harps playing the four-note 'Vyšehrad motif' that will be important throughout the cycle. It is taken up quietly, as if in reverent procession, by horns, then the woodwind, who append a tailpiece of chords rising and falling in a simple arpeggio (a motif taken from *Libuše*). Then the strings take up the Vyšehrad motif, and it builds until it resounds grandly on full orchestra. After this stately tutti, the tempo increases, and the motif passes quietly from instrument to instrument as if setting off on a journey. The arpeggio chords bring in a joyful climax, ant the woodwind introduce a more sweeping phrase that dominates the next passage. A yet greater climax is reached, at which the four-note motif takes on heroic determination. But soon this turns threatening, and collapses. Clarinets quietly intone the motif in the minor, over tremolando strings, and there is a passage of dark uncertainty. But then a corner is turned, and we are back with the harp and horns, and a reprise of the opening. This builds to a confident tutti statement of the motif, after which the movement comes to an end in a spirit of quiet meditation.

2. Vltava
Smetana wrote the most famous of the cycle, 'Vltava', in three weeks in 1874. But there is evidence that ideas for it were forming in his mind several years earlier. These were sparked

by two events: a visit in 1867 to the countryside where two streams flow to join the river Vltava, and a boat trip in 1870 along St John's Rapids (a fast-flowing stretch of the river outside Prague, which was flooded by a reservoir in the twentieth century). It is astonishing that, drawing on these memories, he should have been able to bring this most life-affirming of pieces together at a time of such personal tragedy.

Smetana described 'Vltava' as follows: 'The composition depicts the course of the river, from its beginning where two springs, one cold, the other warm, combine in a stream, running through forests and meadows and lovely countryside where merry feasts are celebrated; water-nymphs dance in the moonlight; on nearby rocks can be seen the silhouettes of ruined castles, proudly soaring into the sky. The Vltava swirls through the St John's Rapids and flows in a broad stream towards Prague. It passes Vyšehrad and disappears majestically into the distance, where it joins the Elbe.'

The piece opens with two flutes, alternating in a rippling pattern over pizzicato strings. This passage is headed, 'The source of the Vltava'. The arrival of the second source of the river is suggested as the clarinets join the flutes. With a delicate touch of the triangle, the rippling moves to the strings, and the violins sing the broad, sweeping melody in E minor that has made this piece famous. Various sources have been suggested for this melody. It resembles a Bohemian children's song and a well-known Swedish folk song, both of which Smetana probably knew; but he makes of them something entirely his own.

As we travel down the river, the melody builds in strength, the rippling becomes swirling and surging, and there are moments of turbulence that suggest rapids. As the swirling continues, there are horn calls, labelled 'Hunt in the woods'. These combine with the river patterns to build to a climax, which fades away.

Now we encounter a 'Country wedding', with a rustic dance (the older Czech recordings give its rhythm a traditional, and delightful, rhythmic lift, a nuance difficult for non-Czech performers to emulate). The dance fades, and over muted string chords the flutes and clarinets resume a gentler version of their rippling: 'Moonlight. Dance of the water-nymphs'. Very softly, the strings play a slow, sweet melody whose shape is derived from the four-note motif. After a while, this is joined by pianissimo horns, trombones, and tuba, in a delicate, insistent march rhythm.

With a crescendo, the swirling flutes and clarinets lead us out into the daylight, and the violins reprise their great melody. This time, it takes an agitated turn as the river enters St John's Rapids. In August 1870, Smetana noted in his diary, 'Today I took an excursion to St John's Rapids, where I sailed in a boat through the huge waves at high water; the view of the landscape on either side was both beautiful and grand.'[3] After a dangerous passage, and a moment of doubt, we emerge into 'The broad flow of the Vltava', as the great melody bursts into a sunny E major. This climaxes with the Vyšehrad motif on full brass. From this grand culmination, the strings emerge with leaping arpeggios that gradually quieten, as if we are looking back to see the river disappearing into the distance. Two full chords bring 'Vltava' to a close.

3. Šárka

When Libuše, the legendary Queen of Bohemia, died, her women warriors declared war on all men. The legend of Šárka, one of the warriors, is a bloody episode in this 'Maidens' War'. Smetana's evocation opens:

... with a portrayal of the enraged girl swearing revenge on the whole race of men for the infidelity of her lover [a detail seemingly added by Smetana]. From the distance is heard the approach of warriors led by Ctirad who has come to punish Šárka and her rebel maidens. From afar Ctirad hears the feigned cries of a young woman (Šárka) who is bound to a tree. When he sees her Ctirad is captivated by her beauty and so inflamed with love that he is moved to free her. With a potion that she has prepared, she drugs him and his warriors, and they fall asleep. As she blows her horn (a prearranged signal), her warrior maidens, hidden in nearby rocks, rush forward and carry out a bloody massacre. The movement ends with the horror of mass slaughter, and the fury of Šárka's fulfilled revenge.

The piece opens with the four-note Vyšehrad motif transformed into an aggressive, thrusting shape and developed in a passionate passage reflecting the anger of Šárka and her women warriors. Out of it emerges a yearning melody, suggesting their mourning for the death of Libuše (or, in Smetana's version of the story, perhaps Šárka's memories of her faithless lover), and a final burst of anger leads to a change of scene.

This is the quiet, stately march of the noble Ctirad and his men. After a while, a pleading clarinet is heard (the cry of Šárka), the march halts, and the clarinet is answered by the cellos (Ctirad). There follows a passionate outpouring of melody, *Tristan*-like in its intensity, as Ctirad falls under the spell of the beautiful Šárka. Then there is an extended passage of dancing joviality, as the men drink and make merry. The music fades as the men fall asleep, low bassoons suggesting their snores. Over tremolando strings a horn calls. Quietly a clarinet reprises the angry melody with which the piece began. There is a great crescendo, and the full orchestra embarks on a passage marked 'frenetico'. With blaring trombone calls and hammering chords the piece comes to an end.

4. From Bohemia's Woods and Fields

Smetana writes: 'This is a painting of the feelings that fill one when gazing at the Bohemian landscape. On all sides, singing, both joyful and melancholy, resounds from fields and woods: the forest regions, depicted on solo horn; the smiling, fertile lowlands of the Elbe valley are the subject of rejoicing. Everyone can draw his own picture according to his own imagination.'

This is the most arresting opening of all six movements, like suddenly being confronted with the grandest of vistas. This is not the cheerful, major-key joy of Beethoven's opening to his 'Pastoral' Symphony, but an imposing minor-key wall of sound. Solid brass chords provide the foundation, while upper strings and woodwind play repeating, swirling patterns that contain hints of cross-rhythms, creating a sense of bewilderment amid all the splendour. As the music fades, woodwind sing a lullaby, first clarinets in the minor, then oboes and bassoons in the major, with flutes elaborating a descant in charmingly rustic style. After a pause, muted violins set off on a fleeting, mysterious fugue, as if we have been transported to Sibelius's frozen north. Each of the five string parts enters in turn, eight bars apart, the texture darkens, but then warms into a new theme. This is a hymn-like melody, sung by clarinets and horns (one could easily imagine it as a national anthem). As they complete the first 'verse', the mysterious fugue resumes briefly, but now with each part entering closer behind the preceding one. A second verse of the hymn is played by all the woodwind, echoed by horns. Again the fugue tries to resume, with the entries bunched even closer than before. But immediately the woodwind break through, the strings remove their mutes, and the whole orchestra joyfully plays the hymn. Its energy is heightened by the woodwind, which accompany with chords in the same swirling pattern that the strings played at the opening of the piece.

At the end of the verse, the woodwind again insist on a change, this time to a polka. At first the strings are unconvinced, and muse solemnly on a phrase of the hymn. At the third attempt, the woodwind persuade the strings to join them, and the polka takes off in high spirits. In a quiet middle section of the dance, clarinets and bassoons play a melodious theme, reminiscent of their entry early in the piece, while the violins delicately continue the polka rhythm. The main polka reasserts itself from time to time, but it is the new theme that predominates for a while. In a quiet moment, the clarinets and bassoons remember the hymn. But the high spirits are not to be suppressed, and the full orchestra sets off on the home straight. Just before the end, the lullaby-like theme from near the beginning is transformed for a moment into a solemn chorale. But the movement ends with a reaffirmation of its joyful spirit.

5. Tábor

Tábor is a city in southern Bohemia, founded in the fifteenth century by the Hussites. Jan Hus was a pioneer of church reform a century before Martin Luther. He was burnt at the stake in 1415, and his followers were subjected to a series of crusades. The Hussites succeeded in repelling these attacks in a series of battles, and at the fourth crusade in 1427 the invading army is said to have broken and run at the sound of the Hussites singing their hymn, 'Ye who are God's warriors'.

Smetana writes: 'The whole composition is based on this majestic hymn. It was certainly in the town of Tábor, the seat of the Hussites, that this stirring chorale resounded most powerfully and most frequently. The movement depicts the determination to win battles, and the dogged perseverance of the Táborites, and it is in this spirit that the poem ends. It cannot be analysed in detail, because it expresses the glory and renown of the Hussite struggle and the indestructible character of the Hussite warriors.'

Over a sustained bass D and a drum roll, the horns intone the stark opening rhythm of the Hussite hymn. In low strings and woodwind, chromatic lines slowly descend, creating dark harmonies, as the horns repeat the rhythm again and again. There is a sudden crescendo, culminating in a fortissimo statement of the first phrase of the hymn (a moment that evokes Siegfried's 'Funeral March' from Wagner's *Götterdämmerung*). Twice the music restarts and climaxes in the same phrase. Then clarinets and bassoons in chorus quietly sing a further phrase of the hymn. The strings develop a striding ascent from the opening rhythm. Woodwind and strings alternate, culminating in a further phrase of the hymn.

Now the pace increases, and a phrase of the hymn is developed with urgency, is interrupted again by the solemn woodwind, and then continues at greater length. Fragments from the hymn are used to create a turbulent drama, full of tension and sudden contrasts, until a climax at which the full brass and woodwind declaim the hymn in majestic chorus. The music fades, a fragment is reiterated by the horns over a persistent D in the bass (an agitated reference back to the opening), and there is one last crescendo. The movement ends with the opening rhythm starkly and persistently hammered again and again.

6. Blaník

Smetana designed 'Tábor' and 'Blaník' to be performed as a complementary pair: *'Blaník* begins where the preceding composition ends. Following their eventual defeat, the Hussite heroes took refuge in the mountain of Blánik where, in a profound sleep, they await the moment when they will be called to the aid of their country. So the chorale *Ye who are God's warriors*, which was used as the basic motif in *Tábor*, forms the foundation of this piece.'

'Blaník' begins with the familiar rhythm of the Hussite hymn once again hammered out. But soon this develops into an ongoing, quietly determined passage which, although in three-time, has a march-like tread, evoking memories of the 'pilgrims' march' from Mendelssohn's 'Italian' Symphony. Eventually this fades away and the woodwind introduce a pastoral oboe solo whose opening phrase is derived from the Vyšehrad motif. Smetana wrote about this passage, 'As a brief intermezzo we hear a short idyll, a description of the Blánik region where a little shepherd boy plays a piece while the echo gently floats back to him.'

The oboe is echoed by a horn, and then joined in counterpoint by clarinet, flute, and horn, over a drone in the strings that suggests bagpipes. A stormy passage follows, which soon lightens into music of more delicate urgency (again rather like Mendelssohn). This grows in insistence, then fades as horn and trombones return to a phrase of the Hussite hymn. The tempo settles into a march. At first jaunty, it grows in dignity as the woodwind play the hymn. There is a quiet moment, then the whole orchestra gathers itself to sing the great hymn. There is one more moment of sombre reflection as the hymn weaves in counterpoint, suggesting the sleep from which the warriors will awake.

For the last time the full orchestra gathers itself to launch into the hymn, urged on by cymbals and triangle. Then the most extraordinary thing happens. The tempo increases, and suddenly the march hymn has metamorphosed into a vigorous polka, as if the warriors have emerged from their long sleep not marching but dancing – a joyful symbol of national renewal that can take the breath away. The polka in turn leads to an *fff* reprise of the great opening of the Hussite hymn on full brass, with the strings adding on to the end of each phrase the Vyšehrad motif (the seed with which the entire work began). At the final climax, the Vyšehrad motif in the brass combines with the arpeggio shape that was its first companion in the strings. There is a final burst of the hymn, followed by fanfares from the brass. Smetana's note concludes, 'With this melody, the Hussite chorale, the resurrection of the Czech nation, its future happiness and glory, will come to pass.'

RICHARD STRAUSS
(1864–1949)

As a young man, Strauss rose to fame as the leading German composer of the new gener-ation. He took the symphonic poem (which he called 'tone poem') of Liszt, and brought it to new heights of daring, imagination, and orchestral virtuosity. His musical language used all the latest post-Wagnerian harmonic developments and elaborated them in a complex but entirely intelligible way. He also brought to a climax the long history of 'programme music', in which the music is tied, explicitly or implicitly, to a narrative. At their best, his tone poems stand entirely on their own as powerful musical structures – though there are undoubtedly moments when the narrative dominates the music in a way that can seem merely clever.

A string of tone poems over five years from 1888 to 1903 – *Don Juan, Tod und Verklärung* (*Death and Transfiguration*), *Till Eulenspiegel, Also sprach Zarathustra, Don Quixote, Ein Heldenleben, Symphonia Domestica* – established Strauss as the great modern virtuoso of orchestral writing. But a composer with such strong roots in literature and storytelling would naturally also be a successful opera-composer. Strauss's operas *Salome* (1905) and *Elektra*

(1909) created a sensation. The orchestral writing, highly complex and at times fiercely dissonant, was combined with vocal lines based on Wagner's principles of 'endless recitative', culminating in soaring lyrical climaxes, particularly for the principal soprano roles. Strauss had
always been a great song-writer, and in opera his combination of song-writing with virtuoso
orchestral scores resulted in compelling music-dramas. After *Elektra*, his next opera was *Der
Rosenkavalier* (1911), and it could hardly have been more different from *Salome* and *Elektra*.
It is a romantic comedy set in 1740s Vienna, and Strauss uses the Viennese waltz and a poignant
harmonic language to evoke an atmosphere that runs from playful parody to nostalgic sweetness. Strauss in his later operas and other works never returned to the acerbic language of
Elektra, and some writers took the view that this was a betrayal of Strauss's modernism, a pragmatic 'selling out' in favour of popular success. Theodor Adorno later went so far as to draw
comparisons with his attitude to the Nazi regime, with which Strauss for a time achieved an
uncomfortable accommodation, both for the sake of his own career and in order to protect his
family (his daughter-in-law was Jewish). Although he privately loathed Hitler and the regime,
his public engagement with the Nazis did not show him in a good light.[1]

As for his musical 'betrayal', this begins to seem, in the twenty-first century, a somewhat empty
accusation. To say that Strauss should have continued to pursue the modernistic course set in
Elektra is not far removed from the supposed Victorian belief that any effective medicine must
necessarily taste bitter. Faced with a murderous revenge-drama, Strauss produced murderous
music. Faced with a period comedy, he produced in *Der Rosenkavalier* a score of unashamed
sweetness, though a sweetness achieved with just the same mercurial skill as the power of *Elektra*.
Which is the real Strauss? One might as well ask which is the real Wagner: the 'modernist' who
wrenched the harmonies of *Tristan* to portray the agonies of a doomed passion, or the composer
who elaborated an utterly consonant major chord to evoke the River Rhine at the opening of *Das
Rheingold*. Strauss was certainly a pragmatist, and not always an attractive one in his personal life,
but he had a musical range that could find the right means of expression at any moment, from
the brutality of *Elektra* through to the valedictory serenity of his Four Last Songs.

His principal orchestral works comprise his series of tone poems, two horn concertos
(his father was a celebrated horn-player), and two works composed in his eighties: an oboe
concerto, and the great lament for strings, *Metamorphosen*.

ALSO SPRACH ZARATHUSTRA (*THUS SPAKE ZARATHUSTRA*), OP. 30
Duration: approx. 35 minutes

The ancient idea that humankind is on a journey, a quest, took on a new lease of life with the
publication of Charles Darwin's *On the Origin of Species* in 1859. Scientists, philosophers, and
churchmen were forced to grapple with the notion that human beings are descended from
apes, and, like all other species, are evolving to an unknown future. In the twentieth century,
science-fiction writers embraced these ideas, notably Arthur C. Clarke in *2001: A Space
Odyssey*, the film that he co-wrote with Stanley Kubrick and then developed into a book. The
film makes impressive use of the opening of Strauss's *Also sprach Zarathustra*, which suddenly
became the most famous passage in all of his music.

The link between the film and the music was wholly appropriate. Strauss's tone poem,
composed in 1896, was inspired by the philosophical-mystical book by Friedrich Nietzsche,
written 1883–5. Nietzsche developed the idea that humanity should strive to evolve into an

'Übermensch', an 'over-human' or 'super-human' (not to be confused with the masculine hero of Wagner's *Ring*, Siegfried, or the 'Superman' of popular fiction). Humanity, on the path from ape to super-human, must overcome all its current prejudices, moral limitations, and ignorance, and must forge its own values and creative purpose. Only the individual can do this: the masses merely take refuge in superstition and tribalism, and it is up to the individual to strive for freedom and the embracing of eternity.

Nietszche's book consists of a series of short chapters in the form of teachings, sermons, and encounters with humanity, cast in a poetical and mystical style. The name, Zarathustra, is a version of Zoroaster, the ancient founder of Zoroastrianism, who preached the individual's freedom to choose right or wrong, and the need to struggle for the truth. Strauss took nine of the chapter titles (not in their original order) as the basis for a great musical structure, beginning with sunrise, and ending in darkness. The music is continuous, so the description that follows gives approximate timings of each section. Each description begins with a summary of the relevant part of Nietszche's poem.

1. Introduction (2 minutes)
After ten years of solitude in the mountains, Zarathustra rises at dawn and addresses the sun, which he has blessed every day, and announces that he will once again descend into the world of humanity.

Over a deep, low C on basses, contrabassoon, and organ, the famous call is declaimed: trumpets rise a fifth, and then to the octave. The rest of the orchestra responds with an arresting upbeat of C major, which immediately switches to a chord of C minor. Timpani beat portentously. The trumpets repeat their call, the orchestra snaps back from C minor to C major. A third time the trumpets call, and the orchestra summons its strength, rising to a splendid climactic chord, which leaves the full organ hanging in mid-air (splendid unless the pitch of orchestra and organ are not perfectly matched). The magnificence of the sunrise seems like an echo of the sunrise in Haydn's *Creation*. But the major-minor-major switching also recalls a mysterious moment in the third movement of Beethoven's Piano Trio in E flat, Opus 70, No. 2. Strauss would have known both, but he creates something strikingly new: a powerful, purposeful uprising – not just a sunrise, but a declaration of Zarathustra's intention.

2. Of Those of the World Beyond (3½ minutes)
God and the afterlife are the creations of human madness, and distractions from the pain of life. Zarathustra urges us instead to base all our beliefs on the physical reality of human beings, and the world in which they live.

There is a moment of darkness and uncertainty. Then a group of solo strings (still supported by the organ) quietly begins a hymn. Gradually, all the other strings join in, until they rise to a warm climax. As the climax falls away, a plangent phrase on cor anglais and bassoon gives a hint of the turbulent emotions to come.

3. Of the Great Longing (2 minutes)
Zarathustra has taught his soul to be free, until it is full of melancholy and longing. He bids it to sing its thanks to him.

The section opens with a newly relaxed, almost dancing theme on violins in duet. Dark reminders of the opening trumpet call, and fragments of the warm string theme from the preceding section, combine with new swirling elements, rising up from below, to suggest the awakening of human desires. A renewed trumpet call leads into:

4. Of Joys and Passions (2 minutes)

Our passions can become our virtues, unique to each individual, but only if we accept their ineffability.

The swirling takes on a regular pattern, creating a tumultuous new theme in C minor, incorporating Strauss's characteristically passionate upward leaps, and building to a powerful climax, with the new theme above, and dark swirlings below.

5. The Grave-Song (3 minutes)

I visited the grave of my youth, and felt the sweetness of the fugitive loves buried there. They died too young.

The passionate theme continues quietly on oboe, with a dark version of the opening trumpet call in cellos and bassoon below. A complex web of melodic lines develops, with harmonies of *Tristan*-like restless anxiety. This resolves onto a long, peaceful chord, with clarinet and cellos falling gently.

6. Of Science (4½ minutes)

Fear is the basis of superstition, but courage is the foundation of true knowledge, subtle, spiritual, and intellectual, with its eagle's wings and serpent's wisdom.

This begins as a very slow fugue based on the opening trumpet call, starting low in the cellos and basses. The fugue subject uses all twelve notes of the chromatic scale, creating mysteriously shifting harmonies in no fixed key, and suggesting humanity stumbling around in the darkness of superstition (and it pre-dates by twenty-five years Schoenberg's 'twelve-note' system). After a time, a bassoon adds to the fugue subject a falling chromatic phrase from the 'Joys and Passions' section, and the fugue subject is played at half tempo by the strings. The music accelerates and grows louder, until it bursts into a fast section.

The violins (and flutes) sing a joyful duet in a major key, echoing their theme at the beginning of 'The Great Longing'. This is joined by a sprightly dotted-rhythm phrase in high woodwind over rapid violins, as if everyone is in flight. There is a sudden shimmering quiet, and the opening call is repeated in trumpet, oboe, and cor anglais. The falling chromatic phrase from 'Joys and Passions' is turned upside down by the clarinets. It is this phrase that bursts out fortissimo on the violins, and a passage incorporating forceful dotted rhythms ends in three abrupt chords, signalling the entry to:

7. The Convalescent (5 minutes)

Zarathustra, with a great cry, challenges the thought from his lowest depths to reveal itself. But the effort causes him to fall into a deep swoon. Recovering slowly, he is tended by his animals, which recognize him as the teacher of the Eternal Return: the truth that all things return, have always existed and recurred, and always will throughout eternity.

The chromatic swirls and dotted rhythms continue above, while, below, trombone, cellos, and basses intone the fugue subject from the beginning of 'Of Science'. This develops into an extended, determined passage, with the fugue subject combined with itself, sometimes at half speed, and the other elements in counterpoint with it. The energy builds, culminating in the trumpet call, intoned over a massive sustained chord on full orchestra and organ. There is a silence, and an abrupt change of key, as if uncertainty has returned. Fragments of the trumpet call, in the minor, and the swirling chromatic phrase, grope around.

Suddenly there is another surge of energy. These two elements are fused together into a confident motif that drives the music upwards over a timpani roll, until the flutes, with viola harmonics, start up a bird-like, repetitive chattering. A trumpet sounds, but its call has been refined into simple leap of an octave, preceded by a dancing dotted rhythm. This new call is taken up by the violins, the swirling motif takes on a joyful air, and the different motifs dart around the orchestra like a whole forest of creatures.

Into this scene steps a solo cello, transforming the rising of the trumpet call and the falling motif, now in a major key, into what could be the introduction to a Viennese waltz. A pair of solo violins take this up, and the mood throughout the orchestra becomes more confident, with a return of the sprightly woodwind theme from 'Of Science', a new, thrusting idea in the strings, and a glockenspiel adding brightness. The chattering is eventually reduced to a trill, creating an expectant moment.

8. The Dance-Song (8 minutes)

Zarathustra comes across a group of maidens dancing in the forest. He urges them to continue, and while they dance he sings a song about Life, the unfathomable woman whom he loves best, even more than that other woman, Wisdom.

This is the longest section of Strauss's work, the culmination in dance. Trumpet and strings answer each other quietly with the opening call. This then swings gently into three-time and becomes a repeated pattern, from which emerges a solo violin, playing what really is the introduction to a waltz. The opening of the waltz's melody is simple, derived from the snappy upbeat right at the beginning of the piece. Accompanied by solo strings, with occasional old-fashioned glissandi specified, the waltz evokes a thoroughly Viennese scene. This develops into a long and complex passage, with motifs from earlier in the piece drawn into the waltz, and the whole brought together to a great climax.

9. Song of the Night Wanderer (4 minutes)

Zarathustra sings a song: The world is full of deep sorrows and deep joys. We cannot wish for eternal recurrence of joy without the eternal recurrence of the sorrow that accompanies it.

At the height of the climax, a bell sounds, striking midnight as the tumult diminishes. The swirling motif gradually calms and becomes elongated. There is a hush, and at a change of key all the violins gently recall the violin duet from 'Of Science', which again becomes a duet of soloists, rising higher and higher. The work ends very quietly, with high, serene chords of B major played by flutes and violins, alternating with low pizzicato reminders of the opening trumpet call, in the original key of C. Despite the seeming accomplishment of serenity, it is the dark bass pizzicato that has the final word.

***DON JUAN*, OP. 20**
Duration: approx. 17 minutes

Strauss wrote his tone poem *Don Juan* in 1887–8, and conducted it himself in his first season as court conductor at Weimar the following year. Strauss himself described the rehearsals:

'The sound was wonderful, with an immense glow and sumptuousness ... The orchestra wheezed and panted, but did their part capitally ... one of the horn-players sat there bathed in sweat, completely out of breath, and sighed, "Dear God! What sin have we committed, for You to send us this rod for our backs (that's me)! And we shan't be rid of it so easily." We all laughed till we cried.'[2] The performance was a triumph. Strauss was twenty-four, and it was this premiere that established his name as the leading composer in Germany.

The inspiration for the work was an unfinished dramatic poem by Nikolaus Lenau, from which Strauss quotes extracts at the beginning of the score. Lenau's Don Juan is a Romantic dreamer, seeking through the intensity of the moment the essence of woman's beauty (he owes more to Goethe's Faust than to Mozart and Da Ponte's Don Giovanni): 'if I could but fly through every place where beauty blossoms, fall on my knees before each one, and, if only for a moment, conquer ... I shun satiety and the exhaustion of pleasure; I keep myself fresh in the service of beauty; and in offending the individual I crave for my devotion to her kind ... passion is always and only the new passion; it cannot be carried from this one to that; it must die here and spring anew there, and when it knows itself, then it knows nothing of repentance.'[3]

Don Juan is an early example of the works that Strauss called a 'tone poem', synonymous with 'symphonic poem', the model established by Liszt. But its marvellously compact structure, and its drawing together of vividly contrasted material, put it as much in the tradition of the concert overtures of Mendelssohn, Brahms, and Tchaikovsky. And although Strauss declares the influence of Lenau's poem, his music has a life and a logic of its own that need no outside explanation.

The opening conveys the joy of passionate abandon, with echoes of the famous moment when Tristan and Isolde rush towards each other in Act 2 of Wagner's *Tristan*. The strings' first flourish is impossible to articulate clearly at the reckless tempo – the need to 'just go for it' seems a fitting start to this portrait of Don Juan (as Strauss said at an early rehearsal, 'fifty notes one way or the other won't really make any difference').[4] In the midst of the outpouring, there are glimpses of the women in his life: a broad, passionate melody, immediately cut off by a coquettish little phrase, like the swirl of a skirt as the girl turns away with a smile, followed by a fragment of a new melody. At last the music rushes to a halt. A quiet held chord and a sweet violin solo suggest a long gaze at the new beloved, and the fragmentary tune we heard a moment ago develops into a great sweeping melody, which builds up through a series of waves to a mighty and satisfying climax.

Scarcely has the climactic chord sounded when fragments of the opening flourish are heard, and the first theme takes off as enthusiastically as before, with a sense of new adventures suggested by moving off into new keys. This, as well as seeming psychologically apt, is the beginning of the development section of the work. After a while, a rising theme in the minor is sung by cellos and violas. This seems new, but it is developed from the opening flourish. It alternates with plaintive sighs from the flute. There is a gradual descent to stillness. Over a chord of G major, the new theme in the minor continues to murmur in the lower strings, and above, the oboe sets off on a beautiful, extended melody. This is a moment of deep contentment, and forms the quiet heart of the work around which all the restless passion of the outer sections seems to make sense. Clarinet and bassoon add to the melody and weave counterpoints, in that manner which Strauss was to make his own in his ecstatic opera ensembles.

The melody quietly sinks to a close. We seem ready for new adventure, and, in conventional procedure, the reprise of the opening. But Strauss here plays a magnificent trump card. The four horns in unison proclaim a heroic melody, opening with a great leap, and ending with a climactic ascent. This seems like a wholly new idea, but it is developed from the sweeping love theme from the opening section. Once again, this is both psychologically apt and musically satisfying. Fragments of the opening, now fully recognizable, soon return, but the new directions they take make it clear that Strauss is not yet ready for the reprise. The mood is playful, at times delicate, with a glockenspiel adding a delightful touch. The tension gradually builds to another huge climax, at which there is a sudden, catastrophic plunge.

From this point to the end, Strauss most clearly echoes the events of Lenau's poem. Don Juan is haunted by ghosts of his past conquests, and as in Mozart and Da Ponte's opera, invites to dinner the statue of a nobleman whom he has killed. The nobleman's son comes to dinner instead of the statue, and challenges Don Juan to a duel. Just as he is about to triumph, Don Juan is overcome by the pointlessness of his life, and allows himself to be killed. In Strauss's musical response, memories of past happy themes flit by. Eventually, tentatively, the opening flourish reappears and builds up, and we are at last into the reprise of the opening paragraph. This time, instead of revisiting all the earlier byways, Strauss heads straight for a last, mighty climax, at which the horns declaim again their heroic melody, and the violins take it up passionately. There is a final burst of energy as the opening flourish is revisited once again. But suddenly it is all over. There is a silence, a quiet chord, a precise stab from two trumpets, and with quivering tremolo, a mournful last breath from the bassoons, and final pizzicato from the strings, this most passionate of works has spent itself.

DON QUIXOTE: FANTASTIC VARIATIONS ON A THEME OF KNIGHTLY CHARACTER, OP. 35
Duration: approx. 40 minutes

Miguel de Cervantes published the two parts of *The ingenious gentleman Don Quixote de la Mancha* in 1605 and 1615. It tells the adventures of a gentleman of La Mancha, aged around fifty. He has devoted all his time to reading books of chivalry, and has become so obsessed by them that he has lost his wits, and conceives the idea of becoming a knight-errant, wandering through the world with his horse and arms in quest of adventures, redressing wrongs and rescuing maidens. He polishes his great-great-grandfather's suit of armour, renames his boney old horse Rosinante, and himself Don Quixote. Since every knight must have a beautiful lady, whose honour he is pledged to defend, he chooses 'a very comely country lass' from a neighbouring village (without her knowing anything about it), and names her Dulcinea del Toboso. He persuades a simple-minded labourer, Sancho Panza, to accompany him on a donkey, promising him the governorship of an island as a reward. In their many adventures together, Don Quixote is fearless in his delusions, and Sancho Panza, though he may be simple, is full of homespun philosophy. Their encounters with all manner of people along the way create a rich tapestry of human life, which is both surreal and touching, and its influence over the centuries has been immense.

Strauss takes some of the most vivid episodes in the story, and uses them as the basis for a set of 'Fantastic variations on a theme of knightly character'. The variations are very freely constructed, some long, others very short. To the listener, they come over as a series of free fantasies on the various themes and motifs that are announced right at the beginning in the

Introduction. The music is full of fantastic effects and virtuoso combinations of instruments. Some of it is rather rambling and fragmented, particularly if the performance is not tightly controlled. But there are also passages of glorious lyricism, with grand climaxes. It is, in a word, quixotic.

Strauss composed *Don Quixote* in 1897. A cello solo represents Don Quixote, with a lesser solo for viola as Sancho Panza, often riding on a donkey-like tuba. Strauss originally intended these solo parts to be performed by the principal players of the orchestra (as he did with the violin solo in *Ein Heldenleben* a year later). But the cello part is so huge that it has usually been performed by a separate soloist, as in a conventional concerto.

Introduction: 'knightly and gallant'. An alert motif on the woodwind permeates the whole work. The two groups of violins enter with elegant phrases, one a step behind the other, as in a courtly dance, and the clarinet rounds it off with a bow and a curtsy. A ruminative viola line leads to a melting melody on oboe, suggesting courtly love for a noble mistress. This is Dulcinea's theme. Fanfares on muted trumpets seem to be riding to rescue her from the threat of the tubas below. Then the beloved's melody rides over the courtly phrases. The texture becomes more complex with several instruments in counterpoint, and it grows in intensity. Brass and strings are all muted, giving a curiously dreamlike quality to the passage. Urgent fanfares and harsh chords bring the passage to a climax, and a pause.

Theme: 'Don Quixote, the Knight of the Sorrowful Countenance'. The solo cello takes up the material of the Introduction, playing the courtly phrases in counterpoint with a solo violin. The cadences with which the theme ends have unexpectedly plangent harmonies, as if to show the deluded seriousness of purpose in the Don. Bass clarinet and tuba solemnly introduce the solo viola of Sancho Panza, who chatters amiably and fusses around his master.

Variation 1: This begins as the cello enters again, in counterpoint with the bass clarinet renewing the Sancho Panza theme, and the violins expanding on the beloved's melody. This is interrupted by the sudden sound of calm octaves, representing the slow turning of windmills. Don Quixote takes these for giants, and charges towards one of them. The turning sail shatters his lance, and horse and rider come crashing to the ground. He sits mournfully contemplating his beloved's theme.

Variation II: His spirits soon restored, Don Quixote sets off enthusiastically in search of fresh adventures. Soon he encounters a flock of sheep. Their bleating is one of the wittiest pieces of imitative writing in the history of music: muted trombones, trumpets, and horns with clarinets are all instructed to 'flutter-tongue' dissonant chords, while the other woodwind play a mock-pastoral tune like the shepherd walking among the flock. Don Quixote takes these to be hostile giants. He charges among them, scattering the flock, and losing some teeth, but nevertheless (according to Strauss's music) emerging triumphant.

Variation III: In a long conversational passage the solo viola (Sancho Panza) seems to be trying to persuade his master of the ordinariness of things. The Don interrupts him forcefully, and embarks on a heartfelt exposition of his noble quest on behalf of his beloved. Her theme rises higher and higher in noble splendour, and comes to rest. In the final bars solo cello and viola rise together in duet, as if even Sancho Panza is for a moment persuaded of the nobility of the cause.

Variation IV: As the pair stride vigorously forth once more, they encounter a religious procession carrying an image of the Virgin Mary (muted trumpets and trombones chanting, with clarinets and oboes muttering). The Don assumes that these are robbers abducting a noble lady. As he challenges them with his sword, one of the bearers strikes out at him, and he falls to the ground, as if dead.

Variation V: There is life in the old knight yet. He spends a sleepless night contemplating the memory of the beautiful Dulcinea, with a long, impassioned recitative.

Variation VI: They come across three peasant girls riding on donkeys (a naive, jolly tune on oboes, made jauntier by switches between two- and three-time). Sancho tells Don Quixote that this is the fair Dulcinea and her companions coming to visit him (the viola plays Dulcinea's theme). Sancho and his master kneel before them. But Don Quixote finds that his beloved has been bewitched into an ugly girl reeking of garlic.

Variation VII: Don Quixote and Sancho Panza mount a flying wooden horse, which (they are told) has been sent so that they can fly to fight the giant Malambruno, who has cast spells on a prince and princess, turning them into a brass monkey and a metal crocodile, and giving their maidservants beards. Blindfolded, the Don is unaware that the wind through which they seem to be flying is provided by bellows. Strauss builds an impressive climax, with the wind suggested by rushing flutes and piccolo, harp glissandi, and a wind machine. The 'flight' is soon over, and leads straight into:

Variation VIII: They come to a river, and find a boat without oars tied to a tree. Despite Sancho's assurance that this is just a fishing boat, Don Quixote insists that it has been placed there so that he can travel across the ocean to rescue some knight in peril. They are carried down the river until they reach a mill, where they are rescued from being crushed by the mill wheel. A complex web of counterpoint reaches another climax, and the cello emerges pizzicato. The variation ends with the woodwind transforming the familiar knightly motif into a chorale, as if in thanks.

Variation IX: The pair set off again and encounter two Benedictine monks riding on mules in company with a lady's carriage. The monks are engaged in peaceful conversation (bassoons in mock-religious counterpoint). Don Quixote takes them to be evil enchanters who have abducted the lady. He charges at one of the monks with his lance, the monk falls in astonishment to the ground, and then Don Quixote gets into a sword fight with the gentleman accompanying the lady in the carriage. Cervantes teasingly leaves the story unfinished, saying that the ending is missing from the historical records, but Strauss suggests a successful outcome to this brief variation with four decisive string chords. These lead straight into:

Variation X: The 'Knight of the White Moon', in full armour, challenges Don Quixote, declaring that his mistress is fairer than Dulcinea. If Don Quixote is vanquished, he must give up his arms and his adventures, and retire to his village. The Knight of the White Moon is a disguised young man from Don Quixote's village, who hopes to cure him of his madness. The Don accepts the challenge, and they joust (much trumpeting of fanfares, and the rumble of a bass drum). He is knocked to the ground (a sudden silence). The stricken Don Quixote persists in asserting that Dulcinea is the most beautiful woman in the world, but agrees to abandon his adventures and return to his village. The music takes on an anguished, processional character. For a moment the Don seems to be revisiting his past follies, as the cor anglais reminds us of the episode with the sheep. The procession resumes, and comes to rest.

Finale: Don Quixote is put to bed with a fever in a state of deep melancholy, with the faithful Sancho by his bedside. After a long sleep, he wakes, and, feeling himself near death, is released from his delusions. He renounces his pseudonym of Don Quixote and his life of folly.

Here, the music becomes noble without any hint of irony, as the cello rises to a glorious climax. The fever threatens (juddering strings). As the cello continues the anguished musings on his former life, the very opening of the work is recalled, like a vision of Don Quixote's youth. The cello falters, and expires with a downward glissando. For the last time the clarinet remembers its opening curtsey, and the final chords are magically touched in with a bell-like glockenspiel. Don Quixote dies peacefully, and entirely sane.

EIN HELDENLEBEN (A HERO'S LIFE), OP. 40

Duration: approx. 47 minutes

In July 1898, Strauss wrote to a friend from the Bavarian Alps, with characteristic irony, 'As Beethoven's Eroica is so very unpopular with our conductors and is therefore seldom performed nowadays, I am meeting a pressing need by composing a great tone poem entitled "A Hero's Life" (true, it has no funeral march, but it is in E flat major and does have lots of horns, horns being quite the thing to express heroism); thanks to the bracing country air, my sketch has progressed well and I hope, if nothing in particular gets in the way, to finish it by New Year's Day.'[5] Strauss dedicated *Ein Heldenleben* to conductor Willem Mengelberg and the Concertgebouw Orchestra of Amsterdam. Mengelberg, at the age of twenty-seven, had in three years transformed the Concertgebouw into an orchestra of exceptional virtuosity, capable of delivering even Strauss's fearsome scores with precision.

Strauss linked *Ein Heldenleben* and *Don Quixote*, saying that he conceived them as 'direct pendants' to each other.[6] But the hero of *Ein Heldenleben* seems portrayed as genuinely heroic, rather than deluded, and the scope and tone of the work suggests a stronger affinity with *Also sprach Zarathustra*. *Ein Heldenleben* is not explicitly linked to Nietzsche, but the hero-figure is inescapably Nietzschean. After conducting a performance in Berlin, Strauss wrote to his father to say that some of the critics were well disposed, but 'the rest spew gall and venom, principally because they have read the analysis ... as meaning that the hideously portrayed "fault-finders and adversaries" are supposed to be themselves, and the Hero me, which is only partly true.'[7] This is revealing: the hero is partly the figure of Nietzsche's *Zarathustra*, struggling towards self-determined fulfilment, but at least partly Strauss himself, if only ironically. Strauss's friend, the author Romain Rolland, wrote in a letter to Strauss in 1905, 'in Heldenleben, with or without a programme, the starting point is a feeling of fervour and heroic joy (no matter who the person may be in whom these passions may be stirring).'[8]

The work falls into six sections, which are played continuously. Approximate timings are given in the following description. The titles were given to each section by Strauss, but then removed before publication of the score.

1. The Hero (4 minutes)

The hero strides forth with an immense sense of purpose (Strauss in his notebook called this 'the primary unfolding of abilities').[9] The theme covers a huge span, full of leaps up and plunges down, like someone ready to overcome any danger or setback, and punctuated by chords like the crack of a whip. Already the score is very 'horn-rich', the opening theme being played by horns and cellos. The theme is immediately extended and developed in a complex web of counterpoint which introduces several motifs that will be important later on, some rhythmically assertive, others lyrical. As the section begins to build towards a climax, the horns are again prominent with a firm descending scale – a motif that will form a grand climax later in the piece. As the sturdy power develops, there is an irresistible suggestion of Wagner's *Die Meistersinger*, together with distinctly Siegfried-like bravura, raising the thought that, if Wagner had written tone poems, this is what they would have sounded like. The section culminates in six repeated gestures of defiance (which Strauss labelled the 'great challenge to the world'). There is a pause and a silence.

2. The Hero's Adversaries (3½ minutes)

The opponents (or critics) are represented as a swarm of argumentative woodwind in a chorus of conflicting, dissonant staccato lines. Beneath this chattering, tubas intone an ominous motto. The hero contemplates this hostile crowd wearily, his majestic theme now in the minor. It rises in the cellos and basses, and develops into a powerful lament (if one has been alerted to Wagnerian suggestions, this passage evokes the guilt-drenched chromaticism of *Parsifal*). The hostile woodwind reappear, even more acerbic than before, but the hero's theme is not to be deterred. It builds in strength, eventually bursting back into the major and resuming its confident stride.

3. The Hero's Female Companion (12 minutes)

As the heroic motifs resume, there enters a solo violin. It introduces a new, falling line with beguiling little turns and unexpected harmonic colours. The hero is stopped in his tracks, his manly gestures slowed. But as soon as he seems to be paying serious attention, the violin turns coquettish, with rapid phrases suggesting a laugh and an evasive skip. This develops into an extensive violin cadenza, in which the mood is continually changing. One moment the violin is seriously playing two-part counterpoint or quoting conventional cadenza figures, as if remembering Mendelssohn's Violin Concerto, the next it is turning sorrowful, or renewing its coquetry. The whole passage evokes a volatile feminine character, with suggestions of the opera singer. Strauss admitted, according to Romain Rolland, that it portrays his wife, Pauline de Ahna, who combined both of these characteristics, and had given up her opera career when their first child was born in 1897, the year before Strauss wrote *Ein Heldenleben*. The hero seems transfixed, from time to time uttering fragments of deep, manly melody. Eventually the cadenza is overwhelmed by the orchestra, which bursts forth with a passionate theme, putting together earlier motifs in a new way. It sounds like a declaration of love, and the solo violin is willingly drawn in. A broad violin melody develops, with tender moments from oboe and clarinet, and sweeping arpeggios in the two harps. As the climax fades away, there is a particularly tender, restful moment, over a sustained bass note. In the distance, the voices of the adversaries are heard. At first, these do not disturb the lovers.

4. The Hero's Battlefield (8 minutes)

When offstage trumpets sound a fanfare, the heroic theme rouses itself, combined with a motif introduced by the solo violin (this is in the minor, as in the earlier episode with the adversaries). A full-blown battle begins, with the adversaries' motif given a new strident edge on trumpet, and an aggressive march rhythm on side drum. If the whole work is thought of as a massive symphonic movement, this is the 'development' section. The themes of the hero and the companion enter the fray, at first seemingly unconcerned, but increasingly dragged into the fight itself. A huge struggle develops. The descending scale motif from the end of the introduction is heard, combined with the other motifs. Eventually the adversaries are beaten off, and the hero emerges triumphant, like a dog shaking itself and barking, but now combined with the companion's theme. This leads to a grand reprise of the hero's theme, now supported by a descant of all eight horns in unison, which magnificently rise to affirm the moment of triumph. As in the introduction, the theme is developed further. But at the point where there was a silence the first time round, the music moves into:

5. The Hero's Works of Peace (5½ minutes)

If Strauss tried to deflect the idea that this piece was all about him, this episode is nevertheless clearly autobiographical. It begins with a quote from his first great success, *Don Juan*, picking up its great horn peroration – the prototype of all Strauss's later horn-drenched climaxes. The ominous, adversarial tubas are heard, but are quickly swept away. Then there is a sustained build-up, beginning delicately and developing in passion, in which there are further quotes from *Don Juan, Don Quixote, Death and Transfiguration, Also sprach Zarathustra,* and other works. This was a bold thing to do at the age of thirty-four, and Strauss's most severe critics hated it for what they saw as its arrogance. But it is done with such tenderness that it has more the effect of a parent cherishing his children than of a man bragging about his achievements.

6. The Hero's Retreat from the World and Fulfilment (12 minutes)

For the last time the tubas intone their dark motto. This time the response is an outburst of sustained anger, as if the hero's tolerance has snapped. The anger gives way to heaviness, and then to a searching cor anglais solo that hints at the heroic theme, but soon metamorphoses into reiterations of calls like a shepherd's pipe. A mood of calm descends. The violins begin a glorious melody that suggests complete fulfilment, soon joined in singing counterpoint by the cellos. There is an eruption of memories of the battle. But these are short-lived, and give way to the solo violin singing the love theme, cleansed of any sense of conflict. This is taken up by solo horn, and a tender dialogue between (heroic) horn and (feminine) violin brings the work to a serene conclusion. This was how *Ein Heldenleben* originally ended. But Strauss then rounded it off with a final blaze, and a sonorous chord from all the wind instruments.

METAMORPHOSEN

Duration: approx. 25 minutes

Adagio ma non troppo – Etwas fliessender – poco più mosso – Agitato – poco accelerando – noch etwas lebhafter – Più allegro – Adagio, tempo primo

Metamorphosen, composed in the last year of the Second World War, is a lament for twenty-three solo strings – in effect, a string orchestra in which each individual has specific responsibility. It was written for the Collegium Musicum, Zürich, and the conductor Paul Sacher, one of the great promoters of new music in the twentieth century. Its commission, in August 1944, was for a suite for strings, but Strauss had already been working on an Adagio for a string ensemble for a year or more, and instead developed this into *Metamorphosen.* The commission had a more than musical purpose: Strauss at the age of eighty was suffering from poor health, and wanted to visit the spa of Baden in Switzerland. But he was unable to get permission from the Nazi authorities to travel, and this commission from Switzerland was intended to help him to obtain it. In the end, Strauss did not complete *Metamorphosen* until May 1945, by which time the war in Europe was over. In October, Strauss finally received permission to travel to Switzerland, and Sacher conducted the premiere in Zürich the following January. Strauss did not attend the concert, but conducted a run-through at the final rehearsal. Willi Schuh reported, 'Strauss knew above all how to achieve magnificently the great sweep of development through powerful increase of dynamic and tempos – an unforgettable experience for the conductor [Sacher], the players of the Collegium, and the very few listeners present.'[10]

Even though sketches for the music go back a long time, there is one event that seems to have spurred Strauss to get the work completed. On 12 March 1945 the Vienna Opera House went the way of those in Munich and Dresden and was destroyed in an Allied bombing raid. Strauss wrote on the score of *Metamorphosen*, 'Begun 13 March 1945'. Ten days earlier, he had written to his librettist, Joseph Gregor, 'I am inconsolable. The Goethe House, the most sacred place on earth, destroyed! My lovely Dresden – Weimar – Munich, all gone!' Strauss completed *Metamorphosen* in May, shortly before Hitler committed suicide and Germany surrendered. Strauss wrote in his diary, 'The most terrible period of human history is at an end, the twelve-year reign of bestiality, ignorance and anti-culture under the greatest criminals, during which Germany's 2000 years of cultural evolution met its doom.'[11]

Strauss's distress at the destruction of the Goethe House in Frankfurt points to a possible source of inspiration for *Metamorphosen*. As he became increasingly isolated in his old age, Strauss embarked on rereading the entire works of Goethe in chronological order: 'I am reading him as he developed and as he finally became ... Now that I am old myself I will be young again with Goethe and then old with him – with his eyes. For he was a man of eyes – he saw what I heard.'[12]

Goethe had been engaged with the idea of metamorphosis as a natural phenomenon ever since publishing *An Essay in Elucidation of the Metamorphosis of Plants* in 1790. This became in his later years a philosophy that could be applied to all aspects of the natural world: 'Form is something mobile, that comes into being and passes away. The science of form is the science of transformation. The doctrine of metamorphosis is the key to all of Nature's signs.'[13] Goethe came increasingly to extend such thinking from the physical world to the world of the mind and the spirit.

Before the war, Strauss had written an opera, *Daphne*, whose plot was derived from Ovid's *Metamorphoses*. But perhaps his title was also an allusion to Goethe's obsession. The themes of *Metamorphosen* do not particularly 'metamorphose' in the way that themes in Liszt or Wagner do. But the way in which they combine and build creates a broader metamorphosis from fragmentary origins to a climax and final dissolution.

There is another possible connection with Goethe. At the time he was beginning working on *Metamorphosen*, Strauss also sketched a setting of a poem by Goethe for male-voice choir, 'Niemand wird sich selber kennen':

No-one can know himself,
Or separate himself from his own self-perception ['Selbst-Ich'];
But he tries every day to test
What is, in the end, clear to others,
What he is, and what he was,
What he can be and what he likes.

The examination of the self, its strivings and possibilities, is a theme running throughout Goethe's work. Perhaps, it has been suggested, there is an element of self-examination in Strauss's *Metamorphosen*. Strauss, at the same time as lamenting the destruction around him, might wonder what has happened to the composer who began as a firebrand and is drawing to the end of his life with his reputation poisoned by accommodation with the hated Nazi regime. Strauss, however, said nothing about the sources of *Metamorphosen*, so we are left with conjecture, and the unmistakable power of the music itself.

One thing that is certain is the care with which Strauss placed the music within the context of German musical culture. Throughout the score there are echoes of great German classics, particularly Wagner. There is one actual quote, from Beethoven's 'Eroica' Symphony, which becomes a dominant element in the music. This was clearly one of the most important pillars of the German heritage for Strauss: he and his sister marked the end of the war by playing a recording of it.

Metamorphosen is scored for ten violins, five violas, five cellos, and three double basses. Although they all have separate parts, they do not act independently all the time (the music would be incomprehensibly elaborate if they did). But it gives Strauss the opportunity to create an infinitely subtle and flexible texture in which individual instruments, or groups of them, become prominent, fade, exchange places with others, so that a web of sound builds up into great paragraphs over a long period of time. It is a distillation of the technique that he had developed in his operas over many years, in which complex counterpoint creates powerful, long crescendos that build to ecstatic climaxes, often with one or more soprano soaring over the top of the orchestra (the climactic scene of *Daphne* was a recent example). Here in *Metamorphosen* the mood is tragic, with the great climaxes seeming like memories of past achievement, or of hopes that are ultimately dashed.

The overall structure of the work falls into three parts. In a typical performance of about 25 minutes, the slow opening section lasts about five minutes. Strauss here presents almost all the thematic material that he uses to build the work. This is followed by a long central section lasting about twelve minutes, in which the themes are elaborated with counterpoints, combined in increasingly elaborate ways, and travel through a succession of keys, gradually accelerating and building. The last section, lasting about seven minutes, returns abruptly to the opening, slow tempo, and the work winds down to a tragic conclusion.

Metamorphosen opens with the five solo cellos and a double bass in sombre chorus. The key is at first uncertain. The harmonies shift poignantly, the melody yearns upwards and descends more calmly, only then settling for a moment into C minor. All this suggests an allusion to the Prelude to Wagner's *Tristan und Isolde*. Two violas enter with the second element: three solemn repeated notes introduce a descending line with the snappy rhythm of the funeral march from Beethoven's 'Eroica' Symphony. This really is a quote, though, according to Strauss, at first an unconscious one. The solemn repeated notes later become an important element in their own right (they could be a reference to the Fugue from Bach's Sonata in G minor for solo violin, but a simple repetition of three notes can be found in many places). Two more violas present the third element, in which the same three repeated notes introduce a line that falls and then leaps, loosening into a winding descent of triplets. This has a Mahlerian character, though it perhaps also suggests an allusion to King Mark in Wagner's *Tristan*. Finally, a trio of violins enter with the fourth element. It begins like the first element, but then blossoms into a moment of free-flowing melody, with a hint of the 'Prize Song' from Wagner's

Die Meistersinger. The different elements (except No. 2, the funeral march) are then revisited in different combinations, and the texture builds up to a sonorous climax at which all twenty-three instruments play together for the first time.

The tempo increases a little. This is the beginning of the long central section of the work, in which an increasingly complex web of counterpoint gradually builds in intensity and in tempo through a series of great waves. At first the emphasis is on the fourth element, which now flows more freely, with filigrees of arpeggio counterpoints rising above it – there are moments that sound almost like Wagner's *Siegfried Idyll*. As other instruments join in, the texture becomes richer, and the first of the waves builds up. As it fades, there is a brief reminder of the funeral-march second element. The texture again becomes light and transparent, with the filigree lines dominating (these elaborate shapes sometimes suggest Schoenberg's *Verklärte Nacht*). The tempo increases again, and the counterpoint develops a complex texture typical of Strauss's later operas. As it builds towards the peak of another wave, five violins sing in unison to cap the resolution, like a soprano in one of Strauss's operatic ensembles. For a moment, Strauss has relaxed into an unambiguous major key.

This moment of relaxation is brief, and the complex web of sound immediately pushes into new keys and develops into a powerful climax. This time, as the music again becomes light and transparent, the funeral-march element, which has not been heard for several minutes, begins to appear in the inner parts. Soon it is echoed in the bass, creating yet another layer in the complex counterpoint. As the music begins to surge forward with increasing power, the funeral-march element is drawn in, losing its doleful quality, and then dropping out to allow a passionate, sustained build-up to develop, driven forward with new energy by running semiquavers in the middle violins.

There is another delicate, transparent passage, at the end of which the funeral march re-enters. This time it is echoed a bar later and a semitone higher, creating a harmonic clash. The music tries to regain its composure. A few bars later, the clashing funeral march reappears. At first the surrounding instruments seem unaffected, but then they arrive at a moment of sudden urgency. The music breaks into a faster tempo, and all twenty-three instruments surge forward gloriously in a burst of sunny C major. This is the great climax of the piece, a rare moment when the darkness has been cast aside and only the glorious things are remembered. But at the very peak of the climax, the clashing funeral march intrudes, and the music is wrenched away from its resolution, towards the darkness of the opening.

The tempo slows to the Adagio with which the piece began. The four elements are revisited in turn, and as they build in strength it seems that we may be able to salvage something of the glories of the past. But once more the music cuts off, the harmonies tug away powerfully, and the clashing funeral march appears with renewed force and persistence. Again there is a moment of delicacy, and the music begins to build. But the harmonies are uncertain, and the mood becomes increasingly anxious.

Eventually, we reach a cadence of C minor, and quietly the cellos and basses quote the opening of Beethoven's funeral march, from which Strauss's funereal theme was taken. Under it in the score Strauss writes, 'IN MEMORIAM!' Even this explicit quotation is not allowed to be itself: over it the violins play the theme in counterpoint, with newly astringent harmonies in the inner parts. The harmonies painfully resolve onto final chords of C minor, and the memories are laid to rest in a spirit of bleak acceptance.

TILL EULENSPIEGEL'S LUSTIGE STREICHE (TILL EULENSPIEGEL'S MERRY PRANKS), OP. 28
Duration: approx. 15 minutes

Till Eulenspiegel was a disruptive figure in medieval German folklore, whose practical jokes punctured the pomposity and hypocrisy of everyone from cobblers to priests. Strauss had planned to write an opera on the story, but eventually settled on this piece, *Till Eulenspiegel's Merry Pranks*, which he composed in 1894–5 as one of his series of 'tone poems' for orchestra. Most of these are long and grand, but *Till Eulenspiegel* is compact and pointed, bringing to the genre a welcome dose of concentrated wit. And although it is scored for Strauss's usual enormous orchestra, he deploys it deftly, making it light on its feet. It is a virtuoso score, often fast and rhythmically complex, and immensely difficult to play and co-ordinate.

The music is a sort of rondo, in which episodes succeed each other, and the two motifs heard right at the beginning recur in different guises. The first motif opens the piece on violins, cast as suave and elegant. The second motif is a horn solo, rising in three phrases and cascading down. There is a build-up, full of sudden bursts of energy, after which a clarinet introduces a third element: a cheeky little tumbling phrase. But this is not really a new theme at all: it is the suave opening motif speeded up. This sort of transformation was a favourite device of Liszt and Wagner: here, Strauss cleverly uses it to suggest Till as the master of disguise.

The music now gets going at an affable trot, which builds again to a sense that excitement lies ahead. The tempo eases to a moment of flirtatious coyness, with the cheeky version of the first motif predominating. Next, there is an expectant tremolo on violins, and a furtive version of the first motif on lower strings, echoed by flute and violins. A sudden crash on the cymbals provokes mayhem (this is presumably the scene in which Till rides his horse through a market). The moment is quickly over, and Till seems to be plotting his next move.

The music softens, and we are back to the suaveness of the opening, now developed into a gentle, courtly dance – Till as the plausible seducer. Muted trumpets tug at the heart strings, and a solo violin pleads convincingly. But suddenly the violin leaps to a high note and runs rapidly down a virtuoso scale. The moment of deception is over, and Till passes jauntily on his way.

He develops a swagger, and the music builds up. There is a sudden hush, and we come across bassoons and contrabassoon in academic debate, or perhaps religious procession. Till's second motif joins in, and becomes mocking as it rises up through the instruments to reach the piccolo. The music now develops momentum and power again, arriving at a climax. Forceful trills evaporate, and we find ourselves dancing a polka. There is a moment of hesitation, as if Till is wondering how to handle this encounter, and the music morphs into a fast waltz. We round a corner, and find ourselves back at the opening horn theme.

This time, the horn repeats the call in a different key (this is one of the trickiest horn solos), and the music seems to be developing in a new direction. But, with Mozartian deftness, Strauss turns another corner, and brings us back to reprise the original build-up. This time, the violins take over the cheeky clarinet phrase, and the music continues to build, with the horn motif developing a four-square rhythm and great momentum. Again, there is a spring in Till's step, and the future looks good. Motifs intertwine delicately, and the music builds yet again to a terrific climax.

But the moment of triumph is broken by a drum roll, and solemn minor chords. The law has caught up with Till, and he must face his execution. He attempts to deflect the inevitable with humour (the cheeky clarinet), and pleading (muted trumpets from the seduction scene), but it is no use. A final shriek from the clarinets, and it is all over. But not quite: an epilogue brings us back to the suave opening, developing the motifs with new charm, as if to suggest that we should remember Till Eulenspiegel with fondness despite (or because of) his roguishness.

IGOR STRAVINSKY
(1882–1971)

Stravinsky grew up in Russia, and was a private pupil of Rimsky-Korsakov. But it was in Paris that he first made his name in the early years of the twentieth century, with a succession of ballet scores for huge orchestra, written for Diaghilev's Ballets Russes – *The Firebird*, *Petrushka*, and the cataclysmic *The Rite of Spring*. The austerity of the First World War put an end to such extravagance, and Stravinsky's next ballet score was for only seven players, *The Soldier's Tale*. From this point on Stravinsky experimented with all sorts of approaches to composition, responding to new ideas and creating others himself. He settled in France in 1920, then emigrated to the United States in 1939. Although he visited Russia in 1962, he never returned to live there.

The artist whom Stravinsky most resembles is Picasso (with whom he collaborated). Like Picasso, he began in a style closely related to nineteenth-century art – in Stravinsky's case, the Russian school of his teacher Rimsky-Korsakov. But later Stravinsky, like Picasso, found a way of writing that seemed to take the world to pieces and reassemble it in a new way. Like a magpie, he picks up whatever catches his ear – Russian folk material, ragtime, baroque music (creating 'neoclassicism'), later still, some of Schoenberg's serial techniques. Stravinsky's music, like Picasso's painting, contains many elements that are familiar. But they are not in their usual context: the perspective has shifted, as if we are looking at the world through prisms or a kaleidoscope.

There is often a powerful ingredient of ritual and the ancient (again suggesting some analogy with Picasso). Already in *The Rite of Spring* the 'primitive' rituals of earth-worship and sacrifice are suggested in the music by insistently repeated patterns and hypnotic rhythms, rather than by conventional musical melodies and forms. Later Stravinsky wrote works called by the traditional names of 'symphony' and 'concerto'; but with their obsessional repetitions and rhythmic tics, they still seem to be haunted by the element of ritual that reached a climax in *The Rite of Spring*.

Stravinsky made a series of declarations about the purpose and power of music over his long career. Most famously, he stated in 1936, 'I consider that music is, by its very nature, essentially powerless to express anything at all, whether a feeling, an attitude of mind, or psychological mood, a phenomenon of nature, etc. . . . Expression has never been an inherent property of music. That is by no means the purpose of its existence.'[1] Later, in lectures delivered in French at Harvard University, and written with the collaboration of his friends Alexis Roland-Manuel and Pyotr Suvchinsky, he enlarged on this: 'the basis of musical creation is a preliminary feeling out, a will moving first in an abstract realm with the object of giving shape to something concrete . . . All music is nothing more than a series of impulses that converge towards a definite point of repose.'[2] However, in the same lectures he declares that the phenomenon of music 'emanates from a complete and well-balanced human being endowed with the resources of his senses and armed with his intellect . . . The central aim of music . . . is to produce a communion, the union of man with his fellow-man and with the Supreme Being.'³

For Stravinsky, therefore, music was not the dry art that he sometimes seems to be describing, but something of immense importance. It might not be 'expressive' in any literal sense, but the ordering of its elements is, for him, nevertheless expressive of the order of God's creation. Such an attitude gives Stravinsky a more profound link to J. S. Bach than 'neoclassicism' does. But this purpose does not mean that Stravinsky saw his music as 'religious', or as a ritual. He visited Bayreuth in 1912 to attend Wagner's *Parsifal*, and recalling it in his *Autobiography* two decades later, he wrote, 'What I find revolting in the whole affair is the underlying conception – the principle of putting a work of art on the same level as the sacred and symbolic ritual which constitutes a religious service.'⁴ Stravinsky was quoted in 1946 as saying, 'As for myself, I need music for hygienic purposes, for the health of my soul. Without music in its best sense there is chaos. For my part, music is a force which gives reason to things, a force which creates organization, which attunes things. Music probably attended the creation of the universe.'⁵

L'OISEAU DE FEU (THE FIREBIRD)
Duration: approx. 44 minutes

Stravinsky was not the first choice for composer of *The Firebird*. When Diaghilev decided that he needed a major new ballet score for the 1910–11 season of the Ballets Russes, he first approached Nikolay Tcherepnin, with whom the company had worked the previous season. Tcherepnin began work, but for some reason withdrew. Anatoly Liadov was then approached, and when he declined, Diaghilev considered Alexander Glazunov. It was only when all of these approaches had come to nothing that he sent a telegram to Stravinsky, who had orchestrated some pieces by Chopin for the previous season's *Les Sylphides*. The subject was to be *The Firebird*, with choreography by Mikhail Fokine. Stravinsky, who had been 'intoxicated' by Fokine's choreography of the dances from Borodin's *Prince Igor*, accepted, and wrote *The Firebird* over the winter of 1909–10. He completed the piano score by the beginning of April, and had orchestrated it by mid-May. The premiere at the Opéra in Paris was on 25 June 1910. Stravinsky was twenty-eight, and this was his great breakthrough.

Stravinsky was, in *The Firebird*, truly the pupil of his master, Rimsky-Korsakov, deploying all the varieties of melody, harmony, rhythm, and orchestration to be found in Rimsky-Korsakov's fantasy-operas. To the harmonic repertoire of Rimsky-Korsakov, he adds new twists and stretchings, including those of his fellow Russian Scriabin (Richard Taruskin goes so far as to identify actual quotes).⁶ The language is at its most chromatic when evoking magic – acerbic when evil, strange and intangible when benign – often with fragmentary little cells rather than themes. By contrast, wholesome elements, particularly human love, are conveyed through simple harmonies and folk-song-like melody (including actual Russian folk songs). The score is, therefore, quite traditional in many ways, and sometimes criticized for it. But, more than a century after its premiere, questions of originality are rather beside the point. *The Firebird* undoubtedly casts a spell, whether in the concert hall or in the ballet theatre, and is the earliest work of Stravinsky to have earned an enduring place in the repertoire, and to have achieved real popularity.

Stravinsky wrote in his *Autobiography* that '[Fokine's] choreography of this ballet always seemed to me to be complicated and overburdened with plastic detail, so that the artists felt, and still feel now, great difficulty in co-ordinating their steps and gestures with the music . . .'[7] Nevertheless, the success of the premiere was overwhelming. Stravinsky was accepted into Parisian cultural circles, and met Debussy, Ravel, Proust, and Sarah Bernhardt. Deciding that this was where his future lay, after a period in Switzerland, Stravinsky and his family settled in Paris in 1920.

The basic scenario for *The Firebird*, in which an intrepid young prince rescues the victims of an evil sorcerer-king with the help of a magic bird, was assembled from various well-known Russian tales. The choreographer, Fokine, the director, Sergei Grigoriev, and Stravinsky himself gave different accounts at various times of how they shared responsibility for its development, but it seems to have involved the three of them, together with the set designer Alexander Benois and Léon Bakst, one of the two costume designers. Fokine provided a detailed scenario in his *Memoirs*.[8] In the following description, the headings are translations of those in the 1911 complete score, and the details of the action are drawn from Fokine's scenario. Stravinsky derived three concert suites from the score in 1911, 1919 and 1945, reducing the orchestra to make it more practical for concert performance.

Introduction
A dark, creeping bass line, low trombone calls, and nervous fluttering in the woodwind, evoke the mountain-top castle of the sinister King Katschei (or Kashchei or Koshchei). But the opening line is not just an evocation: its shifting patterns of major and minor thirds, tones and semitones, are seeds from which several themes in the ballet will grow. It is night. Strings sweep up and down harmonics, and an oboe, in the first transformation of the opening bass line, turns it into a tender moment of melody. Within the stone walls of Katschei's domain there are beautiful princesses whom he has enslaved.

The enchanted garden of Katschei
As the curtain rises, we hear a hesitant passage, as if half-seeing things. Horn and cor anglais sound like mournful bird calls, and glittering celesta suggests the golden fruit in the garden. The strings play a shimmering, scratchy version of the creeping line over dark chords of pizzicato and contrabassoons. In the garden are the petrified statues of Katschei's enemies, including the young knights who attempted to rescue their princesses.

Appearance of the Firebird, pursued by Prince Ivan
The garden is suddenly illuminated by the Firebird. The music is full of fluttering and whooshing effects, from woodwind, harps, and strings, with cymbals rolled with drumsticks, and a flutter-tongued clarinet. A moment of calm, with distant horn calls, suggests the Prince watching in wonder, before the Firebird takes off again and embarks on her dance.

Dance of the Firebird
This is the first of the set-piece dances that are the traditional elements of the ballet. It consists of rapid patterns in the woodwind, riding on a mesh of shimmering effects in the strings. The harmonies are restless and chromatic, strongly suggesting the influence of Scriabin. Despite the almost themeless, 'impressionist' character, the dance is in a traditional three-part form,

with a more agitated middle section, then a return to the opening, which is extended and reaches a climax.

Capture of the Firebird by Prince Ivan – Supplication of the Firebird

The Prince captures the Firebird as she pecks at the golden apples. She begs to be released, and Ivan (who, like all princes in fairy tales, has a kind heart) lets her go. Before she flies off, she gives him one of her feathers, telling him that it will be useful to him. The pursuit of the bird by the Prince combines glittering effect with a regular, more human, tread. The capture of the Firebird is conveyed by anguished chirrups from clarinets over sustained whole-tone harmonies (a classic Russian 'magic' device). A solo viola leads into the bird's supplication. This takes the form of an extended, winding melody, on oboe, bassoon, cor anglais, and flute, enmeshed with the strings. The melody and harmonies continue to shift restlessly and chromatically, again suggesting the influence of Scriabin.

This section too is in three parts, with a slightly faster middle section, and then a return to the opening. As flute and oboe dialogue in the middle section, Debussy's *Prélude à l'après-midi d'un faune* seems not far away. The return is more strongly weighted toward the strings, and rises more passionately. A final tearful appeal (oboe and solo violin) has its effect: the Firebird springs free. Quick switches of mood suggest their conversation, the giving of the magic feather, the warning of danger – shimmering strings, a soft horn solo, a menacing passage with xylophone.

Appearance of the thirteen enchanted princesses

As the Prince is about to leave, the castle door opens, and thirteen beautiful princesses enter the garden. The music suddenly turns sweet and gentle, with a rising phrase that passes between woodwind and strings, and is extended into a melody on muted violins (the original score even has a swooping glissando at one point, an effect that now sounds thoroughly Hollywood).

The princesses' game with the golden apples – Sudden appearance of Prince Ivan

In another set-piece dance, the princesses toss the golden apples to each other, laughing. Like the Firebird's dance, this is full of rapid little phrases creating a kaleidoscopic effect, but the regular tread makes the difference between flying and running. This is another three-part structure. In the middle, a clarinet introduces a folk-song-like melody, before the rapidity of the dance takes over again. The dance ends with the Fairest Princess losing an apple in a bush. As she looks for it, the Prince (represented by a soft horn melody) steps forward, bowing low, and hands it back to her. The princesses are at first frightened, but accept the modest and handsome Prince into their game. The Prince and the Fairest Princess have, of course, fallen in love.

Khorovod (round dance) of the princesses

The princesses dance a khorovod, a traditional circling dance. The melody, too, is traditional, 'In the garden': Stravinsky took it from Rimsky's Collection of 100 Russian Folk Songs, which Rimsky himself had earlier used in his Sinfonietta on Russian Themes.[9] The music is structured to suggest the formality of the traditional dance. The oboe begins the melody, joined by clarinet and bassoon. Then muted strings extend the tune for a more impassioned second section. This concludes with high pianissimo entries on piccolo and flute (very difficult to play quietly enough). The opening returns on the oboe. Then the muted strings take off again, reaching a greater climax than before. The dance ends with fragments of woodwind melody over quiet string tremolando chords. The princesses are so immersed in the dance, and so delighted by their new companion, that they do not notice the coming of daybreak.

Daybreak

The last chord of the khorovod lingers for a magical moment as the dawn is signalled by clashing fanfares on trumpets (in the original score they are offstage). The princesses must return to the castle. There are agitated exchanges as Prince Ivan starts to follow them. The Fairest Princess sadly warns him that it would mean his doom. She locks the golden gates. But he is not to be deterred.

Prince Ivan penetrates Katschei's castle – Magic carillon, appearance of Katschei's monster-guards, and capture of Prince Ivan

As soon as the Prince starts to hack at the gates with his sword, a fearful alarm sounds (low muted trumpets, with piano, bells, and harps, a marvellously threatening effect). The entire castle is awake, monstrous guards appear and surround the Prince, and, after a struggle, he is overpowered. This is a passage of mounting agitation in which the theme associated with Katschei builds up in fragments (he will eventually be forced to dance to it). Xylophone, swirling woodwind, and sinister trombone chords add to the threat.

Arrival of Katschei the Immortal – Dialogue of Katschei and Prince Ivan

The ancient and hideous Katschei appears, to the thud of bass drum, scratchy string tremolo, and low bassoons. The Prince is so overcome by repulsion that he cannot stop himself spitting at him. The court howls with rage.

Intercession of the princesses

The Fairest Princess rushes forward and begs the king to spare Prince Ivan, but to no avail (here, violins and oboe reprise the tender theme from the first appearance of the princesses). Katschei starts the incantation that will turn the Prince to stone (eerie tremolo culminating in brass chords). Then the Prince remembers the feather that the Firebird gave him, and waves it.

Appearance of the Firebird – Dance of Katschei's retinue, enchanted by the Firebird – Infernal dance of all Katschei's subjects

The Firebird appears, blinding Katschei and his henchmen and leading them in a dance. This begins lightly, as if nobody realizes what is happening, but gradually increases in force, with rapid xylophone hammering (the continual xylophone in this scene reminds us that Katschei is often depicted as a skeleton). The crescendo bursts out into the famous Infernal Dance of the entire court, with its sinister, offbeat theme and thwacking chords. Here, Stravinsky pays direct homage to his teacher: the theme (which we have already heard before) is derived from Rimsky-Korsakov's own depiction of Katschei in his opera *Mlada*, though its intervals also relate to the creeping bass with which the ballet began. At the end, the dance becomes faster and faster, wilder and wilder, until the moment when everyone collapses with exhaustion. A mysterious chord is left hanging in the air (muted trumpets, offstage in the original).

Berceuse (the Firebird)

The Firebird flies over the grotesque company, soothing them to sleep as if with a lullaby. A bassoon plays a haunting melody over a static bass, accompanied by a hypnotic four-note pattern marked by harp harmonics. This melody has been shown to be derived from a Ukrainian folk tune. But it too bears a relation to the intervals of the creeping bass line from the Introduction. An impassioned middle passage recalls the Firebird's earlier supplication (and has strong echoes of the 'Prélude à la nuit' from Ravel's recent *Rapsodie espagnole*). The bassoon returns accompanied by delicate high violins.

Katschei's awakening – Katschei's death – profound darkness

Over the dark, deep sound of contrabassoons, the court sleeps. The Firebird leads Prince Ivan to a chest containing an egg. In the egg is the death of Katschei. As the Prince takes the egg, Katschei wakes to a fearsome brass fanfare. The Prince dashes it to the ground, it shatters, and Katschei the Immortal dies. A tremendous crash is followed by the sound of fragments falling. As darkness falls, and the scene changes, a soft chord on muted strings spreads slowly up from the bottom to the top, and then gradually dissolves, narrowing in from bass and treble through a series of tremolando chromatic chords, until all that is left is a shimmering, simple B major.

Second tableau: Disappearance of Katschei's palace and magical creations, return to life of the petrified knights, general rejoicing

The final scene begins quietly, with a horn playing a traditional melody, 'By the gate a pine tree swayed', which Stravinsky took from Rimsky-Korsakov's Collection of 100 Russian Folk Songs. The entire finale is a set of variations on this melody, which gradually builds up, and breaks into a joyous seven-time. A final variation on full orchestra culminates in trumpets, horns, and trombones, reminding us for the last time of the intervals of the creeping line with which the ballet began, now transformed into a triumphant blaze. The petrified princes have found their princesses, and the Prince and the Fairest Princess marry, ready to rule over the liberated kingdom.

PETRUSHKA
Duration: approx. 35 minutes

After the great success of *The Firebird*, Stravinsky and his family spent some years based in Lausanne. It was here, in the autumn of 1910, that Stravinsky began to write an orchestral piece in which the piano would play the most important part: 'In composing the music, I had in my mind a distinct picture of a puppet, suddenly endowed with life, exasperating the patience of the orchestra with diabolical cascades of arpeggi. The orchestra in turn retaliates with menacing trumpet-blasts. The outcome is a terrific noise which reaches its climax and ends in the sorrowful and querulous collapse of the poor puppet.' Soon after, he found the title: 'Petroushka, the immortal and unhappy hero of every fair in all countries'.[10] Petrushka is a traditional puppet character, related to Punch in England, Pulcinella in Italy, and Guignol in France, and dating back at least to the seventeenth century. Stravinsky played the new piece to Diaghilev: 'He was so much pleased with it that he would not leave it alone and began persuading me to develop the theme of the puppet's sufferings and make it into a whole ballet.' Two other ideas followed: the whole story was to take place at the Shrovetide fair in St Petersburg, and, most important of all, the puppets should come to life at the command of a magician, and be capable of real emotions and suffering. The scene in which this takes place particularly impressed Debussy: 'There is a kind of sonorous magic within it, a mysterious transformation of mechanical souls which become human by a sorcery which is, until now, uniquely your invention.'[11]

Stravinsky showed his greatest originality in the characterization of the three puppet characters – the Ballerina, the Moor, and Petrushka. Petrushka is portrayed as a bitter and pathetic character, impotent against the power of the Showman who has magically brought him to life. Petrushka loves the Ballerina, but is rejected by her, and then consumed with jealousy when he finds the Ballerina and the Moor dancing together. In the final scene of the ballet, the Moor kills Petrushka with his scimitar. The Showman assures the crowd that it was just a puppet; but when the crowd disperses, leaving the Showman alone in the dusk, Petrushka's ghost appears, shaking his fist, and the Showman drops the broken puppet and flees in terror. Stravinsky replaced a carnival finale with this evocative ending at a late stage, and thought this scene the best part of the ballet. It premiered at the Théâtre du Châtelet under Pierre Monteux on 13 June 1911, with sets by Alexandre Benois and choreography by Mikhail Fokine. Petrushka was danced by the great Nijinsky, and Stravinsky wrote of 'the perfection with which he became the very incarnation of this character'.[12]

When a suite from *Petrushka* was first performed in Russia in 1913, it was attacked by Rimsky-Korsakov's son, Andrei (to whom Stravinsky had dedicated *The Firebird*), in a stinging review: 'With this piece the historic course of development of Russian music has come to a halt … *Petrushka* glitters with an artificial assortment of bright rags and patches and clatters with ringing rattles. Were it not for the big talents of Benois and Stravinsky, this piece, with its vulgar tunes, would have been a monstrous crime. But then, who knows – might not *Petrushka* be the prelude to some sort of *musical futurism*? If so, then perhaps 'twere better it had never been born.'[13] It was Andrei whom Stravinsky had asked for the music of two such 'vulgar tunes', that is, popular street songs. Stravinsky remembered that Andrei 'did send the music, but with words of his own fitted to it, facetious in intent, but in fact questioning my right to use such "trash" '.[14]

The rift with tradition to which Andrei objected was more than just the choice of songs. The way Stravinsky uses them is quite different from the approach of Rimsky-Korsakov, or for that matter from Stravinsky's own approach in *The Firebird*. In *Petrushka* the borrowed tunes are only occasionally used as real 'themes'. Most of them are thrown into the mix in an almost kaleidoscopic way, like identifiable pieces of newspaper in a collage (Picasso and Braque were beginning to use such techniques around this time). And perhaps this was indeed a portent of a sort of 'musical futurism'. In *The Rite of Spring*, Stravinsky was to develop the use of quotes from traditional tunes (and similar tunes invented by himself) to create a web of 'cells' with which to build the whole work.

The original 1911 version of *Petrushka* has a huge orchestra, including four flutes, four clarinets, pairs of cornets and trumpets, a large percussion section including offstage drums, two harps, glockenspiel, xylophone, celesta, and the all-important piano. In 1947, Stravinsky published a version for slightly reduced (but still large) orchestra, more practical for concert use.

First Tableau: The Shrovetide Fair
We hear the crowds before we see them: over a bustling accompaniment, there are calls from flute and cellos (based on real street vendors' cries). The bustling patterns gradually build up until the curtain rises to reveal the Shrovetide fair in full swing in Admiralty Square, St Petersburg, in 1830. The music comes together into block chords, from which a firm tune

emerges (the first of the many folk tunes Stravinsky quotes), as 'a group of drunken revellers passes by, dancing'. After a burst of five-time, the music breaks back to the bustling opening. Suddenly, a slower tune appears on clarinets, with fluttering flutes, simulating the sound of a street organ. After another interruption, the organ-grinder begins to play continuously a tune called 'Toward evening, in rainy autumn'. Every time the tune includes the note C, the top clarinet is silent, as if one of the organ pipes is malfunctioning. The dancer who accompanies the organ-grinder begins to dance. She plays a triangle, and dances to another tune, this time a saucy French song about Sarah Bernhardt's wooden leg. (Stravinsky had heard this on a barrel organ outside his window in Beaulieu-sur-Mer on the French Riviera, and had not realized it was in copyright.) The organ-grinder puts a cornet to his lips with one hand, and plays as he turns the crank with the other.

A rival musical box and a rival dancer start up (on glockenspiel), playing another tune, 'A wondrous moon plays upon the river', which is combined with the organ-grinder's 'Toward evening' (on clarinets). The triangle-playing dancer resumes with 'The wooden leg', but is interrupted by a resumption of the opening crowd music, and the drunken revellers' tune. (Sporadic reminders of the crowd music give the whole of this opening section something of the shape of a rondo.)

The music is just reaching a climax of energy and complexity when 'two drummers, stepping to the front of the puppet theatre, attract the attention of the crowd by their drumrolls'. There is a silence, and, with grotesque low notes on the contrabassoon, and bassoons in lugubrious duet, 'The old magician steps out in front of the little theatre'. This section is 'The Magic Trick' (the section particularly admired by Debussy). Over the bassoons and clarinets, the celesta, harp, and violins sprinkle mysterious cascades of sound. The old magician plays a languid cadenza on his flute. The curtain of the theatre opens to reveal three puppets: Petrushka, the Moor, and the Ballerina. The mysterious evocation becomes more intense, as filigrees of woodwind join the other instruments (this passage is reminiscent of the evocations of magic in *The Firebird*). There are three little chirrups of the flute, as 'The magician brings them to life by touching them lightly with his flute'. Then, 'Petrushka, the Moor and the Ballerina suddenly begin to dance, to the great astonishment of the crowd'. The Moor is resplendent in turban and pantaloons. The ballerina dances on point all the time. Poor Petrushka is in love with her, but dances clumsily, and the Ballerina has eyes only for the Moor. This is the 'Russian Dance' well known not only from the ballet score, but also in a virtuoso arrangement for solo piano. It is based on two more folk tunes. 'A linden tree is in the field' dominates the first part. A second tune, a 'Song for St John's Eve', dominates the middle section, with frenzied arpeggios in the clarinets and scale patterns in the piano. The dance slows for a moment. Then solo piano, with hammered chords, takes up the first tune again. The rhythm of the dance becomes more disjointed, with offbeat chords, until it reaches a sudden end. 'Darkness: the curtain falls'. A drum roll (offstage in the original version) links to the second part of the ballet.

Second Tableau: Petrushka's Room

'As the curtain rises, the door to Petrushka's room opens suddenly, a foot kicks him onstage. Petrushka falls and the door closes again behind him.' Clarinets play a sourly discordant duet, and bassoon and trumpet play melancholy solos. Flourishes on the piano lead to an outburst as Petrushka curses the magician (fanfares on muted trumpets and trombones against a ferociously agitated background with clashing harmonies). Then Petrushka dances sadly to a brittle, rather oriental-sounding tune, with flute and piano, then cor anglais with a heavy tread, and back to flute.

As the Ballerina enters, the piano warms into the major key. As Petrushka sees her, he leaps into a frantic dance, with music parodying the demure phrase with which she entered. Alarmed, the Ballerina soon escapes, leaving Petrushka alone. Desolate fragments of cadenza on clarinet and piano build up to another outburst of despair and rage, with the dissonant chords and trumpet fanfares. There is a brief reminder of the crowds outside, with *ppp* horns as Petrushka looks out from his room at them – this moment will come to haunt (literally) the magician at the end of the ballet. And the scene ends with an abrupt trumpet fanfare ('Darkness. Curtain'). An offstage drum roll links to the next scene.

Third Tableau: The Moor's Room

In the first production, Benois's set for the Moor's Room was a brightly coloured scene of oriental fantasy, in vivid contrast to Petrushka's sad, dark room. As the curtain rose, Folkine had the Moor reclining on a couch, playing with a coconut. The Moor's dance is a sinister, sinuous line on clarinet and bass clarinet, with processional rhythm on pizzicato strings, bass drum, and cymbal (whatever the staging, the music allows us no escape from the traditional stereotype of the evil Moor). There is then a passage of savage contrasts: in the original staging, the Moor tries to cut the coconut with a scimitar, and when he fails, kneels and worships it as a god. This passage ends with the sinister dance on bassoons.

The Ballerina enters and dances flirtatiously, while playing a toy cornet. The Ballerina and the Moor then dance a slow waltz together. There is an element of parody in the music, with awkwardly phrased bassoon accompaniment, cornet and flute in duet, and with the flute suggesting the Ballerina's teetering steps on her points. Stravinsky here quotes a waltz by Joseph Lanner, and another as the pace increases to that of a Viennese waltz. This is combined with the sinuous melody of the Moor's earlier dance, on low cor anglais and contrabassoon. Savage dissonances return briefly, after which the slow waltz resumes, but with ominous elements on cor anglais and horn below.

There is a sudden hush, with string tremolo as 'The Moor and the Ballerina prick up their ears', and, announced by agitated fragments of trumpet fanfare, the jealous Petrushka appears, interrupting their dance. This leads to 'The fight between the Moor and Petrushka', during which, 'The Ballerina faints'. The melodic fragments and chords in this section once again clash, and are in two keys at once – a technique reminiscent of the 'evil' evocations in *The Firebird*, which Stravinsky was to exploit more systematically in *The Rite of Spring*. The result of this uneven battle is inevitable: the Moor thrashes Petrushka (savage chords), and he flees for his life. An offstage drum roll links to the final scene.

Fourth Tableau: The Shrovetide Fair (Towards Evening)

Like the first tableau, this begins with a vivid evocation of a bustling crowd, even more excited than before. Fragments of earlier themes are heard, most notably a repetitive, rocking motif with an offbeat accent (last heard at the end of the scene in Petrushka's room), and a melodic shape in five-time. The rocking motif quietens, settling into a chattering pattern. This is 'The wet-nurses' dance', the first of a sequence of dances that occupies the first half of this finale. This is the most traditional part of *Petrushka*, echoing the sequences of set-piece dances in the final acts of ballets by Tchaikovsky, Léo Delibes, and others. Phrases of a melody are played first on oboe, then on horn, and finally the whole melody is sung by the violins. This is a Russian folk song, best known as 'Along the Peterskaya Road', and it forms a climax of the celebratory atmosphere. It is the most uncomplicated, lyrical, major-key theme in the whole ballet (though still with some dark undertones in its accompaniment). There is a quirkier middle section to another traditional tune, 'Ah, my doorstep'. When the first melody returns, the two tunes are combined, together with the offbeat rocking motif.

Suddenly 'A peasant enters with a bear. Everyone scatters' – an action vividly evoked by the dispersal of the music. 'The peasant plays a pipe. The bear walks on its hind legs.' Over a heavy tread, clarinets play a high, wailing flourish, evoking the sort of traditional pipe-playing that Stravinsky was to exploit in *The Rite of Spring*. A solo tuba plays a clumsy, slow-motion version of this flourish. This fades away as the peasant and bear leave, and the crowds gradually return (represented by the renewed buzz of activity in the music).

'A revelling merchant and two gypsy women enter. He irresponsibly amuses himself by throwing bank notes to the crowd.' The violins play another folk tune, with thrusting glissandi. 'The gypsy women dance. The merchant plays the accordion.' The music breaks into a fast patter. Earlier elements are drawn in – the murmur of the crowd, and the most recent folk tune. A little fanfare-like phrase, repeated many times, leads in to 'The Dance of the coachmen and the grooms', with its rather stately rhythm. Another traditional tune, 'The snow thaws', passes between trumpets, pizzicato strings, trombones, and horns. After a time, 'Along the Peterskaya Road' returns, as 'The wet-nurses dance with the coachmen and the grooms.' 'The snow thaws' builds to a joyful climax (another straightforward major-key moment).

There is a sudden increase in pace and energy, as a group of masqueraders, including a devil, enters the scene. The music builds in intensity, as if some unspoken anxiety is developing, with the dance reaching its height in a fast five-time. The rest of the crowd joins the dance, and the music settles to a regular metre. 'The crowd continues to dance without taking notice of the cries coming from the little theatre.' Eventually, 'The dance breaks off. Petrushka dashes from the little theatre, pursued by the Moor, whom the Ballerina tries to restrain.' Music earlier associated with Petrushka's rage and jealousy, and the fight between Petrushka and the Moor, builds up frantically, until 'The furious Moor seizes him and strikes him with his sabre.' Throughout this confrontation Stravinsky keeps the music brittle, with no bass line, no trombones, no big orchestral tutti. This preserves the ambiguity of these characters – are they puppets or are they human? Then, with a pianissimo roll of a cymbal, 'Petrushka falls, his head broken.' As the crowd gather round Petrushka, 'He dies, still moaning', to eerie string tremolo, nervous chirrups from flute and piccolo, and mournful phrases from clarinet and bassoon. A policeman (staccato bassoons) brings out the magician, with a return to the grotesque contrabassoon notes and strange, drooping horn phrases from his first appearance.

'He picks up Petrushka's corpse' (sudden muted trumpets), 'shaking it' (agitated muted strings), to demonstrate to the crowd that it is only a puppet. As 'the crowd disperses', the rocking figure with which the ballet began is taken up by pianissimo muted horns, evoking the end of the scene in which Petrushka sadly looked out at the crowds from his room. But sinister bass notes, in an entirely different key, interrupt the uneasy calm. 'The magician remains alone on stage. He drags Petrushka's corpse towards the little theatre.' As the rocking figure resumes, fortissimo muted trumpets snarl out Petrushka's curse. 'Above the little theatre appears the ghost of Petrushka, menacing, thumbing his nose at the magician. The terrified magician lets the puppet-Petrushka drop from his hands, and exits quickly, casting frightened glances over his shoulder.' As the curtain falls, pizzicato strings quietly play a falling phrase, in the remote key of the earlier pizzicato bass, and the ballet ends chillingly unresolved.

PULCINELLA (SUITE)
Duration: approx. 24 minutes

In 1917, Diaghilev's *Ballets Russes* scored a great success in Rome with *The Good-Humoured Ladies*, a ballet choreographed by Léonide Massine, based on a comedy by Carlo Goldoni, with music taken from the harpsichord sonatas of Domenico Scarlatti orchestrated by Vincenzo Tommasini. Diaghilev had acquired from libraries in Naples and London a number of scores of works attributed to another Italian baroque composer, Giovanni Pergolesi (1710–36), though many of them have since been shown to be by other composers. Diaghilev, Massine, and Picasso discussed the possibility of staging a ballet in the style of *commedia dell'arte* based on an eighteenth-century play concerning the rivalry between Pulcinella and the young men of the town, and using Pergolesi's music. Massine had found in a library in Naples a play dating from 1700 called *Quatre Polichinelles Semblables* (this has been identified as probably *I quattro Pollicinelle simili* from a Neapolitan collection of that date).[15] Their first choice of composer was Manuel de Falla, but when he refused the commission, they turned to Stravinsky. Massine drew up a draft scenario, and himself danced the role of Pulcinella. Set and costumes were designed by Picasso who, like Stravinsky, juxtaposed ancient and modern in a fascinating way: his final version of the set shows an internal proscenium arch containing a building formed of incompatible perspectives, cubist-style, while the costumes are in the tradition of the *commedia dell'arte*.

In later years, Stravinsky went on the attack against critics who had found his reworking of Pergolesi disrespectful or sacrilegious, declaring that it was based on love rather than barren respect: 'I am only too familiar with the mentality of those curators and archivists of music who jealously guard the intangibility of relics at which they never so much as look, while resenting any attempt on the part of others to resuscitate these treasures which they themselves regard as dead and sacrosanct. Not only is my conscience clear of having committed sacrilege, but, so far as I can see, my attitude towards Pergolesi is the only one that can usefully be taken up with regard to the music of bygone times.'[16]

Twenty-five years later, he added, 'That the result was to some extent a satire was probably inevitable – who could have treated that material in 1919 without satire? – but even this observation is hindsight; I did not set out to compose a satire and, of course, Diaghilev hadn't even considered the possibility of such a thing. A stylish orchestration was what Diaghilev wanted, and nothing more, and my music so shocked him that he went about for a long time with a look that suggested the Offended Eighteenth Century. In fact, however, the remarkable thing about *Pulcinella* is not how much but how little has been added or changed . . . *Pulcinella* was my discovery of the past, the epiphany through which the whole of my late work became possible. It was a backward look, of course – the first of many love affairs in that direction – but it was a look in the mirror too.'[17]

Stravinsky may have added and changed little, but what he did add and change made the music sound distinctly like Stravinsky. The old music is more or less intact, but coloured with discords, shifts of harmony and rhythm, and confrontational orchestrations as if one is seeing the music through a strange, possibly cubist, pair of spectacles. This creates quite a different effect from Tommasini's more straightforward updating of Scarlatti in *The Good-Humoured Ladies*, or Respighi's First Suite of *Ancient Airs and Dances* from the same year (1917). The term 'neoclassical' has been attached to this approach (though Stravinsky rejected the term), and it was to have considerable influence not only on Stravinsky's later work, but also on other composers, such as Martinů and Hindemith.

The premiere took place in Paris on 15 May 1920, and was conducted by Ernest Ansermet, one of Stravinsky's most faithful and long-standing collaborators. A number of the early reviews were (contrary to what Stravinsky later implied) sympathetic. A French critic commenting on the premiere admired Stravinsky's 'burlesque symphony', with its 'piquant effects', and had no doubt about his right to use Pergolesi's music in this way, since 'his work is charming. In art, the only politics is that of results, and a masterpiece executed at the price of a slight sacrilege is no less admirable for it.'[18]

The principal characters are two young men, Florindo and Caviello, and two young ladies, Prudenza and Rosetta, together with Pulcinella (whom the men see as a dangerous rival) and his beloved, Pimpinella. The first edition of the piano score (which was published before the orchestral score) summarizes the plot: 'All the young girls of the country are in love with Pulcinella. The young men, stung with jealousy, try to kill him. As soon as they think they have accomplished their aim, they put on Pulcinella costumes to present themselves to their beloveds. But Pulcinella has cunningly had himself replaced by a double, who pretended to die under the blows of his enemies. Pulcinella himself dresses as a magician, and comes to resuscitate his double. Just when the young men think they have got rid of him, the real Pulcinella appears, and arranges all their marriages. He himself marries Pimpinella, with the blessing of his double (Fourbo), who, in his turn, takes on the appearance of magician.'[19]

Pulcinella is on a more modest scale than the lavish ballets from before the First World War. It is shorter, and scored for a chamber orchestra: pairs of flutes (the second doubling piccolo), oboes, clarinets, bassoons, and horns, one trumpet, one trombone, and strings. As in an eighteenth-century *concerto grosso*, there is a solo group of strings (string quartet plus double bass), which is contrasted with the full strings. The full ballet score includes vocal music – arias, duets, and trios – as well as instrumental pieces. The work most often heard in the concert hall is the purely instrumental suite that Stravinsky extracted in 1922, and revised in 1949, and it is this that is described below. The composer of the source music (originally thought to be Pergolesi) is given after the title of each movement.[20]

Sinfonia (Domenico Gallo, Trio Sonata No. 1)
Serenata (Giovanni Pergolesi, *Il Flaminio*)
Scherzino – Allegro – Andantino (Gallo, Trio Sonata Nos 2 and 8)
Tarantella (Count Unico van Wassenaer, *Concerti Armonici*, No. 6)
Toccata (Carlo Monza, *Pièces modernes pour le Clavecin*)
Gavotta – Variazione I – Variazione II (Monza, *Pièces modernes pour le Clavecin*)
Vivo (Pergolesi, Sinfonia for cello and basso continuo)
Menuetto – Finale (Pergolesi, *Lo Frate 'nnamorato* – Gallo, Trio Sonata No. 12)

The opening Sinfonia immediately strikes a fascinating balance between ancient and modern. The writing for strings is almost baroque in style, but it is filled out with wind instruments, most noticeably horns. The harmonies are not quite as straightforward as in eighteenth-century music – dissonant notes hang on intriguingly, instead of being immediately resolved. The orchestral textures vary. Sometimes the whole orchestra plays together, the next moment only the strings, then only the wind. There are touches of solo wind instruments, and of solo strings. This gives the impression of an updated baroque *concerto grosso*, but the alternation and balancing of the different elements, combined with the spicy harmonies, result in something characteristically quirky and unpredictable.

The Serenade (which is an aria for tenor in the ballet, taken from an opera by Pergolesi) is a gentle piece in lilting siciliano rhythm, featuring solo oboe and violin (neatly suggesting the two young men serenading the two young ladies). Again, the original music floats on, and in, a stream of modern touches: a keynote that persists, like an internal bagpipe or hurdy-gurdy, spicing the harmonies with clashes; gently 'scrubbed' bowing, giving an effect almost like a brushed cymbal; a variety of pizzicato effects, including plucked harmonics, and more robust chords. These give a changing character to the piece, from charming through ethereal to ironic.

The Scherzino interrupts the languid Serenade. This is the moment of confrontation between the father of one of the girls and the two young men serenading outside the house. There is polite interplay between strings and wind, the 'manly' tones of bassoons and horns perhaps suggesting the father. The confrontation is clearly conducted with decorum. Into this scene bursts a cheeky piccolo, like the piper of a fairground dance, with a drum suggested by chords of pizzicato harmonics. This is the entry of Pulcinella playing a violin, and leads on to the Allegro. A solo violin plays with virtuoso swagger, which proves irresistible to the two girls. A charming decelerating scale accompanies them coming out onto the street. Here, Stravinsky has taken what was a fast movement and turned it into a languid Andantino. The relationship between solo violin, horns, and flutes (sounding demure and feminine) suggests an easy and mutual flirtation.

In the suite, the story now jumps forward. Pulcinella having apparently died, the magician (really Pulcinella) comes to resuscitate the fake Pulcinella. The Tarantella marks the moment when he is brought back to life. Stravinsky prefaces the movement with *Petrushka*-like wild cross-rhythms (was this an ironic reference to the puppet brought back to life?), before settling into the Tarantella. At first, this sounds almost baroque, with its simple string scoring. But soon it acquires dissonant edges and chords with added notes, so the cumulative effect confirms the almost *Petrushka*-like impression with which it started.

This leads straight into the rather stately Toccata. This is another movement in which the juxtaposition of ancient and modern is particularly striking. The solo trumpet has the feel of a 'trumpet voluntary', but the stubbornly unchanging chords beneath it are thoroughly twentieth century. Later, an oboe solo sounds almost baroque, but the high bassoon entry has a mockingly strained effect. The ironical sense is confirmed by the final bar, with an utterly un-baroque last note from the trombone.

The two girls dance with the two young men in Pulcinella costumes, to a Gavotte with two variations. This movement is for wind instruments alone. The first half of each Gavotte is scored with restraint, and is repeated, giving quite an eighteenth-century feel to the dance. But the longer second half in each case acquires more discords and thicker scoring, pulling the music more firmly into the twentieth century.

On the original source of Vivo, Stravinsky scrawled 'Enter the real Pulcinella'. Pulcinella, having faked his own death and resurrection, now reappears as himself and exacts his revenge, throwing Florindo and Caviello in the fountain. This is the most startling transformation in the whole of *Pulcinella*. What was a sonata movement for cello and continuo becomes a raucous trombone solo, with rude glissandi, in awkward dialogue with a solo double bass, which not only plays the bass line but also takes over some of the solo part. They make a comical couple, like a cartoon of an elephant and a hippopotamus dancing together.

Finally, the happy ending. To the strains of a minuet, Pulcinella presides over the uniting of the two men, Florindo and Caviello, with their two girls, Prudenza and Rosetta, while Pulcinella himself is united with Pimpinella. The source of the minuet is an aria from Pergolesi's opera *Lo Frate 'nnamorato*, which, in Stravinsky's ballet, appropriately unites the three singers in a trio. In the suite, after an introduction, the singers' first entries are given to trumpet, horn, and trombone. Stravinsky's slow tempo for the minuet gives it a solemn and sentimental character. Towards the end it builds, with startlingly acerbic discords, until it burst out into the finale.

This is a movement of high spirits, in which Stravinsky allows a thoroughly Russian character to invade the eighteenth-century original: as Richard Taruskin charmingly puts it, 'beady Scythian eyes seem to glint from behind the mask of European urbanity'.[21] And, in the midst of the celebration, Stravinsky cannot resist a sly little quote from Manuel de Falla, with a couple of very Spanish-sounding bars from *The Three-Cornered Hat*. (This was an in-joke: Falla had been the first choice for *Pulcinella*, and it was for *The Three-Cornered Hat* that Diaghilev had first brought Massine and Picasso together in 1919.) At the end, after a moment of lyrical sentiment, Stravinsky obsessively repeats the opening phrase of the movement again and again, with the occasional beat missing. It is as if the stones of a baroque building have been thrown in the air and reassembled to produce a playful folly – like Picasso's cubist set for *Pulcinella*.

LE SACRE DU PRINTEMPS (THE RITE OF SPRING)
Duration: approx. 32 minutes

It was Serge Diaghilev, impresario of the *Ballets Russes*, who staged *The Rite of Spring*, and who claimed much of the credit for it. But the initial idea for a ballet about spring rituals in ancient Russia seems to have originated with Stravinsky himself. Stravinsky, a great self-mythologizer, gave various versions of his original idea over the half century after composing *The Rite*. In his *Autobiography* of 1936, he writes that he was finishing the score of *The Firebird* when he suddenly had 'a fleeting vision ... I saw in imagination a solemn pagan rite: sage elders, seated in a circle, watched a young girl dance herself to death. They were sacrificing her to propitiate the god of spring'.[22] He developed the idea for the ballet in discussion with Nikolai Roerich. Roerich was a Russian artist who had worked with Diaghilev, designing the sets and costumes for Borodin's *Prince Igor* in 1909. He was also an archaeologist with a profound interest in ancient cultures and religion, especially those of ancient Russia. Stravinsky turned to Roerich, explaining, 'who else could help me, who else knows the secret of our ancestors' close feeling for the earth?'[23] It was Roerich who designed sets and costumes for *The Rite of Spring*.

Exactly where Stravinsky and Roerich found their ideas for the ballet is a fascinating topic that scholars have pored over during the last hundred years. The answers are not clear-cut, but, contrary to the impression Stravinsky liked to give, many of the ideas must have come from Roerich rather than Stravinsky. According to the artist Alexander Benois, Roerich was a man 'utterly absorbed in dreams of prehistoric, patriarchal and religious life – of the days when the vast, limitless plains of Russia and the shores of her lakes and rivers were peopled with the fore-fathers of the present inhabitants.'[24] The most important of these forefathers in Russian lore were the Scythians, who occupied a huge area including present-day Russia, whose delicate and beau-tiful artworks are to be found in museums across the world, but of whose culture little is known beyond descriptions in Herodotus's *The Persian Wars*. These include battle with the Amazons. Discovering these ferocious warriors to be women, the Scythians send their young men to mate with them. Stravinsky's sketches for *The Rite of Spring* includes mention of 'Amazons' in relation to what was eventually called 'Glorification of the Chosen One'.[25] But the sacrifice of a woman is not part of Amazon or Scythian ritual, and it is not known where Stravinsky got this idea from. Roerich would have known what sources there were about Scythians, and about pre-Christian Russia, but he also knew that the evidence was sparse. In response to this, Roerich himself in his own writings and paintings had imaginatively fleshed out life in the Stone Age, including rituals of dance and song to greet the arrival of spring.

The Rite of Spring is, of course, not a piece of scholarship or reconstruction, but a work of the creative imagination. Musically, Stravinsky drew on folk material (again, real and imag-ined). In this, *The Rite* stands in a long tradition of Russian music going back all the way to Glinka in the 1840s. It was Glinka who showed how an extended work could be constructed by repetition of a tune, using the simple method of varying its orchestration (see Glinka's *Kamarinskaya*). The next generation of Russian composers, including Stravinsky's teacher, Rimsky-Korsakov, developed this idea in sophisticated ways. With Stravinsky, it reaches a turning point. Fragments of 'folk' melody and rhythm become cells that multiply, divide, and mutate like organic cells in a living creature. These folk-cells preserve some of the character-istics of real folk music – a narrow range of notes, repetitive phrases, irregular rhythmic units – but they are juxtaposed in ways that create clashes of harmony, often giving the impression that the music is in two keys at once. This gives *The Rite* a unique sense of being at the same time highly organized and out of control: organized chaos, you might say. And, crucially, it results in a work that succeeds in sounding both ancient and modern.

This places *The Rite of Spring* firmly in its own time. The relating of the modern and the ancient, the sophisticated and the 'primitive', was one of the most important strands of thought in the early twentieth century, and the study of anthropology was influencing thinking across the arts. James Frazer's *The Golden Bough*, first published in 1890, was enlarged to twelve volumes in 1911–15. It sought to trace the origins of religion to the fertility rites of ancient cultures, with their sacrifice of the priest-king. T. S. Eliot, whose *The Waste Land* (1922) drew on Frazer, found a 1921 performance of *The Rite* 'interesting to anyone who had read *The Golden Bough* and similar works, but hardly more than interesting'.[26] To Eliot, *The Golden Bough* could be read as 'a revelation of that vanished mind of which our mind is a continua-tion', and was as important as the work of Sigmund Freud. Freud followed *The Interpretation of Dreams* (1899) with *Totem and Taboo: Resemblances between the Mental Lives of Savages and Neurotics* in the year of *The Rite of Spring*, 1913. Picasso's fascination with African art was at its height in the period 1906–9, and this fed into his development with Georges Braque of cubism in the years immediately preceding *The Rite of Spring*. Stravinsky and Picasso were to collaborate for Diaghilev on *Pulcinella* in 1920.

The Rite of Spring was undoubtedly an important landmark, which jolted into the open new possibilities for the future direction of music. It was the third of Stravinsky's ballets for

Diaghilev, following *The Firebird* (1910) and *Petrushka* (1911). It is obvious to the ear that it breaks from these earlier scores, but the more one gets to know *The Rite*, the more one can also hear some continuity in the language. Much has been written about the subtleties and complexities of this fascinating topic.[27] But some of the features that *The Rite* does and does not share with those works are relatively straightforward. The nature of the scenario, of the story being told, is quite different. Indeed, *The Rite* does not 'tell a story' at all. It presents a ritual on the stage, as if in real time.

The orchestra, which in *The Firebird* and *Petrushka* evokes scenes and narrative events in a relatively conventional way, in *The Rite* behaves quite differently. The members of the orchestra seem, not like bystanders, but like participants in the ritual. One of the things that make this difference is the make-up of the orchestra itself. As in *The Firebird* and *Petrushka*, it is a huge orchestra. But its composition is significantly changed. The earlier ballets include – as well as strings, woodwind, brass, and the usual percussion – xylophone, glockenspiel, celesta, harps, and piano (apart from the piano, these are also in Ravel's *Daphnis et Chloé*, 1912). *The Rite* has none of these additional instruments, because the traditional evocations of a ballet score are not what Stravinsky and Roerich had in mind. Instead, Stravinsky makes much use of the wind instruments at the top and (particularly) bottom of the range: two piccolos, two cor anglais, two bass clarinets, two contrabassoons, two tubas. The result is an expanded wind palette, particularly in the lower region, giving an exceptionally rich and resonant spread of sonorities. It is like a rural band on a gigantic scale.

The premiere took place at the Théâtre des Champs-Elysées on 29 May 1913. There was uproar (if not quite the 'riot' of popular myth), and at the end supporters and detractors tried to outdo each other in their noise as Stravinsky and Nijinsky took bows. But it is important to remember that this was a ballet audience. The protests began even before the orchestra started playing, and as the ballet got under way the main source of the outrage was the style of the choreography, which was quite unlike traditional, classical (that is to say, nineteenth-century) dance. Jerky movement, stamps, spasms, mass movements, and complex patterns underlined the violence of the music, which, as the performance went on, was partly obscured by the noise of the protests. Later concert performances were a triumph. Now that the work is most often heard in concert, and orchestras are used to playing it, *The Rite* has lost some of its ability to shock. So, nowadays, it helps to have a really visceral choreography to reawaken our understanding of the power of this music, as in the versions by Pina Bausch and Kenneth Macmillan.

First Part: Adoration of the Earth	Second Part: The Sacrifice
Introduction	Introduction
The Augurs of Spring: Dances of the Young Girls	Mystic Circles of the Young Girls
Ritual of Abduction	Glorification of the Chosen One
Spring Rounds	Evocation of the Ancestors
Ritual of the Rival Tribes	Ritual Action of the Ancestors
Procession of the Sage	Sacrificial Dance (The Chosen One)
The Sage	
Dance of the Earth	

The quotations that describe each section are taken from notes that Stravinsky sent to the conductor Serge Koussevitzky for a performance in 1914, together with descriptions that Stravinsky gave in an interview published on the day of the premiere.[28]

First Part: Adoration of the Earth
Introduction

A bassoon in its very highest register plays a free melody, the first of many in the work that have the character of an Eastern European folk tune. This is a Lithuanian traditional melody – Stravinsky claimed that this was the only 'real' folk tune in *The Rite of Spring*, though others have been identified, scattered through the first part of the work. Many of these folk (or folk-like) melodies have features in common – common intervals, a common scale – and this helps to give a sense of coherence to the whole work. To early audiences this opening must have sounded very strange indeed. Bassoonists in modern times have become used to playing difficult, high parts, but in 1913 such writing was most unusual. The sound, particularly on the French bassoon, has a strained reediness. Clarinets, cor anglais, and others join in, immediately evoking a sense of group musical activity. Stravinsky referred to this effect as 'a swarm of *dudki*.'[29] *Dudki* are the traditional pipes (with or without reeds) of rural areas in Eastern Europe, and this interweaving of their melodies vividly suggests a gathering of the communities. But Stravinsky was also quoted as saying (in an interview published the day after the premiere) that he had tried to express in this Introduction 'the fear of nature before the arising of beauty, a sacred terror at the midday sun, a sort of pagan cry . . . And the whole orchestra, all this massing of instruments, should have the significance of The Birth of Spring.'[30]

At the end of this first section, the solo bassoon repeats its opening phrase a semitone lower, and a ticking alternation of two notes in the violins (which has already persisted as an accompanying figure) leads into:

The Augurs of Spring: Dances of the Young Girls

In this first scene, 'Some adolescent boys appear with a very old woman, whose age and even whose century is unknown, who knows the secrets of nature, and who teaches her sons Prediction. She runs, bent over the earth, half-woman, half-beast. The adolescents at her side are Augurs of Spring, who mark in their steps the rhythm of spring, the pulse beat of spring.'

The ticking rhythm suddenly turns into savage repeated chords on the strings. These are in a regular two-time, but are punctuated by sudden offbeats on the horns that cut across the pulse, followed by jagged fanfares and flourishes in the woodwind. The persistent ticking continues in the background. Bassoons and trombones play scale patterns with offbeat accents that suggest processional stamping. After a brief, raucous pause (low trombones), the rhythm starts again. Agitated arpeggios begin in the clarinets. A horn plays another fragment of folk melody, answered by a flute, and then alto flute, interspersed with calls in oboes and trumpet. As the texture begins to build up, four trumpets play a solemn chant. The persistent rhythm becomes more and more hypnotic as other instruments join in, and the music builds into a huge, complex web of sound. At its climax there is a terrifyingly dissonant chord, the rhythm breaks, and we reach:

Ritual of Abduction

'Young girls arrive from the river in single file. They begin the "Dance of the Abduction".'

The strings play shuddering tremolo, and offbeat bass-drum strokes signal a sudden increase in pace and urgency. Trumpet and woodwind play rapid little fanfares, and are answered by whooping horn calls and wild timpani strokes.

This brief section ends with a series of violent chords, and a moment of uneasy calm as flutes hold a long trill.

Spring Rounds

This sequence of sections, up to the arrival of the sage, involves rivalry and conflict between the groups of young men and young women. The girls 'form a circle which mingles with the boys' circle'.

As the flutes sustain their trill, bass clarinet and high clarinet, two octaves apart, play a slow incantation. This is followed by sombre chords in a rising pattern, with offbeats played by two bass clarinets doubling the lower strings, and bass drum and pairs of bassoons and contrabassoons adding weight to the main beats. Soon the solemn chant played by trumpets in 'Augurs of Spring' reappears in different instrumental combinations: violas with flutes (each in four parts), horns with flutes, violins with flutes, and then on full orchestra, with each bar attacked by drums and gong, and ends of phrases marked by a wrenching shift of harmony on trumpets and trombones, with trombone glissando. This grinds to a halt. Flute and piccolos give a whoop of joy, and the rest of the orchestra joins in a brief celebratory passage. It suddenly comes to a halt, leaving trilling flutes and clarinets, as at the beginning of 'Spring Rounds', with the incantation now on alto flute and high clarinet two octaves apart (alto flute replacing the earlier bass clarinet to subtly different effect).

Ritual of the Rival Tribes

'The groups separate and compete, messengers come from one to the other and they quarrel. It is the defining of forces through struggle, that is, through games.'

The incantation gives way to another passage of wild energy, aggressive at first, but developing a more playful character than other sections of the work, partly because of more straightforward harmonies and rhythms. The impression of groups chasing each other is conveyed by contrasts between strings, woodwind, and brass, which accumulate over a bass that grinds out relentlessly. Into this joyful scene intrudes another incantatory chant on trombones, with strokes of bass drum, starkly clashing with the harmonies of the dance (and once again, these clashes have been prefigured earlier in the dance). Without a break or change of tempo, we enter:

Procession of the Sage

'A holy procession leads to the entry of the wise elders, headed by the Sage, who brings the games to a pause and blesses the earth.'

Trombones repeat their incantation again and again, over the heavy tread of bass instruments, timpani, and bass drum. They continue as the arrival of the sage is greeted with a shout from the whole orchestra. There is a sudden cut-off and a silence.

The Sage

'The games stop and the people wait, trembling, for the blessing of the earth. The Sage makes a sign to kiss the earth.'

This section, as the Sage kisses the earth, lasts only a few seconds. Dark chords are sustained by bassoons, and a solo double bass and contrabassoon touch pairs of notes, like some sort of ritual sign. The strings play a quiet, mysterious chord on harmonics.

Dance of the Earth

'The people break into a passionate dance, sanctifying and becoming one with the earth.'

The first stage of the ritual is accomplished, and the whole orchestra gives vent to wild joy. After a passage of violent chords in complex syncopated patterns, with the brazen sound of rolled gong strokes, there is a sudden hush. A rapid pattern of notes gradually emerges from the lower instruments, combining groups of four and three to give an impression of powerful energy bubbling up. Gradually its force increases, building up to an *fff* chord. Abruptly, the first part of *The Rite of Spring* is over.

Second Part: The Sacrifice

Introduction

Stravinsky originally intended to start the second half with the next section, the 'Mystic Circles of the Young Girls', and added this Introduction afterwards. It is one of the most strikingly atmospheric parts of the whole work, evoking a deep sense of mystery. It begins with evocative chords, with a rocking motif, and fragments of a slow melody trying to form itself. When the melody does emerge, it is played by the extraordinary combination of solo violin harmonics with alto flute two octaves below. This melody is another of the 'folk-like' tunes, particularly close in shape to the bassoon solo that opened Part I. The rocking motif reappears on muted trumpets, with a new twist of melody and harmony that makes it even more mysterious. This is repeated again and again, and a delicate network of sounds is built up around it, with little rhythmic points and rapid arpeggios, like things half-heard and half-seen.

Mystic Circles of the Young Girls

'Night. The young girls engage in mysterious games, walking in circles. One of the maidens is chosen for the Sacrifice. Fate points to her twice: twice she is caught in one of the circles without an exit.'

This begins without a break as the violas, divided into six parts, play the new folk melody. At a sudden clarinet trill, the pace increases. The violins play urgent tremolo in another version of the rocking motif from the Introduction. The alto flute plays a folk melody that seems like a variant of the melody it played with the solo violin in the Introduction. Clarinets, dissonantly in sevenths, take it up.

The tempo suddenly slows again, and, over processional pizzicato, flute and viola play sighing phrases, as if the opening of the most recent folk melody has become frozen. The melody resumes, is repeated several times, then comes to a pause with a sudden two-note warning from the horns. The same happens again, with the trumpets calling the warning. This time, the two-note phrase is repeated, accelerating (here we realize the connection to the two-note rocking figure in the Introduction). A sudden violent crescendo is followed by eleven dissonant, fortissimo chords, hammered out by strings, four timpani, and bass drum.

Glorification of the Chosen One
'The girls dance a martial dance honouring the Chosen One.'

The orchestra erupts in whoops of wild celebration, in which a repeated phrase is subjected to ever-changing numbers of beats per bar: 5, 5, 9, 5, 7, 3, 4. It is like dancers trying to dance a regular metre during an earthquake. For a moment there seems to be some regular pattern, with a hypnotically repeating bass, but then once more the irregular whoops, stamping, and brass calls resume, until they are suddenly cut off.

Evocation of the Ancestors
'In a brief dance, the young girls evoke the ancestors.'

There is a thwack of timpani, and over a held bass note, woodwind and brass intone a chordal fanfare. Its top line oscillates between two notes, like the rocking motif from the Introduction to the Second Part. The chords of the fanfare are straightforward consonances, but over a disso-nant bass note. Fortissimo wind and pianissimo strings alternate, followed by four bassoons and contrabassoon, and a final burst of the wind. Bass drum, timpani, and tambourine with horns and pizzicato horns set up a hypnotic treading rhythm that leads without a break into:

Ritual Action of the Ancestors
'The Chosen One is entrusted to the care of the wise old men.'

Over the hypnotic tread, mysterious fragments on cor anglais and alto flute circle around each other. Then the alto flute joins the hypnotic rhythm with another repetitive pattern, again derived from the rocking motif. Muted trumpets and bass trumpet quietly play an incantation (yet another of the folk-like melodies). Quivering tremolando violins heighten the tension. Then horns, with their bells raised, play the incantation fortissimo while the tread persists across the rest of the orchestra. A moment later, the whole orchestra with percussion breaks out, and the horns repeat the incantation *fff*. The section ends with the last quiet moment in the work, as bass trumpet and alto flute, then clarinet and bass clarinet, play a last quasi-improvisation. The treading rhythm falls silent, and a staccato scale on bass clarinet leads into the final section.

Sacrificial Dance (The Chosen One)
'The Chosen One dances to death in the presence of the Ancestors. When she is on the point of falling exhausted, the Ancestors recognize it, and glide towards her like rapacious monsters, so that she may not touch the ground in falling; they raise her and hold her towards the sky.'

Abrupt chords signal the beginning of the end. Here, the fragments of folk material are simplified to almost nothing, as if they have been distilled to create pure rhythm. And yet this is the section of the work that comes closest to conventional structure, as if the ritual of the Sacrificial Dance demands the strongest element of formal expression. It is like a wild rondo. The opening section, with its jagged chords, defies any attempt at regular metre, as if throwing the body of the dancer around mercilessly. A quiet second section has another distorted metre, in which one beat, two beats, three beats, succeed each other in unpredictable patterns. Over this, muted trombones and trumpets play fierce calls, in a descending chromatic shape derived from the top line of the chords that opened the Sacrificial Dance. The rhythmic pattern suddenly increases in volume (and changes in key), and reaches a climax. Then the quiet pattern resumes, a tone lower than the first time.

There is another outburst (and another change of key) with a swirling figure in the violins added to the rhythmic patter. But just as the music seems to progress on, it comes to a juddering halt. The jagged opening section of the dance returns – this is a semitone lower than the first time. Now timpani, gong, and bass drum and trombones set up a mighty rhythmic force, like gigantic waves, against which horns and strings strive to play fragments of melody, derived from the cheerful moments of the Ritual of the Rival Tribes, but now desperate in their attempts to be heard. This comes to a sudden stop.

The opening of the dance returns, now in its original key, but lasts only a few bars before being overwhelmed by the renewed onslaught. Once again the opening of the dance breaks through, but now reduced to the lower instruments, and with the phrases coming more quickly upon each other, as if beginning to stagger. The dance increases in force again, with the sense of desperation resulting in tiny phrase being repeated again and again, still in irregular metres right to the end. The music comes to a halt. Flutes play an upward scale like a last breath, and the final crash descends.

SYMPHONIES OF WIND INSTRUMENTS
Duration: approx. 9 minutes

In 1920 an edition of *La Revue Musicale* was dedicated to the memory of Debussy, who had died two years before. Stravinsky, Ravel, and Falla were among the composers who were each asked to contribute a short piece. Stravinsky's contribution was a chorale for piano. He had been working for some time on sketches for a new piece for strings and harmonium, and it was from these sketches that Stravinsky developed the chorale. The work that eventually emerged from these workings was the Symphonies of Wind Instruments, of which the chorale forms the culmination. The score, like the chorale, is dedicated to the memory of Debussy.

Early performances were not successful. The premiere in London in June 1921 provoked a mixture of applause and hissing, and was followed by an unfortunate public spat between Stravinsky and the conductor, Koussevitzky, who, in response to Stravinsky's criticism of his performance, was quoted as saying that the work 'represents a stage of decline in Mr. Stravinsky's art'.[31] The full score was not published until Stravinsky revised it in 1947. Despite the inauspicious start, the Symphonies of Wind Instruments has come to occupy a special place among Stravinsky's works. Although it lasts less than ten minutes it has been the subject of substantial analytical studies. This is partly because it straddles two distinct phases of Stravinsky's work: the 'Russian' phase of the big ballet scores, and the phase of 'neoclassical' works. It is the first of Stravinsky's works constructed by a technique that seems to strip the music down to essential elements. Blocks of material are placed together in a sort of mosaic, without conventional transitions or developments. The effect is stark and austere, and, with its large ensemble of woodwind and brass instruments, also highly evocative. The question is, evocative of what?

The title has nothing to do with the conventional 'symphony', but refers back to the ancient Greek meaning: the piece consists of 'soundings together' of wind instruments. If the title suggests something of the antique, the music too evokes an atmosphere of ancient ritual, drawing on some of the traditional Russian elements already important in *The Rite of Spring*, *The Soldier's Tale*, and *Les Noces* (which Stravinsky had already completed in a preliminary version). Richard Taruskin has gone so far as to argue that Stravinsky based the shape of the work on the Orthodox memorial service, the *Panikhida*.[32] Even if it cannot be demonstrated in detail (and Taruskin does not claim that it can), this helps the listener to think of this work in terms of the ingredients of Orthodox ritual: the chanting of psalms, alleluiahs, hymns, litanies, responses, acclamations, and, to conclude, the singing of 'Eternal Memory' in which all the congregation joins. Stravinsky himself did not directly make this association, but he did go so far as to describe the work as 'an austere ritual which is unfolded in terms of short litanies between different groups of homogeneous instruments', and even referred to its 'liturgical dialogue'.[33]

The original score is for twenty-four wind instruments, including alto flute and alto clarinet in F. The revised instrumentation of 1947 is as follows: 3 flutes, 2 oboes, cor anglais, 3 clarinets, 3 bassoons (the third doubling contrabassoon), 4 horns, 3 trombones, tuba.

The work opens with a short paragraph consisting of three contrasted elements in quick succession, each of which is important to the whole piece. The first is a call on high clarinets over trumpets and trombones, strongly rhythmic, ending with a decorative flourish. The second is a series of three solemn chords for the whole ensemble. Two of the chords end with a little staccato note, the third leads on to the third element: a rising and falling five-note phrase on the oboe (and horn). The first of these elements is like a call to attention. Taruskin associates it with the introductory phrase of a chant, but one could equally well think of it as akin to the ringing of hand-bells which, in many Orthodox traditions, punctuates the ritual. The second element is the first hint of what will eventually become the solemn chorale. And the third element, the five-note phrase, which is heard from time to time throughout the *Symphonies*, is plausibly associated by Taruskin with the word 'Alleluiah' (which has five syllables in the Russian Orthodox usage).

This little opening paragraph is repeated in a varied form. Then, at a more flowing tempo, three flutes play a meditative melody that winds round on itself, as much like the rustic chanting of a bagpipe as a religious chant (the ambiguous balancing between the rustic and the religious in this piece is one of its chief fascinations). A high bassoon responds with an even more tightly wound melody, circling round three notes. With an abrupt return to the first tempo, the opening 'bell' call and the 'Alleluiah' are reprised.

What follows is a more continuous passage, at the faster tempo. At first this has a forthright, processional character, with the trombones intoning variations on the 'Alleluiah' phrase, and the rest of the ensemble throwing punchy rhythms. After a while this gives way to flute and clarinets playing another rustic melody like the chanting of a bagpipe, which develops a hypnotic, meditative character. Twice oboes and cor anglais interpolate a reminder of the preceding punchy rhythms (Taruskin likens this to the repeated refrain of a hymn).

An interruption brings in a reprise of the opening 'bell' call and the 'Alleluiah', after which the flute and clarinets resume their rustic chanting with further rhythmic interpolations from oboes and cor anglais. Two earlier elements are now reprised in reverse order: the high bassoon melody on three notes, and (after another 'bell' call) the three flutes with their first rustic melody. This time it is brought to a halt by a new element, formed of gently reiterated rocking chords.

After a pause, there is a crucial transitional moment. We hear for the first time two elements of the coming chorale: a first phrase that converts the rocking chords into a poignantly resolved dissonance, and a second phrase built from the 'Alleluiah'. After a variant of the rocking element, there is a sudden burst of a fast tempo (exactly twice the opening tempo). After a momentary hesitation (with the variant rocking figure), this fast tempo gets going, creating the second continuous passage in the piece. Like the rocking element, it centres around two reiterated intervals (a second and a fourth), but now these develop great momentum and energy, with splendid 'block counterpoint' between static treble and running bass, developing material from the earlier, processional section.

This is interrupted by the beginning of the solemn chorale. There is an attempt to return to the energy of the preceding section, but it has now lost its force. The variant of the rocking figure leads in the final chorale. At first, this is scored for brass alone. But gradually the woodwind join in. The chorale, proceeding phrase by phrase, expands in sonority until, in its last phrases, it extends from tuba and contrabassoon at the bottom, to oboes and flutes at the top. And, whatever analogy one chooses, Stravinsky presents us with the contemplation of some sort of completeness – from the depths to the heights, from the beginning to the end (if there is one).

SYMPHONY IN C
Duration: approx. 27 minutes

Moderato alla breve
Larghetto concertante
Allegretto
Largo – Tempo giusto, alla breve

In 1920, Stravinsky drew on eighteenth-century music for his ballet score *Pulcinella*. Over the next thirty years he wrote a series of works that, in more subtle ways, are in dialogue with the 'classical' style of Haydn and Mozart, and are broadly referred to as 'neoclassical'. These include an octet for wind instruments, a concerto for piano and wind, the ballets *Apollon musagète*, *Persephone*, and *Orpheus*, the concerto for chamber orchestra *Dumbarton Oaks*, and two symphonies.

Stravinsky had composed a symphony in traditional Russian style in 1907, while he was still a student of Rimsky-Korsakov. By the late 1930s, with a string of neoclassical works behind him, it was natural that he should return to this most classical of genres, and see what new was to be made of it in the mid-twentieth century. There were, of course, Russian composers who had continued to write symphonies broadly in the Russian tradition – Shostakovich, Rachmaninoff, Prokofiev. Stravinsky, with his Picasso-like ear for deconstruction, set about doing something quite different.

He began work on the Symphony in C in the autumn of 1938, and completed it in the summer of 1940. He had already started it before receiving a commission from Mrs Robert Woods Bliss (Mildred Bliss), for whom he had already composed the *Dumbarton Oaks* Concerto in 1937. The symphony was 'composed to the glory of God, and dedicated to the Chicago Symphony Orchestra on the occasion of the fiftieth anniversary of its existence'. Stravinsky himself conducted that orchestra in the premiere in November 1940.

In a programme note in 1963, Stravinsky himself wrote, 'The Symphony in C was composed during the most tragic year of my life.' In November 1938, while he was composing the first movement, his elder daughter died of tuberculosis at the age of thirty: 'I think it is no exaggeration to say that in the following weeks I myself survived only through my work on the *Symphony in C*.'[34] The following March, his first wife died from the same disease, and then Stravinsky himself spent five months in the same sanatorium in the French Alps being treated for symptoms of 'the family disease'. He reported, 'One of my infrequent absences was to attend the funeral of my mother, who died on June 7. For the third time in half a year I heard the Requiem service chanted for one of my own family, and for the third time walked through the fields to the cemetery of Saint-Geneviève-des-Bois . . . and dropped a handful of dirt in an open grave. And once again I was able to go on only by composing, though no more than before do the parts of the Symphony written in these dark days represent an expression of my feelings of loss.'[35] Stravinsky completed the second movement of the symphony in the sanatorium, and the third in Boston, where he had been invited to deliver the Charles Eliot Norton Lectures at Harvard University. Now remarried, he settled in Beverly Hills, California, where he finished the finale in August 1940.

As for the inspiration for this symphony, Stravinsky's friend, Pierre Suvchinsky, who visited him in the sanatorium, had spotted a score of Tchaikovsky's First Symphony on Stravinsky's piano, and when Stravinsky's symphony became known, a similarity was identified between the first themes of the two symphonies. Stravinsky acknowledged that there were some moments of 'Russian sentiment' in his symphony that would naturally suggest a rapport with Tchaikovsky. He also admitted 'Russian family-likenesses' between '"my" eighteenth century and "Tchaikovsky's"' – Tchaikovsky loved Mozart more than any other composer, and had composed his Suite No. 4 ('Mozartiana') to mark the centenary of Mozart's *Don Giovanni*. But Stravinsky went on, 'If Suvchinsky had reported which Haydn and Beethoven scores were on my desk, no one would have paid any attention, of course, yet both of those composers stand behind at least the first two movements of my Symphony far more profoundly than any music by my much-too-lonely compatriot.'[36]

In his programme note, Stravinsky pours scorn on the critics who 'will find a great deal of nothing to say' about this music 'that is so unmysterious, and so easy to follow at every level and in all relationships'.[37] Stravinsky always liked to be provocative and to deflate the critics, but to describe the symphony as 'unmysterious' and 'easy' is disingenuous, and is liable to make the ordinary music lover feel stupid. The symphony is far from simple or straightforward, and a listener hearing it for the first time is likely to spend much of the time feeling somewhat lost. Analysts draw up neat diagrams of its structures and the relationship between its themes, but unless one has studied the score, it is difficult to follow what is going on.

This is particularly true of the first movement, in which Stravinsky has taken the conventions of a Haydn first movement – with its exposition of themes in different keys, development, and reprise – and has created something analogous, without the clear landmarks or certainty of keys that help to guide one through a movement by Haydn. At times there seem to be echoes of Prokofiev's 'Classical' Symphony. But Prokofiev makes sure that most of the landmarks of Haydn's language are clearly audible (without descending to pastiche), while Stravinsky, with his fracturing of rhythm, phrasing, and key structures, is more enigmatic.

The marking is Moderato alla breve. 'Alla breve' indicates that there are two beats per bar, rather than four, which means that, with all the constant activity going on, the effect is faster than 'Moderato' might imply. The very first gesture is important throughout the movement. Energetic repeated notes culminate in a shape that curls and falls. The curl-and-fall is echoed at half speed in the woodwind. In the following bars, this little idea is played with in counterpoint, and combined with staccato rising scales. Eventually, a solo oboe emerges, and extends the curl-and-fall into a longer melody that is generally taken to be the first real theme of the piece. This idea is further developed, until more abrupt and fractured gestures lead on to a new element: a dotted-rhythm call, announced quietly by trumpets, and then becoming dominant. It is joined by other elements – nervous little twiddles in the strings, staccato chords with a circling melodic pattern in the horns, a rising melody in first horn. Somewhere in there is, perhaps, the second 'theme', though it is more a scattering of ideas. Further play with these elements erupts in a sudden fortissimo, and by now (if not before) we are certainly into the central development section of the movement.

Various elements are combined, with the first theme emerging recognizably on the oboe again. This element drives the music forward, until it culminates in a powerful, rhythmic climax. As this collapses, the solo oboe again steps forward with the first theme, and we are into the reprise. The route through is subtly different, but eventually the dotted rhythms of the second 'theme' become insistent. This time, they develop power, over a treading bass. The climax breaks off, and the first theme quietly reasserts itself on flute and clarinet, and with a series of sharp chords the movement is over.

Incidentally, one of the features of this movement that gives it such an unusual atmosphere is Stravinsky's reluctance to assert the keynote C (of the symphony's title) in a conventionally straightforward way. The final chord is (mostly) a chord of C major; but it also contains a B, and the bass note is E, not C. This echoes the first theme, where the bass note is E, so that the music hovers between C major and E minor. Stravinsky's characteristic harmonies are a whole study in themselves, but one can catch their highly evocative, strangely restless, flavour without needing to analyse exactly what he is doing.

The Larghetto second movement is 'concertante' in the sense that its outer sections feature woodwind solos and duets in dialogue with the strings. Stravinsky described it as using 'Italianate song-and-accompaniment'. The intricate elaborations of the woodwind parts – and at times even the violin parts – certainly evoke opera. But even more, they evoke the expressive floridity of the arias from J. S. Bach's cantatas and passions that have woodwind or violin solos.

The melody begins on solo oboe, soon joined in duet by violins, and answered with increasing floridity by flute and clarinet. As the combinations of melody shift from instrument to instrument, they are accompanied by delicate little trills and rhythmic motifs that introduce a dancing quality to the music. There is a moment of sudden serenity when three solo violas quietly sing a chant-like phrase – one of those touching moments when Stravinsky seems to have dropped his mask.

The middle section of the movement breaks into double speed, with the phrases becoming urgent and spikey, and agitated scrubbing in the accompanying textures. Here, the analogy with the troubled middle section of an operatic aria seems particularly close (as it does in the slow movement of Mozart's Piano Concerto in D minor). The opening tempo returns, the music varied and shortened, and with three solo cellos replacing the moment of solo violas. A duet of oboe and bassoon brings the movement demurely to a close, and the third movement follows without a break.

The first two movements of the symphony were composed in Europe, the third and fourth in America. Commentators have observed that the two halves are very different from each other. Stravinsky himself accepted this 'schism', but then, in his 1963 note distanced himself from this judgement, declaring drily, 'But I am no judge of that.' What is clear is that the third movement is, in comparison to the first two, very restless, with continual changes of metre, and Stravinsky acknowledged that this metrical irregularity was 'the most extreme in the whole of my work'.[38] A symphony of Haydn's day would have a scherzo or minuet and trio at this point, and something of that character and form is echoed here.

The movement opens with agitated chords over a growling bass. Then woodwind, horns, and trumpets answer with a sort of fanfare based on a repetitive melodic pattern. This is written in three-time, as if it were a minuet. But the rhythms within the metre are highly irregular, and they continue to be so as the movement proceeds. The impression is more like a dancer on hot coals, thrown out of any stable rhythm, or of a cubist painting of dancers in which only fragments of feet and hands can clearly be distinguished. It is a fascinating movement, with a succession of vivid effects passing by. At one moment there is a wry bassoon solo over staccato trombone chords, recalling similar textures in Stravinsky's Octet for wind.

The opening chords return, then the tempo slows for the middle section of the movement (the equivalent of the conventional trio), which is a gentle dance. Like the first section, it is based on repetitive melodic fragments, and its metre alternates between three-time and two-time. There is a crescendo and a silence. The fast tempo returns, together with a reference to the 'fanfare' in the woodwind. At the same time a trombone plays a bold, new theme, which turns out to be the subject for a fugue. This is taken up in turn by horn, bass instruments, and oboe with trumpet. It is surrounded by a welter of rushing counterpoints, so that one might describe it as a buried fugue.

The confusion suddenly clears, and the fugue subject is played by violins, then inverted by a clarinet. Stravinsky plays with this combination of right way up and upside down for a few bars. Then, with another shift of gear, the fugue subject becomes a playful fanfare in two keys at once (trumpets in C, horns in D). The playfulness softens, and the movement ends with one last reference to the 'fanfare' in flutes and clarinet over a sustained chord in horns and trumpets – a curiously wistful conclusion, evoking memories of a similar moment in the Symphonies of Wind Instruments.

Memories of that work, with its evocations of religious ritual, recur throughout the finale. It opens with a slow introduction, a sombre, low bassoon duet. The solemn repetitions of its phrases are linked to the first theme of the first movement, and they are punctuated by a repeated, dense chord of horns and trombones. The following Tempo giusto (in effect, Allegro) is, like the first movement, two-in-a-bar (alla breve), and full of determined energy. It too is made of repetitive little phrases, derived from the bassoon duet. Soon it breaks out in a theme more directly related to the first theme of the first movement. Other ideas come from the first movement: running scales, persistent patterns of repeated notes, a gently curling oboe solo. The movement proceeds with tremendous momentum – a relief after all the metrical irregularities of the preceding movement.

Suddenly, it comes to a halt, and the slow bassoon duet returns, now with sustained chords transforming it into a chorale, and more powerfully suggesting a link to the ritualistic Symphonies of Wind Instruments. The music snaps back into the fast tempo, and a combative fugal section develops. Just as it reaches a climax, it is halted in its tracks by the wind chord from the solemn bassoon duet. The tempo slows, with the curling shape of the symphony's first theme in the woodwind, over processional trills in the strings.

Eventually this calms, until the music is reduced to a repeating series of wind chords, surmounted by the curling shape from the first theme. As the chords slowly change, the mood is unmistakably that of the Symphonies of Wind Instruments. But it is the strings that play the last chord, and that chord is very similar to the one that concluded the first movement – a chord of C major, but with an added D and B, and with E in the bass rather than C. This leaves the harmony of the symphony hanging in the air, somewhere between C major and E minor, and resonating with a sense of mystery that Stravinsky would never have wanted to explain. Part of that explanation must surely lie in the dedication, which he omitted from the published score: 'À la gloire de Dieu' ('To the glory of God').

SYMPHONY IN THREE MOVEMENTS
Duration: approx. 22 minutes

I ♩ = 160 (♩ = 80)
II Andante –
Interlude –
III Con moto

As the end of the Second World War came in sight, the New York Philharmonic Orchestra commissioned Stravinsky to compose a work to celebrate the coming Allied victory. But at the premiere of Stravinsky's Symphony in Three Movements in 1946 all that he would say, in a brief note, was that the symphony contained traces of 'this our arduous time of sharp and shifting events, of despair and hope, of continual torments, of tension, and at last cessation and relief'.[39] He reiterated that 'No program is to be found in my musical output.' However, in 1963, Stravinsky, who was renowned for declaring that music was incapable of 'expressing' anything, surprised everyone by admitting, in conversation with Robert Craft, that several parts of this symphony were inspired by particular images associated with the war.[40]

Stravinsky had been asked to write music for news footage during the war, and although the project never came to fruition he retained vivid memories of the filmed scenes, and of the musical ideas that they had provoked, and used them in this symphony. Craft reminded Stravinsky, 'You have at times referred to your Symphony in Three Movements as a "war symphony". In what way is the music marked by the impression of world events?' Stravinsky replied, 'I can say little more than that it was written under the sign of them. It both does and does not "express my feelings" about them, but I prefer to say only that, without participation of what I think of as my will, they excited my musical imagination. And the events that thus activated me were not general, or ideological, but specific: each episode in the Symphony is linked in my imagination with a concrete impression, very often cinematographic in origin, of the war.'

The first movement was inspired by 'a documentary of scorched-earth tactics in China', its middle section 'was conceived as a series of instrumental conversations to accompany a cinematographic scene showing the Chinese people scratching and digging in their fields':

> The third movement actually contains the genesis of a war plot, though I recognized it as such only after completing the composition. The beginning of that movement is partly ... a musical reaction to the newsreel and documentaries that I had seen of goose-stepping soldiers. The square march beat, the brass-band instrumentation, the grotesque *crescendo* in the tuba – these are all related to those repellent pictures ... In spite of contrasting musical episodes, such as the canon for bassoons, the march music is predominant until the fugue, which is the stasis and the turning point. The immobility at the beginning of the fugue is comic, I think – and so, to me, was the overturned arrogance of the Germans when their machine failed. The exposition of the fugue and the end of the Symphony are associated in my plot with the rise of the Allies ...

But after all this confession, Stravinsky concluded by saying, 'But enough of this. In spite of what I have said, the Symphony is not programmatic. Composers combine notes. That is all. How and in what form the things of this world are impressed upon their music is not for them to say.'

The second movement had, according to Stravinsky, a very different origin in film music. In 1943, his friend the writer Franz Werfel asked Stravinsky to compose music for his film project, *The Song of Bernadette*, based on his recent novel. Stravinsky composed music for 'The Apparition of the Virgin'. But the project foundered, and he ended up using the music for the second movement of the symphony.

One thing that is immediately striking about the first movement as it begins is how it seems to inhabit that specifically American, combative style that runs from Copland to Bernstein and beyond. Of course, Copland had already drawn Stravinskian rhythms into his use of popular music, notably in *El Salon Mexico* (1937) and *Billy the Kid* (1939), and Bernstein was to draw heavily on both Copland and Stravinsky in *On the Waterfront* (1954) and *West Side Story* (1957). But here is Stravinsky, in his first work since becoming a naturalized citizen of the United States, wholeheartedly embracing the 'American' musical language that he helped to create.

A rushing upward scale in the strings ends with thrusting leaps, answered by a heavily treading line from the wind. These are the elements that join battle for the opening bars. As the air clears, the thrusting leaps become a horn call, over nervous staccato clarinet chords. The nervousness is caught by strings and piano, with jumpy chords, like gunshot echoing in a courtyard, or the psychological equivalent of involuntary flinching. (This passage, with its combination of piano and strings, is also reminiscent of the second movement of Bartók's Music for Strings, Percussion and Celesta of 1936.) Underneath, the thrusting motif has become a repeating pattern in the bass. At the next fortissimo, the thrusting motif and the treading wind line combine, driving forward relentlessly and joined by running scales in the bass. At another sudden quiet, the horns introduce a new idea, with chords that slide upwards in a menacing gesture. This is echoed in the trumpets, and then builds to a climax, taking us more and more into a savage echo of *The Rite of Spring*.

The threat recedes, and anxious, high wind chords take us into the middle section of the movement. Here the texture thins out to something more like a chamber orchestra, with strings, horns, woodwind, an occasional trumpet, and a prominent piano part. There is an extended quiet passage, in which the familiar elements are passed around. The piano plays patterns based on the thrusting leaps, the violins answer with the rising scale. Nervous fragments of counterpoint develop, held together by persistent staccato chords. Gradually, the fragments coalesce into something firmer and more forceful. There is a sudden stroke of the timpani, and the full force of the orchestra enters with savage offbeat chords. This moment has been likened to the offbeat chords at the climax of the first movement of Beethoven's 'Eroica' Symphony, but the effect is more like one of the sudden eruptions in *The Rite of Spring*. This evocation is confirmed as flutes, clarinets, and piano continue with an eerie passage that develops a ghostly, processional character, with increasingly obsessional repetition of irregular phrases.

Eventually, this unsettling passage culminates in a return of the jumpy, echoing chords from the first part of the movement. The music leaps back and forth between this and the middle section of the movement until the tension is released in a return to the very beginning of the movement. But it too is interrupted, alternating with the eerie processional music, and it is this that brings the movement to a quiet close, with the ticking staccato that has driven the whole movement persisting in the bass clarinet to the end.

A slower ticking staccato opens the Andante, and the bass pizzicato line is made up of leaps that seem closely related to the thrusting leaps from the first movement. According to Stravinsky's later statement, this movement had its origin in a different film score from the rest of the symphony, but these links to the first movement must surely be deliberate, presumably intended to make the movement sound at home in the symphony. The opening theme (if that is what it is) consists of fragments in juxtaposition: the ticking staccato ending with rather baroque-sounding flourishes, followed by a rising staccato scale (another link to the first movement?), with a counterpoint of a falling line in the flute, and a quirky trilling gesture low on clarinets. It is difficult to imagine this as having any connection with the 'Apparition of the Virgin'. The tone seems ironic, balletic, perhaps even puppet-like, with an echo of *Petrushka*. Like the middle section of the first movement, this has the texture of a chamber orchestra, but with a harp replacing the piano. The flute lines become more florid and balletic, and the harp joins in with its own flourishes.

Then a corner is turned into a new key, the elaboration drops away, and the music becomes more fragile. The harp predominates at first, fragments of woodwind coalesce into a chorus that then disperses into duets, and high strings create a sense of mystery and expectation. What follows is strange and dreamlike, with a low flute and harp playing in different keys, and wisps of melody on muted violins (it is easier to imagine this as the 'Apparition of the Virgin'). Passages for strings and woodwind alternate, until high woodwind sing a fragment of a chorale, and a horn holds a long note as strings echo a phrase of the chorale. The moment of mystery is over, and staccato violins usher in a half-remembered reprise of the first section. It comes to a premature end, and woodwind return to a phrase of their chorale. This brief passage is labelled 'Interlude'. It soon becomes urgent, with a crescendo to an expectant chord, and we are into the finale.

Stravinsky immediately plunges back into combat. Harsh chords pit major against minor, with the bass line referring back to the thrusting leaps from the first movement. Once again the similarity to Copland in aggressive mode is striking. The pace increases, and two bassoons engage in squabbling duet, like a fight glimpsed down a side street. Gradually this spreads through the orchestra, including both piano and harp. Relentlessly repeated figures continue the battle between major and minor, punctuated by chords reminding us of the explosive echoes from the first movement.

A crisis is reached. The pace suddenly slows to a tramping march, with bassoons and trumpets in a seemingly confident C major. There are cheerful shouts from the rest of the orchestra. But then the march falters and stutters into silence. A trombone tentatively tries out the beginning of a phrase. The piano takes it up, and extends it into a weird, atonal line. As it continues, the harp enters with a simplified version of the same line, in counterpoint with the piano, and we seem to be into a sort of fugue. In a few bars, the bassoon enters, but already the notion of a fugue is becoming diffuse, and after a few more attempts to sustain the counterpoint, it peters out. Nevertheless something has been released. An agitated rhythm gets going in the strings, and as it grows in strength, we are once more transported back to the world of *The Rite of Spring*. The whole orchestra comes together in a burst of wild rhythms, culminating in a triumphant final chord.

PYOTR ILYICH TCHAIKOVSKY
(1840–93)

Because of the *1812* Overture, with or without cannon, the popular image of Tchaikovsky is of a composer who revelled in grand, even crude, effects, and wore his heart on his sleeve – a sort of precursor to Shostakovich and twentieth-century film scores. But Tchaikovsky's music has an enormous range, encompassing not just the great climaxes but also the most delicate of touches. The composer of the past whom he admired above all others was Mozart, and he loved the delicate and transparent orchestral writing of Mendelssohn – he thought his own orchestration bad by comparison. Of contemporary music, he most admired Bizet's *Carmen* and Delibes's *Sylvia* (he said that if he had known *Sylvia* at the time, he would not have bothered to write *Swan Lake*). He could not stand Wagner, whose talent he regarded as having been paralyzed by theory, and he disliked Brahms, despite the seriousness of his intentions. He had little sympathy for those Russian composers, such as Borodin and Musorgsky, who wished to carve out a Russian music distinct from the great European tradition, though he maintained a fruitful relationship with the leader of 'The Five', Balakirev. In an exchange of letters with his former pupil, Sergei Taneyev, Tchaikovsky set out his approach to folk music, and the whole question of 'Russianness'. Taneyev, elevating the traditional music of Russia to something part-sacred, part-political, had stated that 'only music that has embedded its roots in the people is lasting'. But Tchaikovsky was not to be persuaded by this reductive approach: 'we who use this material will always elaborate it in forms borrowed from Europe – for, though born Russians, we are at the same time even more Europeans, and we have so resolutely and deeply fostered and assimilated their forms that to tear ourselves away from them we would have to strain and do violence to ourselves'.[1]

Tchaikovsky loved Russia, its people, its countryside, and its literature, and much of his music sounds thoroughly Russian, if not always in definable ways. But he saw himself as a craftsman in a tradition of craftsmanship, a view that he expressed in a letter of 1890: 'Ever since I began to compose I have endeavoured to be in my work just what the great masters of music – Mozart, Beethoven and Schubert – were in theirs; not necessarily to be as great as they were, but to work as they did – as the cobbler works at his trade; not in a gentlemanly way, like Glinka, whose genius, however, I by no means deny. Mozart, Beethoven, Schubert, Mendelssohn, Schumann composed their immortal works just as a cobbler makes a pair of boots – by daily work; and more often than not because they were ordered. The result was something colossal.'[2]

As a man, Tchaikovsky was charming and refined, but full of passionate intensity, and subject to periods of nervous exhaustion and melancholy. There were times in his life when his attempts to deal with his homosexuality caused him immense stress. His marriage to a former student was predictably disastrous and short-lived (see note for Symphony No. 4). And it seems possible it was a potential scandal surrounding his sexuality that provoked his death (see note for Symphony No. 6).

1812 OVERTURE, OP. 49
Duration: approx. 15 minutes

In 1880, Tchaikovsky was asked by the conductor and pianist, Nikolai Rubinstein (brother of Anton), to write a work for the Moscow Exhibition of Arts and Industry, which was planned for the following year. The options suggested to him were to celebrate the silver jubilee of Tsar Alexander II, which fell in 1880, to compose an overture for the opening ceremony of the exhibition, or to mark the consecration of the new Cathedral of Christ the Saviour, which was nearing completion. Tchaikovsky replied to the request, 'It is impossible to set about without repugnance such music which is destined for the glorification of something that, in essence, delights me not at all. Neither in the jubilee of the high-ranking person (who has always been fairly antipathetic to me), nor in the Cathedral, which again I don't like at all, is there anything that could stir my inspiration.'[3]

Nevertheless, after further prompting, Tchaikovsky agreed to write a festive overture. He took as his cue the new cathedral, which had been built to commemorate the defeat of Napoleon's army by the Russians in 1812. It is fortunate that he did not choose to celebrate the Tsar's jubilee, because Alexander was to be assassinated the following March, and the exhibition was postponed for a year. The original intention had been to perform the overture in the open air, with church bells and gunfire. But in the event the premiere of the overture took place in a specially built concert hall, without the spectacular effects that have become associated with it. Tchaikovsky wrote the music very quickly, and continued to denigrate it. He wrote to his patron, Nadezhda von Meck, 'The overture will be very noisy. I wrote it without much warmth of enthusiasm; therefore it has no great artistic value.'[4] He nevertheless conducted it on numerous occasions, always to enthusiastic applause, and it became his best-known piece. The score describes it as a 'Solemn Overture' – 'solemn' in the sense of 'ceremonial'.

The ending certainly is 'very noisy', but the earlier parts of the overture are highly effective in more subtle ways, and would not have been out of place in the first movement of a symphony. It is a finer piece of music than its obvious antecedent, Beethoven's *Wellington's Victory*, and it seems that Tchaikovsky was not so detached from the task as he liked to suggest. For Tchaikovsky and his generation of Russians, 1812 was not simply associated with a triumphant event in Russian history, but evoked Tolstoy's great novel, *War and Peace*, published a decade earlier. Perhaps it is not fanciful to suggest that it was partly this that led Tchaikovsky to choose the subject of 1812 for his overture: there is certainly something Tolstoyan about the way in which Tchaikovsky juxtaposes scenes of battle and devastation with others evoking personal aspiration and struggle.

The overture begins with the orthodox chant, 'Save us, oh God', played by a small group of violas and cellos, alternating with woodwind. This simple, small-scale opening suggests a scene of ordinary people at prayer. The prayer increases in intensity, until it gives way to an anxious, restless theme, descending in the oboe, rising in the cellos and basses. This builds up, reaches a climax, and falls away. The *Marseillaise* is heard quietly, on woodwind with side drum, like a scene in *War and Peace* where the massed French armies are seen on the distant hillside. Over it, Tchaikovsky puts a sweeping violin melody, as if attempting to cling on to normal life.

After a silence, sudden activity breaks out, with an agitated figure passing from instrument to instrument. The urgency increases, and more fragments of the *Marseillaise* are brought in. The frantic energy fades away, and the strings play a broad, warm melody, which has the effect of a love theme amid all the threats of war (Tchaikovsky took this from a duet in his early opera, *The Voyevoda*). This is followed by a Russian folk tune, 'At the gate' (one of a collection of tunes that Tchaikovsky had arranged for piano duet in the 1860s). It is a sad, delicate moment, once again evoking memories of the life that is swept away in war.

The moment fades and, pianissimo, the music returns to the agitated passage that preceded the love theme, developing it, and again bringing in the *Marseillaise*. This builds up to a greater battle than before, and fades away to yield once more to the love theme, and to a brief reminiscence of the folk tune. Now, over a sustained bass note and timpani roll, horns play the *Marseillaise*, and the strings respond with fragments of the folk tune, like excited conscripts. Soon, the music builds up to fever pitch, with cannons firing, and we arrive at the grand finale of the overture.

Full brass, *fff*, reprise the chant 'Save us, oh God', while bells cascade (Tchaikovsky specified that these should simulate the festive ringing of church bells), and the strings sweep up and down. In a final Allegro vivace, jaunty phrases of the *Marseillaise* are combined with the bold strains of 'God save the Tsar', the Russian national anthem (of Tchaikovsky's day, not of 1812), with the booming of cannons and the pealing of bells.

Concertos

PIANO CONCERTO NO. 1 IN B FLAT MINOR, OP. 23
Duration: approx. 37 minutes
Allegro non troppo e molto maestoso – Allegro con spirito
Andantino semplice – Prestissimo
Allegro con fuoco

Tchaikovsky completed two piano concertos and began a third. The first is the only one to have found a regular place in the repertoire, though the other two have been revived in recent years.

Tchaikovsky composed this famous concerto over the winter of 1874–5, soon after finishing his opera *Vakula the Smith* (later revised as *Cherivichki*). Hoping that Nikolai Rubinstein would undertake the premiere in Moscow, he played through the concerto to him. Tchaikovsky complained about this experience to his brother Anatoly at the time, but it was three years later, in a letter to Nadezhda von Meck, that he filled in the details:

'As I am not a pianist, it was essential for me to consult a virtuoso-specialist, so that he could point out to me anything that might prove to be technically difficult, awkward, ineffective, etc.' Rubinstein said nothing until Tchaikovsky had reached the end of the third movement. He then let forth a torrent of criticism: 'It turned out that my concerto was worthless and unplayable; passages were so fragmented, so clumsy, so badly written that they were beyond rescue; the work itself was bad, vulgar; in places I had stolen from other composers; only two or three pages were worth preserving; the rest must be thrown away or completely rewritten.' Tchaikovsky, already the composer of two symphonies and a professor at the Moscow Conservatoire, was outraged. Rubinstein later softened his attitude, and offered to play the concerto if it were thoroughly revised according to his demands. Tchaikovsky could not accept this: '"I shall not alter a single note. I shall publish the work exactly as it is!" This I did.'[5]

This is one of the most famous incidents in Tchaikovsky's career. No doubt some of the colourful detail must be taken with a pinch of salt. And it may be that he failed to give a good account of the work when he played it through to Rubinstein (he had studied the piano at the Conservatoire, so was not quite 'not a pianist', but the concerto requires a real virtuoso to do it justice). In any case, Tchaikovsky was sufficiently offended that he offered the premiere instead to Hans von Bülow, who played it in Boston in October 1875 during a tour of the United States. Despite Rubinstein's harsh criticism, he soon came round to the concerto, conducting a performance in Moscow in December that year, and in later years often performing the solo part himself. Meanwhile Tchaikovsky did publish his first version. But, as so often, he later made minor revisions, publishing subsequent editions in 1879 and 1890. It is the final edition that is usually played today.

Tchaikovsky composed a concerto on a grand scale, combining fearsome virtuoso difficulty, beautiful writing for both piano and orchestra, and a command of structure and detail worthy of a symphony. Models for this combination of qualities in a piano concerto are few and far between. Beethoven's 'Emperor' is the most obvious 'heroic' forebear of Tchaikovsky's concerto. More recent concertos by Mendelssohn, Schumann, and Liszt would also have been in his mind. But the most immediate precedent for this concerto's achievement is the one piano concerto by Grieg. Anton Rubinstein had been at its premiere in Copenhagen in 1869, and it had been published in 1872. Assuming that Tchaikovsky knew it, Grieg's concerto might well have given him some ideas about structuring, the incorporation of folk-like material within a grand work, and bold, Liszt-like piano virtuosity made coherent by symphonic thought.

The concerto opens with four horns, fortissimo, declaring three times a stern descending phrase in B flat minor. This sounds as if it might be a motto, as in Beethoven's Fifth Symphony. The piano enters with massive chords, over which violins and cellos extend the horn phrase into a broad, powerful melody, but now in D flat major. The piano takes up the melody, embellishing it with yet more powerful chords and double octaves, until it breaks into a moment of Liszt-style free cadenza. This culminates in another return to the great melody, now on full strings, with the piano driving it on *fff*. Eventually, the power is spent, and the music unwinds to a moment of calm and a pause.

This introduction has been much criticized. Its theme does not return in the rest of the concerto and, furthermore, the great melody is in D flat major, not the B flat minor that is the key of the piece. So the introduction might seem like a grand gesture that has nothing to do with the rest of the concerto. But Tchaikovsky does plant some seeds. The opening horn call contains a three-note descending scale that recurs, either in its original form or upside down, in many later themes. And there is another three-note shape in the middle of the theme (a large descent followed by a little rise) that also recurs. These links might seem insignificant, and they are not obvious to the listener. But they are there nevertheless, and once one becomes aware of them, the concerto seems more coherent, and its introduction more than a gesture. This is just the sort of subtle linking of ideas that Tchaikovsky learned from his great loves, Mozart and Schumann (and, perhaps, from Grieg's concerto).

The Allegro con spirito begins with a playful theme based on a tune that Tchaikovsky had heard in Ukraine, sung by a blind beggar accompanying himself on the hurdy-gurdy ('every blind beggar sings exactly the same tune', according to Tchaikovsky).[6] This is extended energetically, until it relaxes into a lyrical second theme. The opening of this melody (a leap down, and a small rise up) is related to a shape in the grand theme of the introduction. It has also been suggested that the first two notes, D flat–A (in German nomenclature, Des–A) might be code for Désirée Artôt, a singer with whom Tchaikovsky had fallen in love in 1868 and had briefly planned to marry (the only woman ever to have aroused Tchaikovsky's sexual interest, as far as we know).

After the woodwind have played this theme, the piano repeats and extends it, drawing in the opening horn call (played three times, as originally). When the strings continue, it is with the three-note 'cell' from the opening, now ascending. The piano again plays the melody, with rippling accompaniment that gradually becomes more energetic and flamboyant. The music builds to a climax, at which the piano bursts out into a salvo of rapid double octaves, punctuated by orchestral chords. After this has subsided, the violins, now muted, reprise their continuation of the second theme, and, with the piano playing rippling arpeggios, the first section of the Allegro con spirito comes to a peaceful end.

The development begins with a long orchestral build-up, which starts with the continuing second theme on violins combined with chirruping fragments of the first theme on the woodwind. Once again the piano breaks from the orchestral climax with double octaves. In another cadenza-like passage, the piano meditates for a moment, and then bursts out once more, combining phrases from earlier themes. The orchestra enters, and piano and orchestra alternate in passionate dialogue, taking turns in playing the descending phrase, building up over a drum roll. This climaxes with the continuation of the lyrical second theme now transformed into a brazen trombone call.

The mood relaxes, elements of the chirruping first theme begin to enter, and, after another flamboyant piano passage, we are back at the first Allegro con spirito theme for the reprise. This quickly reaches the lyrical second theme. Here, the piano is silent, letting the strings take up *con amore* the theme that they never played the first time round – a particularly beautiful moment. When the piano elaborates the theme, it once again builds gradually to a climax. Out of it emerges, instead of the double octaves, a full-blown cadenza. The lyrical second theme predominates for the first part of the cadenza, culminating in a Liszt-like passage where the continuation of the second theme is surrounded by a delicate filigree of trills. Then bursts of staccato octaves interrupt, and the music develops great power. But it is the quiet second theme that has the last word, before a flourish leads in the flutes and then the violins, with the continuation of the second theme. This develops a grand sweep to propel us towards a last climax, which ends with more double octaves, this time striding triumphantly upwards to meet the orchestra's final chords.

The Andantino is in D flat major, the same key as the grand theme of the first movement's introduction, but it is a feature of the movement that it never stays in one key for long. It begins with very quiet pizzicato chords. A flute plays a lullaby, whose shape is related to the first movement's lyrical second theme. (In most editions, the flute plays the opening phrase with *exactly* the shape of the earlier theme, but the piano then changes it. A correction in the copy of the score prepared for Bülow's premiere suggests that the flute version might be a misprint.)[7] The piano takes the lullaby on to a new key, and flutes play an idea formed of little drooping sighs. A high oboe introduces a third idea, a curling figure over a bagpipe-like drone. As the piano responds to this, the opening phrase of the first theme passes among the wind instruments. The piano's musings evolve into a staccato accompanying pattern, which modulates back to D flat, and beneath which a solo cello reprises the first theme. Then the cello is joined in duet by an oboe. Again, the music changes key, and pauses.

Now the piano very quietly begins the Allegro vivace assai, in a rapid jig metre full of cross-rhythms. Fragments of the earlier drooping sighs emerge from the complex texture. Once more the music modulates for a new theme. This is a French popular tune, 'Il faut s'amuser, danser et rire', a song that Modest Tchaikovsky remembered: the three brothers 'used to sing it constantly during the early seventies', though it was also said to have been a favourite of Désirée Artôt.[8] While the piano keeps up a delicately bubbling patter, the tune passes around the orchestra, as if served by waiters in the liveliest of Parisian cafés.

With a crash, the piano is brought back to earth, and a little cadenza leads in to the reprise of the Andantino. This is elaborated most delicately. And this time, as the music begins to move into another key, it resolves beautifully back into D flat, and harp-like spread chords bring this lovely movement to a close.

The finale begins with a vigorous theme based on a traditional Ukrainian spring song (*vesnyanka*). Its repetitive little descending phrases and strong accents are characteristic of the genre, but it is also related to the motif of the opening horn call (or vice versa: it would be interesting to know what elements of this work Tchaikovsky chose first). The theme begins in B flat minor, with delightful pizzicato accompaniment and woodwind comments, then has a middle passage in D flat major, returns with cross-rhythms in the accompaniment, and ends with a rumbustious tutti. The piano then adds a perky little tailpiece in a different key, which soon slips deftly back to D flat major for the second theme. This movement is full of swift key changes, just like the slow movement.

The second theme is also based on a folk song, its opening phrase being derived from one of the tunes collected by Balakirev that Tchaikovsky had arranged for piano duet: 'I am going to Tsar-gorod'. Tchaikovsky allows it to blossom into a lyrical and expansive melody, before playfully diverting it back to the first theme. This is followed at a slower tempo by a delicate little episode with tripping dotted rhythms, which concludes with a crescendo into a reprise of the rumbustious tutti. The perky tailpiece follows, and the lyrical second theme, in E flat (everything is up a tone this time round). The piano takes over from the violins sooner than before, and drives the melody on to another reprise of the first theme, back in the home key of B flat minor.

This time it is followed by an increase in pace, and a passage of sparkling piano scales and arpeggios up and down the keyboard, moving from key to key, and arriving in B flat major. Here Tchaikovsky lays down an F in the bass, with a quiet timpani roll, creating a sense of anticipation as fragments of the first theme, the tripping dotted rhythms, and the lyrical second theme, gradually build. At the height of the crescendo, the piano once more bursts out with double octaves for a brief but powerful cadenza. Out of it steps the lyrical second theme, with orchestra and piano together creating a splendid peroration, which finally balances the grand introduction with which the concerto began. There is a final increase in speed, and as piano and orchestra hurtle to the finish, the concerto ends with a hair-raising effect popularized by Liszt, in which the hands alternate to create the effect of a rapid chromatic scale in double octaves.

VIOLIN CONCERTO IN D MAJOR, OP. 35

Duration: approx. 37 minutes

Allegro moderato

Canzonetta: Andante

Finale: Allegro vivacissimo

In July 1877, Tchaikovsky married Antonina Ivanovna Milyukova. It was a disaster (see Symphony No. 4). By October, Tchaikovsky had left Russia with his brother Modest to travel and to recover his health and composure. After spending some months in Italy, he settled in a hotel at Clarens, on the shore of Lake Geneva. Having regained his enthusiasm for composing, he completed *Eugene Onegin* and wrote the Fourth Symphony. And now, in March 1878, he was joined by the violinist Iosif Kotek, a close friend and former pupil who had been in Berlin, studying with Joseph Joachim. Kotek brought with him recent music publications for them to explore. One of them was the *Symphonie espagnole* by Édouard Lalo, which Tchaikovsky described as having 'a lot of freshness, lightness, of piquant rhythms, of beautiful and excellently harmonised melodies'. He admired Lalo, because he 'thinks more about *musical beauty* than about observing established traditions, as do the Germans' (Lalo was French).[9] Almost immediately, Tchaikovsky started writing a violin concerto, and completed a first draft within ten days. He then decided, on the advice of Kotek and Modest, to replace the slow movement (the original became the separate piece for violin and piano, *Souvenir d'un lieu cher*). By 11 April, a month after Kotek's arrival, the concerto was complete and fully orchestrated.

The path to performance was much less straightforward. Tchaikovsky dedicated the concerto to the prominent virtuoso Leopold Auer, professor of violin at the St Petersburg Conservatoire, and leader of the Imperial Ballet orchestra. But hopes that Auer would perform the work were to be dashed. Auer considered that the violin part needed revision before it could be played. Tchaikovsky sadly remembered, 'I do not know whether Auer was flattered by my dedication – only that, despite his sincere friendship towards me, he never wanted to master the difficulties of this concerto, and deemed it awkward to play.'[10] The premiere was given in Vienna by Adolf Brodsky in 1881, and the reception was generally hostile, particularly from the fearsome critic Eduard Hanslick. Later, as the work gained acceptance, Auer regretted his decision, and did perform the concerto in his own edition. But it was Auer's pupils, Jascha Heifetz, Nathan Milstein, Mischa Elman, and others, who took the concerto up enthusiastically, making it one of the most frequently performed violin concertos in the twentieth century.

A daunting virtuoso work it may be, but it starts innocently with what could be another 'Rococo Theme'. Within a few bars, a drum roll and fragments of a livelier theme build swiftly to a climax on full orchestra, which falls away in a succession of little pairs of notes. This is all the introduction there is – Tchaikovsky dispenses with the conventional orchestral exposition of themes as thoroughly as Bruch in his First Violin Concerto.

The soloist enters with a graceful little cadenza, and, taking up the earlier phrases in the orchestra, elaborates them into the first theme. This begins lyrically, and then subtly changes in character. Tchaikovsky enlivens the lyricism with piquant dotted rhythms, the theme is repeated with bold chords, and then the dotted rhythms lead on to a new element. Flowing triplets and dotted rhythms alternate at first, then the triplets gain momentum amid a virtuoso flourish. The music builds to a climax, with the dashing of the soloist punctuated by the dotted rhythms in the orchestra.

This falls away to a second main theme. Its lyrical character is similar to that of the first theme, but its development is different. Instead of introducing dotted figures, Tchaikovsky simply builds the intensity of the lyricism up to a high point, then dropping low on the sonorous G string of the violin. Again the melody builds, up and up, until it breaks into rushing scales. This sets off an extended passage of pyrotechnics, and this too builds in excitement. It ends with a series of trills, and the orchestra bursts in to bring the first section of the movement to a close.

This is the first extended orchestral tutti, marking the beginning of the development, and its effect is dramatic. The lyrical first theme is transformed into a grand gesture with polonaise rhythms (though it is in four-time). It is as if the theme has been waiting to achieve this transformation. From here, the orchestra returns to the little pairs of notes with which it first introduced the soloist, and builds an extended passage from them. The soloist reappears, and plays another variation of the first theme, with playful staccato elaboration and chords. This is followed by another grand orchestral statement of the polonaise-like transformation. Further development builds to a climax, out of which the soloist emerges with an extended cadenza. Tchaikovsky here follows the example of Mendelssohn, who pioneered this unusual placing of the cadenza in his Violin Concerto (Sibelius was later to do the same thing). Tchaikovsky had begun the development with the grandest of gestures. Now, at the end of the cadenza he does the opposite. Under the violinist's final trills a flute shyly emerges with the reprise of the lyrical first theme. The melody moves to the violin, and from this point the sequence of themes follows as expected, though with continual new variations. A climactic coda accelerates to an exciting conclusion.

Even the hostile Hanslick was able to appreciate the 'tender Slavonic sadness' of the slow movement. This is unmistakably by the composer of the recently completed *Eugene Onegin*, and it is particularly reminiscent of the yearning, regretful aria that Lensky sings before the duel in which he is killed by Onegin. A solemn wind chorale introduces the movement. The muted solo violin enters and sings the lament in G minor, accompanied by muted strings. A soft horn on the second beat of each bar adds a sad, rocking emphasis. The middle strain of the melody moves to E flat major, and the soloist expands warmly, like Lensky remembering happier times. The melody rises higher and becomes more rhapsodic. The strings creep in below, playing the chorale that opened the movement – a wonderfully subtle touch. And as the solo violin reprises the lament, it is joined by clarinet and flute playing elegant countermelodies. The lament remains unfinished as the opening wind chorale returns. From it the strings derive a little motif that they reiterate sadly, with expectant chords.

Suddenly the full orchestra bursts in *ff*, speeding up this motif to create the introduction to a dance. The soloist enters, toys with the motif in a brief cadenza, and then develops it into the main theme of the finale (this is very similar to the process by which the opening theme of the first movement was revealed). Hanslick was particularly scathing about this finale, 'which plunges us into the brutal, deplorable merriment of a Russian holiday carousal'.[11] His description suggests anti-Russian sentiment beyond the musical: it is precisely its unashamed suggestion of rustic Russian merry-making that gives the movement its charm.

The theme, with its rapid patterns and delicate accompaniment, seems not to touch the ground. Suddenly an upward scale brings a holding of the pace. Over a drone bass, suggesting bagpipes or a hurdy-gurdy, the violin plays a new, sturdy theme. Soon it speeds up to the original pace, and a phrase is repeated again and again with ever-changing orchestration (a device loved by Russians ever since Glinka). The excitement is just beginning to build when an oboe coyly introduces a charming little continuation of the new theme. This too is passed around from instrument to instrument, until the solo violin develops it into another lyrical line.

The moment is soon over, the violin remembers the dance theme, and accelerates into a reprise. This takes new directions and passes through new keys, with rapid-fire interjections from the orchestra raising the excitement, until once again the pace is held, and the drone and the second theme return. The return to tempo elicits yet more variations on the repeated phrase, with the soloist playing in octaves and then in harmonics. Again the oboe introduces the charming continuation, and again the violin develops its lyrical possibilities, this time at greater length and with deeper melancholy. For the last time, the soloist returns to the dance theme. Then, over a held bass note, the orchestra builds a great crescendo, and orchestra and soloist hurl the phrases of the dance back and forth to each other with joyful abandon to bring the concerto to an explosive end.

FRANCESCA DA RIMINI, FANTASIA AFTER DANTE, OP. 32
Duration: approx. 24 minutes

In February 1876, Tchaikovsky revealed in a letter to his brother Modest that he was considering writing an opera about Francesca da Rimini, a woman immortalized in Dante's *Divine Comedy*. He never developed this idea, but four months later wrote, again to Modest, 'This evening in my coach I read the 4th Canto [actually the 5th] of the *Inferno*, and was inflamed by a desire to write a symphonic poem on *Francesca*.'[12] By October he was able to report that he had completed his *Francesca da Rimini*: 'I composed it with love, and love has turned out pretty well, I think [a reference to the repeated word 'Amor' in the speech that Dante puts into Francesca's mouth].'[13]

In the middle of this process, Tchaikovsky attended the first Bayreuth Festival in August 1876, and wrote a series of articles about it, and about Wagner's *Ring*, for the journal *The Russian Register*. He concluded his observations by saying that the experience had left him 'with a vague recollection of many beautiful features, especially of a symphonic kind', but '. . . with misgivings as to whether Wagner's view of opera is correct' and 'it has left me greatly exhausted'.[14] Privately, he had described *Das Rheingold* to Modest as 'an unbelievable muddle in which, from time to time, unusually beautiful and striking details may be fleetingly glimpsed'.[15]

Nikolai Rubinstein conducted the successful first performance of *Francesca da Rimini* in Moscow the following February. Two composers who attended that performance were Sergei Taneyev and César Cui. Taneyev passed on to Tchaikovsky Cui's observation that *Francesca* betrayed the influence of Wagner's *Ring*. To which Tchaikovsky replied, 'The remark that I wrote this work under the impression of the *Nibelungen* is very accurate. I felt this myself while I was working on it. If I am not mistaken, this is particularly noticeable in the introduction. Isn't it strange that I submitted to the influence of an artistic work which I generally dislike?'[16]

Francesca da Polenta, daughter of the Lord of Ravenna, was a historical figure who married Giovanni Malatesta, son of the Lord of Rimini, in about 1275 (when Dante was ten years old). It was a political marriage, bringing together two powerful families. Giovanni Malatesta was crippled, and Francesca fell in love with his younger brother, Paolo, who was also married. Their affair lasted several years, until Giovanni surprised them together, and killed them both.

The published score of Tchaikovsky's *Francesca da Rimini* is headed by lines from Dante's *Inferno*. Dante, accompanied by Virgil, has reached the second circle of hell. In the terrible whirlwind, he notices a man and woman locked in an embrace, and calls to them, asking how they have come to this terrible punishment. Francesca tells him how she and Paolo were reading together the story of Lancelot and Guinevere. At the moment where they read that Guinevere kissed Lancelot, Paolo kissed Francesca, and they were lost. As Francesca tells their story, Paolo weeps, and Dante, overcome by the tragedy of their fate, faints as if dead.

For an understanding of Tchaikovsky's music, the most significant words from Dante are surely those that begin the passage quoted in the score:

Nessun maggior dolore,	There is no greater sorrow
che ricordarsi del tempo felice	than to recollect in misery
ne la miseria …	a time of happiness …

Tchaikovsky's own notes on this passage include the statement that Francesca, already in love with Paolo, was forced against her will to marry his 'hated, twisted' brother. This is not in Dante, and was added to the story by Boccaccio, but it must surely have helped to fire Tchaikovsky's own sympathies for Francesca and her doomed love with Paolo. Tchaikovsky, a man of strong emotional impulses, doubts, and conflicts, was several times drawn to the theme of doomed love to inspire his most powerful works – *Romeo and Juliet*, *Swan Lake*, and *Eugene Onegin*, as well as *Francesca da Rimini*.

In Tchaikovsky's *Romeo and Juliet* and *Hamlet*, faced with a complex plot, he took elements of the story and wove them into a symphonic structure. Here, in *Francesca da Rimini*, the structure of the brief passage in Dante is much more straightforward, and Tchaikovsky's music reflects it with a simple boldness that owes as much to Liszt as to Wagner. The piece begins by evoking the darkness of hell, then the torments of the whirlwind, with increasing ferocity. A long central section is inspired by Francesca's tearful narration, and the music ends with a return to the horrors of the whirlwind.

The slow introduction begins with dark wind chords, emphatic swirls, and the heavy tread of descending scales. As Tchaikovsky acknowledged, these elements have a very Wagnerian feel, as if they have stepped out of *Götterdämmerung*. Soon, the pace increases a little, and indefinite fragments of a theme are heard. This passage is full of little offbeats and syncopations, rhythmically difficult to get hold of (and to play). Its slippery character gives it the feeling of something not clearly distinguished in the darkness. It rises to fortissimo, and dies away to a reminiscence of the opening wind chords. Then the pace increases still further. The indefinite phrases of the earlier passage have become more distinct, and are accompanied by rapid flurries in the woodwind. The music gradually increases in volume and urgency, until it arrives at a ferocious outburst. The violence and rhythmic agitation of this passage recalls Dante's earlier description of the whirlwind:

La bufera infernal, che mai non resta,	The swirling winds of hell, which never rest,
mena li spirti con la sua rapina;	drag the spirits on with their force,
voltando e percotendo li molesta.	painfully twisting and striking them.

Twice the music reaches a climactic outburst, and twice it recedes, the second time arriving at another recall of the dark opening wind chords. Out of the darkness steps forward a solo clarinet, evoking the moment when Francesca speaks. This is the beginning of the long, central section of the Fantasia. After a moment of preparation, the clarinet plays a sorrowful melody in A minor, accompanied by pizzicato. The violins (muted) respond warmly, now in E major, in a rising pattern, full of yearning phrases, but (as so often in Tchaikovsky's most heartfelt moments) pulling against a continuous, unchanging bass note. The melody descends, to end in reiterated little sighs that break up into an accompanying pattern. Over this, flute and oboe take up the sorrowful theme, then violins and cellos. Again the melody breaks up into little sighs. The flutes play an almost dancing phrase, like a reminiscence of happy times. This becomes a pattern, beneath which, for a third time, Francesca's theme begins in the cellos.

But this time it takes a new direction, moving into new keys, and increasing in passion. There is a moment of calm, at which the cor anglais takes a phrase from the cello line and turns it into a new shape. This alternates with harp arpeggios, and is developed into a continuing melody, passing to oboe, and then to flute and clarinet. Calm though this seems, it is syncopated against the pizzicato bass line, giving it a hint of the rhythmic uncertainty from earlier in the Fantasia. Cellos, and then violins, join the melody, with delicately repeating woodwind chords above, and then flurries of rising scales. Eventually, these become a regular pattern in the violins, and Francesca's theme starts once again in flutes and oboe. This is taken up by all the strings, with increasing passion, until finally the brass play the melody *fff*.

As its final sighs die away, distant horn calls intrude, and, with a crash, we are dragged back to the earlier turmoil. After a moment of dark trombone chords, the evocation of the swirling winds is reprised. As before, this builds up tremendous force. At the end, the tempo increases still more, and, in the last bars, crashing gong strokes and stark chords bring the Fantasia to a fearsome close.

HAMLET, FANTASY-OVERTURE, OP. 67
Duration: approx. 18 minutes

The idea of composing an overture or symphonic poem on Shakespeare's *Hamlet* was first suggested to Tchaikovsky by his brother Modest in 1876. Although he tried out ideas for this project from time to time, it was not until June 1888 that he wrote to Nadezhda von Meck, 'I have already prepared in rough a symphony [No. 5] and an overture on the tragedy *Hamlet*, for which I've been collecting materials for some time.'[17] The resurfacing of this idea was prompted by the actor Lucien Guitry (father of Sacha), who asked Tchaikovsky to write an entr'acte for a charity production of part of *Hamlet* in St Petersburg. Although the production was cancelled, this was enough to re-spark Tchaikovsky's interest, and he decided to complete an overture. Three years later he added some incidental music when Guitry staged a full production of *Hamlet* for his last season in St Petersburg. He dedicated the overture to Grieg, with whom he had struck up a friendly relationship, and Tchaikovsky conducted the first performance in St Petersburg in November that year.

The overture *Hamlet*, not surprisingly, shares a quality of dark brooding with the first movement of the Fifth Symphony, and parts of it, including the ending, share the same key (F minor). But, unlike the symphony with its problematic finale, the overture is an unusually tightly constructed work, with an unflagging sense of purpose and drama. Tchaikovsky does not attempt to tell the story of the play, but, as in his *Romeo and Juliet*, builds a coherent symphonic movement from music which, at the same time, vividly evokes characters and atmospheres – Hamlet himself, the ghost of his father, the tragic Ophelia and her love for Hamlet, the warrior-prince Fortinbras, and the death of Hamlet. Permeating all of this is an atmosphere of foreboding, with sudden bursts of violent activity and determined energy, armies on the march, and an overall sense of tragic inevitability. The idea of Fate, which possibly lies behind the Fifth Symphony, is unmistakably a brooding presence in the overture.

F minor may be the key in which *Hamlet* ends, but one of the features that makes this such a powerful overture is the tortuous journey through different keys that it travels in order to get there. It begins Lento lugubre in A minor, a key very remote from F minor, though it barely settles in it before it is off through constantly shifting harmonies. The sombre, restless mood is established straight away, with a crescendo roll of the timpani culminating in a brusque chord, and lamenting phrases on the cellos. After a few bars, this gives way to aggressively swirling patterns rising through the strings, and a plangent response from the woodwind. These contrasting elements carry the music through to a first tutti climax, which cuts off abruptly.

After a silence, muted horns play a single note, at first quietly then gradually louder, while the woodwind play a mysterious series of chords, and string arpeggios rise to an intense, shuddering tremolo. A gong strikes *fff* (one of the most spine-chilling gong strokes in music), and trombones powerfully intone the cellos' phrases from the opening bars (clearly this is the appearance of the ghost). At the start of this section, we are in E minor. After several lurches of harmony it crashes to a halt, and the next theme, a march, sets off in F minor, Allegro vivace. This is a fiercely energetic section, which develops its material at some length, until eventually calming.

There follows the most lyrical section of the overture, beginning with an oboe solo in B minor (Andante). This has a delicate melancholy, and is at one point marked 'plangendo' (weeping) – the association with Ophelia is clear. After a time, it turns to D major, warming to a singing melody, at first in the woodwind, and then in the strings. It begins to extend and develop, but then the distant sound of a military march is heard (Allegro vivace), with side drum. Over a sustained bass note, this gradually builds up, until, as the music turns a corner, we find ourselves in a reprise of the F minor march (which previously followed the 'ghost' music).

This leads on, as before, to the plangent oboe solo, and to the warm melody on woodwind and then strings. Through the reprise of this section, there is a more agitated accompaniment than before. So, although Tchaikovsky has left out any formal 'development section', he maintains the feeling of exploring new possibilities. As the theme extends, it acquires more urgent energy, and as it does so, the 'ghost' theme reappears, first in woodwind and horns, and then *fff* in the trombones.

There is a sudden hush, and the distant military march is heard again. This time it builds up terrific force, through another great gong stroke, to a climactic chord, *fffff* on full brass, dying away to pianissimo. After a silence, the strings play the aggressive swirling patterns from the beginning of the overture, with the plangent response of the woodwind. Cellos play a descending lament, and this leads into the final section, a brief and sorrowful funeral march, which takes us right back to the opening music of the overture, and dies away.

This is one of Tchaikovsky's most impressive works, and deserves to be heard more often. It combines a powerful emotional narrative with a very successful re-imagining of classical formal techniques. It is like a Mozart overture on a massive scale, with themes reprised but with no development section. The way Tchaikovsky reorders the themes at the end for dramatic effect is also something that can be found in Mozart – but the way he combines this classical method with such free exploration of keys is a sign of genius.

ROMEO AND JULIET, FANTASY-OVERTURE
Duration: approx. 20 minutes

Balakirev was only three years older than Tchaikovsky, but exerted considerable influence over him at the time of the composition of *Romeo and Juliet*. Following the death of Glinka in

1857, Balakirev had become the central figure among the group of Russian composers, known as 'The Five', who were dedicated to carrying on Glinka's work, and attempting to forge a Russian school of composition, independent of traditional, academic conservatoire training. Balakirev had in 1862 founded the Free Music School in St Petersburg. Despite Tchaikovsky's conservatoire training, Balakirev was supportive of him, and Tchaikovsky defended Balakirev in his inevitable battles with the conservative establishment.

In 1869, Balakirev suggested that Tchaikovsky might write an overture on Shakespeare's *Romeo and Juliet*. He evidently went into some detail, because in November, Tchaikovsky wrote to Balakirev that much of the overture was already sketched out, and that 'the overall scheme is *yours*: an introduction representing the friar; the struggle – allegro, and love – second theme', and even the sequence of keys was to be as suggested by Balakirev.[18] When Tchaikovsky completed a draft of the overture, Balakirev approved some themes, but not others. A first performance was not unsuccessful, Tchaikovsky revised the overture, and this revision was published in 1871. Nine years later, he returned to it again, and yet another revision was published in 1881. This final version, dedicated to Balakirev, is the work that is usually performed today.

The overture opens with a chant-like theme. This replaced a rather bland melody in the earlier version that did not impress Balakirev – it was his idea that Tchaikovsky should substitute something suggestive of Orthodox chant. It begins low on clarinets and bassoons. String harmonies soon intervene, which are at first poignant, and then reach upwards to radiant chords, with harp arpeggios – though, because they are minor rather than major, they perhaps suggest more a hope of radiance. The chant is repeated higher in the woodwind, over pizzicato. Again the strings reach for radiance. The pace accelerates and the phrases become more urgent, with the chant being drawn into this change of mood. After another brief moment of uneasy calm, the music breaks into the Allegro, with a theme in B minor of abrupt chords and snappy phrases interspersed with rushing strings. Almost immediately this theme is subjected to combative counterpoint (the 'struggle' of Tchaikovsky's draft). The tension rises, and fierce offbeat clashes culminate in the theme on full orchestra.

This dies away, the key slips gently sideways to A flat major, and cor anglais and violas begin the love theme, with its yearning leaps up and down. Murmuring muted strings answer. The theme is taken over by flutes and oboes, and extended onwards and upwards. The tender moment is rounded off by soft strings and harp chords, with fragments of the melody passing from instrument to instrument, and finally coming full circle back to the cor anglais. This is the end of the first section of the overture.

Abruptly, the beginning of the development takes us back to the 'struggle' theme, with its offbeat rhythms and rushing phrases. The opening chant is dragged into this, at first quietly and ominously in the horns. The battle develops in force, and at its climax the chant is blared out by trumpets against the insistent fighting rhythms. The rushing strings are again pitted against offbeat clashes, and we find ourselves back at the 'struggle' theme in its original shape and key.

As this dies away, the music finds its way sooner than before to the murmuring figure, now in the woodwind, and it is the full strings who take up the love theme, and bring it to an intense climax. Then the cellos take the melody in a new direction. Again the full strings rise up, a tone higher than before. But the great melody is never able to find its resolution. The fierce rhythms of the struggle break in. For a moment the strings try to resist it, but they are soon brought into the fight again, and the opening chant is drawn in too, on full brass. The battle becomes desperate, and then falls apart, as if fighters are scattering. The struggle is brought to an end with a fortissimo timpani roll.

After a silence, the rhythm of a funeral march begins, and a fragment of the passionate love theme is transformed into a tragic dirge. The woodwind begin a solemn chorale, which brings in elements of the murmuring figure that led into the love theme. The strings play a final strain of that theme, and the overture ends with a sequence of full chords, in an offbeat pattern taken from the fight, but now enlarged to create a resounding resolution.

SERENADE FOR STRINGS, OP. 48
Duration: approx. 30 minutes

Pezzo in forma di Sonatina: Andante non troppo – Allegro moderato
Valse: Moderato. Tempo di Valse
Élégie: Larghetto elegiaco
Finale (Tema Russo): Andante – Allegro con spirito

In a letter to his brother Anatoly, Tchaikovsky wrote in October 1880, 'I've done quite a lot recently. I've already written the overture for the exhibition, and have also been writing and should finish off a serenade for stringed instruments.'[19] The overture was *1812*, and there could hardly be a greater contrast between the two works. He dashed the overture off more or less as a chore, and never thought highly of it. But the serenade was a work that he developed spontaneously, without a commission. Effective though the overture is, the serenade displays Tchaikovsky's conviction and sheer pleasure in every phrase. As he wrote to Nadezhda von Meck, unlike the overture, 'The Serenade, on the contrary, I wrote from an inner impulse.'[20] At first, in September, he did not know whether it would turn out to be a symphony or a string quartet. By late October it was complete, including the piano-duet arrangement (essential for the domestic market), and Tchaikovsky sent both scores to his publisher with the words, 'I love this Serenade terribly, and fervently hope that it might soon see the light of day.'[21] It was published the following January.

The first movement has the title, 'Piece in the form of a sonatina' – that is, an abbreviated version of 'sonata form' (in which most first movements are written), lacking the 'development section' in the middle. So, in the Allegro, Tchaikovsky presents his two themes, and then presents them again. Although this makes for a simple and clear structure, there are many subtleties and complexities along the way. Tchaikovsky loved Mozart above all other composers, and his inclusion of a sonatina within a serenade might seem a deliberately Mozartian gesture. But the serenade is far from small-scale in effect.

Tchaikovsky prefaces his Allegro with a sonorous introduction, noting in the score: 'The larger the number of players in the string orchestra, the more this will be in accordance with the composer's wishes.' The Allegro's first theme begins with chords as full as those in the introduction, and continues with phrases in the violins echoed half a bar later in violas and cellos. This immediate complexity in a first theme is reminiscent of another of Tchaikovsky's great idols, Schumann. As the theme extends, there is more Schumann-like elaboration, as simple phrases in the violins are accompanied by a complicated counterpoint in the cellos. From this point on, almost continuous running semiquavers are a feature of the rest of the movement. This theme is rounded off by quite a forceful passage in which rapid figures pass from instrument to instrument, before coming to a momentary halt.

The second theme is a contrast, with a quiet melody in violins and violas and light pizzicato below, but this too is made up of rapid semiquavers, now in a pattern with repeated staccato notes. As the texture again becomes more complex, the staccato keeps everything light and transparent, though there are also energetic cross-rhythms. The combination of energy and lightness calls to mind yet another of Tchaikovsky's models, Mendelssohn, and this style is kept up all the way through the extension of the second theme, finishing with a vigorous flourish up an ascending scale.

This is the point where, in a conventional first movement, there would be a development section. But in this 'sonatina', Tchaikovsky immediately cuts to the reprise of the first Allegro theme, elaborated exactly as before. When he reaches the light second theme, this too is as before, except that it is now in the home key (C major). And, once more, it finishes with its vigorous ascending scale. Tchaikovsky rounds off the movement, not with a conventional coda to the Allegro, but with a return to the slow introduction, so that the movement finishes, as it began, grandly and sonorously. In this, Tchaikovsky evokes memories of a yet earlier model, the baroque French Overture.

The second movement is a waltz in G major which is, like the first movement, simple in outline, but subtle and complex in detail. The waltz theme, with its rising scale and elegant phrases, is soon stopped in its tracks, as if transfixed for a moment. It continues, and pauses again, before developing enough momentum to carry on uninterrupted. The melody moves to second violins and cellos, and the first violin decorates it with extravagant arabesques, like a coloratura soprano.

For the middle part of the waltz, the music moves into B minor. Delicate, staccato phrases pass playfully between violins and the bass, and then between first and second violins. Finally, they pass to the violas, just as the first waltz melody returns in the violins, and the violas keep up a complicated patter as a counterpoint. This time round, the end of the melody is charmingly extended by several bars. And at the end, Tchaikovsky rounds off the Waltz with a pianissimo ending of haunting delicacy and grace.

As the Élégie begins, we seem to enter a different world. The rising scale might almost be meant as a wistful memory of the waltz theme. But it is more as if we have entered a cathedral while a choir is chanting – it is the first moment in the serenade that sounds specifically Russian. Four times the chant rises. Only at the fourth attempt does it find a resolution to a sonorous chord of D major.

What follows is in another world again. A pizzicato accompaniment begins, as if a singer is to start serenading. And sure enough, the violins sing, not just a casual serenade, but a melody of wonderful expressive intensity. Violas and cellos sing the second strain, taking the melody higher, while the violins urge them on in counterpoint. Then the cellos embark on the middle section of the melody, with the violins following a bar later. They venture into new keys, but are always held back by a bass note that is sustained all the way through (Tchaikovsky was a master of using an unchanging bass to create tension). Eventually, the violas find the way back, and play the reprise of the first part of the theme. Accompanying them are the pizzicato cellos and bass, with fragments of countermelody in the first violins, but also delicate running semiquavers in the second violins that cut across the triplet rhythm of the pizzicato, creating a beautifully complex texture. Then the violins take the melody to a great climax, and fall back.

Now all the strings are muted for a reprise of the opening chant. This time, it takes longer to find a resolution, passing through poignant harmonies. When it does resolve, violas and cellos in duet attempt to sing the melody again. But now it too is coloured by dark harmonies, and the counterpoints in the violins, which were earlier elegant and playful, now seem anguished. This is the moment when we are reminded that the title of the movement is 'Élégie'. The melody does eventually sink back, and the movement ends with the rising scale of the chant ascending higher and higher, until it reaches a serene chord of D major, played on ethereal harmonics.

The spell is not immediately broken, nor is the key changed, as the slow introduction of the finale begins. From a sustained high D gradually emerges a gentle folk tune, 'On the green meadow'. After a while, the music hesitates, and a phrase of the tune is turned upside down. The players remove the mutes from their instruments, and the Allegro begins, now in C major. This inverted phrase is played at double speed, and we discover that this is the start of a second folk tune, 'Under the apple tree', which forms the first theme of the Allegro (these tunes are both from Balakirev's collection that Tchaikovsky had arranged for piano duet some years earlier). Tchaikovsky plays the tune four times, varying it with countermelodies, and passing it from the violins to the bass.

Then the music slips into E flat major, and there is a more lyrical second theme, not at all like a folk song, first in the cellos then in the violins. But the energy of 'Under the apple tree' is irresistible: soon it returns and, with excursions and developments, rounds off the first section of the Allegro. Then (unlike in the first movement) a development section follows, in which the folk tune and fragments of the second theme are pitted against each other. There is a long crescendo, with the counterpoint becoming more and more exhilarating.

Eventually the music arrives back in C major, and the folk tune in its original form is subjected to more variations. The lyrical second theme once again gives way to the energy of the folk tune. As we reach a pause, the end is clearly in sight. But now Tchaikovsky takes us right back to the beginning, with a reprise of the opening of the slow introduction. This accelerates into a final burst of 'Under the apple tree', and the serenade comes to a joyful finish with a sonorous last chord.

SWAN LAKE, SUITE, OP. 20A
Duration: approx. 25 minutes

In May 1875, while he was working on his Third Symphony, Tchaikovsky received a commission from the Imperial Theatres for a ballet to be performed at the Bolshoi Theatre in Moscow. He completed *Swan Lake* the following April, and it was premiered in February 1877. Two other major ballets followed – *The Sleeping Beauty* in 1890, and *The Nutcracker* in 1892. Of the three, it was *Swan Lake* that had the most difficult birth, and even now it is usually presented in a version very different from Tchaikovsky's intentions. But even in its distorted form, it is a masterpiece.

The origins of *Swan Lake* go back several years. Probably in the summer of 1871, Tchaikovsky made up a ballet, 'The lake of swans', at his sister's house at Kamenka, for his nieces to perform. His brother Modest, who was also staying, danced the prince, their eldest niece Tatyana danced Odette. A nephew, Yuri Davydov, reported his family's memories of this event: 'The staging was done entirely by Uncle Pyotr. It was he who invented the steps and pirouettes, and he danced them himself, showing the performers what he required of them. At such moments, Uncle Pyotr, red in the face, wet with perspiration as he sang the tune, presented a pretty amusing sight. But in the children's eyes he was so perfect in the art of choreography that for many years the memories of this remained with them down to the finest detail.[22]

The ballet company that shared the Bolshoi Theatre in Moscow with Russian and Italian opera companies in Tchaikovsky's day was very different from the Bolshoi Ballet that became famous in the twentieth century. Scenery had to make do for both opera and ballet, and the sets for the first production of *Swan Lake* were 'distinguished by extreme poverty',[23] according to a contemporary critic. Although by the 1870s the ballet company had strong links with St Petersburg, which made it possible to obtain some fine solo dancers, and a new ballet-master had been brought in to improve standards, the corps de ballet was clumsy and aging, 'an army, like the chorus of an opera, little disciplined, that worked carelessly and negligently'.[24] Such a company was used to dancing to straightforward music by second-rate ballet composers. Delibes's *Coppélia* had set a new standard in Paris in 1870, but it had not yet been staged in Russia (when Tchaikovsky heard Delibes's *Sylvia* for the first time in 1877, he said that he would not have bothered to write *Swan Lake* if he had known it). The subtleties of a work like *Swan Lake* were quite new to the Bolshoi dancers – David Brown goes so far as to say that the rhythmic complexity of Tchaikovsky's ballet score was as revolutionary in its day as Stravinsky's *Rite of Spring* in the early twentieth century.[25] And attempting a ballet score was also quite new to Tchaikovsky. He wrote in a letter to Rimsky-Korsakov in September 1875, 'The Opera Direction has commissioned me to write music for the ballet *The Swan Lake*. I accepted the work, partly because I want the money, but also because I have long had a wish to try my hand at this kind of music.'[26]

One of the consequences of the mismatch between the complexities of Tchaikovsky's score and the abilities of the ballet company was that simpler substitutes for his more elaborate numbers were introduced, so that, after a few years, a third of his original score was missing. After his death, a new production with choreography by Marius Petipa was an enormous success, and became the standard version of the work. But, with a revised scenario by Modest Tchaikovsky, new numbers arranged from piano pieces by the composer, and a happy ending, it was not at all the work that Tchaikovsky intended. It is, however, still the most familiar version, and it is only in recent years that attempts have been made to return to something more like the original concept.

The origins of the scenario are unclear, but it seems to have been assembled from a variety of sources, with elements from earlier operas and ballets, and, especially, folk tales.[27]

Act I

It is the eve of Prince Siegfried's coming of age. At a party in the castle park, his friends celebrate, and peasants come to congratulate him. At the prompting of Siegfried's old tutor, Wolfgang, the peasants dance. Siegfried's mother arrives unexpectedly, and tells her son that he must prepare to choose a bride the following day at a ball. Wolfgang's friend Benno commiserates with him. The tutor becomes drunk, and as the guests begin a final dance, a flock of swans flies past, and Benno suggests that they hunt them.

Act II

A moonlit lake in the mountains, with the ruins of a chapel. A swan wearing a crown leads others majestically across the lake. Siegfried enters with Benno, and prepares to fire. But the swans disappear behind the ruins, which are then lit by a magical light. As the men approach the ruins, a young girl wearing the crown comes down the staircase. She tells then that she is Princess Odette, whose stepmother is an evil sorceress who wants to kill her. Her grandfather's crown protects her, but a spell forces her and her friends to become swans by day. The swan-maidens dance, and Siegfried falls in love with Odette. She promises that she will appear at the ball tomorrow, and as dawn breaks, Odette and her companions are transformed back into swans.

Act III

The castle ballroom. Various guests are presented, including six eligible princesses. Siegfried's mother instructs him to choose one, but he cannot. A fanfare announces more guests, and Baron von Rothbart enters with Odile. To Siegfried, she looks like Odette, but Wolfgang cannot see the resemblance. Siegfried and Odile dance together, and he announces that he will marry her. The scene darkens, an owl hoots, and von Rothbart is revealed as a demon. Odette as a swan appears at a window. Siegfried is horrified, and rushes out.

Act IV

At the lake, the swan-maidens are waiting for Odette. She arrives, in despair, and tells then that she has been betrayed. Against their advice, she waits to spend one last moment with Siegfried. A storm breaks, and Siegfried rushes in, asking her to forgive him. But she is powerless, and runs away from him. He vows to stay with her for ever, grasps her crown, and flings it into the lake. An owl carries it away, screeching. Odette dies in the prince's arms as both lovers are engulfed by the flood. As the waters subside, swans are seen gliding across the calm surface of the lake.

The Suite

In 1882, Tchaikovsky wrote to his publisher, Pyotr Jurgenson, to tell him that he intended to extract a concert suite from the ballet score, as Delibes had done with his ballets: 'I want very much to save this music from oblivion, since it contains some fine things.'[28] Jurgenson agreed, and sent the score to Tchaikovsky for him to prepare a suite. But no more was heard of it until 1900, seven years after Tchaikovsky's death, when Jurgenson published the suite that is known today. This may or may not be the selection that Tchaikovsky had in mind, and conductors often add other numbers.

Scène (Act II, No. 10)

This opens Act II, setting the scene for the moonlit lake on which the swans glide majestically. But in the context of the suite, it cleverly substitutes for the introduction to Act I, which, though equally evocative, could not (for reasons of harmony) have been followed so neatly by the Valse. Over shimmering string tremolo and harp arpeggios, an oboe sings a plaintive melody. The rising scale of its first phrase is an inversion of the falling scale that begins the ballet – just the same falling shape that is such a prominent feature of *Eugene Onegin* and the Fourth Symphony, and was associated by Tchaikovsky with the power of Fate. Here its inversion as a rising scale gives a sense of deceptive calm. The second part of the melody is beautifully extended, striving upwards again and again. With increased intensity, four horns take the melody, which is then continued passionately by the strings. This time, it breaks into an agitated triplet pattern, reaching a climax at which the opening phrase is repeated *fff* by tremolando strings, before the music sinks back, with the melody in the bass, the tremolo continuing in the violins to the end. Part of the glorious effect of this brief scene-setter is the way the melody seems constantly to be seeking a resolution, but is unable to find it until the very end.

Valse (Act I, No. 2)

This is the first formal dance on the eve of Siegfried's coming of age. Tchaikovsky greatly admired Delibes, and owes some of the ease and charm of his waltzes to him. But this waltz in A major is a substantial piece on the scale of the waltzes of Johann Strauss II, and has a sweep and power that is Tchaikovsky's own. Its structure begins like a minuet with two trios, but then there are two further new sections before a return to the home key, and a brief reminder of the first section.

The first part of the first theme, on violins, is formed of coy phrases that each begin on the second beat of the bar. At its repeat, it is already decorated with delicate woodwind arpeggios, which also start after the first beat. The second half of the melody, introduced by a timpani roll, is bold and vigorous, twice reaching up to a climax. The second section of the waltz, in F sharp minor, begins with static woodwind chords in a syncopated pattern (which might well have confused the first dancers). This is then accompanied by a swirling pattern in the strings. This swirling pattern is developed by the woodwind into a continuation of the melody, while the strings take over the syncopated chords. The section ends with this combination of elements on full orchestra.

The opening section of the waltz is reprised. Then there is a third section, in F major. Like the first theme, it begins with little phrases starting on the second beat, but these are answered by the woodwind in a murmuring pattern that gently rises and falls. The second half of this section has a cornet solo with violin descant, and then the first half is repeated. The next section of the waltz is in D minor. The melody, on violins, is firmly on the main beat, but the woodwind cut across it with delicate syncopations. The second part of this section is bolder, and rises to a climax, before the first part is repeated. This time, the melody moves on, developing a swirling pattern reminiscent of that in the second section. As the music arrives back in A major, the full orchestra touches on the syncopations of the second section, then moves on to develop a brilliant final tutti, with, at the climax, the very opening phrases of the waltz reappearing in trombones and bass.

Danse des cygnes (Act II, No. 13, Var. 4)

This is from a sequence of dances for the swans, and evokes the charming waddle of young cygnets. The charm lies partly in the varying orchestration. The melody passes from a pair of oboes to pairs of flutes and clarinets. The middle part of the tune begins on violins, which are then joined by flutes an octave higher. Meanwhile, the bass begins on bassoon, but as the violins take over the melody, it passes to pizzicato cellos and basses.

Scène (Act II, No. 13, Var. 5)

This follows on from the preceding piece in the same sequence of dances for the swans. After the humorous charm of the cygnets, the scene suddenly takes on a magical atmosphere, with mysterious woodwind chords and harp arpeggios evoking a mystery. This is the moment at which Odette appears, and she and Siegfried dance a *pas de deux* together. Accompanied by harp chords, a solo violin plays a sad melody, full of aspiring phrases that rise up to a climax in the middle and then fall back. Woodwind chords, a little faster, suggest the response of

Siegfried's heart to what he sees and hears. The violin solo continues, more confidently, and with flamboyant runs. A solo cello joins in, and, returning to the slower tempo, violin and cello sing a duet, the cello taking the melody, the violin adding impassioned counterpoint.

Czardas: Danse hongroise (Act III, No. 20)

After Odile arrives at the ball, and Siegfried is deceived into thinking that she is Odette, there is a sequence of dances by visitors from different nations. This one has the characteristic form of a Hungarian Czárdás: a gloomy, intense first section, and an energetic second section with swirling patterns that becomes increasing wild to its conclusion. Delibes had earlier included a Czárdás in *Coppélia*, but Tchaikovsky did not know it when he wrote *Swan Lake*.

Scène (Act IV, No. 28 and part of No. 29)

This is the tragic final scene of the ballet. The swans are anxiously waiting for Odette. She rushes in, and tells her companions how Siegfried has been tricked into betraying her. The scene begins with an agitated figure passing among the strings and flutes. As Siegfried is seen approaching, there is a sudden tutti, followed by a melancholy passage as Odette waits for him. A drum roll announces the beginning of the storm, followed by swirling woodwind, bass drum, and cymbal. A build-up culminates in the arrival of Siegfried, and a great outburst of impassioned melody. Like many of Tchaikovsky's most powerful moments, this is over an unchanging bass note, so that the harmonies pull against it to create maximum intensity. The moment subsides to final harp chords.

The suite published by Jurgenson finishes there. Some conductors continue to the end of the ballet (another five minutes), giving a more sustained and emphatic conclusion, even if it rather overbalances the rest of the suite in the context of a concert. As the prince asks Odette to forgive him, an oboe plays the melody that appeared at the beginning of the suite (from the beginning of Act II), but at a much more agitated tempo against offbeat string chords. Fragments of the theme are drawn into a passage of increasing tension and desperation. At a drum roll the whole orchestra takes up the melody, *fff*. Again the tension builds until, at a final climax, the great melody bursts from minor to major, though with twisting chromatic harmonies making sure that this is not mistaken for a moment of triumph. As the prince and Odette are overcome by the flood, the music subsides, leaving behind a steady procession of string and harp chords, as the swans glide across the lake.

Symphonies

SYMPHONY NO. 1 IN G MINOR, OP. 13, 'WINTER DAYDREAMS'
Duration: approx. 44 minutes

Daydreams of a winter journey: Allegro tranquillo
Land of gloom, land of mists: Adagio cantabile ma non tanto
Scherzo: Allegro scherzando giocoso
Finale: Andante lugubre – Allegro moderato – Allegro maestoso

In January 1866, Tchaikovsky arrived in Moscow and was immediately installed in the house of Nikolai Rubinstein. Rubinstein's brother, Anton, was director of the St Petersburg Conservatoire, from which Tchaikovsky had recently graduated, and Anton had recommended

Tchaikovsky to teach music theory at Nikolai's newly established Moscow Conservatoire, which was to be inaugurated in September. Over the coming months, Tchaikovsky struggled to write his First Symphony. He was in a state of nervous agitation, assailed by doubts about his ability to compose following a review in which the composer–critic César Cui had described him as 'utterly feeble'; and he was anxious about his health, noting 'the ever present thought that I shall soon die and won't even complete the symphony successfully'.[29] He showed the incomplete symphony to his former teachers in St Petersburg, Anton Rubinstein and Nikolai Zaremba, but they were discouraging, and insisted on changes if they were to consider performing it. He completed the first version in November 1866, but it was not until February 1868 that it was performed, with Nikolai Rubinstein conducting. It was a great success, but Tchaikovsky continued to revise it, reaching a final version only in 1874.

Tchaikovsky gave the symphony and its first two movements evocative titles, though he seems not to have had any extra-musical programme seriously in mind. In this, he was following the examples of two composers whom he particularly admired, Mendelssohn (as in the 'Italian' and 'Scottish' Symphonies) and Schumann (as in the 'Spring' Symphony, and the 'Rhenish' associations of the Third Symphony). These were all works that Tchaikovsky often played on the piano while staying with his sister in the country over the summer of 1866. But there is a strongly Russian character to the entire symphony. Tchaikovsky's themes often have a flavour of either folk music from Russia and its surroundings, or of Russian Orthodox chant, or sometimes a combination of both. In part, this shows a debt to Glinka, but bringing such elements into a symphony was new. Admittedly, Tchaikovsky had been present at the premiere of Rimsky-Korsakov's First Symphony in 1865, conducted by Balakirev at his Free Music School, which includes some folk (and folk-like) material, and is often named as the 'First Russian Symphony'. (Tchaikovsky later expressed admiration for its slow movement, in seven-time, based on a folk melody, but considered its outer movements weak.) But neither Balakirev nor Borodin had yet completed a symphony (though Balakirev had started composing one). Tchaikovsky's First Symphony, therefore, is a remarkable achievement in its integration of specifically Russian elements within a large, four-movement work.

Over gently pulsating violins, flute and bassoon play the first theme. Its rise and fall and its plaintive repetitions have a very Russian feel. As it moves to the violas the flutes introduce a second element, a little staccato call centring around a narrow group of notes. Soon this second element begins to dominate, developing and acquiring accents. These two ideas are used to build an extended paragraph, culminating in a climax at which the staccato element has acquired a forceful edge. It breaks off to reveal a gentle second theme on clarinet. This has a lyrical flow, though its repeating rhythms and shapes still give it a distinctly Russian character, and it builds through beautiful changes of harmony and subsides to another silence. A final climax rounds off the first section, out of which emerge four horns reiterating a little phrase from the climax (Tchaikovsky seems to have recalled this moment when writing his 'Waltz of the Flowers' in *Swan Lake* many years later).

From here the development begins quietly, with fragments of the first two themes re-entering. These gradually build to another climax, more intense and sustained than earlier ones, and this once again breaks off. Out of the silence, lower strings and horns begin mysteriously, very gradually gathering strength, until the violins and violas enter with the reprise of the first theme. At the end of the reprise, Tchaikovsky adds one more climax, before the force ebbs away, leaving the movement back where it started, with one last exchange between the first theme and its staccato companion.

The slow movement, 'Land of gloom, land of mists', is a meditation on a single, long melody, framed by an introduction and conclusion for muted strings alone. This introduction is richly melancholy, but not in the least 'misty'. This is unsurprising, because Tchaikovsky took it from his concert overture, *The Storm*, which was composed two years earlier and based on the play by Alexandr Ostrovsky. Its plot is best known because it also formed the basis of Janáček's opera, *Katya Kabanová*. The melody, in Tchaikovsky's overture, represents what he described as Katya's 'yearnings for true happiness and love'.[30] In the symphony, this introduction leads in to the main theme of the movement, played by the oboe. Like the first theme of the first movement, it sounds intensely Russian, with its continual shifting from C minor to E flat major. Indeed, it seems almost like an extended meditation on that same theme, plaintively returning again and again to the same melodic shapes before ascending to a climax, and then abruptly falling silent. Its poignancy is made all the more telling by the beautiful bassoon counterpoint, and by the bird-like interjections of the flute. With a change of key, the melody moves to the violas, which take it higher, making it less melancholy and more passionate. Then, with another change of key, the violins take over briefly, with the bassoons playing the theme in canon. But then there is a moment's hush, before the theme moves to the cellos for a full reprise of the oboe's theme, rising to a more insistent climax, and with the violins providing a rippling accompaniment. A delicate and hesitant passage follows, until, suddenly, two horns in unison enter fortissimo and begin a full reprise of the theme, back in its original E flat major/C minor, rising to the greatest climax of the movement. When this has ebbed away, the strings conclude with the quote from *The Storm* with which the movement began.

For the third movement, Tchaikovsky took the scherzo from a piano sonata in C sharp minor that he had composed the previous year, transposing it down a semitone and replacing the trio. The scherzo is notated in a fast three-time, but has such persistent cross-rhythms that the metre is thoroughly disguised. The effect is dancing and playful, like some of the Russian and Ukrainian folk dances that Tchaikovsky had encountered. His rewriting of this scherzo shows how thoroughly he was a man of the orchestra, already at the age of twenty-six. The orchestration is subtle and varied, with interplay between strings and woodwind in different combinations, and pizzicato lightening the rhythm. At the quietest point, near the end of the second half, the melody is given to the two flutes, low down, creating a moment of sudden mystery. The newly composed trio is a glorious, heartfelt waltz, which could easily have come from one of Tchaikovsky's mature ballets.

Having based much of the symphony on themes with a distinctly Russian flavour, in the finale he quotes an actual Russian traditional song, 'I am scattering flowers, my little one'. The 'lugubre' (mournful) introduction begins hesitantly, then the tune is played sonorously by the violins over a processional pizzicato bass, while the woodwind add counterpoint and decorations. After another sombre moment of hesitation, the tune moves from minor to major, and to the bass. The music builds up and accelerates to a tutti, with trombones entering for the first time, and culminates in the first theme of the Allegro maestoso.

This is a joyful, straightforward little theme, in danger of sounding banal if Tchaikovsky's 'majestic' instruction is taken too seriously. The theme soon breaks into a fugal passage, with the theme put against a figure of running scales. This leads into the second theme, which is the folk song from the introduction on cellos and horns, now speeded up, and acquiring a determined swagger.

The middle of the movement sets off on a more extended passage of counterpoint. Tchaikovsky no doubt acquired such skills at the St Petersburg Conservatoire under the eyes of his teachers Anton Rubinstein and Zaremba, and in his mature works he learns to use them for dramatic impact. Here, the effect is rather dogged. But this passage is followed by a striking moment. After the first theme has been reprised, we expect the folk song second theme. But, after a brief snatch it comes to a halt, and the Andante lugubre introduction returns. After a few hesitant bars the music enters a mysterious world, with pianissimo horns playing a repeated-note pattern, while chromatic lines creep up and down around it. This passage derives from elements in the first movement – the repeated horns from the lead-in to the reprise, the chromatic lines from the staccato second element (this is the sort of subtle cross-reference that Tchaikovsky would have encountered in Schumann). Through a long stretch of dissonant chord progressions, the music gradually builds up, eventually accelerating to a grand, long peroration to bring the symphony to a blazing conclusion.

SYMPHONY NO. 2 IN C MINOR, OP. 17, 'LITTLE RUSSIAN'
Duration: approx. 33 minutes

Andante sostenuto – Allegro vivo
Andantino marziale quasi moderato
Scherzo: Allegro molto vivace
Finale: Moderato assai – Allegro vivo

Tchaikovsky composed his Second Symphony in 1872. It might seem the most 'Russian' of his symphonies, making use in its outer movements of real folk songs, rather than just composed melodies that sound folk-like. But the three songs Tchaikovsky employs in the symphony are Ukrainian (his sister's house, where he often stayed, was in Ukraine). The title, 'Little Russian', was given to it by friend and critic Nikolai Kashkin, in reference to these Ukrainian themes. Tchaikovsky does not just quote the songs, but uses them as the core of the symphony, particularly the finale. Here, he varies a folk song with constantly changing orchestration and counterpoints, in a manner pioneered by Glinka in his *Kamarinskaya*. Tchaikovsky considered Glinka's piece to be the source of the whole development of the Russian symphony, 'just as the whole oak is in the acorn'.[31]

This radical way to write a symphony met with enthusiastic approval even from Balakirev's circle, who were trying to forge a new Russian way of distancing themselves from traditional, 'academic' musical methods. The premiere was conducted by Nikolai Rubinstein in Moscow, on 7 February 1873, and was so successful that it was repeated twice, in April and May. Nevertheless, Tchaikovsky later came to be dissatisfied with the symphony and revised it in 1879–80, largely rewriting the first movement and shortening the finale. It is this revised version that is usually played, though the original has been recorded, and a number of commentators, from the composer Taneyev to Tchaikovsky's biographer David Brown, have preferred it to the revision.[32] The first version was written by the composer who had recently completed *Romeo and Juliet*, and it shows, particularly in the sustained battles of the first movement. By the time he came to revise the symphony, Tchaikovsky was the composer of *Swan Lake*, and his revision reflects that. He created a first movement that was lighter on its feet, contrasting toughness with grace. Both versions are very fine in their different ways, but as the revised score is the one usually performed, this is the focus of the following description.

Right from the introduction, Glinka's influence can be heard. The melody ('Down my mother Volga') is played three times, with varied orchestration: solo horn, bassoon over pizzicato bass, then back to horn with syncopated figure in woodwind. After further exploration of the melody, with increasingly elaborate orchestration, the introduction ends quietly with two horns.

The first theme of the Allegro is full of brusque, dancing energy, with crisp exchanges between strings and wind. After a short time, the second theme emerges on oboe. This is what had, in Tchaikovsky's original, been the first theme, its rising phrases now transformed so that they are full of romantic yearning. An energetic little rising motif punctuates the theme, and becomes important later on (this phrase is a survival from Tchaikovsky's original second theme). Violas and cellos take up the second theme, with a glorious descant above it in violins. The music mounts up to a recall of the vigorous first theme, and the first section of the Allegro comes to a close.

The development begins with clarinets playing the folk song from the introduction against a counterpoint of the little energetic motif from the second theme. The music builds to a climax, at which the brusque first theme takes over, and, with tremendous energy, leads to a greater climax at which the brass slow the first theme of the Allegro to sound like a chorale. Out of this emerges the first theme, as at the beginning of the Allegro. The reprise continues through the second theme to the tutti, and only then does the folk song from the introduction return (in the first version, it had been prominent through the development). The movement ends with the tempo slowing to the Andante sostenuto, and solo horn and solo bassoon bring the movement to a quiet and sombre close.

In the original version of this movement, the beginning and ending are the same as in the revision. But the original Allegro has two very restless themes, the first with searching upward phrases in the melody, over a bass that descends chromatically. This is the theme that Tchaikovsky later transformed to become the second theme. It grows, reaching abrupt dotted-rhythm chords and agitated exchanges between strings and wind that are reminiscent of the confrontations in *Romeo and Juliet* from three years earlier. The second theme, though mellifluous, is still very restless, and soon culminates in another passage of conflict. The central development of the movement is dominated by the folk song, which provides a massive climax out of which the reprise emerges.

The second and third movements remained substantially the same in the revision. The second movement began life as a wedding march in Act 3 of Tchaikovsky's opera, *Undine* (1869), most of which was destroyed by Tchaikovsky after its rejection by the St Petersburg theatres. It is a charmingly poised little march, set going pianissimo by timpani and woodwind. An episode within the march has a moment of almost operatic melody in the violins, before the opening of the march returns.

The central section of the movement takes another Ukrainian song, 'Spin, my spinner', and varies it in Glinka's 'Russian' style. It begins as a woodwind chorale. The first variation, on clarinet, is accompanied by a fluttering accompaniment on two flutes, perhaps intended to evoke the turning of the spinning-wheel. After other variations and excursions, the march theme returns, now infected by the spirit of variation, until it settles into a reprise, and the movement ends as delicately as it began.

The third movement is the most inventive and striking scherzo in any of Tchaikovsky's symphonies. Like the scherzo of the First Symphony, it is full of cross-rhythms. But here they are not just playful but full of impish mischief and tension. The movement sets off almost like the scherzo of Beethoven's 'Eroica' Symphony, but it is soon assailed by sudden contrasts, little flicks of impossibly fast runs, and swerves of rhythm and harmony. The trio switches from three-time to two-time, as if a troupe of traditional dancers has suddenly encroached on the children's game. At the end, after the reprise of the scherzo, there is a moment when the dancers of the trio are glimpsed again for a moment, before the scherzo's rhythm reasserts itself one last time.

The principal theme of the finale is a third Ukrainian folk song, 'The Crane', in a version that was, according to Tchaikovsky, sung to him by the butler at his sister's house in Ukraine.[33] The introduction presents the elements of the tune cast as a grand entry – the effect is strikingly similar to 'The Great Gate of Kiev' from Musorgsky's *Pictures at an Exhibition*, composed (for piano) two years later. Then the tune takes off at a lively pace, and is treated to a series of variations, once again drawing on the example set by Glinka in his *Kamarinskaya*, in a display of sheer *joie de vivre*. All of this stands for what would be the first theme in a conventional symphonic movement.

The variations come to an end, and without further ado Tchaikovsky launches into a second theme, a gentle lullaby over a held bass note, with a rocking syncopation in its melody. This is soon pushed aside by further variations on 'The Crane' and as the first section of the movement comes to an end, stark octaves in the brass announce the beginning of the development (again, Musorgsky must have been inspired by this moment when writing 'Catacombs' in *Pictures at an Exhibition*). The relentless tread of these octaves underpins the whole development, as it combines with the two themes, separately and in combination. This amasses great power, and, over a sustained bass note, 'The Crane' eventually reaches its original key.

At this point in the original version, Tchaikovsky added some more variations on the tune, but in the revised version he cut this passage, and went straight into the reprise of the gentle second theme. As before, this soon gives way to more variation on 'The Crane' and builds up to a tutti. The music reaches a pause with the brass octaves and a portentous gong stroke. A final presto dashes joyfully to a conclusion.

SYMPHONY NO. 3 IN D MAJOR, OP. 29
Duration: approx. 46 minutes

Introduzione e Allegro: Moderato assai (Tempo di marcia funebre) – Allegro brillante
Alla tedesca: Allegro moderato e semplice
Andante: Andante elegiaco
Scherzo: Allegro vivo
Finale: Allegro con fuoco (Tempo di polacca)

Tchaikovsky composed this symphony in the summer of 1875, less than a year after the First Piano Concerto, and while he was beginning to work on *Swan Lake*. Of his six symphonies, it is the only one in a major key, and it is very unusual in having five movements. The obvious precedent is Schumann's Third Symphony, which Tchaikovsky greatly admired: David Brown suggests that it might have been Tchaikovsky's idea of the symphony that Schumann could have written if he had been Russian.[34] With its many dance elements Tchaikovsky's symphony looks forward to the music of *Swan Lake*, and this combined with the five movements gives it something of the character of a suite on a large scale. It has sometimes been referred to as Tchaikovsky's 'Polish' Symphony because of its polonaise finale. But there is nothing particularly Polish about the earlier movements.

The symphony begins with a funeral march of haunting delicacy, in D minor, with plangent harmonies, tentative phrases with irregular lengths, and subtle orchestration – not the sort of sophistication one expects in a funeral march. An acceleration culminates in the first theme of the Allegro in the major, which is like a grand, marching entry in a ballet. Swirling elements soon join, in the woodwind and then the strings, adding energy to what might have been in danger of becoming stodgy. After another grand tutti, an oboe plays the second theme, a charmingly plaintive melody with falling phrases. Its continuation blossoms in the strings for a moment, before the energy then builds up to another vigorous tutti.

The development becomes contrapuntal, pitting the various elements against each other over a long (possibly too long) paragraph, before arriving at the grand reprise of the first theme. Over the swirling elements, the oboe again introduces the plaintive second theme, which is taken up warmly by the strings, at greater length than before, and rises to a tutti climax. After this, there are two more build-ups, and an increase in pace, before this exuberant movement comes to a close.

Alla tedesca means 'in the German style', that is, like a moderate-tempo waltz. Tchaikovsky's melody has a rather hesitant, perhaps shy, character created by offbeats and unexpected phrase lengths – it seems related to the oboe's second theme in the first movement. Eventually, it warms into a flowing melody on the violins, before demurely stepping back again. The trio is dominated by delicate, chattering triplets that pass between woodwind and strings, a hallmark Tchaikovsky effect. Equally characteristic is the way these triplets persist over the waltz when it returns in the cellos.

In the Andante, two sections loosely alternate. The first, in D minor, begins with two flutes in unison (a haunting sound), playing folk-song-like fragments, and continues with chant-like phrases from bassoon and horn. The second section warms into B flat major, with a flowing violin theme that develops and twice rises to a climax before falling back. The fragments of chant and folk song return. After a while, the woodwind reprise the flowing violin theme, while the triplet rhythm of the chant continues below. The strings again take the melody to two climaxes. The movement ends quietly with even tinier fragments of folk song and chant reiterated over shuddering tremolo.

The fourth movement is a two-time scherzo in B minor, with rapid, fragile, swirling figures passing between strings and woodwind (these are extremely difficult to play and co-ordinate). Beneath the swirling figures, twice a whole-tone scale descends three notes at a time, once in the strings, and then in the horns. This scale had been associated with magical effects in Russian opera ever since Glinka's *Russlan and Ludmilla* thirty year earlier. The trio is a delicate, pointed march – unusually, down a major third from the scherzo, in G minor. There is an atmosphere of mystery and magic about the music, as if it had stepped out of Mendelssohn's music for *A Midsummer Night's Dream*. Two horns alternate to sustain a single note throughout, which has the effect of giving the entire march a feeling of unresolved suspense.

The finale has the character of a polonaise, cast in the form of a rondo, in which the main theme recurs several times interspersed with different episodes. After the initial statement of the grand polonaise, the first episode puts the theme through a passage of playful counterpoint. This leads straight on to a new theme, a rather square tune in the woodwind. The first theme returns briefly. The next episode is charming and delicate, full of the combination of dotted rhythms and triplet figures that Tchaikovsky was so fond of. At the end of this episode the triplet rhythm breaks into semiquavers, and we are back at the main polonaise theme.

The next episode is another passage of counterpoint. Unlike the first episode, this develops into a thoroughgoing fugue, at the end of which, over a sustained bass note, the music builds up, arriving at a majestic, slow-tempo version of the main theme. This then breaks back into the polonaise, and on into a final presto to bring the symphony to a splendid close.

SYMPHONY NO. 4 IN F MINOR, OP. 36

Duration: approx. 44 minutes

Andante sostenuto – Moderato con anima
Andantino in modo di canzona
Scherzo: Pizzicato ostinato
Finale: Allegro con fuoco

In May 1877, Tchaikovsky received a letter from a former student at the Moscow Conservatoire, Antonina Ivanovna Milyukova, in which she declared her love for him. They married in July, but by October they were separated. The marriage was a predictable disaster, and writers have put forward various ideas to help explain why Tchaikovsky might ever have thought it a good idea. These include a way of providing a cover for his homosexuality, a desire for financial security, and confusion in Tchaikovsky's mind between Antonina and Tatiana, the heroine of his opera *Eugene Onegin* – a sensitive, romantic girl who falls in love with the sophisticated Onegin, and suffers the humiliation of being rejected by him. What is certain about the marriage is that it was doomed from the first, and Tchaikovsky already realized it during the wedding ceremony. When the moment came for him to kiss the bride, 'a pain struck my heart and such an anxiety gripped me that I think I began to weep. But I made an effort to master myself quickly and assume an air of calm.'[35] In the aftermath, Tchaikovsky suffered a severe mental breakdown, following which he and his wife separated.

By fortunate coincidence, that autumn Tchaikovsky was suddenly released from financial worries when Nadezhda von Meck, a wealthy widow who admired his music and had engaged in ongoing correspondence with him, began to pay Tchaikovsky an annual allowance. This enabled him to travel over the winter months of 1877–8, and to complete two major works that he had begun before his marriage, *Eugene Onegin* and the Fourth Symphony.

Tchaikovsky wrote the symphony for von Meck, disguising the dedication in the published score with the words, 'To my best friend'. In his letters to her, he referred to it as 'our symphony', and said, 'None of my earlier works for orchestra has given me so much trouble, but on none have I lavished such love and devotion ... In my heart of hearts I feel sure that it is the best thing I have done so far.'[36]

More problematic is the 'programme' for the symphony that Tchaikovsky revealed in one of his letters to von Meck.[37] He begins by a warning against simplistic ideas of 'meaning' in music: 'You ask if in composing this symphony I had a special programme in view. To such questions regarding my symphonic works I generally answer: nothing of the kind. In reality it is very difficult to answer this question. How can one interpret those vague feelings which pass through me during the composition of an instrumental work, without reference to any definite subject? It is a purely lyrical process. A kind of musical shriving of the soul, in which there is an encrustation of material which flows forth again in notes, just as the lyrical poet pours himself out in verse.'

But despite this, Tchaikovsky does provide a detailed programme 'for you – and you alone'. The motto theme opens the symphony: 'This is Fate, the decisive force which prevents our hopes of happiness from being realized, which watches jealously to see that our bliss and peace are not complete and unclouded, and which, like the sword of Damocles, is suspended over our heads and perpetually poisons our souls. This force is inescapable and invincible. There is no other course but to submit and inwardly lament.'

He quotes the secondary themes of the first movement, in which the soul turns from reality and sinks deeper and deeper into dreams, until Fate once more awakens us roughly: 'So all life is but a continual alternation between grim truth and fleeting dreams of happiness. There is no haven. The waves drive us hither and thither, until the sea engulfs us.'

The second movement expresses 'the melancholy which steals over us when at evening we sit indoors alone, weary of work, while the book we have picked up for relaxation slips unheeded from our fingers. A long process of old memories goes by . . . How sad, yet sweet to lose ourselves in them!' In the scherzo, rather than definite feelings we find, 'only capricious arabesques, intangible forms, which come into a man's head when he has been drinking wine and his nerves are rather excited'. Memories are called up – a tipsy peasant, a street song, a military band heard from the distance. And in the finale: 'If you can find no reason for happiness in yourself, look at others. Go to the people. See how they can enjoy life and give themselves up entirely to festivity.' But then, 'Fate reminds us once more of its presence. Others pay no heed to us . . . How merry, how glad they all are! . . . Be glad in others' gladness. This makes life possible.'

To the composer Sergei Taneyev, Tchaikovsky admitted that the symphony had a programme 'so obvious that everyone would understand its meaning', but that to put it into words would be thought 'ludicrous'. But he went on to say, 'In reality my work is a reflection of Beethoven's Fifth Symphony', whose programme 'is so clear that there cannot be the smallest difference of opinion as to what it means'.[38] Beethoven's first biographer, Anton Schindler, had claimed that the composer said of his famous motto theme, 'Thus Fate knocks at the door'. Whether or not Beethoven actually said that, the progress of his Fifth Symphony from some kind of ominous threat to some kind of eventual triumph is, as Tchaikovsky says, obvious, and need not impede our appreciation of the music at all sorts of levels.

Some commentators have found Tchaikovsky's revelation of a programme for his Fourth Symphony unfortunate, and have used it to call into question the quality of the music as a self-sufficient work. Writers have also wondered how much the music of the symphony reflects Tchaikovsky's mental state as he tried to come to terms with the disaster of his marriage. But this is complicated by the fact that he had done most of the work of composition before the wedding. The one specific hint of a connection is in the finale, which Tchaikovsky composed shortly after proposing to Antonina. The second theme is a folk song, 'In the field a little birch tree stood', which Balakirev had already used in an overture. In the song, young women make wreaths from birch twigs and throw them into the river. Those whose wreaths float will marry.

Perhaps the best way to sum up the arguments about this emotional hinterland is to say that the same applies to Tchaikovsky as to Beethoven. We do not need Tchaikovsky's description to appreciate the emotional conflicts and emotional narrative of the music. And the fact that he attempted in a private letter to express something of his thought processes does not take away from the musical achievement.

The symphony opens with the motto, on horns and then full brass. It carries the force of a fanfare, but a fanfare in a minor key accompanied by chromatic harmonies, hence its 'fateful' character. The motto owes an obvious debt not only to Beethoven's Fifth, but also to the (much more cheerful) fanfare that opens the First Symphony ('Spring') of Tchaikovsky's beloved Schumann.

The fanfare fades away, and the Allegro begins. Its first theme is ambivalent in mood. A note instructs that the subdivisions of the bar should be 'in waltz-tempo', but the melody is full of drooping phrases and uncertain rhythms, with dotted rhythms and offbeats in the accompaniment, so that elegance is combined with anxiety. The melody is developed, moves to the bass upside down, and builds to a forceful restatement, with additional swirling at the ends of each phrase. After a yet more agitated statement, a gentle clarinet is heard ('sweetly, gracefully') playing a new major-key version of the theme with hopeful rising phrases. A bassoon responds, and leads in to the second main theme.

This is a strangely hesitant melody in dotted rhythms, in the minor. Each phrase ends with a little bird-like falling phrase, which is answered by the other woodwind. Soon this theme is accompanied by a lyrical descant with a rocking rhythm, first on cellos then on flutes and oboes. The violins take up this rocking melody pianissimo, as taps on the timpani give it a gentle impulse. The woodwind answer with fragments of the first theme, now with a dancing staccato that removes its anxiety. The pace accelerates, the dotted-rhythm elements of the first theme take on an increasingly insistent character. Against this prevailing rhythm, in an *fff* tutti, the strings, and then the horns, play a new, bold major-key melody, to bring the first section of the movement to a gloriously confident close.

But the moment is short-lived. Into this climax breaks the opening fanfare-motto, 'con tutta forza' (with full force), on trumpets and then horns. From this savage interruption, the first theme picks itself up uncertainly, passing between strings and woodwind. Out of this ongoing dialogue, a more hopeful, rising version of the opening phrase of the theme emerges, building higher and higher, until, at its height, the trumpets again enter *fff* with the motto fanfare. But now the more hopeful music will not be silenced, and a tremendous battle develops between these elements. Three times the motto is fought off, until a powerful restatement of the first theme brings a sense of having reached the reprise (in theme, though it is not in the original key). The music calms, and the hesitant second theme follows, now on bassoon. Again the quiet rocking theme accelerates, the music builds, and, more swiftly this time, culminates in the intervention of the motto on trumpets and horns. As the music quietens, the woodwind play a gentle, consoling melody, which is a transformation of a phrase from the threatening motto. Like the confident climax that concluded the first part of the movement, this moment of consolation is also short-lived. The tempo becomes faster, and this phrase from the motto becomes an agitated figure, with the familiar dotted-rhythm pattern.

The agitation builds, the motto again fights for predominance, and at the final *fff* climax the strings play the first theme with ferocious tremolo, as a despairing lament. There is one more surge to the ending, without any sense of triumph – a passage very like the last bars of *Eugene Onegin*, where the distraught Onegin rushes out.

'In the style of a song', says Tchaikovsky's instruction at the head of the Andantino. This is a movement of touching simplicity, in three-part form. An oboe sings a theme in a minor key over pizzicato accompaniment. The melody begins with a straightforward pair of four-bar phrases, like a folk lament; but in the second half, the first phrase is followed not by four bars but by eight, falling gently downwards in a repeating pattern. This extended second half gives the melody great poignancy – it is easy to see how it might have suggested to Tchaikovsky the evocation of old memories (or vice versa). The melody moves to the cellos. Then violins and cellos combine to take it on to a new paragraph. This too begins with regular phrases, each with three firmly repeated notes, but then wanders, moving upwards, changing keys as it goes, arriving at a climax of scale patterns sweeping up and down, over a chord carefully chosen to make the moment seem suspended (again, evoking the idea of sinking into memories). The scales relax into a delicate staccato pattern, under which the first part of the melody is played again, by violas and bassoon, then violins and violas, with the cellos rejoining for the second paragraph.

This time the music moves on to the middle section of the movement, which is a little faster. A new theme consists of a stubborn little phrase that repeats again and again, up and down, up and down, as some folk tunes do. At first this idea seems too dull to be promising, but Tchaikovsky builds it up with countermelodies, enriches its orchestration, and lets it (like the earlier melody) lose itself, and flower into a passionate outpouring. When the original, simple idea comes in at the climax, it no longer seems dull, but like (again) a treasured memory.

The music ebbs away, and leads into a reprise of the first theme of the movement. This starts on violins, and is accompanied by little flourishes in the woodwind. These evoke a specific memory, of the bird-like falling phrases from the second theme of the first movement. The second paragraph of the melody once more wanders off, this time into an extended moment of quiet meditation moving poignantly through new keys. When it finds its way back, the first theme is quietly sung for the last time by a bassoon, with the most delicate of countermelodies touched in sadly by the violins.

The third movement begins and ends as a pizzicato scherzo, a rare thing in a symphony. Since Tchaikovsky himself cited Beethoven's Fifth Symphony as his principal model for this work, it is likely that he was inspired by the pizzicato ending to the scherzo that links to Beethoven's finale. Other possible inspirations are the *Pizzicato Polka* by Johann Strauss II, or the recent *Pizzicati* variation in Delibes's *Sylvia*, a ballet that Tchaikovsky had heard for the first time in November 1877, and loved (he had composed his scherzo in May, but did not orchestrate it until December). However, Tchaikovsky's movement is quite different from any of these, combining the elegance of Delibes and Strauss with a dash and exhilaration all his own.

Like the second movement, the scherzo has a simple structure, but incorporating a great deal of subtlety. It begins with the predominantly soft pizzicato section. One of the pleasures of this music is the way in which Tchaikovsky varies the texture, the melodic line passing playfully from violins to violas, to the cellos and bass, and with sudden surges to forte and unexpected turns of harmony.

As the pizzicato fades away, a note on the oboe announces the middle section of the movement. This is a slower dance for woodwind, with repetitive flourishes that suggest an element of display. The brass section breaks into this scene, returning to the first tempo, but with note values that create a half-speed version of the pizzicato theme, like a march. First a clarinet and then a piccolo add their dance tune (now uncomfortably fast) to the brass. Then the woodwind join in with the pizzicato theme, and this leads to the reprise on the strings. But the wind have not finished yet. Just as the strings seem to be coming to the end, the woodwind join in again, adding their flourishes, and this provokes a crescendo to a climax. As it dies away, there is a final appearance of the brass, disappearing into the distance, and the movement evaporates.

Cymbals and bass drum enter for the first time with the crashing chord that begins the finale. The wildly rushing theme gives way for a moment to a more sombre, almost chant-like, melody. This is the Russian folk song, 'In the field a little birch tree stood'. Tchaikovsky adapts the tune, changing its three-beat phrases into four-beat, to fit his metre for this movement. After the next rushing tutti, the folk tune returns, and is treated to Glinka-style variations of orchestration, building up to another grand tutti, and then back into the first theme.

After this, the folk tune returns for another episode, this time with a difference. The tune starts a third lower in the harmony, with more poignant chords, and a flute decoration above. But this moment of wistfulness is short-lived. Again the energy level of the music increases, reaching a yet more ferocious tutti, until it breaks into the fateful motto from the first movement, on full brass *fff*. This dies away to a mournful moment. Then the first tempo is restored, and over a long bass note there is a great crescendo up to a final reprise of the rushing first theme. A tutti full of wild cheering, with whoops that recall the bird-like flourishes from the first and second movements, brings the symphony to a close.

SYMPHONY NO. 5 IN E MINOR, OP. 64
Duration: approx. 48 minutes

Andante – Allegro con anima
Andante cantabile con alcuna licenza
Valse: Allegro moderato
Finale: Andante maestoso – Allegro vivace

In April 1888, Tchaikovsky jotted down in a notebook sketches of themes for a symphony, together with ideas for a programme for a first movement:[39]

Intro: Total submission before Fate, or, what is the same thing, the inscrutable designs of Providence.
    Allegro: 1. Murmurs, laments, doubts, reproaches against . . . XXX ['X' in Tchaikovsky's diaries is a mysterious code, which might or might not to refer to homosexual yearnings]
    2. Shall I cast myself into the embrace of *faith*???
    A wonderful programme, if only it can be fulfilled.
    [For the slow movement] A ray of light . . . No, there is no hope.

In June, Tchaikovsky wrote that he was working diligently on a symphony 'without a programme'. So it may be that the symphony that he did actually compose in the summer of 1888 has no connection to the fragments of a programme that he had noted in April. As one listens to the symphony, however, it is difficult not to feel that some powerful emotional (if not literal) narrative is being evoked, just as in the *Hamlet* overture that he composed the same summer, or indeed the Fourth Symphony from ten years previously.

Tchaikovsky was constantly worried about his health, and did not expect to live long. And there are one or two other clues to specific ideas. There is a 'motto' theme that begins the symphony, and recurs in each movement. The opening phrase of this motto is a quote (deliberately or by coincidence) from an aria in Act I of Glinka's opera *A Life for the Tsar*, at the words, 'Do not turn our farewell to sorrow.' And in the slow movement, the second theme was associated by Tchaikovsky with the words, 'O que je t'aime! O mon amie!'[40] Since 'amie' is feminine, writers have suggested that this might refer to Tchaikovsky's patroness Nadezhda von Meck, or perhaps to Desirée Artôt, a singer whom he had planned to marry twenty years earlier, and the only woman Tchaikovsky seems genuinely to have loved. They had met again in January 1888, and Tchaikovsky wrote, 'I was inexpressibly glad to see her ... she is just as fascinating as twenty years ago.'[41] But if the words that Tchaikovsky attached to this melody were to be a quote, the feminine 'amie' might equally refer to an 'ami', such as his beloved nephew Bob (Vladimir) Davydov. But we have nothing more to go on than hints, and it is perhaps better to let the music have its unimpeded effect.

Letters during the composition reveal that Tchaikovsky was prey to continual doubts about his ability to compose and the worth of the results. But in September 1888 he reported to his brother Anatoly, 'The symphony has received unanimous approval from all my friends: some even say that it is my best work. It's particularly significant that S. I. Taneyev is wholly enthusiastic' (Taneyev had prepared the piano duet arrangement). By December, after three performances conducted by Tchaikovsky himself, he had lost confidence again, as he wrote to von Meck: 'I am convinced that this symphony is not a success. There is something so repellent about so much excess, insincerity, and artificiality.' But by the following March his feelings had changed yet again after a successful performance in Hamburg, as he wrote to his brother Modest: 'Best of all, I have stopped disliking the symphony. I love it again.'[42]

The symphony opens with a melody like a chant, which is to become the recurring 'motto' of the work. The chanting effect is enhanced by the fact that it is played not by a solo clarinet, but by two in unison, like processing monks. And the tone is made ominous by heavy dotted rhythms, a solemn descending scale, sudden accents and crescendos.

The first theme of the Allegro seems to grow naturally out of the chant. The solemn dotted rhythms now become swung into the lilting 6/8 metre of a siciliano, though still in a dark E minor. This builds to a tutti, at the end of which the strings emerge with pleading phrases. These move to the woodwind. Then there is a sudden increase in tempo, at which the woodwind begin a dance with repeated chords, at last firmly in a major key. But this soon slows to a passionate theme in the violins, still in the major, which sweeps upwards phrase by phrase to a great climax, rounded off by a forceful return to the dance rhythm.

The dance infects the opening of the development, with the first theme moving from instrument to instrument. After a build-up, the music relaxes to the pleading melody in violins. Then there is another climax, another relaxation, and a bassoon leads in the reprise with the first theme. At the end of the reprise, once again the tempo increases, and there is a final climax before the movement ends, as it began, in darkness.

The slow movement is one of Tchaikovsky's most passionate outpourings. It begins with deep, dark chords in the strings, in B minor. But the chords gradually lighten, arriving in D major. A horn plays a sustained solo, which seems constantly to be striving upwards, little phrase by little phrase, and broader phrase by broader phrase (it has this in common with the passionate violin theme from the first movement). A clarinet joins with a countermelody for a time. Then, before the theme has really come to an end, the oboe interrupts with a delicate new idea, and horn and oboe play in duet for a moment (this is the melody that Tchaikovsky associated with the words 'O que je t'aime! O mon amie!'). After another moment of darkness, the cellos then take up the horn theme, raising it higher than before, but seemingly unable to reach their goal as they give way to a plangent wind chord. The violins start the melody again (the marking here is 'con noblezza', 'nobly'), and finally it rises to a great climax and sinks gently back, reaching the conclusion that had eluded the horn.

The middle of the movement begins with a new theme, a meditation over a held bass note, on clarinet and then bassoon (this melancholy moment has a distinct echo of *Eugene Onegin* in it). This too is taken forward by the strings, and begins to develop passion and determination. But just at the moment where it seems to be heading towards a climax, the trumpets break in fortissimo with the motto from the beginning of the first movement, stopping the melody in its tracks. There is a silence, and then uncertain pizzicato chords that find their way back to D major.

The violins return to the horn theme, with a beautiful counterpoint on oboe. As the melody progresses, it becomes gradually more animated, until it culminates in the strings taking up the 'O que je t'aime!' theme, taking it to a huge climax, *ffff*. So the melody that started as a delicate aside on the oboe culminates in the greatest climax of the symphony (emotionally, if not in volume). As it dies away, it too is brutally interrupted by the motto, blasted out on trumpets. There is another silence, and this time the response is sighing phrases that suggest resignation. Very quietly, the strings remember the horn theme for the last time.

For this movement one hardly needs a programme to understand its developing passions, conflicts, rude interruptions, and tender memories. It is, perhaps, a narrative of a passionate life – but that does not have to be Tchaikovsky's.

The third movement is a graceful waltz, scored with subtlety and richness, the melody passing charmingly between strings and woodwind. What is already a dance becomes positively balletic in the middle section, where the violins set off a semiquaver chase in which others join, as in a children's game. When the waltz theme returns in the oboe, the chase continues in the strings until they too rejoin the melody. At the end, Tchaikovsky develops the melody further in a charming coda. Once more the motto intrudes darkly on low clarinets and bassoons, before being swept aside by a series of confident chords.

At the opening of the finale, the motto has ceased to be threatening and fateful and in the minor, and has become 'majestic' and in the major, like a grand, processional entry. But at the end of the Andante introduction, the music turns once more to the minor. The first theme of the Allegro is brusque and vigorous, with elements of Russian dance that have been largely missing from the earlier movements of the symphony. What is less obvious is that it is closely related to the motto: the solemn descending scale of the motto is now hammered out with pairs of repeated notes. Out of this punchy theme emerges a more graceful, dancing element on woodwind, to which the violins respond with a sequence of increasingly passionate falling and rising phrases – these clearly derive their shape from the 'O que je t'aime!' theme from the slow movement.

After this has built up, there is yet another theme in the woodwind, over a persistent, marching bass. The falling scale of the motto is again an ingredient, though speeded up to be unrecognizable. Once more the strings respond passionately, the descending scale now drawn into that passion, and perhaps revealing a link with the great passionate string theme from the first movement. At the next climax, the motto returns, blazing in the brass, still in a major key, and seeming to form part of a general sense of triumph.

As the vigorous first theme of the Allegro returns, the music turns to new keys, and the woodwind's march theme moves to the bass, with clarinet counterpoint above. A tumultuous passage eventually calms, and solemn wind chords and wistful shifts of harmony seem like a memory of past emotions. This moment is short-lived. With a bang, we are brought back to a reprise of the brusque opening Allegro theme, and the other themes follow in their original sequence. As before, this culminates in the reappearance of the motto, in the minor at first, and a great climax is followed by a sudden increase in pace, then a halt.

Now follows the final triumph: the motto, in the major, in grand procession, first on the strings, then on the trumpets, 'con tutta forza' (with full force). A final presto dash brings in other elements from the last movement, and at the very end the trumpets, *ffff*, recall the opening theme of the first movement Allegro, now transformed into a clarion call.

Tchaikovsky was not the only commentator to have doubts about this finale, and particularly its grand peroration. Accepting it wholeheartedly takes a certain leap of faith. It is clear what Tchaikovsky was trying to do. One does not need an explicit programme to hear that the motto, which began the symphony darkly in the minor, and had threatened in each movement, here becomes a triumphant element, having been integrated with other elements from the symphony. Whether the triumph is wholly convincing is a question that continues to hang over the work.

SYMPHONY NO. 6 IN B MINOR, OP. 74, 'PATHÉTIQUE'
Duration: 45–55 minutes

Adagio – Allegro non troppo
Allegro con grazia
Allegro molto vivace
Finale: Adagio lamentoso

On 6 November 1893, Tchaikovsky died in St Petersburg after an illness that lasted only six days. For nearly a century the public version of his death was that he had died of cholera, after drinking a glass of unboiled water. It was not until 1978 that an alternative cause of death was proposed, by the Russian scholar Alexandra Orlova.[43]

According to this version of events, Duke Stenbok-Fermor, who was disturbed by the attention that Tchaikovsky was paying to his young nephew, threatened him with exposure by writing a letter to the Tsar. The civil servant to whom he gave the letter was a fellow pupil at Tchaikovsky's school, and he convened a court of former students to interview the composer and decide his fate. They concluded that the only way for Tchaikovsky and the school to avoid public disgrace was for the composer to kill himself. A few days later, reports emerged that Tchaikovsky was on his deathbed. The details of this terrible story originated from the wife of the civil servant who convened the court. She saw Tchaikovsky leave the house, white as a sheet, and was told what had happened by her husband.

Orlova's reconstruction of events has been accepted by many scholars, but is still hotly disputed.[44] The first performance of the 'Pathétique' Symphony took place three days before that court of honour. Does it have any connection with the tragedy of Tchaikovsky's death? Yes and no. If the story is true, he must have known that he faced possible disgrace. But more importantly, he had spent his life struggling with his homosexuality, and had even gone to the extent of undertaking a disastrous marriage in order to conceal it. Tchaikovsky had sketched out an idea for a symphony in which 'the ultimate essence of the plan of the symphony is *life*', with the final movement representing death.[45] That was before he began work on the 'Pathétique', and long before the events that were to lead to his own death. But it seems very likely that the emotional intensity of the music relates closely to the suffering that his own nature, and the repressive social requirements of the time, had forced upon him throughout his life.

The symphony emerges from darkness: double basses hold a bare fifth, over which a bassoon plays a low, mournful theme in B minor that creeps upwards in sighing phrases. This slow introduction is followed by an Allegro in which the bassoon's mournful theme is speeded up, and then agitated into anxious fragments. There are rapid exchanges between strings and woodwind, sudden outbursts, and a suggestion of military menace in the brass fanfares.

Eventually this dies down, and muted violins and cellos play a second theme, a nostalgically lyrical outpouring of falling phrases, in a warm D major. There is a gentle episode, in which flute and bassoon answer each other. Then the second theme returns, building to an impassioned climax, and lingering before sinking back. This section ends with clarinet and bassoon falling almost to inaudibility – Tchaikovsky's marking is *pppppp*, and a bass clarinet often substitutes for the bassoon to achieve a quieter effect.

The silence is broken by a shattering blow, and fragments of the first theme are roughly thrown around, formed into an agitated fugal passage, and reiterated obsessively. A climax is reached, at which the brass enter *fff* with the opening of the lyrical second theme, now transformed into a despairing cry. There is another descent, at which the trombones briefly quote a Russian Orthodox funeral chant, 'With thy saints, O Christ, grant peace to the soul of thy servant', and then another climax, at which fragments of both themes combine. Again it is the brass that blare out anguished fragments of the second theme, and the passage ends with a great lament building up from the strings, and sinking down once more to pianissimo.

All of this has been so emotionally direct, so wild and so urgent, that we are scarcely aware that it has also formed a traditional, classical development section, just as the opening of the symphony was the classical slow introduction followed by an Allegro. Now we reach the reprise of the opening section. But here Tchaikovsky truncates classical practice, cutting straight to the lyrical second theme. This is at first sweet and hesitant, with nervously shimmering violas and cellos under it. But soon it gains in confidence and sings out passionately. As before, a quiet clarinet meditates on the theme, and this leads to a concluding chorale on brass and woodwind, whose shape is related to the sighing phrases with which the bassoon began the movement, but now in a calm B major.

The second movement in D major is like a gentle minuet sung by the cellos. But it is in five-time instead of the usual three, and the length of the phrases makes it even more complicated than that. The cello line has phrases with beats grouped in a pattern 2+3. But the accompanying instruments group the beats against this pattern, as 3+2. When the woodwind take up the tune, the cellos have a countermelody that alternates 2+3 with 3+2. The result of all this rhythmic variety is a line that seems to float in the air in a charmingly fluid manner. The second half of the quasi-minuet is more balletic in character, with a chorus of strings picking up on the dotted rhythms from the middle of the melody and making them dance.

There is a central section of the movement, corresponding to the conventional trio of a minuet, but still in five-time. This reverts to the B minor of the opening of the symphony, but with the bass repeating the note D throughout, so the music seems suspended. This is given an ominous insistence by the timpani, who tap out the five beats right through the section. The melodic line is sombre, almost chant-like, but with the sighs of the opening bassoon solo. There is then a reprise of the first section, followed by a coda in which the bass again stays on the note D, but now with a more comfortable D major above it, while wistful reminiscences of the repeated phrase from the middle section bring the movement to a close.

The third movement is a very fast scherzo. But although the opening might seem to promise a dancing movement, almost like Mendelssohn, the woodwind are soon cutting against the triplet rhythms with groups of two, to give a chattering effect. A quiet fanfare motif starts up in the oboe, and passes to the brass. At first the strings develop this playfully, but an urgent descending line suddenly breaks through, and the music becomes increasingly tense. The fanfare motif, in brass and timpani, becomes increasingly military in character, and after a climax it is quietly revealed by the clarinets as a real march.

The rest of the movement consists of a series of build-ups, from pianissimo as if the march is in the distance, to increasingly big climaxes. The opening is reprised, and then comes the biggest build-up of all, with the climax thrillingly delayed by blaring brass and swirling strings and woodwind, before the march is hammered out *fff* by the whole orchestra. The intensity is maintained from this point almost constantly until the end of the movement. What began as a playful scherzo ends in sustained triumph, or destruction, or both.

What is to follow this exhausting climax? As Tchaikovsky proudly declared, not a conventional, loud Allegro, but a sustained Adagio, something unprecedented in the nineteenth century. It opens with falling phrases on the strings, reminiscent of the falling phrases of the first movement's second theme. Now, as well as being in the minor, they are terse and anguished, short-breathed, but then rising in sequence and building in intensity. In the background is a counterpoint of bassoons and flutes in unison – a haunting sonority – and they bring the melody to rest. The strings sing their melody again, and this time the bassoons alone round it off, taking it down to the depths from which the opening of the symphony emerged.

Quiet, pulsating horns introduce a second theme. This too consists of a sequence of falling phrases, but now in a warm D major, and formed into a smooth melody. It is as if the first theme has been purged of its anguish, and has become a source of consolation (Tchaikovsky indicates that it should be played 'gently and devoutly'). The sequence of phrases rises gradually to a great climax, breaking off into swirling descending scales, and silence. The consolation has been short-lived, and after a series of halting sighs, the sorrowful first theme returns.

This time horns take over the role of the bassoons, taking the descending counterpoint to a fiercer harmonic twist. Again the strings swirl up to play their first theme, and now it builds relentlessly to an overwhelming climax, the brass instruments rising up to join them. There is a sequence of swirls, over snarling hand-stopped horns, and the theme dies.

A quiet gong stroke brings in a choir of trombones, forming the sighing phrases into a solemn chant. Finally, the second theme, now in B minor and drained of all its consolation, falls steadily back into the darkness, drawn forward by an ominous pulse on the double basses.

Whatever personal anguish went into the writing of this symphony, Tchaikovsky wrote that it was the best and most sincere of all his works: 'I love it as I have never loved any of my other musical offspring.'[46]

VARIATIONS ON A ROCOCO THEME, FOR CELLO AND ORCHESTRA, OP. 33
Duration: approx. 19 minutes

Tchaikovsky's original:	*Fitzhagen's edition:*
Introduction: Moderato assai quasi andante	Introduction: Moderato assai quasi andante
Thema: Moderato semplice	Thema: Moderato semplice
Variation 1: Tempo della tema	Variation 1: Tempo della tema
Variation 2: Tempo della tema	Variation 2: Tempo della tema
Variation 3: Andante	Variation 3 (Tchaikovsky's V. 7): Andante sostenuto
Variation 4: Allegro vivo	Variation 4 (Tchaikovsky's V. 5): Andante grazioso
Variation 5: Andante grazioso	Variation 5 (Tchaikovsky's V. 6): Allegro moderato
Variation 6: Allegro moderato	Variation 6 (Tchaikovsky's V. 3): Andante
Variation 7: Andante sostenuto	Variation 7 (Tchaikovsky's V. 4) e Coda: Allegro vivo
Variation 8 e Coda: Allegro moderato e con anima	(Variation 8 discarded)

In 1876, Tchaikovsky wrote the most vividly descriptive and tempestuous of his symphonic poems, *Francesca da Rimini*. Shortly after finishing it, he endured the disastrous premiere of his opera *Vakula the Smith*, and was already planning another opera, on Shakespeare's *Othello* (which he never wrote). In December he composed the Variations on a Rococo Theme.

Unlike the wild *Francesca da Rimini*, this is music of classical elegance, and on the surface it might seem entirely out of character. But the contrast between *Francesca* and the Variations lays out in the open two strands that lived side by side in Tchaikovsky's musical psyche throughout his life. On the one hand, his music is emotionally intense – sometimes over-whelmingly so. But at the same time he has a touch of great delicacy and refinement. This is most obvious in his ballet music, but all his greatest works manage to fuse these two sides of his character together, even though he often struggled to achieve the synthesis.

The Variations on a Rococo Theme are a tribute to Mozart, whose music Tchaikovsky placed above all other: 'I love everything in Mozart, for we love everything in the man to whom we are truly devoted', he was to write in his diary.[47] But the Variations are not a pastiche of eighteenth-century music. Through their 'elegant detachment', as David Brown puts it, Tchaikovsky expresses essential elements of his own character.[48]

He dedicated the work to his fellow professor at the Moscow Conservatoire, the cellist Wilhelm Fitzhagen. With Nikolai Rubinstein conducting, Fitzhagen gave the very successful first performance in Moscow in November 1877. The cellist wrote to Tchaikovsky after a later performance in Wiesbaden, at which Liszt was present: 'I produced a furore with your varia-tions. I pleased so greatly that I was called three times, and after the Andante Variation (D minor) there was stormy applause.' Afterwards, Liszt said to Fitzhagen, 'Now there, at last, is real music!'[49]

But the work that Fitzhagen played with such success, and that is still familiar today, is not the work as Tchaikovsky wrote it. Fitzhagen made substantial revisions to Tchaikovsky's score, to make it, as he thought, more 'effective'. This meant not only changing details of the solo part (which Tchaikovsky had asked him to look at), but, without consulting Tchaikovsky, completely reordering the sequence of variations. Fitzhagen's version was published, and although Tchaikovsky later expressed his annoyance, he allowed it to stand without public protest. Perhaps if he had not been so preoccupied with his own problems (particularly his disastrous marriage), he would have restored his original version. It was finally published in the 1940s, but only after many years is it beginning to be played and recorded in preference to Fitzhagen's revision.

Tchaikovsky's original has a theme followed without a break by eight linked variations and a coda. Fitzhagen took the variations and placed them in the following order: 1, 2, 7, 5, 6, 3, 4, followed by the coda. Variation 8 was discarded altogether. By removing one of the most vigorous variations and reordering the remainder, Fitzhagen altered the balance between slow and fast music and radically changed the shape of the work. Tchaikovsky's eloquent Variation 7 is the longest, and forms the emotional climax. By moving it forward to become Variation 3, Fitzhagen shifted the heart of the work to near the beginning instead of near the end. With Tchaikovsky's original order restored, we can hear that Tchaikovsky knew exactly what he was doing, and the result is a work of dramatic strength as well as elegance and brilliance.

A brief introduction sets the scene: aspiring string phrases answered by the woodwind, hushed pizzicato, and a horn solo lead us to expect an entry, perhaps of dancers (Tchaikovsky's music so often has a balletic feel). The cellist plays the theme, with its eighteenth-century balance and elegance. But as the soloist finishes, the woodwind add a little tailpiece with entirely modern touches of chromatic melancholy, as if they are the wistful spectators at this courtly dance. The strings and the cello are drawn into this switch of mood and perspective, rounding off the paragraph and linking to the first variation.

Variations 1 and 2 are the same in both editions. Variation 1 continues in the 'Rococo' vein, with the cello elaborating the theme in a charming triplet pattern. The woodwind add their melancholy little coda as before. Variation 2 becomes more energetic, with little fragments of the theme thrown playfully between cello and orchestra, and each phrase rounded off with a virtuoso run-up. The woodwind add their little coda, but in Tchaikovsky's original the strings, instead of responding as before, settle on a repeated chord, and the cello embarks on a cadenza, at first virtuoso, and then increasingly thoughtful. From here it emerges into Variation 3 (Fitzhagen's version shifts this variation, with its cadenza, to become Variation 6).

Tchaikovsky's Variation 3 is an Andante aria in D minor, eloquent and sorrowful. The cello sings over pizzicato accompaniment, with answering phrases from clarinet and flute. The touching little coda in the woodwind takes on an even more melancholy character at this slower tempo, and at the end, the cello ascends to high harmonics.

Variation 4 (which becomes Fitzhagen's final Variation 7) is back to the home key of A major, at a fast tempo. It is a delightful virtuoso dash for both cello and orchestra, with rapid fragments passing between them to create an effect like a high-speed version of Variation 2. It is the first variation to end without the woodwind coda, instead finishing with an arpeggio and a snappy chord.

Variation 5 (placed as No. 4 by Fitzhagen) returns to the Rococo elegance of the theme, but with extra flourishes and virtuoso episodes. The melancholy woodwind coda, which was missing from the preceding variation, is now adapted to alternate with the cello.

Variation 6 (following on as No. 5 in the Fitzhagen) continues this mixture of elegance and virtuosity. The theme is played demurely by a flute while the cello rises through a sequence of trills until it burst out in flamboyant arpeggios. There is a brief orchestral tutti and a little cadenza, then the flute and cello continue their duet. The wistful woodwind coda and the strings' response round off the variation. The cello descends, changing key to prepare for Variation 7.

Variation 7 (placed much earlier as Variation 3 by Fitzhagen) is a great outpouring in C major which, with little adaptation, could take its place as an aria in *Eugene Onegin*. The coy, elegant phrases of the theme have become a continuous, passionate line. After the initial strain of the melody, there is a middle passage in which cello and oboe are in dialogue. And then the great melody is reprised, with delicate accompanying triplets on flute and clarinets. Far from lightening the force of the melody, this delicate accompaniment has the effect of making the melody stand out even more poignantly (Tchaikovsky does something very similar in the first scene of *Eugene Onegin*). The cello's melody never quite finds resolution, but instead wanders gently back to prepare for a return to A major in the final variation, ending, like Variation 3, with high harmonics.

Variation 8 (cut by Fitzhagen) returns to the playful virtuoso style of Variation 4 – this similarity made it possible for Fitzhagen to substitute Variation 4 for the original Variation 8. Awkward figurations and rapid staccato scales, in orchestra as well as cello, make this a particularly challenging variation. It moves seamlessly into a coda in which the woodwind remind us of their own recurring little tailpiece, and on through fearsome cello octaves to a brilliant conclusion.

MICHAEL TIPPETT
(1905–98)

Tippett first studied at the Royal College of Music in London in 1923, and was still composing seventy years later. During this long life he engaged with the world around him to an unusual extent for a composer – not just with music, but with literature, philosophy, psychology, ethics, politics, and the great social issues of the twentieth century. He was a pacifist, and was briefly imprisoned during the Second World War for refusing to work on a farm to support the war effort. During and after the war, he was director of music at Morley College, an adult education college in south London, where he organized concerts of music featuring rarely performed music by Purcell, Monteverdi, and the English madrigalists, as well as conducting an orchestra of out-of-work musicians.

The music that emerged from Tippett's broad engagement with music and the world around him was eclectic but also highly individual. It was open to a wide range of influences without being tied down to any. These ranged from the old music that he revived, through Beethoven (a particular inspiration) to the latest music of Stravinsky and Bartók as well as jazz, blues, and 'folk' music. The work that made his name was the oratorio, *A Child of Our Time*, first performed in 1944. The idea for the work was sparked by an incident in Paris in 1938, in which a young Jewish refugee shot dead a German diplomat, an event that provoked the violent attack on Jews and Jewish buildings throughout Germany in the infamous *Kristallnacht*. Tippett, in his own libretto, explores issues to do with the 'dark side' of human nature, the forces that create violence, and the hope of reconciliation through 'Man's acceptance of his Shadow in relation to his Light'. Throughout the work, Tippett uses spirituals to fulfil the meditative role of the Lutheran chorales in the Passions of J. S. Bach.

Tippett's success was a long time coming. The first work that really made his mark was his Concerto for Double String Orchestra, completed shortly before he began *A Child of Our Time*, when Tippett was thirty-four. His most important later works are the two operas of his middle years: *The Midsummer Marriage* (staged 1955), whose exuberant music triumphs over Tippett's heavily philosophical libretto, and *King Priam* (1962), a powerful tragedy based largely on Homer's *Iliad*.

Although he remained a prominent figure in British musical life, nothing that Tippett wrote in the following three decades equalled the success of those works. And he lived all his career in the shadow of his younger contemporary, Benjamin Britten, whose more accessible music generally made more immediate impact on audiences and critics. The perceived comparison with Britten was not always fair. A telling example is the public reputation of *King Priam* compared with Britten's *War Requiem*. Both were first performed in 1962 to celebrate the consecration of the new Coventry Cathedral, which was built alongside the ruins of the medieval cathedral bombed during the Second World War. Both are fine and major works. Britten's *War Requiem* is frequently performed, and is well known for its links with Coventry Cathedral and its commentary on the senseless destruction of war. Tippett's *King Priam*, also a powerful commentary on war, has rarely been performed, and few people remember its association with Coventry Cathedral. Admittedly this is partly to do with the difference between an opera with a large cast and a choral work with only three soloists that can be performed by a good amateur choral society. But it is striking that, at the time of writing, there are more than thirty recordings of the *War Requiem* available, and only two of *King Priam*.

This does not alter the fact that, at his best, and when not weighed down by over-elaborate philosophical thinking, Tippett produced music of tremendous lyrical energy.

CONCERTO FOR DOUBLE STRING ORCHESTRA
Duration: approx. 22 minutes

Allegro con brio
Adagio cantabile
Allegro molto

Composers in the twentieth century, whether or not consciously 'neo-classical', often looked back to the baroque *concerto grosso* when writing orchestral music. Tippett in this work looks back even further, to the choral works of Monteverdi and the Gabrielis, with their antiphonal effects, and to the English madrigalists (who derived many of their ideas from Monteverdi and the other Italians). He completed it in June 1939, and it was one of the first works to establish him as an important composer with a distinct and confident style. It was premiered in April 1940 at Morley College, where Tippett had recently become director of music. He conducted an orchestra of unemployed musicians, many out of work because of the arrival of sound pictures. A second performance was given at the Wigmore Hall in June 1943, conducted by Walter Goehr. Tippett was unable to attend because he was spending a three-month sentence in prison. He had refused to undertake fire service or land work, as required of conscientious objectors, arguing (supported by Vaughan Williams) that music was his most important contribution to society. He listened to the performance on the radio: 'Goehr gave a smashing performance of the Double Concerto on the Radio. I was v. moved, myself even by the slow movement.'[1]

He further commented on the piece:

In calling the piece a 'concerto', I was harking back to the *Concerti grossi* of Handel, which I knew and loved. I attached myself partly to a special English tradition – that of the Elgar *Introduction and Allegro* and Vaughan Williams's *Fantasia on a Theme of Thomas Tallis*, both of which intermingle the intimacy of the solo string writing with the rich sonority of the full string ensemble. I did not regard the two orchestras as vehicles for concertante writing, such as might be found in the concertino groups of Handel's *Concerti grossi*; they were far more to be considered as antiphonal groups. But the musical forms deployed in my Double Concerto were those of Beethoven: a succinct dramatic sonata allegro, a slow movement virtually modelled on the song–fugue–song layout of the Andante of Beethoven's String Quartet in F minor, Op. 95, and finally a sonata rondo with coda.[2]

The first movement has an unusual time signature: 8/8, that is, eight quavers in a bar. These would conventionally be divided into four groups of two (4/4) or two groups of four (2/2). But Tippett leaves all options open, exploiting all manner of groupings within the eight quavers. These sometimes have a syncopated effect, and at other times they create a rapid shifting of the metre. Tippett himself noted that these syncopations and shifts are characteristic of jazz, but are also to be found in the Elizabethan and Italian madrigalists of the Renaissance: 'What is new is only the pace at which it can take place on modern instruments.'[3]

The concerto opens with the two orchestras in simple octaves playing two ideas simultaneously. Orchestra 1 starts, with a vigorous theme of notes that alternate in a jazzy, syncopated rhythm and then leap up; orchestra 2 enters half a bar later in the bass with a more sustained line that begins with repeated notes and then falls. Then the ideas swap round, with the upward theme in the bass and the falling theme above. These ideas are bounced off each other until the two orchestras both play the falling theme in counterpoint, to bring a short, combative paragraph to a harmonious resolution.

Now there is a new idea: as a pattern of quavers continue quietly, a playful little motif, with a trill and a staccato fall, is passed between violins and cellos in both orchestras. Then the music begins to expand and explore the possibilities of the two principal ideas, by varying their rhythms and metres, extending phrases, turning them upside down, taking the music through different keys, and proceeding in waves from pianissimo to fortissimo. The impression is of restless energy, in which nothing is settled for more than an instant – rhythm, metre, or key. A climax is reached, from which the music fades and comes apart, the opening phrase halved in speed, and then halved again. The music reaches a static point, reduced to little jabbing chords.

Very quietly, the orchestras restart their interplay with the first theme in a new key. It feels somewhat like the start of a conventional development section, though this music has been 'developing' from its first page (as Beethoven often does). As the interplay builds up, there is an ominous new undercurrent that threatens with its sustained, clashing harmonies. But at a climax, the threat is shaken off, as the two themes combine once more, the rising theme high in orchestra 1, the falling theme in the bass in orchestra 2. It is not obvious at first, but this is the reprise.

The sequence of events unfolds rather as before, but with continual new twists, and echoes of the ominous element from time to time emerging with haunting effect. But the driving energy of the music is not to be stopped. The ominous element becomes transformed into a sustained version of the falling theme. Then the orchestras come together in vigorous, rich harmonies, and a final drive takes the music to a resounding chord of bare fifths.

Tippett described the slow movement as 'virtually modelled on the song–fugue–song layout of the Andante [actually Allegretto ma non troppo] of Beethoven's String Quartet in F minor, Op. 95'. Tippett's movement is much slower and more solemn than the Beethoven, and its opening notes are those of an old Scottish song, 'Ca' the yowes' ('Call the ewes'). This is just the start of a broad melody that sweeps in a great arch, first on solo violin, then on full strings. Its deeply nostalgic tone and the rich textures of the accompanying chords are reminiscent of Vaughan Williams' *Fantasia on a Theme of Thomas Tallis*, with its evocation of a rural and ecclesiastical past. Tippett's nostalgia is given a particular poignancy by a 'blues' clash at the height of the second phrase.

The middle of the movement, as in the Beethoven, is a passage of fugue. The tone here is more anxious, with bitter touches in the harmony. Again as in the Beethoven, after the first strain of the fugue the melody is accompanied by a more restless countermelody, and the fugue subject is turned upside down. The music rises to a climax full of anguished harmonies, and then slowly calms, its tensions resolved. As it falls away from the climax, there is a quote from the opening theme of the first movement. A solo cello takes up the reprise of the song, and this quote proceeds with it as an accompaniment. The cello completes the melody, and sad fragments of the fugue return (another echo of the Beethoven). This seems to have the effect of inhibiting a complete reprise of the song by the full strings. The sense of struggling to regain the melody makes the final bars all the more touching.

The finale returns to the restless energy of the first movement, and the restlessness is once again built into its basic time signature. This is expressed as 3/4 – 6/8, meaning that six is divided sometimes as 3 x 2 and sometimes as 2 x 3. The melodic shapes that flit by are related to themes in both the first and second movement, full of intervals of a fourth and a fifth.

The opening paragraph is full of bustle and life, and amid the restlessness phrases of a much simpler tune suddenly emerge with confidence and then vanish. Then the music quietens, and the cellos play a melody that is more lyrical and more extended than anything in the first movement. It could almost be a folk tune, but it has a carefully constructed fluidity, alternating between three beats and four beats in a bar, and rising to a climax before falling gently away. The violins repeat the melody, taking it to a more impassioned climax. Further energetic development of the opening material follows. As this quietens, two phrases of another coherent tune emerge in the violins, as if the cello melody has disguised itself as one of the energetic elements.

A little later this new tune moves to the cellos, and is then thrown around both orchestras as the energy builds. From here the music revisits material from the opening of the movement. There is a reprise of the cello melody, which is again taken up by the violins. Another energetic build-up culminates in a glorious new melody, which Tippett described as a ' "Scottish" tune'.[4] With its rise and fall and 'Scotch snaps' it is in the mould of famous tunes such as 'Ae fond kiss' and 'My love is like a red, red rose'; but, as Tippett also points out, it has affinities with the melodic shapes with which the concerto opened. The tune turns wistful for a moment, and then, with the energetic figures continuing high in the violins, the

'Scottish' tune bursts forth again to bring the concerto to an unashamedly warm-hearted conclusion.

EDGARD VARÈSE
(1883–1965)

Varèse was one of the most innovative and influential figures in early twentieth-century music, but his early training was more or less conventional. He studied composition with Albert Roussel at the Schola Cantorum in Paris, where he developed a particular interest in the complex polyphony of the Renaissance, and then with Charles-Marie Widor at the Paris Conservatoire. But he was always a free spirit, unwilling to be tied down to convention, and eager to pursue new musical worlds and to encourage others to do so. He spent some years in Berlin, inspired by the radical ideas of Busoni. While trying to promote new music, Varèse developed a reputation as a conductor. But finding himself frustrated by the lack of opportunities in Europe, he moved to the United States in 1915.

Two years before his emigration, most of his scores had been destroyed in a fire in Berlin. So in America he started from scratch, composing music even more ambitious and radical than anything he had written before, and expounding his ideas for music of the future: 'We also need new instruments very badly ... Musicians should take up this question in deep earnest with the help of machine specialists.'[1] He conducted concerts of new music, founded organizations for the promotion of contemporary composers, and attracted the attention of a publisher.

Reactions to his music were frequently hostile. But after the Second World War he became a figure of inspiration to a new generation of radical young composers, notably Pierre Boulez and John Cage. Cage wrote, in an essay on Varèse, 'Analytical studies of his work are somehow not relevant to one's experience of it. Though Varèse has defined music as "organized sound", it is unclear how he brings about the organization of his work ... However, more clearly and actively than anyone else of his generation, he established the present nature of music. This nature ... arises from an acceptance of all audible phenomena as material proper to music. While others were still discriminating "musical" tones from noises, Varèse moved into the field of sound itself, not splitting it in two by introducing into the perception of it a mental prejudice.'[2]

In a lecture given in 1936, Varèse expanded on the possibilities of new instruments, and what they might enable: 'When new instruments will allow me to compose music as I conceive it ... the movement of sound-masses, of shifting planes, will be clearly perceived. When these sound-masses collide the phenomena of penetration or repulsion will seem to occur. Certain transmutations taking place on certain planes will seem to be projected onto other planes, moving at different speeds and at different angles. There will no longer be the old conception of melody or interplay of melodies. The entire work will be a melodic totality. The entire work will flow as a river flows.'[3] But Varèse did not see these new developments as a radical break from the past. As he said in another lecture in 1959, 'My fight for the liberation of sound and for my right to make music with any sound and all sounds has sometimes been construed as a desire to disparage and even to discard the great music of the past. But that is where my roots are. No matter how original, how different a composer may seem, he has only grafted a little bit of himself on the old plant. But this he should be allowed to do without being accused of wanting to kill the plant. He only wants to produce a new flower.' The rules of the past are not sacrosanct: 'Listening to music by Perotin, Machaut, Monteverdi, Bach, or Beethoven we are conscious of living substances; they are "alive in the present". But music written in the manner of another century is the result of culture and, desirable and comfortable as culture may be, an artist should not lie down in it.'[4]

One feature of Varèse's music is its rhythmic complexity. For Varèse, rhythm is not principally to do with metre and its subdivisions into beats and accents: 'Rhythm is the element in music that gives life to the work and holds it together. It is the element of stability, the generator of form. In my own works, for instance, rhythm derives from the simultaneous interplay of unrelated elements that intervene at calculated, but not regular time lapses. This corresponds more nearly to the definition of rhythm in physics and philosophy as "a succession of alternate and opposite or correlative states".'[5]

AMÉRIQUES
Duration: approx. 24 minutes

The ideas that Varèse put forward in the quotations above are to be found in embryonic form in the first of his orchestral works to be performed in America, *Amériques* – though 'embryonic' is hardly the word to describe a work for such gargantuan forces. It was composed between 1918 and 1921 before electronic instruments were available, but Varèse uses predominantly conventional instruments in highly unusual ways, and the work remains a milestone of daring and radicalism. Scored for a huge orchestra, even by the standards of the early twentieth century, it was first performed by the Philadelphia Orchestra conducted by Leopold Stokowski in 1926. Varèse revised the score for a slightly smaller (but still huge) orchestra, and this was premiered in Paris in 1929. Interest in the gigantic original version led in 1997 to a corrected edition by Chou Wen-Chung based on Varèse's original autograph.[6] The original version requires thirteen percussion players (even the revision requires nine). The instruments they play include xylophone, glockenspiel, celesta, castanets, chimes, sleigh bells, whip, rattle, siren, and lion's roar (a drum activated by rubbing an attached rosined cord). The most striking difference between the two versions is that, in the original, there is an offstage band of seven brass instruments. This gives a distinct echo of Mahler.

The title is in the plural: 'Americas'. The most famous element in it – the siren – encourages us to concentrate on the references to modern urban life, with the complexity and chaos of New York, where Varèse was now living. But he said, 'I did not think of *Amériques* as purely geographic, but as symbolic of discoveries – new worlds on earth, in the sky, or in the minds of men.'[7]

There are a few thematic elements that recur, but there is little sense of conventional structure. The piece proceeds in a series of waves, jerks, and violent contrasts for about twenty-four continuous minutes. Because there is so little to catch hold of, references to durations are given from time to time in the following description (the timings are to the nearest half-minute). These are based on the 2001 recording of the original score by the Chicago Symphony Orchestra conducted by Pierre Boulez.[8]

Varèse's debt to music of the past is obvious right from the first note. An alto flute reiterates a little phrase, an ornamental flourish, like the chanting of a traditional bagpiper. With its hypnotic, ritualistic character, this evokes the incantations of the alto flute in Stravinsky's *The Rite of Spring* (whose premiere Varèse attended in 1913), with more distant echoes of the alto flute in Ravel's *Daphnis et Chloé* and the flute solo in Debussy's *Prélude à l'après-midi d'un faune*. The reference to the *Rite* becomes unmistakable as the harps begin a repetitive accompaniment and a bassoon interpolates a sliding upward gesture. Horns and trumpets suddenly erupt, and this sets the percussion going in complex interlocking patterns. Chords of harsh trombones and dark horns create a threatening atmosphere. Still the alto flute continues its mournful flourishes, interrupted by shrieking woodwind. With a sweep of harps, bird-like harmonics, and touches of the celesta, we could be back in the forest of Ravel's *Mother Goose*. Violent outbursts alternate with muttering percussion. We hear the siren, menacing at first, and the alto flute's melody is taken up by a muted trumpet. What sounds almost like a snatch of Richard Strauss's *Till Eulenspiegel* provokes another violent outburst, a sudden crisis, and collapse.

Over the siren, a high clarinet plays the alto flute's flourish (5'00"). There is a more sustained forceful passage, which ends with a held trumpet note. The alto flute flourish moves to the violas, timidly playing tremolo and *ppp*. The mutterings and clickings of the percussion are followed by fanfare-like offstage trumpets (a very Mahlerian effect). Low horns, bassoons, and contrabassoons play chords as if from a bottomless pit. There is a moment of mysterious procession, punctuated by a bass drum (7'00"). Trilling woodwind and nervous percussion lead to a volatile and violent passage (this could be out of Schoenberg's Five Orchestral Pieces). Then there is another mysterious procession, this time uncertain and halting, with the rhythm picked out by harps, celesta, and drums, while horns play fragments of a chant (8'00").

There is another volatile outburst, which begins like Schoenberg and continues with the strings playing a passionate, Spanish-style melody over disruptive percussion. From the violent conclusion emerges the siren over tentative chords. After another moment of violence, there are more dark chords for horns and woodwind, and then another procession starts up (10'30"). But this is soon interrupted by agitation and a huge build-up to a sudden halt (these moments of climax and sudden halt are highly characteristic of Varèse). Horns play a chant like a contracted version of the opening alto flute melody (another *Rite*-like moment). High woodwind and percussion break in. More chanting tries to prevail, first on oboe, then on trumpet, quoting the opening alto flute directly.

Then the music breaks into a fast and violent passage (12'00") ending with the siren and lion's roar. Offstage muted trumpets play a new version of the alto flute melody. There is another moment of quiet procession, with the woodwind taking over the chant previously played by horns. Then the music breaks into an agitated passage that soon becomes violent. It develops a menacing swagger and reaches a huge climax. From another sudden cut-off (15'00") emerges a laughing trombone, as if stepping out from a dance band (the instruction 'laugh' is in the score). This is an utterly disorienting moment, and it is almost a relief when the familiar violence erupts again.

The music builds chaotically to a huge, brutal climax (17'00"). Nervous fragments and rattling percussion emerge, as if from the ruins. The opening chant returns on the woodwind (18'00"). Then another processional passage starts up, faster than before, with irregular rhythms, and above it, in the high woodwind, the Spanish-style melody previously played by the strings. This time it is sustained for over a minute (the longest continuous passage in the whole piece), developing Stravinsky-like momentum. There is a series of violent crescendo chords, interspersed with the agitated percussion. From the last of these chords (20'00") the dismal sound of the siren emerges, followed by a series of swirlings. Then a new, determined, thumping rhythm starts up, the beginning of the build-up to the end. The sense of unstoppable force has a similar effect to the end of *The Rite of Spring*, but here multiple forces seem to be converging from many different directions. The end conveys a sense of utter destruction.

RALPH VAUGHAN WILLIAMS
(1872–1958)

Vaughan Williams was taught by the composers Charles Stanford and Hubert Parry at the Royal College of Music in London. Both were rooted in the Austro-German tradition of composition that had been the mainstay of British music throughout the nineteenth century. Stanford's insistence on sticking to his conservative principles is shown by a public lecture that he gave in 1921, called 'On Some Recent Tendencies in Composition'.[1] In it he declared, 'We are not living in the age of beauty, of nature, or of simplicity, but in the days of extravagance.' He specifically objects to the modern use of consecutive fifths (which were an important element in Vaughan Williams' musical language). Vaughan Williams had earlier ruffled Stanford's feathers when he published an essay in the *RCM Magazine* in 1912, 'Who Wants the English Composer?', arguing for the use of folk song and other popular musical 'raw material' as the basis for composition, and against the mere imitation of German models.[2]

Vaughan Williams had joined the English Folk-Song Society in 1904. He became an enthusiastic collector of folk songs, and, with the help of Cecil Sharp, published a collection of sixty-one songs in the *Journal of the English Folk-Song Society*. In 1906 he edited *The English Hymnal*, in which he adapted a number of folk songs for use as hymns.

Vaughan Williams' interest in English folk song and church music was not merely aesthetic. It was part of the search for the cultural roots of Englishness that was at its height in the years leading up to the First World War, when the seeds of destruction of the British Empire and its way of life were first becoming evident. It was also an expression of his deep sense that music should be for everyone, not just an activity for an elite. Amateur music-making was more important to him than professional performance. In the same 1912 article he wrote, 'The composer must not shut himself up and think about art; he must live with his fellows and make his art an expression of the whole life of the community.'[3] His involvement with choral societies and community projects persisted even during wartime. He was a member of a Field Ambulance Unit that was posted to France in 1916. There his team transported wounded soldiers, in dangerous conditions, from the trenches to the field dressing station. Far from being crushed by this experience, Vaughan Williams enjoyed army life, ran a choir for his colleagues and anyone else who wanted to join, and taught them hymns and carols, continuing to do so when they were later posted to Greece.

Folk song provided for Vaughan Williams a healthy foil to the traditional teaching of Stanford and Parry. Equally healthy was his exposure to a composer very different from any he had encountered in England. Over the winter of 1907–8 he spent three months in Paris having lessons with Ravel (who was three years younger than Vaughan Williams). Many years later, Vaughan Williams remembered, 'I learned much from him. For example, that the heavy contrapuntal Teutonic manner was not necessary. "*Complexe, mais pas compliqué*" was his motto. He showed me how to orchestrate in points of colour rather than in lines. It was an invigorating experience to find all artistic problems looked at from what was to me an entirely new angle . . . He was against development for its own sake – one should only develop for the sake of arriving at something better.'[4]

All these various influences – Stanford and Parry, folk song, English hymns, Ravel's refined orchestration – came together in his first masterpiece, the Fantasia on a Theme by Thomas Tallis.

FANTASIA ON A THEME BY THOMAS TALLIS
Duration: approx. 15 minutes

This was composed in 1910, premiered at the Three Choirs Festival in Gloucester Cathedral the same year, and revised in 1919. It was Vaughan Williams' first great success and remains his most famous work, with good reason. It has a powerful and hauntingly mystical atmosphere, bringing together the ecclesiastical and the rural in a masterly way. It is scored for strings, divided into a main orchestra, an echo orchestra, and a string quartet – a division of forces that elaborates those of the *concerto grosso* of Corelli and Handel. These sometimes play all together, at other times separately, sometimes answering each other as if calling across a vast cathedral (as indeed they did at the premiere). The principal theme is a psalm tune by Thomas Tallis (*c.* 1505–85), and part of the haunting atmosphere of the work arises because this tune is in the Phrygian mode (the scale that rises from E on the white notes of the keyboard).

After an opening of hushed chords, the theme is announced hesitantly in the bass, pizzicato, answered by shifting chords that set the elusive mystical atmosphere. The whole hymn is then played sonorously, and repeated passionately, supported by a magnificent texture of wide-spread chords and rippling arpeggios. Fragments of the theme are passed from fortissimo in the main orchestra to pianissimo in the echo orchestra, with sudden shifts of key deepening the sense of mystery.

This subsides, and the viola of the solo quartet plays a rising phrase from the hymn, developing it into a free fantasia like a shepherd using a folk tune to improvise on his pipe. The violin and the other members of the quartet join in, with answering phrases from the main orchestra. Waves pass back and forth between quartet and orchestra, and eventually all combine in a sustained build-up to a mighty climax.

When this has passed, there is a passage in which loud chords from the main orchestra alternate with pianissimo chords from the echo orchestra in remote keys, like sudden glimpses into the distant past. Then the pizzicato bass returns with the theme, as at the opening, and the work winds to a conclusion, with its final, magnificent chord disappearing into the distance.

THE LARK ASCENDING
Duration: approx. 16 minutes

At the beginning of August 1914, Vaughan Williams was on holiday in Margate, walking the chalk cliffs that overlook the English Channel. It was the week in which Britain entered the First World War, and ships of the Royal Navy were exercising. An idea for a piece of music occurred to him, and he started jotting it down in a notebook. A small boy spotted him and reported him to the police as a potential spy, and Vaughan Williams was arrested. (This incident is reminiscent of the occasion when Wordsworth and Coleridge were suspected of spying for the French on the Dorset coast in 1797.)

No doubt larks were singing high over the cliffs, and in any case Vaughan Williams knew the poem by George Meredith, 'The Lark Ascending'. The music that the composer noted down was the beginning of a piece for violin and piano inspired by the poem. A draft of this version was completed soon after, and put aside during the war. Vaughan Williams joined a field ambulance unit of the Royal Army Medical Corps that was posted to France and then Greece. After the war, he returned to *The Lark Ascending* and revised it for violin and orchestra. This version was first performed in 1921 by the violinist Marie Hall, for whom Vaughan Williams composed the piece, and who helped him with the revisions.

Meredith's poem, 'The Lark Ascending', was written in 1881, and it was inspired by the larks on Box Hill in Surrey where he lived, not far from Vaughan Williams' childhood home on Leith Hill. The poem is in the tradition of the seventeenth-century mystical nature-poems of George Herbert and Henry Vaughan, and its portrayal of the innocent lark as a symbol of the eternal landscape chimed perfectly with Vaughan Williams' own feelings for the ancient roots of Englishness.[5]

By the time Vaughan Williams' *The Lark Ascending* was first performed, the war had run its terrible course, and poems expressing nostalgia for the English countryside had acquired particular potency. It was a previous war, the second Boer War, that had made a bestseller of A. E. Housman's 'A Shropshire Lad', with its evocation of a 'land of lost content'. Vaughan Williams had already set a selection of Housman's poems in *On Wenlock Edge* in 1909. Now, in 1921, he presented a portrait of Meredith's ecstatic lark, rising over a landscape that, with its suggestion of folk song, is unmistakably English.

The origins of Vaughan Williams' music have as little to do with the First World War as Gustav Holst's 'Mars' (also composed in the summer of 1914), but it is difficult to unthink the context that both works acquired retrospectively. Larks were, after all, one of the reminders of the natural world that soldiers often described in their letters home from the battlefields of France. Particularly poignant is a report from Lieutenant Rayner of the Devonshire Regiment, who had recently got to know Meredith's poem: 'The larks sing all day here but they are best at dawn. The larks of the morning "stand-to", deserve a poem of their own, they are wonderful after a night of doubt and terror in the trenches, they are the returning light transformed to music; they are the renewed blue trembling into song, they sing of the permanence of the joy of song, of the sweets of light and warmth, and the war-indifferent exquisiteness of Nature.'[6]

At the head of the score, Vaughan Williams placed three extracts from the beginning, middle, and end of Meredith's poem:

He rises and begins to round,
He drops the silver chain of sound,
Of many links without a break,
In chirrup, whistle, slur and shake.
. . .
For singing till his heaven fills,
'Tis love of earth that he instils,
And ever winging up and up,
Our valley is his golden cup,
And he the wine which overflows

To lift us with him when he goes.
...
Till lost on his aerial rings
In light, and then the fancy sings.

Vaughan Williams' music interleaves free cadenza with two more formal themes. This structure might seem simple, but the effect is fluid and organic.

Very softly, the orchestra twice plays a rising sequence of chords over a held bass note. As the strings sustain the final chord *ppp*, the solo violin embarks on an ascending cadenza of trills, scales, and arpeggios that suggests both the song of the lark and its rise from the ground to hover high overhead. Vaughan Williams uses traditional harmonies with great subtlety. The chords that the orchestra plays are in the Dorian mode, a mode in which many folk songs are set (its sharpened sixth gives it a particular flavour). But the violin plays only the notes of a simpler pentatonic (five-note) scale. This contributes to the sense of innocent calm created by the cadenza.

From the highest point, the violin begins to form folk-song-like phrases as it descends, and these coalesce into a coherent theme as the strings join in. There is an extensive meditation on this theme, which passes to oboe, clarinet, and horn, and climaxes on full orchestra (the sound is rich but contained, with woodwind and horns, but no trumpets or trombones). Meanwhile the soloist alternates between fragments of the melody and more florid figuration, at the climax breaking into fortissimo octaves and then sinking back.

The quiet opening chords return, and the soloist plays a briefer cadenza. Now the tempo increases a little, and a flute introduces another folk-song-like tune with a gently dancing lilt. This too passes from instrument to instrument, the soloist sometimes taking up the melody and sometimes playing decorative counterpoints of trills, arpeggios, and scales ('chirrup, whistle, slur and shake', perhaps). Instead of returning to the opening chords, this passage instead leads straight on to a new section with an improvisatory character. The violin trills and a triangle gently strikes. Oboe and clarinet play melodic fragments, as if half-remembering the earlier themes. As other instruments join in, the music acquires the character of a group improvisation (though every detail is written out). It rises to an animated climax and falls away to the trilling and melodic fragments with which it began, and then returns to the flute's folk song, now on solo violin.

There is an oblique reference to the opening chords, the harmonies turn a corner, and blossom into a full-hearted reprise of the opening theme. From here the music gradually winds down to regain the calm of the opening. Once again three chords rise, and as the last is held, the soloist ascends with the cadenza of trills and arpeggio patterns, until, unaccompanied, the final high notes are left hanging in the air.

There is one last subtlety to point out. The piece opened with the orchestra playing chords in the Dorian mode. The chords they play at the end might seem to be the same, but they are not. The sharp sixth of the Dorian mode has been flattened, so that this is now the Aeolian mode. This might seem a technicality, but it has the effect of deepening the sense of calm. The critic of *The Times* wrote of the premiere in 1921 that *The Lark Ascending* 'showed supreme disregard for the ways of today or yesterday. It dreamed itself along.' But when one is made aware of the sensitivity with which Vaughan Williams uses his harmonic palate, one realizes that this is a dream accomplished by supreme craftsmanship.

Symphonies

A LONDON SYMPHONY (SYMPHONY NO. 2)
Duration: approx. 45 minutes (final version)

Lento – Allegro risoluto
Lento
Scherzo (Nocturne): Allegro vivace
Andante con moto – Maestoso alla marcia (quasi lento) – Allegro

This was Vaughan Williams' first purely instrumental symphony. Symphony No. 1, *A Sea Symphony*, premiered in 1910, sets poems by Walt Whitman and is as much a cantata as a symphony. Vaughan Williams had already made some plans for a symphonic poem on London when his friend the composer George Butterworth encouraged him to write an instrumental symphony. So Vaughan Williams redirected his ideas, and *A London Symphony* was given a successful premiere in 1914. This original version was criticized for being too long, and Vaughan Williams himself sought advice from friends and colleagues, including the young Adrian Boult, who conducted it with and without cuts, before Vaughan Williams rewrote the symphony. A revised version was published in 1920, and this edition was widely played, helping to establish Vaughan Williams' reputation as a major British composer. Further revisions followed in 1933.

Vaughan Williams soon became frustrated by people's tendency to take the title too literally and to assume that this was 'programme music' à la Richard Strauss. To counter these misconceptions, he wrote a note for the third performance in February 1915: 'It has been suggested that this Symphony has been misnamed, it should rather be called "Symphony by a Londoner". That is to say it is in no sense descriptive, and though the introduction of the "Westminster Chimes" in the first movement, the slight reminiscence of the "Lavender cry" in the slow movement, and the very faint suggestion of mouth-organs and mechanical pianos in the scherzo give it a tinge of "Local colour", yet it is intended to be listened to as "absolute" music.'[7] One might say that it evokes emotional responses to city life, which are not much different to responses to life in general – the awakening at dawn, the cheerful bustle of people going about their business, a sense of calm before dawn, aspiration when awake, struggles with difficulties, the triumphs of success. When it was first published in 1920, the symphony was dedicated to Vaughan Williams' friend, George Butterworth, who in August 1916 was killed in the Battle of the Somme.

The symphony begins with an introduction of the deepest calm, with quiet rising phrases. Vaughan Williams said that he was 'horrified' when the similarity to the opening of Debussy's *La Mer* was pointed out to him.[8] But the difference is just as striking: Vaughan Williams evokes a sense of deep stillness, as of a city before dawn – very different from the scintillating calm of the sea. A harp plays the Westminster Chimes.

As if at a signal, the orchestra bursts into the Allegro. The first theme that confronts us descends menacingly over discordant harmonies. Even when the force diminishes, what follows is unsettled, with melancholy undulating phrases over a nervous staccato bass. But gradually the melody becomes more spacious, the harmonies more settled, and the threat (whatever it was) recedes. Another moment of tension (with a chord reminiscent of a moment in Holst's 'Mars') is resolved in brass fanfares and a dancing folk-like tune, the first time in the movement that we have heard a cheerful, unclouded theme; this, like the rising phrases that began the symphony, is in a pentatonic (five-note) scale, much used in traditional music. This theme builds to a rousing tutti. But at its climax, the music bursts back to the menacing first theme, with its unsettling harmonies.

Gradually the tension ebbs away, softened by a return to gentle, undulating phrases. From a moment of calm emerge solo cello, violin, and harp, which lead into a passage of richly chorded string sextet. Clarinet and oboe combine rising and undulating phrases from earlier passages, and the strings take them up. The mood is, for a brief moment, rural and dreamlike. The dream ends with solo viola, and a reminiscence of the dancing folk tune on bassoon and clarinet.

Quiet string tremolo and rolling timpani take us back to the unsettling opening chord of the Allegro, and the nervous staccato bass returns with a ghost of the ominous descending phrase. The brass fanfares and the folk dance return, at first quietly, but then bursting into a bold combination of the dance at normal speed in the bass with a half-speed version above. The metre shifts to a broad three-time, and the woodwind play a more expansive version of the rising phrases. From here the music develops momentum, first grandly, then playfully. Just as we move towards the conclusion, the unsettling dissonance returns, but now it resolves into a final burst of G major.

The slow movement starts like a darker anticipation of the opening of *The Lark Ascending*, with a pattern of three rising strings chords that is repeated. The cor anglais sings another melody like a folk song, but with an unfolk-like wrench of harmony in the middle. The brass repeat the chords, and strings take up and develop the cor anglais melody into a lament. The harmonies become warmer, the strings gently pulsate, and a horn plays a rising fourth from the very opening of the symphony (this interval also began the cor anglais's melody). Soon we return to the opening lament, then back to the horn call, and to a silence.

A solo viola meditates (rather as in the Tallis Fantasia), joined by woodwind – there is what Vaughan Williams called 'a slight reminiscence' of a lavender-seller's cry here. A jingle of bells suggests a horse-drawn cab. After a period of searching, the music rises to an ecstatic chorus of wide-spreading chords. This fades away to a return to the dark opening, and final reminiscences by cor anglais, horn, and solo viola.

George Butterworth described this movement as 'an idyll of grey skies and secluded byways'.[9] Vaughan Williams in his programme note said that it 'has been called "Bloomsbury Square on a November afternoon"', characteristically adding, 'This may serve as a clue to the music, but it is not a necessary "explanation" of it.'[10]

The scherzo is subtitled 'Nocturne'. This is not a sleeping city, but an evocation of the bustle of London in the evening. As Vaughan Williams put it, 'If the listener will imagine himself standing on Westminster Embankment at night, surrounded by the distant sounds of The Strand, with its great hotels on one side and the "New Cut" on the other, with its crowded streets and flaring lights, it may serve as a mood in which to listen to this movement.'[11] The music is fleeting, almost like a Mendelssohn fairy-scherzo, but with an earthy element suggested by the steady tread of the rhythm and the folktune-like main theme (first played by a clarinet). After the first part of the scherzo has been repeated, the second part becomes bolder, before returning to the shadowy opening.

A central section (the conventional 'trio') begins with string chords evoking the sound of an accordion, and flutes and oboes play a cheeky tune as if on a mouth organ (though if this were Czech music, we would think it sounded like a village band). There is a moment of bois-terousness, then the cellos transform the cheeky tune into a lyrical melody.

Suddenly we are back in the fleeting music of the scherzo. It rises to a climax and falls away. The scene empties, leaving behind a wistful sadness. Cellos and basses slow down the opening notes of the theme, revealing their shape to be the rising fourth from the start of the symphony and the horn call in the slow movement.

The finale opens with an introduction of sweeping grandeur. The first phrase resolves on a glorious chord of D major, only to break into the descending chromatic line that menaced the opening of the first movement Allegro. After a moment of quiet, a slow march begins. At first, it might be a funeral march, but as melodies and countermelodies are added, it develops a noble character – the climax, with four horns in counterpoint with the violins, is just the sort of splendid effect that was later taken up by composers of film scores to accompany views of the great open spaces of the Wild West. The tempo increases to Allegro, and elements from the first movement are recalled – a new variant of the descending chromatic line, the undulating melodic shape, and the dancing rhythms. The music develops great energy and determination, but the unresolving (often 'whole-tone') harmonies give it all a nervous, agitated character.

The tempo slows, and the march resumes, at first in melancholy mood, then rising nobly. It takes a dark turn, and builds to a massive, tragic climax, surmounted by a gong stroke. A brief burst of Allegro soon fades away. Solo strings, *ppp*, hold a mysterious discord (the same chord that began the first movement Allegro), over which a harp very quietly plays the Westminster Chimes, as if heard from a distance.

Now the symphony reaches its epilogue. Rippling flutes, violins, and violas suggest the water of the Thames. Cellos and basses quietly play the rising-fourth motif, echoed by trombones and then horns and tuba, as the motif rises through a mysterious series of chords (this passage hovers somewhere between Wagner's evocation of the Rhine and Smetana's evocation of the Vltava). Very quietly, the strings restore deep calm with a reminiscence of the opening of the symphony. Pairs of muted trumpets and horns recall whole-tone harmonies. A solo violin rises like a lark, and mysterious chords at last resolve onto G major, as a lingering chord dies away to nothing.

The tragic climax of the finale, and its mysterious epilogue, are not what we might have been expecting at the end of *A London Symphony*, at least if we think of it as some sort of celebration of the city. Vaughan Williams gave a clue to what was in his mind in a letter to Michael Kennedy, nearly half a century after he composed the work: 'For actual coda see end of Wells' *Tono-Bungay*.'[12] This novel by H. G. Wells, published in 1909, charts the attempts of the narrator to save his uncle's corrupt business empire from collapse. It is a parable of England and the British Empire in decline. The nephew's final enterprise is the building of battleships. In the last chapter he sails down the Thames through London in a destroyer and out to the open sea. As he thinks back on this journey, he sees in his mind not only the great panorama, but what lurks behind the elegant facade:

'To run down the Thames so is to run one's hand over the pages in the book of England from end to end ... there come first squalid stretches of mean homes right and left and then the dingy industrialism of the South side, and on the North bank the polite long front of nice houses, artistic, literary, administrative people's residences, that stretches from Cheyne Walk nearly to Westminster and hides a wilderness of slums ...' On through the docks, and on towards the sea: 'Out to the open we go, to windy freedom and trackless ways. Light after light goes down. England and the Kingdom, Britain and the Empire, the old prides and the old devotions, glide abeam, astern, sink down upon the horizon, pass – pass. The river passes – London passes, England passes . . .'[13]

Vaughan Williams was, throughout his life, keen to discourage speculation about any direct programme behind his music, and insisted that the music carried its own meaning. But the revelation of this inspiration for the end of *A London Symphony* seems to indicate that the symphony is as much a lament for what is passing, or what might have been, as it is a celebration of what remains. In this way it is closely linked to the themes that obsessed him throughout his life – the great legacy of the musical and spiritual past, its roots in the music of ordinary people, and the threat posed by the destructive forces of modern life. *A London Symphony*, it seems, is as deeply rooted in these preoccupations as the earlier Tallis Fantasia, and *The Lark Ascending* that was to follow soon after.

PASTORAL SYMPHONY (SYMPHONY NO. 3)

Duration: approx. 35 minutes

Molto moderato
Lento moderato
Moderato pesante
Lento

Vaughan Williams began this symphony after the end of the First World War, and completed it in 1921. It is Vaughan Williams at his most meditative, poised somewhere between serenity and bleakness. As with *The Lark Ascending*, this is best understood as a response to the horrors of war. He wrote to his wife Ursula in 1938, 'It's really wartime music – a great deal of it incubated when I used to go up night after night with the ambulance wagon at Écoivres and we went up a steep hill and there was a wonderful Corot-like landscape in the sunset. It's not really lambkins frisking at all, as most people take for granted.'[14]

The opening could be by Ravel (with whom Vaughan Williams studied): flutes and bassoon gently meander in parallel, giving way subtly to flute and two clarinets. Below, cellos and basses play a solemn theme based on reiterated rising fifths. This will be important throughout the movement. A solo violin enters with arabesques full of falling fifths, with first a horn and then an oboe weaving in counterpoint (there is an echo of *The Lark Ascending* here). Other violins join in, taking up the rising-fifth theme, and this is echoed in the bass. It culminates in quiet, poignant, organ-like chords, from which emerges the cor anglais playing a new melody with a plangent sharpened fourth (the Lydian mode). The cor anglais's melody is taken up in counterpoint by solo viola, clarinet, solo violin, and oboe. This passage too ends with haunting, organ-like chords (with echoes of the Tallis Fantasia), now in a falling pattern, marking the end of the first part of the movement.

This opening paragraph has given us the character and method of the whole movement: melodic shapes in various modes give it the pastoral, folk-like character, but these are continually evolving into different shapes, and are always in counterpoint with accompanying descants and chords that are themselves continually evolving. And, despite the use of the traditional modes, the harmonies often run against each other, producing clashes and moments where the music is in two keys at once. It is this sense of basically simple elements in a fluid and harmonically fragile situation that gives the music such a sense of melancholy.

The return of the initial meandering figure in the flutes signals that we are moving on into the middle of the movement – this would conventionally be called the 'development', but Vaughan Williams' material is in such a fluid state that it has been developing from the very beginning. A horn plays the rising theme, and the strings respond, subdivided into three or four parts to create majestic chords moving in great blocks (perhaps Debussy's processional cloudscape, 'Nuages', was an inspiration, consciously or subconsciously). The harp's gentle but firm chords give crucial definition to the rhythm, as so often in Vaughan Williams. The solo violin takes up the rising-fifth motif, and expands on it. The interweaving counterpoint begins to move on to new keys, reaching a climax and fading away (climaxes in this movement only reach *f*, never *ff*).

More interweaving of woodwind arabesques, and the haunting *pp* string chords, bring us back to a soft G major, the key (or at least, more broadly, the tonality) in which we started. The rising-fifth motif sounds in the bass, and the cor anglais reprises its plangent, Lydian-mode melody. As before, other instruments join in counterpoint, and the melody expands, rising to a second climax and falling away. Now, as the horn plays the rising-fifth theme, the gentle oscillating figure from the opening of the movement appears in the bass, giving a dark, ominous quality. Two more waves of forte bring us to a last, expansive climax. As this falls away and the string chords settle on G major, the cor anglais gives one more plaintive call, and the cellos and basses leave the rising-fifth motif hanging in the air.

The slow movement is scored for strings, woodwind, and horns, without trumpets, trombones or timpani, except for a solo 'natural' trumpet in the centre of the movement. It begins with a dark string chord of F minor. A horn plays a recitative related to the rising-fifth motif from the first movement, in which each phrase ends with sighing, falling thirds. The melody is not in F minor, but in C major (or rather a pentatonic scale on C), clashing with the string chord. This gives a poignant sense of the horn melody being isolated, or of two worlds that co-exist without understanding each other.

The sense of isolation increases as the horn finishes, and the violins rise up over a sustained bass, and echo the sighing phrase ending (this passage is similar to the sorrowful rising violins in the prelude to Act 3 of Wagner's *Tristan*). Oboe and clarinet repeat the horn call, but now the chords shift to accommodate it. There is a touching sense of the isolated being brought in, though the harmonies are still poignant. The horn has the last phrase, and there is a pause.

Over a murmuring accompaniment, solo viola and flute, in unison, meditate on the horn recitative, simplifying and extending it into a developing melody. It acquires yearning leaps, and passes among the woodwind and strings. The development of the melody has much in common with the first movement; but here the process is much simpler, because there is only one evolving melody, supported by shifting harmonies and accompanying figure. This makes it all the more touching when, towards the end of this passage, solo cello, oboe, and clarinet combine in counterpoint, remembering the complex interweaving of the first movement.

The string chords gently come to rest on a chord of E flat major. A solo trumpet quietly plays a cadenza. Opening with a rising fifth, it immediately evokes bugle calls, in particular 'The Last Post', but at the same time it is related to the earlier rising-fifth motif, and the horn recitative. For Vaughan Williams, there was also a specific inspiration for this passage. During the First World War, he was a member of the ambulance crew whose task, in dangerous and appalling conditions, was to evacuate wounded soldiers from the trenches to the military hospital in the village of Écoivres in France, at the bottom of Mont Saint Eloi, near Arras.

There he heard a sound that remained in his memory: 'A bugler used to practise, and this sound became part of that evening landscape and is the genesis of the long trumpet *cadenza* in the second movement of the symphony.'[15] Vaughan Williams asks for it to be played on a trumpet without valves, so that the tuning of the notes is as in the 'natural' harmonic series (the only notes available on a valveless trumpet or bugle). This not only makes the cadenza sound bugle-like, but also produces some notes that are slightly flatter than in the familiar equal-tempered tuning, particularly the seventh, adding to the poignancy of the effect. As the trumpet rises to its highest note, the full orchestra enters, wrenching the harmony back towards F minor and returning to the opening phrase of the movement (marked *ff*, the loudest marking in the symphony so far). This outburst soon fades, leaving the violins rising once again to the desolate, sighing thirds, and descending.

The meditation on the opening melody is reprised, but now embedded in a richer, more complex web of accompanying counterpoint than before. Eventually it descends once again, coming to rest on another quiet string chord, F major. The trumpet cadenza is replayed by a horn, once again without using valves, so that the natural harmonics sound. A clarinet joins it in counterpoint, playing a variant of the recitative that the horn played at the beginning of the movement. As the harmonies slip away beneath them, they persist in F major as if oblivious, like songbirds above the desolate battlefield. As their song comes to an end, violin chords for the last time rise high, ending with two falling sighs that remain unresolved.

The third movement is a heavy scherzo, beginning as a sort of cousin of the sturdy peasant *Ländler* of Mahler and Bruckner. But it is also a profoundly unsettled movement, changing pace and character every few bars. It begins in G minor as a tug between strings and horns, the strings beginning each bar with three notes to a beat, the four horns emphatically answering with two notes to a beat, creating a lurching rhythm. A faster tempo for a few bars culminates in a fortissimo reassertion of the first tempo and rhythmic battle. For a few bars a flute plays delicate arabesques over harp and pianissimo string trills, and is answered by a solo violin. As more violins join in, the heavy scherzo rhythm creeps in below. As it gathers weight, it accelerates, until it breaks into G major (or, more strictly, the Mixolydian mode, with a flattened seventh), and trumpets and trombones launch into a lively three-time dance. After a few bars the pace becomes faster still, then settles back to the dance, and then becomes faster again.

It accelerates, but suddenly breaks back to the heavy first tempo, for the reprise of the initial section. The flute arabesque follows, answered this time by oboe. Once more the heavy scherzo rhythm reasserts itself and accelerates, and again the trumpets play their faster dance in G (Mixolydian). This time it climaxes in disruptive bars of five-time, before fading gradually to a held pianissimo G in the double basses. Over this, the violas lead off a rapid presto contrapuntal dance, like fairies or, more likely, ghosts. Delicately the dance rises up, joined by touches of woodwind and celesta. Shimmering, high violin tremolo accompanies the final descent (with echoes of Holst's 'Mercury'), and the dance fades to nothing as if it has all been a mirage or a dream.

The symphony ends with a slow movement unlike any other finale. Over a pianissimo timpani roll, a distant, offstage soprano (or tenor, though this alternative is rarely chosen) sings a wordless melodic line 'senza misura' (in free time). It has affinities with earlier melodies in the symphony, most obviously the extended trumpet cadenza in the slow movement, but also the many freely evolving melodies in traditional modes and pentatonic scales. The human voice, together with the free rhythm, adds an element of plainchant. Phrase by phrase, the voice rises gradually higher, and then sinks down into silence, lamenting and desolate.

Muted strings enter, the violins rise, and the cor anglais reiterates the soprano's opening phrase, as the bass descends through poignantly clashing harmonies. As the woodwind and harp enter, the mood changes. Rising intervals from the soprano's melody take on the character of a hymn, which expands into a great chorus. As it fades, the music becomes agitated, and the harmonies twist. With the agitation growing, cor anglais, solo violin and flute in turn plaintively remind us of phrases from the soprano melody.

This passage culminates in a great reprise of the soprano melody, played *fff* by strings and woodwind, unaccompanied by any chords, creating a climax that is both forceful and unfulfilled. As it quietens, the hymn is taken up again, and builds to a more complete climax and a brief moment of a clear D major. This too fades away. As at the beginning of the movement, the violins softly rise while the bass descends, pulling the harmonies apart. The violins are left sustaining a high pianissimo A, and the distant soprano returns to her lament, leaving the music unresolved as the violins fade to silence.

SYMPHONY NO. 4 IN F MINOR
Duration: approx. 33 minutes (composer's own recording: 30 minutes)

Allegro
Andante moderato
Scherzo: Allegro molto –
Finale con epilogo fugato: Allegro molto

Vaughan Williams' Fourth Symphony was first performed in 1935 in London by the BBC Symphony Orchestra under its conductor, Adrian Boult. To a friend who had sent an appreciative letter, Vaughan Williams replied, 'I quite got to like it myself in the end. The first rehearsal was unimaginable chaos. But the orchestra & Adrian worked like Trojans for four rehearsals – and things gradually cleared themselves – chiefly owing to Adrian's *real* insight.'[16] Audiences and critics were struck by the symphony's toughness, and assumed that it must have been provoked by the tense international situation (even though the composer had begun work on it in as early as 1931). Vaughan Williams rejected this interpretation: 'I wrote it not as a definite picture of anything external – e.g. the state of Europe – but simply because it occurred to me like this – I can't explain why – I don't think that sitting down and thinking about great things ever produces a great work of art (at least I hope not – because I never do so . . .) – a thing just comes out – or it doesn't – usually doesn't – I always live in hope, as all writers must . . .'[17]

In her biography of the composer, Vaughan Williams' wife, Ursula (who first met him three years after the premiere), wrote about the Fourth Symphony, 'It has often been said that this work is related to the period in which it was written, and, though this must be true to some extent of any work by any composer who does not cut himself off from contemporary life, no one seems to have observed how far more closely it is related to the character of the man who wrote it. The towering furies of which he was capable, his fire, pride and strength are all revealed and so are his imagination and lyricism . . . what emerged has something in common with one of Rembrandt's portraits in middle age.'[18]

The force of the Fourth Symphony might come as a surprise after the comparatively subdued *Pastoral Symphony*. But it is less surprising in the light of the two major works that came immediately before No. 4. The first of these was the ballet *Job, A Masque for Dancing*. Composed in 1930 for Sadler's Wells Ballet, it was inspired by William Blake's engravings to the Book of Job. Much of the force of the symphony, and some specific musical ideas, were developed from Vaughan Williams' music associated with Satan and his destructive force, and with Job's dream of plague, pestilence, famine, and battle. After *Job* came the Piano Concerto of 1931, much of which is tough and dissonant.

Nevertheless, the Fourth Symphony is a tour de force of toughness that Vaughan Williams never repeated. He dedicated it to the composer Arnold Bax. It was the only one of his symphonies that Vaughan Williams recorded himself, conducting the BBC Symphony Orchestra in 1937 with tremendous drive and urgency. He was reported as saying during a rehearsal, 'I don't know if I like it, but it's what I meant.'[19]

Vaughan Williams admitted that he 'deliberately cribbed' the opening of the symphony from the violent start of the finale of Beethoven's Ninth, which begins with a very similar dissonant clash.[20] The difference is that Beethoven's dissonance is a passing challenge that is soon overcome, whereas Vaughan Williams' persists, becoming a motif for the whole symphony and setting its character. At first the falling semitone is strong and aggressive, emphasized by an octave drop and echoed in the bass. Later, it will become a sigh. Three other motifs follow immediately: the second combines two of the initial falling intervals to create a figure of four emphatic notes that curl round on each other chromatically (almost like the famous B-A-C-H motif), then there is a rising chromatic shape, and finally a pattern of rising fourths (first in the brass, then in the woodwind with pizzicato strings). These four motifs permeate the whole work, creating an impression of a symphony of unusually tight logic and emotional intensity. After the opening motifs have fought with each other, the music expands to a sweeping new theme. This has a passionate, heroic character, and it develops powerful momentum, evolving as it goes. Elements from the initial motifs are drawn in, particularly variants of the chromatic 'almost-B-A-C-H' motif. Eventually the music climaxes in a return to the powerful opening clash.

Although the entire movement is in a constant state of fluid evolution, this seems to mark the moment where we enter the central development. For a brief moment, the force is spent. Quiet string tremolo reiterates the falling pair of semitones in a rising pattern, and this is taken up by a bassoon and combined with patterns of falling fourths in the strings. There is a sudden crescendo, and the falling semitones become a heavy, aggressive dance, very similar to Satan's Dance of Triumph in *Job*. The rising fourths culminate in a reprise of the opening clash, which leads on, through a terser version of the tustle at the beginning of the movement, to the sweeping second theme, with the melody now in the bass and a violin descant above it.

A climax falls away, and we enter a quiet epilogue. This refers back to a moment towards the end of the opening struggle, now purged of its force. A chorus of violas and cellos turns the tortuous motifs into something like a hymn, and the continued clashes of harmony with the bass become a thing of mystery (there is a hint of the dark forests of Sibelius's *Tapiola* here). Slowly, the music resolves into serenity, on a chord of D flat major.

The slow movement is very closely tied to material from the first movement. It starts with rising fourths played by the brass and woodwind, creating austere, Hindemith-like chords as they pile on top of each other, culminating in a semitone clash between treble and bass that echoes the first chord of the symphony. Over a pizzicato walking bass, the first violins unfold a melancholy line, whose first phrase hints at the chromatic shapes from the opening of the symphony. Second violins and viola enter with the melody in counterpoint, as in a fugue, and the persisting bass brings something of the quality of a passacaglia. But this is no strict or academic exercise: when the oboe enters, it is with a varied version of the line, incorporating a rocking pattern of fourths, and a further variant of this is taken up by clarinet and bassoon. The level of dissonance, with the music often in two or more keys at once, is something more often encountered in Bartók or Shostakovich than in Vaughan Williams.

The centre of the movement evokes the spirit of Shostakovich particularly vividly. From the first climax, piccolo and oboe emerge, with contrabassoon deep below, giving way to a fragile little flute solo. A little later, a bassoon begins a new fugal passage, with plaintive oboe sighs above. This too builds to an enormous climax. As it fades away, clarinet and violas return to the opening fugue subject, with the ghost of a countersubject high above, *ppp* in the violins. This passage of fugue gradually dissolves, leaving the woodwind bleakly playing the rocking fourths, against which the violins remember the fragile little flute solo. As the music melts into a chord of F major (a rare moment of pure consonance), the flute takes up its solo, with the violas quietly putting the fugue subject against it. This extends into a sorrowful flute cadenza against muted trombone chords, and the movement ends with the flute leaving the melody unresolved on an E. This was an afterthought: in the composer's 1937 recording, the flute resolves onto the keynote, F, as Vaughan Williams had originally written. The unresolved E is doubly touching, as it leaves the attempt at resolution unfulfilled.

The scherzo begins with rapid rising fourths, followed by the 'almost-B-A-C-H' motif played in quick succession three ways: emphatically by the brass, faster by the woodwind, and then as a chattering jig by the strings. The whole scherzo is furious – a friend wrote to Vaughan Williams after the first performance, 'I found your poisonous temper in the *Scherzo*, contrasted with that rollicking lovable opening of the trio, *most* exciting.'[21] (This chimes with Ursula Vaughan Williams' later observation about the symphony as a whole.) The initial momentum is interrupted by a new idea, in which the whole orchestra tears at little offbeat fragments. It sounds like a dog out of control, though the notes themselves are derived from the opening page of the symphony. As this complex rhythm continues quietly in the violins, a jig-like idea is played over it by the woodwind (it is easy to imagine that this must have been one of the most 'chaotic' passages at the first rehearsal). The two elements from the beginning of the scherzo begin to appear, at first sinister and ghostly (with a hint of Holst's 'Mars'), and then in full voice. The offbeat rhythm is combined with the other scherzo themes.

At a slightly slower tempo, tuba and trombones lumber in with the trio, which is also based on the rising fourths. Woodwind and strings make it into something light and playful, and then the whole orchestra joins in. With a crash, the scherzo returns, followed by the beginning of the lumbering trio. But this is swept aside by another burst of the scherzo, and that too soon collapses. Then, as the cellos, basses, and timpani worry away at the offbeat rhythm (now shorn of its chromatic notes), there is a moment of anxious suspense, with the rising fourths, and a sighing motif that momentarily reveals itself as the clash from the opening of the symphony. Suddenly, the tension bursts, and we are propelled headlong into the finale (another 'deliberate crib', this time from the entry to the finale of Beethoven's Fifth Symphony).

The forceful start of the finale might seem new, but it is a full orchestral version of the wistful flute solo from the slow movement. This is the principal theme. The woodwind soon introduce a second element, an emphatically rhythmic version of the sigh that originated in the first bars of the symphony. This opening passage, with its fast marching beat, is the most optimistic and least dissonant music in the symphony so far, though still with a dangerous edge of recklessness. A more relaxed second theme is positively jovial, though it too is immediately drawn into breathlessly energetic complications and cross-rhythms. The woodwind reiterate the rhythmic sigh, more ominously than before, and the music subsides uneasily.

The tempo slows, and the strings quietly remember the ending of the first movement – a haunting moment amid all the frenetic energy. The 'almost-B-A-C-H' motif returns darkly in the low brass, the rising fourths in the bassoon. Once more the tension mounts, with a sustained timpani roll (more homage to Beethoven's Fifth), and the music bursts into the reprise of the opening theme. The familiar elements flash by, but nothing is allowed to impede the rush forward. There is a series of judders, and the trombones declaim the 'almost-B-A-C-H' motif.

We are into the 'Epilogo fugato'. Here, in a tour de force that seems inspired by Mozart's 'Jupiter' Symphony, Vaughan Williams combines all the themes of his finale. Any sense that this might be an academic exercise is swept away by the sheer energy and force of the music, which climaxes in a sudden return to the terrifying opening bars of the symphony. There is a final hammering dissonance, and an abrupt *fff* chord falls like an axe.

SYMPHONY NO. 5 IN D MAJOR

Duration: approx. 35 minutes (score), 36–43 minutes (recordings)

Preludio: Moderato – Allegro – Tempo I
Scherzo: Presto misterioso
Romanza: Lento
Passacaglia: Moderato

Vaughan Williams composed his Fifth Symphony between 1938 and 1943, and conducted the premiere at a Promenade Concert in London in 1943, aged seventy. He dedicated it, 'Without permission and with the sincerest flattery to Jean Sibelius, whose great example is worthy of imitation.' This he shortened in the printed score to: 'To Jean Sibelius, without permission.' When Sibelius heard a performance of the symphony in Stockholm, he wrote to Adrian Boult, 'The Symphony is a marvellous work ... the dedication made me feel proud and grateful ... I wonder if Dr. Williams has any idea of the pleasure he has given me?'[22]

It is a great contrast to the Fourth Symphony – more spacious (though only a little longer), less dissonant, in some ways a return to the Vaughan Williams of the Tallis Fantasia and *The Lark Ascending*. But the work that it most strongly links to is *The Pilgrim's Progress*, the opera, or as Vaughan Williams called it, 'operatic morality', which he worked on for most of his composing life, from about 1906 until its first production in 1951. It was based on the famous book by John Bunyan (1628–88), which narrates, as a dream, the journey of a pilgrim, Christian, from the 'City of Destruction' to the 'Celestial City', and the burdens, fears, and temptations he encounters. Over the years that Vaughan Williams worked on the opera, ideas found their way to and fro between it and other music, particularly the Fifth Symphony, composed at a time when Vaughan Williams had little hope of ever completing the opera. The symphony shares with *The Pilgrim's Progress* specific musical ideas, and, more generally, a sense of deep spirituality. There are struggles along the way, though not nearly as violent as in the Fourth Symphony, but the overall character is one of spiritual aspiration, and the search for serenity. It is scored for a smaller orchestra than the Fourth Symphony, with no percussion apart from timpani.

Even without the dedication, the spacious Preludio would evoke memories of Sibelius. It begins with a quiet horn call in D major, the declared key of the symphony. But under it the cellos and basses sustain a C natural, immediately creating a mysterious seventh chord that pulls away from D (this has echoes of Sibelius's *Tapiola*, whose first and penultimate chord is just such a mysterious harmony with the seventh in the bass). The violins answer with a rising and falling phrase in a pentatonic (five-note) scale that seems to have nothing to do with D major, but could be in C major. This quiet tension between different keys, with folk-like elements struggling against alien harmonies, sets the mood for the movement.

A contrapuntal web gradually opens out, made up of interweaving lines and sometimes of interweaving strings of chords (there are moments when this too sounds as much like Sibelius as Vaughan Williams). For the whole of this opening paragraph – about three minutes – the bass constantly returns to C, as if the orchestra were an enormous, celestial folk band, with C as the drone. There is a hushed moment, and the music shifts into E major. This is hardly a new theme, because it shares so many elements with what has gone before. But these now coalesce into a warm, lyrical outpouring, with violins, violas, and cellos singing together over pizzicato bass, and the woodwind and horns as a complementary chorus. A climactic phrase is very reminiscent of the 'Alleluia' in Vaughan Williams' setting of the hymn, 'For all the saints', which he wrote for *The English Hymnal* in 1906 (the year in which he began working on *The Pilgrim's Progress*).

The great swell of sound subsides, and reminders of the opening search through different keys before alighting on C minor. The music accelerates to Allegro, and the pentatonic phrases in the strings become a continuous texture made up of lines moving up and down independently (this too sounds like a homage to Sibelius). The woodwind introduce an ominous call, a falling semitone. Gradually the tension increases, with the strings eventually breaking into scrubbing tremolo that reaches *fff*, as if we are heading for one of Sibelius's storms. But the gale soon blows out, the music subsides again, and we return to the opening horn call, with the sustained C in the bass.

Once more the rich web of sound builds up, this time breaking straight into a climactic 'Alleluia' phrase of the hymn-like second theme. There is one more great wave, and a final descent. The ominous semitone fall sounds again. The movement ends as it began, with two different keys quietly alternating: the horn call in D major, the cellos and basses repeatedly returning to C. As the final horn call fades away, we are left with the cellos on C, and violas on D, so that nothing is resolved.

The main scherzo theme is built from rising fourths, which were such an important feature of the Fourth Symphony. But here, instead of being stark and Hindemith-like, they are fleeting, on muted strings, first in simple octaves and then in counterpoint. At times the effect is almost like Mendelssohn's fairy music. The woodwind introduce a more flowing element, and there are barbed little snaps and oscillating notes that refer back to the ominous falling semitones from the first movement.

The entry into the central part of the movement (trio) is wonderfully subtle. As the trombones play the rising fourths, a new phrase rounds it off. This then becomes the germ of a sonorous hymn. Fragments of the scherzo in the muted strings continue to flash by as the hymn proceeds, as if the Mendelssohnian fairies have encountered a procession. Trombones and horns stop the hymn in its tracks, on a chord of fourths, and this is the signal for the scherzo to resume. This time the brass inject a fiercer element, breaking into the whirling three-time with a sturdy two-time, and the music rises to a surprising climax. Then the strings take the rising fourths and create of them a passage of yearning wistfulness, after which the fairy-like scherzo vanishes.

The Romanza is the movement that is most explicitly linked to *The Pilgrim's Progress*. At the head of the score, Vaughan Williams placed a quote from Bunyan: 'Upon that place there stood a cross and a little below a sepulchre. Then he [Christian] said, "He hath given us rest by his sorrow and life by his death."' This quote (assembled from two separate quotes) comes from a passage early in Bunyan's narrative. Approaching the cross, struggling under his heavy burden, Christian finds the burden falling from his shoulders, and tumbling into the sepulchre. He then encounters three Shining Ones, who tell him that his sins are forgiven and exchange his rags for new clothes. No doubt because of his earlier experience of people reading too much into extra-musical references, Vaughan Williams removed the quote from the score when it was published. But the links between the music of this movement and that of the opera are unmistakable.

Soft, mystical string chords sound (evoking memories of the Tallis Fantasia), and the cor anglais plays a recitative. Almost note for note, this opens Act I, Scene 2 of *The Pilgrim's Progress*, which is drawn from that passage in Bunyan. We should not make too much of this. Although there are hints of other links with the opera later, the movement develops as a powerful musical structure that stands on its own.

After the cor anglais finishes, the strings, divided into eight parts, sing a chorus that begins with rising fourths, and develops into a half-memory of the warm second theme of the first movement with its 'Alleluia' climax. There is a suggestion of another 'Alleluia', from the Lutheran hymn 'Lasst uns erfreuen' (known in English as 'All creatures of our God and king'), though Vaughan Williams made it clear that this was not a deliberate quotation. Now the music is cleansed of all tension and, in a pure Aeolian mode (A minor with the flat seventh), radiates an atmosphere of deep consolation.

With more rising fourths, flute and oboe exchange calls that evoke birdsong over the peaceful rising and falling string chords. Woodwind and horns return to the string chords that opened the movement, and the strings in unison take up the cor anglais's recitative. But after a few bars they again expand into their consoling eight-part chorus, which rises higher than before. Oboe and cor anglais take up the bird calls, over the peaceful rise and fall, and are joined by the rest of the woodwind.

Then, for the first time in the movement, tension enters the music. The pace increases, the harmonies suddenly move away from the peaceful Aeolian mode, and the woodwind's bird calls become an urgent figure. As the tension increases, there is a sense of anguish that brings to mind Elgar's *Dream of Gerontius* and Wagner's *Parsifal*. A violent string tremolo fades to pianissimo, and a horn plays the recitative, like a distant vision of calm. But the vision is not yet to be recaptured. The tension again mounts, capped by a particularly *Parsifal*-like trumpet. The strings throw the bird call motif in the air, the brass quietly remind us of the serene opening chords, the bird-call motif becomes darker and wearier. But from its lowest point, it gradually rises to a reprise of the consoling string chorus, which mounts to a climax on full orchestra. The chorus fades, and a solo violin takes up the bird call, a muted horn revisits the recitative, and a mood of deep peace floods gently in. The benediction is fulfilled.

The finale is a passacaglia built over a repeating bass line. This old form, also known as a chaconne, evokes memories of J. S. Bach and Henry Purcell, composers very important to Vaughan Williams. In modern times, it had been used by Brahms in his Fourth Symphony and Variations on a Theme of Haydn. But an even more recent model was the slow movement of the piano trio by Ravel, with whom Vaughan Williams studied. Ravel's passacaglia is desolate, Vaughan Williams' is celebratory. But they share a certain 'antique' character, because the bass lines on which they are based pull towards the old modes. Vaughan Williams' passacaglia is in the traditional stately three-time. The bass line consists of seven bars, mostly in the old pentatonic scale. Above the bass, violins and flutes enter with a melody formed of rising and falling phrases in pure D major. This combination of lines has a very fluid character, partly because of the irregular, seven-bar bass unit, partly because of the subtle way in which the melody above relates to it, its phrase endings overlapping with those of the bass, rather than coinciding with them (Purcell excelled in such subtlety in the writing of passacaglias). The violins' melody extends over two statements of the bass, and its second half emphatically repeats one of the 'Alleluia' shapes from the slow movement. The music builds to a forte at which the bass line and violin melody swap with each other. Then the two lines become more fragmented, though they are still held together by the progress of the harmonies.

At a fortissimo, the music breaks into a faster tempo, the trombones enter for the first time, leading a broad, swinging dance in which the melody is played as a canon (round). After a playful excursion into other keys, there is a sudden return to the opening (slower) tempo, and to D major, and the brass play the melody in a blazing chorale, combining once again with the passacaglia bass. A final chord of D major abruptly shifts to a tremolando D minor.

The repeating pattern of the passacaglia has by now been first loosened and then abandoned. What follows is a development of the two themes (bass and melody) in a new four-time metre. As the themes interweave contrapuntally, the music takes on more of the character of earlier movements. The mood becomes urgent and searching, building to a climax at which the brass play the ominous falling semitone from the first movement. We are heading for some sort of resolution, perhaps a return to the passacaglia. But instead, we are taken right back to the very opening of the symphony, the D major horn call over a C in the bass, now in a glorious fortissimo, with fragments of the passacaglia bass below. This is the final climax, which has the effect of purging the music of all remaining tension. Gradually, it finds its way back to D major, and a solo cello leads off the epilogue. The melody from the passacaglia, with its hint of 'Alleluia', gently builds one last, serene web of sound.

SYMPHONY NO. 6 IN E MINOR
Duration: approx. 35 minutes

Allegro –
Moderato –
Scherzo: Allegro vivace –
Epilogue: Moderato

Vaughan Williams began working on this symphony in 1944, though he incorporated two themes that he had written a year earlier for a film score, *Flemish Farm* (the opening of the second and fourth movements). Adrian Boult conducted the premiere with the BBC Symphony Orchestra at the Royal Albert Hall in London on 21 April 1948. They first played it through in December 1947, and the composer Robert Müller-Hartmann, a refugee from Nazi Germany who had become a friend of Vaughan Williams, wrote to him, 'I left the rehearsal of your new symphony rather hurriedly because I would not have been able to talk to you. Although I had heard it twice before on the piano, and certainly excellently played, I never anticipated the overwhelming impression the real thing would make on me.'[23] Deryck Cooke in his book *The Language of Music* remembers that, at the premiere, the effect on him 'was nothing short of cataclysmic', and after the finale, '*pianissimo* throughout, devoid of all warmth and life, a hopeless wandering through a dead world . . . I was no more able to applaud than at the end of Tchaikovsky's *Pathétique* Symphony – less so, in fact, for this seemed to be an ultimate nihilism beyond Tchaikovsky's conceiving: every drop of blood seemed frozen in one's veins.'[24]

The premiere was the greatest success of Vaughan Williams' career. Frank Howes in *The Times* was sure that a future commentator 'will certainly relate the symphony to the experiences of war, its challenges, its sinister import for ultimate values, its physical bombardment even. But what will he make of the ghostly epilogue? Here the composer seems to be seeking not answers but the right questions to ask of human experience.'[25] Vaughan Williams himself wrote to Michael Kennedy about this finale, 'I do NOT BELIEVE IN meanings and mottoes, as you know, but I think we can get in words nearest to the substance of my last movement in "We are such stuff as dreams are made on, and our little life is rounded by [*sic*] a sleep." '[26]

In contrast to the Fifth Symphony, the sixth is scored for a large orchestra including tenor saxophone, a substantial percussion section, and harp 'doubled if possible'. It is played without breaks between movements.

The symphony opens with strings and woodwind playing a defiant rising pattern of three notes, the first three notes of a scale of F minor. The brass slam down a minor chord, but in the wrong key – E minor, a semitone lower than F minor, creating a wrenching discord. But this opening is not just in two keys at once. The top note of the strings, A flat, is, in effect, also G sharp, so that when the chord of E minor joins it, there is a clash between G sharp and G natural, a clash which, in a jazz context, would be a 'blue' effect. So the clash is not just violent, but also contains an ambiguity that is powerfully poignant. The ambiguity is then hammered home in a repeated falling pattern, which straddles the two keys. This scatters into fast cross-rhythms, which tumble chaotically through other keys. Energy of unstoppable power has been unleashed. The opening paragraph of the symphony struggles to find a way out of this conflict. As the rapid patterns continue, the brass threaten with jagged rhythms. The strings find their way to a more sustained melody, but it is still full of rhythmic conflict, and accompanied by continuing agitated patterns and savage brass chords. The new melody moves into the bass. Then a swirl of woodwind, answered by strings, mark the end of the opening paragraph, and the music quietens for the first time.

Over a jaunty rhythm, a repetitive little theme starts up, at last in a clear key, G minor, though with Vaughan Williams' typical modal inflection. What comes as a surprise is the swinging suggestion of a jazz band, enhanced by a tenor saxophone in the mix. At the same time there is a nervous edge to the repetitions, and the brittleness of the accompanying rhythms suggests an affinity with Satan's Dance of Triumph from Vaughan Williams' *Job*. The energy builds and subsides, and as fragments of the jaunty rhythm persist, violins, with flutes and cor anglais below, convert the nervous repetitions into a singing theme, now in a modal B minor, that rises and becomes more lyrical. The swinging rhythms assert themselves again, and this section culminates in the new version of the theme boldly declaimed by trumpets and trombones in (modal) D minor.

Suddenly, with a timpani roll, there is a change of key, and swirling strings and woodwind take us back to the old conflict between E minor and F minor. Soon it subsides, the tempo slows, and for the first time in the movement, we enter the warmth of a major key, E major. Over chords combining harp with gentle trumpets and trombones, strings in unison sing a new and yet more lyrical version of the repetitive theme, which now rises in a great hymn-like outpouring – 'folk hymn', one might say, because Vaughan Williams gives a modal edge to the E major with sharpened fourths and flattened sevenths. So this movement, full of conflict and contradictory elements, culminates in a moment of consolation. But it is short-lived, and proves to be the only such haven in the entire work. As the melody reaches a climax, it breaks back to the opening phrase of the symphony, with its clash between E minor and F minor, and the movement ends ominously on a bass E, which is sustained over to the beginning of the slow movement.

The second movement is not very slow (Moderato), but it is heavy with menace. From the E in the bass, trumpets take over with a sustained B flat, signalling a shift to the remote key of B flat minor. Under the B flat, strings and low woodwind begin a stealthy, creeping theme, whose opening phrases each end with three staccato notes like a sinister tapping. This becomes the dominant motif of the movement, inevitably recalling the similar rhythmic motif that runs through the central section of Holst's 'Mars', and encouraging the war-related interpretation of the symphony. But it is also reminiscent of the ending of Sibelius's Third Symphony. There, the insistent motif is triumphant; here, it is at first sinister and later destructive – so destructive as to invite comparison with another composer, Shostakovich.

At first the music proceeds like a mournful set of variations, which cuts off just as it seems to be approaching a climax. There is a timpani crescendo, and the brass intone a baleful fanfare, in which chords of F minor and E minor alternate in triplet rhythm – the very chords that fought at the opening of the symphony. This has stopped the tapping rhythm in its tracks, but has opened out a new, bleak landscape, through which the music seems to be searching for a way, first in stark octaves, later in a chorus of divided strings.

Trumpets and timpani quietly re-enter with the sinister tapping rhythm on B flat. As the search continues, the rhythm becomes insistent and hypnotic, always on the same note. The search becomes more desperate, the rhythm more hammering. At a climax, there is a sudden cut-off, leaving the hammering and a crescendo on bass drum. High strings play a variant of the baleful fanfare (now chords of G flat major and G minor), as the hammering on B flat continues. Twice more there is a cut-off, twice a mighty climax, but nothing is resolved (there is an echo of the famous unresolved climax in the first movement of Beethoven's Ninth Symphony here). Eventually the menace recedes, leaving cor anglais and strings alone. Beneath the final note of the cor anglais, the sinister rhythm is heard for the last time, like distant gunfire.

The scherzo follows without a break. Here, an interval that has lurked behind the sinister side of the symphony's harmonies comes out into the open. This is the tritone (a semitone less than a fifth), which is boldly stated in the opening bars of the scherzo: B flat to E, then F to B, C to F sharp. A rattling, Shostakovich-like theme gets going in the woodwind, whose agitated character is sharpened by the fact that its scales also outline the tritone. The frantic energy of the scherzo is relentless, its twists of rhythm and cross-rhythm only adding to the sense of something inescapable. Eventually, there is a lightening of mood, and the tenor saxophone plays a solo hinting at the jazzy element that emerged in the first movement. Twice the saxophone attempts its solo, twice the theme is taken up fiercely by the full orchestra, who are not to be deterred from their aggressive drive. The conductor Malcolm Sargent was convinced that this movement 'was all about a night in the war [8 March 1941] when a bomb hit the Café de Paris in London and blew Ken "Snakehips" Johnson and his West Indian Dance Orchestra and dozens of dancers into eternity.' Aged twenty-six, Johnson led the resident dance band at the Café de Paris, and was already famous through his regular radio broadcasts.[27]

There is a sudden string tremolando tritone chord, and a bassoon plays descending tritones. This signals a return to the opening material, with greater contrapuntal chaos than before. As the mayhem reaches a frenzied pitch, suddenly the saxophone's tune reappears, now transformed into a monstrous triumphal march. This dissipates into more tritones, with tremolando chords and descending clarinets and bass clarinet, and the nightmare is gone.

But what remains? Nothing but a ghost of a memory. As the bass clarinet sustains a low E, muted violins begin a wandering attempt at a theme, which incorporates memories of the melodic shapes from the opening of the symphony with more tritone harmonies. As each of the string parts enters, a web of counterpoint builds up. If it resembles anything, it is the mysterious opening of Bartók's Music for Strings, Percussion and Celesta. But here there is no build-up, no climax. Time after time Vaughan Williams instructs 'pp senza crescendo' (pp without crescendo).

There is virtually nothing left, but what there is has no way out, no hope of redemption. The music subsides to a memory of the baleful chords from the end of the second movement, and then rises again. Flutes join the strings, playing the theme at half speed, then the four horns. Their rich chords clash with the continuing strings, now in bleak octaves, as if the two worlds can no longer see each other. Other fragmentary visions pass by: muted brass that could have stepped out of Stravinsky's The Rite of Spring, a solo cello like a lone survivor, ruins of the rich string chords that populate other Vaughan Williams symphonies, a bleak oboe solo.

After further searching, the counterpoint resumes on tremolando strings, with the theme half tempo on harp harmonics. A quartet of solo string players brings in a renewal of the oboe solo. In the final bars, the baleful chords from the second movement rock dismally back and forth – E flat major, E minor, E flat major, E minor – with a last memory of the theme pizzicato below. The symphony ends with a chord of E minor fading to nothing. But, although this is the key-chord of the symphony, it is without its bass note, so it hangs suspended, unresolved.

ANTONIO VIVALDI
(1678–1741)

Vivaldi was one of the great figures who came to prominence at the time of the development of violin-making in northern Italy (see Corelli). From 1703, Vivaldi was employed as violin teacher, and later as overall music director, at the Pio Ospedale della Pietà in Venice. This was one of several institutions that looked after abandoned, orphaned, and illegitimate girls, and gave those who showed talent a musical training. Many stayed on into adult life, and the standard achieved, in both singing and instrumental music, was very high. A German visitor to Venice in the 1720s remarked that the Pietà had 'an orchestra of a quality to be found only at a few large courts'.[1] The level of accomplishment is clear in the works that Vivaldi wrote for them to perform at their regular public performances.

It was while he was in this post that Vivaldi began to make his reputation as a composer. Volumes of sonatas, Opus 1 and 2, were published in 1702 and 1709, and he was meanwhile writing concertos. He also composed choral music for the Pietà, and wrote operas for Venice, Rome, and other cities. But it was as a composer of concertos that he achieved the greatest fame beyond Venice, and on which his reputation principally rests to this day.

If Corelli has the best claim to having set off the fashion for what we call 'orchestral' music, Vivaldi was the composer who greatly extended the range of emotions and effects to be achieved with it. Vivaldi's concertos built on the model first established by Corelli in his set, Opus 6. In particular, he developed subtler ways of using the contrasts between *ripieno* and *concertino* (orchestra and soloists) passages. In Corelli's concertos, the soloists largely continue exploring the same material as the orchestra. In Vivaldi, the soloist(s) typically introduce new material, creating a journey of thematic invention and development that was imitated and enlarged throughout the baroque period, and eventually evolved into the classical concerto of Mozart and Beethoven.

Vivaldi was not working alone in these new developments. Other composers were exploring similar ideas, but it was Vivaldi who was the master in this new genre, and launched it with brilliant success onto the wider world. He was widely imitated through the eighteenth century. Distinct traces of both Corelli and Vivaldi are to be found in Handel. And it was Vivaldi who provided the model for J. S. Bach's orchestral music, and even for several of his solo keyboard works. Bach transcribed several of Vivaldi's concertos, some adapted as concertos for several keyboard instruments, some for solo harpsichord and for organ. His own 'Italian' Concerto for solo harpsichord is modelled closely on Vivaldi.

Part of this enlargement of possibilities was the exploration of a greater range of expressive effects. Corelli's concertos contain contrasts and dramatic juxtapositions, but Vivaldi's contrasts are much more varied and subtle. Corelli gives few markings in the score beyond the notes themselves and indications of tempo: there is the occasional piano and forte, but rarely anything more. Vivaldi's concertos contain many more markings of piano and forte, and occasionally pianissimo, and a much greater range of combinations of instruments; they venture to higher regions of the violin and exploit a greater variety of bowing, including rapid 'scrubbing' effects – most famously in the imitations of nature in *The Four Seasons*.

L'ESTRO ARMONICO
Durations: each concerto 8–12 minutes

In 1711, Vivaldi published his Opus 3, a two-book collection called *L'Estro Armonico* (*Harmonic Inspiration* or *The Gift of Harmony*). This contains twelve concertos, and it was one of the most successful and influential music publications in the eighteenth century, establishing Vivaldi's international reputation as the greatest master of the Italian concerto. It was particularly appreciated in Germany, where J. S. Bach transcribed five of the Opus 3 collection for solo organ or harpsichord, and one as a concerto for four harpsichords. Vivaldi's concertos are for one, two, and four violins – four concertos for each scoring. Some of the concertos for multiple violins also have passages for solo cello, echoing Corelli's practice of a solo *concertino* with its own cello line (the classic *concerto grosso* line-up). In the other concertos there is no solo cello.

CONCERTO NO. 1 IN D MAJOR FOR FOUR VIOLINS, RV 549

Allegro
Largo e spiccato
Allegro

This concerto includes passages of solo cello in the first movement, but these are occasional interventions rather than an integral part of the solo group.

The charm of the opening Allegro lies in the way that Vivaldi deploys the four solo violins, sometimes as individuals, sometimes in pairs, sometimes forte, sometimes piano, with one pair echoing another, and with figures passing round the group. This is particularly effective in live performance, when the 'geography' of this interplay is visible as well as audible. J. S. Bach drew on this method of writing when he came to compose his Third Brandenburg Concerto.

The orchestra opens the slow movement with a theme in solemn dotted notes ('spiccato', 'separated', was used to mean the same as staccato at this period). The strings play in bare octaves, with only the keyboard instrument supplying chords. Between the three statements of this idea, the violas continue to develop the bass line, while the first two solo violins weave a decorative duet above it (the other soloists are silent).

The finale is a jig, with patterns that are so continuous as to form a perpetuum mobile. As in the first movement, material passes around each of the four soloists, alone and in combination. It is all light and cheerful until, over a held bass note, the first violin unexpectedly introduces some poignant touches of harmony. The moment is soon over, and the orchestra restores the cheerful mood for the final tutti.

CONCERTO NO. 2 IN G MINOR FOR TWO VIOLINS AND CELLO, RV 578

Adagio e spiccato
Allegro
Larghetto
Allegro

The solemn Adagio e spiccato builds from the bass upwards, with twists of harmony and unexpected echoes that anticipate the 'frozen' music of *The Four Seasons*. The Allegro is full of bustling energy. Something of the 'frozen' character seems to carry over from the Adagio, with a bass line that rises chromatically in scrubbed repeated notes, echoed in the violins. The ending is particularly charming, where Vivaldi, right at the last minute, introduces a little trilling motif simpler than anything in the rest of the movement to bring it to a close.

The Larghetto begins with bold phrases that echo each other, separated by silences. As the music becomes more coherent, it takes on the character of a sarabande, with passages for the solo trio of two violins and cello.

The final Allegro is in a lively jig rhythm with extended passages for one and two solo violins. But the most striking music is in the orchestral tutti that begins and ends the movement, with its unusually active bass line and quirky harmonies. This brings a quality of nervous edginess to an otherwise cheerful movement.

CONCERTO NO. 3 IN G MAJOR FOR VIOLIN, RV 310

Allegro
Largo
Allegro

This is the first of the concertos that J. S. Bach arranged for solo harpsichord (BWV 978). The first movement is a classic example of the ritornello form that Bach developed so successfully, in which the material heard at the beginning returns, interleaved with episodes. The bold opening tutti has two particularly striking elements – the descending scale that begins the movement, and then the ascending scales that repeat, rising a step at each ascent. The initial, descending scale, punctuates the movement, outlining its basic structure of changing keys – G major, D major, B minor, and back to G major. The sequence of ascending scales occurs only twice, in the first and last tutti, marking the external 'walls' of the movement. In between these landmarks, the soloist plays passages of assorted patterns in a fluid dialogue with the orchestra.

The Largo in E minor begins with alternating bars of simple spiccato (separated) chords and decorative figuration from the soloist. As the movement proceeds, the solo bars become extended and the chords more adventurous in their harmonies.

It is the bass that drives the final Allegro with energetic running semiquavers. These migrate to the soloist, and return to the bass for each ritornello. There is a characteristic touch right at the end, where Vivaldi simplifies the final bars.

CONCERTO NO. 4 IN E MINOR FOR FOUR VIOLINS, RV 550

Andante
Allegro assai
Adagio
Allegro

The opening Andante has the solemn tread of a sarabande. Between each statement of the opening tutti the four soloists enter one at a time, and then play in duet. The final tutti simplifies the theme (one of Vivaldi's favourite ways of ending a movement).

The Allegro assai begins with a forthright ritornello that incorporates a few bars of solo for the first violinist. Between subsequent appearances of the ritornello, each soloist in turn takes up running semiquavers. Then they pair up for duets before the final orchestral tutti.

The Adagio is no more than a few solemn bars to introduce the final movement. This Allegro is in a vigorous three-time. After the first ritornello, soloists 1 and 3 alternate, in the next episode soloists 2 and 4 alternate, and in the final episode they pair up: violins 1 and 2 play in imitative duet, violins 3 and 4 echo them, and then all join in the final ritornello.

CONCERTO NO. 5 IN A MAJOR FOR TWO VIOLINS, RV 519

Allegro
Largo
Allegro

This double concerto must have been one of the most popular of the set, because it exists in many manuscript copies. Although it is scored for two solo violins, the first violin predominates, as if the concerto was designed for a 'senior' and 'junior' player (perhaps for Vivaldi himself to play with a pupil). The Allegro opens with a theme in octaves – a bold statement of the kind that clearly appealed to Handel. The soloists play in duet and then, after the second ritornello, play an echo together. For subsequent episodes, the first violin plays alone.

In the Largo, the second solo violin is silent, and so are the cellos and basses. Soft chords on violins and violas support a highly decorated, but essentially peaceful, violin solo. A tinge of poignancy is added halfway through, as the music moves into a minor key and the accompanying instruments are marked pianissimo.

In the final Allegro, Vivaldi repeats again and again a little rhythmic motif in the bass, moving from a chord of A to a chord of E and back again. Variants of this motif dominate the whole movement, as the two solo violins vie with each other in virtuoso banter. It is the simplest of devices, elevated to a delightful obsession.

CONCERTO NO. 6 IN A MINOR FOR VIOLIN, RV 356

Allegro
Largo
Presto

In the first movement, the role of the solo violin is more dominant than in the earlier solo concerto (No. 3 in G major), and its material is more integrated with that of the orchestral ritornello. The soloist's first entry takes up the tripping first idea and extends it, rather than introducing new material straight away. Later solo entries become more decorative, but the sturdy repeating rhythm in the bass, which was there from the first bar, continues persistently, providing a unifying motif throughout the movement.

In the brief Largo, violins and violas hold pianissimo chords as the soloist plays a singing line. At first simple, and later becoming more highly decorated, its expressive force is heightened by the shifting harmonies beneath.

The playful character of the principal theme of the Presto is created by irregular phrasing: the first phrase is three bars long, the answering phrase is four bars long, giving a subtly lopsided effect. The orchestra continues vigorously with regular phrases, but the continual recurrence of the opening idea gives the whole movement, and the virtuoso solo passages, a delightfully tongue-in-cheek character that is underlined by the surprisingly sudden ending.

CONCERTO NO. 7 IN F MAJOR FOR FOUR VIOLINS AND CELLO, RV 567

Andante
Adagio
Allegro
Adagio
Allegro

The opening Andante is not a slow movement, but, in effect, a more relaxed version of an Allegro movement. There are four bold opening bars over a bass that alternates between F and C, followed by an echo. After a brief solo passage, the orchestra plays one of Vivaldi's characteristic, gently falling chord sequences. Then the bass returns to its alternating F and C while each solo violinist enters in turn with a more animated figure. The bold opening returns.

The next solo entry is more plangent, moving into the minor (the solo cello briefly joins with the solo violinists, but its role is subordinate in this concerto). Finally, the orchestra returns to the falling chord sequence to round off the movement.

The brief Adagio opens with separated chords, probably intended as a basis for embellishment by the first soloist. Then Vivaldi returns to another of his gently falling chord sequences, with unusually poignant harmonies.

The next Allegro is a playful movement. The solo violinists predominate, sometimes in pairs, then chasing each other in solos, at one point in dialogue with the solo cello, and from time to time coming together to form a miniature orchestra of four.

Another brief Adagio leads into the final Allegro. This is a courtly minuet, in which two solo violins and solo cello alternate with the orchestra, in the manner of Corelli's *concerti grossi*.

CONCERTO NO. 8 IN A MINOR FOR TWO VIOLINS, RV 522

Allegro
Larghetto e spiritoso
Allegro

This concerto was arranged by J. S. Bach for solo organ (BWV 593). The opening Allegro is a particularly fine example of a ritornello movement. The material of its opening tutti is unusually varied, with three distinct elements. The first is a vigorous theme of descending and ascending scales, the second works away at a little figure, and the third is made from sighing pairs of notes that acquire a touch of poignancy in their harmonies. The soloists introduce new material, but continually refer back to these elements, and the orchestral ritornelli draw on all three as they move through different keys. The result is a movement that seems both tightly structured and free.

The slow movement opens with another of Vivaldi's bold ideas, a sequence of little phrases with all the strings in octaves ('spiritoso' means 'spirited' or 'vigorous'). This continues pianissimo throughout the movement, while the soloists weave lines above, first individually then in duet. The movement ends with a restatement of the bold opening. J. S. Bach was to build the slow movements of his violin concertos in E major and A minor in a similar way.

The final Allegro opens with the orchestra playing a pattern of simple descending scales, and the soloists answer with rising phrases. Later solo entries develop a more virtuoso dash, including passages written as simple chords that the violinist is expected to elaborate with arpeggios. There is a surprising development halfway through. As the first soloist continues with its vigorous semiquavers, now quietly, the second violin plays a more sustained melody, introducing an unexpectedly lyrical element into the movement (J. S. Bach introduces an equally unexpected lyrical element at a similar point in the finale of his concerto for two violins).

CONCERTO NO. 9 IN D MAJOR FOR VIOLIN, RV 230

Allegro
Larghetto
Allegro

J. S. Bach arranged this violin concerto for solo harpsichord (BWV 972). The first Allegro, with its fanfare-like opening bars and energetic semiquavers in both orchestra and solo part, has a joyful character – one could imagine it with trumpets and drums as the prelude to a Christmas cantata.

The Larghetto begins with two bars of sonorous chords. The solo violin then embarks on a meditation, starting with that same chord sequence, but then exploring through different keys, until it returns to D major. The movement ends with a reprise of the sonorous chords.

The final Allegro returns to the celebratory mood of the opening movement. Orchestral passages in a dancing three-time alternate with solo episodes whose bowing becomes increasingly virtuoso.

CONCERTO NO. 10 IN B MINOR FOR FOUR VIOLINS AND CELLO, RV 580

Allegro
Largo – Larghetto – Largo
Allegro

J. S. Bach arranged several of Vivaldi's concertos for solo harpsichord, but this is the only one that he preserved as a concerto with orchestra, adapting the solo violin parts for four harpsichords (BWV 1065). Although Bach's concerto gives harpsichordists an unusual opportunity, it inevitably removes an important element of the original – Vivaldi's mastery in combining four solo violin lines.

The opening is striking: two solo violins, accompanied only by violas, start the repeated notes and trills of the main theme, like birds calling from adjacent trees (a premonition of the natural effects to come in *The Four Seasons*). The orchestra takes up the theme energetically, and between its entries the third and fourth solo violins respond with running semiquavers. For most of the movement, the four soloists play in a freely developing pattern of solos, duets, trios, and quartet, and a solo cello twice joins them. The orchestra has an accompanying role until the final ritornello.

The Largo, with its stately dotted rhythms, acts as a brief introduction, and even briefer tailpiece, to the central Larghetto. This is one of Vivaldi's most fascinating experiments in string textures. It consists of a slowly evolving pattern of chords, in which each of the four soloists plays a different pattern of arpeggios in a different style of articulation, with the first violin playing at double the speed of the others. The effect is almost hypnotic – one could imagine that it might have inspired the transfixing opening of Handel's great coronation anthem, 'Zadok the Priest'. The arpeggios culminate in a bar of simple chords marked Adagio, which Vivaldi presumably intended to be broken into improvised arpeggios, and the dotted rhythms of the Largo return to round off the movement.

The final Allegro is a lively jig, in which orchestral ritornelli alternate with passages for the soloists in various combinations. At times, the energetic intricacies of this movement seem to look forward to the finale of J. S. Bach's Third Brandenburg Concerto. In a moment of violinistic daring, Vivaldi invites the first violin to play the last solo passage an octave higher than written.

CONCERTO NO. 11 IN D MINOR FOR TWO VIOLINS AND CELLO, RV 565
Allegro – Adagio e spiccato – Allegro
Largo e spiccato
Allegro

This concerto is one of the most celebrated of the set, and was arranged by J. S. Bach for solo organ (BWV 596). The first two sections – Allegro and Adagio e spiccato – form a prelude to the second Allegro.

The concerto opens with the two solo violins 'preluding' together, with overlapping arpeggios and other patterns creating a canon over an insistently repeated D. The cello takes up the semiquaver patterns, bringing the brief movement to a conclusion.

Three bars of Adagio chords announce the Allegro. This is a thoroughly worked-out fugue, a form unusual in Vivaldi's concertos, and an inspiration for Handel's many fugal movements. The fugue has four voices, beginning in the bass and working upwards. After the initial entries, the two solo violins and cello play a freer episode. Another orchestral section returns to more intricate fugue-playing, taking the music through different keys. Another solo episode is followed by a final orchestral tutti, back in the home key of D minor, bringing one of Vivaldi's most concentrated movements to a close.

The Largo e spiccato has the gentle lilt of a siciliano. Between opening and closing orchestral tutti, the first soloist plays a singing melody over pianissimo chords, its lyricism darkened by plangent touches of harmony. Handel and Bach both made frequent use of the siciliano, Handel usually with a pastoral character, Bach more often giving it an expressive intensity that may well have been encouraged by this movement.

The concerto ends with a vigorous movement alternating soloists and orchestra. The two solo violins begin alone, as in the first movement, joined by the solo cello. At first, they play in imitative counterpoint. Later entries range from playful duetting in thirds to more contrapuntal imitation, with a passage of florid semiquavers for the first violin leading into a final, vigorous tutti.

CONCERTO NO. 12 IN E MAJOR FOR VIOLIN, RV 265
Allegro
Largo
Allegro

The last of the set was arranged by J. S. Bach for solo harpsichord (BWV 976). Its first movement is in the classic concerto form that Vivaldi passed on to the next generation, with orchestral ritornelli interspersed with solo passages that start from the orchestra's material and develop them with a mixture of invention and virtuoso display.

The Largo is one of the most subtle of Vivaldi's slow movements. The rising first phrase is echoed in the bass, and this becomes a recurrent motif throughout the movement. The soloist enters with a new version of this rising shape, as a starting point for an extended aria. The use of a motif to create a structure for seemingly free development was one Vivaldi's techniques that inspired J. S. Bach in his own slow movements.

After such subtlety, the final Allegro is straightforward. The opening orchestral tutti is in a brisk three-time. The soloist enters with a rapid display of semiquavers. There is a more extended central tutti, further solo display, some of which is written as simple chords on which the violinist is expected to improvise arpeggios, and the final tutti brings the move-ment to a close as briskly as it began.

LE QUATTRO STAGIONI (THE FOUR SEASONS)
Durations: each concerto approx. 9–11 minutes

Vivaldi's career went hand in hand with the rise of violin-making in northern Italy (see Corelli), and the violin concertos that make up *The Four Seasons* are the most celebrated fruit of that cross-fertilization.

Vivaldi had extended periods away from Venice. Details are sketchy, but it is known that he returned to his post at the Pio Ospedale della Pietà in the summer of 1723, with a new contract to write two concertos a month. Two years later a set of twelve concertos by Vivaldi was published in Amsterdam, under the title, *Il Cimento dell'Armonia e dell'Inventione* (*The Contest between Harmony and Invention*). The first four of them are *The Four Seasons*. The publication is prefaced by a dedication to Count Wenzel von Morzin (or 'Marzin' here), a Bohemian aristocrat and one of Vivaldi's most important patrons (a Count Morzin of the next generation was to employ the young Joseph Haydn). Vivaldi supplied the count with works over a period of at least five years. He describes himself in the dedication as the count's 'maestro di musica in Italia'. He also refers to the 'virtuosissima orchestra' that Morzin main-tains at his court, which gives Vivaldi confidence 'that these poor results of my labours will enjoy prominence that they do not deserve'. He specifically mentions *The Four Seasons* in the dedication, making it clear that these were not new works: 'I beg Your Highness not to be surprised if, among these few and feeble Concerti, you should find the four Seasons, which have been indulged by Your Highness's generosity for so long. But please believe that I have thought them worthy of being printed because, although they are the same works, they have been improved, quite apart from the sonnets which, with absolute clarity, explain everything in them, and so I am confident that they will appear as new.'[2]

For each of the seasons, Vivaldi printed a 'Sonetto Dimostrativo'. The poems are not just an adjunct to the music: extracts from them are quoted throughout the parts, making it clear that Vivaldi was closely following the narrative of the sonnets as he composed. However, it is not known whether he wrote the sonnets before composing the music (if indeed he did write the sonnets), or whether he developed the sonnets from the already vivid narrative of the concertos.

The idea of instrumental music inspired by some sort of outside narrative goes back at least as far as the sixteenth century (William Byrd's keyboard suite, *The Battle*, is a famous example), and the depiction of storms and battles was common in Italian and French opera. But *The Four Seasons* was the first application of such ideas to large-scale orchestral music.

Together, the group of four concertos takes only forty minutes to play, so they are most often performed as a set.

CONCERTO IN E MAJOR, 'SPRING', RV 269

Allegro
Largo
Allegro

Sonetto Dimostrativo:[3]

Allegro

>Spring is here, and the birds
>Welcome her with joyful song,
>While breezes blow and the streams
>Flow with gentle murmur.
>Thunder and lightning announce her,
>Covering the sky with a dark cloak,
>Then as they fall silent, the birds
>Take up once more their enchanting song.

Largo

>Now, on the flower-strewn meadow,
>To the sweet rustling of the leaves
>The goatherd sleeps beside his faithful dog.

Allegro

>To the festive sound of rustic bagpipes
>Nymphs and shepherds dance beneath
>The brilliant canopy of spring.

Spring is announced by a theme that indeed has a spring in its step – similar in effect to the theme representing 'joyful feelings' that was to open Beethoven's 'Pastoral' Symphony a century later. This recurring ritornello alternates with episodes that plot the course of the first eight lines of the sonnet. The soloist enters with birdsong, joined by two other birds (violins) in the orchestra. After the next ritornello, a gentle pattern of semiquavers suggests the breeze and the gentle murmuring of streams. In the next episode, rapid repeated notes, flashing scales, and arpeggio patterns represent the thunder and lightning. After another ritornello, the birds return, and a final ritornello brings the movement to a close.

Throughout the Largo, the violins of the orchestra keep up a gentle pattern in parallel thirds evoking the rustling of leaves. Meanwhile, the violas persistently repeat a pair of notes 'loudly and roughly' to represent the barking of a dog. Over this accompaniment, the violin, as the sleeping goatherd, weaves a slow, sustained melody.

The final Allegro has the lilting rhythm of a siciliano, over sustained bass notes suggesting the drone of bagpipes. As the soloist enters, the dance of the nymphs and shepherds acquires virtuoso flourishes, alternating with moments of calm. A more solemn episode in E minor leads to a contemplative little cadenza, before the final return of the siciliano.

CONCERTO IN G MINOR, 'SUMMER', RV 315

Allegro non molto – Allegro
Adagio – Presto
Presto

Sonetto Dimostrativo:

Allegro non molto – Allegro

>   Under the burning sun
>   Men and flocks languish, and pines scorch.
>   The cuckoo finds its voice, and soon
>   The turtle dove and goldfinch sing.
>   A soft breeze stirs, but suddenly
>   Boreas sweeps it brusquely aside.
>   The shepherd weeps, fearing
>   The violent storms that lie ahead.

Adagio – Presto

>   His limbs are torn from their repose
>   By fear of lightning and of fierce storms
>   And by furious swarms of flies and midges.

Presto

>   Alas, his fears prove justified
>   As the heavens roar, and hailstones
>   Break off the proud heads of standing corn.

For Vivaldi, summer is not a benign season, but a period in which blistering heat is broken by violent storms. The short-breathed phrases of the opening Allegro non troppo evoke exhaustion in the heat. This idea recurs throughout the movement as a ritornello.

At the Allegro the soloist bursts into rapid figuration, the bottom notes of which pick out the call of the cuckoo. The languid opening returns, and the soloist becomes first a turtle dove and then a goldfinch. The upper strings of the orchestra evoke the gentle winds, and then Boreas (the north wind) breaks in powerfully on full orchestra. The sighs of the opening return briefly, and then, in the longest episode of the movement, the soloist expresses the fearful weeping of the shepherd in an aria-like melody over a bass that descends poignantly. Finally, the full orchestra bursts in once more with the north wind, its rapid scales fiercer than before.

In the central movement, Adagio and Presto alternate. In the Adagio sections, the solo violin sings a plaintive melody, while the orchestral violins accompany with a persistent little phrase that represents the midges and flies. Every few bars, the melody is interrupted by furious repeated notes to suggest the fear of thunder and lightning.

The final Presto is a classic storm scene, the kind of evocation that could have stepped straight out of the opera house, and which remained popular through to the nineteenth century (most famously in Beethoven's 'Pastoral' Symphony). The ferocious repeated notes from the second movement and the rapid scales from the first movement are combined to create a violent but structured movement. In solo episodes, the violinist's virtuoso passages convey a sense of desperation.

CONCERTO IN F MAJOR, 'AUTUMN', RV 293

Allegro
Adagio molto
Allegro

Sonetto Dimostrativo:

Allegro

> With song and dance the peasant celebrates
> The pleasure of the harvest gathered in,
> And fired by the wine of Bacchus, many
> End their festival in sleep.

Adagio molto

> The dancers and the singers gradually cease,
> Fanned by pleasant, cooling air,
> And the season invites everyone
> To enjoy the sweetest sleep.

Allegro

> At dawn, the hunters rise, ready for the chase.
> With horns, guns and dogs they venture out,
> Chasing the quarry, following its tracks.
> Terrified and weakened by the noise
> Of guns and dogs, fatally wounded,
> Pitifully it tries to flee, but dies oppressed.

After a violent summer, Vivaldi returns to the happy mood of 'Spring' in the first movement of 'Autumn'. Peasants celebrate the harvest in a cheerful, sturdy dance, whose opening phrases have the same chord sequence as the opening of 'Spring'. At its first entry, the soloist joins in appropriately. But the second and third solo episodes are 'fired by the wine of Bacchus', and break into torrents of arpeggios and dashing scales, interspersed with moments of apparent giddiness (those accompanying the soloist seem to hold their drink better). At the fourth episode, after an attempt at further flamboyance, the violinist is suddenly overcome, and a simple melody, with leaps that suggest heavy breaths, is gradually reduced to a sleeping long note. Enough peasants are still awake to finish the movement with a last round of the dance.

In the slow movement, everyone is asleep, and the Adagio molto consists of a sustained progression of peaceful chords. The harpsichord player is instructed to elaborate the bass line with arpeggios, and much depends on how this is done. Naturally, the simplest arpeggios produce the most peaceful effect.

The leaping intervals of the Allegro's main theme suggest the whooping of hunting horns, the prancing of horses and the invigorating air of dawn. The theme, like that of the first movement, opens with the same chord sequence as the opening of 'Spring'. This is the recurrent ritornello of the movement. The first two solo episodes imitate a pair of hunting horns with two-part chords. At the third episode, the violinist breaks into rapid broken chords to suggest the flight of the quarry. The orchestra answers with aggressive scrubbing – the growling of dogs and the terror of the quarry – and the violin solo becomes more frantic. By now, the persistent repetitions of the orchestral ritornello, which at first seemed benignly energetic, begin to sound menacing. The alternations between solo and orchestra become more intense, until a plaintive rising violin line and a last fall signal the death of the beast. A final, triumphant declaration of the ritornello rounds off the concerto.

CONCERTO IN F MINOR, 'WINTER', RV 297

Allegro non molto
Largo
Allegro – Lento

Sonetto Dimostrativo:

Allegro non molto

> Chilled to the bone by the icy snow
> And the cruel blasts of bitter wind,
> Constantly stamping our feet as we run,
> Teeth chattering uncontrollably.

Largo

> At the fireside, passing happy, peaceful days,
> While the rain drenches those outside.

Allegro

> Walking across the ice, slowly and carefully,
> Afraid of tripping and falling.
> A sudden turn, a fall, and then
> Upright on the ice again, running frantically
> Until the ice cracks and gives way.
> To feel, blasting through the bolted door,
> Sirocco, Boreas and all the winds at war:
> This is winter which, nonetheless, brings joy.

The frozen scene is conjured up by the almost immobile opening pages, with slowly changing pairs of chords surmounted by shivering trills on solo violin. The soloist breaks into rapid figuration (still within the same tempo) as the cruel wind blows, and this alternates with the frozen chords in the orchestra. Then the orchestra introduces a vigorous theme to suggest the stamping of feet. Running scales from the soloist are punctuated by blasts of wind from the orchestra. There is a brief reprise of the frozen opening, then the soloist plays rapidly repeated chords (the chattering of teeth), and the movement ends with a reprise of the foot-stamping theme.

The fireside scene is a beautiful miniature aria for solo violin, with the raindrops outside represented by pizzicato orchestral violins.

The final movement opens with a smooth, even line from the solo violin over a held bass note, evoking careful, steady progress over the ice. The orchestra joins the soloist, and tiptoeing chords build up dissonance, creating an increase in tension. Falling figures are followed by the re-entry of the soloist, now running in staccato semiquavers. There are abrupt phrases and gaps as the ice breaks. The tempo slows to Lento, and calm music depicts the Sirocco (a warm wind from the south). But once again, Boreas, the cold north wind, blasts in, with soloist and orchestra alternating, and the movement ends with a climax of energy to represent the icy joy of winter.

RICHARD WAGNER
(1813–83)

Wagner dominated the music of the late nineteenth century and changed the course of music history. He was to the second half of the nineteenth century what Beethoven had been to the first half. Like Beethoven, he inspired composers to think the unthinkable, to aspire to the impossible. And, as Beethoven had broken the bounds of the symphony with his choral Ninth, so Wagner broke the bounds of opera with his mighty music-dramas. Unlike the unfortunate Beethoven, Wagner led a charmed life, supported for many years by Ludwig II of Bavaria, who made possible the founding of Wagner's own opera festival at Bayreuth.

Wagner's operas are not a topic for a book on orchestral music. But his influence on later composers of orchestral music was profound. The first, and most obvious, influence is the matter of scale and length. *Götterdämmerung*, the final opera of *The Ring*, lasts four and a half hours, more than twice the length of the great model for German opera, Weber's *Der Freischütz*.

Wagner's achievements did not arise out of nowhere. He was, like most great artists, a magpie, taking ideas from wherever he found them and moulding them to his will. Wagner was particularly adept at appropriating other composers' ideas and then making them seem like original thoughts. The composer to whom he owes most is Liszt (whose daughter he married). Liszt was not an opera composer, but his piano music and orchestral works are astonishingly ambitious in ways that have much in common with Wagner's approach to opera. The two composers learned from each other, not only in scale of ambition but in method.

It was Liszt who developed the principle of the transformation of themes. Themes recur throughout a work, and are transformed to create what seem like new themes, so as to provide richness of material with a sense of unity over a substantial piece of music. Wagner took this principle to create the idea of the *Leitmotif* ('guiding motif') in his operas. Each character and feature of an opera – Siegfried, the sword, death, Valhalla – has its own motif that recurs in the orchestra whenever the character appears or the feature is to be evoked. The most important motifs are related by transformation, so that, for example, the mysterious motif symbolizing The Ring is transformed by a change of harmony into the noble motif of Valhalla, the seat of the gods. Over this orchestral tapestry, the voices sing in a sort of stately recitative, without the conventional set pieces of arias and ensembles.

As a composer for orchestra, Wagner started with a great advantage over Liszt. Unlike Liszt, who concentrated on his career as a virtuoso pianist into his thirties, Wagner was already developing his orchestral skills from his early twenties in posts as a conductor. His approach to conducting laid the foundations for the development of the modern conductor, and particularly for the role of the conductor as interpreter of the composer's intentions. Wagner's performances of Beethoven's symphonies were widely regarded as having revealed possibilities in the music in quite a new way. In particular, his performance of Beethoven's Ninth Symphony in Dresden in 1846 was a triumph, demonstrating that this seemingly impossible work could, contrary to the general opinion of the time, be performed successfully.

The influence of Wagner on later generations was immense, and is not over yet. The use of recurring motifs and transformations became widespread in opera and orchestral music after Wagner and Liszt's use of them, and this applies across music of many different cultures – Richard Strauss, Debussy, Messiaen, Smetana, Dvořák, Puccini. The orchestra of Strauss and Smetana may sound richly 'post-Wagnerian', whereas Debussy's subtle orchestral textures might seem positively 'anti-Wagnerian', but the debt to Wagner in all cases is unmistakable.

Sheer scale and ambition have their echoes in the symphonies of Mahler and Bruckner, Schoenberg's *Gurrelieder*, the *Turangalîla Symphony* by Messiaen, and the convention-busting musical landscapes of Ives and Varèse. There are dark sides to this influence: Wagner's all-conquering ambitions were an obvious magnet for figures promoting German cultural and political aggrandisement, and it is only in recent decades that his music (and that of his most ardent disciple, Bruckner) have been able to cast off the resulting shadows.

The harmonies of Wagner's *Tristan* and *Parsifal*, highly chromatic and full of unresolving dissonances, led in different directions. Richard Strauss took the dissonances to an extreme in *Salome* and *Elektra*, Schoenberg and his pupils went from Wagnerian chromaticism through atonality to the 'emancipation of the dissonance' in twelve-note composition. In France, Wagner's chromaticism became dense and rich in Franck, concentrated and austere in late Fauré, evanescent and floating in Debussy and Ravel.

Not just opera, therefore, but the entire history of orchestral music in the last 150 years is saturated with Wagner's influence. Most of what he composed for orchestra is embedded in his mighty operas. Overtures and preludes from them are often played in the concert hall: *Rienzi, The Flying Dutchman, Tannhäuser, Lohengrin, Die Meistersinger*. The Prelude to *Tristan und Isolde* is often paired with an orchestral version of Isolde's *Liebestod* that ends the opera. But this is a terrible thing to do: it makes no sense to bolt the anguished passion of the beginning onto the serene climax of the end without the intervening three and a half hours of tragic development that has made the transition from the Prelude to the *Liebestod* possible.

In the early years of his career Wagner wrote a symphony and a number of concert overtures, of which the most significant is the *Faust Overture*. But the only free-standing orchestral work from his mature years is a piece originally composed for a private occasion, the *Siegfried Idyll*.

SIEGFRIED IDYLL
Duration: approx. 20 minutes

On Christmas morning 1870, members of the Zürich Tonhalle Orchestra and conductor Hans Richter assembled on the stairs of the Wagner home in Switzerland. They were there to present a birthday greeting to Wagner's wife, Cosima. She wrote in her diary, 'As I awoke, my ear caught a sound, which swelled fuller and fuller; no longer could I imagine myself to be dreaming, music was sounding, and such music! When it died away, Richard came into my room with the five children and offered me the score of the symphonic birthday poem. I was in tears, but so was all the rest of the household.'[1]

Cosima was the daughter of Liszt, and the former wife of conductor Hans von Bülow. She had left him for Wagner four years earlier – 'If it had been anyone other than Wagner, I would have shot him,' said Bülow. Two of the five children that Cosima mentions were from her marriage to Bülow; the other three, aged five, three, and eighteen months, were Wagner's. Cosima and Wagner had married in August 1869, so this birthday was the first since their marriage. Wagner's birthday Idyll was intended to remain private. But eight years later, he decided that money was to be made by adapting it for orchestra and publishing it.

Wagner had originally called it 'Triebschen Idyll with Fidi's birdsong and the orange sunrise'. Tribschen (or Triebschen) is the area of Lucerne where the Wagners lived, and Fidi was the parents' pet name for Siegfried, their third child; retitling the piece *Siegfried Idyll* was logical, because of the music's links to the hero of *The Ring*, after whom they had named the boy.

The original scoring is for a small chamber orchestra: flute, oboe, two clarinets, bassoon, two horns, trumpet, and string quartet with double bass. But despite the intimacy of the ensemble and the gentleness of the music, it is a movement on a large scale: surprisingly, it is five minutes longer than Liszt's *Les Préludes*. Wagner greatly admired Liszt's symphonic poems, and the *Siegfried Idyll* is like a symphonic poem for chamber orchestra.

The work opens with music that had begun six years earlier as a string quartet that Wagner never completed. He then reworked it as one of the most tender moments in *The Ring*. In Act III of *Siegfried*, which Wagner had recently composed, the hero fearlessly breaks through the ring of flames to wake Brünnhilde from her sleep. She declares, to this music shared with the *Siegfried Idyll*, 'Ewig war ich, ewig bin ich . . .': 'Always, always, I was and am in a state of sweet, blissful longing, but always for your sake.'

The first violin gently leaps an octave and plays a meditative melody in E major incorporating a rocking figure, while a counterpoint of the other strings descends below (without double bass). After a few bars, the music comes to rest, and begins again, with the first violin leaping higher than before. Again it comes to rest after a few bars, and again it restarts at a higher pitch. This time the music unfolds at greater length, and the violin line rises passionately, before settling once more (the double bass joins in here). Now the first violin returns to the opening octave leap, and as the strings continue to meditate on the theme, the woodwind enter for the first time. The falling phrase that they play is another quotation: the 'slumber' motif from Act III of *Die Walküre*, which appears as Wotan prepares Brünnhilde for her long sleep surrounded by a circle of fire (it reappears in Act III of *Siegfried*, combined with the first theme, as here).

Wind and strings together rise to a climax. As it fades, a new theme appears. A poignant falling interval passes between violin and lower strings. The woodwind answer with a ruminating little melody. Although these are new elements, they derive from the first theme – the falling intervals invert the opening leap, and the rumination is a version of the violin's rocking figure. Further musing on these different elements builds to a climax. It falls away, and the oboe plays a simple little tune, a German lullaby, 'Sleep, little baby, sleep'. This is interleaved with reminiscences of the first theme as the music comes to rest, bringing the first section of the *Idyll* to a close.

We have arrived in B major – a thoroughly conventional key at this point for a work that began in E major. But now, as a sort of development section begins, the key is thrown into doubt. Mysterious arpeggios and trills, evoking for a moment the fire and forests of the *Ring*, lead into a song-like theme on the woodwind in A flat major. This is another quotation from Act III of *Siegfried*, as Brünnhilde continues with the words, 'O Siegfried, Herrlicher! Hort der Welt!' ('O Siegfried, glorious one! Treasure of the world!') The theme develops and builds up, culminating in a cascading clarinet arpeggio. As the strings continue with this theme, continually changing key, the oboe enters with the first theme in counterpoint. These two elements now combine to drive the music on to the biggest climax so far.

From it emerges a horn call in C major, taken from the episode in *Götterdämmerung* known as 'Siegfried's Rhine Journey'. Above it, flute and clarinet interject a fragment of the song of the wood-bird from Act II of *Siegfried*. From here, the music builds to its central climax, combining in counterpoint three elements: the opening theme, the 'slumber' motif, and the woodwind theme ('O Siegfried, Herrliche!'). At the climax itself, the trumpet enters for the first and only time, with a fanfare that is a simplified version of the call of the wood-bird. The trumpet part was played at the first performance by the conductor Hans Richter, who was a horn player.

From this point, the music retraces its steps in a reprise of some of the earlier elements. The theme with poignant falling intervals returns. Then a climax from the first part of the piece is revisited. Eventually, the music finds its way back to the opening theme, by now firmly in E major over a sustained bass note. The tempo slows, and there are reminiscences of the horn call, the song of the wood-bird, and the lullaby. The music is reluctant to tear itself away. The tempo slows further, and the *Idyll* comes to an end in a mood of lingering tenderness, evoking the 'sweet, blissful longing' of Brünnhilde's love-song to Siegfried.

In the first edition of the score, Wagner included a poem to Cosima, and her 'self-sacrificing, noble will':

We nurtured within the bounds of our home
The quiet joy that here became music.

WILLIAM WALTON
(1902–83)

Walton was born in Oldham, Lancashire. Both his parents were singers and singing teachers, and his father was the choirmaster at the local church. When William joined the choir, around the age of five, his father would rap his knuckles if he sang a wrong note. It was a tough upbringing, with little money in the house, but Walton was later grateful that his parents encouraged him in the development of his musical talent.

The first of many strokes of luck in his career occurred when he was ten, and his father spotted an advertisement for probationer choristers at Christ Church, Oxford. He won a scholarship, and spent six years at the choir school. At first, 'It was horrid. The problem was that I had a broad Lancashire accent and the other boys used to sit on my head until I spoke the same as they did, properly, as they thought.'[1]

In 1918 he was admitted to Christ Church as an undergraduate. But he left two years later without completing a degree, having three times failed Responsions (an exam required of all students, which included questions in Greek, Latin, and maths).

In another stroke of luck, Walton had met Sacheverell Sitwell at Oxford, and through him Edith and Osbert. They invited Walton to live with them in their artistic and bohemian house in Chelsea, and even arranged an allowance for him so that he would have time to compose. He stayed with them for over a decade, attended the Russian Ballet, met Stravinsky and Gershwin, heard jazz at the Savoy Hotel, and visited Italy with the Sitwells.

Just as he was becoming established as a composer, he received a third stroke of luck. Samuel and Elizabeth Courtauld, prominent patrons of the arts, were great admirers of Walton, and when Elizabeth died in 1931 she left him a legacy that provided him with an annual income of £500 for life.

Walton never attended a music college, but he had the language of choral music in his veins from his earliest years. His life with the Sitwells brought him up to date with the latest continental trends. At the age of twenty-one, he wrote a string quartet of fearsome modernity that earned the praise of Alban Berg. The same year Walton had a scandalous success with *Façade*. This is an entertainment for speaker and small ensemble that sets surreal poems of Edith Sitwell against music with a broad spectrum of modern influences, including *Pierrot Lunaire*, *The Soldier's Tale*, jazz, and popular dance of the early twenties.

Façade chimed with a taste among a section of the public for outrageous but sophisticated satire (like Satie and Cocteau's *Parade*, which Walton had attended in 1919). But Walton was a reluctant *enfant terrible*, and soon developed a mature style that defies easy comparisons. His first success on a grand scale was the oratorio *Belshazzar's Feast*, which was the highlight of the Leeds Festival in 1931. He became a pillar of the patriotic music establishment, writing coronation marches and music for the wartime film, *The First of the Few* (from which Walton extracted the 'Spitfire' Prelude and Fugue).

He worked hard and sometimes fitfully to forge his style, and the result treads confidently through the minefields of musical history and the twentieth century. As Constant Lambert put it in the mid-1930s, 'Walton . . . by using material that can be related to Handel on the one hand and to Prokofieff on the other, addresses an international audience in easy terms without losing his national and personal qualities.'[2] And those personal qualities, as with Elgar, included a vein of lyrical melancholy lying behind the urbane and confident exterior.

SYMPHONY NO. 1 IN B FLAT MINOR
Duration: approx. 44 minutes

Allegro assai
Presto, con malizia
Andante con malincolia
Maestoso – Brioso ed ardentemente – Vivacissimo – Maestoso

After the tremendous success of his *Belshazzar's Feast* at the Leeds Festival in 1931, Walton began to plan a symphony, at the suggestion of the conductor, Sir Hamilton Harty. Early in 1932 he wrote that he was 'trying to start on a symphony. What a fool I am, treading where so many angels have come a "cropper".'[3]

The score is dedicated to the Baroness Imma Doernberg, widow of Baron Hans-Karl Doernberg, who had died soon after their marriage in 1923. Walton had first met her in 1929, and in August that year he declared, 'I am now fixed up with Imma for life.' Their love affair lasted five years, but marriage never became a serious possibility. Walton, until the lucky windfall of a legacy in 1932, had no money, and, with the rise of the Nazis, Imma found herself a refugee from Germany with no prospects. Staying with friends in Switzerland, Imma was suffering from a serious infection, and Walton wrote, 'life has been very worrying, and such things as symphonies have fallen into the background'.⁴ But there was more than money and illness behind their problems. Many years later, Walton said in an interview about Imma, 'She was a very great friend of mine over several years, and this symphony is about a fearful quarrel we had in the middle of this idyllic … sort of business, and I wrote this rather awful tempestuous work – and it was really all her fault.'⁵ In August 1934 they agreed that they would do better to remain friends than to marry.

At that stage, the symphony still consisted of just three movements, and the premiere, already delayed, went ahead without the finale in December of that year, played by the London Symphony Orchestra under Hamilton Harty. Walton, in another interview much later, said that the symphony's emotional content was to do with 'frustration, in love actually, and it's why I stopped at the end of the slow movement and I couldn't go on until I got a new outlook on the whole thing which was created by another person'.⁶ That 'other person' was Alice Wimborne, the wife of a wealthy industrialist, whom Walton had met through the Sitwells. She and her husband led what would nowadays be called an 'open marriage', each carrying on affairs. Alice was drawn to relationships with younger men, and when she and Walton became lovers, she was fifty-four and Walton was thirty-two. She hosted soirées at the family house in London. As Osbert Sitwell put it, 'Her great beauty, subtle and full of glamour though it was, and the fact that she was the wife of one of the richest men in England, were apt to blind people equally to her political intelligence, interest and experience.'⁷ She inspired Walton to keep going on his symphony, and to compose the last movement. The complete work finally received its premiere in November 1935, with the BBC Symphony Orchestra under Harty.

The symphony opens very quietly with a timpani roll. Four horns enter one by one, building a chord. An urgent repeating rhythmic figure starts up in the second violins. Over it, an oboe plays a plaintively simple melody, consisting of long notes ending in anxious little flicks and turns, which will become important motifs throughout the movement. The texture begins to thicken as other instruments enter. The repeating rhythmic figure moves to the bass, the cellos introduce an element of boldness, violins and violas play an agitated staccato pattern. While all this activity is accumulating, the harmony moves slowly, one long bass note at a time, the harmonic twists creating tension. All of these elements in combination point to Sibelius as Walton's main influence – it could almost be the start of one of Sibelius's evocative journeys drawn from Finnish legend (and Sibelius's reputation in Britain was at its height in the 1930s). But this is no mere imitation. Walton may be deploying Sibelius's method, but he does so with his own voice.

A first climax is reached. Violins and cellos in unison sing a broad new theme, which slowly rises from the agitated surrounding texture, becoming more anguished, and then breaking off. The agitated elements continue. Then cellos and violas attempt another powerful melody, full of yearning leaps. This too is interrupted, and the agitation builds to another climax. Fragments of the different themes continue to sustain the tension, until one crescendo culminates in the first 'flicking' motif, hammered out. At last this does allow a release (though on a very Sibelius-like unresolved chord), and the motifs from the opening lose their agitation and become delicate and lyrical. This marks the end of the first section of the movement.

A high bassoon begins a sustained passage of meditation, which brings together elements from the various motifs and themes, at first gently and simply, then with greater force and complexity. The violins build a powerful melody, which falls away to more delicate musing. Momentum begins to re-establish itself. Over a long passage with the tension rising and the harmonies searching for a way forward, the music builds in a series of waves to the biggest climax of the movement. With an immense struggle, and the opening motif again hammered out, the resolution is found, and as the climax fades the music finds itself back where it started. The opening motif on violins is now accompanied by a newly insistent bass rhythm, led by the tuba, and the music grows much more quickly than before. Another climax is reached, the harmonies become increasingly acerbic, and the tension is finally released into a gallop to the end.

The second movement has rather the character of a Beethoven scherzo, re-imagined in the light of Dukas and Holst: the fleeting quality has something in common with Holst's 'Mercury', and the 'malizia' of the heading sounds like that of a spiteful, mischievous spirit, as in *The Sorcerer's Apprentice*. But again, the recipe is Walton's own, and he is in complete command of his sophisticated musical language. Traditional scherzo rhythms are broken up by frequent disruptions of the metre. And the harmonies, which bring together traditional modes with pungent touches of dissonance, are used to create a sense of momentum – often with sudden changes of direction – just as in the first movement it was the command of harmonies that built the long paragraphs. The scherzo is in one continuous sweep, which barely touches the ground. But there is a ghost of a traditional 'trio' halfway through, when the strings seem transfixed by a nervous little rhythm, as if too terrified to move. This recurs for a moment shortly before the end (another Beethoven-like touch).

'Andante con malincolia' is the marking for the slow movement, an Anglicization of the Italian ('malinconia' is the Italian word for melancholy). A lonely flute plays a melody over soft, sustained horns and strings (Walton had originally intended a faster version of this theme for the first movement). Clarinet and oboes continue, bringing a touch of almost French warmth and piquancy – Walton sounds like Ravel for a moment. The melody unfolds and develops, moving to the strings.

When it returns to the clarinet, it acquires an upward gesture and a falling arpeggio. This new idea passes to flute, oboe, and strings, evolving as it goes, and enriched by lyrical counterpoints. It acquires a dark and increasing intensity, which culminates in a forceful return to the opening theme on the violins and cellos. The last phrase of the melody moves to high violins, with the upward gesture in counterpoint below, a moment that is almost Elgarian in its sweet nostalgia. From this point, over a sustained bass note, the power gradually builds until it reaches a mighty climax. As it falls away, the violins return sorrowfully to the upward gesture, and the movement ends as it began, with a final phrase from a solitary flute.

What could follow this sequence of three intense movements? After a long delay, Walton came up with a finale of unbuttoned celebration that has more in common with his overture *Portsmouth Point* and his oratorio *Belshazzar's Feast* than with the preceding movements of the symphony. It opens with a majestic introduction full of assertive gestures, like an updating of the dotted rhythms of the old French Overture. Suddenly the tempo increases, and what was majestic becomes energetic and brilliant, fulfilling the marking that means 'ardent and full of life'. The gestures continue to be assertive, and as they come together they take on the jazz-inspired rhythmic energy of Walton's earlier works.

The opening paragraph runs its course, and then breaks into a passage of fugue. With its abrupt phrases and its opening of rising fourths it could easily be by Hindemith, a composer Walton greatly admired. This quirkiness saves the fugue from sounding academic, and soon it is interrupted by a brass fanfare, and the counterpoint becomes more loosely energetic.

It is interrupted by a quiet passage of calmer counterpoint in the woodwind, as if the boisterous fugue has encountered a procession of monks. The energy returns, quietly at first, and the opening of the fugue subject is used to build a great crescendo. It reaches a grand climax, as if it is about to return to the majesty of the introduction. Melodic shapes and chords from the first part of the movement do indeed return, but now in a lively three-time (vivacissimo). Other elements return, including the 'monk-like' idea, which for a moment seems about to turn into another fugue.

From a low point, the music starts to build, over another of Walton's favourite unchanging bass notes. A climax is reached, fades, and with a sudden impulse throws us back to the majestic introduction, reinforced with drums and gong, and tugging harmonies in tremolando strings. There is a moment of quiet, then the grandeur reasserts itself. The symphony ends in a blaze of triumph, finishing (like *Belshazzar's Feast* and, before it, Sibelius's Fifth Symphony) with a series of hammer strokes.

VIOLA CONCERTO
Duration: approx. 26 minutes

Andante comodo
Vivo, con molto preciso
Allegro moderato

It was Sir Thomas Beecham who suggested that Walton should write a viola concerto for the great English viola player, Lionel Tertis. But Tertis at first refused to play it, and it was Paul Hindemith (a distinguished violist as well as composer) who played the premiere in 1929, with Walton conducting. Many years later, Tertis wrote, 'With shame and contrition I admit that when the composer offered me the first performance I declined it. I was unwell at the time; but what is also true is that I had not learnt to appreciate Walton's style. The innovations in his musical language, which now [in 1974] seem so logical and so truly in the mainstream of music, then struck me as far-fetched. It took me time to realise what a tower of strength in the literature of the viola is this concerto . . .'[8]

Walton dedicated the concerto 'to Christabel'. Christabel McLaren, a friend of Osbert Sitwell, was happily married to Henry McLaren, who later became Lord Aberconway. She was a beautiful society hostess and patroness of the arts, and Walton was in love with her at this time, treating her as his confidante in his letters.

Constant Lambert, in his often acerbic book on modern music, *Music Ho! A Study of Music in Decline* (1934), wrote of Walton's Viola Concerto: 'One of the most thoughtful and sincerely conceived works of recent years, it refuses to be put into any category from the point of view either of technique or tendency. It is neither English nor cosmopolitan, neo-classical nor neo-romantic. It is just that least sensational and most satisfying of all things, a finished and well-balanced work of art.'[9]

Walton revised the orchestration in 1961, reducing the number of wind instruments and adding a harp, and this is the version that he much preferred and is most often played. The addition of the harp has the effect of softening (in quality, not just volume) many of the textures, and emphasizing the concerto's element of nostalgia.

An elegiac quality is established straight away as the viola sings a long, yearning melody. There are echoes of Elgar's Cello Concerto, whose first movement is in the same, gently swinging metre (9/8), and of the opening of Prokofiev's recent First Violin Concerto. But the bittersweet harmonies are Walton's own, encapsulated after a few bars in a little three-note figure in the flutes that rocks between major and minor. As the viola becomes more agitated, this major-minor figure is reiterated in the woodwind, and passes to the viola in two-part chords as it calms for a moment.

The viola takes up a new theme that swings across the beat and becomes uncertain in metre. Soon, this develops greater energy as the viola plays increasingly virtuosic passages, culminating in hammered chords. There is a burst of full orchestra, and the viola develops the second theme in a rich line of two-part chords. A new rhythmic figure injects another burst of energy, and more virtuoso solo passages culminate in the only substantial orchestral tutti in the movement, with the melancholy opening theme transformed into a sharp little tune in the woodwind. (Each movement of the concerto culminates in a powerful orchestral tutti: Walton thereby solves the problem of how to provide a strong spine to the whole work and yet avoid overpowering the mellow tones of the viola.)

The orchestra reaches a climax and falls away. Over a timpani roll and low tremolo, the viola returns to the nostalgia of the opening with a moment of meditation, like a brief homage to the accompanied cadenza in Elgar's Violin Concerto. As this meditation dissolves into running triplet patterns, an oboe enters with the opening theme, passing it to the flute. The viola line rises to a reminder of the second theme, culminating in yearning repetitions of the major-minor rocking chords. These persist to the end, until we are left with a fading chord of A minor.

The second movement is a scherzo, with the quirkily ungrammatical marking, 'Vivo, con molto preciso' ('preciso' means 'precise', not 'precision'). The brittle theme, beginning with rising fourths, brings Walton close here to Hindemith (as Hindemith himself would certainly have recognised as he played the premiere). A second theme, a little fanfare that first appears on trumpets, takes us back to the French-inspired cheek of Façade. The movement culminates in a long, joyful orchestral tutti, which is not only the climax of this movement, but a vital moment of release at the centre of a work that begins and ends in melancholy. Some of this joyful spirit lingers to the end of the movement, which is thrown playfully into the air.

The finale begins with a rather dandyish theme on bassoon, as if Falstaff were remembering his youth. The theme becomes a little more determined as the viola takes it up, and then the woodwind subject it to a moment of earnest, Hindemith-like counterpoint. A new, anxious idea appears, whose reiterated little motif seems to be searching for something. Over it, a sweeping melody pulls us back towards the nostalgia of the first movement, and the viola responds by returning to a line of lyrical two-part chords.

Soon, the mood is broken by a sudden return to the opening tempo and the first theme. From this point, the music is continually torn between the two opposing characters – the self-confident energy of the first theme and the powerful lyrical pull of the nostalgic legacy from the first movement. The different elements alternate and interweave, twice punctuated by brief orchestral tutti.

Eventually, a third orchestral passage settles over a sustained bass note, with the first theme forming, at half speed, the subject for a fugue. At first this might seem like a disappointingly academic moment, but it soon becomes clear that this is a crucial point of the work. The harmonies twist, the tension rises, and the music builds to a mighty *fff* climax, at which it bursts and settles once more (at such a moment, it is easy to understand how Walton was able to become a fine composer of film scores).

Now the concerto enters its epilogue, a long meditation in which, once again, Walton echoes the accompanied cadenza at the end of Elgar's Violin Concerto, with a hint also of the dying Don Quixote from Richard Strauss's tone poem. It begins with the viola reprising the opening theme from the first movement, with the first theme of the finale forming an accompanying pattern below. As the viola rises higher and higher, it brings in other reminiscences. Now the strings take up the rocking major-minor motif. The viola rises to a final, deeply elegiac outpouring. In the final bars, chords sink down for a final minor-to-major, and as the viola holds the A major chord, pizzicato strings quietly play A minor, leaving the music in a mood of lingering, bittersweet contradiction.

CARL MARIA VON WEBER
(1786–1826)

Weber's importance was primarily as an opera composer and director. He headed the opera houses in Berlin and Dresden, and was a leading figure in the efforts to establish German opera as a central part of German culture, which had for many years been dominated by Italian opera. Weber's own *Der Freischütz*, first staged in Berlin in 1821, was a major landmark. His pupil and biographer, Julius Benedict, observed that, with the exception of the operas of Spohr, which had never become popular, 'Since Beethoven's *Fidelio*, only feeble unmeaning works had been produced in Germany'.[1] *Der Freischütz* was immensely influential in the development of High German Romanticism: it is difficult to imagine Wagner's evocation of the supernatural and heroic in the *Ring* without the example of Weber. Most famous is the scene in the Wolf's Glen from *Der Freischütz*, in which magic bullets are forged with the assistance of demonic powers. The overture to the opera is often performed as a concert piece.

There is nothing in Weber's orchestral music to rival his operas. But there are concertos for clarinet that show off the range and colour of the instrument very effectively, and a brilliant *Konzertstück* for Piano and Orchestra, written for Weber himself to play.

DER FREISCHÜTZ, OVERTURE
Duration: approx. 10 minutes

Mozart and Beethoven had already led the way towards the establishment of opera in German to rival the dominance of Italian opera: Mozart with *Die Entführung aus dem Serail* (*The Abduction from the Seraglio*) and *The Magic Flute*, and Beethoven with *Fidelio*. But it was Weber who succeeded in creating an opera that was serious, in tune with the themes of Romanticism, deeply German in its themes, and brilliantly successful. This was *Der Freischütz*

(*The Marksman*, or *The Freeshooter*). Its overture is unusually dramatic, because Weber, perhaps taking his cue from Beethoven's third *Leonore* overture, creates a piece of music that is not just a scene-setter for the drama, but is like a miniature summary of the opera. Rossini was to draw on this method in his equally famous overture to *William Tell* (1829).

The plot of *Der Freischütz* centres on Max, a young forester, who is in love with Agathe, the old head forester's daughter. A shooting contest is to be held, and the winner will become the new head forester and marry Agathe. Fearing that he will lose, Max is persuaded to make a pact with the devil to ensure that he will win. In the most famous scene in the opera, magic bullets are forged at night in the Wolf's Glen. In the final contest, Max seems to have been tricked into shooting Agathe with a bullet guided by the devil. But the devil is foiled as the bullet is deflected by her bridal wreath. After explanations, recriminations, and forgiveness, the repentant Max escapes banishment, and is allowed to marry Agathe.

In an interview with his biographer, J. C. Lobe, Weber talked at length about the two most important elements of the opera, and the instrumental colours he chose to evoke them. The first element is the forest and hunting life, so strongly associated with German culture and literature. For this, Weber used horns, drawing on traditional tunes though not obviously quoting them. For the second element, Weber quotes a line from Max's aria: 'Dark powers ensnare me': 'I gave a great deal of thought to the question of what was the right principal colouring for this sinister element. Naturally it had to be a dark, gloomy colour – the lowest register of the violins, violas and basses, particularly the lowest register of the clarinet, which seemed especially suitable for depicting the sinister, then the mournful sound of the bassoon, the lowest notes of the horns, the hollow roll of drums or single hollow stroke on them. When you go through the score of the opera, you will find hardly any number in which this sombre principal colour is not noticeable . . .'[2] All of these instrumental colours are to be found in the overture.

The Adagio introduction opens with two simple phrases, which each begin with a long note, rise an octave and then fall gently. Weber gives them portentous expression by starting *pp* with a crescendo that reaches forte at the octave leap. Then, over a soft string accompaniment, the horns play a gentle melody in four parts, just the sort of warm chorale one might associate with relaxation around the fire after a day's hunting. This being composed before the new valve horns came into general use, Weber scores for two pairs of valveless horns, one pitched in C (the key of the piece), the other in F. At the end of the introduction, where the music shifts to C minor, one pair of horns changes from F to E flat, to give the vital note E flat, the third of the new key. As the horns finish their chorale, we hear for the first time Weber's sinister orchestration: low pianissimo tremolo on violins and violas (the chord here is the 'diminished seventh', which was to become a cliché of tension and agitation in the hands of Liszt and others), taps of timpani and pizzicato basses, and yearning phrases on the cellos, rising to an intense *ff* and falling away.

Now begins the Molto vivace, quiet but very agitated, with a rising cello line on the beat and the violins syncopated against it. This is then clarified by the clarinets into a melody that is taken from the concluding section of Max's great aria in Act 1, at the words, 'But dark powers ensnare me'. Here in the overture, it builds to a stormy passage for full orchestra.

As it subsides, moving into a major key, the horns blast out a chord, and over shuddering strings a clarinet plays a haunting solo of sustained notes, taken from later in Max's aria where he sings, 'Does no ray of light shine through these nights?' This leads on to a warm melody on violins and clarinet, taken from Agathe's aria in Act 2, singing of her delight as Max approaches. It concludes with joyful running quavers, which quickly turn back to the agitated music from Max's aria.

Weber now leads this material in new directions, pitting the agitated music against occasional glimpses of Agathe's aria. Then we are back at the opening of the Molto vivace. But instead of a full reprise, Weber touches on the opening passage, reaches a climax, and then arrives dramatically at another shuddering diminished seventh chord, and the yearning cello phrases that ended the introduction, now on violins with bassoon.

The music sinks down to silence. Then a chord of C major bursts out on full orchestra, fortissimo. Weber returns to the music of Agathe's aria, as it will return at the triumphant finale of the opera.

The tumultuous applause that greeted this overture at the premiere was such that Weber was obliged to perform it all again, before the audience had heard a note of singing.

KONZERTSTÜCK IN F MINOR
Duration: approx. 16 minutes

Larghetto affetuoso –
Allegro passionato –
Tempo di marcia –
Presto gioioso

Weber was a very fine pianist, with enormous hands that he was happy to exploit in the works that he wrote for himself to play. He took the latest developments in piano technique and developed them in ways that would later influence Mendelssohn, Chopin, and Liszt. His way of decorating a melody, which is both extravagant and highly expressive, was a stimulus for both Mendelssohn and Chopin. And he showed Liszt the way forward with spectacular effects including glissandi in octaves (much easier to achieve on the pianos of Weber's day, with their lighter and shallower keys, than on the modern piano), and rapid leaps that get wider and wider. Liszt himself used to add extra difficulties and embellishments when performing this piece, converting the glissandi into rapid double octaves, in which he excelled.[3] Weber also gave Liszt in this 'Concert Piece' a successful model for a concerto played without a break: Liszt was to follow this example in his own Second Piano Concerto.

Weber was planning a Concerto in F minor in 1815, as he revealed in a letter of that year: 'But as concertos in the minor without definite, evocative ideas seldom work with the public, I have instinctively inserted into the whole thing a kind of story whose thread will connect and define its character … Allegro, Parting. Adagio, Lament. Finale, Profoundest misery, consolation, reunion, jubilation.'[4] These plans were put on one side for several years as Weber pursued his career in the opera house. But in May 1821, with *Der Freischütz* about to reach the stage, he arrived in Berlin for the premiere bringing with him the sketches of the concerto that was to become his *Konzertstück*. Weber's pupil, Julius Benedict, in his biography of him, remembers that Weber spent the morning of the premiere of *Der Freischütz* putting the finishing touches to his *Konzertstück*:

Entering the room where I was sitting with his wife, and placing himself at the piano, he unrolled to our enchanted ears a musical poem of which he gave us the following outline:

– 'The lady sits in her tower: she gazes sadly into the distance. Her knight has been for years in the Holy Land: shall she ever see him again? Battles have been fought; but no news of him who is so dear to her. In vain have been all her prayers. A fearful vision rises to her mind; – her knight is lying on the battlefield, deserted and alone; his heart's blood is ebbing fast away. Could she be by his side! – Could she but die with him! She falls exhausted and senseless. But hark! What is that distant sound? What glimmers in the sunlight from the wood? What are those forms approaching? Knights and squires with the cross of the Crusades, banner waving, acclamations of the people; and there! – it is he! She sinks into his arms. Love is triumphant. Happiness without end. The very woods and waves sing the song of love; a thousand voices proclaim its victory.' This was the admirable *Concert-Stück* in F minor, which, interpreted by him as by nobody else, left an indelible remembrance. He was certainly one of the greatest pianists who ever lived.[5]

This high-flown narrative was just the latest version of a classic form that can be traced all the way back to Homer's *Odyssey*, and had been most recently used by Beethoven as the basis for his Piano Sonata, Opus 81a, 'Les Adieux'. Beethoven simply labels his movements, 'The Farewell', 'The Absence', and 'The Return', a shape evoked by nothing more Romantic than the departure of his patron and pupil, the Archduke Rudolf. Weber elevates this formula to a quasi-operatic medieval scenario. And, however accurate Benedict's memory of the detailed narrative may have been, the outline of it was well known after Weber's death. The critic Henri Blachard repeated it in a review of a performance by Marie Pleyel in Paris in 1845, observing that Weber had indicated 'a return from the crusade' on the title page of the score, though this did not survive in later editions.[6]

The orchestral introduction could be the prelude to an aria. A solemn chorus of woodwind gives way to the strings. Quietly they lament, rising phrase by phrase, and for a moment warm into a major key. But the mood returns to sadness, and the piano enters. After a brief cadenza, it plays the wind chorus, now as a sustained melody accompanied by dry chords, like pizzicato. The strings enter as before, and the piano begins to elaborate a counterpoint. This soon develops into a wide-ranging fantasy, full of flourishes, some bold and dramatic, others delicate filigree. Tense tremolando strings accompany the piano to a resolving cadence.

From here, a pattern of arpeggios accelerates in a crescendo to a pregnant chord. The wind enter, and we are propelled into the Allegro passionato. The piano's theme alternates falling arpeggios taken from the earlier pattern and bold chords, together with other, agitated patterns. This leads to a fiery orchestral tutti. After another agitated passage from the piano, and another tutti, the piano moves to a major key for a more lyrical theme. This lyricism is combined with continued agitation – runs, leaps, sudden changes of direction. One can imagine Weber's heroine pacing the room restlessly. The fiery opening of the Allegro returns, and becomes wilder and wilder, until it falls away.

The melancholy sound of a bassoon breaks the silence. There is a moment of anxious stillness. Then the distant sound of a march is heard on clarinets and horns (Tempo di marcia). Oboes and bassoons join in. And then the piano, as if waking from its swoon, bursts in with the famous octave glissando, and the whole orchestra takes up the march. The piano responds by breaking into joyful running passages (con molto agitazione), which lead with a trill straight into the final Presto gioioso.

This is the greatest challenge in the whole piece, full of rapid octaves and cascading patterns, but in a dancing rhythm and to be played, Weber instructs, both with great fire (fuoco) and with great lightness (leggierezza). Only a pianist of surpassing skill and judgement can convey what Weber intended: joy that can scarcely be contained.

ANTON WEBERN
(1883–1945)

Born in Vienna, Webern studied musicology at Vienna University from 1902. Shortly before entering the university, he had visited Bayreuth where he had attended performances of *Parsifal* and *The Flying Dutchman*. Webern's early works are in high-Romantic, post-Wagnerian style – *Im Sommerwind*, an idyll for large orchestra, written in 1904, sounds like Richard Strauss at his most voluptuous and orgasmic. So far, he was following the path of many talented young Austrian and German composers at the turn of the century. But all that was to change when, also in 1904, Webern began four years of study with Schoenberg. He became Schoenberg's most devoted pupil, developing his own, highly ordered way of composing, first moving towards atonality, and then adopting Schoenberg's twelve-note technique (see introduction to Schoenberg). He was one of the most intensely intellectual composers, and most of his music still presents enormous challenges to the listener a century after it was written.

But it would be a mistake to think of Webern as a cold intellectual. His music, complex though it is, has roots in the deepest emotions. In September 1906 his mother died from diabetes, two months after Webern had graduated with a PhD in musicology from Vienna University. This catastrophe had a profound effect on his life and music over the following years. To his teacher, Schoenberg, he wrote six years later, 'I would like to tell you that the grief for my mother grows within me more and more. Almost all my compositions have originated in her memory.'[1] And to Alban Berg he specified that, with few exceptions, 'all of my works from the Passacaglia on relate to the death of my mother'. These include not only the Passacaglia, Opus 1, but also 'the first orchestral pieces [Opus 6], and the second set (with a few exceptions) [Opus 10]'. And the associations between music and life experience are, for Webern, quite specific: 'an experience goes around in me, until it becomes music, which quite definitely has to do with the experience. Often down to the details.'[2]

Intimately connected with mourning for his mother were memories of the family estate, the Preglhof, in the southern Austrian countryside of Carinthia, where he spent most summers until his father sold it in 1912, when Webern was twenty-eight. In the same letter to Schoenberg, following the sale of the estate, Webern wrote, 'I must tell you how, almost daily, the longing for our estate simply overwhelms me, especially now in summer. I grieve for this estate as for a dear departed ... Often I wish I could go there and acquire it again. I now see everything in a transfigured light. And in my memory it appears to me like a lost paradise ... The seclusion, the quiet, the house, the forests, the garden, and the cemetery.'[3] For Webern, this was more than just nostalgia. He had a deeply conservative attachment to the countryside, the people, to Austria as a homeland, indeed motherland.

After he finished his studies with Schoenberg, Webern moved towards an almost completely atonal language, composing songs and pieces in a highly condensed style, each often lasting a minute or less. The concentration in these miniatures was to reach such intensity that Schoenberg wrote, in an introduction to Webern's Bagatelles, Opus 9, for string quartet, 'Think what self-denial it takes to cut a long story so short. A glance can always be spun out into a poem, a sigh into a novel. But to convey a novel through a single gesture, or joy by a single catch of the breath: such concentration exists only when emotional self-indulgence is correspondingly absent.'[4] Webern's first instrumental pieces in this new, pared down, atonal style were composed in 1909. These are a set of Five Movements, Opus 5, for string quartet, which he arranged twenty years later for string orchestra. They were followed by his first atonal work for orchestra, the Six Pieces, Opus 6.

For a period of fifteen years, Webern concentrated on songs, finding (like Schoenberg) that it was difficult to sustain an atonal language for extended movements without words to create a sense of structure and narrative. It is not clear when Schoenberg first shared his idea of twelve-note composition, but by the 1920s Webern was beginning to experiment. He composed only two orchestral works after he had adopted Schoenberg's twelve-note method: the Symphony, Opus 21 (1928), and the Variations (1940). Of the two, the Variations are by far the more approachable. The Symphony is extremely complex, even by Webern's standards. Its row of twelve notes is subjected to many different transformations – played in canon, upside down, backwards, in various combinations and transpositions – and these patterns are applied to longer sections as well as to the row. It is an important work in Webern's development, and he himself wrote enthusiastically about the result: 'Greater coherence cannot be achieved. Not even the Netherlanders managed it' (referring to the intricacies of music written by late fifteenth-century composers such as Johannes Ockeghem and Josquin des Prez).[5]

People who are able to grasp the intricacies of Webern's Symphony find extraordinary beauty in it. The composer George Benjamin describes its first movement as 'weightless – a complex, crystal-like object hovering in space'. And he finds the second movement 'infused with intense emotion' in its 'world of rotations and reflections, opening myriad paths for the listener to trace through textures of luminous clarity yet beguiling ambiguity'.[6] But it is impossible for most listeners to detect the ways in which Webern manipulates the twelve notes of his row, and they have to take the word of specialists for what he is doing. Even a specialist needs several hours with the score to begin to understand what is going on. Listeners are left to form what impression they can of a seemingly bewildering succession of notes – they may find the effect beautiful or ugly, but it is difficult to begin to know why.

Webern was one of the most meticulous composers in the history of music. His scores are extremely complex, and as he ventured through atonality to the adoption of Schoenberg's twelve-note technique, they became increasingly intricate while, at the same time, spare and transparent. His mature works are all very short. Even his Symphony, his first twelve-note orchestral work, lasts less than ten minutes. Webern believed that the coherence obtained by this meticulous structuring helped to make his music comprehensible. And, like Schoenberg, he believed that his way of composing was a development of the great German tradition extending back to Beethoven and J. S. Bach.

But the Nazis did not think so. Although he was not Jewish, his music was included in the list of banned 'degenerate' art. Despite this, Webern's fervour for Austrian and German culture led him naively to support Hitler's ascent to power and aspirations (though not his anti-Semitism). After the German occupation of Austria, he accommodated himself to the regime, and even obtained a government grant when his usual sources of income were blocked. He remained in Austria throughout the war, whereas his teacher, Schoenberg, and most of his colleagues and friends fled.

Four months after the end of the war, Webern and his family were living in a village near Salzburg, where they had taken refuge with his daughter's in-laws. The area was occupied by American forces, and as Webern stepped outside after dinner to smoke a cigar (bought on the black market), he was shot and killed by a US army soldier. He was sixty-one.

PASSACAGLIA, OP. 1
Duration: approx. 10 minutes

Webern composed the Passacaglia in 1908 after he had been studying with Schoenberg for almost four years. It is his last tonal work for large orchestra, full of echoes of Mahler and of Schoenberg's early orchestral works. The whole piece is a set of variations on a bass line that is stated slowly at the beginning: eight notes, starting and ending on D. It would be in D minor, as if it were a baroque passacaglia, except that the fourth note (the halfway point of the statement) is not A but A flat. This lurch out of D minor in the middle of the bass series colours the whole work, opening up a swirl of complex, chromatic harmonies, so that there are times when the music does not feel as if it is in a key at all.

Since the variations on this bass flow straight into each other, with the join often disguised, the listener can easily begin to lose track of where one eight-bar section ends and another begins. The theme itself is not always audible, and is sometimes implied in the chord progressions rather than stated. But a sense of coherence is helped by the fact that Webern uses the shape of the theme – which falls once, leaps up, and then falls gradually – to create melodic phrases throughout the piece, quite independent of the (implied) steady tread of the theme in its original form.

There is also a clearly audible overarching structure, which divides the variations into three sections. During the first section (Variations 1–11) the pace gradually increases, reaching a crisis at Variation 7 and then falling back again. The second section (Variations 12–15) returns to the slow tempo of the opening, and is very quiet and dream-like. The third section (Variations 16–23) becomes increasingly stormy, and reaches a climax that is followed by a long concluding coda. This structure echoes that of the most famous passacaglia of recent times, the finale of Brahms's Fourth Symphony, composed only two decades earlier. But it is easy to imagine how this structure might also be interpreted in the light of the death of Webern's mother, which, according to him, inspired the Passacaglia. So one might hear the opening sequence of variations building to a climax of grief, and then giving way to a serene passage of fond memories. Grief reasserts itself and builds to an overwhelming climax before falling away in desolation. Such interpretations of Webern's music were for many years deeply unfashionable in academic circles, until scholars began looking again at what Webern had actually said about the impulses that lay behind his music. The music is not simplistically descriptive (in fact it is not simple at all), but it is certainly deeply rooted in Webern's longings and memories of his childhood.

The theme: a succession of eight notes is played by muted pizzicato strings, beginning and ending on the note D. Variation 1: The theme is in muted trumpet, with flute counterpoint. Variation 2: The theme is on (offbeat) harp, with a counterpoint on clarinet with rising and falling shapes derived from the theme. Variation 3: The theme is on harp, cellos, and basses, with rising and falling counterpoints on strings and horn. Variation 4: The theme is on muted horn, with more agitated rising and falling counterpoints on strings and clarinet. Variation 5: The theme itself is not stated at first, but appears in the bass in the third bar. The counterpoints are now broken into agitated rising and falling arpeggios. Variation 6: There is a cymbal stroke, the strings remove their mutes, and their semiquavers are broken into repeated notes that accelerate as they crescendo, while the woodwind play rising and falling phrases. There is no clear trace of the theme itself here or in the next two variations. Variation 7: maximum tempo has been reached, and the whole orchestra is fortissimo, with plunging arpeggios. Variation 8: The tempo is suddenly held back, and the music reaches a crisis, *fff*. Variation 9: With a stroke of the bass drum, the theme returns in the bass, with lamenting rising and falling phrases in the wind above. Variation 10 (yet slower): The violas play an inversion of the previous wind phrases, now falling and rising. Variation 11: The tempo has now returned to the very slow tempo of the opening. Versions of the falling and rising phrase are scattered round flute, horn, muted trumpet, harp, and cellos (the theme itself is not stated).

Variations 12–15 break from a highly chromatic D minor into an equally chromatic D major. This section has a shimmering, magical atmosphere, reminiscent of passages in Schoenberg's *Gurrelieder* and *Verklärte Nacht*. Variation 12: The scoring is very rich, with high violins at the top, shimmering tremolo below, and yearning phrases on solo viola and solo cello. The theme is (just) audible on trumpet. Variation 13: The principal melody moves to clarinet and then flute, which vary the rising and falling shape. The theme is low on bass clarinet and pizzicato cello. Variation 14: A solo violin plays a sweet variant of the falling and rising idea. The theme is almost buried on cor anglais, its shape echoed by a solo cello. Variation 15: A quiet muted trumpet emerges from the rich texture, playing a simplified version of the falling and rising idea. This brings the central section of the piece to a close. Variation 16: This brings us back to D minor and firmly reminds us of the theme, which is intoned on muted trombones. Variation 17: The music begins once more to accelerate. A fragmented version of the theme is shared between cor anglais and oboe. Little pizzicato figures in triplet rhythm create a sense of unease. Variation 18: The triplet rhythm is drawn into a variant of the falling and rising idea, which passes from instrument to instrument. Variation 19: A new curling twist is added to the familiar phrase, and triplet rhythms cut across it, increasing the tension. Variation 20: the conflict between the two rhythmic figures intensifies. Variation 21: The melody simplifies, and the woodwind and muted trumpet are pursued by whooping horns, all fortissimo. Variation 22: a drum roll and a cymbal crash signal the climactic crisis. The tumult intensifies still further, reaching *fff*, with urgent triplet rhythms pounded out by the timpani. Variation 23: There is another cymbal crash, and the music falls apart. A frantic version of the rising and falling shape peters out, with ominous muted trombones sounding its death knell. There is a pause, followed by a quiet, sonorous chord of simple D minor.

The last three minutes form an epilogue or coda. After a moment of searching, it revisits the sweet violin solo from the D major section, now on muted strings – violas, solo violin, then flute and violins together – passing through various keys as it goes. Gradually, this becomes more and more frenzied, until it arrives at a reprise of the plunging arpeggios of Variation 7, which battle against a mirror of rocketing arpeggios. The music rises to its final, catastrophic *fff* climax, marked by a mighty gong stroke.

From here, it gradually subsides. The unresolved harmonies ensure that there is no sense of any resolution in sight, and the repeated leaping rise of the familiar phrase takes on a tragic character, as if it is the only figure left amid the ruins. Muted cellos, playing tremolo grating against the wood of the bow, take us to a final *ppp* chord of D minor on muted trombones. The arrival back at the home key achieves no sense of fulfilment, but rather exhaustion or defeat.

SIX PIECES, OP. 6
Duration: approx. 12 minutes

1. Langsam (Slow)
2. Bewegt (Animated)
3. Mässig (Moderate tempo)
4. Sehr mässig (Very moderate tempo)
5. Sehr langsam (Very slow)
6. Langsam (Slow)

On 31 March 1913, Schoenberg conducted the premiere of Webern's Opus 6 Pieces in Vienna's Musikverein. It was the first item in a concert of music by Schoenberg and his circle. Famously, the concert culminated in a riot, and already Webern's music provoked laughter and hissing as well as some applause. Demonstrations against the music of Schoenberg and his pupils had become a familiar part of the Viennese scene.

Few in the audience would have known anything about the inspiration for Webern's music, which was far removed from any intention to provoke or shock. The previous year, he had revealed in letters that most of his music was inspired by memories of his mother, and her tragic death. In January 1913, two months before the premiere of the Six Pieces, Webern wrote to Schoenberg explaining specifically what lay behind the music, which he composed in the summer of 1909:

> The first piece is to express my frame of mind when I was still in Vienna, already sensing the disaster [of his mother's death], yet always maintaining the hope that I would find my mother still alive. It was a beautiful day – for a minute I believed quite firmly that nothing had happened. Only during the train ride to Carinthia … did I learn the truth. The third piece conveys the impression of the fragrance of the heather which I gathered at a spot in the forest very meaningful to me and then laid on the bier. The fourth piece I later entitled *Marcia funebre*. Even today I do not understand my feelings as I walked behind the coffin to the cemetery. I only know that I walked the entire way with my head held high, as if to banish everything lowly all around … The evening after the funeral was miraculous. With my wife I went once again to the cemetery and there straightened out the wreaths and flowers on the grave. All the time I had the feeling of my mother's bodily presence – I saw her friendly smile. It was a blissful feeling that lasted moments. Two summers after that I was at our estate again for an extended period; this was the time when I wrote these pieces at summer's end. Daily, towards evening, I was at the grave – often in deep dusk.[7]

For a planned performance in Dortmund 1933, which was cancelled because of Hitler's rise to power in Germany, Webern provided a brief description of all six pieces in a journal: 'they are of a purely lyrical nature – the first expresses the expectation of a calamity, the second the certainty of its fulfilment, the third the most delicate contrast – it is, as it were, the introduction to the fourth, a funeral march. Five and six are an epilogue; remembrance and resignation.'[8]

Webern composed the Six Pieces around the same time as Schoenberg was completing his Five Orchestral Pieces. It has often been suggested that Webern was inspired by Schoenberg's pieces in his bold use of a large orchestra to create constantly changing tone colours and combinations. But since there is no evidence that Webern saw Schoenberg's score before writing his own, it is as likely that teacher and pupil were both thinking along similar lines simultaneously. Webern's first version of the score is for a Mahler-size orchestra including six horns, six trumpets, and six trombones (though they rarely play all together). He arranged the work for a chamber ensemble in 1920, for performances at Schoenberg's recently established Society for Private Musical Performances. And in 1928 he revisited the original score and reduced it to a more manageable orchestra, though still with four each of horns, trumpets, and trombones, and made other revisions including changes to the titles. Webern declared that this revision 'is to be considered the only valid one'. The score is dedicated to 'Arnold Schoenberg my teacher and friend with deepest affection'.

Webern stated in his note, 'They represent short song forms, particularly in the sense of being in three parts. Thematic connections do not exist, not even within the individual pieces. I consciously avoided such connections, since I aimed at a constantly changing mode of expression.'[9] This is similar to Schoenberg's claim that his Five Orchestral Pieces are 'without architecture, without structure'. But, as in the Schoenberg, so in Webern's Pieces there are elements that recur – as you would expect in a composer who spoke of the need for coherence and comprehensibility in music. He continually emphasizes this point in his series of lectures, *The Path to New Music*, given in Vienna in 1932–3. He specifically states, 'What is the easiest way to ensure comprehensibility? Repetition. All formal construction is built up on it, all musical forms are based on this principle.'[10] In the Six Pieces, there is little exact repetition, but there are elements that recur frequently. Two elements are particularly prominent: melodic shapes that rock up and down within a narrow compass of notes, and fleeting arpeggios, up or down. These help the listener to find some way through music that is consistently atonal. Unlike in the earlier Passacaglia, there is never a sense of the music being in a key, and all chords and arpeggios therefore have an atmosphere of strangeness. Occasionally the listener gets a momentary impression of some relation to a familiar chord, as if a distant memory is being evoked. But it is never more than distant.

The first piece opens with two hesitant phrases on flute, first rising and then, after a touch of muted trumpet and celesta, falling. Then a clarinet plays a line that rocks uneasily between higher and lower notes, in counterpoint with the muted trumpet. This rocking idea moves to flutes and oboes, with more agitated figures below, including staccato iterations in the horns, like an obsessive version of the rocking idea, and a more sustained version of the rocking idea high on the violins. As the climax subsides, the obsessive staccato figure passes to clarinets. The piece ends with the muted trumpet playing two falling arpeggios. This seems like a reference back to the two flute phrases with which the piece began – especially once one realizes that the last four (falling) notes on the trumpet are like a mirror image of the four rising notes with which the flute began.

Again, rocking patterns dominate the second piece. It opens with the bass clarinet weaving an uncertain course over a nervous accompaniment. Then flutes weave over a narrower range, with mysterious shimmering strings below. A moment of staccato hesitancy ends with an anxious plea from oboe over muted horns. The rest of the piece consists of violent outbursts interspersed first by panicked or anxious responses, condensed to the repetition of tiny alternations, and latterly by a sort of frozen horror, in which there is only the sound of percussion. A repeated, violent chord finally triumphs.

The third piece was inspired by 'the fragrance of heather' that Webern laid on his mother's coffin. It is the shortest and most elusive of the set. A solo viola plays plaintive fragments of rising and falling melody over a haunting chord of muted trumpets. A clarinet arpeggio descends. Flute, muted horn, and glockenspiel play a staccato rocking pattern. The viola plays a mysterious high harmonic. A bassoon arpeggio rises, the harp alternates two notes, and arpeggios descend in solo viola and celesta. As the harp oscillation continues, a muted trumpet plays a halting attempt at an oscillation, bringing the piece to a close.

The fourth piece, the longest of the set, was originally entitled 'Funeral March', and although Webern removed this from the final version, he still continued to refer to it by that name. It begins with low percussion: a roll of bass drum and strokes of gong and deep bells 'of indeterminate pitch', creating a doleful tread. Chords punctuate the march: flutes and clarinets, muted horns, muted trumpets. There is no sense of key in the chords, but they all contain clashes between major and minor thirds, giving a specific 'spice'. Over a sustained chord of muted trombones, a piccolo plays a chant-like version of the rocking pattern. It lapses into silence, and the tread of the percussion fades away.

Broader melodic patterns pass from clarinet to muted horn and muted trumpet, as the gong and bells are replaced by low, dissonant chords of muted trombones and tuba, like groans. The bells and gong quietly return, together with a side drum roll. The punctuating chords reappear, now extended into melodic fragments. They become gradually louder and more dissonant, until the entire brass section blares out fortissimo, and the piece ends with a massive percussion crescendo. Despite Webern's memory of walking behind his mother's coffin with his head held high, the climax of this funeral march conveys an overwhelming impression of catastrophic horror.

The fifth piece is, according to the metronome indication, the slowest of the six, and its markings range from *p* to *ppp*. But the opening seems not so much peaceful as haunted by terrible memories. A muted trombone plays another fragmentary version of the rocking shape, over acerbic chords in which strings scrape a tremolo with the wood of the bow, alternating with low brass. It is only when an oboe extends the range of the melody, and harp and bass clarinet respond with arpeggios, that a hint of consolation begins to enter the music. Fragments of melody pass from instrument to instrument, until the strings play a mysterious chord and high violins descend.

The atmosphere is changed towards the magical. Rocking patterns combine: a regular pattern on trumpets, celesta, and harp under a delicate melody on glockenspiel. Then low contrabassoon, muted trombones, and string harmonics hold another mysterious chord, while more rocking melodies combine – narrow intervals on flute and oboe, wider intervals on solo violin.

The final piece begins with more fragments of melody on oboe, bassoon, horn, and trumpet. Then a clarinet plays a sustained, oscillating line, over a staccato rocking accompaniment like a ticking, and ultimately faltering, clock. Over a 'barely audible' roll on the deep bell, a solo violin plays a last descending phrase. The piece ends with the celesta playing a strange chord eight times. Despite its strangeness (it is made up of two whole-tone chords, a semitone apart), its repetition makes it seem as if it invites us to find in it some sort of resolution. But we are left floating in the air, as the roll on the bell fades to inaudibility.

VARIATIONS FOR ORCHESTRA, OP. 30

Duration: approx. 7 minutes

Webern composed only two orchestral works after he had adopted Schoenberg's twelve-note method: the Symphony, Opus 21 (1928, see introduction to Webern), and these Variations, written in 1940.

The Variations are somewhat – but only somewhat – more straightforward than the Symphony. At least it is possible to understand some of the basic elements of the score by ear alone. Webern wrote about his new work in a letter to his pupil Willi Reich. He spent 'weeks and weeks' composing the Variations, 'And now, I think, something quite simple and perhaps obvious has emerged.' And he once again explains some of the principle on which the twelve-note method is based. Although it relates the twelve semitones 'only to each other', rather than within the context of traditional, tonal harmonies, he regards himself as *building* a tonality' which does not 'ignore the rules of order provided by the nature of sound – namely the relationship of the overtones to a fundamental [of the harmonic series]. In any case, it's impossible to ignore them, if there is still to be *meaningful* expression in sound!'[11]

Although it is often difficult in a twelve-note composition to sense much relationship with the harmonic series, there is a particular harmonic 'colour' to these Variations. It arises because Webern divides his row into three groups of four notes, and in each of them (and in the complete row) only two intervals occur: semitones and minor thirds. Webern has a habit of leaping freely from one octave to another, which disguises this basic fact. But the overall harmonic sound of the piece is influenced by this predominance of semitones and minor thirds in all its fragmentary melodies, and even in its chords. The music is predominantly dissonant, but the minor thirds within the chords have an intangible softening effect, as if a ghost of traditional harmonies is sometimes to be glimpsed.

As the Variations often run into each other, and it is easy to get lost, approximate timings of each variation are given in the following description.

The piece consists of a theme followed by six variations. It begins with a statement of the complete row in three fragments: four notes on double bass (A, B flat, D flat, C), four notes on oboe (B, D, E flat, G flat), and four notes on trombone (F, E, G, A flat). What matters for the listener is not the specific pitches of the notes, but the intervals that they create within each group and in the gaps between them: semitone, minor third, semitone, (semitone), minor third, semitone, minor third, (semitone), semitone, minor third, semitone. The third group has a shape closely related to the first group.

The theme (0'50") consists of various versions of these four-note shapes, with much leaping between octaves and sudden changes of attack and pace. Twice there are chords: one on pizzicato strings, and right at the end, a staccato chord repeated quietly on muted brass. This chord is also made up of combinations of semitones and minor thirds. Repetitions of the chord continue into:

Variation 1 (1'30"): This is predominantly slow, with occasional bursts of energy that soon drain away. It begins with the brass chords that ended the theme, repeated staccato. These chords pass from group to group throughout the variation: woodwind, lower strings, celesta and harp, and so on. The pitches change, but every chord is made from semitones and minor thirds. Over these chords, the four-note shapes are played, beginning with a solo violin. They become increasingly fragmentary as the variation proceeds.

Variation 2 (0'30") is short, consisting of stabbing chords in a shifting metre, interspersed with a couple of brief moments of pianissimo.

Variation 3 (1'10") reverts to the manner of the theme, with largely unaccompanied fragments of the row leaping from instrument to instrument. They are by turns ghostly and energetic, and at the end a muted trombone sounds for a moment as if it wants to assert the regular rhythm of a brass band. The variation ends with a low held note on double bass that carries over into the next variation.

Variation 4 (1'00"): Webern thought of this as a sort of recapitulation of Variation 1, 'but in a developing manner'. Instead of having separate melodic lines and chords, as Variation 1 did, it builds up a rich texture by overlapping the melodic fragments. It is the most sonorous of the variations, with a mood of tragic intensity that builds to a climax and evaporates.

Variation 5 (0'27"): Webern described this short variation as repeating the manner of the theme (leaping fragments of the row) and of Variation 2 (with its stabbing chords). But it has a brittle atmosphere of its own.

Variation 6 (1'30"): This variation functions as an extended coda or epilogue. It begins with muted brass chords, and ends with a truculent outburst. Between these two events, the music brings together the various elements and moods that have occurred throughout the piece – the fragments of melody, chords that seem to contain a ghostly memory, restless changes of tempo and metre, sudden switches from the tentative to the assertive. There is no sense of this being an end, any more than the start seemed like a beginning. The music is simply there (wherever 'there' is), and we must take it as we find it.

Endnotes

Introduction

1. *A Hundred Years of Music* (London: Methuen, 1938; 3rd edn, 1964), p. 163.
2. Alex Ross, *The Rest is Noise: Listening to the Twentieth Century* (London: Fourth Estate, 2008).

Johann Sebastian Bach

1. 'Christmas with Bach', *Guardian*, 12 December 2005.
2. For discussion of the background to these works, see Malcolm Boyd, *The Brandenburg Concertos* (Cambridge: Cambridge University Press, 1993).
3. Ibid., p. 13.
4. Ibid., p. 61.
5. See Bryan Proksch, 'The Context of the Tromba in F in J. S. Bach's Second Brandenburg Concerto, BWV 1047', *Historic Brass Society Journal* 23 (2011), pp. 43–66.
6. Eva Badura-Skoda, 'Bach, Johann Sebastian', in *The Piano: An Encyclopedia*, ed. Robert Palmieri (New York and London: Routledge, 2003).
7. Letter to Bach's biographer, Johann Nikolaus Forkel, 1774, *The New Bach Reader*, ed. Hans T. David and Arthur Mendel (New York: Norton, 1966), p. 397.

Mily Balakirev

1. Richard Taruskin, *On Russian Music* (Berkeley, CA: University of California Press, 2009), p. 37.
2. Edward Garden, *Balakirev: A Critical Study of His Life and Music* (London: Faber & Faber, 1967).
3. Ibid., p. 195.
4. Nikolai Rimsky-Korsakov, *My Musical Life* (New York: A. A. Knopf, 1925), p. 58.

Samuel Barber

1. John Gruen, 'And where has Samuel Barber been…?', *The New York Times*, 3 October 1971. Quoted in Barbara B. Heyman, *Samuel Barber: The Composer and His Music* (Oxford: Oxford University Press, 1992), p. 513.
2. Ibid., p. 168.
3. Ibid., pp. 171–2.
4. Ibid., p. 174.
5. The writing of the violin concerto is discussed in ibid., pp. 191–201. Links to photographs of this and other relevant letters are provided in the Wikipedia article, 'Violin Concerto (Barber)' (accessed 29 December 2017).
6. Letter of 29 August 1944 in the Piatigorsky Archives, The Colburn School, Los Angeles. Piatigorskyarchives. colburnschool.edu/2016/05/11/letter-from-vernon-duke-vladimir-dukelsky/ (accessed 30 December 2017).

Bèla Bartók

1. 'The Influence of Peasant Music on Modern Music' (1931), in *Béla Bartók Essays*, selected and edited by Benjamin Suchoff (Faber: London, 1976), p. 341.
2. 'Post-War Musical Life in Budapest to February 1920', in *Béla Bartók Essays*, ed. Suchoff, p. 460.

3. *Autobiography* (1921), in *Béla Bartók Essays*, ed. Suchoff, p. 410.
4. Vera Lampert, 'Bartók at the Piano: Lessons from the Composer's Sound Recordings', *The Cambridge Companion to Bartók*, ed. Amanda Bayley (Cambridge: Cambridge University Press, 2001), pp. 236–7.
5. *The Cambridge Companion to Bartók*, ed. Bayley, p. 128.
6. 10 August 1939, quoted in Ulrich Mahlert, Preface to the Breitkopf Urtext edition of the Divertimento (Breitkopf & Härtel, 2016).
7. Interview published in 1919. Julie Brown, *Bartók and the Grotesque* (Abingdon: Routledge, 2016), p. 89.
8. Vera Lampert, '*The Miraculous Mandarin*, Melchior Lengyel, His Pantomime, and His Connections to Béla Bartók', *Bartók and His World*, ed. Peter Laki (Princeton, NJ: Princeton University Press, 1995), p. 163.
9. David Cooper, *Béla Bartók* (New Haven, CT, and London: Yale University Press, 2015), p. 219.
10. Malcolm Gillies, 'A Conversation with Bartók: 1929', *Musical Times*, vol. 128, no. 1736 (October 1987), quoting an interview with M.-D. Calvacoressi published in 1929.
11. *The Cambridge Companion to Bartók*, ed. Bayley, p. 75.
12. Lampert in *Bartók and His World*, p. 163.
13. Ibid., p. 155.
14. Ibid.
15. Brown, *Bartók and the Grotesque*, pp. 88–9.
16. *Béla Bartók Essays*, ed. Suchoff, p. 419.
17. *Bartók and His World*, ed. Laki, p. 192.
18. *Bartók Recordings from Private Collections I*, Hungaroton HCD12334–7.
19. Cooper, *Béla Bartók*, p. 78.
20. Maria Anna Harley, 'Birds in Concert: North American Birdsong in Bartók's Piano Concerto No. 3', *Tempo* no. 189 (June 1994), p. 8.
21. Julie A. Brown, *Bartók and the Grotesque: Studies in Modernity, the Body and Contradiction in Music* (Aldershot: Ashgate, 2007), p. 23.
22. Cooper, *Béla Bartók*, p. 303.
23. Yehudi Menuhin, *Unfinished Journey* (New York: Knopf, 1977), p. 165.

Ludwig van Beethoven

1. *Thayer's Life of Beethoven*, rev. and ed. Elliot Forbes (Princeton, NJ: Princeton University Press, 1967), pp. 173–4.
2. Ibid., p. 329.
3. Carl Czerny, *On the Proper Performance of all Beethoven's Works for the Piano*, ed. Paul Badura-Skoda (Vienna: Universal, 1970), p. 104.
4. Ibid., p. 103.
5. *Thayer's Life of Beethoven*, p. 255.
6. Maynard Solomon, *Beethoven* (London: Cassell, 1978), p. 114.
7. *Thayer's Life of Beethoven*, p. 349.
8. Ibid., p. 375.
9. Ibid., p. 376.
10. O. G. Sonneck, *Beethoven: Impressions by his Contemporaries* (New York: Schirmer, 1926, repr. 1967), p. 54.
11. For a discussion of the origins and development of the Third Symphony, see Lewis Lockwood, *Beethoven's Symphonies: An Artistic Vision* (New York: Norton, 2015), pp. 51–78.
12. *Thayer's Life of Beethoven*, p. 436.
13. Ibid., p. 501.
14. *Louis Spohr's Autobiography* (London: Longman, 1865), pp. 187–8.
15. At the time of writing, conductors Benjamin Zander, David Zinman, and Philippe Herreweghe have so far recorded the Ninth Symphony with this tempo relationship.

Alban Berg

1. To Gian Francesco Malipiero, 27 December 1934, in Mosco Carner, *Alban Berg* (London: Duckworth, rev. ed 1983), p. 83.
2. Douglas Jarman, 'Berg, Alban', in *Grove Music Online*.
3. 8 September 1914, *The Berg–Schoenberg Correspondence: Selected Letters*, ed. Juliane Brand, Christopher Hailey and Donald Harris (Basingstoke and London: Macmillan, 1987), pp. 214–15.

Hector Berlioz

1. Letter to his mother, 15 March 1831, in Sam Morgenstern, *Composers on Music: Eight Centuries of Writings*, expanded edition ed. Josiah Fisk and Jeff William Nichols (Lebanon, NH: Northeastern University Press, 1997), p. 85.
2. Camille Saint-Saëns, *Portraits et Souvenirs* (Paris: Société d'Édition Artistique, 1900), pp. 3–4.
3. *The Memoirs of Berlioz*, trans. David Cairns (London: Gollancz, 1969).
4. Ibid., p. 271.
5. Ibid.
6. Ibid., p. 294.
7. Ibid., p. 295.
8. Ibid., p. 447.
9. Ibid., pp. 109–10.
10. Ibid., p. 112.

11. Richard Wagner, *Mein Leben*, vol. 1, pp. 229–31, trans. Michel Austin, *Hector Berlioz Website*.

12. *The Memoirs of Berlioz*, trans. Cairns, p. 305.

13. Details of the relationship between Berlioz's *Roméo et Juliette* and the various versions of Shakespeare's play are in Julian Rushton, *Berlioz: Roméo et Juliette* (Cambridge: Cambridge University Press, 1994); Ian Kemp, 'Romeo and Juliet and *Roméo et Juliette*', in *Berlioz Studies*, ed. Peter Bloom (Cambridge: Cambridge University Press, 2006).

14. *The Memoirs of Berlioz*, trans. Cairns, p. 109.

15. Jonathan Kregor, *Program Music* (Cambridge: Cambridge University Press, 2015), pp. 71–3.

Alexander Borodin

1. Letter to Nadezhda von Meck, 5 January 1878, in Modeste Tchaikovsky, *The Life and Letters of Peter Ilich Tchaikovsky*, ed. Rosa Newmarch (London: John Lane 1906, repr. 1973), p. 252.

2. Alfred Habets, *Borodin and Liszt*, trans. Rosa Newmarch (London: Digby, Long & Co., 1895), pp. 155–6.

3. The political and 'oriental' background is discussed in Francis Maes, *A History of Russian Music from Kamarinskaya to Babi Yar*, trans. A. J. and E. Pomerans (Berkeley, CA: University of California Press, 2002), p. 81.

4. César Cui, review of a concert given by the Russian Musical Society in *The Voice*, 22 October 1880, from *Russians on Russian Music, 1880–1917: An Anthology*, ed. and trans. Stuart Campbell (Cambridge: Cambridge University Press, 2003), p. 92, adapted.

5. Nikolai Rimsky-Korsakov, *My Musical Life* (New York: A. A. Knopf, 1925), p. 157.

6. Serge Dianin, *Borodin*, trans. Robert Lord (Oxford: Oxford University Press, 1963), pp. 207–8.

7. Ibid.

8. Ibid.

Johannes Brahms

1. Florence May, *The Life of Johannes Brahms* (London: E. Arnold, 1905, 2nd rev. edn 1948), vol. 1, pp. 108–9.

2. *Johannes Brahms: Life and Letters*, ed. Styra Avins (Oxford: Oxford University Press, 1997), p. 48.

3. 'Brahms, Johannes', *A Dictionary of Music and Musicians*, ed. George Grove, vol. 1 (London: Macmillan, 1879), p. 270.

4. Jan Swafford, *Johannes Brahms* (London: Macmillan, 1998), p. 207.

5. To Richard Specht, in Peter Clive, *Brahms and his World: A Biographical Dictionary* (Lanham, MD: Scarecrow Press, 2006), pp. 484–5.

6. 'On the Application of Music to Drama', 1879, in Walter Frisch, *Brahms: The Four Symphonies* (New Haven, CT, and London: Yale University Press, 2003), p. 149.

7. Alan Walker, *Franz Liszt: The Weimar Years, 1848–1861* (Ithaca, NY: Cornell University Press, 1993), p. 340.

8. Berthold Litzmann, *Clara Schumann: An Artist's Life, Based on Material Found in Diaries and Letters*, vol. 2, trans. Grace E. Hadow (1913, repr. Cambridge: Cambridge University Press 2013), p. 392.

9. Michael Musgrave, *A Brahms Reader* (New Haven, CT, and London: Yale University Press, 2000), p. 71.

10. *Johannes Brahms: Life and Letters*, ed. Avins, p. 541.

11. August 1878, in ibid., p. 541.

12. Ulrich Mahlert, preface to Breitkopf & Härtel's study score no. 3693.

13. Carl von Noorden, 1861. Michael Vaillancourt, 'Brahms's "Sinfonie-Serenade" and the Politics of Genre', *The Journal of Musicology*, vol. 26, no. 3 (Summer 2009), p. 387.

14. *Johannes Brahms: Life and Letters*, ed. Avins, p. 488.

15. Michael Musgrave, 'Serenades', in *The Complete Brahms: A Guide to the Musical Works of Johannes Brahms*, ed. Leon Botstein (New York: Norton, 1999), p. 44.

16. Swafford, *Johannes Brahms*, p. 334.

17. Ibid., p. 484.

18. A. Peter Brown, *The Symphonic Repertoire, Volume IV: The Second Golden Age of the Viennese Symphony: Brahms, Bruckner, Dvořák, Mahler, and Selected Contemporaries* (Bloomington and Indianapolis, IN: Indiana University Press, 2003), p. 6.

Benjamin Britten

1. 'Britten, Benjamin', *The New Grove Dictionary of Music and Musicians*, 2nd edn (London: Macmillan, 2001).

2. Neil Powell, *Benjamin Britten* (London: Hutchinson, 2013), p. 184.

3. E. M. Forster, 'George Crabbe: The Poet and the Man', *The Listener*, 29 May 1941.

4. Donald Mitchell, Philip Reed, and Mervyn Cooke, eds, *Letters from a Life: The Selected Letters and Diaries of Benjamin Britten*, vol. 1, 1923–1939 (London: Faber, 1998).

5. Neil Powell, *Benjamin Britten: A Life for Music* (London: Windmill Books, 2014), p. 183.

6. Ibid., p. 190.

7. Mitchell, Reed, and Cooke, eds, *Letters from a Life*, vol. 1, p. 502.

8. 'Britten Looking Back', *Sunday Telegraph*, 17 November 1963, quoted in Michael Kennedy, *Britten* (London: J. M. Dent, 1981), p. 6.

9. Mitchell, Reed, and Cooke, eds, *Letters from a Life*, vol. 1, p. 503.

Max Bruch

1. Christopher Fifield, *Max Bruch: His Life and Work*, 2nd edn (Woodbridge: Boydell Press, 2005), p. 329.

2. Annette. M. Boeckler, 'The Magic of the Moment: *Kol Nidre* in Progressive Judaism', in Lawrence A. Hoffmann, *All These Vows: Kol Nidre* (Woodstock, VT: Jewish Lights Publishing), p. 61.

3. Letter to Fritz Simrock, November 1884, in Fifield, *Max Bruch*, p. 48.

4. Fifield, *Max Bruch*, p. 168.
5. Ibid., p. 62.
6. Ibid., pp. 62–3.
7. Ibid., p. 76.

Anton Bruckner

1. Elisabeth Maier, 'An "inner biography" of Anton Bruckner', *Bruckner Studies*, ed. Timothy L. Jackson and Paul Hawkshaw (Cambridge: Cambridge University Press, 1997), p. 41.
2. Leon Botstein, 'Bruckner's Divided Vienna', 1999 concert note for the American Symphony Orchestra at Lincoln Center, 1 December 1999, americansymphony.org/bruckners-divided-vienna/ (accessed 30 September 2017).
3. Adapted from Andrea Harrandt, 'Bruckner in Vienna', *The Cambridge Companion to Bruckner*, ed. John Williamson (Cambridge: Cambridge University Press, 2004), p. 31.
4. Bruckner's various revisions are discussed in Dermot Gault, *The New Bruckner: Compositional Development and the Dynamics of Revision* (London and New York: Routledge 2016), pp. 73–87.
5. London Classical Players, conducted by Roger Norrington – *EMI* CDC5 56167 2 (1997); Royal Scottish National Orchestra, conducted by Georg Tintner – *Naxos* 8.553454 (1998).
6. Derek Watson, *Bruckner* (New York: Schirmer, 1997), p. 84.
7. John Williamson, 'Programme Symphony and Absolute Music', *The Cambridge Companion to Bruckner*, p. 110.
8. Ibid.
9. Letter to Moritz von Mayfield (13 February 1875), in Gault, *The New Bruckner*, p. 60.
10. Benjamin M. Korstvedt, *Anton Bruckner: Symphony No. 8* (Cambridge: Cambridge University Press, 2000), p. 18. Korstvedt's discussion of Bruckner's correspondence and revisions are summarized here.
11. Eduard Hanslick, *Music Criticisms 1846–99*, trans. Henry Pleasants (Harmondsworth: Penguin, 1963), pp. 288–90.

Emmanuel Chabrier

1. *A Ravel Reader: Correspondence, Articles, Interviews*, ed. Arbie Orenstein (New York, NY: Columbia University Press, 1990, repr. Dover 2003), pp. 391, 303.
2. Francis Poulenc, *Emmanuel Chabrier*, trans. Cynthia Jolly (London: Dobson, 1981), p. 54.
3. Seville, 21 October 1882, 'Lettres inédites d'Emmanuel Chabrier', *Bulletin Français de la S.I.M.*, 15 January 1909, p. 2.
4. Rollo H. Myers, *Chabrier and his Circle* (London: Dent, 1969), p. 28.
5. Francis Poulenc, *J'écris ce que me chante: textes et entretiens réunis, présentés, et annotés par Nicolas Southon* (Paris: Fayard, 2011), p. 56. Poulenc uses the word 'résilles' (hairnets), but is probably referring to the characteristic *mantillas* worn by Spanish dancers.

Frédéric Chopin

1. *Neue Zeitschrift für Musik* 4 (1836), p. 115, quoted in John Rink, *Chopin: The Piano Concertos* (Cambridge: Cambridge University Press, 1997), p. 118, n. 29.
2. *Life and Letters of Sir Charles Hallé* (London: Smith and Elder, 1896), p. 31.
3. *Chopin's Letters*, collected by Henryk Opienski, trans. E. L. Voynich (New York: Alfred A. Knopf, 1931), p. 69.
4. Ibid., pp. 88–9.

Aaron Copland

1. 'Composer from Brooklyn', *Magazine of Art* 1939, quoted in Elizabeth B. Crist, *Music for the Common Man: Aaron Copland during the Depression and War* (Oxford: Oxford University Press, 2005), p. 5.
2. Letter to Arthur Berger, 1943, in ibid., p. 7.
3. The progress of the ballet, and the correspondence between Copland and Graham, are detailed in *Aaron Copland: A Reader: Selected Writings 1923–1972*, ed. Richard Kostelanetz (New York and London: Routledge, 2004), Howard Pollack, *Aaron Copland: The Life and Work of an Uncommon Man*, (Urbana and Chicago, IL: University of Illinois Press, 1999), and Aaron Copland and Vivian Perlis, *Copland*, vol. 1, *1900–42* (London: Faber, 1984).
4. Pollack, *Aaron Copland*, p. 393.
5. Ibid., p. 321.
6. 'Notes on a Cowboy Ballet', *Aaron Copland: A Reader*, pp. 239–40.
7. Boosey & Hawkes, 1938.
8. Letter to Leonard Bernstein, 18 October 1948, *The Selected Correspondence of Aaron Copland*, ed. Elizabeth B. Crist and Wayne Shirley (New Haven, CT, and London: Yale University Press, 2008), p. 189.
9. J. Peter Burkholder, 'A Simple Model for Associative Musical Meaning', *Approaches to Meaning in Music*, ed. Byron Almén and Edward Pearsall (Bloomington and Indianapolis, IN: Indiana University Press, 2006), p. 88.
10. The speech was given at a dinner of the Free World Association in New York City, 8 May 1942. A recording is currently available online in several formats.
11. Letter to Virgil Thomson, in Pollack, *Aaron Copland*, pp. 223–4.
12. Ibid., pp. 298–9.
13. Aaron Copland and Vivian Perlis, *Copland*, vol. 1, *1900–1942* (London: Faber, 1984), p. 246.

Arcangelo Corelli

1. Sir Charles Burney, *A General History of Music from the Earliest Ages to the Present Day*, vol. 3 (London, 1789), pp. 556–7.
2. Ibid., pp. 557–8.

3. John Spitzer and Neal Zaslaw, *The Birth of the Orchestra: History of an Institution, 1650–1815* (Oxford: Oxford University Press, 2004).

4. David D. Boyden, *Violin Playing from its Origins to 1761* (Oxford: Oxford University Press, 1965), p. 256.

Claude Debussy

1. This topic is discussed at length by Edward Lockspeiser in *Debussy: His Life and Mind* (London: Cassell, 1965), vol. 2, pp. 15–32.

2. Ibid., vol. 1, p. 115.

3. *Debussy Letters*, selected and edited by François Lesure and Roger Nichols, trans. Roger Nichols (London: Faber, 1987), p. 140.

4. *A Ravel Reader: Correspondence, Articles, Interviews*, ed. Arbie Orenstein (New York: Columbia University Press, 1990, repr. Dover 2003), p. 45.

5. Williametta Spencer, 'The Relationship between André Caplet and Claude Debussy', *Musical Quarterly*, vol. 66, no. 1 (January 1980), p. 119, adapted.

6. Lockspeiser, *Debussy*, vol. 2, pp. 254–61.

7. Nigel Simeone, 'Debussy and Expression', *The Cambridge Companion to Debussy*, ed. Simon Trezise (Cambridge: Cambridge University Press, 2003), p. 113.

8. *Debussy Letters*, ed. Lesure and Nichols, p. 184.

9. Lockspeiser, *Debussy*, vol. 2, pp. 173–4.

10. Ibid., vol. 2, p. 172.

11. *Debussy Letters*, ed. Lesure and Nichols, p. 288.

12. Ibid., p. 262.

13. Decca SXL 2027 and reissues.

14. Lockspeiser, *Debussy*, vol. 2, p. 119.

15. *Debussy Letters*, ed. Lesure and Nichols, p. 141.

16. Ibid., p. 153.

17. For a study of Debussy's compositional methods in *La Mer*, see Simon Tresize, *Debussy: La Mer* (Cambridge: Cambridge University Press, 1994), and Roy Howat, *Debussy in Proportion: A Musical Analysis* (Cambridge: Cambridge University Press, 1983).

18. Nigel Simeone, 'Debussy and Expression', *The Cambridge Companion to Debussy*, ed. Trezise, p. 104.

19. Simeone, ibid.

20. Ibid.

21. Ibid.

22. Roger Nichols, *The Life of Debussy* (Cambridge: Cambridge University Press, 1998), pp. 83–4, translation adapted.

23. Rosemary Lloyd, 'Debussy, Mallarmé, and "Les Mardis"', *Debussy and His World*, ed. Jane F. Fulcher (Princeton, NJ: Princeton University Press, 2001), p. 256.

24. Lockspeiser, *Debussy*, vol. 1, p. 96.

Frederick Delius

1. Eric Fenby, *Delius as I Knew Him* (Cambridge: Cambridge University Press, 1981), p. 25.

2. *Frederick Delius and Peter Warlock: A Friendship Revealed*, ed. Barry Smith (Oxford: Oxford University Press, 2000), p. 294.

3. Sir Thomas Beecham, *A Mingled Chime* (New York: Putnam, 1943), p. 102.

4. Percy Grainger, programme note for a performance of Delius's *Brigg Fair*, which he conducted at the Hollywood Bowl in August 1928. *The Delius Society Journal* no. 67, April 1980, p. 20.

5. Ibid.

Antonin Dvořák

1. Recollections by Josef Michl, *Antonin Dvořák: Letters and Reminiscences*, ed. Otakar Šourek (Prague: Artia, 1954), p. 23.

2. David Brodbeck, 'Dvorak's Reception in Liberal Vienna: Language Ordinances, National Property, and the Rhetoric of *Deutschtum*', *Journal of the American Musicological Society*, vol. 60, no. 1 (Spring 2007), pp. 71–132.

3. David M. Schiller, 'The "New World" Symphony and *The Wild Dove*', *Rethinking Dvořák: Views from Five Countries*, ed. David R. Beveridge (Oxford: Clarendon Press, 1996), p. 216.

4. Jan Smaczny, *Dvořák: Cello Concerto* (Cambridge: Cambridge University Press, 1999), p. 90.

5. Otakar Šourek, *Antonin Dvořák: Letters and Reminiscences*, trans. Roberta Finlayson Samsour (Prague: Artia, 1954), p. 65.

6. Ludevít Procházka, *Narodni listy*, 23 April 1874. www.antonin-dvorak.cz/en/symphony3 (accessed 11 January 2018).

7. Jerrold Northrop Moore, *Elgar: A Creative Life* (Oxford: Oxford University Press, 1999), p. 109.

8. Michael Beckerman, *Dvořák and his World* (Princeton, NJ: Princeton University Press, 1993), p. 77.

9. Šourek, *Antonin Dvořák*, p. 166.

10. Ibid., p. 167.

11. Kurt Honolka, *Dvořák*, trans. Anne Wyburd (London: Haus Publishing, 2004), p. 83.

Edward Elgar

1. Jerrold Northrop Moore, *Edward Elgar: A Creative Life* (Oxford: Oxford University Press, 1999), p. 349.

2. Jerrold Northrop Moore, *Edward Elgar: Letters of a Lifetime* (Oxford: Clarendon Press, 1990), p. 93.

3. Moore, *Edward Elgar: A Creative Life*, p. 342.

4. Ibid., p. 344.

5. Ibid., p. 580.
6. Robert Philip, *Performing Music in the Age of Recording* (New Haven, CT, and London: Yale University Press, 2004), pp. 146–7.
7. Michael Kennedy, *The Life of Elgar* (Cambridge University Press, 2004), p. 190.
8. Moore, *Edward Elgar: A Creative Life*, p. 585.
9. Edward Elgar, 'Falstaff', *The Musical Times*, vol. 54, no. 847 (1 September 1913), pp. 575–9.
10. *The Musical Times*, vol. 67 (1926), p. 550.
11. Moore, *Edward Elgar: A Creative Life*, p. 425.
12. Ibid., p. 427; 'the drums and tramplings' is a quotation from Sir Thomas Browne (1605–82).
13. Daniel M. Grimley, 'The Chamber Music and Music for Strings', *The Cambridge Companion to Elgar*, ed. Daniel Grimley and Julian Rushton (Cambridge: Cambridge University Press, 2004), p. 125.
14. Moore, *Edward Elgar: A Creative Life*, p. 339.
15. Ibid., p. 348.
16. Ibid., p. 160.
17. Rosa Burley, *Edward Elgar: The Record of a Friendship* (London: Barrie and Jenkins, 1972).
18. *The Cambridge Companion to Elgar*, ed. Grimley and Rushton, p. 61.
19. Moore, *Edward Elgar: Letters of a Lifetime*, p. 205.
20. Letter to Ernest Newman, 4 November 1908, ibid., p. 200.
21. Moore, *Edward Elgar: A Creative Life*, p. 537.
22. William Henry Reed, *Elgar as I Knew Him* (Oxford: Oxford University Press), p. 201.
23. Michael Kennedy, *Portrait of Elgar* (Oxford: Oxford University Press, 1987), p. 238.
24. Ibid., p. 239.
25. Byron Adams, 'Elgar and the Persistence of Memory', *Edward Elgar and His World*, ed. Byron Adams (Princeton, NJ: Princeton University Press, 2007), p. 84.
26. Bernard Shore, *The Orchestra Speaks* (London: Longmans, 1938), p. 135.
27. Michael Kennedy, *Elgar Orchestral Music* (London: British Broadcasting Corporation, 1970), p. 62.
28. Ibid., pp. 247–52.
29. Ibid., p. 270.
30. Edward Elgar, *My Friends Pictured Within* (London: Novello, n.d.). The piano rolls were issued in 1929.
31. Moore, *Edward Elgar: A Creative Life*, p. 259.

Manuel de Falla

1. Douglas Lee, *Masterworks of 20th-Century Music: The Modern Repertoire of the Symphony Orchestra* (New York and London: Routledge, 2002), pp. 140–1.

Gabriel Fauré

1. *Gabriel Fauré: A Life in Letters*, trans. and ed. J. Barrie Jones (London: Batsford, 1989), p. 174.
2. Jean-Michel Nectoux, *Gabriel Fauré: A Musical Life* (Cambridge: Cambridge University Press, 2004), p. 336.
3. *Gabriel Fauré*, trans. and ed. Barrie Jones, p. 181.
4. Jessica Duchen, *Gabriel Fauré* (London: Phaidon, 2000), p. 73.
5. Ibid., p. 74.
6. Edward Lockspeiser, *Debussy: His Life and Mind* (London: Cassell, 1965), vol. 1, p. 76 (translation adapted).
7. Nectoux, *Gabriel Fauré*, p. 152.
8. Mrs Patrick Campbell, *My Life and Some Letters* (New York: Dodd Mead, 1922), p. 165.
9. Nectoux, *Gabriel Fauré*, p. 150 (translation adapted).

César Franck

1. Vincent d'Indy, *César Franck*, trans. Rosa Newmarch (London: Bodley Head, 1910), p. 43.

George Gershwin

1. Howard Pollack, *George Gershwin: His Life and Work* (Berkeley, CA: University of California Press, 2006), p. 37.
2. Ibid., p. 137.
3. Ibid., pp. 119–20.
4. Ibid., p. 431.
5. Hyman Sandow, 'Gershwin Presents a New Work', *Musical America*, vol. 48, no. 18 (18 August 1928), pp. 5, 12.
6. Pollack, *George Gershwin*, p. 346.
7. Ibid., p. 389.
8. Ibid., pp. 351–2.
9. Ibid., p. 347.
10. Ibid., pp. 348–9.
11. Ean Wood, *George Gershwin: His Life and Music* (London: Sanctuary Publishing, 1996), p. 91.
12. Pollack, *George Gershwin*, p. 297.
13. Floyd Levin, *Classic Jazz: A Personal View of the Music and the Musicians* (Berkeley, CA: University of California Press, 2000), pp. 73–4.
14. Ibid., pp. 74–5.
15. Ibid., p. 74.

Mikhail Ivanovich Glinka

1. Modeste Tchaikovsky, *The Life and Letters of Peter Ilich Tchaikovsky*, ed. Rosa Newmarch (1905, repr. New York: Haskell House, 1970), p. 564.
2. Richard Taruskin, *Defining Russia Musically: Historical and Hermeneutical Essays* (Princeton, NJ: Princeton University Press, 2000), p. 116.

Edvard Grieg

1. Roger Nichols, *Ravel* (New Haven, CT, and London: Yale University Press, 2012), p. 276.
2. Frederick J. Marker and Lise-Lone Marker, *Ibsen's Lively Art: A Performance Study of the Major Plays* (Cambridge: Cambridge University Press, 1989), p. 9.
3. Brian Johnston, *The Ibsen Cycle: The Design of the Plays from* Pillars of Society *to* When We Dead Awaken (University Park, PA: Pennsylvania State University Press, 1992), p. 63.
4. Henrik Ibsen, *Peer Gynt: A Dramatic Poem* (Philadelphia, PA: J. P. Lippincott, 1931), p. 9.
5. Roger Fiske, Preface to Grieg, *Peer Gynt, Suite No. 1* (Leipzig: Breitkopf & Härtel, EOS 21473, 2016).
6. Robert Layton, *Grieg* (London: Omnibus Press, 2010), online.

George Frideric Handel

1. Charles Burney, *An Account of the Musical Performances in Westminster Abbey, and the Pantheon, May 26th, 27th, 29th and June the 3d and 5th, 1794, In Commemoration of Handel* (London, 1785), p. 106.
2. For the derivations of Handel's movements and other details of the Concertos, Opus 6, I have relied on the following sources: Donald Burrows, *Handel* (Oxford: Oxford University Press, 2nd edn, 2011); *The Cambridge Companion to Handel*, ed. Donald Burrows (Cambridge: Cambridge University Press, 1997); Paul Henry Lang, *George Frideric Handel* (London: Faber, 1967); and the anonymous (and scholarly) author of the Wikipedia entry, 'Concerti Grossi Op. 6 (Handel)'.
3. Burney, *An Account of the Musical Performances in Westminster Abbey*, p. 102.
4. Ibid., p. 57.
5. Ibid.
6. Ibid., p. 54.
7. Ibid.
8. Ibid., p. 66.
9. Burrows, *Handel*, p. 101.
10. Christopher Hogwood, *Handel: Water Music and Music for the Royal Fireworks* (Cambridge: Cambridge University Press, 2005), p. 12.
11. Both versions are included in the score edited by Roger Fiske (London: Eulenburg, 1973). Other sources of various movements, known or conjectured, are discussed in Christopher Hogwood, *Handel*.
12. Hogwood, *Handel*, p. 31. The recording is by The Academy of Ancient Music, directed by Christopher Hogwood, Decca Editions de L'Oiseau-Lyre, 0289 455 7092 1 (issued 1997).
13. See Hogwood, ibid., pp. 37–8, for the details.
14. Ibid., pp. 41–2.

Franz Joseph Haydn

1. Many details relating to Haydn's orchestral works have been drawn from the first three volumes of H. C. Robbins Landon's survey: H. C. Robbins Landon, *Haydn: Chronicle and Works*, vol. 1, *The Early Years 1732–1765* (Bloomington, IN: Indiana University Press, 1978), vol. 2, *Haydn in Esterháza 1766–1790* (1980), and vol. 3, *Haydn in England 1791–1795* (1976).
2. Karl Geiringer, in collaboration with Irene Geiringer, *Haydn: A Creative Life in Music* (3rd rev. edn, Berkeley, CA: University of California Press, 1982), p. 71.
3. Quoted in Leipzig's *Allgemeine Musikalische Zeitung*, November 1798, p. 116.
4. David Schroeder, 'Orchestral Music: Symphonies and Concertos', *The Cambridge Companion to Haydn*, ed. Caryl Clark (Cambridge: Cambridge University Press, 2005), p. 101.
5. As well as his series of *Chronicles*, I have drawn on H. C. Robbins Landon's *Haydn Symphonies* (London: BBC Publications, 1966).
6. Richard Wigmore, *Haydn* (London: Faber, 2009), p. 103.
7. Georg August Griesinger, *Biographische Notizen über Joseph Haydn*, (Leipzig: Breitkopf & Härtel, 1810). This and the version by Albert Christoph Dies are reproduced in English in Vernon Gotwals, *Haydn: Two Contemporary Portraits* (Madison, WI: University of Wisconsin Press, 1961).
8. Elaine R. Sisman, 'Haydn, Shakespeare and the Rules of Originality', in *Haydn and his World*, ed. Sisman (Princeton, NJ: Princeton University Press, 2012), pp. 26–7. My translation.
9. Robbins Landon, *Haydn Symphonies*, pp. 41–2, my translation. For entries on the Paris Symphonies, I have also drawn on Bernard Harrison, *Haydn: The 'Paris' Symphonies* (Cambridge: Cambridge University Press, 1998).
10. Harrison, *Haydn*, p. 101.
11. Daniel Heartz, *Mozart, Haydn and Early Beethoven: 1781–1802* (New York and London: W. W. Norton and Co., 2008), p. 361.
12. Donald Francis Tovey, *Symphonies and Other Orchestral Works: Selections from Essays in Musical Analysis* (Oxford: Oxford University Press, 1981), p. 341.
13. *The Collected Correspondence and London Notebooks of Joseph Haydn*, ed. H. C. Robbins Landon (London: Barrie and Rockliff, 1959), p. 274.
14. Pauline D. Townsend, *Joseph Haydn* (1884, repr. Cambridge: Cambridge University Press, 2013), p. 95.

15. Fanny Burney, *Memoirs of Doctor Burney: Arranged from His Own Manuscripts, from Family Papers, and from Personal Recollections*, vol. 3 (London 1832, repr. Cambridge: Cambridge University Press 2010), p. 132.
16. Robbins Landon, *Haydn Symphonies*, p. 52.
17. Robbins Landon, *Haydn: Chronicle and Works*, vol. 3: *Haydn in England 1791–1795*, p. 241.
18. Ibid., p. 306.
19. Ibid., p. 308.

Paul Hindemith
1. Giselher Schubert, 'Hindemith, Paul', *Grove Music Online*.
2. *Furtwängler on Music: Essays and Addresses*, ed. and trans. Ronald Taylor (London: Scolar Press, 1991), p. 120.
3. Siglind Bruhn, *The Temptation of Paul Hindemith: Mathis der Maler as a Spiritual Testimony* (Stuyvesant, NY: Pendragon Press, 1998), p. 45.

Gustav Holst
1. Holst's fascination with astrology, together with other background to the composition, is discussed in Richard Greene, *Holst: The Planets* (Cambridge: Cambridge University Press, 1995).
2. Ibid., p. 40.

Charles Ives
1. J. Peter Burkholder, *Charles Ives: The Ideas behind the Music* (New Haven, CT, and London: Yale University Press, 1985), p. 141.
2. Henry Bellamann, 'Charles Ives, the Man and his Music', *Musical Quarterly*, vol. 19, no. 1 (January 1933), p. 47.
3. Charles Ives, *Essays Before a Sonata* (New York: Knickerbocker Press, 1920), repr. *Three Classics in the Aesthetic of Music* (New York: Dover, 1962), p. 179.
4. Ibid., p. 165.
5. *Cage Talk: Dialogues with and about John Cage*, ed. Peter Dickinson (Rochester, New York: University of Rochester Press, 2006), pp. 192–3.
6. Vivian Perlis, *Charles Ives Remembered: An Oral History* (Urbana and Chicago, IL: University of Illinois Press, 2002), p. 224.
7. The Charles Ives Society Performance Edition of the Symphony, based on the Critical Edition realized and edited by Thomas M. Brodhead (New York: Associated Music Publishers, 2011), is, at the time of writing, freely available to read online.
8. Ibid., p. xxvii.
9. Thomas M. Brodhead, 'Ives's *Celestial Railroad* and his Fourth Symphony', *American Music*, vol. 12, no. 4 (Winter 1994), pp. 389–424.
10. Stuart Feder, *The Life of Charles Ives* (Cambridge: Cambridge University Press, 1999), p. 131.
11. Ibid.
12. Burkholder, *Charles Ives*, p. 51.
13. Lorien Foote, *Seeking the One Great Remedy: Francis George Shaw and Nineteenth-Century Reform* (Athens, OH: Ohio University Press, 2003), p. 120.
14. Feder, *The Life of Charles Ives*, p. 117.
15. *Charles Ives and His World*, ed. J. Peter Burkholder (Princeton, NJ: Princeton University Press, 1996), p. 228.

Leoš Janáček
1. 'Moravian Folk Songs from the Musical Point of View', Prague, 1901, in *Composers on Music: Eight Centuries of Writing*, ed. Josiah Fisk and Jeff William Nichols (Boston, MA: Northeastern University Press, 2nd edn, 1997), p. 175.
2. John Tyrrell, *Janáček: Years of a Life, vol. 2, 1914–1928: Tsar of the Forest* (London: Faber, 2011), p. 259.

Franz Liszt
1. Alan Walker, *Franz Liszt*, vol. 2, *The Weimar Years, 1848–1861* (Ithaca, NY: Cornell University Press, 1999), pp. 199–206.
2. Gerald Abraham, *A Hundred Years of Music* (London: Methuen, 1938, 3rd edn 1964), p. 42.
3. English version from *Franz Liszt: Musikalische Werke*, Serie 1, Band 2 (Breitkopf & Härtel, 1908).
4. Walker, *Franz Liszt*, vol. 2, p. 333.
5. Humphrey Searle, *The Music of Liszt* (London: Williams & Norgate 1954, repr. Dover 2012), p. 64.
6. Walker, *Franz Liszt*, vol. 2, pp. 330–3.
7. Ibid., p. 334.

Gustav Mahler
1. Andrew Barnett, *Sibelius* (New Haven, CT, and London: Yale University Press, 2007), p. 185.
2. Quoted by Henry-Louis de la Grange, 'Music about Music in Mahler', in *Mahler Studies*, ed. Stephen E. Hefling (Cambridge: Cambridge University Press, 1997), p. 148.
3. Ernest Jones, *Sigmund Freud, Life and Work*, vol. 2 (New York: Basic Books, 1955), pp. 88–9.
4. Mahler's struggles are vividly detailed in the four volumes of Henry-Louis de la Grange, *Gustav Mahler*: vol. 1, *1860–1901* (New York: Doubleday, 1973); vol. 2, *Vienna: The Years of Challenge (1897–1904)* (rev. edn, Oxford: Oxford University Press, 1995); vol. 3, *Vienna: Triumph and Disillusion (1904–1907)* (rev. edn, Oxford: Oxford University, Press 2000); vol. 4, *A New Life Cut Short (1907–1911)* (rev. edn, Oxford: Oxford University Press, 2008).

5. Alma Mahler, *Gustav Mahler: Memories and Letters*, trans. Basil Creighton (New York: Viking Press, 1946), p. 98.
6. Paul Stefan, *Gustav Mahler: A Study of His Personality and Work*, trans. T. E. Clark (New York: Schirmer, 1913), p. 118.
7. Bruno Walter, *Gustav Mahler*, trans. James Galston (New York: Greystone, 1941) pp. 58–9.
8. The 'porcelain' and 'jade', which Mahler took from the German edition, suggest a ceramic miniature rather than a real scene. But this is the result of mistranslation of the original Chinese poem. See Teng-Leong Chew, 'The Literary Changes in *Das Lied von der Erde*', www.mahlerarchives.net.
9. Stephen E. Hefling, 'Mahler's "Todtenfeir" and the Problem of Program Music', *19th-Century Music*, vol. 12, no. 1 (Summer 1988), pp. 27–53.
10. Edward R. Reilly, 'Todtenfeier and the Second Symphony', *The Mahler Companion*, ed. Donald Mitchell and Andrew Nicholson (Oxford: Oxford University Press, 2002), p. 88.
11. Ibid., 'Three Programmes for the Second Symphony', pp. 123–5.
12. Quoted in *Mahler and His World*, ed. Karen Painter (Princeton, NJ: Princeton University Press, 2002), p. 102.
13. Natalie Bauer-Lechner, *Recollections of Gustav Mahler*, trans. Dika Newlin, ed. Peter Franklin (London: Faber, 1980), pp. 43–4.
14. Peter Franklin, 'A Stranger's Story: Programmes, Politics, and Mahler's Third Symphony', *The Mahler Companion*, ed. Mitchell and Nicholson, pp. 171–86.
15. James L. Zychowicz, *Mahler's Fourth Symphony* (Oxford: Oxford University Press, 2005), p. 35.
16. Robert Philip, *Performing Music in the Age of Recording* (New Haven, CT, and London: Yale University Press), p. 163.
17. De la Grange, *Gustav Mahler*, vol. 2, pp. 418–20.
18. Gilbert Kaplan, 'Adagietto: "From Mahler with Love"', in Jeremy Barham (ed.), *Perspectives on Gustav Mahler* (Aldershot: Ashgate, 2005), pp. 379–400.
19. De la Grange, *Gustav Mahler*, vol. 2, pp. 412–13.
20. Alma Mahler, *Gustav Mahler*, p. 100.
21. Derrick Puffett, 'Berg, Mahler and the Three Orchestral Pieces Op. 6', *The Cambridge Companion to Berg*, ed. Anthony Pople (Cambridge: Cambridge University Press, 1997), pp. 114–15.
22. Alma Mahler, *Gustav Mahler*, p. 322.
23. Arnold Schoenberg, *Letters*, ed. Erwin Stein, trans. Eithne Wilkins and Ernst Kaiser (Berkeley and Los Angeles, CA: University of California Press, 1964), pp. 293–4.
24. De la Grange, *Gustav Mahler*, vol. 3, pp. 426–7.
25. Ibid., pp. 429–30.
26. Stephen E. Hefling, 'Aspects of Mahler's Late Style', *Mahler and his World*, ed. Karen Painter (Princeton: Princeton University Press, 2002), p. 204.
27. Ibid.
28. Ibid.
29. Alma Mahler, *Gustav Mahler*, pp. 260–1.
30. Ibid., p. 135.

Bohuslav Martinů

1. Brian Large, *Martinů* (London: Duckworth, 1975), p. 1.
2. Ibid., p. 74.
3. Miloš Šafránek, *Bohuslav Martinů: The Man and His Music* (New York: Alfred A. Knopf, 1944), p. 46.

Felix Mendelssohn

1. C. Hubert H. Parry, *Studies of Great Composers* (London: George Routledge, 8th edn, 1904), pp. 287–8.
2. Letter to his family, Munich, 6 October 1831, in *Felix Mendelssohn: Letters*, ed. G. Selden-Goth (New York: Pantheon Books, 1945, and Vienna House, 1973), p. 173.
3. Ibid., p. 335.
4. *Felix Mendelssohn*, ed. Selden-Goth, p. 56.
5. Felix Mendelssohn Bartholdy, *Briefe an deutsche Verlege*, ed. Rudolf Elvers (Berlin: Walter der Gruyter & Co., 1968), pp. 25–6.
6. See the letter to his mother, 19 July 1842, in *Felix Mendelssohn*, ed. Selden-Goth, pp. 305–9.
7. Benedict Taylor, *Mendelssohn, Time and Memory: The Romantic Conception of Cyclic Form* (Cambridge: Cambridge University Press, 2011), p. 254.
8. *Felix Mendelssohn*, ed. Selden-Goth, p. 118.
9. John Michael Cooper, 'Mendelssohn and Berlioz: Selective Affinities', in *Mendelssohn Perspectives*, ed. Nicole Grimes and Angela Mace (London: Ashgate 2012), p. 130.
10. *Felix Mendelssohn*, ed. Selden-Goth, pp. 116–17.

Olivier Messiaen

1. Peter Hill and Nigel Simeone, *Messiaen* (New Haven, CT, and London: Yale University Press, 2005), p. 35.
2. Edward Lockspeiser, *Debussy: His Life and Mind, vol. 1* (London: Cassell, 1965), p. 115.
3. Olivier Messiaen, *Music and Color: Conversations with Claude Samuel* (Portland, OR: Amadeus Press, 1994), pp. 30–1. See also Siglind Bruhn, *Messiaen's Explorations of Love and Death: Musico-Poetic Signification in the 'Tristan Trilogy' and Three Related Song Cycles* (Hillsdale, NY: Pendragon Press, 2008).
4. Hill and Simeone, *Messiaen*, p. 173.
5. Ibid., p. 195.

6. From Messiaen's liner notes (trans. Paul Griffiths) for the recording by the Orchestre de l'Opéra Bastille conducted by Myung-Wha Chung. DG 0289 431 7812 9, rec. 1990. These are the source of Messiaen's quotations in the descriptions that follow.
7. Hill and Simeone, *Messiaen*, p. 394, n. 53.
8. Robert Sherlaw Johnson, *Messiaen* (London: Dent, 1975, rev. edn 1989), pp. 89–90.
9. Hill and Simeone, *Messiaen*, p. 167.

Darius Milhaud

1. Darius Milhaud, *My Happy Life*, trans. Donald Evans, George Hall and Christopher Palmer. (London and New York: Marion Boyars, 1995) [originally published in 1973 as *Ma vie heureuse*], p. 69.
2. Ibid., pp. 86–7.
3. Ibid., p. 87.
4. Ibid., p. 88.
5. Background notes and recordings of the tunes can be found at Daniella Thompson, 'Musica Brasiliensis: The *Boeuf* Chronicles. How the Ox Got on the Roof: Darius Milhaud and the Brazilian sources of *Le Boeuf sur le Toit*'. http://daniellathompson.com/Texts/Le_Boeuf/boeuf_chronicles.htm (accessed 16 September 2017).
6. *La revue musicale*, November 1920, quoted in ibid.
7. Milhaud, *My Happy Life*, p. 110.
8. Blaise Cendrars, *Anthologie nègre* (Paris: Éditions de la sirène, 1921).
9. Milhaud, *My Happy Life*, p. 118.
10. Ibid., p. 120.

Wolfgang Amadeus Mozart

1. Hermann Abert, *W. A. Mozart*, trans. Stewart Spencer, ed. Cliff Eisen (Leipzig: Breitkopf & Härtel, 1923–4, repr. New Haven, CT, and London: Yale University Press, 2007), p. 813.
2. Richard Wigmore, *Haydn* (London: Faber, 2009), p. 50, H. C. Robbins Landon, *1791: Mozart's Last Year* (London: Thames & Hudson, 2nd edn, 1989), p. 171.
3. *Mozart's Letters, Mozart's Life*, trans. and ed. Robert Spaethling (London: Faber & Faber 2004), p. 439.
4. 'Mozart and the Clarinet', in Eric Hoeprich, *The Clarinet* (New Haven, CT, and London: Yale University Press, 2008), pp. 100–22.
5. In the *Mercure de France*, April 1770. Reginald Morley-Pegge and Thomas Hiebert, 'Leutgeb [Leitgeb], Joseph [Ignaz]', *Grove Music Online* (accessed 12 January 2018).
6. These include versions by John Humphries, Stephen Roberts, and Robert Levin.
7. Maynard Solomon, *Mozart: A Life* (London: Pimlico, 1995), p. 357.
8. Wolfgang Amadeus Mozart, *Neue Ausgabe sämtlicher Werke*, series V, category 14, vol. 5, ed. Franz Giegling (Kassel: Bärenreiter, 1985), p. xiii; Wolfgang Amadeus Mozart, *Konzert für Horn und Orchester Es-dur KV 495*, ed. Henrik Wiese (Berlin: Breitkopf & Härtel, 2016), pp. v–vi.
9. Otto Erich Deutsch, *Mozart: A Documentary Biography*, trans. Eric Blom, Peter Branscombe and Jeremy Noble (3rd edn, London and New York: Simon & Schuster, 1990), p. 504.
10. The identification was made by Michael Lorenz. See his 'The Jenamy Concerto', *Newsletter of the American Mozart Society*, vol. 9, no. 1 (2005), pp. 1–3.
11. 28 December 1782, in *Mozart's Letters*, ed. Spaethling, p. 116.
12. Ibid., p. 308.
13. Ibid., pp. 364–6.
14. John Irving, *Mozart's Piano Concertos* (Abingdon: Routledge, 2017), p. 210.
15. *Mozart's Letters*, ed. Spaethling, p. 371.
16. Ibid., pp. 364–5.
17. Letter from Leopold to Maria Anna Mozart, 16 February 1785, in Karl Geringer, *Haydn: A Creative Life in Music* (Berkeley, CA: University of California Press, 1982), p. 80.
18. Alfred Einstein, *Mozart: His Character – His Work*, trans. Arthur Mendel and Nathan Broder (London: Cassell, 1946, repr. Oxford: Oxford University Press, 1962), p. 323.
19. *Thayer's Life of Beethoven*, rev. and ed. Elliot Forbes (Princeton: Princeton University Press, 1967), p. 209.
20. Abert, *W. A. Mozart*, p. 276.
21. 11 September 1778, *Mozart's Letters*, ed. Spaethling, p. 185.
22. 23–25 October 1777, ibid., p. 80.
23. Einstein, *Mozart*, p. 249.
24. Stanley Sadie, *Mozart: The Early Years 1756–1781* (Oxford: Oxford University Press, 2006), p. 65.
25. Letter to his father from Paris, 9 July 1778, in *Mozart's Letters*, ed. Spaethling, p. 165.
26. Bernard Harrison, *Haydn: The 'Paris' Symphonies* (Cambridge: Cambridge University Press, 1998), p. 107, n.26
27. 20 July 1782, *Mozart's Letters*, ed. Spaethling, p. 315.
28. 15 February 1783, ibid., p. 343.
29. 7 August 1782, ibid., p. 321.
30. Ibid.
31. Ibid., p. 362.
32. Robbins Landon, *1791*, pp. 31–4.

Modest Musorgsky

1. David Brown, *Musorgsky: His Life and Works* (Oxford: Oxford University Press, 2002), pp. 12–13.
2. Ibid., p. 87.
3. Ibid., p. 90.
4. Alfred Frankenstein, 'Victor Hartmann and Modeste Musorgsky', *Musical Quarterly*, vol. 25 no. 3 (July 1939), pp. 278–9.
5. Interview with M. D. Calvocoressi, *Daily Telegraph*, 12 January 1929.
6. These are gathered together in Alfred Frankenstein, 'Victor Hartmann and Modeste Musorgsky', *Musical Quarterly*, vol. 25, no. 3 (July 1939), pp. 268–91.
7. Brown, *Musorgsky*, pp. 196–7.
8. Richard Taruskin, *On Russian Music* (Berkeley, CA: University of California Press, 2009), p. 198.
9. Brown, *Musorgsky*, p. 238.

Carl Nielsen

1. David Fanning, 'Nielsen, Carl (August)', *Grove Music Online*.
2. Robert Simpson, *Carl Nielsen: Symphonist* (1952, 2nd edn, New York: Taplinger Publishing, 1979), p. 238.
3. Benedikte Brincke, 'The Role of Classical Music in the Construction of Nationalism: An Analysis of Danish Consensus Nationalism and the Reception of Carl Nielsen', *Nations and Nationalism*, vol. 14, issue 4 (October 2008), p. 689.
4. Daniel M. Grimley, *Carl Nielsen and the Idea of Modernism* (Woodbridge: Boydell Press, 2010), p. 96.
5. Preface to the score by Claus Røllum-Larsen, *Carl Nielsen – Vaerker*, Series II, No. 4 (2000), p. xi.
6. Ibid., pp. xiii–xiv.
7. Preface to the score by Michael Fjeldsøe, *Carl Nielsen – Vaerker*, Series II, No. 5 (1998), p. xii.
8. Ibid., pp. xiii–xiv.
9. Ibid., p. xiv.
10. Thomas Michelsen, preface to the score, *Carl Nielsen – Vaerker*, Series II, No. 6 (2001), pp. xi–xii.
11. Andrew Barnett, *Sibelius* (New Haven, CT, and London: Yale University Press, 2007), p. 234.
12. Ludvig Dolleris, *Carl Nielsen, En Musikografi* (Odense: Fyns Boghandels Forlag, 1949), quoted in Thomas Michelsen, preface to the score, p. xvii.
13. Grimley, *Carl Nielsen*, p. 249.
14. Michelsen, preface to the score, *Carl Nielsen – Vaerker*, Series II, No. 6, p. xviii.

Sergei Sergeyevich Prokofiev

1. Israel V. Nestyev, *Prokofiev*, trans. Florence Jonas (Stanford, CA: Stanford University Press, 1960), p. 241.
2. Sergei Prokofiev and S. Shlifstein, *Autobiography, Articles, Reminiscences* (Honolulu: University Press of the Pacific, 2000), pp. 36–7.
3. Simon Morrison, *The People's Artist; Prokofiev's Soviet Years* (Oxford: Oxford University Press 2009, online edn).
4. Prokofiev and Shlifstein, *Autobiography, Articles, Reminiscences*, pp. 84–5.
5. Harlow Robinson, *Sergei Prokofiev: A Biography* (Boston, MA: Northeastern University Press, 1989).
6. 18 August 1912, in *Sergei Prokofiev, Diaries, 1907–1914: Prodigious Youth*, trans. Anthony Phillips (London: Faber, 2006), p. 237.
7. Ibid., p. 258.
8. Ibid., p. 488.
9. Prokofiev and Shlifstein, *Autobiography, Articles, Reminiscences*, p. 33.
10. Nestyev, *Prokofiev*, p. 202.
11. *Selected Letters of Sergei Prokofiev*, ed. and trans. Harrow Robinson (Boston, MA: Northeastern University Press, 1998), 255.
12. Robinson, *Sergei Prokofiev*, p. 166.
13. Prokofiev and Shlifstein, *Autobiography, Articles, Reminiscences*, p. 60.
14. Joseph Szigeti, *With Strings Attached* (New York: Alfred A. Knopf, 1947), p. 199.
15. Nestyev, *Prokofiev*, p. 141.
16. *Selected Letters*, ed. and trans. Robinson, p. 153.
17. The scenario is given in full in Morrison, *The People's Artist*, pp. 395–402.
18. Robinson, *Sergei Prokofiev*, pp. 130–1.
19. Stephen D. Press, *Prokofiev's Ballets for Diaghilev* (Aldershot: Ashgate, 2006), p. 252.
20. Prokofiev and Shlifstein, *Autobiography, Articles, Reminiscences*, pp. 213–14.
21. Nestyev, *Prokofiev*, p. 365.

Sergei Rachmaninoff

1. Barrie Martyn, *Rachmaninoff: Composer, Pianist, Conductor* (Farnham: Ashgate, 1990), p. 96.
2. Ibid., p. 123.
3. Sergei Bertensson and Jay Leyda, *Sergei Rachmaninoff: A Lifetime in Music* (Bloomington, IN: Indiana University Press, 2001), p. 351.
4. Ibid., p. 173.
5. Max Harrison, *Rachmaninoff: Life, Works, Recordings* (London: Bloomsbury, 2006), p. 150.
6. A. J. and K. Swan, 'Rachmaninoff: Personal Reminscences', *The Musical Quarterly*, vol. 30, no. 1 (January 1944), p. 8.
7. Geoffrey Norris, 'Rachmaninoff, Serge', *Grove Music Online*.
8. Bertensson and Leyda, *Rachmaninoff*, p. 95.
9. Robert Rimm, *The Composer-Pianists: Hamelin and the Eight* (Portland, OR: Amadeus Press, 2002), p. 142.

10. Martyn, *Rachmaninoff*, p. 353.
11. Online notes for Los Angeles Philharmonic concert, 8 April 2017. legacy.laphil.com/philpedia/music/symphonic-dances-op-45-sergei-rachmaninoff (accessed 19 September 2017). As this book goes to print (August 2018) the first publication of this recording has been announced: *Rachmaninoff Plays Symphonic Dances: Newly Discovered 1940 Recording*. Marston Records 53022–2.
12. Martyn, *Rachmaninoff*, p. 103.
13. Robert Simpson, *The Symphony*, vol. 2: *Mahler to the Present Day* (New York: Drake Publishers, 1972), pp. 129–30.

Maurice Ravel
1. Roger Nichols, *Ravel* (New Haven, CT, and London: Yale University Press, 2011), p. 24.
2. Arbie Orenstein, *Ravel: Man and Musician* (New York: Columbia University Press, 1975), p. 118.
3. *A Ravel Reader: Correspondence, Articles, Interviews*, ed. Arbie Orenstein (New York: Columbia University Press, 1990), p. 45.
4. *Edgar Allan Poe: Essays and Reviews*, ed. G. R. Thompson (New York: The Library of America, 1984), pp. 14–15.
5. Orenstein, *Ravel*, pp. 200–1.
6. Deborah Mawer, *The Ballets of Maurice Ravel: Creation and Interpretation* (Aldershot: Ashgate, 2006), p. 227.
7. Ibid., p. 224.
8. Ibid., p. 81.
9. Nichols, *Ravel*, p. 143.
10. Roger Nichols, *Ravel Remembered* (New York: Norton, 1988), pp. 41–3.
11. Nichols, *Ravel*, p. 144.
12. Nichols, *Ravel Remembered*, p. 21.
13. M. Robert Rogers, 'Jazz Influence on French Music', *The Musical Quarterly*, vol. 21, no. 1 (January 1935), p. 64.
14. Robert Philip, *Performing Music in the Age of Recording* (New Haven, CT, and London: Yale University Press, 2004), p. 169.
15. *A Ravel Reader*, ed. Orenstein, p. 477.
16. Orenstein, *Ravel*, p. 101.
17. Ibid., p. 102.
18. Nichols, *Ravel*, p. 192.
19. Marguerite Long, *At the Piano with Ravel*, trans. Olive Senior-Ellis (London: J. M. Dent & Sons, 1973), p. 94.
20. Nichols, *Ravel*, p. 59.
21. Ibid., p. 82.
22. Ibid., p. 177.
23. Ibid., p. 205
24. Ibid., pp. 209–10.
25. 'The French Music Festival: An Interview with Ravel', in *De Telegraaf* (30 September 1922), *A Ravel Reader*, ed. Orenstein, p. 423.
26. Ibid., p. 230.
27. Ibid., p. 32.

Nikolai Rimsky-Korsakov
1. Nikolay Andreyevich Rimsky-Korskov, *My Musical Life*, ed. with introduction by Carl van Vechten, trans. Judith A. Joffe (London: Faber & Faber, 1989, first published 1923, original Russian edn 1909), pp. 245–6.
2. Ibid., pp. 291–4.

Gioachino Rossini
1. Undated letter to an unknown correspondent, Luigi Rognoni, *Gioacchino Rossini*, 2nd edn (Turin: Edizioni RAI, 1967), p. 337. Trans. Josiah Fisk and Jeff Nichols (eds), *Composers on Music* (Boston, MA: Northeastern University Press, 1997), p. 67.
2. *Berlioz on Music: Select Criticisms, 1824–1837*, ed. Katherine Kolb, trans. Samuel N. Rosenberg (Oxford: Oxford University Press, 2015), pp. 90–1.

Camille Saint-Saëns
1. Stephen Studd, *Saint-Saëns: A Critical Biography* (London: Cygnus Arts, 1999), p. 46.
2. Ibid., p. 44.
3. *Camille Saint-Saëns: On Music and Musicians*, ed. and trans. Roger Nichols (Oxford: Oxford University Press, 2008), p. 8.
4. 'Camille Saint-Saëns', *Romain Rolland's Essays on Music*, ed. David Ewen (New York: Dover, 1958), p. 370.
5. Saint-Saëns, *Musical Memories*, trans. Edwin Gile Rich (London: John Murray, 1921), p. 2.
6. Camille Saint-Saëns, *Outspoken Essays on Music*, trans. Fred Rothwell (London: Kegan and Paul, 1922), pp. 113–14.
7. Ibid., p. 113.
8. Ibid.

Erik Satie
1. Robert Orledge, *Satie the Composer* (Cambridge: Cambridge University Press, 1990), p. xxii.
2. Ibid., p. 205.
3. Christine Reynolds, '*Parade: ballet réaliste*', in *Erik Satie: Music, Art and Literature*, ed. Caroline Potter (London: Routledge, 2016), pp. 143–4.

4. *Erik Satie: Music, Art and Literature*, ed. Potter, pp. 105–6.
5. Orledge, *Satie the Composer*, p. 224.
6. Norman Peterkin, 'Erik Satie's Parade', *Musical Times*, vol. 60, no. 918 (August 1919), p. 426.
7. *Erik Satie: Music, Art and Literature*, ed. Potter, p. 158.
8. Ibid.
9. Ibid., p. 147.

Arnold Schoenberg

1. H. H. Stuckenschmidt, *Arnold Schoenberg*, trans. Edith Temple Roberts and Humphrey Searle (London: John Calder, 1959), p. 82.
2. Adrian Cedric Boult, *My Own Trumpet* (London: Hamish Hamilton, 1973), p. 147.
3. The political background is discussed by Alex Ross in *The Rest is Noise: Listening to the Twentieth Century* (London: Fourth Estate, 2008), pp. 399–406.
4. Berlin Diary, 28 January 1912, ed. Josef Rufer, quoted by Richard Hoffman, Oberlin Conservatory, for American Symphony Orchestra (1993). Americansymphony.org/five-pieces-for-orchestra-op-16/ (accessed 21 September 2017).
5. Malcolm MacDonald, *Schoenberg* (Oxford: Oxford University Press), p. 9.
6. Michael Kennedy, *Richard Strauss: Man, Musician, Enigma* (Cambridge: Cambridge University Press, 2006), p. 173.
7. Ibid.
8. Arthur Jacobs, *Henry J. Wood: Maker of the Proms* (London: Methuen, 1994), p. 137.
9. Robert Craft, note for recording: Naxos 8.557524.
10. Alma Mahler, *Gustav Mahler, Memories and Letters* (London: John Murray, 1946), p. 153.
11. Craft, ibid.
12. 21 September 1928, *Arnold Schoenberg Letters*, ed. Erwin Stein (London: Faber & Faber, 1964), p. 131.
13. 4 June 1929, ibid., p. 134.
14. 14 April 1934, ibid., p. 185.
15. *Schoenberg's Program Notes and Musical Analyses*, ed. J. Daniel Jenkins (Oxford: Oxford University Press, 2016), p. 297.
16. Recorded 1998. Naxos 8.557522.
17. Richard Dehmel, *Dichtungen, Briefe, Dokumente*, ed. Paul J. Schingler (Hamburg: Hoffmann & Campe, 1963), p. 126.
18. The structure of Schoenberg's *Verklärte Nacht* and its relationship to Dehmel's poem have been much debated. See Walter Frisch, *The Early Works of Arnold Schoenberg, 1893–1909* (Berkeley, CA: University of California Press, 1997), pp. 109–39.

Franz Schubert

1. Schubert's Diary, 16 June 1816, Otto Erich Deutsch, *Schubert: A Documentary Biography* (London: J. M. Dent & Sons, 1946), p. 64.
2. 14 June 1816, ibid., p. 60.
3. *The Musical World of Robert Schumann: A Selection from his Own Writings*, trans. and ed. Henry Pleasants (London: Victor Gollancz, 1965), pp. 166–7.

Robert Schumann

1. Ronald Taylor, *Robert Schumann: His Life and Work* (London: Granada, 1982), p. 62.
2. Eric Frederick Jensen, *Schumann* (Oxford: Oxford University Press, 2001), pp. 34–5.
3. John Worthen, *Robert Schumann: Life and Death of a Musician* (New Haven, CT, and London: Yale University Press, 2007), p. 212.
4. Berthold Litzmann, *Clara Schumann: An Artist's Life, based on Material Found in Diaries and Letters*, vol. 1, trans. Grace E. Hadow (Cambridge: Cambridge University Press, 2013, first published 1913), p. 409.
5. Peter Clive, *Brahms and his World: A Biographical Dictionary* (Lanham, MD: The Scarecrow Press, 2006), p. 406.
6. Letter to Andreas Moser, 5 August 1898, *The Musician's World: Letters of the Great Composers*, ed. Hans Gál (London: Thames & Hudson, 1965), p. 184.
7. Letter to Joachim, 8 October 1853, *The Letters of Robert Schumann*, ed. Karl Storck, trans. Hannah Bryant (London: John Murray, 1907), p. 281.
8. Worthen, *Robert Schumann*, pp. 207–8.
9. Ibid.
10. Ibid.
11. Jensen, *Schumann*, p. 201.
12. *The Letters of Robert Schumann*, ed. Storck, p. 249.
13. Worthen, *Robert Schumann*, p. 270.
14. Litzmann, *Clara Schumann*, vol. 1, p. 435.
15. John Daverio, *Crossing Paths: Schubert, Schumann and Brahms* (Oxford: Oxford University Press, 2002), p. 172.
16. *The Marriage Diaries of Robert and Clara Schumann*, ed. Gerd Nauhaus, trans. Peter Ostwald (Boston, MA: Northeastern University Press, 1993), p. 83.

Alexander Scriabin

1. Boris de Schloezer, *Scriabin: Artist and Mystic* (Oxford: Oxford University Press, 1987, trans. Nicolas Slonimsky from *A. Scriabin*, vol. 1, Berlin, 1923).
2. Ibid.

3. Leonid Sabaneeff, 'A. N. Scriabin – A Memoir', *The Russian Review*, vol. 25, no. 3 (July 1966), p. 263.
4. Faubion Bowers, *Scriabin: A Biography* (New York, Dover: 1996, originally published 1969), vol. 2, p. 61.
5. Ibid., p. 130.
6. Schloezer, *Scriabin*, pp. 231, 149.
7. Bowers, *Scriabin*, vol. 2, p. 131.
8. Hugh MacDonald, 'Words and Music by A. Skryabin', and Alexander Skryabin, *The Poem of Ecstasy*, trans. Hugh MacDonald, *The Musical Times*, vol. 113, no. 1547 (January 1972), pp. 22–5 and 26–7.

Dmitri Shostakovich

1. Shostakovich's humiliating visit to the United States is vividly described by Alex Ross in *The Rest is Noise: Listening to the Twentieth Century* (London: Fourth Estate, 2008), pp. 373–8.
2. Yevgeny Mravinsky, 'Thirty Years of Shostakovich's Music', in L. V. Danilevich, *Dmitri Shostakovich*, pp. 111–14, quoted in Elizabeth Wilson, *Shostakovich: A Life Remembered* (London: Faber & Faber, 1994), p. 139.
3. Wilson, *Shostakovich*, p. 239.
4. 'D. Oistrakh: Great Artist of our Time', *D. Shostakovich: Articles and Other Materials*, ed. G. M. Shneerson (Moscow: Sovetskii Kompozitor, 1976).
5. Victor Juzefovich, *David Oistrakh: Conversations with Igor Oistrakh* (London: Cassell, 1979), p. 172.
6. Ibid., p. 172.
7. Wilson, *Shostakovich*, p. 126.
8. Allan B. Ho and Dmitry Feofanov, *Shostakovich Reconsidered* (London: Toccata Press, 1998), p. 408.
9. Laurel E. Fay, *Shostakovich: A Life* (Oxford: Oxford University Press, 2005), p. 115.
10. The evidence is summarized in Allan B. Ho and Dmitry Feofanov, *The Shostakovich Wars* (online edition, updated 18 September 2011), pp. 134–8.
11. Manashir Iakubov, 'Dmitry Shostakovich's Seventh Symphony: How It Was Composed', *Dmitry Shostakovich New Collected Works*, 1st series, vol. 7, Symphony No. 7, Opus 60, ed. Manashir Iakobiv (Moscow: DSCH Publishers, 2010), p. 260.
12. 18 September 1943, Fay, *Shostakovich*, p. 136.
13. Solomon Volkov, *Testimony: The Memoirs of Dmitri Shostakovich* (London: Hamish Hamilton, 1979), p. 141.
14. Recorded 15 February 1954. *Shostakovich Plays Shostakovich*, vol. 2, Revelation Records, RV 70002 (issued 1997).

Jean Sibelius

1. Byron Adams, ' "Thor's Hammer": Sibelius and British Music Critics, 1905–1957', *Jean Sibelius and his World*, ed. Daniel M. Grimley (Princeton, NJ: Princeton University Press, 2011), p. 154.
2. *Kalevala: The Land of Heroes*, vol. 2, trans. W. F. Kirby (London: Dent, 1910), p. 71.
3. Erik Tawaststjerna (trans Robert Layton), *Sibelius*, vol. 3: *1914–1957* (London: Faber & Faber, 1997), p. 234.
4. Erik Tawaststjerna, *Sibelius*, vol. 1, *1865–1905*, trans. Robert Layton (Berkeley and Los Angeles, CA: University of California Press, 1976), p. 87.
5. Ibid., p. 112.
6. All extracts are taken from *Kalevala: The Land of Heroes*, vol. 2, trans. Kirby.
7. Tawaststjerna, *Sibelius*, vol. 1, p. 130.
8. Interview with A. O. Väisänen, 1921, 'En Saga', Jean Sibelius Website. www.sibelius.fi/english/musiiki/ork_satu.htm (accessed 27 September 2017).
9. Tawaststjerna, *Sibelius*, vol. 1, p. 153.
10. Ibid., p. 244.
11. To Jussi Jalas, 31 December 1943, Jean Sibelius Website. www.sibelius.fi/english/omin_sanoin/17.htm (accessed 27 September 2017).
12. Andrew Barnett, *Sibelius* (New Haven, CT, and London: Yale University Press 2007), p. 185.
13. Letter to his wife, Aino, 8 January 1891, in Tomi Mäkelä, *Jean Sibelius* (Woodbridge: Boydell Press, 2011), p. 343.
14. Barnett, *Sibelius*, p. 184.
15. Ibid., p. 211.
16. London Symphony Orchestra, conducted by Robert Kajanus, rec. 22–23 June, 1932, HMV Sibelius Society, vol. 1, DB1739–1745. Reissue, Naxos 8.111395. Sibelius's metronome markings are discussed in Robert Philip, *Early Recordings and Musical Style: Changing Tastes in Instrumental Performance, 1900–1950* (Cambridge: Cambridge University Press, 1992), pp. 10–11, 33–4.
17. James Hepokoski, *Sibelius: Symphony No. 5* (Cambridge: Cambridge University Press, 1993), p. 36.
18. Veijo Murtomäki, 'Sibelius's Symphonic Ballade *Skoegrået*', *Sibelius Studies*, ed. Timothy L. Jackson, Veijo Murtomäki (Cambridge: Cambridge University Press, 2001), p. 137.
19. Jean Sibelius Website. www.sibelius.fi/english/musiiki/ork_sinf_06.htm (accessed 27 September 2017).
20. To his son-in-law, Jussi Jalas, Jean Sibelius Website. www.sibelius.fi/english/musiiki/ork_sinf_07.htm (accessed 27 September 2017).
21. Donald Francis Tovey, *Concertos and Choral Works: Selections from Essays in Musical Analysis* (Mineola, NY: Dover Publications, 2015), p. 206.
22. Ibid., p. 210.

Bedřich Smetana

1. John Clapham, *Smetana* (London: Dent, 1972), pp. 43–4.
2. Brian Large, *Smetana* (New York and Washington, DC: Praeger, 1970), pp. 270–84.

3. Ibid.

Richard Strauss

1. See Leon Botstein, 'The Enigmas of Richard Strauss: A Revisionist View', *Richard Strauss and his World*, ed. Bryan Gilliam (Princeton, NJ: Princeton University Press, 1992), pp. 7–9.
2. Letters to his father, 7 and 10 November 1889, Willi Schuh, *Richard Strauss: A Chronicle of the Early Years, 1864–1898*, trans. Mary Whittall (Cambridge: Cambridge University Press, 1982, first published in German, 1976), pp. 183–4.
3. The complete extracts are quoted, in German and English, in Norman Del Mar's preface to the 1974 Eulenburg score.
4. Schuh, *Richard Strauss*, p. 183.
5. Ibid., p. 478.
6. Ibid., p. 461.
7. 22 March 1899, ibid., p. 481.
8. 9 July 1905, *Richard Strauss and Romain Rolland: Correspondence* (Berkeley and Los Angeles, CA: University of California Press, 1968), p. 34.
9. Michael Kennedy, *Richard Strauss: Man, Music, Enigma* (Cambridge: Cambridge University Press, 2006), p. 116.
10. Timothy L. Jackson, 'The Metamorphosis of the *Metamorphosen*', *Richard Strauss: New Perspectives on the Composer and his Music* (Durham, NC: Duke University Press, 1997), p. 200.
11. Kennedy, *Richard Strauss*, p. 361.
12. Ibid., p. 357.
13. Nicholas Boyle, *Goethe: Revolution and Renunciation, 1790–1803* (Oxford: Clarendon Press, 2000), p. 459.

Igor Stravinsky

1. Igor Stravinsky, *An Autobiography* (New York: Simon and Schuster, 1936, rep. New York: W. W. Norton & Company, 1962), p. 53.
2. *Poetics of Music in the Form of Six Lessons* (Cambridge, MA, and London: Harvard University Press, 1942/1970), p. 35.
3. Ibid., p. 18.
4. Stravinsky, *An Autobiography*, p. 38.
5. Ingolf Dahl, 'Igor Stravinsky on Film Music', *Musical Digest*, vol. 28 (September 1946).
6. Richard Taruskin, *Stravinsky and the Russian Traditions* (Berkeley and Los Angeles, CA: University of California Press, 1996), vol. 1, pp. 616–22.
7. Stravinsky, *An Autobiography*, p. 30.
8. Taruskin, *Stravinsky and the Russian Traditions*, vol. 1, pp. 561–2.
9. The song is no. 79 of Rimsky-Korsakov's collection, 'Kak' po sadyku', in *Chants nationaux russes*, vol. 2 (St Petersburg: W. Bessel & cie, 1877), p. 88.
10. Stravinsky, *An Autobiography*, pp. 31–2.
11. Letter to Stravinsky, 13 April 1912, in Robert Orledge, *Debussy and the Theatre* (Cambridge: Cambridge University Press, 1982), p. 146.
12. Stravinsky, *An Autobiography*, p. 34.
13. Richard Taruskin: 'Stravinsky's *Petrushka*', in Andrew Wachtel (ed.), *Petrushka: Sources and Contexts* (Evanston, IL: Northwest University Press, 1998), p. 69.
14. Ibid., p. 73. Taruskin examines the origins of many of the traditional tunes in *Petrushka*, and his identifications are used in my description of the score.
15. Maureen A. Carr (ed.), *Stravinsky's Pulcinella: A Facsimile of the Sources and Sketches* (Middleton, WI: A-R Editions, 2010), p. 47, n. 41.
16. Stravinsky, *An Autobiography*, pp. 81–2.
17. In 1962, from Igor Stravinsky and Robert Craft, *Expositions and Developments* (Berkeley and Los Angeles, CA: University of California Press, 1982), pp. 111–14.
18. Carr (ed.), *Stravinsky's Pulcinella*, p. 16.
19. Igor Strawinsky d'après Giambattista Pergolesi, *Pulcinella* (London, J. & W. Chester, 1920).
20. All these sources are detailed, with music examples, in Carr (ed.), *Stravinsky's Pulcinella*.
21. Taruskin, *Stravinsky and the Russian Traditions*, vol. 2, p. 505.
22. Stravinsky, *An Autobiography*, p. 31.
23. Peter Hill, *Stravinsky: The Rite of Spring* (Cambridge: Cambridge University Press, 2000), p. 4.
24. Ibid., pp. 4–5.
25. Ibid., p. 17.
26. Marjorie Garber, *The Muses on their Lunch Hour* (New York: Fordham University Press, 2017), p. 15.
27. See, for example, Pieter van den Toorn, *Stravinsky and the Rite of Spring: The Beginnings of a Musical Language* (Berkeley and Los Angeles, CA: University of California Press, 1987).
28. Hill, *Stravinsky*, pp. 93–5.
29. Ibid., p. 8.
30. Ibid., p. 94.
31. Stephen Walsh, *Igor Stravinsky: A Creative Spring: Russia and France 1882–1934* (Berkeley and Los Angeles, CA: University of California Press, 2003), p. 332.
32. Taruskin, *Stravinsky and the Russian Traditions*, vol. 2, pp. 488–95.
33. Stravinsky, *An Autobiography*, p. 95.
34. Igor Stravinsky and Robert Craft, *Themes and Episodes* (New York: Alfred A. Knopf, 1966), p. 41.
35. Stephen Davies, *Musical Meaning and Expression* (Ithaca, NY, and London: Cornell University Press, 1994), p. 172.

36. Igor Stravinsky, *Themes and Conclusions* (London: Faber & Faber, 1972), pp. 47–51.
37. Ibid., p. 44.
38. Ibid., p. 43.
39. Eric Walter White, *Stravinsky: The Composer and His Work* (Berkeley and Los Angeles, CA: University of California Press, 1984), p. 430.
40. Igor Stravinsky and Robert Craft, *Dialogues and a Diary* (New York: Doubleday, 1963), pp. 83–5.

Pyotr Ilyich Tchaikovsky

1. David Brown, *Tchaikovsky: The Man and his Music* (London: Faber and Faber, 2007), p. 227.
2. Modeste Tchaikovsky, *The Life and Letters of Peter Ilich Tchaikovsky*, ed. Rosa Newmarch (London: John Lane, 1906, New York: Minerva Group, 2004), p. 607.
3. Tchaikovsky Research website: en.tchaikovsky-research.net/pages/The_Year_1812 (accessed 29 September 2017).
4. Tchaikovsky, *The Life and Letters*, p. 390.
5. John Warrack, *Tchaikovsky* (London: Hamish Hamilton, 1973), pp. 78–9.
6. Letter to Nadezhda von Meck, 9 (21) May 1879, in Tchaikovsky, *The Life and Letters*, p. 346.
7. Pianist Stephen Hough drew attention to this correction. See Kirill Gerstein, 'Tchaikovsky's "wrong" Note', *The New York Review of Books*, 13 August 2013. www.nybooks.com/daily/2013/08/13/tchaikovskys-wrong-note (accessed 29 September 2017).
8. Warrack, *Tchaikovsky*, p. 80.
9. Ibid., p. 260.
10. Ibid., p. 262.
11. Tchaikovsky, *The Life and Letters*, p. 415.
12. Tchaikovsky Research Website: en.tchaikovsky-research.net/pages/Francesca_da_Rimini (accessed 29 September 2017).
13. Ibid.
14. 'The Bayreuth Music Festival', *Russian Register*, May–August 1876, trans. Luis Sundkvist, 2009. Tchaikovsky Research Website: en.tchaikovsky-research.net/pages/The_Bayreuth_Music_Festival (accessed 29 September 2017).
15. David Brown, *Tchaikovsky: The Crisis Years, 1874–1878* (London: Gollancz, 1982), p. 97.
16. Tchaikovsky Research Website: en.tchaikovsky-research.net/pages/Richard_Wagner (accessed 29 September 2017).
17. Tchaikovsky Research Website: en.tchaikovsky-research.net/pages/Hamlet_(overture-fantasia) (accessed 29 September 2017).
18. Tchaikovsky Research Website: en.tchaikovsky-research.net/pages/Romeo_and_Juliet (accessed 29 September 2017).
19. Tchaikovsky Research Website: en.tchaikovsky-research.net/pages/Serenade_for_String_Orchestra (accessed 29 September 2017).
20. Ibid.
21. Ibid.
22. David Brown, *Tchaikovsky: The Man and His Music* (London: Faber, 2007), p. 59.
23. Roland John Wiley, *Tchaikovsky's Ballets: Swan Lake, Sleeping Beauty, Nutcracker* (Oxford: Clarendon Press, 1985), p. 27.
24. Ibid., p. 28.
25. Brown, *Tchaikovsky: The Man and His Music*, p. 109.
26. Tchaikovsky, *The Life and Letters*, p. 173.
27. For details, and the full scenario, see Wiley, *Tchaikovsky's Ballets*.
28. Tchaikovsky Research Website: en.tchaikovsky-research.net/pages/Léo_Delibes (accessed 29 September 2017).
29. David Brown, *Tchaikovsky: The Early Years, 1840–1874* (London: Victor Gollancz, 1978), p. 99.
30. Ibid., p. 75.
31. Tchaikovsky, *The Life and Letters*, p. 564.
32. Brown, *Tchaikovsky: The Early Years*, p. 260.
33. Ibid., p. 265.
34. Brown, *Tchaikovsky: The Crisis Years*, p. 44.
35. *Tchaikovsky Through Others' Eyes*, ed. Alexander Poznansky, trans. Ralph C. Burr, Jr., and Robert Bird (Bloomington and Indianapolis, IN: Indiana University Press, 1999), p. 130.
36. Tchaikovsky, *The Life and Letters*, pp. 244, 272.
37. Ibid., pp. 274–8.
38. Ibid., p. 294.
39. Tchaikovsky Research Website: en.tchaikovsky-research.net/pages/Symphony_No._5 (accessed 29 September 2017).
40. David Brown, *Tchaikovsky: The Final Years, 1885–1893* (New York: W. W. Norton, 1991), p. 152.
41. Tchaikovsky, *The Life and Letters*, p. 548. See also Rebecca A. Dixon, 'Reinterpreting the Intended Program of Tchaikovsky's Fifth Symphony'. www.scribd.com/document/189829244/Reinterpreting-the-Programme-of-Tchaikovsky-5 (accessed 30 September 2017).
42. Tchaikovsky Research Website: en.tchaikovsky-research.net/pages/Symphony_No._5 (accessed 29 September 2017).
43. Aleksandra Orlova, 'Tchaikovsky: The Last Chapter', *Music & Letters*, vol. 62 (1981), pp. 125–45.
44. See the closely reasoned rebuttal by Alexander Poznansky on the Tchaikovsky Research Website: en.tchaikovsky-research.net/pages/Tchaikovsky:_A_Life (accessed 29 September 2017).
45. Brown, *Tchaikovsky: The Final Years*, p. 388.
46. Tchaikovsky Research Website: en.tchaikovsky-research.net/pages/Symphony_No._6 (accessed 29 September 2017).
47. Tchaikovsky, *Tchaikovsky: The Life and Letters*, p. 518.

48. Brown, *Tchaikovsky: The Crisis Years*, p. 116.
49. Ibid., p. 121.

Michael Tippett

1. Thomas Schuttenhelm, *The Orchestral Music of Michael Tippett: Creative Development and Compositional Process* (Cambridge: Cambridge University Press, 2014), p. 59.
2. *Tippett on Music*, ed. Meirion Bowen (Oxford: Clarendon Press, 1995), p. 92.
3. Schuttenhelm, *The Orchestral Music of Michael Tippett*, p. 46.
4. Ibid., p. 41.

Edgard Varèse

1. In 1916. Paul Griffiths, 'Varèse, Edgar', *Grove Music Online*.
2. 'Edgard Varèse' in *Silence: Lectures and Writings by John Cage* (Middletown, CT: Wesleyan University Press, 1961), pp. 83–4.
3. 'The Liberation of Sound', compiled and edited by Chou Wen-Chung, *Perspectives of New Music*, vol. 5, no. 1 (Autumn–Winter 1966), p. 11.
4. Ibid., pp. 14–15.
5. Ibid., pp. 15–16.
6. New York, Colfranc Music Publishing Corp., 1973.
7. Fernand Ouellette, *Edgard Varèse* (Montreal: Éditions Segher, 1966), p. 56.
8. Deutsche Grammophon 0289 471 1372 0.

Ralph Vaughan Williams

1. *Proceedings of the Musical Association*, vol. 47 (1920–1), pp. 39–54.
2. David Manning, *Vaughan Williams on Music* (Oxford: Oxford University Press, 2008), pp. 39–42.
3. Ibid., p. 42.
4. Roger Nichols, *Ravel* (New Haven, CT, and London: Yale University Press, 2011), p. 95.
5. For discussion of Vaughan Williams' spiritual and poetic roots, see Wilfrid Mellers, *Vaughan Williams and the Vision of Albion* (Travis and Emery, 2nd edn, 2009).
6. Harold Leslie Rayner, *Letters from France, July 26. 1915 to July 30, 1916* (printed for private circulation by John Bale, Sons, and Danielsson, 1919), p. 195, quoted in John Lewis-Stempel, *Where Poppies Blow: The British Soldier, Nature, The Great War* (London: Hachette, 2016, online edn).
7. Michael Kennedy, *The Works of Ralph Vaughan Williams* (Oxford: Clarendon Press, 2nd edn, 1992), pp. 467–8.
8. Ibid., p. 137.
9. Ibid., p. 138.
10. Ibid., p. 468.
11. Ibid.
12. Ibid., p. 139.
13. Ibid., p. 140.
14. *Letters of Ralph Vaughan Williams*, ed. Hugh Cobbe (Oxford: Oxford University Press, 2008), p. 265.
15. Kennedy, *The Works of Ralph Vaughan Williams*, pp. 170–1.
16. May 1935, *Letters of Ralph Vaughan Williams*, ed. Cobbe, p. ix.
17. Kennedy, *The Works of Ralph Vaughan* Williams, p. 247.
18. Ursula Vaughan Williams, *R.V.W.: A Biography of Ralph Vaughan Williams* (Oxford: Oxford University Press, 1964), p. 190.
19. Michael Kennedy, 'Fluctuations in the Response to the Music of Ralph Vaughan Williams', *The Cambridge Companion to Vaughan Williams*, ed. Alain Frogley and Aidan J. Thomson (Cambridge: Cambridge University Press, 2013), pp. 282–3.
20. Oliver Neighbour, 'The Place of the Eighth among Vaughan Williams' Symphonies', *Vaughan Williams Studies*, ed. Alain Frogley (Cambridge: Cambridge University Press, 1996), p. 222.
21. Kennedy, *The Works of Ralph Vaughan Williams*, p. 245.
22. Jerrold Northrop Moore, *Music and Friends: Seven Decades of Letters to Adrian Boult* (London: Hamish Hamilton, 1979), p. 143.
23. Kennedy, *The Works of Ralph Vaughan Williams*, p. 300.
24. Deryck Cooke, *The Language of Music* (Oxford: Oxford University Press, 1962), p. 253.
25. Kennedy, 'Fluctuations in the Response', p. 285.
26. Kennedy, *The Works of Ralph Vaughan Williams*, p. 302.
27. Michael Kennedy in note for recording by the London Philharmonic Orchestra, cond. Bernard Haitink, EMI Classics 7243 5 567 62 2 1 (1999).

Antonio Vivaldi

1. Joachim Christoph Nemeitz, *Nachlese besonderer Nachrichten von Italien* (Leipzig, 1726), quoted in Karl Heller, *Antonio Vivaldi: The Red Priest of Venice*, trans. David Marinelli (Portland, OR: Amadeus Press, 1997), p. 32.
2. *Il Cimento dell'Armonia e dell'Inventione*, 1st edn (Amsterdam: Michel-Charles Le Cène, [1725]).
3. Translations of the sonnets are by Robert Philip.

Richard Wagner

1. *Cosima Wagner*, vol. 1, trans. Catherine Alison Phillips (New York: Alfred A. Knopf, 1931), p. 438.

William Walton

1. Stephen Lloyd, *William Walton: Muse of Fire* (Woodbridge: Boydell Press, 2001), p. 4.
2. Constant Lambert, *Music Ho! A Study of Music in Decline* (London: Faber, 1934, 3rd edn, 1966), p. 135.
3. Lloyd, *William Walton*, p. 73.
4. Ibid., p. 127.
5. In TV programme, 'Walton at 75', ibid., p. 133.
6. Interview with Hans Keller, 1972, ibid., p. 134.
7. Ibid., p. 135.
8. Lionel Tertis, *My Viola and I: A Complete Autobiography* (London: Paul Elek, 1974), p. 36, quoted in Lloyd, ibid., p. 89.
9. Lambert, *Music Ho!*, pp. 277–8.

Carl Maria von Weber

1. Julius Benedict, *Weber* (London: Sampson Low, Marston & Co., 1881), p. 67.
2. J. C. Lobe, *Gespräche mit Weber*, in *Fliegende Blätter für Musik*, vol. 1 (1853); John Warrack, *Carl Maria von Weber* (Cambridge: Cambridge University Press, 2nd edn, 1976), p. 221.
3. Dana Gooley, *The Virtuoso Liszt* (Cambridge: Cambridge University Press, 2004), p. 103.
4. John Warrack, *Carl Maria von Weber* (Cambridge: Cambridge University Press, 2nd edn, 1976), p. 245.
5. Benedict, *Weber*, p. 66.
6. *Revue et Gazette Musicale*, 6 April 1845, p. 106; Gooley, *The Virtuoso Liszt*, p. 97.

Anton Webern

1. 17 July 1912, Julian Johnson, *Webern and the Transformation of Nature* (Cambridge: Cambridge University Press, 1999), p. 79.
2. 12 July 1912, ibid., p. 84.
3. Ibid., p. 79.
4. Foreword to Webern's Six Bagatelles for String Quartet, Op. 9, June 1924, in Joseph Auner, *A Schoenberg Reader: Documents of a Life* (New Haven, CT, and London: Yale University Press, 2008), p. 184.
5. Hans Moldenhauer and Rosaleen Moldenhauer, *Anton von Webern: A Chronicle of his Life and Work* (New York: Alfred A. Knopf, 1979), p. 328.
6. Quoted by Tom Service in 'Symphony Guide: Webern's Op. 21', *The Guardian*, 17 December 2013.
7. 13 January 1913, Johnson, *Webern and the Transformation of Nature*, p. 104.
8. Allen Forte: *The Atonal Music of Anton Webern* (New Haven, CT, and London: Yale University Press, 1998), p. 91.
9. Ibid.
10. *The Path to the New Music*, trans. Leo Black, ed. Willi Reich (London and Vienna: Universal Edition, 1963), p. 22.
11. Ibid., pp. 60–3.

Index